THE ENCYCLO[PEDIA OF]
INTERNATIONAL CRICKETERS

EVERY TEST & ONE-DAY INTERNATIONAL PLAYER EVER

Mark Fine & Gus Smarrini

Publishing

Published by:

Bas Publishing
ABN 30 106 181 542
F16/171 Collins Street
Melbourne Vic. 3000
Tel: (03) 9650 3200
Fax: (03) 9650 5077
Web: www.baspublishing.com.au
Email: mail@baspublishing.com.au

Copyright © 2006 Gus Smarrini & Mark Fine

This publication is copyright and may not be resold or reproduced in any manner (except excerpts thereof for bona fide study purpose in accordance with the Copyright Act) without the prior consent of the Publisher.

Every effort has been made to ensure that this book is free from error and/or omissions. No responsibility can be accepted by the Publisher, Author or any person involved in the preparation of this book for loss occasioned to any person acting or refraining from action as a result of material in this book.

The National Library of Australia Cataloguing-in-Publication entry

Smarrini, Gus, 1966- .
    The encyclopedia of international cricketers : every test
    and one-day international player ever.

    ISBN 1 920910 74 3.

    1. Cricket - Tournaments - Encyclopedias. 2. Cricket
    matches - Encyclopedias. 3. Cricket players -
    Encyclopedias. I. Fine, Mark. II. Title.

796.3586503

Design & Layout: Ben Graham
Printed in Australian by Griffin Press

Dedications

To my amazing wife Natalie,

I asked you to look at something on the computer a few months ago and you've barely had time to do anything else ever since. Without your efforts this book wouldn't have been published before the 2011 Cricket World Cup.

You are my inspiration. When I succeed it's because of you.

Mark F

To Sarah,

A demanding yet exciting journey which you shared with me along the way.

Gus

Legend

Cap Number (Test players only)

The chronological order of Test players as they make thier debut for their respective countries. Where two or more players are making their debut in the same Test, countries usually assign the 'caps' in alphabetical order. When this situation occurs, Australia, England, India, New Zealand, South Africa, Sri Lanka, West Indies and Zimbabwe assign caps alphabetically by surname whilst Bangladesh and Pakistan assign alphabetically by first name.

Batting

Highest Score: The most number of runs made in one innings.

Asterisk*: denotes a 'not out' score.

No. 50's: The number of half centuries scored. A half century is any score from 50 to 99.

No. 100's: The number of centuries (including double and triple hundreds) scored.

Bowling & Fielding

Wickets: Number of wickets credited to the bowler in either Tests or ODI's. A run out during a bowler's over is not credited as a wicket.

Runs: The total number of runs scored from the player's bowling over his career.

Best Bowling (Innings): The best bowling figures (based on wicket to runs ratio) the player has captured in any one innings ie; 4/100 are better figures than 3/10 as the wickets supercede runs against.

Average: How many runs have been scored per wicket taken. Unlike batting averages, the lower the number, the better the bowling average

5WI: Five wickets in an Innings ie; the number of times the player has taken five wickets or more in an innings.

10WM: Ten wickets in a Match ie: the number of times the player has taken ten or more wickets in a match

Catches: Credited to either wicket-keepers or general fielders.

Stumpings: Only credited to wicket-keepers.

Contents

Introduction 7
About the Authors 8

ICC Test Playing Nations
Australia 9
Bangladesh 128
England 149
India. 310
New Zealand 385
Pakistan 450
South Africa 512
Sri Lanka 587
West Indies 626
Zimbabwe 704

ICC Associate Members - ODI Playing Nations
Bermuda 734
Canada 737
East Africa 743
Holland 745
Ireland 750
Kenya 753
Scotland 758
UAE 762
USA 767

Introduction

Having poured our heart and soul into this project for almost two years, it would surprise some people to hear that for most part the experience has been an absolute pleasure. In writing a book that contains every cricketer to have ever played a Test or One Day International we were expecting to come out the other side with a new depth of cricket knowledge that would confirm our reputations as know-it-alls. Whilst that's true, the totally unexpected bonus in writing about a sport that has had such a long and rich past, is that we received a vivid history lesson through the lives of the more than 3,000 men who fill the pages of our book.

Whilst our subjects were elite sportsmen and national heroes, they were not immune from the world around them. Scores of young cricketers perished in the Boer War and two World Wars, and for many of them it was a national progression to fight for their country after having represented them on the sporting field. It was also startling how many cricketers took their own life in the early years of Test cricket. The fact that it often occurred shortly after retirement paints a bleak picture of the treatment available for people prone to depression at the time.

The history lesson wasn't all doom and gloom though. We looked at the integration of sport in South Africa through the eyes of players like Makhaya Ntini and Ashwell Prince. We saw the emergence of Pakistan not only as a cricketing nation but as an independent country in their own right and more recently how the battling Banglas are the pride of a developing nation. Our cricketers even gave us a first hand look at the changing face of transportation over 130 years. We're sure you'll enjoy reading the book, and if you're not after a history lesson we promise there are tens of thousands of great cricket facts to keep you satisfied.

Mark Fine & Gus Smarrini

About the Authors

Mark Fine is a sports journalist currently working for Australia's only 24 hour sport's radio station - SEN. He produces the 'Beva after Dark' program as well as appearing regularly on the network as a presenter. In 2005 Mark authored his first book - *Urban Footy Legends* and previously worked on television as a segment producer on both *Live & Kicking* and *The Footy Show*. At present he is a contributing writer to *Inside Football*. Away from work Mark divides his time between following his beloved Saints and being chased around by his wife Natalie, three children Anide, Zane and Lucas and pet greyhound Harry.

Although more commonly known as a 'footy tragic' having penned two books - *Team Talk* and *Urban Footy Legends* - Gus Smarrini's passion for the gentlemen's game was inspired during the mid 70s when Kerry Packer's World Series Cricket took on the Test cricket establishment in what would eventually change the face of the game forever. Described as a backyard cricketer at best, Gus has worked on Melbourne radio for the past seven years and continues to talk on the lighter points of the game during his long running segment 'Team Talk' on SEN 1116.

Australia

A'BECKETT, Edward Lambert

Born:	August 11, 1907
Batting:	Right handed
Bowling:	Right arm medium-fast

Tests

Test Career:	1929-31
Cap Number:	128
Tests Played:	4

Test Batting

Innings:	7	Runs:	143
Highest Score:	41	Average:	20.42
No. 50s:	0	No. 100s:	0

Test Bowling & Fielding

Wickets:	3	Runs:	317
Best Bowling:	1/41	Average:	105.66
5 WI:	0	10 WM:	0
Catches:	4	Stumpings:	0

A Victorian all-rounder whose main claim to fame was that his first Test scalp was that of champion English batsman Jack Hobbs. Retired from cricket at only 24 to concentrate on work as a solicitor.

ALDERMAN, Terrence Michael

Born:	June 12, 1956
Batting:	Right handed
Bowling:	Right arm medium-fast

Tests

Test Career:	1981-91
Cap Number:	310
Tests Played:	41

Test Batting

Innings:	53	Runs:	203
Highest Score:	26*	Average:	6.54
No. 50s:	0	No. 100s:	0

Test Bowling & Fielding

Wickets:	170	Runs:	4,616
Best Bowling:	6/47	Average:	27.15
5 WI:	14	10 WM:	1
Catches:	27	Stumpings:	0

One Day Internationals

ODI Career:	1981-91
ODIs Played:	65

ODI Batting

Innings:	18	Runs:	32
Highest Score:	9*	Average:	2.66
No. 50s:	0	No. 100s:	0

ODI Bowling & Fielding

Wickets:	88	Runs:	2,056
Best Bowling:	5/17	Average:	23.36
5 WM:	2	Catches:	29
Stumpings:	0		

Effective on Australian wickets, he was near unplayable on the seaming tracks in England. The tall West Australian enjoyed two outstanding tours to England in 1981 and 1989. On the first of those tours he captured 42 wickets at 21.26 and then he followed up eight years later with 41 victims at an incredible 17.37. Alderman stands 16th on the all time list for Australian Test wicket takers, but he could have been much higher had it not been for a shoulder injury sustained while tackling a English ground invader at Perth in 1982/83 and involvement on the rebel tour to South Africa in 1985.

ALEXANDER, George

Born:	April 22, 1851
Batting:	Right handed

Tests

Test Career:	1880-84
Cap Number:	18
Tests Played:	2

Test Batting

Innings:	4	Runs:	52
Highest Score:	33	Average:	13.00
No. 50s:	0	No. 100s:	0

Test Bowling & Fielding

Wickets:	2	Runs:	93
Best Bowling:	2/69	Average:	46.50
5 WI:	0	10 WM:	0
Catches:	2	Stumpings:	0

An all-rounder from Victoria who took up the position of Australian team manager following his retirement from Test cricket.

ALEXANDER, Harry Houston

Born:	June 9, 1905
Batting:	Right handed
Bowling:	Right arm fast

Tests

Test Career:	1933
Cap Number:	149
Tests Played:	1

Test Batting

Innings:	2	Runs:	17
Highest Score:	17*	Average:	17.00
No. 50s:	0	No. 100s:	0

Test Bowling & Fielding

Wickets:	1	Runs:	154
Best Bowling:	1/129	Average:	154.00
5 WI:	0	10 WM:	0
Catches:	0	Stumpings:	0

A right arm quick from Victoria whose only appearance for Australia was the fifth Test at the MCG during the Bodyline series.

9

ALLAN, Francis Erskine

Born:	December 2, 1849
Batting:	Right handed
Bowling:	Right arm off-break

Tests

Test Career:	1879		
Cap Number:	15		
Tests Played:	1		

Test Batting

Innings:	1	Runs:	5
Highest Score:	5	Average:	5.00
No. 50s:	0	No. 100s:	0

Test Bowling & Fielding

Wickets:	4	Runs:	80
Best Bowling:	2/30	Average:	20.00
5 WI:	0	10 WM:	0
Catches:	0	Stumpings:	0

Though he only played one Test, Frank Allan was considered one of the finest break bowlers in the formative years of Australian cricket. Business and an interest in other sports curtailed his Test career.

ALLAN, Peter John

Born:	December 31, 1935
Batting:	Right handed
Bowling:	Right arm medium-fast

Tests

Test Career:	1965		
Cap Number:	236		
Tests Played:	1		

Test Batting

Innings:	1	Runs:	0
Highest Score:	0	Average:	0.00
No. 50s:	0	No. 100s:	0

Test Bowling & Fielding

Wickets:	2	Runs:	83
Best Bowling:	2/58	Average:	41.50
5 WI:	0	10 WM:	0
Catches:	0	Stumpings:	0

He was a right arm medium pacer from Queensland.

ALLEN, Reginald Charles

Born:	July 2, 1858
Batting:	Right handed
Bowling:	Right arm medium-fast

Tests

Test Career:	1887		
Cap Number:	47		
Tests Played:	1		

Test Batting

Innings:	2	Runs:	44
Highest Score:	30	Average:	22.00
No. 50s:	0	No. 100s:	0

Test Bowling & Fielding

Wickets:	0	Runs:	0
Best Bowling:		Average:	0.00
5 WI:	0	10 WM:	0
Catches:	2	Stumpings:	0

Ex New South Wales. He was the uncle of the great Englishman Gubby Allen.

ANDREWS, Thomas James Edwin

Born:	August 26, 1890
Batting:	Right handed
Bowling:	Right arm leg-break

Tests

Test Career:	1921-26		
Cap Number:	115		
Tests Played:	16		

Test Batting

Innings:	23	Runs:	592
Highest Score:	94	Average:	36.90
No. 50s:	4	No. 100s:	0

Test Bowling & Fielding

Wickets:	1	Runs:	116
Best Bowling:	1/23	Average:	116.00
5 WI:	0	10 WM:	0
Catches:	12	Stumpings:	0

A powerful opening batsman, he failed to reproduce his fine domestic form internationally. Though the New South Welshman never scored a Test century he went close, hitting two scores in the nineties on the tour of England in 1921. Andrews was also an accomplished close in fieldsman.

ANGEL, Jo

Born:	April 22, 1968
Batting:	Left handed
Bowling:	Right arm fast

Tests

Test Career:	1993-95		
Cap Number:	355		
Tests Played:	4		

Test Batting

Innings:	7	Runs:	35
Highest Score:	11	Average:	5.83
No. 50s:	0	No. 100s:	0

Test Bowling & Fielding

Wickets:	10	Runs:	463
Best Bowling:	3/54	Average:	46.30
5 WI:	0	10 WM:	0
Catches:	1	Stumpings:	0

One Day Internationals

ODI Career:	1994-95
ODIs Played:	3

ODI Batting

Innings:	1	Runs:	0
Highest Score:	0	Average:	0.00
No. 50s:	0	No. 100s:	0

ODI Bowling & Fielding

Wickets:	4	Runs:	113
Best Bowling:	2/47	Average:	28.25
5 WM:	0	Catches:	0
Stumpings:	0		

Tall if not a little ungainly, he was one of Australia's most successful domestic bowlers with 419 Shield wickets. Even at Test level Angel was always a chance to get a wicket but it was felt that his bowling was too expensive.

ARCHER, Kenneth Alan

Born:	January 17, 1928
Batting:	Right handed

Tests

Test Career:	1950-51		
Cap Number:	186		
Tests Played:	5		

Test Batting

Innings:	9	Runs:	234
Highest Score:	48	Average:	26.00
No. 50s:	0	No. 100s:	0

Test Bowling & Fielding

Wickets:	0	Runs:	0
Best Bowling:		Average:	0.00
5 WI:	0	10 WM:	0
Catches:	0	Stumpings:	0

An opening batsman from Queensland, he failed to capitalise on a number of good starts to ever score a Test half century. The brother of Test all-rounder Ron.

ARCHER, Ronald Graham

Born:	November 25, 1933
Batting:	Right handed
Bowling:	Right arm fast

Tests

Test Career:	1953-56		
Cap Number:	193		
Tests Played:	19		

Test Batting

Innings:	30	Runs:	713
Highest Score:	128	Average:	24.58
No. 50s:	2	No. 100s:	1

Test Bowling & Fielding

Wickets:	48	Runs:	1,318
Best Bowling:	5/53	Average:	27.45
5 WI:	1	10 WM:	0
Catches:	20	Stumpings:	0

He was a hard hitting batsman and quickish right arm medium pace bowler who crammed his 19 Tests into a four year period. Archer enjoyed a fine tour of England in 1956 taking 18 wickets. On the 1954 tour of the Caribbean Archer impressed with the bat, scoring 84 and 98 before finally cracking it for his only Test century, 128 at Kingston. In retirement he combined a successful career as a TV executive with a role as an ICC Match Referee.

ARMSTRONG, Warwick Winridge

Born:	May 22, 1879
Batting:	Right handed
Bowling:	Right arm slow

Tests

Test Career:	1902-1921		
Cap Number:	80		
Tests Played:	50		

Test Batting

Innings:	84	Runs:	2,863
Highest Score:	159*	Average:	38.68
No. 50s:	8	No. 100s:	6

Test Bowling & Fielding

Wickets:	87	Runs:	2,923
Best Bowling:	6/35	Average:	33.59
5 WI:	3	10 WM:	0
Catches:	44	Stumpings:	0

The expression 'larger than life' may well have been penned with Warwick Armstrong in mind. 'The Big Ship' weighed 22 stone by the end of his career but his girth did nothing to diminish his abilities as a cricketer and leader. He started his sporting life more like a sleek yacht than a big ship, in fact Armstrong played top level Rules football as a slender 20 year old, but over the years a taste for good living saw his weight balloon. In that time he established himself as a fine Test cricketer with his sturdy batting and wily slow bowling. In 1920/21, his final series on home soil, he scored three of his four Test centuries and came away from the series with a Test series average of 77.33. As a captain he enjoyed unparalleled success for his time, winning eight consecutive Tests between 1920 and 1921. An accentric individual, he carried an American Silver Dollar with him and insisted it be used at the toss during Tests in the 1902/21 Ashes series. Following his retirement he made his fortune as a whiskey merchant.

BADCOCK, Clayvel Lindsay (Jack)

Born:	April 10, 1914
Batting:	Right handed

Tests

Test Career:	1936-38		
Cap Number:	155		
Tests Played:	7		

Test Batting

Innings:	12	Runs:	160
Highest Score:	118	Average:	14.54
No. 50s:	0	No. 100s:	1

Test Bowling & Fielding

Wickets:	0	Runs:	0
Best Bowling:		Average:	0.00
5 WI:	0	10 WM:	0
Catches:	3	Stumpings:	0

A precocious youngster, he made his first class debut with Tasmania at only 15. A brilliant batsman in Shield cricket with South Australia he was an abject failure at Test level bar for one innings, 118 at the MCG in the fifth Test of the 1936/37 Ashes series.

BANNERMAN, Alexander Chalmers

Born:	March 21, 1854
Batting:	Right handed
Bowling:	Right arm leg-break

Tests

Test Career:	1879-93		
Cap Number:	16		
Tests Played:	28		

Test Batting

Innings:	50	Runs:	1,108
Highest Score:	94	Average:	23.08
No. 50s:	8	No. 100s:	0

Test Bowling & Fielding

Wickets:	4	Runs:	163
Best Bowling:	3/111	Average:	40.75
5 WI:	0	10 WM:	0
Catches:	21	Stumpings:	0

The Bannermans featured prominently in the early years of Test cricket, yet whilst they were brothers, as batsmen Charles and Alec could not have been less alike. Whilst Charles had the strokeplay to mark him as the game's first century scorer, Alec had the stoic defense that would earn him the nickname Barndoor. His most famous efforts were a score of 91 compiled in seven and a half hours against England, and a laborious four that took 80 minutes at the SCG. Bannerman was an important cricketer for Australia. He played 28 Tests in a career that spanned 15 years, and whilst he was a fine technician and a wonderful fieldsman, Alec Bannermen will always be remembered as Test cricket's first great stonewaller.

BANNERMAN, Charles

Born:	July 3, 1851
Batting:	Right handed

Tests

Test Career:	1877-79
Cap Number:	1
Tests Played:	3

Test Batting

Innings:	6	Runs:	239
Highest Score:	165*	Average:	59.75
No. 50s:	0	No. 100s:	1

Test Bowling & Fielding

Wickets:	0	Runs:	0
Best Bowling:		Average:	0.00
5 WI:	0	10 WM:	0
Catches:	0	Stumpings:	0

English born Bannerman may have had a Test career that spanned only three matches, but his name is remembered by of all keen followers of the game. Charles Bannerman not only faced the first ball bowled in Test cricket, but he went on to score Test cricket's first century. The opener was fortunate to reach double figures in that historic knock as he was dropped before reaching ten. Newspapers at the time described the chance given by the opener as a 'dolly' and Bannerman made the English pay by going on to dominate the bowling to the tune of 165 runs before retiring hurt with a split index finger. Australia's shock victory over England can be directly attributed to Bannerman's innings, given his runs totaled almost 70% of Australia's score and that none of his team mates scored more than 20 for the entire game. Incredibly 140 years later, Bannerman's first Test innings still remains the highest score on debut by an Australian. Whilst he is remembered for that famous knock, Bannerman enjoyed other notable moments in his career. The opening batsman was a member of the touring party that visited England in 1878 and whilst the Australians played no official Test matches, he was the first player on that tour to score a century. Having played only three Tests and with an average of 59.65, Charles Bannerman retired from Test cricket at the age of 28, citing ill-health as the reason. Australia's first century maker would not be lost to Test cricket altogether though, Charles Bannerman stood in 12 Tests as an umpire including two in which his brother Alec was playing.

BARDSLEY, Warren

Born:	December 6, 1882
Batting:	Left handed

Tests

Test Career:	1909-26
Cap Number:	94
Tests Played:	41

Test Batting

Innings:	66	Runs:	2,469
Highest Score:	193*	Average:	40.47
No. 50s:	14	No. 100s:	6

Test Bowling & Fielding

Wickets:	0	Runs:	0
Best Bowling:		Average:	0.00
5 WI:	0	10 WM:	0
Catches:	12	Stumpings:	0

In the first half century of Test cricket, any batsman who ended his career with an average above 40 could rightly be considered a champion. Warren Bardsley was no exception to the rule. The left-handed opener was as comfortable on the front and back foot as he was on Australian or English pitches. His first tour to England in 1909 stamped him as a player of quality with a stand-out performance in the fifth and final Test at The Oval where he scored a century in each innings. Bardsley remained a mainstay of the Test side both before and after World War I. He compiled one of the finest innings ever by an Australian batsman in Test cricket when he carried his bat at Lord's in 1926 for 193 not out.

BARNES, Sidney George

Born:	June 5, 1916
Batting:	Right handed
Bowling:	Right arm leg-break

Tests

Test Career:	1938-48
Cap Number:	163
Tests Played:	13

Test Batting

Innings:	19	Runs:	1,072
Highest Score:	234	Average:	63.05
No. 50s:	5	No. 100s:	3

Test Bowling & Fielding

Wickets:	4	Runs:	218
Best Bowling:	2/25	Average:	54.50
5 WI:	0	10 WM:	0
Catches:	14	Stumpings:	0

Why would a batsman who averaged over 60 in Test cricket play only 17 Tests? In the case of Sid Barnes a number of factors conspired against him, but they did nothing to diminish his reputation as a wonderful batsman. Selected to tour England after only eight first class games, he broke his wrist aboard ship limiting him to only one Test. His career was then interrupted by the Second World War and the limited Test fixturing following the cessation of hostilities. When he did play for his country he was a pugnacious if not all that stylish batsman who took guard in a low crouch and had a propensity for hitting through the off-side. He was capable of compiling large scores and famously hit 234 against England at the SCG in 1946. It was the exact same score as Don Bradman in the same innings and they shared a world record stand of 405 for the fifth wicket along the way. Barnes was an interesting character, cherished for his humour and off beat behaviour. Whilst batting he would play pretend strokes whilst the field was being set and head to the pavillion if he hit the ball into the ground just to tease the crowd. He became a journalist following his career, writing controversial articles on the sport including a scathing report on the 1953 Ashes tour to England. A complex individual he tragically committed suicide in his mid fifties.

BARNETT, Benjamin Arthur

Born:	March 23, 1908
Batting:	Left handed
	Wicket Keeper

Tests

Test Career:	1938
Cap Number:	160
Tests Played:	4

Test Batting

Innings:	8	Runs:	195
Highest Score:	57	Average:	27.85
No. 50s:	1	No. 100s:	0

Test Bowling & Fielding

Wickets:	0	Runs:	0
Best Bowling:		Average:	0.00
5 WI:	0	10 WM:	0
Catches:	3	Stumpings:	2

Australia's second keeper behind Bert Oldfield for many years, he toured to England and South Africa in the mid 30's without playing a Test. In 1938 he finally won the spot as number one keeper, playing all four Tests on the Ashes tour.

BARRETT, John Edward (Jack)

Born:	October 15, 1866
Batting:	Left handed
Bowling:	Right arm medium

Tests

Test Career:	1890
Cap Number:	55
Tests Played:	2

Test Batting

Innings:	4	Runs:	80
Highest Score:	67*	Average:	26.66
No. 50s:	1	No. 100s:	0

Test Bowling & Fielding

Wickets:	0	Runs:	0
Best Bowling:		Average:	0.00
5 WI:	0	10 WM:	0
Catches:	1	Stumpings:	0

A doctor from Victoria, who as his record suggests, would have played more often for his nation had work not stood in the way.

BEARD, Graeme Robert

Born:	August 19, 1950
Batting:	Right handed

Tests

Test Career:	1980
Cap Number:	308
Tests Played:	3

Test Batting

Innings:	5	Runs:	114
Highest Score:	49	Average:	22.80
No. 50s:	0	No. 100s:	0

Test Bowling & Fielding

Wickets:	1	Runs:	109
Best Bowling:	1/26	Average:	109.00
5 WI:	0	10 WM:	0
Catches:	0	Stumpings:	0

One Day Internationals

ODI Career:	1981
ODIs Played:	2

ODI Batting

Innings:	0	Runs:	0
Highest Score:	0	Average:	0.00
No. 50s:	0	No. 100s:	0

ODI Bowling & Fielding

Wickets:	4	Runs:	70
Best Bowling:	2/20	Average:	17.50
5 WM:	0	Catches:	0
Stumpings:	0		

A good spare parts man, Beard could bowl spin or medium pace and was a handy middle order batsman. He played his three Tests on the Australian tour of Pakistan in 1980.

BENAUD, John

Born:	May 11, 1944
Batting:	Right handed
Bowling:	Right arm medium

Tests

Test Career:	1972-73
Cap Number:	261
Tests Played:	3

Test Batting

Innings:	5	Runs:	223
Highest Score:	142	Average:	44.60
No. 50s:	0	No. 100s:	1

Test Bowling & Fielding

Wickets:	2	Runs:	12
Best Bowling:	2/12	Average:	6.00
5 WI:	0	10 WM:	0
Catches:	0	Stumpings:	0

A talented ball striker who lived in the shadow of his older brother Richie, he plundered the Pakistanis to the tune of 142 at the MCG in what was to prove his penultimate Test. Benaud was a highly respected captain of New South Wales and later became a national Test selector.

BENAUD, Richard

Born:	November 6, 1930
Batting:	Right handed
Bowling:	Right arm leg-break

Tests

Test Career:	1952-64
Cap Number:	190
Tests Played:	63

Test Batting

Innings:	97	Runs:	2,201
Highest Score:	122	Average:	24.45
No. 50s:	9	No. 100s:	3

Test Bowling & Fielding

Wickets:	248	Runs:	6,704
Best Bowling:	7/72	Average:	27.03
5 WI:	16	10 WM:	1
Catches:	65	Stumpings:	0

Richie Benaud has lived a life devoted to the game of cricket. The son a grade cricketer from Sydney, Richie and his younger brother John were brought up with a bat in their hands and more importantly for the older brother, with a ball in their fingers. Like his father, Richie was a leg spinner, and after making the New South Wales side at eighteen caught the eye of national selectors. He made his Test debut as a 21 year old against the touring West Indians and while his early Test career was not notable for high scoring or big bags of wickets, he settled well into the national side. His debut Test ton, 121 at Jamaica in 1955 when batting at number eight was just reward for the hard hitting all-rounder. He played a key role in the Australian series win over South Africa in 1957/58 where he took 30 wickets and averaged over fifty with the bat in five Tests. The maturing Benaud was now a key member of the side and when the experiment to appoint youngster Ian Craig as national captain failed the selectors turned to Benaud. The mantle of leader fit perfectly and his sense that the Australian captain should be an ambassador for the game came to light in the wonderful series against the touring West Indians in 1960/61. He and opposing captain Frank Worrell shared a deep mutual respect and the hard fought series was famous for the goodwill that surrounded it. Later that year Benaud led from the front as Australia was forced to fight in order to retain the Ashes. Facing defeat at Old Trafford in the fourth Test, Benaud produced a magical spell of bowling in the second innings to claim six wickets and lead his side to a win. When Benaud scored his 2000th Test run he became the first player to do so having taken 200 Test wickets as well. Since his retirement he has been an integral part of the sport, first as a selector then as a long standing television commentator. His understated style and dry sense of humour have not departed him as he still draws plaudits well in to his seventies.

BENNETT, Murray John

Born:	October 6, 1956
Batting:	Right handed
Bowling:	Left arm off-break

Tests

Test Career:	1984-85
Cap Number:	327
Tests Played:	3

Test Batting

Innings:	5	Runs:	71
Highest Score:	23	Average:	23.66
No. 50s:	0	No. 100s:	0

Test Bowling & Fielding

Wickets:	6	Runs:	325
Best Bowling:	3/79	Average:	54.16
5 WI:	0	10 WM:	0
Catches:	5	Stumpings:	0

One Day Internationals

ODI Career:	1984-85
ODIs Played:	8

ODI Batting

Innings:	4	Runs:	9
Highest Score:	6*	Average:	3.00
No. 50s:	0	No. 100s:	0

ODI Bowling & Fielding

Wickets:	4	Runs:	275
Best Bowling:	2/27	Average:	68.75
5 WM:	0	Catches:	1
Stumpings:	0		

The little known off spinner teamed up with fellow New South Welshman Bob Holland to steamroll the West Indians at the SCG in 1985. He wasn't a prodigious turner of the ball but he did possess a very fine arm ball that clean bowled no less a batsman than Viv Richards in the second innings of that Test.

BEVAN, Michael Gwyl

Born:	May 8, 1970
Batting:	Left handed
Bowling:	Left arm slow

Tests

Test Career:	1994-98
Cap Number:	360
Tests Played:	18

Test Batting

Innings:	30	Runs:	785
Highest Score:	91	Average:	29.07
No. 50s:	6	No. 100s:	0

Test Bowling & Fielding

Wickets:	29	Runs:	703
Best Bowling:	6/82	Average:	24.24
5 WI:	1	10 WM:	1
Catches:	8	Stumpings:	0

One Day Internationals

ODI Career:	1994-2004
ODIs Played:	232

ODI Batting

Innings:	196	Runs:	6,912
Highest Score:	108*	Average:	53.58
No. 50s:	46	No. 100s:	6

ODI Bowling & Fielding

Wickets:	36	Runs:	1,655
Best Bowling:	3/36	Average:	45.97
5 WM:	0	Catches:	69
Stumpings:	0		

A brilliant one day batsman, he bowed out from international cricket with a better one day batting average than Sachin Tendulkar, Brian Lara or Ricky Ponting. Bevan batted in the middle order and could play the role of sheet anchor or risk taker equally well. In one famous innings against the West Indies at the SCG in 1996 he did both, first dragging Australia back from the brink with a succession of ones and twos then securing victory with a swashbuckling finale that included a boundary off the last ball of the match. A fitness fanatic, Bevan used his great endurance to good advantage in the one day game, running tirelessly between wickets. His Test career was less successful, put down mainly to a weakness against fast short pitched bowling. The left hander bowled an extravagant form of leg spin that was dangerous when he got it right. His best return in a Test innings was 6/82 against the West Indians on home soil in 1997/98.

BICHEL, Andrew John

Born: August 27, 1970
Batting: Right handed
Bowling: Right arm medium-fast

Tests
Test Career:	1997-2003		
Cap Number:	371		
Tests Played:	19		

Test Batting
Innings:	22	Runs:	355
Highest Score:	71	Average:	16.90
No. 50s:	1	No. 100s:	0

Test Bowling & Fielding
Wickets:	58	Runs:	1,870
Best Bowling:	5/60	Average:	32.24
5 WI:	1	10 WM:	0
Catches:	16	Stumpings:	0

One Day Internationals
ODI Career:	1997-2004		
ODIs Played:	67		

ODI Batting
Innings:	36	Runs:	471
Highest Score:	64	Average:	20.47
No. 50s:	1	No. 100s:	0

ODI Bowling & Fielding
Wickets:	78	Runs:	2,463
Best Bowling:	7/20	Average:	31.57
5 WM:	2	Catches:	19
Stumpings:	0		

A TV commentator once said that if he had the choice of any Australian cricketer to go to war with it would be Andy Bichel. It perfectly summed up the lion-hearted Queensland bowler cum all-rounder who always gave his all on the cricket field. A regular drinks waiter for the national side, he always performed well when given a chance. He was a member of the 2003 World Cup winning side, starring against England in that series when he took a career best 7 for 20. Now in the twilight of his career, his batting has improved with age and he now regularly bats in his state side's top order.

BISHOP, Glenn Andrew

Born: February 25, 1960
Batting: Right handed

One Day Internationals
ODI Career:	1987		
ODIs Played:	2		

ODI Batting
Innings:	2	Runs:	13
Highest Score:	7	Average:	6.50
No. 50s:	0	No. 100s:	0

ODI Bowling & Fielding
Wickets:	0	Runs:	0
Best Bowling:		Average:	0.00
5 WM:	0	Catches:	1
Stumpings:	0		

A right handed batsman from South Australia who struck a rich vein of form in 1986/87 and was rewarded with a spot in the Australian one day side.

BLACKHAM, John McCarthy (Jack)

Born: May 11, 1854
Batting: Right handed
Wicket Keeper

Tests
Test Career:	1877-94		
Cap Number:	2		
Tests Played:	35		

Test Batting
Innings:	62	Runs:	800
Highest Score:	74	Average:	15.68
No. 50s:	4	No. 100s:	0

Test Bowling & Fielding
Wickets:	0	Runs:	0
Best Bowling:		Average:	0.00
5 WI:	0	10 WM:	0
Catches:	37	Stumpings:	24

Australia's first wicketkeeper had a distinguished Test career that spanned 17 years. Nicknamed 'Black Jack' for his dark beard, the fearless Victorian played 35 Tests including eight as captain. Blackham was at the centre of Test cricket's first major controversy when Australia's great fast bowler Fred Spofforth refused to play because blackham had been selected in preference to Spofforth's New South Wales team mate Billy Murdoch. The demon fast bowler missed out on that historic first Test at the MCG, but eventually relented and went on to play many Tests with the fearless gloveman who stood up to the stumps when keeping to him. A handy lower order batsman known for placing a hefty price on his wicket, Blackham saved his best for his final Test. He was 40 years old when he combined with the great Syd Gregory to put on 154, and in doing so ensure that Gregory become the first player to score a Test double century.

BLACKIE, Donald Dearness

Born: April 5, 1882
Batting: Left handed
Bowling: Right arm off-break

Tests
Test Career:	1928-29		
Cap Number:	126		
Tests Played:	3		

Test Batting
Innings:	6	Runs:	24
Highest Score:	11*	Average:	8.00
No. 50s:	0	No. 100s:	0

Test Bowling & Fielding
Wickets:	14	Runs:	444
Best Bowling:	6/94	Average:	31.71
5 WI:	1	10 WM:	0
Catches:	2	Stumpings:	0

There is a stand at the St. Kilda Cricket Ground in Victoria that bears the name Blackie-Ironmonger and given the similarities they share it is no surprise. Both made their Test debuts in their mid 40's, and whilst Don Blackie only played for his country on three occasions it was still quite an achievement given that he was, and still is, the oldest Australian to represent his country for the first time.

BLEWETT, Gregory Scott
Born:	October 29, 1971
Batting:	Right handed
Bowling:	Right arm medium

Tests
Test Career:	1995-2000		
Cap Number:	363		
Tests Played:	46		

Test Batting
Innings:	79	Runs:	2,552
Highest Score:	214	Average:	34.02
No. 50s:	15	No. 100s:	4

Test Bowling & Fielding
Wickets:	14	Runs:	720
Best Bowling:	2/9	Average:	51.42
5 WI:	0	10 WM:	0
Catches:	45	Stumpings:	0

One Day Internationals
ODI Career:	1995-99		
ODIs Played:	32		

ODI Batting
Innings:	30	Runs:	551
Highest Score:	57*	Average:	20.40
No. 50s:	2	No. 100s:	0

ODI Bowling & Fielding
Wickets:	14	Runs:	646
Best Bowling:	2/6	Average:	46.14
5 WM:	0	Catches:	7
Stumpings:	0		

A top order batsman from South Australia, he was used in various batting spots when playing for his country. His Test career started with a bang, scoring centuries in his first two Tests, and he later hit a double century against South Africa as part of a record 385 run stand with Steve Waugh. Blewett was an elegant batsman, equally comfortable rocking on to the front foot as he was swivelling for pulls and hooks. He had a perceived weakness against slow bowling which counted against him when Australia played sides with a strong spin attack. He was also a clever medium pace bowler who was regularly thrown the ball to either break a partnership or give the front line bowlers a rest. Eventhough he hasn't played international cricket for over five years he still remains an important player for his state.

BONNOR, George John
Born:	February 25, 1855
Batting:	Right handed
Bowling:	Right arm medium

Tests
Test Career:	1880-88		
Cap Number:	19		
Tests Played:	17		

Test Batting
Innings:	30	Runs:	512
Highest Score:	128	Average:	17.06
No. 50s:	2	No. 100s:	1

Test Bowling & Fielding
Wickets:	2	Runs:	84
Best Bowling:	1/5	Average:	42.00
5 WI:	0	10 WM:	0
Catches:	16	Stumpings:	0

George Bonnor was quite literally a giant of the game in its formative years. Though reports of his height vary, it is generally accepted that he stood close to 6ft 6in or 198 centimetres, which at the time was almost unheard of. Bonnor was an opener or number six, and on one occasion in 1882 opened the batting with the diminutive Alec Bannermen, much to the amusement of a large Sydney crowd. His strokeplay befitted his stature and he regularly cleared not only boundary fences but pavilions as well. Whilst capable of large scores, Bonnor was inconsistent at Test level and departed the game with a batting average of just over 17.

BOON, David Clarence
Born:	December 29, 1960
Batting:	Right handed
Bowling:	Right arm slow

Tests
Test Career:	1984-96		
Cap Number:	325		
Tests Played:	107		

Test Batting
Innings:	190	Runs:	7,422
Highest Score:	200	Average:	43.65
No. 50s:	32	No. 100s:	21

Test Bowling & Fielding
Wickets:	0	Runs:	14
Best Bowling:		Average:	0.00
5 WI:	0	10 WM:	0
Catches:	99	Stumpings:	0

One Day Internationals
ODI Career:	1984-95		
ODIs Played:	181		

ODI Batting
Innings:	177	Runs:	5,964
Highest Score:	122	Average:	37.04
No. 50s:	37	No. 100s:	5

For Allan Border to take Australia from easybeats to number one he needed a world class number three. He found that man in David Boon. Shooting to prominence as a teenager in Tasmania, the stocky right hander was elevated into the Test side in 1984 as a 24 year old. His first Test was against the might of the West Indies and possibly the best fast bowling attack in the history of the game. Batting at number six, he stood up to Holding, Marshall, Garner and Walsh to score a half century in the second innings. The selectors liked what they saw and took him to England in 1985 where he struggled to adjust to the change in conditions. Boon went from the the middle order to opening with Geoff Marsh, but it was as a number three that he would become an all-time great. Intense and fearless, he could play every stroke, but was particularly savage on anything short outside off stump. He had boundless mental powers, able to concentrate for an entire days play, pausing only to walk down the wicket, give it a pat or two and glare at the bowler. He hit 21 Test centuries, but it would surprise many to know that he didn't score a Test ton on his first two Ashes tours in 1985 and 1989. He put that statistic behind him on his last trip to the 'old dart', hitting three fine centuries and averaging just under 70. Boon's highest Test score was an even 200 against the Kiwis in 1989/90. He put his ability to concentrate to good use as a short leg fieldsman where he pulled off many fine catches, including a diving take off England's Devon Malcolm at the MCG in 1994 to bring up Shane Warne's only Test hat trick. He was equally at home in the one day arena and top scored with 75 in the final of the 1987 World Cup to lead his country to their first World Championship. Heavily involved in Tasmanian cricket following his retirement in 1996, he became a Test selector in 2000. In 2005, a beer company cashed in on his popularity by producing a talking 'Boonie' doll that proved so popular the company recorded all-time record sales. The little Tasmanian with the bushy moustache never captained his country, but he was a true leader who let his deeds on the field do the talking.

BOOTH, Brian Charles

Born: October 19, 1933
Batting: Right handed
Bowling: Right arm medium

Tests
Test Career: 1961-66
Cap Number: 221
Tests Played: 29

Test Batting
Innings: 48
Highest Score: 169
No. 50s: 10
Runs: 1,773
Average: 42.21
No. 100s: 5

Test Bowling & Fielding
Wickets: 3
Best Bowling: 2/33
5 WI: 0
Catches: 17
Runs: 146
Average: 48.66
10 WM: 0
Stumpings: 0

A tall right handed batsman, Booth was a mainstay of the Australian middle order in the sixties. Though he toured England twice and visited a number of other countries, he enjoyed more success in Australia with four of his five centuries coming on home soil. His highest score of 169 was struck against the South Africans in 1963. When Bob Simpson was unavailable for two Tests against England in 1965/66 Booth filled the breach as Australian captain. Unfortunately that series was to be his last, though he did continue as a fine contributor for his state in Sheffield Shield competition. As well as being a fine strokeplayer he was also a handy bowler and reliable fieldsman.

BORDER, Allan Robert

Born: July 27, 1955
Batting: Left handed
Bowling: Left arm off-break

Tests
Test Career: 1979-94
Cap Number: 299
Tests Played: 156

Test Batting
Innings: 265
Highest Score: 205
No. 50s: 63
Runs: 11,174
Average: 50.56
No. 100s: 27

Test Bowling & Fielding
Wickets: 39
Best Bowling: 7/46
5 WI: 2
Catches: 156
Runs: 1,525
Average: 39.10
10 WM: 1
Stumpings: 0

One Day Internationals
ODI Career: 1979-94
ODIs Played: 273

ODI Batting
Innings: 252
Highest Score: 127*
No. 50s: 39
Runs: 6,524
Average: 30.62
No. 100s: 3

ODI Bowling & Fielding
Wickets: 73
Best Bowling: 3/20
5 WM: 0
Stumpings: 0
Runs: 2,071
Average: 28.36
Catches: 127

One of the most determined cricketers to ever pull on a baggy green cap, Allan Border made his debut in 1978/79 when Australian cricket was at one of its lowest points. The Test side had been ravaged by defections to World Series Cricket and there was little for fans to cheer about bar the emergence of the plucky left handed batsman. Times were just as tough when AB took the captaincy over from Kim Hughes in 1984, with the side having just been thrashed 5-0 by the West

Indies, but as Border would prove many times over the next decade he was the ideal man for a crisis. He captained Australia in 93 tests, leading them to victory on 32 occasions. In the process he began a rebuilding process that would ultimately take Australia back to number one in world cricket. Under his leadership Australia may have not been the undisputed world champions they would become under Steve Waugh, but he did win the World Cup in 1987 and they did regain the Ashes in 1989. He was labeled 'captain grumpy' by the media when the cameras often caught him scowling in the field, but he was always respected by the players under his charge and in the end won over the Australian media and public alike. As a batsman he has a record that suggests he is an all-time great. In 156 test matches he scored 11,174 runs at an average of 50.56 with 27 centuries and a record 63 fifties. There were a number of memorable performances including a defiant 150 in each innings at Lahore in 1979/80 and a career high 205 against New Zealand at Adelaide in 1987. His batting was hardly copybook stuff, but he was always working the ball into gaps and had a deadly cut and heaving pull that ensured the scoreboard always kept ticking over. He wasn't the first captain to underbowl himself, but his slow left arm off-spinners often troubled the best players of spin. He recorded career best figures of 11/96 in an amazing performance against the West Indies at the SCG in 1989. In retirement he has resisted the pull of the media, firstly preferring to coach Australian under age sides and more recently taking over the reins as national chairman of selectors.

BOYLE, Henry Frederick (Harry)

Born:	December 10, 1847
Batting:	Right handed

Tests

Test Career:	1879-84		
Cap Number:	17		
Tests Played:	12		
Test Batting			
Innings:	16	Runs:	153
Highest Score:	36*	Average:	12.75
No. 50s:	0	No. 100s:	0
Test Bowling & Fielding			
Wickets:	32	Runs:	641
Best Bowling:	6/42	Average:	20.03
5 WI:	1	10 WM:	0
Catches:	10	Stumpings:	0

Boyle was a steady bowler who like many early Test players relied on accuracy and length rather than speed. Though he had the fine record of 32 wickets in twelve Test appearances and was a handy lower order batsman, Harry Boyle is best remembered as a fearless fieldsman who thought nothing of fielding just inches from the bat.

BRACKEN, Nathan Wade

Born:	August 12, 1977
Batting:	Right handed
Bowling:	Left arm medium-fast

Tests

Test Career:	2003-		
Cap Number:	387		
Tests Played:	5		
Test Batting			
Innings:	6	Runs:	70
Highest Score:	37	Average:	17.50
No. 50s:	0	No. 100s:	0
Test Bowling & Fielding			
Wickets:	12	Runs:	505
Best Bowling:	4/48	Average:	42.08
5 WI:	0	10 WM:	0
Catches:	2	Stumpings:	0

One Day Internationals

ODI Career:	2001-		
ODIs Played:	38		
ODI Batting			
Innings:	10	Runs:	84
Highest Score:	21*	Average:	21.00
No. 50s:	0	No. 100s:	0
ODI Bowling & Fielding			
Wickets:	65	Runs:	1,377
Best Bowling:	5/67	Average:	21.18
5 WM:	1	Catches:	7
Stumpings:	0		

A tall and talented left arm quick from New South Wales, he currently finds himself in a log jam for spots in the Australian side. He showed glimpses against the touring Indians in 2003/04, but more recently his international appearances have been restricted to the shorter versions of the game.

BRADMAN, Donald George

Born:	August 27, 1908
Batting:	Right handed
Bowling:	Right arm leg-break

Tests

Test Career:	1928-48		
Cap Number:	124		
Tests Played:	52		
Test Batting			
Innings:	80	Runs:	6,996
Highest Score:	334	Average:	99.94
No. 50s:	13	No. 100s:	29
Test Bowling & Fielding			
Wickets:	2	Runs:	72
Best Bowling:	1/8	Average:	36.00
5 WI:	0	10 WM:	0
Catches:	32	Stumpings:	0

Cricket would be one of the few sports where there is no debate as to who holds the title of greatest ever. Likewise Australia would be one of the few countries where there is complete consensus over their best all time sportsperson. Such was, and still is the greatness of Sir Donald Bradman. Born in Cootamundra in 1908, the Bradman family moved to the picturesque New South Wales town of Bowral when young Don was two years old. He excelled at a variety of sports, as he would throughout his life, but it was as a cricketer that he regularly appeared in the local newspaper. Bradman played in the Bowral senior side as a teenager and produced the same type of mammoth innings that would later set him aside from all others in Test cricket. He was 18 when invited to train with the state squad in Sydney and just 19 when he played his first game of Sheffield Shield cricket. His deeds in the bush had not gone unnoticed and there much anticipation when Bradman made his debut against South Australia in 1927. Batting at number seven, the 'boy wonder' as he was known, countered the guile of Clarrie Grimmet to finish with 118. From that moment there was no doubting that the cricketing prodigy would one day play for Australia, and in December of 1928 he fulfilled his destiny against England at the Brisbane Exhibition ground. His first Test return was a disappointing 18 and 1 and the selectors made the young Don cool his heels in the second Test by naming him as twelfth man. He was recalled for the third Test at the MCG, and when he became the youngest ever cricketer to score a Test century, with 112 in the second innings, his illustrious international career was up and running. He played two more Tests at home before heading to England to rewrite the record books and forever change his standing in the game. His first Test on foreign soil was at Trent Bridge, and after another shaky start in the first innings when he scored eight, he was the only Australian batsman to pass 50 in the second dig with a plucky 131 batting at number four. 'The Don' was elevated to number three for the remainder of the tour and reeled off 254 at Lord's, a Test record 334 in Leeds and an Ashes winning 232 at The Oval. It was consistent huge scoring, the like which had never been seen before or has ever been seen since in Test cricket. His 334 at Leed's included over 300 runs in a single day that so defied convention some English newspapers initially refused to run the story, fearing it was a hoax. By the end of his first trip to the much loved 'mother country', he had scored a record 974 runs in five Tests at an average of 139.14. Bradman would tour England three more times. In 1934 he scored 758 runs at 94.75, in 1938 434 runs at 108.50, and in 1948, at the age of almost 40, he hit 508 runs in five Tests at 72.57 per completed innings. His numbers were just as impressive at home where he averaged 98.22 in Tests with five double centuries. Both of his Test triple tons were made in England, though he did come excruciatingly close at Adelaide in 1931/32 when he made 299 not out against South Africa. The only time his output diminished was against the touring English during the controversial 'bodyline' series in 1932/33. The plan to bowl at the batsmen's body, with a stacked on side field, was devised by the English as a direct response to Bradman's brilliance. Whilst he was restricted, he did average over 56 and his unbeaten 103 at the MCG in the second Test is thought by some to be his finest Test knock. The cricket Gods blessed Don Bradman like no other, but even The Don was reminded that he was just a mortal when he made a duck in his final Test innings at The Oval in 1948 needing only four runs to leave Test cricket with an average of 100. Throughout his career, and in retirement, everybody from journalists to scientists searched for the key to his genius. At 5ft 7 inches he hardly stood out from crowd, and with only six Test 6's it certainly wasn't brute strength. His eyes were tested to see if he had been born with some supernatural gift, but they turned out to be annoyingly average. There was no magical secret, Don Bradman was just a batsman with the perfect combination of talent, concentration and determination. He tended to play off the back foot and had sublime timing and placement. There was no quicker scoring batsman in cricket, but he rarely chanced his arm by hitting the ball in the air and his mental powers were so strong that he never went out in the nineties in 80 Test innings. As a leader he didn't lose a series, though he once said he did not "have any special abilities as a captain". There have long been suggestions that there was disharmony in the dressing room under Bradman, with the Test team divided on sectarian lines. Whilst his record as skipper can not be faulted he did have himself in the side to regularly win or save Tests. For the record he was a steady but moderate leg spinner who claimed two Test wickets and an excellent fieldsman. In the years following his retirement historians have analysed not just his cricket career but what role he played in pre-War Australia. It is generally agreed that he was a key figure in two defining moments for Australia. The first was his hand in steering Australia through the Great Depression in the 30's. He gave his countrymen a source of national pride and hope that saw them on the road to recovery and his ability to humble the English, helped a young nation to cut its ties to its Colonial past and forge a new and confident identity. He achievements were recognised shortly after retirement when he became Australian cricket's first knight in a ceremony that was held in his adopted home town of Adelaide. Quantifying Bradman's superiority is no easy task, but an explanation that was given to an American a few years ago makes a good fist of it. The tourist had heard of this amazing cricketer and wanted to know why he was still such a dominant figure so long after his retirement. Not understanding the first thing about the sport he was told that the answer lies in the numbers. It was explained that Test cricket had been played for over a century and in that time over 2000 players have batted for their respective countries. For the sake of the excerise it was decided that the definition of a Test batting career would be the Wisden standard, of a minimum of 20 innings played. And so on to the numbers. In any era a good batsman will average between 35 and 40 for each time he is dismissed. The very good players in that same era average between 40 and 45 and the excellent batsman of that period will average between 45 and 50. The interested Yank was then told that what follows are the champions. Those players will finish their Test careers with an average between 50 and 55. If you doubt that definition of a champion then consider that since 1877 there are only 19 players in the group, amongst them Viv Richards, Sunil Gavaskar and Greg Chappell. And then the American was told that the game enters rarified air. Legends finish their career with averages between 55 and 60 and in the history of the sport only eleven men have had that honour. He was then told the immortals average between 60 and 65 and in a sport that is now played almost daily around the globe and goes all the way back to 1877, there have only ever been three such players. The man who posed the question was then asked to take a seat. He was told that between 65 and 70 there has been no-one, 70 and 75 nobody, and there are no cricketers who left the game with averages between 75 and 80. The pattern continued. He learnt that there was no-one between 80 and 85, or 85 and 90 and there were not a single cricketer who managed to average between 90 and 95 in Tests. He was then told that between 95 and 100 stands the man he was asking about, Sir Donald Bradman with a Test average of 99.94. A cricketer whose ability and results were so superior to every other person to have played the game, that his name will be at the forefront of the sport for as long as it is played.

BRIGHT, Raymond James

Born:	July 13, 1954
Batting:	Right handed
Bowling:	Left arm off-break

Tests

Test Career:	1977-86
Cap Number:	280
Tests Played:	25

Test Batting

Innings:	39	Runs:	445
Highest Score:	33	Average:	14.35
No. 50s:	0	No. 100s:	0

Test Bowling & Fielding

Wickets:	53	Runs:	2,180
Best Bowling:	7/87	Average:	41.13
5 WI:	4	10 WM:	1
Catches:	13	Stumpings:	0

One Day Internationals

ODI Career:	1974-86
ODIs Played:	11

ODI Batting

Innings:	8	Runs:	66
Highest Score:	19*	Average:	16.50
No. 50s:	0	No. 100s:	0

ODI Bowling & Fielding

Wickets:	3	Runs:	350
Best Bowling:	1/28	Average:	116.66
5 WM:	0	Catches:	2
Stumpings:	0		

He was a tidy left handed off-spinner who was in and out of the Test team as the conditions dictated, for almost a decade. Twelfth man for the 1977 Centenary Test at the MCG, he went one better by making the side for the corresponding match in England three years later. The premier spin bowler of the Australian World Series Cricket side, Bright continued his Test career after WSC concluded in 1979, playing a total of 25 Tests and taking ten of the 13 Pakistani wickets to fall at Karachi in 1980.

BROMLEY, Ernest Harvey

Born:	September 2, 1912
Batting:	Left handed
Bowling:	Left arm off-break

Tests

Test Career:	1933-34
Cap Number:	146
Tests Played:	2

Test Batting

Innings:	4	Runs:	38
Highest Score:	26	Average:	9.50
No. 50s:	0	No. 100s:	0

Test Bowling & Fielding

Wickets:	0	Runs:	19
Best Bowling:		Average:	0.00
5 WI:	0	10 WM:	0
Catches:	2	Stumpings:	0

A hard hitting left-hander whose fielding was of such a high standard that it won him a spot on the Ashes tour to England in 1934.

BROWN, William Alfred

Born:	July 31, 1912
Batting:	Right handed

Tests

Test Career:	1934-48
Cap Number:	150
Tests Played:	22

Test Batting

Innings:	35	Runs:	1,592
Highest Score:	206*	Average:	46.82
No. 50s:	9	No. 100s:	4

Test Bowling & Fielding

Wickets:	0	Runs:	0
Best Bowling:		Average:	0.00
5 WI:	0	10 WM:	0
Catches:	14	Stumpings:	0

Originally from Queensland, the NSW opener took the opportunity presented to him following the retirement of first Ponsford then Woodfull.

He was a compact batsman who is often remembered for batting in tandem with fellow New South Welshman Jack Fingleton. Though not as free scoring as Fingleton, he was probably more effective, to which his feat of carrying his bat to score 206 at Lord's in 1938 would testify. He averaged 73.14 in that Ashes series, placing him as the second best Australian batsman behind Bradman. Following the war Brown skippered the side in a one-off Test against New Zealand, a role he passed back to Bradman for the Ashes series in Australia later that year. In 1947/48 Brown became part of cricket folklore when India's Mankad ran him out after he was caught backing up too far at the non-striker's end. In 2000 Bill Brown was awarded the Order of Australia Medal and in 2006 was Australia's oldest living Test cricketer.

BRUCE, William

Born:	May 22, 1864
Batting:	Left handed
Bowling:	Left arm medium

Tests

Test Career:	1885-95
Cap Number:	32
Tests Played:	14

Test Batting

Innings:	26	Runs:	702
Highest Score:	80	Average:	29.25
No. 50s:	5	No. 100s:	0

Test Bowling & Fielding

Wickets:	12	Runs:	440
Best Bowling:	3/88	Average:	36.66
5 WI:	0	10 WM:	0
Catches:	12	Stumpings:	0

An attacking batsman and useful bowler from Victoria, he got his opportunity to play for Australia as a result of a strike by ten Australian cricketers. Bruce scored a memorable 80 at the Adelaide Oval that was particularly well received at the time for no less a reason than he was a left handed batsman.

BURGE, Peter John Parnell

Born:	May 17, 1932
Batting:	Right handed

Tests

Test Career:	1955-66
Cap Number:	200
Tests Played:	42

Test Batting

Innings:	68	Runs:	2,290
Highest Score:	181	Average:	38.16
No. 50s:	12	No. 100s:	4

Test Bowling & Fielding

Wickets:	0	Runs:	0
Best Bowling:		Average:	0.00
5 WI:	0	10 WM:	0
Catches:	23	Stumpings:	0

A powerful and aggressive opening batsman, the Queenslander was the first Australian to tour five other Test cricket playing nations. On the 1961 Ashes tour Burge scored his first Test ton, a blazing 181 at The Oval and three years later was equally impressive scoring 160 at Headingly. It seemed that he saved his best for England, and he struck again at Melbourne during the 1965/66 series with 120 in the first innings. Burge featured near the top of the Australian Test batting averages in a number of series over a sustained period and along with Colin McDonald provided Australia with a fine opening combination for over a decade. In 1997 he was awarded the Medal for the Order of Australia for his services to cricket.

BURKE, James Wallace

Born:	June 12, 1930
Batting:	Right handed
Bowling:	Right arm off-break

Tests

Test Career:	1951-59
Cap Number:	187
Tests Played:	24

Test Batting

Innings:	44	Runs:	1,280
Highest Score:	189	Average:	34.59
No. 50s:	5	No. 100s:	3

Test Bowling & Fielding

Wickets:	8	Runs:	230
Best Bowling:	4/37	Average:	28.75
5 WI:	0	10 WM:	0
Catches:	18	Stumpings:	0

A tall and lean opener from Sydney, he could at best be described as a cautious batsman. Burke made an unbeaten century in his first Test against the English in 1951 and would go on to score big hundreds in Tests against India and South Africa. His near impenetrable defense was used to good effect against the English in 1958 when he crawled to 28 in over four hours at Brisbane. He tragically took his own life at the age of only 48.

BURN, Edwin James Kenneth

Born:	September 17, 1862
Batting:	Right handed

Tests

Test Career:	1890
Cap Number:	56
Tests Played:	2

Test Batting

Innings:	4	Runs:	41
Highest Score:	19	Average:	10.25
No. 50s:	0	No. 100s:	0

Test Bowling & Fielding

Wickets:	0	Runs:	0
Best Bowling:		Average:	0.00
5 WI:	0	10 WM:	0
Catches:	0	Stumpings:	0

His position in the Australian side to tour England in 1890 is surely cricket's greatest selection blunder. Word had found its way to the Australian Test selectors that Tasmania had a talented wicketkeeper by the name of Burn. It was not until 'The Scotsman', as Burn was known, was aboard the ship to England, that he informed team mates that he had never kept wickets in his life. He was however a solid batsman who did play in two of the three Tests on that tour.

BURTON, Frederick John

Born: November 2, 1865
Batting: Right handed
 Wicket Keeper

Tests
Test Career: 1887-88
Cap Number: 48
Tests Played: 2

Test Batting
Innings:	2	Runs:	4
Highest Score:	2*	Average:	2.00
No. 50s:	0	No. 100s:	0

Test Bowling & Fielding
Wickets:	0	Runs:	0
Best Bowling:		Average:	0.00
5 WI:	0	10 WM:	0
Catches:	1	Stumpings:	1

A Victorian wicket keeper who later moved to New South Wales then on to New Zealand.

CALLAWAY, Sydney Thomas

Born: February 6, 1868
Batting: Right handed
Bowling: Right arm medium-fast

Tests
Test Career: 1892-95
Cap Number: 60
Tests Played: 3

Test Batting
Innings:	6	Runs:	87
Highest Score:	41	Average:	17.39
No. 50s:	0	No. 100s:	0

Test Bowling & Fielding
Wickets:	6	Runs:	142
Best Bowling:	5/37	Average:	23.66
5 WI:	1	10 WM:	0
Catches:	0	Stumpings:	0

A Sydney born bowler who performed more than ably in his third and final Test, taking five wickets in an innings and making a brave 41 batting at number 11. Moved to New Zealand shortly after.

CALLEN, Ian Wayne

Born: May 2, 1955
Batting: Left handed
Bowling: Right arm fast

Tests
Test Career: 1978
Cap Number: 291
Tests Played: 1

Test Batting
Innings:	2	Runs:	26
Highest Score:	22*	Average:	0.00
No. 50s:	0	No. 100s:	0

Test Bowling & Fielding
Wickets:	6	Runs:	191
Best Bowling:	3/83	Average:	31.83
5 WI:	0	10 WM:	0
Catches:	1	Stumpings:	0

One Day Internationals
ODI Career: 1978-82
ODIs Played: 5

ODI Batting
Innings:	3	Runs:	6
Highest Score:	3*	Average:	6.00
No. 50s:	0	No. 100s:	0

ODI Bowling & Fielding
Wickets:	5	Runs:	148
Best Bowling:	3/24	Average:	29.60
5 WM:	0	Catches:	2
Stumpings:	0		

A fiery opening bowler from Victoria that went by the nickname 'Mad Dog' whose only Test was on a tour of the Caribbean in 1978. Callen worked in the sporting goods business after his retirement and produced his own line of cricket bats.

CAMPBELL, Gregory Dale

Born: April 10, 1964
Batting: Right handed
Bowling: Right arm medium-fast

Tests
Test Career: 1989-90
Cap Number: 347
Tests Played: 4

Test Batting
Innings:	4	Runs:	10
Highest Score:	6	Average:	2.50
No. 50s:	0	No. 100s:	0

Test Bowling & Fielding
Wickets:	13	Runs:	503
Best Bowling:	3/79	Average:	38.69
5 WI:	0	10 WM:	0
Catches:	1	Stumpings:	0

One Day Internationals
ODI Career: 1989-90
ODIs Played: 12

ODI Batting
Innings:	3	Runs:	6
Highest Score:	4*	Average:	3.00
No. 50s:	0	No. 100s:	0

ODI Bowling & Fielding
Wickets:	18	Runs:	404
Best Bowling:	3/17	Average:	22.44
5 WM:	0	Catches:	4
Stumpings:	0		

A snowy haired paceman from Tasmania, he was a member of the Australian squad that toured England in 1989. Unusually his four career Tests were against four different cricket playing nations; England, Sri Lanka, Pakistan and New Zealand.

CAMPBELL, Ryan John

Born: February 7, 1972
Batting: Right handed
 Wicket Keeper

One Day Internationals
ODI Career: 2002
ODIs Played: 2

ODI Batting
Innings:	2	Runs:	54
Highest Score:	38	Average:	27.00
No. 50s:	0	No. 100s:	0

ODI Bowling & Fielding
Wickets:	0	Runs:	0
Best Bowling:		Average:	0.00
5 WM:	0	Catches:	4
Stumpings:	1		

A punishing top order batsman/wicket keeper from Western Australia who got his chance on the two rare occasions Adam Gilchrist was unavailable for national duty.

CARKEEK, William (Barlow)
Born: October 17, 1878
Batting: Left handed
Wicket Keeper

Tests
Test Career: 1912
Cap Number: 101
Tests Played: 6

Test Batting
Innings:	5	Runs:	16
Highest Score:	6*	Average:	5.33
No. 50s:	0	No. 100s:	0

Test Bowling & Fielding
Wickets:	0	Runs:	0
Best Bowling:		Average:	0.00
5 WI:	0	10 WM:	0
Catches:	6	Stumpings:	0

Reserve wicket keeper on the tour of England in 1909, his moderate and at times obdurate batting kept him from playing more Tests. Also a prominent Rules footballer.

CARLSON, Philip Henry
Born: August 8, 1951
Batting: Right handed
Bowling: Right arm medium

Tests
Test Career: 1979
Cap Number: 300
Tests Played: 2

Test Batting
Innings:	4	Runs:	23
Highest Score:	21	Average:	5.75
No. 50s:	0	No. 100s:	0

Test Bowling & Fielding
Wickets:	2	Runs:	99
Best Bowling:	2/41	Average:	49.50
5 WI:	0	10 WM:	0
Catches:	2	Stumpings:	0

One Day Internationals
ODI Career: 1979
ODIs Played: 4

ODI Batting
Innings:	2	Runs:	11
Highest Score:	11	Average:	5.50
No. 50s:	0	No. 100s:	0

ODI Bowling & Fielding
Wickets:	2	Runs:	70
Best Bowling:	1/21	Average:	35.00
5 WM:	0	Catches:	0
Stumpings:	0		

A chirpy all-rounder from Nundah in Queensland who played all his international cricket in the summer of 1978/79.

CARTER, Hanson (Sammy)
Born: March 15, 1878
Batting: Right handed
Wicket Keeper

Tests
Test Career: 1907-21
Cap Number: 88
Tests Played: 28

Test Batting
Innings:	47	Runs:	873
Highest Score:	72	Average:	22.97
No. 50s:	4	No. 100s:	0

Test Bowling & Fielding
Wickets:	0	Runs:	0
Best Bowling:		Average:	0.00
5 WI:	0	10 WM:	0
Catches:	44	Stumpings:	21

Born in England, Sammy or Sep Carter kept wickets for Australia in an interrupted career that spanned 14 years. The Great War and opposition from other Australian wicket keepers limited him to 28 Tests, but he proved reliable both behind the stumps and with the bat. He toured England on three occasions, a fact which was said to have brought him a great deal of pleasure as it enabled him to visit his native Yorkshire.

CHAPPELL, Gregory Stephen
Born: August 7, 1948
Batting: Right handed
Bowling: Right arm medium

Tests
Test Career: 1970-84
Cap Number: 251
Tests Played: 87

Test Batting
Innings:	151	Runs:	7,110
Highest Score:	247*	Average:	53.86
No. 50s:	31	No. 100s:	24

Test Bowling & Fielding
Wickets:	47	Runs:	1,913
Best Bowling:	5/61	Average:	40.70
5 WI:	1	10 WM:	0
Catches:	122	Stumpings:	0

One Day Internationals
ODI Career: 1971-83
ODIs Played: 74

ODI Batting
Innings:	72	Runs:	2,331
Highest Score:	138*	Average:	40.18
No. 50s:	14	No. 100s:	3

ODI Bowling & Fielding
Wickets:	72	Runs:	2,097
Best Bowling:	5/15	Average:	29.12
5 WM:	2	Catches:	23
Stumpings:	0		

In cricket, style does not always equate with results, but in the case of Greg Chappell it took him to the very top of the tree. Selected in his brother's Australian Test side at the age of 22, he scored a telling century in his first innings. That knock of 108 included the elegant on and off drives that would become the trademark strokes of the master batsman. He could pay any shot, but favoured driving as he said that at the start of any innings he always batted though the 'V', a reference to the area between cover and mid-wicket. For almost fifteen years he was a dominant force in all forms of cricket, including his time against the best in World Series Cricket. His career high Test score of 247 not out was against New Zealand in Wellington in 1974. He scored 133 in the second innings of that game and incredibly his brother Ian also scored a century in both innings. The brilliant top order batsman scored a double century against Pakistan at Brisbane in 1981 then went through an uncharacteristic run of poor form when he scored seven ducks in fifteen innings. Chappell said at the time that when you score ducks you're not out of form you're just not getting a chance to bat, and he proved that theory right with a faultless 176 against New Zealand in the final Test of the 1981/82 summer. His Test career ended as it began, with a perfectly executed century, 182 against Pakistan at the SCG in 1984. When Greg Chappell brought the curtain down on his international career he had a Test average above 50 and ODI average above 40, both marks of a great batsman. He was also a clever change bowler who sent down controlled medium pace with the occasional fast and nasty bouncer thrown in for good measure. Chappell was an intelligent captain, who while lacking the fire of his brother, still had a deep competitive streak. That cricket brain and will to win were at work when he instructed his younger brother Trevor to bowl that famous underarm delivery to Brian McKechnie in 1981. Greg Chappell has resisted the path followed by many former Australia Test captains, and rather than become a commentator, has concentrated on coaching. Today he holds down the challenging position of coach of the Indian national side.

CHAPPELL, Ian Michael

Born:	September 26, 1943
Batting:	Right handed
Bowling:	Right arm leg-break

Tests

Test Career:	1964-80
Cap Number:	231
Tests Played:	75

Test Batting

Innings:	136	Runs:	5,345
Highest Score:	196	Average:	42.42
No. 50s:	26	No. 100s:	14

Test Bowling & Fielding

Wickets:	20	Runs:	1,316
Best Bowling:	2/21	Average:	65.80
5 WI:	0	10 WM:	0
Catches:	105	Stumpings:	0

One Day Internationals

ODI Career:	1971-80
ODIs Played:	16

ODI Batting

Innings:	16	Runs:	673
Highest Score:	86	Average:	48.07
No. 50s:	8	No. 100s:	0

ODI Bowling & Fielding

Wickets:	2	Runs:	23
Best Bowling:	2/14	Average:	11.50
5 WM:	0	Catches:	5
Stumpings:	0		

Seemingly born to represent his country, the grandson of the great Victor Richardson was one of the most influential figures in the history of Australian cricket. A brilliant junior baseballer, Ian Chappell made his Test debut at the age of 21. His early Test record was only moderate and it took him until his tenth Test to make his maiden century, 151 against India at the MCG. It was as captain that Chappell would flourish both as a player and a leader. He took over from Bill Lawry in 1971 and instilled a new aggressiveness to the national side that remains with Australian teams to this day. He was generally a forceful batsman with a penchant for hooking that brought him countless runs and cost him his wicket on a number of occasions. If required however he would temper his natural aggressive streak and employ one of the soundest defences in the game. He starred in the series against the Rest of the World in Australia scoring four centuries and establishing himself as a world class batsman along the way. Under his captaincy Australia would return to the top of the cricketing tree. He secured a draw in the 1972 Ashes series before enjoying series wins against Pakistan and the West Indies. His crowning glory came in 1974/75 when Australia thrashed the English on home soil to regain the Ashes 4-1. In 1975, Australia retained the Ashes 1-0 and Ian Chappell announced his retirement as skipper, scoring 192 at The Oval in his final game at the helm. By the end of 1976 he turned his back on the cricket establishment and became a key player in the creation of World Series Cricket. It was a difficult time for Australian cricket but the outspoken former national captain was steadfast in his belief that cricketers deserved to be better remunerated for their efforts. He worked tirelessly for the breakaway group, both as a player and promoter and has been rewarded to this day by a position with the TV network that was central to its creation. Following the reunification of cricket he made a comeback to the Test arena, scoring 75 in his final Test against England at the MCG. Always willing to speak his mind, Chappelli has polarised opinions from the day he first pulled on a baggy green cap. Whether bearing his backside at the Adelaide Oval or slipping out the magic word whilst calling the game, Ian Chappell has never been far from the spotlight and the game is all the better for it.

CHAPPELL, Trevor Martin

Born:	October 21, 1952
Batting:	Right handed
Bowling:	Right arm medium

Tests
Test Career:	1981
Cap Number:	311
Tests Played:	3

Test Batting
Innings:	6	Runs:	79
Highest Score:	27	Average:	15.80
No. 50s:	0	No. 100s:	0

Test Bowling & Fielding
Wickets:	0	Runs:	0
Best Bowling:		Average:	0.00
5 WI:	0	10 WM:	0
Catches:	2	Stumpings:	0

One Day Internationals
ODI Career:	1980-83
ODIs Played:	20

ODI Batting
Innings:	13	Runs:	229
Highest Score:	110	Average:	17.61
No. 50s:	0	No. 100s:	1

ODI Bowling & Fielding
Wickets:	19	Runs:	538
Best Bowling:	3/31	Average:	28.31
5 WM:	0	Catches:	8
Stumpings:	0		

If living in the shadows of two famous cricketing brothers wasn't enough, Trevor Chappell also has to endure the fact he played a central role in one of the sport's most infamous moments. A talented all-rounder, he was bowling the final over of a one day game between Australia and New Zealand at the MCG in 1981 when his brother, and skipper, Greg instructed him to bowl the final delivery of the game along the pitch. The idea was to prevent the New Zealanders from hitting the six runs required to tie the game, but what ensued was an international incident. Unfortunately the name Trevor Chappell will always be associated with what came to be known as the 'underarm affair'.

CHARLTON, Percie Chater

Born:	April 9, 1867
Batting:	Right handed
Bowling:	Right arm medium-fast

Tests
Test Career:	1890
Cap Number:	57
Tests Played:	2

Test Batting
Innings:	4	Runs:	29
Highest Score:	11	Average:	7.25
No. 50s:	0	No. 100s:	0

Test Bowling & Fielding
Wickets:	3	Runs:	24
Best Bowling:	3/18	Average:	8.00
5 WI:	0	10 WM:	0
Catches:	0	Stumpings:	0

A promising medium pace bowler from New South Wales whose cricket career was curtailed by injuries.

CHIPPERFIELD, Arthur Gordon

Born:	November 17, 1905
Batting:	Right handed
Bowling:	Right arm leg-break

Tests
Test Career:	1934-38
Cap Number:	151
Tests Played:	14

Test Batting
Innings:	20	Runs:	552
Highest Score:	109	Average:	32.47
No. 50s:	2	No. 100s:	1

Test Bowling & Fielding
Wickets:	5	Runs:	437
Best Bowling:	3/91	Average:	87.40
5 WI:	0	10 WM:	0
Catches:	15	Stumpings:	0

A chunky left handed batsman from New South Wales, he stood tall in one of Australia's worst Test performances. In 1936 at the 'Gabba the Aussies were routed in the second innings for only 58 with 'Chipper' left stranded on 26 not out. In 14 Tests his only century was at Durban in 1935/36, scoring 109. He also bowled off spin with limited success.

CLARK, Stuart Rupert

Born:	September 28, 1975
Batting:	Right handed
Bowling:	Right arm medium-fast

Tests
Test Career:	2006-
Cap Number:	396
Tests Played:	4

Test Batting
Innings:	5	Runs:	31
Highest Score:	13*	Average:	10.33
No. 50s:	0	No. 100s:	0

Test Bowling & Fielding
Wickets:	21	Runs:	394
Best Bowling:	5/55	Average:	18.76
5 WI:	1	10 WM:	0
Catches:	2	Stumpings:	0

One Day Internationals
ODI Career:	2006-
ODIs Played:	15

ODI Batting
Innings:	3	Runs:	33
Highest Score:	16*	Average:	33.00
No. 50s:	0	No. 100s:	0

ODI Bowling & Fielding
Wickets:	23	Runs:	688
Best Bowling:	4/55	Average:	29.91
5 WM:	0	Catches:	4
Stumpings:	0		

When little known New South Welshman Stuart Clark was selected for the tour of South Africa in early 2006, cricket fans south of the border were once again crying conspiracy. Convinced that the tall right arm quick had been picked because of the colour of his state cap they overlooked the fact that he had taken over 200 first class wickets at less that 30 runs apiece. By the time he had played in four Tests, two each against South Africa and Bangladesh, they were left in no doubt that the selectors were on a winner. Clark took 21 wickets in those four Tests including the brilliant match figures of 9/89 on debut at Cape Town. With Glenn McGrath set to resume for the 2006/07 Ashes series, fast bowling spots will be at a premium, but no-one will be surprised this time if Stuart Clark gets the nod.

CLARK, Wayne Maxwell

Born: September 19, 1953
Batting: Right handed
Bowling: Right arm medium-fast

Tests
Test Career: 1977-79
Cap Number: 283
Tests Played: 10

Test Batting
Innings:	19	Runs:	98
Highest Score:	33	Average:	5.76
No. 50s:	0	No. 100s:	0

Test Bowling & Fielding
Wickets:	44	Runs:	1,265
Best Bowling:	4/46	Average:	28.75
5 WI:	0	10 WM:	0
Catches:	6	Stumpings:	0

One Day Internationals
ODI Career: 1978
ODIs Played: 2

ODI Batting
Innings:	0	Runs:	0
Highest Score:	0	Average:	0.00
No. 50s:	0	No. 100s:	0

ODI Bowling & Fielding
Wickets:	3	Runs:	61
Best Bowling:	2/39	Average:	20.33
5 WM:	0	Catches:	0
Stumpings:	0		

One of a number of players who was given an opportunity at the highest level by the defection of leading cricketers to World Series Cricket. Clark grasped his opportunity with both hands, taking 44 wickets in ten Tests. It was a fine return for a bowler who was fighting for a spot in his state side not long before making his Test debut. Clark went on to become a successful coach in both England and Australia

CLARKE, Michael John

Born: April 2, 1981
Batting: Right handed
Bowling: Left arm off-break

Tests
Test Career: 2004-
Cap Number: 389
Tests Played: 22

Test Batting
Innings:	34	Runs:	1,123
Highest Score:	151	Average:	36.22
No. 50s:	4	No. 100s:	2

Test Bowling & Fielding
Wickets:	8	Runs:	75
Best Bowling:	6/9	Average:	9.37
5 WI:	1	10 WM:	0
Catches:	18	Stumpings:	0

One Day Internationals
ODI Career: 2003-
ODIs Played: 82

ODI Batting
Innings:	73	Runs:	2,393
Highest Score:	105*	Average:	44.31
No. 50s:	17	No. 100s:	2

ODI Bowling & Fielding
Wickets:	25	Runs:	910
Best Bowling:	5/35	Average:	36.40
5 WM:	1	Catches:	33
Stumpings:	0		

An exuberant middle order batsman from New South Wales, he had been singled out to lead the next generation of Australian cricket from a young age. The former Australian Under 19 captain made his international debut in the one day side as a 22 year old and made an immediate impression as a talent with maturity beyond his years. It was natural that Test selection would follow soon after, but even his most optimistic supporters couldn't imagine that he would score 151 on debut in India. The juggernaut continued with a debut century on home soil against New Zealand at the 'Gabba. Sandwiched between those two fine innings was an amazing spell of left arm off spin in the final Test of the Indian tour when he took 6/9. Test cricket has a habit of giving and taking away and the youngster struggled in subsequent series until he was finally dropped when the West Indies toured Australia in 2005/06. Like Steve Waugh and Ricky Ponting before, his omission was seen as a temporary move and when the Australians toured Bangladesh in 2006 the young gun known to his teammates as 'Pup' was back in the side.

COLLEY, David John

Born: March 15, 1947
Batting: Right handed
Bowling: Right arm medium-fast

Tests
Test Career: 1972
Cap Number: 257
Tests Played: 3

Test Batting
Innings:	4	Runs:	84
Highest Score:	54	Average:	21.00
No. 50s:	1	No. 100s:	0

Test Bowling & Fielding			
Wickets:	6	Runs:	312
Best Bowling:	3/83	Average:	52.00
5 WI:	0	10 WM:	0
Catches:	1	Stumpings:	0

One Day Internationals

ODI Career:	1972		
ODIs Played:	1		
ODI Batting			
Innings:	0	Runs:	0
Highest Score:	0	Average:	0.00
No. 50s:	0	No. 100s:	0
ODI Bowling & Fielding			
Wickets:	0	Runs:	72
Best Bowling:		Average:	0.00
5 WM:	0	Catches:	0
Stumpings:	0		

A fast bowler from New South Wales who played his only three Tests on the Ashes tour to England in 1972.

COLLINS, Herbert Leslie

Born:	January 21, 1888
Batting:	Right handed
Bowling:	Right arm slow

Tests

Test Career:	1920-26		
Cap Number:	106		
Tests Played:	19		
Test Batting			
Innings:	31	Runs:	1,352
Highest Score:	203	Average:	45.06
No. 50s:	6	No. 100s:	4
Test Bowling & Fielding			
Wickets:	49	Runs:	252
Best Bowling:	2/47	Average:	63.00
5 WI:	0	10 WM:	0
Catches:	13	Stumpings:	0

Herbie Collins is one of Australia's lesser known captains, which is unfortunate given he was a fine cricketer possessed of an astute mind. Nicknamed 'Horseshoe', he was a resolute upper order batsman and handy change bowler, but it was as a leader that he made his mark. He took over the reins form Warwick Armstrong for the 1921 tour of South Africa which Australia won 3-0. Collins starred with the bat, averaging 85 for the three Tests and hitting a double ton at the Old Wanderers Ground along the way. He regained the captaincy for the Ashes series of 1924/25 that the Australians won convincingly four Tests to one. His final series as player and captain was the Ashes tour to England in 1926, which Australia lost and in which he failed to play the final two Tests because of illness. Following his retirement from cricket Horseshoe became a leading figure in the Sydney racing industry, first as a bookmaker then later as a stipendary steward.

CONINGHAM, Arthur

Born:	July 14, 1863
Batting:	Left handed
Bowling:	Left arm medium-fast

Tests

Test Career:	1894		
Cap Number:	69		
Tests Played:	1		
Test Batting			
Innings:	2	Runs:	13
Highest Score:	10	Average:	6.50
No. 50s:	0	No. 100s:	0
Test Bowling & Fielding			
Wickets:	2	Runs:	76
Best Bowling:	2/17	Average:	38.00
5 WI:	0	10 WM:	0
Catches:	0	Stumpings:	0

He was surely the most colourful character to have ever played Test cricket, and that includes those modern day players who currently fill the pages of the tabloids. Coningham was a bookmaker and bon vivant who was involved in one of Australia's most famous court cases. He represented himself in his own divorce proceedings during which he claimed and proved that the head of the Australian Catholic Church, Cardinal Moran had an affair with his wife that bore an illegitimate child. He lost the case but became Australia's most talked about cricketer in the process.

CONNOLLY, Norman

Born:	June 29, 1939
Batting:	Right handed
Bowling:	Right arm medium-fast

Tests

Test Career:	1963-71		
Cap Number:	225		
Tests Played:	29		
Test Batting			
Innings:	45	Runs:	260
Highest Score:	37	Average:	10.40
No. 50s:	0	No. 100s:	0
Test Bowling & Fielding			
Wickets:	102	Runs:	2,981
Best Bowling:	6/47	Average:	29.22
5 WI:	4	10 WM:	0
Catches:	17	Stumpings:	0

One Day Internationals

ODI Career:	1971		
ODIs Played:	1		
ODI Batting			
Innings:	0	Runs:	0
Highest Score:	0	Average:	0.00
No. 50s:	0	No. 100s:	0
ODI Bowling & Fielding			
Wickets:	0	Runs:	62
Best Bowling:		Average:	0.00
5 WM:	0	Catches:	0
Stumpings:	0		

A fine servant for state and country, the tall Victorian was a key member of the Australian side throughout the sixties. As the new ball partner for Graham McKenzie he often lived in the shadows, but there were times he stood alone, such as on the the Australian tour of South Africa in in 1969/70 when he took 20 wickets in Tests including a career best 6/47 at Port Elizabeth.

Connolly was plagued by back injuries throughout his career though it did not stop him becoming the first Victorian to pass the 300 wicket mark in state cricket.

COOK, Simon Hewitt
Born: January 29, 1972
Batting: Left handed
Bowling: Right arm medium-fast

Tests
Test Career: 1997
Cap Number: 373
Tests Played: 2

Test Batting
Innings:	2	Runs:	3
Highest Score:	3*	Average:	0.00
No. 50s:	0	No. 100s:	0

Test Bowling & Fielding
Wickets:	7	Runs:	142
Best Bowling:	5/39	Average:	20.28
5 WI:	1	10 WM:	0
Catches:	0	Stumpings:	0

When Simon Cook took seven wickets in his first Test against New Zealand at Perth in 1997 it looked as though a long international career beckoned. Unfortunately he lost his place in the side when Glenn McGrath returned from injury and was never seen at the highest level again.

COOPER, Bransby Beauchamp
Born: March 15, 1844
Batting: Right handed
Wicket Keeper

Tests
Test Career: 1877
Cap Number: 3
Tests Played: 1

Test Batting
Innings:	2	Runs:	18
Highest Score:	15	Average:	9.00
No. 50s:	0	No. 100s:	0

Test Bowling & Fielding
Wickets:	0	Runs:	0
Best Bowling:		Average:	0.00
5 WI:	0	10 WM:	0
Catches:	2	Stumpings:	0

Born in India, Cooper was educated at England's famous Rugby school. A batsman and part time wicket keeper, his only Test was the famous inaugural Test played at the MCG in 1877.

COOPER, William Henry
Born: September 11, 1849
Batting: Right handed
Bowling: Right arm leg-break

Tests
Test Career: 1881-84
Cap Number: 25
Tests Played: 2

Test Batting
Innings:	3	Runs:	13
Highest Score:	7	Average:	6.50
No. 50s:	0	No. 100s:	0

Test Bowling & Fielding
Wickets:	9	Runs:	226
Best Bowling:	6/120	Average:	25.11
5 WI:	1	10 WM:	0
Catches:	1	Stumpings:	0

A slow turning leg-spinner, Cooper's two Tests were both in Australia, though he did tour England in 1884. The great-grandfather of Australian Test batsman Paul Sheahan.

CORLING, Grahame Edward
Born: July 13, 1941
Batting: Right handed
Bowling: Right arm medium-fast

Tests
Test Career: 1964
Cap Number: 228
Tests Played: 5

Test Batting
Innings:	4	Runs:	5
Highest Score:	3	Average:	1.66
No. 50s:	0	No. 100s:	0

Test Bowling & Fielding
Wickets:	12	Runs:	447
Best Bowling:	4/60	Average:	37.25
5 WI:	0	10 WM:	0
Catches:	0	Stumpings:	0

A surprise selction for the Ashes tour in 1964, he was a right arm opening bowler from New South Wales.

COSGROVE, Mark James
Born: June 14, 1984
Batting: Left handed
Bowling: Right arm medium

One Day Internationals
ODI Career: 2006-
ODIs Played: 1

ODI Batting
Innings:	1	Runs:	74
Highest Score:	74	Average:	74.00
No. 50s:	1	No. 100s:	0

ODI Bowling & Fielding
Wickets:	0	Runs:	12
Best Bowling:		Average:	0.00
5 WM:	0	Catches:	0
Stumpings:	0		

The hard hitting middle order batsman made headlines when the South Australian Cricket Association suspended his state contract at the start of the 2005/06 season because he had returned from club cricket in England carrying too much weight. The 21 year old went to work, losing the required five kilograms, and returned to cricket with a century in the domestic one-day competition. Cosgrove scored an impressive 74 in his only ODI and is being touted as a likely member of the Australian 2007 World Cup squad.

COSIER, Gary John
Born: April 25, 1953
Batting: Right handed
Bowling: Right arm medium

Tests
Test Career:	1975-78		
Cap Number:	274		
Tests Played:	18		

Test Batting
Innings:	32	Runs:	897
Highest Score:	168	Average:	28.93
No. 50s:	3	No. 100s:	2

Test Bowling & Fielding
Wickets:	5	Runs:	341
Best Bowling:	2/26	Average:	68.20
5 WI:	0	10 WM:	0
Catches:	14	Stumpings:	0

One Day Internationals
ODI Career:	1975-79		
ODIs Played:	9		

ODI Batting
Innings:	7	Runs:	154
Highest Score:	84	Average:	30.80
No. 50s:	1	No. 100s:	0

ODI Bowling & Fielding
Wickets:	14	Runs:	248
Best Bowling:	5/18	Average:	17.71
5 WM:	1	Catches:	4
Stumpings:	0		

Tall and heavy set, the much travelled Cosier burst onto the Test scene with a debut century at the MCG against the touring West Indies in 1975/76. Holding the bat suspended when taking guard, he was a particularly punishing driver and cutter of the ball. In the years following his impressive debut he was unable to hold down a regular Test spot and despite some fine efforts with the bat and on occasion with the ball he failed to live up to his early potential.

COTTAM, John Thomas
Born:	September 2, 1867
Batting:	Right handed
Bowling:	Right arm leg-break

Tests
Test Career:	1887		
Cap Number:	49		
Tests Played:	1		

Test Batting
Innings:	2	Runs:	4
Highest Score:	3	Average:	2.00
No. 50s:	0	No. 100s:	0

Test Bowling & Fielding
Wickets:	0	Runs:	0
Best Bowling:		Average:	0.00
5 WI:	0	10 WM:	0
Catches:	1	Stumpings:	0

A leg spinner from New South Wales who passed away at the age of 29 in Western Australia.

COTTER, Albert (Tibby)
Born:	December 3, 1884
Batting:	Right handed
Bowling:	Right arm medium-fast

Tests
Test Career:	1904-12		
Cap Number:	85		
Tests Played:	21		

Test Batting
Innings:	37	Runs:	457
Highest Score:	45	Average:	13.05
No. 50s:	0	No. 100s:	0

Test Bowling & Fielding
Wickets:	89	Runs:	2,549
Best Bowling:	7/148	Average:	28.64
5 WI:	7	10 WM:	0
Catches:	8	Stumpings:	0

Tibby Cotter was Australia's fastest bowler at the start of the last century, filling the shoes vacated by Ernie Jones. On his day he could run through any batting line up as proved by his eight wicket haul against England in the MCG Test of 1904. A report at the time described him as having a "powerful spear-throwing action that brings his whole body behind the ball' conjuring up an image of an early Jeff Thomson. He toured England with success in 1905 and 1909, taking five wickets in an innings at Headingly in the latter series. Albert Cotter was killed during World War I whilst serving in the Australian Light Horse.

COULTHARD, George
Born:	August 1, 1856
Batting:	Right handed
Bowling:	Right arm medium

Tests
Test Career:	1882		
Cap Number:	29		
Tests Played:	1		

Test Batting
Innings:	1	Runs:	6
Highest Score:	6*	Average:	6.00
No. 50s:	0	No. 100s:	0

Test Bowling & Fielding
Wickets:	0	Runs:	0
Best Bowling:		Average:	0.00
5 WI:	0	10 WM:	0
Catches:	0	Stumpings:	0

Coulthard was a champion all round sportsman excelling at Australian Rules football as well as cricket. He died of consumption only a year after playing in his only Test.

COWPER, Robert Maskew
Born:	October 5, 1940
Batting:	Left handed
Bowling:	Right arm off-break

Tests
Test Career:	1964-68		
Cap Number:	229		
Tests Played:	27		

Test Batting
Innings:	46	Runs:	2,061
Highest Score:	307	Average:	46.84
No. 50s:	10	No. 100s:	5

Test Bowling & Fielding
Wickets:	36	Runs:	1,139
Best Bowling:	4/48	Average:	31.63
5 WI:	0	10 WM:	0
Catches:	21	Stumpings:	0

Of all the Australian cricketers to have scored a Test triple century Bob Cowper may be the least well known, but to describe him as a one innings wonder would be doing a great injustice to a fine batsman. He made his debut on the Ashes tour of 1964, but it was on the tour of West Indies in 1965 that he truly made a name for himself. He scored two centuries and led the aggregates with 417 runs. Australia's next series was at home against England but poor form saw Cowper dropped for the fourth Test. He celebrated his recall in the fifth and final Test by compiling the highest ever score by a cricketer in a Test on Australian soil. His 307 was a drawn out affair, taking 727 minutes and ensured the match ended in a draw. Following that innings Cowper would continue to score heavily for his country, including two tons against the touring Indians in 1967/68. He was also a handy off spin bowler, who once took seven wickets in a Test against the Indians.

CRAIG, Ian David

Born: June 12, 1935
Batting: Right handed

Tests

Test Career: 1953-58
Cap Number: 194
Tests Played: 11

Test Batting

Innings:	18	Runs:	358
Highest Score:	53	Average:	19.88
No. 50s:	2	No. 100s:	0

Test Bowling & Fielding

Wickets:	0	Runs:	0
Best Bowling:		Average:	0.00
5 WI:	0	10 WM:	0
Catches:	2	Stumpings:	0

In Australian cricket if the question includes the word youngest, the answer most likely is Ian Craig. At 16 years and five months he was the youngest cricketer to play Sheffield Shield cricket, at 17 the youngest ever Australian Test player, and at 22 the youngest player to lead his country. For all those firsts he never reached any great heights as a Test cricketer, scoring only two half centuries with a Test high of 53. Craig enjoyed more success for New South Wales, playing for over a decade and amassing more than 6,500 first class runs.

CRAWFORD, William Patrick Anthony (Pat)

Born: August 3, 1933
Batting: Right handed
Bowling: Right arm fast

Tests

Test Career: 1956
Cap Number: 202
Tests Played: 4

Test Batting

Innings:	5	Runs:	53
Highest Score:	34	Average:	17.66
No. 50s:	0	No. 100s:	0

Test Bowling & Fielding

Wickets:	7	Runs:	107
Best Bowling:	3/28	Average:	15.28
5 WI:	0	10 WM:	0
Catches:	1	Stumpings:	0

A tall right arm quick from New South Wales who starred for his state as a 21 year old. Injuries curtailed his Test career and despite going on the tour of the sub-continent and England in 1956 could only manage four Tests. Went on to later play in England with success.

CULLEN, Dan James

Born: April 10, 1984
Batting: Right handed
Bowling: Right arm off-break

Tests

Test Career: 2006-
Cap Number: 397
Tests Played: 1

Test Batting

Innings:	0	Runs:	0
Highest Score:	0	Average:	0.00
No. 50s:	0	No. 100s:	0

Test Bowling & Fielding

Wickets:	1	Runs:	54
Best Bowling:	1/25	Average:	54.00
5 WI:	0	10 WM:	0
Catches:	0	Stumpings:	0

One Day Internationals

ODI Career: 2006-
ODIs Played: 3

ODI Batting

Innings:	0	Runs:	0
Highest Score:	0	Average:	0.00
No. 50s:	0	No. 100s:	0

ODI Bowling & Fielding

Wickets:	2	Runs:	98
Best Bowling:	2/25	Average:	49.00
5 WM:	0	Catches:	2
Stumpings:	0		

Australia's 397th and latest Test cap got his chance on the tour of Bangladesh in 2006. A promising off-spinner from South Australia, he received the Sir Donald Bradman award for Young Australian Cricketer of the Year in 2005/06.

DALE, Adam Craig

Born: December 30, 1968
Batting: Left handed
Bowling: Right arm medium-fast

Tests

Test Career: 1998-99
Cap Number: 377
Tests Played: 2

Test Batting

Innings:	3	Runs:	6
Highest Score:	5	Average:	2.00
No. 50s:	0	No. 100s:	0

Test Bowling & Fielding

Wickets:	6	Runs:	187
Best Bowling:	3/71	Average:	31.16
5 WI:	0	10 WM:	0
Catches:	0	Stumpings:	0

One Day Internationals	
ODI Career:	1997-2000
ODIs Played:	30

ODI Batting

Innings:	12	Runs:	78
Highest Score:	15*	Average:	19.50
No. 50s:	0	No. 100s:	0

ODI Bowling & Fielding

Wickets:	32	Runs:	979
Best Bowling:	3/18	Average:	30.59
5 WM:	0	Catches:	11
Stumpings:	0		

A sprightly medium pace bowler who had played most of his cricket in Victorian grade ranks before moving to Queensland. He enjoyed immediate success with his adopted state and was quickly noticed by national selectors who rewarded him with a spot in the Australian one day side. At 29, Dale made his Test debut against India at Bangalore, a prospect that would have seemed impossible only a couple of years earlier.

DARLING, Joseph

Born:	November 21, 1870
Batting:	Left handed

Tests

Test Career:	1894-1905		
Cap Number:	64		
Tests Played:	34		

Test Batting

Innings:	60	Runs:	1,657
Highest Score:	178	Average:	28.56
No. 50s:	8	No. 100s:	3

Test Bowling & Fielding

Wickets:	0	Runs:	0
Best Bowling:		Average:	0.00
5 WI:	0	10 WM:	0
Catches:	27	Stumpings:	0

Like George Giffen before him, he was a South Australian who had a huge influence in the early years of international cricket. He toured England on four occasions, the last three as captain and was considered one of Australia's most astute leaders with seven wins and only four losses in 21 Tests. It was in the Ashes series of 1897/98 that Joe Darling shone most brightly. He scored 500 runs, the first time any player reached that mark, plundering three ceturies along the way. One of those innings, 178 at the Adelaide Oval, is still considered to be one of the finest Test knocks of all time. In 1900 he moved to Tasmania where he took up life as a farmer, but continued to play for his country until 1905. Following his retirement from Test cricket he turned his hand to politics, and like his father, became a member of his state's Parliament.

DARLING, Leonard Stuart

Born:	August 14, 1909
Batting:	Left handed
Bowling:	Right arm medium

Tests

Test Career:	1933-37		
Cap Number:	147		
Tests Played:	12		

Test Batting

Innings:	18	Runs:	474
Highest Score:	85	Average:	27.88
No. 50s:	3	No. 100s:	0

Test Bowling & Fielding

Wickets:	0	Runs:	65
Best Bowling:		Average:	0.00
5 WI:	0	10 WM:	0
Catches:	8	Stumpings:	0

Len Darling scored over 3,000 runs for Victoria but failed to carry that good form with him into the Test arena. In 12 Tests he failed to score a century for his country, his highest score being 85 in the final Test of the Bodyline series in 1932/33. He was also an accomplished close in fieldsman.

DARLING, Warrick Maxwell (Rick)

Born:	May 1, 1957
Batting:	Right handed

Tests

Test Career:	1978-79		
Cap Number:	292		
Tests Played:	14		

Test Batting

Innings:	27	Runs:	697
Highest Score:	91	Average:	26.80
No. 50s:	6	No. 100s:	0

Test Bowling & Fielding

Wickets:	0	Runs:	0
Best Bowling:		Average:	0.00
5 WI:	0	10 WM:	0
Catches:	5	Stumpings:	0

One Day Internationals

ODI Career:	1978-82
ODIs Played:	18

ODI Batting

Innings:	18	Runs:	363
Highest Score:	74	Average:	21.35
No. 50s:	1	No. 100s:	0

ODI Bowling & Fielding

Wickets:	0	Runs:	0
Best Bowling:		Average:	0.00
5 WM:	0	Catches:	6
Stumpings:	0		

Related to one of the early greats of the game, Joe Darling, he made his debut as a 20 year old against the likes of Andy Roberts, Colin Croft and Joel Garner on the Caribbean tour of 1978. The courageous opener with bleach blonde hair was once again thrown to the wolves when Australia hosted England the following summer. It was on that tour that he was struck in the chest by Bob Willis and choked on a piece of chewing gum that almost cost him his life.

DAVIDSON, Alan Keith

Born:	June 14, 1929
Batting:	Left handed
Bowling:	Left arm medium-fast

DAVIDSON, Alan Keith

Tests
Test Career:	1953-63		
Cap Number:	195		
Tests Played:	44		

Test Batting
Innings:	61	Runs:	1,328
Highest Score:	80	Average:	24.59
No. 50s:	5	No. 100s:	0

Test Bowling & Fielding
Wickets:	186	Runs:	3,819
Best Bowling:	7/93	Average:	20.53
5 WI:	14	10 WM:	2
Catches:	42	Stumpings:	0

For over a decade Australian cricket could always be assured of a return from Alan Davidson. Despite a relatively short run-up, the left hander was quick through the air, and when he combined that with his ability to gain late movement, he proved to be an irresistable force. He took 33 wickets against the West Indies in the 1960/61 Test series including a telling contribution in the famous tied Test at Brisbane, where he became the first player to score 100 and take 10 wickets in the same Test. His match return of 44 and 80 with the bat and 5/135 and 6/87 with the ball remains one of the great efforts by an all-rounder in a single Test. He took five wickets or more in an innings on 14 occasions, including a career best 7/93 against the Indians in Kanpur. Davidson was also a punishing lower order batsman, and whilst he never scored a Test hundred, he played a key role in many Australian victories. A brilliant out fieldsman, he was a fine Test cricketer who would have unquestionably been a star in one day cricket had he been given the chance.

DAVIS, Ian Charles

Born:	June 25, 1953
Batting:	Right handed

Tests
Test Career:	1974-77		
Cap Number:	266		
Tests Played:	15		

Test Batting
Innings:	27	Runs:	692
Highest Score:	105	Average:	26.61
No. 50s:	4	No. 100s:	1

Test Bowling & Fielding
Wickets:	0	Runs:	0
Best Bowling:		Average:	0.00
5 WI:	0	10 WM:	0
Catches:	9	Stumpings:	0

One Day Internationals
ODI Career:	1974-77
ODIs Played:	3

ODI Batting
Innings:	3	Runs:	12
Highest Score:	11*	Average:	6.00
No. 50s:	0	No. 100s:	0

ODI Bowling & Fielding
Wickets:	0	Runs:	0
Best Bowling:		Average:	0.00
5 WM:	0	Catches:	0
Stumpings:	0		

Great things were predicted for the young New South Welshman when he made his debut at the age of 20, but his career was seemingly short circuited by World Series Cricket. In 1976/77 he enjoyed a very good series against Pakistan, scoring his maiden Test ton at Adelaide and averaging 49. That form saw him earn a spot in the Centenary Test team at the MCG in 1977 and he repaid the selectors faith by scoring a valuable 68 in the second innings. Soon after Davis joined WSC, and whilst the foray into the world of serious professional cricket enhanced the reputation of many of his team mates it did little for his. Following the game's reunification Davis could not force his way back into the national side.

DAVIS, Simon Peter

Born:	November 8, 1959
Batting:	Right handed
Bowling:	Right arm medium-fast

Tests
Test Career:	1986
Cap Number:	336
Tests Played:	1

Test Batting
Innings:	1	Runs:	0
Highest Score:	0	Average:	0.00
No. 50s:	0	No. 100s:	0

Test Bowling & Fielding
Wickets:	0	Runs:	70
Best Bowling:		Average:	0.00
5 WI:	0	10 WM:	0
Catches:	0	Stumpings:	0

One Day Internationals
ODI Career:	1986-88
ODIs Played:	39

ODI Batting
Innings:	11	Runs:	20
Highest Score:	6	Average:	5.00
No. 50s:	0	No. 100s:	0

ODI Bowling & Fielding
Wickets:	44	Runs:	1,133
Best Bowling:	3/10	Average:	25.75
5 WM:	0	Catches:	5
Stumpings:	0		

An accurate paceman from Victoria, he lacked the penetration to play regular Test cricket but was a willing performer in the shorter version of the game.

DE COURCY, James Henry

Born:	April 18, 1927
Batting:	Right handed

Tests
Test Career:	1953
Cap Number:	197
Tests Played:	3

Test Batting				
Innings:	6	Runs:	81
Highest Score:	41	Average:	16.20
No. 50s:	0	No. 100s:	0
Test Bowling & Fielding				
Wickets:	0	Runs:	0
Best Bowling:		Average:	0.00
5 WI:	0	10 WM:	0
Catches:	3	Stumpings:	0

A prolific run scorer for NSW in domestic competition, he was selected to tour England in 1953 but was never able to secure a permanent Test spot.

DELL, Anthony Ross

Born: August 6, 1947
Batting: Right handed
Bowling: Left arm medium-fast

Tests
Test Career: 1971-73
Cap Number: 255
Tests Played: 2

Test Batting				
Innings:	2	Runs:	6
Highest Score:	3*	Average:	6.00
No. 50s:	0	No. 100s:	0
Test Bowling & Fielding				
Wickets:	6	Runs:	160
Best Bowling:	3/65	Average:	26.66
5 WI:	0	10 WM:	0
Catches:	0	Stumpings:	0

A more than handy left arm speedster from Queensland, his meagre return of only two Tests was more a reflection of the strength of Australian fast bowling at the time rather than a comment on his ability.

DI VENUTO, Michael James

Born: December 12, 1973
Batting: Left handed

One Day Internationals
ODI Career: 1997
ODIs Played: 9

ODI Batting				
Innings:	9	Runs:	241
Highest Score:	89	Average:	26.77
No. 50s:	2	No. 100s:	0
ODI Bowling & Fielding				
Wickets:	0	Runs:	0
Best Bowling:		Average:	0.00
5 WM:	0	Catches:	1
Stumpings:	0		

The left handed opener from Tasmania was given his chance at the top of the Australian order in their one day sides during 1997. He performed adequately, but when the emerging Adam Gilchrist put his hand up for the opener's spot it effectively ended Di Venuto's international career. He returned to state cricket and his position as one of the highest scoring players in the domestic game.

DODEMAIDE, Anthony Ian Christopher (Tony)

Born: October 5, 1963
Batting: Right handed
Bowling: Right arm medium-fast

Tests
Test Career: 1987-92
Cap Number: 343
Tests Played: 10

Test Batting				
Innings:	15	Runs:	202
Highest Score:	50	Average:	22.44
No. 50s:	1	No. 100s:	0
Test Bowling & Fielding				
Wickets:	34	Runs:	953
Best Bowling:	6/58	Average:	28.02
5 WI:	1	10 WM:	0
Catches:	6	Stumpings:	0

One Day Internationals
ODI Career: 1988-93
ODIs Played: 24

ODI Batting				
Innings:	16	Runs:	124
Highest Score:	30	Average:	13.77
No. 50s:	0	No. 100s:	0
ODI Bowling & Fielding				
Wickets:	36	Runs:	753
Best Bowling:	5/21	Average:	20.91
5 WM:	1	Catches:	7
Stumpings:	0		

Tony Dodemaide made a spectacular start to his international career, making a half century and taking a 'five for' against New Zealand in his first Test, then following it up a week later with another five wicket bag against Sri Lanka in his first ODI. Unsurprisingly he couldn't maintain that form, but the Victorian all-rounder was a handy performer when called on by his country. Highly educated, he studied and played cricket overseas before returning home to take up the position of CEO for the West Australian Cricket Association.

DONNAN, Henry (Harry)

Born: November 12, 1864
Batting: Right handed
Bowling: Right arm medium

Tests
Test Career: 1892-96
Cap Number: 61
Tests Played: 5

Test Batting				
Innings:	10	Runs:	75
Highest Score:	15	Average:	8.33
No. 50s:	0	No. 100s:	0
Test Bowling & Fielding				
Wickets:	0	Runs:	22
Best Bowling:		Average:	0.00
5 WI:	0	10 WM:	0
Catches:	1	Stumpings:	0

A stand out performer for New South Wales in Shield competition, Harry Donnan failed in numerous appearances for Australia.

DOOLAND, Bruce
Born: November 1, 1923
Batting: Right handed
Bowling: Right arm leg-break

Tests
Test Career: 1947-48
Cap Number: 174
Tests Played: 3

Test Batting
Innings:	5	Runs:	76
Highest Score:	29	Average:	19.00
No. 50s:	0	No. 100s:	0

Test Bowling & Fielding
Wickets:	9	Runs:	419
Best Bowling:	4/69	Average:	46.55
5 WI:	0	10 WM:	0
Catches:	3	Stumpings:	0

A talented leg-spinner and batsman, who like George Tribe in the same era, moved to England to play professionally. Enjoyed great success with Nottinghamshire.

DOREY, Brett Raymond
Born: October 3, 1977
Batting: Right handed
Bowling: Right arm medium-fast

One Day Internationals
ODI Career: 2006-
ODIs Played: 4

ODI Batting
Innings:	1	Runs:	2
Highest Score:	2	Average:	2.00
No. 50s:	0	No. 100s:	0

ODI Bowling & Fielding
Wickets:	2	Runs:	146
Best Bowling:	1/12	Average:	73.00
5 WM:	0	Catches:	0
Stumpings:	0		

At over 200cm he was a surprise selection in the Australian one day side in 2006 having played only a handful of first class games for West Australia.

DUFF, Reginald Alexander
Born: August 17, 1878
Batting: Right handed
Bowling: Right arm medium

Tests
Test Career: 1902-05
Cap Number: 81
Tests Played: 22

Test Batting
Innings:	40	Runs:	1,317
Highest Score:	146	Average:	35.59
No. 50s:	6	No. 100s:	2

Test Bowling & Fielding
Wickets:	4	Runs:	85
Best Bowling:	2/43	Average:	21.25
5 WI:	0	10 WM:	0
Catches:	14	Stumpings:	0

A versatile batsman from New South Wales who scored a century in his first Test at the MCG in 1902. Duff was considered the ideal man for a crisis and held down almost every batting position from opener to number eight.

DUNCAN, John Ross Frederick
Born: March 25, 1944
Batting: Right handed
Bowling: Right arm medium-fast

Tests
Test Career: 1971
Cap Number: 252
Tests Played: 1

Test Batting
Innings:	1	Runs:	3
Highest Score:	3	Average:	3.00
No. 50s:	0	No. 100s:	0

Test Bowling & Fielding
Wickets:	0	Runs:	30
Best Bowling:		Average:	0.00
5 WI:	0	10 WM:	0
Catches:	0	Stumpings:	0

A right arm medium pacer who played his only Test against England at the MCG in 1971.

DYER, Gregory Charles
Born: April 16, 1959
Batting: Right handed
         Wicket Keeper

Tests
Test Career: 1986-88
Cap Number: 339
Tests Played: 6

Test Batting
Innings:	6	Runs:	131
Highest Score:	60	Average:	21.83
No. 50s:	1	No. 100s:	0

Test Bowling & Fielding
Wickets:	0	Runs:	0
Best Bowling:		Average:	0.00
5 WI:	0	10 WM:	0
Catches:	22	Stumpings:	2

One Day Internationals
ODI Career: 1986-88
ODIs Played: 23

ODI Batting
Innings:	13	Runs:	174
Highest Score:	45*	Average:	15.81
No. 50s:	0	No. 100s:	0

ODI Bowling & Fielding
Wickets:	0	Runs:	0
Best Bowling:		Average:	0.00
5 WM:	0	Catches:	24
Stumpings:	4		

A nimble keeper from NSW, he was a member of the Australia side that won the World Cup in 1987. In 1988 at the MCG he claimed a catch off Kiwi batsman Andrew Jones that TV cameras showed had clearly hit the ground. The incident stoked the fires of an already strained relationship between the two cricketing neighbours and by the end of that summer he had played his last Test. Speculation suggested that the incident at the MCG cost Dyer his spot in the team, a harsh punishment given that he was hardly the first cricketer to claim a catch that wasn't. The affair seemed to sour Dyer and he retired from first class cricket altogether the next summer.

DYMOCK, Geoffrey
Born: July 21, 1945
Batting: Left handed
Bowling: Left arm medium-fast

Tests
Test Career:	1974-80		
Cap Number:	268		
Tests Played:	21		

Test Batting
Innings:	32	Runs:	236
Highest Score:	31*	Average:	9.44
No. 50s:	0	No. 100s:	0

Test Bowling & Fielding
Wickets:	78	Runs:	2,116
Best Bowling:	7/67	Average:	27.12
5 WI:	5	10 WM:	1
Catches:	1	Stumpings:	0

One Day Internationals
ODI Career:	1974-80
ODIs Played:	15

ODI Batting
Innings:	7	Runs:	35
Highest Score:	14*	Average:	11.66
No. 50s:	0	No. 100s:	0

ODI Bowling & Fielding
Wickets:	15	Runs:	412
Best Bowling:	2/21	Average:	27.46
5 WM:	0	Catches:	1
Stumpings:	0		

Unlucky to play at a time when Australia had an embarrassment of fast bowling riches, the left handed quick was rated by many opposition batsmen to be as difficult to face as his more illustrious contemporaries. He took five wickets on debut against New Zealand in the second innings of the third Test at Adelaide in 1973/74, but struggled to hold his spot in the side until the advent of World Series Cricket. Dymock enjoyed a purple patch of form in the late 1970's including a single Test against India at Kanpur where he took 12 wickets in a side that was soundly beaten.

DYSON, John
Born: June 11, 1954
Batting: Right handed

Tests
Test Career:	1977-84
Cap Number:	289
Tests Played:	30

Test Batting
Innings:	58	Runs:	1,359
Highest Score:	127*	Average:	26.54
No. 50s:	5	No. 100s:	2

Test Bowling & Fielding
Wickets:	0	Runs:	0
Best Bowling:		Average:	0.00
5 WI:	0	10 WM:	0
Catches:	10	Stumpings:	0

One Day Internationals
ODI Career:	1980-83
ODIs Played:	29

ODI Batting
Innings:	27	Runs:	755
Highest Score:	79	Average:	32.82
No. 50s:	4	No. 100s:	0

ODI Bowling & Fielding
Wickets:	0	Runs:	0
Best Bowling:		Average:	0.00
5 WM:	0	Catches:	12
Stumpings:	0		

A right handed opener from New South Wales, he worked his way into the Australian side in 1977 and was rewarded with a half century on debut. Dyson was a surprise selection to tour England in 1981 and despite a relatively modest tour with the bat he scored his maiden Test century at Headingly with 102 in the first innings. He is probably best remembered for his "catch of the century" at the SCG in 1982 where his flying overhead take dismissed West Indian Sylvester Clarke. In 2004 he was appointed coach of the Sri Lankan national side, a position he would hold until replaced by fellow Australian Tom Moody.

EADY, Charles John
Born: October 29, 1870
Batting: Right handed
Bowling: Right arm fast

Tests
Test Career:	1896-1902
Cap Number:	73
Tests Played:	2

Test Batting
Innings:	4	Runs:	20
Highest Score:	10*	Average:	6.66
No. 50s:	0	No. 100s:	0

Test Bowling & Fielding
Wickets:	7	Runs:	112
Best Bowling:	3/30	Average:	16.00
5 WI:	0	10 WM:	0
Catches:	2	Stumpings:	0

A heavy set Tasmanian batsman who famously scored over 500 in an innings whilst playing domestic cricket in New Zealand in 1902.

EASTWOOD, Kenneth Humphrey
Born: November 23, 1935
Batting: Left handed
Bowling: Left arm leg-break

Tests
Test Career:	1971
Cap Number:	256
Tests Played:	1

Test Batting
Innings:	2	Runs:	5
Highest Score:	5	Average:	2.50
No. 50s:	0	No. 100s:	0

Test Bowling & Fielding
Wickets:	1	Runs:	21
Best Bowling:	1/21	Average:	21.00
5 WI:	0	10 WM:	0
Catches:	0	Stumpings:	0

Picked to make his Test debut on the back of two huge knocks for Victoria against New South

Wales, the opening batsman replaced Bill Lawry for the seventh Test of the 1970/71 Ashes series. The 35 year old needed to enjoy a big match to kick start an unlikely Test career but could manage only 5 and zero.

EBELING, Hans Irvine

Born:	January 1, 1905
Batting:	Right handed
Bowling:	Right arm medium-fast

Tests
Test Career:	1934		
Cap Number:	152		
Tests Played:	1		

Test Batting
Innings:	2	Runs:	43
Highest Score:	41	Average:	21.50
No. 50s:	0	No. 100s:	0

Test Bowling & Fielding
Wickets:	3	Runs:	89
Best Bowling:	3/74	Average:	29.66
5 WI:	0	10 WM:	0
Catches:	0	Stumpings:	0

A Victorian all-rounder whose only Test was at The Oval in in 1934.

EDWARDS, John Dunlop

Born:	June 12, 1860
Batting:	Right handed

Tests
Test Career:	1888		
Cap Number:	52		
Tests Played:	3		

Test Batting
Innings:	6	Runs:	48
Highest Score:	26	Average:	9.59
No. 50s:	0	No. 100s:	0

Test Bowling & Fielding
Wickets:	0	Runs:	0
Best Bowling:		Average:	0.00
5 WI:	0	10 WM:	0
Catches:	1	Stumpings:	0

He was a Victorian whose three Tests all came on the tour of England in 1888.

EDWARDS, Ross

Born:	December 1, 1942
Batting:	Right handed
Bowling:	Right arm medium

Tests
Test Career:	1972-75		
Cap Number:	259		
Tests Played:	20		

Test Batting
Innings:	32	Runs:	1,171
Highest Score:	170*	Average:	40.37
No. 50s:	9	No. 100s:	2

Test Bowling & Fielding
Wickets:	0	Runs:	20
Best Bowling:		Average:	0.00
5 WI:	0	10 WM:	0
Catches:	7	Stumpings:	0

One Day Internationals
ODI Career:	1972-75
ODIs Played:	9

ODI Batting
Innings:	8	Runs:	255
Highest Score:	80*	Average:	36.42
No. 50s:	3	No. 100s:	0

ODI Bowling & Fielding
Wickets:	0	Runs:	0
Best Bowling:		Average:	0.00
5 WM:	0	Catches:	0
Stumpings:	0		

Probably best known as a brilliant cover fieldsman, the West Australian was also a fine middle order batsman who enjoyed success in both the Test and one day arenas. His first Test century and highest score, 170 not out at Trent Bridge actually came when opening the innings during the Ashes tour to England in 1972. He would be a regular part of the Test side for the next three years before making way for younger players such as Gary Cosier and Graham Yallop. Edwards played a key role in getting his side into the final of the innaugural World Cup in 1975 with a fine knock of 80 against Pakistan. A little remembered fact about Ross Edwards is that he also stood in as wicket keeper for his state when Rodney Marsh was on national duty, and in fact toured the West Indies in 1973 as a middle order batsman and second keeper.

EDWARDS, Walter John

Born:	December 23, 1949
Batting:	Right handed

Tests
Test Career:	1974		
Cap Number:	271		
Tests Played:	3		

Test Batting
Innings:	6	Runs:	68
Highest Score:	30	Average:	11.33
No. 50s:	0	No. 100s:	0

Test Bowling & Fielding
Wickets:	0	Runs:	0
Best Bowling:		Average:	0.00
5 WI:	0	10 WM:	0
Catches:	0	Stumpings:	0

One Day Internationals
ODI Career:	1975
ODIs Played:	1

ODI Batting
Innings:	1	Runs:	2
Highest Score:	2	Average:	2.00
No. 50s:	0	No. 100s:	0

ODI Bowling & Fielding
Wickets:	0	Runs:	0
Best Bowling:		Average:	0.00
5 WM:	0	Catches:	0
Stumpings:	0		

An opening batsman from WA, he played three Tests against England in 1974/75. Wally Edwards was a compulsive hooker who regularly fell to the bouncer in his short Test career.

ELLIOTT, Matthew Thomas Gray

Born: September 28, 1971
Batting: Left handed
Bowling: Left arm medium

Tests

Test Career: 1996-2004
Cap Number: 368
Tests Played: 21

Test Batting
Innings:	36	Runs:	1,172
Highest Score:	199	Average:	33.48
No. 50s:	4	No. 100s:	3

Test Bowling & Fielding
Wickets:	0	Runs:	4
Best Bowling:		Average:	0.00
5 WI:	0	10 WM:	0
Catches:	14	Stumpings:	0

One Day Internationals

ODI Career: 1997
ODIs Played: 1

ODI Batting
Innings:	1	Runs:	1
Highest Score:	1	Average:	1.00
No. 50s:	0	No. 100s:	0

ODI Bowling & Fielding
Wickets:	0	Runs:	0
Best Bowling:		Average:	0.00
5 WM:	0	Catches:	0
Stumpings:	0		

Matthew Elliott's Test career started and ended with a disappointing duck, but in between there was plenty of promise. A tall and punishing opening batsman from Victoria, he seemed set for a long Test career when he scored two centuries on his first Ashes tour in 1997 that included a career high 199 at Headingly. The hook shot that served him so well in England let him down when he returned to Australia and after struggling against the South Africans at home he failed dismally in the Caribbean in 1999. Elliott was given a final chance against Sri Lanka in a wintertime Test in Darwin in 2004 but his double failure meant that his Test career was all but over. Elliott conceded that fact when he left Victoria for South Australia in 2005 to start what he described as the final phase of his cricket life.

EMERY, Philip Alan

Born: June 25, 1964
Batting: Left handed
Wicket Keeper

Tests

Test Career: 1994
Cap Number: 362
Tests Played: 1

Test Batting
Innings:	1	Runs:	8
Highest Score:	8*	Average:	0.00
No. 50s:	0	No. 100s:	0

Test Bowling & Fielding
Wickets:	0	Runs:	0
Best Bowling:		Average:	0.00
5 WI:	0	10 WM:	0
Catches:	5	Stumpings:	1

One Day Internationals

ODI Career: 1994
ODIs Played: 1

ODI Batting
Innings:	1	Runs:	11
Highest Score:	11	Average:	11.00
No. 50s:	0	No. 100s:	0

ODI Bowling & Fielding
Wickets:	0	Runs:	0
Best Bowling:		Average:	0.00
5 WM:	0	Catches:	3
Stumpings:	0		

Australia's reserve keeper in the mid nineties, he got his chance when Ian Healy pulled out of the third Test of the 1994/95 tour of Pakistan.

EMERY, Sidney Hand

Born: October 15, 1885
Batting: Right handed
Bowling: Right arm off-break

Tests

Test Career: 1912
Cap Number: 102
Tests Played: 4

Test Batting
Innings:	2	Runs:	6
Highest Score:	5	Average:	3.00
No. 50s:	0	No. 100s:	0

Test Bowling & Fielding
Wickets:	5	Runs:	249
Best Bowling:	2/46	Average:	49.80
5 WI:	0	10 WM:	0
Catches:	2	Stumpings:	0

A New South Wales finger spinner, he got his chance in the triangular series of 1912 after a number of prominent Australian cricketers who were in a dispute with the Board of Control refused to travel to England.

EVANS, Edwin

Born: March 26, 1849
Batting: Right handed
Bowling: Right arm off-break

Tests

Test Career: 1882-86
Cap Number: 26
Tests Played: 6

Test Batting
Innings:	10	Runs:	82
Highest Score:	33	Average:	10.25
No. 50s:	0	No. 100s:	0

Test Bowling & Fielding
Wickets:	7	Runs:	332
Best Bowling:	3/64	Average:	47.42
5 WI:	0	10 WM:	0
Catches:	5	Stumpings:	0

An accurate off-spinner, Evans failed to hold down a regular Test spot depite being a star performer for New South Wales in Sheffield Shield competition.

FAIRFAX, Alan Geoffrey

Born: June 16, 1906
Batting: Right handed
Bowling: Right arm medium-fast
         Wicket Keeper

Tests

Test Career: 1929-31
Cap Number: 131
Tests Played: 10

Test Batting

Innings:	12	Runs:	410
Highest Score:	65	Average:	51.25
No. 50s:	4	No. 100s:	0

Test Bowling & Fielding

Wickets:	21	Runs:	645
Best Bowling:	4/31	Average:	30.71
5 WI:	0	10 WM:	0
Catches:	15	Stumpings:	0

He was an under-rated all rounder who performed well on the Ashes tour of 1930, combining with Tim Wall to take the new ball. On that tour he averaged 50 in Test matches with the bat as well as taking 12 wickets. In 1932 he moved to England where he played professionally in the Lancashire League for Accrington. Fairfax played a key role in one of cricket's more bizarre stories when he called English Test matches from the Eiffel Tower. Poste Parisien was transmitting synthetic Test broadcasts back to England from Paris in the early 30's and used the Australian as their commentator.

FAVELL, Leslie Ernest

Born: November 6, 1929
Batting: Right handed

Tests

Test Career: 1954-61
Cap Number: 198
Tests Played: 19

Test Batting

Innings:	31	Runs:	757
Highest Score:	101	Average:	27.03
No. 50s:	5	No. 100s:	1

Test Bowling & Fielding

Wickets:	0	Runs:	0
Best Bowling:		Average:	0.00
5 WI:	0	10 WM:	0
Catches:	9	Stumpings:	0

One of Australia's finest cricketers at state level where he scored over 12,000 first class runs, he was never quite able to carry that form with him into the Test arena. A punisher of the ball it was that fondness for getting after the bowler that often led to Favell's demise. At Barbados in 1955 he enjoyed a great Test scoring 73 and 55 and looked set for a long Test career but over the next six years found it hard to hold down a regular Test spot. His only century in Test cricket came at Madras in 1960 in an uncharacteristically restrained knock. A state baseballer, Favell used what he learnt in that sport to great effect in cricket where his fielding was of the highest quality.

FERRIS, John James

Born: May 21, 1867
Batting: Left handed
Bowling: Left arm medium

Tests

Test Career: 1887-92
Cap Number: 44
Tests Played: 9

Test Batting

Innings:	17	Runs:	114
Highest Score:	20*	Average:	8.76
No. 50s:	0	No. 100s:	0

Test Bowling & Fielding

Wickets:	61	Runs:	775
Best Bowling:	7/37	Average:	12.70
5 WI:	6	10 WM:	1
Catches:	4	Stumpings:	0

He was a much feared swing bowler in his eight Tests for Australia and single Test for England. His debut Test was the memorable match at the SCG in 1887 when England was sent in and dismissed for only 45. He took 4/27 and along with the great Charlie Turner consigned the 'Old Enemy' to their lowest score in Test history. His strength lay in his ability to move the ball both away and in to the batsman and such was his impact on the game that he was considered amongst Wisden's Cricketers of the Year in 1889. His career best innings figures of 7/37 and match figures of 13/91 were recorded whilst playing for England against South Africa in Cape Town. Sadly that Test was to be his last game at the highest level. J.J. Ferris died in Durban during the Boer War whilst serving as an officer in the British army.

FINGLETON, John Henry Webb (Jack)

Born: April 28, 1908
Batting: Right handed

Tests

Test Career: 1932-38
Cap Number: 142
Tests Played: 18

Test Batting

Innings:	29	Runs:	1,189
Highest Score:	136	Average:	42.46
No. 50s:	3	No. 100s:	5

Test Bowling & Fielding

Wickets:	0	Runs:	0
Best Bowling:		Average:	0.00
5 WI:	0	10 WM:	0
Catches:	13	Stumpings:	0

He opened the batting with distinction during the 30's, fighting back from a disappointing Bodyline series in 1932/33 to be a leading contributor in 1936/37. In that series he hit a century in the first Test and and a masterful 136 in the third when combining with Donald Bradman for a record 346 run partnership. The following year he completed a lifelong ambition when he toured England for the first time. Once retired he became a respected journalist and author with a number of cricket books to his credit.

FLEETWOOD-SMITH, Leslie O'Brien (Chuck)

Born:	August 30, 1908
Batting:	Right handed
Bowling:	Left arm leg-break

Tests

Test Career:	1935-38
Cap Number:	153
Tests Played:	10

Test Batting

Innings:	11	Runs:	54
Highest Score:	16*	Average:	9.00
No. 50s:	0	No. 100s:	0

Test Bowling & Fielding

Wickets:	42	Runs:	1,570
Best Bowling:	6/110	Average:	37.38
5 WI:	2	10 WM:	1
Catches:	0	Stumpings:	0

He was a prodigious spinner of the ball who joined Tiger O'Reilly as Australia's front line spin bowler following the non-selection of Clarrie Grimmett for the 1936/37 tour by England. He was a wicket taker at Test level though England's best batsmen had little trouble playing him. When England scored a then Test record 7/903 against the Aussies in 1938, Fleetwood-Smith bore the brunt of it, returning figures of 1/298. The debonair Victorian with Errol Flynn looks fell on hard times post cricket and did for a time live on the streets of Melbourne. Whilst it had been widely reported that he died homeless, he did in fact pass away in a private hospital after friends who heard of his plight rallied around him.

FLEMING, Damien William

Born:	April 24, 1970
Batting:	Right handed
Bowling:	Right arm medium-fast

Tests

Test Career:	1994-2001
Cap Number:	361
Tests Played:	20

Test Batting

Innings:	19	Runs:	305
Highest Score:	71*	Average:	19.06
No. 50s:	2	No. 100s:	0

Test Bowling & Fielding

Wickets:	75	Runs:	1,942
Best Bowling:	5/30	Average:	25.89
5 WI:	3	10 WM:	0
Catches:	9	Stumpings:	0

One Day Internationals

ODI Career:	1994-2001
ODIs Played:	88

ODI Batting

Innings:	31	Runs:	152
Highest Score:	29	Average:	11.69
No. 50s:	0	No. 100s:	0

ODI Bowling & Fielding

Wickets:	134	Runs:	3,402
Best Bowling:	5/36	Average:	25.38
5 WM:	1	Catches:	14
Stumpings:	0		

Born in Western Australia, making his first class debut in South Australia and coming to prominence in Victoria, the talented swing bowler had a fine strike rate in both Test and one day cricket. He had a dream start in the Test side taking a hat-trick on debut in Rawalpindi in 1994. Fleming played a key role in the 1999 World Cup winning side where he was involved in the last ball run out that knocked the South Africans out of the semi final. He was also a useful all-rounder, with two Test half centuries to his name. Injuries and a tendency to be thought of as mainly a new ball bowler limited a very good player to just 20 Tests.

FRANCIS, Bruce Colin

Born:	February 18, 1948
Batting:	Right handed

Tests

Test Career:	1972
Cap Number:	258
Tests Played:	3

Test Batting

Innings:	5	Runs:	52
Highest Score:	27	Average:	10.40
No. 50s:	0	No. 100s:	0

Test Bowling & Fielding

Wickets:	0	Runs:	0
Best Bowling:		Average:	0.00
5 WI:	0	10 WM:	0
Catches:	1	Stumpings:	0

An opening batsman, he first played for Australia against the Rest of the World XI in 1971/72.

FREEMAN, Eric Walter

Born:	July 13, 1944
Batting:	Right handed
Bowling:	Right arm medium-fast

Tests

Test Career:	1968-70
Cap Number:	244
Tests Played:	11

Test Batting

Innings:	18	Runs:	345
Highest Score:	76	Average:	19.16
No. 50s:	2	No. 100s:	0

Test Bowling & Fielding

Wickets:	34	Runs:	1,128
Best Bowling:	4/52	Average:	33.17
5 WI:	0	10 WM:	0
Catches:	5	Stumpings:	0

A more than handy all-rounder, he put his powerful frame to good use as both a quick bowler and punishing lower order batsman. He was unable to carve out a long Test career but one could easily have imagined him being a very useful one-day cricketer if his time had come a little later.

FREER, Frederick Alfred William

Born: December 4, 1915
Batting: Right handed
Bowling: Right arm medium-fast

Tests

Test Career:	1946
Cap Number:	173
Tests Played:	1

Test Batting

Innings:	1	Runs:	28
Highest Score:	28*	Average:	0.00
No. 50s:	0	No. 100s:	0

Test Bowling & Fielding

Wickets:	3	Runs:	74
Best Bowling:	2/49	Average:	24.66
5 WI:	0	10 WM:	0
Catches:	0	Stumpings:	0

A Victorain right arm quick who performed well when called in to replace Ray Lindwall for the second Test against England at the SCG in 1946/47.

GANNON, John Bryant (Sam)

Born: February 8, 1947
Batting: Right handed
Bowling: Left arm medium-fast

Tests

Test Career:	1977-78
Cap Number:	290
Tests Played:	3

Test Batting

Innings:	5	Runs:	3
Highest Score:	3*	Average:	3.00
No. 50s:	0	No. 100s:	0

Test Bowling & Fielding

Wickets:	11	Runs:	361
Best Bowling:	4/77	Average:	32.81
5 WI:	0	10 WM:	0
Catches:	3	Stumpings:	0

'Sam' Gannon was possibly the least known cricketer to earn national colours as a result of the vacuum created by World Series Cricket. A left arm medium pace bowler from Western Australia, he had played in the state side in the mid 60's as a teenager but was vitually unsighted until a national call up that saw him play three Tests and capture a respectable eleven wickets against the Indians in the summer of 1977/78.

GARRETT, Thomas William

Born: June 25, 1858
Batting: Right handed
Bowling: Right arm medium-fast

Tests

Test Career:	1877-88
Cap Number:	4
Tests Played:	19

Test Batting

Innings:	33	Runs:	339
Highest Score:	51*	Average:	12.55
No. 50s:	1	No. 100s:	0

Test Bowling & Fielding

Wickets:	36	Runs:	970
Best Bowling:	6/78	Average:	26.94
5 WI:	2	10 WM:	0
Catches:	7	Stumpings:	0

Tom Garrett can lay claim to being Australia's first all-rounder. Tall for his time, the six footer bowled sharpish medium, was a hard hitting middle order batsman and a fine fieldsman. In the first Test ever played, Garrett opened the bowling as well as batting at number four in Australia's second innings. It was said that he had no peer when bowling on hard wickets and that his best delivery was a well disguised out swinger. Away from the cricket field Garrett was a renowned sprinter and an accomplished solicitor. He was the last surviving member of Australia's first Test side when he passed away at the age of 85.

GAUNT, Ron Arthur

Born: March 26, 1934
Batting: Left handed
Bowling: Right arm fast

Tests

Test Career:	1958-64
Cap Number:	210
Tests Played:	3

Test Batting

Innings:	4	Runs:	6
Highest Score:	3	Average:	3.00
No. 50s:	0	No. 100s:	0

Test Bowling & Fielding

Wickets:	7	Runs:	310
Best Bowling:	3/53	Average:	44.28
5 WI:	0	10 WM:	0
Catches:	1	Stumpings:	0

A right arm quick from Perth in West Australia who was a surprise selection in his final Test against South Africa at Adelaide in 1964.

GEHRS, Donald Raeburn Algernon

Born: November 29, 1880
Batting: Right handed
Bowling: Right arm leg-break

Tests

Test Career:	1904-1911
Cap Number:	87
Tests Played:	6

Test Batting

Innings:	11	Runs:	221
Highest Score:	67	Average:	20.09
No. 50s:	2	No. 100s:	0

Test Bowling & Fielding

Wickets:	0	Runs:	4
Best Bowling:		Average:	0.00
5 WI:	0	10 WM:	0
Catches:	6	Stumpings:	0

A South Australian, Algy Gehrs failed to bring his fine domestic form with him when playing for his country. His best was reserved for the South Africans against whom he hit his only two Test half centuries.

GIFFEN, George

Born: March 27, 1859
Batting: Right handed
Bowling: Right arm medium

Tests
Test Career:	1882-96		
Cap Number:	27		
Tests Played:	31		

Test Batting
Innings:	53	Runs:	1,238
Highest Score:	161	Average:	23.35
No. 50s:	6	No. 100s:	1

Test Bowling & Fielding
Wickets:	103	Runs:	2,791
Best Bowling:	7/117	Average:	27.09
5 WI:	7	10 WM:	1
Catches:	24	Stumpings:	0

A genuine all-rounder, George Giffen was a dominant force in 19th century cricket with the raw figures telling of a player who was rarely out the game. At Test level he was the first Australian to reach the 1000 run, 100 wicket double and at first class level he is the only Australian to have ever taken 1000 wickets and scored 10,000 runs. He remains the only player to take 16 or more wickets in a game on five seperate occasions and he scored a century and took 10 wickets in the same game an incredible nine times. Giffen made his Test debut in Melbourne at the age of 22 and remained a regular member of the Test team for almost 15 years. In 1894 Giffen played one of the great Tests of all time. He scored 161 and 41 as well as taking eight wickets in a game that the Australians incredibly lost. Giffen captained Australia in four Tests but it was said the he was not as effective a captain as he was a player. Giffen played his last Test at 37, but continued to play first class cricket to the ripe old age of 44, where in his final game for South Australia he took 15 wickets and scored 81 and 97. George Giffen also holds a special place in Australian literary history His book, 'With Bat and Ball' is thought to be the first true Australian autobiography. Giffen's legacy lives on today in the form of a grandstand that bears his name at the picturesque Adelaide Oval.

GIFFEN, Walter Frank

Born: September 20, 1861
Batting: Right handed

Tests
Test Career:	1887-92		
Cap Number:	50		
Tests Played:	3		

Test Batting
Innings:	6	Runs:	11
Highest Score:	3	Average:	1.83
No. 50s:	0	No. 100s:	0

Test Bowling & Fielding
Wickets:	0	Runs:	0
Best Bowling:		Average:	0.00
5 WI:	0	10 WM:	0
Catches:	1	Stumpings:	0

In the modern game it is debatable whether having a highly credentialled brother is a help or a hindrance but in the case of Walter Giffen it certainly didn't hurt. Arguably the worst performed batsman in Test history, it was summised that his famed brother George played a role in him gaining a Test berth. Whatever the case, three Tests seemed three too many for a man of his standing in the sport.

GILBERT, David Robert

Born: December 29, 1960
Batting: Right handed
Bowling: Right arm fast

Tests
Test Career:	1985-86		
Cap Number:	330		
Tests Played:	9		

Test Batting
Innings:	12	Runs:	57
Highest Score:	15	Average:	7.12
No. 50s:	0	No. 100s:	0

Test Bowling & Fielding
Wickets:	16	Runs:	843
Best Bowling:	3/48	Average:	52.68
5 WI:	0	10 WM:	0
Catches:	0	Stumpings:	0

One Day Internationals
ODI Career:	1986		
ODIs Played:	14		

ODI Batting
Innings:	8	Runs:	39
Highest Score:	8	Average:	7.80
No. 50s:	0	No. 100s:	0

ODI Bowling & Fielding
Wickets:	18	Runs:	552
Best Bowling:	5/46	Average:	30.66
5 WI:	1	Catches:	3
Stumpings:	0		

A genuine opening bowler from New South Wales, he made his debut on the 1985 Ashes tour. Following his retirement Gilbert became a leading cricket administrator.

GILCHRIST, Adam Craig

Born: November 14, 1971
Batting: Left handed
Wicket Keeper

Tests
Test Career:	1999-		
Cap Number:	381		
Tests Played:	85		

Test Batting
Innings:	123	Runs:	5,124
Highest Score:	204*	Average:	48.80
No. 50s:	22	No. 100s:	16

Test Bowling & Fielding
Wickets:	0	Runs:	0
Best Bowling:		Average:	0.00
5 WI:	0	10 WM:	0
Catches:	320	Stumpings:	35

One Day Internationals
ODI Career:	1996-		
ODIs Played:	242		

ODI Batting			
Innings:	235	Runs:	8,233
Highest Score:	172	Average:	36.42
No. 50s:	45	No. 100s:	14
ODI Bowling & Fielding			
Wickets:	0	Runs:	0
Best Bowling:		Average:	0.00
5 WM:	0	Catches:	348
Stumpings:	45		

Australia's brilliant wicket keeper/batsman has done much since making his Test debut at the age of 28. He has been universally acclaimed as the best batting gloveman the game has seen and in doing so redefined the role of wicket keeper in international cricket. Gilchrist took over from Ian Healy as the one day keeper in 1996 but had to wait a further three years to make his Test debut. His impact was immediate. Employing the same thrilling strokeplay that brought him so much success in limited over cricket he went about destroying the opposition with his flashing drives, audacious hooks and boundary clearing sweeps. His first Test century was an undefeated 149 at Hobart that gave the Australians an improbable victory against Pakistan. Often at his best in a crisis, he teamed up with Matthew Hayden to punish a powerful Indian spin attack at Mumbai in 2001 after the Aussies had lost five wickets in rapid succession. It was obvious then that the Australian batting line-up had been extended with a world class batsman at number seven. His highest Test score, a blistering 204 not out at the Wanderers in 2001/02, drew comparisons with the great Viv Richards for its savagery. He remains a key member of the powerful Australian side, having fought back from poor form with the bat on the 2005 Ashes tour to hit his 16th Test century in Australia's most recent Test series, an away fixture with Bangladesh. His impact in one day cricket has been just as profound with over 8,000 runs at a strikerate of just under a run a ball. Gilly's elevation to opener freed up a spot in the side for a number of bowling all-rounders and has been central to Australia's success at the last two World Cups. The fact that Gilchrist is a world class batsman sometimes leads critics to question his work behind the stumps, but his keeping has always been of the highest standard, whether working acrobatically to the quicks or in tandem with Shane Warne and co. Highly competitive, he brings his own high standards of sportsmanship to the team and has long been an advocate of walking if he believes he is out. Gilchrist has been vice captain for much of his Test career but he stood in as captain for the injured Ponting on the tour of India in 2004/05 and returned with Australia's first series win there in 35 years. A superstar of the modern game, there are few players who can pull fans through the turnstiles like Adam Gilchrist.

GILLESPIE, Jason Neil

Born:	April 19, 1975
Batting:	Right handed
Bowling:	Right arm fast

Tests

Test Career:	1996-
Cap Number:	370
Tests Played:	71

Test Batting			
Innings:	28	Runs:	1,218
Highest Score:	201*	Average:	18.73
No. 50s:	2	No. 100s:	1
Test Bowling & Fielding			
Wickets:	259	Runs:	6,770
Best Bowling:	7/37	Average:	26.13
5 WI:	8	10 WM:	0
Catches:	27	Stumpings:	0

One Day Internationals

ODI Career:	1996-
ODIs Played:	97

ODI Batting			
Innings:	39	Runs:	289
Highest Score:	44*	Average:	12.56
No. 50s:	0	No. 100s:	0
ODI Bowling & Fielding			
Wickets:	142	Runs:	3,611
Best Bowling:	5/22	Average:	25.42
5 WM:	3	Catches:	10
Stumpings:	0		

In the mid nineties Australia was one piece of the puzzle away from claiming the title as the world's best cricket nation. Already boasting a brilliant batting line-up and the best leg-spinner of all time, the side was crying out for an opening bowler who could capitalise on the pressure that was being created at the other end by Glenn McGrath. Enter Jason Gillespie, a glowering young quick from Adelaide with a kicking short ball, a mean leg cutter and a perfectly manicured mullett. Instantly popular with team mates, he became a regular member of the Australian side and injuries aside, has been there ever since. There is nearly no part of Gillespie's body that has escaped injury, but a broken leg sustained in a sickening outfield collision with Steve Waugh during a Test at Kandy in 1999 when both were running to take a catch, is clearly the best known. Injuries in 2005 interrupted his preparation for the Ashes and he was ultimately overlooked. Gillespie fought back with a number of fine performances at state level and was on hand when Australia played in Bangladesh for the first time. It was on that tour that Gillespie did the unthinkable, hitting a double century after coming in as a nightwatchman. The affable quick has taken 259 Test wickets in his 71 Tests to lie fifth on the all-time list for Australian bowlers, and if he can avoid the physio room, the 300 wicket milestone is not out of the question.

GILMOUR, Gary John

Born: June 26, 1951
Batting: Left handed
Bowling: Left arm medium-fast

Tests
Test Career: 1974-77
Cap Number: 267
Tests Played: 15

Test Batting
Innings:	22	Runs:	483
Highest Score:	101	Average:	23.00
No. 50s:	3	No. 100s:	1

Test Bowling & Fielding
Wickets:	54	Runs:	1,406
Best Bowling:	6/85	Average:	26.03
5 WI:	3	10 WM:	0
Catches:	8	Stumpings:	0

One Day Internationals
ODI Career: 1974-75
ODIs Played: 5

ODI Batting
Innings:	2	Runs:	42
Highest Score:	28*	Average:	42.00
No. 50s:	0	No. 100s:	0

ODI Bowling & Fielding
Wickets:	16	Runs:	165
Best Bowling:	6/14	Average:	10.31
5 WM:	2	Catches:	2
Stumpings:	0		

Always in the game, 'Gus' Gilmour was a regular match winner for the Aussies at both Test and One Day level. His most famous game was the semi final of the first Cricket World Cup tournament when he single handedly lifted the Australians into the finals. He tore through the English with the ball taking 6/14, and with his side teetering in a low run chase hit a furious 28 not out. Injury meant he played only one Test on the Ashes tour of 1975 but his return of nine wickets for the game shows how valuable he was. A true all-rounder he hit a ton against the Kiwis at Christchurch in 1977 batting down at number eight. Later that year Gilmour joined Kerry Packer's World Series Cricket along with other high profile team mates and players from West Indies, South Africa, England and Pakistan. A real country boy, his penchant for a drop of red came back to bite him when he was sidelined with gout at one stage during his career. In later life Gilmour was to endure a health problem of a more serious nature when he required a liver transplant in late 2005.

GLEESON, John William

Born: March 14, 1938
Batting: Right handed
Bowling: Right arm leg-break

Tests
Test Career: 1967-72
Cap Number: 242
Tests Played: 29

Test Batting
Innings:	46	Runs:	395
Highest Score:	45	Average:	10.39
No. 50s:	0	No. 100s:	0

Test Bowling & Fielding
Wickets:	93	Runs:	3,367
Best Bowling:	5/61	Average:	36.20
5 WI:	3	10 WM:	0
Catches:	17	Stumpings:	0

A shrewd spinner with an armory of different deliveries, he could be relied upon to bowl off-spin, leg-spin and arm balls all in the one over. The late bloomer didn't make his Test debut until he was in his late twenties and though at times expensive, he could be relied upon to take wickets at regular intervals. Gleeson performed well on the tour of South Africa in 1969/70 despite Australia losing all four matches. He took 19 wickets including eight in the third Test at Johannesburg.

GRAF, Shaun Francis

Born: May 19, 1957
Batting: Right handed
Bowling: Right arm medium

One Day Internationals
ODI Career: 1980-81
ODIs Played: 11

ODI Batting
Innings:	6	Runs:	24
Highest Score:	8	Average:	4.00
No. 50s:	0	No. 100s:	0

ODI Bowling & Fielding
Wickets:	8	Runs:	345
Best Bowling:	2/23	Average:	43.12
5 WM:	0	Catches:	1
Stumpings:	0		

A strongly built all-rounder from Victoria who didn't do as well as expected with the bat when given a chance in the Australian one day side. Later became a cricket administrator in his home state.

GRAHAM, Henry (Harry)

Born: November 22, 1870
Batting: Right handed

Tests
Test Career: 1893-96
Cap Number: 63
Tests Played: 6

Test Batting
Innings:	10	Runs:	301
Highest Score:	107	Average:	30.10
No. 50s:	0	No. 100s:	0

Test Bowling & Fielding
Wickets:	0	Runs:	0
Best Bowling:		Average:	0.00
5 WI:	0	10 WM:	0
Catches:	3	Stumpings:	0

He was a wonderful hard hitting batsman who scored a century on debut against England at Lords. The consensus at the time was that Harry Graham was an unfulfilled talent who at his best was the equal of any of his peers. In 1900 he moved to New Zealand where he enjoyed great success playing with the Otago XI.

GREGORY, David William

Born:	April 15, 1845
Batting:	Right handed

Tests

Test Career:	1877-79
Cap Number:	5
Tests Played:	3

Test Batting

Innings:	5	Runs:	60
Highest Score:	43	Average:	20.00
No. 50s:	0	No. 100s:	0

Test Bowling & Fielding

Wickets:	0	Runs:	9
Best Bowling:		Average:	0.00
5 WI:	0	10 WM:	0
Catches:	0	Stumpings:	0

It's fitting that Australia's first cricket dynasty would provide the country's first Test captain. Dave Gregory was 31 years of age when he led the Australians into battle against James Lillywhite's Englishmen at the MCG in the March of 1877. The name Gregory featured heavily in the early years of Australian cricket, Dave Gregory had three brothers and three nephews who all played first class cricket. The bearded Sydney-sider was an imposing looking cricketer and whilst his three Tests yielded only 60 runs he will forever be remembered as the man who led the Australians to victory in cricket's first ever Test.

GREGORY, Edward James

Born:	May 29, 1839
Batting:	Right handed

Tests

Test Career:	1877
Cap Number:	6
Tests Played:	1

Test Batting

Innings:	2	Runs:	11
Highest Score:	11	Average:	5.50
No. 50s:	0	No. 100s:	0

Test Bowling & Fielding

Wickets:	0	Runs:	0
Best Bowling:		Average:	0.00
5 WI:	0	10 WM:	0
Catches:	1	Stumpings:	0

Brother of Dave, Ned played in the first ever Test match and has the dubious distinction of scoring Test cricket's first ever duck. His was a life devoted to cricket, as a middle order batsman for New South Wales, curator at what is now the SCG and as father of Australian Test great Syd Gregory. Ned Gregory was also said to have built the game's first permanent scoreboard, located at the Association Ground in Sydney.

GREGORY, John Morrison (Jack)

Born:	August 14, 1895
Batting:	Left handed
Bowling:	Right arm fast

Tests

Test Career:	1920-28
Cap Number:	107
Tests Played:	24

Test Batting

Innings:	34	Runs:	1,146
Highest Score:	119	Average:	36.96
No. 50s:	7	No. 100s:	2

Test Bowling & Fielding

Wickets:	85	Runs:	2,648
Best Bowling:	7/69	Average:	31.15
5 WI:	4	10 WM:	0
Catches:	37	Stumpings:	0

A member of the famous Gregory clan from Sydney, Jack was a powerful all-rounder who at one stage in the early 20's was considered the finest cricketer in the country, if not world. His first Test series was the Ashes tour of 1920/21 where he was his country's second leading wicket taker in Tests with 23 and averaged over 70 with the bat. In the second Test at the MCG he scored a century batting at nine and then took 7/69 in England's first innings. Over the next two years Jack Gregory simply starred with bat and ball. As a bowler his main weapon was sheer speed, though he could be relied upon to move the ball both ways when new. As a batsman he put the power that made him a great fast bowler to good use, and though he batted without gloves it was more often the opposition that was in danger of getting injured whilst he was at the crease. He was also an outstanding slip fieldsman who average almost a catch an innings. Towards the end of his career injury slowed Gregory down, but he should be remembered as one of Australia's greatest all-rounders of all time.

GREGORY, Ross Gerald

Born:	February 28, 1916
Batting:	Right handed
Bowling:	Right arm leg-break

Tests

Test Career:	1937
Cap Number:	159
Tests Played:	2

Test Batting

Innings:	3	Runs:	153
Highest Score:	80	Average:	51.00
No. 50s:	2	No. 100s:	0

Test Bowling & Fielding

Wickets:	0	Runs:	14
Best Bowling:		Average:	0.00
5 WI:	0	10 WM:	0
Catches:	1	Stumpings:	0

No relation to the Gregory clan from Sydney, he was only 20 when he first played for Australia. He performed well in his only two Tests, the fourth and fifth of the 1936/37 Ashes series. He made 80 batting at number six at the MCG but was surprisingly overlooked for the tour of England in 1938 and never played Test cricket again. Ross Gregory was killed during the Second World War whilst serving in the R.A.A.F.

GREGORY, Sydney Edward

Born:	April 14, 1870
Batting:	Right handed
Bowling:	Right arm medium

Tests

Test Career:	1890-1912		
Cap Number:	58		
Tests Played:	58		
Test Batting			
Innings:	100	Runs:	2,282
Highest Score:	201	Average:	24.53
No. 50s:	8	No. 100s:	4
Test Bowling & Fielding			
Wickets:	0	Runs:	33
Best Bowling:		Average:	0.00
5 WI:	0	10 WM:	0
Catches:	25	Stumpings:	0

From the time of his birth on the present day site of the SCG, his was a life devoted to cricket. Both his father and uncle played Test cricket for Australia, the latter being the nation's first Test captain. He played his first Test at the age of 20 and his last some 22 years later. Along the way he broke almost every batting record in the game, becoming the first Australian to pass the 2000 run mark in Test cricket, and the first cricketer to score a double century in Tests. That innings of 201, compiled in only 241 minutes, included a ninth wicket stand of 154 with the keeper Blackham, which still stands as an Australian Test record today. Standing only 5ft 5 inches, Gregory was said to have great footwork and been a master timer who was able to score freely on both sides of the wicket. He was also considered to be the best fieldsman of his era. His last series for Australia was the triangular series in England with South Africa for which he was made captain.

GRIMMETT, Clarence Victor

Born:	December 25, 1891
Batting:	Right handed
Bowling:	Right arm fast

Tests

Test Career:	1925-36		
Cap Number:	121		
Tests Played:	37		
Test Batting			
Innings:	50	Runs:	557
Highest Score:	50	Average:	13.92
No. 50s:	1	No. 100s:	0
Test Bowling & Fielding			
Wickets:	216	Runs:	5,231
Best Bowling:	7/40	Average:	24.21
5 WI:	21	10 WM:	7
Catches:	17	Stumpings:	0

Born on Christmas Day, 1891, in New Zealand the wiry little leg spinner would go on to be one of the greatest bowlers in Test history. Though the record books tell the story of a man who took big bags of wickets on a regular basis and who became the first Australian to capture 200 Test scalps, Clarrie Grimmett was by no means an overnight sensation. Having plied his trade as a young man in New Zealand, Grimmett moved to New South Wales where he failed to make the state side. From there it was on to Victoria where it was said that a prejudice against Kiwis hampered his chances. He then moved to South Australia where he enjoyed success and was finally promoted to the Test side at the age of 34. Grimmett had worked harder than any cricketer before or after to get that baggy green cap and he showed what it meant to him by even wearing it whilst bowling. His impact on the Test arena was immediate, taking 11 wickets on debut in 1925. He was economical for a leg spinner and was able to spin the ball both into and away from the batsman. His greatest weapon though was an entirely new delivery that he had perfected prior to playing Test cricket. It became known as the flipper. A shorter pitched delivery that would rush on to the batsman, it has plagued batsman from the day Grimmett first delivered it to today. Over the next decade he enjoyed enormous succes in tandem with first Arthur Mailey and then Bill O'Reilly. The latter partnership, one of the most famous in Test cricket, yielded an amazing 162 wickets in only 15 Tests. At 44, the man alternatively known as The Scarlet Pimpernel, The Gnome, Grum or The Fox was dropped from the Test side despite having taken 59 wickets in his previous seven Tests. His partner in crime, Tiger Bill O'Reilly was outraged but the little spin master took it in his stride and continued to play for South Australia until he turned 50. It is testiment to Clarrie Grimmett's greatness that leg-spinners today still study the technique that made him a champion over 70 years ago.

GROUBE, Thomas Underwood

Born:	September 2, 1857
Batting:	Right handed
Bowling:	Right arm medium

Tests

Test Career:	1880		
Cap Number:	20		
Tests Played:	1		
Test Batting			
Innings:	2	Runs:	11
Highest Score:	11	Average:	5.50
No. 50s:	0	No. 100s:	0
Test Bowling & Fielding			
Wickets:	0	Runs:	0
Best Bowling:		Average:	0.00
5 WI:	0	10 WM:	0
Catches:	0	Stumpings:	0

A Victorian batsman who was the first New Zealand born Test cricketer.

GROUT, Arthur Theodore Wallace (Wally)
Born: March 20, 1927
Batting: Right handed
Wicket Keeper

Tests
Test Career: 1957-66
Cap Number: 206
Tests Played: 51

Test Batting
Innings:	67	Runs:	890
Highest Score:	67	Average:	15.08
No. 50s:	3	No. 100s:	0

Test Bowling & Fielding
Wickets:	0	Runs:	0
Best Bowling:		Average:	0.00
5 WI:	0	10 WM:	0
Catches:	163	Stumpings:	24

Considered by many to be Australia's finest ever gloveman, Wally Grout had to wait until he was 30 to play his first Test match. By the time he played his last Test at 39, he had broken the then Test record by dismissing six men in an innings against South Africa during the 1957/58 series and had recorded five dismissals in a Test innings on another five occasions. A great mover behind the stumps, he was equally at home keeping to spin or pace and was renowned for his quick movement down leg side. In 1960 Grout broke the first class world record by dismissing eight batsman in an innings against West Australia in a Sheffield Shield game. He was a solid middle order batsman who was the second last wicket to fall in the 1960/61 tied Test against the West Indies. Towards the end of his career he played against medical advice, and in 1968, at only 41 years of age died after suffering a heart attack. Following his passing, Australian cricket great Bob Simpson simply remembered Wally Grout as the best wicket-keeper he had ever seen.

GUEST, Colin Earnest John
Born: October 7, 1937
Batting: Right handed
Bowling: Right arm fast

Tests
Test Career: 1963
Cap Number: 222
Tests Played: 1

Test Batting
Innings:	1	Runs:	11
Highest Score:	11	Average:	11.00
No. 50s:	0	No. 100s:	0

Test Bowling & Fielding
Wickets:	0	Runs:	59
Best Bowling:		Average:	0.00
5 WI:	0	10 WM:	0
Catches:	0	Stumpings:	0

A right arm quick from Victoria. Later played for WA.

HADDIN, Bradley James
Born: October 23, 1977
Batting: Right handed
Wicket Keeper

One Day Internationals
ODI Career: 2001-
ODIs Played: 13

ODI Batting
Innings:	11	Runs:	200
Highest Score:	41	Average:	18.18
No. 50s:	0	No. 100s:	0

ODI Bowling & Fielding
Wickets:	0	Runs:	0
Best Bowling:		Average:	0.00
5 WM:	0	Catches:	13
Stumpings:	4		

Australia's second gloveman, he shares much in common with the man that stands between him and national honours. Like Adam Gilchrist he is a talented ball striker having hit six first class and four one day centuries for New South Wales. He has performed admirably when asked to stand in for Gilchrist, and at the age of 28 seems assured of further national honours.

HAMENCE, Ronald Arthur
Born: November 28, 1915
Batting: Right handed

Tests
Test Career: 1947-48
Cap Number: 176
Tests Played: 3

Test Batting
Innings:	4	Runs:	81
Highest Score:	30*	Average:	27.00
No. 50s:	0	No. 100s:	0

Test Bowling & Fielding
Wickets:	0	Runs:	0
Best Bowling:		Average:	0.00
5 WI:	0	10 WM:	0
Catches:	1	Stumpings:	0

From South Australia, he was a powerful top-order batsman and accomplished fieldsman who played one Test against the English and two against India.

HAMMOND, Jeffrey Robert
Born: April 19, 1950
Batting: Right handed
Bowling: Right arm medium-fast

Tests
Test Career: 1973
Cap Number: 265
Tests Played: 5

Test Batting
Innings:	5	Runs:	28
Highest Score:	19	Average:	9.33
No. 50s:	0	No. 100s:	0

Test Bowling & Fielding
Wickets:	15	Runs:	488
Best Bowling:	4/38	Average:	32.53
5 WI:	0	10 WM:	0
Catches:	2	Stumpings:	0

One Day Internationals

ODI Career:	1972
ODIs Played:	1

ODI Batting

Innings:	1	Runs:	15
Highest Score:	15*	Average:	0.00
No. 50s:	0	No. 100s:	0

ODI Bowling & Fielding

Wickets:	1	Runs:	41
Best Bowling:	1/41	Average:	41.00
5 WM:	0	Catches:	0
Stumpings:	0		

A right arm quick from South Australia he enjoyed a successful tour of the West Indies in 1973 taking 15 wickets. Despite his good form he would never play for Australia again, losing his spot to a young Queenslander by the name of Jeff Thomson.

HARRY, John

Born:	August 1, 1857
Batting:	Right handed
Bowling:	Right arm off-break
	Wicket Keeper

Tests

Test Career:	1895
Cap Number:	70
Tests Played:	1

Test Batting

Innings:	2	Runs:	8
Highest Score:	6	Average:	4.00
No. 50s:	0	No. 100s:	0

Test Bowling & Fielding

Wickets:	0	Runs:	0
Best Bowling:		Average:	0.00
5 WI:	0	10 WM:	0
Catches:	1	Stumpings:	0

A true all-rounder for Victoria where he batted, bowled off-spin, kept wickets and even played interstate baseball.

HARTIGAN, Michael Joseph (Roger)

Born:	December 12, 1879
Batting:	Right handed
Bowling:	Right arm slow

Tests

Test Career:	1908
Cap Number:	92
Tests Played:	2

Test Batting

Innings:	4	Runs:	170
Highest Score:	116	Average:	42.50
No. 50s:	0	No. 100s:	1

Test Bowling & Fielding

Wickets:	0	Runs:	7
Best Bowling:		Average:	0.00
5 WI:	0	10 WM:	0
Catches:	1	Stumpings:	0

He struck a fine century in his second Test, the third of the summer of 1907/08, but unfortunately had to withdraw from the side for the next Test because he could not get time off from the woolbroking firm for which he worked. He toured England in 1909 but lost form and never played Test cricket again. Hartigan served on the Australian Board of Control for 35 years.

HARTKOPF, Albert Ernst Victor

Born:	December 28, 1888
Batting:	Right handed
Bowling:	Right arm leg-break

Tests

Test Career:	1925
Cap Number:	120
Tests Played:	1

Test Batting

Innings:	2	Runs:	80
Highest Score:	80	Average:	40.00
No. 50s:	1	No. 100s:	0

Test Bowling & Fielding

Wickets:	1	Runs:	134
Best Bowling:	1/120	Average:	134.00
5 WI:	0	10 WM:	0
Catches:	0	Stumpings:	0

Though selected as a bowler, he made an 80 in his only Test. Also a fine Rules footballer and medical doctor.

HARVEY, Ian Joseph

Born:	April 10, 1972
Batting:	Right handed
Bowling:	Right arm medium

One Day Internationals

ODI Career:	1997-2004
ODIs Played:	73

ODI Batting

Innings:	51	Runs:	715
Highest Score:	48*	Average:	17.87
No. 50s:	0	No. 100s:	0

ODI Bowling & Fielding

Wickets:	85	Runs:	2,577
Best Bowling:	4/16	Average:	30.31
5 WM:	0	Catches:	17
Stumpings:	0		

An all-rounder with every trick in the book, he earnt the nickname 'Freak' because of his ability to pull off the impossible. His medium pace armoury included swing, seam, off-spin, leggies and a beautifully disguised slow ball that netted him plenty of caught and bowleds. Occasionally mentioned as a possible Test player, he was always better suited to the shorter version of the game, and was a member of the squad that won the World Cup in South Africa in 2003.

HARVEY, Mervyn Roye

Born:	April 29, 1918
Batting:	Right handed

Tests

Test Career:	1947
Cap Number:	175
Tests Played:	1

Test Batting

Innings:	2	Runs:	43
Highest Score:	31	Average:	21.50
No. 50s:	0	No. 100s:	0

Test Bowling & Fielding			
Wickets:	0	Runs:	0
Best Bowling:		Average:	0.00
5 WI:	0	10 WM:	0
Catches:	0	Stumpings:	0

Brother of Neil, his only Test was as opener against England at Adelaide in 1946/47 where he did put on over a hundred for the first wicket with Arthur Morris.

HARVEY, Robert Neil (Neil)

Born:	November 8, 1928
Batting:	Left handed
Bowling:	Right arm off-break

Tests

Test Career:	1948-63
Cap Number:	178
Tests Played:	79

Test Batting			
Innings:	137	Runs:	6,149
Highest Score:	205	Average:	48.41
No. 50s:	24	No. 100s:	21

Test Bowling & Fielding			
Wickets:	3	Runs:	120
Best Bowling:	1/8	Average:	40.00
5 WI:	0	10 WM:	0
Catches:	64	Stumpings:	0

When a precocious young talent makes his Test debut the hype often exceeds the result, but in the case of Neil Harvey the predictions proved to be spot on. He had been the youngest player to score a century in the strong Melbourne district competition and a prolific scorer for his state when called up for the Test side as a 19 year old. After a modest start he took to the Indians in his second Test score a majestic 153 at the MCG. It won him a spot on the tour of England in 1948 and such was the strength of the squad that he had to wait until the fourth Test at Headingly to make his Ashes debut. Still 19 he scored a famous first innings century in a Test considered to be one of the greatest of all time. He was particularly savage on the South Africans averaging over 80 against them in Tests, and hitting them for eight of his 21 Test centuries. They were also the victims when Harvey hit his highest Test score of 205 at the MCG in 1952/53. Throughout his career his exuded class, whether driving perfectly, leaning back to play a scything cut or as a faultless fieldsman. He maintained his involvement with the sport in retirement as a national selector.

HASSETT, Arthur Lindsay

Born:	August 28, 1913
Batting:	Right handed
Bowling:	Right arm medium

Tests

Test Career:	1938-53
Cap Number:	161
Tests Played:	43

Test Batting			
Innings:	69	Runs:	3,073
Highest Score:	198*	Average:	46.56
No. 50s:	11	No. 100s:	10

Test Bowling & Fielding			
Wickets:	0	Runs:	78
Best Bowling:		Average:	0.00
5 WI:	0	10 WM:	0
Catches:	30	Stumpings:	0

In a long and successful career he both bolstered the middle order of a side that was laden with talent, and opened the batting in one that was not. At all times Hassett's wicket was difficult to get, with his trademark full faced bat offered to anything that was on the stumps. Hassett debuted on the 1938 tour to England and whilst he didn't set the world on fire in Tests he batted well enough in other games to secure a regular spot in the side. Over the next 15 years he would go on to score ten Test centuries including a career best 198 not out against India at Adelaide. Hassett also captained his country in 24 Tests for 14 victories, a record that stacks up well against the great Sir Donald Bradman who had 15 wins from the same number of Tests. Upon retiring from the game Hassett became well known as a media figure and owner of a chain of sporting good stores.

HAURITZ, Nathan Michael

Born:	October 18, 1981
Batting:	Right handed
Bowling:	Right arm off-break

Tests

Test Career:	2004-
Cap Number:	390
Tests Played:	1

Test Batting			
Innings:	2	Runs:	15
Highest Score:	15	Average:	7.50
No. 50s:	0	No. 100s:	0

Test Bowling & Fielding			
Wickets:	5	Runs:	103
Best Bowling:	3/16	Average:	20.60
5 WI:	0	10 WM:	0
Catches:	1	Stumpings:	0

One Day Internationals

ODI Career:	2002-
ODIs Played:	8

ODI Batting			
Innings:	4	Runs:	35
Highest Score:	20*	Average:	35.00
No. 50s:	0	No. 100s:	0

ODI Bowling & Fielding			
Wickets:	9	Runs:	308
Best Bowling:	4/39	Average:	34.22
5 WM:	0	Catches:	2
Stumpings:	0		

Australian selectors have always been keen to develop spinners and by selecting Nathan Hauritz for the tour of India in 2004/05 they indicated that he was highly thought of. An off spinner who is willing to flight his deliveries, he played a single Test on that tour claiming five scalps. Since that time he has fallen behind South

Australian Dan Cullen in the pecking order and at the end of the 2005/06 moved from Queensland to New South Wales in order to re-ignite his career.

HAWKE, Neil James Napier

Born:	June 27, 1939
Batting:	Right handed
Bowling:	Right arm medium-fast

Tests

Test Career:	1963-68		
Cap Number:	224		
Tests Played:	27		

Test Batting

Innings:	37	Runs:	365
Highest Score:	45*	Average:	16.59
No. 50s:	0	No. 100s:	0

Test Bowling & Fielding

Wickets:	91	Runs:	2,677
Best Bowling:	7/105	Average:	29.41
5 WI:	6	10 WM:	1
Catches:	9	Stumpings:	0

Muscular and powerful, it came as no surprise to learn that he was a leading Australian Rules footballer as well as Test cricketer. Hawke used a strong upper body to generate surprising pace from a relatively short run up. He made his debut in 1962 and was a regular in the side for the next five years. Hawke enjoyed wickets that provided seam and recorded career best figues of 7/105 against England in Sydney during the 1965/66 Ashes series. He was also a more than handy lower order batsman who amassed more than 3,000 first class runs. Much loved by all in the cricket fraternity he battled illness later in life before passing away in 2000.

HAYDEN, Matthew Lawrence

Born:	October 29, 1971
Batting:	Left handed
Bowling:	Right arm medium

Tests

Test Career:	1994-		
Cap Number:	359		
Tests Played:	84		

Test Batting

Innings:	150	Runs:	7,326
Highest Score:	380	Average:	53.08
No. 50s:	26	No. 100s:	26

Test Bowling & Fielding

Wickets:	0	Runs:	40
Best Bowling:		Average:	0.00
5 WI:	0	10 WM:	0
Catches:	111	Stumpings:	0

One Day Internationals

ODI Career:	1993-		
ODIs Played:	119		

ODI Batting

Innings:	115	Runs:	4,131
Highest Score:	146	Average:	40.10
No. 50s:	26	No. 100s:	5

ODI Bowling & Fielding

Wickets:	0	Runs:	18
Best Bowling:		Average:	0.00
5 WM:	0	Catches:	46
Stumpings:	0		

The run machine from Queensland had a faltering start in Test cricket and for many years it looked as though a handful of Tests would support those critics who claimed that he was not up facing world class bowlers. He had a tough initiation against a strong South African side in 1994 and was dropped after scoring only 15 and 5. He didn't play another Test until the West Indies came to Australia in the summer of 1996/97 and despite scoring a century did little else, and was overlooked for the Ashes tour later that year. Hayden had faith in his technique, so rather than change his game he went back to state cricket looking for big runs to get himself back in to the Test side. His plan worked to prefection and by the end of 1999 the selectors could no longer ignore the powerfully built left hander. In 2000/01 he proved his worth in the three Test series in India. Faced with the spin of Harbhajan Singh and Anil Kumble on dry and dusty wickets he employed his powerful sweep to great effect in scoring a century and double century. A steady stream of runs turned into a flood; in 2001 he scored a record 1391 Test runs for the calendar year and in 2003 he belted the hapless Zimbabweans in Perth for a then world record Test score of 380. The machine eventually slowed, and by mid 2005 he was playing for his place in the side. Like Mark Taylor and Steve Waugh before him he responded with a timely century, hitting a watchful 138 at The Oval. Hayden is back in the swing and it seems that the 35 year old still has plenty of time left at the top of the Australian batting order.

HAZLITT, Gervys Rignold (Gerry)

Born:	September 4, 1888
Batting:	Right handed
Bowling:	Right arm medium

Tests

Test Career:	1907-12		
Cap Number:	89		
Tests Played:	9		

Test Batting

Innings:	12	Runs:	89
Highest Score:	34*	Average:	11.12
No. 50s:	0	No. 100s:	0

Test Bowling & Fielding

Wickets:	23	Runs:	623
Best Bowling:	7/25	Average:	27.08
5 WI:	1	10 WM:	0
Catches:	4	Stumpings:	0

Known as Gerry he came to the fore on the tour of 1912 when Australia travelled to England to compete in a triangular series with their hosts and South Africa. A slow bowler who combined traditional off spin and slow swing, Hazlitt took

7/25 against England at The Oval. Domestically the Victorian moved to NSW following his Test career where he became Master at the prestigious King's College.

HEALY, Ian Andrew

Born:	April 30, 1964
Batting:	Right handed Wicket Keeper

Tests
Test Career:	1988-99		
Cap Number:	344		
Tests Played:	119		

Test Batting
Innings:	182	Runs:	4,356
Highest Score:	161*	Average:	27.39
No. 50s:	22	No. 100s:	4

Test Bowling & Fielding
Wickets:	0	Runs:	0
Best Bowling:		Average:	0.00
5 WI:	0	10 WM:	0
Catches:	366	Stumpings:	29

One Day Internationals
ODI Career:	1988-97
ODIs Played:	168

ODI Batting
Innings:	120	Runs:	1,764
Highest Score:	56	Average:	21.00
No. 50s:	4	No. 100s:	0

ODI Bowling & Fielding
Wickets:	0	Runs:	0
Best Bowling:		Average:	0.00
5 WM:	0	Catches:	194
Stumpings:	39		

Ian Healy was not on most cricket watchers' radars when the selectors chose him to relieve Greg Dyer of the national wicket keeping job in 1988. Australia had been through a number of glovemen since the retirement of Rod Marsh and most thought that the little known Queenslander would soon join the procession. How wrong they would be. Healy held the post for ten years and along the way broke the records for most dismissals and most runs by an Australian keeper. He made his debut in Pakistan in 1988 and despite performing well in difficult conditions didn't win over the entire Australian public. In the second Test against the West Indies at Perth that summer he was jeered by local fans who felt that WA's Tim Zoehrer had deserved a Test recall ahead of Healy. It didn't phase the ever cheerful Healy who top scored for Australia in the second innings of that game with his first Test half century. He would go on to score over 4,000 Test runs including a career high 161 not out against the West Indies at Brisbane in the first Test of the 1996/97 summer. Healy favoured shots square of the wicket with an unconventional lift behind square-leg a particular favourite. His batting copybook was only blemished by occasional runs of poor form where he would struggle to reach double figures for three of four innings in row. A brilliant keeper to Shane Warne, he could read the leg spinner far better than most batsmen. After a shaky start, his keeping to the quick bowlers developed to the point where he was considered the best keeper in Test cricket during the mid nineties. He was vice captain to Mark Taylor for many years and also led the Aussies in a handful of one day games. Like many of his contemporaries he entered the media in retirement and is currently a prominent TV commentator.

HENDRY, Hunter Scott Thomas Laurie (Tom)

Born:	May 24, 1895
Batting:	Right handed
Bowling:	Right arm medium-fast

Tests
Test Career:	1921-29
Cap Number:	116
Tests Played:	11

Test Batting
Innings:	18	Runs:	335
Highest Score:	112	Average:	20.93
No. 50s:	0	No. 100s:	1

Test Bowling & Fielding
Wickets:	16	Runs:	640
Best Bowling:	3/36	Average:	40.00
5 WI:	0	10 WM:	0
Catches:	10	Stumpings:	0

An accomplished all-rounder with long legs and of slim build, he was unsurprisingly nicknamed 'Stork'. Though he didn't live up to his Victorian form when playing for Australia, he did hit a fine century against England at the SCG in 1928. Hendry was part of the first Australian cricket side that toured India in 1936.

HIBBERT, Paul Anthony

Born:	July 23, 1952
Batting:	Left handed
Bowling:	Left arm medium

Tests
Test Career:	1977
Cap Number:	284
Tests Played:	1

Test Batting
Innings:	2	Runs:	15
Highest Score:	13	Average:	7.50
No. 50s:	0	No. 100s:	0

Test Bowling & Fielding
Wickets:	0	Runs:	0
Best Bowling:		Average:	0.00
5 WI:	0	10 WM:	0
Catches:	1	Stumpings:	0

A fine servant for Victoria, the left handed batsman played his only Test against India during their 1977/78 tour to Australia.

HIGGS, James Donald

Born:	July 11, 1950
Batting:	Right handed
Bowling:	Right arm leg-break

Tests
Test Career:	1978-81		
Cap Number:	295		
Tests Played:	22		

Test Batting
Innings:	36	Runs:	111
Highest Score:	16	Average:	5.55
No. 50s:	0	No. 100s:	0

Test Bowling & Fielding
Wickets:	66	Runs:	2,057
Best Bowling:	7/143	Average:	31.16
5 WI:	2	10 WM:	0
Catches:	3	Stumpings:	0

The likeable Victorian leg-spinner had to be good at his art as his batting and fielding did him no favours. And good he was with the ability to bowl not only the leggie, but the wrong 'un and top spinner as well. In 1979 he returned career best figures of 7/143 against India at Madras and in 22 Tests overall, captured a respectable 66 victims.

HILDITCH, Andrew Mark Jefferson
Born:	May 20, 1956
Batting:	Right handed

Tests
Test Career:	1979-85
Cap Number:	302
Tests Played:	18

Test Batting
Innings:	34	Runs:	1,073
Highest Score:	119	Average:	31.55
No. 50s:	6	No. 100s:	2

Test Bowling & Fielding
Wickets:	0	Runs:	0
Best Bowling:		Average:	0.00
5 WI:	0	10 WM:	0
Catches:	13	Stumpings:	0

One Day Internationals
ODI Career:	1979-85
ODIs Played:	8

ODI Batting
Innings:	8	Runs:	226
Highest Score:	72	Average:	28.25
No. 50s:	1	No. 100s:	0

ODI Bowling & Fielding
Wickets:	0	Runs:	0
Best Bowling:		Average:	0.00
5 WM:	0	Catches:	1
Stumpings:	0		

An upright and technically sound opening bat, he made his debut as a result of vacancies created by the exodus of players to World Series Cricket. To his credit he fought hard to regain the spot he had lost when the aforementioned players returned. Hilditch enjoyed his best spell with the bat in 1985 scoring a century against the touring West Indians and then another as a tourist on an Ashes tour. He can lay claim to be one of the few batsmen to be given out 'handled the ball' in a Test match when Pakistan's Safraz Nawaz appealed after he innocently picked up the ball and handed it back to the bowler. Hilditch later became a national Test selector.

HILL, Clement
Born:	March 18, 1877
Batting:	Left handed

Tests
Test Career:	1896-1912
Cap Number:	74
Tests Played:	49

Test Batting
Innings:	89	Runs:	3,412
Highest Score:	191	Average:	39.21
No. 50s:	19	No. 100s:	7

Test Bowling & Fielding
Wickets:	0	Runs:	0
Best Bowling:		Average:	0.00
5 WI:	0	10 WM:	0
Catches:	33	Stumpings:	0

Clem Hill was considered by most judges to be Australia's finest batsman at the turn of the last century. The son of renowned South Australian batsman H.J. Hill, he was possessed of a brilliant eye, with a penchant for leg side play. He plundered seven Test centuries in an era when big scoring was anything but the norm. It was a total that should been added to, given that at one point in his Test career he scored 99,98 and 97 in consecutive innings. His most famous Test knock was at the MCG during the 1897/98 Ashes tour when his 188 rescued Australia who were at one stage 6/58. Hill would go on to captain his country in 1910 but a series of arguments with the Australian Cricket Board, including one that led to him punching selector Peter McAlister in the face, meant that he played his last Test by 1912. After his retirement from cricket he became a leading light in the racing industry, acting as a steward in both Adelaide and Melbourne. He is remembered today at the Adelaide Oval where the large southern grandstand is named in his honour.

HILL, John Charles (Jack)
Born:	June 25, 1923
Batting:	Right handed
Bowling:	Right arm leg-break

Tests
Test Career:	1953-55
Cap Number:	196
Tests Played:	3

Test Batting
Innings:	6	Runs:	21
Highest Score:	8*	Average:	7.00
No. 50s:	0	No. 100s:	0

Test Bowling & Fielding
Wickets:	8	Runs:	273
Best Bowling:	3/35	Average:	34.12
5 WI:	0	10 WM:	0
Catches:	2	Stumpings:	0

A Victorian leg-spinner, Jack Hill toured both England and the West Indies in the mid-fifties.

HOARE, Desmond Edward

Born: October 19, 1934
Batting: Right handed
Bowling: Right arm medium-fast

Tests

Test Career: 1961
Cap Number: 218
Tests Played: 1

Test Batting

Innings:	2	Runs:	35
Highest Score:	35	Average:	17.50
No. 50s:	0	No. 100s:	0

Test Bowling & Fielding

Wickets:	2	Runs:	156
Best Bowling:	2/68	Average:	78.00
5 WI:	0	10 WM:	0
Catches:	2	Stumpings:	0

A fast bowler from West Australia whose only Test was in the nail biter against the West Indies at Adelaide in the 1960/61 series.

HODGE, Bradley John

Born: December 29, 1974
Batting: Right handed
Bowling: Right arm slow

Tests

Test Career: 2005-
Cap Number: 394
Tests Played: 5

Test Batting

Innings:	9	Runs:	409
Highest Score:	203*	Average:	58.42
No. 50s:	1	No. 100s:	1

Test Bowling & Fielding

Wickets:	0	Runs:	8
Best Bowling:		Average:	0.00
5 WI:	0	10 WM:	0
Catches:	9	Stumpings:	0

One Day Internationals

ODI Career: 2005-
ODIs Played: 5

ODI Batting

Innings:	5	Runs:	79
Highest Score:	59	Average:	15.80
No. 50s:	1	No. 100s:	0

ODI Bowling & Fielding

Wickets:	0	Runs:	16
Best Bowling:		Average:	0.00
5 WM:	0	Catches:	1
Stumpings:	0		

After waiting almost a decade to make his Test debut, the Victorian batsman played only five Tests in the Australian summer of 2005/06 before finding himself on the outer again. The treatment seems harsh given that he had scored 60 on debut and then hammered the West Indians in Perth for an unbeaten double century. At present the nuggety right hander has a Test average of 58.42 and it only seems fair that he be given another chance at the top level.

HODGES, John Robart

Born: August 11, 1855
Batting: Right handed
Bowling: Right arm medium-fast

Tests

Test Career: 1877-78
Cap Number: 7
Tests Played: 2

Test Batting

Innings:	4	Runs:	10
Highest Score:	8	Average:	3.33
No. 50s:	0	No. 100s:	0

Test Bowling & Fielding

Wickets:	6	Runs:	84
Best Bowling:	2/7	Average:	14.00
5 WI:	0	10 WM:	0
Catches:	0	Stumpings:	0

A medium fast bowler, the left-handed Hodges had the honour of bowling Australia's first ball in Test cricket. Interestingly Hodges played only four first class games, two of them Test matches.

HOGAN, Tom George

Born: September 23, 1956
Batting: Right handed
Bowling: Left arm off-break

Tests

Test Career: 1983-84
Cap Number: 318
Tests Played: 7

Test Batting

Innings:	12	Runs:	205
Highest Score:	42*	Average:	18.63
No. 50s:	0	No. 100s:	0

Test Bowling & Fielding

Wickets:	15	Runs:	706
Best Bowling:	5/66	Average:	47.06
5 WI:	1	10 WM:	0
Catches:	2	Stumpings:	0

One Day Internationals

ODI Career: 1983-84
ODIs Played: 16

ODI Batting

Innings:	12	Runs:	72
Highest Score:	27	Average:	9.00
No. 50s:	0	No. 100s:	0

ODI Bowling & Fielding

Wickets:	23	Runs:	574
Best Bowling:	4/33	Average:	24.95
5 WM:	0	Catches:	10
Stumpings:	0		

An off spinner and handy lower order bat from West Australia. He was part of an unofficial tour to South Africa in 1985 and never played for his country again.

HOGG, George Bradley

Born: February 6, 1971
Batting: Left handed
Bowling: Left arm leg-break

Tests

Test Career: 1996-
Cap Number: 367
Tests Played: 4

Test Batting
Innings:	5	Runs:	38
Highest Score:	17*	Average:	9.50
No. 50s:	0	No. 100s:	0

Test Bowling & Fielding
Wickets:	9	Runs:	452
Best Bowling:	2/40	Average:	50.22
5 WI:	0	10 WM:	0
Catches:	0	Stumpings:	0

One Day Internationals
ODI Career: 1996-
ODIs Played: 85

ODI Batting
Innings:	49	Runs:	560
Highest Score:	71*	Average:	20.74
No. 50s:	2	No. 100s:	0

ODI Bowling & Fielding
Wickets:	107	Runs:	2,968
Best Bowling:	5/32	Average:	27.73
5 WM:	2	Catches:	25
Stumpings:	0		

In an interesting career he has been selected in the Australian ODI team even when he can't make the West Australian side. Tried unsuccessfully at Test level, his particular brand of quicker leg-spin was well suited to the one day game and the Australian selectors have shown that following the retirement of Shane Warne from the shorter version of the game that George Bradley Hogg will be their man. He was named 'Man of the Series' when Australia met Bangladesh in 2006.

HOGG, Rodney Malcolm
Born: March 5, 1951
Batting: Right handed
Bowling: Right arm fast

Tests
Test Career: 1978-84
Cap Number: 297
Tests Played: 38

Test Batting
Innings:	58	Runs:	439
Highest Score:	52	Average:	9.75
No. 50s:	1	No. 100s:	0

Test Bowling & Fielding
Wickets:	123	Runs:	3,053
Best Bowling:	6/74	Average:	28.47
5 WI:	6	10 WM:	2
Catches:	7	Stumpings:	0

One Day Internationals
ODI Career: 1979-85
ODIs Played: 71

ODI Batting
Innings:	35	Runs:	137
Highest Score:	22	Average:	9.13
No. 50s:	0	No. 100s:	0

ODI Bowling & Fielding
Wickets:	85	Runs:	2,418
Best Bowling:	4/29	Average:	28.44
5 WM:	0	Catches:	8
Stumpings:	0		

Like his run up to the bowling crease, Rodney Hogg's career started slowly but built up momentum as it went. A Victorian, he had to move to South Australia to play first class cricket and then had to wait until the advent of World Series Cricket to finally make the Test side. His debut series against England was nothing short of spectacular. He captured 41 wickets at a cost of only 12.85, despite being part of a side that was trounced 5-1. He took five wickets in an innings in four consecutive innings and by the time he had conquered the English at the MCG in the third Test Australian fans had a new fast bowling hero to idolise. Dennis Lillee's defection to WSC was all but forgotten as 'Hoggy, Hoggy, Hoggy, Oi, Oi, Oi,' rang out around cricket grounds throughout Australia. Over the next six years Rodney Malcolm Hogg would continue to bowl manfully for his country, but injury would prevent him from scaling the heights of 1978/79 again. In 1985 he joined the rebel Australian tour to South Africa and never played an official Test for his country again.

HOHNS, Trevor Victor
Born: January 23, 1954
Batting: Left handed
Bowling: Left arm leg-break

Tests
Test Career: 1989
Cap Number: 345
Tests Played: 7

Test Batting
Innings:	7	Runs:	136
Highest Score:	40	Average:	22.66
No. 50s:	0	No. 100s:	0

Test Bowling & Fielding
Wickets:	17	Runs:	580
Best Bowling:	3/59	Average:	34.11
5 WI:	0	10 WM:	0
Catches:	3	Stumpings:	0

Nicknamed 'Cracker', he was a chinaman bowler from New South Wales who toured England in 1989 playing in all six Tests. At 34 he was never going to be a long term bowling option for Australia and after that Ashes series was passed over for spinners such as Peter Sleep and Peter Taylor. In retirement Hohns became a major player in Australian cricket as national chairman of selectors.

HOLE, Graeme Blake
Born: January 6, 1931
Batting: Right handed
Bowling: Right arm off-break

Tests
Test Career: 1951-55
Cap Number: 188
Tests Played: 18

Test Batting
Innings:	33	Runs:	789
Highest Score:	63	Average:	25.45
No. 50s:	6	No. 100s:	0

Test Bowling & Fielding
Wickets:	3	Runs:	126
Best Bowling:	1/9	Average:	42.00
5 WI:	0	10 WM:	0
Catches:	21	Stumpings:	0

A hard hitting batsman, he was tried in a number of positions in the Australian top-order but failed to show his best at Test level. Interestingly he made six Test half centuries but his highest score was only 63, which he scored against the West Indies during their 1951/52 tour to Australia. Hole was also a fine slip fieldsman.

HOLLAND, Robert George
Born:	October 19, 1946
Batting:	Right handed
Bowling:	Right arm leg-break

Tests
Test Career:	1984-86		
Cap Number:	326		
Tests Played:	11		

Test Batting
Innings:	15	Runs:	35
Highest Score:	10	Average:	3.18
No. 50s:	0	No. 100s:	0

Test Bowling & Fielding
Wickets:	34	Runs:	1,352
Best Bowling:	6/54	Average:	39.76
5 WI:	3	10 WM:	2
Catches:	5	Stumpings:	0

One Day Internationals
ODI Career:	1985		
ODIs Played:	2		

ODI Batting
Innings:	0	Runs:	0
Highest Score:	0	Average:	0.00
No. 50s:	0	No. 100s:	0

ODI Bowling & Fielding
Wickets:	2	Runs:	99
Best Bowling:	2/49	Average:	49.50
5 WM:	0	Catches:	0
Stumpings:	0		

A leg spinner from Newcastle in NSW, he was plucked from relative obscurity to make his Test debut at the age of 38. Deadly on a turning wicket, he mesmerised the West Indians at the SCG in 1985 to capture ten wickets and lead his country to a rare victory over the Windies.

HOOKES, David William
Born:	May 3, 1955
Batting:	Left handed
Bowling:	Left arm slow

Tests
Test Career:	1977-85		
Cap Number:	276		
Tests Played:	23		

Test Batting
Innings:	41	Runs:	1,306
Highest Score:	143*	Average:	34.36
No. 50s:	8	No. 100s:	1

Test Bowling & Fielding
Wickets:	1	Runs:	41
Best Bowling:	1/4	Average:	41.00
5 WI:	0	10 WM:	0
Catches:	12	Stumpings:	0

One Day Internationals
ODI Career:	1977-86		
ODIs Played:	39		

ODI Batting
Innings:	36	Runs:	826
Highest Score:	76	Average:	24.29
No. 50s:	5	No. 100s:	0

ODI Bowling & Fielding
Wickets:	1	Runs:	28
Best Bowling:	1/2	Average:	28.00
5 WM:	0	Catches:	11
Stumpings:	0		

A dashing left hander, he made the Test side on the back of a run of five centuries in six innings for South Australia that had even the great Don Bradman gushing. He made his debut on the biggest of stages, against England in the Centenary Test. Undaunted by the occasion, he took the handle to Tony Greig in the second innings hitting him for 20 runs in one over on the way to an important 56. The dashing left hander had become the hottest property in Australian cricket overnight and he was duly snapped up by the forces behind World Series Cricket. Hookes paid a heavy price for his foray into the 'pyjama' game suffering a sickening injury at the Sydney Showgrounds in 1977 when he had his jaw broken by a bouncer from Andy Roberts. He would continue to play for his country at the top level but he lacked that devil may care attitude that made him an irresistible force prior to the injury. 'Hookesy' was a success in his post playing days making a name for himself as both an administrator and a media figure. In early 2004 David Hookes was killed in a bar-room altercation that left the Australian sporting public in a state of shock. He was only 48 years old.

HOPES, James Redfern
Born:	November 24, 1978
Batting:	Right handed
Bowling:	Right arm medium

One Day Internationals
ODI Career:	2005-		
ODIs Played:	9		

ODI Batting
Innings:	3	Runs:	84
Highest Score:	43	Average:	28.00
No. 50s:	0	No. 100s:	0

ODI Bowling & Fielding
Wickets:	4	Runs:	269
Best Bowling:	1/8	Average:	67.25
5 WM:	0	Catches:	3
Stumpings:	0		

A highly competitive all-rounder who is perfectly suited to the one day team, though his opportunities at national level have been limited thanks to fellow Queenslanders Shane Watson and

Andrew Symonds. Fans can expect to see him in the Australian Twenty/20 side where he has already played and performed with success.

HOPKINS, Albert John Young

Born:	May 3, 1874
Batting:	Right handed
Bowling:	Right arm medium-fast

Tests

Test Career:	1902-09		
Cap Number:	82		
Tests Played:	20		

Test Batting

Innings:	33	Runs:	509
Highest Score:	43	Average:	16.41
No. 50s:	0	No. 100s:	0

Test Bowling & Fielding

Wickets:	26	Runs:	696
Best Bowling:	4/81	Average:	26.76
5 WI:	0	10 WM:	0
Catches:	11	Stumpings:	0

A slow swing bowler he toured England on three seperate occasions as well as being part of Australia's first touring side to South Africa. He surprisingly opened the bowling in The Lord's Test of 1902 capturing two key wickets in the process. hopkins was a hard hitting batsman who saved his best for New South Wales for whom he once scored a double century.

HORAN, Thomas Patrick

Born:	March 8, 1854
Batting:	Right handed
Bowling:	Right arm slow

Tests

Test Career:	1877-85		
Cap Number:	8		
Tests Played:	15		

Test Batting

Innings:	27	Runs:	471
Highest Score:	124	Average:	18.83
No. 50s:	1	No. 100s:	1

Test Bowling & Fielding

Wickets:	11	Runs:	143
Best Bowling:	6/40	Average:	13.00
5 WI:	1	10 WM:	0
Catches:	6	Stumpings:	0

Born in County Cork, Ireland, Tom Horan was considered Victoria's finest bat when selected to represent his country in the first ever Test Match. His Test career spanned 15 Tests and included a fine Test innings of 124 against Shaw's English XI at the MCG. He played over 100 first class matches scoring eight centuries along the way. His best individual effort was a slashing 250 against the Tasmanians whilst playing for East Melbourne at the East Melbourne Cricket Ground. Horan toured England with the Australians in 1882 and fanned the growing rivalry between the two nations by taking no less of a figure than the great W.G. Grace. The revered Englishman had run out Australian Sammy Jones as he strayed from his crease to pat down the pitch during the 1882 Oval Test match, earning a stiff rebuke from Horan: "I do not think it redounds much to any man's credit to endeavor to win a match by resorting to what might not inaptly be called sharp practice." Though not a renowned bowler, Horan took six wickets in an innings at the SCG in 1885 to assist in his country's six run win over the English. It was during that tour to Australia by England that Horan became his country's third Test captain leading his nation in two matches. Upon retirement, Tom Horan's keen cricket knowledge saw him write a regular column for The Australasian newspaper under the nom de plume, Felix.

HORDERN, Herbert Vivian (Ranji)

Born:	February 10, 1883
Batting:	Right handed
Bowling:	Right arm leg-break

Tests

Test Career:	1911-12		
Cap Number:	97		
Tests Played:	7		

Test Batting

Innings:	13	Runs:	254
Highest Score:	50	Average:	23.09
No. 50s:	1	No. 100s:	0

Test Bowling & Fielding

Wickets:	46	Runs:	1,075
Best Bowling:	7/90	Average:	23.36
5 WI:	5	10 WM:	2
Catches:	6	Stumpings:	0

A talented leg-spin bowler, Dr.Herbert Vivian Hordern was nicknamed 'Ranji' because of a simillarity in complexion to the great English Test player K.S. Ranjitsinhji. Hordern was predominately a googly bowler, spinning the ball in the opposite direction to most right hand leg spinners. He did this to great effect, particularly at the SCG in 1911 where he took 12 wickets in the first Test against the English. He unusually honed his cricket in the United States having spent a great deal of time living in and playing for Pennsylvania. A dentist by profession.

HORNIBROOK, Percival Mitchell

Born:	June 27, 1899
Batting:	Left handed
Bowling:	Left arm slow

Tests

Test Career:	1929-30		
Cap Number:	132		
Tests Played:	6		

Test Batting

Innings:	7	Runs:	60
Highest Score:	26	Average:	10.00
No. 50s:	0	No. 100s:	0

Test Bowling & Fielding

Wickets:	17	Runs:	664
Best Bowling:	7/92	Average:	39.05
5 WI:	1	10 WM:	0
Catches:	7	Stumpings:	0

A left armed medium pace bowler from Queensland, he played a key role in Australia winning the Ashes in 1930 when he took 7/92 in the second innings of the fifth and deciding Test. He retired upon returning to Australia, making that his best and last game for his country.

HOWELL, William Peter

Born: December 29, 1869
Batting: Left handed
Bowling: Right arm off-break

Tests

Test Career: 1898-1904
Cap Number: 77
Tests Played: 18

Test Batting

Innings:	27	Runs:	158
Highest Score:	35	Average:	7.52
No. 50s:	0	No. 100s:	0

Test Bowling & Fielding

Wickets:	49	Runs:	1,407
Best Bowling:	5/81	Average:	28.71
5 WI:	1	10 WM:	0
Catches:	12	Stumpings:	0

Though the records show he was an off-spinner, Howell was anything but a slow bowler. Quick through the air, his best return for Australia was on the matting wickets in South Africa where he took 9 wickets in the Cape Town Test. The Sydneysider's most famous effort with the ball was on the 1899 tour of England where he took all ten first innings wickets against Surrey for only 28 runs. Also a powerful middle order batsman.

HUGHES, Kimberley John

Born: January 26, 1954
Batting: Right handed
Bowling: Right arm slow

Tests

Test Career: 1977-84
Cap Number: 281
Tests Played: 70

Test Batting

Innings:	124	Runs:	4,415
Highest Score:	213	Average:	37.41
No. 50s:	22	No. 100s:	9

Test Bowling & Fielding

Wickets:	0	Runs:	28
Best Bowling:	0	Average:	0.00
5 WI:	0	10 WM:	0
Catches:	50	Stumpings:	0

One Day Internationals

ODI Career: 1977-85
ODIs Played: 97

ODI Batting

Innings:	88	Runs:	1,968
Highest Score:	98	Average:	24.00
No. 50s:	17	No. 100s:	0

ODI Bowling & Fielding

Wickets:	0	Runs:	4
Best Bowling:	0	Average:	0.00
5 WM:	0	Catches:	27
Stumpings:	0		

It would be a great injustice if Kim Hughes was just remembered for his tearful resignation as Australian captain in 1983. The elegant West Australian had every shot in the book and on occasion even played some that weren't. After a haltering start to his Test career that saw him play only three Tests over three seperate tours, he made a fighting 129 against England in Brisbane in 1978. That innings won him not only a regular spot in the Test side but also the respect of the men that make decisions, and less than a year later he was leading the Australian Test team at the age of only 25. It was a meteoric rise for the man with baby blonde curls, and he responded with a number of top quality innings. In total he made nine Test tons and a 99 against England in Perth that was the equal of any of his triple figure scores. Hughes was particularly good against spin with quick footwork and a perfectly executed sweep shot, so it was not surprising that his highest Test knock of 213 came up against the Indians on home soil in 1981. Equally at home in the longer or shorter version of the game there was little better sight in the 70's and 80's than Kimberly J Hughes in full flight.

HUGHES, Mervyn Gregory

Born: November 23, 1961
Batting: Right handed
Bowling: Right arm fast

Tests

Test Career: 1985-94
Cap Number: 332
Tests Played: 53

Test Batting

Innings:	70	Runs:	1,032
Highest Score:	72*	Average:	16.64
No. 50s:	2	No. 100s:	0

Test Bowling & Fielding

Wickets:	212	Runs:	6,017
Best Bowling:	8/87	Average:	28.38
5 WI:	7	10 WM:	1
Catches:	23	Stumpings:	0

One Day Internationals

ODI Career: 1988-93
ODIs Played: 33

ODI Batting

Innings:	17	Runs:	100
Highest Score:	20	Average:	11.11
No. 50s:	0	No. 100s:	0

ODI Bowling & Fielding

Wickets:	38	Runs:	1,115
Best Bowling:	4/44	Average:	29.34
5 WM:	0	Catches:	6
Stumpings:	0		

Built more like a long distance truck driver than an opening bowler, the lion-hearted Victorian overcame plenty of early scepticism to become a fine strike bowler for his country. He made his debut against India in 1985 but was soon on the outer once again. Undeterred, he refined his game, shortening his run up and bowling closer to the stumps. He made a successful return to the

Test side, with his finest moment coming at the WACA in 1988 where he claimed 13 West Indian scalps including a career best 8/87 in the second innings. His batting was many things rolled into one, unorthodox, entertaining and at times very effective. In that series 1988 home series against the West Indies he scored a well constructed 72 in Adelaide. It was a vital knock as it enabled his Victorian team mate Dean Jones to record his highest Test score. Larger than life, nearly every cricket biography in recent years has included a couple of 'Merv' stories for light relief. He retired in 1994 having earnt a spot amongst Australia's top ten Test wicket takers with 212 Test scalps. Merv Hughes can rest easy in his retirement knowing that he extracted every last bit from his ample frame. Today he divides his time between countless public appearances and his job as national selector.

ODI Batting
Innings:	4	Runs:	7
Highest Score:	3*	Average:	0.00
No. 50s:	0	No. 100s:	0

ODI Bowling & Fielding
Wickets:	12	Runs:	203
Best Bowling:	5/21	Average:	16.91
5 WM:	1	Catches:	1
Stumpings:	0		

The mustachioed Victorian may have played more Tests had injury not stood in the way. A fast bowler who relied on pace and accuracy rather than sideways movement, he had become a regular member of the side in the era of World Series Cricket until a severe back injury saw him sent home from the 1979/80 tour of India. He would recover but never make it into the Test side again. The unassuming fast bowler has been involved with cricket since his retirement and today acts as a Test referee.

HUNT, William Alfred
Born: August 26, 1908
Batting: Left handed
Bowling: Left arm off-break

Tests
Test Career:	1932
Cap Number:	139
Tests Played:	1

Test Batting
Innings:	1	Runs:	0
Highest Score:	0	Average:	0.00
No. 50s:	0	No. 100s:	0

Test Bowling & Fielding
Wickets:	0	Runs:	39
Best Bowling:		Average:	0.00
5 WI:	0	10 WM:	0
Catches:	1	Stumpings:	0

A left arm medium pace bowler whose only appearance at the highest level was the fourth Test against South Africa at Adelaide in 1931/32.

HURST, Alan George
Born: July 15, 1950
Batting: Right handed
Bowling: Right arm fast

Tests
Test Career:	1974-79
Cap Number:	269
Tests Played:	12

Test Batting
Innings:	20	Runs:	102
Highest Score:	26	Average:	6.00
No. 50s:	0	No. 100s:	0

Test Bowling & Fielding
Wickets:	43	Runs:	1,200
Best Bowling:	5/28	Average:	27.90
5 WI:	2	10 WM:	0
Catches:	3	Stumpings:	0

One Day Internationals
ODI Career:	1975-79
ODIs Played:	8

HURWOOD, Alexander
Born: June 17, 1902
Batting: Right handed
Bowling: Right arm off-break

Tests
Test Career:	1930-31
Cap Number:	135
Tests Played:	2

Test Batting
Innings:	2	Runs:	5
Highest Score:	5	Average:	2.50
No. 50s:	0	No. 100s:	0

Test Bowling & Fielding
Wickets:	11	Runs:	170
Best Bowling:	4/22	Average:	15.45
5 WI:	0	10 WM:	0
Catches:	2	Stumpings:	0

Queensland quick who took 4/22 against the touring West Indies in his second and final Test.

HUSSEY, Michael Edward Killeen
Born: May 27, 1975
Batting: Left handed
Bowling: Right arm medium

Tests
Test Career:	2005-
Cap Number:	393
Tests Played:	11

Test Batting
Innings:	19	Runs:	1,139
Highest Score:	182	Average:	75.93
No. 50s:	4	No. 100s:	4

Test Bowling & Fielding
Wickets:	0	Runs:	18
Best Bowling:		Average:	0.00
5 WI:	0	10 WM:	0
Catches:	3	Stumpings:	0

One Day Internationals
ODI Career:	2004-
ODIs Played:	40

ODI Batting
Innings:	31	Runs:	1,156
Highest Score:	88*	Average:	77.06
No. 50s:	9	No. 100s:	0

ODI Bowling & Fielding

Wickets:	2	Runs:	155
Best Bowling:	1/22	Average:	77.50
5 WM:	0	Catches:	21
Stumpings:	0		

Nicknamed 'Mr. Cricket' because of his all consuming passion for the game, he served a ten year apprenticeship at state and county level before finally getting his chance. With over 15,000 first class runs to his credit, there must have been times when he wondered if that chance would ever come but when Justin Langer was ruled out of the first Test against the West Indies in 20005/06 the call finally came. Things didn't start too well for Hussey, and with 1 and 29 in his first two innings the pressure was on the opener when the series headed to Hobart. A brilliant 137 set his Test career in motion and he followed it with an unbeaten 133 at Adelaide in his very next Test. A versatile batsman who can open or bat in the middle order, Hussey has never looked back and at present boasts an average in the 70's for both Test and one day cricket.

INVERARITY, Robert John

Born:	January 31, 1944
Batting:	Right handed
Bowling:	Left arm slow

Tests

Test Career:	1968-72		
Cap Number:	246		
Tests Played:	6		

Test Batting

Innings:	11	Runs:	174
Highest Score:	56	Average:	17.40
No. 50s:	1	No. 100s:	0

Test Bowling & Fielding

Wickets:	4	Runs:	93
Best Bowling:	3/26	Average:	23.25
5 WI:	0	10 WM:	0
Catches:	4	Stumpings:	0

A prolific run scorer at state level, he was unable to take that form with him into the Test arena. His highest Test score of 56 came against the English on a soft track at The Oval in 1968.

IREDALE, Francis Adams

Born:	June 19, 1867
Batting:	Right handed
Bowling:	Right arm slow

Tests

Test Career:	1894-99		
Cap Number:	65		
Tests Played:	14		

Test Batting

Innings:	23	Runs:	807
Highest Score:	140	Average:	36.68
No. 50s:	4	No. 100s:	2

Test Bowling & Fielding

Wickets:	0	Runs:	3
Best Bowling:		Average:	0.00
5 WI:	0	10 WM:	0
Catches:	16	Stumpings:	0

A leading light for NSW in 19th century cricket, he is rarely mentioned when discussing early Test greats but a batting average of more than 36 suggests otherwise. He played a key role for the Australians in the great 1894/95 series scoring a memorable 81 on debut. Equally at home on English pitches, he scored a fine century at Old Trafford in 1899 on a tour that saw him average over 40. His was a life devoted to cricket; following his retirement he became an Australian Test selector and then became a key committee man with the New South Wales Cricket Association.

IRONMONGER, Herbert

Born:	April 7, 1882
Batting:	Left handed
Bowling:	Left arm slow

Tests

Test Career:	1928-33		
Cap Number:	125		
Tests Played:	14		

Test Batting

Innings:	21	Runs:	42
Highest Score:	12	Average:	2.62
No. 50s:	0	No. 100s:	0

Test Bowling & Fielding

Wickets:	74	Runs:	1,330
Best Bowling:	7/23	Average:	17.97
5 WI:	4	10 WM:	2
Catches:	3	Stumpings:	0

At the age of 45, 'Dainty' Ironmonger is the second oldest Australian to make his Test debut. A finger spinner of sorts, he generated turn by taking advantage of a gap that had been created in his hand by an accident that cost him the top of his middle finger. Despite his late start he played 14 Tests, the last of which was against England at the age of 50. His best Test figures of 7/23 came against the West Indies on their first tour of Australia.

IVERSON, John Brian (Jack)

Born:	July 27, 1915
Batting:	Right handed
Bowling:	Right arm leg-break

Tests

Test Career:	1950-51		
Cap Number:	185		
Tests Played:	5		

Test Batting

Innings:	7	Runs:	3
Highest Score:	1*	Average:	0.75
No. 50s:	0	No. 100s:	0

Test Bowling & Fielding

Wickets:	21	Runs:	320
Best Bowling:	6/27	Average:	15.23
5 WI:	1	10 WM:	0
Catches:	2	Stumpings:	0

Jack Iverson was Australia's secret bowling weapon in the Ashes series against England in 1950/51, bowling a range of slow deliveries that combined both wrist and finger spin. In only five Tests he captured 21 wickets but an ankle injury sustained when he stepped on the ball during a Test match in Adelaide, curtailed what was a promising career.

JACKSON, Archibald Alexander

Born: September 5, 1909
Batting: Right handed

Tests
Test Career: 1929-31
Cap Number: 130
Tests Played: 8

Test Batting
Innings:	11	Runs:	474
Highest Score:	164	Average:	47.40
No. 50s:	2	No. 100s:	1

Test Bowling & Fielding
Wickets:	0	Runs:	0
Best Bowling:		Average:	0.00
5 WI:	0	10 WM:	0
Catches:	7	Stumpings:	0

When the brilliant young New South Welshman made his debut at the age of 20, Australia had unveiled a new batting sensation. His 164 against England in the fourth Test of the Bodyline series went within one run of the highest score on debut by an Australian and confirmed the form he had shown as a teenager with his state. An elegant right hand top order batsman, he never bludgeoned the ball but was said to have near perfect timing and footwork. Noted cricket writer A.G. Moyes described him in glowing terms, saying that he was the closest in style to the great Victor Trumper he had ever seen. Tragically he would be dead only four years after making his Test debut, succumbing to tuberculosis on the very day Australia regained the Ashes in 1933.

JAQUES, Philip Anthony

Born: May 3, 1979
Batting: Left handed

Tests
Test Career: 2005-
Cap Number: 395
Tests Played: 2

Test Batting
Innings:	3	Runs:	96
Highest Score:	66	Average:	32.00
No. 50s:	1	No. 100s:	0

Test Bowling & Fielding
Wickets:	0	Runs:	0
Best Bowling:		Average:	0.00
5 WI:	0	10 WM:	0
Catches:	1	Stumpings:	0

One Day Internationals
ODI Career: 2006
ODIs Played: 2

ODI Batting
Innings:	2	Runs:	94
Highest Score:	94	Average:	47.00
No. 50s:	1	No. 100s:	0

ODI Bowling & Fielding
Wickets:	0	Runs:	0
Best Bowling:		Average:	0.00
5 WM:	0	Catches:	0
Stumpings:	0		

An unconventional opening batsman from New South Wales with an appetite for big scores, he made his debut against South Africa in the 2005/06 Boxing Day Test. Jaques is an attacking batsman who isn't scared to hit over the infield, and whilst he is yet to cement a Test spot, at 26 he has time on his side. In July 2006 he hit a double century and century in the same game while playing for Australia A against India A.

JARMAN, Barrington Noel (Barry)

Born: February 17, 1936
Batting: Right handed
Wicket Keeper

Tests
Test Career: 1959-69
Cap Number: 215
Tests Played: 19

Test Batting
Innings:	30	Runs:	400
Highest Score:	78	Average:	14.81
No. 50s:	2	No. 100s:	0

Test Bowling & Fielding
Wickets:	0	Runs:	0
Best Bowling:		Average:	0.00
5 WI:	0	10 WM:	0
Catches:	50	Stumpings:	4

The affable South Australian had to bide his time as Wally Grout's understudy, but when the opportunity presented itself he took it with both gloves. He made his debut as a fill in for the injured Grout at Melbourne in the 1962/63 Ashes series and showed enough to hold that spot until Grout retired. His experience was put to good use by the Aussies and he captained the side in 1968 when Bill Lawry pulled out of the Headingly Test. Whilst his batting was rarely at its best in Tests, the hard hitter did score 78 against India at Calcutta on the 1964/65 tour.

JARVIS, Arthur Harwood (Affie)

Born: October 19, 1860
Batting: Right handed
Wicket Keeper

Tests
Test Career: 1885-95
Cap Number: 33
Tests Played: 11

Test Batting
Innings:	21	Runs:	303
Highest Score:	82	Average:	16.83
No. 50s:	1	No. 100s:	0

Test Bowling & Fielding
Wickets:	0	Runs:	0
Best Bowling:		Average:	0.00
5 WI:	0	10 WM:	0
Catches:	9	Stumpings:	9

Better known as Affie, he was the first wicket keeper to learn that most difficult of lessons; that being the second best keeper for you country is a frustrating way to earn a living. Despite playing second fiddle to Blackham, the South Australian was said to be a fine gloveman playing eleven Tests and touring England.

JENNER, Terrence James

Born:	September 8, 1944
Batting:	Right handed
Bowling:	Right arm leg-break

Tests
Test Career:	1970-75
Cap Number:	248
Tests Played:	9

Test Batting
Innings:	14	Runs:	208
Highest Score:	74	Average:	23.11
No. 50s:	1	No. 100s:	0

Test Bowling & Fielding
Wickets:	24	Runs:	749
Best Bowling:	5/90	Average:	31.20
5 WI:	1	10 WM:	0
Catches:	5	Stumpings:	0

One Day Internationals
| ODI Career: | 1975 |
| ODIs Played: | 1 |

ODI Batting
Innings:	1	Runs:	12
Highest Score:	12	Average:	12.00
No. 50s:	0	No. 100s:	0

ODI Bowling & Fielding
Wickets:	0	Runs:	28
Best Bowling:		Average:	0.00
5 WM:	0	Catches:	0
Stumpings:	0		

A leg spinner from South Australia, he was often bowled in tandem with his state team mate, Ashley Mallett. Depsite a number of good spells for his country he is probably best remembered for his late innings heroics with the bat against the West Indies at his home ground of Adelaide in 1974/75. He was also batting when struck by a short ball from John Snow in 1970/71 that prompted a savage crowd reaction and a walk off by the English. In recent years he has acted as adviser and coach to Shane Warne.

JENNINGS, Claude Barrow

Born:	June 5, 1884
Batting:	Right handed
	Wicket Keeper

Tests
Test Career:	1912
Cap Number:	103
Tests Played:	6

Test Batting
Innings:	8	Runs:	107
Highest Score:	32	Average:	17.83
No. 50s:	0	No. 100s:	0

Test Bowling & Fielding
Wickets:	0	Runs:	0
Best Bowling:		Average:	0.00
5 WI:	0	10 WM:	0
Catches:	5	Stumpings:	0

An opening batsman from South Australia who failed to seize his chance when presented with a spot in the weakened side that toured England in 1912 for the triangular series with South Africa.

JOHNSON, Ian William Geddes

Born:	December 8, 1917
Batting:	Right handed
Bowling:	Right arm off-break

Tests
Test Career:	1946-56
Cap Number:	164
Tests Played:	45

Test Batting
Innings:	66	Runs:	1,000
Highest Score:	77	Average:	18.51
No. 50s:	6	No. 100s:	0

Test Bowling & Fielding
Wickets:	109	Runs:	3,182
Best Bowling:	7/44	Average:	29.19
5 WI:	3	10 WM:	0
Catches:	30	Stumpings:	0

Ian Johnson is one of a select group of cricketers to have made 1000 Test runs and taken 100 Test wickets though his stats will confirm that it was a close run thing. The Victorian off-spinner was a master of flight and when on song near impossible to score off. At the SCG in 1946 he took 6/42 off 30 eight ball overs in a masterful display of control. His batting was steady rather than spectacular, though he had the ability to hit out if the situation arose. In the mid '50's he was made captain of Australia, and whilst he didn't have the strongest of sides to work with, finished with the respectable record of seven wins and five draws from 17 games at the helm.

JOHNSON, Leonard Joseph

Born:	March 18, 1919
Batting:	Right handed
Bowling:	Right arm medium-fast

Tests
Test Career:	1948
Cap Number:	179
Tests Played:	1

Test Batting
Innings:	1	Runs:	25
Highest Score:	25*	Average:	0.00
No. 50s:	0	No. 100s:	0

Test Bowling & Fielding
Wickets:	6	Runs:	74
Best Bowling:	3/8	Average:	12.33
5 WI:	0	10 WM:	0
Catches:	2	Stumpings:	0

Unlucky not to play more Test cricket, the Queensland right arm quick couldn't break into a side dominated by Lindwall, Johnston and

Miller. His only Test, in which he performed well, was against India.

JOHNSON, Mitchell Guy

Born:	November 2, 1981
Batting:	Left handed
Bowling:	Left arm medium-fast

One Day Internationals

ODI Career:	2005-
ODIs Played:	5

ODI Batting

Innings:	1	Runs:	0
Highest Score:	0*	Average:	0.00
No. 50s:	0	No. 100s:	0

ODI Bowling & Fielding

Wickets:	3	Runs:	174
Best Bowling:	2/24	Average:	58.00
5 WM:	0	Catches:	0
Stumpings:	0		

Big things are expected from the young left arm quick from Queensland who received his first Cricket Australia contract in May, 2006. He has shown a liking for the big stage with career best first class figures of 6/51 in the 2005/06 Australian domestic four day final. He underlined his potential by tearing through the strong Indian top orded in a washed out ODI that was played in Kuala Lumpur in September, 2006.

JOHNSTON, William Arras

Born:	February 26, 1922
Batting:	Left handed
Bowling:	Left arm medium-fast

Tests

Test Career:	1947-55
Cap Number:	177
Tests Played:	40

Test Batting

Innings:	49	Runs:	273
Highest Score:	29	Average:	11.37
No. 50s:	0	No. 100s:	0

Test Bowling & Fielding

Wickets:	160	Runs:	3,826
Best Bowling:	6/44	Average:	23.91
5 WI:	7	10 WM:	0
Catches:	16	Stumpings:	0

Big Bill Johnston was a Victorian left armer with a short run and big heart. He made his debut against the touring Indians in 1947/48 and despite showing good form in the series, the quality of the opposition meant that he was still no certainty to be part of the bowling attack for the Tests in England in 1948. Good early form on the tour saw him make the side for the first Test and from that point there was no turning back. He formed an all-conquering pace trio with Ray Lindwall and Keith Miller taking 27 wickets for the series which equalled Lindwall and eclipsed Miller by 14. With his abbreviated run to the bowling crease he provided the perfect foil for Lindwall. He was mu8ch more than a workhorse though, and he brought up his 100th Test wicket in what was then the quickest time for an Australian. A genuine number 11, he put on 38 with Doug Ring at the MCG to help Australia to an improbable one wicket victory over the West Indies in 1952. In fact Johnston's batting brought his team-mates and fans a great deal of pleasure and on the 1953 tour to England they contrived to get him a Bradman like average. Batting at eleven he only went out once on tour and left England with an average of over 100 for the series!

JONES, Dean Mervyn

Born:	March 24, 1961
Batting:	Right handed
Bowling:	Right arm slow

Tests

Test Career:	1984-92
Cap Number:	324
Tests Played:	52

Test Batting

Innings:	89	Runs:	3,631
Highest Score:	216	Average:	46.55
No. 50s:	14	No. 100s:	11

Test Bowling & Fielding

Wickets:	1	Runs:	64
Best Bowling:	1/5	Average:	64.00
5 WI:	0	10 WM:	0
Catches:	34	Stumpings:	0

One Day Internationals

ODI Career:	1984-94
ODIs Played:	164

ODI Batting

Innings:	161	Runs:	6,068
Highest Score:	145	Average:	44.61
No. 50s:	46	No. 100s:	7

ODI Bowling & Fielding

Wickets:	3	Runs:	81
Best Bowling:	2/34	Average:	27.00
5 WM:	0	Catches:	54
Stumpings:	0		

A dazzling stroke player, there may have been better batsmen to have played the game, but when in full flight there were few better to watch. A superb driver, particularly through the on side, he loved nothing more than charging a fast bowler and hitting him straight back over his head. Jones was equally at home playing Tests or ODI's, thrilling crowds for just over a decade. His first Test innings, a gritty 48 in the Caribbean may not have been an indication of things to come but it showed he had the ability to mix it with the very best. Jones scored two memorable Test double centuries. The first was against India in the famous tied Test at Madras in 1986. Countering severe cramps, vomitting and bouts of diarrhoea, he batted for over 500 minutes to score a wonderful 210. Jones collapsed after being dismissed and was rushed to hospital to be placed on a drip. Two years later he went six runs better against an imposing West Indies attack at the Adelaide Oval in a series that Australia lost 4-0. A member of the World Cup winning side in 1987, he was considered the best one day cricketer in the world at his peak. 'Deano' was never far from controversy and on one famous occasion in 1993 asked Curtly Ambrose to remove his white wristbands whilst bowling in an ODI. "He was definitely trying some form of camouflage," Jones said at the time. A furious Ambrose took off his wristbands and went on to rip through the Australian batting line up in a match winning performance. The opinionated Jones didn't just make headlines on the field. He polarised opinion throughout his career and when he was dropped from the Test side for the final time, many fans thought it had more to do with his attitude than his ability. In retirement Jones continued to entertain as a commentator and print journalist but was once again in hot water when when making a comment about a South African cricketer in 2006. Thinking he was off microphone, Jones referred to Hashim Amla as a terrorist, in a gaffe that cost him his job as a commentator with Ten Sports. .

JONES, Ernest

Born: September 30, 1869
Batting: Right handed
Bowling: Right arm fast

Tests
Test Career: 1894-1902
Cap Number: 66
Tests Played: 19

Test Batting
Innings:	26	Runs:	126
Highest Score:	20	Average:	5.04
No. 50s:	0	No. 100s:	0

Test Bowling & Fielding
Wickets:	64	Runs:	1,857
Best Bowling:	7/88	Average:	29.01
5 WI:	3	10 WM:	1
Catches:	21	Stumpings:	0

The name Ernie Jones is the answer to one of cricket's harder trivia questions: Who was the first player to be no-balled for throwing in a Test match. It would be unfair though to just remember him for that indiscretion at the MCG in 1901, for Jones was considered to be Australia's finest and fastest bowler at the turn of the century. Jonah as he was known, was a miner who put his strength to good use terrorising the English on three separate tours of the mother country. Obviously a man with a good sense of humour, he was introduced to Edward VII on one tour and when asked by the Regent if he attended a famous college in Australia he replied, "Yes, I take the dustcart there regularly".

JONES, Samuel Percy

Born: August 1, 1861
Batting: Right handed
Bowling: Right arm medium-fast

Tests
Test Career: 1882-88
Cap Number: 30
Tests Played: 12

Test Batting
Innings:	24	Runs:	428
Highest Score:	87	Average:	21.39
No. 50s:	1	No. 100s:	0

Test Bowling & Fielding
Wickets:	6	Runs:	112
Best Bowling:	4/47	Average:	18.66
5 WI:	0	10 WM:	0
Catches:	12	Stumpings:	0

An accomplished all-rounder, he is best known for a pivotal role he played in the famous 'Ashes' Test of 1882 at The Oval. Having safely completed a run, Jones left his crease and was run out by WG Grace who was fielding at short leg. The Australians accused the good doctor of unsportsmanlike behaviour claiming that he had summonsed Jones for a conversation prior to running him out. Jones may have also played a role in another legend of Australian cricket. After a series of unfortunate dismissals he fell 13 short of a century in his highest Test innings, leading some cricket historians to nominate him as the player who began the legend of 87 being the devil's number. Following a successful cricket career in Australia he moved to New Zealand.

JOSLIN, Leslie Ronald

Born: December 13, 1947
Batting: Right handed

Tests
Test Career: 1968
Cap Number: 245
Tests Played: 1

Test Batting
Innings:	2	Runs:	9
Highest Score:	7	Average:	4.50
No. 50s:	0	No. 100s:	0

Test Bowling & Fielding
Wickets:	0	Runs:	0
Best Bowling:		Average:	0.00
5 WI:	0	10 WM:	0
Catches:	0	Stumpings:	0

Victorian left hander who made his debut against the touring Indians. Went to England in 1968 but didn't play any Tests.

JULIAN, Brendon Paul

Born: August 10, 1970
Batting: Right handed
Bowling: Left arm medium-fast

Tests
Test Career: 1993-95
Cap Number: 356
Tests Played: 7

Test Batting
Innings:	9	Runs:	128
Highest Score:	56*	Average:	16.00
No. 50s:	1	No. 100s:	0

Test Bowling & Fielding
Wickets:	15	Runs:	599
Best Bowling:	4/36	Average:	39.93
5 WI:	0	10 WM:	0
Catches:	4	Stumpings:	0

One Day Internationals
ODI Career:	1993-99
ODIs Played:	25

ODI Batting
Innings:	17	Runs:	224
Highest Score:	35	Average:	13.17
No. 50s:	0	No. 100s:	0

ODI Bowling & Fielding
Wickets:	22	Runs:	997
Best Bowling:	3/40	Average:	45.31
5 WM:	0	Catches:	8
Stumpings:	0		

Born in New Zealand, the left arm quick was on the periphery of Test and One Day International sides for much of the 90's. He made his debut against England at Manchester in 1993 and after a promising performance in the first innings where he took 2/30 was unlucky to be dropped for the second Test. Recalled for the next Test at Trent Bridge he struggled, and with match figures of 2/194 was back on the outer again. Julian would continue to tantalise with the ball or as a hard hitting lower order batsman and whilst he couldn't nail down a regular spot in the Test or one day sides he was a member of the Australian squad that won the 1999 World Cup. Tall and good looking he turned his hand to television after cricket, working as a sports reporter and presenter on a travel program.

KASPROWICZ, Michael Scott
Born:	February 10, 1972
Batting:	Right handed
Bowling:	Right arm medium-fast

Tests
Test Career:	1996-
Cap Number:	369
Tests Played:	38

Test Batting
Innings:	54	Runs:	445
Highest Score:	25	Average:	10.59
No. 50s:	0	No. 100s:	0

Test Bowling & Fielding
Wickets:	113	Runs:	3,716
Best Bowling:	7/36	Average:	32.88
5 WI:	4	10 WM:	0
Catches:	16	Stumpings:	0

One Day Internationals
ODI Career:	1995-
ODIs Played:	43

ODI Batting
Innings:	13	Runs:	74
Highest Score:	28*	Average:	18.50
No. 50s:	0	No. 100s:	0

ODI Bowling & Fielding
Wickets:	67	Runs:	1,674
Best Bowling:	5/45	Average:	24.98
5 WM:	2	Catches:	13
Stumpings:	0		

The right arm swing bowler from Queensland who made his first class debut as a teenager. He worked hard to earn a Test spot in the mid nineties and equally hard to regain it almost ten years later when many thought his international career was over. Strongly built and possessed of a textbook action for an outswing bowler, he added a well disguised slower ball and an in-cutter to his arsenal when he joined Test ranks. 'Kaspra' has twice captured seven wickets in an innings during his Test career, once against England in 1997 and against Sri Lanka in 2004. Kasprowicz had been overlooked for younger men early in 2005 but fought back with a swag of state wickets and was selected for the Ashes tour. He again proved his worth with the ball on that tour, and so nearly with the bat at Edgbaston, when he was dismissed with Australia two runs shy of a famous Test victory.

KATICH, Simon Mathew
Born:	August 21, 1975
Batting:	Left handed
Bowling:	Left arm leg-break

Tests
Test Career:	2001-
Cap Number:	384
Tests Played:	23

Test Batting
Innings:	38	Runs:	1,260
Highest Score:	125	Average:	36.00
No. 50s:	8	No. 100s:	2

Test Bowling & Fielding
Wickets:	12	Runs:	406
Best Bowling:	6/65	Average:	33.83
5 WI:	1	10 WM:	0
Catches:	15	Stumpings:	0

One Day Internationals
ODI Career:	2001-
ODIs Played:	41

ODI Batting
Innings:	38	Runs:	1,232
Highest Score:	107*	Average:	37.33
No. 50s:	9	No. 100s:	1

ODI Bowling & Fielding
Wickets:	0	Runs:	0
Best Bowling:		Average:	0.00
5 WM:	0	Catches:	12
Stumpings:	0		

Originally from Western Australia the left handed batsman came to notice in the late 90's when he scored over 1,000 runs in a domestic summer. Illness delayed his Test debut but after failing in a single appearance at Headingly on the 2001 Ashes tour it was back to state cricket to bide his time again. The opportunity came against Zimbabwe in 2003/04 where salvation came with ball rather than the bat. He took six wickets in an innings at the SCG with his chinamen, and whilst it was never going to be the birth of a Test bowling career it buoyed his confidence. Later that summer he returned to the SCG to play the Indians and struck his maiden

Test ton. Katich maintained a spot in the middle order until a loss of form against the West Indies in 2005/06 saw him on the outer again. A scrapper for much of his career, he will be hoping to fight his way back into the Test team one more time.

KELLEWAY, Charles
Born: April 25, 1886
Batting: Right handed
Bowling: Right arm medium-fast

Tests
Test Career: 1910-28
Cap Number: 96
Tests Played: 26

Test Batting
Innings:	42	Runs:	1,422
Highest Score:	147	Average:	37.42
No. 50s:	6	No. 100s:	3

Test Bowling & Fielding
Wickets:	52	Runs:	1,683
Best Bowling:	5/33	Average:	32.36
5 WI:	1	10 WM:	0
Catches:	24	Stumpings:	0

With a nickname like 'Rock of Gibraltar' it would come as no surprise to learn that Charles Kellway's only form of attack was in fact defense. He style was best summed up by his turgid 61 in over five hours against England at Lord's in 1912. It was an innings that ensured his country a draw and drew praise from his team mates. He combined wonderfully well with Warren Bardsley both for country and state providing the perfect foil for his more attacking opening partner.

KELLY, James Joseph
Born: May 10, 1867
Batting: Right handed
Wicket Keeper

Tests
Test Career: 1896-1905
Cap Number: 75
Tests Played: 36

Test Batting
Innings:	56	Runs:	664
Highest Score:	46*	Average:	17.02
No. 50s:	0	No. 100s:	0

Test Bowling & Fielding
Wickets:	0	Runs:	0
Best Bowling:		Average:	0.00
5 WI:	0	10 WM:	0
Catches:	43	Stumpings:	20

Australia's second great wicket-keeper he followed in the footsteps of Blackham and like his predecessor had no fear in keeping up to the stumps to fast bowlers. A capable batsman, he retired following a finger injury sustained whilst keeping.

KELLY, Thomas Joseph Dart
Born: May 3, 1884
Batting: Right handed

Tests
Test Career: 1877-79
Cap Number: 12
Tests Played: 2

Test Batting
Innings:	3	Runs:	64
Highest Score:	32	Average:	21.33
No. 50s:	0	No. 100s:	0

Test Bowling & Fielding
Wickets:	0	Runs:	0
Best Bowling:		Average:	0.00
5 WI:	0	10 WM:	0
Catches:	1	Stumpings:	0

An Irish born batsman who was a renowned point fieldsman.

KENDALL, Thomas Kingston
Born: August 24, 1851
Batting: Left handed
Bowling: Left arm slow

Tests
Test Career: 1877
Cap Number: 9
Tests Played: 2

Test Batting
Innings:	4	Runs:	39
Highest Score:	17*	Average:	13.00
No. 50s:	0	No. 100s:	0

Test Bowling & Fielding
Wickets:	14	Runs:	215
Best Bowling:	7/55	Average:	15.35
5 WI:	1	10 WM:	0
Catches:	2	Stumpings:	0

Whilst most cricket fans could tell you that Charles Bannerman batted the Australians to victory in the first ever Test Match, very few could name the bowler that played just as important a role. Tom Kendall was a slow medium break bowler that could turn the ball both into and away from the batsman. A left-hander from Victoria, he beguiled the English in the second innings of the first Test to finish with innings figures of 7/55. Kendall proved it was no fluke by taking six wickets in his second Test. Oddly that was to be his final match for Australia. Kendall was inexplicably left out of the Australian side that toured England in 1878 and though he later played against the English for both Victoria and Tasmania he would never play another Test.

KENT, Martin Francis
Born: November 23, 1953
Batting: Right handed

Tests
Test Career: 1981
Cap Number: 312
Tests Played: 3

Test Batting
Innings:	6	Runs:	171
Highest Score:	54	Average:	28.50
No. 50s:	2	No. 100s:	0

Test Bowling & Fielding			
Wickets:	0	Runs:	0
Best Bowling:		Average:	0.00
5 WI:	0	10 WM:	0
Catches:	6	Stumpings:	0

One Day Internationals

ODI Career:	1981		
ODIs Played:	5		
ODI Batting			
Innings:	5	Runs:	78
Highest Score:	33	Average:	19.50
No. 50s:	0	No. 100s:	0
ODI Bowling & Fielding			
Wickets:	0	Runs:	0
Best Bowling:		Average:	0.00
5 WM:	0	Catches:	4
Stumpings:	0		

If the establishment in Australian cricket had any resentment towards cricketers who had defected to World Series Cricket then Martin Kent could claim he was the prime victim. A tall upper order batsman, he deserved to play more than just three Tests, but after suffering a back injury following the Ashes tour in 1981 he was never seen at the highest level again.

KERR, Robert Byers

Born:	June 16, 1961
Batting:	Right handed

Tests

Test Career:	1985		
Cap Number:	331		
Tests Played:	2		
Test Batting			
Innings:	4	Runs:	31
Highest Score:	17	Average:	7.75
No. 50s:	0	No. 100s:	0
Test Bowling & Fielding			
Wickets:	0	Runs:	0
Best Bowling:		Average:	0.00
5 WI:	0	10 WM:	0
Catches:	1	Stumpings:	0

One Day Internationals

ODI Career:	1985		
ODIs Played:	4		
ODI Batting			
Innings:	4	Runs:	97
Highest Score:	87*	Average:	32.33
No. 50s:	1	No. 100s:	0
ODI Bowling & Fielding			
Wickets:	0	Runs:	0
Best Bowling:		Average:	0.00
5 WM:	0	Catches:	1
Stumpings:	0		

An elegant top order batsman from Queensland who failed to reproduce his impressive state form in the international arena.

KIPPAX, Alan Falconer

Born:	May 25, 1897
Batting:	Right handed
Bowling:	Right arm leg-break

Tests

Test Career:	1925-34		
Cap Number:	122		
Tests Played:	22		
Test Batting			
Innings:	34	Runs:	1,192
Highest Score:	146	Average:	36.12
No. 50s:	8	No. 100s:	2
Test Bowling & Fielding			
Wickets:	0	Runs:	19
Best Bowling:		Average:	0.00
5 WI:	0	10 WM:	0
Catches:	13	Stumpings:	0

He was a star batsman with his state but despite a number of fine innings for his country could not cement a permanent place in the national side. An attacking right hand middle order batsman, his two Test centuries both came at home. The first was exactly 100 against the English at the MCG in 1929 and the second 146 against the inexperienced West Indians a year later. In 1929 he scored 260 for New South Wales against Victoria putting on a world record 307 for the last wicket in the process. The renowned commentator Johnnie Moyes said of Kippax, "He was by nature a charmer, he could cut, drive and hook, there was a beauty about his batting".

KLINE, Lindsay Francis

Born:	September 29, 1934
Batting:	Left handed
Bowling:	Left arm leg-break

Tests

Test Career:	1957-61		
Cap Number:	207		
Tests Played:	13		
Test Batting			
Innings:	16	Runs:	58
Highest Score:	15*	Average:	8.28
No. 50s:	0	No. 100s:	0
Test Bowling & Fielding			
Wickets:	34	Runs:	776
Best Bowling:	7/75	Average:	22.82
5 WI:	1	10 WM:	0
Catches:	9	Stumpings:	0

A left arm wrist spinner from Victoria, he saved his best for matches on foreign soil. Playing against South Africa in Cape Town he got a hat-trick in only his second Test. Kline took 15 wickets in that series for 16.33 and again headed the averages against India and Pakistan in 1959/60 with 16 scalps at only 14.33. Despite those performances with the ball he is remembered as a late order batsman who was left not out in the first ever tied Test. Later in that series with the West Indies, he famously combined with Ken 'Slasher' Mackay at Adelaide in a game saving last wicket stand that lasted 100 minutes.

LAIRD, Bruce Malcolm

Born:	November 21, 1950
Batting:	Right handed
Bowling:	Right arm slow

Tests
Test Career:	1979-82		
Cap Number:	306		
Tests Played:	21		

Test Batting
Innings:	40	Runs:	1,341
Highest Score:	92	Average:	35.28
No. 50s:	11	No. 100s:	0

Test Bowling & Fielding
Wickets:	0	Runs:	12
Best Bowling:		Average:	0.00
5 WI:	0	10 WM:	0
Catches:	16	Stumpings:	0

One Day Internationals
ODI Career:	1979-82
ODIs Played:	23

ODI Batting
Innings:	23	Runs:	594
Highest Score:	117*	Average:	29.70
No. 50s:	2	No. 100s:	1

ODI Bowling & Fielding
Wickets:	0	Runs:	0
Best Bowling:		Average:	0.00
5 WM:	0	Catches:	5
Stumpings:	0		

Nicknamed Stumpy, Laird is surely one of the best batsmen never to have made a Test century. One of the few players without Test experience to sign with World Series Cricket, he had to wait until the reunification of Australian cricket to make his Test debut. His first game turned out to be a baptism of fire, opening the batting in Brisbane against a West Indian attack consisting of Andy Roberts, Michael Holding, Colin Croft and Joel Garner. His innings of 92 against the best, was considered one of the great Test innings of all time, with then commentator Ian Chappell describing it as the finest ever debut by an Australian batsman. Laird followed that courageous knock with 75 in the second innings, and whilst he failed to better that debut innings in 20 subsequent Tests he continued to be a fearless opener for his country.

LANGER, Justin Lee
Born:	November 21, 1970
Batting:	Left handed
Bowling:	Right arm slow

Tests
Test Career:	1993-
Cap Number:	354
Tests Played:	100

Test Batting
Innings:	173	Runs:	7,393
Highest Score:	250	Average:	45.35
No. 50s:	29	No. 100s:	22

Test Bowling & Fielding
Wickets:	0	Runs:	3
Best Bowling:		Average:	0.00
5 WI:	0	10 WM:	0
Catches:	68	Stumpings:	0

One Day Internationals
ODI Career:	1994-97
ODIs Played:	8

ODI Batting
Innings:	7	Runs:	160
Highest Score:	36	Average:	32.00
No. 50s:	0	No. 100s:	0

ODI Bowling & Fielding
Wickets:	0	Runs:	0
Best Bowling:		Average:	0.00
5 WM:	0	Catches:	2
Stumpings:	0		

Justin Langer's picked a momentous Test to make his debut, Australia's painful one run loss to the West Indies at the Adelaide Oval in 1993. Fans can recall the last gasp heroics by Craig McDermott and Tim May as well as the controversial decision that cost the Aussies the match, but what they often forget is that Australia would not have got within cooee of the opposition if not for a courageous 54 by the debutant Langer. He top scored in that nail-biting second innings after having been hit flush on the helmet by an Ian Bishop bouncer earlier in the game. Despite showing maturity beyond his 22 years, he was out of the side less than six months later. Over the next five years he was barely sighted at Test level and seemed destined to be a footnote in Australian Test cricket history, but the youngster from a tough Perth suburb was made of sterner stuff and came again. His debut Test ton in Peshawar in 1998/99 earned him time to prove himself and by the time he landed in Hobart to play Pakistan in October, 1999 he had cemented his Test spot. With Australia facing certain defeat, he and Adam Gilchrist put on 238 and steered their side to a famous victory. He continued to blossom and when Australia needed an opener to fill Michael Slater's shoes he answered the call. He and his partner at the top of the order Matthew Hayden, shared a common history. Both made their Test debuts at 22 and were discarded and seemingly forgotten before resurrecting their careers. Their trust and mutual respect was evident on the field, and they took as much pleasure in the other's successes as their own. By the time he lined up for his 100th Test in 2005/06 his Test record stood at over 7,000 runs at 45.35 with 22 centuries. An incident in that Test would take him back to his debut almost 13 years earlier. He was struck a fearful blow on the helmet by Makhaya Ntini that saw him take no further part in the game and bring his cricket future into question. Langer refuted suggestions that he was jeopardising his health and should retire, and countered critics by heading to England to fulfill his obligations with Somerset. In July, 2006 Langer showed the folly of writing him off when he smashed a club record 342 for his county.

LANGLEY, Gilbert Roche Andrews
Born:	September 14, 1919
Batting:	Right handed
	Wicket Keeper

Tests
Test Career:	1951-56		
Cap Number:	189		
Tests Played:	26		

Test Batting
Innings:	37	Runs:	374
Highest Score:	53	Average:	14.96
No. 50s:	1	No. 100s:	0

Test Bowling & Fielding
Wickets:	0	Runs:	0
Best Bowling:		Average:	0.00
5 WI:	0	10 WM:	0
Catches:	83	Stumpings:	15

He was a very different keeper to most his predecessors in that he was heavily set, but it didn't seem to affect his mobility behind the stumps. Langley's 21 dismissals in a series against the Windies in 1951/52 was a then world record and he left the Test arena with an overall record of almost four victims per Test. As a batsman Langley was effective rather stylish managing only one half century in 21 Tests. He was also an outstanding Australian Rules Footballer in South Australia with the Sturt club.

LAUGHLIN, Trevor John
Born:	January 30, 1951
Batting:	Left handed
Bowling:	Right arm medium

Tests
Test Career:	1978		
Cap Number:	296		
Tests Played:	3		

Test Batting
Innings:	5	Runs:	87
Highest Score:	35	Average:	17.40
No. 50s:	0	No. 100s:	0

Test Bowling & Fielding
Wickets:	6	Runs:	262
Best Bowling:	5/101	Average:	43.66
5 WI:	1	10 WM:	0
Catches:	3	Stumpings:	0

One Day Internationals
ODI Career:	1978-79		
ODIs Played:	6		

ODI Batting
Innings:	5	Runs:	105
Highest Score:	74	Average:	26.25
No. 50s:	1	No. 100s:	0

ODI Bowling & Fielding
Wickets:	8	Runs:	224
Best Bowling:	3/54	Average:	28.00
5 WM:	0	Catches:	0
Stumpings:	0		

A stocky all-rounder from Victoria he got his chance to play Test cricket on the troubled Australian tour to the Caribbean in 1978. The plight of that side is often best summed up by the fact that they were forced to open the bowling the Laughlin's military mediums in the final Test of that series. What is less well known is that he took five wickets in the first innings of that game including four of the West indian top order.

LAVER, Frank Jonas
Born:	December 7, 1869
Batting:	Right handed
Bowling:	Right arm medium

Tests
Test Career:	1899-1909		
Cap Number:	78		
Tests Played:	15		

Test Batting
Innings:	23	Runs:	196
Highest Score:	45	Average:	11.52
No. 50s:	0	No. 100s:	0

Test Bowling & Fielding
Wickets:	37	Runs:	964
Best Bowling:	8/31	Average:	26.05
5 WI:	2	10 WM:	0
Catches:	8	Stumpings:	0

An underrated all-rounder in Australian cricket, Laver shone at both domestic and Test level. He bowled Australia to victory at Trent Bridge in 1909 with first innings figures of 7/64 and repeated the dose at Old Trafford where he took 8/31 in England's first dig. As a batsman he failed to flatter for Australia but was a prodigious scorer in Sheffield Shield cricket where he scored almost 3,000 runs. On the 1909 tour of England he was team manager, a position he maintained following his retirement as a player.

LAW, Stuart Grant
Born:	October 18, 1968
Batting:	Right handed
Bowling:	Right arm medium

Tests
Test Career:	1995		
Cap Number:	365		
Tests Played:	1		

Test Batting
Innings:	1	Runs:	54
Highest Score:	54*	Average:	0.00
No. 50s:	1	No. 100s:	0

Test Bowling & Fielding
Wickets:	0	Runs:	9
Best Bowling:		Average:	0.00
5 WI:	0	10 WM:	0
Catches:	1	Stumpings:	0

One Day Internationals
ODI Career:	1994-99		
ODIs Played:	54		

ODI Batting
Innings:	51	Runs:	1,237
Highest Score:	110	Average:	26.89
No. 50s:	7	No. 100s:	1

ODI Bowling & Fielding
Wickets:	12	Runs:	635
Best Bowling:	2/22	Average:	52.91
5 WM:	0	Catches:	12
Stumpings:	0		

The Queensland captain was a fierce competitor who was unlucky not to have played more than one Test, a game in which he hit an unbeaten half century. Law left Australia in 2005 for England, where he has taken up citizenship and plays for Lancashire.

LAWRY, William Morris

Born: February 11, 1937
Batting: Left handed
Bowling: Left arm medium

Tests
Test Career: 1961-71
Cap Number: 219
Tests Played: 67

Test Batting
Innings:	123	Runs:	5,234
Highest Score:	210	Average:	47.15
No. 50s:	27	No. 100s:	13

Test Bowling & Fielding
Wickets:	0	Runs:	6
Best Bowling:		Average:	0.00
5 WI:	0	10 WM:	0
Catches:	30	Stumpings:	0

One Day Internationals
ODI Career: 1971
ODIs Played: 1

ODI Batting
Innings:	1	Runs:	27
Highest Score:	27	Average:	27.00
No. 50s:	0	No. 100s:	0

ODI Bowling & Fielding
Wickets:	0	Runs:	0
Best Bowling:		Average:	0.00
5 WM:	0	Catches:	1
Stumpings:	0		

The tall opening batsman from Victoria went from precocious teenager to captain of his country in a career marked by one quality above all others, concentration. He made his Test debut on the Ashes tour of 1961 scoring two centuries and averaging above fifty in the five Test series. For the next decade Australia had an ever reliable opening batsman who would go on to make 13 Test centuries. The English press latched on to his nickname 'Phantom' and dubbed him the 'the corpse with pads'. Whilst he had a reputation as a stonewaller Lawry also had a fine array of shots and was particularly savage on any bowler who strayed on to his pads. He replaced Bob Simpson as Australian captain in the summer of 1967/68 and held the post until he was surprisingly dropped for the last Test of the England tour of 1970/71. Not only was Lawry dumped as captain he was also left out of the Test side and never played for his country again. Ironically the man best known for occupying the crease captained Australia's first ever one day side in a one off game at the MCG in 1971. Following his departure from the game he joined the Channel Nine commentary team when the station boss, Kerry Packer created World Series Cricket. Bill Lawry has been a mainstay of the commentary team ever since, coining the much copied phrase "It's all happening" along the way.

LAWSON, Geoffrey Francis

Born: December 7, 1957
Batting: Right handed
Bowling: Right arm fast

Tests
Test Career: 1980-89
Cap Number: 309
Tests Played: 46

Test Batting
Innings:	68	Runs:	894
Highest Score:	74	Average:	15.96
No. 50s:	4	No. 100s:	0

Test Bowling & Fielding
Wickets:	180	Runs:	5,501
Best Bowling:	8/112	Average:	30.56
5 WI:	11	10 WM:	2
Catches:	10	Stumpings:	0

One Day Internationals
ODI Career: 1980-89
ODIs Played: 79

ODI Batting
Innings:	52	Runs:	378
Highest Score:	33*	Average:	11.11
No. 50s:	0	No. 100s:	0

ODI Bowling & Fielding
Wickets:	88	Runs:	2,592
Best Bowling:	4/26	Average:	29.45
5 WM:	0	Catches:	18
Stumpings:	0		

A tall fast bowler from New South Wales who used every bit of his height to advantage, he ably shouldered much of his country's fast bowling workload in the post Dennis Lillee era. He announced himself as a bowler of the future on the Ashes tour in 1981, taking 7/81 in the first innings at Lords. In the years to follow he would show he wasn't scared of marathon spells and would regularly lead the side in overs bowled. His career best figures of 8/112 came off 40 gruelling overs at Adelaide in the summer heat against the West Indies in 1984. Surprisingly erudite for a fast bowler, 'Henry' Lawson was a much respected captain of the New South Wales state side for an extended period.

LEE, Brett

Born: November 8, 1976
Batting: Right handed
Bowling: Right arm fast

Tests
Test Career: 1999-
Cap Number: 383
Tests Played: 54

Test Batting
Innings:	60	Runs:	1,033
Highest Score:	64	Average:	21.08
No. 50s:	3	No. 100s:	0

Test Bowling & Fielding
Wickets:	211	Runs:	6,636
Best Bowling:	5/30	Average:	31.45
5 WI:	7	10 WM:	0
Catches:	15	Stumpings:	0

One Day Internationals
ODI Career: 2000-
ODIs Played: 135

ODI Batting
Innings:	60	Runs:	694
Highest Score:	57	Average:	19.27
No. 50s:	2	No. 100s:	0

ODI Bowling & Fielding

Wickets:	237	Runs:	5,414
Best Bowling:	5/22	Average:	22.84
5 WM:	5	Catches:	34
Stumpings:	0		

When Brett Lee burst onto the Test scene at the MCG in late 1999, cricket had found a new speed sensation. His first scalp, Indian opener Ramesh, had his stumps splayed and at inning's close five batsmen had succumbed to his fearsome pace. Nothing excites cricket fans more than a tearaway fast bowler but they would soon learn that there is a difference between bowling fast and bowling well. A young Lee struggled with the mantle of strike bowler, sacrificing line and length for speed. The result was too many short balls or attempted yorkers and whilst the wickets kept coming they tended to be lower order batsman who didn't have the technique to cope with his pace. Injury gave him time to reassess and by the time he toured England in 2005 he had become a more complete bowler, taking 20 wickets and spearheading an attack that had been depleted by the absence of Glenn McGrath and Jason Gillespie. The added responsibility sat well with Lee who had been in career best form during 2005/06 with a five wicket haul against the touring West Indians and two more in Tests with the South Africans. Lee has been a regular member of the one day side and boasts an ODI hat-trick from an encounter with a shell-shocked Kenyan side during the 2003 World Cup. Just as his bowling has developed over the years so has his batting, with recent good form against England and South Africa suggesting he has almost become an all-rounder.

LEE, Philip Keith

Born:	September 15, 1904
Batting:	Right handed
Bowling:	Right arm medium

Tests

Test Career:	1931-33		
Cap Number:	138		
Tests Played:	2		

Test Batting

Innings:	3	Runs:	57
Highest Score:	42	Average:	19.00
No. 50s:	0	No. 100s:	0

Test Bowling & Fielding

Wickets:	5	Runs:	212
Best Bowling:	4/111	Average:	42.40
5 WI:	0	10 WM:	0
Catches:	1	Stumpings:	0

South Australian finger spinner and handy lower order batsman.

LEE, Shane

Born:	August 8, 1973
Batting:	Right handed
Bowling:	Right arm medium

One Day Internationals

ODI Career:	1995-2001		
ODIs Played:	45		

ODI Batting

Innings:	35	Runs:	477
Highest Score:	47	Average:	17.66
No. 50s:	0	No. 100s:	0

ODI Bowling & Fielding

Wickets:	48	Runs:	1,245
Best Bowling:	5/33	Average:	25.93
5 WM:	1	Catches:	23
Stumpings:	0		

Shorter and more solidly built than his brother Brett, the all-rounder was ideally suited to one-day cricket with hard hitting and aggressive bowling. After showing great potential on home soil he was selected in the 1996 World Cup squad. Lee was a regular fixture in the ODI side until knee injuries prompted an early retirement at the age of only 29.

LEHMANN, Darren Scott

Born:	February 5, 1970
Batting:	Left handed
Bowling:	Left arm off-break

Tests

Test Career:	1998-2004		
Cap Number:	378		
Tests Played:	27		

Test Batting

Innings:	42	Runs:	1,798
Highest Score:	177	Average:	44.95
No. 50s:	10	No. 100s:	5

Test Bowling & Fielding

Wickets:	15	Runs:	412
Best Bowling:	3/42	Average:	27.46
5 WI:	0	10 WM:	0
Catches:	11	Stumpings:	0

One Day Internationals

ODI Career:	1996-2005		
ODIs Played:	117		

ODI Batting

Innings:	101	Runs:	3,078
Highest Score:	119	Average:	38.96
No. 50s:	17	No. 100s:	4

ODI Bowling & Fielding

Wickets:	52	Runs:	1,445
Best Bowling:	4/7	Average:	27.78
5 WM:	0	Catches:	26
Stumpings:	0		

By the time Darren Lehmann made his Test debut at the age of 28 he had done all there was to do at state and county level. The hard hitting South Australian middle order batsman had been a prolific scorer at first class level and only the dominance of the Australian side and a middle order that included Ricky Ponting and the Waugh twins denied him his rightful spot at the highest level. At first Lehmann didn't grasp the opportunity and an inability to convert a start into a big score saw him on the outer again. The man they called 'Boof' had to wait until he was 33 to finally score his maiden Test century, 160 against the West Indies at Port of Spain. From that point on he made hay while the sun shone, hitting two Test tons against both Bangladesh and Sri Lanka. His one day career was even more fruitful where his quick scoring and handy slow bowling won him over 100 national shirts. He was a member of Australia's World Cup winning sides in 1999 and 2003, in fact in 1999 he took enormous pleasure in hitting the winning runs in the final. In 2004 Lehmann surprised the cricket world by announcing his retirement from the international stage. He had been deeply affected by the death of his close friend David Hookes and had said that following his passing he had a new outlook that made him realise that there was more to life than cricket.

LEWIS, Michael Llewellyn

Born:	June 29, 1974
Batting:	Right handed
Bowling:	Right arm medium-fast

One Day Internationals

ODI Career:	2005-06
ODIs Played:	7

ODI Batting

Innings:	1	Runs:	4
Highest Score:	4*	Average:	0.00
No. 50s:	0	No. 100s:	0

ODI Bowling & Fielding

Wickets:	7	Runs:	391
Best Bowling:	3/56	Average:	55.85
5 WM:	0	Catches:	1
Stumpings:	0		

He's a bustling pace bowler from Victoria who was rewarded for a fine domestic career with a spot in the Australian one day side. Unfortunately his last ODI was the historic game against South Africa at the New Wanderers Stadium in Johannesburg in 2006 when the Proteas were set a record 435 to win and reached the target with one ball to go. All of the bowlers received a hiding that day but none more so than Lewis who returned figures of 0/113 off his ten overs.

LILLEE, Dennis Keith

Born:	July 18, 1949
Batting:	Right handed
Bowling:	Right arm fast

Tests

Test Career:	1971-84
Cap Number:	254
Tests Played:	70

Test Batting

Innings:	90	Runs:	905
Highest Score:	73*	Average:	13.71
No. 50s:	1	No. 100s:	0

Test Bowling & Fielding

Wickets:	355	Runs:	8,493
Best Bowling:	7/83	Average:	23.92
5 WI:	23	10 WM:	7
Catches:	23	Stumpings:	0

One Day Internationals

ODI Career:	1972-83
ODIs Played:	63

ODI Batting

Innings:	34	Runs:	240
Highest Score:	42*	Average:	9.23
No. 50s:	0	No. 100s:	0

ODI Bowling & Fielding

Wickets:	103	Runs:	2,145
Best Bowling:	5/34	Average:	20.82
5 WM:	1	Catches:	10
Stumpings:	0		

Regarded as one of the greatest fast bowlers of all time, the brilliant quick took 355 Test wickets in a career interrupted by injury and World Series Cricket. With a long, rhythmical run that culminated in a high delivery stride, Lillee's ball release resembled a striking cobra and was just as venomous. Away swing, leg cutters and in dippers were all delivered at high velocity making him a bowler for all conditions. A West Australian, 'D.K' made his debut in the 1970/71 Ashes series, and while attention was being focused on English firebrand John Snow, Australia was unveiling a lethal weapon of their own. He took 5/84 in his first Test innings and when he tore through the brilliant Rest of the World XI batting line-up in Perth the next summer, a new bowling giant had emerged. Soon after, Australia introduced Queensland speedster Jeff Thomson to the Test side and the Aussies had their best ever opening attack. Together the two plundered the opposition, destroying England at home and away in 1974 and 1975. Between them they took 95 wickets in ten Tests with Lillee capturing 46 and Thomson 49. Lillee found his bunny during those two series, claiming English opener Dennis Amiss six times in five Tests, including a run of three consecutive ducks. All style and speed, there was no better bowler in the world when he put his Test career on hold to join World Series Cricket in 1978. Playing against the best batsmen in the world, on wickets generally prepared for big scores, he took 79 wickets in 'Supertests' to further enhance his reputation. When he returned to the Test arena he continued to lead the Australian attack, though stress fractures in the back that had sidelined him earlier in his career saw him reduce the speed at which he bowled. His most famous moment came at the MCG late in 1981. Playing the West Indies, Australia had been dismissed for 198 during the last session of the first day's play. With just 35 minutes remaining, the West Indies collapsed to be 4/10 with Lillee claiming three wickets including Viv Richards off the last ball of the day. The next day he went on to take career best Test innings figures of 7/83, and in doing so become Test cricket's highest wicket-taker. He broke Lance Gibbs' record of 309 wickets when an outside edge by left hander Larry Gomes found its way into the 'normally' safe hands of Greg Chappell (Chappell had dropped Gomes off Lillee earlier in the day). The demon fast bowler retired in 1984 along with teammates Greg Chappell and keeper Rodney Marsh, who had joined him in 95 of his Test dismissals. Lillee was no stranger to controversy, with one of the most memorable incidents occurring during the formalities prior to the 1977 Centenary Test. As the Australian and English players were being introduced to Queen Elizabeth, the Aussie paceman pulled out a note pad and asked 'Her Majesty' for an autograph. While the Queen politely declined, explaining that if done in public she would be obliged to sign all autograph requests thereafter, she later sent Lillee an autographed photo of the pair from that famous moment. The photo, signed Elizabeth R, remains one of the fast bowler's most treasured possessions. He also twice found himself in hot water at the WACA. Once was in 1979 when he batted with an aluminium bat in a Test against England and then again in 1981 when he made contact with Pakistani captain Javed Miandad. For all the off field shenanigans Dennis Lillee will always be remembered as Australia's greatest ever fast bowler; bounding in with gold chain bouncing, moustache bristling and another wicket not too far away.

LINDWALL, Raymond Russell

Born:	October 3, 1921
Batting:	Right handed
Bowling:	Right arm fast

Tests

Test Career:	1946-60
Cap Number:	165
Tests Played:	61

Test Batting

Innings:	84	Runs:	1,502
Highest Score:	118	Average:	21.15
No. 50s:	5	No. 100s:	2

Test Bowling & Fielding

Wickets:	228	Runs:	5,251
Best Bowling:	7/38	Average:	23.03
5 WI:	12	10 WM:	0
Catches:	26	Stumpings:	0

One of Australia's greatest fast bowlers, he was the first quick to take over 200 Test wickets for his country. Born in Sydney he made his Test debut against New Zealand in 1946 and from quiet beginnings, he took only two wickets in that game, went on to terrorise the best batting line-ups for over a decade. Shorter than six foot, he relied on strength generated through his broad chest and powerful shoulders to plough through defenses. He swung the ball rather than cut it and had genuine pace and bounce for a man of his stature. In 1948 Bradman took a side to England that would become known as 'The Invincibles'. Whilst previous Bradman led sides relied on spin to bowl out the opposition, this team was spearheaded by the genuine pace of Lindwall and the steepling bounce of Bill Johnston. They took 27 wickets apiece in a series the Aussies won 4-0, with Lindwall just snaring the bowling honours by taking his wickets at less that 20 runs each. In the fifth Test of that series England was dismissed for a paltry 52, Lindwall the destroyer taking 6/20 off 16 overs. He would go on to dominate not just Enlgand but India and the West Indies as well. On two occasions he took seven wickets in an innings against the Indians and in two series against the Windies he took over 40 wickets. Strangely though he never took ten wickets or more in a match, eventhough he snared five in an innings on 12 occasions. An excellent tail end bat, Lindwall fell just short of being considered an all-rounder, though he did score two Test centuries.

LOVE, Hampden Stanley Bray

Born:	August 10, 1895
Batting:	Right handed
	Wicket Keeper

Tests

Test Career:	1933
Cap Number:	148
Tests Played:	1

Test Batting

Innings:	2	Runs:	8
Highest Score:	5	Average:	4.00
No. 50s:	0	No. 100s:	0

Test Bowling & Fielding

Wickets:	0	Runs:	0
Best Bowling:		Average:	0.00
5 WI:	0	10 WM:	0
Catches:	3	Stumpings:	0

A fine wicket keeper from Victoria, his only Test was as replacement for the injured Bert Oldfield after that player was famously felled by a Larwood bouncer in Adelaide. Nicknamed 'Hammy'.

LOVE, Martin Lloyd

Born:	March 30, 1974
Batting:	Right handed

Tests

Test Career:	2002-
Cap Number:	385
Tests Played:	5

Test Batting

Innings:	8	Runs:	233
Highest Score:	100*	Average:	46.60
No. 50s:	1	No. 100s:	1

Test Bowling & Fielding

Wickets:	0	Runs:	0
Best Bowling:		Average:	0.00
5 WI:	0	10 WM:	0
Catches:	7	Stumpings:	0

Not many cricketers can boast an unbeaten century in their last Test innings but that seems destined to be Martin Love's lot. A prolific run getter for Queensland, he got his chance during the 2002/03 Ashes series in Australia. After scoring a half century on debut he struggled, and whilst he was recalled for the top end series against Bangladesh in 2003 he was ultimately overlooked for batsmen such as Darren Lehmann, Simon Katich and Michael Clarke.

LOXTON, Samuel John Everett
Born: March 29, 1921
Batting: Right handed
Bowling: Right arm medium-fast

Tests

Test Career: 1948-51
Cap Number: 180
Tests Played: 12

Test Batting
Innings:	15	Runs:	554
Highest Score:	101	Average:	36.93
No. 50s:	3	No. 100s:	1

Test Bowling & Fielding
Wickets:	8	Runs:	349
Best Bowling:	3/55	Average:	43.62
5 WI:	0	10 WM:	0
Catches:	7	Stumpings:	0

Powerful and attacking, the Victorian all-rounder could be described as a poor man's Keith Miller, but given Mller's considerable talent that is no insult. In 12 Tests for Australia he put his powerful hitting to good use, forcing his way into the 'Invincibles' side on the tour of England in 1948 where he was picked for three Tests. His only Test century came a year later at Johannesburg when he scored 101 when batting at number six. Loxton was used sparingly as a bowler for Australia but when given the chance he put his back into it and could bowl at quite a pace. After his playing days were over he became a member of Parliament and later a Test selector. The comparison with Miller doesn't end with cricket, Loxton also played Australian Rules football at the highest level, ironically alongside Miller at the St. Kilda Football Club.

LYONS, John James
Born: May 21, 1863
Batting: Right handed
Bowling: Right arm medium

Tests

Test Career: 1887-97
Cap Number: 51
Tests Played: 14

Test Batting
Innings:	27	Runs:	731
Highest Score:	134	Average:	27.07
No. 50s:	3	No. 100s:	1

Test Bowling & Fielding
Wickets:	6	Runs:	149
Best Bowling:	5/30	Average:	24.83
5 WI:	1	10 WM:	0
Catches:	3	Stumpings:	0

Known as JJ or Jack, he was a fine batsman and medium pace bowler from Gawler in South Australia. Lyons' finest moment came in the Ashes winning second Test at the SCG in 1892, scoring 134 in a match winning second innings opening partnership with Alec 'Barndoor' Bannerman.

MACARTNEY, Charles George
Born: June 27, 1886
Batting: Right handed
Bowling: Left arm slow

Tests

Test Career: 1907-26
Cap Number: 90
Tests Played: 35

Test Batting
Innings:	55	Runs:	2,131
Highest Score:	170	Average:	41.78
No. 50s:	9	No. 100s:	7

Test Bowling & Fielding
Wickets:	45	Runs:	1,240
Best Bowling:	7/58	Average:	27.55
5 WI:	2	10 WM:	1
Catches:	17	Stumpings:	0

The mainstay of the Australian top order for almost two decades, he was an aggressive batsman who had more in common with the modern Test player than he had with the bulk of his peers. Short and powerful, his style of batting is best summed up by his knock in the third Test on the England tour of 1921 when he plundered the opposition for 115, bringing up his century prior to lunch on the opening day. Though he was a fine batsman from the outset, he seemed to improve with age with his final tour being his most successful. In the England summer of '26 he struck three Test centuries and was the Ashes series best batsman with an average of 94.60. Macartney was also a fine orthodox spinner who was originally selected for Australia as a bowler. On his first tour of England he took 71 wickets in all matches, including 11/85 in the Headingly Test.

MACGILL, Stuart Charles Glyndwr
Born: February 25, 1971
Batting: Right handed
Bowling: Right arm leg-break

Tests

Test Career: 1998-
Cap Number: 374
Tests Played: 40

Test Batting
Innings:	45	Runs:	347
Highest Score:	43	Average:	10.20
No. 50s:	0	No. 100s:	0

Test Bowling & Fielding
Wickets:	198	Runs:	5,387
Best Bowling:	8/108	Average:	27.20
5 WI:	12	10 WM:	2
Catches:	16	Stumpings:	0

One Day Internationals

ODI Career: 2000
ODIs Played: 3

ODI Batting
Innings:	2	Runs:	1
Highest Score:	1	Average:	1.00
No. 50s:	0	No. 100s:	0

ODI Bowling & Fielding
Wickets:	6	Runs:	105
Best Bowling:	4/19	Average:	17.50
5 WM:	0	Catches:	2
Stumpings:	0		

The highly talented leg-spinner from New South Wales could be considered the unluckiest bowler in the modern game. Despite the fact that he has taken almost 200 wickets in 40 Tests, he has spent most of his career as a spectator. Selectors have been generally loathe to play two leg spinners, and with Shane Warne assured of a Test spot when available, it has been a case of playing the waiting game for MacGill. He is a different bowler to Shane Warne. MacGill has a lower action, and whilst he does not do a great deal in the air with the ball he is a huge turner on the right track. He may not have his team mates' control, but his strikerate is very similar to that of Warne's. When given his chance he rarely disappoints. During Warne's enforced 12 month lay-off Macgill took 53 wickets in 11 Tests and when used in tandem with the great Victorian he has also performed well. It is fitting the a man called SCG MacGill should perform well at the ground that share his name, and his career best match figures of 12-107 were taken against England at the ground during the fifth Test of the 1998/99 Ashes series. In 2006 he was chosen for tours of South Africa and Bangladesh, and with his side facing a shock loss against the Banglas at Fatullah returned first innings figures of 8/108. The cricket gods may not have always been kind to MacGill, but he has taken it with good grace and remains ready to fill the breach when called upon.

MACKAY, Kenneth Donald (Slasher)

Born:	October 24, 1925
Batting:	Left handed
Bowling:	Right arm medium-fast

Tests
Test Career:	1956-63
Cap Number:	203
Tests Played:	37

Test Batting
Innings:	52	Runs:	1,507
Highest Score:	89	Average:	33.48
No. 50s:	13	No. 100s:	0

Test Bowling & Fielding
Wickets:	50	Runs:	1,721
Best Bowling:	6/42	Average:	34.42
5 WI:	2	10 WM:	0
Catches:	16	Stumpings:	0

Just as Aussie humour decrees that a red-head should be nicknamed Bluey and a bald man be called Curly, Slasher Mackay earnt his handle by being one of the games most watchful batsmen. The Queenslander was a regular part of Australia's middle order in the fifties and early sixties, combining reliable batting with equally conservative and effective medium pace bowling. At the crease he exuded concentration, constantly chewing gum with a determined look plastered on his face. His most famous Test innings was in the nail biting series against the West Indies in 1961 when his last wicket heroics with Lindsay Kline in Adelaide earnt his side a draw. He had previously shown similar resistance against the English in 1956 with a match saving 35 in 264 minutes at Lord's. As a bowler he relied on subtle variations of swing and pace to contain and confound the batsman. His run-up was more amble than run but he had many long and succesful stints at the bowling crease, including a match winning performance in Pakistan where he took 6/42 off an incredible 45 overs. After his retirement from Test cricket he served his state as both selector and coach.

MACLEAN, John Alexander

Born:	April 27, 1946
Batting:	Right handed
	Wicket Keeper

Tests
Test Career:	1978-79
Cap Number:	298
Tests Played:	4

Test Batting
Innings:	8	Runs:	79
Highest Score:	33*	Average:	11.28
No. 50s:	0	No. 100s:	0

Test Bowling & Fielding
Wickets:	0	Runs:	0
Best Bowling:		Average:	0.00
5 WI:	0	10 WM:	0
Catches:	18	Stumpings:	0

One Day Internationals
ODI Career:	1979
ODIs Played:	2

ODI Batting
Innings:	1	Runs:	11
Highest Score:	11	Average:	11.00
No. 50s:	0	No. 100s:	0

ODI Bowling & Fielding
Wickets:	0	Runs:	0
Best Bowling:		Average:	0.00
5 WM:	0	Catches:	0
Stumpings:	0		

A sturdy wicket keeper from Queensland who spent much of the seventies as understudy to Rodney Marsh. He got his chance to play Test cricket when Marsh defected to World Series Cricket in the summer of 1977/78. He scored a brave 33 not out on debut against England, in the First Test at the 'Gabba, when he and Rodney Hogg added 60 for the 8th wicket as Australia plummeted to be all out for 116 in the first innings. He received a serious injury in the fourth Test of the 1978/79 Ashes series at SCG and never played for his country again.

MACLEAY, Kenneth Hervey
Born: April 2, 1950
Batting: Right handed
Bowling: Right arm medium

One Day Internationals
ODI Career: 1983-87
ODIs Played: 16

ODI Batting
Innings:	13	Runs:	139
Highest Score:	41	Average:	12.63
No. 50s:	0	No. 100s:	0

ODI Bowling & Fielding
Wickets:	15	Runs:	626
Best Bowling:	6/39	Average:	41.73
5 WM:	1	Catches:	2
Stumpings:	0		

Whilst it may be common to pick separate Test and one day sides today, when Ken MacLeay was playing cricket he was quite an oddity. The lanky all-rounder from WA never really threatened for a spot in the Australian Test side but was a serviceable performer in the one day team. He was a shock selection in the 1983 World Cup squad but quickly silenced his critics with 6/39 against the Indians in Nottingham.

MADDOCKS, Leonard Victor
Born: May 24, 1926
Batting: Right handed
Wicket Keeper

Tests
Test Career: 1955-56
Cap Number: 199
Tests Played: 7

Test Batting
Innings:	12	Runs:	177
Highest Score:	69	Average:	17.69
No. 50s:	1	No. 100s:	0

Test Bowling & Fielding
Wickets:	0	Runs:	0
Best Bowling:		Average:	0.00
5 WI:	0	10 WM:	0
Catches:	18	Stumpings:	1

The Victorian wicket keeper was Australia's second choice behind Gil Langley and Wally Grout for over a decade. Small and nimble he was a classy batsman and skilled keeper who like many cricketers in his position before and after was considered unlucky not to have played more Test cricket.

MAGUIRE, John Norman
Born: September 15, 1956
Batting: Right handed
Bowling: Right arm medium-fast

Tests
Test Career: 1983-84
Cap Number: 321
Tests Played: 3

Test Batting
Innings:	5	Runs:	28
Highest Score:	15*	Average:	7.00
No. 50s:	0	No. 100s:	0

Test Bowling & Fielding
Wickets:	10	Runs:	323
Best Bowling:	4/57	Average:	32.30
5 WI:	0	10 WM:	0
Catches:	2	Stumpings:	0

One Day Internationals
ODI Career: 1983-84
ODIs Played: 23

ODI Batting
Innings:	11	Runs:	42
Highest Score:	14*	Average:	7.00
No. 50s:	0	No. 100s:	0

ODI Bowling & Fielding
Wickets:	19	Runs:	769
Best Bowling:	3/61	Average:	40.47
5 WM:	0	Catches:	2
Stumpings:	0		

A tall paceman from Queensland, his line and length made him a more effective one day player than Test cricketer. His national career ended when he signed on for the Australian rebel tour to South Africa in 1985.

MAHER, James Patrick
Born: February 27, 1974
Batting: Left handed

One Day Internationals
ODI Career: 1998-2003
ODIs Played: 26

ODI Batting
Innings:	20	Runs:	438
Highest Score:	95	Average:	25.76
No. 50s:	1	No. 100s:	0

ODI Bowling & Fielding
Wickets:	0	Runs:	0
Best Bowling:		Average:	0.00
5 WM:	0	Catches:	18
Stumpings:	0		

A prolific scorer at both state level in Australia and county level in England, it now seems that Jimmy Maher will have to content himself with an international career that amounts to a handful of one day games. Like Stuart Law and Martin Love before him, it is hard justice for a complete opener. In 2005/06 he led his state to the domestic four day title.

MAILEY, Arthur Alfred
Born: January 3, 1886
Batting: Right handed
Bowling: Right arm leg-break

Tests
Test Career: 1920-26
Cap Number: 108
Tests Played: 21

Test Batting
Innings:	29	Runs:	222
Highest Score:	46*	Average:	11.09
No. 50s:	0	No. 100s:	0

Test Bowling & Fielding
Wickets:	99	Runs:	3,358
Best Bowling:	9/121	Average:	33.91
5 WI:	6	10 WM:	2
Catches:	14	Stumpings:	0

His was a life devoted to cricket, both on the field as a gifted leg-spin bowler and off it as a journalist and regular visitor to England and South Africa. His first series was his most impressive. Playing England at home he took a staggering 36 wickets including a 'nine for' in the seconds innings of the fourth Test at the MCG. As his average of 33.91 would suggest he was willing to buy his wickets, but he relied on prodigious spin rather than a batsman's shortcomings to secure his victims.

MALLETT, Ashley Alexander

Born: July 13, 1945
Batting: Right handed
Bowling: Right arm off-break

Tests
Test Career: 1968-80
Cap Number: 247
Tests Played: 38

Test Batting
Innings: 50 Runs: 430
Highest Score: 43* Average: 11.62
No. 50s: 0 No. 100s: 0

Test Bowling & Fielding
Wickets: 132 Runs: 3,940
Best Bowling: 8/59 Average: 29.84
5 WI: 6 10 WM: 1
Catches: 30 Stumpings: 0

One Day Internationals
ODI Career: 1971-75
ODIs Played: 9

ODI Batting
Innings: 3 Runs: 14
Highest Score: 8 Average: 7.00
No. 50s: 0 No. 100s: 0

ODI Bowling & Fielding
Wickets: 11 Runs: 341
Best Bowling: 3/34 Average: 31.00
5 WM: 0 Catches: 4
Stumpings: 0

A tall and lean off spin bowler from South Australia he took time to secure a spot in the Test side after making his debut in 1967. In and out of the side he made a name for himself on the 1970/71 tour of India taking 28 wickets including a haul of 10 in the Test at Madras. Following that series he was a regular member of the side for the next decade in a career that was punctuated by a stint with World Series Cricket. An introspective character with a dry wit, he earnt the nickname 'Rowdy' from his teammates. Mallett was not only one of Australia's finest ever off spin bowlers but he is also remembered as one of his country's best ever gully fieldsmen.

MALONE, Michael Francis

Born: October 9, 1950
Batting: Right handed
Bowling: Right arm medium-fast

Tests
Test Career: 1977
Cap Number: 282
Tests Played: 1

Test Batting
Innings: 1 Runs: 46
Highest Score: 46 Average: 46.00
No. 50s: 0 No. 100s: 0

Test Bowling & Fielding
Wickets: 6 Runs: 77
Best Bowling: 5/63 Average: 12.83
5 WI: 1 10 WM: 0
Catches: 0 Stumpings: 0

One Day Internationals
ODI Career: 1977-82
ODIs Played: 10

ODI Batting
Innings: 7 Runs: 36
Highest Score: 15* Average: 9.00
No. 50s: 0 No. 100s: 0

ODI Bowling & Fielding
Wickets: 11 Runs: 315
Best Bowling: 2/9 Average: 28.63
5 WM: 0 Catches: 1
Stumpings: 0

A bustling right arm quick from WA, he forewent a Test career to join World Series Cricket. Malone was a key player in one of WSC's most famous matches when West Indian number eleven, Wayne Daniel, hit him for six off the last ball of a match at VFL Park Waverly to win the game.

MANN, Anthony Longford

Born: November 8, 1945
Batting: Left handed
Bowling: Left arm leg-break

Tests
Test Career: 1977-78
Cap Number: 285
Tests Played: 4

Test Batting
Innings: 8 Runs: 189
Highest Score: 105 Average: 23.62
No. 50s: 0 No. 100s: 1

Test Bowling & Fielding
Wickets: 4 Runs: 316
Best Bowling: 3/12 Average: 79.00
5 WI: 0 10 WM: 0
Catches: 2 Stumpings: 0

A steady leg spin bowler from Western Australia, he made his name not with the ball but as the first Australia to score a century as a night watchman. Mann etched his name into the records with 105 against India at Perth in 1977, a score that would stand as the highest by a night watchman until Jason Gillespie's double century heroics against Bangladesh almost 30 years later.

MARR, Alfred Percy

Born: March 28, 1862
Batting: Right handed
Bowling: Right arm medium

MARSH, (no first name given on this entry)

Tests
Test Career:	1885		
Cap Number:	34		
Tests Played:	1		

Test Batting
Innings:	2	Runs:	5
Highest Score:	5	Average:	2.50
No. 50s:	0	No. 100s:	0

Test Bowling & Fielding
Wickets:	0	Runs:	14
Best Bowling:		Average:	0.00
5 WI:	0	10 WM:	0
Catches:	0	Stumpings:	0

A New South Wales medium pacer and handy lower order batsman.

MARSH, Geoffrey Robert

Born: December 31, 1958
Batting: Right handed

Tests
Test Career:	1985-92		
Cap Number:	333		
Tests Played:	50		

Test Batting
Innings:	93	Runs:	2,854
Highest Score:	138	Average:	33.18
No. 50s:	15	No. 100s:	4

Test Bowling & Fielding
Wickets:	0	Runs:	0
Best Bowling:		Average:	0.00
5 WI:	0	10 WM:	0
Catches:	38	Stumpings:	0

One Day Internationals
ODI Career:	1986-92		
ODIs Played:	117		

ODI Batting
Innings:	115	Runs:	4,357
Highest Score:	126*	Average:	39.97
No. 50s:	22	No. 100s:	9

ODI Bowling & Fielding
Wickets:	0	Runs:	4
Best Bowling:		Average:	0.00
5 WM:	0	Catches:	31
Stumpings:	0		

Nicknamed Swampy, the laid back country boy from rural Western Australia has had a marked influence on Australian cricket both as a player and coach. Marsh the batsman provided steel to a top order that had gone many years without a reliable opening combination. More circumspect than his partner in crime Mark Taylor, he was the perfect foil not only for Taylor but incoming batsmen such as David Boon and Allan Border. Whilst he never scored a Test 150, he did make nine Test tons and scored an unbeaten triple century for his state. An industrious opening batsman in One Day Internationals, he opened the batting for the team that beat Pakistan to claim the 1987 World Cup. Following his retirement he ventured into coaching and when Bob Simpson gave up the top job with the Australian side, Marsh was appointed. He would enjoy unqualified success, orchestrating the side's memorable win in the 1999 World Cup in England as well as a number of Test series wins. Always one for a challenge, Marsh took up a coaching job with the troubled Zimbabwe cricket side in 2001 and honoured his contract until it expired in 2004.

MARSH, Rodney William

Born: November 4, 1947
Batting: Left handed
Bowling: Right arm off-break
Wicket Keeper

Tests
Test Career:	1970-84		
Cap Number:	249		
Tests Played:	96		

Test Batting
Innings:	150	Runs:	3,633
Highest Score:	132	Average:	26.51
No. 50s:	16	No. 100s:	3

Test Bowling & Fielding
Wickets:	0	Runs:	54
Best Bowling:		Average:	0.00
5 WI:	0	10 WM:	0
Catches:	343	Stumpings:	12

One Day Internationals
ODI Career:	1971-84		
ODIs Played:	92		

ODI Batting
Innings:	76	Runs:	1,225
Highest Score:	66	Average:	20.08
No. 50s:	4	No. 100s:	0

ODI Bowling & Fielding
Wickets:	0	Runs:	0
Best Bowling:		Average:	0.00
5 WM:	0	Catches:	120
Stumpings:	4		

When a wicket keeper starts out with the nickname 'Irongloves', you could hardly expect a long career at the highest level, but not only did Rodney Marsh prove his critics wrong he would win them over and become one of the most popular players to represent his country. Fiercely competitive, he fit perfectly into the tough Australian side that was built under the leadership of Ian Chappell. His keeping to the pace bowlers was nothing short of spectacular and whilst the Aussie quicks fed him many chances over the years it was the combination of court Marsh bowled Lillee that stood out, recording a then record 95 dismissals as double act. Marsh also elevated the status of keeper batsman, becoming the first Australian gloveman to hit a century in a Test. His most important innings was undoubtedly his 110 not out in the second innings of the Centenary Test in 1977, a knock that went a long way to securing victory for his side. He followed the Chappell's and Lillee into World Series Cricket where his big hitting was a feature. Marsh was very much one of the boys, playing hard and celebrating with just as much gusto. He famously ventured into a betting tent when Australia had England on the ropes at Headingly in 1981 and secured enormous odds about an

English win. Ian Botham produced one of the game's great individual performances to win the match for England, and after enduring a storm of controversy Marsh and his good mate D.K. Lillee collected on their bet. In his post playing career Marsh has become a respected coach, holding senior positions both in Australia and abroad.

MARTIN, John Wesley

Born: July 28, 1931
Batting: Left handed
Bowling: Left arm off-break

Tests
Test Career:	1961-67		
Cap Number:	216		
Tests Played:	8		

Test Batting
Innings:	13	Runs:	214
Highest Score:	55	Average:	17.83
No. 50s:	1	No. 100s:	0

Test Bowling & Fielding
Wickets:	17	Runs:	832
Best Bowling:	3/56	Average:	48.94
5 WI:	0	10 WM:	0
Catches:	5	Stumpings:	0

Johnny Martin burst on to the Test scene during the enthralling 1960/61 series against the West Indies. After carrying the drinks in the tied Test he was selected for Melbourne where he scored 55 in the first innings batting at number 10. The left hand chinaman bowler then routed the much vaunted West Indian middle order with three wickets in four balls including the prized scalps of Kanhai and Sobers. Martin would not hit those heights again in Test cricket but the likeable New South Welshman remained a crowd favourite whenever he pulled on a baggy green cap.

MARTYN, Damien Richard

Born: October 21, 1971
Batting: Right handed
Bowling: Right arm medium

Tests
Test Career:	1992-		
Cap Number:	353		
Tests Played:	65		

Test Batting
Innings:	106	Runs:	4,361
Highest Score:	165	Average:	47.40
No. 50s:	23	No. 100s:	13

Test Bowling & Fielding
Wickets:	2	Runs:	168
Best Bowling:	1/0	Average:	84.00
5 WI:	0	10 WM:	0
Catches:	33	Stumpings:	0

One Day Internationals
ODI Career:	1992-		
ODIs Played:	200		

ODI Batting
Innings:	174	Runs:	5,030
Highest Score:	144*	Average:	40.24
No. 50s:	34	No. 100s:	5

ODI Bowling & Fielding
Wickets:	12	Runs:	704
Best Bowling:	2/21	Average:	58.66
5 WM:	0	Catches:	65
Stumpings:	0		

A lightly built middle order batsman from Western Australia, he fought back from the disappointment of being discarded as a 23 year old to become an established Test player of the highest caliber. Selected to play the West Indies in 1992 as a 21 year old he showed enough in four Tests against the world's best pace attack to suggest a long career in the 'baggy green'. Two years later he was blamed for a narrow loss to South Africa, adjudged too reckless for Test cricket and given the boot. It took Martyn almost seven years to win back his Test spot, prompting one journalist to observe that you don't get seven years in Australia for armed robbery but you can get it for a mistimed square drive. When he returned he was still constantly looking to score, but rather than bludgeon the ball he aimed to work it into the gaps and time it to the fence. At times he was almost unobtrusive nestled around the likes of Hayden, Gilchrist and Ponting, but the gifted batsmen always kept the scoreboard ticking over. He hit two tons in the 2001 Ashes series and later that year settled a score by dominating the South Africans. Martyn hit an effortless 117 against the Proteas at the SCG seven years after he faltered against them at the same ground. He has now built his Test average up to a very healthy 47.40 and after again being made the scapegoat, this time for the Ashes loss in 2005, he again fought his way back into the side. Recalled for the tour to South Africa in early 2006 he scored his 13th Test hundred in the third and final Test in Johannesburg. Martyn has also been a fine one day cricketer for his country. After missing out on a spot in the side that won the World Cup in 1999 he led Australia to victory in the 2003 final with an unbeaten 88.

MASSIE, Hugh Hamon

Born: April 11, 1854
Batting: Right handed

Tests
Test Career:	1881-85		
Cap Number:	28		
Tests Played:	9		

Test Batting
Innings:	16	Runs:	249
Highest Score:	55	Average:	15.56
No. 50s:	1	No. 100s:	0

Test Bowling & Fielding
Wickets:	0	Runs:	0
Best Bowling:		Average:	0.00
5 WI:	0	10 WM:	0
Catches:	5	Stumpings:	0

Massie played for Australia on the back of a famous double century for New South Wales but failed to reproduce that form in nine Tests for his country. He did however captain the side for a single Test during the England tour to Australia in 1884/85.

MASSIE, Robert Arnold Lockyer (Bob)
Born: April 14, 1947
Batting: Left handed
Bowling: Right arm medium-fast

Tests
Test Career: 1972-73
Cap Number: 260
Tests Played: 6

Test Batting
Innings:	8	Runs:	78
Highest Score:	42	Average:	11.14
No. 50s:	0	No. 100s:	0

Test Bowling & Fielding
Wickets:	31	Runs:	647
Best Bowling:	8/53	Average:	20.87
5 WI:	2	10 WM:	1
Catches:	1	Stumpings:	0

One Day Internationals
ODI Career: 1972
ODIs Played: 3

ODI Batting
Innings:	1	Runs:	16
Highest Score:	16*	Average:	0.00
No. 50s:	0	No. 100s:	0

ODI Bowling & Fielding
Wickets:	3	Runs:	129
Best Bowling:	2/35	Average:	43.00
5 WM:	0	Catches:	1
Stumpings:	0		

Of all the Australian cricketers to have played less than ten Tests, Bob Massie is arguably the best known. His noteriety centres on one of the games most startling debuts, the second Test at Lord's, during the English summer of 1972. Massie had been playing in England for three seasons prior to the Lord's match, honing his considerable ability as swing bowler in the minor county competition. Whilst the muggy conditions at Lord's were perfect for his style of bowling, Massie nevertheless put in one of the all-time great bowling performances, capturing eight wickets in each innings for a staggering return of 16/137. He punctuated his deadly swing with well placed straight deliveries and had almost the entire compliment of 16 batsmen caught behind the wicket, bowled or LBW. Unfortunately for the West Australian it was not to be the springboard for a long Test career. Possibly weighed down by the burden of expectations, Massie would play only five more Tests, and more relevantly never again lay a batting line-up in ruins.

MATTHEWS, Christopher Darrell
Born: August 22, 1962
Batting: Left handed
Bowling: Left arm fast

Tests
Test Career: 1986-88
Cap Number: 338
Tests Played: 3

Test Batting
Innings:	5	Runs:	54
Highest Score:	32	Average:	10.80
No. 50s:	0	No. 100s:	0

Test Bowling & Fielding
Wickets:	6	Runs:	313
Best Bowling:	3/95	Average:	52.16
5 WI:	0	10 WM:	0
Catches:	1	Stumpings:	0

After a promising Test debut against England in 1986, the broad shouldered quick found himself on the outer until he earnt a recall against the touring West Indians in 1988/89. Struggling for control, his return to the Test arena was a forgettable one, and he never played for Australia again.

MATTHEWS, Gregory John Richard
Born: December 15, 1959
Batting: Left handed
Bowling: Right arm off-break

Tests
Test Career: 1983-93
Cap Number: 322
Tests Played: 33

Test Batting
Innings:	53	Runs:	1,849
Highest Score:	130	Average:	41.08
No. 50s:	12	No. 100s:	4

Test Bowling & Fielding
Wickets:	61	Runs:	2,942
Best Bowling:	5/103	Average:	48.22
5 WI:	2	10 WM:	1
Catches:	17	Stumpings:	0

One Day Internationals
ODI Career: 1984-93
ODIs Played: 59

ODI Batting
Innings:	50	Runs:	619
Highest Score:	54	Average:	16.72
No. 50s:	1	No. 100s:	0

ODI Bowling & Fielding
Wickets:	57	Runs:	2,004
Best Bowling:	3/27	Average:	35.15
5 WM:	0	Catches:	23
Stumpings:	0		

Nicknamed 'Mo', the outspoken off spinner from New South Wales never reached any great heights as a Test bowler, but as a number seven batsman he was a revelation. On his Test debut in 1983, against Pakistan at the MCG, the enigmatic Matthews joined local hero Graham Yallop at the crease as his captain was heading towards a double century. Wearing a white floppy hat, Matthews danced his way to 75, constantly playing up to the crowd. And just when a ton on debut seemed the likely scenario, a thick inside edge on to his pads was poorly adjudged lbw. The party was over, and a disgruntled Matthews and Melbourne crowd expressed their disapproval towards the official in question. Matthews would to make up for the disappointment, and in the Australian summer of 1985/86 he struck three centuries, two of which came against New Zealand and the other at the MCG against India. He would score one more Test ton and finish his career with the average of a good number three - 41.08. Whilst his bowling lacked penetration, he did capture one of the most important wickets in cricket history when he trapped Indian Maninder Singh in line at Madras in 1986 to record the second, and to date, last tie in Test history. Strangely, he was a more effective bowler than batsman in one-day cricket.

MATTHEWS, Thomas James
Born: April 3, 1884
Batting: Right handed
Bowling: Right arm leg-break

Tests
Test Career:	1912		
Cap Number:	99		
Tests Played:	8		

Test Batting
Innings:	10	Runs:	153
Highest Score:	53	Average:	17.00
No. 50s:	1	No. 100s:	0

Test Bowling & Fielding
Wickets:	16	Runs:	419
Best Bowling:	4/29	Average:	26.18
5 WI:	0	10 WM:	0
Catches:	7	Stumpings:	0

Jimmy Matthews holds a unique place in Test history that will be very hard to equal. The Victorian leg-spinner took a hat-trick in each innings of a Test against South Africa at Old Tafford in 1912 as part of a one-off triangular series. He was also a fine Australian Rules footballer playing for the St. Kilda Football Club.

MAY, Timothy Brian Alexander
Born: January 26, 1962
Batting: Right handed
Bowling: Right arm off-break

Tests
Test Career:	1987-95		
Cap Number:	342		
Tests Played:	24		

Test Batting
Innings:	28	Runs:	225
Highest Score:	42*	Average:	14.06
No. 50s:	0	No. 100s:	0

Test Bowling & Fielding
Wickets:	75	Runs:	2,606
Best Bowling:	5/9	Average:	34.74
5 WI:	3	10 WM:	0
Catches:	6	Stumpings:	0

One Day Internationals
ODI Career:	1987-95
ODIs Played:	47

ODI Batting
Innings:	12	Runs:	39
Highest Score:	15	Average:	9.75
No. 50s:	0	No. 100s:	0

ODI Bowling & Fielding
Wickets:	39	Runs:	1,772
Best Bowling:	3/19	Average:	45.43
5 WM:	0	Catches:	3
Stumpings:	0		

An accurate off spinner, he was often used to contain batsmen whilst Australia was attacking at the other end with Shane Warne. The duo enjoyed considerable success on the 1993 Ashes tour, taking 55 Test wickets between them of which May took 21. A popular member of the side, he became concerned with player welfare following his retirement, and became the first CEO of the Australian Cricketer's Association when it was formed.

MAYNE, Edgar Richard
Born: July 2, 1882
Batting: Right handed
Bowling: Right arm medium

Tests
Test Career:	1912-21		
Cap Number:	105		
Tests Played:	4		

Test Batting
Innings:	4	Runs:	64
Highest Score:	25*	Average:	21.33
No. 50s:	0	No. 100s:	0

Test Bowling & Fielding
Wickets:	0	Runs:	1
Best Bowling:		Average:	0.00
5 WI:	0	10 WM:	0
Catches:	2	Stumpings:	0

A fine cricketer at domestic level he captained both Victoria and South Australia. He was unable to cement a spot in the national side, playing four Tests over a nine year period.

MAYNE, Lawrence Charles
Born: January 23, 1942
Batting: Right handed
Bowling: Right arm medium-fast

Tests
Test Career:	1965-70		
Cap Number:	233		
Tests Played:	6		

Test Batting
Innings:	11	Runs:	76
Highest Score:	13	Average:	9.50
No. 50s:	0	No. 100s:	0

Test Bowling & Fielding
Wickets:	19	Runs:	628
Best Bowling:	4/43	Average:	33.05
5 WI:	0	10 WM:	0
Catches:	3	Stumpings:	0

An opening bowler from Western Australia, he was tried on a number of occasions at the highest level but failed to secure a permanent spot in the side.

McALISTER, Peter Alexander

Born:	July 11, 1869
Batting:	Right handed

Tests

Test Career:	1904-09
Cap Number:	86
Tests Played:	8

Test Batting

Innings:	16	Runs:	252
Highest Score:	41	Average:	16.80
No. 50s:	0	No. 100s:	0

Test Bowling & Fielding

Wickets:	0	Runs:	0
Best Bowling:		Average:	0.00
5 WI:	0	10 WM:	0
Catches:	10	Stumpings:	0

Though a competent performer at Shield level, it would have come as a surprise to most Australian cricket fans to have seen McAlister selected as vice captain for the 1909 tour of England. The one person who would not have been in the least bit shocked would have been McAlister himself, given that he was a Test selector at the time. His selection did not sit well with the skipper, Monty Noble, who felt that his was in the touring party simply to spy on the players and report back to the board. Unfortunately he failed to seize upon the opportunity presented by himself and averaged under 20 in eight disappointing Tests.

McCABE, Stanley Joseph

Born:	July 16, 1910
Batting:	Right handed
Bowling:	Right arm medium

Tests

Test Career:	1930-38
Cap Number:	134
Tests Played:	39

Test Batting

Innings:	62	Runs:	2,748
Highest Score:	232	Average:	48.21
No. 50s:	13	No. 100s:	6

Test Bowling & Fielding

Wickets:	36	Runs:	1,543
Best Bowling:	4/13	Average:	42.86
5 WI:	0	10 WM:	0
Catches:	41	Stumpings:	0

The New South Wales batsman broke into the strong Australian line-up at the tender age of 20 and by the end his Test career had worked his way into the 'great top four' standing alongside Woodfull, Ponsford and Bradman. He scored six Test centuries, but is best known for three of the greatest innings ever struck in Test cricket. The first was in the opening Test of the Bodyline series. Bradman was unavailable for the game and when young Stan came into bat Australia was teetering at 3/82. Larwood tested him early with a short ball and rather than duck to protect himself, McCabe rocked on to the back foot smashing it to the square-leg boundary. When Australia was finally dismissed for 360, he remained unbeaten on 187. His second great performance was against the South Africans at the Old Wanderers Ground in Johannesburg where he smashed the Springbok attack for 189 in a game the Aussies were battling to save. The last innings of the trilogy and arguably the best was against England at Trent Bridge in 1938. Australia trailed by an innings and 100 runs when McCabe came to the wicket on the fourth day. Rather than defend, he took to the English attack, scoring 232 at better than a run a minute. His captain Donald Bradman was so taken by the innings that he summoned the rest of the side to join him on the dressing room balcony to watch it. Bradman would later describe the knock as the "best he had ever seen". McCabe scored 2,748 Test runs, but as noted cricket journalist Jim Swanton observed, he would have scored much more had his country needed them.

McCOOL, Colin Leslie

Born:	December 9, 1916
Batting:	Right handed
Bowling:	Right arm slow

Tests

Test Career:	1946-50
Cap Number:	166
Tests Played:	14

Test Batting

Innings:	17	Runs:	459
Highest Score:	104*	Average:	35.30
No. 50s:	1	No. 100s:	1

Test Bowling & Fielding

Wickets:	36	Runs:	958
Best Bowling:	5/41	Average:	26.61
5 WI:	3	10 WM:	0
Catches:	14	Stumpings:	0

An accomplished all-rounder, he made his debut in the one-off Test against New Zealand in 1946. He enjoyed a wonderful Ashes series at home in 1946/47 averaging 54.50 with the bat and taking 18 wickets with his crafty leg-spinners. In that series he made an unbeaten century at the MCG and took a five for at the SCG. The strength of the 1948 Ashes side known as 'The Invincibles' can be best summed up by the fact that Colin McCool made the touring party but failed to play a single Test. Following a fine career in Australia he moved to England where he starred for county side Somerset.

McCORMICK, Ernest Leslie

Born:	May 16, 1906
Batting:	Left handed
Bowling:	Right arm fast

Tests

Test Career:	1935-38
Cap Number:	154
Tests Played:	12

Test Batting

Innings:	14	Runs:	54
Highest Score:	17*	Average:	6.00
No. 50s:	0	No. 100s:	0

Test Bowling & Fielding

Wickets:	36	Runs:	1,079
Best Bowling:	4/101	Average:	29.97
5 WI:	0	10 WM:	0
Catches:	8	Stumpings:	0

The tall Victorian had a promising Test career curtailed by a back injury. When he was fit enough to bowl for his country he was a genuine quick who used his height to either torment batsmen just short of a length or to spear in menacing yorkers. He started with a bang in his first Test against the English taking a wicket with his first ball and finishing the innings with the excellent figures of 3/26.

McCOSKER, Richard Bede (Rick)

Born:	December 11, 1946
Batting:	Right handed

Tests

Test Career:	1975-80
Cap Number:	272
Tests Played:	25

Test Batting

Innings:	46	Runs:	1,622
Highest Score:	127	Average:	39.65
No. 50s:	9	No. 100s:	4

Test Bowling & Fielding

Wickets:	0	Runs:	0
Best Bowling:		Average:	0.00
5 WI:	0	10 WM:	0
Catches:	21	Stumpings:	0

One Day Internationals

ODI Career:	1975-82
ODIs Played:	14

ODI Batting

Innings:	14	Runs:	329
Highest Score:	95	Average:	22.85
No. 50s:	2	No. 100s:	0

ODI Bowling & Fielding

Wickets:	0	Runs:	0
Best Bowling:		Average:	0.00
5 WI:	0	Catches:	3
Stumpings:	0		

Mention the name Rick McCosker and most Australian cricket fans would immediately recall his courageous batting late in the second innings of the Centenary Test. With stakes high in the historic game, the New South Welshman came out to bat carrying a broken jaw, compliments of a mis-timed hook off Bob Willis in the first innings. He scored 25, with each run and defensive stroke earning raptuous applause from the MCG crowd. McCosker was much more than a one Test wonder and he provided Australia with a reliable opener for a sustained period. He joined World Series Cricket in 1977/78, and such was the esteem in which he was held, that when WSC was over he was recalled to the Test side despite being in his early 30's.

McCURDY, Rodney John

Born:	December 30, 1959
Batting:	Right handed
Bowling:	Right arm fast

One Day Internationals

ODI Career:	1985
ODIs Played:	11

ODI Batting

Innings:	6	Runs:	33
Highest Score:	13*	Average:	8.25
No. 50s:	0	No. 100s:	0

ODI Bowling & Fielding

Wickets:	12	Runs:	375
Best Bowling:	3/19	Average:	31.25
5 WM:	0	Catches:	1
Stumpings:	0		

The strongly built Victorian was making an impression for state and country when offered a spot on the rebel tour to South Africa in 1985. His decision to join that side and the ban that followed meant the McCurdy never played for his country at official level again. He performed well on that tour and went on to play first class cricket in South Africa, England and once again in Australia.

McDERMOTT, Craig John

Born:	April 14, 1965
Batting:	Right handed
Bowling:	Right arm fast

Tests

Test Career:	1984-96
Cap Number:	328
Tests Played:	71

Test Batting

Innings:	90	Runs:	940
Highest Score:	42*	Average:	12.20
No. 50s:	0	No. 100s:	0

Test Bowling & Fielding

Wickets:	291	Runs:	8,332
Best Bowling:	8/97	Average:	28.63
5 WI:	14	10 WM:	2
Catches:	19	Stumpings:	0

One Day Internationals

ODI Career:	1985-96
ODIs Played:	138

ODI Batting

Innings:	78	Runs:	432
Highest Score:	37	Average:	7.08
No. 50s:	0	No. 100s:	0

ODI Bowling & Fielding

Wickets:	203	Runs:	5,018
Best Bowling:	5/44	Average:	24.71
5 WM:	1	Catches:	27
Stumpings:	0		

A red headed opening bowler from Queensland, he made his Test debut at the tender age of 19. Nicknamed 'Billy The Kid' he made an inauspicious start in as much that his first Test wicket was a head high full toss that West Indian Richie Richardson could only play on to his stumps. McDermott raised his hand apologetically and sheepishly made his way back to the top of his mark. The youngster quickly recovered and went on to take three wickets in each innings of that debut Test. A promising first series won him a trip to England where he impressed by taking 30 Test wickets. His international career would not bloom for many years though, a combination of injury and indifferent attitude denying him a regular spot in the side. As he matured he became a far better bowler, using his copy book action to out swing and seam as well as pace. From 1990 until his retirement he took five or more wickets in an innings on eleven separate occasions. A brilliant out fielsdman and handy lower order bat, he was almost part of a most unlikely Test win in 1992/93 against the West Indies when he and Tim May put 40 for the last wicket only to fall two runs short.

McDONALD, Colin Campbell

Born:	November 17, 1928
Batting:	Right handed
Bowling:	Right arm slow

Tests

Test Career:	1952-61
Cap Number:	191
Tests Played:	47

Test Batting

Innings:	83	Runs:	3,107
Highest Score:	170	Average:	39.32
No. 50s:	17	No. 100s:	5

Test Bowling & Fielding

Wickets:	0	Runs:	3
Best Bowling:		Average:	0.00
5 WI:	0	10 WM:	0
Catches:	14	Stumpings:	0

Throughout the mid fifties and early sixties, sides that played Australia had a major hurdle to overcome before they could set about the task of dismissing the side. That hurdle was opening batsman Colin McDonald. The Victorian added surety to a top order that came under pace attack from the likes of Frank Tyson and Wes Hall as well as the spin of Jim Laker. Against Laker in the famous Old Trafford Test in 1956 it was McDonald who showed some resistance, scoring 32 out of 84 in the first innings and 89 in the second. He scored five fine Test hundreds, the highest being 170 against England at Adelaide in 1959. As a 33 year old he faced the brunt of the fiery West Indian pace attack in the hard fought 1960/61 series, top scoring with 91 in Australia's decisive fifth Test victory. After his retirement he was a key figure in Australian tennis for many years.

McDONALD, Edgar Arthur

Born:	January 6, 1891
Batting:	Right handed
Bowling:	Right arm fast

Tests

Test Career:	1921
Cap Number:	114
Tests Played:	11

Test Batting

Innings:	12	Runs:	116
Highest Score:	36	Average:	16.57
No. 50s:	0	No. 100s:	0

Test Bowling & Fielding

Wickets:	43	Runs:	1,431
Best Bowling:	5/32	Average:	33.27
5 WI:	2	10 WM:	0
Catches:	3	Stumpings:	0

Tall and lithe he formed one of Australia's finest if not best best known opening bowling combinations with Jack Gregory. It was said that he saved his fastest and best for batsmen of quality and on the 1921 English tour he dominated the enemy taking 27 wickets in five Tests. Work saw him move to England where he enjoyed great success with Lancashire in the English county competition. He died in a car accident at only 45 years of age.

McDONNELL, Percival Stanislaus

Born:	November 13, 1858
Batting:	Right handed
Bowling:	Right arm slow

Tests

Test Career:	1880-88
Cap Number:	21
Tests Played:	19

Test Batting

Innings:	34	Runs:	955
Highest Score:	147	Average:	28.93
No. 50s:	2	No. 100s:	3

Test Bowling & Fielding

Wickets:	0	Runs:	53
Best Bowling:		Average:	0.00
5 WI:	0	10 WM:	0
Catches:	6	Stumpings:	0

Percy McDonnell or 'Greatheart' as he was known had a Test career that would be best described as colourful. A brilliant batsman in all conditions, the English born McDonnell played first class cricket for three states. He scored three fine Test hundreds the best being a 147 at the SCG in 1882 that was part of a then record 199 run stand with Charles Bannerman. McDonnell captained his adopted country and was the first skipper to send the opposition into bat after winning the toss. His decision bore early fruit with the English dismissed for their all-time lowest Test score of only 45, but the tourists fought back and ultimately defeated McDonnell's Australians by 13 runs. Immediately after that game McDonnell came to blows with English bowler William Barnes in an altercation that resulted in Barnes breaking his hand and missing the remainder of the tour. McDonnell played first class cricket until 1895 despite suffering from an illness that claimed his life only a year later.

McGRATH, Glenn Donald

Born:	February 9, 1970
Batting:	Right handed
Bowling:	Right arm medium-fast

Tests
Test Career:	1993-		
Cap Number:	358		
Tests Played:	119		

Test Batting
Innings:	133	Runs:	631
Highest Score:	61	Average:	7.51
No. 50s:	1	No. 100s:	0

Test Bowling & Fielding
Wickets:	542	Runs:	11,684
Best Bowling:	8/24	Average:	21.55
5 WI:	28	10 WM:	3
Catches:	37	Stumpings:	0

One Day Internationals
ODI Career:	1993-		
ODIs Played:	221		

ODI Batting
Innings:	60	Runs:	104
Highest Score:	11	Average:	3.71
No. 50s:	0	No. 100s:	0

ODI Bowling & Fielding
Wickets:	331	Runs:	7,425
Best Bowling:	7/15	Average:	22.43
5 WM:	7	Catches:	34
Stumpings:	0		

Tall and lean, the country boy from New South Wales is a genial character in anything but cricket whites. Ostensibly he is like countless other pace bowlers who have played Test cricket, but with 542 wickets to his name there is much more to the man they call Pigeon. From early on he understood that subtle variation was more likely to get wickets than wild swing or bounce. He bowls an unerring line in what commentators occasionally refer to as the 'corridor of uncertainty'. From that point just outside off stump he can bring the ball back for bowled or LBW or slightly move it away in order to catch the outside edge. Add subtle variations in bounce and pace and it becomes clear that he is no ordinary bowler. He has gone head to head with Brian Lara for over a decade in the ultimate battle of champions. Possessed of a great cricket brain, McGrath detected a weakness Lara had when playing off his hip, and came out on top. His batting is a source of amusement for an entire nation bar one person, McGrath himself. A genuine bunny, he has worked tirelessly on his batting and values his wicket as much as any number three. That dedication paid off in 2004/05 when the number 11 hit 61 in a Test against the Kiwis. He is also durable. 119 Tests for a fast bowler is quite an achievement and it would have been more had he not stood on a ball during the 2005 Ashes series. The subsequent injury forced him out of the side and when he was rushed back prematurely he failed to reach his usual high standard. Late in 2005 McGrath learnt that his wife Jane had suffered a relapse in her fight with cancer and immediately took leave from the game to give her his full support. At 36 years of age he still feels he has plenty to offer and is set to play a key role in the 2006/07 Ashes series.

McILWRAITH, John
Born:	August 7, 1857
Batting:	Right handed

Tests
Test Career:	1886		
Cap Number:	43		
Tests Played:	1		

Test Batting
Innings:	2	Runs:	9
Highest Score:	7	Average:	4.50
No. 50s:	0	No. 100s:	0

Test Bowling & Fielding
Wickets:	0	Runs:	0
Best Bowling:		Average:	0.00
5 WI:	0	10 WM:	0
Catches:	1	Stumpings:	0

A high scoring Victorian batsman who toured England in 1886. He opened the batting in his second and last innings for his country.

McINTYRE, Peter Edward
Born:	April 27, 1966
Batting:	Right handed
Bowling:	Right arm leg-break

Tests
Test Career:	1995-96		
Cap Number:	364		
Tests Played:	2		

Test Batting
Innings:	4	Runs:	22
Highest Score:	16	Average:	7.33
No. 50s:	0	No. 100s:	0

Test Bowling & Fielding
Wickets:	5	Runs:	194
Best Bowling:	3/103	Average:	38.80
5 WI:	0	10 WM:	0
Catches:	0	Stumpings:	0

A right arm leg spinner whose opportunities were strictly limited by the emergence of Shane Warne. Played state cricket for both Victoria and South Australia.

McKENZIE, Graham Douglas (Garth)
Born:	June 24, 1941
Batting:	Right handed
Bowling:	Right arm fast

Tests
Test Career:	1961-71		
Cap Number:	220		
Tests Played:	60		

Test Batting
Innings:	89	Runs:	945
Highest Score:	76	Average:	12.27
No. 50s:	2	No. 100s:	0

Test Bowling & Fielding
Wickets:	246	Runs:	7,328
Best Bowling:	8/71	Average:	29.78
5 WI:	16	10 WM:	3
Catches:	34	Stumpings:	0

One Day Internationals
ODI Career:	1971	
ODIs Played:	1	

ODI Batting

Innings:	1	Runs:	0
Highest Score:	0	Average:	0.00
No. 50s:	0	No. 100s:	0

ODI Bowling & Fielding

Wickets:	2	Runs:	22
Best Bowling:	2/22	Average:	11.00
5 WM:	0	Catches:	1
Stumpings:	0		

'Garth' McKenzie was a powerfully built opening bowler from Western Australia who started his career in tandem with Alan Davidson and ended it by spearheading what was a relatively weak attack by Australian standards. He made his debut in England in 1961 as a 19 year old and despite a solid start didn't come in to his own until the England tour to Australia in 1962/63, taking 20 wickets for the series. Capable of herculean bowling stints he famously took 7/153 off 60 overs against a rampaging England at Old traford in 1964. McKenzie didn't discriminate taking big hauls against all comers. He took 6/69 against Pakistan in 1964 and three 'five fors' on the 1966/67 tour of South Africa. In the New Year's Test at the MCG in 1967/68 he claimed 10 Indian scalps and in the corresponding Test a year later took career best figures of 8/71 in the first innings against the West Indies. While not a renowned batsman he was capable of offering late resistance and hit a Test high of 76 against the South Africans in 1964. He also played county cricket for Leicestershire with fair success. In 1977/78, at age 36, and some six years after his last Test, McKenzie joined Kerry Packer's World Series Cricket but did not partcipate in any of the major matches.

McKIBBIN, Thomas Robert

Born: December 10, 1870
Batting: Left handed
Bowling: Left arm medium

Tests

Test Career:	1895-98
Cap Number:	72
Tests Played:	5

Test Batting

Innings:	8	Runs:	88
Highest Score:	28*	Average:	14.56
No. 50s:	0	No. 100s:	0

Test Bowling & Fielding

Wickets:	17	Runs:	496
Best Bowling:	3/35	Average:	29.17
5 WI:	0	10 WM:	0
Catches:	4	Stumpings:	0

A useful lower order batsman and off-spinner from New South Wales whose suspect bowling action was the cause of much conjecture on the Australian tour of England in 1896.

McLAREN, John William

Born: December 22, 1886
Batting: Right handed
Bowling: Right arm fast

Tests

Test Career:	1912
Cap Number:	100
Tests Played:	1

Test Batting

Innings:	2	Runs:	0
Highest Score:	0*	Average:	0.00
No. 50s:	0	No. 100s:	0

Test Bowling & Fielding

Wickets:	1	Runs:	70
Best Bowling:	1/23	Average:	70.00
5 WI:	0	10 WM:	0
Catches:	0	Stumpings:	0

A Fast bowler from Queensland who toured England in 1912 for the triangular series with South Africa but failed to play a Test. His only cap came in the summer of 1911/12.

McLEOD, Charles Edward

Born: October 24, 1869
Batting: Right handed
Bowling: Right arm medium

Tests

Test Career:	1894-1905
Cap Number:	67
Tests Played:	17

Test Batting

Innings:	29	Runs:	573
Highest Score:	112	Average:	23.87
No. 50s:	4	No. 100s:	1

Test Bowling & Fielding

Wickets:	33	Runs:	1,325
Best Bowling:	5/65	Average:	40.15
5 WI:	2	10 WM:	0
Catches:	9	Stumpings:	0

17 Test appearances in 11 years tells the tale of a talented all-rounder who failed to nail down a regular spot in the Australian side. A reliable batsmen, his slow scoring style often counted against him. In the first Test of the 1897/98 series McLeod was given out in rather unusual circumstances, by the well known umpire Jim Phillips. McLeod, who was almost deaf, had been clean bowled off a no-ball but failed to hear the umpire's call. Whilst making his way back to the pavillion he was caught short of his ground and despite protests by the Australian players was adjudged by Phillips to be out.

McLEOD, Robert William

Born: January 19, 1868
Batting: Left handed
Bowling: Right arm medium

Tests

Test Career:	1892-93
Cap Number:	62
Tests Played:	6

Test Batting
Innings:	11	Runs:	146
Highest Score:	31	Average:	13.27
No. 50s:	0	No. 100s:	0

Test Bowling & Fielding
Wickets:	12	Runs:	382
Best Bowling:	5/53	Average:	31.83
5 WI:	1	10 WM:	0
Catches:	3	Stumpings:	0

Brother of Test cricketer Charlie McLeod, Bob was an accurate medium pace bowler who enjoyed a successful tour of England in 1893.

McSHANE, Patrick George
Born: April 18, 1858
Batting: Left handed
Bowling: Left arm medium

Tests
Test Career:	1885-88
Cap Number:	41
Tests Played:	3

Test Batting
Innings:	6	Runs:	26
Highest Score:	12*	Average:	5.20
No. 50s:	0	No. 100s:	0

Test Bowling & Fielding
Wickets:	1	Runs:	48
Best Bowling:	1/39	Average:	48.00
5 WI:	0	10 WM:	0
Catches:	2	Stumpings:	0

He was unusual for the time given that he was a left hander, but what made George McShane a true cricket oddity was that prior to making his debut in the fifth Test against England in the 1884/85 series he stood as an umpire in the fourth!

MECKIFF, Ian
Born: January 6, 1935
Batting: Right handed
Bowling: Left arm fast

Tests
Test Career:	1957-63
Cap Number:	208
Tests Played:	18

Test Batting
Innings:	20	Runs:	154
Highest Score:	45*	Average:	11.84
No. 50s:	0	No. 100s:	0

Test Bowling & Fielding
Wickets:	45	Runs:	1,423
Best Bowling:	6/38	Average:	31.62
5 WI:	2	10 WM:	0
Catches:	9	Stumpings:	0

While his name is synonymous with the Brisbane Test against South Africa that saw him called for throwing four times it would be grossly unfair if he was just to be remembered as a 'chucker'. Meckiff was a powerful left hand quick from Victoria who was an on and off member of the Test side for six years. Injury curtailed his early career but he shone when England toured in 1958/59 taking 17 Test wickets at just over 17 runs. Unfortunatley for Meckiff there were questions about his action throughout his career, and when umpire Colin Egar called him in that Brisbane Test, it would not only mark the end of his bowling in that match but also the end of his first class career.

MEULEMAN, Kenneth Douglas
Born: September 5, 1923
Batting: Right handed

Tests
Test Career:	1946
Cap Number:	167
Tests Played:	1

Test Batting
Innings:	1	Runs:	0
Highest Score:	0	Average:	0.00
No. 50s:	0	No. 100s:	0

Test Bowling & Fielding
Wickets:	0	Runs:	0
Best Bowling:		Average:	0.00
5 WI:	0	10 WM:	0
Catches:	1	Stumpings:	0

His only Test was against New Zealand where he scored a duck in his only at bat. It was a sad return for a cricketer who amassed almost 8,000 first class runs in a 15 year career.

MIDWINTER, William Evans
Born: June 19, 1851
Batting: Right handed
Bowling: Right arm medium

Tests
Test Career:	1877-87
Cap Number:	10
Tests Played:	12

Test Batting
Innings:	21	Runs:	269
Highest Score:	37	Average:	13.45
No. 50s:	0	No. 100s:	0

Test Bowling & Fielding
Wickets:	24	Runs:	605
Best Bowling:	5/78	Average:	25.20
5 WI:	1	10 WM:	0
Catches:	10	Stumpings:	0

It is fair to say that there has never been a Test career to match that of Billy Midwinter's. A useful medium pace bowler and handy lower order batsman, it wasn't as much what Billy achieved on the field, rather his decisions off it, that make him a standout amongst Test cricketers. Midwinter made his debut for Australia in the first Test at the MCG in 1877, and played his final Test at the SCG in 1887, once again for Australia. In between those two Tests, Billy Midwinter played four Tests for England and was literally kidnapped by W.G. Grace whilst playing for Australia. Midwinter was playing for Australia against Middlesex at Lords in 1878 when he was grabbed by a group of Gloucestershire cricketers acting on the orders of the good doctor. Rather than offend, Midwinter played with his captors and went on to stay in England and represent them in Test cricket. He would play for the

Australians again, but sadly passed away at the age of 39 in a Melbourne mental asylum following the untimely death of his wife and two young children.

MILLER, Colin Reid

Born:	February 6, 1964
Batting:	Right handed
Bowling:	Right arm off-break

Tests

Test Career:	1998-2001
Cap Number:	379
Tests Played:	18

Test Batting

Innings:	24	Runs:	174
Highest Score:	43	Average:	8.28
No. 50s:	0	No. 100s:	0

Test Bowling & Fielding

Wickets:	69	Runs:	1,805
Best Bowling:	5/32	Average:	26.15
5 WI:	3	10 WM:	1
Catches:	6	Stumpings:	0

Nicknamed 'Funky', in no small part because of his penchant to dye his hair a range of unusual colours, the journeyman's persistence was rewarded with 18 Tests at an age when most cricketers are contemplating retirement. For most of his career he was a canny medium pace bowler, but injury and age forced him to re-assess and when he was in his thirties he converted to off-spin. Miller enjoyed great success in the Test side, especially in 2000/01, when he was named the 'Australian Test player of the Year'. That summer saw him return his best Test match figures, 10/113 against the West Indies at the Adelaide Oval. He ultimately lost his Test spot as Australia altered the make-up of the bowling attack, but not before enjoying a most extraordinary end to his playing career.

MILLER, Keith Ross

Born:	November 28, 1919
Batting:	Right handed
Bowling:	Right arm fast

Tests

Test Career:	1946-56
Cap Number:	168
Tests Played:	55

Test Batting

Innings:	87	Runs:	2,958
Highest Score:	147	Average:	36.97
No. 50s:	13	No. 100s:	7

Test Bowling & Fielding

Wickets:	170	Runs:	3,906
Best Bowling:	7/60	Average:	22.97
5 WI:	7	10 WM:	1
Catches:	38	Stumpings:	0

Australia's greatest ever all-rounder, his life could have been lifted straight from the pages of a Boy's Own Annual. He was not only one of the greatest cricketers of all time, he was also an accomplished Australian Rules footballer and war time fighter pilot. Throw in his dashing good looks and a zest for life and you have 'Nugget' Miller. His first Test was against the Kiwis in 1946, but he came to notice in his second when took to England with bat and ball. He scored 79 in the Australia's only at bat and took 9/77 for the match, in a best afield performance that gave him a taste for 'giving' it to the mother country. In that 1947/48 series he hit a spanking 141 not out at Adelaide and four years later bettered that score with 145 not out at the SCG. He continued his great form with the bat against the English in 1953, bringing up another century at Lord's. He was equally savage against England with the ball, taking 87 wickets in 27 Tests at only 22.40. Given his personality it's not surprising that Miller was considered an enigmatic cricketer, brilliant at his best but at times not on song. His greatest disappointment as a player was that he was never chosen to lead his country, ovelooked for the captaincy following Lindsay Hassett's retirement. It could be said that he was not at his most motivated under Ian Johnson but he was always capable of a match winning performance. Another regret may have been that he played prior to the introduction of one-day cricket, for if there was a prototype of the ideal one-day cricketer Keith Miller would have been it. Legendary cricket commentator John Arlott said of the great all-rounder: "If I had my choice of a player to win the match off the last ball, whether it required a catch, a six or a wicket, I would pick one player - Keith Ross Miller". Upon retirement he spent a great deal of time in England where he was much loved. He became a writer and commentator, in 1956 was awarded the MBE for his services to cricket and in 1996 was selected in the foundation XI for the Australian Cricket Hall of Fame. When Keith Miller passed away in 2004 he was honoured with a state funeral in New South Wales. Family, friends and former team-mates paid their respects in a manor befitting the great man; retelling countless 'Nugget' stories over a few cold beers.

MINNETT, Roy Baldwin

Born:	June 13, 1888
Batting:	Right handed
Bowling:	Right arm medium-fast

Tests

Test Career:	1911-12
Cap Number:	98
Tests Played:	9

Test Batting

Innings:	15	Runs:	391
Highest Score:	90	Average:	26.06
No. 50s:	3	No. 100s:	0

Test Bowling & Fielding

Wickets:	11	Runs:	290
Best Bowling:	4/34	Average:	26.36
5 WI:	0	10 WM:	0
Catches:	0	Stumpings:	0

From a talented cricketing family, he scored 90 on debut for Australia against England at the SCG in 1911. He enjoyed a fine debut series in 1911/12 scoring over 300 runs and taking five wickets with his useful medium pace. In that summer he also led NSW to The Sheffield Shield with a match winning 216 not out against the Victorians.

MISSON, Francis Michael

Born: November 19, 1938
Batting: Right handed
Bowling: Right arm fast

Tests
Test Career: 1961
Cap Number: 217
Tests Played: 5

Test Batting
Innings:	5	Runs:	38
Highest Score:	25*	Average:	19.00
No. 50s:	0	No. 100s:	0

Test Bowling & Fielding
Wickets:	16	Runs:	616
Best Bowling:	4/58	Average:	38.50
5 WI:	0	10 WM:	0
Catches:	6	Stumpings:	0

A NSW fast bowler who toured England in 1961. Despite consistent form on that tour he never played for his country again.

MOODY, Thomas Masson

Born: October 2, 1965
Batting: Right handed
Bowling: Right arm medium

Tests
Test Career: 1989-92
Cap Number: 348
Tests Played: 8

Test Batting
Innings:	14	Runs:	456
Highest Score:	106	Average:	32.57
No. 50s:	3	No. 100s:	2

Test Bowling & Fielding
Wickets:	2	Runs:	147
Best Bowling:	1/17	Average:	73.50
5 WI:	0	10 WM:	0
Catches:	9	Stumpings:	0

One Day Internationals
ODI Career: 1987-99
ODIs Played: 76

ODI Batting
Innings:	64	Runs:	1,211
Highest Score:	89	Average:	23.28
No. 50s:	10	No. 100s:	0

ODI Bowling & Fielding
Wickets:	52	Runs:	2,014
Best Bowling:	3/25	Average:	38.73
5 WM:	0	Catches:	21
Stumpings:	0		

The lanky West Australian was a more than handy member of the Australian One Day side for over a decade. An all-rounder, he was a powerful batsman and useful swing bowler who played a major role in Australia's 1999 World Cup victory, joining Steve Waugh as the first Australian to play in two World Cup winning sides. Moody struggled to find a defined role in the Test side and by his final match in 1992 was playing in the unfamiliar position of opening batsman. In 2005 Moody was appointed coach of the Sri Lankan National team.

MORONEY, John (Jack)

Born: July 24, 1917
Batting: Right handed

Tests
Test Career: 1949-51
Cap Number: 183
Tests Played: 7

Test Batting
Innings:	12	Runs:	383
Highest Score:	118	Average:	34.81
No. 50s:	1	No. 100s:	2

Test Bowling & Fielding
Wickets:	0	Runs:	0
Best Bowling:		Average:	0.00
5 WI:	0	10 WM:	0
Catches:	0	Stumpings:	0

Jack Moroney enjoyed incredible highs and lows in his short Test career. In only his fourth Test he scored a century in each innings against South Africa at Johannesburg and only two Tests later he made a pair against England. Despite continuing to enjoy success as an opener for NSW that failure against England would be his second last Test appearance.

MORRIS, Arthur Robert

Born: January 19, 1922
Batting: Left handed
Bowling: Left arm leg-break

Tests
Test Career: 1946-55
Cap Number: 171
Tests Played: 46

Test Batting
Innings:	79	Runs:	3,533
Highest Score:	206	Average:	46.48
No. 50s:	12	No. 100s:	12

Test Bowling & Fielding
Wickets:	2	Runs:	50
Best Bowling:	1/5	Average:	25.00
5 WI:	0	10 WM:	0
Catches:	15	Stumpings:	0

The brilliant left handed opener was destined for greatness from the day he debuted for his state. As an 18 year old he became the first player to score a century in each innings of his first class debut but had to wait six years for national honours due to the war. After serving in New Guinea he resumed his blossoming cricket career and made his debut against England in the 1946/47 series in Australia. He made a stuttering start but hit his straps in the second inings of the third Test at the MCG, smashing the likes of Bedser and Voce for 155. He followed that up in the next Test at Adelaide scoring fine tons in both innings. For the next decade all Australian batting lists were topped by the name A.R. Morris. Of his many Test triumphs, the role he played in Australia's improbable win over England at Leeds in 1948 was his most famous. Needing 404 to win on the final day he and Don Bradman combined for a 303 run partnership in a score of 3/404. Throughout his Test career his nemesis was Alec Bedser of England, though he did manage many fine scores against him including a Test high of 206 at Adelaide in 1950/51. Arthur Morris also holds the record for scoring a hundred on first class debut in four countries, Australia, England, South Africa and the West Indies. He filled in as captain of the Test side on two occasions, unfortunately losing both times. Morris retired at the age of only 33 after the premature passing of his wife, Valerie.

MORRIS, Samuel

Born:	June 22, 1855
Batting:	Right handed

Tests

Test Career:	1885
Cap Number:	35
Tests Played:	1

Test Batting

Innings:	2	Runs:	14
Highest Score:	10*	Average:	14.00
No. 50s:	0	No. 100s:	0

Test Bowling & Fielding

Wickets:	2	Runs:	73
Best Bowling:	2/73	Average:	36.50
5 WI:	0	10 WM:	0
Catches:	0	Stumpings:	0

A Victorian who won a Test spot as result of the player strike in late 1884 but could not hold his position in the side.

MOSES, Henry

Born:	February 13, 1858
Batting:	Left handed

Tests

Test Career:	1887-95
Cap Number:	45
Tests Played:	6

Test Batting

Innings:	10	Runs:	198
Highest Score:	33	Average:	19.80
No. 50s:	0	No. 100s:	0

Test Bowling & Fielding

Wickets:	0	Runs:	0
Best Bowling:		Average:	0.00
5 WI:	0	10 WM:	0
Catches:	1	Stumpings:	0

A fine batsman for New South Wales, who on one occasion scored 297 in Shield cricket. He was involved in a controversial episode, with unsurprisingly WG Grace, when the English skipper denied him a runner after he injured his leg in the SCG Test of 1891/92. Business commitments kept him from playing more than six Tests. He later served as a long standing cricket administrator.

MOSS, Jeffrey Kenneth

Born:	June 29, 1947
Batting:	Left handed

Tests

Test Career:	1979
Cap Number:	305
Tests Played:	1

Test Batting

Innings:	2	Runs:	60
Highest Score:	38*	Average:	60.00
No. 50s:	0	No. 100s:	0

Test Bowling & Fielding

Wickets:	0	Runs:	0
Best Bowling:		Average:	0.00
5 WI:	0	10 WM:	0
Catches:	0	Stumpings:	0

One Day Internationals

ODI Career:	1979
ODIs Played:	1

ODI Batting

Innings:	1	Runs:	7
Highest Score:	7	Average:	7.00
No. 50s:	0	No. 100s:	0

ODI Bowling & Fielding

Wickets:	0	Runs:	0
Best Bowling:		Average:	0.00
5 WM:	0	Catches:	2
Stumpings:	0		

A left hander from Victoria whose only Test was against Pakistan in 1979.

MOULE, William Henry

Born:	January 31, 1858
Batting:	Right handed
Bowling:	Right arm medium

Tests

Test Career:	1880
Cap Number:	22
Tests Played:	1

Test Batting

Innings:	2	Runs:	40
Highest Score:	34	Average:	20.00
No. 50s:	0	No. 100s:	0

Test Bowling & Fielding

Wickets:	3	Runs:	23
Best Bowling:	3/23	Average:	7.66
5 WI:	0	10 WM:	0
Catches:	1	Stumpings:	0

A Victorian who performed admirably for the touring Australians in his only Test.

MULLER, Scott Andrew

Born:	June 11, 1971
Batting:	Right handed
Bowling:	Right arm medium-fast

Tests

Test Career:	1999
Cap Number:	382
Tests Played:	2

Test Batting
Innings:	2	Runs:	6
Highest Score:	6*	Average:	0.00
No. 50s:	0	No. 100s:	0

Test Bowling & Fielding
Wickets:	7	Runs:	258
Best Bowling:	3/68	Average:	36.85
5 WI:	0	10 WM:	0
Catches:	2	Stumpings:	0

Mention the name Scott Muller to an Australian cricket fan and their response will most likely be 'can't bowl, can't throw', a reference to a jibe picked up by a crowd effects microphone during his second and final Test against Pakistan in 1999. Who made that comment became the subject of much speculation, with TV cameraman Joe ultimately claiming responsibility in a move aimed at absolving any of Muller's teammates. It's an unfortunate legacy for a young man who couldn't have fond memories of making the Test side. For the record the right arm pace bowler from Queensland performed admirably in his two Tests, taking seven wickets and sharing a tenth wicket stand of 86 with Shane Warne at his home ground, the 'Gabba.

MURDOCH, William Lloyd (Billy)

Born:	October 18, 1854
Batting:	Right handed
	Wicket Keeper

Tests
Test Career:	1877-92
Cap Number:	13
Tests Played:	19

Test Batting
Innings:	34	Runs:	908
Highest Score:	211	Average:	31.31
No. 50s:	1	No. 100s:	2

Test Bowling & Fielding
Wickets:	0	Runs:	0
Best Bowling:		Average:	0.00
5 WI:	0	10 WM:	0
Catches:	14	Stumpings:	1

Cricketer Billy Murdoch was a giant of the sport, considered by no less a judge than WG Grace to be the Australia's finest batsman of the 19th century. In an extraordinary career spanning two nations and two decades, Murdoch played Test cricket for Australia and England and represented New South Wales and Sussex. Originally selected in the Test side as a wicket keeper, he soon established himself as middle order batsman with a penchant for scoring large totals. At the Oval in 1880 he plundered the English attack to the tune of 153 runs and four years later, when captaining the Australians at the age of 29, he became the first Test cricketer to score a double century. His 211 at The Oval was part of Australia's total of 551 and stood as the highest score in Test cricket for just under twenty years. Stocky and compact, Billy Murdoch was described at the time as a peerless batsman who favoured stroke play along the ground rather than chancing his arm with lofted hitting. Following the 1884 series in England, Murdoch married and played little cricket for five years. He did play in the Australian side that toured England in 1890 but did not to return home with the team, rather choosing to take the position of captain at county team Sussex. He would never play for Australia again but Murdoch did appear in one more Test match, representing England against South Africa at Cape Town in 1892. His single Test for England yielded only 12 runs but an overall average of over in 30 Test cricket supports the notion that at the time there were few if any better batsmen in the game. Billy Murdoch passed away at the age of 55 whilst watching the Australian play South Africa in a Test Match at the MCG.

MUSGROVE, Henry Alfred (Harry)

Born:	November 27, 1858
Batting:	Right handed

Tests
Test Career:	1885
Cap Number:	36
Tests Played:	1

Test Batting
Innings:	2	Runs:	13
Highest Score:	9	Average:	6.50
No. 50s:	0	No. 100s:	0

Test Bowling & Fielding
Wickets:	0	Runs:	0
Best Bowling:		Average:	0.00
5 WI:	0	10 WM:	0
Catches:	0	Stumpings:	0

A Victorian batsman who was part of the inexperienced side that was thrashed by England at the MCG in 1884/85.

NAGEL, Lisle Ernest

Born:	March 6, 1905
Batting:	Right handed
Bowling:	Right arm fast

Tests
Test Career:	1932
Cap Number:	144
Tests Played:	1

Test Batting
Innings:	2	Runs:	21
Highest Score:	21*	Average:	21.00
No. 50s:	0	No. 100s:	0

Test Bowling & Fielding
Wickets:	2	Runs:	110
Best Bowling:	2/110	Average:	55.00
5 WI:	0	10 WM:	0
Catches:	0	Stumpings:	0

A Victorian fast bowler, he stood a towering 6 feet 6 inches. His twin brother Vernon also played state cricket.

NASH, Laurence John

Born:	May 2, 1910
Batting:	Right handed
Bowling:	Right arm fast

Tests

Test Career:	1932-37
Cap Number:	143
Tests Played:	2

Test Batting

Innings:	2	Runs:	30
Highest Score:	17	Average:	15.00
No. 50s:	0	No. 100s:	0

Test Bowling & Fielding

Wickets:	10	Runs:	126
Best Bowling:	4/18	Average:	12.60
5 WI:	0	10 WM:	0
Catches:	6	Stumpings:	0

Laurie Nash was a legendary Australian Rules footballer who would have surely played more Test cricket had he devoted more time to the sport. The Tasmanian was unusual in that he played two Tests without ever playing a game of Sheffield Shield cricket.

NICHOLSON, Matthew James

Born:	October 2, 1974
Batting:	Right handed
Bowling:	Right arm medium-fast

Tests

Test Career:	1998
Cap Number:	380
Tests Played:	1

Test Batting

Innings:	2	Runs:	14
Highest Score:	9	Average:	7.00
No. 50s:	0	No. 100s:	0

Test Bowling & Fielding

Wickets:	4	Runs:	115
Best Bowling:	3/56	Average:	28.75
5 WI:	0	10 WM:	0
Catches:	0	Stumpings:	0

A tall right arm quick from New South Wales, he was a a shock inclusion for the Boxing Day Test against England at MCG in the summer of 1998/99. Despite bowling well, he took three wickets in the second innings of a hard fought game, Nicholson was dropped and has never represented his country again. Since playing for Australia he has moved to Western Australia and back again to NSW.

NITSCHKE, Homesdale Charles (Jack)

Born:	April 14, 1905
Batting:	Left handed

Tests

Test Career:	1931
Cap Number:	137
Tests Played:	2

Test Batting

Innings:	2	Runs:	53
Highest Score:	47	Average:	26.50
No. 50s:	0	No. 100s:	0

Test Bowling & Fielding

Wickets:	0	Runs:	0
Best Bowling:		Average:	0.00
5 WI:	0	10 WM:	0
Catches:	3	Stumpings:	0

He was before his time opening, the batting with the attitude of a modern one-day cricketer. Nitschke falied to flatter for his country but was a star with his state of South Australia.

NOBLE, Montague Alfred

Born:	January 28, 1873
Batting:	Right handed
Bowling:	Right arm medium

Tests

Test Career:	1898-1909
Cap Number:	76
Tests Played:	42

Test Batting

Innings:	73	Runs:	1,997
Highest Score:	133	Average:	30.25
No. 50s:	16	No. 100s:	1

Test Bowling & Fielding

Wickets:	121	Runs:	3,025
Best Bowling:	7/17	Average:	25.00
5 WI:	9	10 WM:	2
Catches:	26	Stumpings:	0

Whilst many a modern cricket fan would have sat in, or at least heard of the M.A. Noble Stand at the SCG, far less would be aware of the on-field feats of the prodigious talent after which it was named. Standing 6ft 2 in, the New South Welshman was an imposing batsman and equally skilled medium pace bowler. His greatest achievements in the Test arena were achieved with ball in hand. He took 6/49 in England's second innings on debut in 1898 and recorded the wonderful match figures of 13/77 against the same opposition during the 1901/02 season. Monty Noble played over a decade of international cricket during which time be became captain of Australia and earnt the reputation as the best all-rounder in the game. It is fitting that his only Test century, 133 against England, was scored at SCG. Following his retirement, Noble maintained a close connection with the game both as a commentator and author of the acclaimed book on Australia-England cricket; Those Ashes.

NOBLET, Geoffrey

Born:	September 14, 1916
Batting:	Right handed
Bowling:	Right arm medium-fast

Tests

Test Career:	1950-53
Cap Number:	184
Tests Played:	3

Test Batting

Innings:	4	Runs:	22
Highest Score:	13*	Average:	7.33
No. 50s:	0	No. 100s:	0

Test Bowling & Fielding
Wickets:	7	Runs:	183
Best Bowling:	3/21	Average:	26.14
5 WI:	0	10 WM:	0
Catches:	1	Stumpings:	0

A pencil thin medium pace bowler from South Australia whose chances were limited by the pace trio of Ray Lindwall, Bill Johnston and Keith Miller.

NOTHLING, Otto Ernest
Born:	August 1, 1900
Batting:	Right handed
Bowling:	Right arm medium-fast

Tests
Test Career:	1928
Cap Number:	127
Tests Played:	1

Test Batting
Innings:	2	Runs:	52
Highest Score:	44	Average:	26.00
No. 50s:	0	No. 100s:	0

Test Bowling & Fielding
Wickets:	0	Runs:	72
Best Bowling:		Average:	0.00
5 WI:	0	10 WM:	0
Catches:	0	Stumpings:	0

A doctor whose only Test was against England. Also represented Australia in Rugby Union.

O'BRIEN, Leo Patrick Joseph
Born:	July 2, 1907
Batting:	Left handed

Tests
Test Career:	1933-36
Cap Number:	145
Tests Played:	5

Test Batting
Innings:	8	Runs:	211
Highest Score:	61	Average:	26.37
No. 50s:	2	No. 100s:	0

Test Bowling & Fielding
Wickets:	0	Runs:	0
Best Bowling:		Average:	0.00
5 WI:	0	10 WM:	0
Catches:	3	Stumpings:	0

A left hand opening batsman from Victoria his finest moment came in the fifth Test of the Bodyline series when he scored a courageous 61 batting at number four. O'Brian remained a keen supporter of cricket in his home state well into his eighties.

O'CONNOR, John Dennis Alphonsus (Jack)
Born:	September 9, 1875
Batting:	Left handed
Bowling:	Right arm medium

Tests
Test Career:	1908-09
Cap Number:	93
Tests Played:	4

Test Batting
Innings:	8	Runs:	86
Highest Score:	20	Average:	12.28
No. 50s:	0	No. 100s:	0

Test Bowling & Fielding
Wickets:	13	Runs:	340
Best Bowling:	5/40	Average:	26.15
5 WI:	1	10 WM:	0
Catches:	3	Stumpings:	0

A right arm quick who starred on debut against England returning match figures of 8/150. Toured England in 1909.

O'DONNELL, Simon Patrick
Born:	January 26, 1963
Batting:	Right handed
Bowling:	Right arm medium-fast

Tests
Test Career:	1985
Cap Number:	329
Tests Played:	6

Test Batting
Innings:	10	Runs:	206
Highest Score:	48	Average:	29.42
No. 50s:	0	No. 100s:	0

Test Bowling & Fielding
Wickets:	6	Runs:	504
Best Bowling:	3/37	Average:	84.00
5 WI:	0	10 WM:	0
Catches:	4	Stumpings:	0

One Day Internationals
ODI Career:	1985-91
ODIs Played:	87

ODI Batting
Innings:	64	Runs:	1,242
Highest Score:	74*	Average:	25.34
No. 50s:	9	No. 100s:	0

ODI Bowling & Fielding
Wickets:	108	Runs:	3,102
Best Bowling:	5/13	Average:	28.72
5 WM:	1	Catches:	22
Stumpings:	0		

Ideally suited to one day cricket, the dynamic all-rounder from Victoria was a key member of the Australian side that won the World Cup in 1987. O'Donnell was diagnosed with cancer in 1987 but made a full recovery and was back playing for his country 18 months later. So good was his form in the shorter version of the game that he won the 'International Cricket of the Year' for the Australian summer of 1990/91 without playing a single Test. Also a brilliant Australian Rules footballer he is the last person to play that sport at the highest level and play Test cricket.

O'KEEFFE, Kerry James
Born:	November 25, 1949
Batting:	Right handed
Bowling:	Right arm leg-break

Tests
Test Career:	1971-77
Cap Number:	253
Tests Played:	24

Test Batting
Innings:	34	Runs:	644
Highest Score:	85	Average:	25.76
No. 50s:	13	No. 100s:	0

Test Bowling & Fielding
Wickets:	53	Runs:	2,018
Best Bowling:	5/101	Average:	38.07
5 WI:	1	10 WM:	0
Catches:	15	Stumpings:	0

One Day Internationals
ODI Career:	19777
ODIs Played:	2

ODI Batting
Innings:	2	Runs:	16
Highest Score:	16*	Average:	16.00
No. 50s:	0	No. 100s:	0

ODI Bowling & Fielding
Wickets:	2	Runs:	79
Best Bowling:	1/36	Average:	39.50
5 WM:	0	Catches:	0
Stumpings:	0		

A tall, blonde leg-spinner from New South Wales who accentuated his height with a hop just prior to delivering the ball. O'Keeffe was in and out of the Test side during the 1970's, often jostling for a position with fellow leggie Terry Jenner. He was also a more than handy lower order batsman who hit a career high 85 against New Zealand at Adelaide in 1974 during a series that saw him average 67. Nicknamed 'Skull', he played an integral role in Australia's 45 run victory against England in the 1977 Centenary Test when he took three wickets in the second innings, including the vital scalp of top scorer Derek Randall. Later that year O'Keefe, along with eight of his team mates from that famous match, joined Kerry Packer's World Series Cricket. In retirement he has gained a cult following for his radio commentary syle that combines match descriptions with humorous anecdotes and occasional rollicking fits of laughter.

O'NEILL, Norman Clifford

Born:	February 19, 1937
Batting:	Right handed
Bowling:	Right arm medium-fast

Tests
Test Career:	1958-65
Cap Number:	211
Tests Played:	42

Test Batting
Innings:	69	Runs:	2,779
Highest Score:	181	Average:	45.55
No. 50s:	15	No. 100s:	6

Test Bowling & Fielding
Wickets:	17	Runs:	667
Best Bowling:	4/41	Average:	39.23
5 WI:	0	10 WM:	0
Catches:	21	Stumpings:	0

The powerfully built New South Welshman was a dominant force in Australian cricket in the fifties and sixties. Tall and with a fondness for rocking on to the back foot to punish the bowling or leaning on to the front to execute a forceful drive, O'Neill played 42 Tests and averaged over 45. His made his debut against England on their 1958/59 Ashes tour and ended the series with an average of 56.40. His maiden Test century was in the famous tied Test in Brisbane in 1960 where he scored 181 in the first innings. O'Neill would go and score five more Test hundreds, two against England, two against India and one when playing Pakistan in Lahore. Norman O'Neill was also a clever spin bowler who was often used as a partnership breaker in Tests. Whilst his batting was brilliant and bowling canny, many feel his fielding in the covers outshone both. In a first class career that spanned 13 years he scored 13,805 runs, an outstanding return for the man once described as 'the new Bradman'.

O'REILLY, William Joseph (Tiger)

Born:	December 20, 1905
Batting:	Left handed
Bowling:	Left arm leg-break

Tests
Test Career:	1932-46
Cap Number:	140
Tests Played:	27

Test Batting
Innings:	39	Runs:	410
Highest Score:	56*	Average:	12.81
No. 50s:	1	No. 100s:	0

Test Bowling & Fielding
Wickets:	144	Runs:	3,254
Best Bowling:	7/54	Average:	22.59
5 WI:	11	10 WM:	3
Catches:	7	Stumpings:	0

In the golden period of Australian cricket that coincided with the career of Don Bradman, the nation had two great weapons; a brilliant top order and incomparable leg-spinners. One of those wrist spiiners was Tiger Bill O'Reilly, a tall, gangly leggie from country New South Wales. Bill O'Reilly moved around a lot as a youngster, on account of his father being a teacher, and came to cricket in the country town of Wingello which he described as cricket 'mad'. During his youth he ran into one Donald Bradman who recalled him as the best bowler he had faced as a junior and for any time thereafter. After making his first class debut in 1927 he had to wait until 1932 to play his first Test. That game was against South Africa and was memorable for the fact that Clarrie Grimmett took 14wickets. Not only was a famous bowling partnership born, but O'Reilly had also found a mentor. In the 1934 Ashes tour he bowled his country to victory taking 28 wickets and followed that up with 23 wickets in four Tests on the 1938 Ashes tour. O'Reilly's last game was against New Zealand and he departed the Test scene with match figures of 8/33. As a bowler he was surprisingly accurate for a leggie, could extract steepling bounce and had a pronounced googly. As a man he was a tenacious competitior, hence the nickname, but a great team player as well. It was well documented that off the field he and Bradman were hardly friends but it was over no particular disagreement, rather they were very different people, O'Reilly was talkative and partial to a drink whilst his skipper was just the opposite. Bill O' Reilly lived to the ripe old age of 86, old enough to sit in the grandstand named in his honour at the SCG and watch a young Shane Warne continue the legacy he and Grimmett had started decades earlier.

OGILVIE, Alan David

Born: June 3, 1951
Batting: Right handed

Tests

Test Career: 1977-78
Cap Number: 286
Tests Played: 5

Test Batting
Innings:	10	Runs:	178
Highest Score:	47	Average:	17.80
No. 50s:	0	No. 100s:	0

Test Bowling & Fielding
Wickets:	0	Runs:	0
Best Bowling:		Average:	0.00
5 WI:	0	10 WM:	0
Catches:	5	Stumpings:	0

The bearded Queenslander was selected in the Test side after scoring over 1,000 runs in a season for his state, but in five Tests failed to reach fifty in any innings.

OLDFIELD, William Albert Stanley (Bert)

Born: September 9, 1894
Batting: Right handed
Wicket Keeper

Tests

Test Career: 1920-37
Cap Number: 109
Tests Played: 54

Test Batting
Innings:	80	Runs:	1,427
Highest Score:	65*	Average:	22.65
No. 50s:	4	No. 100s:	0

Test Bowling & Fielding
Wickets:	0	Runs:	0
Best Bowling:		Average:	0.00
5 WI:	0	10 WM:	0
Catches:	78	Stumpings:	52

The diminutive Oldfield played for his country for almost two decades, but it was the image of the courageous keeper being struck by Harold Larwood in the third Test of the Bodyline series that meant he would play a key role in one of cricket's most famous incidents. Oldfield had come in to bat on the third day of the Adelaide Test following the fall of Victor Richardson with the score at 5/131. He had batted admirably, reaching 41 as the score edged to 7/218, when he attempted to hook a short delivery from the English tearaway. He could only manage to nick the ball which then thundered into his head, fracturing his skull. The sight of Oldfield staggering to square leg, clutching his head, enraged both spectators and the Australians in the dressing room alike. Bert Oldfield had inadvertently turned Bodyline from a bowling theory into a war between two cricketing nations, but for his part Oldfield didn't blame the bowler, saying it was his own fault for missing the hook shot. In fact he became great friends with Larwood who later emigrated to Australia. Of course Oldfield was much more than a key figure in the bodyline series. He was a fine wicket keeper and able lower batsman who had the highest ratio of stumpings to caught of any prominent Australian keeper because of his wonderful glovework to both Bill O'Reilly and Clarrie Grimmett. Bert Oldfield was awarded an OBE in 1970, just reward for a true gentleman and great ambassador of the game.

OXENHAM, Ronald Keven

Born: July 28, 1891
Batting: Right handed
Bowling: Right arm medium

Tests

Test Career: 1929-31
Cap Number: 129
Tests Played: 7

Test Batting
Innings:	10	Runs:	151
Highest Score:	48	Average:	15.10
No. 50s:	0	No. 100s:	0

Test Bowling & Fielding
Wickets:	14	Runs:	522
Best Bowling:	4/39	Average:	37.28
5 WI:	0	10 WM:	0
Catches:	4	Stumpings:	0

Queensland's finest cricketer in the 20's, it was surprising that he failed to make a Test half century or take five wickets in a Test innings, though making his debut at 38, he may have been past his best. He was a right hand medium pacer and handy middle order batsman who took over 150 wickets for his state at just 22 runs apiece.

PALMER, George Eugene (Joey)

Born: February 22, 1859
Batting: Right handed
Bowling: Right arm off-break

Tests

Test Career: 1880-86
Cap Number: 23
Tests Played: 17

Test Batting
Innings:	25	Runs:	296
Highest Score:	48	Average:	14.09
No. 50s:	0	No. 100s:	0

Test Bowling & Fielding			
Wickets:	78	Runs:	1,678
Best Bowling:	7/65	Average:	21.51
5 WI:	6	10 WM:	2
Catches:	13	Stumpings:	0

Joey Palmer was Australia's first great spinner. He was at his most deadly on the sodden wickets that were a feature of early Test match cricket. Called up for the tour of England in 1880, Palmer was a regular in the side until a knee injury curtailed his bowling and virtually ended his Test career. In 1886 Palmer enjoyed great success on the tour of England taking over 100 wickets and scoring almost a thousand runs.

PARK, Roy Lindsay

Born:	July 30, 1892
Batting:	Right handed

Tests
Test Career:	1921
Cap Number:	113
Tests Played:	1

Test Batting
Innings:	1	Runs:	0
Highest Score:	0	Average:	0.00
No. 50s:	0	No. 100s:	0

Test Bowling & Fielding
Wickets:	0	Runs:	9
Best Bowling:		Average:	0.00
5 WI:	0	10 WM:	0
Catches:	0	Stumpings:	0

Sadly Dr Roy Park's only Test innings was a golden duck. It was an unjust return for a fine Shield batsman and equally talented Australian Rules footballer who had been kept up all night prior to his debut by an ill patient. Roy Park was the father in law of Australian Test captain Ian Johnson.

PASCOE, Leonard Stephen

Born:	February 13, 1950
Batting:	Right handed
Bowling:	Right arm fast

Tests
Test Career:	1977-82
Cap Number:	277
Tests Played:	14

Test Batting
Innings:	19	Runs:	106
Highest Score:	30*	Average:	10.60
No. 50s:	0	No. 100s:	0

Test Bowling & Fielding
Wickets:	64	Runs:	1,668
Best Bowling:	5/59	Average:	26.06
5 WI:	1	10 WM:	0
Catches:	2	Stumpings:	0

One Day Internationals
ODI Career:	1977-82
ODIs Played:	29

ODI Batting
Innings:	11	Runs:	39
Highest Score:	15*	Average:	9.75
No. 50s:	0	No. 100s:	0

ODI Bowling & Fielding
Wickets:	53	Runs:	1,066
Best Bowling:	5/30	Average:	20.11
5 WM:	1	Catches:	6
Stumpings:	0		

Born Leonard Durtanovich, he changed his name to Len Pascoe as he made his way through the ranks of grade cricket in Sydney. Lenny played Test cricket either side of a successful stint in World Series Cricket where his reputation as a genuine fast bowler was enhanced. The best selling cricket song, 'C'mon Aussie', included the line 'Pascoe's making divots in the green' and it seemed to inspire the NSW quick who used his considerable strength to terrorise batsmen with a regular battery of short, fast bowling. A good Test bowler and even better one day quick where he had a fine economy rate of only four runs an over, Pascoe was struck down by a series of knee injuries in the early 80's and played his last Test in 1982.

PELLEW, Clarence Everard (Nip)

Born:	September 21, 1893
Batting:	Right handed
Bowling:	Right arm medium

Tests
Test Career:	1920-21
Cap Number:	110
Tests Played:	10

Test Batting
Innings:	14	Runs:	484
Highest Score:	116	Average:	37.23
No. 50s:	1	No. 100s:	2

Test Bowling & Fielding
Wickets:	0	Runs:	34
Best Bowling:		Average:	0.00
5 WI:	0	10 WM:	0
Catches:	4	Stumpings:	0

A strongly built batsman from South Australia, he seemed set for a long career when he struck consecutive Test centuries during the Englishmen's tour of Australia in 1920 /21. However Pellew would struggle after that, both in Australia and on the Ashes tour of '21.

PHILLIPS, Wayne Bentley

Born:	March 1, 1958
Batting:	Right handed
	Wicket Keeper

Tests
Test Career:	1983-86
Cap Number:	320
Tests Played:	27

Test Batting
Innings:	48	Runs:	1,485
Highest Score:	159	Average:	32.28
No. 50s:	7	No. 100s:	2

Test Bowling & Fielding
Wickets:	0	Runs:	0
Best Bowling:		Average:	0.00
5 WI:	0	10 WM:	0
Catches:	52	Stumpings:	0

The Encyclopedia of International Cricketers - Australia

One Day Internationals
ODI Career: 1982-86
ODIs Played: 48

ODI Batting
Innings:	41	Runs:	852
Highest Score:	75*	Average:	24.34
No. 50s:	6	No. 100s:	0

ODI Bowling & Fielding
Wickets:	0	Runs:	0
Best Bowling:		Average:	0.00
5 WM:	0	Catches:	42
Stumpings:	7		

A swashbuckling keeper/batsman from South Australia, he holds the record for the fourth highest score on debut by an Australian, with his 159 against Pakistan at Perth in 1983. Phillips had an interesting philosophy when it came to batting, stating that the reason he liked lofting the ball was because there were more gaps in the air than on the ground! He toured the West Indies in 1983/84 and while he continued to make a valuable contribution with the bat it became clear that he was a batsman keeper rather than the other way around. In 1986 he played a handful of Tests solely as a batsman, but his days at the top level were numbered and he returned to state cricket where he went on to become captain. Today he coaches his beloved South Australia.

PHILLIPS, Wayne Norman
Born: November 7, 1962
Batting: Right handed

Tests
Test Career: 1992
Cap Number: 351
Tests Played: 1

Test Batting
Innings:	2	Runs:	22
Highest Score:	14	Average:	11.00
No. 50s:	0	No. 100s:	0

Test Bowling & Fielding
Wickets:	0	Runs:	0
Best Bowling:		Average:	0.00
5 WI:	0	10 WM:	0
Catches:	0	Stumpings:	0

A neat right handed opener from Victoria who had scored heavily for his state before being selected in the Test side. His only Test was against India on the bouncy WACA wicket in Perth.

PHILPOTT, Peter Ian
Born: November 21, 1934
Batting: Right handed
Bowling: Right arm leg-break

Tests
Test Career: 1965-66
Cap Number: 234
Tests Played: 8

Test Batting
Innings:	10	Runs:	93
Highest Score:	22	Average:	10.33
No. 50s:	0	No. 100s:	0

Test Bowling & Fielding
Wickets:	26	Runs:	1,000
Best Bowling:	5/90	Average:	38.46
5 WI:	1	10 WM:	0
Catches:	5	Stumpings:	0

A right arm leg spin bowler from New South Wales who took 5/90 on debut, playing the English in Brisbane. A fine batsman for his state he was unable to reproduce that form with the bat for his country.

PONSFORD, William Harold
Born: October 19, 1900
Batting: Right handed

Tests
Test Career: 1924-34
Cap Number: 117
Tests Played: 29

Test Batting
Innings:	48	Runs:	2,122
Highest Score:	266	Average:	48.22
No. 50s:	6	No. 100s:	7

Test Bowling & Fielding
Wickets:	0	Runs:	0
Best Bowling:		Average:	0.00
5 WI:	0	10 WM:	0
Catches:	21	Stumpings:	0

Bill Ponsford was a mainstay of the great Australian sides of the 20's and 30's, during which time he formed one of Test cricket's greatest opening combinations with fellow Victorian Bill Woodfull. He made the Test side on the back of a mountain of runs for his state, including a then first class record of 429 against Tasmania. His first Test innings was a century, a feat he repeated again in his second Test. On both occasions he batted in the middle order, in fact it wasn't until 1930 that Ponsford joined Woodfull as an opener. Throughout his Test career he plundered the bowling, though he was said to have been at his best against spin where he combined impenetrible defense with an ability to work the ball into the gaps for countless ones and twos. In his final series, the 1934 tour to England, he outshone even the great Don Bradman scoring 569 Test runs at an average of 94.83 that included a wonderful 266 in his final Test at The Oval. In that innings he combined with Bradman to add a record 451 for the second wicket in a partnership that took only five and a quarter hours to compile. It seems inconceivable by modern standards that Ponsford would retire after that 1934 Ashes tour, but retire he did to concentrate on family and business. He left the Test arena with an average of just under 50, and a Shield average of over 80. Bill Ponsford was honoured when the MCG renamed the Western Stand after him in 1967. In 2006 the MCG was redeveloped and after much discussion it was agreed that the large grandstand at the city end of the ground would continue to be known as the W.H. Ponsford Stand in honour of one of Victoria's finest ever sportsmen.

PONTING, Ricky Thomas

Born: December 19, 1974
Batting: Right handed
Bowling: Right arm medium

Tests

Test Career: 1995-
Cap Number: 366
Tests Played: 105

Test Batting

Innings:	175	Runs:	8,792
Highest Score:	257	Average:	58.22
No. 50s:	34	No. 100s:	31

Test Bowling & Fielding

Wickets:	5	Runs:	231
Best Bowling:	1/0	Average:	46.20
5 WI:	0	10 WM:	0
Catches:	120	Stumpings:	0

One Day Internationals

ODI Career: 1995-
ODIs Played: 252

ODI Batting

Innings:	246	Runs:	9,210
Highest Score:	164	Average:	42.44
No. 50s:	52	No. 100s:	20

ODI Bowling & Fielding

Wickets:	3	Runs:	104
Best Bowling:	1/12	Average:	34.66
5 WM:	0	Catches:	104
Stumpings:	0		

Earmarked for greatness from the time he made his first class debut at the age of 17, the Tasmanian has gone on to become not only one of the best batsmen of his time but captain of the strongest side in Test cricket. With a better Test average than Sachin Tendulkar and Brian Lara, a case could be made that the gifted strokeplayer has been underrated for much of his career, but it seems that the man who scored over 1,500 Test runs in 2005 is finally getting the recognition he deserves. Nicknamed 'Punter' because of his fondness for a bet on his beloved greyhounds, his Test career started against Sri Lanka at the WACA in 1995/96 with an unlucky 96. In his second Test at the MCG he earnt the tag of 'Superboy' with another fine innings, a great outfield catch and an important wicket with his medium pacers. A run of outs saw him miss the first three Tests on the Ashes tour of 1997 but he responded with his first Test hundred in the fourth Test in Leeds. From that point on Ponting has been a regular fixture in the Australian side, scoring big scores with alacrity. He scored consecutive centuries against England in the first two Tests of the 2002/03 Ashes series and went one better with back to back double centuries against the touring Indians a year later. An in-form Ponting became the most dangerous player in world cricket with his ability to turn nearly every delivery into a scoring opportunity. He could mix picket clearing hooks with neat pushes and late cuts to always keep the scoreboard ticking. 2004 was a relatively lean year for Ponting with no triple figure scores, but as though the curse had been lifted on New Year's Eve, he came out in the New Year's Test at the SCG and made 207 against Pakistan. Ponting's ascension to the captaincy was done in two stages, as one day skipper in 2002 and then as Test captain in 2004. He led the side that retained the World Cup in 2003, starring in the final with an unbeaten 140. When it seemed that all he touched turned to gold, he suffered the disappointment of being the first Aussie skipper to lose the Ashes for over 20 years. That series defeat in 2005 burns deep, and in an ominous warning for the rest of the cricketing world, he says it should only serve to deepen his resolve in the future.

POPE, Roland James

Born: February 18, 1864
Batting: Right handed

Tests

Test Career: 1885
Cap Number: 37
Tests Played: 1

Test Batting

Innings:	2	Runs:	3
Highest Score:	3	Average:	1.50
No. 50s:	0	No. 100s:	0

Test Bowling & Fielding

Wickets:	0	Runs:	0
Best Bowling:		Average:	0.00
5 WI:	0	10 WM:	0
Catches:	0	Stumpings:	0

A doctor whose finest moment came when he hit 170 for the famed Melbourne Zingari side.

PORTER, Graeme David

Born: April 18, 1955
Batting: Right handed
Bowling: Right arm medium

One Day Internationals

ODI Career: 1979
ODIs Played: 2

ODI Batting

Innings:	1	Runs:	3
Highest Score:	3	Average:	3.00
No. 50s:	0	No. 100s:	0

ODI Bowling & Fielding

Wickets:	3	Runs:	33
Best Bowling:	2/13	Average:	11.00
5 WM:	0	Catches:	1
Stumpings:	0		

A medium pace bowler who was selected in a 1979 World Cup squad weakened by the defection of leading Australians to World Series Cricket.

RACKEMANN, Carl Gray

Born: June 3, 1960
Batting: Right handed
Bowling: Right arm fast

Test Batting
Innings:	13	Runs:	22
Highest Score:	9	Average:	3.66
No. 50s:	0	No. 100s:	0

Test Bowling & Fielding
Wickets:	23	Runs:	830
Best Bowling:	5/39	Average:	36.08
5 WI:	2	10 WM:	0
Catches:	2	Stumpings:	0

A tall right arm quick from New South Wales, he started impressively in Test cricket, taking 5/39 against India in the second innings of his first Test. From that point on wickets came less easily and despite many stand out performances for his state he failed to secure a regular Test spot. A genuine number eleven, he failed to reach double figures in 13 Test innings.

RICHARDSON, Arthur John
Born:	July 24, 1888
Batting:	Right handed

Tests
Test Career:	1924-26
Cap Number:	118
Tests Played:	9

Test Batting
Innings:	13	Runs:	404
Highest Score:	100	Average:	31.00
No. 50s:	2	No. 100s:	1

Test Bowling & Fielding
Wickets:	12	Runs:	521
Best Bowling:	2/20	Average:	43.41
5 WI:	0	10 WM:	0
Catches:	1	Stumpings:	0

Though he was from the same state as Victor Richardson and made his debut in the same Test, Arthur was no relation to his more illustrious namesake. The tall opener wore glasses whilst batting but it certainly didn't hinder him on debut when he went within a whisker of scoring a century. That second innings 98 against the English at the SCG in 1924 was his highest Test score until his final series, when he scored an even 100 against the same opposition at Headingly. A useful change bowler, he continued in cricket after retiring as a player, coaching in England, New Zealand and Australia and even umpiring Test matches in the West Indies.

RICHARDSON, Victor York
Born:	September 7, 1894
Batting:	Right handed

Tests
Test Career:	1924-36
Cap Number:	119
Tests Played:	19

Test Batting
Innings:	30	Runs:	706
Highest Score:	138	Average:	23.53
No. 50s:	1	No. 100s:	1

Test Bowling & Fielding
Wickets:	0	Runs:	0
Best Bowling:		Average:	0.00
5 WI:	0	10 WM:	0
Catches:	24	Stumpings:	0

Grandfather of the famous Chappell brothers, he was a dominant figure in Australian cricket both on and off the pitch. As a leader he was both successful and well liked, a rare double in Australian pre-war Test match cricket. Having led South Australia for many years and vice captained the Test team he got his opportunity to lead Australia at the age 41 after Bill Woodfull announced his retirement. Under Richardson Australia thrashed the South Africans on their home soil, winning the five Test series 4-0. As a batsman he was effective rather than dominant batting either as an opener or well down the order. His highest score came against the English in 1935 when he hit 138 at the MCG, his only Test century. After retiring he became a journalist and much loved radio commentator with the ABC. Today visitors to the Adelaide Oval can visit the Victor Richardson Gates, named in honour of one of South Australia's greatest sportsmen.

RIGG, Keith Edward
Born:	May 21, 1906
Batting:	Right handed

Tests
Test Career:	1931-37
Cap Number:	136
Tests Played:	8

Test Batting
Innings:	12	Runs:	401
Highest Score:	127	Average:	33.41
No. 50s:	1	No. 100s:	1

Test Bowling & Fielding
Wickets:	0	Runs:	0
Best Bowling:		Average:	0.00
5 WI:	0	10 WM:	0
Catches:	5	Stumpings:	0

The well credentialled Victorian top order batsman battled to break into the talented Australian side of the 30's but did manage eight Tests over a six year period. The highpoint was 127 in the thrashing of South Africa at the SCG in 1931. He top scored in that game, putting on over 200 with Don Bradman in the process.

RING, Douglas Thomas
Born:	October 14, 1918
Batting:	Right handed
Bowling:	Right arm off-break

Tests
Test Career:	1948-53
Cap Number:	181
Tests Played:	13

Test Batting
Innings:	21	Runs:	426
Highest Score:	67	Average:	22.42
No. 50s:	4	No. 100s:	0

Test Bowling & Fielding			
Wickets:	35	Runs:	1,305
Best Bowling:	6/72	Average:	37.28
5 WI:	2	10 WM:	0
Catches:	5	Stumpings:	0

An off spinner who relied on flight and variations in speed rather than vicious turn to get his wickets, he was also a hard hitting tailend batsman. He twice took six wickets in an innings, the first time against the Windies in 1951 and the second just over a year later against South Africa. Both bags were at Brisbane in Tests that Australia just won. He came to the rescue with the bat on more than one occasion with his last wicket partnership with Bill Johnston at the MCG in 1952 being the most famous. Ring went on to become the face of cricket on Australian TV's famous World of Sport.

RITCHIE, Gregory Michael

Born:	January 23, 1960
Batting:	Right handed
Bowling:	Right arm medium

Tests

Test Career:	1982-87
Cap Number:	315
Tests Played:	30

Test Batting

Innings:	53	Runs:	1,690
Highest Score:	146	Average:	35.20
No. 50s:	7	No. 100s:	3

Test Bowling & Fielding

Wickets:	0	Runs:	10
Best Bowling:		Average:	0.00
5 WI:	0	10 WM:	0
Catches:	14	Stumpings:	0

One Day Internationals

| ODI Career: | 1982-87 |
| ODIs Played: | 44 |

ODI Batting

Innings:	42	Runs:	959
Highest Score:	84	Average:	27.40
No. 50s:	6	No. 100s:	0

ODI Bowling & Fielding

Wickets:	0	Runs:	0
Best Bowling:		Average:	0.00
5 WI:	0	Catches:	9
Stumpings:	0		

Nicknamed 'Fatcat' after a rotund children's TV character, the Queenslander enjoyed a fruitful international career, though many of his peers feel he failed to capitalise on his boundless potential. Ritchie made his debut in Pakistan in 1982 and signalled his ability with an unbeaten 106 in the second Test at Faisalabad. Spots were hard to come by in the Australian middle order in the 80's, but when he enjoyed a successful tour of England in 1985 where he scored a brilliant 146 at Old Trafford, it seemed his Test future was assured. Unfortunately he allowed his weight to balloon, and despite still having a fine eye, he made way for fitter men who were less of a liability in the field.

RIXON, Stephen John

Born:	February 25, 1954
Batting:	Right handed
	Wicket Keeper

Tests

Test Career:	1977-85
Cap Number:	287
Tests Played:	13

Test Batting

Innings:	24	Runs:	394
Highest Score:	54	Average:	18.76
No. 50s:	2	No. 100s:	0

Test Bowling & Fielding

Wickets:	0	Runs:	0
Best Bowling:		Average:	0.00
5 WI:	0	10 WM:	0
Catches:	42	Stumpings:	5

One Day Internationals

| ODI Career: | 1978-85 |
| ODIs Played: | 6 |

ODI Batting

Innings:	3	Runs:	40
Highest Score:	20*	Average:	13.33
No. 50s:	0	No. 100s:	0

ODI Bowling & Fielding

Wickets:	0	Runs:	0
Best Bowling:		Average:	0.00
5 WM:	0	Catches:	9
Stumpings:	2		

When Rodney Marsh defected to World Series Cricket the position of national keeper fell to Steve Rixon from New South Wales. The agile glovesman performed well when given the opportunity, though his batting whilst safe, lacked the impact of his predecessor. He went on to become coach of the New South Wales state side and then moved to Surrey in the English county competition where he filled the same position.

ROBERTSON, Gavin Ronald

Born:	May 28, 1966
Batting:	Right handed
Bowling:	Right arm off-break

Tests

Test Career:	1998
Cap Number:	375
Tests Played:	4

Test Batting

Innings:	7	Runs:	140
Highest Score:	57	Average:	20.00
No. 50s:	1	No. 100s:	0

Test Bowling & Fielding

Wickets:	13	Runs:	515
Best Bowling:	4/72	Average:	39.61
5 WI:	0	10 WM:	0
Catches:	1	Stumpings:	0

One Day Internationals

| ODI Career: | 1994-98 |
| ODIs Played: | 13 |

ODI Batting

Innings:	7	Runs:	45
Highest Score:	15	Average:	15.00
No. 50s:	0	No. 100s:	0

ODI Bowling & Fielding		
Wickets:	8	
Best Bowling:	3/29	
5 WM:	0	
Stumpings:	0	
Runs:	430	
Average:	53.75	
Catches:	3	

A steady off-spinner from NSW who performed well when given the chance to tour the sub-continent in 1978.

ROBERTSON, William Roderick (Digger)

Born:	October 6, 1861
Batting:	Right handed
Bowling:	Right arm leg-break

Tests

Test Career:	1885
Cap Number:	38
Tests Played:	1

Test Batting

Innings:	1	Runs:	2
Highest Score:	2	Average:	1.00
No. 50s:	0	No. 100s:	0

Test Bowling & Fielding

Wickets:	0	Runs:	24
Best Bowling:	0	Average:	0.00
5 WI:	0	10 WM:	0
Catches:	0	Stumpings:	0

Leg-spinner from Victoria.

ROBINSON, Rayford Harold

Born:	March 26, 1914
Batting:	Right handed

Tests

Test Career:	1936
Cap Number:	156
Tests Played:	1

Test Batting

Innings:	2	Runs:	5
Highest Score:	3	Average:	2.50
No. 50s:	0	No. 100s:	0

Test Bowling & Fielding

Wickets:	0	Runs:	0
Best Bowling:	0	Average:	0.00
5 WI:	0	10 WM:	0
Catches:	1	Stumpings:	0

An impish top order batsman who played in New Zealand late in his career.

ROBINSON, Richard Darryl

Born:	June 8, 1946
Batting:	Right handed
	Wicket Keeper

Tests

Test Career:	1977
Cap Number:	278
Tests Played:	3

Test Batting

Innings:	6	Runs:	100
Highest Score:	34	Average:	16.66
No. 50s:	0	No. 100s:	0

Test Bowling & Fielding

Wickets:	0	Runs:	0
Best Bowling:	0	Average:	0.00
5 WI:	0	10 WM:	0
Catches:	4	Stumpings:	

One Day Internationals

ODI Career:	1977
ODIs Played:	2

ODI Batting

Innings:	2	Runs:	82
Highest Score:	70	Average:	41.00
No. 50s:	1	No. 100s:	0

ODI Bowling & Fielding

Wickets:	0	Runs:	0
Best Bowling:	0	Average:	0.00
5 WM:	0	Catches:	3
Stumpings:	1		

For so long an understudy to Rodney Marsh, the Victorian keeper finally made it into the Test side as a batsman after a number of fine performances for Victoria. He played three Tests on the Ashes tour in 1977 and whilst he didn't enjoy a great deal of success with the bat he revealed himself to be an excellent close leg fieldsman. On the same tour he made a hard hitting 70 in an ODI at The Oval.

RORKE, Gordon Frederick

Born:	June 27, 1938
Batting:	Left handed
Bowling:	Right arm fast

Tests

Test Career:	1959
Cap Number:	213
Tests Played:	4

Test Batting

Innings:	4	Runs:	9
Highest Score:	7	Average:	4.50
No. 50s:	0	No. 100s:	0

Test Bowling & Fielding

Wickets:	10	Runs:	203
Best Bowling:	3/23	Average:	20.30
5 WI:	0	10 WM:	0
Catches:	1	Stumpings:	0

A 6ft 5 in, opening bowler from NSW, he exploited the back foot no-ball rule by dragging his foot some metres prior to delivery. It was thought his style played a pivotal role in the changing of the no-ball rule to the version we have today. Rorke had his career shortened by a bout of hepatitis.

RUTHERFORD, John Walter (Jack)

Born:	September 25, 1929
Batting:	Right handed
Bowling:	Right arm leg-break

Tests

Test Career:	1956
Cap Number:	204
Tests Played:	1

Test Batting

Innings:	1	Runs:	30
Highest Score:	30	Average:	30.00
No. 50s:	0	No. 100s:	0

Test Bowling & Fielding

Wickets:	1	Runs:	15
Best Bowling:	1/11	Average:	15.00
5 WI:	0	10 WM:	0
Catches:	0	Stumpings:	0

Opening batsman from Western Australia whose only Test was against India in Bombay.

RYDER, John (Jack)
Born: August 8, 1889
Batting: Right handed
Bowling: Right arm medium-fast

Tests
Test Career:	1920-29		
Cap Number:	111		
Tests Played:	20		

Test Batting
Innings:	32	Runs:	1,394
Highest Score:	201*	Average:	51.62
No. 50s:	9	No. 100s:	3

Test Bowling & Fielding
Wickets:	17	Runs:	743
Best Bowling:	2/20	Average:	43.70
5 WI:	0	10 WM:	0
Catches:	17	Stumpings:	0

Jack Ryder's Test average of over 50 rightly marks him as one of his country's finest batsmen in the period between the two World Wars. An attacking and attractive front foot batsman, he made his debut in 1920 and would go onto captain the Aussies for the 28/29' tour by the English. At Adelaide in 1924 he quite simply beat the English off his own bat, making 201 not out in the first innings and 88 in the second to help his side to an 11 run victory. Arguably Ryder's most famous knock was not for Australia but for Victoria. He second top-scored for Victoria with 295 out of 1,107 against New South Wales in 1926/27, a world record first class total that still stands today. In 1930 Jack Ryder became a Test selector, and despite the fact that he had led the Test aggregates as captain in the previous series, his fellow committeemen preferred younger men ahead of him for the English tour later that year. It was said that the 41 year old was deeply disappointed by the decision but he didn't let it sour him. Following the Second World War he rejoined the Australian Test selection committee in a role he held into his eighties.

SAGGERS, Ronald Arthur
Born: May 17, 1917
Batting: Right handed
Wicket Keeper

Tests
Test Career:	1948-50		
Cap Number:	182		
Tests Played:	6		

Test Batting
Innings:	5	Runs:	30
Highest Score:	14	Average:	10.00
No. 50s:	0	No. 100s:	0

Test Bowling & Fielding
Wickets:	0	Runs:	0
Best Bowling:		Average:	0.00
5 WI:	0	10 WM:	0
Catches:	16	Stumpings:	8

An understudy to Don Tallon who got his chance with the gloves when Tallon didn't tour South Africa in 1949/50. Interestingly Saggers completed as many stumpings in six Tests as Tallon did in 21.

SAUNDERS, John Victor
Born: March 21, 1876
Batting: Left handed
Bowling: Left arm medium

Tests
Test Career:	1902-08		
Cap Number:	83		
Tests Played:	14		

Test Batting
Innings:	23	Runs:	39
Highest Score:	11*	Average:	2.29
No. 50s:	0	No. 100s:	0

Test Bowling & Fielding
Wickets:	79	Runs:	1,796
Best Bowling:	7/34	Average:	22.73
5 WI:	6	10 WM:	0
Catches:	5	Stumpings:	0

A tall medium pacer, he burst on to the Test scene with a sparkling debut against England at SCG, taking nine wickets for the match. Saunders flourished on the 1902 tour to England when wet wickets played havoc with the summer's cricket, taking 18 wickets in four Tests. The most memorable of the 18 was the vital of scalp of Tate in the Fourth Test at Old Trafford when the English were just three runs shy of victory. Saunders later moved to New Zealand where he continued to play and coach.

SCOTT, Henry James Herbert (Tup)
Born: December 26, 1858
Batting: Right handed
Bowling: Right arm medium-fast

Tests
Test Career:	1884-86		
Cap Number:	31		
Tests Played:	8		

Test Batting
Innings:	14	Runs:	359
Highest Score:	102	Average:	27.61
No. 50s:	1	No. 100s:	1

Test Bowling & Fielding
Wickets:	0	Runs:	26
Best Bowling:		Average:	0.00
5 WI:	0	10 WM:	0
Catches:	8	Stumpings:	0

A stylish batsman from Victoria, Scott became Australia's sixth Test captain in 1886 when he led his country in three Tests against England. Unfortunately for Scott Australia lost all the matches, but he is best remembered for partnering Billy Murdoch in Test cricket's first ever 200 run partnership, a feat accomplished at The Oval in 1884.

SELLERS, Reginald Hugh Durning

Born: August 20, 1940
Batting: Right handed
Bowling: Right arm leg-break

Tests
Test Career:	1964		
Cap Number:	230		
Tests Played:	1		

Test Batting
Innings:	1	Runs:	0
Highest Score:	0	Average:	0.00
No. 50s:	0	No. 100s:	0

Test Bowling & Fielding
Wickets:	0	Runs:	17
Best Bowling:		Average:	0.00
5 WI:	0	10 WM:	0
Catches:	1	Stumpings:	0

Rex Sellers was an Indian born leg spinner whose only Test was conicidentally in India in 1964.

SERJEANT, Craig Stanton

Born: November 1, 1951
Batting: Right handed

Tests
Test Career:	1977-78		
Cap Number:	279		
Tests Played:	12		

Test Batting
Innings:	23	Runs:	522
Highest Score:	124	Average:	23.72
No. 50s:	2	No. 100s:	1

Test Bowling & Fielding
Wickets:	0	Runs:	0
Best Bowling:		Average:	0.00
5 WI:	0	10 WM:	0
Catches:	13	Stumpings:	0

One Day Internationals
ODI Career:	1977-78
ODIs Played:	3

ODI Batting
Innings:	3	Runs:	73
Highest Score:	46	Average:	24.33
No. 50s:	0	No. 100s:	0

ODI Bowling & Fielding
Wickets:	0	Runs:	0
Best Bowling:		Average:	0.00
5 WM:	0	Catches:	1
Stumpings:	0		

The elegant West Australian played three fine Test innings, but beyond that his Test career was disappointing for a player with plenty of natural ability. Selected in the Test side after only 18 first class matches, he made 81 runs on debut against a strong English attack. His 124 in the Carribean as part of a WSC weakened side was also a standout innings but unfortunately for the affable Western Australian his good Test innings were too few and far between.

SHEAHAN, Andrew Paul

Born: September 30, 1946
Batting: Right handed

Tests
Test Career:	1967-74
Cap Number:	243
Tests Played:	31

Test Batting
Innings:	53	Runs:	1,594
Highest Score:	127	Average:	33.91
No. 50s:	7	No. 100s:	2

Test Bowling & Fielding
Wickets:	0	Runs:	0
Best Bowling:		Average:	0.00
5 WI:	0	10 WM:	0
Catches:	17	Stumpings:	0

One Day Internationals
ODI Career:	1972
ODIs Played:	3

ODI Batting
Innings:	3	Runs:	75
Highest Score:	50	Average:	25.00
No. 50s:	1	No. 100s:	0

ODI Bowling & Fielding
Wickets:	0	Runs:	0
Best Bowling:		Average:	0.00
5 WM:	0	Catches:	0
Stumpings:	0		

A precocious talent, he was a consistent performer for his country though he failed to reach the heights predicted for him. His Test career started promisingly with an 81 in his debut innings against India in 1967 at Adelaide. Over the next four years he was a permanent fixture in the Test side, and though he was unable to make many big scores, he made a solid contribution both in the top order and as a brilliant cover fieldsman. His cricket career came to a premature end in the mid 70's when he chose to concentrate on his career as an educator. Sheahan went on to become Headmaster at the prestigious Geelong and Melbourne Grammar schools.

SHEPHERD, Barry Kenneth

Born: April 23, 1937
Batting: Right handed
Bowling: Right arm off-break

Tests
Test Career:	1963-65
Cap Number:	223
Tests Played:	9

Test Batting
Innings:	14	Runs:	502
Highest Score:	96	Average:	41.83
No. 50s:	5	No. 100s:	0

Test Bowling & Fielding
Wickets:	0	Runs:	9
Best Bowling:		Average:	0.00
5 WI:	0	10 WM:	0
Catches:	2	Stumpings:	0

As his Test average of above 40 would suggest, Shepherd was unfortunate not to play more Test cricket. He scored 71 on debut against England in 1963 and in his first Test against South Africa took to the bowlers with a quickfire 96. The solidly built West Australian continued to be a consistent performer, but his inability to convert many good starts at Test level into a century ultimately counted against him and he would play only nine Tests in total.

SIDDONS, James Darren
Born: April 25, 1964
Batting: Right handed

One Day Internationals
ODI Career: 1988
ODIs Played: 1

ODI Batting
Innings:	1	Runs:	32
Highest Score:	32	Average:	32.00
No. 50s:	0	No. 100s:	0

ODI Bowling & Fielding
Wickets:	0	Runs:	0
Best Bowling:		Average:	0.00
5 WI:	0	Catches:	0
Stumpings:	0		

Generally considered to be the best batsman not to have played Test cricket for Australia in the modern era, Siddons' international career was restricted a single one day game he played as part of the Australian side that toured Pakistan in 1988. As a top order bat for Victoria and South Australia had had few peers and at one stage held the record for most runs in Australian Shield cricket.

SIEVERS, Morris William
Born: April 13, 1912
Batting: Right handed
Bowling: Right arm medium-fast

Tests
Test Career: 1936-37
Cap Number: 157
Tests Played: 3

Test Batting
Innings:	6	Runs:	67
Highest Score:	25*	Average:	13.40
No. 50s:	0	No. 100s:	0

Test Bowling & Fielding
Wickets:	9	Runs:	161
Best Bowling:	5/21	Average:	17.88
5 WI:	1	10 WM:	0
Catches:	4	Stumpings:	0

A tall Victorian right arm quick who played three Tests during the 1936/37 Ashes series. He enjoyed moderate success in that series taking nine wickets at 17.98 with a best of 5/21 on his home track at the MCG.

SIMPSON, Robert Baddeley
Born: February 3, 1936
Batting: Right handed
Bowling: Right arm leg-break

Tests
Test Career: 1957-78
Cap Number: 209
Tests Played: 62

Test Batting
Innings:	111	Runs:	4,869
Highest Score:	311	Average:	46.81
No. 50s:	27	No. 100s:	10

Test Bowling & Fielding
Wickets:	71	Runs:	3,001
Best Bowling:	5/57	Average:	42.26
5 WI:	2	10 WM:	0
Catches:	110	Stumpings:	0

One Day Internationals
ODI Career: 1978
ODIs Played: 2

ODI Batting
Innings:	2	Runs:	36
Highest Score:	23	Average:	18.00
No. 50s:	0	No. 100s:	0

ODI Bowling & Fielding
Wickets:	2	Runs:	95
Best Bowling:	2/30	Average:	47.50
5 WM:	0	Catches:	4
Stumpings:	0		

Three times a leader of his country, Bob Simpson had two distinct spells as Australian captain and another equally influential period as national coach. Originally from New South Wales, he move to Western Australia to advance his first class career in the fifties and was rewarded with Test selection in 1957. For the next seven years he was a fine contributor in the Australian top order but amazingly never scored a Test century. He was appointed captain following the retirement of Richie Benaud in 1963/64 and led the Australians on their Ashes tour to England in 1964. That overdue debut Test ton came in the fourth Test at Old Tafford, a massive 311 that saw the skipper bat for over two days. From that point on the Test hunderds were easier to come by; two in the same Test against Pakistan in November of 1964 and a famous 201 against the fury of Wes Hall and Charlie Griffiths in Bridgetown in 1965. Simpson handed over the leadership reins to Bill Lawry late in 1967 and it seemed a fine Test career had come to an end, but when Australian cricket sent out an SOS during the World Series Cricket years he heeded the call. With most of the country's best and most experienced players defecting to the Kerry Packer led revolution, a 41 year old Simpson was again made Australian captain. He led the side against India and West Indies and whilst his young side was no match for the stronger opposition Simpson added two more centuries to his Test tally. The courage shown by the aging skipper against hostile opposition in the Caribbean put many of the younger players in the side to shame. Simpson stood at first slip for the bulk of his career earning the reputation as one of the best close catchers of all time. He was also an accomplished leg spinner who twice took five wickets in a Test innings. He went into coaching following his retirement and held down the top post in Australia for ten years. His forthright style didn't sit well with some players, but under his tutelage the Australians went from moderate performers to the best cricket playing nation in the world.

SINCOCK, David John

Born:	February 1, 1942
Batting:	Right handed
Bowling:	Left arm leg-break

Tests
Test Career:	1964-66
Cap Number:	232
Tests Played:	3

Test Batting
Innings:	4	Runs:	80
Highest Score:	29	Average:	26.66
No. 50s:	0	No. 100s:	0

Test Bowling & Fielding
Wickets:	8	Runs:	410
Best Bowling:	3/67	Average:	51.25
5 WI:	0	10 WM:	0
Catches:	2	Stumpings:	0

A Chinaman bowler from South Australia, he had the wickedly funny nickname of Evil Dick.

SLATER, Keith Nichol

Born:	March 12, 1936
Batting:	Right handed
Bowling:	Right arm medium

Tests
Test Career:	1959
Cap Number:	212
Tests Played:	1

Test Batting
Innings:	1	Runs:	1
Highest Score:	1*	Average:	1.00
No. 50s:	0	No. 100s:	0

Test Bowling & Fielding
Wickets:	2	Runs:	101
Best Bowling:	2/40	Average:	50.50
5 WI:	0	10 WM:	0
Catches:	0	Stumpings:	0

He was a West Australian off-spinner who may have played more than one Test had he not been called for throwing when playing for his state against NSW in the Sheffield Shield competition.

SLATER, Michael Jonathon

Born:	February 21, 1970
Batting:	Right handed
Bowling:	Right arm medium

Tests
Test Career:	1993-2001
Cap Number:	357
Tests Played:	74

Test Batting
Innings:	131	Runs:	5,312
Highest Score:	219	Average:	42.83
No. 50s:	21	No. 100s:	14

Test Bowling & Fielding
Wickets:	1	Runs:	10
Best Bowling:	1/4	Average:	10.00
5 WI:	0	10 WM:	0
Catches:	33	Stumpings:	0

One Day Internationals
ODI Career:	1993-97
ODIs Played:	42

ODI Batting
Innings:	42	Runs:	987
Highest Score:	73	Average:	24.07
No. 50s:	9	No. 100s:	0

ODI Bowling & Fielding
Wickets:	0	Runs:	11
Best Bowling:	0	Average:	0.00
5 WM:	0	Catches:	9
Stumpings:	0		

Michael Slater was a nimble footed opener from New South Wales who looked to shatter the confidence of any bowler that he faced. His best was pulsating, often launching into cuts and hooks with both feet off the ground. He was particularly savage on England, scoring his first Test hundred at Lord's in 1993 and then repeating the dose when they toured in 1994/95 with 623 runs for the series at an average of 62.30. His highest Test score, 219 against the Sri Lankans at the WACA late in 1995 was a study in savagery with 15 4's and five 6's. It seemed there was no stopping Slater but his uncompromising style would also count against him. When the runs dried up, as they do for all batsmen, he refused to alter his batting style and too often the Australian top order was exposed because of a rash shot by Slater. It cost him his spot in the 1997 Ashes squad and ultimately ended his career in 2001. When the fireworks came to an end he had belted 14 Test centuries and averaged an excellent 42.83. The statistic that best sums up his attitude to batting was the record nine times he went out in the nineties during Tests. It proved that no matter what the scoreboard said, if the ball was there to hit Michael Slater was up for the challenge.

SLEEP, Peter Raymond

Born:	May 4, 1957
Batting:	Right handed
Bowling:	Right arm leg-break

Tests
Test Career:	1979-90
Cap Number:	303
Tests Played:	14

Test Batting
Innings:	21	Runs:	483
Highest Score:	90	Average:	24.15
No. 50s:	3	No. 100s:	0

Test Bowling & Fielding
Wickets:	31	Runs:	1,397
Best Bowling:	5/72	Average:	45.06
5 WI:	1	10 WM:	0
Catches:	4	Stumpings:	0

Used in fits and starts over an eleven year period, 'Sounda' Sleep could extract considerable turn with his leggies, but at times lacked control. Also a very good lower order bat, he occasionally filled a spot in the top order.

SLIGHT, James

Born:	October 20, 1855
Batting:	Right handed

Test Career:	1880		
Cap Number:	24		
Tests Played:	1		

Test Batting

Innings:	2	Runs:	11
Highest Score:	11	Average:	5.50
No. 50s:	0	No. 100s:	0

Test Bowling & Fielding

Wickets:	0	Runs:	0
Best Bowling:		Average:	0.00
5 WI:	0	10 WM:	0
Catches:	0	Stumpings:	0

Victorian batsman who toured England in 1880.

SMITH, David Bertram Miller

Born:	September 14, 1884
Batting:	Right handed

Tests

Test Career:	1912		
Cap Number:	104		
Tests Played:	2		

Test Batting

Innings:	3	Runs:	30
Highest Score:	24*	Average:	15.00
No. 50s:	0	No. 100s:	0

Test Bowling & Fielding

Wickets:	0	Runs:	0
Best Bowling:		Average:	0.00
5 WI:	0	10 WM:	0
Catches:	0	Stumpings:	0

He was a well built Victorian batsman who failed to flatter in his only two Tests.

SMITH, Steven Barry

Born:	October 18, 1961
Batting:	Right handed
Bowling:	Right arm slow

Tests

Test Career:	1984		
Cap Number:	323		
Tests Played:	3		

Test Batting

Innings:	5	Runs:	41
Highest Score:	12	Average:	8.20
No. 50s:	0	No. 100s:	0

Test Bowling & Fielding

Wickets:	0	Runs:	0
Best Bowling:		Average:	0.00
5 WI:	0	10 WM:	0
Catches:	1	Stumpings:	0

One Day Internationals

ODI Career:	1983-85		
ODIs Played:	28		

ODI Batting

Innings:	24	Runs:	861
Highest Score:	117	Average:	39.13
No. 50s:	8	No. 100s:	2

ODI Bowling & Fielding

Wickets:	0	Runs:	5
Best Bowling:		Average:	0.00
5 WM:	0	Catches:	8
Stumpings:	0		

A hard hitting opening batsman from New South Wales, his style was better suited to one day cricket. Also represented Australia in Indoor Cricket.

SPOFFORTH, Frederick Robert

Born:	September 9, 1853
Batting:	Right handed
Bowling:	Right arm medium-fast

Tests

Test Career:	1877-87		
Cap Number:	14		
Tests Played:	18		

Test Batting

Innings:	29	Runs:	217
Highest Score:	50	Average:	9.43
No. 50s:	1	No. 100s:	0

Test Bowling & Fielding

Wickets:	94	Runs:	1,731
Best Bowling:	7/44	Average:	18.41
5 WI:	7	10 WM:	4
Catches:	11	Stumpings:	0

Fred Spofforth's nickname said it all, the 'Demon' was Australia's first great quick bowler who to this day is still regarded as one of his nation's best. Tall and lean with an immaculate black moustache, Spofforth debuted for Australia in the second Test ever played, at the MCG in 1877. He should have been part of Australia's first Test side but stood out in protest over the omission of his New South Wales team mate Billy Murdoch. Though he only played 18 Test matches he was able to take ten wickets in a match on four occasions, including the wonderful match figures of 14/90 against England at The Oval in 1882. The 'Demon' will also be remembered as the man who took Test cricket's first hat-trick, a feat accomplished at the MCG in 1879. Yet it wasn't his first hat-trick against English opposition. In 1878 Australia toured England and played a memorable game against the Marleybone Cricket Club when the MCC were humiliated by their Colonial cousins. Spofforth took six wickets for four runs in the first innings of the game, including a hat-trick, then four wickets for 16 runs in the second. Though a wonderful bowler, the 'Demon' was not as ferocious as his name would suggest. His greatest attributes were accuracy and stamina rather than sheer pace. In fact his first Test wicket was that of Alfred Shaw who was out stumped Blackham bowled Spofforth!

STACKPOLE, Keith Raymond

Born:	July 10, 1940
Batting:	Right handed
Bowling:	Right arm leg-break

Tests

Test Career:	1966-74		
Cap Number:	238		
Tests Played:	43		

Test Batting
Innings:	80	Runs:	2,807
Highest Score:	207	Average:	37.42
No. 50s:	14	No. 100s:	7

Test Bowling & Fielding
Wickets:	15	Runs:	1,001
Best Bowling:	2/33	Average:	66.73
5 WI:	0	10 WM:	0
Catches:	47	Stumpings:	0

One Day Internationals
ODI Career:	1971-74
ODIs Played:	6

ODI Batting
Innings:	6	Runs:	224
Highest Score:	61	Average:	37.33
No. 50s:	3	No. 100s:	0

ODI Bowling & Fielding
Wickets:	3	Runs:	54
Best Bowling:	3/40	Average:	18.00
5 WM:	0	Catches:	1
Stumpings:	0		

Pugnacious and powerful, the stocky Victorian opener lived by the axiom that attack was the best form of defence. A fine performer for his state, he had to wait until he was 25 to play for his country but his early Test career was marked by indifferent form and uncertainty as to what was his best spot in the batting line-up. He didn't secure a regular place in the Test team until he was almost 30, but when given the opener's spot by Bill Lawry in 1969 he grasped the opportunity with both hands. 'Stacky' led the averages against a fomidable English attack in 1970/71, hitting his highest ever Test score of 207 in the first Test at Brisbane. Over the next three seasons he would score five more centuries including a ton at his beloved MCG against the Kiwis in 1973. As his Test career developed he earnt a reputation as the best hooker and puller in world cricket. An exceptional slip fieldsman, Stackpole was a also useful leg-spin bowler who was seemingly under used at Test level. In the thirty plus years following his retirement he has worked as a cricket commentator and befitting the manor in which he played the game has done the job without fear or favour.

STEVENS, Gavin Byron
Born:	February 29, 1932
Batting:	Right handed

Tests
Test Career:	1959-60
Cap Number:	214
Tests Played:	4

Test Batting
Innings:	7	Runs:	112
Highest Score:	28	Average:	16.00
No. 50s:	0	No. 100s:	0

Test Bowling & Fielding
Wickets:	0	Runs:	0
Best Bowling:		Average:	0.00
5 WI:	0	10 WM:	0
Catches:	2	Stumpings:	0

A South Australian who was selected on the tour of the subcontinent in 1959/60 on the back of a purple patch of form for his state in the previous season. Unfortunately the opener failed to fire and could not manage a score of more than 28 in four Tests.

STUART, Anthony Mark
Born:	January 2, 1970
Batting:	Right handed
Bowling:	Right arm medium-fast

One Day Internationals
ODI Career:	1997
ODIs Played:	3

ODI Batting
Innings:	1	Runs:	1
Highest Score:	1	Average:	1.00
No. 50s:	0	No. 100s:	0

ODI Bowling & Fielding
Wickets:	8	Runs:	109
Best Bowling:	5/26	Average:	13.62
5 WM:	1	Catches:	2
Stumpings:	0		

It's hard to cram too many highlights into an international career that consists of only three One Day Internationals but Anthony Stuart will always have the hat-trick he took against Pakistan at the MCG in 1997. An accurate medium paceman from New South Wales, he has gone into coaching following his retirement and is currently in charge of New Zealand first class side, Wellington.

SYMONDS, Andrew
Born:	June 9, 1975
Batting:	Right handed
Bowling:	Right arm off-break

Tests
Test Career:	2004-
Cap Number:	388
Tests Played:	10

Test Batting
Innings:	15	Runs:	286
Highest Score:	72	Average:	19.06
No. 50s:	2	No. 100s:	0

Test Bowling & Fielding
Wickets:	9	Runs:	409
Best Bowling:	3/50	Average:	45.44
5 WI:	0	10 WM:	0
Catches:	10	Stumpings:	0

One Day Internationals
ODI Career:	1998-
ODIs Played:	146

ODI Batting
Innings:	116	Runs:	3,697
Highest Score:	156	Average:	39.32
No. 50s:	18	No. 100s:	5

ODI Bowling & Fielding
Wickets:	114	Runs:	4,148
Best Bowling:	5/18	Average:	36.38
5 WM:	1	Catches:	65
Stumpings:	0		

Naturally gifted rather than a great technician, at present he is thought of mainly as a one day cricketer, despite efforts to utilise his talents in the Test side. For a long time it seemed that even a regular ODI career may be beyond him, but seeing a huge upside, the selectors continued to give him chances. It all came together against Pakistan in the 2003 World Cup. Coming in at 4/86 and with Wasim Akram and Shoaib Akhtar in full flight, Symonds struck the highest ever score by an Australian in a World Cup. His unbeaten 143 won Australia the game and signalled the arrival of the man long considered to be the ideal one day cricketer. With his powerhouse batting and versatile bowling that alternates between medium pace and off spin, Symonds has been part of the ODI side ever since that World Cup. In the summer of 2005/06 he was given every chance to prove himself at Test level, but with the exception of a cracking 72 at the MCG against the Proteas he struggled and was left out of Australia's touring side to Bangladesh in 2006. The man who knocked back the chance to play for his country of birth, England, will be desperate to earn back his spot in time to help his beloved Australia win back the Ashes in 2006/07.

TABER, Headley Brian

Born:	April 29, 1940
Batting:	Right handed
	Wicket Keeper

Tests

Test Career:	1966-70
Cap Number:	240
Tests Played:	16

Test Batting

Innings:	27	Runs:	353
Highest Score:	48	Average:	16.04
No. 50s:	0	No. 100s:	0

Test Bowling & Fielding

Wickets:	0	Runs:	0
Best Bowling:		Average:	0.00
5 WI:	0	10 WM:	0
Catches:	56	Stumpings:	4

Eventhough he played only 16 Tests, many good judges consider him to be one of the best glovemen ever to play for Australia. Equally at home against the quicks or up to the stumps for the spinners, Taber employed copybook technique. His eight dismissals against the South Africans at Johannesburg in 1966/67 was his best haul in a Test. He went on to coach the Australian side following his retirement.

TAIT, Shaun William

Born:	February 22, 1983
Batting:	Right handed
Bowling:	Right arm fast

Tests

Test Career:	2005-
Cap Number:	392
Tests Played:	2

Test Batting

Innings:	3	Runs:	8
Highest Score:	4	Average:	8.00
No. 50s:	0	No. 100s:	0

Test Bowling & Fielding

Wickets:	5	Runs:	210
Best Bowling:	3/97	Average:	42.00
5 WI:	0	10 WM:	0
Catches:	0	Stumpings:	0

He is a genuine fast bowler from South Australia with a powerful slinging action. Tait played two Tests on the 2005 Ashes tour but on returning to Australia suffered a serious shoulder injury that ruled him out of most of the Australian domestic summer.

TALLON, Donald

Born:	February 17, 1916
Batting:	Right handed
	Wicket Keeper

Tests

Test Career:	1946-53
Cap Number:	169
Tests Played:	21

Test Batting

Innings:	26	Runs:	394
Highest Score:	92	Average:	17.13
No. 50s:	2	No. 100s:	0

Test Bowling & Fielding

Wickets:	0	Runs:	0
Best Bowling:		Average:	0.00
5 WI:	0	10 WM:	0
Catches:	50	Stumpings:	8

As is the keepers' lot Don Tallon had to bide his time before being handed the gloves in the national side. First Bert Oldfield, then Ben Barnett and finally World War II kept the man that many believe was Australia's best ever gloveman waiting. When he did get his chance his nimble footwork and lightning reflexes prompted Don Bradman to describe him as the best wicket keeper he had seen. In 21 Tests he kept faultlessly, though his batting was not up to the high standard he managed in state cricket where he scored a number of centuries.

TAYLOR, John Morris

Born:	October 10, 1895
Batting:	Right handed
Bowling:	Right arm medium

Tests

Test Career:	1920-26
Cap Number:	112
Tests Played:	20

Test Batting

Innings:	28	Runs:	997
Highest Score:	108	Average:	35.60
No. 50s:	8	No. 100s:	1

Test Bowling & Fielding

Wickets:	1	Runs:	45
Best Bowling:	1/25	Average:	45.00
5 WI:	0	10 WM:	0
Catches:	11	Stumpings:	0

He was considered the finest young cricketer in Australia prior to the First World War and would have made his Test debut at a much younger age than 25 had Test cricket not been suspended between 1912 and 1920. Persisted with because of his obvious talent, he found form in the 1924/25 Ashes series, scoring his only Test century in the first Test at the SCG. That innings, a match saving knock of 108 included a then record last wicket stand of 127 with Arthur Mailey.

TAYLOR, Mark Anthony

Born: October 27, 1964
Batting: Left handed
Bowling: Right arm slow

Tests

Test Career: 1989-99
Cap Number: 346
Tests Played: 104

Test Batting
Innings:	186	Runs:	7,525
Highest Score:	334*	Average:	43.49
No. 50s:	40	No. 100s:	19

Test Bowling & Fielding
Wickets:	1	Runs:	26
Best Bowling:	1/11	Average:	26.00
5 WI:	0	10 WM:	0
Catches:	157	Stumpings:	0

One Day Internationals

ODI Career: 1989-97
ODIs Played: 113

ODI Batting
Innings:	110	Runs:	3,514
Highest Score:	105	Average:	32.23
No. 50s:	28	No. 100s:	1

ODI Bowling & Fielding
Wickets:	0	Runs:	0
Best Bowling:		Average:	0.00
5 WM:	0	Catches:	56
Stumpings:	0		

The New South Wales country town of Wagga Wagga has produced many fine sportspeople and at the very top of the list is Mark Taylor. Nicknamed 'Tubby', the solidly built left hand opener was not the most stylish of batsman but he had no discernible weaknesses and rarely allowed a loose ball to go unpunished. An astute judge of line and length, he was the perfect opener, who with Geoff Marsh then Michael Slater gave Australia their most successful opening combinations since Ponsford and Woodfull. Taylor made his Test debut against the West Indies in the Australian summer of 1988/89 and despite showing little in his first two Tests was selected to tour England later that year. It was an inspired choice with the opener scoring 839 Test runs at 83.90. He scored his maiden Test century at Headingly in the first Test of the series and a double century at Trent Bridge in the last. For much of that Trent Bridge innings of 216 he had Geoff Marsh for company. Together they put on an Australia/England Test record 329 for the first wicket. When Allan Border played his last Test in March of 1994 the responsibility of leading the country was handed to Mark Taylor. Less intense than his predecessor, the side flourished under his leadership. Under Taylor Australia became the number one Test nation in the world by playing an attacking brand of cricket that revitalised interest in the longer version of the game. Despite a pair in his first match as skipper, Taylor's own form initially didn't waiver but in the summer of 1996/97, with his side playing the West Indies and South Africa, came a form slump that threatened to rob Australia of one of their best ever captains. In nine Tests he scored less than 250 runs, and whilst he was selected to lead the 1997 Ashes tour, the elevation of Steve Waugh to vice captain indicated that he wasn't guaranteed a Test spot. Retained for the first Test at Edgbaston, and clearly playing for his cricketing future, he produced a fighting 129 that stands as one of the game's most courageous knocks. With his spot assured and the Ashes retained, Taylor enjoyed his last two years in the baggy green, smashing four more centuries including a famous triple ton against Pakistan. Playing on a flat, lifeless strip in Peshawar he passed record after record until, when on 334, he declared. Taylor had equaled Sir Donald Bradman's record for the highest score by an Australian in a Test innings and after his respectful declaration he said that being thought of along side 'The Don' was worth more than breaking the record. Taylor spent nearly his entire international career fielding at slip where his concentration and eye enabled him to snare a then record 157 Test catches. Retiring at the age of 34 he joined former Australian Test captains, Richie Benaud, Bill Lawry and Ian Chappell as a television commentator.

TAYLOR, Peter Laurence

Born: August 22, 1956
Batting: Left handed
Bowling: Right arm off-break

Tests

Test Career: 1987-91
Cap Number: 340
Tests Played: 13

Test Batting
Innings:	19	Runs:	431
Highest Score:	87	Average:	26.93
No. 50s:	2	No. 100s:	0

Test Bowling & Fielding
Wickets:	27	Runs:	1,068
Best Bowling:	6/78	Average:	39.55
5 WI:	1	10 WM:	0
Catches:	10	Stumpings:	0

One Day Internationals

ODI Career: 1987-92
ODIs Played: 83

ODI Batting

Innings:	47	Runs:	437
Highest Score:	54*	Average:	19.86
No. 50s:	1	No. 100s:	0

ODI Bowling & Fielding

Wickets:	97	Runs:	2,740
Best Bowling:	4/38	Average:	28.24
5 WM:	0	Catches:	34
Stumpings:	0		

The story surrounding the selection of little known Taylor for the fifth Ashes Test in 1986/87 shows how much of a surprise his choice was. When cricket followers saw Taylor from NSW was to make his debut they assumed it was promising young opener and future national captain Mark Taylor. A TV crew even went to the wrong man's house to interview the debutant. But just as he was on the field, Peter Taylor remained unphased and went on to win the 'Man of the Match' award in his first Test, taking eight wickets and a hitting a very handy 42 in the second innings. From that point on he played mainly in the one day side where his quickish off spin and handy lower order batting were put to good use. For a cricketer who had only played six first class games by the age of 30, his was a most unexpected international career. Possessed of an accute cricket brain Taylor later became a Test selector.

THOMAS, Graham

Born:	March 21, 1938
Batting:	Right handed

Tests

Test Career:	1965-66
Cap Number:	235
Tests Played:	8

Test Batting

Innings:	12	Runs:	325
Highest Score:	61	Average:	29.54
No. 50s:	3	No. 100s:	0

Test Bowling & Fielding

Wickets:	0	Runs:	0
Best Bowling:		Average:	0.00
5 WI:	0	10 WM:	0
Catches:	3	Stumpings:	0

Often on the verge of Test selection, he finally made his Test debut against West Indies at Sabina Park in 1965. He scored 61 in the second Test of that series but would struggle to hold a regular spot in the side. One of the few Australians of Aboriginal heritage to represent the country.

THOMPSON, Nathaniel Frampton Davis

Born:	May 29, 1839
Batting:	Right handed
Bowling:	Right arm slow

Tests

Test Career:	1877
Cap Number:	11
Tests Played:	2

Test Batting

Innings:	4	Runs:	67
Highest Score:	41	Average:	16.75
No. 50s:	0	No. 100s:	0

Test Bowling & Fielding

Wickets:	1	Runs:	31
Best Bowling:	1/14	Average:	31.00
5 WI:	0	10 WM:	0
Catches:	3	Stumpings:	0

Nathaniel 'Nat' Thompson was almost 40 when he lined up for the Australians in the first ever Test Match as an opening batsman. He was bowled by Arthur Hill for one, giving him the 'distinction' of being the first player dismissed in Test cricket.

THOMS, George Ronald

Born:	March 22, 1927
Batting:	Right handed

Tests

Test Career:	1952
Cap Number:	192
Tests Played:	1

Test Batting

Innings:	2	Runs:	44
Highest Score:	28	Average:	22.00
No. 50s:	0	No. 100s:	0

Test Bowling & Fielding

Wickets:	0	Runs:	0
Best Bowling:		Average:	0.00
5 WI:	0	10 WM:	0
Catches:	0	Stumpings:	0

Victorian opening batsman whose only Test was against the West Indies.

THOMSON, Alan Lloyd

Born:	December 2, 1945
Batting:	Right handed
Bowling:	Right arm fast

Tests

Test Career:	1970-71
Cap Number:	250
Tests Played:	4

Test Batting

Innings:	5	Runs:	22
Highest Score:	12*	Average:	22.00
No. 50s:	0	No. 100s:	0

Test Bowling & Fielding

Wickets:	12	Runs:	654
Best Bowling:	3/79	Average:	54.50
5 WI:	0	10 WM:	0
Catches:	0	Stumpings:	0

One Day Internationals

ODI Career:	1971
ODIs Played:	1

ODI Batting

Innings:	0	Runs:	0
Highest Score:	0	Average:	0.00
No. 50s:	0	No. 100s:	0

ODI Bowling & Fielding

Wickets:	1	Runs:	22
Best Bowling:	1/22	Average:	22.00
5 WM:	0	Catches:	0
Stumpings:	0		

Nicknamed 'Froggy' because of his ungainly bowling action, the quick from Victoria struggled with his line when promoted to the national side and could manage only four Tests.

THOMSON, Jeffrey Robert
Born: August 16, 1950
Batting: Right handed
Bowling: Right arm fast

Tests
Test Career: 1972-85
Cap Number: 262
Tests Played: 51

Test Batting
Innings:	73	Runs:	679
Highest Score:	49	Average:	12.81
No. 50s:	0	No. 100s:	0

Test Bowling & Fielding
Wickets:	200	Runs:	5,601
Best Bowling:	6/46	Average:	28.01
5 WI:	8	10 WM:	0
Catches:	20	Stumpings:	0

One Day Internationals
ODI Career: 1975-85
ODIs Played: 50

ODI Batting
Innings:	30	Runs:	181
Highest Score:	21	Average:	7.54
No. 50s:	0	No. 100s:	0

ODI Bowling & Fielding
Wickets:	61	Runs:	2,065
Best Bowling:	4/67	Average:	35.30
5 WM:	0	Catches:	9
Stumpings:	0		

A fearsome fast bowler with a distinctive slinging action, he formed one of cricket's most famous bowling partnerships in tandem with Dennis Lillee. Originally from NSW, he moved to Queensland where his career as an opening bowler flourished. His Test career got off to a haltering start with a single Test against Pakistan in 1973. He played that Test with an injured foot and was not recalled to the team until the 1974/75 season. On rejoining the side Thomson quickly established himself as one of the most dangerous bowlers in the world ,with his ability to deliver balls at frightening pace. The tearaway quick was quoted as saying that if he had no idea where his balls were going what chance did the batsman have, and it was that unpredictablilty as much as his pace that played on the minds of opponents. In the inaugural World Cup held in England in 1975 Thomson wreaked havoc, sending the fledgling Sri Lankan team scurrying with a spell of fast bowling that claimed more injuries than wickets. He and Lillee took on the might of the West Indies in 1975/76 with his 29 wickets helping lead Australia to a convincing Test series win. The following season he crashed with team mate Alan Turner when going for a catch in Adelaide and the resultant shoulder injury ruled him out of that series against Pakistan and the Centenary Test against England.

Thomson initially resisted moves to join World Series Cricket and was clearly Australia's best bowler on the Ashes tour to England in 1977, but he did finally join the rebel cricket association and toured the West Indies with the WSC squad in 1979. When the cricket worlds realigned Thomson was once again Australia's choice as opening bowler and whilst his powers diminished with age he will always be remembered as his country's fastest and most devastating opening bowler.

THURLOW, Hugh Motley (Pud)
Born: January 10, 1903
Batting: Right handed
Bowling: Right arm medium-fast

Tests
Test Career: 1932
Cap Number: 141
Tests Played: 1

Test Batting
Innings:	1	Runs:	0
Highest Score:	0	Average:	0.00
No. 50s:	0	No. 100s:	0

Test Bowling & Fielding
Wickets:	0	Runs:	86
Best Bowling:	0	Average:	0.00
5 WI:	0	10 WM:	0
Catches:	0	Stumpings:	0

A fast bowler from Queensland who was unlucky in as much that his best season, 1929/30, was one when no Tests were played during the Australian summer.

TOOHEY, Peter Michael
Born: April 20, 1954
Batting: Right handed
Bowling: Right arm slow

Tests
Test Career: 1977-79
Cap Number: 288
Tests Played: 15

Test Batting
Innings:	29	Runs:	893
Highest Score:	122	Average:	31.89
No. 50s:	7	No. 100s:	1

Test Bowling & Fielding
Wickets:	0	Runs:	4
Best Bowling:	0	Average:	0.00
5 WI:	0	10 WM:	0
Catches:	9	Stumpings:	0

One Day Internationals
ODI Career: 1978-79
ODIs Played: 5

ODI Batting
Innings:	4	Runs:	105
Highest Score:	54*	Average:	52.50
No. 50s:	1	No. 100s:	0

ODI Bowling & Fielding
Wickets:	0	Runs:	0
Best Bowling:	0	Average:	0.00
5 WM:	0	Catches:	0
Stumpings:	0		

With Australian cricket decimated by the defection of leading players to World Series Cricket, selectors turned to the curly haired New South Welshman to secure the middle order. He performed well in his first series, averaging over 40 against the Indians, but it was an indication of the state of the Australian batting line-up that he batted at numbers three, four and six during that series. He scored his only century, 122, on the tour of the Carribbean that same year but in the Ashes series the following summer Toohey's form deserted him and he averaged only 16.56 in ten innings.

TOSHACK, Ernest Raymond Herbert

Born: December 8, 1914
Batting: Right handed
Bowling: Left arm medium

Tests

Test Career: 1946-48
Cap Number: 170
Tests Played: 12

Test Batting

Innings:	11	Runs:	73
Highest Score:	20*	Average:	14.60
No. 50s:	0	No. 100s:	0

Test Bowling & Fielding

Wickets:	47	Runs:	989
Best Bowling:	6/29	Average:	21.04
5 WI:	4	10 WM:	1
Catches:	4	Stumpings:	0

A tall and angular left handed pace bowler, he relied on line and length in much the same way as Glenn McGrath does in the modern game. He took six wickets on debut against New Zealand and nine in his first Test against the English. Ernie Toshack's career best match figures of 11/31 against India remains a record low runs per wicket return for any Australian who has taken ten or more wickets in a Test. Unfortunately a fine Test career was cut short by recurrent knee injuries.

TRAVERS, Joseph Patrick Francis

Born: January 10, 1871
Batting: Left handed
Bowling: Left arm slow

Tests

Test Career: 1902
Cap Number: 84
Tests Played: 1

Test Batting

Innings:	2	Runs:	10
Highest Score:	9	Average:	5.00
No. 50s:	0	No. 100s:	0

Test Bowling & Fielding

Wickets:	1	Runs:	14
Best Bowling:	1/14	Average:	14.00
5 WI:	0	10 WM:	0
Catches:	1	Stumpings:	0

He was a left-handed spinner from South Australia.

TRIBE, George Edward

Born: October 4, 1920
Batting: Left handed
Bowling: Left arm leg-break

Tests

Test Career: 1946-47
Cap Number: 172
Tests Played: 3

Test Batting

Innings:	3	Runs:	35
Highest Score:	25*	Average:	17.50
No. 50s:	0	No. 100s:	0

Test Bowling & Fielding

Wickets:	2	Runs:	330
Best Bowling:	2/48	Average:	165.00
5 WI:	0	10 WM:	0
Catches:	0	Stumpings:	0

A gifted middle order batsman and leg spinner from Victoria who held the ball behind his back in his approach so as to conceal his delivery type from the batsman. At only 27 he moved to England where he was a dominant player for Northamptonshire for almost a decade. He departed first class cricket with over 10,000 runs and 1,000 wickets.

TRIMBLE, Glenn Samuel

Born: January 1, 1963
Batting: Right handed
Bowling: Right arm medium

One Day Internationals

ODI Career: 1986
ODIs Played: 2

ODI Batting

Innings:	2	Runs:	4
Highest Score:	4	Average:	4.00
No. 50s:	0	No. 100s:	0

ODI Bowling & Fielding

Wickets:	0	Runs:	32
Best Bowling:		Average:	0.00
5 WM:	0	Catches:	0
Stumpings:	0		

Son of legendary Queensland state cricketer Sam, he won a spot in the Australian ODI side after performing well with bat and ball for his state. Unfortunately nerves got the better of the powerfully built youngster and in his national debut at the WACA in 1986 a number of his deliveries failed to hit the pitch. He was given another chance in the Australian one day side later that year when selected as a batsman but could manage only four runs.

TROTT, Albert Edwin

Born: February 6, 1873
Batting: Right handed
Bowling: Right arm slow

Tests

Test Career: 1895-99
Cap Number: 71
Tests Played: 5

Test Batting			
Innings:	9	Runs:	228
Highest Score:	85*	Average:	38.00
No. 50s:	2	No. 100s:	0

Test Bowling & Fielding			
Wickets:	26	Runs:	390
Best Bowling:	8/43	Average:	15.00
5 WI:	2	10 WM:	0
Catches:	4	Stumpings:	0

After a sparkling debut in 1895, he was incredibly left out of the Australian side to tour England the next year in a team that was in fact led by his brother Harry. Known as Alberto, on debut in Adelaide he scored 38 not out and 72 as well as taking 8/43 in England's second innings. He followed that up with an 85 not out at the SCG in what was to be his second last Test for Australia. Upon failing to make the touring party in 1896 he travelled to England on his own steam where he joined Middlesex and eventually played two Tests for his adopted country.

TROTT, George Henry Stevens

Born:	August 5, 1866
Batting:	Right handed
Bowling:	Right arm leg-break

Tests

Test Career:	1888-98
Cap Number:	53
Tests Played:	24

Test Batting			
Innings:	42	Runs:	921
Highest Score:	143	Average:	21.92
No. 50s:	1	No. 100s:	4

Test Bowling & Fielding			
Wickets:	29	Runs:	1,019
Best Bowling:	4/71	Average:	35.13
5 WI:	0	10 WM:	0
Catches:	21	Stumpings:	0

He made his Test debut on the tour of England in 1888 and would visit the 'old country' on four more occasions, the last as captain. Harry Trott was originally selected on the strength of his leg-spin bowling but it was as a batsman that he would make his name in Test cricket. A back foot player with a keen eye, his finest innings was at the Oval in 1896 when he and Sydney Gregory put on 221 against the bowling of Richardson, the English tearaway quick. Though it was not enough to win the game Trott scored a career high of 143 in a knock that won him the respect of his English opposition. Whilst there have been better performing captains to lead Australia to England few were as fondly remembered as Trott, today his memory lives on in the Melbourne suburb of Albert Park with a cricket ground that bears his name.

TRUMBLE, Hugh

Born:	May 12, 1867
Batting:	Right handed
Bowling:	Right arm off-break

Tests

Test Career:	1890-1904
Cap Number:	59
Tests Played:	32

Test Batting			
Innings:	57	Runs:	851
Highest Score:	70	Average:	19.79
No. 50s:	4	No. 100s:	0

Test Bowling & Fielding			
Wickets:	141	Runs:	3,072
Best Bowling:	8/65	Average:	21.78
5 WI:	9	10 WM:	3
Catches:	45	Stumpings:	0

A fine off-spinner, he remains one of only three cricketers to have twice taken a hat-trick in Test matches. The first such occasion came on the 1901/02 English tour of Australia and the second in Trumble's final Test when he recorded innings figures of 7/28. Tall for his time, he generally bowled quickly for a finger spinner with a flighted delivery thrown in as his change up ball. It was that change of pace that often deceived batsmen resulting in his most common form of dismissal, caught and bowled. By the end of his Test career Trumble had taken a staggereing 45 catches in only 32 Tests. He often saved his best for games in which the side lost. His best match figures of 12/89 were recorded in The Oval Test of 1896 when the Australians made only 44 whilst chasing 111 for victory. He was a more than competent batsman who average a respectable 20 in all forms of first class cricket, but it was as a bowler he made his name prompting the call, Trumble, make 'em tumble.

TRUMBLE, John William

Born:	August 16, 1863
Batting:	Right handed
Bowling:	Right arm off-break

Tests

Test Career:	1885-86
Cap Number:	39
Tests Played:	7

Test Batting			
Innings:	7	Runs:	13
Highest Score:	59	Average:	20.25
No. 50s:	1	No. 100s:	0

Test Bowling & Fielding			
Wickets:	10	Runs:	222
Best Bowling:	3/39	Average:	22.20
5 WI:	0	10 WM:	0
Catches:	3	Stumpings:	0

Whilst he could not match the feats of his famed brother Hugh, John was still a more than useful contributor for Australia in a short Test career. An economical off-spinner and handy middle order batsman he played domestic cricket for Victoria.

TRUMPER, Victor Thomas

Born:	November 2, 1877
Batting:	Right handed
Bowling:	Right arm medium

Tests
Test Career:	1899-1912		
Cap Number:	79		
Tests Played:	48		

Test Batting
Innings:	89	Runs:	3,163
Highest Score:	214*	Average:	39.04
No. 50s:	13	No. 100s:	8

Test Bowling & Fielding
Wickets:	8	Runs:	317
Best Bowling:	3/60	Average:	39.62
5 WI:	0	10 WM:	0
Catches:	31	Stumpings:	0

Prior to Bradman, Victor Trumper was considered Australia's greatest ever batsman, and for some even the arrival of 'The Don' did nothing to alter that view. An elegant batsman with exquisite timing, the image of Trumper playing a drive whilst taking a huge stride down the wicket remains one of cricket's most enduring images. By the time he joined the Australians on the tour of 1899 he had already forged a reputation as a batting genius, having scored 292 in a single innings for NSW. In his second Test he scored 135 at Lords: it was an innings that established him as the side's opening batsman for over a decade. Over that period he would flourish in all conditions, scoring on wet tracks when his team mates would flounder. His 104 on a sodden wicket at Old Trafford in 1902 sent cricket scribes into raptures. The Englishman C.B. Fry wrote, "He had no style, yet was all style. Every stroke met the ultimate criterion, the minimum of effort for the maximum effect". His highest Test score was a double century against the touring South Africans in 1910/11 during a series that saw him average over 90. Sadly Trumper was struck down by illness throughout his career, ultimately succumbing to Bright's Disease at the age of 37.

TURNER, Alan
Born:	July 23, 1950
Batting:	Left handed

Tests
Test Career:	1975-77		
Cap Number:	273		
Tests Played:	14		

Test Batting
Innings:	27	Runs:	768
Highest Score:	136	Average:	29.53
No. 50s:	3	No. 100s:	1

Test Bowling & Fielding
Wickets:	0	Runs:	0
Best Bowling:		Average:	0.00
5 WI:	0	10 WM:	0
Catches:	15	Stumpings:	0

One Day Internationals
ODI Career:	1975
ODIs Played:	6

ODI Batting
Innings:	6	Runs:	247
Highest Score:	101	Average:	41.16
No. 50s:	0	No. 100s:	1

ODI Bowling & Fielding
Wickets:	0	Runs:	0
Best Bowling:		Average:	0.00
5 WM:	0	Catches:	3
Stumpings:	0		

A nuggety opening batsman from New South Wales, he was involved in a collision with Jeff Thomson that cost the Queensland quick his spot in the side for the Centenary Test. He was given a number of chances in the Test arena, but apart from a fine century against the West Indies at Adelaide in 1975/76 he failed to reproduce the form that saw his score so prolifically for his state.

TURNER, Charles Thomas Biass
Born:	November 16, 1862
Batting:	Right handed
Bowling:	Right arm medium-fast

Tests
Test Career:	1887-95
Cap Number:	46
Tests Played:	17

Test Batting
Innings:	32	Runs:	323
Highest Score:	29	Average:	11.53
No. 50s:	0	No. 100s:	0

Test Bowling & Fielding
Wickets:	101	Runs:	1,670
Best Bowling:	7/43	Average:	16.53
5 WI:	11	10 WM:	2
Catches:	8	Stumpings:	0

Of all Test cricketers to have taken 100 or more Test wickets, 'The Terror' as Charlie Turner was known, did so with greatest economy, conceding a miserly 16.53 runs per wicket. Though short in statute, he stood only 5 ft and 9 inches, the New South Welshman was considered the finest bowler of his day with a front-on action and long loping run that garnered both swing and bounce. Along with J.J. Ferris he routed the English on more than one occasion, the most famous being on debut in 1887, when after being sent in, the English were skittled for their lowest ever Test innings score of 45. The Terror was the main destroyer with figures of 6/15 off 18 four ball overs. His performance on the tour of England in 1888 was also remarkable given the superiority of the English side. In all matches he took 314 wickets, whilst in Tests he claimed 21 wickets at the cost of 12. It was a performance that saw him earn the title as the best bowler in the world. The great seamer was at his best on uncovered wickets, though he was a danger in all conditions. In 155 first class matches he took 10 or more wickets no less than 35 times. After claiming over 1,000 first class scalps he moved to Queensland for business reasons, and in 1897 retired from the game altogether.

VEIVERS, Thomas Robert

Born: April 6, 1937
Batting: Left handed
Bowling: Right arm off-break

Tests

Test Career: 1963-67
Cap Number: 226
Tests Played: 21

Test Batting

Innings:	30	Runs:	813
Highest Score:	88	Average:	31.26
No. 50s:	7	No. 100s:	0

Test Bowling & Fielding

Wickets:	33	Runs:	1,375
Best Bowling:	4/68	Average:	41.66
5 WI:	0	10 WM:	0
Catches:	7	Stumpings:	0

Australia has never relied too heavily on off spinners, making the effort of Tom Veivers to play 21 Tests all the more commendable. The Queenslander can put his Test career down to a combination of diligent bowling and courageous lower order batting. Whilst his bowling was economical it lacked penetration, so Test level Veivers often needed his batting to guarantee him a spot. He struck two valuable half centuries on the tour to England in 1964 and followed that up with similar scores against India and South Africa. Veivers' highest Test score was against Pakistan at the MCG in 1965 when he fell just 12 runs short of what would have been a well-deserved Test ton.

VELETTA, Michael Robert John

Born: October 30, 1963
Batting: Right handed
 Wicket Keeper

Tests

Test Career: 1987-90
Cap Number: 341
Tests Played: 8

Test Batting

Innings:	11	Runs:	207
Highest Score:	39	Average:	18.81
No. 50s:	0	No. 100s:	0

Test Bowling & Fielding

Wickets:	0	Runs:	0
Best Bowling:		Average:	0.00
5 WI:	0	10 WM:	0
Catches:	12	Stumpings:	0

One Day Internationals

ODI Career: 1987-89
ODIs Played: 20

ODI Batting

Innings:	19	Runs:	484
Highest Score:	68*	Average:	32.26
No. 50s:	2	No. 100s:	0

ODI Bowling & Fielding

Wickets:	0	Runs:	0
Best Bowling:		Average:	0.00
5 WM:	0	Catches:	8
Stumpings:	0		

An opening batsman and occasional wicket keeper, the compact Western Australian was a member of the 1987 World Cup winning team. His knock of 45 of 31 balls that day was in stark contrast to a famous innings he played in a Shield final when he batted for over twelve hours to score a title winning double century.

WAITE, Mervyn George

Born: January 7, 1911
Batting: Right handed
Bowling: Right arm medium

Tests

Test Career: 1938
Cap Number: 162
Tests Played: 2

Test Batting

Innings:	3	Runs:	11
Highest Score:	8	Average:	3.66
No. 50s:	0	No. 100s:	0

Test Bowling & Fielding

Wickets:	1	Runs:	190
Best Bowling:	1/150	Average:	190.00
5 WI:	0	10 WM:	0
Catches:	1	Stumpings:	0

A South Australian all-rounder who failed to flatter on the Ashes tour of 1938.

WALKER, Maxwell Henry Norman

Born: September 12, 1948
Batting: Right handed
Bowling: Right arm medium-fast

Tests

Test Career: 1972-77
Cap Number: 263
Tests Played: 34

Test Batting

Innings:	43	Runs:	586
Highest Score:	78*	Average:	19.53
No. 50s:	1	No. 100s:	0

Test Bowling & Fielding

Wickets:	138	Runs:	3,792
Best Bowling:	8/143	Average:	27.47
5 WI:	6	10 WM:	0
Catches:	12	Stumpings:	0

One Day Internationals

ODI Career: 1974-81
ODIs Played: 17

ODI Batting

Innings:	11	Runs:	79
Highest Score:	20	Average:	9.87
No. 50s:	0	No. 100s:	0

ODI Bowling & Fielding

Wickets:	20	Runs:	546
Best Bowling:	4/19	Average:	27.30
5 WM:	0	Catches:	6
Stumpings:	0		

Nicknamed 'Tanglefoot' or 'Tangles' because of his distinctive wrong-footed bowling style, the lion hearted medium pacer proved the ideal foil for his more illustrious bowling partners, Dennis Lillee and Jeff Thomson. Originally from Tasmania, he moved to Victoria to further his Australian Rules football career with the Melbourne Football Club but quickly caught the eye of state cricket selectors. He was tall and barrel-chested but relied on swing and seam rather than pace and bounce. Maxie Walker followed up an impressive debut series against Pakistan with a memorable tour of the West Indies in 1973, where he took 26 wickets to be the leading Australian wicket taker. Over the next five years he performed admirably taking a career best 8/143 against England in 1974/75 when both Lillee and Thomson were absent. His Test career came to an end with the advent of World Series Cricket, but he would remain in the public eye with his work as a commentator and author of a series of best selling books of cricketing anecdotes.

WALL, Thomas Welbourne (Tim)
Born: May 13, 1904
Batting: Right handed
Bowling: Right arm fast

Tests
Test Career: 1929-34
Cap Number: 133
Tests Played: 18

Test Batting
Innings:	24	Runs:	121
Highest Score:	20	Average:	6.36
No. 50s:	0	No. 100s:	0

Test Bowling & Fielding
Wickets:	56	Runs:	2,010
Best Bowling:	5/14	Average:	35.89
5 WI:	3	10 WM:	0
Catches:	11	Stumpings:	0

The South Australian was his country's dominant fast bowler during a period when spin was Australia's favourite form of attack. A genuine quick, he relied on bounce and sideways movement, meaning that like many Aussie quicks that would come in the years to follow his best was saved for the harder wickets at home. His Test debut against England in the fifth Test in 1928/29 marked a turning point for the team. He took eight wickets for the match and the Aussies broke five successive Test defeats with a win. He led the Australian averages in the Bodyline series with 16 wickets at 25.56. Wall became the first player to take all ten wickets in a Sheffield Shield innings when he routed NSW in 1933. He returned the historic figures of 10/36 including the wickets of Bradman, McCabe, Brown and Fingleton.

WALTERS, Francis Henry
Born: February 9, 1860
Batting: Right handed
Bowling: Right arm medium

Tests
Test Career: 1885
Cap Number: 42
Tests Played: 1

Test Batting
Innings:	2	Runs:	12
Highest Score:	7	Average:	6.00
No. 50s:	0	No. 100s:	0

Test Bowling & Fielding
Wickets:	0	Runs:	0
Best Bowling:		Average:	0.00
5 WI:	0	10 WM:	0
Catches:	2	Stumpings:	0

A capable batsman from Victoria who perished at sea off the coast of India in 1922.

WALTERS, Kevin Douglas (Doug)
Born: December 21, 1945
Batting: Right handed
Bowling: Right arm medium

Tests
Test Career: 1965-81
Cap Number: 237
Tests Played: 74

Test Batting
Innings:	125	Runs:	5,357
Highest Score:	250	Average:	48.26
No. 50s:	33	No. 100s:	15

Test Bowling & Fielding
Wickets:	49	Runs:	1,425
Best Bowling:	5/66	Average:	29.08
5 WI:	1	10 WM:	0
Catches:	43	Stumpings:	0

One Day Internationals
ODI Career: 1971-81
ODIs Played: 28

ODI Batting
Innings:	24	Runs:	513
Highest Score:	59	Average:	28.50
No. 50s:	2	No. 100s:	0

ODI Bowling & Fielding
Wickets:	4	Runs:	273
Best Bowling:	2/24	Average:	68.25
5 WM:	0	Catches:	10
Stumpings:	0		

There may have been better cricketers to play for Australia, but it is hard to imagine that there has been one more popular than Douggie Walters. A star performer for his state in his teens, he was thrust into the limelight at 19 when selected for the Test side. He came into the team with no less a tag than the next Don Bradman, and whilst that sort of pressure would have been enough to defeat most youngsters, the laconic Walters took it in his stride and reached the 1,000 run mark in Test cricket in only 11 Tests. Perennially pictured with a cigarette or beer in hand, he seemed comfortable with the gifts God had given him and wasn't inclined on working too hard to improve upon them. Nevertheless he was a wonderful middle order batsman who scored 15 Test centuries with a top score of 242 against the West Indies at the SCG in 1969. He also scored 103 in the second innings of that game and in doing so became the first Australian to score a double century and century in the same Test. Arguably his most memorable innings was against England at Perth in 1975. Three not out at tea, he took to the English attack in the final session and with one ball remaining on the second day was on 97. A four would bring up his century, but ever the entertainer, Walters went one, or should that read two better. He hooked a short ball from Bob Willis for six and in doing so not only brought up his century but recorded 100 for the session. Despite a promising Test debut on English soil in 1968 when he made 81 and 86, he struggled in English conditions and averaged only 25 over four tours. Walters put his dry wit to good use in describing his form in England when he said that the only 100 he ever scored there was on on a golf course. Walters was also a more than handy medium pace bowler, the quintessential partnership breaker, who took 49 wickets in Test cricket. Kevin Douglas Walters was the fans' favourite. When he played at his home ground, the SCG, fans on the infamous 'Hill' would hold up a bedsheet with the words 'Doug Walters Stand' scrawled on it. It was fitting therefore that when the SCG Hill was replaced with a permanent grandstand it would bear the name of Doug Walters.

WARD, Francis Anthony

Born:	February 23, 1906
Batting:	Right handed
Bowling:	Right arm leg-break

Tests

Test Career:	1936-38
Cap Number:	158
Tests Played:	4

Test Batting

Innings:	8	Runs:	36
Highest Score:	18	Average:	6.00
No. 50s:	0	No. 100s:	0

Test Bowling & Fielding

Wickets:	11	Runs:	574
Best Bowling:	6/102	Average:	52.18
5 WI:	1	10 WM:	0
Catches:	1	Stumpings:	0

In an era when Australia had an abundance of leg-spinners, the talented Ward had to wait until he was in his 30's for a chance at the top level. In 1938 he was controversially chosen ahead of Clarrie Grimmett to tour England but ended up playing only the single Test.

WARNE, Shane Keith

Born:	September 13, 1969
Batting:	Right handed
Bowling:	Right arm leg-break

Tests

Test Career:	1992-
Cap Number:	350
Tests Played:	140

Test Batting

Innings:	194	Runs:	2,958
Highest Score:	99	Average:	16.61
No. 50s:	11	No. 100s:	0

Test Bowling & Fielding

Wickets:	685	Runs:	17,297
Best Bowling:	8/71	Average:	25.25
5 WI:	36	10 WM:	10
Catches:	120	Stumpings:	0

One Day Internationals

ODI Career:	1993-2005
ODIs Played:	194

ODI Batting

Innings:	107	Runs:	1,018
Highest Score:	55	Average:	13.05
No. 50s:	1	No. 100s:	0

ODI Bowling & Fielding

Wickets:	293	Runs:	7,541
Best Bowling:	5/33	Average:	25.73
5 WM:	1	Catches:	80
Stumpings:	0		

Statistics say that Shane Warne is the greatest bowler in Test history, and whilst numbers sometimes lie, in the case of the blonde Victorian they tell only part of the story. A headline maker on and off the field, his ability to pull fans through the gates is unquestioned, and into his late thirties he remains the most recognisable cricketer in the world. Selected on potential rather than outstanding form at state level, he struggled in his first Test against the Indians at the SCG in 1992. His only wicket in that game was a rampaging Ravi Shastri and he finished the Test with figures of 1/150. Over the remainder of that year he was in and out of the Test side but the selectors never lost their faith in the promising young spinner. That faith was repaid against the West Indies in the Boxing Day Test in 1992 when the young leggie took seven second innings wickets. Warne's reputation preceded him when he headed to England for his first Ashes tour in 1993 and the expectant Old Trafford crowd was on the edge of their seats when he was thrown the ball for his first Test delivery on English soil. What happened next is etched in cricket history. Warne sent down a delivery that would become known as the 'ball of the century', a wildly turning leg break that pitched outside leg, traversed a probing Mike Gatting and finally took a good piece of the off stump. The look on a bewildered Gatting's face as he trudged off the ground said it all. With one delivery Warne had cast a spell on English cricket that remains to this day. He took 34 wickets on that Ashes tour and played a key role in a resounding series win. Since that day he has become a dominant figure in international cricket. He has taken five wickets in an innings on over 30 occasions, claimed a hat-trick against the English at the MCG in 1994 and won the 'Man of the Match' award in his side's successful World Cup final in 1999. His control and variety has driven a number of batsmen to distraction, the most famous of whom was Darryl Cullinan who fell to him 12 times. In his 13 years of international cricket Warne has become recognised as the ideal leg spinner. Strong shoulders and wrists allow him to make the ball drift and dip, while nimble fingers let him spin the ball in a variety of ways. His leg break is an exercise in control, turning as much as needs require whilst his under rated wrong 'un has claimed a number of Test scalps. He has a top spinner that kicks and speeds on to the batsman and a trademark 'zooter' that spins low and hard into the batter's pads. Throw in a side spinner that has been developed in recent years and a couple of deliveries that are yet to be christened and you have the most comprehensive armory in the history of spin bowling. Whilst there is nothing he hasn't achieved with the ball, Warne has unfinished business with the bat. A lusty lower order batsman, he can be hit or miss, as his 34 Test ducks would suggest, but when luck runs his way he gets the scoreboard ticking. He's an unconventional batsman who enjoys nothing more than lifting the ball over mid wicket or stepping away to execute an upper-cut. Warne is still desperately looking for a maiden Test century, and until he does he will have to endure the painful memory of holing out to Daniel Vettori on 99 at the WACA in 2001. For every headline he has earnt on the field, there has been another to match it for his misadventures off it. The two most damaging incidents were his involvement with an Indian bookmaker in the mid nineties, and a 12 month ban in 2003 for taking diuretics. In 1994, he and Mark Waugh were both implicated in a betting scandal that whilst never fully substantiated, was seen to have cost him the chance of captaining his country. It was an unofficial sanction that deeply affected Warne, who had the cricket brain and desire to replace Steve Waugh as Test captain. In 2003 he was banned for 12 months after testing positive to a banned diuretic. Warne's explanation was that he had taken a 'slimming pill' given to him by his mother, and whilst the public debated the voracity of his excuse, he announced that the hiatus would mark the end of his international one day career. As he proved with a number of stellar performances in 2006, there are still many years left in Shane Warne if he chooses to continue playing Test cricket. When he finally retires there will be much discussion as to what legacy he will leave behind. For his detractors it will be that of a flawed genius who was in the public spotlight for all the wrong reasons, and for his fans it will be his record as the greatest bowler of all time. What everybody should agree on is how he has changed the face of the cricket. When he burst on to the Test scene there was barely a leg spinner in the game. Wrist spin had been marginalised in an era where speed meant everything and slow bowlers were there just to give the fast bowlers a rest. Today budding young cricketers right around the world love nothing more than trying their hand at wrong'uns, zooters and leggies. The unique art of leg spin is alive and well thanks to Shane Keith Warne.

WATKINS, John Russell

Born: April 16, 1943
Batting: Right handed
Bowling: Right arm leg-break

Tests

Test Career: 1973
Cap Number: 264
Tests Played: 1

Test Batting
Innings:	2	Runs:	39
Highest Score:	36	Average:	39.00
No. 50s:	0	No. 100s:	0

Test Bowling & Fielding
Wickets:	0	Runs:	21
Best Bowling:		Average:	0.00
5 WI:	0	10 WM:	0
Catches:	1	Stumpings:	0

He made his Test debut after only five first class matches, but the meteoric rise and public attention associated with his debut only caused the leg-spinner to tighten up. Whilst he failed with the ball, he did make a valuable 36 and was involved in an unlikely 83 run stand with Bob Massie.

WATSON, Graeme Donald

Born: March 8, 1945
Batting: Right handed
Bowling: Right arm medium-fast

Tests

Test Career: 1967-72
Cap Number: 241
Tests Played: 5

Test Batting
Innings:	9	Runs:	97
Highest Score:	50	Average:	10.77
No. 50s:	1	No. 100s:	0

Test Bowling & Fielding
Wickets:	6	Runs:	254
Best Bowling:	2/67	Average:	42.33
5 WI:	0	10 WM:	0
Catches:	1	Stumpings:	0

One Day Internationals

ODI Career: 1972
ODIs Played: 2

ODI Batting
Innings:	2	Runs:	11
Highest Score:	11*	Average:	11.00
No. 50s:	0	No. 100s:	0

ODI Bowling & Fielding
Wickets:	2	Runs:	28
Best Bowling:	2/28	Average:	14.00
5 WM:	0	Catches:	0
Stumpings:	0		

An all-rounder from Victoria, he was struck in the face by a bean ball from Tony Greig during a Test against the Rest of the World XI and was rushed to hospital where he remained in intensive care for some days. Doctors advised that he never play again, but Watson was made of sterner stuff and he was a member of the Australian side that toured England in 1972.

WATSON, Shane Robert

Born: June 17, 1981
Batting: Right handed
Bowling: Right arm medium-fast

Tests
Test Career: 2005-
Cap Number: 391
Tests Played: 3

Test Batting
Innings:	4	Runs:	81
Highest Score:	31	Average:	20.25
No. 50s:	0	No. 100s:	0

Test Bowling & Fielding
Wickets:	2	Runs:	123
Best Bowling:	1/25	Average:	61.50
5 WI:	0	10 WM:	0
Catches:	0	Stumpings:	0

One Day Internationals
ODI Career: 2002-
ODIs Played: 43

ODI Batting
Innings:	28	Runs:	507
Highest Score:	77*	Average:	31.68
No. 50s:	2	No. 100s:	0

ODI Bowling & Fielding
Wickets:	37	Runs:	1,376
Best Bowling:	4/39	Average:	37.18
5 WM:	0	Catches:	12
Stumpings:	0		

Powerfully built and highly skilled, the blonde all-rounder has been identified as the missing link in the current Australian side. Unfortunately injury has prevented Watson from playing Test cricket with any consistency, but it is hoped that when fit he can emulate the feats of England's Andy Flintoff. His best hasn't been seen at international level yet, but a double century in the 2005/06 Australian domestic cricket final has whet the appetites of Australian cricket fans who hope he will be right to play a major role in the bid to regain the Ashes.

WATSON, William James

Born: January 31, 1931
Batting: Right handed
Bowling: Right arm slow

Tests
Test Career: 1955
Cap Number: 201
Tests Played: 4

Test Batting
Innings:	7	Runs:	106
Highest Score:	30	Average:	17.66
No. 50s:	0	No. 100s:	0

Test Bowling & Fielding
Wickets:	0	Runs:	5
Best Bowling:		Average:	0.00
5 WI:	0	10 WM:	0
Catches:	2	Stumpings:	0

An opening batsman from NSW, he toured the West Indies in 1955 and whilst he performed well in first class games on that tour he failed to reproduce that form in the Test arena.

WAUGH, Mark Edward

Born: June 2, 1965
Batting: Right handed
Bowling: Right arm off-break

Tests
Test Career: 1991-2002
Cap Number: 349
Tests Played: 128

Test Batting
Innings:	209	Runs:	8,029
Highest Score:	153*	Average:	41.81
No. 50s:	47	No. 100s:	20

Test Bowling & Fielding
Wickets:	59	Runs:	2,429
Best Bowling:	5/40	Average:	41.16
5 WI:	1	10 WM:	0
Catches:	181	Stumpings:	0

One Day Internationals
ODI Career: 1988-2002
ODIs Played: 244

ODI Batting
Innings:	236	Runs:	8,500
Highest Score:	173	Average:	39.35
No. 50s:	50	No. 100s:	18

ODI Bowling & Fielding
Wickets:	85	Runs:	2,938
Best Bowling:	5.24	Average:	34.56
5 WM:	1	Catches:	108
Stumpings:	0		

The twin brother of Steve Waugh, he ranks as one of the most gifted batsmen to play the game. Minutes younger than his twin, hence the nickname 'Junior', he played every shot in the textbook with such ease that it was often a shock to see him dismissed. He exerted the same energy lofting a six as playing a late cut and whilst he could play all around the wagon wheel he was particularly savage on any deliveries that strayed full on to his pads. Mark made his Test debut against the England in 1991. He replaced brother Steve who was going through a horror patch with the bat, saying at the time that despite the two sharing a fierce rivalry growing up he had mixed feelings about taking his brother's spot in the side. He became the 15th Australian to score a century on debut when he scored 138 at the Adelaide Oval. Three months later he and Steve played the first of their 108 Tests together in Port of Spain. Over the next ten years the brothers were the star performers in the Australian middle order with the highlight, a series winning stand of 231 against the West Indies at Sabina Park, Kingston in 1995. Mark struck a chanceless 126 against hostile opposition that day and in doing so enhanced his reputation as a big game player. He would play 128 Tests, scoring 20 centuries along the way, and whilst he thrilled cricket lovers with his batting prowess he also frustrated. Mark often went out with the opposition at his mercy, and his highest Test score of 153 seems low for a player of his talent. There was no such frustration when watching him play one day cricket where he was a dominant force not in the middle order but as an opener. He scored three centuries during the 1996 World Cup and was a member of the side that lifted the trophy in 1999. He was also a handy change bowler who alternated between medium pace and off spin and had few peers as a catcher in slips. The man who made a difficult game look easy announced his retirement from international cricket in 2002. A keen racing fan he married racehorse trainer Kim Moore in April, 2005.

WAUGH, Stephen Rodger

Born: June 2, 1965
Batting: Right handed
Bowling: Right arm medium

Tests
Test Career: 1985-2004
Cap Number: 335
Tests Played: 168

Test Batting
Innings:	260	Runs:	10,927
Highest Score:	200	Average:	51.06
No. 50s:	50	No. 100s:	32

Test Bowling & Fielding
Wickets:	92	Runs:	3,445
Best Bowling:	5/28	Average:	37.44
5 WI:	3	10 WM:	0
Catches:	112	Stumpings:	0

One Day Internationals
ODI Career: 1986-2002
ODIs Played: 325

ODI Batting
Innings:	288	Runs:	7,569
Highest Score:	120*	Average:	32.90
No. 50s:	45	No. 100s:	3

ODI Bowling & Fielding
Wickets:	195	Runs:	6,761
Best Bowling:	4/33	Average:	34.67
5 WM:	0	Catches:	111
Stumpings:	0		

Australia's most capped Test cricketer, it was his unyielding will to succeed that transformed a promising young all-rounder into his country's most successful Test captain. As teenagers, he and his twin brother Mark caught the eye of state selectors playing for Bankstown in the Sydney grade competition and were fast tracked into the state side. Steve made his Test debut as a 20 year old in 1985 where his medium pacers made more of an impression than his batting. Over the next five years he held his spot as a number six or seven batsman and useful change bowler, but a run of poor form against New Zealand then England saw him dropped for his twin brother. Steve Waugh went away and studied where he went wrong, coming back determined not to make the same mistakes that saw him relegated back to Shield ranks. After a couple of faltering comeback attempts against the West Indies he may well have been on his last chance when picked for the 1993 Ashes tour. If he was under pressure it didn't show, he finished the six Test series with an average of 83.20, a top score of 157 not out and was part of 332 run partnership with Allan Border at Headingly. The reborn Steve Waugh was never out of the side again. He had eliminated the hook and nearly all pull shots, recognising that whilst they brought runs they also carried a greater risk of dismissal than other strokes. He was a good front foot player, a great square driver and a brilliant worker of the ball. In a stellar career he became the second highest run scorer in Australian Test history, collecting 32 centuries along the way. Perhaps his finest hour came at the SCG against England in 2003. In the twilight of his career and under pressure to retain his spot in the side, he willed himself to a century that was brought up with a boundary off the final over the second day's play. That ton, his 29th in Test cricket, equalled Sir Donald Bradman's record for most Test centuries by an Australian batsman and was described by the attending Australian Prime Minister, John Howrd as his all-time favourite moment in sport. Unsurprisingly Waugh became a complete one day cricketer as well, scoring over 7,500 runs and taking 195 wickets. He played in both the 1987 and 1999 World Cup winning teams as well as countless tri-nation winning sides in Australia. The steely resolve he put to such good use as a batsman served him well as Australian skipper. He inherited a fine side from Mark Taylor but under his leadership they continued to improve and by the time Australia had won a record sixteen consecutive Tests his team was being hailed as the greatest Test side of all time. The ultra competitive Waugh was at his best in the 1999 World Cup where he led his side to victory and was said to have told Herschelle Gibbs "you just dropped the World Cup" after the South African grassed a chance in the nail biting semi final. Steve Waugh finally brought the curtain down on his international career with an 80 against India at the SCG in 2004. A thoughtful character, he was touched by the poverty he had seen on his many cricket tours and in retirement devotes much of his time to raise funds for under-privileged children around the globe.

WELLHAM, Dirk McDonald

Born: March 13, 1959
Batting: Right handed

Tests
Test Career: 1981-87
Cap Number: 314
Tests Played: 6

Test Batting
Innings:	11	Runs:	257
Highest Score:	103	Average:	23.36
No. 50s:	0	No. 100s:	1

Test Bowling & Fielding

Wickets:	0	Runs:	0
Best Bowling:		Average:	0.00
5 WI:	0	10 WM:	0
Catches:	5	Stumpings:	0

One Day Internationals
ODI Career: 1981-87
ODIs Played: 17
ODI Batting

Innings:	17	Runs:	379
Highest Score:	97	Average:	25.26
No. 50s:	1	No. 100s:	0

ODI Bowling & Fielding

Wickets:	0	Runs:	0
Best Bowling:		Average:	0.00
5 WM:	0	Catches:	8
Stumpings:	0		

An intense character, the bespectacled New South Welshman made an immediate impression in first class cricket with a number of high scores as a 19 and 20 year old. He failed to handle the step up to Test cricket, though he did score a century against England at Lord's in 1981.

WESSELS, Kepler Christoffel

Born: September 14, 1957
Batting: Left handed
Bowling: Left arm off-break

Tests
Test Career: 1982-94
Cap Number: 317
Tests Played: 40

Test Batting

Innings:	71	Runs:	2,788
Highest Score:	179	Average:	41.00
No. 50s:	15	No. 100s:	6

Test Bowling & Fielding

Wickets:	0	Runs:	42
Best Bowling:		Average:	0.00
5 WI:	0	10 WM:	0
Catches:	30	Stumpings:	0

One Day Internationals
ODI Career: 1983-94
ODIs Played: 109
ODI Batting

Innings:	105	Runs:	3,367
Highest Score:	107	Average:	34.35
No. 50s:	26	No. 100s:	1

ODI Bowling & Fielding

Wickets:	18	Runs:	666
Best Bowling:	2/16	Average:	37.00
5 WM:	0	Catches:	49
Stumpings:	0		

The expression 'have bat will travel' may well have been coined for Kepler Wessels. Frustrated at the lack of opportunity at Test level brought about by an international ban that had been placed on his native South Africa, he first went to England where he played county cricket for Sussex and then on to Australia. The talented left handed opener was introduced to the Australian public during the second season of World Series Cricket in 1978/79. He grabbed the attention of the media and fans alike when he took a magnificent, one handed catch at mid wicket, to dismiss West Indian opener Desmond Haynes. The catch was a regular feature of the new 'classic catches' competition. He then fulfilled the requirements to play for Australia while playing for Queensland in the Sheffield Shield competition. He celebrated his selection for his adopted country by scoring 162 on debut against England at Brisbane in the 1982/83 Ashes series. His style was hardly textbook, with a stance that had his bat facing point, but he was always brutal on any loose delivery, be they short or overpitched. Kepler returned home to South Africa when they were re-admitted to international cricket and was their first captain after the hiatus.

WHATMORE, Davenell Frederick

Born: March 16, 1954
Batting: Right handed
Bowling: Right arm slow

Tests
Test Career: 1979
Cap Number: 304
Tests Played: 7

Test Batting

Innings:	13	Runs:	293
Highest Score:	77	Average:	22.53
No. 50s:	2	No. 100s:	0

Test Bowling & Fielding

Wickets:	0	Runs:	11
Best Bowling:		Average:	0.00
5 WI:	0	10 WM:	0
Catches:	13	Stumpings:	0

One Day Internationals
ODI Career: 1980
ODIs Played: 1
ODI Batting

Innings:	1	Runs:	2
Highest Score:	2	Average:	2.00
No. 50s:	0	No. 100s:	0

ODI Bowling & Fielding

Wickets:	0	Runs:	0
Best Bowling:		Average:	0.00
5 WM:	0	Catches:	0
Stumpings:	0		

Sri Lankan born, the solidly built Whatmore was given an opportunity to play for his adopted country as a result of the vacancies created by World Series Cricket. His best match was at Delhi in 1979 where he scored 77 and 54 in what was to be his third last Test. He is now a renowned coach having led Sri Lanka to victory in the World Cup in 1996. Whe is currently the coach of the Bangladeshi national side.

WHITE, Cameron Leon

Born: August 18, 1983
Batting: Right handed
Bowling: Right arm leg-break

One Day Internationals
ODI Career: 2005-
ODIs Played: 5

ODI Batting

Innings:	1	Runs:	0
Highest Score:	0	Average:	0.00
No. 50s:	0	No. 100s:	0

ODI Bowling & Fielding

Wickets:	1	Runs:	60
Best Bowling:	1/34	Average:	60.00
5 WM:	0	Catches:	4
Stumpings:	0		

A tall and powerfully built young leg-spinner from Victoria who is biding his time as he waits for an opportunity with either bat or ball at national level. He was appointed captain of his state at the tender of age 20, an indication of the high esteem in which he is held.

WHITNEY, Michael Roy

Born: February 24, 1959
Batting: Right handed
Bowling: Right arm fast

Tests

Test Career:	1981-92		
Cap Number:	313		
Tests Played:	12		

Test Batting

Innings:	19	Runs:	68
Highest Score:	13	Average:	6.18
No. 50s:	0	No. 100s:	0

Test Bowling & Fielding

Wickets:	39	Runs:	1,325
Best Bowling:	7/27	Average:	33.97
5 WI:	2	10 WM:	1
Catches:	2	Stumpings:	0

One Day Internationals

ODI Career:	1973-93		
ODIs Played:	38		

ODI Batting

Innings:	13	Runs:	40
Highest Score:	9*	Average:	6.66
No. 50s:	0	No. 100s:	0

ODI Bowling & Fielding

Wickets:	46	Runs:	1,249
Best Bowling:	4/34	Average:	27.15
5 WM:	0	Catches:	11
Stumpings:	0		

When any young cricketer travels overseas to further their career they dream of doing a 'Mike Whitney'. Playing for tiny Fleetwood in the minor counties competition he was seconded into the Test side when his country suffered a series of injuries to fast bowlers in 1981. With his head spinning Whitney took two wickets in both innings of his debut Test and in doing so put his name in front of selectors for the next decade. His Test and one day appearances were relatively infrequent from that day on, but whenever he pulled on the baggy green cap he gave his all. That fighting spirit was never more evident than in 1987 when Whitney, a genuine batting bunny, held out the great Richard Hadlee to earn his country a draw at the MCG.

WHITTY, William James

Born: August 15, 1886
Batting: Right handed
Bowling: Left arm medium-fast

Tests

Test Career:	1909-12		
Cap Number:	95		
Tests Played:	14		

Test Batting

Innings:	19	Runs:	161
Highest Score:	39*	Average:	13.41
No. 50s:	0	No. 100s:	0

Test Bowling & Fielding

Wickets:	65	Runs:	1,373
Best Bowling:	6/17	Average:	21.12
5 WI:	3	10 WM:	0
Catches:	4	Stumpings:	0

Bill Whitty was a versatile left arm bowler from NSW who could take the new ball with good effect and yet was equally comfortable bowling finger spin later in the innings. He was at his most effective during the triangular series in 1912 where he took 13 wickets against the South Africans and 12 against the English to be the leading wicket-taker for his country. Moved to South Australia later in his career.

WIENER, Julien Mark

Born: May 1, 1955
Batting: Right handed
Bowling: Right arm off-break

Tests

Test Career:	1979-80		
Cap Number:	307		
Tests Played:	6		

Test Batting

Innings:	11	Runs:	281
Highest Score:	93	Average:	25.54
No. 50s:	2	No. 100s:	0

Test Bowling & Fielding

Wickets:	0	Runs:	41
Best Bowling:		Average:	0.00
5 WI:	0	10 WM:	0
Catches:	4	Stumpings:	0

One Day Internationals

ODI Career:	1979-80		
ODIs Played:	7		

ODI Batting

Innings:	7	Runs:	140
Highest Score:	50	Average:	20.00
No. 50s:	1	No. 100s:	0

ODI Bowling & Fielding

Wickets:	0	Runs:	34
Best Bowling:		Average:	0.00
5 WM:	0	Catches:	2
Stumpings:	0		

Nicknamed 'Schnitzel', it is a common misconception that Wiener got his chance to play at Test level thanks to World Series Cricket. The athletically built opener in fact forced his way in to a full strength Australian side in 1979/80 on the back of consistent heavy scoring for his state. He scored 93 in the third Test at Lahore in 1980 but was surprisingly never picked for his country again.

WILLIAMS, Brad Andrew

Born: November 20, 1974
Batting: Right handed
Bowling: Right arm fast

Tests
Test Career: 2003-04
Cap Number: 386
Tests Played: 4

Test Batting
Innings:	6	Runs:	23
Highest Score:	10*	Average:	7.66
No. 50s:	0	No. 100s:	0

Test Bowling & Fielding
Wickets:	9	Runs:	406
Best Bowling:	4/53	Average:	45.11
5 WI:	0	10 WM:	0
Catches:	4	Stumpings:	0

One Day Internationals
ODI Career: 2002-04
ODIs Played: 25

ODI Batting
Innings:	6	Runs:	27
Highest Score:	13*	Average:	13.50
No. 50s:	0	No. 100s:	0

ODI Bowling & Fielding
Wickets:	35	Runs:	814
Best Bowling:	5/22	Average:	23.25
5 WM:	2	Catches:	4
Stumpings:	0		

A powerfully built opening bowler from Victoria, he was an under rated one day performer who twice took five wickets in an innings for his country. Hampered by injuries, he looked to rekindle his career by moving to Western Australia in 2005 but the move ended acrimoniously and by the end of the season he had retired from first class cricket.

WILSON, John William (Jack)

Born: August 20, 1921
Batting: Right handed
Bowling: Right arm off-break

Tests
Test Career: 1956
Cap Number: 205
Tests Played: 1

Test Batting
Innings:	0	Runs:	0
Highest Score:	0	Average:	0.00
No. 50s:	0	No. 100s:	0

Test Bowling & Fielding
Wickets:	1	Runs:	64
Best Bowling:	1/25	Average:	64.00
5 WI:	0	10 WM:	0
Catches:	0	Stumpings:	0

A left arm finger spinner whose only Test was against India in Bombay. From Victoria.

WILSON, Paul

Born: January 12, 1972
Batting: Right handed
Bowling: Right arm medium-fast

Tests
Test Career: 1998
Cap Number: 376
Tests Played: 1

Test Batting
Innings:	2	Runs:	0
Highest Score:	0*	Average:	0.00
No. 50s:	0	No. 100s:	0

Test Bowling & Fielding
Wickets:	0	Runs:	50
Best Bowling:		Average:	0.00
5 WI:	0	10 WM:	0
Catches:	0	Stumpings:	0

One Day Internationals
ODI Career: 1997-98
ODIs Played: 11

ODI Batting
Innings:	5	Runs:	4
Highest Score:	2	Average:	1.33
No. 50s:	0	No. 100s:	0

ODI Bowling & Fielding
Wickets:	13	Runs:	450
Best Bowling:	3/39	Average:	34.61
5 WM:	0	Catches:	1
Stumpings:	0		

Nicknamed 'Blocker', the hard working opening bowler from South Australia played his only Test against India on the Australian tour of India in 1998. In 2006 he turned his hand to umpiring hoping to emulate the success of fellow Australian quick Paul Reiffel.

WOOD, Graeme Malcolm

Born: November 6, 1956
Batting: Left handed

Tests
Test Career: 1978-88
Cap Number: 293
Tests Played: 59

Test Batting
Innings:	112	Runs:	3,374
Highest Score:	172	Average:	31.83
No. 50s:	13	No. 100s:	9

Test Bowling & Fielding
Wickets:	0	Runs:	0
Best Bowling:		Average:	0.00
5 WI:	0	10 WM:	0
Catches:	41	Stumpings:	0

One Day Internationals
ODI Career: 1978-89
ODIs Played: 83

ODI Batting
Innings:	77	Runs:	2,219
Highest Score:	114*	Average:	33.62
No. 50s:	11	No. 100s:	3

ODI Bowling & Fielding
Wickets:	0	Runs:	0
Best Bowling:		Average:	0.00
5 WM:	0	Catches:	17
Stumpings:	0		

The compact West Australian opener was a member of the national side over a ten year period despite a reputation for being a dreadful runner between wickets that earnt him the nickname 'The Kamikaze Kid'. Debuting in 1978, he was one of the few cricketers who maintained his spot in the side following the return of players from World Series Cricket. His debut ton, run out for 126 at Georgetown in 1978 was one of the few highlights by an Australian batsman on that ill fated tour to the Caribbean. Wood in fact scored almost 200 more runs than any other Australian on that tour, in a performance that saw him recognised as a batsman of note. Unfortunately his running between wickets was not as well regarded and it was said to have cost him a spot in the World Cup side in 1979. He fought his way back into the team and repaid the selectors faith by scoring a century in the 1980 Centenary Test against England at Lord's. Wood followed that with a ton against the Kiwis, but three consecutive ducks saw him on the outer again. He was in and out of the side for much of the 80's with his career ending in much the same way as it started, by scoring a ton against the might of the West Indies on a hard fast track at Perth. With nine Test centuries and three more in One Day Internationals, Graeme Wood was much more than a bad judge of a single.

WOODCOCK, Ashley James

Born: February 27, 1947
Batting: Right handed

Tests

Test Career: 1974
Cap Number: 270
Tests Played: 1

Test Batting

Innings:	1	Runs:	27
Highest Score:	27	Average:	27.00
No. 50s:	0	No. 100s:	0

Test Bowling & Fielding

Wickets:	0	Runs:	0
Best Bowling:		Average:	0.00
5 WI:	0	10 WM:	0
Catches:	1	Stumpings:	0

One Day Internationals

ODI Career: 1974
ODIs Played: 1

ODI Batting

Innings:	1	Runs:	53
Highest Score:	53	Average:	53.00
No. 50s:	1	No. 100s:	0

ODI Bowling & Fielding

Wickets:	0	Runs:	0
Best Bowling:		Average:	0.00
5 WM:	0	Catches:	0
Stumpings:	0		

An accomplished batsman from South Australia whose only Test was at his home ground in 1974 against New Zealand.

WOODFULL, William Maldon

Born: August 22, 1897
Batting: Right handed

Tests

Test Career: 1926-34
Cap Number: 123
Tests Played: 35

Test Batting

Innings:	54	Runs:	2,300
Highest Score:	161	Average:	46.00
No. 50s:	13	No. 100s:	7

Test Bowling & Fielding

Wickets:	0	Runs:	0
Best Bowling:		Average:	0.00
5 WI:	0	10 WM:	0
Catches:	7	Stumpings:	0

The great opener of the pre-war era was a leader of the highest quality who steered his country through the 'bodyline' series and on to cricket greatness. The Victorian hailed from the small country town of Maldon and moved to the city in his early 20's. In Melbourne he would meet another young opener by the name of Bill Ponsford and together they would form one of their country's finest opening combinations of all time. Woodfull joined the Australian side on the Ashes tour of 1926 and after rain ruined his debut and two failures marred his second game he moved to the opening slot for the third Test. His 141 against the great Maurice Tate anouced the arrival of the heavy set right handed batsman and it was confirmed with another fine century in the fourth Test. He was an established member of the Test side when Jack Ryder was relieved of the captaincy in 1930. The man known as the 'great unbowlable' was offered the job of leading his country and after initial doubts he took over the reins. Respected by his team mates he was at the helm when the visiting English employed the now famous bodyline tactics on the Ashes tour of 1932/33. Woodfull's steely resolve resonated through the side and whilst he didn't allow the series to denegrate into farce he let the feelings of a nation be known. His famous quote, "there are two teams out there, but only one of them is playing cricket", was meant for private consumption but perfectly summed up the sentiments of the Australian public. Woodfull retired from Test cricket in 1934 but he left behind a mature side that would soon develop into one of the best the game has ever seen.

WOODS, Samuel Moses James

Born: April 13, 1867
Batting: Right handed
Bowling: Right arm medium-fast

Tests

Test Career: 1888-96
Cap Number: 54
Tests Played: 6

Test Batting

Innings:	10	Runs:	154
Highest Score:	53	Average:	15.40
No. 50s:	1	No. 100s:	0

Test Bowling & Fielding
Wickets:	10	Runs:	250
Best Bowling:	3/28	Average:	25.00
5 WI:	0	10 WM:	0
Catches:	5	Stumpings:	0

He was an all-round sportsman in the truest sense and whilst he didn't shine at Test level he was still considered to be a very fine batsman and medium pace bowler. He played Test cricket for both Australia and England, represented England 13 times in Rugby, played Association Football or soccer for Sussex and was even considered more than capable when on one occasion asked to step into the boxing ring!

WOOLLEY, Roger Douglas
Born: September 16, 1954
Batting: Right handed
Wicket Keeper

Tests
Test Career: 1983-84
Cap Number: 319
Tests Played: 2

Test Batting
Innings:	2	Runs:	21
Highest Score:	13	Average:	10.50
No. 50s:	0	No. 100s:	0

Test Bowling & Fielding
Wickets:	0	Runs:	0
Best Bowling:		Average:	0.00
5 WI:	0	10 WM:	0
Catches:	7	Stumpings:	0

One Day Internationals
ODI Career: 1983
ODIs Played: 4

ODI Batting
Innings:	3	Runs:	31
Highest Score:	16	Average:	31.00
No. 50s:	0	No. 100s:	0

ODI Bowling & Fielding
Wickets:	0	Runs:	0
Best Bowling:		Average:	0.00
5 WM:	0	Catches:	1
Stumpings:	1		

Tasmania made their Sheffield Shield debut in 1977/78, but had to wait until 1983 to see a home grown player make the Test side. That player was Roger Woolley, a fine wicketkeeper batsman who got his opportunity when injury forced Rodney Marsh to pull out of the inaugural Test against Sri Lanka at Kandy in 1983.

WORRALL, John
Born: June 20, 1860
Batting: Right handed
Bowling: Right arm slow

Tests
Test Career: 1885-99
Cap Number: 40
Tests Played: 11

Test Batting
Innings:	22	Runs:	478
Highest Score:	76	Average:	25.15
No. 50s:	5	No. 100s:	0

Test Bowling & Fielding
Wickets:	1	Runs:	127
Best Bowling:	1/97	Average:	127.00
5 WI:	0	10 WM:	0
Catches:	13	Stumpings:	0

A brilliant sportsman who was not only a dominant Victorian cricketer but also one of the most important figures in the early years of Australian Rules football. Worrall played his first Test in the controversial MCG Test of 1884/85 when ten regular team members went on strike. Over the next fourteen years unavailabilty for a variety of reasons limited his Test appearances but he continued to play for Victoria and played his final Test at the age of 39 in 1899.

WRIGHT, Kevin John
Born: December 27, 1953
Batting: Right handed
Wicket Keeper

Tests
Test Career: 1979
Cap Number: 301
Tests Played: 10

Test Batting
Innings:	18	Runs:	219
Highest Score:	55*	Average:	16.84
No. 50s:	1	No. 100s:	0

Test Bowling & Fielding
Wickets:	0	Runs:	0
Best Bowling:		Average:	0.00
5 WI:	0	10 WM:	0
Catches:	31	Stumpings:	4

One Day Internationals
ODI Career: 1979
ODIs Played: 5

ODI Batting
Innings:	2	Runs:	29
Highest Score:	23	Average:	0.00
No. 50s:	0	No. 100s:	0

ODI Bowling & Fielding
Wickets:	0	Runs:	0
Best Bowling:		Average:	0.00
5 WM:	0	Catches:	8
Stumpings:	0		

Small in stature, he got his chance with the gloves when John MacLean was injured in the 1978/79 summer. He was part of the Australian side at the 1979 World Cup.

YALLOP, Graham Neil
Born: October 7, 1952
Batting: Left handed
Bowling: Left arm fast

Tests
Test Career: 1976-84
Cap Number: 275
Tests Played: 39

Test Batting
Innings:	70	Runs:	2,756
Highest Score:	268	Average:	41.13
No. 50s:	9	No. 100s:	8

Test Bowling & Fielding

Wickets:	1	Runs:	116
Best Bowling:	1/21	Average:	116.00
5 WI:	0	10 WM:	0
Catches:	23	Stumpings:	0

One Day Internationals

ODI Career:	1978-84		
ODIs Played:	30		

ODI Batting

Innings:	27	Runs:	823
Highest Score:	66*	Average:	39.19
No. 50s:	7	No. 100s:	0

ODI Bowling & Fielding

Wickets:	3	Runs:	119
Best Bowling:	2/28	Average:	39.66
5 WM:	0	Catches:	5
Stumpings:	0		

There were two distinct aspects of Graham Yallop's Test career. One was as a middle order batsman of the highest calibre and the other as captain of an Australian side ravaged by defections to World Series Cricket. Yallop the batsman started his Test career against the West Indies in the mid 70's, breaking into a strong middle order. He was in and out of the Test side until the final Test of the 1976/77 season when he hit 121 against India at Adelaide. Yallop resisted offers to join Kerry Packer's rebel cricket tour and was rewarded with the national captaincy following the retirement of Bobby Simpson. The captaincy appeared to not suit Yallop and under his leadership a weakened Australian line-up were thrashed at home by England. Yallop's thoughts on the state of Australian Test cricket were documented in his controversial book, 'Lambs to the Slaughter' where he laid the blame for the state of Australian cricket on the very people who had appointed him to the top job. He continued to perform well with the bat but upon the return of Australia's best from World Series Cricket, Yallop was relieved of the captaincy. His Test position was no longer guaranteed, but Yallop fought hard for a spot in the national side and was rewarded with a fine series at home against Pakistan in 1983/84 where he scored 554 runs at an average of 92.33 including a top score of 268. Having passed up on a chance to join WSC he agreed to lead an Australian team on a rebel tour of South Africa in 1985. That decision and the subsequent ban ended the international career of one of Australia's most complex captains.

YARDLEY, Bruce

Born:	September 5, 1947
Batting:	Right handed
Bowling:	Right arm off-break

Tests

Test Career:	1978-83
Cap Number:	294
Tests Played:	33

Test Batting

Innings:	54	Runs:	978
Highest Score:	74	Average:	19.56
No. 50s:	4	No. 100s:	0

Test Bowling & Fielding

Wickets:	126	Runs:	3,986
Best Bowling:	7/98	Average:	31.63
5 WI:	6	10 WM:	1
Catches:	31	Stumpings:	0

One Day Internationals

ODI Career:	1978-83		
ODIs Played:	7		

ODI Batting

Innings:	4	Runs:	58
Highest Score:	28	Average:	14.50
No. 50s:	0	No. 100s:	0

ODI Bowling & Fielding

Wickets:	7	Runs:	130
Best Bowling:	3/28	Average:	18.57
5 WM:	0	Catches:	1
Stumpings:	0		

A right arm off spinner, his bowling bordered on medium pace at times with bounce as much of a weapon as turn. Yardley was an under rated bowler who performed so well in the summer of 1981/82 that he was awarded the International Cricketer of the Year. He took 20 wickets in the three Test series against the West Indies eclipsing the likes of Dennis Lillee, Jeff Thomson and Len Pascoe. His best figures in a Test innings, 7/98 were recorded at Sydney in that series. Yardley was also a more than competent lower order batsman with four Test half centuries to his name.

YOUNG, Bradley Evan

Born:	February 23, 1973
Batting:	Right handed
Bowling:	Left arm off-break

One Day Internationals

ODI Career:	1998-1999
ODIs Played:	6

ODI Batting

Innings:	3	Runs:	31
Highest Score:	18	Average:	15.50
No. 50s:	0	No. 100s:	0

ODI Bowling & Fielding

Wickets:	1	Runs:	251
Best Bowling:	1/26	Average:	251.00
5 WM:	0	Catches:	2
Stumpings:	0		

A feisty off spinner from South Australia, his surprise call-up to the Australian one day side may have had as much to do with his smart lower order batting as his bowling. In recent years has been overlooked for his promising state team mate Dan Cullen.

YOUNG, Shaun

Born:	June 13, 1970
Batting:	Left handed
Bowling:	Right arm medium-fast

Tests
Test Career:	1997		
Cap Number:	372		
Tests Played:	1		

Test Batting
Innings:	2	Runs:	4
Highest Score:	4*	Average:	4.00
No. 50s:	0	No. 100s:	0

Test Bowling & Fielding
Wickets:	0	Runs:	13
Best Bowling:		Average:	0.00
5 WI:	0	10 WM:	0
Catches:	0	Stumpings:	0

A Tasmanian all-rounder who earnt a spot on the 1997 Ashes tour on the back of many fine performances for his state. He was not expected to play a Test on that tour, but injury and unavailability meant he was selected to play at The Oval. Given little opportunity with the ball, it was his last Test appearance.

ZESERS, Andris Karlis (Andrew)
Born:	March 11, 1967
Batting:	Right handed
Bowling:	Right arm medium-fast

One Day Internationals
ODI Career:	1987		
ODIs Played:	2		

ODI Batting
Innings:	2	Runs:	10
Highest Score:	8*	Average:	0.00
No. 50s:	0	No. 100s:	0

ODI Bowling & Fielding
Wickets:	1	Runs:	74
Best Bowling:	1/37	Average:	74.00
5 WM:	0	Catches:	1
Stumpings:	0		

At the age of 21 Zesers had become the youngest Australian to take 100 first class wickets and was rewarded with a spot in the Australian 1987 World Cup side. He played two games in that series, but a serious shoulder injury severely hampered him thereafter, and by 23 he had given the game away.

ZOEHRER, Timothy Joseph
Born:	September 25, 1961
Batting:	Right handed
	Wicket Keeper

Tests
Test Career:	1986-87		
Cap Number:	337		
Tests Played:	10		

Test Batting
Innings:	14	Runs:	246
Highest Score:	52*	Average:	20.50
No. 50s:	1	No. 100s:	0

Test Bowling & Fielding
Wickets:	0	Runs:	0
Best Bowling:		Average:	0.00
5 WI:	0	10 WM:	0
Catches:	18	Stumpings:	1

One Day Internationals
ODI Career:	1986-94		
ODIs Played:	22		

ODI Batting
Innings:	15	Runs:	130
Highest Score:	50	Average:	10.83
No. 50s:	1	No. 100s:	0

ODI Bowling & Fielding
Wickets:	0	Runs:	0
Best Bowling:		Average:	0.00
5 WM:	0	Catches:	21
Stumpings:	2		

A keeper batsman from West Australia who replaced Rod Marsh but was in turn replaced by Greg Dyer and ultimately Ian Healy. His batting was more than acceptable but his footwork behind the stumps let him down on occasion. The versatile Zoehrer turned his hand to leg spin when he returned to state ranks.

Bangladesh

ABEDIN, Minhajul (Nannu)
Born: September 25, 1965
Batting: Right handed
Bowling: Right arm off-break

One Day Internationals
ODI Career: 1986-99
ODIs Played: 27

ODI Batting
Innings: 26 Runs: 453
Highest Score: 68* Average: 18.87
No. 50s: 2 No. 100s: 0

ODI Bowling & Fielding
Wickets: 13 Runs: 511
Best Bowling: 2/39 Average: 39.30
5 WM: 0 Catches: 0
Stumpings: 0

A member of Bangladesh's inaugural (official) one-day international, against Pakistan at Moratuwa, in 1986, Minhajul Abedin was a useful middle order batsman who enjoyed a thirteen year career at the highest level. He captained the side on two occasions and played an important part in Bangladesh's first ever ODI victory over a Test-playing nation in Pakistan, when he took the vital wicket of all-rounder Wasim Akram during their 1999 World Cup encounter. It was Abedin's last match and a fitting way to end his international career considering the number of losses he endured along the journey.

ABEDIN, Nurul
Born: September 7, 1964
Batting: Right handed
Bowling: Right arm medium

One Day Internationals
ODI Career: 1986-90
ODIs Played: 4

ODI Batting
Innings: 4 Runs: 15
Highest Score: 13 Average: 3.75
No. 50s: 0 No. 100s: 0

ODI Bowling & Fielding
Wickets: 0 Runs: 0
Best Bowling: Average: 0.00
5 WM: 0 Catches: 0
Stumpings: 0

A stylish right hand batsman, he opened the innings in Bangladesh's inaugural one-day international against Pakistan, at Moratuwa in 1986. Unfortunately he was out for a duck and managed just three ODI appearances.

AHMED, Faruk
Born: July 24, 1966
Batting: Right handed
Bowling: Right arm off-break

One Day Internationals
ODI Career: 1988-89
ODIs Played: 7

ODI Batting
Innings: 7 Runs: 105
Highest Score: 57 Average: 15.00
No. 50s: 1 No. 100s: 0

ODI Bowling & Fielding
Wickets: 0 Runs: 0
Best Bowling: Average: 0.00
5 WM: 0 Catches: 2
Stumpings: 0

A right hand batsman who could either open or bat at number three. Faruk Ahmed made one fifty in his seven ODI's for Bangladesh.

AHMED, Jamaluddin
Born: January 5, 1977
Batting: Right handed
Bowling: Right arm off-break

One Day Internationals
ODI Career: 2003
ODIs Played: 1

ODI Batting
Innings: 1 Runs: 18
Highest Score: 18* Average: 18.00
No. 50s: 0 No. 100s: 0

ODI Bowling & Fielding
Wickets: 0 Runs: 28
Best Bowling: Average: 0.00
5 WM: 0 Catches: 0
Stumpings: 0

An injury to regular spinner, Mohammad Rafique in 2003, opened the door for the virtually unknown Jamaluddin Ahmed. He made his ODI debut against England at Chittagong and while he failed to take a wicket coming on as a second change bowler, Jamaluddin unexpectedly, impressed with the bat when he made 18 not out in a 37 run partnership for the last wicket with Tapash Baisya. However, his effort could not earn him another international cap.

AHMED, Nasir
Born: January 1, 1964
Batting: Right handed
  Wicket Keeper

One Day Internationals
ODI Career: 1988-90
ODIs Played: 7

ODI Batting

Innings:	4	Runs:	25
Highest Score:	11	Average:	12.50
No. 50s:	0	No. 100s:	0

ODI Bowling & Fielding

Wickets:	0	Runs:	0
Best Bowling:		Average:	0.00
5 WM:	0	Catches:	1
Stumpings:	1		

A wicket-keeper who played in seven ODI's after making his debut against India, at Chittagong in 1988.

AHMED, Sajjad

Born:	May 20, 1974
Batting:	Right handed
Bowling:	Right arm off-break

One Day Internationals

ODI Career:	1995
ODIs Played:	2

ODI Batting

Innings:	2	Runs:	15
Highest Score:	11	Average:	7.50
No. 50s:	0	No. 100s:	0

ODI Bowling & Fielding

Wickets:	0	Runs:	0
Best Bowling:		Average:	0.00
5 WM:	0	Catches:	0
Stumpings:	0		

A right hand batsman from Dhaka who made his ODI debut against India at Sharjah in 1995. Made just the two ODI appearances.

AHMED, Shafiuddin

Born:	June 1, 1973
Batting:	Right handed
Bowling:	Right arm medium-fast

One Day Internationals

ODI Career:	1997-00
ODIs Played:	11

ODI Batting

Innings:	10	Runs:	22
Highest Score:	11	Average:	5.50
No. 50s:	0	No. 100s:	0

ODI Bowling & Fielding

Wickets:	11	Runs:	426
Best Bowling:	3/42	Average:	38.72
5 WM:	0	Catches:	0
Stumpings:	0		

A right arm pace bowler, 'Babu' Ahmed regularly opened the bowling for Bangladesh over his three year career. Although he enjoyed a career best 3/42 against Zimbabwe, Babu was quite often very expensive as his bowling average of 38.72 indicates.

AHMED, Sheikh Salahuddin

Born:	February 10, 1969
Batting:	Right handed
Bowling:	Right arm off-break

One Day Internationals

ODI Career:	1997
ODIs Played:	6

ODI Batting

Innings:	5	Runs:	24
Highest Score:	12	Average:	12.00
No. 50s:	0	No. 100s:	0

ODI Bowling & Fielding

Wickets:	4	Runs:	249
Best Bowling:	2/48	Average:	62.25
5 WM:	0	Catches:	0
Stumpings:	0		

A right arm off-break bowler from Khulna, Ahmed made his ODI debut in an Asia Cup match against Pakistan at Colombo in 1997.

AHMED CHOWDHURY, Aftab

Born:	November 10, 1985
Batting:	Right handed
Bowling:	Right arm medium

Tests

Test Career:	2004-06
Cap Number:	39
Tests Played:	10

Test Batting

Innings:	20	Runs:	395
Highest Score:	82*	Average:	20.78
No. 50s:	1	No. 100s:	0

Test Bowling & Fielding

Wickets:	3	Runs:	176
Best Bowling:	1/28	Average:	58.66
5 WI:	0	10 WM:	0
Catches:	0	Stumpings:	0

One Day Internationals

ODI Career:	2004-06
ODIs Played:	31

ODI Batting

Innings:	31	Runs:	680
Highest Score:	81*	Average:	25.18
No. 50s:	5	No. 100s:	0

ODI Bowling & Fielding

Wickets:	10	Runs:	487
Best Bowling:	5/31	Average:	48.70
5 WM:	1	Catches:	5
Stumpings:	0		

A talented but rather inconsistent right hand batsman, Aftab Ahmed made his Test debut against New Zealand at Chittagong in 2004. An exciting limited overs player, Ahmed is best remembered for his aggressive batting display in Bangladesh's historic win over the Australians at Cardiff in 2005.

AL-SAHARIAR, Mohammad

Born:	April 23, 1978
Batting:	Right handed
Bowling:	Right arm leg-break

Tests

Test Career:	2000-03
Cap Number:	2
Tests Played:	15

Test Batting

Innings:	30	Runs:	683
Highest Score:	71	Average:	22.76
No. 50s:	4	No. 100s:	0

Test Bowling & Fielding

Wickets:	0	Runs:	0
Best Bowling:		Average:	0.00
5 WI:	0	10 WM:	0
Catches:	10	Stumpings:	0

One Day Internationals

ODI Career:	1999-03		
ODIs Played:	29		

ODI Batting

Innings:	29	Runs:	374
Highest Score:	62*	Average:	13.35
No. 50s:	2	No. 100s:	0

ODI Bowling & Fielding

Wickets:	0	Runs:	0
Best Bowling:		Average:	0.00
5 WM:	0	Catches:	7
Stumpings:	0		

A talented right hand middle order batsman who has also opens, Al-Sahariar played in Bangladesh's inaugural Test against India in 2000 but never really lived up to expectations and has been overlooked for international selection since 2003.

ALAM, Jahangir

Born:	March 5, 1973
Batting:	Right handed
	Wicket Keeper

One Day Internationals

ODI Career:	1997-99		
ODIs Played:	3		

ODI Batting

Innings:	3	Runs:	4
Highest Score:	3	Average:	1.33
No. 50s:	0	No. 100s:	0

ODI Bowling & Fielding

Wickets:	0	Runs:	0
Best Bowling:		Average:	0.00
5 WM:	0	Catches:	0
Stumpings:	1		

A talented wicket-keeper from Narayanganj, Jahangir Alam made his international debut against Kenya at Nairobi in 1997.

ALAM, Rafiqul

Born:	March 5, 1973
Batting:	Right handed

One Day Internationals

ODI Career:	1986		
ODIs Played:	2		

ODI Batting

Innings:	2	Runs:	24
Highest Score:	14	Average:	12.00
No. 50s:	0	No. 100s:	0

ODI Bowling & Fielding

Wickets:	0	Runs:	0
Best Bowling:		Average:	0.00
5 WM:	0	Catches:	0
Stumpings:	0		

A middle order batsman who scored 14 in Bangladesh's inaugural (official) ODI against Pakistan at Moratuwa in 1986.

ALAM TALUKDAR, Mohammad Jahangir

Born:	December 4, 1968
Batting:	Right handed
Bowling:	Left arm medium

One Day Internationals

ODI Career:	1990		
ODIs Played:	2		

ODI Batting

Innings:	1	Runs:	7
Highest Score:	7	Average:	7.00
No. 50s:	0	No. 100s:	0

ODI Bowling & Fielding

Wickets:	0	Runs:	36
Best Bowling:		Average:	0.00
5 WM:	0	Catches:	0
Stumpings:	0		

A left arm medium pacer who made his ODI debut against Australia at Sharjah in 1990.

ALI KHAN, Athar

Born:	February 10, 1962
Batting:	Right handed
Bowling:	Right arm medium

One Day Internationals

ODI Career:	1988-98		
ODIs Played:	19		

ODI Batting

Innings:	19	Runs:	532
Highest Score:	82	Average:	29.55
No. 50s:	3	No. 100s:	0

ODI Bowling & Fielding

Wickets:	6	Runs:	365
Best Bowling:	2/33	Average:	60.83
5 WM:	0	Catches:	2
Stumpings:	0		

A right hand middle order batsman who could also open the batting when required, Athar Ali Khan played his first ODI against India at Chittigong in 1988. A useful medium pace bowler, he scored three 50's in a career that lasted just over a decade.

ALI KHAN, Mohammad Morshed

Born:	May 14, 1972
Batting:	Left handed
Bowling:	Left arm medium

One Day Internationals

ODI Career:	1998		
ODIs Played:	3		

ODI Batting

Innings:	1	Runs:	2
Highest Score:	2*	Average:	2.00
No. 50s:	0	No. 100s:	0

ODI Bowling & Fielding

Wickets:	2	Runs:	85
Best Bowling:	1/26	Average:	42.50
5 WM:	0	Catches:	2
Stumpings:	0		

A left arm medium pacer who made his ODI debut against India at Chandigarh in 1998. Ali Khan took the just the one wicket in his three matches, that of former Indian captain Sourav Ganguly.

ASHRAF, Gazi

Batting: Right handed
Bowling: Right arm off-break

One Day Internationals
ODI Career: 1986-90
ODIs Played: 7

ODI Batting
Innings:	7	Runs:	59
Highest Score:	18	Average:	8.42
No. 50s:	0	No. 100s:	0

ODI Bowling & Fielding
Wickets:	2	Runs:	33
Best Bowling:	1/7	Average:	16.50
5 WM:	0	Catches:	1
Stumpings:	0		

Bangladesh's inaugural One Day captain, Gazi Ashraf played in his country's first official limited overs international against Pakistan at Moratuwa. Although he unfortunately made a duck batting at number three, he did manage to take the prize wicket of Javed Miandad.

ASHRAFUL, Mohammad

Born: July 7, 1984
Batting: Right handed
Bowling: Right arm leg-break

Tests
Test Career: 2001-06
Cap Number: 17
Tests Played: 33

Test Batting
Innings:	65	Runs:	1,511
Highest Score:	158*	Average:	24.33
No. 50s:	6	No. 100s:	3

Test Bowling & Fielding
Wickets:	9	Runs:	623
Best Bowling:	2/42	Average:	69.22
5 WI:	0	10 WM:	0
Catches:	10	Stumpings:	0

One Day Internationals
ODI Career: 2001-06
ODIs Played: 68

ODI Batting
Innings:	65	Runs:	1,222
Highest Score:	100	Average:	19.38
No. 50s:	8	No. 100s:	1

ODI Bowling & Fielding
Wickets:	10	Runs:	317
Best Bowling:	3/26	Average:	32.70
5 WM:	0	Catches:	8
Stumpings:	0		

Mohammad Ashraful stunned the cricket world when at 17 years and 63 days, he became the youngest player to score a Test century, breaking a forty year record held by former Pakistan captain Mustaq Mohammad. The fact that Ashraful made his maiden Test hundred - 114 on debut - while continually facing one of the world's best bowlers in Murali Muralitharan, makes the feat even more remarkable. Both men, the experienced campaigner Murali and 'new kid on the block' Ashraful shared 'Man of the Match' honours as Sri Lanka cruised to an innings and 137 run victory. But like in many 'shooting star' cases before him, the young middle order batsman was prone to inconsistency. After a short lapse of form, Ashraful recaptured his form and in late 2004 registered his second Test century with a sizzling 158 not out in a losing side against India, at Chittagong. On this occasion, Ashraful enjoyed sole rights to the 'Man of the Match' trophy. When he notched up his third ton, 136 against Sri Lanka at Chittagong in early 2006, he joined captain Habibul Bashar as equal record holder for most Test centuries. An exciting player in limited overs cricket, where he has scored eight fifties and a memorable century against Australia at Cardiff in 2005, Mohammad Ashraful is clearly the most exciting prospect to hit the Bangladesh cricket scene in their short history to date.

AZIZ, Mohammad Tareq

Born: September 4, 1983
Batting: Right handed
Bowling: Right arm medium-fast

Tests
Test Career: 2004
Cap Number: 37
Tests Played: 3

Test Batting
Innings:	6	Runs:	22
Highest Score:	10*	Average:	11.00
No. 50s:	0	No. 100s:	0

Test Bowling & Fielding
Wickets:	1	Runs:	261
Best Bowling:	1/76	Average:	261.00
5 WI:	0	10 WM:	0
Catches:	1	Stumpings:	0

One Day Internationals
ODI Career: 2002-04
ODIs Played: 10

ODI Batting
Innings:	8	Runs:	26
Highest Score:	11*	Average:	26.00
No. 50s:	0	No. 100s:	0

ODI Bowling & Fielding
Wickets:	13	Runs:	424
Best Bowling:	3/19	Average:	32.61
5 WM:	0	Catches:	4
Stumpings:	0		

A fiery right arm pace bowler, Tareq Aziz made an impressive start to his international career when he snared 3/19 against Pakistan in his first ODI in 2002. Aziz made his Test debut two years later when he was selected on the tour of the West Indies in 2004.

BAISYA, Tapash Kumar

Born: December 15, 1982
Batting: Right handed
Bowling: Right arm medium-fast

Tests
Test Career:	2002-05		
Cap Number:	27		
Tests Played:	21		

Test Batting
Innings:	40	Runs:	384
Highest Score:	66	Average:	11.29
No. 50s:	2	No. 100s:	0

Test Bowling & Fielding
Wickets:	36	Runs:	2,137
Best Bowling:	4/72	Average:	59.36
5 WI:	0	10 WM:	0
Catches:	6	Stumpings:	0

One Day Internationals
ODI Career:	2002-06		
ODIs Played:	52		

ODI Batting
Innings:	39	Runs:	318
Highest Score:	35*	Average:	11.77
No. 50s:	0	No. 100s:	0

ODI Bowling & Fielding
Wickets:	56	Runs:	2,267
Best Bowling:	4/16	Average:	40.48
5 WM:	0	Catches:	7
Stumpings:	0		

A tall and slender right arm pace bowler, Tapash Baisya was 19 when he took just the one wicket in his maiden Test match against Sri Lanka at Colombo in 2002. But it was his 52 not out, batting at number nine, which captured the attention of the selectors who, in many opinion, had fast tracked the youngster. In his 21 Tests, Baisya has struggled for consistency with both bat and ball but his undoubted potential suggests that he is one that the Bangladesh 'brains trust' will perservere with.

BASHAR, Habibul
Born:	August 17, 1972
Batting:	Right handed
Bowling:	Right arm off-break

Tests
Test Career:	2000-06		
Cap Number:	4		
Tests Played:	42		

Test Batting
Innings:	83	Runs:	2,838
Highest Score:	113	Average:	34.60
No. 50s:	24	No. 100s:	3

Test Bowling & Fielding
Wickets:	0	Runs:	195
Best Bowling:		Average:	0.00
5 WI:	0	10 WM:	0
Catches:	19	Stumpings:	0

One Day Internationals
ODI Career:	1995-06		
ODIs Played:	82		

ODI Batting
Innings:	80	Runs:	1,663
Highest Score:	74	Average:	21.59
No. 50s:	12	No. 100s:	0

ODI Bowling & Fielding
Wickets:	1	Runs:	142
Best Bowling:	1/31	Average:	142.00
5 WM:	0	Catches:	16
Stumpings:	0		

Considered, and with good reason, Bangladesh's premier player in their short history to date, Habibul Bashar holds just about every Bangladesh Test record on offer. A member of Bangladesh's inaugural Test team of 2000 where he scored 71 on debut, Bashar has represented Bangladesh in more Tests than any other player and has led his country on more occasions than his three predecessors. He has also scored the most Test runs and his batting average of 34.60, albeit modest by Test standards, is the highest by any Bangladesh batsman and shares the 'most centuries' honour (three) with Mohammad Ashraful. Of the three centuries, Bashar scored 108 twice (against Zimbabwe at Chittagong & Pakistan at Karachi) and his third, his highest score of 113, was made in trying conditions against the West Indies in the Caribbean in 2004. A technically gifted player who is partial to the hook shot, Bashar was awarded the captaincy in 2004 when he took over from Khaled Mahmud and led his country to a memorable win over the all conquering Australians at Cardiff during the Natwest Series in 2005.

DAS, Bikash Ranjan
Born:	July 14, 1982
Batting:	Right handed
Bowling:	Left arm medium-fast

Tests
Test Career:	2000		
Cap Number:	10		
Tests Played:	1		

Test Batting
Innings:	2	Runs:	2
Highest Score:	2	Average:	1.00
No. 50s:	0	No. 100s:	0

Test Bowling & Fielding
Wickets:	1	Runs:	72
Best Bowling:	1/64	Average:	72.00
5 WI:	0	10 WM:	0
Catches:	1	Stumpings:	0

A genuine left arm pace bowler who opened the bowling with Hasibul Hossain in Bangladesh's first ever Test match against India at Dhaka in 2000, Ranjan Das failed to convince the selectors that he was worthy of another chance at international level. He therefore became Bangladesh's inaugural member of the unofficial 'One Test' club.

FARUQ, Gholam
Batting:	Right handed
Bowling:	Right arm medium

One Day Internationals
ODI Career:	1986-90		
ODIs Played:	5		

ODI Batting
Innings:	4	Runs:	44
Highest Score:	23*	Average:	22.00
No. 50s:	0	No. 100s:	0

ODI Bowling & Fielding

Wickets:	2	Runs:	116
Best Bowling:	1/22	Average:	58.00
5 WM:	0	Catches:	0
Stumpings:	0		

One of the eleven who played in Bangladesh's inaugural ODI against Pakistan, at Moratuwa, in 1986. He played just the five ODI's, taking his best figures of 1/22 against New Zealand at Sharjah in his last match in 1990.

GANI, Wahidul

Batting: Right handed
Bowling: Right arm off-break

One Day Internationals
ODI Career: 1988
ODIs Played: 1

ODI Batting

Innings:	0	Runs:	0
Highest Score:	0	Average:	0.00
No. 50s:	0	No. 100s:	0

ODI Bowling & Fielding

Wickets:	0	Runs:	32
Best Bowling:	0/32	Average:	0.00
5 WM:	0	Catches:	0
Stumpings:	0		

A right arm off spinner and useful lower order batsman, Wahidul Ghani played just the solitary ODI against Pakistan at Chittagong in the Asia Cup Competition in 1988 but didn't get the opportunity to bat. While his stint on the international scene was brief and uneventful, post retirement, Ghani has devoted his energy towards developing junior players as he runs a well regarded cricket-coaching academy called "Ankur".

HAQUE, Ehsanul

Born: December 1, 1979
Batting: Right handed
Bowling: Right arm off-break

Tests
Test Career: 2002
Cap Number: 23
Tests Played: 1

Test Batting

Innings:	2	Runs:	7
Highest Score:	5	Average:	3.50
No. 50s:	0	No. 100s:	0

Test Bowling & Fielding

Wickets:	0	Runs:	18
Best Bowling:	0/18	Average:	0.00
5 WI:	0	10 WM:	0
Catches:	0	Stumpings:	0

One Day Internationals
ODI Career: 2002-03
ODIs Played: 6

ODI Batting

Innings:	6	Runs:	57
Highest Score:	20	Average:	9.50
No. 50s:	0	No. 100s:	0

ODI Bowling & Fielding

Wickets:	3	Runs:	113
Best Bowling:	2/34	Average:	37.66
5 WM:	0	Catches:	0
Stumpings:	0		

A right hand batsman who failed to reach double figures in both innings during his solitary Test against Sri Lanka at Colombo in 2002.

HAQUE, Enamul

Born: February 27, 1966
Batting: Left handed
Bowling: Left arm off-break

Tests
Test Career: 2001-03
Cap Number: 16
Tests Played: 10

Test Batting

Innings:	19	Runs:	180
Highest Score:	24*	Average:	12.00
No. 50s:	0	No. 100s:	0

Test Bowling & Fielding

Wickets:	18	Runs:	1,027
Best Bowling:	4/136	Average:	57.05
5 WI:	0	10 WM:	0
Catches:	1	Stumpings:	0

One Day Internationals
ODI Career: 1990-02
ODIs Played: 29

ODI Batting

Innings:	26	Runs:	236
Highest Score:	32	Average:	11.23
No. 50s:	0	No. 100s:	0

ODI Bowling & Fielding

Wickets:	19	Runs:	1,083
Best Bowling:	2/40	Average:	57.00
5 WM:	0	Catches:	6
Stumpings:	0		

A hard working and honest left arm off-break bowler who played his first of ten Tests against Zimbabwe at Harare in 2001. He took a career best 4/136 against Pakistan at Dhaka, in 2001.

HAQUE, Shariful

Born: January 15, 1976
Batting: Right handed
Bowling: Right arm off-break

One Day Internationals
ODI Career: 1988
ODIs Played: 1

ODI Batting

Innings:	1	Runs:	10
Highest Score:	10	Average:	10.00
No. 50s:	0	No. 100s:	0

ODI Bowling & Fielding

Wickets:	0	Runs:	21
Best Bowling:	0/21	Average:	0.00
5 WM:	0	Catches:	0
Stumpings:	0		

An off-break bowler from Mymensingh, Shariful Haque, played just the solitary ODI against India at Dhaka in 1988. Haque, coming in at number eleven in his only ODI innings, smashed a huge six and while an entertaining cameo was looming, he was run out for 10.

HAQUE CHOWDHURI, Mohammad Mazharul
Born: July 3, 1980
Batting: Right handed
Bowling: Right arm off-break

One Day Internationals
ODI Career: 2002
ODIs Played: 1

ODI Batting
Innings:	1	Runs:	3
Highest Score:	3	Average:	3.00
No. 50s:	0	No. 100s:	0

ODI Bowling & Fielding
Wickets:	0	Runs:	4
Best Bowling:	0/4	Average:	0.00
5 WM:	0	Catches:	0
Stumpings:	0		

A right handed batsman from Narayanganj, Haque is yet another member of the one match club after playing his only ODI against Australia at Colombo in 2002.

HAQUE JNR, Enamul
Born: December 5, 1986
Batting: Right handed
Bowling: Left arm, off-break

Tests
Test Career: 2003-06
Cap Number: 34
Tests Played: 10

Test Batting
Innings:	18	Runs:	28
Highest Score:	9	Average:	4.00
No. 50s:	0	No. 100s:	0

Test Bowling & Fielding
Wickets:	32	Runs:	1,198
Best Bowling:	7/95	Average:	37.43
5 WI:	3	10 WM:	1
Catches:	2	Stumpings:	0

One Day Internationals
ODI Career: 2005
ODIs Played: 3

ODI Batting
Innings:	2	Runs:	4
Highest Score:	4*	Average:	4.00
No. 50s:	0	No. 100s:	0

ODI Bowling & Fielding
Wickets:	4	Runs:	129
Best Bowling:	2/37	Average:	32.25
5 WM:	0	Catches:	5
Stumpings:	0		

Since making made his Test debut against England at Dhaka in 2004, left arm off spinner Enamul Haque seems destined for a prosperous and exciting international career. In his ten Tests he has taken five wickets in an innings on three occasions and took a record twelve wickets in a match when he ripped through the Zimbabwean batting line up in January 2005 taking 7/95 in the first innings and another five in the second. He was also impressive during the First Test against Australia in April 2006 where he took three wickets.

HASAN, Mohammad Zakir
Born: September 1, 1972
Batting: Right handed
Bowling: Right arm medium-fast

One Day Internationals
ODI Career: 1997-98
ODIs Played: 2

ODI Batting
Innings:	1	Runs:	0
Highest Score:	0	Average:	0.00
No. 50s:	0	No. 100s:	0

ODI Bowling & Fielding
Wickets:	0	Runs:	35
Best Bowling:		Average:	0.00
5 WM:	0	Catches:	0
Stumpings:	0		

A right arm pace bowler, Zakir Hasan made his ODI debut against India at Colombo during the 1997 Asia Cup series. He didn't get the opportunity to bat on debut and in his second, and last ODI, he was out first ball.

HASAN, Raqibul
Born: January 1, 1953
Batting: Right handed
Wicket Keeper

One Day Internationals
ODI Career: 1986
ODIs Played: 2

ODI Batting
Innings:	2	Runs:	17
Highest Score:	12	Average:	8.50
No. 50s:	0	No. 100s:	0

ODI Bowling & Fielding
Wickets:	0	Runs:	0
Best Bowling:		Average:	0.00
5 WM:	0	Catches:	0
Stumpings:	0		

A right hand opening batsman who opened the innings for Bangladesh in their inaugural ODI against Pakistan, at Moratuwa, in 1986.

HOSSAIN, Azhar
Born: March 15, 1964
Batting: Right handed
Bowling: Right arm off-break

One Day Internationals
ODI Career: 1988-90
ODIs Played: 7

ODI Batting
Innings:	7	Runs:	96
Highest Score:	54	Average:	13.71
No. 50s:	1	No. 100s:	0

ODI Bowling & Fielding
Wickets:	4	Runs:	209
Best Bowling:	1/20	Average:	52.25
5 WM:	0	Catches:	2
Stumpings:	0		

A right hand opening batsman and useful off break bowler, Azhar Hossain scored one fifty in his seven ODI's for Bangladesh.

HOSSAIN, Faisal

Born:	October 26, 1978
Batting:	Left handed
Bowling:	Right arm medium-fast

Tests
Test Career: 2004
Cap Number: 36
Tests Played: 1

Test Batting
Innings:	2	Runs:	7
Highest Score:	5	Average:	3.50
No. 50s:	0	No. 100s:	0

Test Bowling & Fielding
Wickets:	0	Runs:	0
Best Bowling:		Average:	0.00
5 WI:	0	10 WM:	0
Catches:	0	Stumpings:	0

One Day Internationals
ODI Career: 2004
ODIs Played: 4

ODI Batting
Innings:	4	Runs:	35
Highest Score:	17	Average:	8.75
No. 50s:	0	No. 100s:	0

ODI Bowling & Fielding
Wickets:	0	Runs:	0
Best Bowling:		Average:	0.00
5 WM:	0	Catches:	2
Stumpings:	0		

An elegant left hand batsman, Faisal Hossain played his only Test on the tour of the West Indies in 2004.

HOSSAIN, Kazi Shahadat

Born:	August 7, 1986
Batting:	Right handed
Bowling:	Right arm medium-fast

Tests
Test Career: 2005-06
Cap Number: 42
Tests Played: 7

Test Batting
Innings:	14	Runs:	55
Highest Score:	13	Average:	6.11
No. 50s:	0	No. 100s:	0

Test Bowling & Fielding
Wickets:	16	Runs:	793
Best Bowling:	5/86	Average:	49.56
5 WI:	1	10 WM:	0
Catches:	0	Stumpings:	0

One Day Internationals
ODI Career: 2006
ODIs Played: 10

ODI Batting
Innings:	4	Runs:	9
Highest Score:	5*	Average:	9.00
No. 50s:	0	No. 100s:	0

ODI Bowling & Fielding
Wickets:	11	Runs:	311
Best Bowling:	3/34	Average:	28.27
5 WM:	0	Catches:	0
Stumpings:	0		

After a forgettable Test debut against England at Lord's in 2005, Shahadat Hossain regrouped superbly to become a key strike bowler in 2006, his best effort 5/86 against Sri Lanka at Bogra. The solidly built, right arm pace bowler has shown enough to suggest that he could become a long term member of both Test and One Day teams.

HOSSAIN, Mehrab

Born:	September 22, 1978
Batting:	Right handed
Bowling:	Right arm medium

Tests
Test Career: 2000-03
Cap Number: 7
Tests Played: 9

Test Batting
Innings:	18	Runs:	241
Highest Score:	71	Average:	13.38
No. 50s:	1	No. 100s:	0

Test Bowling & Fielding
Wickets:	0	Runs:	5
Best Bowling:	0/5	Average:	0.00
5 WI:	0	10 WM:	0
Catches:	6	Stumpings:	0

One Day Internationals
ODI Career: 1998-03
ODIs Played: 18

ODI Batting
Innings:	18	Runs:	449
Highest Score:	101	Average:	24.94
No. 50s:	21	No. 100s:	1

ODI Bowling & Fielding
Wickets:	0	Runs:	42
Best Bowling:		Average:	0.00
5 WM:	0	Catches:	6
Stumpings:	0		

One of three 'Hossains' to play in Bangladesh's first Test against India at Dhaka in 2000, Mehrab Hossain opened the batting with namesake Shahrir but failed to reach double figures in either innings. While his Test career was at best, modest, he was a valuable contributor in limted overs competition and has the honour of being the first Bangladesh player to score an ODI century when he scored 101 against Zimbabwe in 1999.

HOSSAIN, Mohammad Anwar

Born:	December 10, 1983
Batting:	Right handed
	Wicket Keeper

Tests
Test Career: 2002
Cap Number: 30
Tests Played: 1

Test Batting
Innings:	2	Runs:	14
Highest Score:	12	Average:	7.00
No. 50s:	0	No. 100s:	0

Test Bowling & Fielding
Wickets:	0	Runs:	0
Best Bowling:		Average:	0.00
5 WI:	0	10 WM:	0
Catches:	0	Stumpings:	0

One Day Internationals
ODI Career: 2002
ODIs Played: 1

ODI Batting

Innings:	1	Runs:	42
Highest Score:	42	Average:	42.00
No. 50s:	0	No. 100s:	0

ODI Bowling & Fielding

Wickets:	0	Runs:	0
Best Bowling:		Average:	0.00
5 WM:	0	Catches:	0
Stumpings:	0		

An injury to number one gloveman Khaled Mashud, opened the door for Anwar Hossain to make his Test debut in the first Test of the 2002 series against West Indies at Dhaka. While Hossain did not do too much wrong in his one and only Test appearance, he was merely keeping Mashud's seat warm. He impressed in his maiden ODI where he scored a solid 42 as an opener.

HOSSAIN, Mohammad Hasibul

Born:	June 3, 1977
Batting:	Right handed
Bowling:	Right arm medium-fast

Tests

Test Career:	2000-01		
Cap Number:	5		
Tests Played:	5		

Test Batting

Innings:	10	Runs:	97
Highest Score:	31	Average:	10.77
No. 50s:	0	No. 100s:	0

Test Bowling & Fielding

Wickets:	6	Runs:	571
Best Bowling:	2/125	Average:	95.16
5 WI:	0	10 WM:	0
Catches:	1	Stumpings:	0

One Day Internationals

ODI Career:	1995-04		
ODIs Played:	32		

ODI Batting

Innings:	26	Runs:	172
Highest Score:	21*	Average:	8.60
No. 50s:	0	No. 100s:	0

ODI Bowling & Fielding

Wickets:	29	Runs:	1,338
Best Bowling:	4/56	Average:	46.13
5 WM:	0	Catches:	0
Stumpings:	0		

A right arm pace bowler, Hasibul Hossain opened the bowling in Bangladesh's inaugural Test against India at Dhaka in 2000, but didn't capture a wicket until the second innings where he took the only wicket, that of opener Ramesh, as India cruised to a nine wicket victory. A member of the 1999 World Cup 1999 squad, Hossain went on to become Bangladesh's leading wicket taker in ODI competition.

HOSSAIN, Mohammad Nazmul

Born:	October 5, 1987
Batting:	Right handed
Bowling:	Right arm medium-fast

Tests

Test Career:	2004		
Cap Number:	40		
Tests Played:	1		

Test Batting

Innings:	2	Runs:	8
Highest Score:	8*	Average:	8.00
No. 50s:	0	No. 100s:	0

Test Bowling & Fielding

Wickets:	2	Runs:	114
Best Bowling:	2/114	Average:	57.00
5 WI:	0	10 WM:	0
Catches:	0	Stumpings:	0

One Day Internationals

ODI Career:	2006		
ODIs Played:	17		

ODI Batting

Innings:	11	Runs:	30
Highest Score:	6*	Average:	7.50
No. 50s:	0	No. 100s:	0

ODI Bowling & Fielding

Wickets:	18	Runs:	731
Best Bowling:	4/40	Average:	40.61
5 WM:	0	Catches:	4
Stumpings:	0		

A stylish right arm pace bowler, Nazmul Hossain looks to have been prematurely pigeon-holed as a limited overs specialist after being selected for just the one Test - against India at Chittagong in 2004. He has performed admirably at ODI level with a best to date performance of 4/40 and clearly has both time and potential to develop into a premier bowler for his country.

HOSSAIN, Mohammad Sanwar

Born:	August 5, 1973
Batting:	Right handed
Bowling:	Right arm off-break

Tests

Test Career:	2001-03		
Cap Number:	20		
Tests Played:	9		

Test Batting

Innings:	18	Runs:	345
Highest Score:	49	Average:	19.16
No. 50s:	0	No. 100s:	0

Test Bowling & Fielding

Wickets:	5	Runs:	310
Best Bowling:	2/128	Average:	62.00
5 WI:	0	10 WM:	0
Catches:	1	Stumpings:	0

One Day Internationals

ODI Career:	1998-03		
ODIs Played:	27		

ODI Batting

Innings:	27	Runs:	290
Highest Score:	52	Average:	11.60
No. 50s:	1	No. 100s:	0

ODI Bowling & Fielding

Wickets:	10	Runs:	327
Best Bowling:	3/49	Average:	32.70
5 WM:	0	Catches:	11
Stumpings:	0		

A middle order batsman who made an impressive 45 in his first Test outing against New Zealand at

Hamilton in 2001, Sanwar Hossain rarely recaptured his debut form and therefore struggled to cement a regular spot in the Test side.

HOSSAIN, Mohammad Shahriar

Born: June 1, 1976
Batting: Right handed

Tests
Test Career: 2000-04
Cap Number: 11
Tests Played: 3

Test Batting
Innings:	5	Runs:	99
Highest Score:	48	Average:	19.80
No. 50s:	0	No. 100s:	0

Test Bowling & Fielding
Wickets:	0	Runs:	0
Best Bowling:		Average:	0.00
5 WI:	0	10 WM:	0
Catches:	0	Stumpings:	1

One Day Internationals
ODI Career: 1997-04
ODIs Played: 20

ODI Batting
Innings:	19	Runs:	362
Highest Score:	95	Average:	19.05
No. 50s:	0	No. 100s:	0

ODI Bowling & Fielding
Wickets:	0	Runs:	0
Best Bowling:		Average:	0.00
5 WM:	0	Catches:	5
Stumpings:	0		

A right handed batsman who opened the batting with namesake Mehrab Hossain in Bangladesh's first Test match against India, at Dhaka, in 2000. Shahriar could only manage a further two Tests but became a regular member of the ODI side.

IMRAN, Tushar

Born: December 20, 1983
Batting: Right handed
Bowling: Right arm medium

Tests
Test Career: 2002-05
Cap Number: 28
Tests Played: 4

Test Batting
Innings:	8	Runs:	55
Highest Score:	28	Average:	6.87
No. 50s:	0	No. 100s:	0

Test Bowling & Fielding
Wickets:	0	Runs:	0
Best Bowling:		Average:	0.00
5 WI:	0	10 WM:	0
Catches:	1	Stumpings:	0

One Day Internationals
ODI Career: 2001-06
ODIs Played: 35

ODI Batting
Innings:	34	Runs:	545
Highest Score:	65	Average:	16.02
No. 50s:	2	No. 100s:	0

ODI Bowling & Fielding
Wickets:	1	Runs:	66
Best Bowling:	1/24	Average:	66.00
5 WM:	0	Catches:	5
Stumpings:	0		

A right hand middle order batsman, Tushar Imran, was yet another who was fast tracked onto the international arena during a bleak period in Bangladesh cricket. With a top score of 28 and a less than modest average of 6.87, the selectors retracted their initial thoughts and decided to develop young Imran through the One Day side where he has shown improvement with every match.

IQBAL KHAN, Nafees

Born: October 31, 1985
Batting: Right handed
Bowling: Right arm medium-fast

Tests
Test Career: 2004-06
Cap Number: 38
Tests Played: 11

Test Batting
Innings:	22	Runs:	518
Highest Score:	121	Average:	23.54
No. 50s:	2	No. 100s:	1

Test Bowling & Fielding
Wickets:	0	Runs:	0
Best Bowling:		Average:	0.00
5 WI:	0	10 WM:	0
Catches:	2	Stumpings:	0

One Day Internationals
ODI Career: 2003-05
ODIs Played: 16

ODI Batting
Innings:	16	Runs:	309
Highest Score:	58	Average:	19.31
No. 50s:	2	No. 100s:	0

ODI Bowling & Fielding
Wickets:	0	Runs:	0
Best Bowling:		Average:	0.00
5 WM:	0	Catches:	2
Stumpings:	0		

In early 2005, the exciting right hand opener became the seventh Bangladesh batsman to register a Test century when he took to the Zimbabwean bowling in the second Test at Dhaka. His knock of 121 went a long way to saving the match thus providing Bangladesh with their first ever series win.

ISLAM, Mohammad Aminul

Born: April 1, 1975
Batting: Right handed
Bowling: Right arm medium-fast

One Day Internationals
ODI Career: 1999
ODIs Played: 1

ODI Batting
Innings:	1	Runs:	1
Highest Score:	1	Average:	1.00
No. 50s:	0	No. 100s:	0

ODI Bowling & Fielding			
Wickets:	1	Runs:	33
Best Bowling:	1/33	Average:	1.00
5 WM:	0	Catches:	0
Stumpings:	0		

An energetic right arm pace bowler from Rajshahi who played just the sole ODI against Kenya at Dhaka in 1999.

ISLAM, Mohammad Aminul

Born: February 2, 1968
Batting: Right handed
Bowling: Right arm off-break

Tests
Test Career: 2000-02
Cap Number: 3
Tests Played: 13

Test Batting
Innings:	26	Runs:	530
Highest Score:	145	Average:	21.20
No. 50s:	2	No. 100s:	1

Test Bowling & Fielding
Wickets:	1	Runs:	149
Best Bowling:	1/66	Average:	149.00
5 WI:	0	10 WM:	0
Catches:	5	Stumpings:	0

One Day Internationals
ODI Career: 1988-02
ODIs Played: 39

ODI Batting
Innings:	39	Runs:	794
Highest Score:	70	Average:	23.35
No. 50s:	3	No. 100s:	0

ODI Bowling & Fielding
Wickets:	7	Runs:	411
Best Bowling:	3/57	Average:	58.71
5 WM:	0	Catches:	13
Stumpings:	0		

Some twelve years after first representing Bangladesh at One Day level, the diminutive Aminul Islam made an impact in Bangladesh's inaugural Test against India at Dhaka in 2000, when he carved out a gruelling 145 on debut. While this was to be a historic moment in Bangladesh cricket, it was to remain Aminul's only Test century in his 13 Tests. Previously he had captained Bangladesh in the 1999 World Cup.

ISLAM, Mohammad Manjural

Born: November 7, 1979
Batting: Left handed
Bowling: Left arm medium-fast

Tests
Test Career: 2001-04
Cap Number: 13
Tests Played: 17

Test Batting
Innings:	33	Runs:	81
Highest Score:	21	Average:	3.63
No. 50s:	0	No. 100s:	0

Test Bowling & Fielding
Wickets:	28	Runs:	1,605
Best Bowling:	6/81	Average:	53.32
5 WI:	1	10 WM:	0
Catches:	4	Stumpings:	0

One Day Internationals
ODI Career: 1999-03
ODIs Played: 34

ODI Batting
Innings:	22	Runs:	53
Highest Score:	13	Average:	5.80
No. 50s:	0	No. 100s:	0

ODI Bowling & Fielding
Wickets:	24	Runs:	1,284
Best Bowling:	3/37	Average:	53.50
5 WM:	0	Catches:	8
Stumpings:	0		

A member of the 1999 World Cup squad, left-arm seamer Manjural Islam's Test debut was one of the most memorable by a Bangladesh bowler where he took an incredible 6/71 against Zimbabwe in 2001.

ISLAM, Mohammad Rafiqul

Born: November 7, 1977
Batting: Right handed

Tests
Test Career: 2002
Cap Number: 29
Tests Played: 1

Test Batting
Innings:	2	Runs:	7
Highest Score:	6	Average:	3.50
No. 50s:	0	No. 100s:	0

Test Bowling & Fielding
Wickets:	0	Runs:	0
Best Bowling:		Average:	0.00
5 WI:	0	10 WM:	0
Catches:	0	Stumpings:	0

One Day Internationals
ODI Career: 2002
ODIs Played: 1

ODI Batting
Innings:	1	Runs:	0
Highest Score:	0	Average:	0.00
No. 50s:	0	No. 100s:	0

ODI Bowling & Fielding
Wickets:	0	Runs:	0
Best Bowling:		Average:	0.00
5 WM:	0	Catches:	0
Stumpings:	0		

A right arm batsman, Rafiqul Islam was called up to play just the solitary Test and ODI - both against South Africa in 2002.

ISLAM, Saiful

Born: April 14, 1969
Batting: Right handed
Bowling: Right arm medium

One Day Internationals
ODI Career: 1990-97
ODIs Played: 7

ODI Batting
Innings:	4	Runs:	37
Highest Score:	22*	Average:	18.50
No. 50s:	0	No. 100s:	0

ODI Bowling & Fielding
Wickets:	6	Runs:	256
Best Bowling:	4/36	Average:	42.66
5 WM:	0	Catches:	0
Stumpings:	0		

A right arm medium pacer who opened the bowling for Bangladesh in ODI competition. Islam's batting average of 18.50 suggests that he was probably a touch better than what his usual 'number 11' position suggested.

ISLAM RANA, Qazi Manjural

Born: May 4, 1984
Batting: Left handed
Bowling: Left arm off-break

Tests

Test Career: 2004
Cap Number: 35
Tests Played: 6

Test Batting

Innings:	11	Runs:	257
Highest Score:	69	Average:	25.70
No. 50s:	1	No. 100s:	0

Test Bowling & Fielding

Wickets:	5	Runs:	401
Best Bowling:	3/84	Average:	80.20
5 WI:	0	10 WM:	0
Catches:	3	Stumpings:	0

One Day Internationals

ODI Career: 2003-06
ODIs Played: 25

ODI Batting

Innings:	21	Runs:	331
Highest Score:	63	Average:	20.68
No. 50s:	1	No. 100s:	0

ODI Bowling & Fielding

Wickets:	23	Runs:	689
Best Bowling:	4/34	Average:	29.95
5 WM:	0	Catches:	6
Stumpings:	0		

A left arm off break bowler, Manjural Islam Rana made his Test debut against Zimbabwe at Harare in 2004. Although he took just two wickets for the match, Islam Rana unexpectedly impressed with his batting scoring in the thirties in both innings. And while his batting has been promising for an aspiring all-rounder, having scored 50's at both forms of the game, it is form with the ball, or lack thereof, that has kept him out of the Test eleven.

JUBAIR, Talha

Born: December 10, 1985
Batting: Right handed
Bowling: Right arm medium

Tests

Test Career: 2002-04
Cap Number: 25
Tests Played: 7

Test Batting

Innings:	14	Runs:	52
Highest Score:	31	Average:	6.50
No. 50s:	0	No. 100s:	0

Test Bowling & Fielding

Wickets:	14	Runs:	771
Best Bowling:	3/135	Average:	55.07
5 WI:	0	10 WM:	0
Catches:	1	Stumpings:	0

One Day Internationals

ODI Career: 2002-03
ODIs Played: 6

ODI Batting

Innings:	5	Runs:	5
Highest Score:	4*	Average:	2.50
No. 50s:	0	No. 100s:	0

ODI Bowling & Fielding

Wickets:	6	Runs:	255
Best Bowling:	4/65	Average:	42.50
5 WM:	0	Catches:	1
Stumpings:	0		

Arguably the fastest bowler to represent Bangladesh, the slightly built Talha Jubair opened the bowling in his Test debut against Sri Lanka at Colombo in 2002. He struggled with consistency and was rather expensive over his short career.

KABIR, Mohammad Alamgir

Born: January 10, 1981
Batting: Right handed
Bowling: Right arm medium-fast

Tests

Test Career: 2002-04
Cap Number: 22
Tests Played: 3

Test Batting

Innings:	5	Runs:	8
Highest Score:	4	Average:	2.00
No. 50s:	0	No. 100s:	0

Test Bowling & Fielding

Wickets:	0	Runs:	221
Best Bowling:		Average:	0.00
5 WI:	0	10 WM:	0
Catches:	0	Stumpings:	0

A right arm medium pacer who had quite a forgetful debut against Sri Lanka at Colombo in 2002 where he made a 'pair' and took 0/82. Even though Kabir remained wicket-less after three Test appearances, his line and length did improve in his last two Tests.

KAMAL, Shaker Ahmed

Born: June 15, 1977
Batting: Right handed
Bowling: Right arm medium-fast

One Day Internationals

ODI Career: 1999
ODIs Played: 1

ODI Batting

Innings:	1	Runs:	11
Highest Score:	11	Average:	11.00
No. 50s:	0	No. 100s:	0

ODI Bowling & Fielding

Wickets:	1	Runs:	39
Best Bowling:	1/39	Average:	39.00
5 WM:	0	Catches:	0
Stumpings:	0		

Nicknamed the 'Colonel', Shaker Ahmed Kamal was selected in just the one ODI against the West Indies at Dhaka in 1999 where he took the wicket of opener Sherwin Campbell.

KAPALI, Alok

Born:	January 1, 1984
Batting:	Right handed
Bowling:	Right arm leg-break

Tests

Test Career:	2002-06
Cap Number:	26
Tests Played:	17

Test Batting

Innings:	34	Runs:	584
Highest Score:	85	Average:	17.69
No. 50s:	2	No. 100s:	0

Test Bowling & Fielding

Wickets:	6	Runs:	709
Best Bowling:	3/3	Average:	118.16
5 WI:	0	10 WM:	0
Catches:	5	Stumpings:	0

One Day Internationals

ODI Career:	2002-06
ODIs Played:	53

ODI Batting

Innings:	50	Runs:	931
Highest Score:	89*	Average:	19.80
No. 50s:	5	No. 100s:	0

ODI Bowling & Fielding

Wickets:	15	Runs:	783
Best Bowling:	2/29	Average:	58.20
5 WM:	0	Catches:	21
Stumpings:	0		

For a bowler who averages over 118 runs per Test wicket, it is quite ironic that leg spinner Alok Kapali became the first Bangladesh bowler to take a Test match 'hat trick' when he captured a record breaking 3/3 against Pakistan at Peshawar in 2003. Touted as an all rounder, Kapali has scored fifties in both forms of the game but it will be his form with the ball that will determine if he is to be recalled to the Test arena.

KHAN, Mohammad Akram Hussain

Born:	November 1, 1968
Batting:	Right handed
Bowling:	Right arm medium

Tests

Test Career:	2000-03
Cap Number:	1
Tests Played:	8

Test Batting

Innings:	16	Runs:	259
Highest Score:	44	Average:	16.18
No. 50s:	0	No. 100s:	0

Test Bowling & Fielding

Wickets:	0	Runs:	0
Best Bowling:		Average:	0.00
5 WI:	0	10 WM:	0
Catches:	3	Stumpings:	0

One Day Internationals

ODI Career:	1998-03
ODIs Played:	44

ODI Batting

Innings:	44	Runs:	976
Highest Score:	65	Average:	23.23
No. 50s:	0	No. 100s:	0

ODI Bowling & Fielding

Wickets:	0	Runs:	138
Best Bowling:		Average:	0.00
5 WM:	0	Catches:	8
Stumpings:	0		

A burly middle order batsman, Akram Khan was vice captain of Bangladesh's World Cup side of 1999 and later went on to captain his country in limited overs competition. Khan played in Bangladesh's inaugural Test against India in 2000, and thus has the honour of the holding the 'number one' Test cap. Played just the eight Tests but represented Bangladesh in over 40 ODI's.

MAHMUD, Khaled

Born:	July 26, 1971
Batting:	Right handed
Bowling:	Right arm medium

Tests

Test Career:	2001-03
Cap Number:	18
Tests Played:	12

Test Batting

Innings:	23	Runs:	266
Highest Score:	45	Average:	12.09
No. 50s:	0	No. 100s:	0

Test Bowling & Fielding

Wickets:	13	Runs:	832
Best Bowling:	4/37	Average:	64.00
5 WI:	0	10 WM:	0
Catches:	2	Stumpings:	0

One Day Internationals

ODI Career:	1998-06
ODIs Played:	77

ODI Batting

Innings:	72	Runs:	991
Highest Score:	50	Average:	14.36
No. 50s:	1	No. 100s:	0

ODI Bowling & Fielding

Wickets:	67	Runs:	2,865
Best Bowling:	4/19	Average:	42.76
5 WM:	0	Catches:	17
Stumpings:	0		

A right-arm seam blower, Khaled Mahmud was an integral part of Bangladesh's first ever ODI victory - against a Test playing nation - when they defeated Pakistan by 62 runs during their 1999 World Cup encounter. Mahmud made a handy 27 coming in at number seven, and then followed up with 3/31 taking the vital wickets of top line batsmen Shahid Afridi, Inzamam-ul-Huq and Salim Malik and thus earning the 'Man of the Match' award. The victory no doubt helped Bangladesh's cause to be elevated Test status, which was granted a year later. In 2001, Mahmud made his Test debut in a rain interrupted match against Zimbabwe at Dhaka. A popular member of the side, Mahmud succeeded wicket-keeper Khaled Mashud as Bangladesh captain after the 2003 World Cup. He captained his country in eleven Tests for no victories and his own form waned. By the end of 2003, Mahmud was dropped and retired. He reversed his decision not long after and has been a regular member of the One Day side ever since. He slowly started to regain form and took a career-best 4/19 against Zimbabwe in early 2004, but whether he gets another chance at Test level is debatable.

MASHUD, Khaled

Born: February 8, 1976
Batting: Right handed
Wicket Keeper

Tests
Test Career:	2000-06		
Cap Number:	6		
Tests Played:	41		

Test Batting
Innings:	79	Runs:	1,361
Highest Score:	103*	Average:	19.44
No. 50s:	3	No. 100s:	1

Test Bowling & Fielding
Wickets:	0	Runs:	0
Best Bowling:		Average:	0.00
5 WI:	0	10 WM:	0
Catches:	75	Stumpings:	8

One Day Internationals
ODI Career:	1995-06		
ODIs Played:	112		

ODI Batting
Innings:	102	Runs:	1,671
Highest Score:	71*	Average:	21.42
No. 50s:	7	No. 100s:	0

ODI Bowling & Fielding
Wickets:	0	Runs:	0
Best Bowling:		Average:	0.00
5 WM:	0	Catches:	73
Stumpings:	27		

Bangladesh's first Test wicket-keeper, Khaled Mashud made an impressive debut in his country's inaugural Test against India at Dhaka in 2000 when he scored 32 in the first innings followed up with 21 not out in the second. A dour competitor, Mashud was awarded the captaincy after Naimur Rahman was dumped in late 2001. He led Bangladesh during the 2003 World Cup but resigned from the post shortly afterwards. Over the years he forged a reputation as a quality wicketkeeper and handy batsman scoring three fifties and a match saving century against the West Indies at St Lucia in 2004 where he helped secure a draw in Bangladesh's first-ever Test in the Caribbean. Mashud has also performed well at ODI level having clocked up seven fifties including a memorable 71 not out against Australia in the final of the Nat West series in 2005.

MONIR, Anwar Hossain

Born: December 31, 1981
Batting: Right handed
Bowling: Right arm medium-fast

Tests
Test Career:	2003-05		
Cap Number:	32		
Tests Played:	3		

Test Batting
Innings:	6	Runs:	22
Highest Score:	13	Average:	7.33
No. 50s:	0	No. 100s:	0

Test Bowling & Fielding
Wickets:	0	Runs:	307
Best Bowling:		Average:	0.00
5 WI:	0	10 WM:	0
Catches:	0	Stumpings:	0

One Day Internationals
ODI Career:	2002		
ODIs Played:	1		

ODI Batting
Innings:	1	Runs:	0
Highest Score:	0*	Average:	0.00
No. 50s:	0	No. 100s:	0

ODI Bowling & Fielding
Wickets:	0	Runs:	45
Best Bowling:	0/45	Average:	0.00
5 WM:	0	Catches:	0
Stumpings:	0		

An energetic medium pacer who made his Test debut against Australia at Cairns, North Queensland, in 2003. Monir did not claim a wicket in his three Test and solitary ODI appearances.

MONIRUZZAMAN, Al Mohammad

Born: October 25, 1976
Batting: Right handed

One Day Internationals
ODI Career:	2003		
ODIs Played:	2		

ODI Batting
Innings:	2	Runs:	1
Highest Score:	1	Average:	0.50
No. 50s:	0	No. 100s:	0

ODI Bowling & Fielding
Wickets:	0	Runs:	0
Best Bowling:		Average:	0.00
5 WM:	0	Catches:	0
Stumpings:	0		

A right hand batsman, Moniruzzaman was selected for two ODI matches against England in 2003 when Bangladesh decided to 'rest' their premier batsman Habibul Bashar. Moniruzzaman made a duck on debut and just one in his second and last ODI.

MORTAZA, Mashrafe Bin

Born: January 5, 1983
Batting: Right handed
Bowling: Right arm medium-fast

Tests
Test Career:	2001-06		
Cap Number:	19		
Tests Played:	20		

Test Batting
Innings:	37	Runs:	283
Highest Score:	48	Average:	8.57
No. 50s:	0	No. 100s:	0

Test Bowling & Fielding

Wickets:	50	Runs:	1,871
Best Bowling:	4/60	Average:	37.42
5 WI:	0	10 WM:	0
Catches:	0	Stumpings:	0

One Day Internationals

ODI Career:	2001-06		
ODIs Played:	34		

ODI Batting

Innings:	28	Runs:	307
Highest Score:	44*	Average:	13.34
No. 50s:	0	No. 100s:	0

ODI Bowling & Fielding

Wickets:	37	Runs:	1,434
Best Bowling:	3/38	Average:	38.75
5 WM:	0	Catches:	10
Stumpings:	0		

A fiery right arm pace bowler Mashrafe bin Mortaza took four wickets on his Test debut against Zimbabwe at Dhaka in 2001. Mortaza has added a bit of sting to the Bangladesh bowling attack in both Tests and ODI's and with a highest score of 48 in Tests and 44 not out in limited overs competition, he has proven to be a more than capable lower order batsman.

MUNTASIR RAHMAN, Fahim

Born:	November 1, 1980
Batting:	Right handed
Bowling:	Right arm off-break

Tests

Test Career:	2002		
Cap Number:	21		
Tests Played:	3		

Test Batting

Innings:	6	Runs:	52
Highest Score:	33	Average:	8.66
No. 50s:	0	No. 100s:	0

Test Bowling & Fielding

Wickets:	5	Runs:	342
Best Bowling:	3/131	Average:	68.40
5 WI:	0	10 WM:	0
Catches:	1	Stumpings:	0

One Day Internationals

ODI Career:	2001-02		
ODIs Played:	3		

ODI Batting

Innings:	3	Runs:	6
Highest Score:	5	Average:	3.00
No. 50s:	0	No. 100s:	0

ODI Bowling & Fielding

Wickets:	0	Runs:	111
Best Bowling:		Average:	0.00
5 WM:	0	Catches:	2
Stumpings:	0		

Off-spinner Fahim Muntasir was off to quite a forgettable debut against Pakistan at Dhaka in 2002, having made a duck in the first innings and taking 0/109 when plying his trade with the ball. He somewhat atoned in the second innings when he made a dour 33, batting at number nine.

NAFEES AHMED, Shahriar

Born:	January 25, 1986
Batting:	Left handed

Tests

Test Career:	2005-06		
Cap Number:	43		
Tests Played:	6		

Test Batting

Innings:	12	Runs:	402
Highest Score:	138	Average:	55.60
No. 50s:	2	No. 100s:	1

Test Bowling & Fielding

Wickets:	0	Runs:	0
Best Bowling:		Average:	0.00
5 WI:	0	10 WM:	0
Catches:	6	Stumpings:	0

One Day Internationals

ODI Career:	2005-06		
ODIs Played:	17		

ODI Batting

Innings:	17	Runs:	496
Highest Score:	91	Average:	29.17
No. 50s:	4	No. 100s:	0

ODI Bowling & Fielding

Wickets:	0	Runs:	0
Best Bowling:		Average:	0.00
5 WM:	0	Catches:	5
Stumpings:	0		

An exciting prospect, Shahriar Nafees is a left hand opening batsman who made his Test debut against Sri Lanka at Colombo in 2005. Although he made just three and 13 in both innings on debut, it didn't take long for the youngster to find his true form as he scored a half century in his second Test. But it was against the highly regarded Australians at Fatullah, in early 2006, that captured the attention of the cricketing fraternity when the aspiring batsman scored a magnificent 138 - his maiden Test century and third highest score by a Bangladesh batsman. With a Test average of just over 55, Shahriar Nafees has the opportunity to establish himself as not just a regular Test player but also one of the Bangladesh's finest openers at both forms of the game.

NOUSHER, Gholam Mohammad

Born:	October 6, 1964
Batting:	Left handed
Bowling:	Left arm medium

One Day Internationals

ODI Career:	1986-90		
ODIs Played:	9		

ODI Batting

Innings:	3	Runs:	8
Highest Score:	4	Average:	8.00
No. 50s:	0	No. 100s:	0

ODI Bowling & Fielding

Wickets:	5	Runs:	314
Best Bowling:	1/27	Average:	62.80
5 WM:	0	Catches:	0
Stumpings:	0		

Nousher was a left arm medium pace bowler who opened the bowling in Bangladesh's first ever (official) One Day International against Pakistan at

Moratuwa. He took just five wickets in his nine matches.

OMAR, Mohammad Javed
Born: November 25, 1976
Batting: Right handed
Bowling: Right arm leg-break

Tests
Test Career: 2001-06
Cap Number: 12
Tests Played: 35

Test Batting
Innings:	70	Runs:	1,525
Highest Score:	119	Average:	22.10
No. 50s:	6	No. 100s:	1

Test Bowling & Fielding
Wickets:	0	Runs:	12
Best Bowling:	0/12	Average:	0.00
5 WI:	0	10 WM:	0
Catches:	7	Stumpings:	0

One Day Internationals
ODI Career: 1995-06
ODIs Played: 50

ODI Batting
Innings:	50	Runs:	1,142
Highest Score:	85*	Average:	24.82
No. 50s:	9	No. 100s:	0

ODI Bowling & Fielding
Wickets:	0	Runs:	0
Best Bowling:		Average:	0.00
5 WM:	0	Catches:	9
Stumpings:	0		

Javed Omar burst onto the Test scene when he made his debut against Zimbabwe at Bulawayo in 2001. The highly talented opener scored 62 in the first innings and then carried his bat in the second with a superb 85 not out. He became only the third player in Test history to do so and his effort earned him the 'Man of the Match' award even though Bangladesh were thrashed by an innings and 32 runs. A few months later he scored his maiden Test century, 119 against Pakistan, at Peshawar. An entertaining batsmen at both versions of the game, Omar has represented Bangladesh on 50 occasions at ODI level.

RAFIQUE, Mohammad
Born: May 9, 1970
Batting: Left handed
Bowling: Left arm slow

Tests
Test Career: 2000-06
Cap Number: 8
Tests Played: 26

Test Batting
Innings:	50	Runs:	982
Highest Score:	111	Average:	21.82
No. 50s:	4	No. 100s:	1

Test Bowling & Fielding
Wickets:	87	Runs:	3,184
Best Bowling:	6/77	Average:	36.59
5 WI:	7	10 WM:	0
Catches:	6	Stumpings:	0

One Day Internationals
ODI Career: 1995-06
ODIs Played: 95

ODI Batting
Innings:	85	Runs:	977
Highest Score:	77	Average:	13.56
No. 50s:	2	No. 100s:	0

ODI Bowling & Fielding
Wickets:	89	Runs:	3,532
Best Bowling:	5/47	Average:	39.18
5 WM:	0	Catches:	22
Stumpings:	0		

Bangladesh's Cricketer of the Year for 2004/05, Mohammad Rafique was a member of Bangladesh's inaugural Test side against India at Dhaka in 2001. A slow but tidy left arm bowler, Rafique was one of the better performers on both his, and his country's, Test debut where he captured 3/117 and scored 22 as a tail ender. Shortly afterwards, Rafique became yet another bowler from the sub continent to have their bowling action questioned but after an initial inquiry, he was cleared to play. After this short hiccup, Rafique went on to become one of Bangladesh's most prominent bowlers taking five wickets in an innings on seven occasions - his career best 6/77 against South Africa in 2003. He was also a key contributor in Bangladesh's first ever Test win taking 5/65 against Zimbabwe at Chittagong. While primarily a bowler, Rafique has performed admirably with the bat having scored four fifties and an inspiring century - 111 against the West Indies in 2004 when coming in at number nine. Rafique's talent is not limited to the Test arena as he has been a regular member of Bangladesh's One Day team over the duration of his career.

RAHIM, Mohammad Mushfiqur
Born: September 1, 1988
Batting: Right handed
Wicket Keeper

Tests
Test Career: 2005-06
Cap Number: 41
Tests Played: 2

Test Batting
Innings:	4	Runs:	24
Highest Score:	19	Average:	6.00
No. 50s:	0	No. 100s:	0

Test Bowling & Fielding
Wickets:	0	Runs:	0
Best Bowling:		Average:	0.00
5 WI:	0	10 WM:	0
Catches:	1	Stumpings:	0

A talented young wicket-keeper who was surprisingly selected for the tour of England in 2005, Mushfiqur Rahim was only 16 years old when he made his Test debut against England at Lord's. He scored 19 in the first innings and while he didn't get the opportunity to don the keeper's gloves in either of his two Tests, as he was selected as a reserve keeper to Khaled Mashud, the youngster definitely profited from the experience and is rated an exciting prospect.

RAHMAN, Anisur
Born: March 1, 1971
Batting: Left handed
Bowling: Left arm medium-fast

One Day Internationals
ODI Career: 1995-98
ODIs Played: 2

ODI Batting
Innings:	2	Runs:	2
Highest Score:	2	Average:	1.00
No. 50s:	0	No. 100s:	0

ODI Bowling & Fielding
Wickets:	0	Runs:	68
Best Bowling:		Average:	0.00
5 WM:	0	Catches:	0
Stumpings:	0		

A left arm opening pace bowler who didn't capture a wicket in his two ODI appearances. Rahman made his debut against India at Sharjah in 1995.

RAHMAN, Hafizur
Batting: Right handed
Wicket Keeper

One Day Internationals
ODI Career: 1986
ODIs Played: 2

ODI Batting
Innings:	1	Runs:	8
Highest Score:	8	Average:	8.00
No. 50s:	0	No. 100s:	0

ODI Bowling & Fielding
Wickets:	0	Runs:	0
Best Bowling:		Average:	0.00
5 WM:	0	Catches:	2
Stumpings:	0		

Hafizur Rahman officially became Bangladesh's first ever wicket-keeper at international level when he was selected to represent his country in their inaugural ODI against Pakistan at Moratuwa in 1986. Rahman took just the one catch behind the stumps on his debut - his victim, Pakistan legend Javed Miandad. He played just the one more ODI against Sri Lanka at Kandy a month later.

RAHMAN, Mafizur
Born: November 10, 1978
Batting: Right handed
Bowling: Right arm medium-fast

One Day Internationals
ODI Career: 1997
ODIs Played: 4

ODI Batting
Innings:	4	Runs:	53
Highest Score:	16	Average:	17.66
No. 50s:	0	No. 100s:	0

ODI Bowling & Fielding
Wickets:	0	Runs:	73
Best Bowling:		Average:	0.00
5 WM:	0	Catches:	1
Stumpings:	0		

A right arm fast-medium pacer, 'Munna' Rahman played four ODI's in 1997 after making his debut in an Asia Cup match against Sri Lanka at Colombo.

RAHMAN, Mahbubur
Born: February 1, 1969
Batting: Right handed
Bowling: Right arm off-break

One Day Internationals
ODI Career: 1999
ODIs Played: 1

ODI Batting
Innings:	1	Runs:	3
Highest Score:	3	Average:	3.00
No. 50s:	0	No. 100s:	0

ODI Bowling & Fielding
Wickets:	0	Runs:	0
Best Bowling:		Average:	0.00
5 WM:	0	Catches:	0
Stumpings:	0		

A middle order batsman from Mymensingh, Rahman was selected in just one ODI against Zimbabwe at Dhaka, in 1999.

RAHMAN, Mushfiqur
Born: January 1, 1980
Batting: Right handed
Bowling: Right arm medium-fast

Tests
Test Career: 2001-04
Cap Number: 15
Tests Played: 10

Test Batting
Innings:	19	Runs:	232
Highest Score:	46*	Average:	13.64
No. 50s:	0	No. 100s:	0

Test Bowling & Fielding
Wickets:	13	Runs:	823
Best Bowling:	4/65	Average:	63.30
5 WI:	0	10 WM:	0
Catches:	6	Stumpings:	0

One Day Internationals
ODI Career: 2000-04
ODIs Played: 28

ODI Batting
Innings:	25	Runs:	360
Highest Score:	49	Average:	16.36
No. 50s:	0	No. 100s:	0

ODI Bowling & Fielding
Wickets:	19	Runs:	983
Best Bowling:	2/21	Average:	51.73
5 WM:	0	Catches:	6
Stumpings:	0		

A right arm pace bowler, Mushfiqur Rahman struggled to cement a regular Test spot in his early years and was used predominantly in limited overs competition. He managed to regain his place in 2003 but his modest averages with both bat and ball make it difficult for selectors to consider him a long term proposition.

RAHMAN, Naimur

Born:	September 19, 1974
Batting:	Right handed
Bowling:	Right arm off-break

Tests

Test Career:	2000-02		
Cap Number:	9		
Tests Played:	8		

Test Batting

Innings:	15	Runs:	210
Highest Score:	48	Average:	15.00
No. 50s:	0	No. 100s:	0

Test Bowling & Fielding

Wickets:	12	Runs:	718
Best Bowling:	6/132	Average:	59.83
5 WI:	0	10 WM:	0
Catches:	4	Stumpings:	0

One Day Internationals

ODI Career:	1995-02		
ODIs Played:	29		

ODI Batting

Innings:	27	Runs:	488
Highest Score:	47	Average:	19.52
No. 50s:	0	No. 100s:	0

ODI Bowling & Fielding

Wickets:	10	Runs:	904
Best Bowling:	2/51	Average:	90.40
5 WM:	0	Catches:	7
Stumpings:	0		

The tiny but stocky off-break bowler, Naimur 'Durjoy' Rahman became Bangladesh's first Test captain when he led the side in their inaugural match against India at Dhaka in 2000. He led from the front taking a career best 6/132 on debut, which included the prize scalps of Tendulkar and Ganguly. Rahman captained his country in seven Tests but was replaced by wicket-keeper Khaled Mashud after Bangladesh's poor showing against Zimbabwe on home soil in 2001.

RAHMAN, Samiur

Batting:	Right handed
Bowling:	Right arm medium-fast

One Day Internationals

ODI Career:	1986		
ODIs Played:	2		

ODI Batting

Innings:	2	Runs:	4
Highest Score:	4	Average:	2.00
No. 50s:	0	No. 100s:	0

ODI Bowling & Fielding

Wickets:	0	Runs:	0
Best Bowling:		Average:	0.00
5 WM:	0	Catches:	1
Stumpings:	0		

A pace bowler who opened the bowling with Gholam Nousher in Bangladesh's inaugural ODI against Pakistan in 1986, at Moratuwa. Rahman didn't take a wicket but did well to contain the star studded Pakistani batting line up with his 0/15 from seven overs.

RAHMAN, Shaheedur

Batting:	Right handed

One Day Internationals

ODI Career:	1986		
ODIs Played:	2		

ODI Batting

Innings:	2	Runs:	62
Highest Score:	37	Average:	31.00
No. 50s:	0	No. 100s:	0

ODI Bowling & Fielding

Wickets:	0	Runs:	0
Best Bowling:		Average:	0.00
5 WM:	0	Catches:	0
Stumpings:	0		

A capable middle order batsman, Shaheedur Rahman top scored with 37 in Bangladesh's inaugural ODI against Pakistan at Moratuwa in 1986. He followed up with a handy 25 against Sri Lanka in Bangladesh's next match showing plenty of poise against a formidable pace attack.

RASEL, Syed

Born:	July 3, 1984
Batting:	Left handed
Bowling:	Left arm medium-fast

Tests

Test Career:	2005-06		
Cap Number:	44		
Tests Played:	4		

Test Batting

Innings:	8	Runs:	30
Highest Score:	19	Average:	5.00
No. 50s:	0	No. 100s:	0

Test Bowling & Fielding

Wickets:	9	Runs:	360
Best Bowling:	4/129	Average:	40.00
5 WI:	0	10 WM:	0
Catches:	0	Stumpings:	0

One Day Internationals

ODI Career:	2005-06		
ODIs Played:	11		

ODI Batting

Innings:	6	Runs:	26
Highest Score:	15	Average:	5.20
No. 50s:	0	No. 100s:	0

ODI Bowling & Fielding

Wickets:	15	Runs:	396
Best Bowling:	3/28	Average:	26.40
5 WM:	0	Catches:	3
Stumpings:	0		

A left arm pace bowler with the ability to swing the ball, Syed Rasel was selected on the tour of Sri Lanka in 2005 on the back of several eye-catching performances at domestic level. He took a respectable 4/129 on debut where he was given the new ball, and has since been a valuable addition to the One Day squad. Rasel's genuine pace and natural ability suggests that he will be persevered with and could become a permanent member of Bangladesh's bowling attack.

RASHID, Mohammad Harunur

Born: November 30, 1968
Batting: Right handed
Bowling: Right arm leg-break

One Day Internationals

ODI Career: 1988
ODIs Played: 2

ODI Batting

Innings:	2	Runs:	0
Highest Score:	0	Average:	0.00
No. 50s:	0	No. 100s:	0

ODI Bowling & Fielding

Wickets:	0	Runs:	0
Best Bowling:		Average:	0.00
5 WM:	0	Catches:	0
Stumpings:	0		

A right hand opening batsman from Mymensingh who failed to trouble the scorers in both his ODI appearances in 1988.

RASHID, Mohammad Niamur

Born: January 1, 1975
Batting: Right handed
Bowling: Right arm medium-fast

One Day Internationals

ODI Career: 1999
ODIs Played: 2

ODI Batting

Innings:	2	Runs:	5
Highest Score:	4	Average:	5.00
No. 50s:	0	No. 100s:	0

ODI Bowling & Fielding

Wickets:	1	Runs:	66
Best Bowling:	1/46	Average:	66.00
5 WM:	0	Catches:	1
Stumpings:	0		

Niamur Rashid was a right arm pace bowler who on debut, took one wicket that of Zimbabwean great Andy Flower.

RAZZAK, Abdur

Born: June 15, 1982
Batting: Left handed
Bowling: Left arm off-break

Tests

Test Career: 2006
Cap Number: 45
Tests Played: 1

Test Batting

Innings:	2	Runs:	15
Highest Score:	15	Average:	7.50
No. 50s:	0	No. 100s:	0

Test Bowling & Fielding

Wickets:	0	Runs:	99
Best Bowling:		Average:	0.00
5 WI:	0	10 WM:	0
Catches:	0	Stumpings:	0

One Day Internationals

ODI Career: 2004-06
ODIs Played: 14

ODI Batting

Innings:	11	Runs:	45
Highest Score:	21	Average:	7.50
No. 50s:	0	No. 100s:	0

ODI Bowling & Fielding

Wickets:	18	Runs:	482
Best Bowling:	3/17	Average:	26.77
5 WM:	0	Catches:	1
Stumpings:	0		

A tallish, left arm off spinner who was tried at one day level prior to making his Test debut against Australia at Chittagong in 2006. Although wicketless, the 24 year old Razak has the goods to develop into a regular Test player.

RAZZAK, Zahid

Batting: Right handed

One Day Internationals

ODI Career: 1988-90
ODIs Played: 3

ODI Batting

Innings:	3	Runs:	14
Highest Score:	6	Average:	4.66
No. 50s:	0	No. 100s:	0

ODI Bowling & Fielding

Wickets:	0	Runs:	0
Best Bowling:		Average:	0.00
5 WM:	0	Catches:	0
Stumpings:	0		

A right hand middle order batsman who made his ODI debut against India at Chittagong in 1988.

SALEH ALAM, Rajin

Born: January 20, 1983
Batting: Right handed
Bowling: Right arm off-break

Tests

Test Career: 2003-06
Cap Number: 33
Tests Played: 17

Test Batting

Innings:	33	Runs:	930
Highest Score:	89	Average:	29.06
No. 50s:	6	No. 100s:	0

Test Bowling & Fielding

Wickets:	2	Runs:	244
Best Bowling:	1/9	Average:	122.00
5 WI:	0	10 WM:	0
Catches:	11	Stumpings:	0

One Day Internationals

ODI Career: 2003-06
ODIs Played: 37

ODI Batting

Innings:	37	Runs:	875
Highest Score:	108*	Average:	24.30
No. 50s:	5	No. 100s:	1

ODI Bowling & Fielding

Wickets:	9	Runs:	400
Best Bowling:	3/48	Average:	44.44
5 WM:	0	Catches:	8
Stumpings:	0		

Since making his Test debut against Pakistan in Karachi in 2003, Rajin Saleh has gone from strength to strength. Alongside captain Habibul Bashar, Saleh is considered Bangladesh's most talented batsman. Equally adept at both forms of the game, Saleh has scored a century and five fifties at ODI level and although to date is yet to notch up his maiden Test century, his current form suggests that day is not too far away.

SALIM, Mohammad
Born: October 15, 1981
Batting: Right handed
Wicket Keeper

Tests
Test Career: 2003
Cap Number: 31
Tests Played: 2

Test Batting
Innings:	4	Runs:	49
Highest Score:	26	Average:	16.33
No. 50s:	0	No. 100s:	0

Test Bowling & Fielding
Wickets:	0	Runs:	0
Best Bowling:		Average:	0.00
5 WI:	0	10 WM:	0
Catches:	3	Stumpings:	1

One Day Internationals
ODI Career: 2003
ODIs Played: 1

ODI Batting
Innings:	1	Runs:	9
Highest Score:	9	Average:	9.00
No. 50s:	0	No. 100s:	0

ODI Bowling & Fielding
Wickets:	0	Runs:	0
Best Bowling:		Average:	0.00
5 WM:	0	Catches:	1
Stumpings:	0		

A stand in wicket-keeper, Salim performed reasonably well with both bat and ball in two Tests against South Africa in 2003.

SARKAR, Abdul Hannan
Born: December 1, 1982
Batting: Right handed
Bowling: Right arm medium

Tests
Test Career: 2002-04
Cap Number: 24
Tests Played: 17

Test Batting
Innings:	33	Runs:	662
Highest Score:	76	Average:	20.06
No. 50s:	5	No. 100s:	0

Test Bowling & Fielding
Wickets:	0	Runs:	0
Best Bowling:		Average:	0.00
5 WI:	0	10 WM:	0
Catches:	7	Stumpings:	0

One Day Internationals
ODI Career: 2002-04
ODIs Played: 20

ODI Batting
Innings:	20	Runs:	383
Highest Score:	61	Average:	19.15
No. 50s:	3	No. 100s:	0

ODI Bowling & Fielding
Wickets:	0	Runs:	13
Best Bowling:	0/13	Average:	0.00
5 WM:	0	Catches:	8
Stumpings:	0		

A dour right hand opening batsman, Hannan Sarkar scored his first of five fifties on debut when he was selected to replace regular opener Javed Omar against Sri Lanka at Colombo in 2002. Whilst a technically correct batsman, adept at playing shots on both side of the wicket, Sarkar's form after his debut was inconsistent. So much so, that he earned the distinction of being dismissed 'first ball' in consecutive Test matches, when touring the Caribbean in 2004. His Test average of just over 20, tested the resolve of the selectors thus driving them to wield the axe and drop him for the New Zealand series later that year.

SHAH, Jahangir Badsha
Batting: Right handed
Bowling: Right arm medium-fast

One Day Internationals
ODI Career: 1986-90
ODIs Played: 5

ODI Batting
Innings:	4	Runs:	16
Highest Score:	8*	Average:	8.00
No. 50s:	0	No. 100s:	0

ODI Bowling & Fielding
Wickets:	2	Runs:	172
Best Bowling:	2/23	Average:	86.00
5 WM:	0	Catches:	1
Stumpings:	0		

A right arm pace bowler, Jahangir Shah was a member of Bangladesh's inaugural One Day side that took on Pakistan in the Asia Cup at Moratuwa, in 1986. Shah took two of Bangladesh's three wickets when he captured both Mohsin Khan and Rameez Raja leg before wicket.

SHARIF, Mohammad
Born: December 12, 1985
Batting: Right handed
Bowling: Right arm medium-fast

Tests
Test Career: 2001-02
Cap Number: 14
Tests Played: 8

Test Batting
Innings:	16	Runs:	86
Highest Score:	24*	Average:	6.14
No. 50s:	0	No. 100s:	0

Test Bowling & Fielding
Wickets:	14	Runs:	911
Best Bowling:	4/98	Average:	65.07
5 WI:	0	10 WM:	0
Catches:	5	Stumpings:	0

One Day Internationals
ODI Career: 2001-02
ODIs Played: 8

ODI Batting
Innings:	8	Runs:	47
Highest Score:	13*	Average:	15.66
No. 50s:	0	No. 100s:	0

ODI Bowling & Fielding

Wickets:	9	**Runs:**	371
Best Bowling:	3/40	**Average:**	41.22
5 WM:	0	**Catches:**	1
Stumpings:	0		

A tiny but effective swing bowler, Mohammad Sharif holds a unique record of capturing the same batsman as his first wicket in both Tests and ODI's - that being Zimbabwe's Alistair Campbell. While on coincidences, Sharif played the same number of Tests as ODI's - eight - over a two year period.

England

ABEL, Robert
Born:	November 30, 1857
Batting:	Right handed
Bowling:	Right arm off-break

Tests

Test Career:	1888-1902
Cap Number:	57
Tests Played:	13

Test Batting

Innings:	22	Runs:	744
Highest Score:	132*	Average:	37.20
No. 50s:	2	No. 100s:	2

Test Bowling & Fielding

Wickets:	0	Runs:	0
Best Bowling:		Average:	0.00
5 WI:	0	10 WM:	0
Catches:	13	Stumpings:	0

Nicknamed the Guv'nor, he was a punishing batsman from Surrey with a glorious first class career that saw him amass over 30,000 first class runs. The opening batsman appeared in 13 Tests scoring a century against both Australia and South Africa. His ton against the South Africans, the first in Tests between the two nations was struck on the mats in the second Test at Cape Town in 1888/89. His Test average of 37.20 marks him as one of England's finest batsmen of the 19th century.

ABSOLOM, Charles Alfred
Born:	June 7, 1846
Batting:	Right handed
Bowling:	Right arm medium

Tests

Test Career:	1879
Cap Number:	12
Tests Played:	1

Test Batting

Innings:	2	Runs:	58
Highest Score:	52	Average:	29.00
No. 50s:	1	No. 100s:	0

Test Bowling & Fielding

Wickets:	0	Runs:	0
Best Bowling:		Average:	0.00
5 WI:	0	10 WM:	0
Catches:	0	Stumpings:	0

Chosen to tour Australia for the one off Test in 1879, the bearded all-rounder came in at number nine and rescued his side with a fine half century. It was to be his only Test appearance.

ADAMS, Christopher John
Born:	May 6, 1970
Batting:	Right handed
Bowling:	Right arm off-break

Tests

Test Career:	1999-2000
Cap Number:	598
Tests Played:	5

Test Batting

Innings:	8	Runs:	104
Highest Score:	31	Average:	13.00
No. 50s:	0	No. 100s:	0

Test Bowling & Fielding

Wickets:	1	Runs:	59
Best Bowling:	1/42	Average:	59.00
5 WI:	0	10 WM:	0
Catches:	6	Stumpings:	0

One Day Internationals

ODI Career:	1998-2000
ODIs Played:	5

ODI Batting

Innings:	4	Runs:	71
Highest Score:	42	Average:	17.75
No. 50s:	0	No. 100s:	0

ODI Bowling & Fielding

Wickets:	0	Runs:	0
Best Bowling:		Average:	0.00
5 WM:	0	Catches:	3
Stumpings:	0		

The hard hitting Sussex captain toured South Africa in 1999/2000 and could manage only 104 runs despite playing in all five Tests.

AFZAAL, Usman
Born:	June 9, 1977
Batting:	Left handed
Bowling:	Left arm off-break

Tests

Test Career:	2001
Cap Number:	606
Tests Played:	3

Test Batting

Innings:	6	Runs:	83
Highest Score:	54	Average:	16.60
No. 50s:	1	No. 100s:	0

Test Bowling & Fielding

Wickets:	1	Runs:	49
Best Bowling:	1/49	Average:	49.00
5 WI:	0	10 WM:	0
Catches:	0	Stumpings:	0

A middle order batsman and left arm off spinner who was born in Rawalpindi Pakistan. He played three Tests against the Australians in 2001, scoring 54 and dismissing Adam Gilchrist at The Oval. That performance earnt him a spot for the tour to India later that year but he wasn't selected for any of the Tests and has been on the outer ever since.

AGNEW, Jonathan Philip

Born: April 4, 1960
Batting: Right handed
Bowling: Right arm fast

Tests
Test Career: 1984-85
Cap Number: 508
Tests Played: 3

Test Batting
Innings:	4	Runs:	10
Highest Score:	5	Average:	10.00
No. 50s:	0	No. 100s:	0

Test Bowling & Fielding
Wickets:	4	Runs:	373
Best Bowling:	2/51	Average:	93.25
5 WI:	0	10 WM:	0
Catches:	0	Stumpings:	0

One Day Internationals
ODI Career: 1985
ODIs Played: 3

ODI Batting
Innings:	1	Runs:	2
Highest Score:	2*	Average:	0.00
No. 50s:	0	No. 100s:	0

ODI Bowling & Fielding
Wickets:	3	Runs:	120
Best Bowling:	3/38	Average:	40.00
5 WM:	0	Catches:	1
Stumpings:	0		

One of the most identifiable voices in the cricket media, the right arm speedster played three Tests during the mid eighties.

ALI, Kabir

Born: November 24, 1980
Batting: Right handed
Bowling: Right arm medium-fast

Tests
Test Career: 2003
Cap Number: 618
Tests Played: 1

Test Batting
Innings:	2	Runs:	10
Highest Score:	9	Average:	5.00
No. 50s:	0	No. 100s:	0

Test Bowling & Fielding
Wickets:	5	Runs:	136
Best Bowling:	3/80	Average:	27.20
5 WI:	0	10 WM:	0
Catches:	0	Stumpings:	0

One Day Internationals
ODI Career: 2003-
ODIs Played: 14

ODI Batting
Innings:	9	Runs:	93
Highest Score:	39*	Average:	15.50
No. 50s:	0	No. 100s:	0

ODI Bowling & Fielding
Wickets:	20	Runs:	682
Best Bowling:	4/45	Average:	34.10
5 WM:	0	Catches:	1
Stumpings:	0		

An accurate medium pace bowler and hard hitter with a good eye, he seems set for a long career in England's one day side. The willing worker also played a single Test against South Africa at Leeds in 2003.

ALLEN, David Arthur

Born: October 29, 1935
Batting: Right handed
Bowling: Right arm off-break

Tests
Test Career: 1960-66
Cap Number: 398
Tests Played: 39

Test Batting
Innings:	51	Runs:	918
Highest Score:	88	Average:	25.50
No. 50s:	5	No. 100s:	0

Test Bowling & Fielding
Wickets:	122	Runs:	3,779
Best Bowling:	5/30	Average:	30.97
5 WI:	4	10 WM:	0
Catches:	10	Stumpings:	0

He was one of many talented off spinners who was vying for a spot in the English side through the early 1960's. A slowish spinner who was hard to play if the wicket was taking turn, he also played a number of good Test innings coming in at eight or nine. He struggled on his first tour to the Caribbean but bounced back well by taking 13 wickets against the touring Australians in 1961. Allen's best series were on the grassless tracks in the subcontinent with his best match figures of 9/162 coming in a Test at Calcutta. His batting was often an unexpected bonus for the English. The man who averaged only 18.80 at county level scored five half tons for England including an 88 against the New Zealanders in 1966.

ALLEN, George Oswald Browning

Born: July 31, 1902
Batting: Right handed
Bowling: Right arm fast

Tests
Test Career: 1930-48
Cap Number: 255
Tests Played: 25

Test Batting
Innings:	33	Runs:	750
Highest Score:	122	Average:	24.19
No. 50s:	3	No. 100s:	1

Test Bowling & Fielding
Wickets:	81	Runs:	2,379
Best Bowling:	7/80	Average:	29.37
5 WI:	5	10 WM:	1
Catches:	20	Stumpings:	0

The Australian born Allen was a fine all-rounder for England as much respected for his sportsmanship as he was for his talent on the field He made his Test debut in 1930 in the 2nd Test against Australia at Lord's and even though he struggled with the ball he made a fighting 57 in the second innings of a game Australia won comfortably. In his very next match he scored 122 against New Zealand as part of the all-time Test record partnership for the 8th wicket with Leslie Ames. He played a key role in Australia during the 'bodyline' series taking 21 wickets and even more famously announcing his displeasure at the tactics employed by his captain Douglas Jardine. After retiring from all forms of the game in Allen chaired the Test selection panel and in 1986 was knighted as reward for a live devoted to cricket.

ALLEYNE, Mark Wayne

Born:	May 23, 1968		
Batting:	Right handed		
Bowling:	Right arm medium		
	Wicket Keeper		

One Day Internationals

ODI Career:	1999-00		
ODIs Played:	10		

ODI Batting

Innings:	8	Runs:	151
Highest Score:	53	Average:	21.57
No. 50s:	1	No. 100s:	0

ODI Bowling & Fielding

Wickets:	10	Runs:	280
Best Bowling:	3/27	Average:	28.00
5 WM:	0	Catches:	3
Stumpings:	0		

London born, Barbados raised, Mark Alleyne was a wicket-keeper by trade but played as an all-rounder in all of his ten ODI's between 1999 and 2000 while Alec Stewart or Chris Read kept wickets. His finest performance was against South Africa, at Buffalo Park in February 2000, where he scored his only ODI half century, 53, and took the wickets of Kallis, Cronje and Klusener, thus giving him 3/55 and the 'Man of the Match' award.

ALLOM, Maurice James Carrick

Born:	March 23, 1906		
Batting:	Right handed		
Bowling:	Right arm medium-fast		

Tests

Test Career:	1930-31		
Cap Number:	246		
Tests Played:	5		

Test Batting

Innings:	3	Runs:	14
Highest Score:	8*	Average:	14.00
No. 50s:	0	No. 100s:	0

Test Bowling & Fielding

Wickets:	14	Runs:	265
Best Bowling:	5/38	Average:	18.92
5 WI:	1	10 WM:	0
Catches:	0	Stumpings:	0

Whilst he played only five Tests there have been few more sensational debuts than Allom's first match at Christchurch in New Zealand. He not only took a hat-trick but followed it up with another scalp two balls later to be one of the few cricketers to have taken four wickets in the same Test over. He finished with 5/38 and though he never reached those heights again, traded off the fame from that famous debut with a number of entertaining cricket books.

ALLOTT, Paul John Walter

Born:	September 14, 1956		
Batting:	Right handed		
Bowling:	Right arm medium-fast		

Tests

Test Career:	1981-85		
Cap Number:	491		
Tests Played:	13		

Test Batting

Innings:	18	Runs:	213
Highest Score:	52*	Average:	14.20
No. 50s:	1	No. 100s:	0

Test Bowling & Fielding

Wickets:	26	Runs:	1,084
Best Bowling:	6/61	Average:	41.69
5 WI:	1	10 WM:	0
Catches:	4	Stumpings:	0

One Day Internationals

ODI Career:	1982-85		
ODIs Played:	13		

ODI Batting

Innings:	6	Runs:	15
Highest Score:	8	Average:	3.00
No. 50s:	0	No. 100s:	0

ODI Bowling & Fielding

Wickets:	15	Runs:	552
Best Bowling:	3/41	Average:	36.80
5 WM:	0	Catches:	2
Stumpings:	0		

An opening bowler from Lancashire who at 6ft 4in and with the ability to move the ball, looked set for a long international career. He made an excellent start in Test cricket, scoring a surprise 52 and taking four wickets in his debut against Australia at Old Trafford. Allott was a good trier who ultimately was just not quick enough to be considered top class. His best effort in an innings came against the West Indies in Leeds, when he claimed Desmond Haynes and Viv Richards in a haul of 6/61. Quick witted and intelligent he is now one of cricket's most respected commentators.

AMES, Leslie Ethelbert George

Born:	December 3, 1905		
Batting:	Right handed		
Bowling:	Right arm leg-break		
	Wicket Keeper		

Tests

Test Career:	1929-39		
Cap Number:	244		
Tests Played:	47		

Test Batting

Innings:	72	Runs:	2,434
Highest Score:	149	Average:	40.56
No. 50s:	7	No. 100s:	8

Test Bowling & Fielding

Wickets:	0	Runs:	0
Best Bowling:		Average:	0.00
5 WI:	0	10 WM:	0
Catches:	74	Stumpings:	23

It's been said that great English wicket keepers can be counted on one hand and if that is the case then Les Ames must surely take up one of the digits. A world class batsman in his own right he was the first true keeper batsman in the mould of modern stars such as Adam Gilchrist and Kumar Sangakkara. He toured the West Indies in 1929/30 averaging just under 60 for the series and scoring his highest Test score of 149 in Jamaica. In all Ames scored eight Test centuries including a famous 120 against the all-conquering Australians at Lord's in 1934. As a keeper he was equally effective to medium pace or the cunning spin of Hedley Verity, and whilst there may have been better gloveman to play for his country there have been precious few who were the equal as all round cricketers.

AMISS, Dennis Leslie

Born:	April 7, 1943
Batting:	Right handed

Tests

Test Career:	1966-77
Cap Number:	434
Tests Played:	50

Test Batting

Innings:	88	Runs:	3,612
Highest Score:	262*	Average:	46.30
No. 50s:	11	No. 100s:	11

Test Bowling & Fielding

Wickets:	0	Runs:	0
Best Bowling:		Average:	0.00
5 WI:	0	10 WM:	0
Catches:	24	Stumpings:	0

One Day Internationals

ODI Career:	1972-77
ODIs Played:	18

ODI Batting

Innings:	18	Runs:	859
Highest Score:	137	Average:	47.72
No. 50s:	1	No. 100s:	4

ODI Bowling & Fielding

Wickets:	0	Runs:	0
Best Bowling:		Average:	0.00
5 WM:	0	Catches:	2
Stumpings:	0		

To most Australian cricket fans Dennis Amiss was no more than Dennis Lillee's bunny, but the man who averaged 46.30 in Test cricket and played one of the finest innings in English Test history deserves far better. He made his national debut as a 23 year old against a powerhouse West Indian attack that included Hall, Griffiths and Sobers and although brave was out of his depth. It took him 13 Tests to make his first half century, but until his famous failure at the hands of Lillee there were few better top order batsmen in the world. His biggest and best knock was an undefeated 262 against the West Indies in Jamaica that denied the home side a certain victory. In the twilight of his career he was offered a lucrative World Series Cricket contract and whilst the money may have been good it was hard earned given the opener had to face the likes of D.K. Lillee, Michael Holding, Andy Roberts and Garth Le Roux on a regular basis.

ANDERSON, James Michael

Born:	July 30, 1982
Batting:	Left handed
Bowling:	Right arm medium-fast

Tests

Test Career:	2003-
Cap Number:	613
Tests Played:	13

Test Batting

Innings:	18	Runs:	89
Highest Score:	21*	Average:	14.83
No. 50s:	0	No. 100s:	0

Test Bowling & Fielding

Wickets:	41	Runs:	1,353
Best Bowling:	5/73	Average:	33.00
5 WI:	2	10 WM:	0
Catches:	4	Stumpings:	0

One Day Internationals

ODI Career:	2002-
ODIs Played:	50

ODI Batting

Innings:	19	Runs:	69
Highest Score:	12*	Average:	6.90
No. 50s:	0	No. 100s:	0

ODI Bowling & Fielding

Wickets:	75	Runs:	1,972
Best Bowling:	4/25	Average:	26.29
5 WM:	0	Catches:	11
Stumpings:	0		

An athletic fast bowler from Lancashire who has provided useful back up for the England side in recent years. Behind the likes of Harmison, Hoggard and Jones in the pecking order, he was recalled to the side for the third Test against India at Mumbai in early 2006. Anderson had a fine match taking 4/40 and 2/39 but has since suffered a back injury and hasn't played another Test.

ANDREW, Keith Vincent

Born:	December 15, 1929
Batting:	Right handed
Bowling:	Right arm leg-break
	Wicket Keeper

Tests

Test Career:	1954-63
Cap Number:	378
Tests Played:	2

Test Batting

Innings:	4	Runs:	29
Highest Score:	15	Average:	9.66
No. 50s:	0	No. 100s:	0

Test Bowling & Fielding
Wickets:	0	Runs:	0
Best Bowling:		Average:	0.00
5 WI:	0	10 WM:	0
Catches:	1	Stumpings:	0

Back up wicket keepers need boundless patience, and that's what Keith Andrew had in a two Test career that spanned almost nine years.

APPLEYARD, Robert
Born: June 27, 1924
Batting: Right handed

Tests
Test Career:	1954-56
Cap Number:	373
Tests Played:	9

Test Batting
Innings:	9	Runs:	51
Highest Score:	19*	Average:	17.00
No. 50s:	0	No. 100s:	0

Test Bowling & Fielding
Wickets:	31	Runs:	554
Best Bowling:	5/51	Average:	17.87
5 WI:	1	10 WM:	0
Catches:	4	Stumpings:	0

He overcame immense personal tragedy as a youngster when he lost his family in a murder/suicide, and then survived a bout of tuberculosis to become a fine Test cricketer. A fast finger spinner, he thrived on soft wickets taking 5/51 on debut against Pakistan at Trent Bridge in 1954. He was particularly effective on the short tour to New Zealand in 1955 taking nine wickets at less than nine runs apiece. Ill-health forced an early retirement from the game, but now in his early 80's he still lives in his native Yorkshire.

ARCHER, Alfred German
Born: December 6, 1872
Batting: Right handed
Wicket Keeper

Tests
Test Career:	1899
Cap Number:	120
Tests Played:	1

Test Batting
Innings:	2	Runs:	31
Highest Score:	24*	Average:	31.00
No. 50s:	0	No. 100s:	0

Test Bowling & Fielding
Wickets:	0	Runs:	0
Best Bowling:		Average:	0.00
5 WI:	0	10 WM:	0
Catches:	0	Stumpings:	0

Alfie Archer kept wickets for Worcestershire, but in his only Test at Cape Town in 1899 batted at number 10 and didn't stand behind the stumps.

ARMITAGE, Thomas
Born: April 25, 1848
Batting: Right handed
Bowling: Right arm medium

Tests
Test Career:	1877
Cap Number:	1
Tests Played:	2

Test Batting
Innings:	3	Runs:	33
Highest Score:	21	Average:	11.00
No. 50s:	0	No. 100s:	0

Test Bowling & Fielding
Wickets:	0	Runs:	15
Best Bowling:		Average:	0.00
5 WI:	0	10 WM:	0
Catches:	0	Stumpings:	0

A slow bowler from Yorkshire, he was a member of the English side that played in the first Test in Melbourne in 1877.

ARNOLD, Edward George
Born: November 7, 1876
Batting: Right handed
Bowling: Right arm medium-fast

Tests
Test Career:	1903-07
Cap Number:	136
Tests Played:	10

Test Batting
Innings:	15	Runs:	160
Highest Score:	40	Average:	13.33
No. 50s:	0	No. 100s:	0

Test Bowling & Fielding
Wickets:	31	Runs:	788
Best Bowling:	5/37	Average:	25.41
5 WI:	1	10 WM:	0
Catches:	8	Stumpings:	0

One of many all-rounders to get a game with England at the turn of the last century, he was a medium pace bowler with a good outswinger and a forceful middle order batsman. His batting never amounted to much in his ten Tests but he bowled manfully on the successful Ashes tour of 1903/04 where he took 18 wickets.

ARNOLD, Geoffrey Graham (Ted)
Born: September 3, 1944
Batting: Right handed
Bowling: Right arm medium-fast

Tests
Test Career:	1967-75
Cap Number:	436
Tests Played:	34

Test Batting
Innings:	46	Runs:	421
Highest Score:	59	Average:	12.02
No. 50s:	1	No. 100s:	0

Test Bowling & Fielding
Wickets:	115	Runs:	3,254
Best Bowling:	6/45	Average:	28.29
5 WI:	6	10 WM:	0
Catches:	9	Stumpings:	0

One Day Internationals
ODI Career:	1972-75
ODIs Played:	14

ODI Batting			
Innings:	6	Runs:	48
Highest Score:	18*	Average:	16.00
No. 50s:	0	No. 100s:	0
ODI Bowling & Fielding			
Wickets:	19	Runs:	339
Best Bowling:	4/27	Average:	17.84
5 WM:	0	Catches:	2
Stumpings:	0		

He was a fine contributor for the English cricket side with his dangerous seam and swing bowling for almost a full decade. Nicknamed 'Orse' from his initials G.G. Arnold could make the ball move away and into the batsmen and was most likely an exponent of reverse swing before the term existed. He claimed 115 wickets in 34 Tests at the respectable cost of 28.29 apiece.

ARNOLD, John

Born:	November 30, 1907
Batting:	Right handed
Bowling:	Right arm slow

Tests

Test Career:	1931		
Cap Number:	259		
Tests Played:	1		
Test Batting			
Innings:	2	Runs:	34
Highest Score:	34	Average:	17.00
No. 50s:	0	No. 100s:	0
Test Bowling & Fielding			
Wickets:	0	Runs:	0
Best Bowling:		Average:	0.00
5 WI:	0	10 WM:	0
Catches:	0	Stumpings:	0

He played a single Test against New Zealand in 1931 and whilst he never played for England again he was regular in the Hampshire side until 1950.

ASTILL, William Ewart

Born:	March 1, 1888
Batting:	Right handed

Tests

Test Career:	1927-30		
Cap Number:	226		
Tests Played:	9		
Test Batting			
Innings:	15	Runs:	190
Highest Score:	40	Average:	12.66
No. 50s:	0	No. 100s:	0
Test Bowling & Fielding			
Wickets:	25	Runs:	856
Best Bowling:	4/58	Average:	34.24
5 WI:	0	10 WM:	0
Catches:	7	Stumpings:	0

The slightly built Astill was a giant with Leicestershire where he became the first professional captain in 1935. Whilst he didn't play Test cricket until he was 39, and enjoyed only moderate success against weak opposition, he should be remembered as one of the few cricketers to make over 20,000 runs and take over 2,000 wickets in first class cricket.

ATHERTON, Michael Andrew

Born:	March 23, 1968
Batting:	Right handed
Bowling:	Right arm leg-break

Tests

Test Career:	1989-2001		
Cap Number:	538		
Tests Played:	115		
Test Batting			
Innings:	212	Runs:	7,728
Highest Score:	185*	Average:	37.69
No. 50s:	46	No. 100s:	16
Test Bowling & Fielding			
Wickets:	2	Runs:	302
Best Bowling:	1/20	Average:	151.00
5 WI:	0	10 WM:	0
Catches:	83	Stumpings:	0

One Day Internationals

ODI Career:	1990-98		
ODIs Played:	54		
ODI Batting			
Innings:	54	Runs:	1,791
Highest Score:	127	Average:	35.11
No. 50s:	12	No. 100s:	2
ODI Bowling & Fielding			
Wickets:	0	Runs:	0
Best Bowling:		Average:	0.00
5 WM:	0	Catches:	15
Stumpings:	0		

England's 71st and longest standing Test captain was earmarked for the position from the day he first stepped out for his county. Nicknamed FEC or 'future England captain', the Lancashire batsman took over from Graham Gooch in 1993 and held the position until 2001. His leadership was steady rather than inspiring, and whilst the team had some respectable series under Atherton such as the 2-2 draw with the West Indies in 1995, his time at the top was marked by the huge turnover of players in the side. His batting was not dissimilar to his captaincy, more persistent than brilliant. The number three valued his wicket and often provided the only resistance as lesser known batsmen were falling around him. His highest Test score, 185 against South Africa at Johannesburg in 1995/96 was a case in point. He batted for over ten hours to save the Test against a strong South African line-up that was spearheaded by an Allan Donald. If there was a query over Atherton it was his record against arch rivals Australia. In 33 Tests he scored only the single century and averaged less than 30. His edginess against the Aussies seemed to spread through the side who were unsuccessful in four Ashes series under him. Atherton's ability to endure saw him play 115 Tests and score 7728 runs to lie fifth on the list of all time Test scorers for England. As a TV commentator he has opened the door on an engaging personality that remained hidden throughout his long and at times successful career.

ATHEY, Charles William Jeffrey (Bill)
Born: September 27, 1957
Batting: Right handed
Bowling: Right arm off-break

Tests
Test Career: 1980-88
Cap Number: 487
Tests Played: 23

Test Batting
Innings:	41	Runs:	919
Highest Score:	123	Average:	22.97
No. 50s:	4	No. 100s:	1

Test Bowling & Fielding
Wickets:	0	Runs:	0
Best Bowling:		Average:	0.00
5 WI:	0	10 WM:	0
Catches:	13	Stumpings:	0

One Day Internationals
ODI Career: 1980-88
ODIs Played: 31

ODI Batting
Innings:	30	Runs:	848
Highest Score:	142*	Average:	31.40
No. 50s:	4	No. 100s:	2

ODI Bowling & Fielding
Wickets:	0	Runs:	10
Best Bowling:		Average:	0.00
5 WM:	0	Catches:	16
Stumpings:	0		

England regularly turned to him as an opening option over an eight year period, but apart from his 123 against Pakistan at Lord's in 1987 he was generally disappointing. The industrious opener fared better in the shorter version of the game where he scored two hundreds for his country.

ATTEWELL, William
Born: June 12, 1861
Batting: Right handed
Bowling: Right arm medium

Tests
Test Career: 1884-92
Cap Number: 46
Tests Played: 10

Test Batting
Innings:	15	Runs:	150
Highest Score:	43*	Average:	16.66
No. 50s:	0	No. 100s:	0

Test Bowling & Fielding
Wickets:	28	Runs:	626
Best Bowling:	4/42	Average:	22.35
5 WI:	0	10 WM:	0
Catches:	9	Stumpings:	0

A medium-pace bowler from Notts in the county competition, he was an exponent of off-theory that involved bowling wide of the off stump to a packed field. That plan served him well in his ten match Test career, taking 28 wickets and going for only 1.31 runs per over.

AUSTIN, Ian David
Born: May 30, 1966
Batting: Left handed
Bowling: Right arm medium

One Day Internationals
ODI Career: 1998-99
ODIs Played: 9

ODI Batting
Innings:	6	Runs:	34
Highest Score:	11*	Average:	6.80
No. 50s:	0	No. 100s:	0

ODI Bowling & Fielding
Wickets:	6	Runs:	360
Best Bowling:	2/25	Average:	60.00
5 WM:	0	Catches:	0
Stumpings:	0		

A chunky right arm seamer from Lancashire who played a further eight ODI's after taking two wickets on debut against Sri Lanka at Lord's in 1998.

BAILEY, Robert John
Born: October 28, 1963
Batting: Right handed
Bowling: Right arm off-break

Tests
Test Career: 1988-90
Cap Number: 531
Tests Played: 4

Test Batting
Innings:	8	Runs:	119
Highest Score:	43	Average:	14.87
No. 50s:	0	No. 100s:	0

Test Bowling & Fielding
Wickets:	0	Runs:	0
Best Bowling:		Average:	0.00
5 WI:	0	10 WM:	0
Catches:	0	Stumpings:	0

One Day Internationals
ODI Career: 1985-90
ODIs Played: 4

ODI Batting
Innings:	4	Runs:	137
Highest Score:	43*	Average:	68.50
No. 50s:	0	No. 100s:	0

ODI Bowling & Fielding
Wickets:	0	Runs:	25
Best Bowling:		Average:	0.00
5 WM:	0	Catches:	1
Stumpings:	0		

A right hand bat from Northants who played all of his Test cricket against the powerful West Indians. In one Test at home and three away he struggled and averaged less than 15. He is currently umpiring first class cricket in the UK.

BAILEY, Trevor Edward
Born: December 3, 1923
Batting: Right handed
Bowling: Right arm medium-fast

Tests
Test Career: 1949-59
Cap Number: 342
Tests Played: 61

Test Batting
Innings:	91	Runs:	2,290
Highest Score:	134*	Average:	29.74
No. 50s:	10	No. 100s:	1

Test Bowling & Fielding

Wickets:	132	Runs:	3,856
Best Bowling:	7/34	Average:	29.21
5 WI:	5	10 WM:	1
Catches:	32	Stumpings:	0

One in a long history of great English all-rounders, the powerful Bailey was at once an attacking opening bowler and a dour opening batsman. Bailey the bowler was a typical English paceman, short on pace but high on movement both in the air and off the wicket. His career best figure of 7/34 came against the West Indies at Sabina Park in 1954 when the home side won the toss and looked set for a long stay on a batter's wicket. Bailey the batsman was a study in concentration, often standing up when wickets were tumbling around him. He once scored a fifty in 357 minutes for the M.C.C. and his highest Test score of 134 not out against New Zealand took over six hours to compile. In retirement he continued to give pleasure to his legion of fans via the BBC commentary box.

BAIRSTOW, David Leslie

Born:	September 1, 1951
Batting:	Right handed
Bowling:	Right arm medium
	Wicket Keeper

Tests

Test Career:	1979-81		
Cap Number:	481		
Tests Played:	4		

Test Batting

Innings:	7	Runs:	125
Highest Score:	59	Average:	20.83
No. 50s:	1	No. 100s:	0

Test Bowling & Fielding

Wickets:	0	Runs:	0
Best Bowling:		Average:	0.00
5 WI:	0	10 WM:	0
Catches:	12	Stumpings:	1

One Day Internationals

ODI Career:	1979-84
ODIs Played:	21

ODI Batting

Innings:	20	Runs:	206
Highest Score:	23*	Average:	14.71
No. 50s:	0	No. 100s:	0

ODI Bowling & Fielding

Wickets:	0	Runs:	0
Best Bowling:		Average:	0.00
5 WM:	0	Catches:	17
Stumpings:	4		

The pugnacious Yorkshireman regularly toured as England's second keeper but played in only four Tests. He tragically took his own life in 1998 at the age of 46.

BAKEWELL, Alfred Harry

Born:	November 2, 1908
Batting:	Right handed
Bowling:	Right arm medium

Tests

Test Career:	1931-35		
Cap Number:	260		
Tests Played:	6		

Test Batting

Innings:	9	Runs:	409
Highest Score:	107	Average:	45.44
No. 50s:	3	No. 100s:	1

Test Bowling & Fielding

Wickets:	0	Runs:	8
Best Bowling:		Average:	0.00
5 WI:	0	10 WM:	0
Catches:	3	Stumpings:	0

The brilliant young batsman from Northampton had a promising Test career cut short when he was seriously injured in a car accident in 1936. He had played six Tests to that point the best of which was against the West Indies at The Oval in 1934 when he rescued England with a timely century. He was an industrious batsman known for having one of the finest late cuts the game had ever seen.

BALDERSTONE, John Christopher (Chris)

Born:	November 16, 1940
Batting:	Right handed
Bowling:	Left arm off-break

Tests

Test Career:	1976		
Cap Number:	467		
Tests Played:	2		

Test Batting

Innings:	4	Runs:	39
Highest Score:	35	Average:	9.75
No. 50s:	0	No. 100s:	0

Test Bowling & Fielding

Wickets:	1	Runs:	80
Best Bowling:	1/80	Average:	80.00
5 WI:	0	10 WM:	0
Catches:	1	Stumpings:	0

Better known as a professional footballer with Carlisle Untied, he played both of his Tests against the West Indies in 1976. He later turned his hand to umpiring, standing in two ODI's during the 80's.

BARBER, Robert William

Born:	September 26, 1935
Batting:	Left handed
Bowling:	Left arm leg-break

Tests

Test Career:	1960-68		
Cap Number:	399		
Tests Played:	28		

Test Batting

Innings:	45	Runs:	1,495
Highest Score:	185	Average:	35.59
No. 50s:	9	No. 100s:	1

Test Bowling & Fielding

Wickets:	42	Runs:	1,806
Best Bowling:	4/132	Average:	43.00
5 WI:	0	10 WM:	0
Catches:	21	Stumpings:	0

In 28 Tests, Bob Barber was nearly always good for runs or wickets. As a leg spinner he was willing to concede runs in the chase of wickets, and he took that adventurous attitude with him when he went in to bat. Generally used as an opener, he often fell in the fifties or sixties, but on one memorable occasion against Australia at the SCG he went on with it. It was the opening day of the third Test in 1965/66 and the Warwickshire leftie blasted a scintillating 185 against Garth McKenzie and Neil Hawke. He would have played more Tests for England had business commitments not meant he was often unavailable for selection.

BARBER, Wilfred
Born: April 18, 1901
Batting: Right handed
Bowling: Right arm medium-fast

Tests
Test Career: 1935
Cap Number: 284
Tests Played: 2
Test Batting
Innings: 4 Runs: 83
Highest Score: 44 Average: 20.75
No. 50s: 0 No. 100s: 0
Test Bowling & Fielding
Wickets: 1 Runs: 0
Best Bowling: 1/0 Average: 0.00
5 WI: 0 10 WM: 0
Catches: 1 Stumpings: 0

A right handed batsman from Yorkshire who played two Tests against the touring South Africans in 1935.

BARLOW, Graham Derek
Born: March 26, 1950
Batting: Left handed
Bowling: Right arm medium

Tests
Test Career: 1976-77
Cap Number: 470
Tests Played: 3
Test Batting
Innings: 5 Runs: 17
Highest Score: 7* Average: 4.25
No. 50s: 0 No. 100s: 0
Test Bowling & Fielding
Wickets: 0 Runs: 0
Best Bowling: Average: 0.00
5 WI: 0 10 WM: 0
Catches: 0 Stumpings: 0

One Day Internationals
ODI Career: 1976-77
ODIs Played: 6
ODI Batting
Innings: 6 Runs: 149
Highest Score: 80* Average: 29.80
No. 50s: 1 No. 100s: 0
ODI Bowling & Fielding
Wickets: 0 Runs: 0
Best Bowling: Average: 0.00
5 WM: 0 Catches: 4
Stumpings: 0

An opening batsman from Middlesex who scored only 17 runs in his three Tests, but did hit a fine 80 not out in his ODI debut playing the West Indies in 1976.

BARLOW, Richard Gordon
Born: May 28, 1851
Batting: Right handed
Bowling: Left arm medium

Tests
Test Career: 1882-87
Cap Number: 29
Tests Played: 17
Test Batting
Innings: 30 Runs: 591
Highest Score: 62 Average: 22.73
No. 50s: 2 No. 100s: 0
Test Bowling & Fielding
Wickets: 34 Runs: 767
Best Bowling: 7/40 Average: 22.55
5 WI: 3 10 WM: 0
Catches: 14 Stumpings: 0

A leading all-rounder in the early days of Test cricket who made a valuable contribution as either a middle order batsman or clever left arm medium pace bowler. His finest moment came at Old Trafford in 1886 when he bowled his country to victory against the Australians with a bag of seven wickets in the second innings. Barlow later turned his hand to umpiring, standing in a single Test in 1899.

BARNES, Sydney Francis
Born: April 19, 1873
Batting: Right handed

Tests
Test Career: 1901-14
Cap Number: 129
Tests Played: 27
Test Batting
Innings: 39 Runs: 242
Highest Score: 38* Average: 8.06
No. 50s: 0 No. 100s: 0
Test Bowling & Fielding
Wickets: 189 Runs: 3,106
Best Bowling: 9/103 Average: 16.43
5 WI: 24 10 WM: 7
Catches: 12 Stumpings: 0

Almost a century after he played his final Test, it is still questionable as to whether England has seen a better bowler than Sid Barnes. He made his Test debut in Australia at the age of 28 in 1901/02 and despite missing two out of five Tests due to injury still took 19 wickets for the series to be his country's second leading wicket taker. The right handed paceman was near unplayable on the mats in South Africa, and in 1913/14 took 49 wickets in only four Tests. The South Africans were no longer easy beats yet Barnes dominated the series and took the then Test record match figures of 17/159 at Johannesburg in the second Test. A medium fast opening bowler, his strength lay in his ability to make the ball move off the wicket like a spinner. In all he took 189 wickets in 27 Tests at an average of 16.43. The esteem in which he was held is best summed by an anecdote from the legendary Sir Neville Carduss long after Barnes retired. Former Test great Wilfred Rhodes was asked to rate the modern English bowlers by Carduss and replied that they were half as good as Barnes. The Yorkshireman then went on to say it was meant as a compliment to the current day bowlers!

BARNES, William

Born: May 27, 1852
Batting: Right handed
Bowling: Right arm medium-fast

Tests

Test Career: 1880-90
Cap Number: 21
Tests Played: 21

Test Batting
Innings:	33	Runs:	725
Highest Score:	134	Average:	23.38
No. 50s:	5	No. 100s:	1

Test Bowling & Fielding
Wickets:	51	Runs:	793
Best Bowling:	6/28	Average:	15.54
5 WI:	3	10 WM:	0
Catches:	19	Stumpings:	0

He was a wonderful all-rounder from Nottinghamshire, who single handedly guided England to victory on more that one occasion. His 134 in the first Test ever played in Adelaide in 1884/85 was quickly followed by a half century and six wicket haul at the MCG. England were victorious on both occasions with Billy Barnes clearly the best player for either side. As a batsman he was a forceful stroke player and a fastish medium pace bowler who took over 50 Test wickets. On occasions he had been admonished by his county side for arriving at matches affected by alcohol, so it was no surprise when he became a publican following his retirement.

BARNETT, Charles John

Born: July 3, 1910
Batting: Right handed
Bowling: Right arm medium

Tests

Test Career: 1933-48
Cap Number: 269
Tests Played: 20

Test Batting
Innings:	35	Runs:	1,098
Highest Score:	129	Average:	35.41
No. 50s:	5	No. 100s:	2

Test Bowling & Fielding
Wickets:	0	Runs:	93
Best Bowling:		Average:	0.00
5 WI:	0	10 WM:	0
Catches:	14	Stumpings:	0

England's search for an opener for an opener in the era immediately following the retirement of Sutcliffe and Hobbs produced Len Hutton and the hard hitting Charlie Barnett from Glocestershire. He saved his best for Tests against Australia averaging just over 43 in both the series in Australia in 1936/37 and at home in 1938. His first Test ton was 129 at The Adelaide Oval in 1937 and his second 126 against the Aussies at Trent Bridge a year later. Unfortunately the Second World War when Barnett was at his peak and even though he played against the Australians in 1948 his best years had been lost to the War.

BARNETT, Kim John

Born: July 17, 1960
Batting: Right handed

Tests

Test Career: 1988-89
Cap Number: 533
Tests Played: 4

Test Batting
Innings:	7	Runs:	207
Highest Score:	80	Average:	29.57
No. 50s:	2	No. 100s:	0

Test Bowling & Fielding
Wickets:	0	Runs:	32
Best Bowling:		Average:	0.00
5 WI:	0	10 WM:	0
Catches:	1	Stumpings:	0

One Day Internationals

ODI Career: 1988
ODIs Played: 1

ODI Batting
Innings:	1	Runs:	84
Highest Score:	84	Average:	84.00
No. 50s:	1	No. 100s:	0

ODI Bowling & Fielding
Wickets:	0	Runs:	0
Best Bowling:		Average:	0.00
5 WM:	0	Catches:	0
Stumpings:	0		

England seemed to have made the right choice when they selected the balding Barnett for the first Test of the 1989 Ashes series. He scored 80, and was part of a big stand with Allan Lamb for the third wicket. Like most of his team mates he struggled from that point on and by the fourth Test he was out of the side.

BARRATT, Fred

Born: April 12, 1894
Batting: Right handed
Bowling: Right arm fast

Tests

Test Career: 1929-30
Cap Number: 243
Tests Played: 5

Test Batting
Innings:	4	Runs:	28
Highest Score:	17	Average:	9.33
No. 50s:	0	No. 100s:	0

Test Bowling & Fielding

Wickets:	5	Runs:	235
Best Bowling:	1/8	Average:	47.00
5 WI:	0	10 WM:	0
Catches:	2	Stumpings:	0

An opening bowler from Nottinghamshire, he toured New Zealand and despite playing in four Tests could manage only three wickets for the series.

BARRINGTON, Kenneth Frank

Born: November 24, 1930
Batting: Right handed
Bowling: Right arm leg-break

Tests

Test Career: 1955-68
Cap Number: 380
Tests Played: 82

Test Batting

Innings:	131	Runs:	6,806
Highest Score:	256	Average:	58.67
No. 50s:	35	No. 100s:	20

Test Bowling & Fielding

Wickets:	29	Runs:	1,300
Best Bowling:	3/4	Average:	44.82
5 WI:	0	10 WM:	0
Catches:	58	Stumpings:	0

When commentators list cricket's all time great batsmen, the name Ken Barrington rarely gets a mention. It seems an injustice for a man who scored 20 Test centuries and averaged 58.67 in Tests. After a taste of Test cricket in 1955 he earnt a regular spot in the England side from 1959 when he was almost 30 years old. He scored consecutive Test tons in the West Indies in 1959/60 and was equally impressive with three large hundreds in India and Pakistan during a tour in 1961/62. It wasn't until 1964 that Barrington scored his first century on home soil when taking on the Australians at Old Trafford. He was obviously savouring the moment, as the hundred turned into a 256 that took 683 minutes to compile. It was copybook Barrington, safety came first but at times he loosened the shackles to hit 26 boundaries. In the end he scored hundreds against all opposition and in all conditions, placing a high price on his wicket at all times. In 1968 a heart attack forced him to retire from cricket, and only 13 years later he passed away while acting as team manager for Ian Botham's England side in the West Indies. His infectious smile is missed by everyone who he met through the game that was his life.

BARTON, Victor Alexander

Born: October 6, 1867
Batting: Right handed

Tests

Test Career: 1892
Cap Number: 73
Tests Played: 1

Test Batting

Innings:	1	Runs:	23
Highest Score:	23	Average:	23.00
No. 50s:	0	No. 100s:	0

Test Bowling & Fielding

Wickets:	0	Runs:	0
Best Bowling:		Average:	0.00
5 WI:	0	10 WM:	0
Catches:	0	Stumpings:	0

A number of English cricketers played their only Tests on the 1892 tour of South Africa because a stronger national side was touring Australia at the time. One of those players was Victor Barton, a clean stiker of the ball from Kent.

BATES, Willie

Born: November 9, 1855
Batting: Right handed
Bowling: Right arm off-break

Tests

Test Career: 1882-87
Cap Number: 30
Tests Played: 15

Test Batting

Innings:	26	Runs:	656
Highest Score:	64	Average:	27.33
No. 50s:	5	No. 100s:	0

Test Bowling & Fielding

Wickets:	50	Runs:	821
Best Bowling:	7/28	Average:	16.42
5 WI:	4	10 WM:	1
Catches:	9	Stumpings:	0

A right arm off spinner of considerable talent, his cricket career was cut short when he was struck in the face while bowling in the nets at the MCG in 1887. The blow damaged his eyesight and for a time he was so depressed at the thought of never playing cricket again that he attempted suicide. It was a sad end for Bates who took England's first Test hat trick five years earlier. That match at the MCG proved a triumph for Bates who claimed 14 of the 20 wickets to fall.

BATTY, Gareth Jon

Born: October 13, 1977
Batting: Right handed
Bowling: Right arm off-break

Tests

Test Career: 2003-
Cap Number: 619
Tests Played: 7

Test Batting

Innings:	8	Runs:	144
Highest Score:	38	Average:	20.57
No. 50s:	0	No. 100s:	0

Test Bowling & Fielding

Wickets:	11	Runs:	733
Best Bowling:	3/55	Average:	66.63
5 WI:	0	10 WM:	0
Catches:	3	Stumpings:	0

One Day Internationals

ODI Career: 2002-
ODIs Played: 7

ODI Batting

Innings:	5	Runs:	6
Highest Score:	3	Average:	1.50
No. 50s:	0	No. 100s:	0

ODI Bowling & Fielding

Wickets:	4	Runs:	294
Best Bowling:	2/40	Average:	73.50
5 WM:	0	Catches:	4
Stumpings:	0		

One in a procession of faceless off-spinners who have come and gone in the English side in recent years. Batty is nagging rather than threatening, and in three Tests against Bangladesh managed only three wickets.

BEAN, George

Born:	March 7, 1864
Batting:	Right handed
Bowling:	Right arm medium

Tests

Test Career:	1892		
Cap Number:	72		
Tests Played:	3		

Test Batting

Innings:	5	Runs:	92
Highest Score:	50	Average:	18.40
No. 50s:	1	No. 100s:	0

Test Bowling & Fielding

Wickets:	0	Runs:	0
Best Bowling:		Average:	0.00
5 WI:	0	10 WM:	0
Catches:	4	Stumpings:	0

An accomplished all-rounder from the strong Notts side who disappointed in three Tests on the tour of Australia in 1891/92. It came as a surprise when he wasn't thrown the ball in any of the Tests on that tour.

BEDSER, Alec Victor

Born:	July 4, 1918
Batting:	Right handed
Bowling:	Right arm medium-fast

Tests

Test Career:	1946-55		
Cap Number:	311		
Tests Played:	51		

Test Batting

Innings:	71	Runs:	714
Highest Score:	79	Average:	12.75
No. 50s:	1	No. 100s:	0

Test Bowling & Fielding

Wickets:	236	Runs:	5,876
Best Bowling:	7/44	Average:	24.89
5 WI:	15	10 WM:	5
Catches:	26	Stumpings:	0

Like his identical twin Eric, he came to prominence with Surrey just prior to the outbreak of the Second World War. With his short run and seemingly effortless action, there is no doubt that many a batsman were initially lulled into a false sense of security by the bowling of Alec Bedser. What would have soon become apparent was that the powerfully built speedster was not only deceptively quick, but he could also move the ball both in the air and off the seam. His chief weapon was a leg cutter that would square the batsman up and offer chance after chance to the catchers behind the wicket. He made his debut immediately after the War in a home series against the Indians, establishing himself with 11 wickets in his first two Tests. He loved battling against the Australians, and after struggling in his first series on Australian soil in 1946/47 generally had the better of his colonial cousins. He had many a fine tussle with Australian opener Arthur Morris, and whilst Morris boasted a number of large innings against the English he often fell to his good friend Bedser. After a decade of lion-hearted service as a bowler he became an English selector, serving as chairman between 1969 and 1981. In 1966 the immensely popular bowler was knighted for his services to the game.

BELL, Ian Ronald

Born:	April 11, 1982
Batting:	Right handed
Bowling:	Right arm medium

Tests

Test Career:	2004-		
Cap Number:	625		
Tests Played:	17		

Test Batting

Innings:	30	Runs:	1,269
Highest Score:	162*	Average:	48.80
No. 50s:	7	No. 100s:	5

Test Bowling & Fielding

Wickets:	1	Runs:	64
Best Bowling:	1/33	Average:	64.00
5 WI:	0	10 WM:	0
Catches:	18	Stumpings:	0

One Day Internationals

ODI Career:	2004-		
ODIs Played:	18		

ODI Batting

Innings:	16	Runs:	556
Highest Score:	80	Average:	39.71
No. 50s:	4	No. 100s:	0

ODI Bowling & Fielding

Wickets:	6	Runs:	78
Best Bowling:	3/9	Average:	13.00
5 WM:	0	Catches:	2
Stumpings:	0		

As a teenager he had the reputation of being the best young batsman in England but by the end of the 2005 Ashes series Ian Bell's Test career was hanging by a thread. He came into the series against Australia having played three Tests and with an inflated average of almost 300 courtesy of Bangladesh but quickly came back to earth with only 171 runs in ten innings including a pair at The Oval. Bell's response to his Ashes disappointment has been emphatic, a century at Faisalabad in November of 2005 righted the ship and three hundreds in consecutive Tests against the touring Pakistanis in 2006 has him primed for another tilt at the Australians in 2006/07 and the chance to exorcise his demons.

BENJAMIN, Joseph Emmanuel

Born: February 2, 1961
Batting: Right handed
Bowling: Right arm medium-fast

Tests
Test Career: 1994
Cap Number: 570
Tests Played: 1

Test Batting
Innings:	1	Runs:	0
Highest Score:	0	Average:	0.00
No. 50s:	0	No. 100s:	0

Test Bowling & Fielding
Wickets:	4	Runs:	80
Best Bowling:	4/42	Average:	20.00
5 WI:	0	10 WM:	0
Catches:	0	Stumpings:	0

One Day Internationals
ODI Career: 1994-95
ODIs Played: 2

ODI Batting
Innings:	1	Runs:	0
Highest Score:	0	Average:	0.00
No. 50s:	0	No. 100s:	0

ODI Bowling & Fielding
Wickets:	1	Runs:	47
Best Bowling:	1/22	Average:	47.00
5 WM:	0	Catches:	0
Stumpings:	0		

Born in St.Kitts, Joey Benjamin was a paceman who got the call up for his only Test against South Africa in 1994 as a 33 year old.

BENSON, Mark Richard

Born: July 6, 1958
Batting: Left handed
Bowling: Right arm off-break

Tests
Test Career: 1986
Cap Number: 518
Tests Played: 1

Test Batting
Innings:	2	Runs:	51
Highest Score:	30	Average:	25.50
No. 50s:	0	No. 100s:	0

Test Bowling & Fielding
Wickets:	0	Runs:	0
Best Bowling:		Average:	0.00
5 WI:	0	10 WM:	0
Catches:	0	Stumpings:	0

One Day Internationals
ODI Career: 1986
ODIs Played: 1

ODI Batting
Innings:	1	Runs:	24
Highest Score:	24	Average:	24.00
No. 50s:	0	No. 100s:	0

ODI Bowling & Fielding
Wickets:	0	Runs:	0
Best Bowling:		Average:	0.00
5 WM:	0	Catches:	0
Stumpings:	0		

On opening batsman from Kent who scored 30 and 21 in his only Test which was against India at Edgbaston in 1986.

BERRY, Robert

Born: January 29, 1926
Batting: Left handed
Bowling: Left arm off-break

Tests
Test Career: 1950
Cap Number: 346
Tests Played: 2

Test Batting
Innings:	4	Runs:	6
Highest Score:	4*	Average:	3.00
No. 50s:	0	No. 100s:	0

Test Bowling & Fielding
Wickets:	9	Runs:	228
Best Bowling:	5/63	Average:	25.33
5 WI:	1	10 WM:	1
Catches:	2	Stumpings:	0

A left arm off spinner whose chance at Test level were limited by the likes of Jim Laker. He took nine wickets on debut against the West Indies at Old Trafford in 1950, and whilst that effort earnt him a spot to tour Australia in 1950/51, he wasn't given a Test and never played for his country again.

BICKNELL, Martin Paul

Born: January 14, 1969
Batting: Right handed
Bowling: Right arm medium-fast

Tests
Test Career: 1993-2003
Cap Number: 565
Tests Played: 4

Test Batting
Innings:	7	Runs:	45
Highest Score:	15	Average:	6.42
No. 50s:	0	No. 100s:	0

Test Bowling & Fielding
Wickets:	14	Runs:	543
Best Bowling:	4/84	Average:	38.78
5 WI:	0	10 WM:	0
Catches:	2	Stumpings:	0

One Day Internationals
ODI Career: 1990-91
ODIs Played: 7

ODI Batting
Innings:	6	Runs:	96
Highest Score:	31*	Average:	24.00
No. 50s:	0	No. 100s:	0

ODI Bowling & Fielding
Wickets:	13	Runs:	347
Best Bowling:	3/55	Average:	26.69
5 WM:	0	Catches:	2
Stumpings:	0		

The Surrey speedster would have thought his Test career was over after two unspectacular Tests against the Aussies in 1993, but he received an unexpected recall to the national side more than ten years later. He repaid the selectors with ten wickets in two Tests, including a valuable six wickets at The Oval that denied the Proteas a series victory.

BINKS, James Graham
Born: October 5, 1935
Batting: Right handed
Bowling: Right arm leg-break
Wicket Keeper

Tests
Test Career: 1964
Cap Number: 419
Tests Played: 2

Test Batting
Innings:	4	Runs:	91
Highest Score:	55	Average:	22.75
No. 50s:	1	No. 100s:	0

Test Bowling & Fielding
Wickets:	0	Runs:	0
Best Bowling:		Average:	0.00
5 WI:	0	10 WM:	0
Catches:	8	Stumpings:	0

The Yorkshire keeper played two Tests in India in 1964 when regular keeper John Murray was sent home with an injury. He scored a game saving 55 in the second innings of his first Test at Bombay.

BIRD, Morice Carlos
Born: March 25, 1888
Batting: Right handed
Bowling: Right arm medium

Tests
Test Career: 1910-14
Cap Number: 164
Tests Played: 10

Test Batting
Innings:	16	Runs:	280
Highest Score:	61	Average:	18.66
No. 50s:	2	No. 100s:	0

Test Bowling & Fielding
Wickets:	8	Runs:	120
Best Bowling:	3/11	Average:	15.00
5 WI:	0	10 WM:	0
Catches:	5	Stumpings:	0

A famous schoolboy cricketer who got his chance to play for England by making himself available to tour South Africa, which he did on two separate occasions. Though he was no great shakes as a Test cricketer he did captain the famous Surrey side in the 1910's.

BIRKENSHAW, Jack
Born: November 13, 1940
Batting: Left handed
Bowling: Right arm off-break

Tests
Test Career: 1973-74
Cap Number: 456
Tests Played: 5

Test Batting
Innings:	7	Runs:	148
Highest Score:	64	Average:	21.14
No. 50s:	1	No. 100s:	0

Test Bowling & Fielding
Wickets:	13	Runs:	469
Best Bowling:	5/57	Average:	36.07
5 WI:	1	10 WM:	0
Catches:	3	Stumpings:	0

He was a right arm off spinner who had to wait until he was 33 to play the first of his five Tests. Birkenshaw wasn't a huge spinner of the ball, but his excellent control garnered him over 1000 first class wickets. Like a number of English Test cricketers before and after he turned to umpiring in retirement and was rewarded with two Tests and six ODI's.

BLACKWELL, Ian David
Born: June 10, 1978
Batting: Left handed
Bowling: Left arm off-break

Tests
Test Career: 2006-
Cap Number: 629
Tests Played: 1

Test Batting
Innings:	1	Runs:	4
Highest Score:	4	Average:	4.00
No. 50s:	0	No. 100s:	0

Test Bowling & Fielding
Wickets:	0	Runs:	71
Best Bowling:		Average:	0.00
5 WI:	0	10 WM:	0
Catches:	0	Stumpings:	0

One Day Internationals
ODI Career: 2002-
ODIs Played: 34

ODI Batting
Innings:	29	Runs:	403
Highest Score:	82	Average:	14.92
No. 50s:	1	No. 100s:	0

ODI Bowling & Fielding
Wickets:	24	Runs:	877
Best Bowling:	3/26	Average:	36.54
5 WM:	0	Catches:	8
Stumpings:	0		

A steady off spinner and lusty lower order batsman, he seems destined to play most of his international cricket in the shorter versions of the game.

BLAKEY, Richard John
Born: January 15, 1967
Batting: Right handed
Wicket Keeper

Tests
Test Career: 1993
Cap Number: 558
Tests Played: 2

Test Batting
Innings:	4	Runs:	7
Highest Score:	6	Average:	1.75
No. 50s:	0	No. 100s:	0

Test Bowling & Fielding
Wickets:	0	Runs:	0
Best Bowling:		Average:	0.00
5 WI:	0	10 WM:	0
Catches:	2	Stumpings:	0

One Day Internationals
ODI Career: 1992-93
ODIs Played: 3

ODI Batting
Innings:	2	Runs:	25
Highest Score:	25	Average:	12.50
No. 50s:	0	No. 100s:	0

ODI Bowling & Fielding
Wickets:	0	Runs:	0
Best Bowling:		Average:	0.00
5 WM:	0	Catches:	2
Stumpings:	0		

The Yorkshire wicket keeper was given a chance on the tour of Pakistan and India in 1992/93 where he played two Tests and a handful of ODI's.

BLIGH, Ivo Francis Walter
Born: March 13, 1859
Batting: Right handed

Tests
Test Career:	1882-83		
Cap Number:	38		
Tests Played:	4		

Test Batting
Innings:	7	Runs:	62
Highest Score:	19	Average:	10.33
No. 50s:	0	No. 100s:	0

Test Bowling & Fielding
Wickets:	0	Runs:	0
Best Bowling:		Average:	0.00
5 WI:	0	10 WM:	0
Catches:	7	Stumpings:	0

The Honourable Ivo Bligh was a London nobleman who excelled not only in cricket, but tennis and golf as well. Later to be known as The 8th Earl of Darnley, he captained his country in all four Tests played in Australia in 1882/83, and despite performing only moderately returned home with the newly created 'Ashes'. He later became president of the Marleybone Cricket Club.

BLYTHE, Colin
Born: May 30, 1879
Batting: Right handed
Bowling: Left arm off-break

Tests
Test Career:	1901-10		
Cap Number:	130		
Tests Played:	19		

Test Batting
Innings:	31	Runs:	183
Highest Score:	27	Average:	9.63
No. 50s:	0	No. 100s:	0

Test Bowling & Fielding
Wickets:	100	Runs:	1,863
Best Bowling:	8/59	Average:	18.63
5 WI:	9	10 WM:	4
Catches:	6	Stumpings:	0

He was a fine left arm off spinner from Kent who took ten or more wickets in a Test match on four occasions. In 1909 he led England to a comfortable victory over Australia at Edgbaston with 11 wickets for the game and later that series took seven in a match at Old Trafford. He recorded career best Test figures of 15/99 at Lord's in 1907 during South Africa's first series on English soil. Blythe holds a first class record that has stood for a century and will probably never be broken. Playing for Northamptonshire against Kent, he took 17 wickets in a single day, capturing 10/30 in the first innings and 7/18 in the second. 'Charlie' Blythe was killed in France during World War I whilst serving his country.

BOARD, John Henry (Jack)
Born: February 23, 1867
Batting: Right handed
Wicket Keeper

Tests
Test Career:	1899-1906		
Cap Number:	111		
Tests Played:	6		

Test Batting
Innings:	12	Runs:	108
Highest Score:	29	Average:	10.80
No. 50s:	0	No. 100s:	0

Test Bowling & Fielding
Wickets:	0	Runs:	0
Best Bowling:		Average:	0.00
5 WI:	0	10 WM:	0
Catches:	8	Stumpings:	3

A wicket keeper from Gloucestershire who played all his Test cricket in South Africa.

BOLUS, John Brian (Brian)
Born: January 31, 1934
Batting: Right handed
Bowling: Left arm medium

Tests
Test Career:	1963-64		
Cap Number:	417		
Tests Played:	7		

Test Batting
Innings:	12	Runs:	496
Highest Score:	88	Average:	41.33
No. 50s:	4	No. 100s:	0

Test Bowling & Fielding
Wickets:	0	Runs:	16
Best Bowling:		Average:	0.00
5 WI:	0	10 WM:	0
Catches:	2	Stumpings:	0

With an average of over 40 he may have been unlucky not to have played more than seven Tests. The Yorkshireman captained both Nottinghamshire and Derbyshire in county cricket.

BOOTH, Major William
Born: December 10, 1886
Batting: Right handed
Bowling: Right arm medium-fast

Tests
Test Career:	1913-14		
Cap Number:	179		
Tests Played:	2		

Test Batting
Innings:	2	Runs:	46
Highest Score:	32	Average:	23.00
No. 50s:	0	No. 100s:	0

Test Bowling & Fielding

Wickets:	7	Runs:	130
Best Bowling:	4/49	Average:	18.57
5 WI:	0	10 WM:	0
Catches:	0	Stumpings:	0

A promising bowler/batsman who played just two Tests prior to going off to fight in the First World War. He was killed in action on the Somme in 1916.

BOSANQUET, Bernard James Tindal

Born:	October 13, 1877
Batting:	Right handed
Bowling:	Right arm leg-break

Tests

Test Career:	1903-05
Cap Number:	137
Tests Played:	7

Test Batting

Innings:	14	Runs:	147
Highest Score:	27	Average:	13.36
No. 50s:	0	No. 100s:	0

Test Bowling & Fielding

Wickets:	25	Runs:	604
Best Bowling:	8/107	Average:	24.16
5 WI:	2	10 WM:	0
Catches:	9	Stumpings:	0

A tallish leg spinner whose name will live on in the ball he was said to have introduced to the game. Bernard Bosanquet started out as a medium pace bowler but upon changing to leg spin introduced a delivery that would spin back into the right hand batsman. Christened the 'Bosie' in his honour and also referred to as the googly or the wrong'un in Australia, he allegedly learnt how to master this form of opposite spin from a game with a tennis ball that was popular at the turn of the 19th century. Called 'twisti twosti', it involved spinning a tennis ball on a table top and taught the Middlesex man the soon to be famous 'Bosie'. He used it to great effect against the Australians at the SCG in 1903/04, taking 6/51 in the series deciding Test. The Bosie was on display again when he routed Australia at Trent Bridge in 1905, capturing 8 wickets in an innings. He was also an accomplished batsman with a good technique who scored 21 first class centuries.

BOTHAM, Ian Terence

Born:	November 24, 1955
Batting:	Right handed
Bowling:	Right arm medium-fast

Tests

Test Career:	1977-92
Cap Number:	474
Tests Played:	102

Test Batting

Innings:	161	Runs:	5,200
Highest Score:	208	Average:	33.54
No. 50s:	22	No. 100s:	14

Test Bowling & Fielding

Wickets:	383	Runs:	10,878
Best Bowling:	8/34	Average:	28.40
5 WI:	27	10 WM:	4
Catches:	120	Stumpings:	0

One Day Internationals

ODI Career:	1976-92
ODIs Played:	116

ODI Batting

Innings:	106	Runs:	2,113
Highest Score:	79	Average:	23.21
No. 50s:	9	No. 100s:	0

ODI Bowling & Fielding

Wickets:	145	Runs:	4,139
Best Bowling:	4/31	Average:	28.54
5 WM:	0	Catches:	36
Stumpings:	0		

As brash as he was brilliant, Ian Botham sits atop a long list of great English all-rounders. The brutal ballet that was his batting was hardly elegant but he had an excellent technique and rock solid defence when he applied himself. He may not have been the greatest bowler of all time, but he was close to the most competitive. There was no thought of containment when Botham had the ball, just attack via his copybook outswinger or by whatever means he deemed suitable at the time. He burst on to the Test scene with a five wicket innings haul against the Australians in this first Test in 1977 and stayed there. Botham holds a number of Test records as an all-rounder, including being the fastest to achieve the doubles of 1,000 runs and 100 wickets, 2,000 runs and 200 wickets, and 3,000 runs and 300 wickets. He was the first player to score 5,000 runs and take 300 wickets in Tests, and the first to score a century and take 10 wickets in the same Test match. He scored a century and took five wickets in an innings in the same Test match on a record five occasions. His most famous moment came in the legendary third Ashes Test at Headingly in 1981 when his amazing feats saw England become the first side to win a Test after following on. Mike Brearley had replaced Botham as England captain, and despite the former skipper taking 6/95 Australia were able to reach 9/401 in their first innings. The next day was a disaster for England, the top order was out cheaply and with only Botham making a half century they scored 174 and were forced to follow on. By the time England was 4/41 in their second innings all seemed lost. Dennis Lillee and Rodney Marsh had notoriously taken 500/1 about England winning and were surely contemplating tearing up their tickets. A handy partnership between Peter Willey and Geoff Boycott lifted the score to 105 when Willey's dismissal brought Ian Botham out to the middle. At first he placed, then he plundered and when Bob Willis was dismissed for two, 'Beefy' Botham stood undefeated at the other end on 149. Chasing 130 the Australians fell to a ramping Bob Willis. England had won an impossible match that would be forever known as 'Botham's Test'. That game encapsulated the man, brilliant with bat and ball and with a self belief that could make him rise above any adversity. He's outspoken and outgoing and in his time rubbed some people the wrong way, but the former champion cricketer and current commentator has earnt his place amongst the greatest cricketers to ever play.

BOWDEN, Montague Parker
Born: November 1, 1865
Batting: Right handed
Wicket Keeper

Tests
Test Career:	1889		
Cap Number:	61		
Tests Played:	2		

Test Batting
Innings:	2	Runs:	25
Highest Score:	25	Average:	12.50
No. 50s:	0	No. 100s:	0

Test Bowling & Fielding
Wickets:	0	Runs:	0
Best Bowling:		Average:	0.00
5 WI:	0	10 WM:	0
Catches:	1	Stumpings:	0

Monty Parker played in only two Tests, both in the foundation series against South Africa in 1889. The 23 year old wicket keeper captained the side in the second of those Tests and in doing so became England's youngest ever captain at the time. He remained in South Africa, playing first class cricket and pursuing a love of adventure. Unfortunately he died of injuries suffered while on safari at the age of 26.

BOWES, William Eric
Born: July 25, 1908
Batting: Right handed

Tests
Test Career:	1932-46		
Cap Number:	264		
Tests Played:	15		

Test Batting
Innings:	11	Runs:	28
Highest Score:	10*	Average:	4.66
No. 50s:	0	No. 100s:	0

Test Bowling & Fielding
Wickets:	68	Runs:	1,519
Best Bowling:	6/33	Average:	22.33
5 WI:	6	10 WM:	0
Catches:	2	Stumpings:	0

Throughout the thirties nothing filled English cricket fans with more hope than the sight of a bespectacled Bill Bowes galloping towards the delivery crease. The fast medium bowler spearheaded the English attack against the might of Bradman's Australians and whilst he came in for his share of treatment he always took his share of wickets as well. In the 1934 Ashes series he took 19 wickets in only three Tests included a bag of six in Australia's only innings at Headingly and nine in the next match at The Oval. A batting bunny of the highest order, in Tests he took 68 wickets but made only 28 runs.

BOWLEY, Edward Henry
Born: June 6, 1890
Batting: Right handed
Bowling: Right arm leg-break

Tests
Test Career:	1929-30		
Cap Number:	242		
Tests Played:	5		

Test Batting
Innings:	7	Runs:	252
Highest Score:	109	Average:	36.00
No. 50s:	0	No. 100s:	1

Test Bowling & Fielding
Wickets:	0	Runs:	116
Best Bowling:		Average:	0.00
5 WI:	0	10 WM:	0
Catches:	2	Stumpings:	0

An opening batsman from Sussex, he scored a century at Auckland in 1930 as part of the first English side to tour New Zealand.

BOYCOTT, Geoffrey
Born: October 21, 1940
Batting: Right handed
Bowling: Right arm medium

Tests
Test Career:	1964-82		
Cap Number:	422		
Tests Played:	108		

Test Batting
Innings:	193	Runs:	8,114
Highest Score:	246*	Average:	47.72
No. 50s:	42	No. 100s:	22

Test Bowling & Fielding
Wickets:	7	Runs:	382
Best Bowling:	3/47	Average:	54.57
5 WI:	0	10 WM:	0
Catches:	33	Stumpings:	0

One Day Internationals
ODI Career:	1971-81		
ODIs Played:	36		

ODI Batting
Innings:	34	Runs:	1,082
Highest Score:	105	Average:	36.06
No. 50s:	9	No. 100s:	1

ODI Bowling & Fielding
Wickets:	5	Runs:	105
Best Bowling:	2/14	Average:	21.00
5 WM:	0	Catches:	5
Stumpings:	0		

There has long been an argument as to whether Test cricket is a team sport or a game played by a group of individuals. Those who propose the latter would no doubt present Geoffrey Boycott as their main argument. Always resolute in defense and determined to protect his wicket at all costs, the man often described as selfish only played in 20 losing sides during his 108 Test career. It was his belief that if he did his job then the rest would take care of itself. Boycott made his Test debut against Australia at Trent Bridge in 1964 and his careful 48 in 149 was a portent of things to come. The first of his 22 Test hundreds came less than a year later in Port Elizabeth with a 117 against the South Africans that took more than seven hours to compile. The dye had been cast, England had an opener who would take the shine off not one but two or three new balls. The iron willed Yorkshireman played no Test cricket between June 1974 and August 1977, standing down in protest at being overlooked for the Test captaincy. The move did little to quell public opinion against a man perceived as self centred, but when he did return to the Test arena it was that personal pride that drove him to 442 in three Tests against the touring Australians at an average of 147.33. The match at Trent Bridge in that series saw him become the first cricketer to bat in all five days of a Test where his aggregate score of 187 took 730 minutes to compile. Boycott had the ability to make time stand still at the crease and holds the record for the highest Test score without a boundary; 77 at the WACA in Perth in 1978. He played on in to his forties, scoring the last of his Test centuries in typically slow style at Delhi. That last ton took seven hours and twenty minutes and he was even outscored by notorious stonewaller Chris Tavare who scored 40 more runs in the same time. Throughout his career Boycott had more than his share of detractors but with over 8,000 Test runs at an average of just under 48 he remains one of the best openers the game has seen.

BRADLEY, Walter Morris (Bill)

Born:	January 2, 1875
Batting:	Right handed
Bowling:	Right arm fast

Tests

Test Career:	1899
Cap Number:	127
Tests Played:	2

Test Batting

Innings:	2	Runs:	23
Highest Score:	23*	Average:	23.00
No. 50s:	0	No. 100s:	0

Test Bowling & Fielding

Wickets:	6	Runs:	233
Best Bowling:	5/67	Average:	38.83
5 WI:	1	10 WM:	0
Catches:	0	Stumpings:	0

Bill Bradley burst on to the Test scene in 1899, taking five wickets in his first Test innings. The unlikely combination of Bill Bradley and Sailor Young dismissed a powerful Australian side that included Victor Trumper and Monty Noble for only 196 in the first innings of the fourth Test at Old Trafford. Like Young, his feats were soon forgotten and he played only one more Test.

BRAUND, Leonard Charles

Born:	October 18, 1875
Batting:	Right handed
Bowling:	Right arm leg-break

Tests

Test Career:	1901-08
Cap Number:	131
Tests Played:	23

Test Batting

Innings:	41	Runs:	987
Highest Score:	104	Average:	25.97
No. 50s:	2	No. 100s:	3

Test Bowling & Fielding

Wickets:	47	Runs:	1,810
Best Bowling:	8/81	Average:	38.51
5 WI:	3	10 WM:	0
Catches:	39	Stumpings:	0

England had two great all-rounders in the early 20th century. One, Wilfred Rhodes is known to most cricket fans, but the other, Len Braund has been all but forgotten. Establishing himself at Somerset after Surrey inexplicably let him go, he joined the England side that toured Australia in 1901/02. He made 58 in his first Test innings at the SCG and scored his maiden Test century only two Tests later in Adelaide. He relished playing in Australia and on his next visit scored another century, this time at the SCG. He also captured eight wickets in an innings in Melbourne in the same series. An all-rounder in the truest sense of the word, he became a Test umpire once his playing days were over.

BREARLEY, John Michael (Mike)

Born:	April 28, 1942
Batting:	Right handed
Bowling:	Right arm medium

Tests

Test Career:	1976-81
Cap Number:	465
Tests Played:	39

Test Batting

Innings:	66	Runs:	1,442
Highest Score:	91	Average:	22.88
No. 50s:	9	No. 100s:	0

Test Bowling & Fielding

Wickets:	0	Runs:	0
Best Bowling:		Average:	0.00
5 WI:	0	10 WM:	0
Catches:	52	Stumpings:	0

One Day Internationals

ODI Career:	1977-80
ODIs Played:	25

ODI Batting

Innings:	24	Runs:	510
Highest Score:	78	Average:	24.28
No. 50s:	3	No. 100s:	0

ODI Bowling & Fielding

Wickets:	0	Runs:	0
Best Bowling:		Average:	0.00
5 WM:	0	Catches:	12
Stumpings:	0		

With 39 Tests for no centuries and an average of only 22.88, there must have been something very

special about Mike Brearley's captaincy. To some he was the finest thinker to have led England and with a Test record of 18 wins and only four losses from 31 Tests, he has the record to support the claim. Brearley took over the reigns from Tony Greig after the South African's involvement with World Series Cricket became public knowledge. He led his country in ten Test series for just one loss, with his finest hour coming in his final series at the helm when he inspired Ian Botham to lead the charge as England regained the Ashes in 1981.

BREARLEY, Walter
Born: March 11, 1876
Batting: Right handed
Bowling: Right arm fast

Tests
Test Career: 1905-12
Cap Number: 144
Tests Played: 4

Test Batting
Innings:	5	Runs:	21
Highest Score:	11*	Average:	7.00
No. 50s:	0	No. 100s:	0

Test Bowling & Fielding
Wickets:	17	Runs:	359
Best Bowling:	5/110	Average:	21.11
5 WI:	1	10 WM:	0
Catches:	0	Stumpings:	0

A right arm opening bowler from Lancashire, he played in only four Tests but was a highly regarded bowler for his county for whom he took over 800 first class wickets. Such was his standing in England that he was nominated as one of Wisden's five Cricketers of the Year in 1909.

BRENNAN, Donald Vincent
Born: February 10, 1920
Batting: Right handed
 Wicket Keeper

Tests
Test Career: 1951
Cap Number: 359
Tests Played: 2

Test Batting
Innings:	2	Runs:	16
Highest Score:	16	Average:	8.00
No. 50s:	0	No. 100s:	0

Test Bowling & Fielding
Wickets:	0	Runs:	0
Best Bowling:		Average:	0.00
5 WI:	0	10 WM:	0
Catches:	0	Stumpings:	1

A wicket keeper from Yorkshire who played both his Tests against South Africa in 1951.

BRESNAN, Timothy Thomas
Born: February 28, 1985
Batting: Right handed
Bowling: Right arm medium-fast

One Day Internationals
ODI Career: 2006
ODIs Played: 4

ODI Batting
Innings:	4	Runs:	51
Highest Score:	20	Average:	17.00
No. 50s:	0	No. 100s:	0

ODI Bowling & Fielding
Wickets:	2	Runs:	169
Best Bowling:	1/38	Average:	84.50
5 WM:	0	Catches:	1
Stumpings:	0		

A young up and coming all-rounder from Yorkshire who played in four ODI's against the touring Sri Lankans in mid 2006. Bresnan looks destined for a promising international career.

BRIGGS, John
Born: October 3, 1862
Batting: Right handed
Bowling: Left arm off-break

Tests
Test Career: 1884-99
Cap Number: 47
Tests Played: 33

Test Batting
Innings:	50	Runs:	815
Highest Score:	121	Average:	18.11
No. 50s:	2	No. 100s:	1

Test Bowling & Fielding
Wickets:	118	Runs:	2,095
Best Bowling:	8/11	Average:	17.75
5 WI:	9	10 WM:	4
Catches:	12	Stumpings:	0

The chirpy Lancashire all-rounder had a number of notable highlights in his 33 Test career, but none to surpass his effort in a Test against South Africa in 1888/89. The South Africans were playing in only their second ever Test and fell to a rampaging Briggs who took 15 wickets in the Test for only 28 runs. The breakdown was 7/17 in the first innings and a then Test record 8/11 in the second. It was not the only time his left arm off spin wreaked havoc, he also had three match hauls of ten or more wickets against the Australians. Briggs was originally chosen to represent his country as a batsman on the tour to Australia in 1884/85. He scored a century in that series, 121 at the MCG, but amazingly did not bowl a single over. An epileptic, he suffered a fit while playing at Lord's in 1899, and such was the ignorance of the condition at the time that he was sent to the Cheadle Asylum. Sadly his health deteriorated in the confines of the mad house and he passed away there in 1903.

BROAD, Brian Christopher (Chris)
Born: September 29, 1957
Batting: Left handed
Bowling: Right arm medium

Tests
Test Career:	1984-89		
Cap Number:	506		
Tests Played:	25		

Test Batting
Innings:	44	Runs:	1,661
Highest Score:	162	Average:	39.54
No. 50s:	6	No. 100s:	6

Test Bowling & Fielding
Wickets:	0	Runs:	4
Best Bowling:		Average:	0.00
5 WI:	0	10 WM:	0
Catches:	10	Stumpings:	0

One Day Internationals
ODI Career:	1987-88		
ODIs Played:	34		

ODI Batting
Innings:	34	Runs:	1,361
Highest Score:	106	Average:	40.02
No. 50s:	11	No. 100s:	1

ODI Bowling & Fielding
Wickets:	0	Runs:	6
Best Bowling:		Average:	0.00
5 WM:	0	Catches:	10
Stumpings:	0		

The tall opening batsman from Notts via Gloucestershire had a spectacular southern summer when he toured Australia in 1986/87. A powerful batsman on the off side, he scored centuries in three consecutive Tests to end the series with 487 runs and an average just under 70. His love affair with Australia continued in the one-off Test the next year at the SCG where he hit triple figures again with 139. All of Chris Broad's six Test centuries came on foreign soil, and by 1989 the player who struggled at home had played his last Test. He currently serves as an ICC match referee.

BROCKWELL, William
Born:	January 21, 1865
Batting:	Right handed
Bowling:	Right arm medium

Tests
Test Career:	1893-99		
Cap Number:	87		
Tests Played:	7		

Test Batting
Innings:	12	Runs:	202
Highest Score:	49	Average:	16.83
No. 50s:	0	No. 100s:	0

Test Bowling & Fielding
Wickets:	5	Runs:	309
Best Bowling:	3/33	Average:	61.80
5 WI:	0	10 WM:	0
Catches:	6	Stumpings:	0

He was a leading player for the dominant Surrey side in the late 19th century and toured Australia in 1894/95. A free scoring batsman and equally proficient medium pace bowler, his best efforts were 49 in the first Test at the SCG and 3/33 at the MCG in the second.

BROMLEY-DAVENPORT, Hugh Richard
Born:	August 18, 1870
Batting:	Right handed
Bowling:	Left arm fast

Tests
Test Career:	1896-99		
Cap Number:	93		
Tests Played:	4		

Test Batting
Innings:	6	Runs:	128
Highest Score:	84	Average:	21.33
No. 50s:	1	No. 100s:	0

Test Bowling & Fielding
Wickets:	4	Runs:	98
Best Bowling:	2/46	Average:	24.50
5 WI:	0	10 WM:	0
Catches:	1	Stumpings:	0

All of his four Tests were played on two tours of South Africa in the 1890's, suggesting that he belonged to the second tier of English cricketers. His highest Test score was an 84 at Johannesburg in 1896.

BROOKES, Dennis
Born:	October 29, 1915
Batting:	Right handed
Bowling:	Right arm medium

Tests
Test Career:	1948		
Cap Number:	327		
Tests Played:	1		

Test Batting
Innings:	2	Runs:	17
Highest Score:	10	Average:	8.50
No. 50s:	0	No. 100s:	0

Test Bowling & Fielding
Wickets:	0	Runs:	0
Best Bowling:		Average:	0.00
5 WI:	0	10 WM:	0
Catches:	1	Stumpings:	0

A legendary cricketer with Northampton, he played only the one Test despite a first class career that yielded over 30,000 runs.

BROWN, Alan
Born:	October 17, 1935
Batting:	Right handed
Bowling:	Right arm medium-fast

Tests
Test Career:	1961		
Cap Number:	404		
Tests Played:	2		

Test Batting
Innings:	1	Runs:	3
Highest Score:	3*	Average:	0.00
No. 50s:	0	No. 100s:	0

Test Bowling & Fielding
Wickets:	3	Runs:	150
Best Bowling:	3/27	Average:	50.00
5 WI:	0	10 WM:	0
Catches:	1	Stumpings:	0

A quick bowler from Kent who played two Tests on England's tour of the subcontinent in 1961.

BROWN, Alistair Duncan (Ally)

Born: February 11, 1970
Batting: Right handed
Bowling: Right arm off-break

One Day Internationals

ODI Career: 1996-01
ODIs Played: 16

ODI Batting

Innings:	16	Runs:	354
Highest Score:	118	Average:	22.12
No. 50s:	1	No. 100s:	1

ODI Bowling & Fielding

Wickets:	0	Runs:	5
Best Bowling:		Average:	0.00
5 WM:	0	Catches:	6
Stumpings:	0		

Arguably, the most entertaining batsman to have never played Test cricket, Ally Brown was the quintessential limited overs cricketer - an attacking batsman, economical bowler and brilliant fielder. Brown made his ODI debit against India at The Oval in 1996, and made a century in his third appearance at Old Trafford. However, his form was at extremes thereafter and managed only a handful of ODI's over a five-year period.

BROWN, David John

Born: January 30, 1942
Batting: Right handed
Bowling: Right arm medium-fast

Tests

Test Career: 1965-69
Cap Number: 429
Tests Played: 26

Test Batting

Innings:	34	Runs:	342
Highest Score:	44*	Average:	11.79
No. 50s:	0	No. 100s:	0

Test Bowling & Fielding

Wickets:	79	Runs:	2,237
Best Bowling:	5/42	Average:	28.31
5 WI:	2	10 WM:	0
Catches:	7	Stumpings:	0

A tall and talented all-rounder from Warwickshire, he was a regular member of the English side in the late 60's. When Australia was bundled out for an embarrassing 78 at Lord's in 1968 it was Brown who was the chief destroyer taking 5/24.

BROWN, Douglas Robert

Born: October 29, 1969
Batting: Right handed
Bowling: Right arm medium-fast

One Day Internationals

ODI Career: 1997-06
ODIs Played: 11

ODI Batting

Innings:	10	Runs:	114
Highest Score:	21	Average:	19.00
No. 50s:	0	No. 100s:	0

ODI Bowling & Fielding

Wickets:	9	Runs:	344
Best Bowling:	2/28	Average:	38.22
5 WM:	0	Catches:	1
Stumpings:	0		

Scottish born Dougie Brown made his ODI debut for England against India at Sharjah in 1997. As a promising pace bowler, he played in nine ODI's for England between 1997 and 1998 and after an eight year hiatus made his ODI debut for Scotland in August 2006.

BROWN, Frederick Richard

Born: December 16, 1910
Batting: Right handed
Bowling: Right arm leg-break

Tests

Test Career: 1931-53
Cap Number: 261
Tests Played: 22

Test Batting

Innings:	30	Runs:	734
Highest Score:	79	Average:	25.31
No. 50s:	5	No. 100s:	0

Test Bowling & Fielding

Wickets:	45	Runs:	1,398
Best Bowling:	5/49	Average:	31.06
5 WI:	1	10 WM:	0
Catches:	22	Stumpings:	0

The stocky Englishman played 22 Tests in a career that spanned over two decades that saw him go from a promising young all-rounder to a much respected captain of the side. In the early 30's he won a spot in the side that toured Australia for the infamous 'bodyline' series and whilst he didn't play a Test on that tour the ill-feeling between the two countries must have made a great impression on him. Nearly 20 years later he was chosen to captain the side that toured Australia for the 1950/51 Ashes series and eventhough England lost 4-1, he ensured that his charges played the game in the right spirit. As a result there was a great thawing in the relationship between the two Test playing nations and Freddie Brown earnt the title as the most popular English captain who ever took a side to Australia.

BROWN, George

Born: October 6, 1887
Batting: Left handed
Bowling: Right arm medium
Wicket Keeper

Tests

Test Career: 1921-23
Cap Number: 199
Tests Played: 7

Test Batting

Innings:	12	Runs:	299
Highest Score:	84	Average:	29.90
No. 50s:	2	No. 100s:	0

Test Bowling & Fielding

Wickets:	0	Runs:	0
Best Bowling:		Average:	0.00
5 WI:	0	10 WM:	0
Catches:	9	Stumpings:	3

The Hampshire man was a larger than life character who bowled, batted and kept wickets for his county side. He was used in the English side as a batsman keeper to good effect, averaging almost 30 runs per innings in his seven Tests.

BROWN, John Thomas (Jack)

Born:	August 20, 1869
Batting:	Right handed
Bowling:	Right arm leg-break

Tests

Test Career:	1894-99		
Cap Number:	89		
Tests Played:	8		

Test Batting

Innings:	16	Runs:	470
Highest Score:	140	Average:	36.15
No. 50s:	1	No. 100s:	1

Test Bowling & Fielding

Wickets:	0	Runs:	22
Best Bowling:		Average:	0.00
5 WI:	0	10 WM:	0
Catches:	7	Stumpings:	0

When cricket lovers talk of the greatest Test innings of all time it is fair to say that Jack Brown's effort at MCG in March of 1895 is almost never mentioned. It should be. The Yorkshireman had enjoyed only a moderate tour and with his side at 2/28 and the skies threatening, he made his way to the crease in the second innings of the deciding fifth Test. England required 270 more runs to regain the Ashes and Brown was instructed by captain Stoddart to chase the runs before rain ended the game. He made 50 in 28 minutes, then 100 in just over one and a half hours before finally being dismissed for 140 in 145 minutes. England won the Test and the series with J.T. Brown the hero. The masterful batsman and occasional leg-spinner continued playing for Yorkshire until a heart condition claimed his life at the age of only 35.

BROWN, Simon John Emmerson

Born:	June 29, 1969
Batting:	Right handed
Bowling:	Left arm medium-fast

Tests

Test Career:	1996		
Cap Number:	581		
Tests Played:	1		

Test Batting

Innings:	2	Runs:	11
Highest Score:	10*	Average:	11.00
No. 50s:	0	No. 100s:	0

Test Bowling & Fielding

Wickets:	2	Runs:	138
Best Bowling:	1/60	Average:	69.00
5 WI:	0	10 WM:	0
Catches:	1	Stumpings:	0

As England searched for success in the mid 90's the call went out to a number of cricketers who could have hardly have been contemplating Test cricket. One of them 'Chubby' Brown was a given a Test against Pakistan in 1996. He returned match figures of 2/138.

BUCKENHAM, Claude Percival

Born:	January 16, 1876
Batting:	Right handed
Bowling:	Right arm fast

Tests

Test Career:	1910		
Cap Number:	165		
Tests Played:	4		

Test Batting

Innings:	7	Runs:	43
Highest Score:	17	Average:	6.14
No. 50s:	0	No. 100s:	0

Test Bowling & Fielding

Wickets:	21	Runs:	593
Best Bowling:	5/115	Average:	28.23
5 WI:	1	10 WM:	0
Catches:	2	Stumpings:	0

A beanpole opening bowler form Essex, he toured South Africa in 1910 and had a good time of it on the mats taking 21 wickets in his only ever four Tests.

BUTCHER, Alan Raymond

Born:	January 7, 1954
Batting:	Left handed

Tests

Test Career:	1979		
Cap Number:	482		
Tests Played:	1		

Test Batting

Innings:	2	Runs:	34
Highest Score:	20	Average:	17.00
No. 50s:	0	No. 100s:	0

Test Bowling & Fielding

Wickets:	0	Runs:	9
Best Bowling:		Average:	0.00
5 WI:	0	10 WM:	0
Catches:	0	Stumpings:	0

One Day Internationals

ODI Career:	1980		
ODIs Played:	1		

ODI Batting

Innings:	1	Runs:	14
Highest Score:	14	Average:	14.00
No. 50s:	0	No. 100s:	0

ODI Bowling & Fielding

Wickets:	0	Runs:	0
Best Bowling:		Average:	0.00
5 WM:	0	Catches:	0
Stumpings:	0		

The father of Test player Mark Butcher, he played a single Test against India at The Oval in 1979.

BUTCHER, Mark Alan

Born:	August 23, 1972
Batting:	Left handed
Bowling:	Right arm medium

Tests
Test Career:	1997-2004		
Cap Number:	584		
Tests Played:	71		

Test Batting
Innings:	131	Runs:	4,288
Highest Score:	173*	Average:	34.58
No. 50s:	23	No. 100s:	8

Test Bowling & Fielding
Wickets:	15	Runs:	541
Best Bowling:	4/42	Average:	36.06
5 WI:	0	10 WM:	0
Catches:	61	Stumpings:	0

Anyone who witnessed Mark Butcher's brilliant 173 not out against the Australians at Headingly in 2001 would be in no doubt of his ability as a Test batsman. Set 315 to win by a confident Steve Waugh, Butcher set about demolishing an Australian attack that contained Glenn McGrath, Jason Gillespie and Shane Warne. England won the game comfortably and Butcher was being hailed as the best batsman in the English side. It was not his only sparkling Test innings, he hit two other fine centuries against Australia and made eight Test tons in total. Interspersed amongst the good was a fair smattering of bad. Between November 1998 and August 2001 he could manage only 509 in 28 completed Test innings at an average of only 18.17. Interestingly the attacking batsman and useful slow bowler never played a one day game for his country.

BUTCHER, Roland Orlando
Born:	October 14, 1953
Batting:	Right handed
Bowling:	Right arm leg-break

Tests
Test Career:	1981
Cap Number:	489
Tests Played:	3

Test Batting
Innings:	5	Runs:	71
Highest Score:	32	Average:	14.20
No. 50s:	0	No. 100s:	0

Test Bowling & Fielding
Wickets:	0	Runs:	0
Best Bowling:		Average:	0.00
5 WI:	0	10 WM:	0
Catches:	3	Stumpings:	0

One Day Internationals
ODI Career:	1980-81
ODIs Played:	3

ODI Batting
Innings:	3	Runs:	58
Highest Score:	52	Average:	19.33
No. 50s:	1	No. 100s:	0

ODI Bowling & Fielding
Wickets:	0	Runs:	0
Best Bowling:		Average:	0.00
5 WM:	0	Catches:	0
Stumpings:	0		

The Barbados born batsman was England's first West Indian born cricketer when he lined up against the Windies at Bridgetown in 1981. He played his only three Tests on that tour of the Caribbean.

BUTLER, Harold James
Born:	March 12, 1913
Batting:	Right handed
Bowling:	Right arm medium-fast

Tests
Test Career:	1947-48
Cap Number:	323
Tests Played:	2

Test Batting
Innings:	2	Runs:	15
Highest Score:	15*	Average:	15.00
No. 50s:	0	No. 100s:	0

Test Bowling & Fielding
Wickets:	12	Runs:	215
Best Bowling:	4/34	Average:	17.91
5 WI:	0	10 WM:	0
Catches:	1	Stumpings:	0

A brilliant debut saw him return match figures of 7/66 off 52 overs against South Africa in 1947 and earnt him a trip to the West Indies the following year. In his only Test on that tour he took another five wickets but he never played for England again.

BUTT, Henry Rigden (Harry)
Born:	December 27, 1865
Batting:	Right handed
	Wicket Keeper

Tests
Test Career:	1896
Cap Number:	94
Tests Played:	3

Test Batting
Innings:	4	Runs:	22
Highest Score:	13	Average:	7.33
No. 50s:	0	No. 100s:	0

Test Bowling & Fielding
Wickets:	0	Runs:	0
Best Bowling:		Average:	0.00
5 WI:	0	10 WM:	0
Catches:	1	Stumpings:	1

One of the many wicket keepers given a taste of Test cricket in the 19th century, he played all of his three Tests on the mats in South Africa during the 1896 tour.

CADDICK, Andrew Richard
Born:	November 21, 1968
Batting:	Right handed
Bowling:	Right arm medium-fast

Tests
Test Career:	1993-2003
Cap Number:	559
Tests Played:	62

Test Batting
Innings:	95	Runs:	861
Highest Score:	49*	Average:	10.37
No. 50s:	0	No. 100s:	0

Test Bowling & Fielding

Wickets:	234	Runs:	6,999
Best Bowling:	7/46	Average:	29.91
5 WI:	13	10 WM:	1
Catches:	21	Stumpings:	0

One Day Internationals

ODI Career: 1993-2003
ODIs Played: 54

ODI Batting

Innings:	38	Runs:	249
Highest Score:	36	Average:	12.45
No. 50s:	0	No. 100s:	0

ODI Bowling & Fielding

Wickets:	69	Runs:	1,965
Best Bowling:	4/19	Average:	28.47
5 WM:	0	Catches:	9
Stumpings:	0		

For much of the 90's England's new ball duties fell to Somerset's Andy Caddick. The long legged quick responded with a number of fine efforts, but the fact he was called upon so often reflects the paucity of English fast bowlers at the time. He took 18 wickets in four Tests on the tour to the West Indies in 1993/94 to be England's leading bowler. England lost that series 3-1 and whilst it was no reflection on Caddick it did highlight the limitations of using him as a strike bowler. Throughout his Test career, the New Zealand born quickly gave his all against the Australians and it was fitting that he should record his best Test figures against the Aussies in his final Test. He took ten wickets for the match and for once had the best of the powerful Australian top order.

CALTHORPE, Frederick Somerset Gough

Born: May 27, 1892
Batting: Right handed
Bowling: Right arm medium

Tests

Test Career: 1930
Cap Number: 252
Tests Played: 4

Test Batting

Innings:	7	Runs:	129
Highest Score:	49	Average:	18.42
No. 50s:	0	No. 100s:	0

Test Bowling & Fielding

Wickets:	1	Runs:	91
Best Bowling:	1/38	Average:	91.00
5 WI:	0	10 WM:	0
Catches:	3	Stumpings:	0

He had taken an M.C.C side to the Caribbean in 1926 and was rewarded when the M.C.C. sent a squad their again in 1930. The 38 year old played in four matches that were eventually recognised as Tests.

CAPEL, David John

Born: February 6, 1963
Batting: Right handed
Bowling: Right arm medium-fast

Tests

Test Career: 1987-90
Cap Number: 526
Tests Played: 15

Test Batting

Innings:	25	Runs:	374
Highest Score:	98	Average:	15.58
No. 50s:	2	No. 100s:	0

Test Bowling & Fielding

Wickets:	21	Runs:	1,064
Best Bowling:	3/88	Average:	50.66
5 WI:	0	10 WM:	0
Catches:	6	Stumpings:	0

One Day Internationals

ODI Career: 1987-90
ODIs Played: 23

ODI Batting

Innings:	19	Runs:	327
Highest Score:	50*	Average:	19.23
No. 50s:	1	No. 100s:	0

ODI Bowling & Fielding

Wickets:	17	Runs:	805
Best Bowling:	3/38	Average:	47.35
5 WM:	0	Catches:	6
Stumpings:	0		

A lightly built medium pace bowler and quick scoring batsman whose claim to fame was dismissing Viv Richards three times in Tests. He also scored 98 against Pakistan at Karachi in 1987/88.

CARR, Arthur William

Born: May 21, 1893
Batting: Right handed
Bowling: Right arm medium

Tests

Test Career: 1922-29
Cap Number: 206
Tests Played: 11

Test Batting

Innings:	13	Runs:	237
Highest Score:	63	Average:	19.75
No. 50s:	1	No. 100s:	0

Test Bowling & Fielding

Wickets:	0	Runs:	0
Best Bowling:		Average:	0.00
5 WI:	0	10 WM:	0
Catches:	3	Stumpings:	0

The famous Notts captain played in eleven Tests for England, but with the exception of a single knock of 63 against South Africa in 1922/23, he was never able to reproduce the form that saw him score over 20,000 first class runs with 45 centuries. He captained the side in six of his Tests, for one win and five draws. Whilst he was an astute leader his poor form with the bat cost him his spot in the side.

CARR, Donald Bryce

Born: December 28, 1926
Batting: Right handed
Bowling: Left arm off-break

172

Tests
Test Career:	1951-52		
Cap Number:	362		
Tests Played:	2		

Test Batting
Innings:	4	Runs:	135
Highest Score:	76	Average:	33.75
No. 50s:	1	No. 100s:	0

Test Bowling & Fielding
Wickets:	2	Runs:	140
Best Bowling:	2/84	Average:	70.00
5 WI:	0	10 WM:	0
Catches:	0	Stumpings:	0

Donald Carr toured India in 1951/52, and although scoring 76 in the second innings of his first Test, played only once more for England. He served as an ICC match referee in the early 1990's.

CARR, Douglas Ward
Born:	March 17, 1872
Batting:	Right handed
Bowling:	Right arm leg-break

Tests
Test Career:	1909		
Cap Number:	162		
Tests Played:	1		

Test Batting
Innings:	1	Runs:	0
Highest Score:	0	Average:	0.00
No. 50s:	0	No. 100s:	0

Test Bowling & Fielding
Wickets:	7	Runs:	282
Best Bowling:	5/146	Average:	40.28
5 WI:	1	10 WM:	0
Catches:	0	Stumpings:	0

A googly bowler from Kent, he performed well in his only Test taking seven wickets against the Australians at The Oval in 1909.

CARTWRIGHT, Thomas William
Born:	July 22, 1935
Batting:	Right handed
Bowling:	Right arm medium

Tests
Test Career:	1964-65		
Cap Number:	424		
Tests Played:	5		

Test Batting
Innings:	7	Runs:	26
Highest Score:	9	Average:	5.20
No. 50s:	0	No. 100s:	0

Test Bowling & Fielding
Wickets:	15	Runs:	544
Best Bowling:	6/94	Average:	36.26
5 WI:	1	10 WM:	0
Catches:	2	Stumpings:	0

The medium pacer played four Tests against Australia in 1964 but could manage only five wickets. He had a more successful summer the following year when he took six wickets in an innings against the touring Springboks at Trent Bridge. A lusty lower order batsman he once scored a double century for Warwickshire.

CHAPMAN, Arthur Percy Frank (Percy)
Born:	September 3, 1900
Batting:	Left handed

Tests
Test Career:	1924-31		
Cap Number:	213		
Tests Played:	26		

Test Batting
Innings:	36	Runs:	925
Highest Score:	121	Average:	28.90
No. 50s:	5	No. 100s:	1

Test Bowling & Fielding
Wickets:	0	Runs:	20
Best Bowling:	0	Average:	0.00
5 WI:	0	10 WM:	0
Catches:	32	Stumpings:	0

A hard hitting left hander from Kent who was a renowned clubber of sixes, he captained England in 17 Tests for a record of nine wins and only two losses. His very first match as skipper was the famous fifth Test at the Oval in 1926. In a damp summer the first four matches of the series had resulted in a draw and Chapman had been handed the reins when an out of form Arthur Carr was omitted from the side. England won the match convincingly and he retained the captaincy until the corresponding match at the same ground in 1930. His best result at the helm was the Ashes series in Australia in 1928/29 which the English won 4-1. Whilst he was an inconsistent batsman in Tests, he did score 121 against the Australians at Lord's in 1930 in a typically forceful innings.

CHAPPLE, Glen
Born:	January 23, 1974
Batting:	Right handed
Bowling:	Right arm medium-fast

One Day Internationals
ODI Career:	2006		
ODIs Played:	1		

ODI Batting
Innings:	1	Runs:	14
Highest Score:	14	Average:	14.00
No. 50s:	0	No. 100s:	0

ODI Bowling & Fielding
Wickets:	0	Runs:	14
Best Bowling:	0	Average:	0.00
5 WM:	0	Catches:	0
Stumpings:	0		

A respected County veteran, Yorkshire born paceman Glen Chapple, at 32, played his first and to date, only ODI against Ireland at Belfast in 2006,

CHARLWOOD, Henry Rupert James
Born:	December 19, 1846
Batting:	Right handed

Tests
Test Career:	1877
Cap Number:	2
Tests Played:	2

Test Batting			
Innings:	4	Runs:	63
Highest Score:	36	Average:	15.75
No. 50s:	0	No. 100s:	0
Test Bowling & Fielding			
Wickets:	0	Runs:	0
Best Bowling:		Average:	0.00
5 WI:	0	10 WM:	0
Catches:	0	Stumpings:	0

One of four brothers who played for Sussex, he played in the first ever Test match and performed admirably making 36 in the first innings when batting at number three.

CHATTERTON, William
Born: December 27, 1861
Batting: Right handed

Tests
Test Career:	1892		
Cap Number:	74		
Tests Played:	1		
Test Batting			
Innings:	1	Runs:	48
Highest Score:	48	Average:	48.00
No. 50s:	0	No. 100s:	0
Test Bowling & Fielding			
Wickets:	0	Runs:	0
Best Bowling:		Average:	0.00
5 WI:	0	10 WM:	0
Catches:	0	Stumpings:	0

Eventhough his only Test was as part of the weakened side that toured South Africa in 1892, he was a champion batsman with Derbyshire for whom he scored ten centuries. Noted as a cautious batsman and smart lob bowler, he played first class cricket into his forties until overcome by ill-health. Chatterton died of consumption at the age of 51.

CHILDS, John Henry
Born: August 15, 1951
Batting: Left handed
Bowling: Left arm off-break

Tests
Test Career:	1988		
Cap Number:	528		
Tests Played:	2		
Test Batting			
Innings:	4	Runs:	2
Highest Score:	2*	Average:	0.00
No. 50s:	0	No. 100s:	0
Test Bowling & Fielding			
Wickets:	3	Runs:	183
Best Bowling:	1/13	Average:	61.00
5 WI:	0	10 WM:	0
Catches:	1	Stumpings:	0

A surprise selection to tour the West Indies in 1988, the left arm off spinner played in two Tests but could manage only three wickets.

CHRISTOPHERSON, Stanley
Born: November 11, 1861
Batting: Right handed
Bowling: Right arm fast

Tests
Test Career:	1884		
Cap Number:	45		
Tests Played:	1		
Test Batting			
Innings:	1	Runs:	17
Highest Score:	17	Average:	17.00
No. 50s:	0	No. 100s:	0
Test Bowling & Fielding			
Wickets:	1	Runs:	69
Best Bowling:	1/52	Average:	69.00
5 WI:	0	10 WM:	0
Catches:	0	Stumpings:	0

One of ten cricketing brothers from Kent, he was a fast bowler who took one wicket in his only Test but did score a handy 17 coming in at number eleven.

CLARK, Edward Winchester
Born: August 9, 1902
Batting: Left handed
Bowling: Left arm fast

Tests
Test Career:	1929-34		
Cap Number:	245		
Tests Played:	8		
Test Batting			
Innings:	9	Runs:	36
Highest Score:	10	Average:	9.00
No. 50s:	0	No. 100s:	0
Test Bowling & Fielding			
Wickets:	32	Runs:	899
Best Bowling:	5/98	Average:	28.09
5 WI:	1	10 WM:	0
Catches:	0	Stumpings:	0

The fair haired fast bowler from Northampton had his finest moment for England in his final Test at The Oval in 1934. The left hander known as 'Nobby' took five wickets in the second innings including the prized scalps of Don Bradman and Stan McCabe. Whilst he never played for his country again he continued for another ten years in county cricket.

CLARKE, Rikki
Born: September 29, 1981
Batting: Right handed
Bowling: Right arm medium-fast

Tests
Test Career:	2003		
Cap Number:	620		
Tests Played:	2		
Test Batting			
Innings:	3	Runs:	96
Highest Score:	55	Average:	32.00
No. 50s:	1	No. 100s:	0
Test Bowling & Fielding			
Wickets:	4	Runs:	60
Best Bowling:	2/7	Average:	15.00
5 WI:	0	10 WM:	0
Catches:	1	Stumpings:	0

One Day Internationals
ODI Career:	2003-04
ODIs Played:	17

The Encyclopedia of International Cricketers - England

ODI Batting

Innings:	10	Runs:	99
Highest Score:	37	Average:	9.90
No. 50s:	0	No. 100s:	0

ODI Bowling & Fielding

Wickets:	10	Runs:	351
Best Bowling:	2/28	Average:	35.10
5 WM:	0	Catches:	11
Stumpings:	0		

The gangly youngster from Surrey may look ungainly but he is a talented batsman and equally impressive first change bowler. His two Tests against Bangladesh were encouraging with a high score of 55 at Chittagong, and he remains in contention for a spot in the English one day side.

CLAY, John Charles

Born:	March 18, 1898
Batting:	Right handed
Bowling:	Right arm off-break

Tests

Test Career:	1935
Cap Number:	288
Tests Played:	1

Test Batting

Innings:	0	Runs:	0
Highest Score:	0	Average:	0.00
No. 50s:	0	No. 100s:	0

Test Bowling & Fielding

Wickets:	0	Runs:	75
Best Bowling:		Average:	0.00
5 WI:	0	10 WM:	0
Catches:	1	Stumpings:	0

A Welsh born off-spinner who played a single Test against South Africa at Lord's in 1935.

CLOSE, Dennis Brian (Brian)

Born:	February 24, 1931
Batting:	Left handed

Tests

Test Career:	1949-76
Cap Number:	344
Tests Played:	22

Test Batting

Innings:	37	Runs:	887
Highest Score:	70	Average:	25.34
No. 50s:	4	No. 100s:	0

Test Bowling & Fielding

Wickets:	18	Runs:	532
Best Bowling:	4/35	Average:	29.55
5 WI:	0	10 WM:	0
Catches:	24	Stumpings:	0

One Day Internationals

ODI Career:	1972
ODIs Played:	3

ODI Batting

Innings:	3	Runs:	49
Highest Score:	43	Average:	16.33
No. 50s:	0	No. 100s:	0

ODI Bowling & Fielding

Wickets:	0	Runs:	21
Best Bowling:		Average:	0.00
5 WM:	0	Catches:	1
Stumpings:	0		

Very few cricketers can boast a Test career that spans 27 years, but the fact that Brian Close played only 22 Tests in that period shows that he and controversy were never far apart. He made his debut as an 18 year old on home soil against New Zealand and played a single Test against Australia 18 months later in 1950/51. Close was played more as an all-rounder than batsman in those Tests, but a return of just one run in three innings saw him relegated to county cricket for four seasons. He was an in infrequent performer in the late fifties paying the price for pursuing a professional football career. It wasn't until 1963 that he held down a regular Test spot and 1966 that he was handed the captaincy. England flourished under his leadership winning six of seven Tests, but just as it seemed as player and country were finally comfortable he ran foul of authorities. A controversy that stemmed from county cricket saw him stripped of the English captaincy. He moved from Yorkshire to Somerset in the 1970's rekindling his career and earning a recall to the Test side against the might of the West Indies in 1976. The then 45 year old batted with enormous courage scoring 60 and 46 in the second Test at Lord's to be England's highest scorer for the match.

COLDWELL, Leonard John

Born:	January 10, 1933
Batting:	Right handed
Bowling:	Right arm medium-fast

Tests

Test Career:	1962-64
Cap Number:	411
Tests Played:	7

Test Batting

Innings:	7	Runs:	9
Highest Score:	6*	Average:	4.50
No. 50s:	0	No. 100s:	0

Test Bowling & Fielding

Wickets:	22	Runs:	610
Best Bowling:	6/85	Average:	27.72
5 WI:	1	10 WM:	0
Catches:	1	Stumpings:	0

The medium fast bowler from Worcester made his Test debut against Pakistan in 1962, taking 13 wickets in his first two Tests. Caldwell struggled from that point on capturing only nine wickets in five more Tests.

COLLINGWOOD, Paul David

Born:	May 26, 1976
Batting:	Right handed
Bowling:	Right arm medium

Tests

Test Career:	2003-
Cap Number:	622
Tests Played:	14

Test Batting

Innings:	26	Runs:	996
Highest Score:	186	Average:	41.50
No. 50s:	3	No. 100s:	2

Test Bowling & Fielding

Wickets:	1	Runs:	216
Best Bowling:	1/33	Average:	216.00
5 WI:	0	10 WM:	0
Catches:	19	Stumpings:	0

One Day Internationals

ODI Career:	2001-		
ODIs Played:	95		

ODI Batting

Innings:	85	Runs:	2,119
Highest Score:	112*	Average:	32.60
No. 50s:	11	No. 100s:	2

ODI Bowling & Fielding

Wickets:	48	Runs:	1,830
Best Bowling:	6/31	Average:	38.12
5 WM:	1	Catches:	51
Stumpings:	0		

The persistent Collingwood has gone from one day specialist to regular Test batsman against the predictions of most experts. His early Test career was a haltering affair that returned just four matches over a two year period. He finally turned the corner on the tour of Pakistan and India in 2005/06 with a 96 and 80 at Lahore that he quickly followed with a maiden Test century in Nagpur. Collingwood made good on that form with a career high 186 against Pakistan at Lord's later in 2006. His medium pace, so effective in one day cricket, has been less so at Test level and it wasn't until his 14th Test that he finally took his first wicket.

COMPTON, Denis Charles Scott

Born:	May 23, 1918
Batting:	Right handed
Bowling:	Left arm medium

Tests

Test Career:	1937-57
Cap Number:	297
Tests Played:	78

Test Batting

Innings:	131	Runs:	5,807
Highest Score:	278	Average:	50.06
No. 50s:	28	No. 100s:	17

Test Bowling & Fielding

Wickets:	25	Runs:	1,410
Best Bowling:	5/70	Average:	56.40
5 WI:	1	10 WM:	0
Catches:	49	Stumpings:	0

A champion cricketer and footballer, he was the embodiment of the British sporting gentleman. Just as Sir Donald Bradman had lifted Australian spirits through that country's debilitating depression in the 30's, Compton was chosen as the man to rekindle hope in the years following World War II. As a cricketer he had the application and talent to become one of the best batsmen the game has seen. He was an imperious timer of the ball, needing only to lean on a cover drive to send them rushing to the boundary. He employed the sweep whenever possible and whilst it brought countless runs there were times it caused his downfall when he seemed impossible to remove. He made his Test debut just prior to the war and even though there was only time for seven Tests he scored two fine centuries and established his spot in the English side. When cricket resumed he took little time in re-establishing himself. He scored a century in each innings of the Adelaide Test on the 1946/47 Ashes tour and later that year destroyed the visiting South Africans with 753 in five runs that included two centuries and a double century. Compton was not only at the height of his powers as a Test cricketer, he was also a leading light for Arsenal FC in the English first division. His football came at a cost with knee injuries starting to affect his availability for the Tests side. He was unhindered in 1948 when his 562 runs against Bradman's Australians was the best effort by an Englishman. Over the next decade he was the mainstay of the English middle order, wonky knee permitting. He scored 17 Test centuries with a career high 278 against Pakistan at Trent Bridge in 1954. He was also a handy part chinaman bowler who once took five wickets in an innings against South Africa. For all of his talents on-field Compton's greatest legacy might be his place as England's first marketable cricketer. The man who sold Brylcream to millions paved the way for countless others to make more out of the sport than just match payments and a goodbye testimonial.

COOK, Alastair

Born:	December 25, 1984
Batting:	Left handed
Bowling:	Right arm slow

Tests

Test Career:	2006-
Cap Number:	630
Tests Played:	8

Test Batting

Innings:	14	Runs:	638
Highest Score:	127	Average:	53.16
No. 50s:	2	No. 100s:	3

Test Bowling & Fielding

Wickets:	0	Runs:	0
Best Bowling:		Average:	0.00
5 WI:	0	10 WM:	0
Catches:	6	Stumpings:	0

One Day Internationals

ODI Career:	2006-
ODIs Played:	2

ODI Batting

Innings:	2	Runs:	80
Highest Score:	41	Average:	40.00
No. 50s:	0	No. 100s:	0

ODI Bowling & Fielding

Wickets:	0	Runs:	0
Best Bowling:		Average:	0.00
5 WM:	0	Catches:	0
Stumpings:	0		

The dark haired batsman has done nothing but impress since scoring 60 and 104 not out on debut against India Nagpur at the start of 2006. In eight Tests he's hit three centuries and has looked at home either opening the batting in Marcus Trescothick absence at batting at number three. His greatest Test will come on the tour of Australia at the end of 2006 but the 21 year old gives every indication that he'll be up to the task.

COOK, Cecil
Born: August 23, 1921
Batting: Right handed
Bowling: Left arm off-break

Tests
Test Career: 1947
Cap Number: 317
Tests Played: 1

Test Batting
Innings:	2	Runs:	4
Highest Score:	4	Average:	2.00
No. 50s:	0	No. 100s:	0

Test Bowling & Fielding
Wickets:	0	Runs:	127
Best Bowling:		Average:	0.00
5 WI:	0	10 WM:	0
Catches:	0	Stumpings:	0

A right arm 'offie' known as Sam, he played one Test against South Africa in 1947 but failed to flatter.

COOK, Geoffrey
Born: October 9, 1951
Batting: Right handed
Bowling: Left arm off-break

Tests
Test Career: 1982-83
Cap Number: 493
Tests Played: 7

Test Batting
Innings:	13	Runs:	203
Highest Score:	66	Average:	15.61
No. 50s:	2	No. 100s:	0

Test Bowling & Fielding
Wickets:	0	Runs:	27
Best Bowling:		Average:	0.00
5 WI:	0	10 WM:	0
Catches:	9	Stumpings:	0

One Day Internationals
ODI Career: 1981-83
ODIs Played: 6

ODI Batting
Innings:	6	Runs:	106
Highest Score:	32	Average:	17.66
No. 50s:	0	No. 100s:	0

ODI Bowling & Fielding
Wickets:	0	Runs:	0
Best Bowling:		Average:	0.00
5 WM:	0	Catches:	2
Stumpings:	0		

With a number of players suspended because of their involvement on a rebel tour to South Africa, the Northants opener was given a chance at level in 1982. He struggled in his seven Tests averaging just over 15.

COOK, Nicholas Grant Billson
Born: June 17, 1956
Batting: Right handed
Bowling: Left arm off-break

Tests
Test Career: 1983-89
Cap Number: 501
Tests Played: 15

Test Batting
Innings:	25	Runs:	179
Highest Score:	31	Average:	8.52
No. 50s:	0	No. 100s:	0

Test Bowling & Fielding
Wickets:	52	Runs:	1,689
Best Bowling:	6/65	Average:	32.48
5 WI:	4	10 WM:	0
Catches:	5	Stumpings:	0

One Day Internationals
ODI Career: 1984-89
ODIs Played: 3

ODI Batting
Innings:	0	Runs:	0
Highest Score:	0	Average:	0.00
No. 50s:	0	No. 100s:	0

ODI Bowling & Fielding
Wickets:	5	Runs:	95
Best Bowling:	2/18	Average:	19.00
5 WI:	0	Catches:	2
Stumpings:	0		

A left arm off spinner who played for both Leicestershire and Northants. He made his debut against the Kiwis at Lord's in 1983 with 5/35 in the first innings. Cook's best bowling in a Test match was against Pakistan in Karachi in 1983/84 where he finished with 11/83.

COPE, Geoffrey Alan
Born: February 23, 1947
Batting: Right handed
Bowling: Right arm off-break

Tests
Test Career: 1977-78
Cap Number: 475
Tests Played: 3

Test Batting
Innings:	3	Runs:	40
Highest Score:	22	Average:	13.33
No. 50s:	0	No. 100s:	0

Test Bowling & Fielding
Wickets:	8	Runs:	277
Best Bowling:	3/102	Average:	34.62
5 WI:	0	10 WM:	0
Catches:	1	Stumpings:	0

One Day Internationals
ODI Career: 1977-78
ODIs Played: 2

ODI Batting
Innings:	1	Runs:	1
Highest Score:	1*	Average:	0.00
No. 50s:	0	No. 100s:	0

ODI Bowling & Fielding
Wickets:	2	Runs:	35
Best Bowling:	1/16	Average:	17.50
5 WM:	0	Catches:	0
Stumpings:	0		

An off spinner who had altered his action on more than occasion after it was deemed illegal by authorities. He played three Tests on the tour of Pakistan in 1978/79.

COPSON, William Henry
Born: April 27, 1908
Batting: Right handed
Bowling: Right arm medium-fast

Tests
Test Career: 1939-47
Cap Number: 309
Tests Played: 3

Test Batting
Innings:	1	Runs:	6
Highest Score:	6	Average:	6.00
No. 50s:	0	No. 100s:	0

Test Bowling & Fielding
Wickets:	15	Runs:	297
Best Bowling:	5/85	Average:	19.80
5 WI:	1	10 WM:	0
Catches:	1	Stumpings:	0

The red headed paceman from Derbyshire took 15 wickets in a three Test career that was interrupted by the Second World War.

CORK, Dominic Gerald
Born: August 7, 1971
Batting: Right handed
Bowling: Right arm medium-fast

Tests
Test Career: 1995-2002
Cap Number: 572
Tests Played: 37

Test Batting
Innings:	56	Runs:	864
Highest Score:	59	Average:	18.00
No. 50s:	3	No. 100s:	0

Test Bowling & Fielding
Wickets:	131	Runs:	3,906
Best Bowling:	7/43	Average:	29.81
5 WI:	5	10 WM:	0
Catches:	18	Stumpings:	0

One Day Internationals
ODI Career: 1992-2002
ODIs Played: 32

ODI Batting
Innings:	21	Runs:	180
Highest Score:	31*	Average:	10.00
No. 50s:	0	No. 100s:	0

ODI Bowling & Fielding
Wickets:	41	Runs:	1,368
Best Bowling:	3/27	Average:	33.36
5 WM:	0	Catches:	6
Stumpings:	0		

Lean and athletic, the speedster had the cricket world at his feet when he burst onto the Test scene against the West Indies at Lord's in 1995. With the visitors at 2/124 in their second innings and chasing 296 runs for victory Cork took matters into his own hands taking 7/43 to dismiss the West Indies 73 runs short. He took 26 wickets in five Tests against the Windies to be named 'Man of the Series'. In his very next series against South Africa he took 19 wickets to secure an opening bowlers spot alongside Darren Gough. When fit he had pace and lift to trouble any batsman as his 131 Test wickets suggest.

CORNFORD, Walter Latter
Born: December 25, 1900
Batting: Right handed
Wicket Keeper

Tests
Test Career: 1930
Cap Number: 247
Tests Played: 4

Test Batting
Innings:	4	Runs:	36
Highest Score:	18	Average:	9.00
No. 50s:	0	No. 100s:	0

Test Bowling & Fielding
Wickets:	0	Runs:	0
Best Bowling:		Average:	0.00
5 WI:	0	10 WM:	0
Catches:	5	Stumpings:	3

Standing only five foot tall, Tich Cornford was even 'tichier' than his contemporary Tich Freeman. The Sussex keeper played in only four Tests, standing up to the stumps to pacemen and spinners alike. Whilst he was a fine gloveman he had a horror Test in Auckland in 1930 when he let through 31 byes in a single innings.

COTTAM, Robert Michael Henry
Born: October 16, 1944
Batting: Right handed
Bowling: Right arm medium-fast

Tests
Test Career: 1969-73
Cap Number: 441
Tests Played: 4

Test Batting
Innings:	5	Runs:	27
Highest Score:	13	Average:	6.75
No. 50s:	0	No. 100s:	0

Test Bowling & Fielding
Wickets:	14	Runs:	327
Best Bowling:	4/50	Average:	23.35
5 WI:	0	10 WM:	0
Catches:	2	Stumpings:	0

A tall medium pace bowler from Hampshire, he toured Pakistan then later India where his willingness to work hard was put to good use.

COVENTRY, Charles John
Born: February 26, 1867
Batting: Right handed

Tests
Test Career: 1889
Cap Number: 62
Tests Played: 2

Test Batting
Innings:	2	Runs:	13
Highest Score:	12	Average:	13.00
No. 50s:	0	No. 100s:	0

Test Bowling & Fielding

Wickets:	0	Runs:	0
Best Bowling:		Average:	0.00
5 WI:	0	10 WM:	0
Catches:	0	Stumpings:	0

Like many of the cricketers who toured South Africa in 1888/89 he only got a spot in the side because he was able to pay for his travel to the colonial outpost. His two Tests were in fact his only first class games.

COWANS, Norman George

Born: April 17, 1961
Batting: Right handed
Bowling: Right arm fast

Tests

Test Career:	1982-85
Cap Number:	500
Tests Played:	19

Test Batting

Innings:	29	Runs:	175
Highest Score:	36	Average:	7.95
No. 50s:	0	No. 100s:	0

Test Bowling & Fielding

Wickets:	51	Runs:	2,003
Best Bowling:	6/77	Average:	39.27
5 WI:	2	10 WM:	0
Catches:	9	Stumpings:	0

One Day Internationals

ODI Career:	1983-85
ODIs Played:	23

ODI Batting

Innings:	8	Runs:	13
Highest Score:	4*	Average:	2.60
No. 50s:	0	No. 100s:	0

ODI Bowling & Fielding

Wickets:	23	Runs:	913
Best Bowling:	3/44	Average:	39.69
5 WM:	0	Catches:	5
Stumpings:	0		

The Jamaican born Cowans was selected to tour Australia in 1982/83 on potential rather than performance. His took 11 wickets in four Tests, with the standout effort coming at Melbourne where his 6/77 in the second innings gave England a surprise victory. He would struggle to regain the rhythm he had in that match again was out of international cricket by 1985.

COWDREY, Christopher Stuart

Born: October 20, 1957
Batting: Right handed

Tests

Test Career:	1984-88
Cap Number:	510
Tests Played:	6

Test Batting

Innings:	8	Runs:	101
Highest Score:	38	Average:	14.42
No. 50s:	0	No. 100s:	0

Test Bowling & Fielding

Wickets:	4	Runs:	309
Best Bowling:	2/65	Average:	77.25
5 WI:	0	10 WM:	0
Catches:	5	Stumpings:	0

One Day Internationals

ODI Career:	1985
ODIs Played:	3

ODI Batting

Innings:	3	Runs:	51
Highest Score:	46*	Average:	25.50
No. 50s:	0	No. 100s:	0

ODI Bowling & Fielding

Wickets:	2	Runs:	55
Best Bowling:	1/3	Average:	27.50
5 WM:	0	Catches:	0
Stumpings:	0		

The son of English great Colin Cowdrey played only six Tests but controversially captained England in one of them against the West Indies in 1988. He was a solid if unspectacular top order batsman.

COWDREY, Michael Colin

Born: December 24, 1932
Batting: Right handed
Bowling: Right arm leg-break

Tests

Test Career:	1954-75
Cap Number:	379
Tests Played:	114

Test Batting

Innings:	188	Runs:	7,624
Highest Score:	182	Average:	44.06
No. 50s:	38	No. 100s:	22

Test Bowling & Fielding

Wickets:	0	Runs:	104
Best Bowling:		Average:	0.00
5 WI:	0	10 WM:	0
Catches:	120	Stumpings:	0

One Day Internationals

ODI Career:	1971
ODIs Played:	1

ODI Batting

Innings:	1	Runs:	1
Highest Score:	1	Average:	1.00
No. 50s:	0	No. 100s:	0

ODI Bowling & Fielding

Wickets:	0	Runs:	0
Best Bowling:		Average:	0.00
5 WM:	0	Catches:	0
Stumpings:	0		

There were many famous firsts in the career of Colin Cowdrey. He was the first Englishman to play 100 Tests, the first cricketer to receive a peerage and the first man called on when his country was suffering at the hands of the Dennis Lillee and Jeff Thomson. Colin, or Michael as he was then known, came to prominence as a schoolboy prodigy in 1946. He was playing first class cricket for Kent by the age of 17 and made his Test debut as a 21 year on the Ashes tour in 1954. That what would the first of six visits to Australia over a 20 year period. The youngster impressed in the close fought series, scoring over 300 runs, including a maiden Test hundred at the MCG in the third Test. He would go on to score 22 Test centuries, reaching triple figures against all the other Test playing nations. Firstly as a middle order batsman then later as an opener, he had a flawless defensive technique and was often at his best when the side was facing adversity. He led a losing battle against Australia away in 1958/59 with over 300 runs at an average of 43.44. The fact he had an impenetrable defense didn't mean that he was a stonewaller, with punishing strokeplay the feature of many of his hundreds. Cowdrey's 159 against Pakistan in 1962 took just over four hours, and his Test high 182 at The Oval in the same series contained over a century in boundaries. The 42 year old was enjoying the spoils of middle age when asked to provide some backbone to a brittle English batting line-up in 1974/75. The side had been trounced by Australia in the first Test of that Ashes series at Brisbane when Sir Colin received the call. The notion of on overweight, retired cricketer being called out to save the side may have been a sign of surrender by the English, but he not only came to Australia, he performed admirably. In his first Test innings for over three years, the portly number three resisted Lillee and Thomson for over two hours to score a brave 22. He played out the remained of the series, providing stout resistance to the formidable Australian speed attack. Cowdrey, captained England in 27 Tests and played almost 700 games of first class cricket. It was a life consumed by cricket, and the man dubbed a modern day W. G. Grace was elevated to the House of Lords in 1997.

COXON, Alexander (Alec)
Born: January 18, 1916
Batting: Right handed
Bowling: Right arm medium-fast

Tests
Test Career: 1948
Cap Number: 334
Tests Played: 1

Test Batting
Innings:	2	Runs:	19
Highest Score:	19	Average:	9.50
No. 50s:	0	No. 100s:	0

Test Bowling & Fielding
Wickets:	3	Runs:	172
Best Bowling:	2/90	Average:	57.33
5 WI:	0	10 WM:	0
Catches:	0	Stumpings:	0

His Test career started promisingly, dismissing Sid Barnes for a duck in his first spell, but by the end of the match he had recorded figures of 3/172 and never played for England again.

CRANSTON, James
Born: January 9, 1859
Batting: Left handed

Tests
Test Career: 1890
Cap Number: 69
Tests Played: 1

Test Batting
Innings:	2	Runs:	31
Highest Score:	16	Average:	15.50
No. 50s:	0	No. 100s:	0

Test Bowling & Fielding
Wickets:	0	Runs:	0
Best Bowling:		Average:	0.00
5 WI:	0	10 WM:	0
Catches:	1	Stumpings:	0

His one Test, against the Australians in 1890, was a close fought match that the English won in no small part because of his brave 16 in the second innings. A promising career was cut short when he took ill on the field whilst playing for Gloucestershire.

CRANSTON, Kenneth
Born: October 20, 1917
Batting: Right handed
Bowling: Right arm medium

Tests
Test Career: 1947-48
Cap Number: 321
Tests Played: 8

Test Batting
Innings:	14	Runs:	209
Highest Score:	45	Average:	14.92
No. 50s:	0	No. 100s:	0

Test Bowling & Fielding
Wickets:	18	Runs:	461
Best Bowling:	4/12	Average:	25.61
5 WI:	0	10 WM:	0
Catches:	3	Stumpings:	0

The Navy man had risen from virtual obscurity in 1946 to national selection in 1947. He had been playing minor county cricket when Lancashire not only selected him, but made him captain. Test honours soon followed but a promising career was abandoned when Cranston chose to concentrate on his dental practice.

CRAPP, John Frederick (Jack)
Born: October 14, 1912
Batting: Left handed

Tests
Test Career: 1948-49
Cap Number: 335
Tests Played: 7

Test Batting
Innings:	13	Runs:	319
Highest Score:	56	Average:	29.00
No. 50s:	3	No. 100s:	0

Test Bowling & Fielding
Wickets:	0	Runs:	0
Best Bowling:		Average:	0.00
5 WI:	0	10 WM:	0
Catches:	7	Stumpings:	0

A natty left handed batsman from Gloucs, he struggled against the Australians in 1948 but enjoyed more success when touring to South Africa the next year. He umpired four Tests in the mid sixties.

CRAWFORD, John Neville (Jack)

Born: December 1, 1866
Batting: Right handed

Tests
Test Career: 1906-08
Cap Number: 146
Tests Played: 12

Test Batting
Innings:	23	Runs:	469
Highest Score:	74	Average:	22.33
No. 50s:	2	No. 100s:	0

Test Bowling & Fielding
Wickets:	39	Runs:	1,150
Best Bowling:	5/48	Average:	29.48
5 WI:	3	10 WM:	0
Catches:	13	Stumpings:	0

The bespectacled Crawford was a leading all-rounder who was lost to English cricket after tangling with authorities at his county club Surrey. That prompted a move to Australia, but prior to that he had played 12 Tests for England in which he took 39 wickets and scored almost 500 runs. A genuine fast medium bowler he was also a clean hitter of the ball who once landed a six on the top balcony of the Lord's pavilion.

CRAWLEY, John Paul

Born: September 21, 1971
Batting: Right handed
Bowling: Right arm medium

Tests
Test Career: 1994-2003
Cap Number: 569
Tests Played: 37

Test Batting
Innings:	61	Runs:	1,800
Highest Score:	156*	Average:	34.61
No. 50s:	9	No. 100s:	4

Test Bowling & Fielding
Wickets:	0	Runs:	0
Best Bowling:		Average:	0.00
5 WI:	0	10 WM:	0
Catches:	29	Stumpings:	0

One Day Internationals
ODI Career: 1994-1999
ODIs Played: 13

ODI Batting
Innings:	12	Runs:	235
Highest Score:	73	Average:	21.36
No. 50s:	2	No. 100s:	0

ODI Bowling & Fielding
Wickets:	0	Runs:	0
Best Bowling:		Average:	0.00
5 WM:	0	Catches:	1
Stumpings:	1		

First with Lancashire, and then with Hampshire his heavy scoring in county cricket has always meant that John Crawley demands attention. He made his Test debut against South Africa at Lord's 1994 and despite moderate form was selected to tour Australia at the end of the year. The jury was still out after three Tests for 172 runs but over the next decade it became clear that whilst he could hit some attacks for big scores he was just short of world class. His test tons, two against India and one against Sri Lanka and Zimbabwe suggest that he is more comfortable against attacks that lack a genuine fast bowler. Nevertheless each time he's dropped from the Test side he goes back to county cricket and scores heavily. An excellent 2006 season for Hampshire had the 34 year old in line for another trip to Australia for the 2006-07 Ashes series, but when the squad was named he had just missed out.

CROFT, Robert Damien Bale

Born: May 25, 1970
Batting: Right handed
Bowling: Right arm off-break

Tests
Test Career: 1996-2001
Cap Number: 582
Tests Played: 21

Test Batting
Innings:	34	Runs:	421
Highest Score:	37*	Average:	16.19
No. 50s:	0	No. 100s:	0

Test Bowling & Fielding
Wickets:	49	Runs:	1,825
Best Bowling:	5/95	Average:	37.24
5 WI:	1	10 WM:	0
Catches:	10	Stumpings:	0

One Day Internationals
ODI Career: 1996-2001
ODIs Played: 50

ODI Batting
Innings:	36	Runs:	345
Highest Score:	32	Average:	14.37
No. 50s:	0	No. 100s:	0

ODI Bowling & Fielding
Wickets:	45	Runs:	1,743
Best Bowling:	3/51	Average:	38.73
5 WM:	0	Catches:	11
Stumpings:	0		

The cricketer, once facetiously referred to as the best Welsh off-spinner in the world, may not have been the biggest turner of the ball but he was a handy servant in 21 Tests. His best return in a Test innings was 5/95 against New Zealand at Lancaster Park, Christchurch in 1997. In November 2001 he was chosen to tour India but pulled out amid the fear that surrounded air travel following the September 11 attacks in the USA. He never played for England again.

CURTIS, Timothy Stephen

Born: January 15, 1960
Batting: Right handed
Bowling: Right arm leg-break

Tests
Test Career: 1988-89
Cap Number: 529
Tests Played: 5

Test Batting
Innings:	9	Runs:	140
Highest Score:	41	Average:	15.55
No. 50s:	0	No. 100s:	0

Test Bowling & Fielding
Wickets:	0	Runs:	7
Best Bowling:		Average:	0.00
5 WI:	0	10 WM:	0
Catches:	3	Stumpings:	0

He played all of his Test cricket against the touring West Indians in 1988 and the Australians in 1989. The opening batsman's top score in nine Test innings was a 41 against the Aussie at Edgbaston.

CUTTELL, Willis Robert
Born:	September 13, 1863
Batting:	Right handed
Bowling:	Right arm slow

Tests
Test Career:	1899
Cap Number:	112
Tests Played:	2

Test Batting
Innings:	4	Runs:	65
Highest Score:	21	Average:	16.25
No. 50s:	0	No. 100s:	0

Test Bowling & Fielding
Wickets:	6	Runs:	73
Best Bowling:	3/17	Average:	12.16
5 WI:	0	10 WM:	0
Catches:	2	Stumpings:	0

He was a right-arm off spinner who showed enough for his county side Lancashire to receive a nomination as one of Wisden's Cricketers of the Year in 1898. His only two Tests were in South Africa in 1899.

D'OLIVEIRA, Basil Lewis
Born:	October 4, 1931
Batting:	Right handed
Bowling:	Right arm medium

Tests
Test Career:	1966-72
Cap Number:	432
Tests Played:	44

Test Batting
Innings:	70	Runs:	2,484
Highest Score:	158	Average:	40.06
No. 50s:	15	No. 100s:	5

Test Bowling & Fielding
Wickets:	47	Runs:	1,859
Best Bowling:	3/46	Average:	39.55
5 WI:	0	10 WM:	0
Catches:	29	Stumpings:	0

One Day Internationals
ODI Career:	1971-72
ODIs Played:	4

ODI Batting
Innings:	4	Runs:	30
Highest Score:	17	Average:	10.00
No. 50s:	0	No. 100s:	0

ODI Bowling & Fielding
Wickets:	3	Runs:	140
Best Bowling:	1/19	Average:	46.66
5 WM:	0	Catches:	1
Stumpings:	0		

Destructive with the bat, frugal with ball and an important figure in international sport are all apt descriptions of Basil D'Oliveira. Born in Cape Town, he came to England at the behest of John Allot and made an immediate impression with Worcestershire. He was an able contributor in his first Test series scoring three half centuries against the West Indies and chiming in with eight wickets. His output would not diminish in his next 40 Tests for England. A quick scorer with a flashing square drive, he scored five Test tons including a career high 158 against the Aussies at The Oval in 1968. He highlighted the injustices of the apartheid system in South Africa when his inclusion in the Test squad meant that he would have to travel separately from the side once back in his native South Africa. England pulled out of the tour, and by 1970 South Africa had been banned from Test cricket altogether. The all-rounder was a part of the Test side until 1972 when he was replaced, somewhat ironically, by former South African Tony Greig.

DALRYMPLE, James William
Born:	January 21, 1981
Batting:	Right handed
Bowling:	Right arm off-break

One Day Internationals
ODI Career:	2006
ODIs Played:	6

ODI Batting
Innings:	6	Runs:	219
Highest Score:	67	Average:	36.50
No. 50s:	1	No. 100s:	0

ODI Bowling & Fielding
Wickets:	5	Runs:	256
Best Bowling:	2/44	Average:	51.20
5 WM:	0	Catches:	4
Stumpings:	0		

Born in Nairobi, Kenya, Jamie Dalrymple is an exciting all-rounder who made his ODI debut against Ireland at Belfast in mid 2006. A handy off-spinner, he later played in five ODI's against Sri Lanka in the Nat West Series, where he averaged 40.40. He will definitely add to his tally of six ODI'S.

DAWSON, Edward William
Born:	February 13, 1904
Batting:	Right handed

Tests
Test Career:	1928-30
Cap Number:	233
Tests Played:	5

Test Batting
Innings:	9	Runs:	175
Highest Score:	55	Average:	19.44
No. 50s:	1	No. 100s:	0

Test Bowling & Fielding
Wickets:	0	Runs:	0
Best Bowling:		Average:	0.00
5 WI:	0	10 WM:	0
Catches:	0	Stumpings:	0

A one time Cambridge captain, he may have not been in England's best XI, but when players were required to tour South Africa and New Zealand in the late 20's he made himself available and performed admirably.

DAWSON, Richard Kevin James

Born: August 4, 1980
Batting: Right handed
Bowling: Right arm off-break

Tests

Test Career: 2001-03
Cap Number: 608
Tests Played: 7

Test Batting
Innings:	13	Runs:	114
Highest Score:	19*	Average:	11.40
No. 50s:	0	No. 100s:	0

Test Bowling & Fielding
Wickets:	11	Runs:	677
Best Bowling:	4/134	Average:	61.54
5 WI:	0	10 WM:	0
Catches:	3	Stumpings:	0

An off spinner from Yorkshire who played all of his Tests on foreign soil. He celebrated his Test debut with four wickets against India at Chandigarh in 2001 but struggled thereafter. The Australian media pointed to the fact that he was playing in the 2002/03 Ashes series as proof of England's fallibility. Dawson bowled with control but lacked penetration and took only five wickets in four Tests.

DEAN, Harry

Born: August 13, 1884
Batting: Left handed
Bowling: Left arm medium-fast

Tests

Test Career: 1912
Cap Number: 178
Tests Played: 3

Test Batting
Innings:	4	Runs:	10
Highest Score:	8	Average:	5.00
No. 50s:	0	No. 100s:	0

Test Bowling & Fielding
Wickets:	11	Runs:	153
Best Bowling:	4/19	Average:	13.90
5 WI:	0	10 WM:	0
Catches:	2	Stumpings:	0

A pace bowler from Lancashire, he played three Tests in the ill-conceived triangular series between England, Australia and South Africa that was held in England in 1912.

DEFREITAS, Phillip Anthony Jason

Born: February 18, 1966
Batting: Right handed
Bowling: Right arm medium-fast

Tests

Test Career: 1986-95
Cap Number: 522
Tests Played: 44

Test Batting
Innings:	68	Runs:	934
Highest Score:	88	Average:	14.82
No. 50s:	4	No. 100s:	0

Test Bowling & Fielding
Wickets:	140	Runs:	4,700
Best Bowling:	7/70	Average:	33.57
5 WI:	4	10 WM:	0
Catches:	14	Stumpings:	0

One Day Internationals

ODI Career: 1987-97
ODIs Played: 103

ODI Batting
Innings:	66	Runs:	690
Highest Score:	67	Average:	16.04
No. 50s:	1	No. 100s:	0

ODI Bowling & Fielding
Wickets:	115	Runs:	3,775
Best Bowling:	4/35	Average:	32.82
5 WM:	0	Catches:	26
Stumpings:	0		

An energetic fast medium bowler, he was one of many West Indian born Englishman to break into the Test side during the 80's. DeFreitas was never scared of hard work and put in many good long spells for his country. His best effort in a Test innings was a 7/70 against Sri Lanka at Lord's in 1991. The industrious tailender was well suited to one day cricket and made more than 100 appearances for England in the shorter version of the game. He was part of the squad that finished second in the 1989 World Cup.

DENNESS, Michael Henry

Born: December 1, 1940
Batting: Right handed

Tests

Test Career: 1969-75
Cap Number: 444
Tests Played: 28

Test Batting
Innings:	45	Runs:	1,667
Highest Score:	188	Average:	39.69
No. 50s:	7	No. 100s:	4

Test Bowling & Fielding
Wickets:	0	Runs:	0
Best Bowling:		Average:	0.00
5 WI:	0	10 WM:	0
Catches:	28	Stumpings:	0

One Day Internationals

ODI Career: 1973-75
ODIs Played: 12

ODI Batting
Innings:	11	Runs:	264
Highest Score:	66	Average:	29.33
No. 50s:	1	No. 100s:	0

ODI Bowling & Fielding
Wickets:	0	Runs:	0
Best Bowling:		Average:	0.00
5 WM:	0	Catches:	1
Stumpings:	0		

The gentlemanly Scotsman presided over the English team in the mid 70's and whist his side played a meritorious drawn series against the West Indies in the Caribbean and thrashed India at home, he will unfortunately be remembered for an ignominious loss to Australia in 1974/75. Denness struggled with the bat in the first three Tests of that series and dropped himself for the fourth and ultimately deciding Test. It was a baffling decision that earnt him a barrage of criticism back home. Despite a fine 188, in the last Test at the MCG, his card had been marked and he played his final Test by mid 1975. Denness coached and managed a number of teams in his post playing days and latterly served as an ICC match referee.

DENTON, David

Born:	July 4, 1874
Batting:	Right handed
Bowling:	Right arm medium-fast

Tests

Test Career:	1905-10
Cap Number:	142
Tests Played:	11

Test Batting

Innings:	22	Runs:	424
Highest Score:	104	Average:	20.19
No. 50s:	1	No. 100s:	1

Test Bowling & Fielding

Wickets:	0	Runs:	0
Best Bowling:		Average:	0.00
5 WI:	0	10 WM:	0
Catches:	8	Stumpings:	0

Nicknamed 'Lucky', he was a bubbly batsman and brilliant fieldsman who made his Test debut on his 31st birthday. Denton scored a single Test century at Johannesburg in the 3rd Test of the 1909/10 series.

DEWES, John Gordon

Born:	October 11, 1926
Batting:	Left handed
Bowling:	Right arm medium

Tests

Test Career:	1948-50
Cap Number:	337
Tests Played:	5

Test Batting

Innings:	10	Runs:	121
Highest Score:	67	Average:	12.10
No. 50s:	1	No. 100s:	0

Test Bowling & Fielding

Wickets:	0	Runs:	0
Best Bowling:		Average:	0.00
5 WI:	0	10 WM:	0
Catches:	0	Stumpings:	0

The left handed opener made his Test as a 21 year old against the touring Australians in 1948 and whilst he was a fine batsman for Middlesex he struggled when elevated to the national side.

DEXTER, Edward Ralph

Born:	May 15, 1935
Batting:	Right handed
Bowling:	Right arm medium

Tests

Test Career:	1958-68
Cap Number:	388
Tests Played:	62

Test Batting

Innings:	102	Runs:	4,502
Highest Score:	205	Average:	47.89
No. 50s:	27	No. 100s:	9

Test Bowling & Fielding

Wickets:	66	Runs:	2,306
Best Bowling:	4/10	Average:	34.93
5 WI:	0	10 WM:	0
Catches:	29	Stumpings:	0

Surely the finest cricketer ever born in Italy, he was a powerful stroke maker who enjoyed nothing more than singling out the best bowler in the opposition attack for particularly savage treatment. He made a double century against Pakistan at Karachi in 1961/62, but his two most famous innings were both against Australia. The first of those was 180 at Edgbaston in 1961 when England avoided defeat after trailing on the first innings by over 300 runs, and the second 174 at Old Trafford after Australia had scored 656 in the first innings of the game. Dexter was also a fine medium pace bowler who was under used by most of his captains including himself. As skipper he led England in thirty Tests, for a record of nine wins and seven losses. Ted Dexter served as English chairman of selectors from 1989 to 1993.

DILLEY, Graham Roy

Born:	May 18, 1959
Batting:	Left handed
Bowling:	Right arm fast

Tests

Test Career:	1979-89
Cap Number:	483
Tests Played:	41

Test Batting

Innings:	58	Runs:	521
Highest Score:	56	Average:	13.35
No. 50s:	2	No. 100s:	0

Test Bowling & Fielding

Wickets:	138	Runs:	4,107
Best Bowling:	6/38	Average:	29.76
5 WI:	6	10 WM:	0
Catches:	10	Stumpings:	0

One Day Internationals

ODI Career:	1979-88
ODIs Played:	36

ODI Batting

Innings:	18	Runs:	114
Highest Score:	31*	Average:	11.40
No. 50s:	0	No. 100s:	0

ODI Bowling & Fielding

Wickets:	48	Runs:	1,291
Best Bowling:	4/23	Average:	26.89
5 WM:	0	Catches:	4
Stumpings:	0		

The blonde bombshell burst on to the Test scene when selected to tour Australia in 1979/80. Whilst he didn't set the world on fire, he was able to generate plenty of pace with his long delivery stride and energetic action. He played a major role in England retaining the Ashes in 1986/87 with 16 wickets for the series. In his debut at Perth he was a part of cricket's best loved scorebook entry when his second Test wicket read; Lillee ct. Willey bl. Dilley.

DIPPER, Alfred Ernest

Born: November 9, 1885
Batting: Right handed
Bowling: Right arm medium

Tests

Test Career: 1921
Cap Number: 195
Tests Played: 1

Test Batting
Innings: 2   Runs: 51
Highest Score: 40   Average: 25.50
No. 50s: 0   No. 100s: 0

Test Bowling & Fielding
Wickets: 0   Runs: 0
Best Bowling: Average: 0.00
5 WI: 0   10 WM: 0
Catches: 0   Stumpings: 0

A dour opening batsman from Gloucestershire, his only Test was against Australia at Lord's in London when he scored a fighting 40 in the second innings.

DOGGART, George Hubert Graham (Hubert)

Born: July 18, 1925
Batting: Right handed
Bowling: Right arm off-break

Tests

Test Career: 1950
Cap Number: 347
Tests Played: 2

Test Batting
Innings: 4   Runs: 76
Highest Score: 29   Average: 19.00
No. 50s: 0   No. 100s: 0

Test Bowling & Fielding
Wickets: 0   Runs: 0
Best Bowling: Average: 0.00
5 WI: 0   10 WM: 0
Catches: 3   Stumpings: 0

A right hand batsman from Sussex, he played both of his Tests against the touring West Indians in 1950.

DOLLERY, Horace Edgar (Tom)

Born: October 14, 1914
Batting: Right handed
         Wicket Keeper

Tests

Test Career: 1947-50
Cap Number: 318
Tests Played: 4

Test Batting
Innings: 7   Runs: 72
Highest Score: 37   Average: 10.28
No. 50s: 0   No. 100s: 0

Test Bowling & Fielding
Wickets: 0   Runs: 0
Best Bowling: Average: 0.00
5 WI: 0   10 WM: 0
Catches: 1   Stumpings: 0

He was a brilliant schoolboy cricketer who was intermittently selected for England between 1947 and 1950 but showed none of the form that later won him selection as one of Wisden's five Cricketer's of the Year in 1952.

DOLPHIN, Arthur

Born: December 24, 1885
Batting: Right handed
         Wicket Keeper

Tests

Test Career: 1921
Cap Number: 188
Tests Played: 1

Test Batting
Innings: 2   Runs: 1
Highest Score: 1   Average: 0.50
No. 50s: 0   No. 100s: 0

Test Bowling & Fielding
Wickets: 0   Runs: 0
Best Bowling: Average: 0.00
5 WI: 0   10 WM: 0
Catches: 1   Stumpings: 0

The Yorkshire keeper had involvement in seven Test matches. One was as a player against Australia in 1921 and the other six were as an umpire in the 1930's.

DOUGLAS, John William Henry Tyler

Born: September 3, 1882
Batting: Right handed
Bowling: Right arm medium-fast

Tests

Test Career: 1911-25
Cap Number: 170
Tests Played: 23

Test Batting
Innings: 35   Runs: 962
Highest Score: 119 Average: 29.15
No. 50s: 6   No. 100s: 1

Test Bowling & Fielding
Wickets: 45   Runs: 1,486
Best Bowling: 5/46 Average: 33.02
5 WI: 1   10 WM: 0
Catches: 9   Stumpings: 0

He hailed from a famous boxing family and employed that sport's training methods to become the fittest Test player of his time. A quick bowler and resolute batsman, he captained England in 18 Tests, finishing with a record of eight wins and eight losses. He presided over the side that was soundly thrashed by the Aussies in the years immediately after the First World War, but with an average of over 30 in those Tests and a healthy bag of wickets in both the 1920/21 series in Australia and the 1921 series in England he could hardly be held to blame. Whilst he was a consistent performer, he scored only the one Test century, 119 against the South Africans at Durban in 1914. A famous sportsman, he won an Olympic gold medal in 1908 for boxing and represented England at football. Douglas died in a boating accident off the coast of Denmark at the age of 48.

DOWNTON, Paul Rupert

Born:	April 4, 1957
Batting:	Right handed
Bowling:	Right arm off-break
	Wicket Keeper

Tests

Test Career:	1981-88
Cap Number:	488
Tests Played:	30

Test Batting

Innings:	48	Runs:	785
Highest Score:	71	Average:	19.62
No. 50s:	4	No. 100s:	0

Test Bowling & Fielding

Wickets:	0	Runs:	0
Best Bowling:		Average:	0.00
5 WI:	0	10 WM:	0
Catches:	70	Stumpings:	5

One Day Internationals

ODI Career:	1977-88
ODIs Played:	28

ODI Batting

Innings:	20	Runs:	242
Highest Score:	44*	Average:	16.13
No. 50s:	0	No. 100s:	0

ODI Bowling & Fielding

Wickets:	0	Runs:	0
Best Bowling:		Average:	0.00
5 WM:	0	Catches:	26
Stumpings:	3		

The Middlesex keeper replaced an aging Bob Taylor in the Test side in 1981 and the two shared the position until Taylor finally retired in 1984. Tall for a keeper, he was a safe gloveman and adequate lower order bat who was a member of the English side the lost the 1987 World Cup final.

DRUCE, Norman Frank

Born:	January 1, 1875
Batting:	Right handed

Tests

Test Career:	1897-98
Cap Number:	107
Tests Played:	5

Test Batting

Innings:	9	Runs:	252
Highest Score:	64	Average:	28.00
No. 50s:	1	No. 100s:	0

Test Bowling & Fielding

Wickets:	0	Runs:	0
Best Bowling:		Average:	0.00
5 WI:	0	10 WM:	0
Catches:	5	Stumpings:	0

All of his five Tests were on the 1897/98 tour to Australia. Batting in the middle order he performed well, scoring 252 runs including a Test high of 64 at the SCG in the fifth and final Test.

DUCAT, Andrew

Born:	February 16, 1886
Batting:	Right handed

Tests

Test Career:	1921
Cap Number:	200
Tests Played:	1

Test Batting

Innings:	2	Runs:	5
Highest Score:	3	Average:	2.50
No. 50s:	0	No. 100s:	0

Test Bowling & Fielding

Wickets:	0	Runs:	0
Best Bowling:		Average:	0.00
5 WI:	0	10 WM:	0
Catches:	1	Stumpings:	0

The Surrey man played one Test against Australia at Headingly in 1921 but was a renowned footballer who played for England and skippered Aston Villa to victory in the 1920 FA Cup.

DUCKWORTH, George

Born:	May 9, 1901
Batting:	Right handed
	Wicket Keeper

Tests

Test Career:	1924-36
Cap Number:	219
Tests Played:	24

Test Batting

Innings:	28	Runs:	234
Highest Score:	39*	Average:	14.62
No. 50s:	0	No. 100s:	0

Test Bowling & Fielding

Wickets:	0	Runs:	0
Best Bowling:		Average:	0.00
5 WI:	0	10 WM:	0
Catches:	45	Stumpings:	15

An enthusiastic gloveman from Lancashire he will be remembered as one the game's great appealers if not for anything else. Duckworth played in 24 Tests, and whilst he was only a moderate batsman he enjoyed a good time of it behind the stumps with his keen footwork. In retirement he worked as a steward for the English Test side.

DULEEPSINHJI, Kumar Shri (Duleep)

Born:	June 13, 1905
Batting:	Right handed
Bowling:	Right arm leg-break

Tests

Test Career:	1929-31
Cap Number:	238
Tests Played:	12

Test Batting

Innings:	19	Runs:	995
Highest Score:	173	Average:	58.52
No. 50s:	5	No. 100s:	3

Test Bowling & Fielding
Wickets:	0	Runs:	7
Best Bowling:		Average:	0.00
5 WI:	0	10 WM:	0
Catches:	10	Stumpings:	0

Like his uncle Ranji before him, Duleep was an immensely popular cricketer who brought an inimitable sense of style and occasion to the English side. He played in only 12 Tests, but his innings at Lord's in 1930 goes down as one of the finest in Test history. He scored 173 out of 425, with his footwork and timing off Clarrie Grimmett the feature. He made two more hundreds, both against New Zealand, leaving Test cricket with the formidable average of 58.52.

DURSTON, Frederick John (Jack)
Born: July 11, 1893
Batting: Right handed
Bowling: Right arm medium-fast

Tests
Test Career: 1921
Cap Number: 196
Tests Played: 1

Test Batting
Innings:	2	Runs:	8
Highest Score:	6*	Average:	8.00
No. 50s:	0	No. 100s:	0

Test Bowling & Fielding
Wickets:	5	Runs:	136
Best Bowling:	4/102	Average:	27.20
5 WI:	0	10 WM:	0
Catches:	0	Stumpings:	0

He was a hard working opening bowler from Middlesex who played a single Test against Australia in 1921.

EALHAM, Mark Alan
Born: August 27, 1969
Batting: Right handed
Bowling: Right arm medium-fast

Tests
Test Career: 1996-98
Cap Number: 580
Tests Played: 8

Test Batting
Innings:	13	Runs:	210
Highest Score:	53*	Average:	21.00
No. 50s:	2	No. 100s:	0

Test Bowling & Fielding
Wickets:	17	Runs:	488
Best Bowling:	4/21	Average:	28.70
5 WI:	0	10 WM:	0
Catches:	4	Stumpings:	0

One Day Internationals
ODI Career: 1996-2001
ODIs Played: 64

ODI Batting
Innings:	45	Runs:	716
Highest Score:	45	Average:	17.46
No. 50s:	0	No. 100s:	0

ODI Bowling & Fielding
Wickets:	67	Runs:	2,197
Best Bowling:	5/15	Average:	32.79
5 WM:	2	Catches:	9
Stumpings:	0		

A nagging one day bowler and lusty late order hitter who played the bulk of his representative cricket in ODI's.

EDMONDS, Phillippe-Henri
Born: March 8, 1951
Batting: Right handed
Bowling: Left arm off-break

Tests
Test Career: 1975-87
Cap Number: 464
Tests Played: 51

Test Batting
Innings:	65	Runs:	875
Highest Score:	64	Average:	17.50
No. 50s:	2	No. 100s:	0

Test Bowling & Fielding
Wickets:	125	Runs:	4,273
Best Bowling:	7/66	Average:	34.18
5 WI:	2	10 WM:	0
Catches:	42	Stumpings:	0

One Day Internationals
ODI Career: 1977-87
ODIs Played: 29

ODI Batting
Innings:	18	Runs:	116
Highest Score:	20	Average:	10.54
No. 50s:	0	No. 100s:	0

ODI Bowling & Fielding
Wickets:	26	Runs:	965
Best Bowling:	3/39	Average:	37.11
5 WM:	0	Catches:	6
Stumpings:	0		

Born in what was then Rhodesia, he was a left arm finger spinner with a high action and good control. He provided good contrast to Derek Underwood with his slower more tempting form of off spin and captured 125 wickets in his 51 Test appearances. He took five or more wickets in a Test innings only twice in his career, one being in his very first at bowl for England when he captured five Australian wickets for only 28 runs. With two Test half centuries to his name, Phil Edmonds was also a resolute lower order batsman.

EDRICH, John Hugh
Born: June 21, 1937
Batting: Left handed
Bowling: Right arm medium

Tests
Test Career: 1963-76
Cap Number: 415
Tests Played: 77

Test Batting
Innings:	127	Runs:	5,138
Highest Score:	310*	Average:	43.54
No. 50s:	24	No. 100s:	12

Test Bowling & Fielding

Wickets:	0	Runs:	23
Best Bowling:		Average:	0.00
5 WI:	0	10 WM:	0
Catches:	43	Stumpings:	0

One Day Internationals

ODI Career:	1971-75		
ODIs Played:	7		

ODI Batting

Innings:	6	Runs:	223
Highest Score:	90	Average:	37.16
No. 50s:	2	No. 100s:	0

ODI Bowling & Fielding

Wickets:	0	Runs:	0
Best Bowling:		Average:	0.00
5 WM:	0	Catches:	0
Stumpings:	0		

A cousin of Bill Edrich, he was a masterful back foot batsman who was the backbone of the English top order for over a decade. His first Test century was a fighting 120 against the touring Australians in 1964 at Lord's. Opening the batting, he was the eighth man out and his 120 counted for almost half of the English score. His next Test at Lord's was just as memorable but for a much different reason. Playing South Africa he ducked into a bouncer from Peter Pollock and was knocked out cold. He didn't play for England again until the tour of Australia later that year but seemed to take no ill effect from the blow, scoring 375 in five Tests at an average of 46.88. In all he scored 12 Test centuries, that included a triple ton against New Zealand at home in 1965. The courageous number three played 77 Tests in all, finally calling it a day after facing up to the might of the West Indies at the age of 39.

EDRICH, William John

Born:	March 26, 1916
Batting:	Right handed

Tests

Test Career:	1938-55		
Cap Number:	300		
Tests Played:	39		

Test Batting

Innings:	63	Runs:	2,440
Highest Score:	219	Average:	40.00
No. 50s:	13	No. 100s:	6

Test Bowling & Fielding

Wickets:	41	Runs:	1,693
Best Bowling:	4/68	Average:	41.29
5 WI:	0	10 WM:	0
Catches:	39	Stumpings:	0

Short in stature but high on courage, Bill Edrich was for much of his Test career the workmanlike ying to Denis Compton's dashing yang. Like his Middlesex teammate Compton, he had a short burst of Test cricket prior to World War II, scoring his highest Test knock of 219 against South Africa in the famous timeless Test at Durban. When England returned to Test cricket in 1946 he resumed his spot in the middle order and whilst the side initially struggled Edrich had lost none of his old sparkle. The back foot player was still capable of executed his punishing hooks and cuts to perfection, enjoying a fine Australian summer in 1946/47 with 462 runs to be England leading scorer for the series. He and Compton demolished the visiting South Africans in 1947 and Edrich was again at the ready when Australia toured in 1948, though his average of 31 for the series was below his best. In all he averaged exactly 40 in Tests for England and took 41 wickets with his surprisingly nippy medium pace.

ELLIOTT, Harry

Born:	November 2, 1891
Batting:	Right handed Wicket Keeper

Tests

Test Career:	1928-34		
Cap Number:	234		
Tests Played:	4		

Test Batting

Innings:	5	Runs:	61
Highest Score:	37*	Average:	15.25
No. 50s:	0	No. 100s:	0

Test Bowling & Fielding

Wickets:	0	Runs:	0
Best Bowling:		Average:	0.00
5 WI:	0	10 WM:	0
Catches:	8	Stumpings:	3

A wicket keeper from Derbyshire, he had an interesting career playing Tests in England and India as well as standing as an umpire in seven Tests during the fifties.

ELLISON, Richard Mark

Born:	September 21, 1959
Batting:	Left handed
Bowling:	Right arm medium-fast

Tests

Test Career:	1984-86		
Cap Number:	509		
Tests Played:	11		

Test Batting

Innings:	16	Runs:	202
Highest Score:	41	Average:	13.46
No. 50s:	0	No. 100s:	0

Test Bowling & Fielding

Wickets:	35	Runs:	1,048
Best Bowling:	6/77	Average:	29.94
5 WI:	3	10 WM:	1
Catches:	2	Stumpings:	0

One Day Internationals

ODI Career:	1984-86		
ODIs Played:	14		

ODI Batting

Innings:	12	Runs:	86
Highest Score:	24	Average:	10.75
No. 50s:	0	No. 100s:	0

ODI Bowling & Fielding

Wickets:	12	Runs:	510
Best Bowling:	3/42	Average:	42.50
5 WM:	0	Catches:	2
Stumpings:	0		

A right arm medium pace bowler from Kent whose recall to the Test side in 1984/85 was the main reason England retained the Ashes. He took ten wickets in the fifth Test and seven in the final test at The Oval in a remarkable two week spell. Unfortunately for Ellison he was struck down by injury in 1987.

EMBUREY, John Ernest

Born:	August 20, 1952
Batting:	Right handed
Bowling:	Right arm off-break

Tests

Test Career:	1978-95		
Cap Number:	480		
Tests Played:	64		

Test Batting

Innings:	96	Runs:	1,713
Highest Score:	75	Average:	22.53
No. 50s:	10	No. 100s:	0

Test Bowling & Fielding

Wickets:	147	Runs:	5,646
Best Bowling:	7/78	Average:	38.40
5 WI:	6	10 WM:	0
Catches:	34	Stumpings:	0

One Day Internationals

ODI Career:	1980-93		
ODIs Played:	61		

ODI Batting

Innings:	45	Runs:	501
Highest Score:	34	Average:	14.31
No. 50s:	0	No. 100s:	0

ODI Bowling & Fielding

Wickets:	76	Runs:	2,346
Best Bowling:	4/37	Average:	30.86
5 WM:	0	Catches:	19
Stumpings:	0		

Selected and set aside more times than he'd care to remember, John Emburey was an able servant in the English Test side for almost 17 years. He was a right handed off spinner who relied more on flight than turn, but rarely failed if given the job to either contain or chase wickets. He took 147 Test wickets, and whilst he didn't often run through sides, he did take 6/33 in the second innings of Sri Lanka's historic first ever Test and also captured seven wickets in an innings at the SCG in 1987. Emburey was a stubborn lower order bat who was happy to swat a boundary as the field closed in around him. In the same Test at the SCG where he captured career best figures of 7/78 he also scored 69 in the first innings, coming in at number eight. Even though he visited South Africa twice on unauthorised tours he never was never suspended by the M.C.C.

EMMETT, George Malcolm

Born:	December 2, 1912
Batting:	Right handed
Bowling:	Left arm off-break

Tests

Test Career:	1948		
Cap Number:	336		
Tests Played:	1		

Test Batting

Innings:	2	Runs:	10
Highest Score:	10	Average:	5.00
No. 50s:	0	No. 100s:	0

Test Bowling & Fielding

Wickets:	0	Runs:	0
Best Bowling:		Average:	0.00
5 WI:	0	10 WM:	0
Catches:	0	Stumpings:	0

An opener from Gloucs, he played a single Test against the Australians at Old Trafford in 1948.

EMMETT, Thomas

Born:	September 3, 1841
Batting:	Left handed
Bowling:	Left arm fast

Tests

Test Career:	1877-82		
Cap Number:	3		
Tests Played:	7		

Test Batting

Innings:	13	Runs:	160
Highest Score:	48	Average:	13.33
No. 50s:	0	No. 100s:	0

Test Bowling & Fielding

Wickets:	9	Runs:	284
Best Bowling:	7/68	Average:	31.55
5 WI:	1	10 WM:	0
Catches:	9	Stumpings:	0

A Yorkshireman who played in the first ever Test at the MCG in 1877. He was a prolific run scorer and wicket taker for Yorkshire where he was captain from 1878 to 1882.

EVANS, Alfred John

Born:	May 1, 1889
Batting:	Right handed
Bowling:	Right arm medium-fast

Tests

Test Career:	1921		
Cap Number:	197		
Tests Played:	1		

Test Batting

Innings:	2	Runs:	18
Highest Score:	14	Average:	9.00
No. 50s:	0	No. 100s:	0

Test Bowling & Fielding

Wickets:	0	Runs:	0
Best Bowling:		Average:	0.00
5 WI:	0	10 WM:	0
Catches:	0	Stumpings:	0

One of many English cricketers who got a taste of Test cricket in 1921 against the Australians. Test cricket had just resumed after the First World War, and in the process of rebuilding England tried 30 players in the five Test series.

EVANS, Thomas Godfrey

Born: August 18, 1920
Batting: Right handed
Bowling: Right arm leg-break
Wicket Keeper

Tests
Test Career: 1946-59
Cap Number: 315
Tests Played: 91

Test Batting
Innings:	133	Runs:	2,439
Highest Score:	104	Average:	20.49
No. 50s:	8	No. 100s:	2

Test Bowling & Fielding
Wickets:	0	Runs:	0
Best Bowling:		Average:	0.00
5 WI:	0	10 WM:	0
Catches:	173	Stumpings:	46

Modern wicket keepers are also required to be frontline batmen, but when it was glovework that decided who stood behind the stumps Godfrey Evans had no peer. He did his work with a flourish, often tumbling down leg side or removing the bails with a giant sweep, but if there was a little showman in the Londoner it never came at the expense of taking the ball safely. He played in a then record 91 Tests, with over 200 dismissals of which a high proportion were stumpings. He regularly stood up to the stumps when Alec Bedser was bowling and executed a number of great catches including a famous leg side take off Neil Harvey in 1950/51. Whilst his batting wasn't lifted from the pages of a teaching manual, his good eye served him well, and he scored 104 against both India and the West Indies on home soil in 1950 and 1952 respectively.

FAGG, Arthur Edward

Born: June 18, 1915
Batting: Right handed
Bowling: Right arm medium
Wicket Keeper

Tests
Test Career: 1936-39
Cap Number: 291
Tests Played: 5

Test Batting
Innings:	8	Runs:	150
Highest Score:	39	Average:	18.75
No. 50s:	0	No. 100s:	0

Test Bowling & Fielding
Wickets:	0	Runs:	0
Best Bowling:		Average:	0.00
5 WI:	0	10 WM:	0
Catches:	5	Stumpings:	0

The promising opening batsman played five Tests immediately prior to the Second World War bat failed to reach 40 in any single innings. He had a long a successful career with Kent, scoring over 25,000 runs playing until he was well into his forties.

FAIRBROTHER, Neil Harvey

Born: September 9, 1963
Batting: Left handed
Bowling: Left arm medium

Tests
Test Career: 1987-93
Cap Number: 525
Tests Played: 10

Test Batting
Innings:	15	Runs:	219
Highest Score:	83	Average:	15.64
No. 50s:	1	No. 100s:	0

Test Bowling & Fielding
Wickets:	0	Runs:	9
Best Bowling:		Average:	0.00
5 WI:	0	10 WM:	0
Catches:	4	Stumpings:	0

One Day Internationals
ODI Career: 1987-99
ODIs Played: 75

ODI Batting
Innings:	71	Runs:	2,092
Highest Score:	113	Average:	39.47
No. 50s:	16	No. 100s:	1

ODI Bowling & Fielding
Wickets:	0	Runs:	9
Best Bowling:		Average:	0.00
5 WM:	0	Catches:	33
Stumpings:	0		

A useful all-rounder who played the bulk of his representative cricket for the one day side. Fairbrother bowled accurate military mediums, was a good worker of the ball as a batsman and a very good field. His only English century was in an ODI against the West Indies at Lord's in 1991. He represented England in three World Cup campaigns between 1989 and 1996.

FANE, Frederick Luther

Born: April 27, 1875
Batting: Right handed

Tests
Test Career: 1906-10
Cap Number: 147
Tests Played: 14

Test Batting
Innings:	27	Runs:	682
Highest Score:	143	Average:	26.23
No. 50s:	3	No. 100s:	1

Test Bowling & Fielding
Wickets:	0	Runs:	0
Best Bowling:		Average:	0.00
5 WI:	0	10 WM:	0
Catches:	6	Stumpings:	0

England's 19th Test captain, he led his country in five Tests against the South Africans. An opening batsman, he scored 143 on his first tour to South Africa where he took to the slower bowlers on the mats.

FARNES, Kenneth

Born: July 8, 1911
Batting: Right handed
Bowling: Right arm fast

FARNES, Kenneth

Tests
Test Career:	1934-39		
Cap Number:	274		
Tests Played:	15		

Test Batting
Innings:	17	Runs:	58
Highest Score:	20	Average:	4.83
No. 50s:	0	No. 100s:	0

Test Bowling & Fielding
Wickets:	60	Runs:	1,719
Best Bowling:	6/96	Average:	28.65
5 WI:	3	10 WM:	1
Catches:	1	Stumpings:	0

The young speedster made his debut against the Australians at Trent Bridge in 1934. Hardly overawed by the prospect of bowling to the powerful batting line up he took five wickets in each innings including the scalps of captain Woodfull for just 26 and 2 and Don Bradman in the second innings for 25. He toured Australia in 1936/37 taking career best figures of 6/96 at the MCG and in 1938 led the English wicket takers against the touring Australians with 17. A successful tour of South Africa followed but then the War intervened where Farnes was tragically killed after his plane was downed over a field in Oxfordshire. He was only 30 years of age.

FARRIMOND, William

Born:	May 23, 1903
Batting:	Right handed
	Wicket Keeper

Tests
Test Career:	1931-35		
Cap Number:	257		
Tests Played:	4		

Test Batting
Innings:	7	Runs:	116
Highest Score:	35	Average:	16.57
No. 50s:	0	No. 100s:	0

Test Bowling & Fielding
Wickets:	0	Runs:	0
Best Bowling:	0	Average:	0.00
5 WI:	0	10 WM:	0
Catches:	5	Stumpings:	2

A reserve wicket keeper for Lancashire and England over many years, he played four Tests over a five year period when either George Duckworth was injured or Les Ames was used solely as a batsman.

FENDER, Percy George Herbet

Born:	August 22, 1892
Batting:	Right handed
Bowling:	Right arm leg-break

Tests
Test Career:	1921-29		
Cap Number:	187		
Tests Played:	13		

Test Batting
Innings:	21	Runs:	380
Highest Score:	60	Average:	19.00
No. 50s:	2	No. 100s:	0

Test Bowling & Fielding
Wickets:	29	Runs:	1,185
Best Bowling:	5/90	Average:	40.86
5 WI:	2	10 WM:	0
Catches:	14	Stumpings:	0

A famous cricket writer in his post playing days, he was a long standing captain of Surrey who played in 13 Tests. Fender bowled a variety of over the wrist medium pace along with genuine spin and whilst he was always a chance to take a wicket his fondness for experimentation made him an expensive commodity at Test level. His 12 wickets against Australia on the unsuccessful 1920/21 Ashes tour was second only to Ciss Parkin.

FERRIS, John James

Born:	May 21, 1867
Batting:	Left handed
Bowling:	Left arm medium

Tests
Test Career:	1887-92		
Cap Number:	75		
Tests Played:	9		

Test Batting
Innings:	17	Runs:	114
Highest Score:	20*	Average:	0.00
No. 50s:	0	No. 100s:	0

Test Bowling & Fielding
Wickets:	61	Runs:	775
Best Bowling:	7/37	Average:	12.70
5 WI:	6	10 WM:	1
Catches:	4	Stumpings:	0

He was a much feared swing bowler in his eight Tests for Australia and single Test for England. His debut Test was the memorable match at the SCG in 1887 when England was sent in and dismissed for only 45. He took 4/27 and along with the great Charlie Turner consigned the 'Old Enemy' to their lowest score in Test history. His strength lay in his ability to move the ball both away and in to the batsman and such was his impact on the game that he was considered amongst Wisden's Cricketers of the Year in 1889. His career best innings figures of 7/37 and match figures of 13/91 were recorded whilst playing for England against South Africa in Cape Town. Sadly that Test was to be his last game at the highest level. J.J. Ferris died in Durban during the Boer War whilst serving as an officer in the British army.

FIELDER, Arthur

Born:	July 19, 1877
Batting:	Right handed
Bowling:	Right arm fast

Tests
Test Career:	1904-08
Cap Number:	140
Tests Played:	6

Test Batting			
Innings:	12	Runs:	78
Highest Score:	20	Average:	11.14
No. 50s:	0	No. 100s:	0
Test Bowling & Fielding			
Wickets:	26	Runs:	711
Best Bowling:	6/82	Average:	27.34
5 WI:	1	10 WM:	0
Catches:	4	Stumpings:	0

The fast bowler from Kent played all of his six Tests in Australia over two separate tours. His best effort was in 1907/08 when he took a most respectable 25 wickets in four appearances.

FISHLOCK, Laurence Barnard
Born: January 2, 1907
Batting: Left handed
Bowling: Left arm off-break

Tests

Test Career:	1936-47
Cap Number:	292
Tests Played:	4

Test Batting			
Innings:	5	Runs:	47
Highest Score:	19*	Average:	11.75
No. 50s:	0	No. 100s:	0
Test Bowling & Fielding			
Wickets:	0	Runs:	0
Best Bowling:		Average:	0.00
5 WI:	0	10 WM:	0
Catches:	1	Stumpings:	0

A left handed batsman from Surrey who played two Tests either side of the Second World War.

FLAVELL, John Alfred (Jack)
Born: May 15, 1929
Batting: Left handed
Bowling: Right arm medium-fast

Tests

Test Career:	1961-64
Cap Number:	403
Tests Played:	4

Test Batting			
Innings:	6	Runs:	31
Highest Score:	14	Average:	7.75
No. 50s:	0	No. 100s:	0
Test Bowling & Fielding			
Wickets:	7	Runs:	367
Best Bowling:	2/65	Average:	52.42
5 WI:	0	10 WM:	0
Catches:	0	Stumpings:	0

A fine first class bowler for Worcestershire, he was unfortunate to play at the same time as Trueman, Statham and Tyson. Whilst he did little in his four Tests he did take nine wickets in an innings three times for his county.

FLEMING, Matthew Valentine
Born: December 12, 1964
Batting: Right handed
Bowling: Right arm medium

One Day Internationals

ODI Career:	1997-98
ODIs Played:	11

ODI Batting			
Innings:	10	Runs:	139
Highest Score:	33	Average:	15.44
No. 50s:	0	No. 100s:	0
ODI Bowling & Fielding			
Wickets:	17	Runs:	434
Best Bowling:	4/45	Average:	25.52
5 WM:	0	Catches:	1
Stumpings:	0		

A medium pacer from Kent whose great grandfather, all-rounder Charles Leslie played four Tests for England way back in 1882-83. Fleming played in eleven ODI'S from 1997-98, taking a personal best 4/45 on debut against India.

FLETCHER, Keith William Robert
Born: May 20, 1944
Batting: Right handed
Bowling: Right arm leg-break

Tests

Test Career:	1968-82
Cap Number:	439
Tests Played:	59

Test Batting			
Innings:	96	Runs:	3,272
Highest Score:	216	Average:	39.90
No. 50s:	19	No. 100s:	7
Test Bowling & Fielding			
Wickets:	2	Runs:	193
Best Bowling:	1/6	Average:	96.50
5 WI:	0	10 WM:	0
Catches:	54	Stumpings:	0

One Day Internationals

ODI Career:	1971-82
ODIs Played:	24

ODI Batting			
Innings:	22	Runs:	757
Highest Score:	131	Average:	39.84
No. 50s:	5	No. 100s:	1
ODI Bowling & Fielding			
Wickets:	0	Runs:	0
Best Bowling:		Average:	0.00
5 WM:	0	Catches:	4
Stumpings:	0		

A compact top order batsman from Essex, he experienced the high and lows of cricket in a Test career that spanned 14 years. At his best he was a complete shot maker who was particularly good against spin bowling, where he could use his quick footwork to good effect. He struck a maiden Test century at Bombay in 1973 against the great Indian trio of Bedi, Venkataraghavan, and Chandrasekhar batting for almost five hours in a match saving innings. Whilst he may have had a number of torrid days against quicks from Australia and the West Indies he did score hundreds against both. Fletcher seemed to save his best for the Kiwis with 173 at Lord's in 1974 and 216 at Eden Park in 1975. The quietly spoken Fletcher was handed the captaincy in India in 1981/82, but he seemed uncomfortable in the position and not only was he relieved after seven Tests, he never played for England again.

FLINTOFF, Andrew

Born: December 6, 1977
Batting: Right handed
Bowling: Right arm fast

Tests

Test Career:	1998-		
Cap Number:	591		
Tests Played:	62		

Test Batting

Innings:	100	Runs:	3,127
Highest Score:	167	Average:	32.91
No. 50s:	22	No. 100s:	5

Test Bowling & Fielding

Wickets:	185	Runs:	5,827
Best Bowling:	5/58	Average:	31.32
5 WI:	2	10 WM:	0
Catches:	44	Stumpings:	0

One Day Internationals

ODI Career:	1999-		
ODIs Played:	102		

ODI Batting

Innings:	90	Runs:	2,674
Highest Score:	123	Average:	34.28
No. 50s:	15	No. 100s:	3

ODI Bowling & Fielding

Wickets:	110	Runs:	2,840
Best Bowling:	4/14	Average:	25.81
5 WM:	0	Catches:	33
Stumpings:	0		

As strong as the Australian Test side has been throughout history, they have always been susceptible to a good English all-rounder. In 1902 Wilfred Rhodes captured 7/17 in Birmingham as Australia tumbled to their lowest ever Test score of 36. The off spinner proved his worth as a batsman in the same game by outscoring Australia with a first innings 38. 79 years later Australia became the first side to lose a Test after enforcing the follow-on in what has since become known as 'Botham's Test'. So it should have come as no surprise that when Australia finally lost the Ashes in 2005 it would be an all-rounder that proved to be the difference. 'Freddie' Flintoff was named as man of the series along with Shane Warne, taking 24 wickets and scoring 402 runs at an average of 40.20. He is a true all-rounder in that he is a frontline bowler yet he extends the top order batting by one. Flintoff was just a big kid when he made his debut as a 20 year old and whilst his potential was there for all to see, the results were not forthcoming. He made five ducks in his first 20 innings with a top score of 42, and whilst his bowling was more encouraging his chances must have been wearing thin. The relief was palpable when he finally broke the shackles at Jade Stadium in Christchurch in 2002. He made 137 off only 163 balls with all but 27 of the runs coming in boundaries. Since then Flintoff has reveled in the role of match winner, either with the bat where he has passed 50 on 27 occasions or with the ball where he has taken four or more wickets in an innings 11 times. He signaled his intention to win back the Ashes in 2005 and backed up those words by performing in every Test. He was named man of the match twice, firstly at Edgbaston where he took seven wickets and made 68 and 73, then in Nottingham where he made a century and claimed three more wickets. More importantly, England won both of those Tests and went on to regain the Ashes for the first time in over 20 years. In 2006 he took over the captaincy from the injured Michael Vaughan but in turn had to stand down when he injured his ankle whilst playing Sri Lanka at Trent Bridge. Freddie took the rest of the summer off but is aiming to play a key role when England first defends the Ashes in Australia, then heads to the Caribbean for the 2007 World Cup.

FLOWERS, Wilfred

Born: December 7, 1856
Batting: Right handed
Bowling: Right arm off-break

Tests

Test Career:	1884-93		
Cap Number:	48		
Tests Played:	8		

Test Batting

Innings:	14	Runs:	254
Highest Score:	56	Average:	18.14
No. 50s:	1	No. 100s:	0

Test Bowling & Fielding

Wickets:	14	Runs:	296
Best Bowling:	5/46	Average:	21.14
5 WI:	1	10 WM:	0
Catches:	2	Stumpings:	0

He was a smart all rounder from Nottinghamshire who could make a respectable contribution either as a bowler of slow off-spin or as a middle order batsman. His finest hour came at the SCG in 1885 where he took five wickets in Australia's first innings then scored a fighting 56 as England fell just six runs short of victory. He went on to serve as a first class umpire until failing eyesight forced him to retire.

FORD, Francis Gilbert Justice

Born: December 14, 1866
Batting: Left handed
Bowling: Left arm off-break

Tests

Test Career:	1894-95		
Cap Number:	90		
Tests Played:	5		

Test Batting

Innings:	9	Runs:	168
Highest Score:	48	Average:	18.66
No. 50s:	0	No. 100s:	0

Test Bowling & Fielding

Wickets:	1	Runs:	129
Best Bowling:	1/47	Average:	129.00
5 WI:	0	10 WM:	0
Catches:	5	Stumpings:	0

A beanpole off spinner from Middlesex nicknamed 'Stork', he played every Test on the 1894/95 Ashes tour but disappointed with only one wicket.

FOSTER, Frank Rowbotham

Born:	January 31, 1889
Batting:	Right handed
Bowling:	Left arm medium-fast

Tests

Test Career:	1911-12
Cap Number:	171
Tests Played:	11

Test Batting

Innings:	15	Runs:	330
Highest Score:	71	Average:	23.57
No. 50s:	3	No. 100s:	0

Test Bowling & Fielding

Wickets:	45	Runs:	926
Best Bowling:	6/91	Average:	20.57
5 WI:	4	10 WM:	0
Catches:	11	Stumpings:	0

A left arm swing bowler, he opened the bowling with Sid Barnes on the 1911/12 Ashes tour taking 32 wickets in five Tests. Between them the two medium pacers claimed 66 victims and were the key to England's comfortable series win. Foster was also a more than competent batsman who batted at number six in that series and impressed with three half centuries that included a 71 at The Adelaide Oval. Unfortunately a wartime motorcycle accident forced a premature retirement for a player who had the potential to join the all-time greats of he game.

FOSTER, James Savin

Born:	April 15, 1980
Batting:	Right handed
	Wicket Keeper

Tests

Test Career:	2001-02
Cap Number:	609
Tests Played:	7

Test Batting

Innings:	12	Runs:	226
Highest Score:	48	Average:	25.11
No. 50s:	0	No. 100s:	0

Test Bowling & Fielding

Wickets:	0	Runs:	0
Best Bowling:		Average:	0.00
5 WI:	0	10 WM:	0
Catches:	17	Stumpings:	1

One Day Internationals

ODI Career:	2001-02
ODIs Played:	11

ODI Batting

Innings:	6	Runs:	41
Highest Score:	13	Average:	13.66
No. 50s:	0	No. 100s:	0

ODI Bowling & Fielding

Wickets:	0	Runs:	0
Best Bowling:		Average:	0.00
5 WM:	0	Catches:	13
Stumpings:	7		

One of three English wicket keepers given an opportunity following the retirement of Alec Stewart. He played seven Tests in 2001 and 2002 but has since been replaced by both Geraint Jones and Chris Read.

FOSTER, Neil Alan

Born:	May 6, 1962
Batting:	Right handed
Bowling:	Right arm medium-fast

Tests

Test Career:	1983-93
Cap Number:	502
Tests Played:	29

Test Batting

Innings:	45	Runs:	446
Highest Score:	39	Average:	11.73
No. 50s:	0	No. 100s:	0

Test Bowling & Fielding

Wickets:	88	Runs:	2,891
Best Bowling:	8/107	Average:	32.85
5 WI:	5	10 WM:	0
Catches:	7	Stumpings:	0

One Day Internationals

ODI Career:	1984-89
ODIs Played:	48

ODI Batting

Innings:	25	Runs:	150
Highest Score:	24	Average:	11.53
No. 50s:	0	No. 100s:	0

ODI Bowling & Fielding

Wickets:	59	Runs:	1,836
Best Bowling:	3/20	Average:	31.11
5 WM:	0	Catches:	12
Stumpings:	0		

A serviceable medium pacer from Essex whose career was plagued by a succession of knee injuries. When right, the seamer with a copybook action was an automatic selection in the English side, as his 11 wickets against India at Madras proved. He toured South Africa on the rebel tour in 1989 and after serving a three year ban played a single Test against Australia in 1993.

FOSTER, Reginald Erskine

Born:	April 16, 1878
Batting:	Right handed
Bowling:	Right arm fast

Tests

Test Career:	1903-07
Cap Number:	138
Tests Played:	8

Test Batting

Innings:	14	Runs:	602
Highest Score:	287	Average:	46.30
No. 50s:	1	No. 100s:	1

Test Bowling & Fielding

Wickets:	0	Runs:	0
Best Bowling:		Average:	0.00
5 WI:	0	10 WM:	0
Catches:	13	Stumpings:	0

Known as Tip, he is the only person to have captained England at both cricket and football having led his country in three of his eight Test matches. Reg Foster made his debut at the SCG in 1903/04 and no batsman before or since has performed as well. His 287 took 419 minutes, included 37 boundaries and eclipsed Australia's entire first innings total by two runs. His short but spectacular Test career saw him finish with an average of 46.30. Unfortunately he suffered from diabetes and with the limited treatment available in the early 1900's died when only 36.

FOTHERGILL, Arnold James

Born: August 26, 1854
Batting: Left handed
Bowling: Left arm medium

Tests

Test Career:	1889
Cap Number:	63
Tests Played:	2

Test Batting

Innings:	2	Runs:	33
Highest Score:	32	Average:	16.50
No. 50s:	0	No. 100s:	0

Test Bowling & Fielding

Wickets:	8	Runs:	90
Best Bowling:	4/19	Average:	11.25
5 WI:	0	10 WM:	0
Catches:	0	Stumpings:	0

An all rounder form Somerset, his only Tests were as part of the side that toured South Africa in 1889.

FOWLER, Graeme

Born: April 20, 1957
Batting: Left handed
Bowling: Right arm medium
 Wicket Keeper

Tests

Test Career:	1982-85
Cap Number:	498
Tests Played:	21

Test Batting

Innings:	37	Runs:	1,307
Highest Score:	201	Average:	35.32
No. 50s:	8	No. 100s:	3

Test Bowling & Fielding

Wickets:	0	Runs:	11
Best Bowling:		Average:	0.00
5 WI:	0	10 WM:	0
Catches:	10	Stumpings:	0

One Day Internationals

ODI Career:	1983-86
ODIs Played:	26

ODI Batting

Innings:	26	Runs:	744
Highest Score:	81*	Average:	31.00
No. 50s:	4	No. 100s:	0

ODI Bowling & Fielding

Wickets:	0	Runs:	0
Best Bowling:		Average:	0.00
5 WM:	0	Catches:	4
Stumpings:	2		

A left hand opening batsman from Lancashire whose best for England was very good indeed. He scored 105 against New Zealand at The Oval in 1983 and followed that up with a superb 106 against the West Indies at Lord's in 1984 when Malcolm Marshall tore through the rest of the English batting line up. He was not a recognised player of spin but he confounded his critics with 201 at Madras in 1985 in his second last Test innings. Fowler scored 69 in his final Test knock but upon the side's return home was demoted back to the county scene for good.

FRANKS, Paul John

Born: February 3, 1979
Batting: Left handed
Bowling: Right arm medium-fast

One Day Internationals

ODI Career:	2000
ODIs Played:	1

ODI Batting

Innings:	1	Runs:	4
Highest Score:	4	Average:	4.00
No. 50s:	0	No. 100s:	0

ODI Bowling & Fielding

Wickets:	0	Runs:	48
Best Bowling:		Average:	0.00
5 WM:	0	Catches:	1
Stumpings:	0		

An injury plagued pace bowler from Nottinghamshire who played just the one ODI against the West Indies on his home ground at Trent Bridge in 2000.

FRASER, Angus Robert Charles

Born: August 8, 1965
Batting: Right handed
Bowling: Right arm medium-fast

Tests

Test Career:	1989-98
Cap Number:	537
Tests Played:	46

Test Batting

Innings:	67	Runs:	388
Highest Score:	32	Average:	7.46
No. 50s:	0	No. 100s:	0

Test Bowling & Fielding

Wickets:	177	Runs:	4,836
Best Bowling:	8/53	Average:	27.32
5 WI:	13	10 WM:	2
Catches:	9	Stumpings:	0

One Day Internationals

ODI Career:	1989-99
ODIs Played:	42

ODI Batting

Innings:	20	Runs:	141
Highest Score:	38*	Average:	12.81
No. 50s:	0	No. 100s:	0

ODI Bowling & Fielding

Wickets:	47	Runs:	1,412
Best Bowling:	4/22	Average:	30.04
5 WM:	0	Catches:	5
Stumpings:	0		

Big Angus Fraser was a lion hearted seamer who shouldered much of the work in the English side throughout the 90's. Through that period, injury and form troughs meant that he was in an out of the team, but as his 8/53 in the first innings at Port of Spain in 1998 shows he was a dangerous bowler when right. A counter to the argument that all fast bowlers are a bit thick, he has become an insightful cricket journalist in retirement.

FREEMAN, Alfred Percy

Born:	May 17, 1888
Batting:	Right handed
Bowling:	Right arm leg-break

Tests

Test Career:	1924-29
Cap Number:	222
Tests Played:	12

Test Batting

Innings:	16	Runs:	154
Highest Score:	50*	Average:	14.00
No. 50s:	1	No. 100s:	0

Test Bowling & Fielding

Wickets:	66	Runs:	1,707
Best Bowling:	7/71	Average:	25.86
5 WI:	5	10 WM:	3
Catches:	4	Stumpings:	0

Universally known as 'Tich,' the little leg-spinner from Kent is remembered as one of England's greatest slow bowlers even though he only played in 12 Tests. Joining the first class seen in his mid twenties, his career had to be put on hold with the advent of World War I, but when cricket resumed he quickly regained the mantle as the best leg spinner in county cricket. He was a fearless leggie who constantly tempted the batsmen to come forward by flighting the ball. If his opponents didn't get their feet in the right position it was generally fatal as his landing deliveries would turn appreciably. The Australians took to him on the Ashes tour of 1924/25 and he was shielded from them thereafter. The West Indies and South Africans seemed clueless against him and he led the averages in series against both nations. It was as a county cricketer however that Tich will be best remembered, taking over 3,000 wickets and claiming 10 wickets in a match more than 100 times.

FRENCH, Bruce Nicholas

Born:	August 13, 1959
Batting:	Right handed
	Wicket Keeper

Tests

Test Career:	1986-88
Cap Number:	517
Tests Played:	16

Test Batting

Innings:	21	Runs:	308
Highest Score:	59	Average:	18.11
No. 50s:	1	No. 100s:	0

Test Bowling & Fielding

Wickets:	0	Runs:	0
Best Bowling:		Average:	0.00
5 WI:	0	10 WM:	0
Catches:	38	Stumpings:	1

One Day Internationals

ODI Career:	1685-88
ODIs Played:	13

ODI Batting

Innings:	8	Runs:	34
Highest Score:	9*	Average:	6.80
No. 50s:	0	No. 100s:	0

ODI Bowling & Fielding

Wickets:	0	Runs:	0
Best Bowling:		Average:	0.00
5 WM:	0	Catches:	13
Stumpings:	3		

Like most wicket keepers he served a long apprenticeship as England's second keeper before finally getting his chance against India at Headingly in 1986. An excellent gloveman his moderate batting limited his Test career to just 16 matches.

FRY, Charles Burgess (C.B.)

Born:	April 25, 1872
Batting:	Right handed
Bowling:	Right arm medium-fast

Tests

Test Career:	1896-1912
Cap Number:	95
Tests Played:	26

Test Batting

Innings:	41	Runs:	1,223
Highest Score:	144	Average:	32.18
No. 50s:	7	No. 100s:	2

Test Bowling & Fielding

Wickets:	0	Runs:	3
Best Bowling:		Average:	0.00
5 WI:	0	10 WM:	0
Catches:	17	Stumpings:	0

His was a life most extraordinary, and whilst his cricket exploits made him the equal of any in his generation, they counted for only a fraction of his achievements. As a batsman he played mainly off the back foot, but from that stance was able to dispatch the ball to any corner of the ground. In a Test career that lasted over 15 years he scored more than 1,200 Test runs, including a career high 144 at The Oval in 1905 against the likes of Tibby Cotter and Monty Noble from Australia. A long standing skipper at Sussex, he also captained England in six Test for four wins. Fry would have played more than 26 Tests if he had the time, but his other interests meant that he only played on home soil. A brilliant scholar, he played Association Football for Southampton and England, held the world long jump record for 21 years, stood as a member of Parliament and wrote prolifically yet still had time to score more than 30,000 first class runs in an amazing career.

GALLIAN, Jason Edward Riche

Born:	June 25, 1971
Batting:	Right handed
Bowling:	Right arm medium

Tests
Test Career:	1995		
Cap Number:	573		
Tests Played:	3		

Test Batting
Innings:	6	Runs:	74
Highest Score:	28	Average:	12.33
No. 50s:	0	No. 100s:	0

Test Bowling & Fielding
Wickets:	0	Runs:	62
Best Bowling:		Average:	0.00
5 WI:	0	10 WM:	0
Catches:	1	Stumpings:	0

The Australian's move to England paid off with three Tests in 1995. Unfortunately for the Lancashire batsman he let the opportunity slip when he could only manage 74 runs in six completed innings.

GATTING, Michael William
Born: June 6, 1957
Batting: Right handed
Bowling: Right arm medium

Tests
Test Career:	1978-95		
Cap Number:	477		
Tests Played:	79		

Test Batting
Innings:	138	Runs:	4,409
Highest Score:	207	Average:	35.55
No. 50s:	21	No. 100s:	10

Test Bowling & Fielding
Wickets:	4	Runs:	317
Best Bowling:	1/14	Average:	79.25
5 WI:	0	10 WM:	0
Catches:	59	Stumpings:	0

One Day Internationals
ODI Career:	1977-93		
ODIs Played:	92		

ODI Batting
Innings:	88	Runs:	2,095
Highest Score:	115*	Average:	29.50
No. 50s:	9	No. 100s:	1

ODI Bowling & Fielding
Wickets:	10	Runs:	336
Best Bowling:	3/32	Average:	33.60
5 WM:	0	Catches:	22
Stumpings:	0		

England's 65th captain may have won only two Tests out of the 23 at the helm, but they were both against Australia and secured the Ashes in 1986/87 for what would be the last time in twenty years. The Middlesex man had a Test career that spanned 17 years and whilst he only averaged in the mid thirties in Tests there were many impressive innings such as his 207 against India at Madras in 1984/85 where he showed his mastery over spin bowling, or his 117 at Adelaide in 1995 as a 37 year old. He was a forthright skipper who at times seemed moody. His confrontation with Pakistani umpire Shakoor Rana raised questions about his control on the field and whilst he retained the job for another year, it was not forgotten by English authorities.

GAY, Leslie Hewitt
Born: March 24, 1871
Batting: Right handed
Wicket Keeper

Tests
Test Career:	1894		
Cap Number:	91		
Tests Played:	1		

Test Batting
Innings:	2	Runs:	37
Highest Score:	33	Average:	18.50
No. 50s:	0	No. 100s:	0

Test Bowling & Fielding
Wickets:	0	Runs:	0
Best Bowling:		Average:	0.00
5 WI:	0	10 WM:	0
Catches:	3	Stumpings:	1

A wicket keeper for the English cricket side and goalkeeper for the national football side, his only Test was at the SCG in 1894. Gay scored a bright 33 batting at number ten and completed four dismissals but was replaced by Punch Philipson for the remainder of the tour and never played Test cricket again.

GEARY, George
Born: July 9, 1893
Batting: Right handed
Bowling: Right arm medium-fast

Tests
Test Career:	1924-34		
Cap Number:	220		
Tests Played:	14		

Test Batting
Innings:	20	Runs:	249
Highest Score:	66	Average:	15.56
No. 50s:	2	No. 100s:	0

Test Bowling & Fielding
Wickets:	46	Runs:	1,353
Best Bowling:	7/70	Average:	29.41
5 WI:	4	10 WM:	1
Catches:	13	Stumpings:	0

He was a smart off spinner and useful lower order batsman from Leicestershire who nearly had his cricket career cut short when his shoulder was slashed by a spinning airplane propellor in 1914. Geary recovered and put in one of the great marathon stints bowling at the MCG in 1929 when he took 5/106 off 81 overs.

GIBB, Paul Antony
Born: July 11, 1913
Batting: Right handed
Wicket Keeper

Tests
Test Career:	1938-46	
Cap Number:	305	
Tests Played:	8	

Test Batting
Innings:	13	Runs:	581
Highest Score:	120	Average:	44.69
No. 50s:	3	No. 100s:	2

Test Bowling & Fielding
Wickets:	0	Runs:	0
Best Bowling:		Average:	0.00
5 WI:	0	10 WM:	0
Catches:	3	Stumpings:	1

A right hand bat batsman and good reserve wicket keeper, he was selected to tour South Africa in 1938 and made an immediate impression by scoring 93 and 106 on debut in Johannesburg. He hit another century at Durban to end the tour with 473 runs at 59.12. Unfortunately for Gibbs the war intervened, and whilst he was selected for Tests against Australia and India in the mid 40's, he would never regain the sparkling form he showed on his first tour.

GIDDINS, Edward Simon Hunter
Born: July 20, 1971
Batting: Right handed
Bowling: Right arm medium-fast

Tests
Test Career: 1999-2000
Cap Number: 596
Tests Played: 4

Test Batting
Innings:	7	Runs:	10
Highest Score:	7	Average:	2.50
No. 50s:	0	No. 100s:	0

Test Bowling & Fielding
Wickets:	12	Runs:	240
Best Bowling:	5/15	Average:	20.00
5 WI:	1	10 WM:	0
Catches:	0	Stumpings:	0

A controversial figure in English cricket who was banned for betting against his side in a county game. Giddins took 5/15 against Zimbabwe in the most memorable of his four Tests.

GIFFORD, Norman
Born: March 30, 1940
Batting: Left handed
Bowling: Left arm off-break

Tests
Test Career: 1964-73
Cap Number: 423
Tests Played: 15

Test Batting
Innings:	20	Runs:	179
Highest Score:	25*	Average:	16.27
No. 50s:	0	No. 100s:	0

Test Bowling & Fielding
Wickets:	33	Runs:	1,026
Best Bowling:	5/55	Average:	31.09
5 WI:	1	10 WM:	0
Catches:	8	Stumpings:	0

One Day Internationals
ODI Career: 1985
ODIs Played: 2

ODI Batting
Innings:	1	Runs:	0
Highest Score:	0	Average:	0.00
No. 50s:	0	No. 100s:	0

ODI Bowling & Fielding
Wickets:	4	Runs:	50
Best Bowling:	4/23	Average:	12.50
5 WM:	0	Catches:	1
Stumpings:	0		

A left arm off spinner, he was forced to play second fiddle to Derek Underwood for much of his career. Twelve years after his final Test, he led an English one day side to Sharjah in 1985 at the age of 44 where he showed that there was fight in the old dog yet with 4/23 off 10 overs against Pakistan.

GILES, Ashley Fraser
Born: March 19, 1973
Batting: Right handed
Bowling: Left arm off-break

Tests
Test Career: 1998-
Cap Number: 590
Tests Played: 52

Test Batting
Innings:	77	Runs:	1,347
Highest Score:	59	Average:	20.72
No. 50s:	4	No. 100s:	0

Test Bowling & Fielding
Wickets:	140	Runs:	5,544
Best Bowling:	5/57	Average:	39.60
5 WI:	5	10 WM:	0
Catches:	32	Stumpings:	0

One Day Internationals
ODI Career: 1997-
ODIs Played: 62

ODI Batting
Innings:	35	Runs:	385
Highest Score:	41	Average:	17.50
No. 50s:	0	No. 100s:	0

ODI Bowling & Fielding
Wickets:	55	Runs:	2,069
Best Bowling:	5/57	Average:	37.61
5 WM:	1	Catches:	22
Stumpings:	0		

The Warwickshire off-spinner has had his knockers over the years but has always been able to prove them wrong. He has never been a big spinner of the ball, but over the years has become more adventurous, willing to add flight and bounce to his accurate deliveries. He was discarded after a single Test against South Africa in 1998 and had to wait until the end of 2000 for another chance. Selected to tour Pakistan, he captured 17 wickets in three Tests and almost overnight had become England's front line spinner. For the next five years he provided steady service for England and certainly played his part when England regained the Ashes in 2005. Australia planned to attack the affable offie, but he was up to the task, taking eleven wickets and bowling plenty of economical overs. For all his successes he has always had to prove himself, and with the emergence of Monty Panesar in the summer of 2006 the challenge is once again squarely at Giles' feet. He has always been a crowd favourite and his cult status received a boost when an issue of mugs that was supposed to read 'Ashley Giles - King of Spin' arrived from China reading ' Ashley Giles - King of Spain'.

GILLIGAN, Alfred Herbert Harold

Born:	June 29, 1896
Batting:	Right handed
Bowling:	Right arm leg-break

Tests

Test Career:	1930
Cap Number:	248
Tests Played:	4

Test Batting

Innings:	4	Runs:	71
Highest Score:	32	Average:	17.75
No. 50s:	0	No. 100s:	0

Test Bowling & Fielding

Wickets:	0	Runs:	0
Best Bowling:		Average:	0.00
5 WI:	0	10 WM:	0
Catches:	0	Stumpings:	0

The leg spinning all rounder from Sussex played only four Tests all against New Zealand and two of them as skipper.

GILLIGAN, Arthur Edward Robert

Born:	December 23, 1894
Batting:	Right handed
Bowling:	Right arm medium-fast

Tests

Test Career:	1922-25
Cap Number:	207
Tests Played:	11

Test Batting

Innings:	16	Runs:	209
Highest Score:	39*	Average:	16.07
No. 50s:	0	No. 100s:	0

Test Bowling & Fielding

Wickets:	36	Runs:	1,046
Best Bowling:	6/7	Average:	29.05
5 WI:	2	10 WM:	1
Catches:	3	Stumpings:	0

Arthur Gilligan may have played only eleven Tests for England but he led the side in nine of them for the respectable record of four wins and four losses. Rare for a captain in that he was an opening bowler, he tore through the South Africans at Edgbaston in 1924 with Maurice Tate, dismissing the tourists for a then record low innings score of 30. Gilligan followed up his 6/7 in the first innings with 5/83 in the second. Later that year he led the side to Australia and by his own admission the burden of captaincy affected his bowling. He took only ten wickets for the series which his side lost four Tests to one. Following his retirement he was one of the early pioneers of radio commentary, teaming up with former Australian captain Victor Richardson.

GIMBLETT, Harold

Born:	October 19, 1914
Batting:	Right handed
Bowling:	Right arm medium

Tests

Test Career:	1936-39
Cap Number:	290
Tests Played:	3

Test Batting

Innings:	5	Runs:	129
Highest Score:	67*	Average:	32.25
No. 50s:	1	No. 100s:	0

Test Bowling & Fielding

Wickets:	0	Runs:	0
Best Bowling:		Average:	0.00
5 WI:	0	10 WM:	0
Catches:	1	Stumpings:	0

An attacking batsman from Somerset who had a promising Test career cut short by World War II. He scored 67 not out against India on debut at Lord's in 1936 but played only two more Tests before the war intervened. Whilst he was not considered for the Test side after the resumption in 1946 he continued to be a fine player for Somerset and ended his career with 50 first class centuries.

GLADWIN, Clifford

Born:	April 3, 1916
Batting:	Right handed
Bowling:	Right arm medium-fast

Tests

Test Career:	1947-49
Cap Number:	322
Tests Played:	8

Test Batting

Innings:	11	Runs:	170
Highest Score:	51*	Average:	28.33
No. 50s:	1	No. 100s:	0

Test Bowling & Fielding

Wickets:	15	Runs:	571
Best Bowling:	3/21	Average:	38.06
5 WI:	0	10 WM:	0
Catches:	2	Stumpings:	0

The accurate medium pace bowler had an extraordinary start to his Test career taking 2/58 off 50 overs against South Africa in the first innings of his first Test at Old Trafford in 1947. He toured South Africa later that year, but 13 wickets in five Tests was a disappointing return and he would play ony one more Test for his country.

GODDARD, Thomas William John

Born:	October 1, 1900
Batting:	Right handed
Bowling:	Right arm off-break

Tests

Test Career:	1930-39
Cap Number:	256
Tests Played:	8

Test Batting

Innings:	5	Runs:	13
Highest Score:	8	Average:	6.50
No. 50s:	0	No. 100s:	0

Test Bowling & Fielding

Wickets:	22	Runs:	588
Best Bowling:	6/29	Average:	26.72
5 WI:	1	10 WM:	0
Catches:	3	Stumpings:	0

The towering off spinner from Gloucestershire took almost 3,000 first class wickets and was considered unlucky not have played more than just eight Tests. Goddard took six first class hat-tricks, one of which came in a Test at Johannesburg in 1938. Goddard was the mainstay of the Gloucestershire attack for three decades, playing his last game for the club in 1952.

GOOCH, Graham Alan

Born:	July 23, 1953
Batting:	Right handed
Bowling:	Right arm medium

Tests

Test Career:	1975-95
Cap Number:	461
Tests Played:	118

Test Batting

Innings:	215	Runs:	8,900
Highest Score:	333	Average:	42.58
No. 50s:	46	No. 100s:	20

Test Bowling & Fielding

Wickets:	23	Runs:	1,069
Best Bowling:	3/39	Average:	46.47
5 WI:	0	10 WM:	0
Catches:	103	Stumpings:	0

One Day Internationals

ODI Career:	1976-95
ODIs Played:	125

ODI Batting

Innings:	122	Runs:	4,290
Highest Score:	142	Average:	36.98
No. 50s:	23	No. 100s:	8

ODI Bowling & Fielding

Wickets:	36	Runs:	1,516
Best Bowling:	3/19	Average:	42.11
5 WM:	0	Catches:	45
Stumpings:	0		

Very few cricketers who score a pair on debut go on to have long Test careers. Not only did Graham Gooch have a long career it was also one of the game's most successful. That pair came against a speed laden Australian attack at Edgbaston in 1975 and after being given one more chance in the very next Test, Gooch was sent back to Essex for almost three years. Upon returning he had added strength and power to his considerable frame and this time there were no false starts. He performed consistently without starring for over 20 Tests until he finally broke through for his maiden Test century in 1980. It was a just reward for Gooch who had scored 99 at the MCG earlier in the year. That innings of 126 against the West Indies at Lord's would be the first of 20 Test hundreds for England but by no means the largest. In July 1990 England faced India at Lord's under the leadership of Gooch. He had assumed the captaincy in 1988 and at first it appeared that the added burden of responsibility had affected his batting. He struggled against the touring New Zealanders 1990 until the final Test in Birmingham where he scored 154 in the first innings. With the shackles lifted he wrought havoc on the Indian attack at Lord's, hitting the highest score by an Englishman in Tests since Walter Hammond's 336 almost 60 years earlier. His 333 took over 10 hours and contained 46 boundaries. Throughout the marathon stay he was at his powerful best, with that trademark high backlift slamming down on anything that was overpitched or a quick pivot sending any short delivery either racing to, or soaring over the ropes. He followed up the triple ton with 123 in the second innings to break the record for most runs in a single Test by any batsman. There was another double century against New Zealand as a 40 year old and when he retired at the end of the Ashes series in 1994/95 he had scored exactly 8,900 runs at an average of 42.58. Gooch was for the most part an outwardly serious character who led his country in 34 Tests for ten wins and 12 losses. With 118 Tests for England, he lies second only to Alec Stewart on the all time list, but given that he toured South Africa in 1981 and suffered a three year ban he should be sitting at number one. Today the former English skipper works as a TV commentator and with the pressures of international cricket behind him, comes across as a witty and likeable individual.

GOUGH, Darren

Born:	September 18, 1970
Batting:	Right handed
Bowling:	Right arm fast

Tests

Test Career:	1994-2003
Cap Number:	568
Tests Played:	58

Test Batting

Innings:	86	Runs:	855
Highest Score:	65	Average:	12.57
No. 50s:	2	No. 100s:	0

Test Bowling & Fielding

Wickets:	229	Runs:	6,503
Best Bowling:	6/42	Average:	28.39
5 WI:	9	10 WM:	0
Catches:	13	Stumpings:	0

One Day Internationals

ODI Career:	1994-
ODIs Played:	157

ODI Batting

Innings:	85	Runs:	590
Highest Score:	46*	Average:	12.55
No. 50s:	0	No. 100s:	0

ODI Bowling & Fielding

Wickets:	235	Runs:	6,137
Best Bowling:	5/44	Average:	26.11
5 WM:	2	Catches:	25
Stumpings:	0		

The likeable quick from Yorkshire gave his all for England whether steaming in with ball, haring around the boundary to make a diving save or flinging his bat at the end of an innings. It was always 100% effort for Gough who burst onto the Test scene with 14 wickets in his first two Tests. England must have thought they had got an all-rounder in Gough as well, but his debut knock of 65 against the Kiwis in Manchester was to be his highest score in 86 Test innings. His bowling however was no illusion, as Gough would go on to lead England to victory in a number of Tests. His seven wickets at the MCG in 1998/99 gave the English a rare Ashes Test win in a series that saw him capture 21 wickets. Twenty five wickets against the West Indies at home was the difference between the two sides in 2000 and he was equally effective against Pakistan the following summer. Whilst he hasn't played a Test since 2003, Gough is far from a spent force and was named in the England one day squad for the Champion's Trophy in India at the end of 2006. Unfortunately an injury sustained whilst playing a twenty/20 game in August may mean the end of his international aspirations.

GOULD, Ian James

Born: August 19, 1957
Batting: Left handed
Wicket Keeper

One Day Internationals

ODI Career: 1983
ODIs Played: 18

ODI Batting

Innings:	14	Runs:	155
Highest Score:	42	Average:	12.91
No. 50s:	0	No. 100s:	0

ODI Bowling & Fielding

Wickets:	0	Runs:	0
Best Bowling:		Average:	0.00
5 WM:	0	Catches:	15
Stumpings:	3		

A hardworking wicket-keeper who was unfortunate not to be given a chance at Test level, Ian Gould made his ODI debut against New Zealand at the 'Gabba, during the Australian one day triangular series in 1983. Later that year he represented England in seven World Cup matches including the semi final against India at Old Trafford.

GOVER, Alfred Richard

Born: February 29, 1908
Batting: Right handed
Bowling: Right arm fast

Tests

Test Career: 1936-46
Cap Number: 293
Tests Played: 4

Test Batting

Innings:	1	Runs:	2
Highest Score:	2*	Average:	0.00
No. 50s:	0	No. 100s:	0

Test Bowling & Fielding

Wickets:	8	Runs:	359
Best Bowling:	3/85	Average:	44.87
5 WI:	0	10 WM:	0
Catches:	1	Stumpings:	0

An opening bowler from Surrey who had his Test career interrupted by the Second World War. Gover ran England's best known cricket school for 40 years. The academy located in south London boasted many well known students including a young Viv Richards who attended prior to playing first class cricket in England.

GOWER, David Ivon

Born: April 1, 1957
Batting: Left handed
Bowling: Right arm off-break

Tests

Test Career: 1978-92
Cap Number: 479
Tests Played: 117

Test Batting

Innings:	204	Runs:	8,231
Highest Score:	215	Average:	44.25
No. 50s:	39	No. 100s:	18

Test Bowling & Fielding

Wickets:	1	Runs:	20
Best Bowling:	1/1	Average:	20.00
5 WI:	0	10 WM:	0
Catches:	74	Stumpings:	0

One Day Internationals

ODI Career: 1978-91
ODIs Played: 114

ODI Batting

Innings:	111	Runs:	3,170
Highest Score:	158	Average:	30.77
No. 50s:	12	No. 100s:	7

ODI Bowling & Fielding

Wickets:	0	Runs:	14
Best Bowling:		Average:	0.00
5 WM:	0	Catches:	44
Stumpings:	0		

A brilliant if not sometimes frustrating batsman, David Gower played with a gentle ease that belied the dangers that face Test batsmen. A wristy driver and loose limbed puller and hooker, one had a sense that if there really was a 'good old days' then they used to bat like Gower during it. For all his elegance there were times when his laconic nature seemed to work against him, playing strokes that had no place in Test cricket. He scored his maiden Test century in his first summer of international cricket in a match against New Zealand at The Oval. His first tour to Australia in 1978/79 was outstanding. He topped the aggregates and the averages and made an excellent ton on the bouncy WACA wicket along the way. A double century the next English summer against India was to be his highest Test score until he played an innings of supreme mastery at Edgbaston in 1985 to record a career high 215. That summer started poorly for Gower with scores of three, one and zero in the limited over openers and before long the English tabloids were calling for his sacking. A century in the final one-dayer and 732 runs in the six Test series reaffirmed his reputation as England's best batsman in the 80's. In all his 8,231 Test runs sees him third on the all time list for England and even though an average off 44.25 may seem low for a player of his boundless ability, he still ranks as one of England finest batsmen. Though he was well liked by the players, he seemed to lack the drive to be a great captain with a record of five wins in 32 Tests providing proof. Like most modern former Test captains he now works on television as a commentator.

GRACE, Edward Mills

Born: November 28, 1841
Batting: Right handed
Bowling: Right arm slow

Tests

Test Career: 1880
Cap Number: 22
Tests Played: 1

Test Batting
Innings:	2	Runs:	36
Highest Score:	36	Average:	18.00
No. 50s:	0	No. 100s:	0

Test Bowling & Fielding
Wickets:	0	Runs:	0
Best Bowling:		Average:	0.00
5 WI:	0	10 WM:	0
Catches:	1	Stumpings:	0

The oldest of the three Grace brothers to have appeared for England, Edward may have played only the single Test but he was a legendary player for Gloucestershire where he score ten thousand first class runs. In one famous match for the M.C.C. in 1862 he made 192 not out and took ten wickets in a single innings with his well guided round arm lobs.

GRACE, George Frederick

Born: December 13, 1850
Batting: Right handed
Bowling: Right arm slow

Tests

Test Career: 1880
Cap Number: 23
Tests Played: 1

Test Batting
Innings:	2	Runs:	0
Highest Score:	0	Average:	0.00
No. 50s:	0	No. 100s:	0

Test Bowling & Fielding
Wickets:	0	Runs:	0
Best Bowling:		Average:	0.00
5 WI:	0	10 WM:	0
Catches:	2	Stumpings:	0

The youngest of the three Grace brothers to play Test cricket, his only outing for England was a distinct disappointment scoring a pair against the Australians at The Oval in 1880. Tragically the talented batsman with eight first class centuries to his name would not get the chance to redeem himself as he died of pneumonia only two weeks later.

GRACE, William Gilbert (W.G.)

Born: July 18, 1848
Batting: Right handed
Bowling: Right arm slow

Tests

Test Career: 1880-99
Cap Number: 24
Tests Played: 22

Test Batting
Innings:	36	Runs:	1,098
Highest Score:	170	Average:	32.29
No. 50s:	5	No. 100s:	2

Test Bowling & Fielding
Wickets:	9	Runs:	236
Best Bowling:	2/12	Average:	26.22
5 WI:	0	10 WM:	0
Catches:	39	Stumpings:	0

The Doctor was such an imposing figure in cricket's formative years that almost 100 years after he passed away his proud whiskered face is still one of the game's most recognizable images. His numbers are mind boggling, 43 years as a first class cricketer, 54,211 first class runs and 2809 first class wickets. He scored over 1,000 first class runs in a season 28 times. He was already 32 when he played his first Test but in 22 appearances for England he scored over 1,000 runs with two fine centuries and was the first cricketer to score a hundred on English soil. He captained in England in 13 Tests both at home and in Australia for eight wins and three losses. As impressive as his statistics were his greatness lay in the way he conducted himself. The doctor carried an air of superiority on the field that not only served him well but raised the status of the game. W.G. was the epitome of an English gentleman and the fact that he derived so much pleasure out of the sport encouraged others of his station to abandon their smoker's clubs and take to the sporting field. For each of his innings, which numbered almost 1,500 there was an accompanying tale, some tall and some true. He famously replaced the bails after being bowled in a charity, telling the bowler "They came to see me bat, not to see you bowl". He was credited with having a quick wit and it was said that on his way to the cricket one day, he was accosted by a woman who asked if he could attend her two sons who had measles. "Can you come?" "Not just now," Grace replied. "But contact me at the ground if their temperatures reach 210 for two." The first great of the game passed away during an air raid in 1915, he was sixty-seven and only seven years out of the game.

GRAVENEY, Thomas William

Born: June 16, 1927
Batting: Right handed
Bowling: Right arm leg-break

Tests

Test Career: 1951-69
Cap Number: 358
Tests Played: 79

Test Batting

Innings:	123	Runs:	4,882
Highest Score:	258	Average:	44.38
No. 50s:	20	No. 100s:	11

Test Bowling & Fielding

Wickets:	1	Runs:	167
Best Bowling:	1/34	Average:	167.00
5 WI:	0	10 WM:	0
Catches:	80	Stumpings:	0

There was certainly something special about Tom Graveney's first Test century. Playing in only his second Test, the tall number three from Gloucestershire took almost 500 minutes to craft a 175 against an imposing Indian attack in Bombay. In what would become commonplace for almost the next two decades he denied the opposition and staved off defeat. As a batsman he was a fine technician using his long batting stride to either drive forcefully or defend safely. His Test career seemed over at the end of 1962 when at 35 he was thought too old. But a move to Worcestershire as captain rekindled interest in Graveney and he not only rejoined the Test team in 1966 but went on to add four more Test centuries to the seven he had already scored. Of those 11 tons, the highest was 258 against the West Indies at Trent Bridge in 1957. He celebrated his 42nd birthday during his final Test and went on to become a member of BBC TV's commentary team. His son David currently serves as English chairman of selectors.

GRAYSON, Adrian Paul

Born: March 31, 1971
Batting: Right handed
Bowling: Left arm slow

One Day Internationals

ODI Career: 2000-01
ODIs Played: 2

ODI Batting

Innings:	2	Runs:	6
Highest Score:	6	Average:	3.00
No. 50s:	0	No. 100s:	0

ODI Bowling & Fielding

Wickets:	3	Runs:	60
Best Bowling:	3/40	Average:	20.00
5 WM:	0	Catches:	1
Stumpings:	0		

An all-rounder from York, Grayson was selected on the ICC knockout tournament in Kenya in 2000 but was out first ball on debut against South Africa. He played his next ODI a year later against Zimbabwe, at Bulawayo, where he improved his average by just three runs.

GREENHOUGH, Thomas

Born: November 9, 1931
Batting: Right handed
Bowling: Right arm leg-break

Tests

Test Career: 1959-60
Cap Number: 393
Tests Played: 4

Test Batting

Innings:	4	Runs:	4
Highest Score:	2	Average:	1.33
No. 50s:	0	No. 100s:	0

Test Bowling & Fielding

Wickets:	16	Runs:	357
Best Bowling:	5/35	Average:	22.31
5 WI:	1	10 WM:	0
Catches:	1	Stumpings:	0

A leg spinner from Rochdale near Manchester, his stock ball was a big turning googly. In Greenough's second Test at Lord's he took 5/35 in India's first innings.

GREENWOOD, Andrew

Born: August 20, 1847
Batting: Right handed

Tests

Test Career: 1877
Cap Number: 4
Tests Played: 2

Test Batting

Innings:	4	Runs:	77
Highest Score:	49	Average:	19.25
No. 50s:	0	No. 100s:	0

Test Bowling & Fielding

Wickets:	0	Runs:	0
Best Bowling:		Average:	0.00
5 WI:	0	10 WM:	0
Catches:	2	Stumpings:	0

A top order batsman from Yorkshire who played in the first two Tests of all time. He performed particularly well in the second where he made 49 and 22 batting at number three.

GREIG, Anthony William

Born: October 6, 1946
Batting: Right handed
Bowling: Right arm medium

Tests

Test Career: 1972-77
Cap Number: 452
Tests Played: 58

Test Batting

Innings:	93	Runs:	3,599
Highest Score:	148	Average:	40.43
No. 50s:	20	No. 100s:	8

Test Bowling & Fielding

Wickets:	141	Runs:	4,541
Best Bowling:	8/86	Average:	32.20
5 WI:	6	10 WM:	2
Catches:	87	Stumpings:	0

One Day Internationals

ODI Career: 1972-77
ODIs Played: 22

ODI Batting

Innings:	19	Runs:	269
Highest Score:	48	Average:	16.81
No. 50s:	0	No. 100s:	0

ODI Bowling & Fielding

Wickets:	19	Runs:	619
Best Bowling:	4/45	Average:	32.57
5 WM:	0	Catches:	7
Stumpings:	0		

Cricket's bad guy may have had the ability to rile opposition players and fans like no other, but he could back up his bad boy antics with some very fine cricket. When South Africa became a sporting pariah because of their apartheid policy Greig headed to England in search of Test cricket. He not only won a spot in the side, but was later made the national captain. Looking to counter the Australians and West Indians, the English selectors abandoned their policy of making the best thinker in the country the skipper and went for the aggressive Greig as a replacement for Mike Denness in 1975. He led from the front, and whilst he was unable to secure a series win over Australia or the West Indies, he succeeded with both the bat and the ball. He was generally an attacking batsman, who with bat held high, clouted many fine Test centuries. He made consecutive tons on the tour of the West Indies in 1973/74 and a fighting 110 at Brisbane in 1974/75 against a rampaging Dennis Lillee and Jeff Thomson. Greig was also a dangerous bowler who used his considerable height to good use whether bowling medium pace or well flighted off-spin. At Port of Spain in 1974 he took 13 wickets in a single Test to help England to a famous victory. He was still very much a member of the English side when he assisted Kerry Packer in the creation of World Series Cricket. By the time the breakaway group went public, Greig had moved to Australia and abandoned the country that gave him a chance to play Test cricket. It was an acrimonious parting but Tony Greig prospered from his decision and still works for the network that he quietly assisted almost 30 years ago.

GREIG, Ian Alexander

Born:	December 8, 1955
Batting:	Right handed
Bowling:	Right arm medium

Tests

Test Career:	1982		
Cap Number:	496		
Tests Played:	2		

Test Batting

Innings:	4	Runs:	26
Highest Score:	14	Average:	6.50
No. 50s:	0	No. 100s:	0

Test Bowling & Fielding

Wickets:	4	Runs:	114
Best Bowling:	4/53	Average:	28.50
5 WI:	0	10 WM:	0
Catches:	0	Stumpings:	0

The younger brother of Tony, he was an all-rounder who played two Tests against the touring Pakistanis in 1982.

GRIEVE, Basil Arthur Firebrace

Born:	May 28, 1864
Batting:	Right handed

Tests

Test Career:	1889		
Cap Number:	64		
Tests Played:	2		

Test Batting

Innings:	3	Runs:	40
Highest Score:	14*	Average:	40.00
No. 50s:	0	No. 100s:	0

Test Bowling & Fielding

Wickets:	0	Runs:	0
Best Bowling:		Average:	0.00
5 WI:	0	10 WM:	0
Catches:	0	Stumpings:	0

One of many English cricketers whose entire first class career comprised of the two Tests he played under Major Warton on the tour of South Africa in 1889. He opened the bowling for Harrow but was used solely as a batsman in his two Tests.

GRIFFITH, Stewart Cathie (Billy)

Born:	June 16, 1914
Batting:	Right handed
	Wicket Keeper

Tests

Test Career:	1948-49		
Cap Number:	332		
Tests Played:	3		

Test Batting

Innings:	5	Runs:	157
Highest Score:	140	Average:	31.40
No. 50s:	0	No. 100s:	1

Test Bowling & Fielding

Wickets:	0	Runs:	0
Best Bowling:		Average:	0.00
5 WI:	0	10 WM:	0
Catches:	5	Stumpings:	0

The Surrey wicket keeper was used as a batsman on the tour of the West Indies in 1948 when he was selected for the second Test at Port of Spain. He opened the batting and his 140 in the first innings was his first ever first class century. Billy, as he was known played two more Tests, but never again found the form that saw him shock English fans in his first Test.

GUNN, George

Born:	June 13, 1879
Batting:	Right handed
Bowling:	Right arm slow

Tests

Test Career:	1907-30		
Cap Number:	153		
Tests Played:	15		

Test Batting

Innings:	29	Runs:	1,120
Highest Score:	122*	Average:	40.00
No. 50s:	7	No. 100s:	2

Test Bowling & Fielding			
Wickets:	0	Runs:	8
Best Bowling:		Average:	0.00
5 WI:	0	10 WM:	0
Catches:	15	Stumpings:	0

A star batsman from county side Notts who scored over 35,000 first class runs. George Gunn had an excellent Test career scoring over 1,000 runs in only 15 Tests and he was the best performed batsman in the side that got trounced by the Australians 4-1 on the Ashes tour of 1907/08. He played all five Tests that series scoring 462 runs at 51.33 with two centuries. He was related to William Gunn of cricket bat fame.

GUNN, John Richmond

Born: July 19, 1876
Batting: Left handed

Tests

Test Career: 1901-05
Cap Number: 132
Tests Played: 6

Test Batting

Innings:	10	Runs:	85
Highest Score:	24	Average:	10.62
No. 50s:	0	No. 100s:	0

Test Bowling & Fielding

Wickets:	18	Runs:	387
Best Bowling:	5/76	Average:	21.50
5 WI:	1	10 WM:	0
Catches:	3	Stumpings:	0

A nephew of Test cricketer William Gunn, he was a skillful left-arm off spinner. He played all five Tests in Archie MacLaren's side that toured Australia in 1901/02 taking 17 wickets at just over 21 runs apiece.

GUNN, William

Born: December 4, 1858
Batting: Right handed

Tests

Test Career: 1887-99
Cap Number: 52
Tests Played: 11

Test Batting

Innings:	20	Runs:	392
Highest Score:	102*	Average:	21.77
No. 50s:	1	No. 100s:	1

Test Bowling & Fielding

Wickets:	0	Runs:	0
Best Bowling:		Average:	0.00
5 WI:	0	10 WM:	0
Catches:	5	Stumpings:	0

He was a fine batsman from Notts who played in eleven Tests over a 12 year period. Possessed of a fine technique, Gunn played a renowned innings for a side known as Players when Australia toured in 1890. His 228 against the tourists won him high praise and he followed it up in a Test against the Australians three years later at Old Tafford with his only Test century. His availability for the Test side was restricted because of a growing sporting goods business that would make him a wealthy man. The name of that buisness was Gunn and Moore and it survives today as one of the sport's leading manufacturer of bats and other equipment.

HABIB, Aftab

Born: February 7, 1972
Batting: Right handed
Bowling: Right arm medium-fast

Tests

Test Career: 1999
Cap Number: 594
Tests Played: 2

Test Batting

Innings:	3	Runs:	26
Highest Score:	19	Average:	8.66
No. 50s:	0	No. 100s:	0

Test Bowling & Fielding

Wickets:	0	Runs:	0
Best Bowling:		Average:	0.00
5 WI:	0	10 WM:	0
Catches:	0	Stumpings:	0

A journeyman in county cricket, the top order batsman was tried in two Tests against New Zealand in 1999 but could manage only 26 runs in three at bats.

HAIG, Nigel Esme

Born: December 12, 1887
Batting: Right handed
Bowling: Right arm medium-fast

Tests

Test Career: 1921-30
Cap Number: 198
Tests Played: 5

Test Batting

Innings:	9	Runs:	126
Highest Score:	47	Average:	14.00
No. 50s:	0	No. 100s:	0

Test Bowling & Fielding

Wickets:	13	Runs:	448
Best Bowling:	3/73	Average:	34.46
5 WI:	0	10 WM:	0
Catches:	4	Stumpings:	0

Tall and athletic, the all-rounder from Middlesex appeared briefly against Australia in 1921. He wasn't seen again in international cricket until he toured the West Indies in 1929/30 where he played a further four Tests.

HAIGH, Schofield

Born: March 19, 1871
Batting: Right handed
Bowling: Right arm medium-fast

Tests

Test Career: 1899-1912
Cap Number: 113
Tests Played: 11

Test Batting

Innings:	18	Runs:	113
Highest Score:	25	Average:	7.53
No. 50s:	0	No. 100s:	0

Test Bowling & Fielding			
Wickets:	24	Runs:	622
Best Bowling:	6/11	Average:	25.91
5 WI:	1	10 WM:	0
Catches:	8	Stumpings:	0

A medium pace bowler from Yorkshire, he made his debut for England as part of Lord Hawke's side that toured South Africa in 1899. In the second Test at Cape Town he tore through the home side in the second innings to take 6/11 as they tumbled to be all out for 35. However those tours to South Africa were considered to be inferior to the Tests played between England and Australia and Haigh did not appear in the Test side for another six years. In all his 11 Tests were spread out over a 13 year period.

HALLOWS, Charles

Born:	April 4, 1895
Batting:	Left handed
Bowling:	Left arm off-break

Tests

Test Career:	1921-28
Cap Number:	203
Tests Played:	2

Test Batting

Innings:	2	Runs:	42
Highest Score:	26	Average:	42.00
No. 50s:	0	No. 100s:	0

Test Bowling & Fielding

Wickets:	0	Runs:	0
Best Bowling:		Average:	0.00
5 WI:	0	10 WM:	0
Catches:	0	Stumpings:	0

An opening batsman from Lancashire, he played two Tests for England separated by a break of seven years. He was a prolific scorer for his county, but was unfortunate to have played at the same time as Jack Hobbs and Herb Sutcliffe.

HAMILTON, Gavin Mark

Born:	September 16, 1974
Batting:	Left handed
Bowling:	Right arm medium-fast

Tests

Test Career:	1999
Cap Number:	599
Tests Played:	1

Test Batting

Innings:	2	Runs:	0
Highest Score:	0	Average:	0.00
No. 50s:	0	No. 100s:	0

Test Bowling & Fielding

Wickets:	0	Runs:	63
Best Bowling:		Average:	0.00
5 WI:	0	10 WM:	0
Catches:	0	Stumpings:	0

One Day Internationals

| ODI Career: | 1999- |
| ODIs Played: | 6 |

ODI Batting

Innings:	6	Runs:	226
Highest Score:	76	Average:	45.20
No. 50s:	2	No. 100s:	0

ODI Bowling & Fielding

Wickets:	3	Runs:	149
Best Bowling:	2/36	Average:	49.66
5 WM:	0	Catches:	1
Stumpings:	0		

The Scottish born Hamilton toured South Africa in 1999 where he played his only Test. Unfortunately with a pair and 0/63 of 15 overs it's highly unlikely he'll ever play another.

HAMMOND, Walter Reginald

Born:	June 19, 1903
Batting:	Right handed
Bowling:	Right arm medium-fast

Tests

Test Career:	1927-47
Cap Number:	227
Tests Played:	85

Test Batting

Innings:	140	Runs:	7,249
Highest Score:	336*	Average:	58.45
No. 50s:	24	No. 100s:	22

Test Bowling & Fielding

Wickets:	83	Runs:	3,138
Best Bowling:	5/36	Average:	37.80
5 WI:	2	10 WM:	0
Catches:	110	Stumpings:	0

It seems only fair that at the same time as Australia was blessed with the great Don Bradman, England had their own master batsman in Walter Hammond. He was a commanding cricketer who strode out to bat with an aura of authority and once in the middle left no-one in doubt as to the depths of his talent. His first two series were impressive enough, but it was on the tour of Australia in 1928/29 that he announced his greatness. His first Test century was a glorious 251 at the SCG that single handedly won the Test for his country and left spectators and media searching for superlatives. The shell-shocked Australians had little time to regroup, in the next Test at Melbourne he hit another double century and then followed it up in Adelaide with an unbeaten 119 and 177. Walter Hammond had arrived with a record breaking 905 runs for the series at an average well in excess of 100. With a taste for records he broke Don Bradman's highest score in Tests when he took to the fledgling New Zealand side in 1932/33. His 336 not out at Auckland was a study in sustained savagery, taking only 318 minutes with 34 fours and a record 10 sixes. Of all his leviathan innings, his 240 against Australia at Lord's is said to have been his best. Bradman himself was in awe of the Gloucs great who handled the spin of O'Reilly and Fleetwood-Smith with ludicrous ease. By the time he played his last Test in 1947, he had made 22 big Test hundreds and finished with a champion's average of 58.45. His batting prowess overshadowed his not inconsiderable ability with the ball. The powerfully built Hammond put his shoulder into his work bowling above medium pace and taking five wickets in an innings twice in Tests. Hammond retired to South Africa where he lived in relative anonymity until his passing at the age of 62.

HAMPSHIRE, John Harry

Born:	February 10, 1941
Batting:	Right handed
Bowling:	Right arm leg-break

Tests
Test Career:	1969-75		
Cap Number:	442		
Tests Played:	8		

Test Batting
Innings:	16	Runs:	403
Highest Score:	107	Average:	26.86
No. 50s:	2	No. 100s:	1

Test Bowling & Fielding
Wickets:	0	Runs:	0
Best Bowling:		Average:	0.00
5 WI:	0	10 WM:	0
Catches:	9	Stumpings:	0

One Day Internationals
ODI Career:	1971-72		
ODIs Played:	3		

ODI Batting
Innings:	3	Runs:	48
Highest Score:	25*	Average:	24.00
No. 50s:	0	No. 100s:	0

ODI Bowling & Fielding
Wickets:	0	Runs:	0
Best Bowling:		Average:	0.00
5 WM:	0	Catches:	0
Stumpings:	0		

His Test career started in a blaze of glory with a Test hundred on debut against the West Indies at Lord's but he was inexplicably dropped for the very next Test. Despite regaining his place in the side Hampshire never seemed to recover from the lack of faith shown in him and played only 8 Tests in total. He went on to become a highly respected international umpire.

HARDINGE, Harold Thomas William (Wally)

Born:	February 25, 1886
Batting:	Right handed
Bowling:	Left arm off-break

Tests
Test Career:	1921		
Cap Number:	201		
Tests Played:	1		

Test Batting
Innings:	2	Runs:	30
Highest Score:	25	Average:	15.00
No. 50s:	0	No. 100s:	0

Test Bowling & Fielding
Wickets:	0	Runs:	0
Best Bowling:		Average:	0.00
5 WI:	0	10 WM:	0
Catches:	0	Stumpings:	0

He was on opening batsman from Kent who played a single Test against the Australians at Leeds in 1921. Hardinge was also a famous footballer, playing with Sheffield United, Newcastle United and Arsenal in the English FA.

HARDSTAFF, Joseph (Jnr)

Born:	July 3, 1911
Batting:	Right handed
Bowling:	Right arm medium

Tests
Test Career:	1935-48		
Cap Number:	285		
Tests Played:	23		

Test Batting
Innings:	38	Runs:	1,636
Highest Score:	205*	Average:	46.74
No. 50s:	10	No. 100s:	4

Test Bowling & Fielding
Wickets:	0	Runs:	0
Best Bowling:		Average:	0.00
5 WI:	0	10 WM:	0
Catches:	9	Stumpings:	0

The son of Joseph senior, he too was a forceful right handed batsman with a penchant for scoring freely. He toured Australia with moderate success in 1936/37, but it was on Australia's return tour in 1938 that he came into his own. He teamed up with Len Hutton at The Oval to put on a record 215 for the sixth wicket. Jospeh junior scored 169 not out as England compiled a then world record innings score of 7 declared for 903. Whilst his best years in terms of cricket were lost to the Second World War he did return to the Test side in 1946 scoring 205 not out against the touring Indians at Lord's.

HARDSTAFF, Joseph (Snr)

Born:	November 9, 1882
Batting:	Right handed
Bowling:	Right arm medium-fast

Tests
Test Career:	1907-08		
Cap Number:	154		
Tests Played:	5		

Test Batting
Innings:	10	Runs:	311
Highest Score:	72	Average:	31.10
No. 50s:	3	No. 100s:	0

Test Bowling & Fielding
Wickets:	0	Runs:	0
Best Bowling:		Average:	0.00
5 WI:	0	10 WM:	0
Catches:	1	Stumpings:	0

A member of the side that was soundly beaten 4-1 in the 1907/08 Ashes series in Australia, he played all five Tests and returned a respectable 311 runs from his ten at bats.

HARMISON, Stephen James

Born:	October 23, 1978
Batting:	Right handed
Bowling:	Right arm fast

Tests
Test Career:	2002-
Cap Number:	611
Tests Played:	44

Test Batting

Innings:	59	Runs:	497
Highest Score:	42	Average:	11.29
No. 50s:	0	No. 100s:	0

Test Bowling & Fielding

Wickets:	175	Runs:	5,032
Best Bowling:	7/12	Average:	28.75
5 WI:	8	10 WM:	1
Catches:	6	Stumpings:	0

One Day Internationals

ODI Career:	2002-		
ODIs Played:	44		

ODI Batting

Innings:	20	Runs:	64
Highest Score:	13*	Average:	8.00
No. 50s:	0	No. 100s:	0

ODI Bowling & Fielding

Wickets:	64	Runs:	1,978
Best Bowling:	5/33	Average:	30.90
5 WI:	1	Catches:	8
Stumpings:	0		

The menacing speedster from county Durham is a decidedly un-English bowler in that he prefers pace and bounce to swing and seam. When he is focused on removing batsmen rather than their heads he is as effective as any fast bowler in modern cricket. Harmison doesn't possess a classical action rather a squarish ball release that takes advantage of his height and considerable power. When he's good, he's very very good. He humbled the home side at Sabina Park in 2004 with a terrifying spell of fast bowling that reminded locals of a time when it was their quicks that had batsman ducking for their lives. The West Indians were skittled for 47 and Harmison finished with career best figures of 7/12. When he's bad he is probably playing South Africa. He struggled against the touring South Africans early in his career and was keen to make amends on the tour of 2004/05. Unfortunately his radar was off for the entire series and despite complaining of a leg injury he played in all five Tests. A return of nine expensive wickets was disappointing and the quick had plenty to work on before the arrival of the Australians for the Ashes series in 2005. Ten wickets in two Tests against Bangladesh was a nice tune up and when he took eight wickets in Australia's comfortable first Test win it seemed that England's main strike bowler was back on song. He took only two wickets at Edgbaston in the second Test but one of them was that that touch by Michael Kasprowicz down leg side to Geraint Jones. It gave England victory by two runs and put them back in a series that they eventually won. He took 17 wickets in that hard fought series, and as much as they were vital, it was his aggressive bowling setting up opportunities for his teammates that mattered most. It was more of the same in 2006 with the year meandering along until the big man took matters into his own hands against Pakistan at Old Trafford with a match winning 11/76 that consigned Pakistan to one of their worst ever losses to England. No-one is ever quite sure of which Steve Harmison is going to turn up, but if it's the one that means business then the opposition better watch out.

HARRIS, George Robert Canning

Born:	February 3, 1851
Batting:	Right handed
Bowling:	Right arm medium

Tests

Test Career:	1879-1884
Cap Number:	13
Tests Played:	4

Test Batting

Innings:	6	Runs:	145
Highest Score:	52	Average:	29.00
No. 50s:	1	No. 100s:	0

Test Bowling & Fielding

Wickets:	0	Runs:	29
Best Bowling:	0	Average:	0.00
5 WI:	0	10 WM:	0
Catches:	2	Stumpings:	0

The 4th Lord Harris is best known for his work in spreading the game to the four corners of the globe. A fine all rounder who captained England in their first Test on home soil, the much travelled peer took the game to Australia, America, Canada and most famously India where he promoted the game amongst the local population. As a player he scored almost 10,000 first class runs as a top order batsman and was renowned as one of the finest fielders of his day.

HARTLEY, John Cabourn

Born:	November 15, 1874
Batting:	Right handed
Bowling:	Right arm leg-break

Tests

Test Career:	1906
Cap Number:	151
Tests Played:	2

Test Batting

Innings:	4	Runs:	15
Highest Score:	9	Average:	3.75
No. 50s:	0	No. 100s:	0

Test Bowling & Fielding

Wickets:	1	Runs:	115
Best Bowling:	1/62	Average:	115.00
5 WI:	0	10 WM:	0
Catches:	2	Stumpings:	0

An orthodox leg spinner he toured South Africa in 1905/06 and played two Tests.

HAWKE, Martin Bladen

Born:	August 16, 1860
Batting:	Right handed

Tests

Test Career:	1896-99
Cap Number:	96
Tests Played:	5

HAYES, Ernest George (continued stats)

Test Batting
Innings:	8	Runs:	55
Highest Score:	30	Average:	7.85
No. 50s:	0	No. 100s:	0

Test Bowling & Fielding
Wickets:	0	Runs:	0
Best Bowling:		Average:	0.00
5 WI:	0	10 WM:	0
Catches:	3	Stumpings:	0

Lord Hawke had a huge impact on cricket in the late 19th century and many of the luxuries enjoyed by the modern player can be attributed directly to him. A champion of cricketer's rights, he worked tirelessly to ensure players were paid fairly and received enough income to last them through the year. As a player he led the Yorkshire side for 28 years and took two touring sides to South Africa in 1896 and 1899. In four Tests as English captain he was never beaten and whilst his record with the bat was only moderate, his impact on the game can never be under estimated.

HAYES, Ernest George

Born:	November 6, 1876
Batting:	Right handed
Bowling:	Right arm leg-break

Tests
Test Career:	1906-12
Cap Number:	148
Tests Played:	5

Test Batting
Innings:	9	Runs:	86
Highest Score:	35	Average:	10.75
No. 50s:	0	No. 100s:	0

Test Bowling & Fielding
Wickets:	1	Runs:	52
Best Bowling:	1/28	Average:	52.00
5 WI:	0	10 WM:	0
Catches:	2	Stumpings:	0

He was a leg break bowler who had a marvelous first class career that spanned 30 seasons. Unfortunately he couldn't reproduce that form in any of his five Tests where took only the single wicket and never reached fifty in any of his nine innings.

HAYES, Frank Charles

Born:	December 6, 1946
Batting:	Right handed
Bowling:	Right arm medium

Tests
Test Career:	1973-76
Cap Number:	458
Tests Played:	9

Test Batting
Innings:	17	Runs:	244
Highest Score:	106*	Average:	15.25
No. 50s:	0	No. 100s:	1

Test Bowling & Fielding
Wickets:	0	Runs:	0
Best Bowling:		Average:	0.00
5 WI:	0	10 WM:	0
Catches:	7	Stumpings:	0

One Day Internationals
ODI Career:	1973-75
ODIs Played:	6

ODI Batting
Innings:	6	Runs:	128
Highest Score:	52	Average:	25.60
No. 50s:	1	No. 100s:	0

ODI Bowling & Fielding
Wickets:	0	Runs:	0
Best Bowling:		Average:	0.00
5 WM:	0	Catches:	0
Stumpings:	0		

When Frank Hayes hit 106 not out in his second Test innings hopes were high that a long Test career lay ahead. He had prospered against a strong West Indian attack whilst players of the ilk of Boycott, Fletcher and Greig had fallen around him. Unfortunately it was a false dawn and he departed the Test after nine Tests with a disappointing average of 15.25

HAYWARD, Thomas Walter

Born:	April 29, 1871
Batting:	Right handed
Bowling:	Right arm medium

Tests
Test Career:	1896-1909
Cap Number:	97
Tests Played:	35

Test Batting
Innings:	60	Runs:	1,999
Highest Score:	137	Average:	34.46
No. 50s:	12	No. 100s:	3

Test Bowling & Fielding
Wickets:	14	Runs:	514
Best Bowling:	4/22	Average:	36.71
5 WI:	0	10 WM:	0
Catches:	19	Stumpings:	0

One of England's leading lights in the early days of Test cricket, he went within a whisker of becoming the first Englishman to score 2,000 runs in Test cricket. A giant with the powerful Surrey side, he made his debut in South Africa in 1896 but came to the fore against Australia in 1899 when he scored a fine 130 at Old Tafford. His first class record placed him on a par with the legendary W.G. Grace. He scored over 1,000 first class runs in 20 consecutive seasons and became only the second player behind the good Doctor to record 100 first class centuries. His 3,518 runs in 1906 stood as an English record for over 40 years.

HEADLEY, Dean Warren

Born:	January 27, 1970
Batting:	Right handed
Bowling:	Right arm medium-fast

Tests
Test Career:	1997-99
Cap Number:	585
Tests Played:	15

Test Batting			
Innings:	26	Runs:	186
Highest Score:	31	Average:	8.45
No. 50s:		No. 100s:	0

Test Bowling & Fielding			
Wickets:	60	Runs:	1,671
Best Bowling:	6/60	Average:	27.85
5 WI:	1	10 WM:	0
Catches:	7	Stumpings:	0

One Day Internationals
ODI Career:	1996-99		
ODIs Played:	13		

ODI Batting			
Innings:	6	Runs:	22
Highest Score:	10*	Average:	11.00
No. 50s:	0	No. 100s:	0

ODI Bowling & Fielding			
Wickets:	11	Runs:	520
Best Bowling:	2/38	Average:	47.27
5 WM:	0	Catches:	3
Stumpings:	0		

The grandson of West Indian great George Headley bowled with plenty of verve in his short Test career. He proved a surprise packet in the Caribbean in 1997/98 with 19 Test wickets and backed it up a year later with another 19 wickets in three Tests against Australia. Just when it looked as though England had unearthed a long term bowling prospect Headley suffered a serious back injury and had to give the game away.

HEARNE, Alec
Born:	June 22, 1863
Batting:	Right handed

Tests
Test Career:	1892
Cap Number:	76
Tests Played:	1

Test Batting			
Innings:	1	Runs:	9
Highest Score:	9	Average:	9.00
No. 50s:	0	No. 100s:	0

Test Bowling & Fielding			
Wickets:	0	Runs:	0
Best Bowling:		Average:	0.00
5 WI:	0	10 WM:	0
Catches:	1	Stumpings:	0

One of three brothers to have played Test cricket for England, his single Test fails to tell the story of a giant of the game. He played county cricket for Kent for over a quarter of a century scoring over 16,000 runs and taking over 1,100 first class wickets and following his retirement went on to coach his county for many years more.

HEARNE, Frank
Born:	November 23, 1858
Batting:	Right handed
Bowling:	Right arm fast

Tests
Test Career:	1889-96
Cap Number:	65
Tests Played:	6

Test Batting			
Innings:	10	Runs:	168
Highest Score:	30	Average:	16.80
No. 50s:	0	No. 100s:	0

Test Bowling & Fielding			
Wickets:	2	Runs:	40
Best Bowling:	2/40	Average:	20.00
5 WI:	0	10 WM:	0
Catches:	3	Stumpings:	0

Only a shade taller than the stumps, Hearne was a fine top order batsman and useful slow bowler who played Test cricket for both England and South Africa. He toured South Africa in 1888/89, and so enjoyed his time there that he emigrated and played in four Tests for his adopted country when England returned in 1891/92.

HEARNE, George
Born:	July 7, 1856
Batting:	Left handed

Tests
Test Career:	1892
Cap Number:	77
Tests Played:	1

Test Batting			
Innings:	1	Runs:	0
Highest Score:	0	Average:	0.00
No. 50s:	0	No. 100s:	0

Test Bowling & Fielding			
Wickets:	0	Runs:	0
Best Bowling:		Average:	0.00
5 WI:	0	10 WM:	0
Catches:	0	Stumpings:	0

The eldest of three brothers who played for England, his only Test match was against South Africa in Cape Town where he scored a duck in his only at bat.

HEARNE, John Thomas (Jack)
Born:	May 3, 1867
Batting:	Right handed
Bowling:	Right arm medium

Tests
Test Career:	1892-99
Cap Number:	78
Tests Played:	12

Test Batting			
Innings:	18	Runs:	126
Highest Score:	40	Average:	9.00
No. 50s:	0	No. 100s:	0

Test Bowling & Fielding			
Wickets:	49	Runs:	1,082
Best Bowling:	6/41	Average:	22.08
5 WI:	4	10 WM:	1
Catches:	4	Stumpings:	0

Unlike his two brothers who played for Kent, 'Old Jack' was a Middlesex man in a first class career that spanned an amazing 35 years. He enjoyed a successful three Test series against the Australians in 1896 when he claimed 15 wickets at 14.07 to guide England to victory along with Tom Richardson. His finest moment in the Test arena came at Headingly in 1899 when he claimed a hat trick against a strong Australian top order, dismissing the powerful trio of Clem Hill, Syd Gregory and Monty Noble all for ducks. John Thomas Hearne was not directly related to the three Hearne brothers who played for England at the same time.

HEARNE, John William

Born:	February 11, 1891
Batting:	Right handed
Bowling:	Right arm leg-break

Tests

Test Career:	1911-26
Cap Number:	172
Tests Played:	24

Test Batting

Innings:	36	Runs:	806
Highest Score:	114	Average:	26.00
No. 50s:	2	No. 100s:	1

Test Bowling & Fielding

Wickets:	30	Runs:	1,462
Best Bowling:	5/49	Average:	48.73
5 WI:	1	10 WM:	0
Catches:	13	Stumpings:	0

English cricket was dominated by all-rounders at the start of the 20th century and 'Young Jack' Hearne could be counted amongst the best of them. A leg break bowler and middle order batsman from Middlesex, he played in twenty four Tests over a 15 year period that was interrupted by World War I. He scored his only Test century as a 20 year old, 115 at the MCG, with batting described as effective rather than brilliant. Hearne toured with the M.C.C. on five separate occasions, visiting not only Australia but South Africa and the West Indies as well.

HEGG, Warren Kevin

Born:	February 23, 1968
Batting:	Right handed
	Wicket Keeper

Tests

Test Career:	1998-99
Cap Number:	593
Tests Played:	2

Test Batting

Innings:	4	Runs:	30
Highest Score:	15	Average:	7.50
No. 50s:	0	No. 100s:	0

Test Bowling & Fielding

Wickets:	0	Runs:	0
Best Bowling:		Average:	0.00
5 WI:	0	10 WM:	0
Catches:	8	Stumpings:	0

A wicket keeper from Lancashire who toured Australia in 1998/99, paying two Tests when the selectors felt that the burden of keeping was affecting Alec Stewart's batting.

HEMMINGS, Edward Ernest

Born:	February 20, 1949
Batting:	Right handed
Bowling:	Right arm off-break

Tests

Test Career:	1982-91
Cap Number:	497
Tests Played:	16

Test Batting

Innings:	21	Runs:	383
Highest Score:	95	Average:	22.52
No. 50s:	2	No. 100s:	0

Test Bowling & Fielding

Wickets:	43	Runs:	1,825
Best Bowling:	6/58	Average:	42.44
5 WI:	1	10 WM:	0
Catches:	5	Stumpings:	0

One Day Internationals

ODI Career:	1982-91
ODIs Played:	33

ODI Batting

Innings:	12	Runs:	30
Highest Score:	8*	Average:	5.00
No. 50s:	0	No. 100s:	0

ODI Bowling & Fielding

Wickets:	37	Runs:	1,294
Best Bowling:	4/52	Average:	34.97
5 WM:	0	Catches:	5
Stumpings:	0		

Big Eddie Hemmings had the last laugh on Australian fans who were sniggering at his selection on the Ashes tour in 1982/83. The off spinner scored a pair in third Test, so it came as a surprise when he was given the job of night watchman in the deciding Test at the SCG. He not only survived but went on to score 95 the next day. He played his last Test at 41 and continued in county cricket till the ripe old age of 46.

HENDREN, Elias Henry

Born:	February 5, 1889
Batting:	Right handed
Bowling:	Right arm leg-break

Tests

Test Career:	1920-35
Cap Number:	181
Tests Played:	51

Test Batting

Innings:	83	Runs:	3,525
Highest Score:	205*	Average:	47.63
No. 50s:	21	No. 100s:	7

Test Bowling & Fielding

Wickets:	1	Runs:	31
Best Bowling:	1/27	Average:	31.00
5 WI:	0	10 WM:	0
Catches:	33	Stumpings:	0

A powerfully built Londoner of Irish decent, hence the nickname Patsy, he may not have been the most elegant batsman of his time but there were few as effective. His first appearance in English colours was on the Australian tour of 1920/21. England received a five to nil drubbing but the determined Hendren could leave with his head held high and a batting average of over 30. He was retained for the return series against the Australians in England later that year but struggled in two Tests and found himself on the outer until the South Africans toured England in 1924.

Scores of 132 and 142 in the third and fifth Tests finally saw the Middlesex man cement his spot in the side, and there he remained until the mid 1930's. In all he scored over 3,000 Test runs with six centuries and a single double century which came against the West Indies in Port of Spain during the 1929/30 tour. His finest Test innings came towards the end of his career when he blunted the Australian spin duo of Grimmett and O'Reilly to score a 132 at Old Trafford in 1934. He was also a footballer of note playing in the top division for both Brentford and Manchester City.

HENDRICK, Michael

Born:	October 22, 1948
Batting:	Right handed
Bowling:	Right arm medium-fast

Tests

Test Career:	1974-81
Cap Number:	459
Tests Played:	30

Test Batting

Innings:	35	Runs:	128
Highest Score:	15	Average:	6.40
No. 50s:	0	No. 100s:	0

Test Bowling & Fielding

Wickets:	87	Runs:	2,248
Best Bowling:	4/28	Average:	25.83
5 WI:	0	10 WM:	0
Catches:	25	Stumpings:	0

One Day Internationals

ODI Career:	1973-81
ODIs Played:	22

ODI Batting

Innings:	10	Runs:	6
Highest Score:	2*	Average:	1.20
No. 50s:	0	No. 100s:	0

ODI Bowling & Fielding

Wickets:	35	Runs:	681
Best Bowling:	5/31	Average:	19.45
5 WM:	1	Catches:	5
Stumpings:	0		

A hardworking seam bowler who often toiled into the breeze or with the old ball, he was a fine foil for Bob Willis throughout the '70's. The economical swing bowler never took five wickets in a Test innings but he did come close on a number of occasions with five bags of four. His Test career came to an abrupt halt in 1981 when he joined an unauthorised tour to South Africa that earned him a three year ban on his return.

HESELTINE, Christopher

Born:	November 29, 1869
Batting:	Right handed
Bowling:	Right arm fast

Tests

Test Career:	1896
Cap Number:	102
Tests Played:	2

Test Batting

Innings:	2	Runs:	18
Highest Score:	18	Average:	9.00
No. 50s:	0	No. 100s:	0

Test Bowling & Fielding

Wickets:	5	Runs:	84
Best Bowling:	5/38	Average:	16.80
5 WI:	1	10 WM:	0
Catches:	3	Stumpings:	0

A tall fast bowler from Hampshire, he toured South Africa with Lord Hawke's side in 1895/96. Heseltine served in both the Boer War and World War I as a Lieutenant Colonel.

HICK, Graeme Ashley

Born:	May 23, 1966
Batting:	Right handed
Bowling:	Right arm off-break

Tests

Test Career:	1991-2001
Cap Number:	548
Tests Played:	65

Test Batting

Innings:	114	Runs:	3,383
Highest Score:	178	Average:	31.32
No. 50s:	18	No. 100s:	6

Test Bowling & Fielding

Wickets:	23	Runs:	1,306
Best Bowling:	4/126	Average:	56.78
5 WI:	0	10 WM:	0
Catches:	90	Stumpings:	0

One Day Internationals

ODI Career:	1991-2001
ODIs Played:	120

ODI Batting

Innings:	118	Runs:	3,846
Highest Score:	126*	Average:	37.33
No. 50s:	27	No. 100s:	5

ODI Bowling & Fielding

Wickets:	30	Runs:	1,026
Best Bowling:	5/33	Average:	34.20
5 WM:	1	Catches:	64
Stumpings:	0		

One of the heaviest scorers in first class cricket over the past twenty years, he failed to consistently deliver when elevated to Test level. The Zimbabwean born Hick had already scored over fifty first class centuries when he became eligible to play for England with expectations high that he could single handedly turn around the fortunes of a flagging nation. Scores of six in his first two Test innings did little to dampen the enthusiasm, but by the time he had played a dozen Tests with a top score of just 51, people began to reassess their predictions for the strongly built batsman. His first Test ton and highest score at top level finally came against India at Mumbai in 1992/93. Rather than silence his detractors, they said it confirmed that whilst a mighty player of slow bowling with a majestic sweep, he couldn't succeed against a world class pace attack. Over the next eight years Hick had plenty of chances to prove the critics wrong but with an average of 31.32 in Tests and no hundreds against Australia he failed to do so. Through it all the runs always flowed at county level with his most famous feat an unbeaten 405 for Worcestershire against Somerset in 1988.

HIGGS, Kenneth
Born: January 14, 1937
Batting: Left handed
Bowling: Right arm medium-fast

Tests
Test Career: 1965-68
Cap Number: 430
Tests Played: 15

Test Batting
Innings:	19	Runs:	185
Highest Score:	63	Average:	11.56
No. 50s:	1	No. 100s:	0

Test Bowling & Fielding
Wickets:	71	Runs:	1,473
Best Bowling:	6/91	Average:	20.74
5 WI:	2	10 WM:	0
Catches:	4	Stumpings:	0

On sheer numbers alone Ken Higgs should have played far more than his 15 Tests. The whippy right arm bowler took 71 Test wickets relying on accuracy and deceptive pace as his main weapons. He enjoyed an excellent series against the West Indies in 1966 claiming 24 wickets and famously putting on 128 with John Snow in a last wicket stand at The Oval. More success followed when Pakistan visited the next summer with Higgs taking 17 wickets in the three Tests series. In his Test career he played only two Tests against Australia, and his record of four wickets at a cost of 55 runs apiece against the arch enemy may have been what counted against him.

HILL, Allen
Born: November 14, 1843
Batting: Right handed
Bowling: Right arm fast

Tests
Test Career: 1877
Cap Number: 5
Tests Played: 2

Test Batting
Innings:	4	Runs:	101
Highest Score:	49	Average:	50.50
No. 50s:	0	No. 100s:	0

Test Bowling & Fielding
Wickets:	7	Runs:	130
Best Bowling:	4/27	Average:	18.57
5 WI:	0	10 WM:	0
Catches:	1	Stumpings:	0

Allen Hill holds a special place in cricket as the man who took the first Test wicket. On March 15th, 1877 he bowled Australia opener Nathaniel Thompson to take his place in the history books. The right arm seam bowler from Yorkshire only took one wicket in that famous first Test but performed well a month later in the second when he took 4/27 in Australia's first innings.

HILL, Arthur James Ledger
Born: July 26, 1871
Batting: Right handed
Bowling: Right arm medium-fast

Tests
Test Career: 1896
Cap Number: 98
Tests Played: 3

Test Batting
Innings:	4	Runs:	251
Highest Score:	124	Average:	62.75
No. 50s:	1	No. 100s:	1

Test Bowling & Fielding
Wickets:	4	Runs:	8
Best Bowling:	4/8	Average:	2.00
5 WI:	0	10 WM:	0
Catches:	1	Stumpings:	0

He played all of his three Tests on the South African tour of 1896, and whilst he had a brief Test career, he crammed a great deal into it. He averaged 62.75, scored a century at Cape Town and was one of the last cricketers to take a Test wicket bowling underarm with a bag of four in the third Test of that series.

HILTON, Malcolm Jameson
Born: August 2, 1928
Batting: Right handed
Bowling: Left arm off-break

Tests
Test Career: 1950-52
Cap Number: 351
Tests Played: 4

Test Batting
Innings:	6	Runs:	37
Highest Score:	15	Average:	7.40
No. 50s:	0	No. 100s:	0

Test Bowling & Fielding
Wickets:	14	Runs:	477
Best Bowling:	5/61	Average:	34.07
5 WI:	1	10 WM:	0
Catches:	1	Stumpings:	0

A left arm off spinner from Lancashire who came to public notice when he dismissed Donald Bradman twice during a tour match. His best bowling analysis in a Test was at Kanpur in 1952 where he took nine Indian wickets for only 93 runs.

HIRST, George Herbert
Born: September 7, 1871
Batting: Right handed
Bowling: Left arm medium-fast

Tests
Test Career: 1897-1909
Cap Number: 108
Tests Played: 24

Test Batting
Innings:	38	Runs:	790
Highest Score:	85	Average:	22.57
No. 50s:	5	No. 100s:	0

Test Bowling & Fielding

Wickets:	59	Runs:	1,770
Best Bowling:	5/48	Average:	30.00
5 WI:	3	10 WM:	0
Catches:	18	Stumpings:	0

Yorkshire born and bred, he was unusual for his time in that he batted right handed and bowled with his left. He famously teamed up with Wilfred Rhodes in 1902 to dismiss the Australians for a paltry 36, their lowest ever score in Test history. To prove it was no fluke he repeated the dose when Australia was playing Yorkshire the following week. Hirst captured 5/9 and the Aussies longed for the day they made 36 as the side compounded for just 23. In his 24 Tests he surprisingly failed to hit a century, but when batting for his county he was a formidable striker of the ball who scored over 30,000 runs.

HITCH, John William

Born:	May 7, 1886
Batting:	Right handed
Bowling:	Right arm fast

Tests

Test Career:	1912-21
Cap Number:	175
Tests Played:	7

Test Batting

Innings:	10	Runs:	103
Highest Score:	51*	Average:	14.71
No. 50s:	1	No. 100s:	0

Test Bowling & Fielding

Wickets:	7	Runs:	325
Best Bowling:	2/31	Average:	46.42
5 WI:	0	10 WM:	0
Catches:	4	Stumpings:	0

Bill Hitch played in only seven Tests over a ten year period, and though the First World War was mainly to blame, he can also look at a poor tour of Australia in 1911/12 as the cause. He was a quick bowler and hard hitting lower order batsman but in three Tests in Australia he could manage only eight runs and five wickets.

HOBBS, John Berry (Jack)

Born:	December 16, 1882
Batting:	Right handed
Bowling:	Right arm medium

Tests

Test Career:	1908-1930
Cap Number:	157
Tests Played:	61

Test Batting

Innings:	102	Runs:	5,410
Highest Score:	211	Average:	56.94
No. 50s:	28	No. 100s:	15

Test Bowling & Fielding

Wickets:	1	Runs:	165
Best Bowling:	1/19	Average:	165.00
5 WI:	0	10 WM:	0
Catches:	17	Stumpings:	0

Simply known as 'The Master', Jack Hobbs was one of the greatest batsman to ever wield the willow. His Test record of over 5,000 runs at an average of 56.94 would be impressive enough if he played today, but in the years just prior to and after the First World War it was unprecedented. He played on uncovered wickets against strong attacks in an era when the very best batsman struggled to average forty. He made his Test debut at the MCG in 1908 and whilst he was a productive batsman in the early stages of his Test career, his first century didn't come until his twelfth Test. He was playing South Africa on the mats at Cape Town and though unaccustomed to the surface scored 187. His batting was literally copybook. Whilst there were varying batting methods employed in the early years of Test cricket it was Hobbs' easily flowing upright style that became the ideal. His technique was deemed as 'correct' and whilst the likes of Victor Trumper punished the bowling with a long stride down the crease it was the Jack Hobbs' style that endured. He was an opening batsman who most famously teamed with Herbert Sutcliffe and Wilfred Rhodes over many years. He combined with Sutcliffe for a then record 15 opening partnerships of over 100 and with Wilfred Rhodes for the then world record opening stand of 323 at the MCG in 1911/12. Hobbs hit his highest Test score of 211 against South Africa at Lord's in 1924 as a 42 year old. His was a life devoted to cricket and Jack Hobbs was rewarded when knighted in 1953 for services to the game.

HOBBS, Robin Nicholas Stuart

Born:	May 8, 1942
Batting:	Right handed
Bowling:	Right arm leg-break

Tests

Test Career:	1967-71
Cap Number:	435
Tests Played:	7

Test Batting

Innings:	8	Runs:	34
Highest Score:	15*	Average:	6.80
No. 50s:	0	No. 100s:	0

Test Bowling & Fielding

Wickets:	12	Runs:	481
Best Bowling:	3/25	Average:	40.08
5 WI:	0	10 WM:	0
Catches:	8	Stumpings:	0

A handy leg spinner from Essex, he played all of his Test cricket against either India or Pakistan. Experienced against spin, Hobbs' Test opponents had little trouble with his gentle leggies and he took only 12 wickets in seven Tests.

HOGGARD, Matthew James

Born:	December 31, 1976
Batting:	Right handed
Bowling:	Right arm medium-fast

Tests

Test Career:	2000-		
Cap Number:	602		
Tests Played:	57		

Test Batting

Innings:	78	Runs:	411
Highest Score:	38	Average:	7.90
No. 50s:	0	No. 100s:	0

Test Bowling & Fielding

Wickets:	219	Runs:	6,483
Best Bowling:	7/61	Average:	29.60
5 WI:	6	10 WM:	1
Catches:	22	Stumpings:	0

One Day Internationals

ODI Career:	2001-		
ODIs Played:	26		

ODI Batting

Innings:	6	Runs:	17
Highest Score:	7	Average:	4.25
No. 50s:	0	No. 100s:	0

ODI Bowling & Fielding

Wickets:	32	Runs:	1,152
Best Bowling:	5/49	Average:	36.00
5 WM:	1	Catches:	5
Stumpings:	0		

Powerfully built and with an appetite for hard work, he may not have got the plaudits of teammates Steve Harmison and Andy Flintoff in recent years, but he has been just as important. The Yorkshireman isn't express pace but he can swing the ball late in the air and in the right conditions is deadly. He got those conditions in the vital fourth Test of England's tour to South Africa in 2004/05. With the series locked at one apiece the home side required 325 runs for victory in their second innings. Enter Hoggard who had taken five wickets in the first innings. He demolished the South African top order taking the first six wickets to fall, to finish with 7/61 and match figures of 12/205. Hoggard left South Africa with 26 Test scalps to be England's chief wicket taker and in the process went from being seen as a workhorse to a strike bowler. Fourteen wickets in two Tests against Bangladesh had him primed for the 2005 Ashes series and he played his part with 15 wickets at 29.56. Since then Hoggard has stood up while his fellow quicks have gone down with a succession of injuries. It is that durability, combined with plenty of natural talent that now makes him so important to the English side.

HOLLIES, William Eric

Born:	June 5, 1912
Batting:	Right handed
Bowling:	Right arm leg-break

Tests

Test Career:	1935-50		
Cap Number:	277		
Tests Played:	13		

Test Batting

Innings:	15	Runs:	37
Highest Score:	18*	Average:	5.28
No. 50s:	0	No. 100s:	0

Test Bowling & Fielding

Wickets:	44	Runs:	1,332
Best Bowling:	7/50	Average:	30.27
5 WI:	5	10 WM:	0
Catches:	2	Stumpings:	0

Eric Hollies will forever be remembered as the man who rained on cricket's greatest parade. With Donald Bradman needing four runs in his last innings to leave Test cricket with an average of 100 he was bowled for nought by Hollies. Hollies had bowled a regulation leg spinner to Bradman the previous ball and then made a well pitched googly spin through the gate to claim the must famous duck in Test history. The fair haired leg spinner was far more than a one ball wonder though. Accurate, and with a turning googly, he took five wickets in a Test innings on five separate occasions, including career best figures of 7/50 against the West Indies in only his second Test. In fact that famous Bradman dismissal was part of a marathon spell of 56 overs for a return of 5/131. The Second World War cut a large swathe into what would have been a fine Test career, but he should still be remembered as one of the best leg spinners to have played for England.

HOLLIOAKE, Adam John

Born:	September 5, 1971
Batting:	Right handed
Bowling:	Right arm medium

Tests

Test Career:	1997-98		
Cap Number:	587		
Tests Played:	4		

Test Batting

Innings:	6	Runs:	65
Highest Score:	45	Average:	10.83
No. 50s:	0	No. 100s:	0

Test Bowling & Fielding

Wickets:	2	Runs:	67
Best Bowling:	2/31	Average:	33.50
5 WI:	0	10 WM:	0
Catches:	4	Stumpings:	0

One Day Internationals

ODI Career:	1996-99		
ODIs Played:	35		

ODI Batting

Innings:	30	Runs:	606
Highest Score:	83*	Average:	25.25
No. 50s:	3	No. 100s:	0

ODI Bowling & Fielding

Wickets:	32	Runs:	1,019
Best Bowling:	4/23	Average:	31.84
5 WM:	0	Catches:	13
Stumpings:	0		

The Australian born all-rounder played four Tests for his adopted country but was a more important figure in their one day side. He not only played 35 ODI's for England but he captained the side when Michael Atherton stood down to concentrate on his Test leadership.

HOLLIOAKE, Benjamin Caine
Born: November 11, 1977
Batting: Right handed
Bowling: Right arm medium-fast

Tests
Test Career: 1997-98
Cap Number: 588
Tests Played: 2

Test Batting
Innings:	4	Runs:	44
Highest Score:	28	Average:	11.00
No. 50s:	0	No. 100s:	0

Test Bowling & Fielding
Wickets:	4	Runs:	199
Best Bowling:	2/105	Average:	49.75
5 WI:	0	10 WM:	0
Catches:	2	Stumpings:	0

One Day Internationals
ODI Career: 1997-2002
ODIs Played: 20

ODI Batting
Innings:	17	Runs:	309
Highest Score:	63	Average:	20.60
No. 50s:	2	No. 100s:	0

ODI Bowling & Fielding
Wickets:	8	Runs:	532
Best Bowling:	2/37	Average:	66.50
5 WM:	0	Catches:	6
Stumpings:	0		

The younger brother of Adam, he played two Tests in the late 90's but like his brother seemed better suited to the shorter version of the game. Having represented England in a one day competition in India early in 2002, he went to Perth to visit his family prior to returning to England. Tragically he was involved in a car crash whilst in Perth and lost his life. The gifted cricketer was only 24 years old.

HOLMES, Errol Reginald Thorold
Born: August 21, 1905
Batting: Right handed
Bowling: Right arm fast

Tests
Test Career: 1935
Cap Number: 278
Tests Played: 5

Test Batting
Innings:	9	Runs:	114
Highest Score:	85*	Average:	16.28
No. 50s:	1	No. 100s:	0

Test Bowling & Fielding
Wickets:	2	Runs:	76
Best Bowling:	1/10	Average:	38.00
5 WI:	0	10 WM:	0
Catches:	4	Stumpings:	0

In Test cricket he managed only 114 runs of which 85 came in a single unbeaten knock at Port of Spain in 1934/35. He was also a speedy opening bowler for Surrey in county competition.

HOLMES, Percy
Born: November 25, 1886
Batting: Right handed

Tests
Test Career: 1921-32
Cap Number: 190
Tests Played: 7

Test Batting
Innings:	14	Runs:	357
Highest Score:	88	Average:	27.46
No. 50s:	4	No. 100s:	0

Test Bowling & Fielding
Wickets:	0	Runs:	0
Best Bowling:		Average:	0.00
5 WI:	0	10 WM:	0
Catches:	3	Stumpings:	0

Whilst not the most famous opening batsman from Yorkshire to play for England, he was nonetheless a fine county cricketer, with over 30,000 first class runs and a triple century to his name. His best series was against South Africa in 1927/28 when he scored 302 runs including his best Test effort of 88. His final match for England was India's historic first ever Test played at Lord's in 1932.

HONE, Leland
Born: January 30, 1853
Batting: Right handed
        Wicket Keeper

Tests
Test Career: 1879
Cap Number: 14
Tests Played: 1

Test Batting
Innings:	2	Runs:	13
Highest Score:	7	Average:	6.50
No. 50s:	0	No. 100s:	0

Test Bowling & Fielding
Wickets:	0	Runs:	0
Best Bowling:		Average:	0.00
5 WI:	0	10 WM:	0
Catches:	2	Stumpings:	0

A wicket keeper batsman from Ireland, he was chosen to tour Australia in 1879 despite never having previously played first class cricket.

HOPWOOD, John Leonard
Born: October 30, 1903
Batting: Right handed
Bowling: Left arm medium

Tests
Test Career: 1934
Cap Number: 275
Tests Played: 2

Test Batting
Innings:	3	Runs:	12
Highest Score:	8	Average:	6.00
No. 50s:	0	No. 100s:	0

Test Bowling & Fielding
Wickets:	0	Runs:	155
Best Bowling:		Average:	0.00
5 WI:	0	10 WM:	0
Catches:	0	Stumpings:	0

A medium pacer who played two Tests against the touring Australians in 1934 but failed to take a wicket.

HORNBY, Albert Neilson

Born: February 10, 1847
Batting: Right handed
Bowling: Right arm medium

Tests
Test Career: 1879-1884
Cap Number: 15
Tests Played: 3

Test Batting
Innings:	6	Runs:	21
Highest Score:	9	Average:	3.50
No. 50s:	0	No. 100s:	0

Test Bowling & Fielding
Wickets:	1	Runs:	0
Best Bowling:	1/0	Average:	0.00
5 WI:	0	10 WM:	0
Catches:	0	Stumpings:	0

A slightly built batsman from Lancashire, he enjoyed little success when playing for England but was a leading figure in first class cricket at the time. Nicknamed 'Monkey', he captained England in two of his three Tests and led his county to the Championship on no less than four occasions.

HORTON, Martin John

Born: April 21, 1934
Batting: Right handed
Bowling: Right arm off-break

Tests
Test Career: 1959
Cap Number: 394
Tests Played: 2

Test Batting
Innings:	2	Runs:	60
Highest Score:	58	Average:	30.00
No. 50s:	1	No. 100s:	0

Test Bowling & Fielding
Wickets:	2	Runs:	59
Best Bowling:	2/24	Average:	29.50
5 WI:	0	10 WM:	0
Catches:	2	Stumpings:	0

He was on off spinner from Worcester who played two Tests against India in 1959.

HOWARD, Nigel David

Born: May 18, 1925
Batting: Right handed

Tests
Test Career: 1951-52
Cap Number: 363
Tests Played: 4

Test Batting
Innings:	6	Runs:	86
Highest Score:	23	Average:	17.20
No. 50s:	0	No. 100s:	0

Test Bowling & Fielding
Wickets:	0	Runs:	0
Best Bowling:		Average:	0.00
5 WI:	0	10 WM:	0
Catches:	4	Stumpings:	0

A right handed batsman from Lancashire, he played four Tests on England's tour of India in 1951/52.

HOWELL, Henry (Harry)

Born: November 29, 1890
Batting: Right handed
Bowling: Right arm fast

Tests
Test Career: 1921-24
Cap Number: 185
Tests Played: 5

Test Batting
Innings:	8	Runs:	15
Highest Score:	5	Average:	7.50
No. 50s:	0	No. 100s:	0

Test Bowling & Fielding
Wickets:	7	Runs:	559
Best Bowling:	4/115	Average:	79.85
5 WI:	0	10 WM:	0
Catches:	0	Stumpings:	0

The opening bowler from Warwickshire once captured all wickets in an innings during a county game but in five Tests for England could manage only seven dismissals at almost 80 runs apiece

HOWORTH, Richard

Born: April 26, 1909
Batting: Left handed
Bowling: Left arm off-break

Tests
Test Career: 1947-48
Cap Number: 325
Tests Played: 5

Test Batting
Innings:	10	Runs:	145
Highest Score:	45*	Average:	18.12
No. 50s:	0	No. 100s:	0

Test Bowling & Fielding
Wickets:	19	Runs:	635
Best Bowling:	6/124	Average:	33.42
5 WI:	1	10 WM:	0
Catches:	2	Stumpings:	0

Dick Howorth was a left arm off spinner from Worcestershire who is a member of the exclusive group of cricketers who took a wicket with their first ball in Test cricket. That was against South Africa in 1947 and good form in the Test earnt him a spot on the subsequent tour of the West Indies where he played the remainder of his representative cricket.

HUMPAGE, Geoffrey William

Born: April 24, 1954
Batting: Right handed
Bowling: Right arm medium
Wicket Keeper

One Day Internationals
ODI Career: 1981
ODIs Played: 3

217

ODI Batting
Innings:	2	Runs:	11
Highest Score:	6	Average:	5.50
No. 50s:	0	No. 100s:	0

ODI Bowling & Fielding
Wickets:	0	Runs:	0
Best Bowling:		Average:	0.00
5 WI:	0	Catches:	2
Stumpings:	0		

A wicket-keeper, who was also an accomplished batsman at County level, Humpage played in three ODI's against Australia in 1981. Averaging just over five with the bat he later joined the rebel tour of South Africa.

HUMPHRIES, Joseph
Born:	May 19, 1876
Batting:	Right handed
	Wicket Keeper

Tests
Test Career:	1908
Cap Number:	158
Tests Played:	3

Test Batting
Innings:	6	Runs:	44
Highest Score:	16	Average:	8.80
No. 50s:	0	No. 100s:	0

Test Bowling & Fielding
Wickets:	0	Runs:	0
Best Bowling:		Average:	0.00
5 WI:	0	10 WM:	0
Catches:	7	Stumpings:	0

He played three Tests on the tour of Australia in 1907/08 sharing the wicket keeping duties with Dick Young of Sussex.

HUNTER, Joe
Born:	August 3, 1855
Batting:	Right handed
	Wicket Keeper

Tests
Test Career:	1884-85
Cap Number:	49
Tests Played:	5

Test Batting
Innings:	7	Runs:	93
Highest Score:	39*	Average:	18.60
No. 50s:	0	No. 100s:	0

Test Bowling & Fielding
Wickets:	0	Runs:	0
Best Bowling:		Average:	0.00
5 WI:	0	10 WM:	0
Catches:	8	Stumpings:	3

A wicket keeper from Yorkshire, he played in all five Tests on the tour to Australia in 1884/85. Batting at number 11 in the second Test he scored an unbeaten 39, combining with Johnny Briggs to put on a record 96 for the last wicket.

HUSSAIN, Nasser
Born:	March 28, 1968
Batting:	Right handed
Bowling:	Right arm leg-break

Tests
Test Career:	1990-2004
Cap Number:	542
Tests Played:	96

Test Batting
Innings:	171	Runs:	5,764
Highest Score:	207	Average:	37.18
No. 50s:	33	No. 100s:	14

Test Bowling & Fielding
Wickets:	0	Runs:	15
Best Bowling:		Average:	0.00
5 WI:	0	10 WM:	0
Catches:	67	Stumpings:	0

One Day Internationals
ODI Career:	1989-2003
ODIs Played:	88

ODI Batting
Innings:	87	Runs:	2,332
Highest Score:	115	Average:	30.28
No. 50s:	16	No. 100s:	1

ODI Bowling & Fielding
Wickets:	0	Runs:	0
Best Bowling:		Average:	0.00
5 WI:	0	Catches:	40
Stumpings:	0		

The Indian born Hussain rose from a battling Test batsman to the leader who reinvigorated a flagging Test nation. He made his debut against the West Indies in 1989/90 but after just three Tests found himself on the outer and wondering if his Test career was over. Recalled to the side to play Australia at home in 1993, he established himself as first a fighting middle order batsman then later a prolific run scorer closer to the top of the order. A sound front foot player, he preferred to rock back scoring at will square of the wicket on the off side. Hussain got England off to a flying start in the 1997 Ashes series with a masterful 207 at Edgbaston. His handling of Shane Warne was a sight to behold and whilst his countrymen seemed mesmerised by the champion leg spinner, Nasser had the technique and temperament to prosper against him. His resolve impressed selectors and in 1999 he took over the captaincy from Michael Atherton. The new skipper publicly announced that there would be no more honourable losses for the English side and on more than occasion stated that he wanted his team to be more like the Australians. Under Hussain England won more Tests than they lost, and by the time he played his last Test in 2004 his goal had been achieved; England had the resolve of a side that could one day be the best in the world.

HUTCHINGS, Kenneth Lotherington
Born:	December 7, 1882
Batting:	Right handed
Bowling:	Right arm fast

Tests
Test Career:	1907-09
Cap Number:	155
Tests Played:	7

Test Batting

Innings:	12	Runs:	341
Highest Score:	126	Average:	28.41
No. 50s:	1	No. 100s:	1

Test Bowling & Fielding

Wickets:	1	Runs:	81
Best Bowling:	1/5	Average:	81.00
5 WI:	0	10 WM:	0
Catches:	9	Stumpings:	0

The high ranking military man lost his life during the First World War and it was said at the time that of all the cricketers England lost in the Great War he was the best credentialed. A brilliant stroke player from Kent, he played only seven Tests but amongst them was a match at the MCG in 1907 in which he made a chanceless 126. His final Test knock was 59 at The Oval in 1909.

HUTTON, Leonard

Born:	June 23, 1916
Batting:	Right handed
Bowling:	Right arm leg-break

Tests

Test Career:	1937-55
Cap Number:	294
Tests Played:	79

Test Batting

Innings:	138	Runs:	6,971
Highest Score:	364	Average:	56.67
No. 50s:	33	No. 100s:	19

Test Bowling & Fielding

Wickets:	3	Runs:	232
Best Bowling:	1/2	Average:	77.33
5 WI:	0	10 WM:	0
Catches:	57	Stumpings:	0

The third and last of the three great 'H's to play for England, he was less attacking than Hobbs and Hammond but no less successful. Len Hutton's Test career started meekly with a double failure against the touring New Zealanders in 1937, but he quickly put the disappointment of scoring 0 and 1 in his first Test behind him with a century in his next outing at Old Trafford. The selectors had seen enough to realise that the young Yorkshireman was going to be a key player in the upcoming Ashes series in England and he was retained to open the batting with Charlie Barnett. The right hander scored a century in his first Ashes Test at Trent Bridge, failed in both innings at Lord's, and missed the fourth Test at Headingley because of a broken finger. Whilst he had shown that he had the patience and technique to wear down the best of bowlers, no-one could have been prepared for what he had in store at The Oval. Hutton batted for over 13 hours, made 364 and re-wrote the record books. His was the highest ever score in Test cricket and his marathon innings still stands as the best by a batsman in an Ashes Test. He and his team mates ground the Aussies into the dust, and when the Test was over the home side had won by an incredible innings and 579 runs. Over the next 12 months he would continue to compile big scores, first against South Africa and then in a three Test series with the West Indies where he averaged 96.00. When Test cricket went into recess for the Second World War, Hutton had played 13 Tests, scoring 1345 runs at an average of 67.25. During the war he seriously injured his arm in a military training accident, yet he recovered to be part of the first side to play following the resumption of Test cricket. Whilst his post war numbers were not as impressive as his achievements in the 30's, he remained one of the game's great batsman. Hutton led the English averages in Australia 1946/47, and after being inexplicably dropped for the start of the 1948 Ashes series, fought back to score 342 runs at an average of 42.75. He scored double centuries at home against New Zealand and the West Indies in 1949 and 1950, and played one of his most famous innings against Australia in 1953, when as a 37 year old he opened the batting and made 145 against the likes of Ray Lindwall, Bill Johnston and Keith Miller. In 1952 Hutton became the first professional to captain England. He was a much respected leader and in 23 Tests had the excellent record of 11 wins and eight draws. Sir Colin Cowdrey recalled that he went out of his way to make new players feel at home. "I was just so lucky to play my earlier matches in the England side under his captaincy. He took all the trouble in the world to help me on my way". The great batsman and leader announced his retirement from all cricket at the start of 1956, and his enormous contribution to the game was swiftly recognised with a knighthood in June of that year.

HUTTON, Richard Anthony

Born:	September 6, 1942
Batting:	Right handed
Bowling:	Right arm medium-fast

Tests

Test Career:	1971
Cap Number:	450
Tests Played:	5

Test Batting

Innings:	8	Runs:	219
Highest Score:	81	Average:	36.50
No. 50s:	2	No. 100s:	0

Test Bowling & Fielding

Wickets:	9	Runs:	257
Best Bowling:	3/72	Average:	28.55
5 WI:	0	10 WM:	0
Catches:	9	Stumpings:	0

An all-rounder, he played Test cricket despite the pressure of being the son of the great Sir Leonard Hutton. His highest Test score was 81 against India in 1971.

IDDON, John (Jack)

Born: July 8, 1902
Batting: Right handed
Bowling: Left arm off-break

Tests

Test Career:	1935
Cap Number:	279
Tests Played:	5

Test Batting

Innings:	7	Runs:	170
Highest Score:	73	Average:	28.33
No. 50s:	2	No. 100s:	0

Test Bowling & Fielding

Wickets:	0	Runs:	27
Best Bowling:		Average:	0.00
5 WI:	0	10 WM:	0
Catches:	0	Stumpings:	0

A right handed batsman from Lancashire who toured the West Indies in 1935. His highest Test score was a 73 in the first innings at Port of Spain. Iddons was style playing class cricket when he was killed in a car accident at the age of 44.

IGGLESDEN, Alan Paul

Born: October 8, 1964
Batting: Right handed
Bowling: Right arm medium-fast

Tests

Test Career:	1989-94
Cap Number:	540
Tests Played:	3

Test Batting

Innings:	5	Runs:	6
Highest Score:	3*	Average:	3.00
No. 50s:	0	No. 100s:	0

Test Bowling & Fielding

Wickets:	6	Runs:	329
Best Bowling:	2/91	Average:	54.83
5 WI:	0	10 WM:	0
Catches:	1	Stumpings:	0

One Day Internationals

ODI Career:	1994
ODIs Played:	4

ODI Batting

Innings:	3	Runs:	20
Highest Score:	18	Average:	10.00
No. 50s:	0	No. 100s:	0

ODI Bowling & Fielding

Wickets:	2	Runs:	122
Best Bowling:	2/12	Average:	61.00
5 WM:	0	Catches:	1
Stumpings:	0		

A medium pace bowler from Kent who could manage only six wickets in the his three Tests.

IKIN, John Thomas (Jack)

Born: March 7, 1918
Batting: Left handed
Bowling: Left arm leg-break

Tests

Test Career:	1946-55
Cap Number:	312
Tests Played:	18

Test Batting

Innings:	31	Runs:	606
Highest Score:	60	Average:	20.89
No. 50s:	3	No. 100s:	0

Test Bowling & Fielding

Wickets:	3	Runs:	354
Best Bowling:	1/38	Average:	118.00
5 WI:	0	10 WM:	0
Catches:	31	Stumpings:	0

A leg spinner and middle order batsman who played in 18 Tests immediately after the Second World War. He failed to reproduce the form that he had shown with Lancashire in the county competition, but the brilliant close-in fieldsman did take 31 Test catches.

ILLINGWORTH, Raymond

Born: June 8, 1932
Batting: Right handed
Bowling: Right arm off-break

Tests

Test Career:	1958-73
Cap Number:	389
Tests Played:	61

Test Batting

Innings:	90	Runs:	1,836
Highest Score:	113	Average:	23.24
No. 50s:	5	No. 100s:	2

Test Bowling & Fielding

Wickets:	122	Runs:	3,807
Best Bowling:	6/29	Average:	31.20
5 WI:	3	10 WM:	0
Catches:	45	Stumpings:	0

One Day Internationals

ODI Career:	1971-73
ODIs Played:	3

ODI Batting

Innings:	2	Runs:	5
Highest Score:	4	Average:	2.50
No. 50s:	0	No. 100s:	0

ODI Bowling & Fielding

Wickets:	4	Runs:	84
Best Bowling:	3/50	Average:	21.00
5 WM:	0	Catches:	1
Stumpings:	0		

England's skipper from 1969 to 1973 was a shrewd leader, talented off spinner and under rated middle order batsman. 'Illy' the cricketer thrived on the challenge, whether it be containing a class batsman with his accurate off spin or denying a world class bowler with his at oft times infuriating batting. He took five wickets in an innings on only three occasions but it was his economy rate of less that two runs per over that was his main asset. He made test hundreds against India and the West Indies but it was a fighting 15 or 20 that was often more important. Illingworth took over the captaincy from Colin Cowdrey in 1969 and under his leadership England won a hard fought Ashes series in Australia in 1970/71. During that series Illingworth led his team off the SCG after his players were pelted with beer cans by a hostile local crowd. Illingworth hardly presided over a golden era in

English cricket, yet he boasted a record of 12 wins and 5 losses from 31 Tests. He served as English chairman of selectors for three years, but spent most of the time at loggerheads with captain Mike Atherton.

ILLINGWORTH, Richard Keith

Born: August 23, 1963
Batting: Right handed
Bowling: Left arm off-break

Tests
Test Career: 1991-95
Cap Number: 551
Tests Played: 9

Test Batting
Innings:	14	Runs:	128
Highest Score:	28	Average:	18.28
No. 50s:	0	No. 100s:	0

Test Bowling & Fielding
Wickets:	19	Runs:	615
Best Bowling:	4/96	Average:	32.36
5 WI:	0	10 WM:	0
Catches:	5	Stumpings:	0

One Day Internationals
ODI Career: 1991-96
ODIs Played: 25

ODI Batting
Innings:	11	Runs:	68
Highest Score:	14	Average:	11.33
No. 50s:	0	No. 100s:	0

ODI Bowling & Fielding
Wickets:	30	Runs:	1,059
Best Bowling:	3/33	Average:	35.30
5 WM:	0	Catches:	8
Stumpings:	0		

A left arm off spinner who relied on accuracy rather than rip. Whilst he was good enough to play in nine Tests for England he obviously did little to impress the great Viv Richards who was asked if he turned the ball after facing him in a county game. Richards responded by saying that the only time Illingworth turned was at the top of his mark.

ILOTT, Mark Christopher

Born: August 27, 1970
Batting: Right handed
Bowling: Left arm medium-fast

Tests
Test Career: 1993-95
Cap Number: 561
Tests Played: 5

Test Batting
Innings:	6	Runs:	28
Highest Score:	15	Average:	7.00
No. 50s:	0	No. 100s:	0

Test Bowling & Fielding
Wickets:	12	Runs:	542
Best Bowling:	3/48	Average:	45.16
5 WI:	0	10 WM:	0
Catches:	0	Stumpings:	0

One of a number of medium pacers tried by England in the mid 90's, he took four wickets on debut against the Australians at Trent Bridge.

INSOLE, Douglas John

Born: April 18, 1926
Batting: Right handed
Bowling: Right arm medium
Wicket Keeper

Tests
Test Career: 1950-57
Cap Number: 349
Tests Played: 9

Test Batting
Innings:	17	Runs:	408
Highest Score:	110*	Average:	27.20
No. 50s:	1	No. 100s:	1

Test Bowling & Fielding
Wickets:	0	Runs:	0
Best Bowling:		Average:	0.00
5 WI:	0	10 WM:	0
Catches:	8	Stumpings:	0

The Essex batsman played in nine Tests for his country with the highlight clearly being an unbeaten 110 against South Africa at Durban in 1956/57. He made a far greater impact on English cricket in retirement serving as an English selector for 19 years.

IRANI, Ronald Charles

Born: October 26, 1971
Batting: Right handed

Tests
Test Career: 1996-99
Cap Number: 577
Tests Played: 3

Test Batting
Innings:	5	Runs:	86
Highest Score:	41	Average:	17.20
No. 50s:	0	No. 100s:	0

Test Bowling & Fielding
Wickets:	3	Runs:	112
Best Bowling:	1/22	Average:	37.33
5 WI:	0	10 WM:	0
Catches:	2	Stumpings:	0

One Day Internationals
ODI Career: 1996-2003
ODIs Played: 31

ODI Batting
Innings:	30	Runs:	360
Highest Score:	53	Average:	14.40
No. 50s:	1	No. 100s:	0

ODI Bowling & Fielding
Wickets:	24	Runs:	989
Best Bowling:	5/26	Average:	41.20
5 WM:	1	Catches:	6
Stumpings:	0		

A busy all-rounder who played the bulk of his representative cricket in ODI's. He was a member of the England squad at the 2003 World Cup but played in only two games.

JACKMAN, Robin David

Born: August 13, 1945
Batting: Right handed
Bowling: Right arm medium-fast

Tests
Test Career:	1981-82		
Cap Number:	490		
Tests Played:	4		

Test Batting
Innings:	6	Runs:	42
Highest Score:	17	Average:	7.00
No. 50s:	0	No. 100s:	0

Test Bowling & Fielding
Wickets:	14	Runs:	445
Best Bowling:	4/110	Average:	31.78
5 WI:	0	10 WM:	0
Catches:	0	Stumpings:	0

One Day Internationals
ODI Career:	1974-83
ODIs Played:	15

ODI Batting
Innings:	9	Runs:	54
Highest Score:	14	Average:	6.75
No. 50s:	0	No. 100s:	0

ODI Bowling & Fielding
Wickets:	19	Runs:	598
Best Bowling:	3/41	Average:	31.47
5 WM:	0	Catches:	4
Stumpings:	0		

A slightly built fast medium bowler who played four Tests for England in 1981 and 1982. Jackman was at the centre of a controversy in the Caribbean that saw the cancellation of a Test when the Guyanese government objected to him playing in the second Test at Georgetown because of his strong ties with South Africa and Rhodesia. He had played and coached in Africa for many years, but England refused to drop Jackman and the match was ultimately called off.

JACKSON, Frank Stanley
Born:	November 21, 1870
Batting:	Right handed
Bowling:	Right arm medium-fast

Tests
Test Career:	1893-1905
Cap Number:	82
Tests Played:	20

Test Batting
Innings:	33	Runs:	1,415
Highest Score:	144*	Average:	48.79
No. 50s:	6	No. 100s:	5

Test Bowling & Fielding
Wickets:	24	Runs:	799
Best Bowling:	5/52	Average:	33.29
5 WI:	1	10 WM:	0
Catches:	10	Stumpings:	0

Unlike many of the noblemen who represented England in the first twenty years of Test cricket who got their chance due to their station in life, Sir Stanley Jackson was truly worthy of national honours. The son of cabinet member Lord Allerton, he made his debut against the Australians in 1893 with a fine 91 at Lord's. That innings was followed up with 103 at The Oval in his second Test. In all Jackson scored five centuries in a twenty Test career that was interrupted only by service in South Africa during the Boer War. His Test career finished on a high, scoring un unbeaten 144 against the Australians at Headingly in the third Test of the 1905 Ashes series. 'Jacker' scored 492 runs in that five Test series at 70.92 and took thirteen wickets with his medium pace at a cost of only 15.46. Retiring from the game at the top of his powers in 1907, he took over the reins in his native Yorkshire as Chairman and later served as Chairman of Selectors for the English Test side.

JACKSON, Herbert Leslie
Born:	April 5, 1921
Batting:	Right handed
Bowling:	Right arm fast

Tests
Test Career:	1949-61
Cap Number:	345
Tests Played:	2

Test Batting
Innings:	2	Runs:	15
Highest Score:	8	Average:	15.00
No. 50s:	0	No. 100s:	0

Test Bowling & Fielding
Wickets:	7	Runs:	155
Best Bowling:	2/26	Average:	22.14
5 WI:	0	10 WM:	0
Catches:	1	Stumpings:	0

An opening bowler from Derbyshire, he played in two Tests both against Australia. What makes Les Jackson's Test career extraordinary is that those two Tests were 12 years apart.

JAMES, Stephen Peter
Born:	September 7, 1967
Batting:	Right handed
Bowling:	Right arm medium

Tests
Test Career:	1998
Cap Number:	589
Tests Played:	2

Test Batting
Innings:	4	Runs:	71
Highest Score:	36	Average:	17.75
No. 50s:	0	No. 100s:	0

Test Bowling & Fielding
Wickets:	0	Runs:	0
Best Bowling:		Average:	0.00
5 WI:	0	10 WM:	0
Catches:	0	Stumpings:	0

The Glamorgan right hander played two Tests for England in 1998 but with a high score of only 36 couldn't retain his post in the side. In 2000 he became the first Glamorgan player to hit a triple century when he scored an unbeaten 309 against Sussex.

JAMESON, John Alexander
Born:	June 30, 1941
Batting:	Right handed

Tests
Test Career:	1971-74		
Cap Number:	451		
Tests Played:	4		

Test Batting
Innings:	8	Runs:	214
Highest Score:	82	Average:	26.75
No. 50s:	1	No. 100s:	0

Test Bowling & Fielding
Wickets:	1	Runs:	17
Best Bowling:	1/17	Average:	17.00
5 WI:	0	10 WM:	0
Catches:	0	Stumpings:	0

One Day Internationals
ODI Career:	1973-75		
ODIs Played:	3		

ODI Batting
Innings:	3	Runs:	60
Highest Score:	28	Average:	20.00
No. 50s:	0	No. 100s:	0

ODI Bowling & Fielding
Wickets:	0	Runs:	3
Best Bowling:		Average:	0.00
5 WM:	0	Catches:	0
Stumpings:	0		

An attacking opening batsman from Warwickshire, he did himself no favours by being run out in his 2nd, 3rd and 4th Test innings. He represented England in the first world Cup which was held on home soil in 1975.

JARDINE, Douglas Robert
Born:	October 23, 1900
Batting:	Right handed
Bowling:	Right arm leg-break

Tests
Test Career:	1928-34		
Cap Number:	235		
Tests Played:	22		

Test Batting
Innings:	33	Runs:	1,296
Highest Score:	127	Average:	48.00
No. 50s:	10	No. 100s:	1

Test Bowling & Fielding
Wickets:	0	Runs:	10
Best Bowling:		Average:	0.00
5 WI:	0	10 WM:	0
Catches:	26	Stumpings:	0

If television and movie portrayals of Douglas Jardine are to be believed, then he should have taken to the cricket field wearing a black hat and sidearms rather than the traditional whites. An Oxford man, he led the team to Australia in 1932/33 and is held primarily responsible for the acrimony that surrounded what became known as the 'bodyline' series. Whilst it is true that he devised a plan to bowl fast leg theory at the Australians, his intention was to curb the brilliance of Bradman and co rather than send them to an early grave. Unfortunately for Jardine his austere exterior made him unpopular with spectators and he was soon cast as the villain in the piece. What can not be disputed is that under his leadership, England beat one of the greatest teams on their own patch, and so effective were his tactics, that the rules of the game had to be changed. His role in the historic series means that few people remember Jardine the cricketer, but he was an excellent batsman with a fine defense who averaged 48 in Test cricket.

JARVIS, Paul William
Born:	June 29, 1965
Batting:	Right handed
Bowling:	Right arm medium-fast

Tests
Test Career:	1988-93		
Cap Number:	527		
Tests Played:	9		

Test Batting
Innings:	15	Runs:	132
Highest Score:	29*	Average:	10.15
No. 50s:	0	No. 100s:	0

Test Bowling & Fielding
Wickets:	21	Runs:	965
Best Bowling:	4/107	Average:	45.95
5 WI:	0	10 WM:	0
Catches:	2	Stumpings:	0

One Day Internationals
ODI Career:	1988-93		
ODIs Played:	16		

ODI Batting
Innings:	8	Runs:	31
Highest Score:	16*	Average:	5.16
No. 50s:	0	No. 100s:	0

ODI Bowling & Fielding
Wickets:	24	Runs:	672
Best Bowling:	5/35	Average:	28.00
5 WM:	1	Catches:	1
Stumpings:	0		

A nippy opening bowler form Yorkshire, he made his debut against New Zealand at Christchurch in 1988 and whilst he was a consistent performer most of his Test wickets were lower order batsmen.

JENKINS, Roland Oliver
Born:	November 24, 1918
Batting:	Right handed
Bowling:	Right arm leg-break

Tests
Test Career:	1948-52		
Cap Number:	339		
Tests Played:	9		

Test Batting
Innings:	12	Runs:	198
Highest Score:	39	Average:	18.00
No. 50s:	0	No. 100s:	0

Test Bowling & Fielding
Wickets:	32	Runs:	1,098
Best Bowling:	5/116	Average:	34.31
5 WI:	1	10 WM:	0
Catches:	4	Stumpings:	0

A big turning leg spinner who always bowled in his cap, Roly Jenkins was always willing to surrender a few runs in search of a wicket. A few turned into many against the West Indies at Lord's in 1950 when his career high Test match total of nine scalps cost him no less than 290 runs. He had a wicked sense of humour that saw him occasionally run foul of authorities but he produced a number of gems such as the time he was bowling to Reverend Jim Aitchison in a county game. The good Reverend had played and missed on a number of occasions prompting Roly to come down the wicket and offer, "They say you're a vicar. Well, with your luck, you'll soon be the Archbishop of Canterbury.'"

JESSOP, Gilbert Laird

Born:	May 19, 1874
Batting:	Right handed
Bowling:	Right arm fast

Tests

Test Career:	1899-1912
Cap Number:	122
Tests Played:	18

Test Batting

Innings:	26	Runs:	569
Highest Score:	104	Average:	21.88
No. 50s:	3	No. 100s:	1

Test Bowling & Fielding

Wickets:	10	Runs:	354
Best Bowling:	4/68	Average:	35.40
5 WI:	0	10 WM:	0
Catches:	11	Stumpings:	0

Even though he played almost a century before the advent of one day cricket, there are many keen historians who still believe that 'Croucher' Jessop was the hardest hitting batsman to ever play the game. Nicknamed 'Croucher' because of an unusual stance that had him ready to pounce on any delivery, he attacked from the very first ball he faced in first class cricket. Coming in on a hat-trick for Gloucestershire in his first game he ploughed the ball to the boundary for four and in doing so laid the foundations for his amazing career. He scored a 268 for his county in less than three hours and obliterated a touring West Indian side in 1900 with a century that if reports are to be believed, took less than 60 minutes. He played 18 Tests for England, and while his blazing style generally brought about his downfall, he famously won a Test off his own bat in 1902. England were facing defeat at the hands of the Australians at The Oval until 'The Croucher' hit 104 in 75 minutes to see his side home by just one wicket.

JESTY, Trevor Edward

Born:	June 2, 1948
Batting:	Right handed
Bowling:	Right arm medium

One Day Internationals

ODI Career:	1983
ODIs Played:	10

ODI Batting

Innings:	10	Runs:	127
Highest Score:	52*	Average:	21.16
No. 50s:	1	No. 100s:	0

ODI Bowling & Fielding

Wickets:	1	Runs:	93
Best Bowling:	1/23	Average:	93.00
5 WM:	0	Catches:	5
Stumpings:	0		

An all-rounder who played in ten ODI's during the 1982/83 Triangular Series between host nation Australia, New Zealand and England. A medium pacer, Jesty's only wicket was that of Australian captain, Kim Hughes, whom he dismissed for a duck.

JOHNSON, Richard Leonard

Born:	December 29, 1974
Batting:	Right handed
Bowling:	Right arm medium

Tests

Test Career:	2003
Cap Number:	615
Tests Played:	3

Test Batting

Innings:	4	Runs:	59
Highest Score:	26	Average:	14.75
No. 50s:	0	No. 100s:	0

Test Bowling & Fielding

Wickets:	16	Runs:	275
Best Bowling:	6/33	Average:	17.18
5 WI:	2	10 WM:	0
Catches:	0	Stumpings:	0

One Day Internationals

ODI Career:	2003
ODIs Played:	10

ODI Batting

Innings:	4	Runs:	16
Highest Score:	10	Average:	5.33
No. 50s:	0	No. 100s:	0

ODI Bowling & Fielding

Wickets:	11	Runs:	239
Best Bowling:	3/22	Average:	21.72
5 WM:	0	Catches:	0
Stumpings:	0		

A chirpy medium pace bowler from Somerset via Middlesex who does plenty with the ball in the air. He had a fine start to international career taking nine wickets in his first Test against Zimbabwe and six in his second a year later against Bangladesh. Unfortunately for Johnson, England has an abundance of good fast bowlers at the moment making it near impossible for him to regain his Test spot.

JONES, Arthur Owen

Born:	August 16, 1872
Batting:	Right handed
Bowling:	Right arm leg-break

Tests

Test Career:	1899-1909
Cap Number:	128
Tests Played:	12

Test Batting

Innings:	21	Runs:	291
Highest Score:	34	Average:	13.85
No. 50s:	0	No. 100s:	0

Test Bowling & Fielding

Wickets:	3	Runs:	133
Best Bowling:	3/73	Average:	44.33
5 WI:	0	10 WM:	0
Catches:	15	Stumpings:	0

He was a highly rated all-rounder from Nottinghamshire who was considered to be the best fieldsman in England at the turn of the last century. A top order bat and useful leg-spinner, he played 12 times for England but generally was disappointing and never scored over 34. Jones played county cricket until his premature death at the age of 42.

JONES, Geraint Owen

Born:	July 14, 1976
Batting:	Right handed
	Wicket Keeper

Tests

Test Career:	2004-		
Cap Number:	623		
Tests Played:	31		

Test Batting

Innings:	47	Runs:	1,109
Highest Score:	100	Average:	25.79
No. 50s:	6	No. 100s:	1

Test Bowling & Fielding

Wickets:	0	Runs:	0
Best Bowling:		Average:	0.00
5 WI:	0	10 WM:	0
Catches:	119	Stumpings:	5

One Day Internationals

ODI Career:	2004-		
ODIs Played:	49		

ODI Batting

Innings:	41	Runs:	815
Highest Score:	80	Average:	24.69
No. 50s:	4	No. 100s:	0

ODI Bowling & Fielding

Wickets:	0	Runs:	0
Best Bowling:		Average:	0.00
5 WM:	0	Catches:	68
Stumpings:	4		

Born in Papua New Guinea, raised in Queensland and living in England, Jones is one of the new breed of Test keepers whose batting is considered good enough to cover a multitude of sins. He is a hard hitting number seven, who whilst not in the Adam Gilchrist class has still scored a Test century and averages over 25. His keeping on the other hand fluctuates from spectacular to appalling, though when it counted most he took a leg side catch to dismiss Michael Kasprowicz and keep England in the chase for the 2005 Ashes. In the summer of 2006 he was replaced in the England side by former Test keeper Chris Read.

JONES, Ivor Jeffrey

Born:	December 10, 1941
Batting:	Right handed
Bowling:	Left arm fast

Tests

Test Career:	1964-68		
Cap Number:	420		
Tests Played:	15		

Test Batting

Innings:	17	Runs:	38
Highest Score:	16	Average:	4.75
No. 50s:	0	No. 100s:	0

Test Bowling & Fielding

Wickets:	44	Runs:	1,769
Best Bowling:	6/118	Average:	40.20
5 WI:	1	10 WM:	0
Catches:	4	Stumpings:	0

The Glamorgan speedster had a successful tour of Australia in 1965/66 taking 15 wickets in four Tests. His best effort was 6/118 at the Adelaide Oval in the fourth Test. A serious elbow injury caused his premature retirement.

JONES, Simon Philip

Born:	December 25, 1978
Batting:	Left handed
Bowling:	Right arm medium-fast

Tests

Test Career:	2002-		
Cap Number:	610		
Tests Played:	18		

Test Batting

Innings:	18	Runs:	205
Highest Score:	44	Average:	15.76
No. 50s:	0	No. 100s:	0

Test Bowling & Fielding

Wickets:	59	Runs:	1,666
Best Bowling:	6/53	Average:	28.23
5 WI:	3	10 WM:	0
Catches:	4	Stumpings:	0

One Day Internationals

ODI Career:	2004-		
ODIs Played:	8		

ODI Batting

Innings:	1	Runs:	1
Highest Score:	1	Average:	1.00
No. 50s:	0	No. 100s:	0

ODI Bowling & Fielding

Wickets:	7	Runs:	275
Best Bowling:	2/43	Average:	39.28
5 WM:	0	Catches:	0
Stumpings:	0		

A tall and talented fast medium who is capable of that most valuable of modern commodities, reverse swing. The son of Test cricketer Jeff, he has been plagued by knee injuries throughout his career, but when fit is an integral member of the English attack. Simon Jones was the surprise packet of the successful 2005 Ashes campaign with 18 wickets in four Tests that included two five wicket hauls. There was no more important dismissal in the Ashes series than when he caught Ricky Ponting in front of his stumps for just one at Trent Bridge. His 5/44 in the first innings of that fourth Test set up a series winning victory and confirmed his importance in the team. Unfortunately for Jones, he is again fighting injury and looks likely to miss England's defense of the Ashes in Australia in 2006/07.

JOYCE, Edmund Christopher
Born: September 22, 1978
Batting: Left handed
Bowling: Right arm medium

One Day Internationals
ODI Career: 2006
ODIs Played: 1
ODI Batting
Innings: 1 Runs: 10
Highest Score: 10 Average: 10.00
No. 50s: 0 No. 100s: 0
ODI Bowling & Fielding
Wickets: 0 Runs: 0
Best Bowling: Average: 0.00
5 WI: 0 Catches: 1
Stumpings: 0

Dublin born and raised, Ed Joyce made his ODI debut for England against his former countrymen at Belfast, in 2006. A left hander, he opened with Marcus Trescothick but was dismissed for just 10. If it wasn't ironic enough playing his first ODI against his home nation, Joyce's brother, Dominick, opened the batting for Ireland in that same match. Definitely one for the trivia buffs.

JUPP, Harry
Born: November 19, 1841
Batting: Right handed
Wicket Keeper

Tests
Test Career: 1877
Cap Number: 6
Tests Played: 2
Test Batting
Innings: 4 Runs: 68
Highest Score: 63 Average: 17.00
No. 50s: 1 No. 100s: 0
Test Bowling & Fielding
Wickets: 0 Runs: 0
Best Bowling: Average: 0.00
5 WI: 0 10 WM: 0
Catches: 2 Stumpings: 0

An opening batsman from Surrey, he had already had a long and successful first class career when selected to join Lillywhite's team for the first ever Test match. Nicknamed 'Young Stonewall' he was the only Englishman to record a double century in that historic first Test with 63 in the first innings.

JUPP, Vallance William Crisp
Born: March 27, 1891
Batting: Right handed
Bowling: Right arm off-break

Tests
Test Career: 1921-28
Cap Number: 191
Tests Played: 8

Test Batting
Innings: 13 Runs: 208
Highest Score: 38 Average: 17.33
No. 50s: 0 No. 100s: 0
Test Bowling & Fielding
Wickets: 28 Runs: 616
Best Bowling: 4/37 Average: 22.00
5 WI: 0 10 WM: 0
Catches: 5 Stumpings: 0

He was an off spinner and fine front foot batsman who scored 1,000 runs and took 100 wickets in the one season with both Northamptonshire and Sussex. He played Test cricket against Australia, South Africa and the West Indies.

KEETON, William Walter
Born: April 30, 1905
Batting: Right handed

Tests
Test Career: 1934-39
Cap Number: 276
Tests Played: 2
Test Batting
Innings: 4 Runs: 57
Highest Score: 25 Average: 14.25
No. 50s: 0 No. 100s: 0
Test Bowling & Fielding
Wickets: 0 Runs: 0
Best Bowling: Average: 0.00
5 WI: 0 10 WM: 0
Catches: 0 Stumpings: 0

A long standing player with Notts, his two Tests for England were against Australia in 1934 and the West Indies in 1939.

KENNEDY, Alexander Stuart
Born: January 24, 1891
Batting: Right handed
Bowling: Right arm medium

Tests
Test Career: 1922-23
Cap Number: 208
Tests Played: 5
Test Batting
Innings: 8 Runs: 93
Highest Score: 41* Average: 15.50
No. 50s: 0 No. 100s: 0
Test Bowling & Fielding
Wickets: 31 Runs: 599
Best Bowling: 5/76 Average: 19.32
5 WI: 2 10 WM: 0
Catches: 5 Stumpings: 0

Born in Scotland he was a seam bowler and handy lower order batsman. He played all of his Test cricket in five Tests on the tour of South Africa in 1922/23 enjoying a fine series with 31 wickets.

KENYON, Donald
Born: May 15, 1924
Batting: Right handed
Bowling: Right arm medium

Tests

Test Career:	1951-55		
Cap Number:	364		
Tests Played:	6		

Test Batting

Innings:	15	Runs:	192
Highest Score:	87	Average:	12.80
No. 50s:	1	No. 100s:	0

Test Bowling & Fielding

Wickets:	0	Runs:	0
Best Bowling:		Average:	0.00
5 WI:	0	10 WM:	0
Catches:	5	Stumpings:	0

A legend with the Worcestershire, he played a staggering 643 first class matches. The middle order batsman was given a number of chances in the England side but could manage only the one half century, an 87 against South Africa at Trent Bridge in 1955.

KEY, Robert William Trevor

Born:	May 12, 1979
Batting:	Right handed
Bowling:	Right arm off-break

Tests

Test Career:	2002-		
Cap Number:	612		
Tests Played:	15		

Test Batting

Innings:	26	Runs:	775
Highest Score:	221	Average:	31.00
No. 50s:	3	No. 100s:	1

Test Bowling & Fielding

Wickets:	0	Runs:	0
Best Bowling:		Average:	0.00
5 WI:	0	10 WM:	0
Catches:	11	Stumpings:	0

One Day Internationals

ODI Career:	2003-04		
ODIs Played:	5		

ODI Batting

Innings:	5	Runs:	54
Highest Score:	19	Average:	10.80
No. 50s:	0	No. 100s:	0

ODI Bowling & Fielding

Wickets:	0	Runs:	0
Best Bowling:		Average:	0.00
5 WM:	0	Catches:	0
Stumpings:	0		

The bulk of his Test runs came in a single knock against the West Indies at Lord's in 2004. His 221 has counted for more than a quarter of all runs scored at Test level and whilst the promising batsman was appointed Kent captain in 2006 he lost ground to fellow countrymen Ian Bell and Paul Collingwood in the last 18 months.

KILLIACK, Edgar Thomas

Born:	May 9, 1907
Batting:	Right handed

Tests

Test Career:	1929		
Cap Number:	239		
Tests Played:	2		

Test Batting

Innings:	4	Runs:	81
Highest Score:	31	Average:	20.25
No. 50s:	0	No. 100s:	0

Test Bowling & Fielding

Wickets:	0	Runs:	0
Best Bowling:		Average:	0.00
5 WI:	0	10 WM:	0
Catches:	2	Stumpings:	0

The Reverend Tom Killick played two Tests for his country against South Africa in 1929.

KILNER, Roy

Born:	October 17, 1890
Batting:	Left handed
Bowling:	Left arm off-break

Tests

Test Career:	1924-26		
Cap Number:	214		
Tests Played:	9		

Test Batting

Innings:	8	Runs:	233
Highest Score:	74	Average:	33.28
No. 50s:	2	No. 100s:	0

Test Bowling & Fielding

Wickets:	24	Runs:	734
Best Bowling:	4/51	Average:	30.58
5 WI:	0	10 WM:	0
Catches:	6	Stumpings:	0

The left hander was a constant member of the Yorkshire side from the age of 20 and his good form saw him force his way into the Test side. The off spinner toured Australia in 1924/25, performing particularly well at the MCG in the fourth Test where he made 74 and took five wickets for the match. At 37 he was still very much in contention for a Test spot when he visited India for a coaching commitment and contracted a fatal bout of enteric fever.

KING, John Herbert

Born:	April 16, 1871
Batting:	Left handed
Bowling:	Left arm medium

Tests

Test Career:	1909		
Cap Number:	160		
Tests Played:	1		

Test Batting

Innings:	2	Runs:	64
Highest Score:	60	Average:	32.00
No. 50s:	1	No. 100s:	0

Test Bowling & Fielding

Wickets:	1	Runs:	99
Best Bowling:	1/99	Average:	99.00
5 WI:	0	10 WM:	0
Catches:	0	Stumpings:	0

A fine batsman from Leicestershire with over 25,000 first class runs, he could count himself most unlucky to have played only the one Test. That came against Australia at Lord's in 1909 and he top scored for England in their first innings with 60.

KINNEIR, Septimus Paul

Born: May 13, 1871
Batting: Left handed
Bowling: Right arm medium

Tests

Test Career:	1911		
Cap Number:	173		
Tests Played:	1		

Test Batting

Innings:	2	Runs:	52
Highest Score:	30	Average:	26.00
No. 50s:	0	No. 100s:	0

Test Bowling & Fielding

Wickets:	0	Runs:	0
Best Bowling:		Average:	0.00
5 WI:	0	10 WM:	0
Catches:	0	Stumpings:	0

He was a well known first class cricketer at the turn of the last century with Warwickshire, but played only the one Test at the SCG in 1911.

KIRTLEY, Robert James

Born: January 10, 1975
Batting: Right handed
Bowling: Right arm medium-fast

Tests

Test Career:	2003		
Cap Number:	616		
Tests Played:	4		

Test Batting

Innings:	7	Runs:	32
Highest Score:	12	Average:	5.33
No. 50s:	0	No. 100s:	0

Test Bowling & Fielding

Wickets:	19	Runs:	561
Best Bowling:	6/34	Average:	29.52
5 WI:	1	10 WM:	0
Catches:	3	Stumpings:	0

One Day Internationals

ODI Career:	2001-04		
ODIs Played:	11		

ODI Batting

Innings:	2	Runs:	2
Highest Score:	1	Average:	1.00
No. 50s:	0	No. 100s:	0

ODI Bowling & Fielding

Wickets:	9	Runs:	481
Best Bowling:	2/33	Average:	53.44
5 WM:	0	Catches:	5
Stumpings:	0		

A pencil thin paceman from Sussex who sits just outside the top bracket of English fast bowlers. His Test debut could not have been more impressive, bowling England to victory over South Africa in 2003 at Trent Bridge with 6/34 in the second innings. Opportunities have been few and far between since then but he remains in the wings should England's fast bowling stocks be depleted by injury.

KNIGHT, Albert Ernest

Born: October 8, 1872
Batting: Right handed

Tests

Test Career:	1904		
Cap Number:	141		
Tests Played:	3		

Test Batting

Innings:	6	Runs:	81
Highest Score:	70*	Average:	16.20
No. 50s:	1	No. 100s:	0

Test Bowling & Fielding

Wickets:	0	Runs:	0
Best Bowling:		Average:	0.00
5 WI:	0	10 WM:	0
Catches:	1	Stumpings:	0

He was a middle order batsman who played three Tests in 'Plum' Warner's side that toured Australia in 1903/04. Most of his 81 Test runs came in one knock at the SCG when he top scored with an unbeaten 70 in the first innings of the fourth test. It was a game England won and that innings went a long way to securing the Ashes for Knight's side.

KNIGHT, Barry Rolfe

Born: February 18, 1938
Batting: Right handed
Bowling: Right arm medium-fast

Tests

Test Career:	1961-69		
Cap Number:	408		
Tests Played:	29		

Test Batting

Innings:	38	Runs:	812
Highest Score:	127	Average:	26.19
No. 50s:	0	No. 100s:	2

Test Bowling & Fielding

Wickets:	70	Runs:	2,223
Best Bowling:	4/38	Average:	31.75
5 WI:	0	10 WM:	0
Catches:	14	Stumpings:	0

Seventy wickets and two centuries in Test cricket was just reward for the industrious all-rounder from Leicestershire. The hard hitting lower order batsman hit 125 against New Zealand at Eden Park in 1963 coming in at number eight and repeated the dose 12 months later against India at Kanpur. Both his Tests on the Ashes tour of 1965/66 were at the MCG where he claimed eight wickets with his nippy medium pace. He moved to Australia post retirement and opened a successful indoor cricket centre.

KNIGHT, Donald John

Born: May 12, 1894
Batting: Right handed

Tests

Test Career:	1921		
Cap Number:	192		
Tests Played:	2		

Test Batting

Innings:	4	Runs:	54
Highest Score:	38	Average:	13.50
No. 50s:	0	No. 100s:	0

Test Bowling & Fielding			
Wickets:	0	Runs:	0
Best Bowling:		Average:	0.00
5 WI:	0	10 WM:	0
Catches:	1	Stumpings:	0

One of many English cricketers to struggle against the Australians upon the resumption of Test cricket in 1920, the Surrey man could score only 54 runs in his two Tests on home soil in 1921.

KNIGHT, Nicholas Verity

Born: November 28, 1969
Batting: Right handed
Bowling: Right arm medium

Tests

Test Career: 1995-2001
Cap Number: 574
Tests Played: 17

Test Batting			
Innings:	30	Runs:	719
Highest Score:	113	Average:	23.96
No. 50s:	4	No. 100s:	1

Test Bowling & Fielding			
Wickets:	0	Runs:	0
Best Bowling:		Average:	0.00
5 WI:	0	10 WM:	0
Catches:	26	Stumpings:	0

One Day Internationals

ODI Career: 1996-2003
ODIs Played: 100

ODI Batting			
Innings:	100	Runs:	3,637
Highest Score:	125*	Average:	40.41
No. 50s:	25	No. 100s:	5

ODI Bowling & Fielding			
Wickets:	0	Runs:	0
Best Bowling:		Average:	0.00
5 WM:	0	Catches:	44
Stumpings:	0		

A multi faceted all-rounder ideally suited to one day cricket, Knight fittingly ended his career as a member of England's World Cup squad in South Africa in 2003. An opening batsman in the ODI side he hit five one day centuries to go with his single century in the longer version off the game. That ton, 113 against Pakistan at Headingly in 1996 suggests that he should have played more than 17 Tests. He was also an outstanding out fielder who took a number of spectacular catches for his country.

KNOTT, Alan Philip Eric

Born: April 9, 1946
Batting: Right handed
Bowling: Right arm off-break
Wicket Keeper

Tests

Test Career: 1967-81
Cap Number: 437
Tests Played: 95

Test Batting			
Innings:	149	Runs:	4,389
Highest Score:	135	Average:	32.75
No. 50s:	30	No. 100s:	5

Test Bowling & Fielding			
Wickets:	0	Runs:	0
Best Bowling:		Average:	0.00
5 WI:	0	10 WM:	0
Catches:	250	Stumpings:	19

One Day Internationals

ODI Career: 1971-77
ODIs Played: 20

ODI Batting			
Innings:	14	Runs:	200
Highest Score:	50	Average:	20.00
No. 50s:	1	No. 100s:	0

ODI Bowling & Fielding			
Wickets:	0	Runs:	0
Best Bowling:		Average:	0.00
5 WM:	0	Catches:	15
Stumpings:	1		

As a keeper he was capable of flying takes and swift stumpings. With the bat he was brave and reliable. In all Alan Knott has been England's finest gloveman in 130 years of Test cricket. Whether keeping or batting he was equally at home to speed or spin scoring heavily against Pakistan in England in 1971 and sitting second in the series aggregates against the Australians in 1974/75. He scored 364 runs against an attack spearheaded by Lillee and Thomson including a classic 106 not out at The Adelaide Oval. Overall he scored five Test centuries to go with his record 269 Test dismissals. Knott joined World Series Cricket in 1977 where he had the opportunity to keep to the game's fastest bowlers as part of a World XI.

KNOX, Neville Alexander

Born: October 10, 1884
Batting: Right handed
Bowling: Right arm fast

Tests

Test Career: 1907
Cap Number: 152
Tests Played: 2

Test Batting			
Innings:	4	Runs:	24
Highest Score:	8*	Average:	8.00
No. 50s:	0	No. 100s:	0

Test Bowling & Fielding			
Wickets:	3	Runs:	105
Best Bowling:	2/39	Average:	35.00
5 WI:	0	10 WM:	0
Catches:	0	Stumpings:	0

A fast bowler from the powerful Surrey side, he played against the South Africans on their first tour to England in 1907.

LAKER, James Charles

Born: February 9, 1922
Batting: Right handed
Bowling: Right arm off-break

Tests

Test Career: 1948-59
Cap Number: 328
Tests Played: 46

Test Batting

Innings:	63	Runs:	676
Highest Score:	63	Average:	14.08
No. 50s:	2	No. 100s:	0

Test Bowling & Fielding

Wickets:	193	Runs:	4,101
Best Bowling:	10/53	Average:	21.24
5 WI:	9	10 WM:	3
Catches:	12	Stumpings:	0

The wicket that was prepared for the Old Trafford Test in 1956 was unquestionably tailored to suit the English spin duo of Jim Laker and Tony Lock. It was devoid of grass and developing cracks by the second morning, but even of most ardent followers of Laker could not predict the what toll he would take on it. 10/53 in the first innings was staggering enough but by the time he had returned match figures of 19/90 Australia had been defeated by an innings and 170 runs and Laker had set a record that one doubts will ever be beaten. He finished the five Test series with a record 46 Test wickets at a bewildering cost of only 9.61 runs but was certainly more than a one series wonder with a fine high action and strong spinning fingers, Laker took 193 Test wickets in 43 Tests. After retiring from cricket he joined the BBC where he worked as a much respected commentator.

LAMB, Allan Joseph

Born:	June 20, 1954
Batting:	Right handed
Bowling:	Right arm medium

Tests

Test Career:	1982-92
Cap Number:	494
Tests Played:	79

Test Batting

Innings:	139	Runs:	4,656
Highest Score:	142	Average:	36.09
No. 50s:	18	No. 100s:	14

Test Bowling & Fielding

Wickets:	1	Runs:	23
Best Bowling:	1/6	Average:	23.00
5 WI:	0	10 WM:	0
Catches:	75	Stumpings:	0

One Day Internationals

ODI Career:	1982-92
ODIs Played:	122

ODI Batting

Innings:	118	Runs:	4,010
Highest Score:	118	Average:	39.31
No. 50s:	26	No. 100s:	4

ODI Bowling & Fielding

Wickets:	0	Runs:	3
Best Bowling:		Average:	0.00
5 WM:	0	Catches:	31
Stumpings:	0		

He was a punishing top order batsman who was savage on anything short or wide of the wickets. Allan Lamb had moved to England in 1978 to play with Northants, and when he realised that a Test career might pass him by because of the sporting ban imposed on his native country, he chose to become an English citizen. He made his Test debut just ten days shy of his 28th birthday and gave England wonderful service over the next decade. Lamb made 14 Test centuries, the best of which were successive hundreds he made on the tour of the West Indies in 1989/90 against the best pace attack in the world. If there was one criticism that can be leveled at him it was that he saw making triple figures as a license to throw all caution to the wind, and as a result never went on to make a single 150 in Tests. Lamb captained the side in three Tests but lost them all.

LANGRIDGE, James

Born:	July 10, 1906
Batting:	Left handed
Bowling:	Left arm off-break

Tests

Test Career:	1933-46
Cap Number:	268
Tests Played:	8

Test Batting

Innings:	9	Runs:	242
Highest Score:	70	Average:	26.88
No. 50s:	1	No. 100s:	0

Test Bowling & Fielding

Wickets:	19	Runs:	413
Best Bowling:	4/56	Average:	21.73
5 WI:	2	10 WM:	0
Catches:	6	Stumpings:	0

He was a left arm off spinner and more than capable middle order batsman who had a fine debut for England taking seven wickets in the second innings of his first Test against the West Indies. Wickets were harder to come by for Langridge after that taking only 11 in seven further Test appearances.

LARKINS, Wayne

Born:	November 22, 1953
Batting:	Right handed
Bowling:	Right arm medium

Tests

Test Career:	1980-91
Cap Number:	484
Tests Played:	13

Test Batting

Innings:	25	Runs:	493
Highest Score:	64	Average:	20.54
No. 50s:	3	No. 100s:	0

Test Bowling & Fielding

Wickets:	0	Runs:	0
Best Bowling:		Average:	0.00
5 WI:	0	10 WM:	0
Catches:	8	Stumpings:	0

One Day Internationals

ODI Career:	1979-91
ODIs Played:	25

ODI Batting

Innings:	24	Runs:	591
Highest Score:	124	Average:	24.62
No. 50s:	0	No. 100s:	1

ODI Bowling & Fielding

Wickets:	0	Runs:	22
Best Bowling:		Average:	0.00
5 WM:	0	Catches:	8
Stumpings:	0		

The moustachioed Larkins was given a number of opportunities by English selectors to show the form that made him a star at Durham but could manage only three half centuries in 25 innings.

LARTER, John David Frederick

Born:	April 24, 1940
Batting:	Right handed
Bowling:	Right arm medium-fast

Tests

Test Career:	1962-65
Cap Number:	413
Tests Played:	10

Test Batting

Innings:	7	Runs:	16
Highest Score:	10	Average:	3.20
No. 50s:	0	No. 100s:	0

Test Bowling & Fielding

Wickets:	37	Runs:	941
Best Bowling:	5/57	Average:	25.43
5 WI:	2	10 WM:	0
Catches:	5	Stumpings:	0

The Scottish speedster started with a bang taking nine wickets in his first Test against Pakistan. At the time of his debut he was thought to have been the tallest cricketer to play for England.

LARWOOD, Harold

Born:	November 14, 1904
Batting:	Right handed
Bowling:	Right arm fast

Tests

Test Career:	1926-33
Cap Number:	225
Tests Played:	21

Test Batting

Innings:	28	Runs:	485
Highest Score:	98	Average:	19.40
No. 50s:	2	No. 100s:	0

Test Bowling & Fielding

Wickets:	78	Runs:	2,212
Best Bowling:	6/32	Average:	28.35
5 WI:	4	10 WM:	1
Catches:	15	Stumpings:	0

Short but powerful, the miner for Nuncargate in Nottinghamshire will forever be known as the man who delivered the thunderbolts that made the 1932/33 series between Australia and England the most infamous in Test history. Larwood made his debut against Australia in 1926 and despite his lack of inches proved a genuine threat with his long run up and raw speed. In 1928/29 he visited Australia for the first time and impressed with 18 wickets, but when Australia regained the Ashes in 1930, Larwood struggled and could manage only four wickets for the series. Enter the calculating Douglas Jardine in 1932/33 and a tactic that had been previously referred to as 'leg theory'. The English captain famously instructed Larwood and fellow opener Bill Voce to bowl short and fast with a bolstered leg side field. It was Larwood who provided the knockout blows, literally. In Adelaide he struck Bill Woodfull a fearsome blow just under the heart and caught Bert Oldfield in the side of the head after the Australian keeper top edged an attempted hook. Through the furore that was dubbed 'bodyline', Larwood remained focused and followed his captain's instructions. In five Tests he took 33 wickets at less than 20 runs apiece and won his country back the Ashes. Far from being cast as the villain by the Australians who held the English captain and team management responsible, Larwood was seen as a fine competitor who had been taken advantage of by less scrupulous men. To English supporters he was the only bowler who ever made Donald Bradman look mortal and single handedly rested back the Ashes from one of the greatest sides to ever play the game. In 1950 Larwood emigrated to Australia, living out his days quietly in the Sydney suburb of Randwick.

LATHWELL, Mark Nicholas

Born:	December 26, 1971
Batting:	Right handed
Bowling:	Right arm medium

Tests

Test Career:	1993
Cap Number:	562
Tests Played:	2

Test Batting

Innings:	4	Runs:	78
Highest Score:	33	Average:	19.50
No. 50s:	0	No. 100s:	0

Test Bowling & Fielding

Wickets:	0	Runs:	0
Best Bowling:		Average:	0.00
5 WI:	0	10 WM:	0
Catches:	0	Stumpings:	0

England turned over a number of players during the 1993 Ashes series of which promising Somerset batsman Lathwell was one. The youngster struggled in two Tests and never played for England again.

LAWRENCE, David Valentine

Born:	January 28, 1964
Batting:	Right handed
Bowling:	Right arm fast

Tests

Test Career:	1988-92
Cap Number:	534
Tests Played:	5

Test Batting

Innings:	6	Runs:	60
Highest Score:	34	Average:	10.00
No. 50s:	0	No. 100s:	0

Test Bowling & Fielding
Wickets:	18	Runs:	676
Best Bowling:	5/106	Average:	37.55
5 WI:	1	10 WM:	0
Catches:	0	Stumpings:	0

One Day Internationals
ODI Career: 1991
ODIs Played: 1

ODI Batting
Innings:	0	Runs:	0
Highest Score:	0	Average:	0.00
No. 50s:	0	No. 100s:	0

ODI Bowling & Fielding
Wickets:	4	Runs:	67
Best Bowling:	4/67	Average:	16.75
5 WM:	0	Catches:	0
Stumpings:	0		

A right arm speedster who fell to the ground with a crippling knee injury whilst playing against New Zealand in 1992. The Gloucs fast bowler had played in five Tests and shown a great deal of promise with his best effort a 'five for' against the West Indies at The Oval in 1991 that included the prized scalps of Haynes, Richards and Richardson. Lawrence recovered from the snapped tendon but never played for England again.

LEADBEATER, Edric (Eddie)
Born: August 15, 1927
Batting: Right handed
Bowling: Right arm leg-break

Tests
Test Career: 1951-52
Cap Number: 367
Tests Played: 2

Test Batting
Innings:	2	Runs:	40
Highest Score:	38	Average:	20.00
No. 50s:	0	No. 100s:	0

Test Bowling & Fielding
Wickets:	2	Runs:	218
Best Bowling:	1/38	Average:	109.00
5 WI:	0	10 WM:	0
Catches:	3	Stumpings:	0

He was a surprise call up to the squad that was touring India in 1951/52 to replace the injured Harold Rhodes. The leg spinner played two Tests for two wickets and 40 runs.

LEE, Henry William (Harry)
Born: October 26, 1890
Batting: Right handed

Tests
Test Career: 1931
Cap Number: 258
Tests Played: 1

Test Batting
Innings:	2	Runs:	19
Highest Score:	18	Average:	9.50
No. 50s:	0	No. 100s:	0

Test Bowling & Fielding
Wickets:	0	Runs:	0
Best Bowling:		Average:	0.00
5 WI:	0	10 WM:	0
Catches:	0	Stumpings:	0

He was a batsman from Middlesex who played a single Test against South Africa at the Old Wanderers ground in 1931.

LEES, Walter Scott
Born: December 25, 1875
Batting: Right handed
Bowling: Right arm medium-fast

Tests
Test Career: 1906
Cap Number: 149
Tests Played: 5

Test Batting
Innings:	9	Runs:	66
Highest Score:	25*	Average:	11.00
No. 50s:	0	No. 100s:	0

Test Bowling & Fielding
Wickets:	26	Runs:	467
Best Bowling:	6/78	Average:	17.96
5 WI:	2	10 WM:	0
Catches:	2	Stumpings:	0

Lees was a medium fast bowler from the strong Surrey side who played all of his Test cricket on the mats in South Africa in 1906.

LEGGE, Geoffrey Bevington
Born: January 26, 1903
Batting: Right handed
Bowling: Right arm leg-break

Tests
Test Career: 1927-30
Cap Number: 228
Tests Played: 5

Test Batting
Innings:	7	Runs:	299
Highest Score:	196	Average:	49.83
No. 50s:	0	No. 100s:	1

Test Bowling & Fielding
Wickets:	0	Runs:	34
Best Bowling:		Average:	0.00
5 WI:	0	10 WM:	0
Catches:	1	Stumpings:	0

He played against New Zealand in their inaugural Test series and starred at Auckland where he scored 196 in the first innings. A Lieutenant in the English army, he died over Devon during the Second World War.

LESLIE, Charles Frederick Henry
Born: December 8, 1861
Batting: Right handed
Bowling: Right arm fast

Tests
Test Career: 1882-83
Cap Number: 39
Tests Played: 4

Test Batting
Innings:	7	Runs:	106
Highest Score:	54	Average:	15.14
No. 50s:	1	No. 100s:	0

Test Bowling & Fielding
Wickets:	4	Runs:	44
Best Bowling:	3/31	Average:	11.00
5 WI:	0	10 WM:	0
Catches:	1	Stumpings:	0

A noted batsman from Middlesex, he toured Australia as part of the side that regained the Ashes in 1882/83. He played his part taking three wickets in the first Test and scoring a valuable 54 in the second.

LEVER, John Kenneth

Born:	January 24, 1949
Batting:	Right handed
Bowling:	Left arm medium-fast

Tests
Test Career:	1976-86		
Cap Number:	471		
Tests Played:	21		

Test Batting
Innings:	31	Runs:	306
Highest Score:	53	Average:	11.76
No. 50s:	1	No. 100s:	0

Test Bowling & Fielding
Wickets:	73	Runs:	1,951
Best Bowling:	7/46	Average:	26.72
5 WI:	3	10 WM:	1
Catches:	11	Stumpings:	0

One Day Internationals
ODI Career:	1976-82		
ODIs Played:	22		

ODI Batting
Innings:	11	Runs:	56
Highest Score:	27*	Average:	8.00
No. 50s:	0	No. 100s:	0

ODI Bowling & Fielding
Wickets:	24	Runs:	713
Best Bowling:	4/29	Average:	29.70
5 WM:	0	Catches:	6
Stumpings:	0		

A left arm quick from Essex, he made a startling debut as a 27 year old when he took ten wickets in his first Test. Playing India at Delhi, he claimed 7/46 in the first innings and 3/24 in the second for match figures of 10/70. That tour produced 26 wickets, and whilst he didn't ever reach those heights again he gave his country hearty service for almost a decade.

LEVER, Peter

Born:	September 17, 1940
Batting:	Right handed
Bowling:	Right arm medium-fast

Tests
Test Career:	1970-75		
Cap Number:	447		
Tests Played:	17		

Test Batting
Innings:	18	Runs:	350
Highest Score:	88*	Average:	21.87
No. 50s:	2	No. 100s:	0

Test Bowling & Fielding
Wickets:	41	Runs:	1,509
Best Bowling:	6/38	Average:	36.80
5 WI:	2	10 WM:	0
Catches:	11	Stumpings:	0

One Day Internationals
ODI Career:	1971-75		
ODIs Played:	10		

ODI Batting
Innings:	3	Runs:	17
Highest Score:	8*	Average:	17.00
No. 50s:	0	No. 100s:	0

ODI Bowling & Fielding
Wickets:	11	Runs:	261
Best Bowling:	4/35	Average:	23.72
5 WM:	0	Catches:	2
Stumpings:	0		

A perky right arm quick from Lancashire, he was unrelated to John Lever who played for England at the same time. In 1971 he was playing for England against New Zealand in Auckland when he bowled a bouncer that struck tailender Ewen Chatfield in the head. Lever was left to pray at the bowler's end as medicos fought to revive the Kiwi. Chatfield made a full recovery and Lever went on to bowl manfully for his country in many more Tests.

LEVESON-GOWER, Henry Dudley Gresham

Born:	May 8, 1873
Batting:	Right handed
Bowling:	Right arm leg-break

Tests
Test Career:	1910		
Cap Number:	166		
Tests Played:	3		

Test Batting
Innings:	6	Runs:	95
Highest Score:	31	Average:	23.75
No. 50s:	0	No. 100s:	0

Test Bowling & Fielding
Wickets:	0	Runs:	0
Best Bowling:		Average:	0.00
5 WI:	0	10 WM:	0
Catches:	1	Stumpings:	0

Slightly built and nicknamed 'Shrimp', he toured South Africa in 1910 playing three Tests. Though the talented batsman he never played for England in Tests again he went on a number of 'unofficial' tours playing matches in America, Canada and the West Indies.

LEVETT, William Howard Vincent

Born:	January 25, 1908
Batting:	Right handed
	Wicket Keeper

Tests
Test Career:	1934
Cap Number:	273
Tests Played:	1

Test Batting			
Innings:	2	Runs:	7
Highest Score:	5	Average:	7.00
No. 50s:	0	No. 100s:	0
Test Bowling & Fielding			
Wickets:	0	Runs:	0
Best Bowling:		Average:	0.00
5 WI:	0	10 WM:	0
Catches:	3	Stumpings:	0

Nicknamed 'Hopper', the Kent wicketkeeper played his only Test against England in Calcutta in 1934. The farmer got his nickname because amongst other crops he grew hops for beer.

LEWIS, Anthony Robert

Born:	July 6, 1938
Batting:	Right handed
Bowling:	Right arm leg-break

Tests

Test Career:	1972-73
Cap Number:	454
Tests Played:	9

Test Batting			
Innings:	16	Runs:	457
Highest Score:	125	Average:	32.64
No. 50s:	3	No. 100s:	1
Test Bowling & Fielding			
Wickets:	0	Runs:	0
Best Bowling:		Average:	0.00
5 WI:	0	10 WM:	0
Catches:	0	Stumpings:	0

Tony Lewis crammed a lot into his short Test career. He skippered the side on debut at Delhi in 1972, scoring a valuable 70 in the second innings to secure victory for his side. He hit a century at Kanpur in the same series but by mid 1973 had played his last Test courtesy of a knee injury. Retirement didn't force him out of the game he loved, rather he became an insightful journalist and polished commentator with the BBC.

LEWIS, Clairmonte Christopher

Born:	February 14, 1968
Batting:	Right handed
Bowling:	Right arm medium-fast

Tests

Test Career:	1990-96
Cap Number:	544
Tests Played:	32

Test Batting			
Innings:	51	Runs:	1,105
Highest Score:	117	Average:	23.02
No. 50s:	4	No. 100s:	1
Test Bowling & Fielding			
Wickets:	93	Runs:	3,490
Best Bowling:	6/111	Average:	37.52
5 WI:	3	10 WM:	0
Catches:	25	Stumpings:	0

One Day Internationals

| ODI Career: | 1990-98 |
| ODIs Played: | 53 |

ODI Batting			
Innings:	40	Runs:	374
Highest Score:	33	Average:	14.38
No. 50s:	0	No. 100s:	0
ODI Bowling & Fielding			
Wickets:	66	Runs:	1,942
Best Bowling:	4/30	Average:	29.42
5 WM:	0	Catches:	20
Stumpings:	0		

Promise can only take a cricketer so far, and whilst he showed glimpses of his best at Test level, Chris Lewis was ultimately a disappointment. With his lively fast medium pace and hard hitting batting it was hoped that England had found a replacement for Ian Botham in the Guyanese born all-rounder, but apart from a single Test century against India in 1993 and the occasional four wicket haul he didn't live up to expectations.

LEWIS, Jonathan

Born:	August 26, 1975
Batting:	Right handed
Bowling:	Right arm medium

Tests

Test Career:	2006-
Cap Number:	634
Tests Played:	1

Test Batting			
Innings:	2	Runs:	27
Highest Score:	20	Average:	13.50
No. 50s:	0	No. 100s:	0
Test Bowling & Fielding			
Wickets:	3	Runs:	122
Best Bowling:	3/68	Average:	40.66
5 WI:	0	10 WM:	0
Catches:	0	Stumpings:	0

One Day Internationals

| ODI Career: | 2005- |
| ODIs Played: | 3 |

ODI Batting			
Innings:	1	Runs:	7
Highest Score:	7*	Average:	0.00
No. 50s:	0	No. 100s:	0
ODI Bowling & Fielding			
Wickets:	4	Runs:	124
Best Bowling:	3/32	Average:	31.00
5 WM:	0	Catches:	0
Stumpings:	0		

The medium pace bowler from Gloucestershire played a single Test against Sri Lanka in 2006 after playing three ODI's the previous year.

LEYLAND, Maurice

Born:	July 20, 1900
Batting:	Left handed
Bowling:	Left arm off-break

Tests

Test Career:	1928-38
Cap Number:	237
Tests Played:	41

Test Batting			
Innings:	65	Runs:	2,764
Highest Score:	187	Average:	46.06
No. 50s:	10	No. 100s:	9

Test Bowling & Fielding			
Wickets:	6	Runs:	585
Best Bowling:	3/91	Average:	97.50
5 WI:	0	10 WM:	0
Catches:	13	Stumpings:	0

One of many fine pre-war batsman from Yorkshire, he may be lost to Test cricket after a single failure on debut against the West Indies had selectors not taken a risk with him and put him on the boat to Australia in 1928. England dominated the 1928/29 Ashes series winning the first four Tests, and their ascendancy allowed selectors the chance to give the 29 year old Yorkshireman a chance in the final Test. Leyland scored 137 and 53 and in doing so extended his Test career by almost a decade. Over 41 Tests the powerful left hander hit nine more centuries, scored 2,764 runs at an average of 46.06 and clearly led the averages against the powerful Australians in 1934.

LILLEY, Arthur Fredrick Augustus (Dick)

Born:	November 28, 1866
Batting:	Right handed
Bowling:	Right arm medium
	Wicket Keeper

Tests

Test Career:	1896-1909		
Cap Number:	104		
Tests Played:	35		
Test Batting			
Innings:	52	Runs:	903
Highest Score:	84	Average:	20.52
No. 50s:	4	No. 100s:	0
Test Bowling & Fielding			
Wickets:	1	Runs:	23
Best Bowling:	1/23	Average:	23.00
5 WI:	0	10 WM:	0
Catches:	70	Stumpings:	22

A goveman from Warwickshire, he held down position of English wicket keeper for over a decade. He was a consistent batsman who scored over 15,000 first class runs including 16 centuries.

LILLYWHITE (JNR), James

Born:	February 23, 1842
Batting:	Left handed
Bowling:	Left arm slow

Tests

Test Career:	1877		
Cap Number:	7		
Tests Played:	2		
Test Batting			
Innings:	3	Runs:	16
Highest Score:	10	Average:	8.00
No. 50s:	0	No. 100s:	0
Test Bowling & Fielding			
Wickets:	8	Runs:	126
Best Bowling:	4/70	Average:	15.75
5 WI:	0	10 WM:	0
Catches:	1	Stumpings:	0

England's first ever Test captain hailed from a famous cricketing family, all of whom play for Sussex in the county competition. A left arm bowler with fine control, he had toured Australia in the 1873/74 when no official Tests were played, and was given the captaincy for the first Test side in the absence of W.G. Grace. In his second and last Test, Lillywhite not only led England to victory but enjoyed great success with the ball taking six wickets for the match.

LLOYD, David

Born:	March 18, 1947
Batting:	Left handed
Bowling:	Left arm off-break

Tests

Test Career:	1974-75		
Cap Number:	460		
Tests Played:	9		
Test Batting			
Innings:	15	Runs:	552
Highest Score:	214*	Average:	42.46
No. 50s:	0	No. 100s:	1
Test Bowling & Fielding			
Wickets:	0	Runs:	17
Best Bowling:		Average:	0.00
5 WI:	0	10 WM:	0
Catches:	11	Stumpings:	0

One Day Internationals

ODI Career:	1973-80		
ODIs Played:	8		
ODI Batting			
Innings:	8	Runs:	285
Highest Score:	116*	Average:	40.71
No. 50s:	0	No. 100s:	1
ODI Bowling & Fielding			
Wickets:	1	Runs:	3
Best Bowling:	1/3	Average:	3.00
5 WM:	0	Catches:	3
Stumpings:	0		

The left handed Lancastrian holds a unique place in Test cricket as the only man to score a double century, with no other centuries or half centuries. His opus came in his second Test when England hosted India at Edgbaston in 1974. He was expected to perform well on the tour of Australia in 1974/75 but less than 200 runs in four Tests was deemed as a failure and he never played Test cricket again. He was appointed England coach in 1996 and after three years at the helm returned to his role as a TV commentator.

LLOYD, Graham David

Born:	July 1, 1969
Batting:	Right handed
Bowling:	Right arm medium

One Day Internationals

ODI Career:	1996-98		
ODIs Played:	6		
ODI Batting			
Innings:	5	Runs:	39
Highest Score:	22	Average:	9.75
No. 50s:	0	No. 100s:	0

ODI Bowling & Fielding
Wickets:	0	Runs:	0
Best Bowling:		Average:	0.00
5 WM:	0	Catches:	2
Stumpings:	0		

The son of former Test opener and current day Sky Sports commentator, David Lloyd, middle order batsman Graham played in six ODI's, between 1996 and 1998, with moderate success.

LLOYD, Timothy Andrew

Born:	November 5, 1956
Batting:	Left handed
Bowling:	Right arm medium

Tests
Test Career:	1984
Cap Number:	505
Tests Played:	1

Test Batting
Innings:	1	Runs:	10
Highest Score:	10*	Average:	0.00
No. 50s:	0	No. 100s:	0

Test Bowling & Fielding
Wickets:	0	Runs:	0
Best Bowling:		Average:	0.00
5 WI:	0	10 WM:	0
Catches:	0	Stumpings:	0

One Day Internationals
ODI Career:	1984
ODIs Played:	3

ODI Batting
Innings:	3	Runs:	101
Highest Score:	49	Average:	33.66
No. 50s:	0	No. 100s:	0

ODI Bowling & Fielding
Wickets:	0	Runs:	0
Best Bowling:		Average:	0.00
5 WM:	0	Catches:	0
Stumpings:	0		

His only Test ended in disaster when he was struck on the head by a bouncer from West Indian speedster Malcolm Marshall. Andy Lloyd was ruled out of the remainder of the Test by doctors and never played for England again.

LOADER, Peter James

Born:	October 25, 1929
Batting:	Right handed
Bowling:	Right arm fast

Tests
Test Career:	1954-58
Cap Number:	376
Tests Played:	13

Test Batting
Innings:	19	Runs:	76
Highest Score:	17	Average:	5.84
No. 50s:	0	No. 100s:	0

Test Bowling & Fielding
Wickets:	39	Runs:	878
Best Bowling:	6/36	Average:	22.51
5 WI:	1	10 WM:	0
Catches:	2	Stumpings:	0

A fast bowler from Surrey, his Tests chances were limited by the likes of Brian Statham and Fred Trueman. In all he played 13 Tests including his most memorable game against the West Indies at Leeds in 1957 when he captured 6/36 including a hat-trick. He later emigrated to Australia, playing for Western Australia in the Sheffield Shield competition.

LOCK, Graham Anthony Richard (Tony)

Born:	July 5, 1929
Batting:	Right handed
Bowling:	Left arm off-break

Tests
Test Career:	1952-68
Cap Number:	370
Tests Played:	49

Test Batting
Innings:	63	Runs:	742
Highest Score:	89	Average:	13.74
No. 50s:	3	No. 100s:	0

Test Bowling & Fielding
Wickets:	174	Runs:	4,451
Best Bowling:	7/35	Average:	25.58
5 WI:	9	10 WM:	3
Catches:	59	Stumpings:	0

The left arm finger spinner was picked out for greatness at a young age, making his first class debut for Surrey when he was only 16. Whilst his receding hairline belied his youthfulness, he made his English debut as a 23 year old and quickly stamped himself as a class bowler, taking 4/36 in his first innings of Test cricket. Better suited to the softer English wickets, he would work in tandem with Jim Laker to wreak havoc on touring sides. Lock took 13 wickets in three Tests against the touring South Africans in 1955 and 18 against the Australians in 1956. His single wicket at Old Trafford during that series denied Laker the opportunity of taking all 20 for the match. He took 11 wickets in a Test on three separate occasions, and such was his control that each time it was for less than 100 runs. In 1963 he moved to Western Australia, captaining the state side to victory in the Sheffield Shield competition.

LOCKWOOD, William Henry

Born:	April 25, 1868
Batting:	Right handed
Bowling:	Right arm fast

Tests
Test Career:	1893-1902
Cap Number:	83
Tests Played:	12

Test Batting
Innings:	16	Runs:	231
Highest Score:	52*	Average:	17.76
No. 50s:	1	No. 100s:	0

Test Bowling & Fielding
Wickets:	43	Runs:	883
Best Bowling:	7/71	Average:	20.53
5 WI:	5	10 WM:	1
Catches:	4	Stumpings:	0

He was a highly skilled fast bowler who was said to have had the ability to move that ball one way in the air then cut it back the other way off the seam. Not at his best on the tour to Australia in 1894/95, he found form in the 1902 Ashes Test series where he took 17 wickets. His best performance was in the nail biting fourth Test at Old Trafford where Australia won by a mere three runs despite Lockwood's brilliant match figures of 11/76.

LOHMANN, George Alfred

Born:	June 2, 1865
Batting:	Right handed
Bowling:	Right arm medium-fast

Tests

Test Career:	1886-96
Cap Number:	51
Tests Played:	18

Test Batting

Innings:	26	Runs:	213
Highest Score:	62*	Average:	8.87
No. 50s:	1	No. 100s:	0

Test Bowling & Fielding

Wickets:	112	Runs:	1,205
Best Bowling:	9/28	Average:	10.75
5 WI:	9	10 WM:	5
Catches:	28	Stumpings:	0

A dashing blonde medium pace bowler from Surrey, he can lay claim to the title of England's first great pace bowler. He took eight wickets in a Test innings on four occasions including 8/7 on the mats at Port Elizabeth in 1895/96 as part of match figures of 15/45. He dominated the two Test series against Australia in 1886/87, taking 16 wickets including 8/35 at the SCG in the second Test. He was not an express bowler, rather he got his wickets by making the ball move in what was described at the time as a variety of deceptive ways. With 112 Test wickets at 10.75 he has a record that suggests he should be considered as one of the very best bowlers in the history of Test cricket. He contracted tuberculosis on a tour of South Africa, and despite moving there in the hope that the warmer weather would improve his health he passed away aged only 36.

LOUDON, Alexander Guy Rushworth

Born:	September 6, 1980
Batting:	Right handed
Bowling:	Right arm off-break

One Day Internationals

ODI Career:	2006
ODIs Played:	1

ODI Batting

Innings:	1	Runs:	0
Highest Score:	0	Average:	0.00
No. 50s:	0	No. 100s:	0

ODI Bowling & Fielding

Wickets:	0	Runs:	36
Best Bowling:		Average:	0.00
5 WM:	0	Catches:	0
Stumpings:	0		

A champion school-boy cricketer, all-rounder Loudon was unfortunately run out for a duck in his one ODI to date against Sri Lanka at Chester-le-Street, in June 2006. Loudon has enough potential to warrant future ODI selection as well a possible Test berth.

LOVE, James

Born:	April 22, 1955
Batting:	Right handed
Bowling:	Right arm medium

One Day Internationals

ODI Career:	1981
ODIs Played:	3

ODI Batting

Innings:	3	Runs:	61
Highest Score:	43	Average:	20.33
No. 50s:	0	No. 100s:	0

ODI Bowling & Fielding

Wickets:	0	Runs:	0
Best Bowling:		Average:	0.00
5 WM:	0	Catches:	1
Stumpings:	0		

A middle order batsman from Yorkshire who played in three ODIs against the touring Australians in 1981. His best effort was 43 in his second ODI at Edgbaston.

LOWSON, Frank Anderson

Born:	July 1, 1925
Batting:	Right handed
Bowling:	Right arm off-break

Tests

Test Career:	1951-55
Cap Number:	360
Tests Played:	7

Test Batting

Innings:	13	Runs:	245
Highest Score:	68	Average:	18.84
No. 50s:	2	No. 100s:	0

Test Bowling & Fielding

Wickets:	0	Runs:	0
Best Bowling:		Average:	0.00
5 WI:	0	10 WM:	0
Catches:	5	Stumpings:	0

He was a prolific run scorer from Yorkshire who disappointed when given a number of chances in the Test side.

LUCAS, Alfred Perry

Born:	February 20, 1857
Batting:	Right handed
Bowling:	Right arm slow

Tests

Test Career:	1879-1884
Cap Number:	16
Tests Played:	5

Test Batting

Innings:	9	Runs:	157
Highest Score:	55	Average:	19.62
No. 50s:	1	No. 100s:	0

Test Bowling & Fielding			
Wickets:	0	Runs:	54
Best Bowling:		Average:	0.00
5 WI:	0	10 WM:	0
Catches:	1	Stumpings:	0

'Bunny' Lucas was first selected to play for his country when only 21 years old but the opening batsman failed to perform in any of his five Tests. He enjoyed a long and fruitful first class career that saw him captain the MCC against the touring Australians at Lord's in 1902, some 23 years after making his Test debut.

LUCKHURST, Brian William

Born: February 5, 1939
Batting: Right handed
Bowling: Left arm off-break

Tests

Test Career: 1970-74
Cap Number: 445
Tests Played: 21

Test Batting

Innings:	41	Runs:	1,298
Highest Score:	131	Average:	36.05
No. 50s:	5	No. 100s:	4

Test Bowling & Fielding

Wickets:	1	Runs:	32
Best Bowling:	1/9	Average:	32.00
5 WI:	0	10 WM:	0
Catches:	14	Stumpings:	0

One Day Internationals

ODI Career: 1975
ODIs Played: 3

ODI Batting

Innings:	3	Runs:	15
Highest Score:	14	Average:	5.00
No. 50s:	0	No. 100s:	0

ODI Bowling & Fielding

Wickets:	0	Runs:	0
Best Bowling:		Average:	0.00
5 WM:	0	Catches:	0
Stumpings:	0		

He was one of a handful of English cricketers who had their Test careers halted by an unsuccessful series against a Dennis Lillee and Jeff Thomson led Australia. The stocky Kent opening batsman arrived in Australia in 1974/75 with a reputation as a fighter on the back of a successful visit in 1970/71. He averaged 56.88 during that Ashes series and scored two hundreds, but two Tests and only 54 runs later his international career was over.

LYNCH, Monte

Born: May 21, 1958
Batting: Right handed

One Day Internationals

ODI Career: 1988
ODIs Played: 3

ODI Batting

Innings:	3	Runs:	8
Highest Score:	6	Average:	2.66
No. 50s:	0	No. 100s:	0

ODI Bowling & Fielding

Wickets:	0	Runs:	0
Best Bowling:		Average:	0.00
5 WM:	0	Catches:	1
Stumpings:	0		

Born in Guyana, Lynch was a member of the 'rebel' West Indian squad that toured South Africa in 1983/84. A right hand batsman, in 1988 he was chosen to represent England in three ODI's, ironically against the West Indies, but failed to reach double figures on any occasion.

LYTTELTON, Alfred

Born: February 7, 1857
Batting: Right handed
Bowling: Right arm leg-break
Wicket Keeper

Tests

Test Career: 1880-84
Cap Number: 25
Tests Played: 4

Test Batting

Innings:	7	Runs:	94
Highest Score:	31	Average:	15.66
No. 50s:	0	No. 100s:	0

Test Bowling & Fielding

Wickets:	4	Runs:	19
Best Bowling:	4/19	Average:	4.75
5 WI:	0	10 WM:	0
Catches:	2	Stumpings:	0

He was a brilliant all round sportsman who was considered the finest tennis player of his time and also played football for his country. Such was his versatility, that the batsman keeper had only one spell with the ball for England, at the Oval in 1884, but returned the handsome figures of 4/19.

MACAULAY, George Gibson

Born: December 7, 1897
Batting: Right handed

Tests

Test Career: 1923-33
Cap Number: 211
Tests Played: 8

Test Batting

Innings:	10	Runs:	112
Highest Score:	76	Average:	18.66
No. 50s:	1	No. 100s:	0

Test Bowling & Fielding

Wickets:	24	Runs:	662
Best Bowling:	5/64	Average:	27.58
5 WI:	1	10 WM:	0
Catches:	5	Stumpings:	0

The Yorkshire spinner made his debut on the tour to South Africa in 1922/23 and is one of the few crickets to have taken a wicket with his first delivery in Test cricket. He played a single Test against Australia in 1926, and while he took only the one wicket at a cost of 132, the tailender scored 76 coming in at number ten. A member of the Royal Air Force, he died serving his country in the Second World War.

MACBRYAN, John Crawford William (Jack)
Born: July 22, 1892
Batting: Right handed

Tests
Test Career:	1924
Cap Number:	221
Tests Played:	1

Test Batting
Innings:	0	Runs:	0
Highest Score:	0	Average:	0.00
No. 50s:	0	No. 100s:	0

Test Bowling & Fielding
Wickets:	0	Runs:	0
Best Bowling:		Average:	0.00
5 WI:	0	10 WM:	0
Catches:	0	Stumpings:	0

The one time Somerset captain was selected for a single Test against South Africa in 1924, but bad weather prevented him from batting or bowling in the match.

MACGREGOR, Gregor
Born: August 31, 1869
Batting: Right handed
Wicket Keeper

Tests
Test Career:	1890-93
Cap Number:	68
Tests Played:	8

Test Batting
Innings:	11	Runs:	96
Highest Score:	31	Average:	12.00
No. 50s:	0	No. 100s:	0

Test Bowling & Fielding
Wickets:	0	Runs:	0
Best Bowling:		Average:	0.00
5 WI:	0	10 WM:	0
Catches:	14	Stumpings:	3

Considered England's finest gloveman of the 19th century, he emmulated the feats of Australia's Jack Blackham by standing up to the stumps to the opening bowlers. Though his Test record suggests otherwise, he was a very useful batsman for Middlesex for whom he scored three centuries.

MACKINNON, Francis Alexander
Born: April 9, 1848
Batting: Right handed

Tests
Test Career:	1879
Cap Number:	17
Tests Played:	1

Test Batting
Innings:	2	Runs:	5
Highest Score:	5	Average:	2.50
No. 50s:	0	No. 100s:	0

Test Bowling & Fielding
Wickets:	0	Runs:	0
Best Bowling:		Average:	0.00
5 WI:	0	10 WM:	0
Catches:	0	Stumpings:	0

A nobleman who played much of his first class cricket for Kent, his only Test was against Australia at the MCG in 1879. MacKinnon was no match for Fred Spofforth who cleaned bowled him for a golden duck on his first visit to the crease.

MACLAREN, Archibald Campbell
Born: December 1, 1871
Batting: Right handed

Tests
Test Career:	1894-1909
Cap Number:	92
Tests Played:	35

Test Batting
Innings:	61	Runs:	1,931
Highest Score:	140	Average:	33.87
No. 50s:	8	No. 100s:	5

Test Bowling & Fielding
Wickets:	0	Runs:	0
Best Bowling:		Average:	0.00
5 WI:	0	10 WM:	0
Catches:	29	Stumpings:	0

He was a leading figure in English cricket at the turn of the century, captaining the side in 22 matches and featuring as a leading batsman. He made five centuries in a Test career that spanned 15 years, four of which were struck in Australia. Archie MacLaren was at his best on tour in 1897/98 when he topped the aggregates in the five Test series with 488 runs and an average of 54.22. A right hand batsman with a high backlift typical of the era, his most famous innings was not for England but his county Lancashire when he hit a record 424 against Somerset in 1895.

MADDY, Darren Lee
Born: May 23, 1974
Batting: Right handed
Bowling: Right arm medium

Tests
Test Career:	1999-2000
Cap Number:	597
Tests Played:	3

Test Batting
Innings:	4	Runs:	46
Highest Score:	24	Average:	11.50
No. 50s:	0	No. 100s:	0

Test Bowling & Fielding
Wickets:	0	Runs:	40
Best Bowling:		Average:	0.00
5 WI:	0	10 WM:	0
Catches:	4	Stumpings:	0

One Day Internationals
ODI Career:	1998-2000
ODIs Played:	8

ODI Batting
Innings:	6	Runs:	113
Highest Score:	53	Average:	18.83
No. 50s:	1	No. 100s:	0

ODI Bowling & Fielding
Wickets:	0	Runs:	0
Best Bowling:		Average:	0.00
5 WM:	0	Catches:	1
Stumpings:	0		

An opening batsman from Leicestershire who has had a number of chances in both the Test and one day sides but is yet to consolidate a spot in either.

MAHMOOD, Sajid Iqbal

Born:	December 21, 1981
Batting:	Right handed
Bowling:	Right arm medium-fast

Tests
Test Career:	2006-		
Cap Number:	633		
Tests Played:	4		

Test Batting
Innings:	4	Runs:	48
Highest Score:	34	Average:	16.00
No. 50s:	0	No. 100s:	0

Test Bowling & Fielding
Wickets:	13	Runs:	397
Best Bowling:	4/22	Average:	30.53
5 WI:	0	10 WM:	0
Catches:	0	Stumpings:	0

One Day Internationals
ODI Career:	2004-		
ODIs Played:	8		

ODI Batting
Innings:	5	Runs:	30
Highest Score:	9	Average:	6.00
No. 50s:	0	No. 100s:	0

ODI Bowling & Fielding
Wickets:	8	Runs:	414
Best Bowling:	3/37	Average:	51.75
5 WM:	0	Catches:	0
Stumpings:	0		

An exuberant pace bowler who was plucked form obscurity to play first for Lancashire and then for England. He played four Tests in the summer of 2006, and with a return of 13 wickets, is in line for a spot on the Ashes tour later in the year.

MAKEPEACE, Joseph William Henry

Born:	August 22, 1881
Batting:	Right handed
Bowling:	Right arm leg-break

Tests
Test Career:	1921		
Cap Number:	186		
Tests Played:	4		

Test Batting
Innings:	8	Runs:	279
Highest Score:	117	Average:	34.87
No. 50s:	2	No. 100s:	1

Test Bowling & Fielding
Wickets:	0	Runs:	0
Best Bowling:		Average:	0.00
5 WI:	0	10 WM:	0
Catches:	0	Stumpings:	0

His international career may have lasted only four Tests but he excelled in one of them coming in at number three. England showed little in their whitewash at the hands of the Australians in 1920/21 but at least Makepeace's effort in the fourth Test where he scored 117 and 54 gave them some cause for joy. The talented sportsman also represented England at football and was a member of the Everton side that won the 1906 F.A. Cup.

MALCOLM, Devon Eugene

Born:	February 22, 1963
Batting:	Right handed
Bowling:	Right arm fast

Tests
Test Career:	1989-97		
Cap Number:	539		
Tests Played:	40		

Test Batting
Innings:	58	Runs:	236
Highest Score:	29	Average:	6.05
No. 50s:	0	No. 100s:	0

Test Bowling & Fielding
Wickets:	128	Runs:	4,748
Best Bowling:	9/57	Average:	37.09
5 WI:	5	10 WM:	2
Catches:	7	Stumpings:	0

One Day Internationals
ODI Career:	1990-94		
ODIs Played:	10		

ODI Batting
Innings:	5	Runs:	9
Highest Score:	4	Average:	3.00
No. 50s:	0	No. 100s:	0

ODI Bowling & Fielding
Wickets:	16	Runs:	404
Best Bowling:	3/40	Average:	25.25
5 WM:	0	Catches:	1
Stumpings:	0		

The Jamaican born speedster was genuinely quick and whilst the there was an appreciable difference between his best and worst, when on song there were few as lethal. After an inauspicious debut against Australia in 1989 he was chosen to tour the West Indies later in the year, enjoying an excellent series where he took 19 wickets in four Tests including ten at Port of Spain. The hulking speedster had been eligible to play Test cricket for either nation and by the time he returned home authorities in the Caribbean were ruing the fact that they hadn't tried harder to regain his services. They had seen Malcolm at his best, and whilst he was capable of great spells such as his 9/57 against the Proteas at The Oval in 1994, there were times when his lack of control made him an expensive commodity. A shocking batsman, it was fitting that he should be the third victim in Shane Warne's only Test hat-trick.

MALLENDER, Neil Alan

Born:	August 13, 1961
Batting:	Right handed
Bowling:	Right arm medium-fast

Tests
Test Career:	1992		
Cap Number:	556		
Tests Played:	2		

Test Batting
Innings:	3	Runs:	8
Highest Score:	4	Average:	2.66
No. 50s:	0	No. 100s:	0

Test Bowling & Fielding
Wickets:	10	Runs:	215
Best Bowling:	5/50	Average:	21.50
5 WI:	1	10 WM:	0
Catches:	0	Stumpings:	0

The balding paceman made his debut against Pakistan at Headingly in 1992 with eight wickets for the match. He was retained for the final Test of that series but was never selected for England again.

MANN, Francis George
Born: September 6, 1917
Batting: Right handed

Tests
Test Career:	1948-49
Cap Number:	340
Tests Played:	7

Test Batting
Innings:	12	Runs:	376
Highest Score:	136*	Average:	37.60
No. 50s:	0	No. 100s:	1

Test Bowling & Fielding
Wickets:	0	Runs:	0
Best Bowling:		Average:	0.00
5 WI:	0	10 WM:	0
Catches:	3	Stumpings:	0

He captained England in all of his seven Tests, and whilst the side only won two of them, they avoided defeat in the other five. He was a right hand bat who saved his best for his country, scoring his highest ever first class score of 136 not out against South Africa at Port Elizabeth in 1948/49.

MANN, Francis Thomas
Born: March 3, 1888
Batting: Right handed

Tests
Test Career:	1922-23
Cap Number:	209
Tests Played:	5

Test Batting
Innings:	9	Runs:	281
Highest Score:	84	Average:	35.12
No. 50s:	2	No. 100s:	0

Test Bowling & Fielding
Wickets:	0	Runs:	0
Best Bowling:		Average:	0.00
5 WI:	0	10 WM:	0
Catches:	4	Stumpings:	0

He led the tour to South Africa in 1922/23, captaining the side in all five Tests and scoring 281 runs. His highest score for the series was an 84 in the third Test when he batted at number seven. Whilst he never played another Test for England, he is one of the few captains in international cricket who can boast a 100 per cent record for series wins.

MARKS, Victor James
Born: June 25, 1955
Batting: Right handed
Bowling: Right arm off-break

Tests
Test Career:	1982-84
Cap Number:	499
Tests Played:	6

Test Batting
Innings:	10	Runs:	249
Highest Score:	83	Average:	27.66
No. 50s:	3	No. 100s:	0

Test Bowling & Fielding
Wickets:	11	Runs:	484
Best Bowling:	3/78	Average:	44.00
5 WI:	0	10 WM:	0
Catches:	2	Stumpings:	0

One Day Internationals
ODI Career:	1980-88
ODIs Played:	34

ODI Batting
Innings:	24	Runs:	285
Highest Score:	44	Average:	13.57
No. 50s:	0	No. 100s:	0

ODI Bowling & Fielding
Wickets:	44	Runs:	1,135
Best Bowling:	5/20	Average:	25.79
5 WM:	2	Catches:	8
Stumpings:	0		

Those who enjoy the articulate Marks on radio and television may be surprised to know he was an accomplished international cricketer. The off spinner didn't give the ball a big rip, but he was accurate and well suited to ODI's where he represented England on 34 occasions.

MARRIOTT, Charles Stowell
Born: September 14, 1895
Batting: Right handed
Bowling: Right arm leg-break

Tests
Test Career:	1933
Cap Number:	270
Tests Played:	1

Test Batting
Innings:	1	Runs:	0
Highest Score:	0	Average:	0.00
No. 50s:	0	No. 100s:	0

Test Bowling & Fielding
Wickets:	11	Runs:	96
Best Bowling:	6/59	Average:	8.72
5 WI:	2	10 WM:	1
Catches:	1	Stumpings:	0

A clever little leg spin bowler he played a single Test against the touring West Indians at The Oval in 1933.

MARTIN, Frederick
Born: October 12, 1861
Batting: Left handed
Bowling: Left arm medium

Tests
Test Career:	1890-92		
Cap Number:	70		
Tests Played:	2		

Test Batting
Innings:	2	Runs:	14
Highest Score:	13	Average:	7.00
No. 50s:	0	No. 100s:	0

Test Bowling & Fielding
Wickets:	14	Runs:	141
Best Bowling:	6/50	Average:	10.07
5 WI:	2	10 WM:	1
Catches:	2	Stumpings:	0

A left arm opening bowler from Kent, he played only two Tests but excelled in one of them returning match figures of 12/102 against the Australians at The Oval in 1890.

MARTIN, John William
Born:	February 16, 1917
Batting:	Right handed
Bowling:	Right arm fast

Tests
Test Career:	1947		
Cap Number:	319		
Tests Played:	1		

Test Batting
Innings:	2	Runs:	26
Highest Score:	26	Average:	13.00
No. 50s:	0	No. 100s:	0

Test Bowling & Fielding
Wickets:	1	Runs:	129
Best Bowling:	1/111	Average:	129.00
5 WI:	0	10 WM:	0
Catches:	0	Stumpings:	0

An opening bowler from Kent, he played a single Test against South Africa in 1947.

MARTIN, Peter James
Born:	November 15, 1968
Batting:	Right handed
Bowling:	Right arm medium-fast

Tests
Test Career:	1995-97		
Cap Number:	571		
Tests Played:	8		

Test Batting
Innings:	13	Runs:	115
Highest Score:	29	Average:	8.84
No. 50s:	0	No. 100s:	0

Test Bowling & Fielding
Wickets:	17	Runs:	580
Best Bowling:	4/60	Average:	34.11
5 WI:	0	10 WM:	0
Catches:	6	Stumpings:	0

One Day Internationals
ODI Career:	1995-98		
ODIs Played:	20		

ODI Batting
Innings:	13	Runs:	38
Highest Score:	6	Average:	6.33
No. 50s:	0	No. 100s:	0

ODI Bowling & Fielding
Wickets:	27	Runs:	806
Best Bowling:	4/44	Average:	29.85
5 WM:	0	Catches:	1
Stumpings:	0		

A medium pace bowler from Lancashire who started his international career in fine style with 4/44 against the West Indies in an ODI at The Oval in 1995. From that point it was steady rather than spectacular going for Martin who gave good service over a three year period.

MASON, John Richard
Born:	March 26, 1874
Batting:	Right handed
Bowling:	Right arm medium-fast

Tests
Test Career:	1897-98		
Cap Number:	109		
Tests Played:	5		

Test Batting
Innings:	10	Runs:	129
Highest Score:	32	Average:	12.90
No. 50s:	0	No. 100s:	0

Test Bowling & Fielding
Wickets:	2	Runs:	149
Best Bowling:	1/8	Average:	74.50
5 WI:	0	10 WM:	0
Catches:	3	Stumpings:	0

A skillful all-rounder from Kent, he played all five Tests on the Ashes tour in 1897/98 but failed to reproduce his county form and was never selected for England again.

MATTHEWS, Austin David George
Born:	May 3, 1904
Batting:	Right handed
Bowling:	Right arm medium-fast

Tests
Test Career:	1937		
Cap Number:	298		
Tests Played:	1		

Test Batting
Innings:	1	Runs:	2
Highest Score:	2*	Average:	0.00
No. 50s:	0	No. 100s:	0

Test Bowling & Fielding
Wickets:	2	Runs:	65
Best Bowling:	1/13	Average:	32.50
5 WI:	0	10 WM:	0
Catches:	1	Stumpings:	0

The Welshman played a single Test against New Zealand in 1937.

MAY, Peter Barker Howard
Born:	December 31, 1929
Batting:	Right handed

Tests
Test Career:	1951-61		
Cap Number:	361		
Tests Played:	66		

Test Batting
Innings:	106	Runs:	4,537
Highest Score:	285*	Average:	46.77
No. 50s:	22	No. 100s:	13

Test Bowling & Fielding
Wickets:	0	Runs:	0
Best Bowling:		Average:	0.00
5 WI:	0	10 WM:	0
Catches:	42	Stumpings:	0

In the 1950's school masters and cricket coaches generally had a single instruction for their charges; bat like Peter May. The square shouldered batsman from Surrey had the perfect technique, an upright stance, keen footwork and the full face of the bat whether defending or driving. He captained England in 41 Tests, a record that survived until passed by Michael Atherton in 2001 and scored a then record 13 Test centuries for his country. He played many memorable Test innings. He hit 138 on debut against South Africa in 1951, 285 against the West Indies at Edgbaston in 1957 when he and Colin Cowdrey put on 411 runs for the fourth wicket and 113 at the SCG in 1958/59 when the rest of the English side was crumbling around him. The gentlemanly May retired from first class cricket in 1961 and went on to become an English chairman of selectors and an ICC Match referee. When Peter May passed away at the age of only 64 in 1994 he was fondly remembered as the embodiment of English cricket values at their finest.

MAYNARD, Matthew Peter
Born: March 21, 1966
Batting: Right handed
Bowling: Right arm medium

Tests
Test Career:	1988-94
Cap Number:	532
Tests Played:	4

Test Batting
Innings:	8	Runs:	87
Highest Score:	35	Average:	10.87
No. 50s:	0	No. 100s:	0

Test Bowling & Fielding
Wickets:	0	Runs:	0
Best Bowling:		Average:	0.00
5 WI:	0	10 WM:	0
Catches:	3	Stumpings:	0

One Day Internationals
ODI Career:	1994-2000
ODIs Played:	14

ODI Batting
Innings:	12	Runs:	156
Highest Score:	41	Average:	14.18
No. 50s:	0	No. 100s:	0

ODI Bowling & Fielding
Wickets:	0	Runs:	0
Best Bowling:		Average:	0.00
5 WM:	0	Catches:	4
Stumpings:	0		

A hard hitting batsman from Glamorgan who played a single Test against the West Indies in 1988 and then was recalled against the Australians for the 1993 Ashes series. He could manage only 39 runs in four innings in that series, falling to the spin of Shane Warne and Tim May.

McCAGUE, Martin John
Born: May 24, 1969
Batting: Right handed
Bowling: Right arm fast

Tests
Test Career:	1993-94
Cap Number:	563
Tests Played:	3

Test Batting
Innings:	5	Runs:	21
Highest Score:	11	Average:	4.20
No. 50s:	0	No. 100s:	0

Test Bowling & Fielding
Wickets:	6	Runs:	390
Best Bowling:	4/121	Average:	65.00
5 WI:	0	10 WM:	0
Catches:	1	Stumpings:	0

Raised in Australia and a member of the West Australian state side, he saw his chances for Test cricket in Australia as slim so he headed to England where he was eligible for selection by dint of his British heritage. He played all of his three Tests against Australia, but after showing promise in England, failed both physically and mentally in Brisbane in 1994/95 and was sent home.

McCONNON, James Edward
Born: June 21, 1922
Batting: Right handed
Bowling: Right arm off-break

Tests
Test Career:	1954
Cap Number:	374
Tests Played:	2

Test Batting
Innings:	3	Runs:	18
Highest Score:	11	Average:	9.00
No. 50s:	0	No. 100s:	0

Test Bowling & Fielding
Wickets:	4	Runs:	74
Best Bowling:	3/19	Average:	18.50
5 WI:	0	10 WM:	0
Catches:	4	Stumpings:	0

An off-spinner from Glamorgan, he played his only two Tests against the touring Pakistanis in 1954.

McGAHEY, Charles Percy
Born: February 12, 1871
Batting: Right handed
Bowling: Right arm leg-break

Tests
Test Career:	1902
Cap Number:	133
Tests Played:	2

Test Batting
Innings:	4	Runs:	38
Highest Score:	18	Average:	9.50
No. 50s:	0	No. 100s:	0

Test Bowling & Fielding
Wickets:	0	Runs:	0
Best Bowling:		Average:	0.00
5 WI:	0	10 WM:	0
Catches:	1	Stumpings:	0

A hard hitting batsman from Essex, he played two Tests in Australia in 1901/02 but failed to show his best and was never selected in the national side again.

McGRATH, Anthony
Born:	October 6, 1975
Batting:	Right handed
Bowling:	Right arm medium

Tests
Test Career:	2003
Cap Number:	614
Tests Played:	4

Test Batting
Innings:	5	Runs:	201
Highest Score:	81	Average:	40.20
No. 50s:	2	No. 100s:	0

Test Bowling & Fielding
Wickets:	4	Runs:	56
Best Bowling:	3/16	Average:	14.00
5 WI:	0	10 WM:	0
Catches:	3	Stumpings:	0

One Day Internationals
ODI Career:	2003-04
ODIs Played:	14

ODI Batting
Innings:	12	Runs:	166
Highest Score:	52	Average:	16.60
No. 50s:	1	No. 100s:	0

ODI Bowling & Fielding
Wickets:	4	Runs:	175
Best Bowling:	1/13	Average:	43.75
5 WM:	0	Catches:	4
Stumpings:	0		

A capable all-rounder from Yorkshire, his chances at international level have been limited due to the emergence of Andy Flintoff. McGrath performed well in his four Tests with a batting average of 40.20 and scores of 69 and 81 against Zimbabwe.

McINTYRE, Arthur John William
Born:	May 14, 1918
Batting:	Right handed
Bowling:	Right arm leg-break
	Wicket Keeper

Tests
Test Career:	1950-55
Cap Number:	352
Tests Played:	3

Test Batting
Innings:	6	Runs:	19
Highest Score:	7	Average:	3.16
No. 50s:	0	No. 100s:	0

Test Bowling & Fielding
Wickets:	0	Runs:	0
Best Bowling:		Average:	0.00
5 WI:	0	10 WM:	0
Catches:	8	Stumpings:	0

The wicketkeeper for the all-conquering Surrey side in the fifties, he had to play second fiddle to Godfrey Evans and subsequently played only three Tests.

McMASTER, Joseph Emile Patrick
Born:	March 16, 1861
Batting:	Right handed

Tests
Test Career:	1889
Cap Number:	67
Tests Played:	1

Test Batting
Innings:	1	Runs:	0
Highest Score:	0	Average:	0.00
No. 50s:	0	No. 100s:	0

Test Bowling & Fielding
Wickets:	0	Runs:	0
Best Bowling:		Average:	0.00
5 WI:	0	10 WM:	0
Catches:	0	Stumpings:	0

McMaster holds the dubious honour of having the least impressive record of any player to have ever played Test cricket. His entire first class career consisted of just one Test in South Africa in which he scored a second ball duck.

MEAD, Charles Philip
Born:	March 9, 1887
Batting:	Left handed
Bowling:	Left arm off-break

Tests
Test Career:	1911-28
Cap Number:	174
Tests Played:	17

Test Batting
Innings:	26	Runs:	1,185
Highest Score:	182*	Average:	49.37
No. 50s:	3	No. 100s:	4

Test Bowling & Fielding
Wickets:	0	Runs:	0
Best Bowling:		Average:	0.00
5 WI:	0	10 WM:	0
Catches:	4	Stumpings:	0

With over 55,000 first class runs and a Test average of a just under 50, it is fair to describe Mead as one of the forgotten greats of English cricket. A Hampshire player for over 30 years, he represented England in Tests both before and after the War to great effect. He scored two centuries against South Africa just prior to the cessation of Test cricket and scored two more upon its resumption. One of those hundreds was a fighting 182 not out against a dominant Australian side at The Oval in 1921. John Arlott described him as a perfect timer of the ball who always got himself into the right position prior to playing a shot. It was said he had the same routine before facing any delivery where he would touch his cap four times then tap his bat four times on the crease. Bowlers would have found Phil Mead very annoying as much for his enormous talent as for his idiosyncratic habits.

MEAD, Walter

Born:	April 1, 1868
Batting:	Right handed
Bowling:	Right arm slow

Tests

Test Career:	1899
Cap Number:	123
Tests Played:	1

Test Batting

Innings:	2	Runs:	7
Highest Score:	7	Average:	3.50
No. 50s:	0	No. 100s:	0

Test Bowling & Fielding

Wickets:	1	Runs:	91
Best Bowling:	1/91	Average:	91.00
5 WI:	0	10 WM:	0
Catches:	1	Stumpings:	0

A slow bowler from Essex, his only Test was against the Australians at Lord's in 1899.

MIDWINTER, William Evans

Born:	June 19, 1851
Batting:	Right handed

Tests

Test Career:	1877-87
Cap Number:	31
Tests Played:	12

Test Batting

Innings:	21	Runs:	269
Highest Score:	37	Average:	13.45
No. 50s:	0	No. 100s:	0

Test Bowling & Fielding

Wickets:	24	Runs:	605
Best Bowling:	5/78	Average:	25.20
5 WI:	1	10 WM:	0
Catches:	10	Stumpings:	0

It is fair to say that there has never been a Test career to match that of Billy Midwinter's. A useful medium pace bowler and handy lower order batsman, it wasn't as much what Billy achieved on the field, rather his decisions off it, that make him a standout amongst Test cricketers. Midwinter made his debut for Australia in the first Test at the MCG in 1877, and played his final Test at the SCG in 1887, once again for Australia. In between those two Tests, Billy Midwinter played four Tests for England and was literally kidnapped by W.G. Grace whilst playing for Australia. Midwinter was playing for Australia against Middlesex at Lords in 1878 when he was grabbed by a group of Gloucestershire cricketers acting on the orders of the good doctor. Rather than offend, Midwinter played with his captors and went on to stay in England and represent them in Test cricket. He would play for the Australians again, but sadly passed away at the age of 39 in a Melbourne mental asylum following the untimely death of his wife and two young children.

MILBURN, Colin

Born:	October 23, 1941
Batting:	Right handed
Bowling:	Right arm medium

Tests

Test Career:	1966-69
Cap Number:	431
Tests Played:	9

Test Batting

Innings:	16	Runs:	654
Highest Score:	139	Average:	46.71
No. 50s:	2	No. 100s:	2

Test Bowling & Fielding

Wickets:	0	Runs:	0
Best Bowling:		Average:	0.00
5 WI:	0	10 WM:	0
Catches:	7	Stumpings:	0

English fans were left to ponder what might have been when Colin Milburn lost an eye in a car accident in 1969. The likeable lad from Northampton had won a spot in the Test side despite his generous proportions. 'Ollie' made his Test debut in 1966 with a clattering 94 in the second innings of the Old Trafford Test against the West Indies and followed it up with 126 a week later. Milburn had strength to go with his size and he thrilled fans with a power laden 83 against Australia at Lord's in 1968 that came at faster than a run a minute. There was one more Test century, 136 in Karachi and then that fateful car crash. He tried a first class comeback in 1973 but could not overcome his impaired vision and retired in 1974. Literally the next big thing in English cricket, Milburn passed away after suffering a heart attack in 1990 at the age of 48.

MILLER, Audley Montague

Born:	October 19, 1869
Batting:	Right handed

Tests

Test Career:	1896
Cap Number:	99
Tests Played:	1

Test Batting

Innings:	2	Runs:	24
Highest Score:	20*	Average:	0.00
No. 50s:	0	No. 100s:	0

Test Bowling & Fielding

Wickets:	0	Runs:	0
Best Bowling:		Average:	0.00
5 WI:	0	10 WM:	0
Catches:	0	Stumpings:	0

His only Test was at Port Elizabeth in 1896, one of only five first class games he ever played.

MILLER, Geoffrey

Born:	September 8, 1952
Batting:	Right handed
Bowling:	Right arm off-break

Tests
Test Career:	1976-84		
Cap Number:	469		
Tests Played:	34		

Test Batting
Innings:	51	Runs:	1,213
Highest Score:	98*	Average:	25.80
No. 50s:	7	No. 100s:	0

Test Bowling & Fielding
Wickets:	60	Runs:	1,859
Best Bowling:	5/44	Average:	30.98
5 WI:	1	10 WM:	0
Catches:	17	Stumpings:	0

One Day Internationals
ODI Career:	1977-84		
ODIs Played:	25		

ODI Batting
Innings:	18	Runs:	136
Highest Score:	46	Average:	8.50
No. 50s:	0	No. 100s:	0

ODI Bowling & Fielding
Wickets:	25	Runs:	813
Best Bowling:	3/27	Average:	32.52
5 WM:	0	Catches:	4
Stumpings:	0		

A steady right arm off spinner and talented lower order batsman who represented England in 34 Tests. 'Dusty' Miller could count himself most unlucky to have never scored a Test century with two 98's and an 89.

MILLIGAN, Frank William
Born:	March 19, 1870
Batting:	Right handed
Bowling:	Right arm fast

Tests
Test Career:	1899		
Cap Number:	114		
Tests Played:	2		

Test Batting
Innings:	4	Runs:	58
Highest Score:	38	Average:	14.50
No. 50s:	0	No. 100s:	0

Test Bowling & Fielding
Wickets:	0	Runs:	29
Best Bowling:		Average:	0.00
5 WI:	0	10 WM:	0
Catches:	1	Stumpings:	0

Frank Milligan was one of many players who only got their chance at Test level because England sent virtual second XI's to visit South Africa at the turn of the last century. He played both of his Tests under Lord Hawke in 1899.

MILLMAN, Geoffrey
Born:	October 2, 1934
Batting:	Right handed
Bowling:	Right arm off-break
	Wicket Keeper

Tests
Test Career:	1962		
Cap Number:	409		
Tests Played:	6		

Test Batting
Innings:	7	Runs:	60
Highest Score:	32*	Average:	12.00
No. 50s:	0	No. 100s:	0

Test Bowling & Fielding
Wickets:	0	Runs:	0
Best Bowling:		Average:	0.00
5 WI:	0	10 WM:	0
Catches:	13	Stumpings:	2

A stand in wicketkeeper who played all his Tests against Pakistan and India in 1961/62 when first choice keeper John Murray went home with an injury.

MILTON, Clement Arthur
Born:	March 10, 1928
Batting:	Right handed
Bowling:	Right arm medium

Tests
Test Career:	1958-59		
Cap Number:	387		
Tests Played:	6		

Test Batting
Innings:	9	Runs:	204
Highest Score:	104*	Average:	25.50
No. 50s:	0	No. 100s:	1

Test Bowling & Fielding
Wickets:	0	Runs:	12
Best Bowling:		Average:	0.00
5 WI:	0	10 WM:	0
Catches:	5	Stumpings:	0

One of the last people to have played for England in cricket and football, the well known Arsenal right-half marked his Test debut with a century against New Zealand at Headingly in 1958. Whilst there were to be no more highlights in his six Test career he did captain Gloucs in the late 60's.

MITCHELL, Arthur
Born:	September 13, 1902
Batting:	Right handed

Tests
Test Career:	1933-36		
Cap Number:	271		
Tests Played:	6		

Test Batting
Innings:	10	Runs:	298
Highest Score:	72	Average:	29.80
No. 50s:	2	No. 100s:	0

Test Bowling & Fielding
Wickets:	0	Runs:	4
Best Bowling:		Average:	0.00
5 WI:	0	10 WM:	0
Catches:	9	Stumpings:	0

A right hand top order batsman from Yorkshire, he was steady rather than spectacular. Nicknamed 'ticker', he was called up at the last minute to play South Africa in Leeds in 1935 and enjoyed his best result in a Test scoring 58 and 72. He was no relation of Thomas Mitchell who played for England at the same time.

MITCHELL, Frank
Born: August 13, 1872
Batting: Right handed
Bowling: Right arm medium
Wicket Keeper

Tests
Test Career:	1899-1912		
Cap Number:	115		
Tests Played:	5		

Test Batting
Innings:	10	Runs:	116
Highest Score:	41	Average:	11.60
No. 50s:	0	No. 100s:	0

Test Bowling & Fielding
Wickets:	0	Runs:	0
Best Bowling:		Average:	0.00
5 WI:	0	10 WM:	0
Catches:	2	Stumpings:	0

An England cap in cricket and rugby, he visited South Africa as part of Lord Hawke's touring party in 1899. He served in South Africa during the Boer War and then returned there to captain their cricket side. He led the South African side that toured England in both 1904 and 1912.

MITCHELL, Thomas Bignall
Born: September 4, 1902
Batting: Right handed
Bowling: Right arm leg-break

Tests
Test Career:	1933-35		
Cap Number:	266		
Tests Played:	5		

Test Batting
Innings:	6	Runs:	20
Highest Score:	9	Average:	5.00
No. 50s:	0	No. 100s:	0

Test Bowling & Fielding
Wickets:	8	Runs:	498
Best Bowling:	2/49	Average:	62.25
5 WI:	0	10 WM:	0
Catches:	1	Stumpings:	0

A bespectacled leg-spinner from Derbyshire, he played five Tests in the mid thirties but could manage only eight wickets. He was England's oldest living Test cricketer just prior to passing away at the age of 93 in 1996.

MITCHELL-INNES, Norman Stewart
Born: September 7, 1914
Batting: Right handed

Tests
Test Career:	1935		
Cap Number:	283		
Tests Played:	1		

Test Batting
Innings:	1	Runs:	5
Highest Score:	5	Average:	5.00
No. 50s:	0	No. 100s:	0

Test Bowling & Fielding
Wickets:	0	Runs:	0
Best Bowling:		Average:	0.00
5 WI:	0	10 WM:	0
Catches:	0	Stumpings:	0

The Indian born Mitchell-Innes played a single Test against the touring South Africans in 1935. In 2006 he was England's oldest living Test cricketer.

MOLD, Athur Webb
Born: May 27, 1863
Batting: Right handed
Bowling: Right arm fast

Tests
Test Career:	1893		
Cap Number:	84		
Tests Played:	3		

Test Batting
Innings:	3	Runs:	0
Highest Score:	0	Average:	0.00
No. 50s:	0	No. 100s:	0

Test Bowling & Fielding
Wickets:	7	Runs:	234
Best Bowling:	3/44	Average:	33.42
5 WI:	0	10 WM:	0
Catches:	1	Stumpings:	0

A fast bowler with a questionable action from Lancashire, his three Tests were all against the touring Australians in 1893. In 1900 he was called for throwing in a county game and the 12 county captains were called to vote on the legitimacy of his bowling action. They voted against Mold eleven votes to one and his cricket career was over.

MOON, Leonard James
Born: February 9, 1878
Batting: Right handed

Tests
Test Career:	1906		
Cap Number:	150		
Tests Played:	4		

Test Batting
Innings:	8	Runs:	182
Highest Score:	36	Average:	22.75
No. 50s:	0	No. 100s:	0

Test Bowling & Fielding
Wickets:	0	Runs:	0
Best Bowling:		Average:	0.00
5 WI:	0	10 WM:	0
Catches:	4	Stumpings:	0

A military man, he played all of his four Tests in South Africa on the 1905/06 tour. He died serving his country in the First World War.

MORLEY, Frederick
Born: December 16, 1850
Batting: Left handed
Bowling: Left arm medium-fast

Tests
Test Career:	1880-83		
Cap Number:	26		
Tests Played:	4		

Test Batting
Innings:	6	Runs:	6
Highest Score:	2*	Average:	1.50
No. 50s:	0	No. 100s:	0

Test Bowling & Fielding
Wickets:	16	Runs:	296
Best Bowling:	5/56	Average:	18.50
5 WI:	1	10 WM:	0
Catches:	4	Stumpings:	0

An opening bowler from Nottinghamshire, he was considered the fastest bowler in England in the 1870's. Morley starred with the ball in the first Test on English soil taking five wickets in australia's first innings and finishing with eight for the match. He was injured on the ship's journey to Australia in 1882/83 and sadly died in the summer of 1884.

MORRIS, Hugh
Born:	October 5, 1963
Batting:	Left handed
Bowling:	Right arm medium

Tests
Test Career:	1991		
Cap Number:	552		
Tests Played:	3		

Test Batting
Innings:	6	Runs:	115
Highest Score:	44	Average:	19.16
No. 50s:	0	No. 100s:	0

Test Bowling & Fielding
Wickets:	0	Runs:	0
Best Bowling:		Average:	0.00
5 WI:	0	10 WM:	0
Catches:	3	Stumpings:	0

A fine captain for Glamorgan his excellent leadership was put to good use by the English selectors who put him in charge of a number of England A sides in the 90's. He played all of his three Tests in 1991.

MORRIS, John Edward
Born:	April 1, 1964
Batting:	Right handed
Bowling:	Right arm medium

Tests
Test Career:	1990		
Cap Number:	545		
Tests Played:	3		

Test Batting
Innings:	5	Runs:	71
Highest Score:	32	Average:	23.66
No. 50s:	0	No. 100s:	0

Test Bowling & Fielding
Wickets:	0	Runs:	0
Best Bowling:		Average:	0.00
5 WI:	0	10 WM:	0
Catches:	3	Stumpings:	0

One Day Internationals
ODI Career:	1990-91		
ODIs Played:	8		

ODI Batting
Innings:	8	Runs:	167
Highest Score:	63*	Average:	23.85
No. 50s:	1	No. 100s:	0

ODI Bowling & Fielding
Wickets:	0	Runs:	0
Best Bowling:		Average:	0.00
5 WM:	0	Catches:	2
Stumpings:	0		

The Derbyshire batsman was given three Tests against the touring Indians in 1990 but with a top score of only 32 was quickly sent back to county ranks.

MORTIMORE, John Brian
Born:	May 14, 1933
Batting:	Right handed
Bowling:	Right arm off-break

Tests
Test Career:	1959-64		
Cap Number:	392		
Tests Played:	9		

Test Batting
Innings:	12	Runs:	243
Highest Score:	73*	Average:	24.30
No. 50s:	1	No. 100s:	0

Test Bowling & Fielding
Wickets:	13	Runs:	733
Best Bowling:	3/36	Average:	56.38
5 WI:	0	10 WM:	0
Catches:	3	Stumpings:	0

An all-rounder from Gloucestershire with a fine record at county level, he was given a number of chances in the Test side. His 44 not out on debut against Australia in 1958/59 and a smart unbeaten 73 against India at Chennai in 1963/64 were his two best efforts at Test level.

MOSS, Alan Edward
Born:	November 14, 1930
Batting:	Right handed
Bowling:	Right arm medium-fast

Tests
Test Career:	1954-60		
Cap Number:	371		
Tests Played:	9		

Test Batting
Innings:	7	Runs:	61
Highest Score:	26	Average:	10.16
No. 50s:	0	No. 100s:	0

Test Bowling & Fielding
Wickets:	21	Runs:	626
Best Bowling:	4/35	Average:	29.80
5 WI:	0	10 WM:	0
Catches:	1	Stumpings:	0

A right arm medium pace bowler from Middlesex who was in and out of the Test team over a six year period.

MOXON, Martyn Douglas
Born:	May 4, 1960
Batting:	Right handed
Bowling:	Right arm medium

Tests
Test Career:	1986-89
Cap Number:	520
Tests Played:	10

Test Batting				
Innings:	17	Runs:	455	
Highest Score:	99	Average:	28.43	
No. 50s:	3	No. 100s:	0	

Test Bowling & Fielding
Wickets:	0	Runs:	30
Best Bowling:		Average:	0.00
5 WI:	0	10 WM:	0
Catches:	10	Stumpings:	0

One Day Internationals
ODI Career: 1985-88
ODIs Played: 8

ODI Batting
Innings:	8	Runs:	174
Highest Score:	70	Average:	21.75
No. 50s:	1	No. 100s:	0

ODI Bowling & Fielding
Wickets:	0	Runs:	0
Best Bowling:		Average:	0.00
5 WM:	0	Catches:	15
Stumpings:	0		

An opening batsman from Yorkshire, he went close to scoring a Test hundred with 99 against New Zealand in 1988.

MULLALLY, Alan David
Born: July 12, 1969
Batting: Right handed
Bowling: Left arm medium-fast

Tests
Test Career: 1996-2001
Cap Number: 578
Tests Played: 19

Test Batting
Innings:	27	Runs:	127
Highest Score:	24	Average:	5.52
No. 50s:	0	No. 100s:	0

Test Bowling & Fielding
Wickets:	58	Runs:	1,812
Best Bowling:	5/105	Average:	31.24
5 WI:	1	10 WM:	0
Catches:	6	Stumpings:	0

One Day Internationals
ODI Career: 1996-2001
ODIs Played: 50

ODI Batting
Innings:	25	Runs:	86
Highest Score:	20	Average:	5.73
No. 50s:	0	No. 100s:	0

ODI Bowling & Fielding
Wickets:	63	Runs:	1,728
Best Bowling:	4/18	Average:	27.42
5 WM:	0	Catches:	8
Stumpings:	0		

A towering left arm speedster who was born in England but moved with his family to Australia at a young age. After a tussle for his services England won out and selected him in his first against India in 1996 and whilst he gave good service in 19 Tests lacked the penetration to be an effective strike bowler. Apart for a 'five for' against Australia in the first innings of the 1998/99 Ashes series he never took more than three wickets in a Test innings.

MUNTON, Timothy Alan
Born: July 30, 1965
Batting: Right handed
Bowling: Right arm medium-fast

Tests
Test Career: 1992
Cap Number: 555
Tests Played: 2

Test Batting
Innings:	2	Runs:	25
Highest Score:	25*	Average:	25.00
No. 50s:	0	No. 100s:	0

Test Bowling & Fielding
Wickets:	4	Runs:	200
Best Bowling:	2/22	Average:	50.00
5 WI:	0	10 WM:	0
Catches:	0	Stumpings:	0

The tall paceman from Warwickshire played in two Tests against Pakistan on their 1992 tour of England.

MURDOCH, William Lloyd (Billy)
Born: October 18, 1854
Batting: Right handed
         Wicket Keeper

Tests
Test Career: 1877-1892
Cap Number: 79
Tests Played: 19

Test Batting
Innings:	34	Runs:	908
Highest Score:	211	Average:	31.31
No. 50s:	1	No. 100s:	2

Test Bowling & Fielding
Wickets:	0	Runs:	0
Best Bowling:		Average:	0.00
5 WI:	0	10 WM:	0
Catches:	14	Stumpings:	1

One of the few cricketers to play for two nations, Billy Murdoch was a giant of the sport, considered by no less a judge than WG Grace to be the Australia's finest batsman of the 19th century. In an extraordinary career spanning two nations and two decades Murdoch played Test cricket for Australia and England and represented New South Wales and Sussex. Originally selected in the Test side as a wicket keeper he soon established himself as middle order batsman with a penchant for scoring large totals. At the Oval in 1880 he plundered the English attack to the tune of 153 runs and four years later, when captaining the Australians at the age of 29, he became the first Test cricketer to score a double century. His 211 at the Oval was part of Australia's total of 551 and stood as the highest score in Test cricket for just under twenty years. Stocky and compact, Billy Murdoch was described at the time as a peerless batsman who favoured stroke play along the ground rather than chancing his arm with lofted hitting. Following the 1884 series in England, Murdoch married and played little cricket for five years. He did play in the Australian side that toured England in 1890 but did not to return home with the team, rather choosing to take the position of captain at county team Sussex. He would never play for Australia again but Murdoch did appear in one more Test match, representing England against South Africa at Cape Town in 1892. His single Test for England yielded only 12 runs but an overall average of over in 30 Test cricket supports the notion that at the time there were few if any better batsmen in the game. Billy Murdoch passed away at the age of 55 whilst watching the Australian play South Africa in a Test Match at the MCG.

MURRAY, John Thomas
Born: April 1, 1935
Batting: Right handed
Bowling: Right arm medium
Wicket Keeper

Tests
Test Career: 1961-67
Cap Number: 402
Tests Played: 21

Test Batting
Innings: 28 Runs: 506
Highest Score: 112 Average: 22.00
No. 50s: 2 No. 100s: 1

Test Bowling & Fielding
Wickets: 0 Runs: 0
Best Bowling: Average: 0.00
5 WI: 0 10 WM: 0
Catches: 52 Stumpings: 3

One of the finest glovemen to play for England he was renowned for his neat work off the spinners. Murray was also a sturdy lower order batsman who scored a single century for England against the West Indies in 1966.

NEWHAM, William
Born: December 12, 1860
Batting: Right handed

Tests
Test Career: 1888
Cap Number: 55
Tests Played: 1

Test Batting
Innings: 2 Runs: 26
Highest Score: 17 Average: 13.00
No. 50s: 0 No. 100s: 0

Test Bowling & Fielding
Wickets: 0 Runs: 0
Best Bowling: Average: 0.00
5 WI: 0 10 WM: 0
Catches: 0 Stumpings: 0

An accomplished batsman from Sussex who scored over 14,000 first class runs but could manage only the one Test for his country against Australia at the SCG in 1888.

NEWPORT, Philip John
Born: October 11, 1962
Batting: Right handed
Bowling: Right arm medium-fast

Tests
Test Career: 1988-91
Cap Number: 535
Tests Played: 3

Test Batting
Innings: 5 Runs: 110
Highest Score: 40* Average: 27.50
No. 50s: 0 No. 100s: 0

Test Bowling & Fielding
Wickets: 10 Runs: 417
Best Bowling: 4/87 Average: 41.70
5 WI: 0 10 WM: 0
Catches: 1 Stumpings: 0

An upright medium pacer who was flown to Australia for a single Test in 1990/981 as a replacement for the injured Angus Fraser. In all he played three Tests with a match return of seven wickets on debut against Sri Lanka in 1988 clearly the standout.

NICHOLS, Morris Stanley
Born: October 6, 1900
Batting: Left handed
Bowling: Right arm fast

Tests
Test Career: 1930-39
Cap Number: 249
Tests Played: 14

Test Batting
Innings: 19 Runs: 355
Highest Score: 78* Average: 29.58
No. 50s: 2 No. 100s: 0

Test Bowling & Fielding
Wickets: 41 Runs: 1,152
Best Bowling: 6/35 Average: 28.09
5 WI: 2 10 WM: 0
Catches: 11 Stumpings: 0

An opening bowler and middle order batsman from Essex, he was a dominant force in county cricket during the 1930's. Nichols was the first English cricketer to have played against five Test nations when he lined up against the touring South Africans in 1935.

O'BRIEN, Timothy Carew
Born: November 5, 1861
Batting: Right handed

Tests
Test Career: 1884-96
Cap Number: 44
Tests Played: 5

Test Batting
Innings: 8 Runs: 59
Highest Score: 20 Average: 7.37
No. 50s: 0 No. 100s: 0

Test Bowling & Fielding
Wickets: 0 Runs: 0
Best Bowling: Average: 0.00
5 WI: 0 10 WM: 0
Catches: 4 Stumpings: 0

A belligerent batsman whose attacking attitude brought him undone on many occasions. Born in Ireland, his five Test career was spread out over a twelve year period. O'Brien caught the eye with a

92 for Oxford against the visiting Australians in 1884 and he was selected in the English Test side under Lord Harris, but failed to reproduce the dashing form that had won him his praise only a few weeks earlier. Statistics suggest he struggled at the highest level with a Test average of only 7.37.

O'CONNOR, Jack
Born: November 6, 1897
Batting: Right handed

Tests
Test Career:	1929-30		
Cap Number:	240		
Tests Played:	4		

Test Batting
Innings:	7	Runs:	153
Highest Score:	51	Average:	21.85
No. 50s:	1	No. 100s:	0

Test Bowling & Fielding
Wickets:	1	Runs:	72
Best Bowling:	1/31	Average:	72.00
5 WI:	0	10 WM:	0
Catches:	2	Stumpings:	0

He played in four Tests in 1929 and 1930, one at home against South Africa and three against the West Indies in the Caribbean. Those three Tests were originally classified as first class games for the M.C.C but were later recognised as official Test matches.

OAKMAN, Alan Stanley Myles
Born: April 20, 1930
Batting: Right handed
Bowling: Right arm off-break

Tests
Test Career:	1956		
Cap Number:	383		
Tests Played:	2		

Test Batting
Innings:	2	Runs:	14
Highest Score:	10	Average:	7.00
No. 50s:	0	No. 100s:	0

Test Bowling & Fielding
Wickets:	0	Runs:	21
Best Bowling:		Average:	0.00
5 WI:	0	10 WM:	0
Catches:	7	Stumpings:	0

A beanpole all-rounder from Sussex who did little with bat or ball in his only two Tests. The short leg did however take five catches at Old Trafford in 1956 to play his part in Jim Laker's record breaking match figures of 19/90.

OLD, Christopher Middleton
Born: December 22, 1948
Batting: Left handed
Bowling: Right arm medium-fast

Tests
Test Career:	1973-81		
Cap Number:	455		
Tests Played:	46		

Test Batting
Innings:	66	Runs:	845
Highest Score:	65	Average:	14.82
No. 50s:	2	No. 100s:	0

Test Bowling & Fielding
Wickets:	143	Runs:	4,020
Best Bowling:	4/50	Average:	28.11
5 WI:	4	10 WM:	0
Catches:	22	Stumpings:	0

One Day Internationals
ODI Career:	1973-81		
ODIs Played:	32		

ODI Batting
Innings:	25	Runs:	338
Highest Score:	51*	Average:	18.77
No. 50s:	1	No. 100s:	0

ODI Bowling & Fielding
Wickets:	45	Runs:	999
Best Bowling:	4/8	Average:	22.20
5 WM:	0	Catches:	8
Stumpings:	0		

Nicknamed 'Chilly' because of his name, C. Old was one of a group of fine English swing bowlers in the 70's. Along with Geoff Arnold and Mike Hendricks he offered able support to England's main act during that period, Bob Willis, and in 46 Tests took 143 wickets. Like Willis he never took ten wickets in a Test match but went close with 9/88 against India at Lord's in 1974 and 8/88 against Pakistan at Edgbaston in 1978. His Test career came to an end in 1981 when he joined a rebel tour to South Africa and was subsequently suspended for three years.

OLDFIELD, Norman
Born: May 5, 1911
Batting: Right handed

Tests
Test Career:	1939		
Cap Number:	310		
Tests Played:	1		

Test Batting
Innings:	2	Runs:	99
Highest Score:	80	Average:	49.50
No. 50s:	1	No. 100s:	0

Test Bowling & Fielding
Wickets:	0	Runs:	0
Best Bowling:		Average:	0.00
5 WI:	0	10 WM:	0
Catches:	0	Stumpings:	0

A batsman relies on timing to succeed and in the case of Buddy Oldfield his couldn't have been worse. He was selected to play in the final Test against the touring West Indians in 1939 and stood out with an 80 in his first at bat as part of a stand of 131 with the great Walter Hammond. Unfortunately that was to be England's last Test prior to the outbreak of World War II and the Lancashire batsman would never play for his country again.

ORMOND, James
Born: August 20, 1977
Batting: Right handed
Bowling: Right arm medium-fast

Tests
Test Career:	2001		
Cap Number:	607		
Tests Played:	2		

Test Batting
Innings:	4	Runs:	38
Highest Score:	18	Average:	12.66
No. 50s:	0	No. 100s:	0

Test Bowling & Fielding
Wickets:	2	Runs:	185
Best Bowling:	1/70	Average:	92.50
5 WI:	0	10 WM:	0
Catches:	0	Stumpings:	0

A tall swing bowler from Surrey who struggled in his only two Tests taking just two wickets at 92.50 runs apiece.

PADGETT, Douglas Ernest Vernon
Born: July 20, 1934
Batting: Right handed
Bowling: Right arm medium

Tests
Test Career:	1960		
Cap Number:	401		
Tests Played:	2		

Test Batting
Innings:	4	Runs:	51
Highest Score:	31	Average:	12.75
No. 50s:	0	No. 100s:	0

Test Bowling & Fielding
Wickets:	0	Runs:	8
Best Bowling:		Average:	0.00
5 WI:	0	10 WM:	0
Catches:	0	Stumpings:	0

A batsman from Yorkshire who played two Tests on home soil against South Africa in 1960.

PAINE, George Alfred Edward
Born: June 11, 1908
Batting: Right handed
Bowling: Left arm off-break

Tests
Test Career:	1935		
Cap Number:	280		
Tests Played:	4		

Test Batting
Innings:	7	Runs:	97
Highest Score:	49	Average:	16.16
No. 50s:	0	No. 100s:	0

Test Bowling & Fielding
Wickets:	17	Runs:	467
Best Bowling:	5/168	Average:	27.47
5 WI:	1	10 WM:	0
Catches:	5	Stumpings:	0

A left arm off spinner who played all of his four Tests in the Caribbean in 1935.

PALAIRET, Lionel Charles Hamilton
Born: May 27, 1870
Batting: Right handed
Bowling: Right arm medium

Tests
Test Career:	1902		
Cap Number:	134		
Tests Played:	2		

Test Batting
Innings:	4	Runs:	49
Highest Score:	20	Average:	12.25
No. 50s:	0	No. 100s:	0

Test Bowling & Fielding
Wickets:	0	Runs:	0
Best Bowling:		Average:	0.00
5 WI:	0	10 WM:	0
Catches:	2	Stumpings:	0

He was a versatile cricketer for Somerset where he opened the batting, bowled leg-spin and occasionally filled in as wicketkeeper. He played two Test on home soil against the Australians in 1902.

PALMER, Charles Henry
Born: May 15, 1919
Batting: Right handed
Bowling: Right arm off-break

Tests
Test Career:	1954		
Cap Number:	342		
Tests Played:	1		

Test Batting
Innings:	2	Runs:	22
Highest Score:	22	Average:	11.00
No. 50s:	0	No. 100s:	0

Test Bowling & Fielding
Wickets:	0	Runs:	15
Best Bowling:		Average:	0.00
5 WI:	0	10 WM:	0
Catches:	0	Stumpings:	0

His only Test was against the West Indies at Bridgetown in 1954.

PALMER, Kenneth Ernest
Born: April 22, 1937
Batting: Right handed
Bowling: Right arm medium-fast

Tests
Test Career:	1965		
Cap Number:	427		
Tests Played:	1		

Test Batting
Innings:	1	Runs:	10
Highest Score:	10	Average:	10.00
No. 50s:	0	No. 100s:	0

Test Bowling & Fielding
Wickets:	1	Runs:	189
Best Bowling:	1/113	Average:	189.00
5 WI:	0	10 WM:	0
Catches:	0	Stumpings:	0

His only Test as a player was in Durban in 1965, but he did appear in 23 more as an umpire between 1977 and 2001.

PANESAR, Mudhsuden Singh (Monty)
Born: April 25, 1982
Batting: Left handed
Bowling: Left arm off-break

Tests
Test Career:	2006-
Cap Number:	631
Tests Played:	9

Test Batting
Innings:	12	Runs:	51
Highest Score:	26	Average:	12.75
No. 50s:	0	No. 100s:	0

Test Bowling & Fielding
Wickets:	31	Runs:	934
Best Bowling:	5/72	Average:	30.12
5 WI:	2	10 WM:	0
Catches:	2	Stumpings:	0

Even though his international career isn't yet 12 months old Monty Panesar gives every indication that he will be a part of the Test side for many years to come. England have been searching for a golden-armed spinner ever since Derek Underwood retired, and after what seems like hundreds of auditions, they may have finally found their man. Like Underwood he is a left arm offie, but the similarity ends there with Panesar flighting the ball far more than his predecessor. He had plenty of support in his Test debut at Nagpur with a number of family members who still live in India attending the game, and whilst he was steady it appeared he was still finding his feet. With a tour under his belt it was a far more relaxed Panesar who played six home Tests in 2006, and he prospered, taking ten wickets against Sri Lanka and 16 against Pakistan. He's a genuine wicket-taker with plenty of tricks, but the likeable Monty faces his sternest Test on his first tour to Australia where the hard bouncy wickets have been a notorious graveyard for off spinners.

PARFITT, Peter Howard

Born:	December 8, 1936
Batting:	Left handed
Bowling:	Right arm off-break

Tests
Test Career:	1962-72
Cap Number:	410
Tests Played:	37

Test Batting
Innings:	52	Runs:	1,882
Highest Score:	131*	Average:	40.91
No. 50s:	6	No. 100s:	7

Test Bowling & Fielding
Wickets:	12	Runs:	574
Best Bowling:	2/5	Average:	47.83
5 WI:	0	10 WM:	0
Catches:	42	Stumpings:	0

Peter Parfitt's Pakistani purple patch may read like a schoolyard tongue twister but it aptly describes his run of form in 1962. Playing against Pakistan both home and away he scored four centuries in five Tests to seemingly secure a spot at the top of the English batting order. However poor form at home against Australia in 1964, and the emergence of Geoff Boycott meant that he was constantly in and out of the Test side until his last Test which was against Australia in 1972.

PARKER, Charles Warrington Leonard

Born:	October 14, 1882
Batting:	Right handed
Bowling:	Left arm off-break

Tests
Test Career:	1921
Cap Number:	204
Tests Played:	1

Test Batting
Innings:	1	Runs:	3
Highest Score:	3*	Average:	0.00
No. 50s:	0	No. 100s:	0

Test Bowling & Fielding
Wickets:	2	Runs:	32
Best Bowling:	2/32	Average:	16.00
5 WI:	0	10 WM:	0
Catches:	0	Stumpings:	0

He played only the one Test for his country, against Australia at Manchester in 1921. It seems a skinny return for a player who took over 3,000 first class wickets in a marathon career that lasted over 30 years.

PARKER, Paul William Giles

Born:	January 15, 1956
Batting:	Right handed

Tests
Test Career:	1981
Cap Number:	492
Tests Played:	1

Test Batting
Innings:	2	Runs:	13
Highest Score:	13	Average:	6.50
No. 50s:	0	No. 100s:	0

Test Bowling & Fielding
Wickets:	0	Runs:	0
Best Bowling:		Average:	0.00
5 WI:	0	10 WM:	0
Catches:	0	Stumpings:	0

The Rhodesian born Parker played just a single Test, against Australia at The Oval in 1981.

PARKHOUSE, William Gilbert Anthony

Born:	October 12, 1925
Batting:	Right handed
Bowling:	Right arm medium

Tests
Test Career:	1950-59
Cap Number:	348
Tests Played:	7

Test Batting
Innings:	13	Runs:	373
Highest Score:	78	Average:	28.69
No. 50s:	2	No. 100s:	0

Test Bowling & Fielding
Wickets:	0	Runs:	0
Best Bowling:		Average:	0.00
5 WI:	0	10 WM:	0
Catches:	3	Stumpings:	0

A well credentialed Welsh cricketer, his form with Glamorgan earnt him a Test spot against the West Indies in 1950. Whilst he never reached the heights for England that he did for his county he did score an elegant 78 against India at Leeds in 1959 when opening the batting.

PARKIN, Cecil Harry (Ciss)

Born: February 18, 1886
Batting: Right handed

Tests

Test Career: 1920-24
Cap Number: 182
Tests Played: 10

Test Batting

Innings:	16	Runs:	160
Highest Score:	36	Average:	12.30
No. 50s:	0	No. 100s:	0

Test Bowling & Fielding

Wickets:	32	Runs:	1,128
Best Bowling:	5/38	Average:	35.25
5 WI:	2	10 WM:	0
Catches:	3	Stumpings:	0

When Test cricket resumed after the First World War, England was on the receiving end of two heavy series defeats at the hands of the Australians. The only bowler who presented any danger to the Aussies in those 10 Tests was 'Ciss' Parkin from Yorkshire. The off-spinner was a renowned joker on and off the field, but he was also a canny spinner with a well disguised slower and quicker ball. In nine Tests against the 'old enemy' he captured 32 wickets, leading the aggregates for both the 1920/21 series in Australia and the return series on home soil in 1921.

PARKS, James Horace

Born: May 12, 1903
Batting: Right handed

Tests

Test Career: 1937
Cap Number: 295
Tests Played: 1

Test Batting

Innings:	2	Runs:	29
Highest Score:	22	Average:	14.50
No. 50s:	0	No. 100s:	0

Test Bowling & Fielding

Wickets:	3	Runs:	36
Best Bowling:	2/26	Average:	12.00
5 WI:	0	10 WM:	0
Catches:	0	Stumpings:	0

An all-rounder from Sussex who enjoyed an extraordinary year in 1937 scoring 3,003 runs and taking 101 wickets. Whilst his efforts were more a reflection on the amount of cricket being played at the time than anything else, he was rewarded with a Test against New Zealand during June of that year.

PARKS, James Michael

Born: October 21, 1931
Batting: Right handed
Bowling: Right arm leg-break
Wicket Keeper

Tests

Test Career: 1954-68
Cap Number: 375
Tests Played: 46

Test Batting

Innings:	68	Runs:	1,962
Highest Score:	108*	Average:	32.16
No. 50s:	9	No. 100s:	2

Test Bowling & Fielding

Wickets:	1	Runs:	51
Best Bowling:	1/43	Average:	51.00
5 WI:	0	10 WM:	0
Catches:	103	Stumpings:	11

The son of James Parks who played for England in the 30's, he started his English career as a batsman in 1954, but it was not until he replaced John Murray as keeper in 1960 that he had a regular spot. Whilst his glovework may have not been as good as the very best, his batting made him an invaluable part of the time for much of the 60's. He scored two Test centuries, the highest of which was an unbeaten 108 against South Africa at Durban in 1964.

PATAUDI SNR (NAWAB OF), Iftikhar Ali Khan

Born: March 16, 1910
Batting: Right handed

Tests

Test Career: 1932-46
Cap Number: 265
Tests Played: 6

Test Batting

Innings:	10	Runs:	199
Highest Score:	102	Average:	19.89
No. 50s:	0	No. 100s:	1

Test Bowling & Fielding

Wickets:	0	Runs:	0
Best Bowling:		Average:	0.00
5 WI:	0	10 WM:	0
Catches:	0	Stumpings:	0

The only cricketer to have played Test cricket for both England and India. Pataudi scored a hundred on debut, for England, against Australia at the SCG, but was subsequently dropped for the next Test following a difference in opinion with Douglas Jardine. Later captained India but his best cricket was well and truly behind him. His son, Mansur Ali Khan Pataudi, captained India in 40 Tests during the 1960's and early 70's.

PATEL, Minal Mahesh

Born: July 7, 1970
Batting: Right handed
Bowling: Left arm off-break

Tests

Test Career:	1996		
Cap Number:	579		
Tests Played:	2		

Test Batting

Innings:	2	Runs:	45
Highest Score:	27	Average:	22.50
No. 50s:	0	No. 100s:	0

Test Bowling & Fielding

Wickets:	1	Runs:	180
Best Bowling:	1/101	Average:	180.00
5 WI:	0	10 WM:	0
Catches:	2	Stumpings:	0

A left arm off spinner who played two Tests against the touring Indians in 1996.

PAYNTER, Edward

Born:	November 5, 1901
Batting:	Left handed
Bowling:	Right arm medium

Tests

Test Career:	1931-39		
Cap Number:	263		
Tests Played:	20		

Test Batting

Innings:	31	Runs:	1,540
Highest Score:	243	Average:	59.23
No. 50s:	7	No. 100s:	4

Test Bowling & Fielding

Wickets:	0	Runs:	0
Best Bowling:		Average:	0.00
5 WI:	0	10 WM:	0
Catches:	7	Stumpings:	0

A good bar bet would be to ask which Englishman holds the record for the best batting average in Tests against Australia. Only the keenest of cricket buffs would know the answer is Eddie Paynter with 84.42 in seven outings. The Lancs middle order batsman made his debut for England just three months shy of his 30th birthday when picked to play against the visiting New Zealanders in 1931. He came to the fore during the 'bodyline' series in 1932/33 scoring a gritty 77 in the third Test and a brave 83 in the fourth, when he left his hospital bed to come to his side's rescue. Paynter was suffering from a severe bout of tonsillitis and wouldn't have batted had England fared well, but at 6/216 the call went out for the left hander. He not only batted for four hours, he then took the field when England was finally dismissed. In 1938 and 1939 he scored two Test double centuries. The first was an unbeaten 216 against the Australian leg spinning duo of Fleetwood-Smith and O'Reilly at Trent Bridge and the second a Test high of 243 against South Africa in Durban. The slightly built Paynter played only 20 Tests but with an overall average of 59.23 he remains one of the finest batsmen to ever play for England.

PEATE, Edmund

Born:	March 2, 1855
Batting:	Left handed
Bowling:	Left arm leg-break

Tests

Test Career:	1881-86		
Cap Number:	32		
Tests Played:	9		

Test Batting

Innings:	14	Runs:	70
Highest Score:	13	Average:	11.66
No. 50s:	0	No. 100s:	0

Test Bowling & Fielding

Wickets:	31	Runs:	683
Best Bowling:	6/85	Average:	22.03
5 WI:	2	10 WM:	0
Catches:	2	Stumpings:	0

Peate was a leg spinner from Yorkshire who enjoyed great success for England taking four or more wickets in an innings on four occasions. His finest hour came at The Oval in 1881/82 where he took eight wickets for the Test at a cost of only 58 runs. A colourful character, he played club cricket in Leeds till his passing at the age of 45.

PEEBLES, Ian Alexander Ross

Born:	January 20, 1908
Batting:	Right handed
Bowling:	Right arm leg-break

Tests

Test Career:	1927-31		
Cap Number:	229		
Tests Played:	13		

Test Batting

Innings:	17	Runs:	98
Highest Score:	26	Average:	10.88
No. 50s:	0	No. 100s:	0

Test Bowling & Fielding

Wickets:	45	Runs:	1,391
Best Bowling:	6/63	Average:	30.91
5 WI:	3	10 WM:	0
Catches:	5	Stumpings:	0

The Scottish born leg-spinner played in 13 Tests for England but is best remembered for dismissing Donald Bradman for 14 at Old Trafford in 1930. That failure by the Don was sandwiched between innings of 334 and 232, and at least for one Test England could claim to have a bowler that had the better of the great Australian.

PEEL, Robert

Born:	February 12, 1857
Batting:	Left handed
Bowling:	Left arm off-break

Tests

Test Career:	1884-96		
Cap Number:	50		
Tests Played:	20		

Test Batting

Innings:	33	Runs:	427
Highest Score:	83	Average:	14.72
No. 50s:	3	No. 100s:	0

Test Bowling & Fielding

Wickets:	101	Runs:	1,715
Best Bowling:	7/31	Average:	16.98
5 WI:	5	10 WM:	1
Catches:	17	Stumpings:	0

A stout Yorkshireman, he was an all-rounder of note who played all of his twenty Tests against Australia. The leftie bowled slow off spin which he used to great effect when combining with fellow northerner Johnny Briggs at the SCG in 1894 He took six second innings wickets, bowling his side to an improbable victory after Australia had scored 568 in their first at bat. His best return in a Test match came about some six years earlier when he took 11 wickets against the Australians playing at Old Trafford. Despite being a slow bowler, Peel was held in such high regard that he regularly opened the attack for England. He was also a fine batsman with a Test high score of 83 at The Adelaide Oval in 1892.

PENN, Frank

Born: March 7, 1851
Batting: Right handed
Bowling: Right arm slow

Tests

Test Career: 1880
Cap Number: 27
Tests Played: 1

Test Batting

Innings:	2	Runs:	50
Highest Score:	27*	Average:	50.00
No. 50s:	0	No. 100s:	0

Test Bowling & Fielding

Wickets:	0	Runs:	2
Best Bowling:		Average:	0.00
5 WI:	0	10 WM:	0
Catches:	0	Stumpings:	0

A fine top order batsman from Kent who played in the first Test on English soil in 1880.

PERKS, Reginald Thomas David

Born: October 4, 1911
Batting: Right handed
Bowling: Right arm medium-fast

Tests

Test Career: 1939
Cap Number: 308
Tests Played: 2

Test Batting

Innings:	2	Runs:	3
Highest Score:	2*	Average:	0.00
No. 50s:	0	No. 100s:	0

Test Bowling & Fielding

Wickets:	11	Runs:	355
Best Bowling:	5/100	Average:	32.27
5 WI:	2	10 WM:	0
Catches:	1	Stumpings:	0

A right arm paceman, he played in the timeless Test against South Africa in 1939 that spanned an incredible 12 days.

PHILIPSON, Hylton

Born: June 8, 1866
Batting: Right handed
 Wicket Keeper

Tests

Test Career: 1892-95
Cap Number: 81
Tests Played: 5

Test Batting

Innings:	8	Runs:	63
Highest Score:	30	Average:	9.00
No. 50s:	0	No. 100s:	0

Test Bowling & Fielding

Wickets:	0	Runs:	0
Best Bowling:		Average:	0.00
5 WI:	0	10 WM:	0
Catches:	8	Stumpings:	3

Prior to the turn of the century England employed a number of different wicketkeepers to stand behind the stumps in its Test sides. One of those keepers was 'Punch' Philipson from Middlesex who twice toured Australia and performed admirably with the gloves on both occasions.

PIETERSEN, Kevin Peter

Born: June 27, 1980
Batting: Right handed
Bowling: Right arm off-break

Tests

Test Career: 2005-
Cap Number: 626
Tests Played: 17

Test Batting

Innings:	32	Runs:	1,501
Highest Score:	158	Average:	48.41
No. 50s:	5	No. 100s:	5

Test Bowling & Fielding

Wickets:	1	Runs:	67
Best Bowling:	1/11	Average:	67.00
5 WI:	0	10 WM:	0
Catches:	11	Stumpings:	0

One Day Internationals

ODI Career: 2004-
ODIs Played: 33

ODI Batting

Innings:	27	Runs:	1,268
Highest Score:	116	Average:	60.38
No. 50s:	9	No. 100s:	3

ODI Bowling & Fielding

Wickets:	1	Runs:	52
Best Bowling:	1/4	Average:	52.00
5 WM:	0	Catches:	18
Stumpings:	0		

In sporting terms it seems as though Kevin Pietersen was put on this planet for just one reason, to grab games of cricket by the scruff of the neck. A hard hitter who is comfortable clearing the ropes on either the back or front foot, he's no flat track bully, rather preferring to belt the opposition's best bowlers out of the attack. For someone who hits the ball with such power he's surprisingly sound in defense, with the only thing streaky about him the blonde tips that run through his hair. KP loves a challenge and he faced the biggest of all when he lined up against the Proteas in 2005 for seven one day internationals. South African born and raised, he responded to a hostile home crowd by smashing hundreds at Blomfontein, East London and Centurion. One day innings are often taken with a grain of salt by selectors, but Pietersen's performance in South Africa convinced everybody that he was worthy of a spot in the English top order. He made his Test debut during the riveting 2005 Ashes contest, and in a series where every run was valuable, he scored 473 runs at an average of 52.55 With England needing a draw to win the Ashes he hit an amazing 158 on the final day of the series. Rather than bat for time he chose to hit the Australians out of the game and his blazing knock included seven 6's. Since then it has been more of the same for Pietersen with two hundreds against both Sri Lanka and Pakistan. When England head to Australia to defend the Ashes at the end of 2006 fans can Kevin Pietersen to once again lead the charge.

PIGOTT, Anthony Charles Shackleton

Born: June 4, 1958
Batting: Right handed
Bowling: Right arm medium-fast

Tests

Test Career: 1984
Cap Number: 504
Tests Played: 1

Test Batting
Innings:	2	Runs:	12
Highest Score:	8*	Average:	12.00
No. 50s:	0	No. 100s:	0

Test Bowling & Fielding
Wickets:	2	Runs:	75
Best Bowling:	2/75	Average:	37.50
5 WI:	0	10 WM:	0
Catches:	0	Stumpings:	0

The medium pacer was playing for Wellington in New Zealand when the touring English sent an SOS for another bowler. He heeded the call and took two wickets in his only Test.

PILLING, Richard

Born: August 11, 1855
Batting: Right handed
Wicket Keeper

Tests

Test Career: 1882-88
Cap Number: 33
Tests Played: 8

Test Batting
Innings:	13	Runs:	91
Highest Score:	23	Average:	7.58
No. 50s:	0	No. 100s:	0

Test Bowling & Fielding
Wickets:	0	Runs:	0
Best Bowling:		Average:	0.00
5 WI:	0	10 WM:	0
Catches:	10	Stumpings:	4

A highly regarded wicketkeeper from Lancashire who would have played more Tests if not for failing health. he passed away at the age of 36.

PLACE, Winston

Born: December 7, 1914
Batting: Right handed

Tests

Test Career: 1948
Cap Number: 329
Tests Played: 3

Test Batting
Innings:	6	Runs:	144
Highest Score:	107	Average:	28.80
No. 50s:	0	No. 100s:	1

Test Bowling & Fielding
Wickets:	0	Runs:	0
Best Bowling:		Average:	0.00
5 WI:	0	10 WM:	0
Catches:	0	Stumpings:	0

He toured the West Indies in 1948 playing in three Tests. Place failed in five of his Test innings but in the other scored 107.

PLUNKETT, Liam Edward

Born: April 6, 1985
Batting: Right handed
Bowling: Right arm medium-fast

Tests

Test Career: 2005-
Cap Number: 628
Tests Played: 6

Test Batting
Innings:	9	Runs:	69
Highest Score:	28	Average:	8.62
No. 50s:	0	No. 100s:	0

Test Bowling & Fielding
Wickets:	16	Runs:	601
Best Bowling:	3/17	Average:	37.56
5 WI:	0	10 WM:	0
Catches:	2	Stumpings:	0

One Day Internationals

ODI Career: 2005-
ODIs Played: 16

ODI Batting
Innings:	15	Runs:	200
Highest Score:	56	Average:	20.00
No. 50s:	1	No. 100s:	0

ODI Bowling & Fielding
Wickets:	16	Runs:	727
Best Bowling:	3/51	Average:	45.43
5 WM:	0	Catches:	4
Stumpings:	0		

An emerging paceman from Durham who got his chance in recent times with injuries to a number of England's frontline bowlers. After struggling in the first Test against Pakistan at Lord's he was dropped the up and coming Sajid Mahmood.

POCOCK, Patrick Ian

Born: September 24, 1946
Batting: Right handed
Bowling: Right arm off-break

Tests
Test Career: 1968-85
Cap Number: 438
Tests Played: 25

Test Batting
Innings:	37	Runs:	206
Highest Score:	33	Average:	6.24
No. 50s:	0	No. 100s:	0

Test Bowling & Fielding
Wickets:	67	Runs:	2,976
Best Bowling:	6/79	Average:	44.41
5 WI:	3	10 WM:	0
Catches:	15	Stumpings:	0

One Day Internationals
ODI Career: 1985
ODIs Played: 1

ODI Batting
Innings:	1	Runs:	4
Highest Score:	4	Average:	4.00
No. 50s:	0	No. 100s:	0

ODI Bowling & Fielding
Wickets:	0	Runs:	20
Best Bowling:		Average:	0.00
5 WM:	0	Catches:	0
Stumpings:	0		

In and out of the Test side over a 17 year period, he was an off spinner with a nice languid action. Interestingly he played only one Test against Australia, but in that match at Old Trafford in 1968 returned his best Test innings figures of 6/79.

POLLARD, Richard

Born: June 19, 1912
Batting: Right handed
Bowling: Right arm medium-fast

Tests
Test Career: 1946-48
Cap Number: 314
Tests Played: 4

Test Batting
Innings:	3	Runs:	13
Highest Score:	10*	Average:	13.00
No. 50s:	0	No. 100s:	0

Test Bowling & Fielding
Wickets:	15	Runs:	378
Best Bowling:	5/24	Average:	25.20
5 WI:	1	10 WM:	0
Catches:	3	Stumpings:	0

A handy quick bowler from Lancashire, he made his debut against India at Old Trafford in 1946, taking 5/24 off 27 overs in the first innings.

POOLE, Cyril John

Born: March 13, 1921
Batting: Left handed
Bowling: Left arm medium
 Wicket Keeper

Tests
Test Career: 1952
Cap Number: 368
Tests Played: 3

Test Batting
Innings:	5	Runs:	161
Highest Score:	69*	Average:	40.25
No. 50s:	2	No. 100s:	0

Test Bowling & Fielding
Wickets:	0	Runs:	0
Best Bowling:		Average:	0.00
5 WI:	0	10 WM:	0
Catches:	1	Stumpings:	0

Selected as a batsman on the tour of India in 1951/52, the occasional keeper from Notts performed well averaging over 40 in the three Tests that he played.

POPE, George Henry

Born: January 27, 1911
Batting: Right handed
Bowling: Right arm medium-fast

Tests
Test Career: 1947
Cap Number: 320
Tests Played: 1

Test Batting
Innings:	1	Runs:	8
Highest Score:	8*	Average:	0.00
No. 50s:	0	No. 100s:	0

Test Bowling & Fielding
Wickets:	1	Runs:	85
Best Bowling:	1/49	Average:	85.00
5 WI:	0	10 WM:	0
Catches:	0	Stumpings:	0

The Debyshire all-rounder had a fine record in county cricket but was given only the one Test against South Africa at Lord's in 1947.

POUGHER, Arthur Dick

Born: April 19, 1865
Batting: Right handed
Bowling: Right arm medium-fast

Tests
Test Career: 1892
Cap Number: 80
Tests Played: 1

Test Batting
Innings:	1	Runs:	17
Highest Score:	17	Average:	17.00
No. 50s:	0	No. 100s:	0

Test Bowling & Fielding
Wickets:	3	Runs:	26
Best Bowling:	3/26	Average:	8.66
5 WI:	0	10 WM:	0
Catches:	2	Stumpings:	0

Dick Pougher was a fine bowler batsman from Leicestershire whose only appearance for England was as part of the side that toured South Africa in 1892. Whilst his Test record is only moderate, he had may fine spells for his county including a famous haul of 7/8 against Warwickshire in 1886.

PRICE, John Sidney Ernest
Born: July 22, 1937
Batting: Left handed
Bowling: Right arm medium-fast

Tests
Test Career: 1964-72
Cap Number: 421
Tests Played: 15

Test Batting
Innings:	15	Runs:	66
Highest Score:	32	Average:	7.33
No. 50s:	0	No. 100s:	0

Test Bowling & Fielding
Wickets:	40	Runs:	1,401
Best Bowling:	5/73	Average:	35.02
5 WI:	1	10 WM:	0
Catches:	7	Stumpings:	0

He was a powerful quick bowler from Middlesex who would have played more than 15 Tests if not for a constant stream of injuries. He toured South Africa in 1964/65 and would have thought that the final Test at Johannesburg would have been his last, but a recall against India and Pakistan in 1971 saw him back in the side and bowling well in his mid thirties.

PRICE, Wilfred Frederick Frank (Fred)
Born: April 25, 1902
Batting: Right handed
Wicket Keeper

Tests
Test Career: 1938
Cap Number: 303
Tests Played: 1

Test Batting
Innings:	2	Runs:	6
Highest Score:	6	Average:	3.00
No. 50s:	0	No. 100s:	0

Test Bowling & Fielding
Wickets:	0	Runs:	0
Best Bowling:		Average:	0.00
5 WI:	0	10 WM:	0
Catches:	2	Stumpings:	0

He was county wicketkeeper for over 20 years with Middlesex who played a single Test against Australia at Leeds in 1938. He also umpired eight Tests between 1964 and 1967.

PRIDEAUX, Roger Malcolm
Born: July 31, 1939
Batting: Right handed
Bowling: Right arm medium

Tests
Test Career: 1968-69
Cap Number: 440
Tests Played: 3

Test Batting
Innings:	6	Runs:	102
Highest Score:	64	Average:	20.40
No. 50s:	1	No. 100s:	0

Test Bowling & Fielding
Wickets:	0	Runs:	0
Best Bowling:		Average:	0.00
5 WI:	0	10 WM:	0
Catches:	0	Stumpings:	0

The Londoner played three Tests for England in 1968 and 1969 but apart from a fine 64 against the Australians at Headingly on debut showed little. He played Currie Cup in South Africa in the early 70's.

PRINGLE, Derek Raymond
Born: September 18, 1958
Batting: Right handed
Bowling: Right arm medium

Tests
Test Career: 1982-92
Cap Number: 495
Tests Played: 30

Test Batting
Innings:	50	Runs:	695
Highest Score:	63	Average:	15.10
No. 50s:	1	No. 100s:	0

Test Bowling & Fielding
Wickets:	70	Runs:	2,518
Best Bowling:	5/95	Average:	35.97
5 WI:	3	10 WM:	0
Catches:	10	Stumpings:	0

One Day Internationals
ODI Career: 1982-93
ODIs Played: 44

ODI Batting
Innings:	30	Runs:	425
Highest Score:	49*	Average:	23.61
No. 50s:	0	No. 100s:	0

ODI Bowling & Fielding
Wickets:	44	Runs:	1,677
Best Bowling:	4/42	Average:	38.11
5 WM:	0	Catches:	11
Stumpings:	0		

A tall, almost awkward speedster he gave England good service in 30 Tests during the 80's. Pringle had been born in Kenya and came under notice at Cambridge University as a batsman. It was as a bowler though that he made his way through the ranks, ultimately making his debut for England in 1982. He took four wickets in his first Test and captured five wickets in an innings in Tests on three occasions thereafter. The big lad was often the subject to heckling by opposition fans but he always took it in good spirits and ended up a crowd favourite.

PRIOR, Matthew
Born: February 26, 1982
Batting: Right handed
Wicket Keeper

One Day Internationals
ODI Career: 2004-06
ODIs Played: 12

ODI Batting
Innings:	12	Runs:	240
Highest Score:	45	Average:	20.00
No. 50s:	0	No. 100s:	0

ODI Bowling & Fielding
Wickets:	0	Runs:	0
Best Bowling:		Average:	0.00
5 WM:	0	Catches:	4
Stumpings:	1		

A South African born wicket-keeper, Matt Prior was selected on the 2004/05 tour of Zimbabwe where he made his ODI debut as an opener scoring 35 while regular keeper Geraint Jones donned the gloves. He has since played in 12 ODI's, where he has kept wickets in just two of them. He averages 20 with the bat and should continue to press for selection.

PULLAR, Geoffrey

Born:	August 1, 1935
Batting:	Left handed
Bowling:	Left arm leg-break

Tests

Test Career:	1959-63
Cap Number:	396
Tests Played:	28

Test Batting

Innings:	49	Runs:	1,974
Highest Score:	175	Average:	43.86
No. 50s:	12	No. 100s:	4

Test Bowling & Fielding

Wickets:	1	Runs:	37
Best Bowling:	1/1	Average:	37.00
5 WI:	0	10 WM:	0
Catches:	2	Stumpings:	0

A laconic character nicknamed 'Noddy', he was a tall and talented left hander from Lancashire. He made 75 on debut against India and continued his fine form in his second Test with a maiden century. He averaged over 40 in his 29 Tests but indifferent form against arch rivals Australia saw him play his last Test by January of 1963.

QUAIFE, William George

Born:	March 17, 1872
Batting:	Right handed
Bowling:	Right arm leg-break

Tests

Test Career:	1899-1902
Cap Number:	125
Tests Played:	7

Test Batting

Innings:	13	Runs:	228
Highest Score:	68	Average:	19.00
No. 50s:	1	No. 100s:	0

Test Bowling & Fielding

Wickets:	0	Runs:	6
Best Bowling:		Average:	0.00
5 WI:	0	10 WM:	0
Catches:	4	Stumpings:	0

The diminutive Quaife stood just over five foot tall yet scored over 36,000 first class runs in both England and South Africa. His forays into Test cricket were generally unsuccessful, though he did enjoy a good Test at the Adelaide Cricket Ground in the Australian summer of 1901/02 when he scored 68 and 44. He was also known as a brilliant cover fieldsman.

RADFORD, Neal Victor

Born:	June 7, 1957
Batting:	Right handed
Bowling:	Right arm medium-fast

Tests

Test Career:	1986-88
Cap Number:	519
Tests Played:	3

Test Batting

Innings:	4	Runs:	21
Highest Score:	12*	Average:	7.00
No. 50s:	0	No. 100s:	0

Test Bowling & Fielding

Wickets:	4	Runs:	351
Best Bowling:	2/131	Average:	87.75
5 WI:	0	10 WM:	0
Catches:	0	Stumpings:	0

One Day Internationals

ODI Career:	1988
ODIs Played:	6

ODI Batting

Innings:	3	Runs:	0
Highest Score:	0*	Average:	0.00
No. 50s:	0	No. 100s:	0

ODI Bowling & Fielding

Wickets:	2	Runs:	230
Best Bowling:	1/32	Average:	115.00
5 WM:	0	Catches:	2
Stumpings:	0		

The Rhodesian born Radford played three Tests between 1986 and 1988 but could manage only four wickets in total.

RADLEY, Clive Thornton

Born:	May 13, 1944
Batting:	Right handed
Bowling:	Right arm leg-break

Tests

Test Career:	1978
Cap Number:	478
Tests Played:	8

Test Batting

Innings:	10	Runs:	481
Highest Score:	158	Average:	48.10
No. 50s:	2	No. 100s:	2

Test Bowling & Fielding

Wickets:	0	Runs:	0
Best Bowling:		Average:	0.00
5 WI:	0	10 WM:	0
Catches:	4	Stumpings:	0

One Day Internationals

ODI Career:	1978
ODIs Played:	4

ODI Batting

Innings:	4	Runs:	250
Highest Score:	117*	Average:	83.33
No. 50s:	1	No. 100s:	1

ODI Bowling & Fielding

Wickets:	0	Runs:	0
Best Bowling:		Average:	0.00
5 WI:	0	Catches:	0
Stumpings:	0		

A late beginner, the round faced Radley played eight Tests for England after making his debut as a 34 year old. With time against him he quickly got to work scoring 158 at Auckland in his second Test and scored another century later that year when England hosted Pakistan. Whilst he wasn't a hard hitter, he scored a third century for England in an ODI against Pakistan.

RAMPRAKASH, Mark Ravin

Born:	September 5, 1969
Batting:	Right handed
Bowling:	Right arm off-break

Tests

Test Career:	1991-2002
Cap Number:	549
Tests Played:	52

Test Batting

Innings:	92	Runs:	2,350
Highest Score:	154	Average:	27.32
No. 50s:	12	No. 100s:	2

Test Bowling & Fielding

Wickets:	4	Runs:	477
Best Bowling:	1/2	Average:	119.25
5 WI:	0	10 WM:	0
Catches:	39	Stumpings:	0

One Day Internationals

ODI Career:	1991-2001
ODIs Played:	18

ODI Batting

Innings:	18	Runs:	376
Highest Score:	51	Average:	26.85
No. 50s:	1	No. 100s:	0

ODI Bowling & Fielding

Wickets:	4	Runs:	108
Best Bowling:	3/28	Average:	27.00
5 WM:	0	Catches:	8
Stumpings:	0		

England called on the skilful top order batsman a number of times, but whilst he was capable of the sublime, as he showed with tons against the West Indies and Australia on foreign soil, he was generally not the answer the team was looking for. The free scoring Ramprakash remains a formidable county cricketer but his Test average of less than 28 means that he is unlikely to play for his country again.

RANDALL, Derek William

Born:	February 24, 1951
Batting:	Right handed
Bowling:	Right arm medium

Tests

Test Career:	1977-84
Cap Number:	472
Tests Played:	47

Test Batting

Innings:	79	Runs:	2,470
Highest Score:	174	Average:	33.37
No. 50s:	12	No. 100s:	7

Test Bowling & Fielding

Wickets:	0	Runs:	3
Best Bowling:		Average:	0.00
5 WI:	0	10 WM:	0
Catches:	31	Stumpings:	0

One Day Internationals

ODI Career:	1976-85
ODIs Played:	49

ODI Batting

Innings:	45	Runs:	1,067
Highest Score:	88	Average:	26.67
No. 50s:	5	No. 100s:	0

ODI Bowling & Fielding

Wickets:	1	Runs:	2
Best Bowling:	1/2	Average:	2.00
5 WM:	0	Catches:	25
Stumpings:	0		

He was a fidgety batsman and perpetually moving cover fieldsman from Notts in the north of England. Randall top scored in the Centenary Test at the MCG in 1977 with a 174 that won him the award for 'Man of the Match'. During the innings he famously doffed his cap at Dennis Lillee after the Australian quick almost struck him in the head with a bouncer. He had no peer in the field where he would run rather than walk in with the bowler. Randall scored seven Test centuries and 12 half centuries but an average of 33.37 tells the tale of a batsman who was susceptible early. A crowd favourite, he was nicknamed 'Arkle' after the famous English racehorse.

RANJITSINHJI, Kumar Shri (Ranji)

Born:	September 10, 1872
Batting:	Right handed

Tests

Test Career:	1896-1902
Cap Number:	105
Tests Played:	15

Test Batting

Innings:	26	Runs:	989
Highest Score:	175	Average:	44.95
No. 50s:	6	No. 100s:	2

Test Bowling & Fielding

Wickets:	1	Runs:	39
Best Bowling:	1/23	Average:	39.00
5 WI:	0	10 WM:	0
Catches:	13	Stumpings:	0

A prince by birth, the famous Ranji can lay claim to being the first Test cricketer from the sub-continent. From Rajput in India, he studied at Cambridge where he quickly excelled at cricket and was soon playing for Sussex. He made his debut against Australia in 1896 and could not have been more impressive making 62 and 154 not out. He toured Australia once to much acclaim scoring 175 at the SCG in his first Test and averaging 50.77 for the series. The cricket world were at once fascinated and besotted by the Indian nobleman. His batting was all style, relying on wristy flicks forward of the wicket and delicate glances behind. Unfortunately commitments in his native India limited his Test career to just 15 Tests, but he did return to play on for his county until 1920. Ranji famously lost an eye in a shooting accident towards the end of his playing days but simply modified his stance and continued to play the game he loved.

READ, Christopher Mark Wells
Born: August 10, 1978
Batting: Right handed
Wicket Keeper

Tests
Test Career:	1999-		
Cap Number:	595		
Tests Played:	12		

Test Batting
Innings:	18	Runs:	292
Highest Score:	55	Average:	19.46
No. 50s:	1	No. 100s:	0

Test Bowling & Fielding
Wickets:	0	Runs:	0
Best Bowling:		Average:	0.00
5 WI:	0	10 WM:	0
Catches:	35	Stumpings:	5

One Day Internationals
ODI Career:	2000-04		
ODIs Played:	28		

ODI Batting
Innings:	17	Runs:	239
Highest Score:	30*	Average:	21.72
No. 50s:	0	No. 100s:	0

ODI Bowling & Fielding
Wickets:	0	Runs:	0
Best Bowling:		Average:	0.00
5 WM:	0	Catches:	36
Stumpings:	2		

A highly skilled wicket keeper from Nottinghamshire who lost his place in the Test side when selectors felt Geraint Jones provided the better batting option. Clearly the better keeper, he fought back in 2006 to regain his spot during the home series against Pakistan.

READ, Holcombe Douglas
Born: January 28, 1910
Batting: Right handed
Bowling: Right arm fast

Tests
Test Career:	1935		
Cap Number:	289		
Tests Played:	1		

Test Batting
Innings:	0	Runs:	0
Highest Score:	0	Average:	0.00
No. 50s:	0	No. 100s:	0

Test Bowling & Fielding
Wickets:	6	Runs:	200
Best Bowling:	4/136	Average:	33.33
5 WI:	0	10 WM:	0
Catches:	0	Stumpings:	0

Nicknamed 'Hopper', he was an express bowler who played a single Test against South Africa in 1935. He took six wickets and was impressive enough to earn a spot in an MCC squad that toured Australia and New Zealand later that year but retired soon after.

READ, John Maurice
Born: February 9, 1859
Batting: Right handed

Tests
Test Career:	1882-93		
Cap Number:	36		
Tests Played:	17		

Test Batting
Innings:	29	Runs:	461
Highest Score:	57	Average:	0.00
No. 50s:	0	No. 100s:	0

Test Bowling & Fielding
Wickets:	0	Runs:	0
Best Bowling:		Average:	0.00
5 WI:	0	10 WM:	0
Catches:	8	Stumpings:	0

Better known as an accumulator of great scores for his county Surrey, Read toured Australia on two occasions and was part of the side that visited South Africa for that country's first Test. His highest ever first class score was an unbeaten 186 for Surrey against the touring Australians in 1886.

READ, Walter William
Born: November 23, 1855
Batting: Right handed
Bowling: Right arm medium-fast

Tests
Test Career:	1883-93		
Cap Number:	40		
Tests Played:	18		

Test Batting
Innings:	27	Runs:	720
Highest Score:	117	Average:	27.69
No. 50s:	5	No. 100s:	1

Test Bowling & Fielding
Wickets:	0	Runs:	63
Best Bowling:		Average:	0.00
5 WI:	0	10 WM:	0
Catches:	16	Stumpings:	0

Simply known as W.W., the hard hitting batsman from Surrey enjoyed a colourful career for England that saw him earn the wrath of his captains on some occasions and lead his country on others. A bold character, Lord Harris had demoted him to number 10 for the Third Test at The Oval in 1884 with England needing a win or draw to retain the Ashes. Read was furious with his skipper's decision and let his anger out on the Australian bowlers, scoring 117 in the process. He skippered England to victory in a one-off Test against the Australians in 1887/88 and enjoyed similar success when he took an inexperienced side to South Africa four years later. Read scored over 22,000 first class runs, including a triple century when playing for Surrey against Oxford University.

REEVE, Dermot Alexander
Born: April 2, 1963
Batting: Right handed
Bowling: Right arm medium

Tests

Test Career:	1992		
Cap Number:	553		
Tests Played:	3		

Test Batting
Innings:	5	Runs:	124
Highest Score:	59	Average:	24.80
No. 50s:	1	No. 100s:	0

Test Bowling & Fielding
Wickets:	2	Runs:	60
Best Bowling:	1/4	Average:	30.00
5 WI:	0	10 WM:	0
Catches:	1	Stumpings:	0

One Day Internationals

ODI Career:	1991-96		
ODIs Played:	29		

ODI Batting
Innings:	21	Runs:	291
Highest Score:	35	Average:	24.25
No. 50s:	0	No. 100s:	0

ODI Bowling & Fielding
Wickets:	20	Runs:	820
Best Bowling:	3/20	Average:	41.00
5 WM:	0	Catches:	12
Stumpings:	0		

The Hong Kong born Reeve was the ideal one day cricketer with his nagging medium pace bowling and clever late innings batting. The all-rounder played in the 1992 World Cup where he performed admirably. Reeve skippered Warwickshire for many seasons and was in charge when Brian Lara scored his world record 501 against Durham.

RELF, Albert Edward

Born: June 26, 1874
Batting: Right handed

Tests

Test Career:	1903-14		
Cap Number:	139		
Tests Played:	13		

Test Batting
Innings:	21	Runs:	416
Highest Score:	63	Average:	23.11
No. 50s:	1	No. 100s:	0

Test Bowling & Fielding
Wickets:	25	Runs:	624
Best Bowling:	5/85	Average:	24.96
5 WI:	1	10 WM:	0
Catches:	14	Stumpings:	0

An all-rounder from Sussex, he first appeared for England in Australia under Archie MacLaren in 1903/04. He bowled gentle medium pace relying on accuracy and a nagging length. As a batsman he boosted the England lower order with a number of timely innings and important partnerships. Such was his longevity that as a 39 year old he was still playing in the Test side and was named as one of Wisden's five Cricketers of the Year. He took his own life in tragic circumstances at the age of 62 believing his wife was terminally ill.

RHODES, Harold James (Dusty)

Born: July 22, 1936
Batting: Right handed
Bowling: Right arm fast

Tests

Test Career:	1959		
Cap Number:	397		
Tests Played:	2		

Test Batting
Innings:	1	Runs:	0
Highest Score:	0*	Average:	0.00
No. 50s:	0	No. 100s:	0

Test Bowling & Fielding
Wickets:	9	Runs:	244
Best Bowling:	4/50	Average:	27.11
5 WI:	0	10 WM:	0
Catches:	0	Stumpings:	0

A medium pacer from Derbyshire who played in two Tests in 1959. When he was no-balled for throwing in a county game in 1960 his international career was over.

RHODES, Steven John

Born: June 17, 1964
Batting: Right handed
Wicket Keeper

Tests

Test Career:	1994-95		
Cap Number:	566		
Tests Played:	11		

Test Batting
Innings:	17	Runs:	294
Highest Score:	65*	Average:	24.50
No. 50s:	1	No. 100s:	0

Test Bowling & Fielding
Wickets:	0	Runs:	0
Best Bowling:	0	Average:	0.00
5 WI:	0	10 WM:	0
Catches:	46	Stumpings:	3

One Day Internationals

ODI Career:	1989-95		
ODIs Played:	9		

ODI Batting
Innings:	8	Runs:	107
Highest Score:	56	Average:	17.83
No. 50s:	1	No. 100s:	0

ODI Bowling & Fielding
Wickets:	0	Runs:	0
Best Bowling:	0	Average:	0.00
5 WM:	0	Catches:	9
Stumpings:	2		

A wicket keeper who would have played more Test and one day cricket had the selectors not been satisfied with the glovework of batsman Alec Stewart. A gifted keeper, his strike rate of over four dismissals per Test is one of the best in Test cricket.

RHODES, Wilfred

Born: October 29, 1877
Batting: Right handed
Bowling: Left arm off-break

Tests

Test Career:	1899-1930		
Cap Number:	121		
Tests Played:	58		

Test Batting

Innings:	98	Runs:	2,325
Highest Score:	179	Average:	30.19
No. 50s:	11	No. 100s:	2

Test Bowling & Fielding

Wickets:	127	Runs:	3,425
Best Bowling:	15/124	Average:	26.96
5 WI:	6	10 WM:	1
Catches:	60	Stumpings:	0

The great Wilfred Rhodes was a steely competitor for both county and country for over 30 years. He made his debut for England as a 21 year old against Australia in the summer of 1899, and whilst he showed little with the bat in three Tests during that series, he did take 13 wickets with his canny left arm off spinners. That ability to perform well in one facet of the game if the other was not up to par would be the hallmark of one of England's best ever cricketers. He made two big Test hundreds, the first of which came 12 years after he made his English debut. He scored 179 when opening at the MCG in 1911 as part of a record 323 run opening partnership with the great Jack Hobbs. Rhodes scored 463 runs that series at 57.88 in a side that many still consider to be one of England's finest. His second and last Test ton was a masterful 152 at Johannesburg in 1914. As a bowler there was no-one better at thinking the opponent out. His most famous effort for his country was during the rain soaked summer of 1902 when in the very first innings of the Test series, he condemned Australia to their lowest ever Test score. Rhodes took 7/17 at Edgbaston as the tourists tumbled to be all out for just 36. His best return in a match was 15 wickets, which he claimed at the MCG in 1904. He played his last Test on England's first Test tour of the West Indies in 1930 as a fifty two year old. In the years following his retirement he was a regular cricket goer who maintained a close link with the sport until his passing at the age of 95. The Yorkshireman who was as economical with words as he was at the bowling crease, was once asked to rate Victor Trumper by the great cricketer writer Sir Neville Cardus. Rhodes had seen none better but could offer no more than "E were a good bat were Trumper".

RICHARDS, Clifton James (Jack)

Born:	August 10, 1958
Batting:	Right handed
Bowling:	Right arm medium
	Wicket Keeper

Tests

Test Career:	1986-88		
Cap Number:	523		
Tests Played:	8		

Test Batting

Innings:	13	Runs:	285
Highest Score:	133	Average:	21.92
No. 50s:	0	No. 100s:	1

Test Bowling & Fielding

Wickets:	0	Runs:	0
Best Bowling:		Average:	0.00
5 WI:	0	10 WM:	0
Catches:	20	Stumpings:	1

One Day Internationals

ODI Career:	1981-88		
ODIs Played:	22		

ODI Batting

Innings:	16	Runs:	154
Highest Score:	50	Average:	11.84
No. 50s:	1	No. 100s:	0

ODI Bowling & Fielding

Wickets:	0	Runs:	0
Best Bowling:		Average:	0.00
5 WM:	0	Catches:	16
Stumpings:	1		

The curly haired Jack Richards was an eager wicketkeeper who played five of his eight Tests on the Ashes tour of 1986/87. He not only kept well but had a fine series with the bat that included a career high 133 at the WACA.

RICHARDSON, Derek Walter (Dick)

Born:	November 3, 1934
Batting:	Left handed
Bowling:	Left arm medium

Tests

Test Career:	1957		
Cap Number:	385		
Tests Played:	1		

Test Batting

Innings:	1	Runs:	33
Highest Score:	33	Average:	33.00
No. 50s:	0	No. 100s:	0

Test Bowling & Fielding

Wickets:	0	Runs:	0
Best Bowling:		Average:	0.00
5 WI:	0	10 WM:	0
Catches:	1	Stumpings:	0

The brother of Peter, he played one Test against the West Indies at Trent Bridge in 1957.

RICHARDSON, Peter Edward

Born:	July 4, 1931
Batting:	Left handed
Bowling:	Right arm medium

Tests

Test Career:	1956-63		
Cap Number:	382		
Tests Played:	34		

Test Batting

Innings:	56	Runs:	2,061
Highest Score:	126	Average:	37.47
No. 50s:	9	No. 100s:	5

Test Bowling & Fielding

Wickets:	3	Runs:	48
Best Bowling:	2/10	Average:	16.00
5 WI:	0	10 WM:	0
Catches:	6	Stumpings:	0

A blonde headed opening batsman from Worcestershire, he burst on to the Test scene with an outstanding debut series at home against Australia in 1956. Averaging 45.50 in five Tests, he brought up his maiden Test century at Old Tafford with 104 in England's only at bat. After a fine series at home against the West Indies in 1957 when he scored 411 runs at average of almost 60, he tended to struggle and despite a number of chances couldn't cement a regular spot in the side.

RICHARDSON, Thomas

Born: August 11, 1870
Batting: Right handed
Bowling: Right arm fast

Tests

Test Career:	1893-88		
Cap Number:	88		
Tests Played:	14		

Test Batting

Innings:	24	Runs:	177
Highest Score:	25*	Average:	11.06
No. 50s:	0	No. 100s:	0

Test Bowling & Fielding

Wickets:	88	Runs:	2,220
Best Bowling:	8/94	Average:	25.22
5 WI:	11	10 WM:	4
Catches:	5	Stumpings:	0

Richardson can lay claim to being England's first genuine fast bowler of quality with 88 Test wickets at an average of over six per game. His first Test was against Australia at Old Tafford in 1893 and the swarthy six footer with a bristling black moustache made an immediate impression. He took ten wickets for the match which earnt him the reputation of being England's number one strike bowler. He lived up to that billing as part of Stoddart's team that toured Australia in 1894/95 with a brilliant 32 wickets in the five Test series. Clearly England's best bowler, he almost single handedly brought the Ashes home with a six wicket haul in the second innings of the deciding fifth Test at the MCG. He was even more impressive on home soil against the Australians in 1896 where he took 24 wickets in three Tests including a career best 13 in the second at Old Trafford. 22 more wickets in Australia the next year saw out the great quick who from that point on faded quickly, as he began to put on weight. At his best he bowled with genuine speed, making the ball cut an appreciable margin either away or into the batsman. In the final years of the 19th century there was no better bowler in the game than Tom Richardson.

RICHMOND, Thomas Leonard

Born: June 23, 1890
Batting: Right handed
Bowling: Right arm slow

Tests

Test Career:	1921		
Cap Number:	193		
Tests Played:	1		

Test Batting

Innings:	2	Runs:	6
Highest Score:	4	Average:	3.00
No. 50s:	0	No. 100s:	0

Test Bowling & Fielding

Wickets:	2	Runs:	86
Best Bowling:	2/69	Average:	43.00
5 WI:	0	10 WM:	0
Catches:	0	Stumpings:	0

A googly bowler from Notts, his only Test was against the Australia on his home track at Trent Bridge in 1921.

RIDGWAY, Frederick

Born: August 10, 1923
Batting: Right handed
Bowling: Right arm medium-fast

Tests

Test Career:	1951-52		
Cap Number:	365		
Tests Played:	5		

Test Batting

Innings:	6	Runs:	49
Highest Score:	24	Average:	8.16
No. 50s:	0	No. 100s:	0

Test Bowling & Fielding

Wickets:	7	Runs:	379
Best Bowling:	4/83	Average:	54.14
5 WI:	0	10 WM:	0
Catches:	3	Stumpings:	0

A fast medium bowler form Kent, he toured India in 1951/52 where he played all of his five career Tests. In 1951 he took four wickets in four balls for his county in a game against Derbyshire.

ROBERTSON, John David Benbow

Born: February 22, 1917
Batting: Right handed
Bowling: Right arm off-break

Tests

Test Career:	1947-52		
Cap Number:	326		
Tests Played:	11		

Test Batting

Innings:	21	Runs:	881
Highest Score:	133	Average:	46.36
No. 50s:	6	No. 100s:	2

Test Bowling & Fielding

Wickets:	2	Runs:	58
Best Bowling:	2/17	Average:	29.00
5 WI:	0	10 WM:	0
Catches:	6	Stumpings:	0

Jack Robertson's omission from the English side after scoring a 121 against New Zealand at Lord's still ranks as one of Test cricket's most puzzling selection decisions. The stylish opener from Middlesex had teamed up with Len Hutton to great effect in the years following the Second World War and had scored another century whilst touring the West Indies. He was ultimately recalled to the side for the tour of India in 1951/52 but after scoring a half century in each innings at Madras, Robertson was dropped again. And so with two test centuries and an average of 46.36 in only 11 Tests he never played for England again.

ROBINS, Robert Walter Vivian

Born: June 3, 1906
Batting: Right handed
Bowling: Right arm leg-break

Tests
Test Career: 1929*-37
Cap Number: 241
Tests Played: 19

Test Batting
Innings:	27	Runs:	612
Highest Score:	108	Average:	26.60
No. 50s:	4	No. 100s:	1

Test Bowling & Fielding
Wickets:	64	Runs:	1,758
Best Bowling:	6/32	Average:	27.46
5 WI:	1	10 WM:	0
Catches:	12	Stumpings:	0

A free scoring batsman and right arm leg spinner from Middlesex he played in 19 Tests for England which included three against New Zealand in 1937 as captain. He could be relied upon to make a contribution at the some point in all games either with bat, ball or as a spectacular cover fieldsman. He scored a single Test century in the 1935 series against South Africa when the rest of the English side struggled. He was also a well known footballer who played in the first XI for Nottingham Forest.

ROBINSON, Robert Timothy

Born: November 21, 1958
Batting: Right handed
Bowling: Right arm medium

Tests
Test Career: 1984-89
Cap Number: 511
Tests Played: 29

Test Batting
Innings:	49	Runs:	1,601
Highest Score:	175	Average:	36.38
No. 50s:	6	No. 100s:	4

Test Bowling & Fielding
Wickets:	0	Runs:	0
Best Bowling:		Average:	0.00
5 WI:	0	10 WM:	0
Catches:	8	Stumpings:	0

One Day Internationals
ODI Career: 1984-88
ODIs Played: 26

ODI Batting
Innings:	26	Runs:	597
Highest Score:	83	Average:	22.96
No. 50s:	3	No. 100s:	0

ODI Bowling & Fielding
Wickets:	0	Runs:	0
Best Bowling:		Average:	0.00
5 WM:	0	Catches:	6
Stumpings:	0		

An opening batsman from Nottinghamshire who seemed set for a long English career when he scored a commanding 175 against the Australians at Headingly in 1985. He ended that series with 490 runs at an average of 61.25 but was soon back to earth after suffering a horror run in the Caribbean where he scored only 72 runs in eight Test innings. The plucky Robinson bounced back with 166 against Pakistan on home soil the following summer.

ROOPE, Graham Richard James

Born: July 12, 1946
Batting: Right handed
Bowling: Right arm medium

Tests
Test Career: 1973-78
Cap Number: 458
Tests Played: 21

Test Batting
Innings:	32	Runs:	860
Highest Score:	77	Average:	30.71
No. 50s:	7	No. 100s:	0

Test Bowling & Fielding
Wickets:	0	Runs:	76
Best Bowling:		Average:	0.00
5 WI:	0	10 WM:	0
Catches:	35	Stumpings:	0

One Day Internationals
ODI Career: 1973-78
ODIs Played: 8

ODI Batting
Innings:	8	Runs:	173
Highest Score:	44	Average:	21.62
No. 50s:	0	No. 100s:	0

ODI Bowling & Fielding
Wickets:	0	Runs:	0
Best Bowling:		Average:	0.00
5 WM:	0	Catches:	2
Stumpings:	0		

A middle order batsman from Surrey who never quite nailed down a permanent spot in the national side. His highest score in 32 Test innings was a determined 77 against an Australian pace attack in 1975 that boasted Dennis Lillee and Jeff Thomson.

ROOT, Charles Frederick

Born: April 16, 1890
Batting: Right handed
Bowling: Right arm medium-fast

Tests
Test Career: 1926
Cap Number: 224
Tests Played: 3

Test Batting
Innings:	0	Runs:	0
Highest Score:	0	Average:	0.00
No. 50s:	0	No. 100s:	0

Test Bowling & Fielding
Wickets:	8	Runs:	194
Best Bowling:	4/84	Average:	24.25
5 WI:	0	10 WM:	0
Catches:	1	Stumpings:	0

He played three Tests against Australia in 1926 of which his best performance was 4/84 at Old Trafford.

ROSE, Brian Charles
Born: June 4, 1950
Batting: Left handed
Bowling: Left arm medium

Tests
Test Career: 1977-81
Cap Number: 476
Tests Played: 9

Test Batting
Innings:	16	Runs:	358
Highest Score:	70	Average:	25.57
No. 50s:	2	No. 100s:	0

Test Bowling & Fielding
Wickets:	0	Runs:	0
Best Bowling:		Average:	0.00
5 WI:	0	10 WM:	0
Catches:	4	Stumpings:	0

One Day Internationals
ODI Career: 1977
ODIs Played: 2

ODI Batting
Innings:	2	Runs:	99
Highest Score:	54	Average:	49.50
No. 50s:	1	No. 100s:	0

ODI Bowling & Fielding
Wickets:	0	Runs:	0
Best Bowling:		Average:	0.00
5 WM:	0	Catches:	1
Stumpings:	0		

He was a left handed top order batsman who averaged almost 50 against the touring West Indians in 1980.

ROYLE, Vernon Peter Fanshawe Archer
Born: January 29, 1854
Batting: Right handed
Bowling: Right arm medium

Tests
Test Career: 1879
Cap Number: 18
Tests Played: 1

Test Batting
Innings:	2	Runs:	21
Highest Score:	18	Average:	10.50
No. 50s:	0	No. 100s:	0

Test Bowling & Fielding
Wickets:	0	Runs:	6
Best Bowling:		Average:	0.00
5 WI:	0	10 WM:	0
Catches:	2	Stumpings:	0

The good Reverand played only one Test for England but was a much revered figure in county cricket with Lancashire where he delighted onlookers by alternating between a right and left hand batting stance.

RUMSEY, Frederick Edward
Born: December 4, 1935
Batting: Right handed
Bowling: Left arm medium-fast

Tests
Test Career: 1964-65
Cap Number: 425
Tests Played: 5

Test Batting
Innings:	5	Runs:	30
Highest Score:	21*	Average:	15.00
No. 50s:	0	No. 100s:	0

Test Bowling & Fielding
Wickets:	17	Runs:	461
Best Bowling:	4/25	Average:	27.11
5 WI:	0	10 WM:	0
Catches:	0	Stumpings:	0

A fast bowler from Somerset via Worcester who took 15 wickets in 1965 against the touring New Zealanders and South Africans but never played Test cricket again. Later played county cricket for Derbyshire.

RUSSELL, Charles Albert George (Jack)
Born: October 7, 1887
Batting: Right handed

Tests
Test Career: 1920-23
Cap Number: 183
Tests Played: 10

Test Batting
Innings:	18	Runs:	910
Highest Score:	140	Average:	56.87
No. 50s:	2	No. 100s:	5

Test Bowling & Fielding
Wickets:	0	Runs:	0
Best Bowling:		Average:	0.00
5 WI:	0	10 WM:	0
Catches:	8	Stumpings:	0

He was one of the early great cricketers from county side Essex and holds a place in the history books as the first English batsman to score a century in each innings of a single Test. 'Jack' Russell achieved the feat at Durban in 1923 when he scored first 140 then 111 against the South Africans. What is most curious about his effort is that it was to be his last Test appearance. They were not his first centuries either, in fact he had already scored three against the powerful Australian side in 1920 and 1921. In only ten Tests he averaged 56.87, and even though he was ill in South Africa, it remains a mystery as to why he didn't represent his country again.

RUSSELL, Robert Charles (Jack)
Born: August 15, 1963
Batting: Left handed
Bowling: Right arm off-break
Wicket Keeper

Tests
Test Career: 1988-98
Cap Number: 536
Tests Played: 54

Test Batting
Innings:	86	Runs:	1,897
Highest Score:	128*	Average:	27.10
No. 50s:	6	No. 100s:	2

Test Bowling & Fielding

Wickets:	0	Runs:	0
Best Bowling:		Average:	0.00
5 WI:	0	10 WM:	0
Catches:	153	Stumpings:	12

One Day Internationals

ODI Career:	1987-98		
ODIs Played:	40		

ODI Batting

Innings:	31	Runs:	423
Highest Score:	50	Average:	17.62
No. 50s:	1	No. 100s:	0

ODI Bowling & Fielding

Wickets:	0	Runs:	0
Best Bowling:		Average:	0.00
5 WM:	0	Catches:	41
Stumpings:	6		

Little 'Jack' Russell may have looked scruffy with his floppy hat and untucked cricket shirt, but he was a competitior of the highest order. The industrious Russell was always in the game, either flinging himself around behind the stumps or proving a thorn in the opposition's side with the bat. He was often in and out of the side as England looked to bolster their batting by handing Alec Stewart the gloves, but as his 128 against the Australians in 1989 proved, Russell may have been the better option all the time. He hit another century almost a decade later when England met India at Lord's in 1996. Russell rarely missed a chance when keeping, and holds the record for most dismissals by a keeper ever in a Test, with 11 against South Africa at Johannesburg in 1995/96. A talented painter, he can regularly be found at the cricket today with easel and paints in hand, creating a permanent record of the game he took so much pleasure in playing.

RUSSELL, William Eric

Born:	July 3, 1936
Batting:	Right handed
Bowling:	Right arm medium

Tests

Test Career:	1961-67		
Cap Number:	405		
Tests Played:	10		

Test Batting

Innings:	18	Runs:	362
Highest Score:	70	Average:	21.29
No. 50s:	2	No. 100s:	0

Test Bowling & Fielding

Wickets:	0	Runs:	44
Best Bowling:		Average:	0.00
5 WI:	0	10 WM:	0
Catches:	4	Stumpings:	0

An opening batsman from Middlesex who was slated for big things after his fine 70 against South Africa at The Oval in 1965 but in eight subsequent Tests only made one more half century.

SAGGERS, Martin John

Born:	May 23, 1972
Batting:	Right handed
Bowling:	Right arm medium-fast

Tests

Test Career:	2003-04		
Cap Number:	621		
Tests Played:	3		

Test Batting

Innings:	3	Runs:	1
Highest Score:	1	Average:	0.33
No. 50s:	0	No. 100s:	0

Test Bowling & Fielding

Wickets:	7	Runs:	247
Best Bowling:	2/29	Average:	35.28
5 WI:	0	10 WM:	0
Catches:	1	Stumpings:	0

A change bowler form Kent whose three Tests in 2003 and 2004 against Bangladesh and New Zealand netted him seven wickets.

SALISBURY, Ian David Kenneth

Born:	January 21, 1970
Batting:	Right handed
Bowling:	Right arm leg-break

Tests

Test Career:	1992-2000		
Cap Number:	554		
Tests Played:	15		

Test Batting

Innings:	25	Runs:	368
Highest Score:	50	Average:	16.72
No. 50s:	1	No. 100s:	0

Test Bowling & Fielding

Wickets:	20	Runs:	1,539
Best Bowling:	4/163	Average:	76.95
5 WI:	0	10 WM:	0
Catches:	5	Stumpings:	0

One Day Internationals

ODI Career:	1993-94		
ODIs Played:	4		

ODI Batting

Innings:	2	Runs:	7
Highest Score:	5	Average:	7.00
No. 50s:	0	No. 100s:	0

ODI Bowling & Fielding

Wickets:	5	Runs:	177
Best Bowling:	3/41	Average:	35.40
5 WM:	0	Catches:	1
Stumpings:	0		

One of the few leg spinners to have played for England, his twenty wickets in 15 Tests indicate that selectors were willing to persist with him more in hope than anything else.

SANDHAM, Andrew

Born:	July 6, 1890
Batting:	Right handed

Tests

Test Career:	1921-30
Cap Number:	205
Tests Played:	14

Test Batting
Innings:	23	Runs:	879
Highest Score:	325	Average:	38.21
No. 50s:	3	No. 100s:	2

Test Bowling & Fielding
Wickets:	0	Runs:	0
Best Bowling:		Average:	0.00
5 WI:	0	10 WM:	0
Catches:	4	Stumpings:	0

Andy Sandham may have played second fiddle to his more famous opening partner Jack Hobbs, but on one famous day in 1930 it was he who made headlines. England was playing the final Test on their tour of the West Indies when he became the first Test triple-centurion, compiling a mammoth 325 out of England's equally imposing total of 849. The timeless match was abandoned as a draw after nine days, but Sandham had still had time to make 50 in the second innings. That was Sandham's final match at Test level, and his 325 is the highest score by anyone in their final appearance. That innings boosted his Test average to above 38 and also gave him a permanent place in the record books.

SCHOFIELD, Christopher Paul
Born:	October 6, 1978
Batting:	Left handed
Bowling:	Left arm leg-break

Tests
Test Career:	2000
Cap Number:	601
Tests Played:	2

Test Batting
Innings:	3	Runs:	67
Highest Score:	57	Average:	22.33
No. 50s:	1	No. 100s:	0

Test Bowling & Fielding
Wickets:	0	Runs:	73
Best Bowling:		Average:	0.00
5 WI:	0	10 WM:	0
Catches:	0	Stumpings:	0

A leg spinner from Rochdale in Lancashire, who played two Tests against Zimbabwe in 2000 but failed to take a wicket.

SCHULTZ, Sandford Spence
Born:	August 29, 1857
Batting:	Right handed
Bowling:	Right arm fast

Tests
Test Career:	1879
Cap Number:	19
Tests Played:	1

Test Batting
Innings:	2	Runs:	20
Highest Score:	20	Average:	20.00
No. 50s:	0	No. 100s:	0

Test Bowling & Fielding
Wickets:	1	Runs:	26
Best Bowling:	1/16	Average:	26.00
5 WI:	0	10 WM:	0
Catches:	0	Stumpings:	0

A member of Lord Harris' team that toured Australia in 1879, he made a brave 20 batting at number 11 in the second innings of the one-off Test. He changed his German sounding surname to Storey during World War I.

SCOTTON, William Henry
Born:	January 15, 1856
Batting:	Left handed
Bowling:	Left arm medium-fast

Tests
Test Career:	1882-87
Cap Number:	34
Tests Played:	15

Test Batting
Innings:	25	Runs:	510
Highest Score:	90	Average:	22.17
No. 50s:	3	No. 100s:	0

Test Bowling & Fielding
Wickets:	0	Runs:	20
Best Bowling:		Average:	0.00
5 WI:	0	10 WM:	0
Catches:	4	Stumpings:	0

He was a cautious left hand batsman from Nottinghamshire who was first used in the middle order, then as opener in his 15 Tests. Scotton's 90 against the Australians at The Oval in 1884 took over five hours to compile and went a long to securing an important draw for his country. In 1893 he tragically took his own life, due in no small part to the fact that he had lost his place in his county side.

SELBY, John
Born:	July 1, 1849
Batting:	Right handed

Tests
Test Career:	1877-82
Cap Number:	8
Tests Played:	6

Test Batting
Innings:	12	Runs:	256
Highest Score:	70	Average:	23.27
No. 50s:	2	No. 100s:	0

Test Bowling & Fielding
Wickets:	0	Runs:	0
Best Bowling:		Average:	0.00
5 WI:	0	10 WM:	0
Catches:	1	Stumpings:	0

A right handed batsman from Nottinghamshire, he was a member of England's first ever Test side. He enjoyed a fine Test against the Australians in 1881 at the MCG when he scored 55 and 70 batting at number three.

SELVEY, Michael Walter William
Born:	April 25, 1948
Batting:	Right handed
Bowling:	Right arm medium-fast

Tests
Test Career:	1976-77
Cap Number:	466
Tests Played:	3

Test Batting			
Innings:	5	Runs:	15
Highest Score:	5*	Average:	7.50
No. 50s:	0	No. 100s:	0
Test Bowling & Fielding			
Wickets:	6	Runs:	343
Best Bowling:	4/41	Average:	57.16
5 WI:	0	10 WM:	0
Catches:	1	Stumpings:	0

The swing bowler played only three Tests for England but in one rattled a strong West Indian top order returning match figures of 4/41. He went on to become a well renowned cricket journalist and commentator.

SHACKLETON, Derek
Born: August 12, 1924
Batting: Right handed
Bowling: Right arm medium

Tests
Test Career:	1950-53		
Cap Number:	350		
Tests Played:	7		
Test Batting			
Innings:	13	Runs:	113
Highest Score:	42	Average:	18.83
No. 50s:	0	No. 100s:	0
Test Bowling & Fielding			
Wickets:	18	Runs:	768
Best Bowling:	4/72	Average:	42.66
5 WI:	0	10 WM:	0
Catches:	1	Stumpings:	0

An accurate medium pace bowler from Hampshire who could best be described as a workhorse. Shackleton took seven wickets against the West Indies at Lord's in 1963 as a 39 year old, but more importantly came in at number 11 on the last day of that Test to face 20 nail-biting deliveries and deny the visitors victory.

SHAH, Owais Alam
Born: October 22, 1978
Batting: Right handed
Bowling: Right arm off-break

Tests
Test Career:	2006-		
Cap Number:	632		
Tests Played:	1		
Test Batting			
Innings:	2	Runs:	126
Highest Score:	88	Average:	63.00
No. 50s:	1	No. 100s:	0
Test Bowling & Fielding			
Wickets:	0	Runs:	0
Best Bowling:		Average:	0.00
5 WI:	0	10 WM:	0
Catches:	1	Stumpings:	0

One Day Internationals
ODI Career:	2001-		
ODIs Played:	18		
ODI Batting			
Innings:	18	Runs:	294
Highest Score:	62	Average:	18.37
No. 50s:	2	No. 100s:	0
ODI Bowling & Fielding			
Wickets:	0	Runs:	0
Best Bowling:		Average:	0.00
5 WM:	0	Catches:	6
Stumpings:	0		

The right handed batsman from Middlesex would have been a Test regular had he born a decade earlier, but with a high price on spots in the English top order he has played just one Test. He batted at number three at Mumbai in March 2006 and impressed with a first innings 88 against the spin duo of Anil Kumble and Harbhajan Singh. With the emergence of Alastair Cook and Ian Bell he is a little down the pecking order but, there is no doubt he will get another chance to prove his worth in the Test side.

SHARP, John (Jack)
Born: February 15, 1878
Batting: Right handed
Bowling: Left arm medium-fast

Tests
Test Career:	1909		
Cap Number:	161		
Tests Played:	3		
Test Batting			
Innings:	6	Runs:	188
Highest Score:	105	Average:	47.00
No. 50s:	1	No. 100s:	1
Test Bowling & Fielding			
Wickets:	3	Runs:	111
Best Bowling:	3/67	Average:	37.00
5 WI:	0	10 WM:	0
Catches:	1	Stumpings:	0

Jack Sharp was a smart all-rounder from Hereford who had a long and distinguished career with Lancashire but played only three Tests. He showed his worth in his final game for England scoring a 105 against the Australians at The Oval. A leading footballer, he was member of the Everton side the won the FA Cup in 1906.

SHARPE, John William
Born: December 9, 1866
Batting: Right handed
Bowling: Right arm medium-fast

Tests
Test Career:	1890-92		
Cap Number:	71		
Tests Played:	3		
Test Batting			
Innings:	6	Runs:	44
Highest Score:	26	Average:	22.00
No. 50s:	0	No. 100s:	0
Test Bowling & Fielding			
Wickets:	11	Runs:	305
Best Bowling:	6/84	Average:	27.72
5 WI:	1	10 WM:	0
Catches:	2	Stumpings:	0

Unhindered by the loss of an eye as a young man, the fast bowler from Notts and Surrey performed well on the Australian tour of 1891/92. He opened the bowling in the first Test at the MCG and was clearly England's best bowler with six wickets. Upon his return to England he struggled to make the strong Surrey side.

SHARPE, Philip John
Born: December 27, 1936
Batting: Right handed
Bowling: Right arm off-break

Tests
Test Career: 1963-69
Cap Number: 416
Tests Played: 12

Test Batting
Innings:	21	Runs:	786
Highest Score:	111	Average:	46.23
No. 50s:	4	No. 100s:	1

Test Bowling & Fielding
Wickets:	0	Runs:	0
Best Bowling:		Average:	0.00
5 WI:	0	10 WM:	0
Catches:	17	Stumpings:	0

He is probably best remembered as one of England's finest slip fieldsman, though the handy batsman did score one Test century, 112 against New Zealand at Trent Bridge in 1969.

SHAW, Alfred
Born: August 29, 1842
Batting: Right handed
Bowling: Right arm slow

Tests
Test Career: 1877-82
Cap Number: 9
Tests Played: 7

Test Batting
Innings:	12	Runs:	111
Highest Score:	40	Average:	10.09
No. 50s:	0	No. 100s:	0

Test Bowling & Fielding
Wickets:	12	Runs:	285
Best Bowling:	5/38	Average:	23.75
5 WI:	1	10 WM:	0
Catches:	4	Stumpings:	0

The bearded Shaw was a member of England's very first Test side under James Lillywhite in 1877 and four years later led the English side that played four Tests in Australia. He typified cricket's earliest bowlers, accurate and sturdy but hardly prone to great bursts of energy. The result for Shaw was a slow medium pace that garnered him over 2,000 first class wickets in a long and successful career. He played with Nottinghamshire in his youth, later moving to Sussex where he became coach.

SHEPPARD, David Stuart
Born: March 6, 1929
Batting: Right handed
Bowling: Left arm off-break

Tests
Test Career: 1950-63
Cap Number: 353
Tests Played: 22

Test Batting
Innings:	33	Runs:	1,172
Highest Score:	119	Average:	37.80
No. 50s:	6	No. 100s:	3

Test Bowling & Fielding
Wickets:	0	Runs:	0
Best Bowling:		Average:	0.00
5 WI:	0	10 WM:	0
Catches:	12	Stumpings:	0

The good Reverend played his first Test against the West Indies in 1950 and made a hard fought 29 that was the top score in England's paltry second innings score of 109. That effort was enough to earn him a spot on the tour to Australia in 1950/51 but he struggled down-under, playing only two Tests. In 1952 he scored his maiden Test century at The Oval with 119 against the touring Indians. Sheppard was in and out of the Test side until 1963, the year in which he played his finest Test innings, a match winning 113 against the Australians in Melbourne. He also captained his country for two Tests in 1954 against Pakistan. The minister retired after the 1962/63 tour to Australia and rose to the position of Bishop of Liverpool.

SHERWIN, Mordecai
Born: February 26, 1851
Batting: Right handed
 Wicket Keeper

Tests
Test Career: 1887-88
Cap Number: 53
Tests Played: 3

Test Batting
Innings:	6	Runs:	30
Highest Score:	21*	Average:	15.00
No. 50s:	0	No. 100s:	0

Test Bowling & Fielding
Wickets:	0	Runs:	0
Best Bowling:		Average:	0.00
5 WI:	0	10 WM:	0
Catches:	5	Stumpings:	2

One of the many Notts cricketers to represent England in the 19th century, he was known as much for his great weight as he was for his fine glovework. A talented sportsman he also played Association Football for Notts County where unsurprisingly he was also a keeper.

SHREWSBURY, Arthur
Born: April 11, 1856
Batting: Right handed
Bowling: Right arm slow

Tests
Test Career: 1882-93
Cap Number: 35
Tests Played: 23

Test Batting
Innings:	40	Runs:	1,277
Highest Score:	164	Average:	35.47
No. 50s:	4	No. 100s:	3

Test Bowling & Fielding			
Wickets:	0	Runs:	2
Best Bowling:		Average:	0.00
5 WI:	0	10 WM:	0
Catches:	29	Stumpings:	0

Arthur Shrewsbury can lay claim to being England's first great Test batsman, outstripping even the good Doctor W.G. Grace in career average and centuries scored. A right handed batsman from Notts, he toured Australia in 1881/82, scoring 82 and 47 in the third Test at the SCG. He would visit Australia on three more occasions, scoring an unbeaten century at the MCG in 1884/85. A fluent stroke maker who could score runs on any wicket, his most famous innings, and one of the finest in Test history, was struck at Lord's in 1886. Facing an attack including Fred Spofforth and Hugh Trumble, he amassed 164 runs on a sodden pitch to lead his side to an innings victory. Shrewsbury was a successful Test captain whose record stood at five wins from seven matches. He played his last series for England in 1893, when as a 37 year old his hit his third and final century, once again at Lord's. W.G. Grace was once said to have been asked who he would be his first choice to join him in the English side to which he responded, "give me Arthur". Shrewsbury played for his county for another ten years until he took his own life in 1903.

SHUTER, John

Born:	February 9, 1855
Batting:	Right handed

Tests

Test Career:	1888		
Cap Number:	58		
Tests Played:	1		
Test Batting			
Innings:	1	Runs:	28
Highest Score:	28	Average:	28.00
No. 50s:	0	No. 100s:	0
Test Bowling & Fielding			
Wickets:	0	Runs:	0
Best Bowling:		Average:	0.00
5 WI:	0	10 WM:	0
Catches:	0	Stumpings:	0

A renowned cricketer for both Kent and Surrey, his only Test was against Australia at The Oval in 1988.

SHUTTLEWORTH, Kenneth

Born:	November 13, 1944
Batting:	Right handed
Bowling:	Right arm fast

Tests

Test Career:	1970-71		
Cap Number:	446		
Tests Played:	5		
Test Batting			
Innings:	6	Runs:	46
Highest Score:	21	Average:	7.66
No. 50s:	0	No. 100s:	0
Test Bowling & Fielding			
Wickets:	12	Runs:	427
Best Bowling:	5/47	Average:	35.58
5 WI:	1	10 WM:	0
Catches:	1	Stumpings:	0

One Day Internationals

ODI Career:	1971		
ODIs Played:	1		
ODI Batting			
Innings:	1	Runs:	7
Highest Score:	7	Average:	7.00
No. 50s:	0	No. 100s:	0
ODI Bowling & Fielding			
Wickets:	1	Runs:	29
Best Bowling:	1/29	Average:	29.00
5 WM:	0	Catches:	1
Stumpings:	0		

After a fine debut against Australia at Brisbane in 1970 where he took 5/47 in the second innings, the tall right arm quick found Test wickets hard to come by. He played his final Test less than seven months later.

SIDEBOTTOM, Arnold

Born:	April 1, 1954
Batting:	Right handed
Bowling:	Right arm medium-fast

Tests

Test Career:	1985		
Cap Number:	512		
Tests Played:	1		
Test Batting			
Innings:	1	Runs:	2
Highest Score:	2	Average:	2.00
No. 50s:	0	No. 100s:	0
Test Bowling & Fielding			
Wickets:	1	Runs:	65
Best Bowling:	1/65	Average:	65.00
5 WI:	0	10 WM:	0
Catches:	0	Stumpings:	0

A well credentialed footballer who once played with Manchester Untied, Sidebottom played a single Test against Australia at Trent Bridge in 1985.

SIDEBOTTOM, Ryan Jay

Born:	January 15, 1978
Batting:	Left handed
Bowling:	Left arm medium-fast

Tests

Test Career:	2001-		
Cap Number:	604		
Tests Played:	1		
Test Batting			
Innings:	1	Runs:	4
Highest Score:	4	Average:	4.00
No. 50s:	0	No. 100s:	0
Test Bowling & Fielding			
Wickets:	0	Runs:	64
Best Bowling:		Average:	0.00
5 WI:	0	10 WM:	0
Catches:	0	Stumpings:	0

One Day Internationals

ODI Career:	2001-
ODIs Played:	2

ODI Batting			
Innings:	1	Runs:	2
Highest Score:	2*	Average:	0.00
No. 50s:	0	No. 100s:	0
ODI Bowling & Fielding			
Wickets:	2	Runs:	84
Best Bowling:	1/42	Average:	42.00
5 WM:	0	Catches:	0
Stumpings:	0		

The mop topped speedster from Yorkshire played his only Test against Pakistan at Lord's in 2001. He'll be hoping to add to that number to at least outstrip his father Arnie, who also played a single Test for England back in 1985.

SILVERWOOD, Christopher Eric Wilfred

Born:	March 5, 1975
Batting:	Right handed
Bowling:	Right arm medium-fast

Tests

Test Career:	1996-2002
Cap Number:	583
Tests Played:	6

Test Batting

Innings:	7	Runs:	29
Highest Score:	10	Average:	7.25
No. 50s:	0	No. 100s:	0

Test Bowling & Fielding

Wickets:	11	Runs:	444
Best Bowling:	5/91	Average:	40.36
5 WI:	1	10 WM:	0
Catches:	2	Stumpings:	0

One Day Internationals

ODI Career:	1996-2001
ODIs Played:	7

ODI Batting

Innings:	4	Runs:	17
Highest Score:	12	Average:	4.25
No. 50s:	0	No. 100s:	0

ODI Bowling & Fielding

Wickets:	6	Runs:	244
Best Bowling:	3/43	Average:	40.66
5 WM:	0	Catches:	0
Stumpings:	0		

A whole-hearted paceman who played four Tests on the tour to South Africa in 1999/2000 but could manage only seven wickets.

SIMPSON, Reginald Thomas

Born:	February 27, 1920
Batting:	Right handed
Bowling:	Right arm off-break

Tests

Test Career:	1948-55
Cap Number:	341
Tests Played:	27

Test Batting

Innings:	45	Runs:	1,401
Highest Score:	156*	Average:	33.35
No. 50s:	6	No. 100s:	4

Test Bowling & Fielding

Wickets:	2	Runs:	22
Best Bowling:	2/4	Average:	11.00
5 WI:	0	10 WM:	0
Catches:	5	Stumpings:	0

A tall and upright opening batsman from Nottinghamshire, he took full advantage of a good start to score four centuries for England. His highest Test score came at the MCG in 1951 when his unbeaten 156 led England to their first win over Australia in 13 years.

SIMPSON-HAYWARD, George Hayward Thomas

Born:	June 7, 1875
Batting:	Right handed

Tests

Test Career:	1910
Cap Number:	167
Tests Played:	5

Test Batting

Innings:	8	Runs:	105
Highest Score:	29*	Average:	15.00
No. 50s:	0	No. 100s:	0

Test Bowling & Fielding

Wickets:	23	Runs:	420
Best Bowling:	6/43	Average:	18.26
5 WI:	2	10 WM:	0
Catches:	1	Stumpings:	0

One of the last underarm or lob bowlers to play in Tests, he was suited to bowling on the mats and took 23 wickets in five Tests in the series against South Africa in 1910.

SIMS, James Morton

Born:	May 13, 1903
Batting:	Right handed
Bowling:	Right arm leg-break

Tests

Test Career:	1935-37
Cap Number:	286
Tests Played:	4

Test Batting

Innings:	4	Runs:	16
Highest Score:	12	Average:	4.00
No. 50s:	0	No. 100s:	0

Test Bowling & Fielding

Wickets:	11	Runs:	480
Best Bowling:	5/73	Average:	43.63
5 WI:	1	10 WM:	0
Catches:	6	Stumpings:	0

Jim Sims was a steady leg spinner from Middlesex who earnt a trip to Australia in 1936/37 after a good Test against India earlier that year. His seven wickets in that game was clearly his best effort in Tests with only four wickets his three other appearances for England.

SINFIELD, Reginald Albert

Born:	December 24, 1900
Batting:	Right handed
Bowling:	Right arm slow

Tests

Test Career:	1938		
Cap Number:	301		
Tests Played:	1		

Test Batting

Innings:	1	Runs:	6
Highest Score:	6	Average:	6.00
No. 50s:	0	No. 100s:	0

Test Bowling & Fielding

Wickets:	2	Runs:	123
Best Bowling:	1/51	Average:	61.50
5 WI:	0	10 WM:	0
Catches:	0	Stumpings:	0

He was an off spinner from Gloucs who played a single Test against the touring Australians in 1938.

SLACK, Wilfred Norris

Born:	December 12, 1954
Batting:	Left handed
Bowling:	Right arm medium

Tests

Test Career:	1986		
Cap Number:	516		
Tests Played:	3		

Test Batting

Innings:	6	Runs:	81
Highest Score:	52	Average:	13.50
No. 50s:	1	No. 100s:	0

Test Bowling & Fielding

Wickets:	0	Runs:	0
Best Bowling:		Average:	0.00
5 WI:	0	10 WM:	0
Catches:	3	Stumpings:	0

One Day Internationals

ODI Career:	1986
ODIs Played:	2

ODI Batting

Innings:	2	Runs:	43
Highest Score:	34	Average:	21.50
No. 50s:	0	No. 100s:	0

ODI Bowling & Fielding

Wickets:	0	Runs:	0
Best Bowling:		Average:	0.00
5 WM:	0	Catches:	0
Stumpings:	0		

The West Indian born Slack toured the West Indies in 1985 making his Test high score of 52 in the fifth Test of the series. He had a history of passing out on the cricket field but with doctors unable to identify the cause he continued to play. In 1989 he was playing in The Gambia when he collapsed and died whilst batting. Wilf Slack was only 34 years old.

SMAILES, Thomas Francis

Born:	March 27, 1910
Batting:	Left handed
Bowling:	Right arm medium

Tests

Test Career:	1946
Cap Number:	313
Tests Played:	1

Test Batting

Innings:	1	Runs:	25
Highest Score:	25	Average:	25.00
No. 50s:	0	No. 100s:	0

Test Bowling & Fielding

Wickets:	3	Runs:	62
Best Bowling:	3/44	Average:	20.66
5 WI:	0	10 WM:	0
Catches:	0	Stumpings:	0

A medium pacer who played a single Test against India at Lord's in 1947.

SMALL, Gladstone Cleophas

Born:	October 18, 1961
Batting:	Right handed
Bowling:	Right arm medium-fast

Tests

Test Career:	1986-91
Cap Number:	521
Tests Played:	17

Test Batting

Innings:	24	Runs:	263
Highest Score:	59	Average:	15.47
No. 50s:	1	No. 100s:	0

Test Bowling & Fielding

Wickets:	55	Runs:	1,871
Best Bowling:	5/48	Average:	34.01
5 WI:	2	10 WM:	0
Catches:	9	Stumpings:	0

One Day Internationals

ODI Career:	1987-92
ODIs Played:	53

ODI Batting

Innings:	24	Runs:	98
Highest Score:	18*	Average:	6.53
No. 50s:	0	No. 100s:	0

ODI Bowling & Fielding

Wickets:	58	Runs:	1,942
Best Bowling:	4/31	Average:	33.48
5 WM:	0	Catches:	7
Stumpings:	0		

Born in Barbados, he was a hard toiling pace bowler who at times suffered from a distinct lack of control. He teamed up brilliantly with Ian Botham at the MCG in 1986 to dismiss the Australians for 141 and 194 claiming seven wickets for the match. The distinctively built Small copped a lot of ribbing throughout his career for his strong yet neckless physique.

SMITH, Alan Christopher

Born:	October 25, 1936
Batting:	Right handed
Bowling:	Right arm medium-fast
	Wicket Keeper

Tests

Test Career:	1962-63
Cap Number:	414
Tests Played:	6

Test Batting

Innings:	7	Runs:	118
Highest Score:	69*	Average:	29.50
No. 50s:	1	No. 100s:	0

Test Bowling & Fielding			
Wickets:	0	Runs:	0
Best Bowling:		Average:	0.00
5 WI:	0	10 WM:	0
Catches:	20	Stumpings:	0

He bowled, batted and kept wickets in fine style for Warwickshire but it came as a surprise when he was chosen to tour Australia and New Zealand in 1962/63. He played as wicketkeeper in six of the eight Tests on that tour and whilst he performed well with both bat and gloves, he was never chosen to represent England again.

SMITH, Andrew Michael (Mike)

Born: October 1, 1967
Batting: Right handed
Bowling: Left arm medium-fast

Tests
Test Career:	1997		
Cap Number:	586		
Tests Played:	1		

Test Batting
Innings:	2	Runs:	4
Highest Score:	4*	Average:	4.00
No. 50s:	0	No. 100s:	0

Test Bowling & Fielding
Wickets:	0	Runs:	89
Best Bowling:		Average:	0.00
5 WI:	0	10 WM:	0
Catches:	0	Stumpings:	0

The Gloucs swing bowler played a single Test for England against Australia at Headingly in 1997.

SMITH, Cedric Ivan James

Born: August 25, 1906
Batting: Right handed
Bowling: Right arm fast

Tests
Test Career:	1935-37		
Cap Number:	281		
Tests Played:	5		

Test Batting
Innings:	10	Runs:	102
Highest Score:	27	Average:	10.20
No. 50s:	0	No. 100s:	0

Test Bowling & Fielding
Wickets:	15	Runs:	393
Best Bowling:	5/16	Average:	26.20
5 WI:	1	10 WM:	0
Catches:	1	Stumpings:	0

An opening bowler and hefty hitter of the ball, 'Big Jim' Smith toured the West Indies in 1934/35 taking 5/15 on debut at Bridgetown. He played four Tests on that tour and a single Test against the fledgling New Zealand side more than two years later.

SMITH, Charles Aubrey

Born: July 21, 1863
Batting: Right handed
Bowling: Right arm fast

Tests
Test Career:	1889		
Cap Number:	66		
Tests Played:	1		

Test Batting
Innings:	1	Runs:	3
Highest Score:	3	Average:	3.00
No. 50s:	0	No. 100s:	0

Test Bowling & Fielding
Wickets:	7	Runs:	61
Best Bowling:	5/19	Average:	8.71
5 WI:	1	10 WM:	0
Catches:	0	Stumpings:	0

English cricket captain, Hollywood actor, raconteur and Knight of the Realm, it was quite the life for the former Cambridge blue. His only Test was the first ever between England and South Africa, a game in which he captained and took seven wickets with his cunning medium pacers. Nicknamed 'Round the Corner' for his unusual run up to the wicket, he stayed in South Africa to work as a stockbroker after that series in 1889 before moving to Hollywood where he played the role of the perfect English gentleman in a number of movies. Smith famously formed the Hollywood Cricket Club where he got the likes of Errol Flynn, Sir John Barrymore and David Niven to pull on the flanels.

SMITH, Christopher Lyall

Born: October 15, 1958
Batting: Right handed
Bowling: Right arm off-break

Tests
Test Career:	1983-86		
Cap Number:	503		
Tests Played:	8		

Test Batting
Innings:	14	Runs:	392
Highest Score:	91	Average:	30.15
No. 50s:	2	No. 100s:	0

Test Bowling & Fielding
Wickets:	3	Runs:	39
Best Bowling:	2/31	Average:	13.00
5 WI:	0	10 WM:	0
Catches:	5	Stumpings:	0

One Day Internationals
ODI Career:	1984		
ODIs Played:	4		

ODI Batting
Innings:	4	Runs:	109
Highest Score:	70	Average:	27.25
No. 50s:	1	No. 100s:	0

ODI Bowling & Fielding
Wickets:	2	Runs:	28
Best Bowling:	2/8	Average:	14.00
5 WM:	0	Catches:	0
Stumpings:	0		

The South African born Smith was a handy top order batsman who was eligible to play for England because his parents were English. In eight Tests his highest score was a 91 at Eden Park in New Zealand in 1984. The older brother of Robin.

SMITH, David Mark

Born:	January 9, 1956
Batting:	Left handed
Bowling:	Right arm medium

Tests

Test Career:	1986		
Cap Number:	514		
Tests Played:	2		

Test Batting

Innings:	4	Runs:	80
Highest Score:	47	Average:	20.00
No. 50s:	0	No. 100s:	0

Test Bowling & Fielding

Wickets:	0	Runs:	0
Best Bowling:		Average:	0.00
5 WI:	0	10 WM:	0
Catches:	0	Stumpings:	0

One Day Internationals

ODI Career:	1986-90		
ODIs Played:	2		

ODI Batting

Innings:	2	Runs:	15
Highest Score:	10*	Average:	15.00
No. 50s:	0	No. 100s:	0

ODI Bowling & Fielding

Wickets:	0	Runs:	0
Best Bowling:		Average:	0.00
5 WM:	0	Catches:	0
Stumpings:	0		

The tall top order batsman toured the West Indies in 1985/86 where he top scored in both innings in the second Test at Port of Spain. Unfortunately for Smith he sustained an injury in that match and never played for England again.

SMITH, David Robert

Born:	October 5, 1934
Batting:	Right handed
Bowling:	Right arm medium

Tests

Test Career:	1961-62		
Cap Number:	407		
Tests Played:	5		

Test Batting

Innings:	5	Runs:	38
Highest Score:	34	Average:	9.50
No. 50s:	0	No. 100s:	0

Test Bowling & Fielding

Wickets:	6	Runs:	359
Best Bowling:	3/60	Average:	59.83
5 WI:	0	10 WM:	0
Catches:	2	Stumpings:	0

One of many medium pacers in the early 60's to have their opportunities severely limited by the presence of Fred Trueman and Brian Statham. His five Tests were all played in the sub-continent in 1961/62.

SMITH, Denis

Born:	January 24, 1907
Batting:	Left handed
Bowling:	Right arm medium
	Wicket Keeper

Tests

Test Career:	1935		
Cap Number:	287		
Tests Played:	2		

Test Batting

Innings:	4	Runs:	128
Highest Score:	57	Average:	32.00
No. 50s:	1	No. 100s:	0

Test Bowling & Fielding

Wickets:	0	Runs:	0
Best Bowling:		Average:	0.00
5 WI:	0	10 WM:	0
Catches:	1	Stumpings:	0

One of 15 Smiths to play for England, the opening batsman and back up keeper had a fine debut, scoring 75 against South Africa in Leeds in 1935.

SMITH, Donald Victor

Born:	June 14, 1923
Batting:	Left handed
Bowling:	Left arm medium

Tests

Test Career:	1957		
Cap Number:	384		
Tests Played:	3		

Test Batting

Innings:	4	Runs:	25
Highest Score:	16*	Average:	8.33
No. 50s:	0	No. 100s:	0

Test Bowling & Fielding

Wickets:	1	Runs:	97
Best Bowling:	1/12	Average:	97.00
5 WI:	0	10 WM:	0
Catches:	0	Stumpings:	0

A medium pace bowler and handy batsman from Sussex who played three Tests against the touring West Indians in 1957.

SMITH, Edward Thomas

Born:	June 19, 1977
Batting:	Right handed
Bowling:	Right arm medium-fast

Tests

Test Career:	2003		
Cap Number:	617		
Tests Played:	3		

Test Batting

Innings:	5	Runs:	87
Highest Score:	64	Average:	17.40
No. 50s:	1	No. 100s:	0

Test Bowling & Fielding

Wickets:	0	Runs:	0
Best Bowling:		Average:	0.00
5 WI:	0	10 WM:	0
Catches:	5	Stumpings:	0

The Cambridge University graduate came to prominence on the back of a rich vein of form for Kent in 2003. He was rewarded with three Tests against South Africa, but after a promising 64 in the first at Trent Bridge, struggled and quickly faded from view.

SMITH, Ernest James
Born: February 6, 1886
Batting: Right handed
Wicket Keeper

Tests
Test Career:	1912-13		
Cap Number:	176		
Tests Played:	11		

Test Batting
Innings:	14	Runs:	113
Highest Score:	22	Average:	8.69
No. 50s:	0	No. 100s:	0

Test Bowling & Fielding
Wickets:	0	Runs:	0
Best Bowling:		Average:	0.00
5 WI:	0	10 WM:	0
Catches:	17	Stumpings:	3

Nicknamed 'Tiger', the Birmingham born Smith kept brilliantly to the opening combination of Sid Barnes and Frank Foster in the 1911/12 Ashes series in Australia. He stood up to the stumps to the two medium pacers and the pressure he applied contributed in no small part to their success. Following his retirement from first class cricket in 1930 he became an umpire and eventually went on to stand in eight Tests.

SMITH, Harry
Born: May 21, 1891
Batting: Right handed

Tests
Test Career:	1928		
Cap Number:	236		
Tests Played:	1		

Test Batting
Innings:	1	Runs:	7
Highest Score:	7	Average:	7.00
No. 50s:	0	No. 100s:	0

Test Bowling & Fielding
Wickets:	0	Runs:	0
Best Bowling:		Average:	0.00
5 WI:	0	10 WM:	0
Catches:	1	Stumpings:	0

He was a batsman for Gloucestershire who played a single Test against the visiting West Indies side in 1928.

SMITH, Michael John
Born: January 4, 1942
Batting: Right handed
Bowling: Left arm slow

One Day Internationals
ODI Career:	1973-74		
ODIs Played:	5		

ODI Batting
Innings:	5	Runs:	70
Highest Score:	31	Average:	14.00
No. 50s:	0	No. 100s:	0

ODI Bowling & Fielding
Wickets:	0	Runs:	0
Best Bowling:		Average:	0.00
5 WM:	0	Catches:	1
Stumpings:	0		

He opened the batting with Geoff Boycott on his ODI debut against the West Indies, at Headingley in 1973. He scored an impressive 31 while his more senior and more famous counterpart made a duck. Smith played in a further four ODI's but also could not manage to break into the Test eleven.

SMITH, Michael John Knight
Born: June 30, 1933
Batting: Right handed

Tests
Test Career:	1958-72		
Cap Number:	386		
Tests Played:	50		

Test Batting
Innings:	78	Runs:	2,278
Highest Score:	121	Average:	31.63
No. 50s:	11	No. 100s:	3

Test Bowling & Fielding
Wickets:	1	Runs:	128
Best Bowling:	1/10	Average:	128.00
5 WI:	0	10 WM:	0
Catches:	53	Stumpings:	0

He was a quietly spoken Test captain who was an honest if unspectacular batsman. Easily identifiable in cap and glasses, he played mainly through the on side and whilst he did score three Test centuries, his Test average of just over 30 shows his greatest worth was as a leader. Known by the three initials of his given names, MJK also played a single rugby Test for England.

SMITH, Neil Michael Knight
Born: July 27, 1967
Batting: Right handed
Bowling: Right arm off-break

One Day Internationals
ODI Career:	1996		
ODIs Played:	7		

ODI Batting
Innings:	6	Runs:	100
Highest Score:	31	Average:	20.00
No. 50s:	0	No. 100s:	0

ODI Bowling & Fielding
Wickets:	6	Runs:	190
Best Bowling:	3/29	Average:	31.66
5 WM:	0	Catches:	1
Stumpings:	0		

A right hand batsman and off-spinner from Warwickshire, Smith played in seven ODI's in 1996, including three World Cup matches in Pakistan. He performed solidly while opening the batting with Alec Stewart and Michael Atherton.

SMITH, Robin Arnold
Born: September 13, 1963
Batting: Right handed
Bowling: Right arm leg-break

Tests
Test Career:	1988-96
Cap Number:	530
Tests Played:	62

Test Batting
Innings:	112	Runs:	4,236
Highest Score:	175	Average:	43.67
No. 50s:	28	No. 100s:	9

Test Bowling & Fielding
Wickets:	0	Runs:	6
Best Bowling:		Average:	0.00
5 WI:	0	10 WM:	0
Catches:	39	Stumpings:	0

One Day Internationals
ODI Career:	1988-96
ODIs Played:	71

ODI Batting
Innings:	70	Runs:	2,419
Highest Score:	167*	Average:	39.01
No. 50s:	15	No. 100s:	4

ODI Bowling & Fielding
Wickets:	0	Runs:	0
Best Bowling:		Average:	0.00
5 WM:	0	Catches:	26
Stumpings:	0		

The younger brother of Chris, he provided England with much needed dash and vigour at the top of the order for almost a decade. He was clearly England's best batsman in the 4-0, 1989 Ashes drubbing at the hands of the Australians. Smith scored 553 runs at an average of 61.44 to outscore his nearest English rival by almost 150 runs. English batsmen scored only five centuries in that series and he scored two of them, 143 at Old Trafford in the fourth Test and 101 in the next Test at Trent Bridge. The South African born batsman had another run of successive hundreds the following summer against India with centuries at Lord's and Old Trafford in the first and second Tests of the series. A hard hitter of the ball, he was most comfortable against quick bowling and as far as he was concerned the faster and shorter the better. His highest Test score of 175 was against a West Indian attack fronted by Curtley Ambrose and Courtney Walsh. Smith's record of over 4,000 runs at 43.67 marks him as one of England's best batsman in the last 20 years.

SMITH, Thomas Peter Bromley
Born:	October 30, 1908
Batting:	Right handed
Bowling:	Right arm leg-break

Tests
Test Career:	1946-47
Cap Number:	316
Tests Played:	4

Test Batting
Innings:	5	Runs:	33
Highest Score:	24	Average:	6.60
No. 50s:	0	No. 100s:	0

Test Bowling & Fielding
Wickets:	3	Runs:	319
Best Bowling:	2/172	Average:	106.33
5 WI:	0	10 WM:	0
Catches:	1	Stumpings:	0

He was an Essex all-rounder for over two decades where his leg-spinners earnt him selection as one Widsden's five Cricketers of the Year in 1947.

SMITHSON, Gerald Arthur
Born:	November 1, 1926
Batting:	Right handed
Bowling:	Right arm medium

Tests
Test Career:	1948
Cap Number:	330
Tests Played:	2

Test Batting
Innings:	3	Runs:	70
Highest Score:	35	Average:	23.33
No. 50s:	0	No. 100s:	0

Test Bowling & Fielding
Wickets:	0	Runs:	0
Best Bowling:		Average:	0.00
5 WI:	0	10 WM:	0
Catches:	0	Stumpings:	0

The left handed batsman from Leicestershire played two Tests in the Caribbean in 1948.

SNAPE, Jeremy Nicholas
Born:	April 27, 1973
Batting:	Right handed
Bowling:	Right arm off-break

One Day Internationals
ODI Career:	2001-02
ODIs Played:	10

ODI Batting
Innings:	7	Runs:	118
Highest Score:	38	Average:	29.50
No. 50s:	0	No. 100s:	0

ODI Bowling & Fielding
Wickets:	13	Runs:	403
Best Bowling:	3/43	Average:	31.00
5 WM:	0	Catches:	5
Stumpings:	0		

A right arm off-spinner who dismissed both Flower brothers on his ODI debut against Zimbabwe, at Harare in 2001. Snape was serviceable in ten ODI's between 2001-02.

SNOW, John Augustine
Born:	October 13, 1941
Batting:	Right handed
Bowling:	Right arm medium-fast

Tests
Test Career:	1965-76
Cap Number:	428
Tests Played:	49

Test Batting
Innings:	71	Runs:	772
Highest Score:	73	Average:	13.54
No. 50s:	2	No. 100s:	0

Test Bowling & Fielding
Wickets:	202	Runs:	5,387
Best Bowling:	7/40	Average:	26.66
5 WI:	8	10 WM:	1
Catches:	16	Stumpings:	0

One Day Internationals
ODI Career:	1971-75
ODIs Played:	9

ODI Batting

Innings:	4	Runs:	9
Highest Score:	5*	Average:	4.50
No. 50s:	0	No. 100s:	0

ODI Bowling & Fielding

Wickets:	14	Runs:	232
Best Bowling:	4/11	Average:	16.57
5 WM:	0	Catches:	1
Stumpings:	0		

The term white line fever may have been penned with John Snow in mind. Off the field the son of a clergyman was retiring to the point of being aloof, but on it he was a firebrand who once knocked India's Sunil Gavaskar off his feet whilst the batting maestro was trying to take a run. Snow the bowler was genuinely quick, with the scent of blood always in his nostrils. He tore through the West Indians in the Caribbean in 1967/68, taking 7/49 in a single innings at Sabina Park and finishing the series as England's number one bowler with 27 victims. His reputation preceded him when he toured Australia under Ray Illingworth in 1970/71 and he didn't let the expectant throng down. Snow played the role of baddie to perfection, incensing the Australian crowds with a powerhouse display of fast bowling. He famously felled Australian tailender Terry Jenner at the SCG in an incident that saw England taken off the field by skipper Illingworth after the crowd showed their displeasure by hurling beer cans on to the ground. Snow wasn't just quick during that series he was also very effective, finishing with 31 wickets and spearheading England to a 3-0 victory. In retirement the man that ran foul of authorities on a number of occasions let the title of his autobiography say it all; Cricket Rebel.

SOLANKI, Vikram Singh

Born:	April 1, 1976
Batting:	Right handed
Bowling:	Right arm off-break

One Day Internationals

ODI Career:	2000-06
ODIs Played:	51

ODI Batting

Innings:	46	Runs:	1,097
Highest Score:	106	Average:	26.75
No. 50s:	5	No. 100s:	2

ODI Bowling & Fielding

Wickets:	1	Runs:	105
Best Bowling:	1/17	Average:	105.00
5 WM:	0	Catches:	16
Stumpings:	0		

Born in India and raised in Wolverhampton, right hand middle order batsman Vikram Solanki made his ODI debut against South Africa at Bloemfontein in 2000. With his average just hovering around the 16-run mark after his first two series against South Africa and Zimbabwe, Solanki was unsurprisingly dropped. He remained in the wilderness for almost three years until he was recalled for the NatWest Challenge against the touring Pakistanis in 2003. His average dramatically improved and has been a regular member of the ODI side ever since, scoring two ODI centuries - 106 against South Africa, at The Oval in 2003, and 100 against Zimbabwe, at Bulawayo in 2005. However, now on the wrong side of 30, the jury is still out as to whether Solanki will ever get to wear that elusive Test cap.

SOUTHERTON, James

Born:	November 16, 1827
Batting:	Right handed
Bowling:	Left arm off-break

Tests

Test Career:	1877
Cap Number:	10
Tests Played:	2

Test Batting

Innings:	3	Runs:	7
Highest Score:	6	Average:	3.50
No. 50s:	0	No. 100s:	0

Test Bowling & Fielding

Wickets:	7	Runs:	107
Best Bowling:	4/46	Average:	15.28
5 WI:	0	10 WM:	0
Catches:	2	Stumpings:	0

When James Southerton played in the first ever Test side, his long first class career was near an end. The 49 year old had played for Surrey, Sussex and Hampshire for almost a quarter of a century, but his slow off breaks were still effective and he took seven wickets in his only two Tests.

SPOONER, Reginald Herbert

Born:	October 21, 1880
Batting:	Right handed

Tests

Test Career:	1905-12
Cap Number:	145
Tests Played:	10

Test Batting

Innings:	15	Runs:	481
Highest Score:	119	Average:	32.06
No. 50s:	4	No. 100s:	1

Test Bowling & Fielding

Wickets:	0	Runs:	0
Best Bowling:		Average:	0.00
5 WI:	0	10 WM:	0
Catches:	4	Stumpings:	0

An elegant top order batsman from Lancashire, he would have played far more Test cricket had his career not been interrupted by three years service in the Boer War. He scored a single Test century, against South Africa at Lord's in 1912.

SPOONER, Richard Thompson

Born:	December 30, 1919
Batting:	Left handed
	Wicket Keeper

Tests
Test Career:	1951-55		
Cap Number:	366		
Tests Played:	7		

Test Batting
Innings:	14	Runs:	354
Highest Score:	92	Average:	27.23
No. 50s:	3	No. 100s:	0

Test Bowling & Fielding
Wickets:	0	Runs:	0
Best Bowling:		Average:	0.00
5 WI:	0	10 WM:	0
Catches:	10	Stumpings:	2

Spooner was a wicketkeeper from Warwickshire who spent the bulk of his career waiting in line behind Godfrey Evans for a chance to play Test cricket. He played all five Tests in India in 1951/52 as a keeper and opening batsman, performing particularly well at Calcutta in the third Test where he scored 71 and 92.

STANYFORTH, Ronald Thomas (Rory)

Born:	May 30, 1892
Batting:	Right handed
	Wicket Keeper

Tests
Test Career:	1927-28
Cap Number:	230
Tests Played:	4

Test Batting
Innings:	6	Runs:	13
Highest Score:	6*	Average:	2.60
No. 50s:	0	No. 100s:	0

Test Bowling & Fielding
Wickets:	0	Runs:	0
Best Bowling:		Average:	0.00
5 WI:	0	10 WM:	0
Catches:	7	Stumpings:	2

When captain George Jackson pulled out of the 1927/28 South African tour due to illness, the job of leading the team was given to sometime Yorkshire keeper Rory Stanyforth. An able keeper and limited batsman, he led England to a series win and never played for his country again.

STAPLES, Samuel James

Born:	September 18, 1892
Batting:	Right handed
Bowling:	Right arm off-break

Tests
Test Career:	1928
Cap Number:	232
Tests Played:	3

Test Batting
Innings:	5	Runs:	65
Highest Score:	39	Average:	13.00
No. 50s:	0	No. 100s:	0

Test Bowling & Fielding
Wickets:	15	Runs:	435
Best Bowling:	3/50	Average:	29.00
5 WI:	0	10 WM:	0
Catches:	0	Stumpings:	0

An off spinner and competent lower order batsman, he played three Tests in South Africa in 1928.

STATHAM, John Brian

Born:	June 17, 1930
Batting:	Left handed
Bowling:	Right arm medium-fast

Tests
Test Career:	1951-65
Cap Number:	356
Tests Played:	70

Test Batting
Innings:	87	Runs:	675
Highest Score:	38	Average:	11.44
No. 50s:	0	No. 100s:	0

Test Bowling & Fielding
Wickets:	252	Runs:	6,261
Best Bowling:	7/39	Average:	24.84
5 WI:	9	10 WM:	1
Catches:	28	Stumpings:	0

A rare commodity in English cricket in that he was a genuine fast bowler, he combined with first Frank Tyson then Fred Trueman to spearhead the English attack for almost 15 years. Statham was a stump to stump bowler who used to say "if the batsman misses, I hit" and on many occasions that's exactly what happened. He made his Test debut at Christchurch in 1951 but didn't come to the fore until almost three years later when he was the leading wicket taker in the Caribbean. In 1954/55 England retained the Ashes on the back of the efforts of Statham and Tyson, with the pair taking 46 wickets between them of which Statham took 18. From that point on his output never wavered. Fast and economical, he dominated the touring South Africans in 1960, taking 27 wickets for the series including career best figures of 11/97 at Lord's. In all he took 252 Test wickets and he still lies fifth on England's all-time list. Brian Statham may have been a fine fast bowler but he was also a true gentleman, liked by all who played with and against him.

STEEL, Allan Gibson

Born:	September 24, 1858
Batting:	Right handed
Bowling:	Right arm medium

Tests
Test Career:	1880-88
Cap Number:	28
Tests Played:	13

Test Batting
Innings:	20	Runs:	600
Highest Score:	148	Average:	35.29
No. 50s:	0	No. 100s:	2

Test Bowling & Fielding
Wickets:	29	Runs:	605
Best Bowling:	3/27	Average:	20.86
5 WI:	0	10 WM:	0
Catches:	5	Stumpings:	0

He was a masterful all-rounder from Lancashire who became the first Englishman to score a century at home and abroad when he followed up his ton at the SCG in 1882/83 with a wonderful 148 at Lord's in 1884. He was also a wily slow bowler who took over 1,000 first class wickets. In his latter years with England, Steel skippered the side in four Tests for three victories.

STEELE, David Stanley
Born: September 29, 1941
Batting: Right handed
Bowling: Left arm off-break

Tests
Test Career:	1975-76		
Cap Number:	462		
Tests Played:	8		

Test Batting
Innings:	16	Runs:	673
Highest Score:	106	Average:	42.06
No. 50s:	5	No. 100s:	1

Test Bowling & Fielding
Wickets:	2	Runs:	39
Best Bowling:	1/1	Average:	19.50
5 WI:	0	10 WM:	0
Catches:	7	Stumpings:	0

One Day Internationals
ODI Career:	1976		
ODIs Played:	1		

ODI Batting
Innings:	1	Runs:	8
Highest Score:	8	Average:	8.00
No. 50s:	0	No. 100s:	0

ODI Bowling & Fielding
Wickets:	0	Runs:	9
Best Bowling:		Average:	0.00
5 WM:	0	Catches:	0
Stumpings:	0		

David Steele was perfectly named. With his steel rimmed glasses, steely grey hair and equally steely resolve, he was plucked from obscurity to take on the might of the rampaging Australians at home in 1975. He scored 50 and 45 on debut to the rapturous applause of the fans at Lord's, and followed it up with an even better performance in his next Test in Leeds, making 73 and 92. Australia has rarely had a better pace attack but Lillee, Thomson, Gilmour and Walker couldn't budge the 34 year old from Northants. He finished that series with an average of over 60 but wasn't called on again until the following season when England was once again under fire at home. This time it was the West Indies and Steele answered the call with 106 at Trent Bridge against Andy Roberts and Michael Holding. In all the courageous Steele played in only eight Tests but gave a fine account of himself in every one.

STEPHENSON, John Patrick
Born: March 14, 1965
Batting: Right handed
Bowling: Right arm medium

Tests
Test Career:	1989		
Cap Number:	541		
Tests Played:	1		

Test Batting
Innings:	2	Runs:	36
Highest Score:	25	Average:	18.00
No. 50s:	0	No. 100s:	0

Test Bowling & Fielding
Wickets:	0	Runs:	0
Best Bowling:		Average:	0.00
5 WI:	0	10 WM:	0
Catches:	0	Stumpings:	0

An all-rounder from Essex who played his only Test against Australia at The Oval in 1989.

STEVENS, Greville Thomas Scott
Born: January 7, 1901
Batting: Right handed
Bowling: Right arm leg-break

Tests
Test Career:	1922-30		
Cap Number:	210		
Tests Played:	10		

Test Batting
Innings:	17	Runs:	263
Highest Score:	69	Average:	15.47
No. 50s:	1	No. 100s:	0

Test Bowling & Fielding
Wickets:	20	Runs:	648
Best Bowling:	5/90	Average:	32.40
5 WI:	2	10 WM:	1
Catches:	9	Stumpings:	0

A wonderful all-rounder who played the bulk of his cricket for Oxford University and Middlesex, he would have played many more Tests for England had business commitments not meant he was often unavailable for selection. The middle order batsman and leg spinner scored 149 for Middlesex against the touring Australians in 1926 and in doing so won a spot in the powerful side that regained the Ashes at The Oval later that season.

STEVENSON, Graham Barry
Born: December 16, 1955
Batting: Right handed
Bowling: Right arm medium

Tests
Test Career:	1980-81		
Cap Number:	485		
Tests Played:	2		

Test Batting
Innings:	2	Runs:	28
Highest Score:	27*	Average:	28.00
No. 50s:	0	No. 100s:	0

Test Bowling & Fielding
Wickets:	5	Runs:	183
Best Bowling:	3/111	Average:	36.60
5 WI:	0	10 WM:	0
Catches:	0	Stumpings:	0

One Day Internationals
ODI Career:	1980-81		
ODIs Played:	4		

ODI Batting
Innings:	4	Runs:	43
Highest Score:	28*	Average:	43.00
No. 50s:	0	No. 100s:	0

ODI Bowling & Fielding
Wickets:	7	Runs:	125
Best Bowling:	4/33	Average:	17.85
5 WM:	0	Catches:	2
Stumpings:	0		

An all-rounder from Yorkshire who played two Tests in the early 80's.

STEWART, Alec James
Born: April 8, 1963
Batting: Right handed
Bowling: Right arm medium
Wicket Keeper

Tests
Test Career:	1990-2003		
Cap Number:	543		
Tests Played:	133		

Test Batting
Innings:	235	Runs:	8,463
Highest Score:	190	Average:	39.54
No. 50s:	45	No. 100s:	15

Test Bowling & Fielding
Wickets:	0	Runs:	13
Best Bowling:		Average:	0.00
5 WI:	0	10 WM:	0
Catches:	263	Stumpings:	14

One Day Internationals
ODI Career:	1989-2003		
ODIs Played:	170		

ODI Batting
Innings:	162	Runs:	4,677
Highest Score:	116	Average:	31.60
No. 50s:	28	No. 100s:	4

ODI Bowling & Fielding
Wickets:	0	Runs:	0
Best Bowling:		Average:	0.00
5 WM:	0	Catches:	159
Stumpings:	15		

No cricketer has played more Tests for England than Alec Stewart, which is as much a tribute to his fighting spirit as his ability. He was neither a world class batsman nor a world class keeper but combined his version of the two to provide England with sterling service for 13 years. Stewart the batsman took a number of Tests to adjust to Test cricket, but after scoring his maiden hundred against Sri Lanka at Lord's in 1992 went on a spree that saw him belt three more tons in his next four Tests. Hardly a classical batsman, he had the canny knack of sending any loose ball to the boundary by whatever means. His shots could be described as a collection of swats, slaps and hoiks but the result was generally effective as his 15 Test centuries prove. His keeping was similarly unorthodox. Often described as a backstop rather than wicket keeper, he was always brave and took many a blow on the body when his hands weren't up to the task. Alec Stewart played his cricket more like an Australian than an Englishman, happy to give as good as he got in the verbal stakes and never willing to surrender. He acted as captain in 15 Tests before and after Michael Atherton's tenure, and as with his batting and keeping, never said die.

STEWART, Michael James
Born: September 16, 1932
Batting: Right handed
Bowling: Right arm medium

Tests
Test Career:	1962-64		
Cap Number:	412		
Tests Played:	8		

Test Batting
Innings:	12	Runs:	385
Highest Score:	87	Average:	35.00
No. 50s:	2	No. 100s:	0

Test Bowling & Fielding
Wickets:	0	Runs:	0
Best Bowling:		Average:	0.00
5 WI:	0	10 WM:	0
Catches:	6	Stumpings:	0

Mickey Stewart short Test career included one fine innings of 87 against Pakistan at Headingly in 1962, but he is best known as a former long standing Surrey captain, a one time England team manager and as the father of Alec.

STODDART, Andrew Ernest
Born: April 11, 1863
Batting: Right handed
Bowling: Right arm medium

Tests
Test Career:	1888-98		
Cap Number:	56		
Tests Played:	16		

Test Batting
Innings:	30	Runs:	996
Highest Score:	173	Average:	35.57
No. 50s:	3	No. 100s:	2

Test Bowling & Fielding
Wickets:	2	Runs:	94
Best Bowling:	1/10	Average:	47.00
5 WI:	0	10 WM:	0
Catches:	6	Stumpings:	0

Stoddard's reputation preceded him into first class cricket on the back of an extraordinary 485 he hit in a game of village geen cricket in 1886. A captain at Middlesex who also led his country into battle, he was at the helm when England won the Ashes in Australia in 1894/95. He enjoyed a fine tour and scored a then record 173 in the second Test at the MCG. Known as Stod, the fine all round sportsman also captained England in Rugby.

STORER, William
Born: January 25, 1867
Batting: Right handed
Bowling: Right arm leg-break
Wicket Keeper

Tests

Test Career:	1897-99		
Cap Number:	110		
Tests Played:	6		

Test Batting

Innings:	11	Runs:	215
Highest Score:	51	Average:	19.54
No. 50s:	1	No. 100s:	0

Test Bowling & Fielding

Wickets:	2	Runs:	108
Best Bowling:	1/24	Average:	54.00
5 WI:	0	10 WM:	0
Catches:	11	Stumpings:	0

An all round sportsman who also played football for Derby County, he kept wickets in the five Tests on the 1897/98 Ashes tour. Interestingly he took off the keepers gloves in two of those Tests to bowl leg spin and enjoyed success taking a wicket on both occasions.

STRAUSS, Andrew John

Born:	March 2, 1977
Batting:	Left handed
Bowling:	Left arm medium

Tests

Test Career:	2004-		
Cap Number:	624		
Tests Played:	30		

Test Batting

Innings:	56	Runs:	2,505
Highest Score:	147	Average:	46.38
No. 50s:	6	No. 100s:	10

Test Bowling & Fielding

Wickets:	0	Runs:	0
Best Bowling:		Average:	0.00
5 WI:	0	10 WM:	0
Catches:	37	Stumpings:	0

One Day Internationals

ODI Career:	2003-		
ODIs Played:	56		

ODI Batting

Innings:	55	Runs:	1,682
Highest Score:	152	Average:	35.04
No. 50s:	9	No. 100s:	2

ODI Bowling & Fielding

Wickets:	0	Runs:	0
Best Bowling:		Average:	0.00
5 WM:	0	Catches:	16
Stumpings:	0		

It's hard to believe that Andrew Strauss has only been playing Test cricket since May 2004. In the space of just over two years the left handed batsman from Middlesex has scored over two and a half thousand Tests runs, hit ten Test centuries and captained the national side against Sri Lanka and Pakistan. His first Test was against New Zealand at Lord's and Strauss took no time in claiming the opening spot alongside Marcus Trescothick. He made 112 and 83 on debut and since that time has shown an amazing propensity for stamping his authority when facing a new opponent. His first Test innings against the West Indies was 137, he made 126 on debut against South Africa and has already compiled three figure scores against Australia, India and Pakistan. Strauss' batting comes in two distinct phases. His defense is resolute and gives no suggestion that there is quick scorer lurking within, but when in control he keeps the scoreboard moving by constantly working the ball into gaps and to the boundary. With Michael Vaughan and Andy Flintoff out of the 2006 English summer due to injury, the South African born Strauss was handed the captaincy, and as he did with his Test batting, fitted seamlessly into the role.

STREET, George Benjamin

Born:	December 6, 1889
Batting:	Right handed
	Wicket Keeper

Tests

Test Career:	1923		
Cap Number:	212		
Tests Played:	1		

Test Batting

Innings:	2	Runs:	11
Highest Score:	7*	Average:	11.00
No. 50s:	0	No. 100s:	0

Test Bowling & Fielding

Wickets:	0	Runs:	0
Best Bowling:		Average:	0.00
5 WI:	0	10 WM:	0
Catches:	0	Stumpings:	1

A wicketkeeper from Sussex, he played a single Test against South Africa at Durban in 1923.

STRUDWICK, Herbert

Born:	January 28, 1880
Batting:	Right handed
	Wicket Keeper

Tests

Test Career:	1910-26		
Cap Number:	168		
Tests Played:	28		

Test Batting

Innings:	42	Runs:	230
Highest Score:	24	Average:	7.93
No. 50s:	0	No. 100s:	0

Test Bowling & Fielding

Wickets:	0	Runs:	0
Best Bowling:		Average:	0.00
5 WI:	0	10 WM:	0
Catches:	61	Stumpings:	12

In a 25 year career, the Surrey keeper had the amazing record of over 1,500 first class dismissals behind the stumps. A genuine number eleven batsman, it was a measure of how good a keeper he was that he played 28 Tests. Agile and compact 'Struddie' is thought to have resembled modern day keepers more than any other gloveman of his era.

STUDD, Charles Thomas

Born:	December 2, 1860
Batting:	Right handed
Bowling:	Right arm medium-fast

Tests

Test Career:	1882-83
Cap Number:	37
Tests Played:	5

Test Batting

Innings:	9	Runs:	160
Highest Score:	48	Average:	20.00
No. 50s:	0	No. 100s:	0

Test Bowling & Fielding

Wickets:	3	Runs:	98
Best Bowling:	2/35	Average:	32.66
5 WI:	0	10 WM:	0
Catches:	5	Stumpings:	0

An all rounder of note who captained Cambridge University in first class games, he achieved the double of 1,000 runs and 100 wickets in a first class season on two occasions. A promising cricket career was cut short when he found God and headed to the Belgian Congo to work as a missionary.

STUDD, George Brown

Born:	October 20, 1859
Batting:	Right handed

Tests

Test Career:	1882-83
Cap Number:	41
Tests Played:	4

Test Batting

Innings:	7	Runs:	31
Highest Score:	9	Average:	0.00
No. 50s:	0	No. 100s:	0

Test Bowling & Fielding

Wickets:	0	Runs:	0
Best Bowling:		Average:	0.00
5 WI:	0	10 WM:	0
Catches:	8	Stumpings:	0

The brother of Charles Studd, he toured Australia in 1882/83, and whilst he played in all four Tests showed none of the form that made him a formidable batsman for Middlesex in county competition.

SUBBA ROW, Raman

Born:	January 29, 1932
Batting:	Left handed
Bowling:	Left arm leg-break

Tests

Test Career:	1958-61
Cap Number:	390
Tests Played:	13

Test Batting

Innings:	22	Runs:	984
Highest Score:	137	Average:	46.85
No. 50s:	4	No. 100s:	3

Test Bowling & Fielding

Wickets:	0	Runs:	2
Best Bowling:		Average:	0.00
5 WI:	0	10 WM:	0
Catches:	5	Stumpings:	0

In a short Test career the Surrey batsman scored three excellent Test centuries. He scored an even 100 against the West Indies at Georgetown in 1959/60 to deny the home team a victory and chance to level the series. He also scored two hundreds against the touring Australians in 1961, 112 at Edgbaston and 137 at The Oval in the final Test. Subba Row scored 468 runs in that series at an average of 46.80 but retired immediately after citing business as the reason.

SUCH, Peter Mark

Born:	June 12, 1964
Batting:	Right handed
Bowling:	Right arm off-break

Tests

Test Career:	1993-99
Cap Number:	560
Tests Played:	11

Test Batting

Innings:	16	Runs:	67
Highest Score:	14*	Average:	6.09
No. 50s:	0	No. 100s:	0

Test Bowling & Fielding

Wickets:	37	Runs:	1,242
Best Bowling:	6/67	Average:	33.56
5 WI:	2	10 WM:	0
Catches:	4	Stumpings:	0

A steady right arm off spinner who played for a number of county sides in a first class career that spanned 20 years. His highlight as a Test cricketer was clearly the 6/67 he took in his first Test against the touring Australians in 1993. His victims included no less a quartet than Mark Taylor, David Boon, Allan Border and Steve Waugh.

SUGG, Frank Howe

Born:	January 11, 1862
Batting:	Right handed

Tests

Test Career:	1888
Cap Number:	59
Tests Played:	2

Test Batting

Innings:	2	Runs:	55
Highest Score:	31	Average:	27.50
No. 50s:	0	No. 100s:	0

Test Bowling & Fielding

Wickets:	0	Runs:	0
Best Bowling:		Average:	0.00
5 WI:	0	10 WM:	0
Catches:	0	Stumpings:	0

An accomplished right hand bat with over 10,000 first class runs to his name, he was one of Derbyshire's few Test representatives in the early years of Test cricket.

SUTCLIFFE, Herbert

Born:	November 24, 1894
Batting:	Right handed
Bowling:	Right arm medium

Tests

Test Career:	1924-35
Cap Number:	215
Tests Played:	54

Test Batting
Innings:	84	Runs:	4,555
Highest Score:	194	Average:	60.73
No. 50s:	23	No. 100s:	16

Test Bowling & Fielding
Wickets:	0	Runs:	0
Best Bowling:		Average:	0.00
5 WI:	0	10 WM:	0
Catches:	23	Stumpings:	0

Of all the Test batsmen who have scored over 2,000 runs, only four finished their careers with an average above 60. One of them was the famed English opener Herb Sutcliffe. The opening batsman from Yorkshire who put a great price on his wicket with a near impenetrable defense, could also attack and was never accused of putting his own interests before that of the team. He made his debut against the touring South Africans in 1924 and was paired at the top of the order with Jack Hobbs. Within two Tests England had found one of cricket's great opening combinations, they put on 136 in their first outing at Edgbaston and 268 at Lord's in their second. There was much anticipation when Sutcliffe made his first visit to Australia in 1924/25 and he didn't disappoint with 734 runs in nine Test innings. His first Test on foreign soil was at the SCG where he scored 59 and 115. If the Australian public was impressed, they were soon to be in awe. Sutcliffe scored 176 and 127 in a losing side at the MCG in the second Test and along with Hobbs, England suddenly had batsmen to rival the likes of Ponsford, Ryder and Richardson. In all he scored 16 Test centuries, often saving his best for the Australians. He scored 440 during the 'bodyline' series in 1932/33 to top the aggregates for both sides along with Walter Hammond. Sutcliffe scored his Test high of 194 at the SCG in the first Test of that acrimonious series. The pugnacious opener played his final Test for England at the age of 40 and in retirement became an English Test selector. Whilst he played with and against many greats, there is no doubting who he held in the highest regard. The answer lies in the naming of his son who went on to captain Yorkshire; William Herbert Hobbs Sutcliffe.

SWANN, Graeme Peter
Born:	March 24, 1979
Batting:	Right handed
Bowling:	Right arm off-break

One Day Internationals
ODI Career:	2000
ODIs Played:	1

ODI Batting
Innings:	0	Runs:	0
Highest Score:	0	Average:	0.00
No. 50s:	0	No. 100s:	0

ODI Bowling & Fielding
Wickets:	0	Runs:	24
Best Bowling:		Average:	0.00
5 WM:	0	Catches:	0
Stumpings:	0		

A blonde off-spinner who was also a competent batsman, Swann didn't take a wicket nor get the chance to bat in his solitary ODI against South Africa at Bloemfontein in 2000.

SWETMAN, Roy
Born:	October 25, 1933
Batting:	Right handed
Bowling:	Right arm off-break
	Wicket Keeper

Tests
Test Career:	1959-60
Cap Number:	391
Tests Played:	11

Test Batting
Innings:	17	Runs:	254
Highest Score:	65	Average:	16.93
No. 50s:	1	No. 100s:	0

Test Bowling & Fielding
Wickets:	0	Runs:	0
Best Bowling:		Average:	0.00
5 WI:	0	10 WM:	0
Catches:	24	Stumpings:	2

The neat wicketkeeper and competent lower order batsman played a handful of games for England in 1959 and 1960 but couldn't consolidate a place in the Test side.

TATE, Frederick William
Born:	July 24, 1867
Batting:	Right handed
Bowling:	Right arm medium

Tests
Test Career:	1902-05
Cap Number:	135
Tests Played:	1

Test Batting
Innings:	2	Runs:	9
Highest Score:	5*	Average:	9.00
No. 50s:	0	No. 100s:	0

Test Bowling & Fielding
Wickets:	2	Runs:	51
Best Bowling:	2/7	Average:	25.50
5 WI:	0	10 WM:	0
Catches:	2	Stumpings:	0

He was a medium pace bowler from Sussex who played one Test against Australia in 1902. Unfortunately for Tate, England lost that game by three runs and he missed a catch at a vital stage. He never played for England again

TATE, Maurice William
Born:	May 30, 1895
Batting:	Right handed

Tests
Test Career:	1924-35
Cap Number:	216
Tests Played:	39

Test Batting			
Innings:	52	Runs:	1,198
Highest Score:	100*	Average:	25.48
No. 50s:	5	No. 100s:	1

Test Bowling & Fielding			
Wickets:	155	Runs:	4,055
Best Bowling:	6/42	Average:	26.16
5 WI:	7	10 WM:	1
Catches:	11	Stumpings:	0

The son of Fred Tate, he was a gifted swing bowler who was marked for greatness at a young age. He made his debut for Sussex as a 17 year old and it seemed only a matter of time before he would join Test ranks. The First World War intervened and that matter of time turned out to be 12 long years. When Maurice Tate finally did make his debut he was already 29 years of age, and as though he knew he had no time to spare, he quickly went about breaking records. In his first series against South Africa he was clearly his side's best bowler with 27 wickets at only 15.60 runs apiece and that performance earnt him a spot in the side that toured Australia at the end of that year. He duly rewrote the record books, taking 38 Test wickets at a cost of 23.18. It was a Herculean performance by the strongly built southerner who bowled near twice as many overs as any other Englishman during that series. Tate came to the fore again when the Aussies toured in 1926, claiming 13 wickets in the rain interrupted series to once again be the leading English wicket taker. In all he took 155 wickets in 39 Tests and as important as that was, his greatest strength was his ability to contain batsmen. With a relatively short run up he regularly bowled mammoth spells, but never seemed to tire and conceded less that two runs per over in his brilliant Test career.

TATTERSALL, Roy

Born: August 17, 1922
Batting: Left handed
Bowling: Right arm off-break

Tests

Test Career: 1951-54
Cap Number: 355
Tests Played: 16

Test Batting			
Innings:	17	Runs:	50
Highest Score:	10*	Average:	5.00
No. 50s:	0	No. 100s:	0

Test Bowling & Fielding			
Wickets:	58	Runs:	1,513
Best Bowling:	7/52	Average:	26.08
5 WI:	4	10 WM:	1
Catches:	8	Stumpings:	0

He was a high stepping right arm finger spinner from Lancashire who would have been the ideal one day bowler. Accurate and quick through the air, he maintained an economy rate of barely two runs per over throughout a first class career that spanned three different decades. In the right conditions he was also a wicket taker as his 12/101 against South Africa at Lord's in 1951 proves.

TAVARE, Christopher James

Born: October 27, 1954
Batting: Right handed
Bowling: Right arm off-break

Tests

Test Career: 1980-89
Cap Number: 486
Tests Played: 31

Test Batting			
Innings:	56	Runs:	1,755
Highest Score:	149	Average:	32.50
No. 50s:	12	No. 100s:	2

Test Bowling & Fielding			
Wickets:	0	Runs:	11
Best Bowling:		Average:	0.00
5 WI:	0	10 WM:	0
Catches:	20	Stumpings:	0

One Day Internationals

ODI Career: 1980-84
ODIs Played: 29

ODI Batting			
Innings:	28	Runs:	720
Highest Score:	83*	Average:	27.69
No. 50s:	4	No. 100s:	0

ODI Bowling & Fielding			
Wickets:	0	Runs:	3
Best Bowling:		Average:	0.00
5 WM:	0	Catches:	7
Stumpings:	0		

A notoriously slow batsman, he infuriated opposition bowlers and supporters alike. His highest Test score of 149 was played in tandem with Geoff Boycott in a partnership that lasted almost twelve hours.

TAYLOR, Jonathan Paul

Born: August 8, 1964
Batting: Left handed
Bowling: Left arm medium-fast

Tests

Test Career: 1993-94
Cap Number: 557
Tests Played: 2

Test Batting			
Innings:	4	Runs:	34
Highest Score:	17	Average:	17.00
No. 50s:	0	No. 100s:	0

Test Bowling & Fielding			
Wickets:	3	Runs:	156
Best Bowling:	1/18	Average:	52.00
5 WI:	0	10 WM:	0
Catches:	0	Stumpings:	0

One Day Internationals

ODI Career: 1993
ODIs Played: 1

ODI Batting			
Innings:	1	Runs:	1
Highest Score:	1	Average:	1.00
No. 50s:	0	No. 100s:	0

ODI Bowling & Fielding
Wickets:	0	Runs:	20
Best Bowling:		Average:	0.00
5 WM:	0	Catches:	0
Stumpings:	0		

A surprise selection to tour India in 1993, he played just the one Test at Kolkata. He played in one more Test a year later at Lord's but with only three Test wickets was quickly replaced.

TAYLOR, Kenneth
Born: August 21, 1935
Batting: Right handed

Tests
Test Career: 1959-64
Cap Number: 395
Tests Played: 3

Test Batting
Innings:	5	Runs:	57
Highest Score:	24	Average:	11.40
No. 50s:	0	No. 100s:	0

Test Bowling & Fielding
Wickets:	0	Runs:	6
Best Bowling:		Average:	0.00
5 WI:	0	10 WM:	0
Catches:	1	Stumpings:	0

The Yorkshire batsman played three Tests for England without much success, but along with his time as a footballer with Huddersfield Town, it gave the gifted painter plenty of material for his sporting portraits

TAYLOR, Leslie Brian
Born: October 25, 1953
Batting: Right handed
Bowling: Right arm medium-fast

Tests
Test Career: 1985
Cap Number: 513
Tests Played: 2

Test Batting
Innings:	1	Runs:	1
Highest Score:	1*	Average:	0.00
No. 50s:	0	No. 100s:	0

Test Bowling & Fielding
Wickets:	4	Runs:	178
Best Bowling:	2/34	Average:	44.50
5 WI:	0	10 WM:	0
Catches:	1	Stumpings:	0

One Day Internationals
ODI Career: 1986
ODIs Played: 2

ODI Batting
Innings:	1	Runs:	1
Highest Score:	1*	Average:	0.00
No. 50s:	0	No. 100s:	0

ODI Bowling & Fielding
Wickets:	0	Runs:	47
Best Bowling:		Average:	0.00
5 WM:	0	Catches:	0
Stumpings:	0		

The strongly built Taylor performed adequately in his only two Tests taking four wickets against the Australians at home in 1985.

TAYLOR, Robert William
Born: July 17, 1941
Batting: Right handed
Bowling: Right arm medium
Wicket Keeper

Tests
Test Career: 1971-84
Cap Number: 449
Tests Played: 57

Test Batting
Innings:	83	Runs:	1,156
Highest Score:	97	Average:	16.28
No. 50s:	3	No. 100s:	0

Test Bowling & Fielding
Wickets:	0	Runs:	6
Best Bowling:		Average:	0.00
5 WI:	0	10 WM:	0
Catches:	167	Stumpings:	7

One Day Internationals
ODI Career: 1973-84
ODIs Played: 27

ODI Batting
Innings:	17	Runs:	130
Highest Score:	26*	Average:	13.00
No. 50s:	0	No. 100s:	0

ODI Bowling & Fielding
Wickets:	0	Runs:	0
Best Bowling:		Average:	0.00
5 WM:	0	Catches:	26
Stumpings:	6		

The Derbyshire keeper was an enthusiastic understudy to Alan Knott for many years and when presented with an opportunity courtesy of World Series Cricket he grabbed it with both gloves. Originally preferred to Knott because of his superior work behind the stumps, Taylor ultimately was relegated because of his competitor's fine batting. Superbly fit, he stayed on in the Test side long after WSC playing his last Test at 42. Nicknamed 'Chat', the gregarious keeper was a gutsy bat who was often thrust into the role of nightwatchman. He was desperately unlucky not to record a Test ton with two scores of 97 to his name.

TENNYSON, Lionel Hallam
Born: November 7, 1889
Batting: Right handed
Bowling: Right arm fast

Tests
Test Career: 1913-21
Cap Number: 180
Tests Played: 9

Test Batting
Innings:	125	Runs:	345
Highest Score:	74*	Average:	31.36
No. 50s:	4	No. 100s:	0

Test Bowling & Fielding
Wickets:	0	Runs:	1
Best Bowling:		Average:	0.00
5 WI:	0	10 WM:	0
Catches:	6	Stumpings:	0

The solidly built 3rd Baron Tennyson may not have enjoyed the greatest success at Test level, but he was well respected for his keen cricket brain, and was rewarded with the English captaincy in 1921. He failed to win any of his three games at the helm but it did nothing to quell his leadership aspirations and upon losing his Test spot his took his own sides to India, The West Indies and North America.

TERRY, Vivian Paul
Born:	January 14, 1959
Batting:	Right handed
Bowling:	Right arm medium

Tests
Test Career:	1984
Cap Number:	507
Tests Played:	2

Test Batting
Innings:	3	Runs:	16
Highest Score:	8	Average:	5.33
No. 50s:	0	No. 100s:	0

Test Bowling & Fielding
Wickets:	0	Runs:	0
Best Bowling:		Average:	0.00
5 WI:	0	10 WM:	0
Catches:	2	Stumpings:	0

A batsman from Hampshire who disappointed in his only two Tests with a top score of only eight.

THOMAS, John Gregory
Born:	August 12, 1960
Batting:	Right handed
Bowling:	Right arm fast

Tests
Test Career:	1986
Cap Number:	515
Tests Played:	5

Test Batting
Innings:	10	Runs:	83
Highest Score:	31*	Average:	13.83
No. 50s:	0	No. 100s:	0

Test Bowling & Fielding
Wickets:	10	Runs:	504
Best Bowling:	4/70	Average:	50.40
5 WI:	0	10 WM:	0
Catches:	0	Stumpings:	0

One Day Internationals
ODI Career:	1986-87
ODIs Played:	3

ODI Batting
Innings:	3	Runs:	1
Highest Score:	1*	Average:	1.00
No. 50s:	0	No. 100s:	0

ODI Bowling & Fielding
Wickets:	3	Runs:	144
Best Bowling:	2/59	Average:	48.00
5 WM:	0	Catches:	0
Stumpings:	0		

A fast bowler from Wales who made his debut against the West Indies in Jamaica in 1986. He was part of Mike Gatting's side that toured South Africa for unofficial Tests in 1989/90.

THOMPSON, George Joseph
Born:	October 27, 1877
Batting:	Right handed
Bowling:	Right arm medium-fast

Tests
Test Career:	1909-10
Cap Number:	159
Tests Played:	6

Test Batting
Innings:	10	Runs:	273
Highest Score:	63	Average:	30.33
No. 50s:	2	No. 100s:	0

Test Bowling & Fielding
Wickets:	23	Runs:	638
Best Bowling:	4/50	Average:	27.73
5 WI:	0	10 WM:	0
Catches:	5	Stumpings:	0

The mustachioed Thompson was one of an incredible 25 Englishmen to play in the five Test series against the Australians in 1909. He did little in his single Test but toured South Africa the next season, making over 300 runs and taking 23 wickets.

THOMSON, Norman Ian
Born:	January 23, 1929
Batting:	Right handed
Bowling:	Right arm medium

Tests
Test Career:	1964-65
Cap Number:	426
Tests Played:	5

Test Batting
Innings:	4	Runs:	69
Highest Score:	39	Average:	23.00
No. 50s:	0	No. 100s:	0

Test Bowling & Fielding
Wickets:	9	Runs:	568
Best Bowling:	2/55	Average:	63.11
5 WI:	0	10 WM:	0
Catches:	3	Stumpings:	0

A typical English seam bowler, he toured South Africa in 1964/65 playing in all five Tests for a return of just nine wickets.

THORPE, Graham Paul
Born:	August 1, 1969
Batting:	Left handed
Bowling:	Right arm medium

Tests
Test Career:	1993-2005
Cap Number:	564
Tests Played:	100

Test Batting
Innings:	179	Runs:	6,744
Highest Score:	200*	Average:	44.66
No. 50s:	39	No. 100s:	16

Test Bowling & Fielding
Wickets:	0	Runs:	37
Best Bowling:		Average:	0.00
5 WI:	0	10 WM:	0
Catches:	105	Stumpings:	0

One Day Internationals
ODI Career:	1993-2002
ODIs Played:	82

ODI Batting

Innings:	77	Runs:	2,380
Highest Score:	89	Average:	37.18
No. 50s:	21	No. 100s:	0

ODI Bowling & Fielding

Wickets:	2	Runs:	97
Best Bowling:	2/15	Average:	48.50
5 WM:	0	Catches:	42
Stumpings:	0		

A left-hander from Surrey he made his Test debut against Australia at Trent Bridge in 1993. Thorpe scored a 114 in the second innings of that match and as he did throughout his career proved to the hardest batsman fo the Australians to remove. A gritty individual who always seemed to be urging himself to concentrate during his innings, he provided much needed backbone to the English batting for over a decade. In 2002 he withdrew from cricket citing personal problems but returned for the fifth Test agaisnt South Africa at The Oval in 2003. Thorpe scored a century, and remained in the side until he played his 100th Test against Bangladesh in June 2005. He hadn't intended that 100th Test to be his last, but when he was overlooked for the first Ashes Test in 2005 he announced his retirement. Thorpe moved to Australia later that year to coach in New South Wales and by the end of the season was guiding that state's best youngsters in the NSW 2nd XI.

TITMUS, Frederick John

Born:	November 24, 1932
Batting:	Right handed
Bowling:	Right arm off-break

Tests

Test Career:	1955-1975
Cap Number:	381
Tests Played:	53

Test Batting

Innings:	76	Runs:	1,449
Highest Score:	84*	Average:	22.29
No. 50s:	10	No. 100s:	0

Test Bowling & Fielding

Wickets:	153	Runs:	4,931
Best Bowling:	7/79	Average:	32.22
5 WI:	4	10 WM:	0
Catches:	35	Stumpings:	0

One Day Internationals

ODI Career:	1975
ODIs Played:	2

ODI Batting

Innings:	1	Runs:	11
Highest Score:	11	Average:	11.00
No. 50s:	0	No. 100s:	0

ODI Bowling & Fielding

Wickets:	3	Runs:	53
Best Bowling:	3/53	Average:	17.66
5 WM:	0	Catches:	1
Stumpings:	0		

He enjoyed a long and hearty Test career, rolling out his reliable right arm off breaks for almost two decades. Titmus broke into the Test side as a 22 year old and after two rather inglorious Tests against a touring South African side wasn't seen again at the highest level for another seven years. When he returned, the more seasoned bowler enjoyed great success taking 21 wickets on the Ashes tour of 1962/63, including a career best 7/79 in a single innings at the SCG. Hardly athletic to begin with his, cause was not helped when he lost four toes in a boating accident in 1968 that threatened to end his career. He was able to fight back and regain his spot in the Test side that toured Australia in the mid 70's. Titmus was also an obstinate lower order batsman who made 10 Test half centuries, including an unbeaten 84 against India at Bombay in 1984.

TOLCHARD, Roger William

Born:	June 15, 1946
Batting:	Right handed
Bowling:	Right arm off-break
	Wicket Keeper

Tests

Test Career:	1977
Cap Number:	473
Tests Played:	4

Test Batting

Innings:	7	Runs:	129
Highest Score:	67	Average:	25.80
No. 50s:	1	No. 100s:	0

Test Bowling & Fielding

Wickets:	0	Runs:	0
Best Bowling:	0	Average:	0.00
5 WI:	0	10 WM:	0
Catches:	5	Stumpings:	0

One Day Internationals

ODI Career:	1979
ODIs Played:	1

ODI Batting

Innings:	0	Runs:	0
Highest Score:	0	Average:	0.00
No. 50s:	0	No. 100s:	0

ODI Bowling & Fielding

Wickets:	0	Runs:	0
Best Bowling:	0	Average:	0.00
5 WM:	0	Catches:	1
Stumpings:	0		

A safe wicket keeper, he was third choice behind Alan Knott and Bob Taylor but actually played in his four Tests as a batsman only.

TOWNSEND, Charles Lucas

Born:	November 7, 1876
Batting:	Left handed
Bowling:	Left arm leg-break

Tests

Test Career:	1899
Cap Number:	124
Tests Played:	2

Test Batting

Innings:	3	Runs:	51
Highest Score:	38	Average:	17.00
No. 50s:	0	No. 100s:	0

Test Bowling & Fielding			
Wickets:	3	Runs:	75
Best Bowling:	3/50	Average:	25.00
5 WI:	0	10 WM:	0
Catches:	0	Stumpings:	0

An orthodox leg spinner and left hand batsman, he impressed in his first Test taking three wickets in Australia's first inning during the second Test of the 1899 Ashes series. He did not play again until the fifth Test where he went wicketless.

TOWNSEND, David Charles Humphrey

Born:	April 20, 1912
Batting:	Right handed
Bowling:	Right arm medium

Tests
Test Career:	1935
Cap Number:	282
Tests Played:	3

Test Batting
Innings:	6	Runs:	77
Highest Score:	36	Average:	12.83
No. 50s:	0	No. 100s:	0

Test Bowling & Fielding
Wickets:	0	Runs:	9
Best Bowling:		Average:	0.00
5 WI:	0	10 WM:	0
Catches:	1	Stumpings:	0

The Oxford University man was the last cricketer to represent England without ever playing county cricket. The right hand batsman played in three Tests against The West Indies during the 1934/35 tour of the Caribbean.

TOWNSEND, Leslie Fletcher

Born:	June 8, 1903
Batting:	Right handed
Bowling:	Right arm medium

Tests
Test Career:	1930-34
Cap Number:	254
Tests Played:	4

Test Batting
Innings:	6	Runs:	97
Highest Score:	40	Average:	16.16
No. 50s:	0	No. 100s:	0

Test Bowling & Fielding
Wickets:	6	Runs:	205
Best Bowling:	2/22	Average:	34.16
5 WI:	0	10 WM:	0
Catches:	2	Stumpings:	0

He played all of his Tests on foreign soil with a single appearance on the tour of West Indies in 1930 then three more when England toured India for the first time in 1933. He later emigrated to New Zealand where he played first class cricket for Auckland.

TREMLETT, Christopher Timothy

Born:	September 2, 1981
Batting:	Right handed
Bowling:	Right arm medium-fast

One Day Internationals
ODI Career:	2005
ODIs Played:	3

ODI Batting
Innings:	1	Runs:	8
Highest Score:	8	Average:	8.00
No. 50s:	0	No. 100s:	0

ODI Bowling & Fielding
Wickets:	5	Runs:	111
Best Bowling:	4/32	Average:	22.20
5 WM:	0	Catches:	0
Stumpings:	0		

The grandson of Somerset legend, Maurice Tremlett who opened the bowling for England in three Tests back in 1948, Chris, like his grandfather, is also a right arm pace bowler. At 6ft 7, Tremlett has impressed at ODI level taking 4/32 on debut, against Bangladesh at Trent Bridge in 2005. Although wicket-less in the follow up match at Headingley, Tremlett ability warrants further international ODI selection.

TREMLETT, Maurice Fletcher

Born:	July 5, 1923
Batting:	Right handed
Bowling:	Right arm medium-fast

Tests
Test Career:	1948
Cap Number:	331
Tests Played:	3

Test Batting
Innings:	5	Runs:	20
Highest Score:	18*	Average:	6.66
No. 50s:	0	No. 100s:	0

Test Bowling & Fielding
Wickets:	4	Runs:	226
Best Bowling:	2/98	Average:	56.50
5 WI:	0	10 WM:	0
Catches:	0	Stumpings:	0

The Somerset captain had a huge impact on county cricket throughout the fifties but played only three Tests for England. They were all on the tour of the West Indies in 1948 and whilst Tremlett was a fine bat he could manage only 20 runs in five innings.

TRESCOTHICK, Marcus Edward

Born:	December 25, 1975
Batting:	Left handed
Bowling:	Right arm medium

Tests
Test Career:	2000-
Cap Number:	603
Tests Played:	75

Test Batting
Innings:	141	Runs:	5,815
Highest Score:	219	Average:	44.38
No. 50s:	29	No. 100s:	14

Test Bowling & Fielding
Wickets:	1	Runs:	155
Best Bowling:	1/34	Average:	155.00
5 WI:	0	10 WM:	0
Catches:	93	Stumpings:	0

One Day Internationals

ODI Career:	2000-		
ODIs Played:	120		

ODI Batting

Innings:	119	Runs:	4,313
Highest Score:	137	Average:	38.16
No. 50s:	21	No. 100s:	12

ODI Bowling & Fielding

Wickets:	4	Runs:	219
Best Bowling:	2/7	Average:	54.75
5 WM:	0	Catches:	48
Stumpings:	0		

When England needed a stand-in one-day opener in 2000, England coach Duncan Fletcher turned to Marcus Trescothick. The imposing gent from Somerset was retained for the Test team that met the touring West Indians in August and cemented his place in the side after scoring a typically solid 66 on debut. That innings was 268 minutes in the making but showed selectors that if it was a bulwark they wanted at the top of the order then Trescothick was their man. Even though he has 14 Test centuries to his name, that number could be far great given the number of times he has been out in the 60's and 70's. One occasion he did grind the opposition into the ground was against South Africa at The Oval in 2003. His 219 in the first innings and unbeaten 69 in the second steered England to a victory and in turn secured a 2-2 series result. He has little trouble against the weaker Test attacks, scoring a century in each of his innings at Edgbaston against the West Indies in 2004 and successive 150's against Bangladesh in 2005. Against Australia however the hundreds have been harder to come by, and in 15 Tests his highest score is 90. Trescothick led England in two Tests during Michael Vaughan's reign, but was overlooked in favour of first Andy Flintoff then Andrew Strauss when the skipper was out of action in 2006.

TROTT, Albert Edwin

Born:	February 6, 1873
Batting:	Right handed
Bowling:	Right arm slow

Tests

Test Career:	1895-99		
Cap Number:	116		
Tests Played:	5		

Test Batting

Innings:	9	Runs:	228
Highest Score:	85*	Average:	38.00
No. 50s:	2	No. 100s:	0

Test Bowling & Fielding

Wickets:	26	Runs:	390
Best Bowling:	8/43	Average:	15.00
5 WI:	2	10 WM:	0
Catches:	4	Stumpings:	0

After a sparkling debut in 1895, he was incredibly left out of the Australian side to tour England the next year in a team that was in fact led by his brother Harry. Known as Alberto, on debut in Adelaide he scored 38 not out and 72 as well as taking 8/43 in England's second innings. He followed that up with an 85 not out at the SCG in what was to be his second last Test for Australia. Upon failing to make the touring party in 1896 he travelled to England on his own steam where he joined Middlesex and eventually played two Tests for his adopted country.

TROUGHTON, Jamie Oliver (Jim)

Born:	March 2, 1979
Batting:	Left handed
Bowling:	Left arm slow

One Day Internationals

ODI Career:	2003		
ODIs Played:	6		

ODI Batting

Innings:	5	Runs:	36
Highest Score:	20	Average:	9.00
No. 50s:	0	No. 100s:	0

ODI Bowling & Fielding

Wickets:	0	Runs:	0
Best Bowling:		Average:	0.00
5 WM:	0	Catches:	1
Stumpings:	0		

A dapper looking middle order batsman, Jim Troughton struggled to make an impact during his six ODI's in 2003.

TRUEMAN, Frederick Sewards

Born:	February 6, 1931
Batting:	Right handed
Bowling:	Right arm fast

Tests

Test Career:	1952-65		
Cap Number:	369		
Tests Played:	67		

Test Batting

Innings:	85	Runs:	981
Highest Score:	39*	Average:	13.81
No. 50s:	0	No. 100s:	0

Test Bowling & Fielding

Wickets:	307	Runs:	6,625
Best Bowling:	8/31	Average:	21.57
5 WI:	17	10 WM:	3
Catches:	64	Stumpings:	0

The first man to take 300 Test wickets, he was one of the great characters to have played and observed the game of cricket. The brash youngster burst on to the scene against India in 1952 taking 29 wickets in only four Tests. He almost single handedly blasted out the tourists at Old Trafford, taking 8/31 as India was dismissed for only 58. For over a decade he would open the English bowling, often saving his best for arch rivals Australia. His finest hour came against the Aussies during the third Test at Headingly in 1961. With Australia one nil up in the series and seemingly cruising at 2/183 in the first innings, Trueman produced a speed of fearsome fast bowling that had the opposition all out of 237. He followed his 5/58 with 6/30 in the second innings to lead

England to a comfortable eight wicket victory. He matched that 11 wicket haul with a similar effort against the West Indies at Lord's in 1963, then bettered it in the very next Test with match figures of 12/119 in Birmingham. Fiery Fred's greatness stemmed from a textbook technique that took advantage of his natural strength and allowed for his lack of height. Standing at only 5ft 10ins, he relied on out swing rather than bounce, with many of his victims falling to catches behind the wickets. His 307 Test scalps stood as a world record till passed by West Indian spinner Lance Gibbs in the 70's. Trueman made the transition from player to commentator in the 60's and his willingness to speak his mind, combined with a wicked sense of humour, made him a favourite with cricket followers around the globe. There are countless quotes from the great man, such as his definition of a gentleman as "being someone who gets out of the bath to take a pee". His could put that wit to cutting use in the commentary box and on one occasion chastised an out of form English bowler with, "E' can now be called an all-rounder because e' bowls as bad as e' bats". Fred Trueman passed away in his native Yorkshire in 2006 at the age of 75.

TUDOR, Alex Jeremy

Born: October 23, 1977
Batting: Right handed
Bowling: Right arm fast

Tests
Test Career:	1998-2002
Cap Number:	592
Tests Played:	10

Test Batting
Innings:	16	Runs:	229
Highest Score:	99*	Average:	19.08
No. 50s:	1	No. 100s:	0

Test Bowling & Fielding
Wickets:	28	Runs:	963
Best Bowling:	5/44	Average:	34.39
5 WI:	1	10 WM:	0
Catches:	3	Stumpings:	0

One Day Internationals
ODI Career:	2002
ODIs Played:	3

ODI Batting
Innings:	2	Runs:	9
Highest Score:	6	Average:	9.00
No. 50s:	0	No. 100s:	0

ODI Bowling & Fielding
Wickets:	4	Runs:	136
Best Bowling:	2/30	Average:	34.00
5 WM:	0	Catches:	1
Stumpings:	0		

An opening bowler from Surrey who would have played more cricket for England had he not been injury prone. Whilst he was very much a bowler, Tudor made the highest score in Test history by an English night watchman when he scored 99 not out against New Zealand at Edgbaston in 1999.

TUFNELL, Neville Charsley

Born: June 13, 1887
Batting: Right handed
Bowling: Right arm slow
Wicket Keeper

Tests
Test Career:	1910
Cap Number:	169
Tests Played:	1

Test Batting
Innings:	1	Runs:	14
Highest Score:	14	Average:	14.00
No. 50s:	0	No. 100s:	0

Test Bowling & Fielding
Wickets:	0	Runs:	0
Best Bowling:		Average:	0.00
5 WI:	0	10 WM:	0
Catches:	0	Stumpings:	1

A reserve keeper at Surrey behind Albert Strudwick, he played a single Test in South Africa in 1910.

TUFNELL, Philip Clive Roderick

Born: April 29, 1966
Batting: Right handed
Bowling: Left arm off-break

Tests
Test Career:	1990-2001
Cap Number:	547
Tests Played:	42

Test Batting
Innings:	59	Runs:	153
Highest Score:	22*	Average:	5.10
No. 50s:	0	No. 100s:	0

Test Bowling & Fielding
Wickets:	121	Runs:	4,560
Best Bowling:	7/47	Average:	37.68
5 WI:	5	10 WM:	2
Catches:	12	Stumpings:	0

One Day Internationals
ODI Career:	1990-97
ODIs Played:	20

ODI Batting
Innings:	10	Runs:	15
Highest Score:	5*	Average:	15.00
No. 50s:	0	No. 100s:	0

ODI Bowling & Fielding
Wickets:	19	Runs:	699
Best Bowling:	4/22	Average:	36.78
5 WM:	0	Catches:	4
Stumpings:	0		

Always the lad, Phil Tufnell may have been happy playing the fool, but when he did concentrate on his bowling he was a dangerous left arm off spinner. He was in and out of the side for a decade as selectors wrestled with the value of playing someone who couldn't bat, couldn't field, and seemed to take Test cricket too casually. On the up side was a crafty spinner who single handedly bowled England to victory against the Australians at The Oval in 1997 with the stunning match figures of 11/93. In retirement Tufnell has become a media darling, appearing in reality TV shows and espousing his opinion on talkback radio. He prodded England/Australia rivalry when he released a comical video during the 2005 Ashes series denigrating members of the Australian side.

TURNBULL, Maurice Joseph Lawson
Born: March 16, 1906
Batting: Right handed
Bowling: Right arm off-break

Tests
Test Career: 1930-36
Cap Number: 250
Tests Played: 9

Test Batting
Innings:	13	Runs:	224
Highest Score:	61	Average:	20.36
No. 50s:	1	No. 100s:	0

Test Bowling & Fielding
Wickets:	0	Runs:	0
Best Bowling:		Average:	0.00
5 WI:	0	10 WM:	0
Catches:	1	Stumpings:	0

He was a slashing batsman who could be regarded as Glamorgan's first world class cricketer. Turnbull toured the West Indies and India and following his Test career acted as a national selector. A Major in the Welsh National Guard he was killed in action in Normandy.

TYLDESLEY, George Ernest
Born: February 5, 1889
Batting: Right handed

Tests
Test Career: 1921-29
Cap Number: 194
Tests Played: 14

Test Batting
Innings:	20	Runs:	990
Highest Score:	122	Average:	55.00
No. 50s:	6	No. 100s:	3

Test Bowling & Fielding
Wickets:	0	Runs:	2
Best Bowling:		Average:	0.00
5 WI:	0	10 WM:	0
Catches:	2	Stumpings:	0

He was the younger brother of Test cricketer Johnny, but at 16 years his junior never played alongside him for England. Like his brother he was an attacking batsman, equally at home on the front or back foot. He made his debut against the Australians in 1921 and whilst he scored an unbeaten 78 in that series he never seemed comfortable against a strong Australian attack. He did flourish however against weaker Test opposition, scoring two centuries on the tour of South Africa in 1927/28 and another when the West Indies toured England in the summer of '28. Those innings bolstered his Test average and when he completed his last Test against the Australians at the MCG in 1929 he left Test cricket with a batting average of 55.

TYLDESLEY, John Thomas
Born: November 22, 1873
Batting: Right handed

Tests
Test Career: 1899-1909
Cap Number: 117
Tests Played: 31

Test Batting
Innings:	55	Runs:	1,661
Highest Score:	138	Average:	30.75
No. 50s:	9	No. 100s:	4

Test Bowling & Fielding
Wickets:	0	Runs:	0
Best Bowling:		Average:	0.00
5 WI:	0	10 WM:	0
Catches:	16	Stumpings:	0

Whilst he might have been short in stature standing at only 5ft 6ins the Lancashire stalwart was an attacking batsman who held down the number three spot in the English batting line up for a decade. He made his debut in Lord Hawke's side that played in South Africa in 1899 and whilst many of the members of that touring party were never seen again at Test level, Johnny Tyldesley would go on to give his country fine service. He scored the first of four Test centuries against the South Africans at Cape Town in 1899. The remainder of his Test tons were against the Australians on home soil including two during the 1905 summer in which he scored 424 Test runs at average of 53.

TYLDESLEY, Richard Knowles
Born: March 11, 1897
Batting: Right handed
Bowling: Right arm leg-break

Tests
Test Career: 1924-30
Cap Number: 218
Tests Played: 7

Test Batting
Innings:	7	Runs:	47
Highest Score:	29	Average:	7.83
No. 50s:	0	No. 100s:	0

Test Bowling & Fielding
Wickets:	19	Runs:	619
Best Bowling:	3/50	Average:	32.57
5 WI:	0	10 WM:	0
Catches:	1	Stumpings:	0

Whilst he had two brothers who played first class cricket for Lancashire, the right handed leg spinner was not related to the Tyldesleys who played for England. Heavy set as a youngster and with an ever increasing girth he wasn't a big turner of the ball but did capture many batsmen LBW with a well worked top spinner. He toured Australia in 1924/25 but only played in one Test for the disappointing return of 0/136.

TYLECOTE, Edmund Ferdinando Sutton

Born:	June 23, 1849
Batting:	Right handed
	Wicket Keeper

Tests

Test Career:	1883-86		
Cap Number:	42		
Tests Played:	6		

Test Batting

Innings:	9	Runs:	152
Highest Score:	66	Average:	19.00
No. 50s:	0	No. 100s:	0

Test Bowling & Fielding

Wickets:	0	Runs:	0
Best Bowling:		Average:	0.00
5 WI:	0	10 WM:	0
Catches:	5	Stumpings:	5

A wicketkeeper whose century for Kent against the touring Australians in 1882 earned him a spot in Bligh's side that visited Australia later that year. With the series tied at one apiece he scored a vital 66 in the third Test to enable England to win the Test and ultimately the series.

TYLER, Edwin James

Born:	October 13, 1864
Batting:	Left handed
Bowling:	Left arm off-break

Tests

Test Career:	1896		
Cap Number:	103		
Tests Played:	1		

Test Batting

Innings:	1	Runs:	0
Highest Score:	0	Average:	0.00
No. 50s:	0	No. 100s:	0

Test Bowling & Fielding

Wickets:	4	Runs:	65
Best Bowling:	3/49	Average:	16.25
5 WI:	0	10 WM:	0
Catches:	0	Stumpings:	0

An off spinner from Somerset whose only Test was against the South Africans at Cape Town in 1896.

TYSON, Frank Holmes

Born:	June 6, 1930
Batting:	Right handed
Bowling:	Right arm fast

Tests

Test Career:	1954-59		
Cap Number:	377		
Tests Played:	17		

Test Batting

Innings:	24	Runs:	230
Highest Score:	37*	Average:	10.95
No. 50s:	0	No. 100s:	0

Test Bowling & Fielding

Wickets:	76	Runs:	1,411
Best Bowling:	7/27	Average:	18.56
5 WI:	4	10 WM:	1
Catches:	4	Stumpings:	0

Bald and quick is a simple but accurate way to describe possibly England's fastest bowler of all time. A series of debilitating injuries meant the 'Typhoon' played only 17 Tests but within that short career there were some famous spells of bowling. He was at his best in Australia in 1954/55 and at the MCG during the third Test unleashed a spell of wind assisted bowling that old timers still say is the fastest ever seen at the historic ground. He took 7/27 in the home side's second innings as a batting line up that included Arthur Morris, Keith Miller, Neil Harvey and Richie Benaud fell for only 111. Tyson took 28 wickets for the series teaming with Brian Statham to win the Ashes for England. In retirement Tyson emigrated to Australia where he worked as a television and radio commentator.

UDAL, Shaun David

Born:	March 18, 1969
Batting:	Right handed
Bowling:	Right arm off-break

Tests

Test Career:	2005-		
Cap Number:	627		
Tests Played:	4		

Test Batting

Innings:	7	Runs:	109
Highest Score:	33*	Average:	18.16
No. 50s:	0	No. 100s:	0

Test Bowling & Fielding

Wickets:	8	Runs:	344
Best Bowling:	4/14	Average:	43.00
5 WI:	0	10 WM:	0
Catches:	1	Stumpings:	0

One Day Internationals

ODI Career:	1994-		
ODIs Played:	11		

ODI Batting

Innings:	7	Runs:	35
Highest Score:	11*	Average:	11.66
No. 50s:	0	No. 100s:	0

ODI Bowling & Fielding

Wickets:	9	Runs:	400
Best Bowling:	2/37	Average:	44.44
5 WM:	0	Catches:	1
Stumpings:	0		

In the decade between Shaun Udal's last ODI and first Test the right arm off spinner must have thought his days of international cricket were over. He had played a handfiul of one day games in 1994/95 and would have been shocked to get a call up to the Test side in 2005. His best performance during his comeback was a memorable effort in Mumbai when his 4/14 on the final day gave England a series saving win. Udal's Indian summer lasted for four Tests but with the emergence of Monty Panesar there will surely be no more amazing resurrections.

ULYETT, George

Born:	October 21, 1851
Batting:	Right handed
Bowling:	Right arm fast

Tests

Test Career:	1877-90
Cap Number:	11
Tests Played:	25

Test Batting

Innings:	39	Runs:	949
Highest Score:	149	Average:	24.33
No. 50s:	7	No. 100s:	1

Test Bowling & Fielding

Wickets:	50	Runs:	1,020
Best Bowling:	7/36	Average:	20.40
5 WI:	1	10 WM:	0
Catches:	19	Stumpings:	0

English cricket's first all-rounder, the genial Yorkshireman played in his country's first Test side and unlike most of his team mates went on to play for England for over a decade. Nicknamed 'Hapy Jack', he hit a famous 149 at the MCG in 1882 after surviving a strenuous appeal for caught behind when he was on 30. The hallmarks of his batting that day were fluent drives and a series of lusty strokes to leg. Ulyett followed up that fine form with 64 in the second dig to become the first Englishman to score over 200 runs in the one Test. His quickish bowling off a short run was also of the highest order and he led England to a comfortable victory against the Australians at Lord's in 1884 with figures of 7/36 in the second innings. Ulyett played in the first Test between England and South Africa in 1888/89, the only member of that first ever Test side to do so.

UNDERWOOD, Derek Leslie

Born:	June 8, 1945
Batting:	Right handed
Bowling:	Left arm off-break

Tests

Test Career:	1966-82
Cap Number:	433
Tests Played:	86

Test Batting

Innings:	116	Runs:	937
Highest Score:	45*	Average:	11.56
No. 50s:	0	No. 100s:	0

Test Bowling & Fielding

Wickets:	297	Runs:	7,674
Best Bowling:	8/51	Average:	25.83
5 WI:	17	10 WM:	6
Catches:	44	Stumpings:	0

One Day Internationals

ODI Career:	1973-82
ODIs Played:	26

ODI Batting

Innings:	13	Runs:	53
Highest Score:	17	Average:	5.88
No. 50s:	0	No. 100s:	0

ODI Bowling & Fielding

Wickets:	32	Runs:	734
Best Bowling:	4/44	Average:	22.93
5 WM:	0	Catches:	6
Stumpings:	0		

When Derek Underwood was able to bowl his zippy left arm off spin on a damp track the result was more often than not 'Deadly'. The Kent bowler made a modest start to his Test career, claiming only one wicket in his first two Tests, but by the time Australia left for home without the Ashes in 1968 England had unearthed a slow bowler to rival the likes of Hedley Verity and Jim Laker. With a rhythmic bowling action that he was able to reproduce each time he got to the bowling crease, his main form of attack was to stifle the batsman, then tempt him into error. That tactic went out the door on soft tracks when he could turn the ball wildly away from right handers or confound them with a well disguised arm ball. After Lord's was soaked by constant rain in 1974 he bundled out 13 Pakistan batsmen for only 71 runs, and was similarly dangerous against New Zealand five years earlier when a wet summer helped him to take 23 wickets in only three Tests. Underwood was also a brave lower order batsman who was often sent in before nervous batsmen to act as nightwatchman.

VALENTINE, Bryan Herbert

Born:	January 17, 1908
Batting:	Right handed
Bowling:	Right arm medium

Tests

Test Career:	1933-39
Cap Number:	272
Tests Played:	7

Test Batting

Innings:	9	Runs:	454
Highest Score:	136	Average:	64.85
No. 50s:	1	No. 100s:	2

Test Bowling & Fielding

Wickets:	0	Runs:	0
Best Bowling:		Average:	0.00
5 WI:	0	10 WM:	0
Catches:	2	Stumpings:	0

He was a hard hitter from Kent who had a promising Test career cut short by the Second World War. When cricket took a forced hiatus in 1939 his seven Tests had yielded two quick fire centuries and a batting average of 64.85. His two tons were a 136 in Bombay that took less than three hours and a 112 at Cape Town that was belted in less than 120 minutes.

VAUGHAN, Michael Paul

Born:	October 29, 1974
Batting:	Right handed
Bowling:	Right arm off-break

Tests

Test Career:	1999-
Cap Number:	600
Tests Played:	64

Test Batting
Innings:	115	Runs:	4,595
Highest Score:	197	Average:	42.94
No. 50s:	14	No. 100s:	15

Test Bowling & Fielding
Wickets:	6	Runs:	537
Best Bowling:	2/71	Average:	89.50
5 WI:	0	10 WM:	0
Catches:	37	Stumpings:	0

One Day Internationals
ODI Career:	2001-
ODIs Played:	74

ODI Batting
Innings:	71	Runs:	1,730
Highest Score:	90*	Average:	28.36
No. 50s:	15	No. 100s:	0

ODI Bowling & Fielding
Wickets:	12	Runs:	562
Best Bowling:	4/22	Average:	46.83
5 WM:	0	Catches:	20
Stumpings:	0		

If Michael Vaughan did nothing else in his Test career other than regain the Ashes as England skipper in 2005 that would be enough for most English fans. As it is the right hander is not only a fine captain but also an iron willed top order batsman. Prior to his first Test hundred, 120 against Pakistan in 2001, he had only shown glimpses with the bat, but from that point the big scores have kept coming. He helped himself to 900 runs in the summer of 2002 against the visiting Sri Lankans and Indians. A double century just eluded him with scores of 195 and 197, but until he repeated that form in Australia later that year there were still those who were unconvinced. By the time he made 177 in Adelaide, 145 in Melbourne and 183 in Sydney, there was no doubt that Michael Vaughan was a world class opening batsman. As captain he has done more than just win the Ashes, he has taken a talented group of cricketers and turned them into a side with self belief. A knee injury has seen him miss all of 2006 and with England set to defend the Ashes without him it will become clearer as to what his captaincy means to the side.

VERITY, Hedley
Born:	May 18, 1905
Batting:	Right handed
Bowling:	Left arm off-break

Tests
Test Career:	1931-39
Cap Number:	262
Tests Played:	40

Test Batting
Innings:	44	Runs:	669
Highest Score:	66*	Average:	20.90
No. 50s:	3	No. 100s:	0

Test Bowling & Fielding
Wickets:	144	Runs:	3,510
Best Bowling:	8/43	Average:	24.37
5 WI:	5	10 WM:	2
Catches:	30	Stumpings:	0

A right handed batsman and left arm off spinner who stands alongside Wilfred Rhoses, Jim Laker and Derek Underwood as the best slow bowler to ever play for England. A late starter in first class cricket who didn't get a game with Yorkshire until he was 25, he made an immediate impression and was playing for England only a year later. Verity played in 40 Tests between 1931 and 1939 with his most memorable moment coming at Lord's in 1934 when his 15-104 against Australia helped his side to their only victory over the 'old enemy during the 20th century at the famous ground. Fourteen of those 15 wickets came in a one day, still a record in Test cricket and he also holds the record for dismissing Don Bradman on eight occasions, more than any other player in Tests. As good as he was for England, Verity may be best remembered for his exceptional record with Yorkshire. He took ten wickets in an innings on two occasions; once against Warwickshire at Headingley when he conceded 36 runs and then at the same ground against Nottinghamshire for an extraordinary cost of ten runs. Those figures of 10/10 stand as a record in first class cricket and included a hat-trick. As war swept through Europe, Verity joined a brigade called the 'Green Howards' and fought with distinction until tragically dying of injuries sustained in Italy in 1943. The brilliant cricketer and much respected military man had only just turned 38.

VERNON, George Frederick
Born:	June 20, 1856
Batting:	Right handed

Tests
Test Career:	1883
Cap Number:	43
Tests Played:	1

Test Batting
Innings:	2	Runs:	14
Highest Score:	11*	Average:	14.00
No. 50s:	0	No. 100s:	0

Test Bowling & Fielding
Wickets:	0	Runs:	0
Best Bowling:		Average:	0.00
5 WI:	0	10 WM:	0
Catches:	0	Stumpings:	0

A right handed batsman from Middlesex who played his only Test against Australia at the MCG in 1882.

VINE, Joseph
Born:	May 15, 1875
Batting:	Right handed
Bowling:	Right arm leg-break

Tests
Test Career:	1912
Cap Number:	177
Tests Played:	2

Test Batting				
Innings:	3	Runs:	46
Highest Score:	36	Average:	46.00
No. 50s:	0	No. 100s:	0

Test Bowling & Fielding				
Wickets:	0	Runs:	0
Best Bowling:		Average:	0.00
5 WI:	0	10 WM:	0
Catches:	0	Stumpings:	0

A famous batsman and leg-spin bowler for Sussex, he played two Tests in Australia under Johnny Douglas in 1912.

VOCE, William

Born: August 8, 1909
Batting: Right handed
Bowling: Left arm medium-fast

Tests

Test Career: 1930-47
Cap Number: 253
Tests Played: 27

Test Batting				
Innings:	38	Runs:	308
Highest Score:	66	Average:	13.39
No. 50s:	1	No. 100s:	0

Test Bowling & Fielding				
Wickets:	98	Runs:	2,733
Best Bowling:	7/70	Average:	27.88
5 WI:	3	10 WM:	2
Catches:	15	Stumpings:	0

He was a left arm bowler from a harsh coal mining town near Nottingham who played a role in the formation and execution of bodyline bowling. Following England's demolition at the hands of Donald Bradman in 1930 he met with the future English captain Douglas Jardine and Nottinghamshire captain Arthur Carr to devise a tactic to counter the brilliant Australian. It was agreed that Voce and fellow Nottingham bowler Harold Larwood would set a field that would allow them to bowl short rising balls at the body of batsmen on the tour of Australia in 1932/33. Although not as quick as Larwood, his line and height meant that batsmen got no relief when facing him and he did a fine job on the tour taking fifteen wickets in four matches. In all an excellent record of 98 wickets in 27 matches meant that he was much more than just a 'bodyline' bully.

WADDINGTON, Abraham

Born: February 4, 1893
Batting: Right handed
Bowling: Left arm medium-fast

Tests

Test Career: 1920-21
Cap Number: 184
Tests Played: 2

Test Batting				
Innings:	4	Runs:	16
Highest Score:	7	Average:	4.00
No. 50s:	0	No. 100s:	0

Test Bowling & Fielding				
Wickets:	1	Runs:	119
Best Bowling:	1/35	Average:	119.00
5 WI:	0	10 WM:	0
Catches:	1	Stumpings:	0

He was a seam bowler from Yorkshire who toured Australia in 1920/21 playing two Tests but taking only one wicket.

WAINWRIGHT, Edward

Born: April 8, 1865
Batting: Right handed
Bowling: Right arm off-break

Tests

Test Career: 1893-98
Cap Number: 85
Tests Played: 5

Test Batting				
Innings:	9	Runs:	132
Highest Score:	49	Average:	14.66
No. 50s:	0	No. 100s:	0

Test Bowling & Fielding				
Wickets:	0	Runs:	73
Best Bowling:		Average:	0.00
5 WI:	0	10 WM:	0
Catches:	2	Stumpings:	0

A right arm off spinner from Yorkshire where he took over 1,000 wickets, Wainwright was given five Tests to prove his worth for his country but failed to take a single Test wicket.

WALKER, Peter Michael

Born: February 17, 1936
Batting: Right handed
Bowling: Left arm medium

Tests

Test Career: 1960
Cap Number: 400
Tests Played: 3

Test Batting				
Innings:	4	Runs:	128
Highest Score:	52	Average:	32.00
No. 50s:	1	No. 100s:	0

Test Bowling & Fielding				
Wickets:	0	Runs:	34
Best Bowling:		Average:	0.00
5 WI:	0	10 WM:	0
Catches:	5	Stumpings:	0

English born and South African raised, he played all of his three Tests against the touring Springboks in 1960.

WALTERS, Cyril Frederick

Born: August 28, 1905
Batting: Right handed

Tests

Test Career: 1933-34
Cap Number: 267
Tests Played: 11

Test Batting				
Innings:	18	Runs:	784
Highest Score:	102	Average:	52.56
No. 50s:	7	No. 100s:	1

Test Bowling & Fielding			
Wickets:	0	Runs:	0
Best Bowling:		Average:	0.00
5 WI:	0	10 WM:	0
Catches:	6	Stumpings:	0

A superbly fit Welsh athlete who unsurprisingly played Rugby as a young man, he averaged over 50 in a Test career that lasted little more than 12 months. Walters made his Test debut against an inexperienced West Indian side at Lord's in 1933 and retained his spot in the national side when they toured India in 1933/34. His highest Test innings of 102 came at Madras in a match where he also scored a half century. If being selected for his first Ashes Test in 1934 wasn't enough he was thrown the captaincy for one Test after the skipper R.E.S. Wyatt pulled out with a hand injury. He performed well in that Test and for the rest of the series, scoring over 400 runs against the deadly Aussie spin duo of O'Reilly and Grimmett. Having made such a positive start to his Test career it came as a great shock to English fans when he announced his retirement in 1935 due to family and business commitments.

WARD, Alan

Born:	August 10, 1947
Batting:	Right handed
Bowling:	Right arm fast

Tests

Test Career:	1969-76
Cap Number:	443
Tests Played:	5

Test Batting			
Innings:	6	Runs:	40
Highest Score:	21	Average:	8.00
No. 50s:	0	No. 100s:	0
Test Bowling & Fielding			
Wickets:	14	Runs:	453
Best Bowling:	4/61	Average:	32.35
5 WI:	0	10 WM:	0
Catches:	3	Stumpings:	0

The strongly built fast bowler was trumpeted as England's new speed tyro when he made his Test debut as a 21 year old against New Zealand in 1969. After a promising start when he took 10 wickets in three Tests, Ward suffered an injury that saw him on the sidelines for much of the next summer and sent home from the tour of Australia in 1970/71. A single Test when recalled in 1976 marked the end of his international career.

WARD, Albert

Born:	November 21, 1865
Batting:	Right handed

Tests

Test Career:	1893-95
Cap Number:	86
Tests Played:	7

Test Batting			
Innings:	13	Runs:	487
Highest Score:	117	Average:	37.46
No. 50s:	0	No. 100s:	0
Test Bowling & Fielding			
Wickets:	0	Runs:	0
Best Bowling:		Average:	0.00
5 WI:	0	10 WM:	0
Catches:	1	Stumpings:	0

A tall and upright batsman with a fine technique, he had an extremely successful tour of Australia in 1894/95. He scored a double century against South Australia then made good on that form with 75 and 117 in the first Test at the SCG. Ward top scored in that Test series for England with 419 runs but such were the vaguaries of Test selection at the time that he never played for England again.

WARD, Ian James

Born:	September 30, 1972
Batting:	Left handed
Bowling:	Right arm medium

Tests

Test Career:	2001-
Cap Number:	605
Tests Played:	5

Test Batting			
Innings:	9	Runs:	129
Highest Score:	39	Average:	16.12
No. 50s:	0	No. 100s:	0
Test Bowling & Fielding			
Wickets:	0	Runs:	0
Best Bowling:		Average:	0.00
5 WI:	0	10 WM:	0
Catches:	1	Stumpings:	0

He was given his chance to play Test cricket in 2005 with five Tests against Pakistan and Australia. After an encouraging start when he scored 39 against Pakistan at Lord's it was all downhill and he departed the Test scene with an average of only 16.12.

WARDLE, John Henry

Born:	January 8, 1923
Batting:	Left handed
Bowling:	Left arm slow

Tests

Test Career:	1948-57
Cap Number:	333
Tests Played:	28

Test Batting			
Innings:	41	Runs:	653
Highest Score:	66	Average:	19.78
No. 50s:	2	No. 100s:	0
Test Bowling & Fielding			
Wickets:	102	Runs:	2,080
Best Bowling:	7/36	Average:	20.39
5 WI:	5	10 WM:	1
Catches:	12	Stumpings:	0

He was a canny left arm spinner from Yorkshire who interspersed his well flighted off-spin with the occasional chinaman. Wardle was often forced to carry the drinks with selectors preferring the combination of Laker and Lock, but when presented with opportunities he rarely disappointed. In 1956/57 he toured South Africa with great success, taking 26 wickets in four Tests including an innings haul of 7/36 at Cape Town. An accomplished writer, his autobiography Happy Go Johnny was published in 1957.

WARNER, Pelham Francis (Plum)
Born: October 2, 1873
Batting: Right handed

Tests
Test Career: 1899-1912
Cap Number: 118
Tests Played: 15

Test Batting
Innings:	28	Runs:	622
Highest Score:	132*	Average:	23.92
No. 50s:	3	No. 100s:	1

Test Bowling & Fielding
Wickets:	0	Runs:	0
Best Bowling:		Average:	0.00
5 WI:	0	10 WM:	0
Catches:	3	Stumpings:	0

As a cricketer 'Plum' Warner achieved more for his county side Middlesex than he did for England. In fact the man who scored almost 30,000 first class runs at an average in excess of 36, could manage an average of only 23.92 when playing for his country. His finest hour at Test level was unbeaten 132 at Johannesburg in his very first Test. It was as team manager of the side that toured Australia in 1932/33 that he gained greater fame. That was the infamous 'bodyline' series and whilst his exact role may never be known, it is clear that he didn't have a great deal of influence over what English captain Douglas Jardine did on the field. Warner's was a life devoted to cricket and he was duly recognized with a knighthood for his services to the game and a stand named in his honour at Lord's, where his Ashes were scattered when he passed away in 1963.

WARR, John James
Born: July 16, 1927
Batting: Right handed
Bowling: Right arm medium-fast

Tests
Test Career: 1951
Cap Number: 354
Tests Played: 2

Test Batting
Innings:	4	Runs:	4
Highest Score:	4	Average:	1.00
No. 50s:	0	No. 100s:	0

Test Bowling & Fielding
Wickets:	1	Runs:	281
Best Bowling:	1/76	Average:	281.00
5 WI:	0	10 WM:	0
Catches:	0	Stumpings:	0

A medium pace bowler who toured Australia in 1950/51. He played two Tests but could manage only the one wicket.

WARREN, Arnold
Born: April 2, 1875
Batting: Right handed
Bowling: Right arm fast

Tests
Test Career: 1905
Cap Number: 143
Tests Played: 10

Test Batting
Innings:	1	Runs:	7
Highest Score:	7	Average:	7.00
No. 50s:	0	No. 100s:	0

Test Bowling & Fielding
Wickets:	6	Runs:	113
Best Bowling:	5/57	Average:	18.83
5 WI:	1	10 WM:	0
Catches:	1	Stumpings:	0

The Derbyshire opening bowler was given only a single Test in which took six wickets including a five wicket haul in the first innings. His victims that day included Victor Trumper, Joe Darling and Monty Noble making it all the more surprising that he never played for his country again.

WASHBROOK, Cyril
Born: December 6, 1914
Batting: Right handed
Bowling: Right arm medium

Tests
Test Career: 1937-56
Cap Number: 299
Tests Played: 37

Test Batting
Innings:	66	Runs:	2,569
Highest Score:	195	Average:	42.81
No. 50s:	12	No. 100s:	6

Test Bowling & Fielding
Wickets:	1	Runs:	33
Best Bowling:	1/25	Average:	33.00
5 WI:	0	10 WM:	0
Catches:	12	Stumpings:	0

The dapper right hander from Lancashire opened the English batting with distinction in the years immediately following the Second World War. As Sir Leonard Hutton's partner he often had to play second fiddle, but as his 62 and 112 at the MCG in 1947 showed he was a more than capable batsman in his own right. That second innings century took over six hours to compile and staved off a certain victory for the Australians. His 148 against Bradman's Australians at Headingly in 1948 was described as near faultless by Wisden and in that same year he scored a career high 195 against South Africa in Johannesburg. That knock was part of an English record first wicket partnership of 359 with Hutton that confirmed their place amongst the all time great Test opening combinations. A crowd favourite for his stylish strokeplay and fighting attitude, Washbrook played for his country until he was 41.

WATKIN, Steven Llewellyn

Born:	September 15, 1964
Batting:	Right handed
Bowling:	Right arm medium-fast

Tests

Test Career:	1991-93
Cap Number:	550
Tests Played:	3

Test Batting

Innings:	5	Runs:	25
Highest Score:	13	Average:	5.00
No. 50s:	0	No. 100s:	0

Test Bowling & Fielding

Wickets:	11	Runs:	305
Best Bowling:	4/65	Average:	27.72
5 WI:	0	10 WM:	0
Catches:	1	Stumpings:	0

One Day Internationals

ODI Career:	1994
ODIs Played:	4

ODI Batting

Innings:	2	Runs:	4
Highest Score:	4	Average:	2.00
No. 50s:	0	No. 100s:	0

ODI Bowling & Fielding

Wickets:	7	Runs:	193
Best Bowling:	4/49	Average:	27.57
5 WI:	0	Catches:	0
Stumpings:	0		

The Welshman made a promising start to his international career taking five wickets against the West Indies in a winning side at Leeds in 1991. He was equally impressive in his last Test two years later when he took six wickets against the visiting Australians.

WATKINS, Albert John

Born:	April 21, 1922
Batting:	Left handed
Bowling:	Left arm medium-fast

Tests

Test Career:	1948-52
Cap Number:	338
Tests Played:	15

Test Batting

Innings:	24	Runs:	810
Highest Score:	137*	Average:	40.50
No. 50s:	4	No. 100s:	2

Test Bowling & Fielding

Wickets:	11	Runs:	554
Best Bowling:	3/20	Average:	50.36
5 WI:	0	10 WM:	0
Catches:	17	Stumpings:	0

One of two Welsh Watkins to play for England, he may have struggled against the strong Australian side but he had little problem when facing India and South Africa. He played the bulk of his cricket against those two countries and scored one Test century against each. As well as being a fine and forceful middle order batsman he was also a handy swing bowler.

WATKINSON, Michael

Born:	August 1, 1961
Batting:	Right handed
Bowling:	Right arm medium

Tests

Test Career:	1995-96
Cap Number:	575
Tests Played:	4

Test Batting

Innings:	6	Runs:	167
Highest Score:	82*	Average:	33.40
No. 50s:	1	No. 100s:	0

Test Bowling & Fielding

Wickets:	10	Runs:	348
Best Bowling:	3/64	Average:	34.80
5 WI:	0	10 WM:	0
Catches:	1	Stumpings:	0

One Day Internationals

ODI Career:	1996
ODIs Played:	1

ODI Batting

Innings:	0	Runs:	0
Highest Score:	0	Average:	0.00
No. 50s:	0	No. 100s:	0

ODI Bowling & Fielding

Wickets:	0	Runs:	43
Best Bowling:	0	Average:	0.00
5 WM:	0	Catches:	0
Stumpings:	0		

He had been a regular traveler up and down the highways of England for over a decade as a county cricketer when given a chance to strut his stuff against the West Indies in 1995. Watkinson responded in typically professional style by taking eight wickets and scoring 176 runs in three Tests. Time was against the aging all-rounder, and despite being selected to tour South Africa later that year, he played only one more Test.

WATSON, Willie

Born:	March 7, 1920
Batting:	Left handed

Tests

Test Career:	1951-59
Cap Number:	357
Tests Played:	23

Test Batting

Innings:	37	Runs:	879
Highest Score:	116	Average:	25.85
No. 50s:	3	No. 100s:	2

Test Bowling & Fielding

Wickets:	0	Runs:	0
Best Bowling:		Average:	0.00
5 WI:	0	10 WM:	0
Catches:	8	Stumpings:	0

One of England's great all round sportsmen, he played in 23 Test matches as well as being a member of England's squad for the 1950 Football World Cup in Brazil. It was that football commitment that delayed his Test career, but when he finally made his debut in 1951 against South Africa he made an immediate impression. 57 in his first Test was followed by 79 in his second, and whilst he found it hard to hold down a regular spot in the strong English batting lineup, he did go on to score centuries against both Australia and the West Indies.

WEBBE, Alexander Josiah
Born: January 16, 1855
Batting: Right handed

Tests
Test Career: 1879
Cap Number: 20
Tests Played: 1

Test Batting
Innings:	2	Runs:	4
Highest Score:	4	Average:	2.00
No. 50s:	0	No. 100s:	0

Test Bowling & Fielding
Wickets:	0	Runs:	0
Best Bowling:		Average:	0.00
5 WI:	0	10 WM:	0
Catches:	2	Stumpings:	0

A single Test for only four runs is a poor return for Webbe who was considered one of the finest 19th century batsmen by no less a figure than W.G. Grace. He skippered Middlesex for 15 seasons and is still remembered today as that county's most influential early cricketer.

WELLARD, Arthur William
Born: April 8, 1902
Batting: Right handed
Bowling: Right arm medium-fast

Tests
Test Career: 1937-38
Cap Number: 296
Tests Played: 2

Test Batting
Innings:	4	Runs:	47
Highest Score:	38	Average:	11.75
No. 50s:	0	No. 100s:	0

Test Bowling & Fielding
Wickets:	7	Runs:	237
Best Bowling:	4/81	Average:	33.85
5 WI:	0	10 WM:	0
Catches:	2	Stumpings:	0

A paceman from Somerset who was known in the late 30's as the hardest hitting tailender in the game. He was credited with belting over 500 6's in a first class career that spanned 23 seasons.

WELLS, Alan Peter
Born: October 2, 1961
Batting: Right handed
Bowling: Right arm medium

Tests
Test Career: 1995
Cap Number: 576
Tests Played: 1

Test Batting
Innings:	2	Runs:	3
Highest Score:	3*	Average:	3.00
No. 50s:	0	No. 100s:	0

Test Bowling & Fielding
Wickets:	0	Runs:	0
Best Bowling:		Average:	0.00
5 WI:	0	10 WM:	0
Catches:	0	Stumpings:	0

One Day Internationals
ODI Career: 1995
ODIs Played: 1

ODI Batting
Innings:	1	Runs:	15
Highest Score:	15	Average:	15.00
No. 50s:	0	No. 100s:	0

ODI Bowling & Fielding
Wickets:	0	Runs:	0
Best Bowling:		Average:	0.00
5 WM:	0	Catches:	0
Stumpings:	0		

A right handed batsman who toured South Africa in 1990 under Mike Gatting. He would have thought his chance to play Test cricket had passed him by but was selected for one Test against the West Indies at The Oval in 1995.

WELLS, Colin Mark
Born: March 3, 1960
Batting: Right handed
Bowling: Right arm medium

One Day Internationals
ODI Career: 1985
ODIs Played: 2

ODI Batting
Innings:	2	Runs:	22
Highest Score:	17	Average:	11.00
No. 50s:	0	No. 100s:	0

ODI Bowling & Fielding
Wickets:	0	Runs:	0
Best Bowling:		Average:	0.00
5 WM:	0	Catches:	0
Stumpings:	0		

Sussex born Colin Wells was a right hand middle order batsman who played in two ODI's - against Australia and Pakistan - at Sharjah in 1985.

WELLS, Vince John
Born: August 6, 1965
Batting: Right handed
Bowling: Right arm medium
Wicket Keeper

One Day Internationals
ODI Career: 1999
ODIs Played: 9

ODI Batting
Innings:	7	Runs:	141
Highest Score:	39	Average:	20.14
No. 50s:	0	No. 100s:	0

ODI Bowling & Fielding
Wickets:	8	Runs:	189
Best Bowling:	3/30	Average:	23.62
5 WM:	0	Catches:	7
Stumpings:	0		

An all-rounder of sorts, Vince Wells was a handy medium pacer, solid right hand batsman and competent wicket-keeper, even though he never kept wickets at international level. At age 33 he made his ODI debut against Australia, at the

'Gabba in 1999, and played in nine ODI's during that year. His best figures were 3/30 against Australia at the SCG, where he took the wickets of Mark Waugh, Darren Lehmann and Ricky Ponting.

WHARF, Alex George

Born:	June 4, 1975
Batting:	Right handed
Bowling:	Right arm medium-fast

One Day Internationals

ODI Career:	2004-05
ODIs Played:	13

ODI Batting

Innings:	5	Runs:	19
Highest Score:	9	Average:	9.50
No. 50s:	0	No. 100s:	0

ODI Bowling & Fielding

Wickets:	18	Runs:	428
Best Bowling:	4/24	Average:	23.77
5 WM:	0	Catches:	1
Stumpings:	0		

A pace bowler from Yorkshire who had an impressive ODI debut against India at Trent Bridge where he took the wickets of Ganguly, Laxman and Dravid. Wharf took his best figures of 4/24 against Zimbabwe at Harare in 2004/05.

WHARTON, Alan

Born:	April 30, 1923
Batting:	Right handed
Bowling:	Right arm medium

Tests

Test Career:	1949
Cap Number:	343
Tests Played:	1

Test Batting

Innings:	2	Runs:	20
Highest Score:	13	Average:	10.00
No. 50s:	0	No. 100s:	0

Test Bowling & Fielding

Wickets:	0	Runs:	0
Best Bowling:	0	Average:	0.00
5 WI:	0	10 WM:	0
Catches:	0	Stumpings:	0

His solitary Test was against the visiting Kiwis in 1949. He was a competitive county cricketer for Lancashire and then Leicestershire for 18 seasons.

WHITAKER, John James

Born:	May 5, 1962
Batting:	Right handed
Bowling:	Right arm off-break

Tests

Test Career:	1986
Cap Number:	524
Tests Played:	1

Test Batting

Innings:	1	Runs:	11
Highest Score:	11	Average:	11.00
No. 50s:	0	No. 100s:	0

Test Bowling & Fielding

Wickets:	0	Runs:	0
Best Bowling:		Average:	0.00
5 WI:	0	10 WM:	0
Catches:	1	Stumpings:	0

One Day Internationals

ODI Career:	1987
ODIs Played:	2

ODI Batting

Innings:	2	Runs:	48
Highest Score:	44*	Average:	48.00
No. 50s:	0	No. 100s:	0

ODI Bowling & Fielding

Wickets:	0	Runs:	0
Best Bowling:		Average:	0.00
5 WM:	0	Catches:	1
Stumpings:	0		

A long and prosperous career with Leicestershire was rewarded with a trip to Australia in 1986/87. He played his one Test at the Adelaide Oval, scoring 11 in his only at bat.

WHITE, Craig

Born:	December 16, 1969
Batting:	Right handed

Tests

Test Career:	1994-2002
Cap Number:	567
Tests Played:	30

Test Batting

Innings:	50	Runs:	1,052
Highest Score:	121	Average:	24.46
No. 50s:	5	No. 100s:	1

Test Bowling & Fielding

Wickets:	59	Runs:	2,220
Best Bowling:	5/32	Average:	37.62
5 WI:	3	10 WM:	0
Catches:	14	Stumpings:	0

One Day Internationals

ODI Career:	1994-2003
ODIs Played:	51

ODI Batting

Innings:	41	Runs:	568
Highest Score:	57*	Average:	15.77
No. 50s:	1	No. 100s:	0

ODI Bowling & Fielding

Wickets:	65	Runs:	1,726
Best Bowling:	5/21	Average:	26.55
5 WM:	1	Catches:	12
Stumpings:	0		

The Yorkshire all-rounder was exactly the sort of bits and pieces player that one day cricket was made for. A nagging medium pacer and innovative batsman, his 30 Tests were probably too many and his 51 ODI's too few. His stand out effort in whites for England was his 121 at Ahmedabad against India in 2001.

WHITE, David William

Born:	December 14, 1935
Batting:	Left handed
Bowling:	Right arm fast

Tests			
Test Career:	1961-62		
Cap Number:	406		
Tests Played:	2		
Test Batting			
Innings:	2	Runs:	0
Highest Score:	0	Average:	0.00
No. 50s:	0	No. 100s:	0
Test Bowling & Fielding			
Wickets:	4	Runs:	119
Best Bowling:	3/65	Average:	29.75
5 WI:	0	10 WM:	0
Catches:	0	Stumpings:	0

A speedster from Hampshire who played two Tests against Pakistan in 1961. Nicknamed Butch, he later transferred to Glamorgan.

WHITE, John Cornish

Born:	February 19, 1891
Batting:	Right handed
Bowling:	Left arm off-break

Tests			
Test Career:	1921-31		
Cap Number:	202		
Tests Played:	15		
Test Batting			
Innings:	22	Runs:	239
Highest Score:	29	Average:	18.38
No. 50s:	0	No. 100s:	0
Test Bowling & Fielding			
Wickets:	49	Runs:	1,581
Best Bowling:	8/126	Average:	32.26
5 WI:	3	10 WM:	1
Catches:	6	Stumpings:	0

The slow left arm finger spinner from Somerset had been a leading bowler in the county competition for almost 20 years before securing a regular spot for England. When he finally did he was in his late thirties, but age proved no barrier and White enjoyed a successful Ashes tour in 1928/29 where he took 25 wickets and outbowled the likes of Maurice Tate. His best effort in Test cricket came at Adelaide during the fourth Test when his eight second innings wickets helped his side to a narrow 12 run win.

WHYSALL, William Wilfrid

Born:	October 31, 1887
Batting:	Right handed
Bowling:	Right arm medium Wicket Keeper

Tests			
Test Career:	1925-30		
Cap Number:	223		
Tests Played:	4		
Test Batting			
Innings:	7	Runs:	209
Highest Score:	76	Average:	29.85
No. 50s:	2	No. 100s:	0
Test Bowling & Fielding			
Wickets:	0	Runs:	9
Best Bowling:		Average:	0.00
5 WI:	0	10 WM:	0
Catches:	7	Stumpings:	0

Nicknamed Dodger, he was a late bloomer who enjoyed success on the tour of Australia in 1924/25 and then fought his way back into the side as a 42 year old in 1930. He played in the final Test of that series in August and by November was dead having succumbed to an elbow infection he suffered after injuring himself in a fall on a dancefloor.

WILKINSON, Leonard Litton

Born:	November 5, 1916
Batting:	Right handed
Bowling:	Right arm leg-break

Tests			
Test Career:	1938-39		
Cap Number:	306		
Tests Played:	3		
Test Batting			
Innings:	2	Runs:	3
Highest Score:	2	Average:	3.00
No. 50s:	0	No. 100s:	0
Test Bowling & Fielding			
Wickets:	7	Runs:	271
Best Bowling:	4/115	Average:	38.71
5 WI:	0	10 WM:	0
Catches:	0	Stumpings:	0

He was an orthodox leg-spinner who played three Tests on the tour of South Africa in 1938.

WILLEY, Peter

Born:	December 6, 1949
Batting:	Right handed
Bowling:	Right arm off-break

Tests			
Test Career:	1976-86		
Cap Number:	468		
Tests Played:	26		
Test Batting			
Innings:	50	Runs:	1,184
Highest Score:	102*	Average:	26.90
No. 50s:	5	No. 100s:	2
Test Bowling & Fielding			
Wickets:	7	Runs:	456
Best Bowling:	2/73	Average:	65.14
5 WI:	0	10 WM:	0
Catches:	3	Stumpings:	0
One Day Internationals			
ODI Career:	1977-86		
ODIs Played:	26		
ODI Batting			
Innings:	24	Runs:	538
Highest Score:	64	Average:	23.39
No. 50s:	5	No. 100s:	0
ODI Bowling & Fielding			
Wickets:	13	Runs:	659
Best Bowling:	3/33	Average:	50.69
5 WM:	0	Catches:	4
Stumpings:	0		

The all-rounder from Northants played 26 Tests for England and whilst he was a tight off spinner it was his resolute batting that served his country best. His two-eyed stance meant he was compelled to get behind every delivery but he was highly effective and particularly harsh on anything short and wide. Willey's courage was put to good use in a number of Tests against the West Indians and both of his Test centuries were against the men from the Caribbean. After a long and successful first class career he became an umpire representing England on the international panel in 25 Tests.

WILLIAMS, Neil FitzGerald

Born:	July 2, 1962
Batting:	Right handed
Bowling:	Right arm medium-fast

Tests

Test Career:	1990
Cap Number:	546
Tests Played:	1

Test Batting

Innings:	1	Runs:	38
Highest Score:	38	Average:	38.00
No. 50s:	0	No. 100s:	0

Test Bowling & Fielding

Wickets:	2	Runs:	148
Best Bowling:	2/148	Average:	74.00
5 WI:	0	10 WM:	0
Catches:	0	Stumpings:	0

A medium pace bowler from St. Vincent in the West Indies, he played a single Test against India at The Oval in 1990 when Chris Lewis pulled out with a migraine. He suffered a serious stroke in 2006 and passed away at the age of 43.

WILLIS, Robert George Dylan

Born:	May 30, 1949
Batting:	Right handed
Bowling:	Right arm fast

Tests

Test Career:	1971-84
Cap Number:	448
Tests Played:	90

Test Batting

Innings:	128	Runs:	840
Highest Score:	28*	Average:	11.50
No. 50s:	0	No. 100s:	0

Test Bowling & Fielding

Wickets:	325	Runs:	8,190
Best Bowling:	8/43	Average:	25.20
5 WI:	16	10 WM:	0
Catches:	39	Stumpings:	0

One Day Internationals

ODI Career:	1973-84
ODIs Played:	64

ODI Batting

Innings:	22	Runs:	83
Highest Score:	24	Average:	10.37
No. 50s:	0	No. 100s:	0

ODI Bowling & Fielding

Wickets:	80	Runs:	1,968
Best Bowling:	4/11	Average:	24.60
5 WM:	0	Catches:	22
Stumpings:	0		

Tall, talented, and just a little mad, he spearheaded the English attack for over a decade and in the process became his country's greatest Test wicket taker of all time. Willis made his Test debut as willowy youngster when he was flown to Australia to replace the injured Alan Ward in 1971. Twelve wickets in four Tests was a decent return for the 21 year old but he would not earn a regular Test spot until he returned to Australia in 1974/75. His 17 wickets in that series were enough to share the honours with Derek Underwood and Tony Greig and set him on the road to a long and successful career. He would take five or more wickets in a Test innings on 16 occasions including 8/43 in the 1981 Ashes Test at Headingly when he and Ian Botham turned certain defeat into a miraculous victory. Willis may have never taken ten wickets in a Test match, but he was the leading wicket taker in a number of series including the tour of India in 1976/77 with 20, the Ashes series at home in 1977 with 27 and the Ashes series of 1981 with 31. He became one of the few fast bowlers to lead his country when he was handed the captaincy in 1982 and enjoyed immediate success on a tour of the subcontinent. In an era of famous fast bowlers, England's Bob Willis could be counted amongst the very best.

WILSON, Clement Eustace Macro

Born:	May 15, 1875
Batting:	Right handed

Tests

Test Career:	1899
Cap Number:	119
Tests Played:	2

Test Batting

Innings:	4	Runs:	42
Highest Score:	18	Average:	14.00
No. 50s:	0	No. 100s:	0

Test Bowling & Fielding

Wickets:	0	Runs:	0
Best Bowling:		Average:	0.00
5 WI:	0	10 WM:	0
Catches:	0	Stumpings:	0

He was an all-rounder from Yorkshire who played both of his Tests in Lord Hawke's side that was undefeated in South Africa in 1899. Reverend Clement Wilson later served as Vicar at Litchfield Cathedral till his passing in 1944.

WILSON, Donald

Born:	August 7, 1937
Batting:	Left handed
Bowling:	Left arm off-break

Tests

Test Career:	1964-71
Cap Number:	418
Tests Played:	6

Test Batting

Innings:	7	Runs:	75
Highest Score:	42	Average:	12.50
No. 50s:	0	No. 100s:	0

Test Bowling & Fielding
Wickets:	11	Runs:	466
Best Bowling:	2/17	Average:	42.36
5 WI:	0	10 WM:	0
Catches:	1	Stumpings:	0

A left arm off spinner with almost two decades experience in county cricket, he was used intermittently as a replacement for Fred Titmus in the English side.

WILSON, Evelyn Rockley
Born: March 25, 1879
Batting: Right handed
Bowling: Right arm leg-break

Tests
Test Career: 1921
Cap Number: 189
Tests Played: 1

Test Batting
Innings:	2	Runs:	10
Highest Score:	5	Average:	5.00
No. 50s:	0	No. 100s:	0

Test Bowling & Fielding
Wickets:	3	Runs:	36
Best Bowling:	2/28	Average:	12.00
5 WI:	0	10 WM:	0
Catches:	0	Stumpings:	0

He was a slow bowler who played the bulk of his first class cricket in his time at Cambridge University. His only Test was against Australia at the SCG in 1921.

WOOD, Arthur
Born: August 25, 1898
Batting: Right handed
Wicket Keeper

Tests
Test Career: 1938-39
Cap Number: 304
Tests Played: 4

Test Batting
Innings:	5	Runs:	80
Highest Score:	53	Average:	20.00
No. 50s:	1	No. 100s:	0

Test Bowling & Fielding
Wickets:	0	Runs:	0
Best Bowling:		Average:	0.00
5 WI:	0	10 WM:	0
Catches:	10	Stumpings:	1

A sprightly keeper who played over 400 first class games for Yorkshire, he scored 53 on debut for England as a part of their record score of 7/903 against the Australians at The Oval in 1938.

WOOD, Barry
Born: December 6, 1942
Batting: Right handed
Bowling: Right arm medium

Tests
Test Career: 1972-78
Cap Number: 453
Tests Played: 12

Test Batting
Innings:	21	Runs:	454
Highest Score:	90	Average:	21.61
No. 50s:	2	No. 100s:	0

Test Bowling & Fielding
Wickets:	0	Runs:	50
Best Bowling:		Average:	0.00
5 WI:	0	10 WM:	0
Catches:	6	Stumpings:	0

One Day Internationals
ODI Career: 1972-82
ODIs Played: 13

ODI Batting
Innings:	12	Runs:	314
Highest Score:	78*	Average:	31.40
No. 50s:	2	No. 100s:	0

ODI Bowling & Fielding
Wickets:	9	Runs:	224
Best Bowling:	2/14	Average:	24.88
5 WM:	0	Catches:	6
Stumpings:	0		

A pugnacious opening batsman from northern England, he made 90 in his first Test against an Australian side that boasted Dennis Lillee and Bob Massie. He was used to fill gaps in the national side thereafter enjoying more success in the one day team where he averaged over 30.

WOOD, George Edward Charles
Born: August 22, 1893
Batting: Right handed
Bowling: Right arm medium
Wicket Keeper

Tests
Test Career: 1924
Cap Number: 217
Tests Played: 3

Test Batting
Innings:	2	Runs:	7
Highest Score:	6	Average:	3.50
No. 50s:	0	No. 100s:	0

Test Bowling & Fielding
Wickets:	0	Runs:	0
Best Bowling:		Average:	0.00
5 WI:	0	10 WM:	0
Catches:	5	Stumpings:	1

An old style keeper who stood up to the stumps to all bowlers, he played three Tests against South Africa in 1924.

WOOD, Henry
Born: December 14, 1853
Batting: Right handed
Wicket Keeper

Tests
Test Career: 1888-92
Cap Number: 60
Tests Played: 4

Test Batting
Innings:	4	Runs:	204
Highest Score:	134*	Average:	68.00
No. 50s:	1	No. 100s:	1

Test Bowling & Fielding			
Wickets:	0	Runs:	0
Best Bowling:		Average:	0.00
5 WI:	0	10 WM:	0
Catches:	2	Stumpings:	1

Harry Wood was a fine wicketkeeper who played the bulk of his first class career with Surrey, though he did also appear in the Kent side for a short period. He was selected on England's second tour of South Africa and scored the only first class century of his career in the Test at Cape Town when he took advantage of a weak attack with an unbeaten 134.

WOOD, Reginald

Born: March 7, 1860
Batting: Left handed

Tests

Test Career:	1887
Cap Number:	54
Tests Played:	1

Test Batting

Innings:	2	Runs:	6
Highest Score:	6	Average:	3.00
No. 50s:	0	No. 100s:	0

Test Bowling & Fielding

Wickets:	0	Runs:	0
Best Bowling:		Average:	0.00
5 WI:	0	10 WM:	0
Catches:	0	Stumpings:	0

Hardly an imposing cricketer, he played only six games with Lancashire before emigrating to Australia in the 1880's. He was called up by the tourists for one Test when Billy Barnes was injured in a brawl, but scored only six and a duck.

WOODS, Samuel Moses James

Born: April 13, 1867
Batting: Right handed
Bowling: Right arm medium-fast

Tests

Test Career:	1888-96
Cap Number:	100
Tests Played:	6

Test Batting

Innings:	10	Runs:	154
Highest Score:	53	Average:	15.40
No. 50s:	1	No. 100s:	0

Test Bowling & Fielding

Wickets:	10	Runs:	250
Best Bowling:	3.28	Average:	25.00
5 WI:	0	10 WM:	0
Catches:	5	Stumpings:	0

He was an all-round sportsman in the truest sense, and whilst he didn't shine at Test level, he was still considered to be a very fine batsman and medium pace bowler. Sammy Woods played Test cricket for both Australia and England, represented England 13 times in Rugby, played Association Football or soccer for Sussex and was even considered more than capable when on one occasion asked to step into the boxing ring!

WOOLLEY, Frank Edward

Born: May 27, 1887
Batting: Left handed

Tests

Test Career:	1909-34
Cap Number:	163
Tests Played:	64

Test Batting

Innings:	98	Runs:	3,283
Highest Score:	154	Average:	36.07
No. 50s:	23	No. 100s:	5

Test Bowling & Fielding

Wickets:	83	Runs:	2,815
Best Bowling:	7/76	Average:	33.91
5 WI:	4	10 WM:	1
Catches:	64	Stumpings:	0

The left handed all-rounder had a long and successful Test career, appearing for England in 64 Tests over a 25 year period. He made his debut at The Oval in 1909, and unlike many of the English players tried in that series maintained his spot in the Test side. He averaged above 48 on his first tour to Australia in 1911/12, bringing up his maiden Test century in the process. That 133 not out helped his side to a comfortable 4-1 series victory and marked the start of a great run he had with both bat and ball. Woolley played in the triangular series in England in 1912, and whilst Australia failed to send their best side, he showed his worth for one Test with a ten wicket return for the match against the 'old enemy' at The Oval. He bowled off spin and was said to have a near perfect action that allowed him to pitch the ball wherever he chose. With no cricket played between 1915 and 1919 due to the War, Woolley's career was put on hold but when Test matches resumed his output was undiminished. In total he scored five Test hundreds, the last of which was 154 against South Africa at Manchester when he 42 years old. As well as being a world class batsman and bowler he was one of England's best ever slip fieldsman and averaged a catch per Test throughout his long career. The Kent man kept his spot in the Test side until he was 47 and throughout maintained the highest traditions of great English all-rounders.

WOOLMER, Robert Andrew

Born: May 14, 1948
Batting: Right handed
Bowling: Right arm medium

Tests

Test Career:	1975-81
Cap Number:	463
Tests Played:	19

Test Batting

Innings:	34	Runs:	1,059
Highest Score:	149	Average:	33.09
No. 50s:	2	No. 100s:	3

Test Bowling & Fielding
Wickets:	4	Runs:	299
Best Bowling:	1/8	Average:	74.75
5 WI:	0	10 WM:	0
Catches:	10	Stumpings:	0

One Day Internationals
ODI Career: 1972-76
ODIs Played: 6

ODI Batting
Innings:	4	Runs:	21
Highest Score:	9	Average:	5.25
No. 50s:	0	No. 100s:	0

ODI Bowling & Fielding
Wickets:	9	Runs:	260
Best Bowling:	3/33	Average:	28.88
5 WM:	0	Catches:	3
Stumpings:	0		

The current Pakistan coach gave away a promising Test career to play World Series Cricket and unsanctioned cricket in South Africa in 1981. He had made an immediate impact in 1975, when in only his second Test, he scored 149 against a strong Australian side at The Oval. In all he made three Test hundreds, all of which were scored against the Aussies.

WORTHINGTON, Thomas Stanley
Born: August 21, 1905
Batting: Right handed
Bowling: Right arm medium-fast

Tests
Test Career: 1930-37
Cap Number: 251
Tests Played: 9

Test Batting
Innings:	11	Runs:	321
Highest Score:	128	Average:	29.18
No. 50s:	1	No. 100s:	1

Test Bowling & Fielding
Wickets:	8	Runs:	316
Best Bowling:	2/19	Average:	39.50
5 WI:	0	10 WM:	0
Catches:	8	Stumpings:	0

The Derbyshire all rounder was selected predominately as a batsman when picked to tour Australia in 1936/37. He struggled against the strong Australian attack and on his return to England found himself back in county ranks. Stan Worthington was recalled to the side to face the visiting Indians in 1938 and prospered against the fledgling Test nation with 128 at The Oval in an innings that saw him add 266 for the fourth wicket with Walter Hammond.

WRIGHT, Charles William
Born: May 27, 1863
Batting: Right handed
         Wicket Keeper

Tests
Test Career: 1896
Cap Number: 101
Tests Played: 3

Test Batting
Innings:	4	Runs:	125
Highest Score:	71	Average:	31.25
No. 50s:	1	No. 100s:	0

Test Bowling & Fielding
Wickets:	0	Runs:	0
Best Bowling:		Average:	0.00
5 WI:	0	10 WM:	0
Catches:	0	Stumpings:	0

A member of Lord Hawke's side that toured South Africa in 1895/96, he was a some time wicket keeper who performed well with the bat in his three Tests, averaging above 30.

WRIGHT, Douglas Vivian Parson
Born: August 21, 1914
Batting: Right handed

Tests
Test Career: 1938-51
Cap Number: 302
Tests Played: 34

Test Batting
Innings:	39	Runs:	289
Highest Score:	45	Average:	11.11
No. 50s:	0	No. 100s:	0

Test Bowling & Fielding
Wickets:	108	Runs:	4,224
Best Bowling:	7/105	Average:	39.11
5 WI:	6	10 WM:	1
Catches:	10	Stumpings:	0

A zippy leg-spinner from Kent, he actually started out as a medium pace bowler in county cricket who would bowl some of his deliveries over the wrist and turned into one of England's best leg spinners of all time. Wright played briefly prior to World War II and upon the resumption of Test cricket was selected to tour Australia in 1946/47. England was soundly beaten in the series and took only 60 wickets in five Tests but the leg spinner was the best of a disappointing bowling attack with 23. He took a further 19 wickets against South Africa at home in 1947 and ended his Test career with a tour of Australia that saw him pass the 100 mark in Test wickets. Wright also took a staggering seven first class hat-tricks.

WYATT, Robert Elliott Storey
Born: May 2, 1901
Batting: Right handed
Bowling: Right arm medium

Tests
Test Career: 1927-37
Cap Number: 231
Tests Played: 40

Test Batting
Innings:	64	Runs:	1,839
Highest Score:	149	Average:	31.70
No. 50s:	12	No. 100s:	2

Test Bowling & Fielding
Wickets:	18	Runs:	642
Best Bowling:	3/4	Average:	35.66
5 WI:	0	10 WM:	0
Catches:	16	Stumpings:	0

He was an accomplished all rounder either opening the batting, coming in at number six or bowling his steady swinging medium pace. As a cricketer he was possibly just short of top class, but he had a keen cricket brain and spent the bulk of his career as either Vice Captain or Captain of the national side. Wyatt took over the reins as Test captain during the 1934 Ashes series and retained the leadership in series against the West Indies and South Africa that England lost. His highest Test score came in a loss to South Africa in 1935 when he scored 149 at Trent Bridge. An influential figure in the game for much of his 93 years, he wrote books on the sport as well as serving as English Chairman of Selectors.

WYNYARD, Edward George (Teddy)

Born:	April 1, 1861
Batting:	Right handed

Tests

Test Career:	1896-1906
Cap Number:	106
Tests Played:	3

Test Batting

Innings:	6	Runs:	72
Highest Score:	30	Average:	12.00
No. 50s:	0	No. 100s:	0

Test Bowling & Fielding

Wickets:	0	Runs:	17
Best Bowling:		Average:	0.00
5 WI:	0	10 WM:	0
Catches:	0	Stumpings:	0

Standing over six foot tall, Major Wynyard was a commanding individual who played in three official Tests for his country. He also led an English tour to New Zealand in 1906.

YARDLEY, Norman Walter Dransfield

Born:	March 19, 1915
Batting:	Right handed
Bowling:	Right arm medium

Tests

Test Career:	1938-50
Cap Number:	307
Tests Played:	20

Test Batting

Innings:	34	Runs:	812
Highest Score:	99	Average:	25.37
No. 50s:	4	No. 100s:	0

Test Bowling & Fielding

Wickets:	21	Runs:	707
Best Bowling:	3/67	Average:	33.66
5 WI:	0	10 WM:	0
Catches:	14	Stumpings:	0

The Yorkshire man may not have been England's greatest all-rounder, but in the years immediately following the Second World War he gave great service as both player and captain. He was an accurate medium pace bowler and smart batsman who performed well in the disappointing side that toured Australia in 1946/47, averaging over 30 with the bat and taking ten wickets. Three of those dismissals were Donald Bradman, and whilst the Don was hardly anyone's bunny, Yardley did dismiss him for less than a hundred in both innings at the MCG during the third Test. Whilst he never made a Test century he went awfully close with 99 against South Africa in 1947.

YOUNG, Harding Issac (Sailor)

Born:	February 5, 1876
Batting:	Right handed
Bowling:	Left arm medium

Tests

Test Career:	1899
Cap Number:	126
Tests Played:	2

Test Batting

Innings:	2	Runs:	43
Highest Score:	43	Average:	21.50
No. 50s:	0	No. 100s:	0

Test Bowling & Fielding

Wickets:	12	Runs:	262
Best Bowling:	4/30	Average:	24.83
5 WI:	0	10 WM:	0
Catches:	1	Stumpings:	0

Known as Sailor, he played twice during the 1899 Ashes series in England and performed well taking a total of twelve wickets. Young who bowled left arm medium pace that relied heavily on swing, took over 500 wickets with Essex in the county competition. He was a member of the ground staff at Lord's and later stood in three Tests as an umpire.

YOUNG, John Albert (Jack)

Born:	October 14, 1912
Batting:	Right handed
Bowling:	Left arm off-break

Tests

Test Career:	1947-49
Cap Number:	324
Tests Played:	8

Test Batting

Innings:	10	Runs:	28
Highest Score:	10*	Average:	5.60
No. 50s:	0	No. 100s:	0

Test Bowling & Fielding

Wickets:	17	Runs:	757
Best Bowling:	3/65	Average:	44.52
5 WI:	0	10 WM:	0
Catches:	5	Stumpings:	0

The left arm off spinner had a great record for Middlesex, but when called up for England he failed to sparkle and could manage only 17 wickets in eight Tests.

YOUNG, Richard Alfred

Born:	September 16, 1885
Batting:	Right handed
	Wicket Keeper

Tests

Test Career:	1907-08
Cap Number:	156
Tests Played:	2

Test Batting

Innings:	4	**Runs:**	27
Highest Score:	13	**Average:**	6.75
No. 50s:	0	**No. 100s:**	0

Test Bowling & Fielding

Wickets:	0	**Runs:**	0
Best Bowling:		**Average:**	0.00
5 WI:	0	**10 WM:**	0
Catches:	6	**Stumpings:**	0

Unusual for a wicket keeper in that he wore glasses, he played his only two matches for England in Australia in 1907/08. Dick Young also played Association Football for England.

India

ABID ALI, Syed

Born:	September 9, 1941
Batting:	Right handed
Bowling:	Right arm medium-fast

Tests

Test Career:	1967-74
Cap Number:	116
Tests Played:	29

Test Batting

Innings:	53	Runs:	1,018
Highest Score:	81	Average:	20.35
No. 50s:	6	No. 100s:	0

Test Bowling & Fielding

Wickets:	47	Runs:	1,980
Best Bowling:	6/55	Average:	42.20
5 WI:	1	10 WM:	0
Catches:	32	Stumpings:	0

One Day Internationals

ODI Career:	1974-75
ODIs Played:	5

ODI Batting

Innings:	3	Runs:	93
Highest Score:	70	Average:	31.00
No. 50s:	1	No. 100s:	0

ODI Bowling & Fielding

Wickets:	7	Runs:	187
Best Bowling:	2/22	Average:	26.71
5 WM:	0	Catches:	0
Stumpings:	0		

Although of stocky build, Abid was a tremendous athlete with incredible endurance. An all rounder he could bat, bowl both medium/fast and leg spin and occasionally keep wickets when required. He took an impressive 6/55 on debut against Australia in Adelaide, but found it difficult to cement a permanent spot in the side due to the plethora of top line spinners at the time. He had the honour of hitting the winning runs against England at The Oval in 1971, which was India's first ever win in England.

ADHIKARI, Hemchandra Ramachandra

Born:	July 31, 1919
Batting:	Right handed

Tests

Test Career:	1947-59
Cap Number:	36
Tests Played:	21

Test Batting

Innings:	36	Runs:	872
Highest Score:	114*	Average:	31.14
No. 50s:	4	No. 100s:	1

Test Bowling & Fielding

Wickets:	3	Runs:	82
Best Bowling:	3/68	Average:	27.33
5 WI:	0	10 WM:	0
Catches:	8	Stumpings:	0

Serviceable player over his 12 year Test career and captained India on one occasion. Adhikari was a member of the Indian teams that played inaugural Tests against Australia, West Indies and Pakistan. He became national coach and was team manager when India won their first series in England in 1971.

AGARKAR, Ajit Bhalchandra

Born:	December 4, 1977
Batting:	Right handed
Bowling:	Right arm medium-fast

Tests

Test Career:	1998-06
Cap Number:	216
Tests Played:	26

Test Batting

Innings:	39	Runs:	571
Highest Score:	109*	Average:	16.79
No. 50s:	0	No. 100s:	1

Test Bowling & Fielding

Wickets:	58	Runs:	2,745
Best Bowling:	6/41	Average:	47.32
5 WI:	1	10 WM:	0
Catches:	0	Stumpings:	0

One Day Internationals

ODI Career:	1998-06
ODIs Played:	164

ODI Batting

Innings:	99	Runs:	1,116
Highest Score:	95	Average:	15.94
No. 50s:	3	No. 100s:	0

ODI Bowling & Fielding

Wickets:	252	Runs:	6,842
Best Bowling:	6/42	Average:	27.15
5 WM:	2	Catches:	47
Stumpings:	0		

An aggressive pace bowler with plenty of unearthed talent, Ajit Agarkar made an immediate impact in ODI competition. He was selected in a one off Test against Zimbabwe at Harare, in 1998 where he opened the bowling with seasoned campaigner Javagal Srinath. But inconsistency has plagued the best part of Agarkar's career and he unfortunately had to endure the baggage of collecting five consecutive Test ducks against the Australians on the 1999/2000 tour. Apart from this unenviable blotch on his resume, Agarkar has proven to be a handy lower order batsman in both Tests and

ODI's. He scored his maiden Test century against England at Lords in 2002.

AHMED, Ghulam

Born: July 4, 1922
Batting: Right handed
Bowling: Right arm off-break

Tests
Test Career: 1949-1959
Cap Number: 49
Tests Played: 22

Test Batting
Innings:	31	Runs:	192
Highest Score:	50	Average:	8.72
No. 50s:	1	No. 100s:	0

Test Bowling & Fielding
Wickets:	68	Runs:	2,052
Best Bowling:	7/49	Average:	30.17
5 WI:	4	10 WM:	1
Catches:	0	Stumpings:	0

Part of the highly regarded Indian 'spin trio' when combining with Vinoo Mankad and Subash Gupte. A quality off spinner who also captained India on three occasions. Scored his only Test 50 when coming in at number 11 against Pakistan at New Delhi in 1952-53. Together with Hemu Adhikari they scored a record 109 runs for the last wicket.

ALI, Syed Mushtaq

Born: December 17, 1914
Batting: Right handed
Bowling: Left arm off-break

Tests
Test Career: 1934-52
Cap Number: 19
Tests Played: 11

Test Batting
Innings:	20	Runs:	612
Highest Score:	112	Average:	32.21
No. 50s:	2	No. 100s:	3

Test Bowling & Fielding
Wickets:	3	Runs:	202
Best Bowling:	1/45	Average:	67.33
5 WI:	0	10 WM:	0
Catches:	7	Stumpings:	0

A class batsman who endured controversy over his non-selection later in his career, Mushtaq has the unique honour of being the first Indian to score a century offshore - against England at Old Trafford in 1936. He had a successful batting partnership with Vijay Merchant. A true gentleman both on and off the field and highly respected by the Indian and cricketing public of the time.

ALI, Syed Nazir

Born: June 8, 1906
Batting: Right handed
Bowling: Right arm medium-fast

Tests
Test Career: 1932-34
Cap Number: 8
Tests Played: 2

Test Batting
Innings:	4	Runs:	13
Highest Score:	13	Average:	7.50
No. 50s:	0	No. 100s:	0

Test Bowling & Fielding
Wickets:	4	Runs:	83
Best Bowling:	4/83	Average:	20.75
5 WI:	0	10 WM:	0
Catches:	0	Stumpings:	0

Younger brother of Wazir, and a member of India's first ever Test team that played against England, at Lord's in 1932, Nazir Ali's modest average of 7.50 was not a true reflection of his batting ability. And ironically it was his bowling feat of 4/83 for which he is best remembered for at Test level. Like many of his Indian contemporaries, Ali went on to play at County level with plenty of success.

ALI, Syed Wazir

Born: September 15, 1903
Batting: Right handed
Bowling: Right arm medium

Tests
Test Career: 1932-36
Cap Number: 11
Tests Played: 7

Test Batting
Innings:	14	Runs:	237
Highest Score:	42	Average:	16.92
No. 50s:	0	No. 100s:	0

Test Bowling & Fielding
Wickets:	0	Runs:	25
Best Bowling:	0/25	Average:	0.00
5 WI:	0	10 WM:	0
Catches:	1	Stumpings:	0

Like younger brother Nazir Ali, Syed Wazir Ali also played in India's first ever Test against England, in 1932. A classical batsman, his highest score of 42 was littered with shots to all parts of the ground.

AMARNATH, Lala (Nanik)

Born: January 9, 1920
Batting: Right handed
Bowling: Right arm medium
       Wicket Keeper

Tests
Test Career: 1933-52
Cap Number: 12
Tests Played: 24

Test Batting
Innings:	40	Runs:	878
Highest Score:	118	Average:	24.38
No. 50s:	4	No. 100s:	1

Test Bowling & Fielding
Wickets:	45	Runs:	1,481
Best Bowling:	5/96	Average:	32.91
5 WI:	2	10 WM:	0
Catches:	13	Stumpings:	0

One of the most famous names in Indian cricket, Lala Amarnath was a cricketing patriarch in his own right. Father of Test players Surinder and the highly talented Mohinder, Lala was an aggressive and free flowing batsman. He made a memorable test century on debut (India's first in Test cricket) - a swashbuckling 118 against England in even time after coming in with the score at 2/21. Conservatism was not in his vocabulary and even though he was not to score another test hundred, there was an air of expectation whenever Lala took guard. He was no slouch with the ball either as his 45 wickets at an average of 32.91 would indicate. And if that wasn't enough he could also keep wickets with aplomb. Controversial at times, and a headache for the establishment on various occasions, Amarnath captained India in 1948 against the Bradman led Australians before retiring from the Test arena in 1952. He later became a respected selector and commentator. A true legend of Indian cricket.

AMARNATH, Mohinder

Born: September 26, 1950
Batting: Right handed
Bowling: Right arm medium

Tests
Test Career: 1969-88
Cap Number: 125
Tests Played: 69

Test Batting
Innings:	113	Runs:	4,378
Highest Score:	138	Average:	42.50
No. 50s:	24	No. 100s:	11

Test Bowling & Fielding
Wickets:	32	Runs:	1,781
Best Bowling:	4/63	Average:	55.68
5 WI:	0	10 WM:	0
Catches:	47	Stumpings:	0

One Day Internationals
ODI Career: 1975-89
ODIs Played: 85

ODI Batting
Innings:	75	Runs:	1,924
Highest Score:	102*	Average:	30.53
No. 50s:	13	No. 100s:	2

ODI Bowling & Fielding
Wickets:	46	Runs:	1,971
Best Bowling:	3/12	Average:	42.82
5 WM:	0	Catches:	0
Stumpings:	0		

The son of the great Lala Amarnath, Mohinder Amarnath fell off the cricketing radar shortly after making his Test debut against Australia in 1969. He reappeared on the Test scene some six years later in 1975/76. Handsome, and definitely the pin up boy of Indian cricket at the time, Amarnath got better with age and went on to record 11 centuries and 24 fifties at Test level as well as being named 'Man of the Match' in India's victorious World Cup side of 1983.

AMARNATH, Surinder (Bhardwaj)

Born: December 30, 1948
Batting: Left handed
Bowling: Right arm medium-fast

Tests
Test Career: 1976-78
Cap Number: 137
Tests Played: 10

Test Batting
Innings:	18	Runs:	550
Highest Score:	124	Average:	30.55
No. 50s:	3	No. 100s:	1

Test Bowling & Fielding
Wickets:	1	Runs:	5
Best Bowling:	1/5	Average:	0.00
5 WI:	0	10 WM:	0
Catches:	4	Stumpings:	0

One Day Internationals
ODI Career: 1978
ODIs Played: 3

ODI Batting
Innings:	3	Runs:	100
Highest Score:	62	Average:	33.33
No. 50s:	1	No. 100s:	0

ODI Bowling & Fielding
Wickets:	0	Runs:	0
Best Bowling:		Average:	0.00
5 WM:	0	Catches:	1
Stumpings:	0		

Eldest son of Indian legend Lala and brother of the stylish Mohinder, Surinder Amarnath had a dream start to Test cricket when he scored 124 on debut against New Zealand, at Auckland in 1975. While it seemed that Amarnath legend would continue to prosper, the left-hander could only manage a further nine Tests as he was unable to recapture his debut form.

AMRE, Pravin Kalyan

Born: August 14, 1968
Batting: Right handed
Bowling: Right arm leg-break

Tests
Test Career: 1992-93
Cap Number: 195
Tests Played: 11

Test Batting
Innings:	13	Runs:	425
Highest Score:	103	Average:	42.50
No. 50s:	3	No. 100s:	1

Test Bowling & Fielding
Wickets:	0	Runs:	0
Best Bowling:		Average:	0.00
5 WI:	0	10 WM:	0
Catches:	9	Stumpings:	0

One Day Internationals
ODI Career: 1991-94
ODIs Played: 37

ODI Batting
Innings:	30	Runs:	513
Highest Score:	84*	Average:	20.51
No. 50s:	2	No. 100s:	0

ODI Bowling & Fielding
Wickets:	0	Runs:	0
Best Bowling:		Average:	0.00
5 WM:	0	Catches:	12
Stumpings:	0		

A right handed batsman from Mumbai, Amre belongs to that elite band of players who have scored a Test century on debut - 103 against Sth Africa at Durban in 1992. He was suprisingly dumped from the Test side after only 11 matches.

ANAND (RAJKUMAR OF VIZIANAGRAM), Vijaya

Born: December 28, 1905
Batting: Right handed

Tests

Test Career: 1936
Cap Number: 23
Tests Played: 3

Test Batting
Innings:	6	Runs:	33
Highest Score:	19*	Average:	8.25
No. 50s:	0	No. 100s:	0

Test Bowling & Fielding
Wickets:	0	Runs:	0
Best Bowling:		Average:	0.00
5 WI:	0	10 WM:	0
Catches:	1	Stumpings:	0

More commonly known as 'Vizzy'. It was suggested that while he was an ordinary cricketer at best, Vizzy used his wealth and influence to promote his standing amongst the cricket elite. He captained India during the 1936 tour of England and was involved in the Lala Amarnath controversy having ordered the respected champion to 'go home'. As the purists pondered how a man of such limited talent could play at the highest level but let alone lead the national team, Vizzy was subsequently knighted and hence became known as Sir Gajapatairaj Vijaya Ananda, the Maharajkumar of Vizianagram.

ANKOLA, Salil Ashok

Born: March 1, 1968
Batting: Right handed
Bowling: Right arm medium-fast

Tests

Test Career: 1989-90
Cap Number: 186
Tests Played: 1

Test Batting
Innings:	1	Runs:	6
Highest Score:	6	Average:	6.00
No. 50s:	0	No. 100s:	0

Test Bowling & Fielding
Wickets:	2	Runs:	128
Best Bowling:	1/35	Average:	64.00
5 WI:	0	10 WM:	0
Catches:	0	Stumpings:	0

One Day Internationals

ODI Career: 1989-97
ODIs Played: 20

ODI Batting
Innings:	13	Runs:	34
Highest Score:	9	Average:	3.77
No. 50s:	0	No. 100s:	0

ODI Bowling & Fielding
Wickets:	13	Runs:	615
Best Bowling:	3/33	Average:	47.30
5 WM:	0	Catches:	2
Stumpings:	0		

A fast bowler from Maharashtra, with movie star good looks. He played just the one Test against Pakistan at Karachi but was serviceable as a one day player for just under a decade. Not surprisingly he later pursued an acting career.

APTE, Arvindrao Laxmanrao

Born: October 24, 1934
Batting: Right handed
Bowling: Right arm medium

Tests

Test Career: 1959
Cap Number: 92
Tests Played: 1

Test Batting
Innings:	2	Runs:	15
Highest Score:	8	Average:	7.50
No. 50s:	0	No. 100s:	0

Test Bowling & Fielding
Wickets:	0	Runs:	0
Best Bowling:		Average:	0.00
5 WI:	0	10 WM:	0
Catches:	0	Stumpings:	0

An opening batsman who played the one Test against England at Headingley, in 1959. Younger brother of Madhav Apte.

APTE, Madhavrao Laxmanrao

Born: October 5, 1932
Batting: Right handed
Bowling: Right arm medium

Tests

Test Career: 1952-53
Cap Number: 64
Tests Played: 7

Test Batting
Innings:	13	Runs:	542
Highest Score:	163*	Average:	49.27
No. 50s:	3	No. 100s:	1

Test Bowling & Fielding
Wickets:	0	Runs:	3
Best Bowling:	0/3	Average:	0.00
5 WI:	0	10 WM:	0
Catches:	2	Stumpings:	0

A dour opening batsman who rarely put a foot wrong in his short Test career. After making an impressive debut against Pakistan, he was selected to tour the Caribbean where he averaged just over 50 for the series and scored a magnificent 163 not out. Amazingly, upon his return home, he was dropped from the national side and never played another Test.

ARUN, Bharathi

Born: December 14, 1962
Batting: Right handed
Bowling: Right arm medium-fast

Tests
Test Career:	1986-87		
Cap Number:	176		
Tests Played:	2		

Test Batting
Innings:	2	Runs:	4
Highest Score:	2*	Average:	4.00
No. 50s:	0	No. 100s:	0

Test Bowling & Fielding
Wickets:	4	Runs:	116
Best Bowling:	3/76	Average:	29.00
5 WI:	0	10 WM:	0
Catches:	2	Stumpings:	0

One Day Internationals
ODI Career:	1986-87		
ODIs Played:	4		

ODI Batting
Innings:	3	Runs:	21
Highest Score:	8	Average:	10.50
No. 50s:	0	No. 100s:	0

ODI Bowling & Fielding
Wickets:	1	Runs:	103
Best Bowling:	1/43	Average:	103.00
5 WM:	0	Catches:	0
Stumpings:	0		

A powerful right arm medium-fast bowler who made his Test debut against Sri Lanka at Kanpur in 1986 where he took 3/76 in the first innings. He played just the one more Test and a handful of ODI appearances.

ARUN LAL, Jagdishlal
Born:	August 1, 1955
Batting:	Right handed
Bowling:	Right arm medium

Tests
Test Career:	1982-89		
Cap Number:	159		
Tests Played:	16		

Test Batting
Innings:	29	Runs:	729
Highest Score:	93	Average:	26.03
No. 50s:	6	No. 100s:	0

Test Bowling & Fielding
Wickets:	0	Runs:	7
Best Bowling:		Average:	0.00
5 WI:	0	10 WM:	0
Catches:	13	Stumpings:	0

One Day Internationals
ODI Career:	1982-89		
ODIs Played:	13		

ODI Batting
Innings:	13	Runs:	122
Highest Score:	51	Average:	9.38
No. 50s:	1	No. 100s:	0

ODI Bowling & Fielding
Wickets:	0	Runs:	0
Best Bowling:		Average:	0.00
5 WM:	0	Catches:	4
Stumpings:	0		

Hard working right hand batsman from Moradabad, Uttar Pradesh, Lal had to wait until age 27 before making his Test debut against Sri Lanka, at Chennai in 1982, where he scored an impressive 63.

AYUB, Arshad
Born:	August 2, 1958
Batting:	Right handed
Bowling:	Right arm off-break

Tests
Test Career:	1987-89		
Cap Number:	178		
Tests Played:	13		

Test Batting
Innings:	19	Runs:	257
Highest Score:	57	Average:	17.13
No. 50s:	1	No. 100s:	0

Test Bowling & Fielding
Wickets:	41	Runs:	1,438
Best Bowling:	5/50	Average:	35.07
5 WI:	3	10 WM:	0
Catches:	2	Stumpings:	0

One Day Internationals
ODI Career:	1987-90		
ODIs Played:	32		

ODI Batting
Innings:	17	Runs:	116
Highest Score:	31*	Average:	11.59
No. 50s:	0	No. 100s:	0

ODI Bowling & Fielding
Wickets:	31	Runs:	1,216
Best Bowling:	5/21	Average:	39.22
5 WM:	1	Catches:	5
Stumpings:	0		

A right arm off-spinner from Hyderabad, Ayub made his Test debut against West Indies at Delhi, in 1987 but gained more prominence as a One Day International player. His most memorable and best bowling performance was his 5/21 which helped steer India to victory against Pakistan in the Asia Cup final, at Dhaka, in 1988.

AZAD, Kirtivardhan Bhagwat Jha
Born:	January 2, 1959
Batting:	Right handed
Bowling:	Right arm off-break

Tests
Test Career:	1981-83		
Cap Number:	150		
Tests Played:	7		

Test Batting
Innings:	12	Runs:	135
Highest Score:	24	Average:	1.25
No. 50s:	0	No. 100s:	0

Test Bowling & Fielding
Wickets:	3	Runs:	373
Best Bowling:	2/84	Average:	124.33
5 WI:	0	10 WM:	0
Catches:	3	Stumpings:	0

One Day Internationals
ODI Career:	1980-86		
ODIs Played:	25		

ODI Batting
Innings:	21	Runs:	269
Highest Score:	39*	Average:	14.15
No. 50s:	0	No. 100s:	0

ODI Bowling & Fielding
Wickets:	7	Runs:	273
Best Bowling:	2/48	Average:	39.00
5 WM:	0	Catches:	7
Stumpings:	0		

An off-spinner who made his Test debut against New Zealand in 1980, Azad could only manage a further six Tests but made his name as a limited overs player, having played 25 ODI's over six years. He was a member of India's successful World Cup side of 1983.

AZHARUDDIN, Mohammad

Born: February 8, 1963
Batting: Right handed
Bowling: Right arm medium

Tests
Test Career: 1985-00
Cap Number: 169
Tests Played: 99

Test Batting
Innings:	147	Runs:	6,215
Highest Score:	199	Average:	45.03
No. 50s:	21	No. 100s:	22

Test Bowling & Fielding
Wickets:	0	Runs:	16
Best Bowling:	0/16	Average:	0.00
5 WI:	0	10 WM:	0
Catches:	105	Stumpings:	0

One Day Internationals
ODI Career: 1985-00
ODIs Played: 334

ODI Batting
Innings:	308	Runs:	9,378
Highest Score:	153*	Average:	36.92
No. 50s:	58	No. 100s:	7

ODI Bowling & Fielding
Wickets:	12	Runs:	479
Best Bowling:	3/19	Average:	39.91
5 WM:	0	Catches:	156
Stumpings:	0		

At age 21, Mohammad Azharuddin, a classical and elegant right hand batsman from Hyderabad, took Indian cricket by storm. He not only scored a Test century on debut with 110 against England at Kolkata, in 1984, but followed up with centuries in his next two Tests - 105 at Chennai then 122 at Kanpur - thus making him the only player in Test history to score a century in each of his first three Test matches. Shortly afterwards he was being touted as "the jewel in India's crown" and the next great batsman since Sunil Gavaskar. Scoring centuries was almost second nature to him as cricket fans all over the world waited for the 'mother of all innings' to arrive. Amazingly enough in his 99 Tests, Azharuddin never scored a Test double century. He fell one short when he hit a superb 199 against Sri Lanka at Kanpur in 1986 and then got close again when he scored 192 against New Zealand in Auckland in 89/90. With 22 Test hundreds and 21 fifties along side his name, Azharuddin's conversion rate - of 50's into 100s - was as good, if not marginally better than that of Gavaskar and Tendulkar. If dominating the Test scene wasn't enough, Azharuddin's record in ODI was also impressive. Averaging just under 37, his 62-ball century against New Zealand in 1988 still remains the fastest ODI century by an Indian. An exceptional fielder, Azharuddin captained India in 47 Tests from 1989 to 1999 - allowing for a brief stint in 1996 when Tendulkar took over the reins. With 6215 Test runs, Azharuddin is the fifth highest run scorer in India's history. However, with all the accolades that one could possibly dream of having bestowed upon them, sadly, Azharuddin's reputation was tarnished after his retirement when he was embroiled in a match fixing scandal. The end result - a life ban that was imposed in 2000. Beyond 2006, Azharuddin still aims to clear his name.

BADANI, Hemang Kamal

Born: November 14, 1976
Batting: Left handed
Bowling: Left arm off-break

Tests
Test Career: 2001
Cap Number: 237
Tests Played: 4

Test Batting
Innings:	7	Runs:	94
Highest Score:	38	Average:	15.66
No. 50s:	0	No. 100s:	0

Test Bowling & Fielding
Wickets:	0	Runs:	7
Best Bowling:	0/7	Average:	0.00
5 WI:	0	10 WM:	0
Catches:	6	Stumpings:	0

One Day Internationals
ODI Career: 2000-04
ODIs Played: 40

ODI Batting
Innings:	36	Runs:	867
Highest Score:	100	Average:	33.34
No. 50s:	4	No. 100s:	1

ODI Bowling & Fielding
Wickets:	3	Runs:	149
Best Bowling:	1/7	Average:	49.60
5 WM:	0	Catches:	13
Stumpings:	0		

A middle order batsman from Tamil Nadu who started his Test career as an opener against Zimbabwe at Harare, in 2001. His first inning score of two suggested that it may not have been the wisest of moves, so Badani was moved down the order and batted at seven in the second innings where he looked alot more comfortable and made 16 not out. Played just the four Tests but was valuable contributor over his 40 game One Day International career.

BAHUTULE, Sairaj Vasant

Born: January 6, 1973
Batting: Left handed
Bowling: Left arm leg-break

Tests
Test Career: 2001
Cap Number: 235
Tests Played: 2

Test Batting			
Innings:	4	Runs:	39
Highest Score:	21*	Average:	13.00
No. 50s:	0	No. 100s:	0

Test Bowling & Fielding
Wickets:	3	Runs:	203
Best Bowling:	1/32	Average:	67.66
5 WI:	0	10 WM:	0
Catches:	1	Stumpings:	0

One Day Internationals
ODI Career: 1997-03
ODIs Played: 8

ODI Batting
Innings:	4	Runs:	23
Highest Score:	11	Average:	7.66
No. 50s:	0	No. 100s:	0

ODI Bowling & Fielding
Wickets:	2	Runs:	283
Best Bowling:	1/31	Average:	141.50
5 WM:	0	Catches:	3
Stumpings:	0		

A leg break bowler from Mumbai who was given his chance due to an injury to Anil Kumble. He made his debut against Australia at Chennai in 2000 but could only add one more Test cap to his tally.

BAIG, Abbas Ali
Born: March 19, 1939
Batting: Right handed
Bowling: Right arm leg-break

Tests
Test Career: 1959-67
Cap Number: 93
Tests Played: 10

Test Batting
Innings:	18	Runs:	428
Highest Score:	112	Average:	23.77
No. 50s:	2	No. 100s:	1

Test Bowling & Fielding
Wickets:	0	Runs:	15
Best Bowling:		Average:	0.00
5 WI:	0	10 WM:	0
Catches:	6	Stumpings:	0

Originally from Hyderabad and considered by many unlucky not to have played in more Tests considering his unlimited talent. Baig scored a century, 112 on debut against England, at Old Trafford, in 1959, after replacing the injured Vijay Manjrekar. At the time, he was the youngest Indian to get a Test hundred. Thereafter his performances ranged from admirable to disappointing hence his 112 on debut was to remain his highest score and only Test century. He played his last Test against the West Indies at Kolkata in 1966/67.

BALAJI, Lakshmipathy
Born: September 27, 1981
Batting: Right handed
Bowling: Right arm medium-fast

Tests
Test Career: 2003-05
Cap Number: 245
Tests Played: 8

Test Batting
Innings:	9	Runs:	51
Highest Score:	31	Average:	5.66
No. 50s:	0	No. 100s:	0

Test Bowling & Fielding
Wickets:	27	Runs:	1,004
Best Bowling:	5/76	Average:	37.18
5 WI:	1	10 WM:	0
Catches:	1	Stumpings:	0

One Day Internationals
ODI Career: 2002-05
ODIs Played: 29

ODI Batting
Innings:	15	Runs:	113
Highest Score:	21*	Average:	12.55
No. 50s:	0	No. 100s:	0

ODI Bowling & Fielding
Wickets:	24	Runs:	1,312
Best Bowling:	4/48	Average:	38.58
5 WM:	0	Catches:	11
Stumpings:	0		

A right arm pace bowler from Chennai, Balaji made an uneventful debut against New Zealand in 2003 but emerged as a fast bowler to be reckoned with after a successful tour of Pakistan. It wasn't just the wickets he took, it was also the many unplayable deliveries that made his spells a pure delight to watch. Amazingly, he was omitted from the side after the tour of Sri Lanka and then missed quite a bit of cricket due to injury. However, being the passionate competitor that he is, he made it back into the side in 2005 where he performed admirably against Pakistan on home soil taking a career best 5/76 at Chanidgarh.

BANERJEE, Sarobindu Nath
Born: October 3, 1911
Batting: Right handed

Tests
Test Career: 1949
Cap Number: 52
Tests Played: 1

Test Batting
Innings:	2	Runs:	13
Highest Score:	8	Average:	6.50
No. 50s:	0	No. 100s:	0

Test Bowling & Fielding
Wickets:	5	Runs:	127
Best Bowling:	4/54	Average:	25.39
5 WI:	0	10 WM:	0
Catches:	0	Stumpings:	0

Making his debut at age 35, against the West Indies at Mumbai, most would have thought that Banerjee's five wickets, including his 4/54 in the second innings, would have been enough to grant him at least another Test appearance. Unfortunately, the selectors had other ideas.

BANERJEE, Subroto Tara

Born: February 13, 1969
Batting: Right handed
Bowling: Right arm medium-fast

Tests
Test Career: 1992
Cap Number: 194
Tests Played: 1

Test Batting
Innings:	1	Runs:	3
Highest Score:	3	Average:	3.00
No. 50s:	0	No. 100s:	0

Test Bowling & Fielding
Wickets:	3	Runs:	47
Best Bowling:	3/47	Average:	15.66
5 WI:	0	10 WM:	0
Catches:	0	Stumpings:	0

One Day Internationals
ODI Career: 1991-92
ODIs Played: 6

ODI Batting
Innings:	5	Runs:	49
Highest Score:	25*	Average:	24.50
No. 50s:	0	No. 100s:	0

ODI Bowling & Fielding
Wickets:	5	Runs:	202
Best Bowling:	3/30	Average:	40.39
5 WM:	0	Catches:	3
Stumpings:	0		

A right arm medium fast bowler who took a respectable 3/47 in his one and only Test appearance against Australia, at the SCG in 1991. Was also a solid performer in his six ODI appearances.

BANERJEE, Sudangsu Abinash

Born: November 1, 1919
Batting: Right handed
Bowling: Right arm medium

Tests
Test Career: 1948-49
Cap Number: 48
Tests Played: 1

Test Batting
Innings:	1	Runs:	0
Highest Score:	0	Average:	0.00
No. 50s:	0	No. 100s:	0

Test Bowling & Fielding
Wickets:	5	Runs:	181
Best Bowling:	4/120	Average:	36.20
5 WI:	0	10 WM:	0
Catches:	0	Stumpings:	0

Played the one Test and performed well taking 4/120. Although he didn't trouble the scorers while batting, he was considered quite unlucky not to be selected for any future tests.

BANGAR, Sanjay Bapusaheb

Born: October 11, 1972
Batting: Right handed
Bowling: Right arm medium-fast

Tests
Test Career: 2001-02
Cap Number: 240
Tests Played: 12

Test Batting
Innings:	18	Runs:	470
Highest Score:	100*	Average:	29.37
No. 50s:	3	No. 100s:	1

Test Bowling & Fielding
Wickets:	7	Runs:	343
Best Bowling:	2/23	Average:	49.00
5 WI:	0	10 WM:	0
Catches:	4	Stumpings:	0

One Day Internationals
ODI Career: 2002-04
ODIs Played: 15

ODI Batting
Innings:	15	Runs:	180
Highest Score:	57*	Average:	13.84
No. 50s:	1	No. 100s:	0

ODI Bowling & Fielding
Wickets:	7	Runs:	384
Best Bowling:	2/39	Average:	54.85
5 WM:	0	Catches:	4
Stumpings:	0		

An energetic all-rounder from Maharashtra, Sanjay Bangar added a touch of excitement to the Indian line up after making his debut against England at Chandigarh in 2002. An excellent mover of the ball however his bowling average of 49.00 doesn't really reflect his true talent. Just as exciting when batting, Bangar, in his second Test hit a memorable 100 not out against Zimbabwe, coming in at number seven. Has also been a valuable member of India's ODI side.

BEDADE, Atul Chandrakant

Born: September 24, 1966
Batting: Left handed
Bowling: Right arm medium

One Day Internationals
ODI Career: 1994
ODIs Played: 13

ODI Batting
Innings:	10	Runs:	158
Highest Score:	51	Average:	22.57
No. 50s:	1	No. 100s:	0

ODI Bowling & Fielding
Wickets:	0	Runs:	0
Best Bowling:		Average:	0.00
5 WM:	0	Catches:	4
Stumpings:	0		

A hard hiting batsman who made his ODI debut against United Arab Emirates in the Pepsi Austral-Asia Cup Competition at Sharjah in 1994.

BEDI, Bishan Singh

Born: September 25, 1946
Batting: Right handed
Bowling: Left arm off-break

Tests
Test Career: 1967-79
Cap Number: 113
Tests Played: 67

Test Batting
Innings:	101	Runs:	656
Highest Score:	50*	Average:	8.98
No. 50s:	1	No. 100s:	0

Test Bowling & Fielding			
Wickets:	266	Runs:	7,637
Best Bowling:	7/98	Average:	28.71
5 WI:	14	10 WM:	1
Catches:	26	Stumpings:	0

One Day Internationals

ODI Career:	1974-79		
ODIs Played:	10		
ODI Batting			
Innings:	7	Runs:	31
Highest Score:	13	Average:	6.20
No. 50s:	0	No. 100s:	0
ODI Bowling & Fielding			
Wickets:	7	Runs:	340
Best Bowling:	2/44	Average:	48.57
5 WM:	0	Catches:	4
Stumpings:	0		

A majestic left arm off spinner who inadvertently made the turban a fashion statement during the 1970's. Bedi was part of the spin quartet comprising of Chandrasekhar, Prasanna and Venkat. It was a purist's delight when he and Chandrasekhar worked in tandem as a more artistic display of spin bowling could not be imagined. Always thinking, and constantly testing the batsman with variations in drift and loop, Bedi amassed 266 wickets at 28.71, with a personal best of 7/98 against Australia at Kolkata, in 69/70. He also has a Test 50 not out alongside his name, which is a considerable effort for a number ten batsman batting with spectacles. Bedi captained India in 22 Tests between 1975 to '79 and displayed tremendous leadership. Never taking a backward step, he spoke his mind even if it meant ruffling a few feathers. He objected to the use of vaseline strips by two English bowlers during the Madras Test of 1976 and then in Jamaica protested against West Indian bowling tactics by declaring India's first and second innings closed. However, controversy didn't affect Bedi's performances. He continued to take wickets and enjoyed success even in the twilight of his career. In the 1977/78 Australian tour, where he became a popular figure amongst the Australian fans, Bedi took 31 wickets at 23.87 and by the time he retired in 1979, he was India's highest wicket taker. Today he sits in third place behind Anil Kumble and Kapil Dev.

BHANDARI, Amit

Born:	October 1, 1978
Batting:	Right handed
Bowling:	Right arm medium-fast

One Day Internationals

ODI Career:	2000-04		
ODIs Played:	2		
ODI Batting			
Innings:	1	Runs:	0
Highest Score:	0*	Average:	0.00
No. 50s:	0	No. 100s:	0
ODI Bowling & Fielding			
Wickets:	5	Runs:	106
Best Bowling:	3/31	Average:	21.19
5 WM:	0	Catches:	0
Stumpings:	0		

A right arm fast bowler from Delhi who made his ODI debut against Pakistan at Dhaka in 2000, then played his second ODI four years later against Zimbabwe.

BHANDARI, Prakash

Born:	November 27, 1935
Batting:	Right handed
Bowling:	Right arm off-break

Tests

Test Career:	1955-56		
Cap Number:	73		
Tests Played:	3		
Test Batting			
Innings:	4	Runs:	77
Highest Score:	39	Average:	19.25
No. 50s:	0	No. 100s:	0
Test Bowling & Fielding			
Wickets:	0	Runs:	39
Best Bowling:		Average:	0.00
5 WI:	0	10 WM:	0
Catches:	1	Stumpings:	0

Originally from Delhi, Bhandari made his debut in 1954/55 against Pakistan as a highly talented all rounder but never lived up to the expectations of the Indian cricketing public.

BHARADWAJ, Raghvendrarao Vijay

Born:	August 15, 1975
Batting:	Right handed
Bowling:	Right arm off-break

Tests

Test Career:	1999-00		
Cap Number:	223		
Tests Played:	3		
Test Batting			
Innings:	3	Runs:	28
Highest Score:	22	Average:	9.33
No. 50s:	0	No. 100s:	0
Test Bowling & Fielding			
Wickets:	1	Runs:	107
Best Bowling:	1/26	Average:	107.00
5 WI:	0	10 WM:	0
Catches:	3	Stumpings:	0

One Day Internationals

ODI Career:	1999-02		
ODIs Played:	10		
ODI Batting			
Innings:	9	Runs:	136
Highest Score:	41*	Average:	27.19
No. 50s:	0	No. 100s:	0
ODI Bowling & Fielding			
Wickets:	16	Runs:	307
Best Bowling:	3/34	Average:	19.18
5 WM:	0	Catches:	4
Stumpings:	0		

A middle order batsman from Karnataka who made his Test debut against New Zealand at Chandigarh, Bharadwaj, who was also known as Vijay, enjoyed greater success as a limited overs player where he averaged 27 with the bat and an impressive 19.18 runs per wicket with the ball.

BHAT, Adwai Raghuram

Born: April 16, 1958
Batting: Left handed
Bowling: Left arm off-break

Tests
Test Career: 1983
Cap Number: 165
Tests Played: 2

Test Batting
Innings:	3	Runs:	6
Highest Score:	6	Average:	3.00
No. 50s:	0	No. 100s:	0

Test Bowling & Fielding
Wickets:	4	Runs:	151
Best Bowling:	2/65	Average:	37.75
5 WI:	0	10 WM:	0
Catches:	0	Stumpings:	0

An off-spinner from Puttur Mysore, Bhat played his first Test match against Pakistan, at Nagpur in 1983, where he took the wickets of Javed Miandad and Mudassar Nazar. He played his last ODI a fortnight later against the West Indies.

BINNY, Roger Michael Humphrey

Born: July 19, 1955
Batting: Right handed
Bowling: Right arm medium

Tests
Test Career: 1979-87
Cap Number: 148
Tests Played: 27

Test Batting
Innings:	41	Runs:	830
Highest Score:	83*	Average:	23.05
No. 50s:	5	No. 100s:	0

Test Bowling & Fielding
Wickets:	47	Runs:	1,534
Best Bowling:	6/56	Average:	32.63
5 WI:	2	10 WM:	0
Catches:	11	Stumpings:	0

One Day Internationals
ODI Career: 1980-87
ODIs Played: 72

ODI Batting
Innings:	49	Runs:	629
Highest Score:	57	Average:	16.12
No. 50s:	1	No. 100s:	0

ODI Bowling & Fielding
Wickets:	77	Runs:	2,260
Best Bowling:	4/29	Average:	29.35
5 WM:	0	Catches:	12
Stumpings:	0		

A tall and powerful all-rounder who burst onto the scene in 1979, Roger Binny was an excitement machine when in full swing. He was just as comfortable when plying his trade in limited overs competition as he was in Tests. Binny provided India with batting versatility as he could either play the hard hitting cameo role late in the innings and at other times open the batting. As a bowler, he could swing the ball either way and captured a personal best of 6/56 against Pakistan at Kolkata in 1987. A member of India's victorious 1983 World Cup side Binny took 18 wickets in the competition, which was a record at the time. Upon closer inspection, it was noticed that Binny had quite a unique bowling action, but not in the controversial sense. When landing in his delivery stride, his back (right) foot would point backwards, instead of forward.

BORDE, Chandrakant Gulabrao (Chandu)

Born: July 21, 1934
Batting: Right handed
Bowling: Right arm leg-break

Tests
Test Career: 1958-69
Cap Number: 83
Tests Played: 55

Test Batting
Innings:	97	Runs:	3,061
Highest Score:	177*	Average:	35.59
No. 50s:	18	No. 100s:	5

Test Bowling & Fielding
Wickets:	52	Runs:	2,417
Best Bowling:	5/88	Average:	46.48
5 WI:	1	10 WM:	0
Catches:	37	Stumpings:	0

A quality all rounder and brilliant fielder. Borde was the only Indian selected in the Rest of the World team that played Barbados in a commemoration match in 1967. He scored five Test centuries, including an unbeaten 177 against Pakistan at Chennai in 1960/61. Accompanying his healthy batting average of 35.59 was his success as a leg spin bowler, even though a shoulder injury restricted his bowling towards the latter part of his career. He later became Chairman of Selectors.

BOSE, Gopal Krishna

Born: May 20, 1947
Batting: Right handed
Bowling: Right arm off-break

One Day Internationals
ODI Career: 1974
ODIs Played: 1

ODI Batting
Innings:	1	Runs:	13
Highest Score:	13	Average:	13.00
No. 50s:	0	No. 100s:	0

ODI Bowling & Fielding
Wickets:	1	Runs:	39
Best Bowling:	1/39	Average:	39.00
5 WM:	0	Catches:	0
Stumpings:	0		

A bespectacled opener vying for the position of partner to the great Sunil Gavaskar but could only manage the sole ODI against England at The Oval in 1974 where he made 13. Took just the one wicket that of current commentator David Lloyd.

CHANDRASEKHAR, Bhagwat Subramanya

Born:	May 17, 1945
Batting:	Right handed
Bowling:	Right arm leg-break

Tests
Test Career:	1964-79
Cap Number:	106
Tests Played:	58

Test Batting
Innings:	80	Runs:	167
Highest Score:	22	Average:	4.07
No. 50s:	0	No. 100s:	0

Test Bowling & Fielding
Wickets:	242	Runs:	7,199
Best Bowling:	8/79	Average:	29.74
5 WI:	16	10 WM:	2
Catches:	25	Stumpings:	0

One Day Internationals
ODI Career:	1976
ODIs Played:	1

ODI Batting
Innings:	1	Runs:	11
Highest Score:	11*	Average:	11.00
No. 50s:	0	No. 100s:	0

ODI Bowling & Fielding
Wickets:	3	Runs:	36
Best Bowling:	3/36	Average:	12.00
5 WM:	0	Catches:	0
Stumpings:	0		

Suffering polio as a child, Chandrasekhar became one of India's greatest bowlers. Part of the famous spin quartet of the late 60's and 70's (Bedi, Prasanna Venkataraghavan & Chandrasekhar) his bouncy run up combined with a quick, fizzing action produced a variety of unplayable googlies and leg breaks. Of the four spinners, he combined beautifully and best with Bishen Bedi. Even today, their 'partnership' is widely heralded as one of the best spin bowling combinations the game has seen. He was clearly India's most successful bowler abroad. He was instrumental in providing India with their first ever series win in England when he captured 6/38 at The Oval. Later in that decade he toured Australia in 1978 and the Aussie crowds warmed to him. His 12/104 at the MCG was the catalyst for India's first win in Australia. He played the solitary One Day International against New Zealand, at Auckland, in 1976 and with 242 wickets at 29.74, Bhagwat Chandrasekhar is considered as one of the best leg spinners of all time.

CHANDRASEKHAR, Vakkadai Biksheswaran

Born:	August 21, 1961
Batting:	Right handed
	Wicket Keeper

One Day Internationals
ODI Career:	1988-90
ODIs Played:	7

ODI Batting
Innings:	7	Runs:	88
Highest Score:	53	Average:	12.57
No. 50s:	1	No. 100s:	0

ODI Bowling & Fielding
Wickets:	0	Runs:	0
Best Bowling:		Average:	0.00
5 WM:	0	Catches:	0
Stumpings:	0		

An exciting batsman from Chennai suited to the shorter version of the game. He made his debut against New Zealand in 1988/89. A firm believer in cultivating youthful talent, these days Chandrasekhar runs a cricket academy in Chennai.

CHATTERJEE, Utpal Subodh

Born:	July 13, 1964
Batting:	Left handed

One Day Internationals
ODI Career:	1995
ODIs Played:	3

ODI Batting
Innings:	2	Runs:	6
Highest Score:	3*	Average:	6.00
No. 50s:	0	No. 100s:	0

ODI Bowling & Fielding
Wickets:	3	Runs:	117
Best Bowling:	2/35	Average:	39.00
5 WM:	0	Catches:	1
Stumpings:	0		

A suprise selection, Chatterjee made his ODI debut as a 30 year old against Bangladesh at Sharjah in 1995. Played just the three ODI's without raising too many eyebrows.

CHAUHAN, Chetandra Pratap Singh (Chetan)

Born:	July 21, 1947
Batting:	Right handed
Bowling:	Right arm off-break

Tests
Test Career:	1968-81
Cap Number:	118
Tests Played:	40

Test Batting
Innings:	68	Runs:	2,084
Highest Score:	97	Average:	31.57
No. 50s:	16	No. 100s:	0

Test Bowling & Fielding
Wickets:	2	Runs:	106
Best Bowling:	1/4	Average:	53.00
5 WI:	0	10 WM:	0
Catches:	38	Stumpings:	0

One Day Internationals
ODI Career:	1978-81
ODIs Played:	7

ODI Batting
Innings:	7	Runs:	153
Highest Score:	46	Average:	21.85
No. 50s:	0	No. 100s:	0

ODI Bowling & Fielding

Wickets:	0	Runs:	0
Best Bowling:		Average:	0.00
5 WM:	0	Catches:	3
Stumpings:	0		

The tiny opener with the fixed smile, Chetan Chauhan will always be remembered as Sunil Gavaskar's partner in crime for the better part of seventies and early eighties. Together they managed ten century partnerships - which remains a record in Indian cricket. Their most memorable being their 213 run stand against England at The Oval, in 1979, passing the previous highest partnership of 203 set way back in 1936 by Merchant and Ali. A patient batsman and a fine exponent of the cut shot, Chauhan came to age as a batsman during the 1977/78 Australian tour where he notched up a memorable 88 against the Aussie pace attack in Perth. Although scoring over 2,000 runs at Test level, surprisingly Chauhan never hit a test ton and was the first player to reach the 2000 milestone without a century next to his name - an interesting trivia question but no consolation for one who batted so courageously for his country for over such a long period of time.

CHAUHAN, Rajesh Kumar

Born:	December 19, 1966
Batting:	Right handed
Bowling:	Right arm off-break

Tests

Test Career:	1993-98		
Cap Number:	197		
Tests Played:	21		
Test Batting			
Innings:	17	Runs:	98
Highest Score:	23	Average:	7.00
No. 50s:	0	No. 100s:	0
Test Bowling & Fielding			
Wickets:	47	Runs:	857
Best Bowling:	4/48	Average:	39.51
5 WI:	0	10 WM:	0
Catches:	12	Stumpings:	0

One Day Internationals

ODI Career:	1993-97		
ODIs Played:	35		
ODI Batting			
Innings:	18	Runs:	132
Highest Score:	32	Average:	10.15
No. 50s:	0	No. 100s:	0
ODI Bowling & Fielding			
Wickets:	29	Runs:	1,216
Best Bowling:	3/29	Average:	41.93
5 WM:	0	Catches:	10
Stumpings:	0		

Right arm off spinner from Madhya Pradesh, Chauhan was serviceable in both forms of the game. A suspect bowling action may have hindered his opportunity to play more International cricket.

CHAWLA, Piyush

Born:	December 24, 1988
Batting:	Left handed
Bowling:	Left arm leg-break

Tests

Test Career:	2006		
Cap Number:	255		
Tests Played:	1		
Test Batting			
Innings:	1	Runs:	1
Highest Score:	1	Average:	1.00
No. 50s:	0	No. 100s:	0
Test Bowling & Fielding			
Wickets:	1	Runs:	53
Best Bowling:	1/8	Average:	53.00
5 WI:	0	10 WM:	0
Catches:	0	Stumpings:	0

A talented left arm leg-break bowler who is touted as a future all-rounder, Piyush Chawla's solitary Test appearance to date, was in early 2006 where India comfortably accounted for England by nine wickets at Chandigarh. Chawla took just the one wicket for the match, albeit an important one, that of Andrew 'Freddie' Flintoff.

CHOPRA, Aakash

Born:	September 19, 1977
Batting:	Right handed
Bowling:	Right arm medium

Tests

Test Career:	2003-04		
Cap Number:	246		
Tests Played:	10		
Test Batting			
Innings:	19	Runs:	437
Highest Score:	60	Average:	23.00
No. 50s:	2	No. 100s:	0
Test Bowling & Fielding			
Wickets:	0	Runs:	0
Best Bowling:		Average:	0.00
5 WI:	0	10 WM:	0
Catches:	15	Stumpings:	0

A hard-working opener from Uttar Pradesh who made his Test debut against New Zealand at Ahmedabad, in 2003-04, where he made a respectable 42 & 31. Struggled to make runs against the Australian star studded attack but earned the reputation as one who was patient enough to see out the new ball in order to make life easier for batsmen up the order.

CHOPRA, Nikhil

Born:	December 26, 1973
Batting:	Right handed
Bowling:	Right arm off-break

Tests

Test Career:	2000		
Cap Number:	227		
Tests Played:	1		
Test Batting			
Innings:	2	Runs:	7
Highest Score:	4	Average:	3.50
No. 50s:	0	No. 100s:	0

Test Bowling & Fielding
Wickets:	0	Runs:	78
Best Bowling:		Average:	0.00
5 WI:	0	10 WM:	0
Catches:	0	Stumpings:	0

One Day Internationals
ODI Career:	1998-00
ODIs Played:	39

ODI Batting
Innings:	26	Runs:	310
Highest Score:	61	Average:	15.50
No. 50s:	1	No. 100s:	0

ODI Bowling & Fielding
Wickets:	46	Runs:	1,286
Best Bowling:	5/21	Average:	27.95
5 WM:	1	Catches:	16
Stumpings:	0		

A talented off break bowler and hard hitting late order batsmen, surprisingly Chopra was only considered for one Test match against South Africa at Bangalore, in 2000. He was highly rated as an ODI bowler and went on to represent his country in 39 limited over matches. His best bowling of 5/21 is complimented with a highest score of 61.

CHOWDHURY, Nirode Ranjan
Born:	May 23, 1923
Batting:	Right handed

Tests
Test Career:	1949-51
Cap Number:	50
Tests Played:	2

Test Batting
Innings:	2	Runs:	3
Highest Score:	3*	Average:	3.00
No. 50s:	0	No. 100s:	0

Test Bowling & Fielding
Wickets:	1	Runs:	205
Best Bowling:	1/130	Average:	205.00
5 WI:	0	10 WM:	0
Catches:	0	Stumpings:	0

A medium pacer who played his first Test against the West Indies in 1948 and took his only career wicket, that of opener and future captain Jeff Stolmeyer. He had to wait three years to play his next, and final Test, against England at Delhi.

COLAH, Sorabji
Born:	September 22, 1902
Batting:	Right handed
Bowling:	Right arm medium

Tests
Test Career:	1932-33
Cap Number:	2
Tests Played:	2

Test Batting
Innings:	4	Runs:	69
Highest Score:	31	Average:	17.25
No. 50s:	0	No. 100s:	0

Test Bowling & Fielding
Wickets:	0	Runs:	0
Best Bowling:		Average:	0.00
5 WI:	0	10 WM:	0
Catches:	0	Stumpings:	0

Regarded as an aggressive batsman who liked to take on the bowling, Colah was a member of India's inaugural Test team of 1932 that played England at Lord's. Although highly rated, he played just the two Tests, his second and last, against England at Mumbai which was the first Test match on Indian soil.

CONTRACTOR, Nariman Jamshedji (Nari)
Born:	March 7, 1934
Batting:	Left handed
Bowling:	Right arm medium

Tests
Test Career:	1955-62
Cap Number:	77
Tests Played:	31

Test Batting
Innings:	52	Runs:	1,611
Highest Score:	108	Average:	31.58
No. 50s:	11	No. 100s:	1

Test Bowling & Fielding
Wickets:	1	Runs:	80
Best Bowling:	1/9	Average:	80.00
5 WI:	0	10 WM:	0
Catches:	18	Stumpings:	0

One of India's finest and most courageous players. Contractor was a dour opening batsman who played under duress at various times during his career. The most prominent was the time he was struck on the skull by West Indian speedster Charlie Griffith during a tour game against Barbados in 1962. Having to undergo a number of operations, Contractor thankfully survived and made a comeback to first class cricket some two years later - even though he was never the same player. Prior to the sickening incident, he scored his only Test century against Australia in 1959-60 at Bombay. At 26, he was appointed skipper against Pakistan in 1960-61, thus making him the youngest ever Indian captain.

DAHIYA, Vijay
Born:	May 10, 1973
Batting:	Right handed
	Wicket Keeper

Tests
Test Career:	2000
Cap Number:	232
Tests Played:	2

Test Batting
Innings:	1	Runs:	2
Highest Score:	2*	Average:	2.00
No. 50s:	0	No. 100s:	0

Test Bowling & Fielding
Wickets:	0	Runs:	0
Best Bowling:		Average:	0.00
5 WI:	0	10 WM:	0
Catches:	6	Stumpings:	0

One Day Internationals
ODI Career:	2000-01		
ODIs Played:	19		

ODI Batting
Innings:	15	Runs:	216
Highest Score:	51	Average:	16.61
No. 50s:	1	No. 100s:	0

ODI Bowling & Fielding
Wickets:	0	Runs:	0
Best Bowling:		Average:	0.00
5 WM:	0	Catches:	19
Stumpings:	5		

A wicket-keeper from Delhi who made his Test debut against Zimbabwe in front of his home crowd. He was given an opportunity when the Indian selectors were combing the nation for the next number one gloveman.

DANI, Hemchandra Tukaram (Bal)
Born:	May 24, 1933
Batting:	Right handed
Bowling:	Right arm off-break

Tests
Test Career:	1952-53		
Cap Number:	65		
Tests Played:	1		

Test Batting
Innings:	0	Runs:	0
Highest Score:	0	Average:	0.00
No. 50s:	0	No. 100s:	0

Test Bowling & Fielding
Wickets:	1	Runs:	19
Best Bowling:	1/9	Average:	19.00
5 WI:	0	10 WM:	0
Catches:	0	Stumpings:	0

Yet another story of a player who excelled in Ranji Trophy competition but hardly got a chance to make an impact at Test level. He didn't get to bat in his only Test appearance against Pakistan at Mumbai, 1952 and managed just the one wicket from limited opportunities. Dani later became a national selector.

DAS, Shiv Sunder
Born:	November 5, 1977
Batting:	Right handed
Bowling:	Right arm medium

Tests
Test Career:	2000-02		
Cap Number:	229		
Tests Played:	23		

Test Batting
Innings:	40	Runs:	1,326
Highest Score:	110	Average:	34.89
No. 50s:	9	No. 100s:	2

Test Bowling & Fielding
Wickets:	0	Runs:	35
Best Bowling:		Average:	0.00
5 WI:	0	10 WM:	0
Catches:	34	Stumpings:	0

One Day Internationals
ODI Career:	2001-02
ODIs Played:	4

ODI Batting
Innings:	4	Runs:	39
Highest Score:	30	Average:	13.00
No. 50s:	0	No. 100s:	0

ODI Bowling & Fielding
Wickets:	0	Runs:	0
Best Bowling:		Average:	0.00
5 WM:	0	Catches:	0
Stumpings:	0		

A technically sound opening batsman from Orissa, Das scored his two centuries against Zimbabwe at Nagpur but struggled against more talented bowling attacks. Played 23 Tests and just a handful of ODI's.

DASGUPTA, Deep
Born:	June 7, 1977
Batting:	Right handed
	Wicket Keeper

Tests
Test Career:	2001-02		
Cap Number:	238		
Tests Played:	8		

Test Batting
Innings:	13	Runs:	344
Highest Score:	100	Average:	28.66
No. 50s:	2	No. 100s:	1

Test Bowling & Fielding
Wickets:	0	Runs:	0
Best Bowling:		Average:	0.00
5 WI:	0	10 WM:	0
Catches:	13	Stumpings:	0

One Day Internationals
ODI Career:	2001
ODIs Played:	5

ODI Batting
Innings:	4	Runs:	51
Highest Score:	24*	Average:	17.00
No. 50s:	0	No. 100s:	0

ODI Bowling & Fielding
Wickets:	0	Runs:	0
Best Bowling:		Average:	0.00
5 WM:	0	Catches:	2
Stumpings:	1		

A keeper who could also open the batting, Dasgupta got his chance at international level when regular keeper Sameer Dighe fell out of favour with the selectors after the Zimbabwe and Sri Lankan series in 2001. Dasgupta was invited on the 2001/02 tour of South Africa and made his Test debut at Bloemfontein. An accomplished batsman at domestic level, Dasgupta scored his maiden Test century against England at Chandigarh as an opening batsman.

DAVID, Noel Arthur
Born:	February 26, 1971
Batting:	Right handed
Bowling:	Right arm off-break

One Day Internationals
ODI Career:	1997
ODIs Played:	4

ODI Batting			
Innings:	2	Runs:	9
Highest Score:	8*	Average:	9.00
No. 50s:	0	No. 100s:	0
ODI Bowling & Fielding			
Wickets:	4	Runs:	133
Best Bowling:	3/21	Average:	33.25
5 WM:	0	Catches:	0
Stumpings:	0		

An off-break bowler from Hyderabad who had scored a double century at domestic level. Made his ODI debut against the West Indies at Port of Spain covering for the injured Javagal Srinath.

DESAI, Ramakant Bhikaji (Tiny)
Born: June 20, 1939
Batting: Right handed

Tests

Test Career: 1959-68
Cap Number: 90
Tests Played: 28

Test Batting
Innings:	44	Runs:	418
Highest Score:	85	Average:	13.48
No. 50s:	1	No. 100s:	0

Test Bowling & Fielding
Wickets:	74	Runs:	2,761
Best Bowling:	6/56	Average:	37.31
5 WI:	2	10 WM:	0
Catches:	9	Stumpings:	0

Standing at 5.4, there was no irony in Ramakant Desai's nickname. 'Tiny' utilised a healthy run up to generate the pace required to bowl at the highest level. Courageous and tireless his best haul was 6/56 but arguably, his major career highlight occurred in 1961 when he scored 85 against Pakistan, coming in at number 10. After retiring at age 30 he was later appointed chairman of selectors and was embroiled in controversy when he dismissed Sachin Tendulkar as Indian captain.

DEV, Kapil dev Ramlal Nikhanj
Born: January 6, 1959
Batting: Right handed
Bowling: Right arm medium-fast

Tests

Test Career: 1978-94
Cap Number: 141
Tests Played: 131

Test Batting
Innings:	184	Runs:	5,248
Highest Score:	163	Average:	31.05
No. 50s:	27	No. 100s:	8

Test Bowling & Fielding
Wickets:	434	Runs:	12
Best Bowling:	9/83	Average:	29.64
5 WI:	23	10 WM:	2
Catches:	64	Stumpings:	0

One Day Internationals

ODI Career: 1978-94
ODIs Played: 225

ODI Batting			
Innings:	198	Runs:	3,783
Highest Score:	175*	Average:	23.79
No. 50s:	14	No. 100s:	1
ODI Bowling & Fielding			
Wickets:	253	Runs:	6,945
Best Bowling:	5/43	Average:	27.45
5 WM:	0	Catches:	71
Stumpings:	0		

During the 1970's and 80's international cricket was blessed with a plethora of great all rounders such as Imran Khan, Richard Hadlee and Ian Botham. And India's contribution to the cause, Kapil Dev, was held in just as high esteem. Although not super quick, Dev's ability to consistently swing the ball, and his amazing endurance were the attributes, which eventually saw him overtake Sir Richard Hadlee as Test cricket's highest wicket taker. Dev got five wickets in an innings on 23 occasions, his best 9/83 against West Indies in 1983, and finished with 434 scalps. While he was touted as India's best ever pace bowler, his batting record as an all rounder, is just as impressive. He made eight Test hundreds with a highest score of 163 against Sri Lanka, at Nagpur in 1986. Dev was also just as good at the shorter version of the game and captained India to their renowned 'boilover' World Cup victory in 1983 against the powerful West Indies. His 175 not out against Zimbabwe during that same tournament remained the highest ODI score by any Indian until 2006. Dev captained India in 34 Tests from 1982-87. In 2002 he received the highest individual honour in Indian cricket when voted India's 'Cricketer of the Century'.

DHARMANI, Pankaj
Born: September 27, 1974
Batting: Right handed
Wicket Keeper

One Day Internationals

ODI Career: 1996-97
ODIs Played: 1

ODI Batting			
Innings:	1	Runs:	8
Highest Score:	8	Average:	8.00
No. 50s:	0	No. 100s:	0
ODI Bowling & Fielding			
Wickets:	0	Runs:	0
Best Bowling:	0	Average:	0.00
5 WM:	0	Catches:	0
Stumpings:	0		

A wicket-keeper from Delhi who played his one and only ODI as a batsmen while regular keeper Mongia kept wickets.

DHONI, Mahendra Singh (MS)
Born: July 7, 1981
Batting: Right handed
Bowling: Right arm medium
Wicket Keeper

Tests
Test Career:	2005-06		
Cap Number:	251		
Tests Played:	13		

Test Batting
Innings:	20	Runs:	602
Highest Score:	148	Average:	13.68
No. 50s:	3	No. 100s:	1

Test Bowling & Fielding
Wickets:	0	Runs:	13
Best Bowling:		Average:	0.00
5 WI:	0	10 WM:	0
Catches:	38	Stumpings:	9

One Day Internationals
ODI Career:	2004-06		
ODIs Played:	47		

ODI Batting
Innings:	43	Runs:	1,467
Highest Score:	183*	Average:	48.90
No. 50s:	8	No. 100s:	2

ODI Bowling & Fielding
Wickets:	0	Runs:	0
Best Bowling:		Average:	0.00
5 WM:	0	Catches:	44
Stumpings:	9		

Regarded as a 'breath of fresh air' in Indian cricket, MS Dhoni is a competent and aggressive batsman capable of scoring quick runs. Since making his Test debut against Sri Lanka at Chennai in 2005, Dhoni has continued to impress with both bat and gloves and at both forms of the game. His 183 not out against Sri Lanka in 2005 became the highest score by a wicket-keeper in One Day Internationals breaking the record previously held by Australian Adam Gilchrist.

DIGHE, Sameer Sudhakar
Born:	October 8, 1968
Batting:	Right handed
	Wicket Keeper

Tests
Test Career:	2001		
Cap Number:	236		
Tests Played:	6		

Test Batting
Innings:	10	Runs:	141
Highest Score:	47	Average:	15.66
No. 50s:	0	No. 100s:	0

Test Bowling & Fielding
Wickets:	0	Runs:	0
Best Bowling:		Average:	0.00
5 WI:	0	10 WM:	0
Catches:	12	Stumpings:	2

One Day Internationals
ODI Career:	2000-01		
ODIs Played:	23		

ODI Batting
Innings:	17	Runs:	256
Highest Score:	94*	Average:	23.27
No. 50s:	1	No. 100s:	0

ODI Bowling & Fielding
Wickets:	0	Runs:	0
Best Bowling:		Average:	0.00
5 WM:	0	Catches:	19
Stumpings:	5		

A late bloomer who made his international debut at age 31, Dighe was used mainly in ODI's and once held the record for the highest score by an Indian wicket-keeper at ODI level with his unbeaten 94 against the West Indies, in Zimbabwe, in 2001. He won the respect of peers and held the number one keeping position for a 12-month period but could only manage six Tests in his short but entertaining career.

DIVECHA, Ramesh Vithaldas
Born:	October 18, 1927
Batting:	Right handed

Tests
Test Career:	1951-52		
Cap Number:	57		
Tests Played:	5		

Test Batting
Innings:	5	Runs:	60
Highest Score:	26	Average:	12.00
No. 50s:	0	No. 100s:	0

Test Bowling & Fielding
Wickets:	11	Runs:	361
Best Bowling:	3/102	Average:	32.81
5 WI:	0	10 WM:	0
Catches:	5	Stumpings:	0

A strongly built medium pacer who could also bowl off-spin, Divecha was a member of India's first Test win at Chennai in 1952. He played just five Tests but had a successful career in English County cricket.

DOSHI, Dilip Rasiklal
Born:	December 22, 1947
Batting:	Left handed
Bowling:	Left arm off-break

Tests
Test Career:	1979-83		
Cap Number:	146		
Tests Played:	33		

Test Batting
Innings:	38	Runs:	129
Highest Score:	20	Average:	4.60
No. 50s:	0	No. 100s:	0

Test Bowling & Fielding
Wickets:	114	Runs:	3,502
Best Bowling:	6/102	Average:	30.71
5 WI:	6	10 WM:	0
Catches:	10	Stumpings:	0

One Day Internationals
ODI Career:	1980-82		
ODIs Played:	15		

ODI Batting
Innings:	5	Runs:	9
Highest Score:	5*	Average:	3.00
No. 50s:	0	No. 100s:	0

ODI Bowling & Fielding
Wickets:	22	Runs:	524
Best Bowling:	4/30	Average:	23.81
5 WM:	0	Catches:	3
Stumpings:	0		

It was not until age 32 that Dilip Doshi received his first invitation to represent his country at Test level. Prior to making his debut against Australia at Chennai in 1979, the bespectacled off spinner had to watch from sidelines as Indian great, Bishen Bedi and counterparts Erapally Prasanna & Venkat shared the off spinning duties. Much maligned for his fielding, (as it was said at times that the captain would try and 'hide' him in the field) Doshi's bowling ability would have no doubt earned him many more Test appearances, and an earlier debut, had he been born in another time or another place. His son Nayan, who is also a left arm off spinner, plays first class cricket in England.

DRAVID, Rahul Sharad

Born: January 11, 1973
Batting: Right handed
Bowling: Right arm off-break
Wicket Keeper

Tests

Test Career:	1996-06		
Cap Number:	206		
Tests Played:	104		

Test Batting

Innings:	176	Runs:	9,049
Highest Score:	270	Average:	58.75
No. 50s:	46	No. 100s:	23

Test Bowling & Fielding

Wickets:	1	Runs:	39
Best Bowling:	1/18	Average:	39.00
5 WI:	0	10 WM:	0
Catches:	146	Stumpings:	0

One Day Internationals

ODI Career:	1996-06		
ODIs Played:	292		

ODI Batting

Innings:	271	Runs:	9,528
Highest Score:	153	Average:	40.20
No. 50s:	71	No. 100s:	12

ODI Bowling & Fielding

Wickets:	4	Runs:	170
Best Bowling:	2/43	Average:	42.50
5 WM:	0	Catches:	174
Stumpings:	0		

A right hand batsman who oozes class, Rahul Dravid's elegant strokeplay is complimented with a technically flawless defence. By the time his career draws to a close, he well may be considered one of the finest batsmen of world cricket. With over 9,000 runs alongside his name, Dravid is headed only by the dual 'little masters' in Tendulkar and Gavaskar for most Test runs scored for India. However his Test average of 58.75 stands alone at the top. Unlucky not to score a century on debut, when he was dismissed for 95 when batting at number seven against England at Lords, Dravid has well and truly made up for the oversight since, scoring 23 Test tons including five double centuries. His 270 against Pakistan at Rawalpindi in 2004 is the third highest score by any Indian. But it was his 180 when playing second fiddle to VVS Laxman's epic 281 against Australia, which is considered by many as his finest performance.

Dravid has a been a consistent performer also at one day level where he averages over 40 with the bat and handles himself competently as a part time wicket-keeper. He is the current Indian captain after replacing long time team mate, Sourav Ganguly.

DURANI, Salim Aziz

Born: December 11, 1934
Batting: Left handed
Bowling: Left arm off-break

Tests

Test Career:	1960-73		
Cap Number:	95		
Tests Played:	29		

Test Batting

Innings:	50	Runs:	1,202
Highest Score:	104	Average:	25.04
No. 50s:	7	No. 100s:	1

Test Bowling & Fielding

Wickets:	75	Runs:	2,657
Best Bowling:	6/73	Average:	35.42
5 WI:	3	10 WM:	1
Catches:	14	Stumpings:	0

Born in Kabul, Afghanistan, the tall and rather dapper, Salim Durrani was an old fashioned all rounder who loved nothing better than to smash the bowling to all parts of the ground. Rather laconic in style but a match winner on his day, he steered India to a series victory over England in 1961-62 by collecting eight wickets at Kolkata and then a bag of ten at Chennai. His highest score of 104 was scored against West Indies in 1962.

ELAHI, Amir

Born: September 1, 1908
Batting: Right handed
Bowling: Right arm medium

Tests

Test Career:	1947-52		
Cap Number:	40		
Tests Played:	6		

Test Batting

Innings:	9	Runs:	82
Highest Score:	47	Average:	10.25
No. 50s:	0	No. 100s:	0

Test Bowling & Fielding

Wickets:	7	Runs:	248
Best Bowling:	4/134	Average:	35.42
5 WI:	0	10 WM:	0
Catches:	0	Stumpings:	0

One of a handful of players who played Test cricket for both India and Pakistan. He represented India against Australia in 1947, and then his remaining five Tests for Pakistan were all against India in 1952/53, including Pakistan's inaugural Test at Delhi.

ENGINEER, Farokh Maneksha

Born:	February 25, 1938
Batting:	Right handed
Bowling:	Right arm leg-break
	Wicket Keeper

Tests

Test Career:	1961-75
Cap Number:	102
Tests Played:	46

Test Batting

Innings:	87	Runs:	2,611
Highest Score:	121	Average:	31.08
No. 50s:	16	No. 100s:	2

Test Bowling & Fielding

Wickets:	0	Runs:	0
Best Bowling:		Average:	0.00
5 WI:	0	10 WM:	0
Catches:	0	Stumpings:	0

One Day Internationals

ODI Career:	1974-75
ODIs Played:	5

ODI Batting

Innings:	4	Runs:	114
Highest Score:	54*	Average:	38.00
No. 50s:	1	No. 100s:	0

ODI Bowling & Fielding

Wickets:	0	Runs:	0
Best Bowling:		Average:	0.00
5 WM:	0	Catches:	3
Stumpings:	1		

One of the best keepers going around in his day, Farokh Engineer was also an accomplished batsman who was promoted to opener early in his career. He scored two test centuries, his first, 109 against the West Indies at Chennai in 1967 and then against England in 1973, he scored a career best 121 at Mumbai. Testament to his ability was his selection as first-choice keeper for the Rest of the World XI series in England and Australia in the early 1970's where he again shone with the bat scoring 192 against a combined eleven at Hobart. He kept to Indian spin masters of Bedi, Prasanna, Chandrasekhar and Venkataraghavan. Engineer was a natural to the shorter version of the game when One Day Internationals were introduced in the early seventies. Along with his understudy Syed Kirmani, Engineer is regarded as one of India's finest wicket-keepers.

GADKARI, Chandrasekhar Vaman

Born:	February 3, 1928
Batting:	Right handed

Tests

Test Career:	1953-55
Cap Number:	69
Tests Played:	6

Test Batting

Innings:	10	Runs:	129
Highest Score:	50*	Average:	21.50
No. 50s:	1	No. 100s:	0

Test Bowling & Fielding

Wickets:	0	Runs:	45
Best Bowling:		Average:	0.00
5 WI:	0	10 WM:	0
Catches:	0	Stumpings:	0

A right handed batsman who enjoyed taking on the bowling. He would have played more than his six tests if not for his commitment to the armed forces. His 50 not out, coming in at number nine against the West Indies, was clearly the highlight of his career.

GAEKWAD, Aunshuman Dattajirao

Born:	September 23, 1952
Batting:	Right handed
Bowling:	Right arm off-break

Tests

Test Career:	1974-84
Cap Number:	135
Tests Played:	40

Test Batting

Innings:	70	Runs:	1,985
Highest Score:	201	Average:	30.07
No. 50s:	10	No. 100s:	2

Test Bowling & Fielding

Wickets:	2	Runs:	187
Best Bowling:	1/4	Average:	93.50
5 WI:	0	10 WM:	0
Catches:	15	Stumpings:	0

One Day Internationals

ODI Career:	1975-87
ODIs Played:	15

ODI Batting

Innings:	14	Runs:	269
Highest Score:	78*	Average:	20.69
No. 50s:	1	No. 100s:	0

ODI Bowling & Fielding

Wickets:	1	Runs:	39
Best Bowling:	1/39	Average:	39.00
5 WM:	0	Catches:	6
Stumpings:	0		

A bespectacled right hand batsman from Baroda, Gaekwad is the son of Datta Gaekwad who captained India in the 1950's. Although he never reached the heights of many of his more higher profile contemporaries such as Gavaskar, Viswanath and Vengsarker, he did score a double century late in his career - 201 against Pakistan at Jalandhar, in 1983/84, but at the time was the slowest double century in Test history. Like quite a few former players, he became a national selector after retiring.

GAEKWAD, Dattajirao Krishnarao (Datta)

Born:	October 27, 1928
Batting:	Right handed

Tests

Test Career:	1952-61
Cap Number:	60
Tests Played:	11

Test Batting (Gaekwad)

Innings:	20	Runs:	350
Highest Score:	52	Average:	18.42
No. 50s:	1	No. 100s:	0

Test Bowling & Fielding

Wickets:	0	Runs:	12
Best Bowling:	0/12	Average:	0.00
5 WI:	0	10 WM:	0
Catches:	5	Stumpings:	0

A solid batsman who earned a reputation as an outstanding fieldsmen, Gaekwad, could only manage 11 Tests in just under a decade - even though he captained India on their English tour of 1959. Although a modest Test record, like many of his contemporaries, Gaekwad was a standout when playing in the Ranji Trophy. His son, Anshuman Gaekwad, played Test cricket for India in the 1970's and 80's.

GAEKWAD, Hiralal Ghasulal

Born: August 29, 1923
Batting: Left handed
Bowling: Left arm medium

Tests

Test Career: 1952-53
Cap Number: 62
Tests Played: 1

Test Batting

Innings:	2	Runs:	22
Highest Score:	14	Average:	11.00
No. 50s:	0	No. 100s:	0

Test Bowling & Fielding

Wickets:	0	Runs:	47
Best Bowling:	0/47	Average:	0.00
5 WI:	0	10 WM:	0
Catches:	0	Stumpings:	0

Played his one and only Test in 1952 against Pakistan, at Lucknow, when selected to replace Vinoo Mankad.

GAMBHIR, Gautam

Born: October 14, 1981
Batting: Left handed
Bowling: Left arm leg-break

Tests

Test Career: 2004-05
Cap Number: 249
Tests Played: 13

Test Batting

Innings:	21	Runs:	684
Highest Score:	139	Average:	36.00
No. 50s:	3	No. 100s:	1

Test Bowling & Fielding

Wickets:	0	Runs:	0
Best Bowling:		Average:	0.00
5 WI:	0	10 WM:	0
Catches:	12	Stumpings:	0

One Day Internationals

ODI Career: 2003-06
ODIs Played: 16

ODI Batting

Innings:	16	Runs:	409
Highest Score:	103	Average:	25.56
No. 50s:	1	No. 100s:	1

ODI Bowling & Fielding

Wickets:	0	Runs:	13
Best Bowling:		Average:	0.00
5 WM:	0	Catches:	6
Stumpings:	0		

After an impressive apprenticeship at One Day level, left handed opener Gambhir was given his chance at Test level in 2004. However he found the Australian pace attack of McGrath, Gillespie and co somewhat overwhelming. His 139 against Bangladesh at Chittagong later that year remains his only Test century.

GANDHI, Devang Jayant

Born: September 6, 1971
Batting: Right handed
Bowling: Right arm medium

Tests

Test Career: 1999-06
Cap Number: 221
Tests Played: 4

Test Batting

Innings:	7	Runs:	204
Highest Score:	88	Average:	34.00
No. 50s:	2	No. 100s:	0

Test Bowling & Fielding

Wickets:	0	Runs:	0
Best Bowling:		Average:	0.00
5 WI:	0	10 WM:	0
Catches:	3	Stumpings:	0

One Day Internationals

ODI Career: 1999-00
ODIs Played: 3

ODI Batting

Innings:	3	Runs:	49
Highest Score:	30	Average:	16.13
No. 50s:	0	No. 100s:	0

ODI Bowling & Fielding

Wickets:	0	Runs:	0
Best Bowling:		Average:	0.00
5 WM:	0	Catches:	0
Stumpings:	0		

An opening batsman, Gandhi made his Test debut against New Zealand at Chandigarh in 1999. Although he performed solidly against the Kiwis, Gandhi struggled against the Australians on the following tour and was eventually dropped. He retired in April 2006.

GANDOTRA, Ashok

Born: November 24, 1948
Batting: Left handed
Bowling: Left arm off-break

Tests

Test Career: 1969
Cap Number: 122
Tests Played: 2

Test Batting

Innings:	4	Runs:	54
Highest Score:	18	Average:	13.50
No. 50s:	0	No. 100s:	0

Test Bowling & Fielding
Wickets:	0	Runs:	5
Best Bowling:	0/5	Average:	0.00
5 WI:	0	10 WM:	0
Catches:	0	Stumpings:	0

Brazilian born left hander, Gandotra played his two Tests on home soil against New Zealand and Australia in 1969/70.

GANESH, Doddanarasiah (Dodda)
Born:	June 30, 1973
Batting:	Right handed
Bowling:	Right arm medium

Tests
Test Career:	1997		
Cap Number:	210		
Tests Played:	4		

Test Batting
Innings:	7	Runs:	25
Highest Score:	8	Average:	6.25
No. 50s:	0	No. 100s:	0

Test Bowling & Fielding
Wickets:	5	Runs:	287
Best Bowling:	2/28	Average:	57.39
5 WI:	0	10 WM:	0
Catches:	0	Stumpings:	0

One Day Internationals
ODI Career:	1997		
ODIs Played:	1		

ODI Batting
Innings:	1	Runs:	4
Highest Score:	4	Average:	4.00
No. 50s:	0	No. 100s:	0

ODI Bowling & Fielding
Wickets:	1	Runs:	20
Best Bowling:	1/20	Average:	20.00
5 WM:	0	Catches:	0
Stumpings:	0		

Dodda Ganesh played one ODI and four Tests in his short career. He made his Test debut against Sth Africa in Cape Town in 1996. Originally from Karnataka.

GANGULY, Sourav Chandidas
Born:	July 8, 1972
Batting:	Left handed
Bowling:	Right arm fast

Tests
Test Career:	1996-06		
Cap Number:	207		
Tests Played:	88		

Test Batting
Innings:	140	Runs:	5,221
Highest Score:	173	Average:	40.78
No. 50s:	25	No. 100s:	12

Test Bowling & Fielding
Wickets:	26	Runs:	1,419
Best Bowling:	3/28	Average:	54.57
5 WI:	0	10 WM:	0
Catches:	59	Stumpings:	0

One Day Internationals
ODI Career:	1992-05		
ODIs Played:	279		

ODI Batting
Innings:	270	Runs:	10,123
Highest Score:	183	Average:	40.65
No. 50s:	60	No. 100s:	22

ODI Bowling & Fielding
Wickets:	93	Runs:	3,470
Best Bowling:	5/16	Average:	37.31
5 WM:	2	Catches:	96
Stumpings:	0		

After taking over the captaincy from Sachin Tendulkar in 2000, Sourav Ganguly has not only captained India in more Tests than any of his predecessors (49) but can also boast the best win/loss ratio. However a six (later reduced to four) match ban by ICC match referee Clive Lloyd in 2005, for a slow over rate against Pakistan and a public fall out with coach Greg Chappell led to Ganguly being asked to stand down as skipper. He was replaced by long standing teammate Rahul Dravid whom he debuted with against England at Lord's in 1996. It was to be a dawning of a new era in Indian cricket as both men have gone on to become two of India's finest batsmen. While Dravid fell five short of scoring a ton on debut, Ganguly's 131 was the highest score in the match, which eventually petered out to a draw. Ganguly's batting record may not have not reached the prestigious heights of Dravid however his 12 centuries and 25 fifties at Test level have been more than serviceable. As a one day batsman, Ganguly has few peers. His swashbuckling performances when opening with Sachin Tendulkar have been as entertaining as they have been damaging. He has scored 22 centuries, at an average of just over 40, with a highest score of 183 against Sri Lanka during the 1999 World Cup. A handy right arm seamer, Ganguly's best haul at ODI level occurred at Toronto in 1997 where he captured five Pakistan wickets for just 16 runs.

GAVASKAR, Rohan Sunil
Born:	February 20, 1976
Batting:	Left handed
Bowling:	Left arm off-break

One Day Internationals
ODI Career:	2004		
ODIs Played:	11		

ODI Batting
Innings:	10	Runs:	151
Highest Score:	54	Average:	18.87
No. 50s:	1	No. 100s:	0

ODI Bowling & Fielding
Wickets:	1	Runs:	74
Best Bowling:	1/56	Average:	74.00
5 WM:	0	Catches:	5
Stumpings:	0		

As the son of arguably India's most famous cricketer of all time, Sunil Gavaskar, the spotlight was on young Rohan from the outset. He took one wicket and made two not out in an uneventful ODI debut against Australia at Brisbane, in

2004. Unlike his father, Rohan is a left hander. He bowls reasonable off spin and if his form continues to impress at domestic level, he should add to his tally of 11 ODI's.

GAVASKAR, Sunil Manohar

Born:	July 10, 1949
Batting:	Right handed
Bowling:	Right arm medium

Tests

Test Career:	1971-87		
Cap Number:	128		
Tests Played:	125		
Test Batting			
Innings:	214	Runs:	10
Highest Score:	236*	Average:	51.12
No. 50s:	45	No. 100s:	34
Test Bowling & Fielding			
Wickets:	1	Runs:	206
Best Bowling:	1/34	Average:	206.00
5 WI:	0	10 WM:	0
Catches:	108	Stumpings:	0

One Day Internationals

ODI Career:	1974-87		
ODIs Played:	108		
ODI Batting			
Innings:	102	Runs:	3,092
Highest Score:	103*	Average:	35.13
No. 50s:	27	No. 100s:	1
ODI Bowling & Fielding			
Wickets:	1	Runs:	25
Best Bowling:	1/10	Average:	25.00
5 WM:	0	Catches:	22
Stumpings:	0		

Standing at just 5.4', he may have been small in stature, but Sunil Gavaskar became one of the biggest names in world cricket. In many corners, he is regarded as the best opening batsman the game has seen. Facing the pace attack of the West Indies on their home soil would be considered a 'baptism of fire' for many entering the Test arena for the first time, however Gavaskar's debut in the 2nd Test at Port of Spain, Trinidad, back in 1971, was an indication of things to come. He opened with an impressive 65 and then followed up with an unbeaten 67 in the second innings, which saw India score a rare victory in the Caribbean. While some waited to see whether the debutante's performance was a 'flash in the pan', Gavaskar just went about his business of scoring runs, thus silencing the critics and cynics alike. Taking a liking to the Port of Spain venue, Queen's Park Oval, he brought up his third century of the series with 124 in the first and 220 in the second innings of the Fifth Test. By the end of the series, Gavaskar had amassed an incredible 774 runs in four Tests, averaging an unprecedented 154 for the series. From then he was appropriately dubbed the 'Little Master'. Unlike many of his past, and even latter sub continent compatriots, Gavaskar was more than comfortable against genuine pace bowling and, in fact was hailed as the best player of fast bowling in the early seventies. He was awarded the captaincy in 1975 and skippered India in 47 Tests but was considered a rather conservative tactician as his nine-eight win/loss ratio and 30 draws record would later indicate. While he was smashing records ad nauseam, Gavaskar's unflattering 30 draws as captain also made the record books. He relinquished the leadership to Bishen Bedi in 1978 but was reappointed at various stages later in his career. Throughout his career he continued to let his batting do the talking and of his record-breaking 34 Test tons, there are many standouts. His 221 against England at Old Trafford in 1979, when India was set 438 to win, was one of the most memorable. Gavaskar scored an amazing 179 of his 221 on the last day, to draw the match, which remains an Indian Test record. In the early part of the 80's, he relegated himself lower in the batting order. In 1983 at Chennai when the West Indies had India reeling at two wickets for none - dismissing both Gaekwad and Vengsarker for ducks - Gavaskar came in and took on the new ball, but on this occasion as a number four batsman. He went on to score a career best 236 not out and ensured that India would not endure yet another demoralising defeat. Although his One Day International record plays second fiddle to his brilliant Test career, Gavaskar played over 100 ODI's and was a member of the 1983 World Cup side that caused one of the biggest boilovers in cricket history when India defeated the unbackable West Indies in the final. A year later, in the 1984/85 tour of England, Gavaskar was reappointed captain. His tenure was short lived but he continued to pile on the runs during the twilight of his illustrious career. His crowning moment occurred in March 1987 during the fourth, and his penultimate Test, against Pakistan at Ahmedabad. A stylish late cut for two took the 'Little Master's' score to 58 and he became the first batsman to reach 10,000 runs in Test cricket. This sent the crowd into a frenzy, which saw the pitch invaded for almost half an hour. The following Test at Bangalore would be his last and on a pitch that could be best described as a minefield, Gavaskar scored a dour and patient 96 in his last innings, thus earning him the 'Man of the Match' award. As he headed towards the pavilion for the last time, Gavaskar had amassed 10,122 runs alongside his name with a healthy average of 51.12. He also held the record as the most prolific run scorer in Test cricket until Australian captain Allan Border overtook him in 1993. He is the first Indian (non wicket keeper) fielder to reach 100 catches and remains one of five players to have reached the magical 10,000 run figure. A true ornament of the game, Sunil Gavaskar, now a highly respected commentator, will long remain one of the finest cricketers the game has seen.

GHAI, Rajinder Singh
Born: June 12, 1960
Batting: Right handed
Bowling: Right arm medium-fast

One Day Internationals
ODI Career: 1984-86
ODIs Played: 6

ODI Batting
Innings:	1	Runs:	1
Highest Score:	1	Average:	1.00
No. 50s:	0	No. 100s:	0

ODI Bowling & Fielding
Wickets:	3	Runs:	260
Best Bowling:	1/38	Average:	86.66
5 WM:	0	Catches:	0
Stumpings:	0		

A quickish bowler from Jalandhar who struggled for wickets in his six ODI's in two years. He played his last against Australia at Rajkot and never got the opportunity to play at Test level.

GHAVRI, Karsan Devjibhai
Born: February 28, 1951
Batting: Left handed
Bowling: Left arm medium

Tests
Test Career: 1975-81
Cap Number: 136
Tests Played: 39

Test Batting
Innings:	57	Runs:	913
Highest Score:	86	Average:	21.23
No. 50s:	2	No. 100s:	0

Test Bowling & Fielding
Wickets:	109	Runs:	3,656
Best Bowling:	5/33	Average:	33.54
5 WI:	4	10 WM:	0
Catches:	16	Stumpings:	0

One Day Internationals
ODI Career: 1975-81
ODIs Played: 19

ODI Batting
Innings:	16	Runs:	114
Highest Score:	20	Average:	11.40
No. 50s:	0	No. 100s:	0

ODI Bowling & Fielding
Wickets:	15	Runs:	708
Best Bowling:	3/40	Average:	47.20
5 WM:	0	Catches:	2
Stumpings:	0		

A hard working, left-arm medium pacer who partnered as an opening bowler with Kapil Dev during the late 1970's. The two seamers complimented the highly rated spin attack of the day in Bedi, Chandrasekhar and Prasanna. A member of India's 1975 & '79 World Cup squads and with a Test batting average of just over 21, Ghavri was considered somewhat of an all rounder and played some fine cameo innings at both Test and One Day level. His highest Test score of 86 was made against Australia at Mumbai, where he and wicket keeper Syed Kirmani put on 127 for the eighth wicket, which at the time was a Test record.

GHORPADE, Jaysinghrao Mansinghrao
Born: October 2, 1930
Batting: Right handed
Bowling: Right arm leg-break

Tests
Test Career: 1953-59
Cap Number: 70
Tests Played: 8

Test Batting
Innings:	15	Runs:	229
Highest Score:	41	Average:	15.26
No. 50s:	0	No. 100s:	0

Test Bowling & Fielding
Wickets:	0	Runs:	131
Best Bowling:		Average:	0.00
5 WI:	0	10 WM:	0
Catches:	4	Stumpings:	0

Bespectacled 'leggy' who showed quite a bit of dash when batting. He made his debut against the West Indies at Port of Spain in 1953 and was a serviceable contibutor over his six years career.

GOPALAN, Morappakam Joysam
Born: June 6, 1909
Batting: Right handed
Bowling: Right arm medium-fast

Tests
Test Career: 1934
Cap Number: 18
Tests Played: 1

Test Batting
Innings:	2	Runs:	18
Highest Score:	11*	Average:	18.00
No. 50s:	0	No. 100s:	0

Test Bowling & Fielding
Wickets:	1	Runs:	39
Best Bowling:	1/39	Average:	39.00
5 WI:	0	10 WM:	0
Catches:	3	Stumpings:	0

A right arm fast-medium bowler who played one Test against England, at Kolkata in 1934. He also represented India at hockey.

GOPINATH, Coimbatarao Doraikannu
Born: March 1, 1930
Batting: Right handed

Tests
Test Career: 1951-60
Cap Number: 55
Tests Played: 8

Test Batting
Innings:	12	Runs:	242
Highest Score:	50*	Average:	22.00
No. 50s:	1	No. 100s:	0

Test Bowling & Fielding
Wickets:	1	Runs:	11
Best Bowling:	1/11	Average:	11.00
5 WI:	0	10 WM:	0
Catches:	2	Stumpings:	0

Gopinath made his highest score of 50 not out on debut against England at Mumbai, in 1952 but struggled thereafter and was in and out of the Test side for the remainder fo his career. Later became chairman of the national selection committee.

GUARD, Ghulam Mustafa

Born: December 12, 1925
Batting: Left handed
Bowling: Left arm medium-fast

Tests

Test Career: 1958-60
Cap Number: 84
Tests Played: 2

Test Batting
Innings:	2	Runs:	11
Highest Score:	7	Average:	5.50
No. 50s:	0	No. 100s:	0

Test Bowling & Fielding
Wickets:	3	Runs:	182
Best Bowling:	2/69	Average:	60.66
5 WI:	0	10 WM:	0
Catches:	2	Stumpings:	0

Making his debut against West Indies, at Mumbai in 1958 at the ripe old age of 33, Guard picked up the prize scalp of Sir Garfield Sobers. He went on to play just one more Test - against Australia - but left the game with a fantastic story to tell his grand-kids.

GUHA, Subrata

Born: January 31, 1946
Batting: Right handed
Bowling: Right arm medium-fast

Tests

Test Career: 1967-69
Cap Number: 114
Tests Played: 4

Test Batting
Innings:	7	Runs:	17
Highest Score:	6	Average:	3.39
No. 50s:	0	No. 100s:	0

Test Bowling & Fielding
Wickets:	3	Runs:	311
Best Bowling:	2/55	Average:	103.66
5 WI:	0	10 WM:	0
Catches:	2	Stumpings:	0

A right arm, medium pace swing bowler from Kolkata. He made his debut against England at Headingley in 1967 and played four Tests in total with moderate success.

GUPTE, Balkrishna Pandharinath (Baloo)

Born: August 30, 1934
Batting: Right handed
Bowling: Right arm leg-break

Tests

Test Career: 1961-65
Cap Number: 100
Tests Played: 3

Test Batting
Innings:	3	Runs:	28
Highest Score:	17*	Average:	28.00
No. 50s:	0	No. 100s:	0

Test Bowling & Fielding
Wickets:	3	Runs:	349
Best Bowling:	1/54	Average:	116.33
5 WI:	0	10 WM:	0
Catches:	0	Stumpings:	0

Baloo Gupte made his debut against Pakistan at Chennai, in 1961. Played only the three Tests and lived in the shadow of older brother Subash Gupte.

GUPTE, Subhashchandra Pandharinath (Fergie)

Born: December 11, 1929
Batting: Right handed
Bowling: Right arm leg-break

Tests

Test Career: 1951-61
Cap Number: 58
Tests Played: 36

Test Batting
Innings:	42	Runs:	183
Highest Score:	21	Average:	6.31
No. 50s:	0	No. 100s:	0

Test Bowling & Fielding
Wickets:	149	Runs:	4,403
Best Bowling:	9/102	Average:	29.55
5 WI:	12	10 WM:	1
Catches:	14	Stumpings:	0

Long before Abdul Qadir, Bhagwat Chandrasekhar and Shane Warne, Subhash Gupte was considered the premier leg break/googly bowler of his day. Apart from giving the ball an 'almighty tweak', he was like Warne, deadly accurate. He captured five wickets in an innings on a dozen occasions, with his most memorable performance being his 5/18 against Pakistan at Dhaka in 1955 and his career best 9/102 against West Indies at Kanpur, three years later. Gupte married and settled in the West Indies midway through his career and played for Trinidad as well as continuing to represent India. In 1961, his final year of Test cricket, he created cricket history when his 4/6 off 18 balls, at Kanpur, enforced England to follow on for the first time against India.

HARDIKAR, Manohar Shankar

Born: February 8, 1936
Batting: Right handed
Bowling: Right arm medium

Tests

Test Career: 1958
Cap Number: 85
Tests Played: 2

Test Batting
Innings:	4	Runs:	56
Highest Score:	32*	Average:	18.66
No. 50s:	0	No. 100s:	0

Test Bowling & Fielding				
Wickets:	1	Runs:		55
Best Bowling:	1/9	Average:		55.00
5 WI:	0	10 WM:		0
Catches:	3	Stumpings:		0

A medium pacer who played two Tests against West Indies in the 1958/59 series. On debut he trapped West Indian legend Rohan Kanhai lbw with his third ball. His only Test wicket, but a memorable one.

HAZARE, Vijay Samuel

Born:	March 11, 1915
Batting:	Right handed
Bowling:	Right arm medium

Tests

Test Career:	1946-53
Cap Number:	28
Tests Played:	30

Test Batting				
Innings:	52	Runs:		2,192
Highest Score:	164*	Average:		47.65
No. 50s:	9	No. 100s:		7
Test Bowling & Fielding				
Wickets:	20	Runs:		1,220
Best Bowling:	4/29	Average:		61.00
5 WI:	0	10 WM:		0
Catches:	11	Stumpings:		0

An Indian run machine who amassed over 2,000 runs with a healthy average of 47.65. He scored a century in each innings of the Adelaide Test, during the 1947/48 tour. Although a part time bowler, Hazare's main claim to fame is that he dismissed the great Don Bradman on two occasions.

HINDLEKAR, Dattaram Dharmaji

Born:	January 1, 1909
Batting:	Right handed
	Wicket Keeper

Tests

Test Career:	1936-46
Cap Number:	22
Tests Played:	4

Test Batting				
Innings:	7	Runs:		71
Highest Score:	26	Average:		14.19
No. 50s:	0	No. 100s:		0
Test Bowling & Fielding				
Wickets:	0	Runs:		0
Best Bowling:		Average:		0.00
5 WI:	0	10 WM:		0
Catches:	3	Stumpings:		0

Touted as one of India's finest wicket-keepers, alongside Farokh Engineer and Syed Kirmani, Hindlekar was one of the most popular members of the team during the early years. He toured England at age 37 but sadly died three years later.

HIRWANI, Narendra Deepchand

Born:	October 18, 1968
Batting:	Right handed
Bowling:	Right arm leg-break

Tests

Test Career:	1988-96
Cap Number:	180
Tests Played:	17

Test Batting				
Innings:	22	Runs:		54
Highest Score:	17	Average:		5.40
No. 50s:	0	No. 100s:		0
Test Bowling & Fielding				
Wickets:	66	Runs:		1,987
Best Bowling:	8/61	Average:		30.10
5 WI:	4	10 WM:		1
Catches:	5	Stumpings:		0

One Day Internationals

| ODI Career: | 1988-92 |
| ODIs Played: | 18 |

ODI Batting				
Innings:	7	Runs:		8
Highest Score:	4	Average:		2.00
No. 50s:	0	No. 100s:		0
ODI Bowling & Fielding				
Wickets:	23	Runs:		719
Best Bowling:	4/43	Average:		31.26
5 WM:	0	Catches:		2
Stumpings:	0			

A leg spiner from Madhya Pradesh, Narendra Hirwani could not have dreamed of a better start to his Test career after taking 8/61 - and 16 wickets for the match - on debut against the West Indies, at Chennai in 1988. It did though, prove to be a hard act to follow as he struggled to emulate his feat and thus hold a regular Test spot after his first series.

HUSSAIN, Dilawar

| Born: | March 19, 1907 |
| Batting: | Right handed |

Tests

Test Career:	1934-36
Cap Number:	17
Tests Played:	3

Test Batting				
Innings:	6	Runs:		254
Highest Score:	59	Average:		42.33
No. 50s:	3	No. 100s:		0
Test Bowling & Fielding				
Wickets:	0	Runs:		0
Best Bowling:		Average:		0.00
5 WI:	0	10 WM:		0
Catches:	6	Stumpings:		1

A talented wicket-keeper who could also bat, Hussain was asked at times to open for his country. He was the first Indian to score two 50's in the same test and his average of 42.33 for a 'keeper' was more than impressive in India's early days as a Test nation.

IBRAHIM, Khanmohammad Cassumbhoy

| Born: | January 26, 1919 |
| Batting: | Right handed |

Tests

Test Career:	1948-49		
Cap Number:	45		
Tests Played:	4		

Test Batting

Innings:	8	Runs:	169
Highest Score:	85	Average:	21.12
No. 50s:	1	No. 100s:	0

Test Bowling & Fielding

Wickets:	0	Runs:	0
Best Bowling:		Average:	0.00
5 WI:	0	10 WM:	0
Catches:	0	Stumpings:	0

A highly regarded domestic cricketer who kicked off his Test career in a blaze of glory with scores of 85 and 44 but struggled to make an impact thereafter.

INDRAJITSINHJI, Kumar Shri Madhavsinhji Jadeja

Born:	June 15, 1937
Batting:	Right handed
	Wicket Keeper

Tests

Test Career:	1964-69		
Cap Number:	109		
Tests Played:	4		

Test Batting

Innings:	7	Runs:	51
Highest Score:	23	Average:	8.50
No. 50s:	0	No. 100s:	0

Test Bowling & Fielding

Wickets:	0	Runs:	0
Best Bowling:		Average:	0.00
5 WI:	0	10 WM:	0
Catches:	6	Stumpings:	3

A.K.A Prince Indrajitsinhji and cousin of Suryaveer Singh and Hanumant Singh. Highly regarded wicketkeeper who played second fiddle to the likes of Engineer and Kunderan therefore being utilised as a 'stop gap measure' as indicated by his four Test appearances in five years.

IRANI, Jamshed Khudadad

Born:	August 18, 1923
Batting:	Right handed
	Wicket Keeper

Tests

Test Career:	1947		
Cap Number:	37		
Tests Played:	2		

Test Batting

Innings:	3	Runs:	3
Highest Score:	2*	Average:	3.00
No. 50s:	0	No. 100s:	0

Test Bowling & Fielding

Wickets:	0	Runs:	0
Best Bowling:		Average:	0.00
5 WI:	0	10 WM:	0
Catches:	2	Stumpings:	1

A wicketkeeper who played his two Tests in Australia during the 1947/48 series. He Later became an umpire.

JADEJA, Ajaysingh

Born:	February 1, 1971
Batting:	Right handed
Bowling:	Right arm medium

Tests

Test Career:	1992-00		
Cap Number:	196		
Tests Played:	15		

Test Batting

Innings:	24	Runs:	576
Highest Score:	96	Average:	26.18
No. 50s:	4	No. 100s:	0

Test Bowling & Fielding

Wickets:	0	Runs:	0
Best Bowling:		Average:	0.00
5 WI:	0	10 WM:	0
Catches:	5	Stumpings:	0

One Day Internationals

ODI Career:	1992-00
ODIs Played:	196

ODI Batting

Innings:	179	Runs:	5,359
Highest Score:	119	Average:	37.47
No. 50s:	30	No. 100s:	6

ODI Bowling & Fielding

Wickets:	20	Runs:	1,094
Best Bowling:	3/3	Average:	54.70
5 WM:	0	Catches:	59
Stumpings:	0		

A big hitting athlete from Gujarat, Ajay Jadeja was tailor made for the One Day game. In all he represented India on 196 occasions in limited overs competition and scored over 5,000 runs with a healthy average of 37.47. Because of his Bollywood good looks, he was a favourite amongst the female contingent and his potential both on and off the field was unlimited. Unfortunately, it all went pear-shaped in December 2000 when he was given a five-year ban following an inconclusive finding on a match-fixing enquiry.

JAFFER, Wasim

Born:	February 16, 1978
Batting:	Right handed

Tests

Test Career:	2000-06		
Cap Number:	225		
Tests Played:	14		

Test Batting

Innings:	26	Runs:	883
Highest Score:	212	Average:	33.96
No. 50s:	6	No. 100s:	2

Test Bowling & Fielding

Wickets:	2	Runs:	18
Best Bowling:	2/18	Average:	9.00
5 WI:	0	10 WM:	0
Catches:	15	Stumpings:	0

Big things were expected from this stylish opening batsman from Mumbai. However his debut against the South Africans in 2000 did not go according to plan and the talented youngster was discarded shortly afterwards. He was recalled to the Test team in early 2006 to take on the English at home. In the First Test at Nagpur, he vindicated the selectors' faith in him by scoring 81 in the first innings and 100 exactly, his maiden Test century, in the second. Averaging 41.66 for the series was enough to book him a ticket to the Caribbean where he continued to impress scoring a career best 212 in the First Test at St.Johns, Antigua. Currently one of the form batsmen of Indian cricket.

JAI, Laxmidas Purshottamdas
Born: April 1, 1902
Batting: Right handed

Tests
Test Career: 1933
Cap Number: 13
Tests Played: 1

Test Batting
Innings:	2	Runs:	19
Highest Score:	19	Average:	9.50
No. 50s:	0	No. 100s:	0

Test Bowling & Fielding
Wickets:	0	Runs:	0
Best Bowling:		Average:	0.00
5 WI:	0	10 WM:	0
Catches:	0	Stumpings:	0

Jai was originally selected on the inaugural tour of England in 1932 but declined because of political reasons. He played the one Test - against England at Mumbai a year later. A highly regarded batsman at domestic level, he later became a national selector.

JAISIMHA, Motganhalli Laxmanarsu
Born: March 3, 1939
Batting: Right handed
Bowling: Right arm off-break

Tests
Test Career: 1959-71
Cap Number: 91
Tests Played: 339

Test Batting
Innings:	71	Runs:	2,056
Highest Score:	129	Average:	30.68
No. 50s:	12	No. 100s:	3

Test Bowling & Fielding
Wickets:	9	Runs:	829
Best Bowling:	2/54	Average:	92.11
5 WI:	0	10 WM:	0
Catches:	17	Stumpings:	0

Classical in every sense of the word, right hand opener Jaisimha, was a pleasure to watch during his 39 Tests. Caressed strokes through all parts of the ground was common place just about every time he took guard. A superb fielder, he made three Test centuries, with a highest score of 129 against England, in 1964. With a Test average of 30.68, Jaisimha did not reach the dizzy heights of a Tendulkar or a Gavaskar, but for sheer entertainment value, Jaisimha had very few peers. After retiring, he later became manager of the national team.

JAMSHEDJI, Rustomji D
Born: November 18, 1892
Batting: Right handed
Bowling: Left arm off-break

Tests
Test Career: 1933-34
Cap Number: 14
Tests Played: 1

Test Batting
Innings:	2	Runs:	5
Highest Score:	4*	Average:	5.00
No. 50s:	0	No. 100s:	0

Test Bowling & Fielding
Wickets:	3	Runs:	137
Best Bowling:	3/137	Average:	45.60
5 WI:	0	10 WM:	0
Catches:	2	Stumpings:	0

Still holds the 'honourable' record as the oldest Indian debutant. Jamshedji was 41 years, 27 days when he played his first and only Test for India, against England at Mumbai in 1933. He took an impressive 3/137 with his left arm 'offies'.

JAOOMAL, Naoomal
Born: April 17, 1904
Batting: Right handed
Bowling: Right arm leg-break

Tests
Test Career: 1932-34
Cap Number: 5
Tests Played: 3

Test Batting
Innings:	5	Runs:	108
Highest Score:	43	Average:	27.00
No. 50s:	0	No. 100s:	0

Test Bowling & Fielding
Wickets:	2	Runs:	68
Best Bowling:	1/4	Average:	34.00
5 WI:	0	10 WM:	0
Catches:	0	Stumpings:	0

A dour and meticulous batsman, Naoomal opened the batting for India in their inaugural Test match at Lord's in 1932. He performed well on debut scoring 33 and 25 but played just the three Tests. He became Pakistan's national coach in the 1950's and later an umpire.

JAYANTILAL, Hirji Kenia
Born: January 13, 1948
Batting: Right handed
Bowling: Right arm off-break

Tests
Test Career: 1971
Cap Number: 126
Tests Played: 1

Test Batting
Innings:	1	Runs:	5
Highest Score:	5	Average:	5.00
No. 50s:	0	No. 100s:	0

Test Bowling & Fielding
Wickets:	0	Runs:	0
Best Bowling:		Average:	0.00
5 WI:	0	10 WM:	0
Catches:	0	Stumpings:	0

Originally from Hyderabad, opener Jayantilal played his one and only Test in 1971 against the West Indies at Kingston. He was overlooked thereafter mainly due to the emergence of one Sunil Gavaskar.

JILANI, Mohammed Baqa
Born: July 20, 1911
Batting: Right handed
Bowling: Right arm medium-fast

Tests
Test Career: 1936
Cap Number: 26
Tests Played: 1

Test Batting
Innings:	2	Runs:	16
Highest Score:	12	Average:	16.00
No. 50s:	0	No. 100s:	0

Test Bowling & Fielding
Wickets:	0	Runs:	55
Best Bowling:		Average:	0.00
5 WI:	0	10 WM:	0
Catches:	0	Stumpings:	0

A medium-fast bowler from Jalandhar, Jilani played just the one Test against England at The Oval, in 1936. He died at the tender age of 29.

JOHNSON, David Jude
Born: October 16, 1971
Batting: Right handed
Bowling: Right arm medium

Tests
Test Career: 1996
Cap Number: 208
Tests Played: 2

Test Batting
Innings:	3	Runs:	8
Highest Score:	5	Average:	4.00
No. 50s:	0	No. 100s:	0

Test Bowling & Fielding
Wickets:	3	Runs:	143
Best Bowling:	2/52	Average:	47.66
5 WI:	0	10 WM:	0
Catches:	0	Stumpings:	0

A medium pacer from Karnataka, Johnson made his Test debut against Australia at Delhi, in 1996 when he was called to replace the injured Srinath. Earned a spot a few months later on the upcoming South African tour where he played his second and final Test.

JOSHI, Padmanabh Govind
Born: October 27, 1926
Batting: Right handed
Wicket Keeper

Tests
Test Career: 1951-60
Cap Number: 53
Tests Played: 12

Test Batting
Innings:	20	Runs:	207
Highest Score:	52*	Average:	10.89
No. 50s:	1	No. 100s:	0

Test Bowling & Fielding
Wickets:	0	Runs:	0
Best Bowling:		Average:	0.00
5 WI:	0	10 WM:	0
Catches:	0	Stumpings:	0

A wicket-keeper who struggled to string together consistent performances during his 12 match career. He scored his only 50 in his last Test against Pakistan, at Mumbai, in 1960.

JOSHI, Sunil Bandacharya
Born: June 6, 1970
Batting: Left handed
Bowling: Left arm off-break

Tests
Test Career: 1996-00
Cap Number: 202
Tests Played: 15

Test Batting
Innings:	19	Runs:	352
Highest Score:	92	Average:	20.70
No. 50s:	1	No. 100s:	0

Test Bowling & Fielding
Wickets:	41	Runs:	1,470
Best Bowling:	5/142	Average:	35.85
5 WI:	1	10 WM:	0
Catches:	7	Stumpings:	0

One Day Internationals
ODI Career: 1996-01
ODIs Played: 69

ODI Batting
Innings:	45	Runs:	584
Highest Score:	61*	Average:	17.17
No. 50s:	1	No. 100s:	0

ODI Bowling & Fielding
Wickets:	69	Runs:	2,509
Best Bowling:	5/6	Average:	36.36
5 WM:	1	Catches:	19
Stumpings:	0		

A left arm orthodox spinner from Karnataka, Joshi was likened to Bishen Bedi in his early days. He played his first Test match against England, at Lord's in 1996 and was handy with a highest Test score of 92 at Test level and 61 in ODI's. It was with the ball in limited overs cricket where he enjoyed his finest moment when he snared an extraordinary 5/6 in his ten over allotment against South Africa. His memorable spell included six maidens.

KAIF, Mohammad
Born: December 1, 1980
Batting: Right handed
Bowling: Right arm off-break

Tests
Test Career: 2000-06
Cap Number: 228
Tests Played: 13

Test Batting
Innings:	22	Runs:	624
Highest Score:	148*	Average:	32.84
No. 50s:	3	No. 100s:	1

Test Bowling & Fielding

Wickets:	0	Runs:	4
Best Bowling:	0/4	Average:	0.00
5 WI:	0	10 WM:	0
Catches:	14	Stumpings:	0

One Day Internationals

ODI Career:	2002-06
ODIs Played:	18

ODI Batting

Innings:	104	Runs:	2,673
Highest Score:	111*	Average:	33.00
No. 50s:	17	No. 100s:	2

ODI Bowling & Fielding

Wickets:	0	Runs:	0
Best Bowling:		Average:	0.00
5 WM:	0	Catches:	54
Stumpings:	0		

A well accomplished player in one day competition, where he has scored two tons and 17 fifties, Mohammad Kaif has struggled to cement a place in the Test eleven over his six years at the elite level. He scored his maiden Test century, 148 not out against the West Indies in 2006.

KALE, Abhijit Vasant

Born:	July 3, 1973
Batting:	Right handed
Bowling:	Right arm off-break

One Day Internationals

ODI Career:	2003
ODIs Played:	1

ODI Batting

Innings:	1	Runs:	10
Highest Score:	10	Average:	10.00
No. 50s:	0	No. 100s:	0

ODI Bowling & Fielding

Wickets:	0	Runs:	0
Best Bowling:		Average:	0.00
5 WM:	0	Catches:	0
Stumpings:	0		

A right hander from Ahmednagar, Maharashtra, Kale made his ODI debut as a 30 year old when he was selected to play against Bangladesh at Dhaka in 2003. It was the only ODI he was to play as, shortly afterwards, he was embroiled in controversy where it was suggested that he had offered bribes to Indian selectors. As a result, he was banned until 31 December 2004.

KAMBLI, Vinod Ganpat

Born:	January 18, 1972
Batting:	Left handed
Bowling:	Right arm off-break

Tests

Test Career:	1993-95
Cap Number:	198
Tests Played:	17

Test Batting

Innings:	21	Runs:	1,084
Highest Score:	227	Average:	54.20
No. 50s:	3	No. 100s:	4

Test Bowling & Fielding

Wickets:	0	Runs:	0
Best Bowling:		Average:	0.00
5 WI:	0	10 WM:	0
Catches:	7	Stumpings:	0

One Day Internationals

ODI Career:	1991-00
ODIs Played:	104

ODI Batting

Innings:	97	Runs:	2,477
Highest Score:	106	Average:	32.59
No. 50s:	14	No. 100s:	2

ODI Bowling & Fielding

Wickets:	1	Runs:	7
Best Bowling:	1/7	Average:	7.00
5 WM:	0	Catches:	15
Stumpings:	0		

To say Vinod Kambli enjoyed a dream start to Test cricket would be a huge understatement. The stylish left hander scored two double centuries and two centuries in his first seven Tests. His 224 against England, at Mumbai in 1992/93 was shortly followed by a personal best of 227 against Zimbabwe at Delhi. Because of the precedent he had set, his two centuries, 120 & 125, against Sri Lanka were considered almost innocuous. With the sky seemingly the limit, Kambli played only a further 14 Tests without registering another century. By 1995, two years after his meteoric rise, Kambli's Test career was over. He then struggled to hold a permanent spot in the one day team.

KANITKAR, Hemant Shamsunder

Born:	December 8, 1942
Batting:	Right handed
	Wicket Keeper

Tests

Test Career:	1974
Cap Number:	133
Tests Played:	2

Test Batting

Innings:	4	Runs:	111
Highest Score:	65	Average:	27.75
No. 50s:	1	No. 100s:	0

Test Bowling & Fielding

Wickets:	0	Runs:	0
Best Bowling:		Average:	0.00
5 WI:	0	10 WM:	0
Catches:	0	Stumpings:	0

A right-handed batsmen who could also keep wickets, Kantikar made his Test debut against the West Indies at Bangalore in 1974 where he scored a dashing 65, batting at number three. His son Hrishikesh also played two Tests for India.

KANITKAR, Hrishikesh Hemant

Born:	November 14, 1974
Batting:	Left handed
Bowling:	Right arm off-break

Tests

Test Career:	1999-00
Cap Number:	224
Tests Played:	2

KANITKAR, Hrishikesh Hemant

Test Batting			
Innings:	4	Runs:	74
Highest Score:	45	Average:	18.50
No. 50s:	0	No. 100s:	0

Test Bowling & Fielding			
Wickets:	0	Runs:	2
Best Bowling:	0/2	Average:	0.00
5 WI:	0	10 WM:	0
Catches:	0	Stumpings:	0

One Day Internationals

ODI Career:	1997-00
ODIs Played:	34

ODI Batting			
Innings:	24	Runs:	339
Highest Score:	57	Average:	17.84
No. 50s:	1	No. 100s:	0

ODI Bowling & Fielding			
Wickets:	17	Runs:	803
Best Bowling:	2/22	Average:	47.23
5 WM:	0	Catches:	14
Stumpings:	0		

The son of Hemant Kanitkar, who played in two Tests against West Indies in 1974/75, Kantikar jnr was an all rounder who many believe, did not live up to expectations. A dour left-hand batsman, capable off-spinner and quite adept in the field, Kanitkar, like his father, managed just the two Tests. He made his debut against Australia, at the MCG in 1999.

KAPOOR, Aashish Rakesh

Born:	March 25, 1971
Batting:	Right handed
Bowling:	Right arm off-break

Tests

Test Career:	1994-96
Cap Number:	201
Tests Played:	4

Test Batting			
Innings:	6	Runs:	97
Highest Score:	42	Average:	19.39
No. 50s:	0	No. 100s:	0

Test Bowling & Fielding			
Wickets:	6	Runs:	255
Best Bowling:	2/19	Average:	42.50
5 WI:	0	10 WM:	0
Catches:	1	Stumpings:	0

One Day Internationals

ODI Career:	1994-00
ODIs Played:	17

ODI Batting			
Innings:	6	Runs:	43
Highest Score:	19	Average:	7.16
No. 50s:	0	No. 100s:	0

ODI Bowling & Fielding			
Wickets:	8	Runs:	612
Best Bowling:	2/33	Average:	76.50
5 WM:	0	Catches:	1
Stumpings:	0		

A right arm off-spinner who could bat as well, Kapoor was a member of the 1996 World Cup squad. But upon his return home he struggled to hold a regular place in the ODI side. He played six Tests in total after making his debut against the West Indies, at Chandigarh in 1994.

KARDAR, Abdul Hafeez

Born:	January 17, 1925
Batting:	Left handed
Bowling:	Left arm off-break

Tests

Test Career:	1946-58
Cap Number:	29
Tests Played:	26

Test Batting			
Innings:	42	Runs:	927
Highest Score:	93	Average:	23.76
No. 50s:	5	No. 100s:	0

Test Bowling & Fielding			
Wickets:	0	Runs:	0
Best Bowling:		Average:	0.00
5 WI:	0	10 WM:	0
Catches:	10	Stumpings:	0

Abdul Kardar played his first of three Tests for India, at Lords in 1946 but finished his career donning the green cap of Pakistan in 1958. Kardar played in Pakistan's inaugural Test against India, at Delhi in 1952, and was Pakistan's first captain. He went on to play in 23 Tests for Pakistan and his highest score of 93 was ironically made against India at Karachi, in 1955. A pioneer of Pakistan cricket, Kardar, (who in earlier days played under the name Hafeez) became chairman of selectors, and President of Pakistan's Board of Control from 1972 to 1977. Originally from Lahore, he was an outspoken advocate about introducing neutral umpires in Test cricket. (In the early part of his career he played under the name Abdul Hafeez)

KARIM, Syed Saba

Born:	November 14, 1967
Batting:	Right handed
	Wicket Keeper

Tests

Test Career:	2000
Cap Number:	230
Tests Played:	1

Test Batting			
Innings:	1	Runs:	15
Highest Score:	15	Average:	15.00
No. 50s:	0	No. 100s:	0

Test Bowling & Fielding			
Wickets:	0	Runs:	0
Best Bowling:		Average:	0.00
5 WI:	0	10 WM:	0
Catches:	1	Stumpings:	0

One Day Internationals

ODI Career:	1997-00
ODIs Played:	34

ODI Batting			
Innings:	24	Runs:	362
Highest Score:	55	Average:	15.73
No. 50s:	1	No. 100s:	0

ODI Bowling & Fielding			
Wickets:	0	Runs:	0
Best Bowling:		Average:	0.00
5 WM:	0	Catches:	27
Stumpings:	3		

Syed Saba Karim looked like making his international debut almost six years before he actually did when he was chosen as reserve wicket-keeper for the West Indies tour of 1989. But the aspiring wicketkeeper could only watch from the stands as the long awaited nod from the selectors never eventuated. It was not until 1996 that he was again considered for potential International duties when he was selected for the tour of South Africa. This time he was given a chance and scored an impressive 55 in his first ODI at Bloemfontein. He became a regular with the One Day squad and then eventually was given a chance at Test level in 2000 against Bangladesh at Dhaka. A serious eye injury, which required surgery, plus the competition around the number one keeper job in India, put pay to any further Test opportunities.

KARTHIK, Krishnakumar Dinesh

Born: June 1, 1985
Batting: Right handed
Wicket Keeper

Tests
Test Career: 2004-05
Cap Number: 250
Tests Played: 10

Test Batting
Innings:	13	Runs:	245
Highest Score:	93	Average:	18.84
No. 50s:	1	No. 100s:	0

Test Bowling & Fielding
Wickets:	0	Runs:	0
Best Bowling:		Average:	0.00
5 WI:	0	10 WM:	0
Catches:	29	Stumpings:	4

One Day Internationals
ODI Career: 2004-06
ODIs Played: 3

ODI Batting
Innings:	1	Runs:	1
Highest Score:	1	Average:	1.00
No. 50s:	0	No. 100s:	0

ODI Bowling & Fielding
Wickets:	0	Runs:	0
Best Bowling:		Average:	0.00
5 WM:	0	Catches:	6
Stumpings:	1		

A polished wicket-keeper and competent right hand batsman, Dinesh Karthik has played the role as reserve wicket-keeper for the best part of his career after making his Test debut against Australia, at Mumbai in 2004, but is now slowly establishing himself as a premier gloveman.

KARTIK, Murali

Born: September 11, 1976
Batting: Left handed
Bowling: Left arm off-break

Tests
Test Career: 2000-04
Cap Number: 226
Tests Played: 8

Test Batting
Innings:	10	Runs:	88
Highest Score:	43	Average:	9.77
No. 50s:	0	No. 100s:	0

Test Bowling & Fielding
Wickets:	24	Runs:	820
Best Bowling:	4/44	Average:	34.16
5 WI:	0	10 WM:	0
Catches:	2	Stumpings:	0

One Day Internationals
ODI Career: 2002-06
ODIs Played: 30

ODI Batting
Innings:	11	Runs:	89
Highest Score:	32*	Average:	12.71
No. 50s:	0	No. 100s:	0

ODI Bowling & Fielding
Wickets:	27	Runs:	1,312
Best Bowling:	3/36	Average:	48.59
5 WM:	0	Catches:	10
Stumpings:	0		

Apart from a career best 4/44 against Australia in 2005, left arm off-spinner Murali Kartik has found the going tough as he tries to establish himself in a side containing the likes of Anil Kumble and Harbhajan Singh. He has not played a Test since 2004 but has been a regular member of the One Day side.

KENNY, Ramnath Baburao

Born: September 29, 1930
Batting: Right handed
Bowling: Right arm off-break

Tests
Test Career: 1959-60
Cap Number: 87
Tests Played: 5

Test Batting
Innings:	10	Runs:	245
Highest Score:	62	Average:	27.22
No. 50s:	3	No. 100s:	0

Test Bowling & Fielding
Wickets:	0	Runs:	0
Best Bowling:		Average:	0.00
5 WI:	0	10 WM:	0
Catches:	1	Stumpings:	0

Originally from Mumbai, Kenny played five Tests - debuting against West Indies at Kolkata in 1959 and then four Tests against Australia during the 1959/60 series. He scored three 50's and made his highest score of 62 in his last innings where it all started for him - at Kolkata.

KHAN, Dr Mohammad Jahangir

Born: February 1, 1910
Batting: Right handed
Bowling: Right arm medium-fast

Tests
Test Career: 1932-36
Cap Number: 3
Tests Played: 4

Test Batting
Innings:	7	Runs:	39
Highest Score:	13	Average:	5.57
No. 50s:	0	No. 100s:	0

Test Bowling & Fielding

Wickets:	4	Runs:	225
Best Bowling:	4/60	Average:	63.75
5 WI:	0	10 WM:	0
Catches:	4	Stumpings:	0

A member of India's inaugural 1932 Test team, Khan's contribution to cricket extends way beyond his four Test caps. A doctor by profession, Khan later became a highly noted administrator and key figure in the development of cricket in Pakistan. The Khan dynasty continued long after the good doctor's playing career was over as his son, Majid, and nephews, the high profile Imran Khan, and Javed Burki all went on to captain Pakistan. Khan is also fondly remembered as the 'bowler' in the Lord's 'sparrow story'. While it is noted that no one actually witnessed the incident, it is alleged that while playing for Cambridge against the MCC at Lord's, Khan bowled the ball that struck a bird, which in turn dislodged the bails. After the shoulder shrugging and pondering subsided the bird was subsequently stuffed and displayed in the Memorial Gallery at Lord's.

KHAN, Zaheer

Born:	October 7, 1978
Batting:	Right handed
Bowling:	Left arm medium-fast

Tests

Test Career:	2000-06		
Cap Number:	231		
Tests Played:	42		

Test Batting

Innings:	54	Runs:	507
Highest Score:	75	Average:	12.67
No. 50s:	1	No. 100s:	0

Test Bowling & Fielding

Wickets:	121	Runs:	4,398
Best Bowling:	5/29	Average:	36.34
5 WI:	3	10 WM:	0
Catches:	10	Stumpings:	0

One Day Internationals

ODI Career:	2000-06		
ODIs Played:	107		

ODI Batting

Innings:	58	Runs:	453
Highest Score:	34*	Average:	13.32
No. 50s:	0	No. 100s:	0

ODI Bowling & Fielding

Wickets:	155	Runs:	4,335
Best Bowling:	4/19	Average:	27.96
5 WM:	0	Catches:	25
Stumpings:	0		

A sharp, left arm pace bowler Zaheer Khan made his debut against Bangladesh in their inaugural Test at Dhaka in 2000. He took the early wicket of opener Mehrab Hossain thus giving him the 'honour' of dismissing the first Bangladeshi batsman at Test level.

KHANNA, Surinder Chamanlal

Born:	June 3, 1956
Batting:	Right handed
	Wicket Keeper

One Day Internationals

ODI Career:	1979-84		
ODIs Played:	10		

ODI Batting

Innings:	10	Runs:	176
Highest Score:	56	Average:	22.00
No. 50s:	2	No. 100s:	0

ODI Bowling & Fielding

Wickets:	0	Runs:	0
Best Bowling:		Average:	0.00
5 WM:	0	Catches:	4
Stumpings:	4		

Khanna was selected for the tour of England in 1979 to replace the ageing Syed Kirmani. He played in all three World Cup games against West Indies, New Zealand and Sri Lanka but could not break into the Test side as Bharath Reddy became the preferred option.

KHODA, Gagan Kishanlal

Born:	October 12, 1974
Batting:	Right handed

One Day Internationals

ODI Career:	1998		
ODIs Played:	2		

ODI Batting

Innings:	2	Runs:	115
Highest Score:	89	Average:	57.50
No. 50s:	1	No. 100s:	0

ODI Bowling & Fielding

Wickets:	0	Runs:	0
Best Bowling:		Average:	0.00
5 WM:	0	Catches:	0
Stumpings:	0		

An opening batsman from Rajasthan who many thought would eventually play Test cricket. Khoda scored an impressive 89 against Kenya in his second and last ODI.

KHURASIYA, Amay Ramsevak

Born:	May 18, 1972
Batting:	Left handed
Bowling:	Left arm off-break

One Day Internationals

ODI Career:	1999-01		
ODIs Played:	12		

ODI Batting

Innings:	11	Runs:	149
Highest Score:	57	Average:	13.54
No. 50s:	1	No. 100s:	0

ODI Bowling & Fielding

Wickets:	0	Runs:	0
Best Bowling:		Average:	0.00
5 WM:	0	Catches:	3
Stumpings:	0		

A dashing left hand opener from Madhya Pradesh, Amay Khurasiya scored a memorable 50 in his first one day outing against Sri Lanka at Pune in 1999. He was serviceable in the dozen times he represented India at ODI level and was also a member of their 1999 World Cup squad.

KIRMANI, Syed Mujtaba Hussein

Born: December 29, 1949
Batting: Right handed
Bowling: Right arm off-break
Wicket Keeper

Tests
Test Career: 1976-86
Cap Number: 138
Tests Played: 88

Test Batting
Innings:	124	Runs:	2,759
Highest Score:	102	Average:	27.04
No. 50s:	12	No. 100s:	12

Test Bowling & Fielding
Wickets:	1	Runs:	13
Best Bowling:	1/9	Average:	13.00
5 WI:	0	10 WM:	0
Catches:	160	Stumpings:	38

One Day Internationals
ODI Career: 1976-86
ODIs Played: 49

ODI Batting
Innings:	31	Runs:	373
Highest Score:	48*	Average:	20.72
No. 50s:	0	No. 100s:	0

ODI Bowling & Fielding
Wickets:	0	Runs:	0
Best Bowling:		Average:	0.00
5 WM:	0	Catches:	27
Stumpings:	9		

A master keeper of spin having kept wicket to the likes of Bedi, Prasanna and Chandrasekhar while at their prime, Kirmani took over the reins from his respected mentor, Farokh Engineer in 1976. He whipped off the bails on 38 occasions and made 160 catches during his ten year Test career. With a respectable batting average of 27, Kirmani hit two centuries, both at Mumbai. The first, 101 not out, against Australia in 79/80 and his highest score of 102 against England in 84/85. Kirmani was a vital member of India's victorious 1983 World Cup side. He is still regarded by many, even outside India, as the finest keeper of spin bowling the game has seen.

KISHENCHAND (HARISINGHANI), Gogumal

Born: April 14, 1925
Batting: Right handed
Bowling: Right arm leg-break

Tests
Test Career: 1947-52
Cap Number: 38
Tests Played: 5

Test Batting
Innings:	10	Runs:	89
Highest Score:	44	Average:	8.90
No. 50s:	0	No. 100s:	0

Test Bowling & Fielding
Wickets:	0	Runs:	0
Best Bowling:		Average:	0.00
5 WI:	0	10 WM:	0
Catches:	1	Stumpings:	0

A short defensive batsman from Karachi whose single-figured average would yield him only five Test appearances.

KRISHNAMURTHY, Pochiah

Born: July 12, 1947
Batting: Right handed
Bowling: Right arm leg-break

Tests
Test Career: 1971
Cap Number: 127
Tests Played: 5

Test Batting
Innings:	6	Runs:	33
Highest Score:	20	Average:	5.50
No. 50s:	0	No. 100s:	0

Test Bowling & Fielding
Wickets:	0	Runs:	0
Best Bowling:		Average:	0.00
5 WI:	0	10 WM:	0
Catches:	7	Stumpings:	1

One Day Internationals
ODI Career: 1976
ODIs Played: 1

ODI Batting
Innings:	1	Runs:	6
Highest Score:	6	Average:	6.00
No. 50s:	0	No. 100s:	0

ODI Bowling & Fielding
Wickets:	0	Runs:	0
Best Bowling:		Average:	0.00
5 WM:	0	Catches:	1
Stumpings:	1		

A lanky wicket-keeper who enjoyed standing up to the quicks. Struggled to hold his Test place as Farokh Engineer was also on the scene. Also known as Pallemoni Krishnamurthy.

KULKARNI, Nilesh Moreshwar

Born: April 3, 1973
Batting: Left handed
Bowling: Left arm off-break

Tests
Test Career: 1997-01
Cap Number: 212
Tests Played: 3

Test Batting
Innings:	2	Runs:	5
Highest Score:	4	Average:	5.00
No. 50s:	0	No. 100s:	0

Test Bowling & Fielding
Wickets:	2	Runs:	332
Best Bowling:	1/70	Average:	166.00
5 WI:	0	10 WM:	0
Catches:	1	Stumpings:	0

One Day Internationals
ODI Career: 1997-98
ODIs Played: 10

ODI Batting

Innings:	5	Runs:	11
Highest Score:	5*	Average:	5.50
No. 100s:	0	No. 100s:	0

ODI Bowling & Fielding

Wickets:	11	Runs:	357
Best Bowling:	3/27	Average:	32.54
5 WM:	0	Catches:	2
Stumpings:	0		

One of only 12 bowlers in Test history, and the only Indian, to have taken a wicket with his first ball against Sri Lanka at Colombo in 1997. Played just the one more Test and a handful of ODI's.

KULKARNI, Rajiv Ramesh

Born:	September 25, 1962
Batting:	Right handed
Bowling:	Right arm medium-fast

Tests

Test Career:	1986-87
Cap Number:	175
Tests Played:	3

Test Batting

Innings:	2	Runs:	2
Highest Score:	2	Average:	1.00
No. 50s:	0	No. 100s:	0

Test Bowling & Fielding

Wickets:	5	Runs:	227
Best Bowling:	3/85	Average:	45.39
5 WI:	0	10 WM:	0
Catches:	1	Stumpings:	0

One Day Internationals

ODI Career:	1983-87
ODIs Played:	10

ODI Batting

Innings:	5	Runs:	33
Highest Score:	15	Average:	16.50
No. 50s:	0	No. 100s:	0

ODI Bowling & Fielding

Wickets:	10	Runs:	345
Best Bowling:	3/42	Average:	34.50
5 WM:	0	Catches:	2
Stumpings:	0		

A pace bowler from Mumbai, Kulkarni took 3/85 on his Test debut against Australia, in his hometown, in 1986. He played three Tests in a just over 12 months and was a fringe player in the ODI side for around five years.

KULKARNI, Umesh Narayan

Born:	March 7, 1942
Batting:	Left handed
Bowling:	Left arm medium-fast

Tests

Test Career:	1967-68
Cap Number:	117
Tests Played:	4

Test Batting

Innings:	8	Runs:	13
Highest Score:	7	Average:	4.33
No. 50s:	0	No. 100s:	0

Test Bowling & Fielding

Wickets:	5	Runs:	238
Best Bowling:	2/37	Average:	47.60
5 WI:	0	10 WM:	0
Catches:	0	Stumpings:	0

A left arm medium pacer from Alibagh. Kulkarni played all four Tests abroad - three against Australia and his last against New Zealand in Christchurch, in 1968.

KUMAR, Vaman Viswanath

Born:	June 22, 1935
Batting:	Right handed
Bowling:	Right arm leg-break

Tests

Test Career:	1961
Cap Number:	101
Tests Played:	2

Test Batting

Innings:	2	Runs:	6
Highest Score:	6	Average:	3.00
No. 50s:	0	No. 100s:	0

Test Bowling & Fielding

Wickets:	7	Runs:	202
Best Bowling:	5/64	Average:	28.85
5 WI:	1	10 WM:	0
Catches:	2	Stumpings:	0

A highly skilled leg spinner from Chennai. Kumar made his debut against Pakistan at Delhi in 1961 and although did exceptionally well taking 5/64, he could only manage one more Test which surprised many at the time.

KUMARAN, Thirunavukkarasu (Kenny)

Born:	December 30, 1975
Batting:	Right handed
Bowling:	Right arm medium

One Day Internationals

ODI Career:	1999-00
ODIs Played:	8

ODI Batting

Innings:	3	Runs:	19
Highest Score:	8	Average:	6.33
No. 50s:	0	No. 100s:	0

ODI Bowling & Fielding

Wickets:	9	Runs:	348
Best Bowling:	3/24	Average:	38.66
5 WM:	0	Catches:	3
Stumpings:	0		

A medium pacer from Chennai whose best figures of 3/24 at ODI level suggests that he could have been a tad unlucky not be selected on a few more occasions. He made his ODI debut against New Zealand, at Guwahati in 1999.

KUMBLE, Anil

Born:	October 17, 1970
Batting:	Right handed
Bowling:	Right arm leg-break

Tests

Test Career:	1990-06
Cap Number:	192
Tests Played:	110

Test Batting
Innings:	140	Runs:	2,025
Highest Score:	88	Average:	17.92
No. 50s:	4	No. 100s:	0

Test Bowling & Fielding
Wickets:	533	Runs:	15,329
Best Bowling:	10/74	Average:	28.75
5 WI:	33	10 WM:	8
Catches:	50	Stumpings:	0

One Day Internationals
ODI Career:	1990-05		
ODIs Played:	264		

ODI Batting
Innings:	131	Runs:	930
Highest Score:	26	Average:	10.94
No. 50s:	0	No. 100s:	0

ODI Bowling & Fielding
Wickets:	329	Runs:	10
Best Bowling:	6/12	Average:	30.76
5 WM:	2	Catches:	84
Stumpings:	0		

Second Test, India v Pakistan, Delhi, 1999, and VVS Laxman, while fielding at bat pad, holds onto a sharp chance off Pakistan captain Wasim Akram. The catch has not only secured a 212 run victory for India but holds even greater significance for leg spinner Anil Kumble as he becomes only the second bowler in Test history to claim all ten wickets in an innings. Not since 1956 had any bowler managed to emulate Jim Laker's demolition of Australia at Old Trafford. Chasing 420 for victory, openers Shahid Afridi and Saeed Anwar got Pakistan off to a flyer, scoring 101 off 140 balls. Enter Anil Kumble. It is noticed very early on that Kumble has forgone his familiar quick, sharp action for a slower style and there is a lot more loop in his deliveries. Within minutes after the lunch interval, Kumble has Afridi caught behind by wicket keeper Mongia, and then traps Ijaz Ahmed lbw the very next ball. Surviving the hat-trick delivery, Inzamam-ul-Haq adds 14 with opener Anwar before a Kumble googly easily passes through Inzamam's laconic defensive prod. Two balls later, and Yousuf Youhana is adjudged plumb in front - 4/115. When Saqlain Mushtaq becomes Kumble's ninth victim, and with the score at 198, victory is all but assured. However, the parochial Indian crowd are high on anticipation. They only have to wait for a further nine runs to be scored before the figures of 26.3 overs, 9 maidens, 10 for 74, are etched in the history books alongside the name of one of their favourite sons, 'Anil Kumble'. In an interview shortly after his amazing feat, Kumble humbly recalls the moment; "I just went totally blank. My first thought was that we had won the Test match. And the next thought was oh, I have taken all the ten wickets". A tireless contributor, Kumble has been a consistent performer for over 15 years since making his debut against England, ironically at the same ground Jim Laker took his famous haul - Old Trafford. He has amassed 533 Test wickets to become India's all time leading wicket taker and fourth in Tests overall, behind Shane Warne, Muttiah Muralitharan and Glenn McGrath.

KUNDERAN, Budhisagar Krishnappa (Kunderam)

Born:	October 2, 1939
Batting:	Right handed
Bowling:	Right arm medium
	Wicket Keeper

Tests
Test Career:	1960-67
Cap Number:	96
Tests Played:	18

Test Batting
Innings:	34	Runs:	981
Highest Score:	192	Average:	32.70
No. 50s:	3	No. 100s:	2

Test Bowling & Fielding
Wickets:	0	Runs:	13
Best Bowling:	0/13	Average:	0.00
5 WI:	0	10 WM:	0
Catches:	23	Stumpings:	7

A.K.A Budhisagar Krishnappa Kunderam from 1964. Describing Kunderan as an all rounder is quite an understatement. He not only kept wickets and was an accomplished batsman, he opened the batting later in his career and also once opened the bowling for his country when playing against England in 1967. Although he shared keeping duties with Engineer during his career, his 192 at Chennai, is still the highest Test score by an Indian keeper. Like quite a few of his era and before, Kunderan was dropped at two stages during his career in what many believed to be unreasonable circumstances.

KURUVILLA, Abey

Born:	August 8, 1968
Batting:	Right handed
Bowling:	Right arm medium-fast

Tests
Test Career:	1997
Cap Number:	211
Tests Played:	10

Test Batting
Innings:	11	Runs:	66
Highest Score:	35*	Average:	6.59
No. 50s:	0	No. 100s:	0

Test Bowling & Fielding
Wickets:	25	Runs:	829
Best Bowling:	5/68	Average:	35.67
5 WI:	1	10 WM:	0
Catches:	0	Stumpings:	0

One Day Internationals
ODI Career:	1997
ODIs Played:	25

ODI Batting
Innings:	11	Runs:	26
Highest Score:	7	Average:	3.71
No. 50s:	0	No. 100s:	0

ODI Bowling & Fielding

Wickets:	25	Runs:	890
Best Bowling:	4/43	Average:	35.60
5 WM:	0	Catches:	4
Stumpings:	0		

Standing at 6'6", Kuruvilla made his Test debut against West Indies at Kingston in 1997. He captured 6/97 in the Third Test at Bridgetown with an excellent display of swing bowling.

LAMBA, Raman

Born:	January 2, 1960
Batting:	Right handed

Tests

Test Career:	1986-87		
Cap Number:	177		
Tests Played:	4		

Test Batting

Innings:	5	Runs:	102
Highest Score:	53	Average:	20.39
No. 50s:	1	No. 100s:	0

Test Bowling & Fielding

Wickets:	0	Runs:	0
Best Bowling:		Average:	0.00
5 WI:	0	10 WM:	0
Catches:	5	Stumpings:	0

One Day Internationals

ODI Career:	1986-89		
ODIs Played:	32		

ODI Batting

Innings:	31	Runs:	783
Highest Score:	102	Average:	27.00
No. 50s:	6	No. 100s:	1

ODI Bowling & Fielding

Wickets:	1	Runs:	20
Best Bowling:	1/9	Average:	20.00
5 WM:	0	Catches:	10
Stumpings:	0		

An attacking right hand batsman, Raman Lamba played four Tests after making his debut against Sri Lanka at Kanpur, in 1986. However, he made his name as a limited overs specialist when he was named 'Man of the Series' after scoring 64, 74 ad 102 during the 1986/87 One Day International series against Australia. Sadly, it would be during a club match at the Bangabandhu Stadium, Dhaka in 1998 that would provide an even bigger headline than his Man of the Series feat a decade earlier. While playing for Abahani against Mohammedans, the then 38 year old Lamba was fielding at forward short leg and was accidentally struck in the temple. He was not wearing a helmet. While it was quite evident from the outset that the blow was severe, after a few minutes, he left the ground unaided. Tragically, Raman Lamba suffered an internal haemorrhage and died three days later. The cricket public in both India and Bangladesh mourned the loss of the man who was a popular and respected figure in both countries. The unfortunate batsman at the time was Mehrab Hossain who was deeply affected by incident and decided to stay away from the game for a short while. Hossain went on to represent Bangladesh.

LAXMAN, Vangipurappu Venkata Sai (VVS)

Born:	November 1, 1974
Batting:	Right handed
Bowling:	Right arm off-break

Tests

Test Career:	1996-06		
Cap Number:	209		
Tests Played:	77		

Test Batting

Innings:	124	Runs:	4,698
Highest Score:	281	Average:	42.70
No. 50s:	25	No. 100s:	10

Test Bowling & Fielding

Wickets:	1	Runs:	100
Best Bowling:	1/32	Average:	100.00
5 WI:	0	10 WM:	0
Catches:	81	Stumpings:	0

One Day Internationals

ODI Career:	1998-05		
ODIs Played:	85		

ODI Batting

Innings:	82	Runs:	2,338
Highest Score:	131	Average:	31.17
No. 50s:	10	No. 100s:	6

ODI Bowling & Fielding

Wickets:	0	Runs:	40
Best Bowling:		Average:	0.00
5 WM:	0	Catches:	39
Stumpings:	0		

An elegant stroke-player and superb timer, Vangipurappu Venkata Sai Laxman - or more commonly known as VVS Laxman started his career as a middle order batsman. He made an impressive debut scoring 50 against South Africa in 1996 but had to wait almost four years before he registered his first Test century. The moment occurred in January 2000 when Laxman, now being tried as an opener, made a patient 167 against Australia at the SCG. However, it was his effort a few months later that made the cricketing world stand up and take notice of the rather underrated and unassuming Laxman. In the 2nd Test at Kolkata, India was forced to follow on, and the signs were ominous early in the second innings. With the score at 3/115 and with Tendulkar back in the pavilion, it seemed only a matter of time before Warne, McGrath and co would arrest control and subsequently wrap up the middle order and tail. But VVS had other ideas. Batting at first drop, rather than his usual opening position, he added 117 with skipper Ganguly. In what developed into a marathon innings, he continued the run fest with the classy Rahul Dravid, as the pair added a record breaking 376 for the fifth wicket before VVS was dismissed for 281. With a style likened to Mohammad Azharuddin, Laxman is the quintessential Test batsman and a delight to watch. He has currently ten Test 100's with an average of 42.70.

MADAN LAL, Udhouram Sharma
Born: March 20, 1951
Batting: Right handed
Bowling: Right arm medium

Tests
Test Career: 1974-86
Cap Number: 130
Tests Played: 39

Test Batting
Innings:	62	Runs:	1,042
Highest Score:	74	Average:	22.65
No. 50s:	1	No. 100s:	0

Test Bowling & Fielding
Wickets:	71	Runs:	2,846
Best Bowling:	5/23	Average:	40.08
5 WI:	4	10 WM:	0
Catches:	15	Stumpings:	0

One Day Internationals
ODI Career: 1974-87
ODIs Played: 67

ODI Batting
Innings:	35	Runs:	401
Highest Score:	53*	Average:	19.09
No. 50s:	1	No. 100s:	0

ODI Bowling & Fielding
Wickets:	73	Runs:	2,137
Best Bowling:	4/20	Average:	0.00
5 WM:	0	Catches:	18
Stumpings:	0		

An all rounder from Punjab, Madan Lal was a solid all rounder in both Tests and ODI for his country during his 13 year career. A medium pacer who batted in the middle order he was an important member in the 1983 World Cup winning side, taking the prize wickets of Desmond Haynes, Viv Richards and Larry Gomes which helped India on their way to their first ever World Cup title. With an average of 22 with the bat in Tests, Madan Lal was a regular member of the Indian eleven however was out favour towards the end of the 1970's. He was recalled after two years in the wilderness and played his last Test against England at Headingley in 1986. Upon retirement, he became national coach and eventually a selector.

MAKA, Ebrahim Suleman
Born: March 5, 1922
Batting: Right handed
       Wicket Keeper

Tests
Test Career: 1952-53
Cap Number: 67
Tests Played: 2

Test Batting
Innings:	1	Runs:	2
Highest Score:	2*	Average:	2.00
No. 50s:	0	No. 100s:	0

Test Bowling & Fielding
Wickets:	0	Runs:	0
Best Bowling:		Average:	0.00
5 WI:	0	10 WM:	0
Catches:	2	Stumpings:	1

A reserve wicketkeeper who managed two catches and one stumping on debut against Pakistan at Chennai in 1952. Toured the West Indies in 1953.

MALHOTRA, Ashok Omprakash
Born: January 26, 1957
Batting: Right handed
Bowling: Right arm medium

Tests
Test Career: 1982-85
Cap Number: 155
Tests Played: 7

Test Batting
Innings:	10	Runs:	226
Highest Score:	72*	Average:	25.11
No. 50s:	1	No. 100s:	0

Test Bowling & Fielding
Wickets:	0	Runs:	3
Best Bowling:	0/3	Average:	0.00
5 WI:	0	10 WM:	0
Catches:	2	Stumpings:	0

One Day Internationals
ODI Career: 1982-86
ODIs Played: 20

ODI Batting
Innings:	19	Runs:	457
Highest Score:	65	Average:	30.46
No. 50s:	1	No. 100s:	0

ODI Bowling & Fielding
Wickets:	0	Runs:	0
Best Bowling:	0/0	Average:	0.00
5 WM:	0	Catches:	4
Stumpings:	0		

A middle order batsman from Amritsar Punjab, Malhotra made his highest Test score of 72 not out against West Indies at Mumbai. He was a member of the Indian team that won the World Championship of Cricket in Australia in 1985.

MANJREKAR, Sanjay Vijay
Born: July 12, 1965
Batting: Right handed
Bowling: Right arm off-break

Tests
Test Career: 1987-96
Cap Number: 179
Tests Played: 37

Test Batting
Innings:	61	Runs:	2,043
Highest Score:	218	Average:	37.14
No. 50s:	9	No. 100s:	4

Test Bowling & Fielding
Wickets:	0	Runs:	15
Best Bowling:	0/15	Average:	0.00
5 WI:	0	10 WM:	0
Catches:	25	Stumpings:	1

One Day Internationals
ODI Career: 1988-96
ODIs Played: 74

ODI Batting

Innings:	70	Runs:	1,994
Highest Score:	105	Average:	33.23
No. 50s:	15	No. 100s:	1

ODI Bowling & Fielding

Wickets:	1	Runs:	10
Best Bowling:	1/2	Average:	10.00
5 WM:	0	Catches:	23
Stumpings:	0		

A part time wicket-keeper and son of the renowned Vijay Manjrekar, Sanjay Manjrekar, like many who follow in their father's footsteps, was heavily scrutinised, especially early in his career. An undoubted talent, Manjrekar hit four Test centuries including a double century against Pakistan at Lahore in 1989/90. However his form deserted him shortly afterwards and struggled for consistency for the remainder of his career.

MANJREKAR, Vijay Laxman

Born:	September 26, 1931
Batting:	Right handed
Bowling:	Right arm off-break

Tests

Test Career:	1951-62
Cap Number:	59
Tests Played:	55

Test Batting

Innings:	92	Runs:	3,208
Highest Score:	189*	Average:	39.12
No. 50s:	15	No. 100s:	7

Test Bowling & Fielding

Wickets:	1	Runs:	44
Best Bowling:	1/16	Average:	44.00
5 WI:	0	10 WM:	0
Catches:	19	Stumpings:	2

A fine player of fast bowling - a rarity for many Indian batsmen at the time - Vijay Manjrekar, compiled over 3,000 runs including seven hundreds and 15 fifties in his 12 year Test career. Small in stature and an exceptional cutter, Vijay loved to take on the bowling and would hook when the opportunity presented itself. A jack-of-all trades, Vijay moonlighted as an off spinner, wicketkeeper and specialist cover fielder. His son, Sanjay, also represented India in Tests.

MANKAD, Ashok Vinoo

Born:	October 12, 1946
Batting:	Right handed
Bowling:	Right arm medium

Tests

Test Career:	1969-78
Cap Number:	119
Tests Played:	22

Test Batting

Innings:	42	Runs:	991
Highest Score:	97	Average:	25.41
No. 50s:	6	No. 100s:	0

Test Bowling & Fielding

Wickets:	0	Runs:	43
Best Bowling:		Average:	0.00
5 WI:	0	10 WM:	0
Catches:	12	Stumpings:	0

One Day Internationals

ODI Career:	1974
ODIs Played:	1

ODI Batting

Innings:	1	Runs:	44
Highest Score:	44	Average:	44.00
No. 50s:	0	No. 100s:	0

ODI Bowling & Fielding

Wickets:	1	Runs:	47
Best Bowling:	1/47	Average:	47.00
5 WM:	0	Catches:	0
Stumpings:	0		

Son of Vinoo Mankad, Ashok unfortunately did not go on to achieve the heights of his famous father. A technically correct right hand batsman, Mankad was played up and down the batting order, including opener, for the best part of his Test career and thus never really settled in the one position. He was unlucky to miss out on what would have been his only Test century when he scored a gritty 97 against Australia in 1970. His was to encounter further heartache in 1974, when on 43, and looking comfortable against England at Edgbaston, his attempt to avoid a Chris Old bouncer saw his cap fall from his crown and crash into the stumps.

MANKAD, Mulvantrai Himmatlal (Vinoo)

Born:	April 12, 1912
Batting:	Right handed
Bowling:	Left arm off-break

Tests

Test Career:	1946-59
Cap Number:	30
Tests Played:	44

Test Batting

Innings:	72	Runs:	2,109
Highest Score:	231	Average:	31.47
No. 50s:	6	No. 100s:	5

Test Bowling & Fielding

Wickets:	162	Runs:	5,236
Best Bowling:	8/52	Average:	32.32
5 WI:	8	10 WM:	2
Catches:	33	Stumpings:	0

One of India's finest all-rounders but best remembered, these days at least, for having a type of run out named after him. It was an incident involving Australian opener Bill Brown at the SCG in 1947, that later became known as the 'Mankad run out'. After warning Brown for backing up at the non strikers end during a tour match, 'Vinoo' ran out the Australian as he came in to bowl. He repeated the dose a month later during the first test at the SCG - but this time there was no warning issued. This sparked debate as to whether the action was within the spirit of the game. Mankad's 'run out' has had an obvious, and in some many ways, a positive effect on the game as these days batsmen at the non strikers end are well aware of the consequences of backing up too far and take on being 'mankaded' at their own peril. Although quite versatile, Mankad usually opened the innings in his 44 Tests for India. His 413 run stand, with the bespectacled Pankaj Roy against New Zealand, at Chennai in 1956, remains a Test record for the first wicket. Mankad's 231 in that innings was his second double-century for the series and as well as being his highest score, it was also the highest score by any Indian batsman. It would take a supreme effort from the great Sunil Gavaskar, some 30 years later, to claim the title from Mankad. A natural talent, Mankad, a left arm orthodox off-spinner, took 162 wickets at 32 and took eight wickets in an innings on two occasions. His 8/55 against England at Chennai in 1952, was followed up with a career best 8/52 against Pakistan at Delhi, later that year. Again, Mankad monopolised the record books as his quinella of 'eights' were the best bowling figures by an Indian until Subhash Gupte's haul of 9/102 against the West Indies in 1958/59. Vinoo captained India in Pakistan in 1954/55 and later, he and son Ashook accomplished a rare feat in cricket when they both represented India in the same match.

MANTRI, Madhav Krishnaji

Born: September 1, 1921
Batting: Right handed
Bowling: Right arm medium
Wicket Keeper

Tests

Test Career: 1951-55
Cap Number: 56
Tests Played: 4

Test Batting

Innings:	8	Runs:	67
Highest Score:	39	Average:	9.57
No. 50s:	0	No. 100s:	0

Test Bowling & Fielding

Wickets:	0	Runs:	0
Best Bowling:		Average:	0.00
5 WI:	0	10 WM:	0
Catches:	8	Stumpings:	1

Caught between a rock and hard place, Mantri was an opening batsman while being asked to keep wickets and hence could not consolidate either position. He played four Tests but his greater claim to fame is that he is the uncle of Sunil Gavaskar.

MARTIN, Jacob Joseph

Born: May 11, 1972
Batting: Right handed
Bowling: Right arm leg-break

One Day Internationals

ODI Career: 1999-01
ODIs Played: 10

ODI Batting

Innings:	8	Runs:	158
Highest Score:	39	Average:	22.57
No. 50s:	0	No. 100s:	0

ODI Bowling & Fielding

Wickets:	0	Runs:	0
Best Bowling:		Average:	0.00
5 WM:	0	Catches:	6
Stumpings:	0		

A highly competitive right arm batsman from Baroda who made his ODI debut against the West Indies in Toronto in 1999. A prolific run scorer in the Ranji Trophy competition.

MEHERHOMJI, Khershed

Born: August 9, 1911
Batting: Right handed
Wicket Keeper

Tests

Test Career: 1936
Cap Number: 24
Tests Played: 1

Test Batting

Innings:	1	Runs:	0
Highest Score:	0*	Average:	0.00
No. 50s:	0	No. 100s:	0

Test Bowling & Fielding

Wickets:	0	Runs:	0
Best Bowling:		Average:	0.00
5 WI:	0	10 WM:	0
Catches:	1	Stumpings:	0

Meherhomji was reserve to regular keeper Hindlekar during the 1936 tour of England. He played in the second Test at Old Trafford where he took one catch.

MEHRA, Vijay Laxman

Born: March 12, 1938
Batting: Right handed

Tests

Test Career: 1955-64
Cap Number: 78
Tests Played: 8

Test Batting

Innings:	14	Runs:	329
Highest Score:	62	Average:	23.50
No. 50s:	2	No. 100s:	0

Test Bowling & Fielding

Wickets:	0	Runs:	6
Best Bowling:		Average:	0.00
5 WI:	0	10 WM:	0
Catches:	1	Stumpings:	0

At 17 years and 265 days, opening batsmen Vijay Mehra held the record for quite a number of years as the youngest to play Test cricket for India. The record stood until Maninder Singh made his debut in 1982/83. After a slow start he was dropped form the test team but recalled some six years later against England in 1961/62. Later became a national selector.

MERCHANT, Vijaysingh Madhavji

Born: October 12, 1911
Batting: Right handed
Bowling: Right arm medium

Tests
Test Career: 1933-51
Cap Number: 15
Tests Played: 10

Test Batting
Innings:	18	Runs:	859
Highest Score:	154	Average:	47.72
No. 50s:	3	No. 100s:	3

Test Bowling & Fielding
Wickets:	0	Runs:	40
Best Bowling:		Average:	0.00
5 WI:	0	10 WM:	0
Catches:	7	Stumpings:	0

Also known as Vijay Madhavji Thakersey. Merchant was a classy opening batsman whose average of 47.72 was considered by many a misrepresentation of his true talent as he was, in some circles, likened to a lesser Bradman. Although he stood at 5.7, Merchant had all the shots complimented with elegant footwork. He was a sheer delight to watch throughout a career that spanned almost two decades. He played his last Test at age 40 and amassed his highest score of 154. After retiring, he became a national selector and commentator.

MHAMBREY, Paras Laxmikant

Born: June 20, 1972
Batting: Right handed
Bowling: Right arm medium

Tests
Test Career: 1996
Cap Number: 203
Tests Played: 2

Test Batting
Innings:	3	Runs:	58
Highest Score:	28	Average:	29.00
No. 50s:	0	No. 100s:	0

Test Bowling & Fielding
Wickets:	2	Runs:	148
Best Bowling:	1/43	Average:	74.00
5 WI:	0	10 WM:	0
Catches:	1	Stumpings:	0

One Day Internationals
ODI Career: 1996-98
ODIs Played: 3

ODI Batting
Innings:	1	Runs:	7
Highest Score:	7*	Average:	7.00
No. 50s:	0	No. 100s:	0

ODI Bowling & Fielding
Wickets:	3	Runs:	120
Best Bowling:	2/69	Average:	40.00
5 WM:	0	Catches:	0
Stumpings:	0		

A right arm medium pacer from Mumbai who made an impressive Test debut against England at Edgbaston in 1996 where he made 28 handy runs in the first innings after coming in at number 10. As a second change bowler he took the wicket of English captain Michael Atherton and finished with the respectable figures of 1/43.

MILKHA SINGH, Amritsar Govindsingh

Born: December 31, 1941
Batting: Left handed
Bowling: Right arm medium

Tests
Test Career: 1960-61
Cap Number: 97
Tests Played: 4

Test Batting
Innings:	6	Runs:	92
Highest Score:	35	Average:	15.33
No. 50s:	0	No. 100s:	0

Test Bowling & Fielding
Wickets:	0	Runs:	2
Best Bowling:		Average:	0.00
5 WI:	0	10 WM:	0
Catches:	2	Stumpings:	0

Originally from Chennai and part of the famous Singh family of Indian cricket, Milkha Singh made his Test debut shortly after his 18th birthday. But by age 20, and three Tests later, his international career was over.

MISHRA, Amit

Born: November 24, 1982
Batting: Right handed
Bowling: Right arm leg-break

One Day Internationals
ODI Career: 2003
ODIs Played: 3

ODI Batting
Innings:	0	Runs:	0
Highest Score:	0	Average:	0.00
No. 50s:	0	No. 100s:	0

ODI Bowling & Fielding
Wickets:	2	Runs:	67
Best Bowling:	1/29	Average:	33.50
5 WM:	0	Catches:	0
Stumpings:	0		

An attacking leg spinner from Delhi, Mishra made his ODI debut against South Africa at Dhaka in 2003. An exciting prospect and also rated as a brilliant fieldsman, Mishra has been overlooked for the past few years but is still young enough to push for future selection.

MODI, Rusitomji Sheriyar

Born: November 11, 1924
Batting: Right handed
Bowling: Right arm medium

Tests
Test Career: 1946-52
Cap Number: 31
Tests Played: 10

Test Batting
Innings:	17	Runs:	736
Highest Score:	112	Average:	46.00
No. 50s:	6	No. 100s:	1

Test Bowling & Fielding

Wickets:	0	Runs:	14
Best Bowling:		Average:	0.00
5 WI:	0	10 WM:	0
Catches:	3	Stumpings:	0

A lanky batsman from Mumbai, Modi was a consistent and elegant stroke player during his six year Test career. Averaged a respectable 46.00.

MOHAMMAD, Gul

Born:	October 15, 1921
Batting:	Left handed
Bowling:	Left arm medium

Tests

Test Career:	1946-56		
Cap Number:	27		
Tests Played:	9		

Test Batting

Innings:	17	Runs:	205
Highest Score:	34	Average:	12.81
No. 50s:	0	No. 100s:	0

Test Bowling & Fielding

Wickets:	2	Runs:	24
Best Bowling:	2/21	Average:	12.00
5 WI:	0	10 WM:	0
Catches:	3	Stumpings:	0

An elegant left handed batsmen and outstanding fielder in his day, Gul Mohammad made his debut against England at Lord's in 1946 and played a further seven Tests for India. One of the few to play Test cricket for two nations, he finished his career playing one Test for Pakistan in 1956-57 against Australia.

MOHANTY, Debasis Sarbeswar

Born:	July 20, 1976
Batting:	Right handed
Bowling:	Right arm medium

Tests

Test Career:	1997		
Cap Number:	213		
Tests Played:	2		

Test Batting

Innings:	0	Runs:	0
Highest Score:	0*	Average:	0.00
No. 50s:	0	No. 100s:	0

Test Bowling & Fielding

Wickets:	4	Runs:	239
Best Bowling:	4/78	Average:	59.75
5 WI:	0	10 WM:	0
Catches:	0	Stumpings:	0

One Day Internationals

ODI Career:	1997-01
ODIs Played:	45

ODI Batting

Innings:	11	Runs:	28
Highest Score:	18	Average:	5.59
No. 50s:	0	No. 100s:	0

ODI Bowling & Fielding

Wickets:	57	Runs:	1,662
Best Bowling:	4/56	Average:	29.15
5 WM:	0	Catches:	10
Stumpings:	0		

Although he only played the two Tests, making his debut against Sri Lanka at Colombo in 1997, Mohanty was a regular at ODI level, representing India on 45 occasions. He was a member of the 1999 World Cup squad where he took a career best 4/56 against Kenya.

MONGIA, Dinesh

Born:	April 17, 1977
Batting:	Left handed
Bowling:	Left arm off-break

One Day Internationals

ODI Career:	2001-05
ODIs Played:	51

ODI Batting

Innings:	45	Runs:	1,073
Highest Score:	159*	Average:	27.51
No. 50s:	3	No. 100s:	1

ODI Bowling & Fielding

Wickets:	8	Runs:	370
Best Bowling:	3/31	Average:	46.25
5 WM:	0	Catches:	21
Stumpings:	0		

After a humble start to his ODI career against Australia in 2001, the jury was out as to whether the prolific run scorer from Chandigarh would become a permanent fixture in the one-day side. Contemporary history would show that Mongia would go on to play a handy 51 ODI's, scoring over 1000 runs, including a hard-hitting 159 not out against Zimbabwe, at Guwahati in March 2002. But like many before him, Mongia fell out of favour with the selectors and was left out of the side for awhile. He was recalled for the 2003 World Cup squad, but did little to restore confidence in the selectors' minds and thus, in 2006, attempts to once again reaffirm his place.

MONGIA, Nayan Ramlal

Born:	December 19, 1969
Batting:	Right handed
	Wicket Keeper

Tests

Test Career:	1994-01
Cap Number:	200
Tests Played:	44

Test Batting

Innings:	68	Runs:	1,442
Highest Score:	152	Average:	24.03
No. 50s:	6	No. 100s:	1

Test Bowling & Fielding

Wickets:	0	Runs:	0
Best Bowling:		Average:	0.00
5 WI:	0	10 WM:	0
Catches:	99	Stumpings:	8

One Day Internationals

ODI Career:	1994-00
ODIs Played:	140

ODI Batting

Innings:	96	Runs:	1,272
Highest Score:	69	Average:	20.19
No. 50s:	2	No. 100s:	0

ODI Bowling & Fielding

Wickets:	0	Runs:	0
Best Bowling:		Average:	0.00
5 WM:	0	Catches:	110
Stumpings:	44		

An enthusiastic competitor from Baroda, Mongia was another who was earmarked as eventual successor to wicket-keeper Kiran More. Eventually it boiled down to a two horse race between him and Yadav with the selectors preferring Mongia. He vindicated their decision by holding the position for 44 Tests over an eight year period. A handy middle order batsman, Mongia was asked at times to open the innings. And it was as an opener when he registered his maiden Test century and highest score of 152, against Australia, at New Delhi in 1996. Mongia also enjoyed playing the shorter version of the game and in fact racked up 140 appearances in the gold and blue uniform. But unfortunately his reputation was somewhat tarnished towards the end of his career and was subsequently banned after being involved in match-fixing scandals.

MORE, Kiran Shankar

Born:	September 4, 1962
Batting:	Right handed
Bowling:	Right arm off-break
	Wicket Keeper

Tests

Test Career:	1986-93		
Cap Number:	173		
Tests Played:	49		

Test Batting

Innings:	64	Runs:	1,285
Highest Score:	73	Average:	25.69
No. 50s:	7	No. 100s:	0

Test Bowling & Fielding

Wickets:	0	Runs:	12
Best Bowling:	0/12	Average:	0.00
5 WI:	0	10 WM:	0
Catches:	110	Stumpings:	20

One Day Internationals

ODI Career:	1984-93		
ODIs Played:	94		

ODI Batting

Innings:	65	Runs:	563
Highest Score:	42*	Average:	13.09
No. 50s:	0	No. 100s:	0

ODI Bowling & Fielding

Wickets:	0	Runs:	0
Best Bowling:		Average:	0.00
5 WM:	0	Catches:	63
Stumpings:	27		

When long standing and highly respected keeper Syed Kirmani was nearing retirement, the Indian selectors combed the nation for the most suitable successor. Having sampled a number of the most promising domestic keepers, the eventual 'nod' went to the young Kiran More from Baroda. The energetic More was Kirmani's understudy during the West Indies tour of 1982/83 and followed the master to Australia in 1985/86. He took over the number one mantle in 1986 and eventually became Indian vice captain in 1990. Playing in 49 Tests and 94 ODI's history confirms that the Indian brains trust got it right as More became the most successful Indian Test keeper after Kirmani.

MUDDIAH, Venatappa Musandra

Born:	June 8, 1929
Batting:	Right handed
Bowling:	Right arm off-break

Tests

Test Career:	1959-60		
Cap Number:	94		
Tests Played:	2		

Test Batting

Innings:	3	Runs:	11
Highest Score:	11	Average:	5.50
No. 50s:	0	No. 100s:	0

Test Bowling & Fielding

Wickets:	3	Runs:	134
Best Bowling:	2/40	Average:	44.66
5 WI:	0	10 WM:	0
Catches:	0	Stumpings:	0

An off spinner from Bangalore who played two tests - his first against Australia at Delhi, in 1959, and his second, and last, a year later against Pakistan at Kanpur.

MUKHERJEE, Saradindu Purnendu

Born:	October 5, 1964
Batting:	Right handed

One Day Internationals

ODI Career:	1990-91		
ODIs Played:	3		

ODI Batting

Innings:	1	Runs:	2
Highest Score:	2*	Average:	2.00
No. 50s:	0	No. 100s:	0

ODI Bowling & Fielding

Wickets:	2	Runs:	98
Best Bowling:	1/30	Average:	49.00
5 WM:	0	Catches:	1
Stumpings:	0		

An off-break bowler from Kolkata who was selected for the Asia Cup in 1990/91. He made his ODI debut against Bangladesh at Chandigarh but could only manage two more appearances, both against Sri Lanka. His only victim was Aravinda de Silva who he dismissed twice.

NADKARNI, Rameshchandra Gangaram (Bapu)

Born:	April 4, 1933
Batting:	Left handed
Bowling:	Left arm off-break

Tests

Test Career:	1955-68
Cap Number:	80
Tests Played:	41

Test Batting

Innings:	67	Runs:	1,414
Highest Score:	122*	Average:	25.70
No. 50s:	7	No. 100s:	1

Test Bowling & Fielding

Wickets:	88	Runs:	2,559
Best Bowling:	6/43	Average:	29.07
5 WI:	4	10 WM:	1
Catches:	0	Stumpings:	0

Although considered one of the premier orthodox spinners of his time, Bapu could make a claim for a place in the 'all rounder' category. He retired with a healthy Test average of 25.70 and scored just under 1,500 runs, including an unbeaten 122 against England at Kanpur in 1963-64. But his strength was his bowling and was renowned for his tightness in making batsmen earn every run they scored from his left arm off-spinners.

NAIK, Sudhir Sakharam

Born: February 21, 1945
Batting: Right handed

Tests

Test Career: 1974-75
Cap Number: 132
Tests Played: 3

Test Batting

Innings:	6	Runs:	141
Highest Score:	77	Average:	23.50
No. 50s:	0	No. 100s:	0

Test Bowling & Fielding

Wickets:	0	Runs:	0
Best Bowling:		Average:	0.00
5 WI:	0	10 WM:	0
Catches:	0	Stumpings:	0

One Day Internationals

ODI Career: 1974
ODIs Played: 2

ODI Batting

Innings:	2	Runs:	38
Highest Score:	20	Average:	19.00
No. 50s:	0	No. 100s:	0

ODI Bowling & Fielding

Wickets:	0	Runs:	0
Best Bowling:		Average:	0.00
5 WM:	0	Catches:	0
Stumpings:	0		

A dour batsmen from Mumbai, Naik made his highest score of 77 on debut against England at Lord's in 1974.

NAVLE, Janardan

Born: December 7, 1902
Batting: Right handed

Tests

Test Career: 1932-33
Cap Number: 6
Tests Played: 2

Test Batting

Innings:	4	Runs:	42
Highest Score:	13	Average:	10.50
No. 50s:	0	No. 100s:	0

Test Bowling & Fielding

Wickets:	0	Runs:	0
Best Bowling:		Average:	0.00
5 WI:	0	10 WM:	0
Catches:	1	Stumpings:	0

Apart from being India's first ever wicket keeper, Navle also had the honour of facing India's first ever ball at Test level when he opened the batting with Naoomal Jaoomal against England in 1932. Could only manage one further test due to age, as he was already 30 on debut.

NAYAK, Surendra Vithal

Born: October 20, 1954
Batting: Left handed
Bowling: Right arm medium

Tests

Test Career: 1982
Cap Number: 158
Tests Played: 2

Test Batting

Innings:	3	Runs:	19
Highest Score:	11	Average:	9.50
No. 50s:	0	No. 100s:	0

Test Bowling & Fielding

Wickets:	1	Runs:	132
Best Bowling:	1/16	Average:	132.00
5 WI:	0	10 WM:	0
Catches:	1	Stumpings:	0

One Day Internationals

ODI Career: 1981-82
ODIs Played: 4

ODI Batting

Innings:	1	Runs:	3
Highest Score:	3	Average:	3.00
No. 50s:	0	No. 100s:	0

ODI Bowling & Fielding

Wickets:	1	Runs:	161
Best Bowling:	1/51	Average:	161.00
5 WM:	0	Catches:	1
Stumpings:	0		

Toured England in 1982 playing just the two Tests and four One Day Internationals.

NAYUDU, Cottari Kanakaiya

Born: October 31, 1895
Batting: Right handed
Bowling: Right arm medium

Tests

Test Career: 1932-36
Cap Number: 7
Tests Played: 7

Test Batting

Innings:	14	Runs:	350
Highest Score:	81	Average:	25.00
No. 50s:	2	No. 100s:	0

Test Bowling & Fielding

Wickets:	9	Runs:	386
Best Bowling:	3/40	Average:	42.88
5 WI:	0	10 WM:	0
Catches:	4	Stumpings:	0

India's first ever Test captain, the tall and athletic Nayudu led from the front against England at Lord's in 1932 when he top scored with 40 in the first innings. Nayudu was an all round cricketer as his batting was complimented by fine fielding and astute bowling. His talent was not restricted to the cricket arena as he was also a more than handy hockey player and footballer.

NAYUDU, Cottari Subbanna

Born: April 18, 1914
Batting: Right handed
Bowling: Right arm leg-break

Tests
Test Career: 1934-52
Cap Number: 20
Tests Played: 11

Test Batting
Innings:	19	Runs:	147
Highest Score:	36	Average:	9.18
No. 50s:	0	No. 100s:	0

Test Bowling & Fielding
Wickets:	2	Runs:	359
Best Bowling:	1/19	Average:	179.50
5 WI:	0	10 WM:	0
Catches:	3	Stumpings:	0

Younger brother of India's first Test captain, CK Nayudu, Cottaru Subbanna made his Test debut at age 19. Played most of his Test cricket in England and Australia. A fine domestic cricketer with a modest Test record.

NEHRA, Ashish

Born: April 29, 1979
Batting: Right handed
Bowling: Left arm medium-fast

Tests
Test Career: 1999-04
Cap Number: 220
Tests Played: 17

Test Batting
Innings:	25	Runs:	77
Highest Score:	19	Average:	5.50
No. 50s:	0	No. 100s:	0

Test Bowling & Fielding
Wickets:	44	Runs:	1,866
Best Bowling:	4/72	Average:	42.40
5 WI:	0	10 WM:	0
Catches:	5	Stumpings:	0

One Day Internationals
ODI Career: 2001-05
ODIs Played: 72

ODI Batting
Innings:	26	Runs:	87
Highest Score:	24	Average:	7.25
No. 50s:	0	No. 100s:	0

ODI Bowling & Fielding
Wickets:	92	Runs:	2,859
Best Bowling:	6/23	Average:	31.07
5 WM:	2	Catches:	10
Stumpings:	0		

Considered the shining light in India's pace attack after his tour of Zimbabwe, Ashish Nehra, the talented left arm pace bowler from Delhi, worried batsmen in both forms of the game in his early days. He was a member of the 2003 World Cup where he collected his best ODI's figures of 6/23 when he single-handedly tore the English battling line up apart. Unfortunately, Nehra became injury riddled midway through his career. He was forced to return home during India's tour to Pakistan in 2004 due to an injury in the webbing in his right hand and a year later, history would repeat itself, when a back problem had him packing up early and heading home during the Test series against Zimbabwe. An excitement machine when on song, Nehra underwent extensive physiotherapy in Australia in 2006 and has not given up returning to international cricket.

NISSAR, Mohammad

Born: August 1, 1910
Batting: Right handed
Bowling: Right arm medium-fast

Tests
Test Career: 1932-36
Cap Number: 9
Tests Played: 6

Test Batting
Innings:	11	Runs:	55
Highest Score:	14	Average:	6.87
No. 50s:	0	No. 100s:	0

Test Bowling & Fielding
Wickets:	25	Runs:	707
Best Bowling:	5/90	Average:	28.28
5 WI:	3	10 WM:	0
Catches:	2	Stumpings:	0

A member of India's inaugural Test team of 1932, against England at Lord's, Nissar opened the bowling with Amar Singh and many pundits have retrospectively likened to the Lillee/Thomson combination some forty years later. Nissar was genuine pace and one of India's quickest in their history.

NYALCHAND, Shah

Born: September 14, 1919
Batting: Left handed
Bowling: Left arm medium

Tests
Test Career: 1952-53
Cap Number: 63
Tests Played: 1

Test Batting
Innings:	2	Runs:	7
Highest Score:	6*	Average:	7.00
No. 50s:	0	No. 100s:	0

Test Bowling & Fielding
Wickets:	3	Runs:	97
Best Bowling:	3/97	Average:	32.33
5 WI:	0	10 WM:	0
Catches:	0	Stumpings:	0

A left arm medium pacer from Kathiawar who played his first and only Test against Pakistan at Lucknow in 1952 where he took 3/97.

PAI, Ajit Manohar

Born: April 28, 1945
Batting: Left handed
Bowling: Right arm medium-fast

Tests

Test Career:	1969		
Cap Number:	120		
Tests Played:	1		

Test Batting

Innings:	2	Runs:	10
Highest Score:	9	Average:	5.00
No. 50s:	0	No. 100s:	0

Test Bowling & Fielding

Wickets:	2	Runs:	31
Best Bowling:	2/29	Average:	15.50
5 WI:	0	10 WM:	0
Catches:	0	Stumpings:	0

A wiry framed fast bowler from Mumbai, Pai played just the one Test against New Zealand, at Mumbai in 1969.

PAL, Rajinder

Born:	November 18, 1937
Batting:	Right handed
Bowling:	Right arm medium-fast

Tests

Test Career:	1964		
Cap Number:	107		
Tests Played:	1		

Test Batting

Innings:	2	Runs:	6
Highest Score:	3	Average:	6.00
No. 50s:	0	No. 100s:	0

Test Bowling & Fielding

Wickets:	0	Runs:	22
Best Bowling:		Average:	0.00
5 WI:	0	10 WM:	0
Catches:	0	Stumpings:	0

A right arm fast-medium pacer from Delhi, Pal played only the one Test against England, at Mumbai in 1964, but failed to convince the selectors that he was worthy of an another opportunity.

PALIA, Phiroze Edulji

Born:	September 5, 1910
Batting:	Left handed
Bowling:	Left arm off-break

Tests

Test Career:	1932-36		
Cap Number:	10		
Tests Played:	2		

Test Batting

Innings:	4	Runs:	29
Highest Score:	16	Average:	9.66
No. 50s:	0	No. 100s:	0

Test Bowling & Fielding

Wickets:	0	Runs:	13
Best Bowling:	0/13	Average:	0.00
5 WI:	0	10 WM:	0
Catches:	0	Stumpings:	0

Palia was a left hand batsman and member of India's inaugural Test team of 1932 that played against England at Lord's. A middle order batsman and handy slow bowler, Palia, after sustaining a leg injury in the field, batted at number eleven in the second innings of the first Test in order to save the match for India. But his heroics were in vain as England cruised to a 158 run victory. He became a Test selector and respected commentator after his retirement from first class cricket.

PANDEY, Gyanendrakumar Kedarnath

Born:	August 12, 1972
Batting:	Left handed
Bowling:	Left arm off-break

One Day Internationals

ODI Career:	1999		
ODIs Played:	2		

ODI Batting

Innings:	2	Runs:	4
Highest Score:	4*	Average:	4.00
No. 50s:	0	No. 100s:	0

ODI Bowling & Fielding

Wickets:	0	Runs:	60
Best Bowling:		Average:	0.00
5 WM:	0	Catches:	0
Stumpings:	0		

A left arm off-break bowler from Uttar Pradesh who played two ODI's against Pakistan in the 1999 Pepsi Cup.

PANDIT, Chandrakant Sitaram

Born:	September 30, 1961
Batting:	Right handed
	Wicket Keeper

Tests

Test Career:	1986-92		
Cap Number:	174		
Tests Played:	5		

Test Batting

Innings:	8	Runs:	171
Highest Score:	39	Average:	24.42
No. 50s:	0	No. 100s:	0

Test Bowling & Fielding

Wickets:	0	Runs:	0
Best Bowling:		Average:	0.00
5 WI:	0	10 WM:	0
Catches:	14	Stumpings:	2

One Day Internationals

ODI Career:	1986-92		
ODIs Played:	36		

ODI Batting

Innings:	23	Runs:	290
Highest Score:	33*	Average:	20.71
No. 50s:	0	No. 100s:	0

ODI Bowling & Fielding

Wickets:	0	Runs:	0
Best Bowling:		Average:	0.00
5 WM:	0	Catches:	15
Stumpings:	15		

Although selected as a batsman in his debut Test against England at Headingley in 1986, Pandit was one among several who were tried as possible successors to the great Syed Kirmani. In his five Test appearances he got the opportunity to show his keeping wares in only two of them - and this was because of the preferred Kiran More's unavailability. While things didn't work out at Test level, Pandit was a valuable contributor in 36 ODI's over his six year career.

PARANJPE, Jatin Vasudeo

Born: April 17, 1972
Batting: Left handed
Bowling: Left arm off-break

One Day Internationals

ODI Career: 1998
ODIs Played: 4

ODI Batting

Innings:	4	Runs:	54
Highest Score:	27	Average:	18.00
No. 50s:	0	No. 100s:	0

ODI Bowling & Fielding

Wickets:	0	Runs:	0
Best Bowling:		Average:	0.00
5 WM:	0	Catches:	2
Stumpings:	0		

A middle-order batsman from Mumbai who made his ODI debut against Kenya, at Gwalior in 1998. Played just the four ODI's.

PARKAR, Ghulam Ahmed Hasan Mohammed

Born: October 25, 1955
Batting: Right handed
Bowling: Right arm medium

Tests

Test Career: 1982
Cap Number: 157
Tests Played: 1

Test Batting

Innings:	2	Runs:	7
Highest Score:	6	Average:	3.50
No. 50s:	0	No. 100s:	0

Test Bowling & Fielding

Wickets:	0	Runs:	0
Best Bowling:		Average:	0.00
5 WI:	0	10 WM:	0
Catches:	1	Stumpings:	0

One Day Internationals

ODI Career: 1982-84
ODIs Played: 10

ODI Batting

Innings:	10	Runs:	165
Highest Score:	42	Average:	18.33
No. 50s:	0	No. 100s:	0

ODI Bowling & Fielding

Wickets:	0	Runs:	0
Best Bowling:		Average:	0.00
5 WM:	0	Catches:	4
Stumpings:	0		

A right hand opening batsman from Kaluste, Maharashtra, Parkar struggled at Test level and played just the one Test against England, at Lord's in 1982.

PARKAR, Ramnath Dhondu

Born: October 31, 1946
Batting: Right handed

Tests

Test Career: 1972-73
Cap Number: 129
Tests Played: 2

Test Batting

Innings:	4	Runs:	80
Highest Score:	35	Average:	20.00
No. 50s:	0	No. 100s:	0

Test Bowling & Fielding

Wickets:	0	Runs:	0
Best Bowling:		Average:	0.00
5 WI:	0	10 WM:	0
Catches:	0	Stumpings:	0

An outstanding cover fieldsman, Parkar was Sunil Gavaskar's opening partner in the first two Tests against England in 1972/73. However he was unfortunately not given another opportunity at Test level.

PARSANA, Dhiraj Devshibhai

Born: December 2, 1947
Batting: Left handed

Tests

Test Career: 1979
Cap Number: 143
Tests Played: 2

Test Batting

Innings:	4	Runs:	46
Highest Score:	20	Average:	9.19
No. 50s:	0	No. 100s:	0

Test Bowling & Fielding

Wickets:	1	Runs:	50
Best Bowling:	1/32	Average:	50.00
5 WI:	0	10 WM:	0
Catches:	0	Stumpings:	0

A left arm seam bowler from Gujarat, Parsana played two Tests, making his debut against the West Indies at Chennai in 1979.

PATANKAR, Chandrakant Trimbak

Born: November 24, 1930
Batting: Right handed
Wicket Keeper

Tests

Test Career: 1955-56
Cap Number: 82
Tests Played: 1

Test Batting

Innings:	2	Runs:	14
Highest Score:	13	Average:	14.00
No. 50s:	0	No. 100s:	0

Test Bowling & Fielding

Wickets:	0	Runs:	0
Best Bowling:		Average:	0.00
5 WI:	0	10 WM:	0
Catches:	0	Stumpings:	0

A reserve wicket-keeper given a chance at Test level against the touring Kiwis in 1955/56. With regular keepers Tambane and Joshi on the scene, further opportunities for Patankar were limited and eventually non existent.

PATAUDI JNR (NAWAB OF PATAUDI), Mansur Ali Khan

Born: January 5, 1941
Batting: Right handed
Bowling: Right arm medium

Tests

Test Career:	1961-75		
Cap Number:	104		
Tests Played:	46		

Test Batting

Innings:	83	Runs:	2,793
Highest Score:	203*	Average:	34.91
No. 50s:	16	No. 100s:	6

Test Bowling & Fielding

Wickets:	1	Runs:	88
Best Bowling:	1/10	Average:	88.00
5 WI:	0	10 WM:	0
Catches:	0	Stumpings:	0

Previoulsy known as The Nawab of Pataudi, Mansur Ali Khan is considered by many as India's greatest captain. At 21, and shortly after being involved in a car accident that impaired the sight in one eye, Pataudi was awarded the captaincy and led the side with inspirational leadership over 40 Tests. Under his reign India won their first first overseas Test, against New Zealand in 1967. His philosophy fully endorsed playing three spinners, which paved a new direction for Indian cricket over the next decade. His father, Iftikhar Ali Khan, is the only man in Test history to have represented both England and India in Tests.

PATAUDI SNR (NAWAB OF), Iftikhar Ali Khan

Born:	March 16, 1910
Batting:	Right handed

Tests

Test Career:	1932-46		
Cap Number:	32		
Tests Played:	6		

Test Batting

Innings:	10	Runs:	199
Highest Score:	102	Average:	19.89
No. 50s:	0	No. 100s:	1

Test Bowling & Fielding

Wickets:	0	Runs:	0
Best Bowling:		Average:	0.00
5 WI:	0	10 WM:	0
Catches:	0	Stumpings:	0

The only cricketer to have played Test cricket for both England and India. Pataudi scored a hundred on debut, for England, against Australia at the SCG, but was subsequently dropped for the next Test following a difference in opinion with Douglas Jardine. Later captained India but his best cricket was well and truly behind him. His son, Mansur Ali Khan Pataudi, captained India in 40 Tests during the 1960's and early 70's.

PATEL, Ashok Kurjibhai

Born:	March 6, 1957
Batting:	Right handed
Bowling:	Right arm off-break

One Day Internationals

ODI Career:	1984-85
ODIs Played:	8

ODI Batting

Innings:	2	Runs:	6
Highest Score:	6	Average:	3.00
No. 50s:	0	No. 100s:	0

ODI Bowling & Fielding

Wickets:	7	Runs:	263
Best Bowling:	3/43	Average:	37.57
5 WM:	0	Catches:	0
Stumpings:	0		

A slender off-spinner from Saurashtra who managed a respectable personal best of 3/43 from the eight ODI's he participated in.

PATEL, Brijesh Pursuram

Born:	November 24, 1952
Batting:	Right handed
Bowling:	Right arm off-break

Tests

Test Career:	1974-77		
Cap Number:	131		
Tests Played:	21		

Test Batting

Innings:	38	Runs:	972
Highest Score:	115*	Average:	29.45
No. 50s:	5	No. 100s:	1

Test Bowling & Fielding

Wickets:	0	Runs:	0
Best Bowling:		Average:	0.00
5 WI:	0	10 WM:	0
Catches:	1	Stumpings:	0

One Day Internationals

ODI Career:	1974-79
ODIs Played:	10

ODI Batting

Innings:	9	Runs:	243
Highest Score:	82	Average:	30.37
No. 50s:	0	No. 100s:	0

ODI Bowling & Fielding

Wickets:	0	Runs:	0
Best Bowling:		Average:	0.00
5 WM:	0	Catches:	1
Stumpings:	0		

A talented middle-order batsman and swing bowler who completely dominated the domestic competition but could not live up to expectations at Test level. Scored his only Test hundred, 115 not out, against West Indies, at Port of Spain, and was selected in the World Cup squads of 1975 & 79 as his style was better suited to the one day game.

PATEL, Jasubhai Motibhai

Born:	November 26, 1924
Batting:	Right handed
Bowling:	Right arm off-break

Tests

Test Career:	1955-60		
Cap Number:	74		
Tests Played:	7		

Test Batting

Innings:	10	Runs:	25
Highest Score:	12	Average:	2.77
No. 50s:	0	No. 100s:	0

Test Bowling & Fielding

Wickets:	29	Runs:	637
Best Bowling:	9/69	Average:	21.96
5 WI:	2	10 WM:	1
Catches:	2	Stumpings:	0

Although he only played seven Tests in total, off-spinner Jasubhai Patel's 9/69 against Australia at Kanpur in 1959, were the best figures by an Indian bowler until Anil Kumble's 10/74 against Pakistan at Delhi in 1999. Originally from Gujarat, his 14/124, from that same match, are also the second best match figures by an Indian bowler.

PATEL, Munaf Musa

Born:	July 12, 1983
Batting:	Right handed
Bowling:	Right arm medium-fast

Tests

Test Career:	2006		
Cap Number:	254		
Tests Played:	6		

Test Batting

Innings:	7	Runs:	32
Highest Score:	13	Average:	6.40
No. 50s:	0	No. 100s:	0

Test Bowling & Fielding

Wickets:	24	Runs:	680
Best Bowling:	4/25	Average:	28.33
5 WI:	0	10 WM:	0
Catches:	3	Stumpings:	0

One Day Internationals

ODI Career:	2006		
ODIs Played:	5		

ODI Batting

Innings:	3	Runs:	3
Highest Score:	2*	Average:	3.00
No. 50s:	0	No. 100s:	0

ODI Bowling & Fielding

Wickets:	2	Runs:	235
Best Bowling:	1/48	Average:	117.50
5 WM:	0	Catches:	2
Stumpings:	0		

An exciting right arm fast medium pacer who has the good looks to go with his natural ability. Patel impressed in his first Test against England when he caught & bowled English 'guns' Pietersen and Flintoff to set him on his way to a respectable 3/72. He followed up in the second innings with 4/25 and in his six Tests to date has done enough to suggest that he could become a regular in India's pace attack.

PATEL, Parthiv Ajay

Born:	March 9, 1985
Batting:	Left handed
	Wicket Keeper

Tests

Test Career:	2002-04		
Cap Number:	244		
Tests Played:	19		

Test Batting

Innings:	28	Runs:	669
Highest Score:	69	Average:	31.85
No. 50s:	4	No. 100s:	0

Test Bowling & Fielding

Wickets:	0	Runs:	0
Best Bowling:		Average:	0.00
5 WI:	0	10 WM:	0
Catches:	39	Stumpings:	7

One Day Internationals

ODI Career:	2003-04		
ODIs Played:	14		

ODI Batting

Innings:	10	Runs:	132
Highest Score:	28	Average:	14.66
No. 50s:	0	No. 100s:	0

ODI Bowling & Fielding

Wickets:	0	Runs:	0
Best Bowling:		Average:	0.00
5 WM:	0	Catches:	12
Stumpings:	3		

At 17 years, 153 days, Parthiv Patel became Test cricket's youngest wicketkeeper when he made his debut against England, at Trent Bridge in 2002 as a replacement for the injured Ajay Ratra. A handy batsman he made four fifties in his 19 Tests including a highest score of 69 when he opened the batting against the Pakistan pace attack in 2003/04. Unfortunately, his inconsistency and frequent 'clangers' behind the stumps were well documented and thus the selectors lost patience with the tiny, but energetic keeper. He was eventually replaced by Dinesh Karthik.

PATEL, Rashid Ghulam Mohammed

Born:	June 1, 1964
Batting:	Left handed
Bowling:	Left arm medium-fast

Tests

Test Career:	1988		
Cap Number:	183		
Tests Played:	1		

Test Batting

Innings:	2	Runs:	0
Highest Score:	0	Average:	0.00
No. 50s:	0	No. 100s:	0

Test Bowling & Fielding

Wickets:	0	Runs:	51
Best Bowling:	0/51	Average:	0.00
5 WI:	0	10 WM:	0
Catches:	1	Stumpings:	0

One Day Internationals

ODI Career:	1988		
ODIs Played:	1		

ODI Batting

Innings:	0	Runs:	0
Highest Score:	0	Average:	0.00
No. 50s:	0	No. 100s:	0

ODI Bowling & Fielding

Wickets:	0	Runs:	58
Best Bowling:	0/58	Average:	0.00
5 WM:	0	Catches:	0
Stumpings:	0		

A medium pacer from Baroda who made a pair of ducks and failed to take a wicket in his only Test against New Zealand at Mumbai in 1988.

PATHAN, Irfan Khan

Born: October 27, 1984
Batting: Left handed
Bowling: Left arm medium-fast

Tests
Test Career: 2003-06
Cap Number: 248
Tests Played: 25

Test Batting
Innings:	32	Runs:	835
Highest Score:	93	Average:	27.83
No. 50s:	6	No. 100s:	0

Test Bowling & Fielding
Wickets:	91	Runs:	2,802
Best Bowling:	7/59	Average:	30.79
5 WI:	7	10 WM:	2
Catches:	8	Stumpings:	0

One Day Internationals
ODI Career: 2004-06
ODIs Played: 63

ODI Batting
Innings:	46	Runs:	858
Highest Score:	83	Average:	26.00
No. 50s:	4	No. 100s:	0

ODI Bowling & Fielding
Wickets:	108	Runs:	2,651
Best Bowling:	5/27	Average:	24.54
5 WM:	1	Catches:	10
Stumpings:	0		

A highly talented and energetic left arm swing bowler who is fast developing into a world-class paceman. A fine exponent of reverse swing, Pathan made his Test debut against Australia in Adelaide in 2003 and on the tour of Zimbabwe in 2005 took a career best 7/59 in India's ten wicket win in the 2nd Test. Pathan took 21 wickets in the two Tests and was aptly named 'Player of the Series'.

PATIL, Sadashiv Raoji

Born: October 10, 1933
Batting: Right handed
Bowling: Right arm medium-fast

Tests
Test Career: 1955-56
Cap Number: 79
Tests Played: 1

Test Batting
Innings:	1	Runs:	14
Highest Score:	14*	Average:	14.00
No. 50s:	0	No. 100s:	0

Test Bowling & Fielding
Wickets:	2	Runs:	51
Best Bowling:	1/15	Average:	25.50
5 WI:	0	10 WM:	0
Catches:	1	Stumpings:	0

He played his first and only Test against New Zealand at Mumbai in 1955, but again, another case of a player who showed considerable potential but was not given another opportunity after making his debut.

PATIL, Sandeep Madhusudan

Born: August 18, 1956
Batting: Right handed
Bowling: Right arm medium

Tests
Test Career: 1980-84
Cap Number: 149
Tests Played: 29

Test Batting
Innings:	47	Runs:	1,588
Highest Score:	174	Average:	36.93
No. 50s:	7	No. 100s:	4

Test Bowling & Fielding
Wickets:	9	Runs:	240
Best Bowling:	2/28	Average:	26.66
5 WI:	0	10 WM:	0
Catches:	12	Stumpings:	0

One Day Internationals
ODI Career: 1980-86
ODIs Played: 45

ODI Batting
Innings:	42	Runs:	1,005
Highest Score:	84	Average:	24.51
No. 50s:	9	No. 100s:	0

ODI Bowling & Fielding
Wickets:	15	Runs:	589
Best Bowling:	2/28	Average:	39.26
5 WM:	0	Catches:	0
Stumpings:	0		

A hard hitting all rounder, Sandip Patil provided ultimate entertainment value just about every time he entered the arena. The only difference between playing Test and One Day Cricket was the uniform as his attitude towards both forms of the game was almost identical. Patil took on the Dennis Lillee led pace attack in Adelaide, in 1980, to score a breath-taking 174, his highest score in Test cricket. Just over a year later, he smashed an undefeated 129 at Old Trafford, taking 24 runs off a Bob Willis over. A vital member of India's 1983 victorious World Cup team, Patil, after retiring, became coach of the national team and later coach of Kenya and took the cricketing minnows to the semi-final of the 2003 World Cup.

PHADKAR, Dattatraya Gajanan

Born: December 12, 1925
Batting: Right handed
Bowling: Right arm medium-fast

Tests
Test Career: 1947-58
Cap Number: 41
Tests Played: 31

Test Batting
Innings:	45	Runs:	1,229
Highest Score:	123	Average:	33.34
No. 50s:	8	No. 100s:	2

Test Bowling & Fielding
Wickets:	62	Runs:	2,285
Best Bowling:	7/159	Average:	36.85
5 WI:	3	10 WM:	0
Catches:	0	Stumpings:	0

A hard hitting all rounder who could also move the ball. Renowned pin up boy of Indian cricket, Phadkar became a regular member of the Indian team after touring Australia in 1947. He scored two Test centuries and eight fifties.

POWAR, Ramesh Rajaram
Born:	May 20, 1978
Batting:	Right handed
Bowling:	Right arm off-break

One Day Internationals
ODI Career:	2004-06		
ODIs Played:	14		

ODI Batting
Innings:	9	Runs:	107
Highest Score:	54	Average:	21.40
No. 50s:	1	No. 100s:	0

ODI Bowling & Fielding
Wickets:	16	Runs:	544
Best Bowling:	3/34	Average:	34.00
5 WM:	0	Catches:	0
Stumpings:	0		

A right arm off-break bowler and handy lower order batsman, Ramesh Powar has been a valuable contributor in his 14 ODI's averaging just over 21 with the bat and best bowling figures of 3/34.

PRABHAKAR, Manoj
Born:	March 15, 1963
Batting:	Right handed
Bowling:	Right arm medium-fast

Tests
Test Career:	1984-95		
Cap Number:	168		
Tests Played:	39		

Test Batting
Innings:	58	Runs:	1,600
Highest Score:	120	Average:	32.65
No. 50s:	9	No. 100s:	1

Test Bowling & Fielding
Wickets:	96	Runs:	3,581
Best Bowling:	6/132	Average:	37.30
5 WI:	3	10 WM:	0
Catches:	20	Stumpings:	0

One Day Internationals
ODI Career:	1984-96		
ODIs Played:	130		

ODI Batting
Innings:	98	Runs:	1,858
Highest Score:	106	Average:	24.12
No. 50s:	11	No. 100s:	2

ODI Bowling & Fielding
Wickets:	157	Runs:	4,534
Best Bowling:	5/33	Average:	28.87
5 WM:	2	Catches:	27
Stumpings:	0		

For just over a decade Manoj Prabhakar provided India with quality and consistent performances as a batsman and a swing bowler - in both forms of the game. With versatility as his key attribute, Prabhakar was asked to open the batting at one stage of his career and scored centuries in both Tests (highest score of 120 v West Indies at Mohali 94/95) and One Day Internationals. A tireless bowler he captured 96 Test scalps and over 150 in ODI's.

PRASAD, Bapu Krishnarao Venkatesh
Born:	August 5, 1969
Batting:	Right handed
Bowling:	Right arm medium-fast

Tests
Test Career:	1996-01		
Cap Number:	204		
Tests Played:	33		

Test Batting
Innings:	47	Runs:	203
Highest Score:	30*	Average:	7.51
No. 50s:	0	No. 100s:	0

Test Bowling & Fielding
Wickets:	96	Runs:	3,360
Best Bowling:	6/33	Average:	35.00
5 WI:	7	10 WM:	1
Catches:	6	Stumpings:	0

One Day Internationals
ODI Career:	1994-01		
ODIs Played:	161		

ODI Batting
Innings:	63	Runs:	221
Highest Score:	19	Average:	6.90
No. 50s:	0	No. 100s:	0

ODI Bowling & Fielding
Wickets:	196	Runs:	6,332
Best Bowling:	5/27	Average:	32.30
5 WM:	1	Catches:	37
Stumpings:	0		

Partner in crime with Javagal Srinath during the 90's when India's pace attack was arguably at its best. Prasad was a more than useful seam bowler and although he played only 33 Tests in all, he enjoyed one of the most memorable spells in Test cricket when he captured six Pakistani wickets for 33 at Chennai in 1999 - and at one stage he had 5/0. Prasad played over 160 ODI's for his country and will be remembered as one who gave his all for his country anytime he took the field.

PRASAD, Mannava Sri Kanth
Born:	April 25, 1975
Batting:	Right handed
	Wicket Keeper

Tests
Test Career:	1999-00		
Cap Number:	222		
Tests Played:	6		

Test Batting
Innings:	10	Runs:	106
Highest Score:	19	Average:	11.77
No. 50s:	0	No. 100s:	0

Test Bowling & Fielding
Wickets:	0	Runs:	0
Best Bowling:		Average:	0.00
5 WI:	0	10 WM:	0
Catches:	15	Stumpings:	0

One Day Internationals

ODI Career:	1998-99
ODIs Played:	17

ODI Batting

Innings:	11	Runs:	131
Highest Score:	63	Average:	14.55
No. 50s:	1	No. 100s:	0

ODI Bowling & Fielding

Wickets:	0	Runs:	0
Best Bowling:		Average:	0.00
5 WM:	0	Catches:	14
Stumpings:	7		

An injury to regular keeper, Nayan Mongia, after the 1999 World Cup provided Prasad with an opportunity to experience cricket at the highest level. After his debut Test against New Zealand at Chandigarh in 1999/00 he played a further five Tests and became a regular in the ODI side. He will need to improve on his batting if he is to seriously push for further international selection.

PRASANNA, Erapalli Anatharao Srinivas

Born:	May 22, 1940
Batting:	Right handed
Bowling:	Right arm off-break

Tests

Test Career:	1962-78
Cap Number:	105
Tests Played:	49

Test Batting

Innings:	84	Runs:	735
Highest Score:	37	Average:	11.48
No. 50s:	0	No. 100s:	0

Test Bowling & Fielding

Wickets:	189	Runs:	5,742
Best Bowling:	8/76	Average:	30.38
5 WI:	10	10 WM:	2
Catches:	0	Stumpings:	0

Part of the great Indian spin quartet of the seventies comprising of (Bedi, Chandrasekhar and Venkat), Prasanna was the 'thinking man's' bowler. Although vying with Venkat for the third spinning position at various times, Prasanna could flight the ball better than most and lured many a batsman into mistiming relatively straight forward strokes. After taking a sabbatical in the early sixties, to pursue an academic qualification, Prasanna returned to the Test arena finishing with 189 wickets at 30.38. Although not the most high profile players the game has known, Prasanna's bowling ability is still regarded as exceptional highly amongst many of his former opponents.

PUNJABI, Pananmal Hotchand

Born:	September 20, 1921
Batting:	Right handed
	Wicket Keeper

Tests

Test Career:	1955
Cap Number:	71
Tests Played:	5

Test Batting

Innings:	10	Runs:	164
Highest Score:	33	Average:	16.39
No. 50s:	0	No. 100s:	0

Test Bowling & Fielding

Wickets:	0	Runs:	0
Best Bowling:		Average:	0.00
5 WI:	0	10 WM:	0
Catches:	5	Stumpings:	0

Opener and part time keeper, Punjabi managed to squeeze his five test appearances into a three month period between January and March 1955.

RAI SINGH, Kanwar

Born:	February 24, 1922
Batting:	Right handed

Tests

Test Career:	1947-48
Cap Number:	42
Tests Played:	1

Test Batting

Innings:	2	Runs:	26
Highest Score:	24	Average:	13.00
No. 50s:	0	No. 100s:	0

Test Bowling & Fielding

Wickets:	0	Runs:	0
Best Bowling:		Average:	0.00
5 WI:	0	10 WM:	0
Catches:	0	Stumpings:	0

Played the one Test against Australia at MCG in 1947/48. Originally from Southern Punjab.

RAINA, Suresh Kumar

Born:	November 27, 1986
Batting:	Left handed
Bowling:	Right arm off-break

One Day Internationals

ODI Career:	2005-06
ODIs Played:	26

ODI Batting

Innings:	19	Runs:	481
Highest Score:	81*	Average:	32.06
No. 50s:	3	No. 100s:	0

ODI Bowling & Fielding

Wickets:	1	Runs:	37
Best Bowling:	1/23	Average:	37.00
5 WM:	0	Catches:	10
Stumpings:	0		

Hailed as an exciting all rounder, Suresh Raina made his international debut against Sri Lanka at Dambulla in 2005. He was selected for the West Indies tour of 2006 and as he is in his early 20's, the talented youngster has plenty of time to develop.

RAJINDERNATH, N

Born:	January 7, 1928
Batting:	Right handed
	Wicket Keeper

Tests
Test Career: 1952-53
Cap Number: 66
Tests Played: 1
Test Batting
Innings: 0 Runs: 0
Highest Score: 0 Average: 0.00
No. 50s: 0 No. 100s: 0
Test Bowling & Fielding
Wickets: 0 Runs: 0
Best Bowling: Average: 0.00
5 WI: 0 10 WM: 0
Catches: 0 Stumpings: 4

A wicket-keeper who was called in for one Test against Pakistan at Mumbai, in 1952. He didn't get the opportunity to bat, but managed four stumpings on debut. Unlucky not to receive nother chance at Test level.

RAJPUT, Lalchand Sitaram
Born: December 18, 1961
Batting: Right handed
Tests
Test Career: 1985
Cap Number: 171
Tests Played: 2
Test Batting
Innings: 4 Runs: 105
Highest Score: 61 Average: 26.25
No. 50s: 1 No. 100s: 0
Test Bowling & Fielding
Wickets: 0 Runs: 0
Best Bowling: Average: 0.00
5 WI: 0 10 WM: 0
Catches: 1 Stumpings: 0
One Day Internationals
ODI Career: 1985-87
ODIs Played: 4
ODI Batting
Innings: 4 Runs: 9
Highest Score: 8 Average: 3.00
No. 50s: 0 No. 100s: 0
ODI Bowling & Fielding
Wickets: 0 Runs: 42
Best Bowling: 0/42 Average: 0.00
5 WM: 0 Catches: 2
Stumpings: 0

An opening batsman from Mumbai, Rajput had an impressive start to his Test career (61 v Sri Lanka at Colombo) but failed to hold a regular place.

RAJU, Sagi Lakshmi Venkatapathy
Born: July 9, 1969
Batting: Right handed
Bowling: Left arm off-break
Tests
Test Career: 1990-01
Cap Number: 189
Tests Played: 28
Test Batting
Innings: 34 Runs: 240
Highest Score: 31 Average: 10.00
No. 50s: 0 No. 100s: 0
Test Bowling & Fielding
Wickets: 93 Runs: 2,857
Best Bowling: 6/12 Average: 30.72
5 WI: 1 10 WM: 0
Catches: 6 Stumpings: 0
One Day Internationals
ODI Career: 1990-96
ODIs Played: 53
ODI Batting
Innings: 16 Runs: 32
Highest Score: 8 Average: 4.00
No. 50s: 0 No. 100s: 0
ODI Bowling & Fielding
Wickets: 63 Runs: 2,014
Best Bowling: 4/46 Average: 31.96
5 WM: 0 Catches: 8
Stumpings: 0

A finger spinner from Hyderabad, Raju made his debut against New Zealand at Christchurch in 1990 and partnered well with fellow spinner Anil Kumble. Nicknamed 'Muscles', Raju was a solid contributor at both Test and ODI competition.

RAMAN, Woorkeri Venkat
Born: May 23, 1965
Batting: Left handed
Bowling: Left arm leg-break
Tests
Test Career: 1988-97
Cap Number: 181
Tests Played: 11
Test Batting
Innings: 19 Runs: 448
Highest Score: 96 Average: 24.88
No. 50s: 4 No. 100s: 0
Test Bowling & Fielding
Wickets: 2 Runs: 129
Best Bowling: 1/7 Average: 64.50
5 WI: 0 10 WM: 0
Catches: 6 Stumpings: 0
One Day Internationals
ODI Career: 1988-96
ODIs Played: 27
ODI Batting
Innings: 27 Runs: 617
Highest Score: 114 Average: 23.73
No. 50s: 3 No. 100s: 1
ODI Bowling & Fielding
Wickets: 2 Runs: 170
Best Bowling: 1/23 Average: 85.00
5 WM: 0 Catches: 2
Stumpings: 0

A left hand batsman from Chennai who made his Test debut against West Indies at Chennai, 1988. Just missed out on a Test hundred with a well made 96 against New Zealand in 1990, but did reach triple figures at ODI level, scoring 114 against South Africa in 1992/93.

RAMASWAMI, Cotar
Born: June 16, 1896
Batting: Left handed
Bowling: Right arm medium

Tests
Test Career:	1936		
Cap Number:	25		
Tests Played:	2		
Test Batting			
Innings:	4	Runs:	170
Highest Score:	60	Average:	56.66
No. 50s:	1	No. 100s:	0
Test Bowling & Fielding			
Wickets:	0	Runs:	0
Best Bowling:		Average:	0.00
5 WI:	0	10 WM:	0
Catches:	0	Stumpings:	0

The multi talented Ramaswami played Davis Cup in the 1920s and went on to represent India at Test level on the 1936 tour of England. Ramaswami made his debut in the second Test at Old Trafford, aged 40 years, 37 days, only second to Rustomji Jamshedji who made his debut some three years earlier, aged 41. Later became manager of the first Indian team to tour the West Indies and then, like quite a few of his era, became a national selector.

RAMCHAND, Gulabrai Sipahimalani
Born: July 26, 1927
Batting: Right handed

Tests
Test Career:	1952-60		
Cap Number:	61		
Tests Played:	33		
Test Batting			
Innings:	53	Runs:	1,180
Highest Score:	109	Average:	24.58
No. 50s:	1	No. 100s:	2
Test Bowling & Fielding			
Wickets:	41	Runs:	1,899
Best Bowling:	6/49	Average:	46.31
5 WI:	1	10 WM:	0
Catches:	20	Stumpings:	0

A hard hitting all rounder who also opened the bowling. Agile in the field, Ramchand scored two Test centuries, his first against New Zealand in 1955, then followed up with his highest score of 109 against Australia in 1956. He went on to lead India to their first ever win against Australia in 1959.

RAMESH, Sadagoppan
Born: October 16, 1975
Batting: Left handed
Bowling: Right arm off-break

Tests
Test Career:	1991-01		
Cap Number:	219		
Tests Played:	19		
Test Batting			
Innings:	37	Runs:	1,367
Highest Score:	143	Average:	37.97
No. 50s:	8	No. 100s:	2
Test Bowling & Fielding			
Wickets:	0	Runs:	43
Best Bowling:		Average:	0.00
5 WI:	0	10 WM:	0
Catches:	18	Stumpings:	0

One Day Internationals
ODI Career:	1999		
ODIs Played:	24		
ODI Batting			
Innings:	24	Runs:	646
Highest Score:	82	Average:	28.08
No. 50s:	6	No. 100s:	0
ODI Bowling & Fielding			
Wickets:	1	Runs:	38
Best Bowling:	1/23	Average:	38.00
5 WM:	0	Catches:	3
Stumpings:	0		

A highly competent left hand opening batsman who made his Test debut against Pakistan at Chennai in 1989 where he looked more than comfortable against the formidable Pakistan pace attack. Scored his first Test hundred and highest score of 143 against Sri Lanka at Colombo but the runs seemed to dry up shortly after his second and last ton of 110 against New Zealand in 1999. He played some useful knocks at one day level where he averaged 28.08.

RAMJI, Ladha
Born: February 10, 1900
Batting: Right handed
Bowling: Right arm fast

Tests
Test Career:	1933-34		
Cap Number:	16		
Tests Played:	1		
Test Batting			
Innings:	2	Runs:	1
Highest Score:	1	Average:	0.50
No. 50s:	0	No. 100s:	0
Test Bowling & Fielding			
Wickets:	0	Runs:	64
Best Bowling:	0/64	Average:	0.00
5 WI:	0	10 WM:	0
Catches:	1	Stumpings:	0

The older brother of Amar Singh who played in the inaugural Test team in 1932, Ramji hardly troubled the scorers in his one Test for India against England at Mumbai, in 1933, which was the the first ever Test match on Indian soil.

RANGACHARI, Commandur Rajagopalachari
Born: April 14, 1916
Batting: Right handed
Bowling: Right arm fast

Tests
Test Career:	1948		
Cap Number:	44		
Tests Played:	4		
Test Batting			
Innings:	6	Runs:	8
Highest Score:	8*	Average:	2.66
No. 50s:	0	No. 100s:	0

Test Bowling & Fielding

Wickets:	9	Runs:	493
Best Bowling:	5/107	Average:	54.77
5 WI:	1	10 WM:	0
Catches:	0	Stumpings:	0

A police officer and fast bowler from Chennai who made his debut against Australia at Adelaide in 1948. Rangachari played just the six Tests and his best performance was his 5/107 against the West Indies in 1948/49.

RANGNEKAR, Khanderao Moreshwar

Born: June 27, 1917
Batting: Left handed
Bowling: Right arm medium

Tests

Test Career:	1947-48		
Cap Number:	39		
Tests Played:	3		

Test Batting

Innings:	6	Runs:	33
Highest Score:	18	Average:	5.50
No. 50s:	0	No. 100s:	0

Test Bowling & Fielding

Wickets:	0	Runs:	0
Best Bowling:		Average:	0.00
5 WI:	0	10 WM:	0
Catches:	1	Stumpings:	0

A left handed batsmen and right arm medium pacer, Rangnekar played all three career Tests during the 1947-48 tour of Australia. Later became President of the Bombay Cricket Association.

RANJANE, Vasant Baburao

Born: July 22, 1937
Batting: Right handed
Bowling: Right arm medium-fast

Tests

Test Career:	1958-64		
Cap Number:	86		
Tests Played:	7		

Test Batting

Innings:	9	Runs:	40
Highest Score:	16	Average:	6.66
No. 50s:	0	No. 100s:	0

Test Bowling & Fielding

Wickets:	19	Runs:	649
Best Bowling:	4/72	Average:	34.15
5 WI:	0	10 WM:	0
Catches:	1	Stumpings:	0

A medium pacer from Maharashtra who could never cement a permanent spot in the Test team over his six year career. Best figures of 4/72 against the West Indies in 1962 where he picked up the wickets of Kanhai and Sobers.

RAO, Modireddy Venkat Narasimha (Bobjee)

Born: August 11, 1954
Batting: Right handed
Bowling: Right arm leg-break

Tests

Test Career:	1978-79		
Cap Number:	142		
Tests Played:	4		

Test Batting

Innings:	6	Runs:	46
Highest Score:	20*	Average:	9.19
No. 50s:	0	No. 100s:	0

Test Bowling & Fielding

Wickets:	0	Runs:	0
Best Bowling:		Average:	0.00
5 WI:	0	10 WM:	0
Catches:	8	Stumpings:	0

A leg spiner and middle order batsmen, 'Bobjee' debuted against West Indies in 1978 but his time at Test level was restricted due the emergence of the great Bhagwat Chandrsekhar.

RATHOUR, Vikram

Born: March 26, 1969
Batting: Right handed
Wicket Keeper

Tests

Test Career:	1996-97		
Cap Number:	205		
Tests Played:	6		

Test Batting

Innings:	10	Runs:	131
Highest Score:	44	Average:	13.09
No. 50s:	0	No. 100s:	0

Test Bowling & Fielding

Wickets:	0	Runs:	0
Best Bowling:		Average:	0.00
5 WI:	0	10 WM:	0
Catches:	12	Stumpings:	0

One Day Internationals

ODI Career:	1996-97		
ODIs Played:	7		

ODI Batting

Innings:	7	Runs:	193
Highest Score:	54	Average:	27.57
No. 50s:	2	No. 100s:	0

ODI Bowling & Fielding

Wickets:	0	Runs:	0
Best Bowling:		Average:	0.00
5 WM:	0	Catches:	4
Stumpings:	0		

A wicketkeeper, originally from Jalandhar who opened the batting in his six Tests. He made his Test debut against England at Lord's in 1996.

RATRA, Ajay

Born: December 13, 1981
Batting: Right handed
Bowling: Right arm off-break
Wicket Keeper

Tests

Test Career:	2002		
Cap Number:	243		
Tests Played:	6		

Test Batting

Innings:	10	Runs:	163
Highest Score:	115*	Average:	18.11
No. 50s:	0	No. 100s:	1

Test Bowling & Fielding
Wickets: 0
Best Bowling: 0/1
5 WI: 0
Catches: 11
Runs: 1
Average: 0.00
10 WM: 0
Stumpings: 2

One Day Internationals
ODI Career: 2002
ODIs Played: 12
ODI Batting
Innings: 8
Highest Score: 30
No. 50s: 0
Runs: 90
Average: 12.85
No. 100s: 0
ODI Bowling & Fielding
Wickets: 0
Best Bowling:
5 WM: 0
Stumpings: 5
Runs: 0
Average: 0.00
Catches: 11

A wicket-keeper from Haryana, who in 2002, at age 20, scored 115 not out against West Indies, at Antigua therefore making him the youngest wicket-keeper to score a Test century. Unfortunately, he could not hold his place due to the emergence of Parthiv Patel.

RAUL, Sanjay Susanta
Born: October 6, 1976
Batting: Right handed

One Day Internationals
ODI Career: 1998
ODIs Played: 2
ODI Batting
Innings: 2
Highest Score: 8
No. 50s: 0
Runs: 8
Average: 4.00
No. 100s: 0
ODI Bowling & Fielding
Wickets: 1
Best Bowling: 1/13
5 WM: 0
Stumpings: 0
Runs: 27
Average: 27.00
Catches: 0

A middle order batsman from Orissa who played both his ODI's against Pakistan at the Sahara 'Friendship' Cup Tournament, held in Toronto, in 1998.

RAZDAN, Vivek
Born: August 25, 1969
Batting: Right handed
Bowling: Right arm medium-fast

Tests
Test Career: 1989
Cap Number: 188
Tests Played: 2
Test Batting
Innings: 2
Highest Score: 6*
No. 50s: 0
Runs: 6
Average: 6.00
No. 100s: 0
Test Bowling & Fielding
Wickets: 5
Best Bowling: 5/79
5 WI: 1
Catches: 0
Runs: 141
Average: 28.19
10 WM: 0
Stumpings: 0

One Day Internationals
ODI Career: 1989-90
ODIs Played: 3
ODI Batting
Innings: 3
Highest Score: 18
No. 50s: 0
Runs: 23
Average: 11.50
No. 100s: 0
ODI Bowling & Fielding
Wickets: 1
Best Bowling: 1/37
5 WM: 0
Stumpings: 0
Runs: 77
Average: 77.00
Catches: 4

A fast bowler from Delhi who netted an impressive 5/79 against Pakistan in his second and final Test. His one and only wicket at ODI level was Pakistan's highest Test run scorer Javed Miandad.

REDDY, Bharath
Born: November 12, 1954
Batting: Right handed

Tests
Test Career: 1979
Cap Number: 144
Tests Played: 4
Test Batting
Innings: 5
Highest Score: 21
No. 50s: 0
Runs: 38
Average: 9.50
No. 100s: 0
Test Bowling & Fielding
Wickets: 0
Best Bowling:
5 WI: 0
Catches: 9
Runs: 0
Average: 0.00
10 WM: 0
Stumpings: 2

One Day Internationals
ODI Career: 1978-81
ODIs Played: 3
ODI Batting
Innings: 2
Highest Score: 8*
No. 50s: 0
Runs: 11
Average: 8.00
No. 100s: 0
ODI Bowling & Fielding
Wickets: 0
Best Bowling:
5 WM: 0
Stumpings: 0
Runs: 0
Average: 0.00
Catches: 2

A wicket-keeper from Chennai who replaced veteran keeper Syed Kirmani in 1979. He played all his four Tests in England but could not consolidate a regular spot in the side. Reddy was omitted when the selectors had a change of heart and reinstated Kirmani.

REGE, Madhusudan Ramachandra
Born: March 18, 1924
Batting: Right handed
Bowling: Right arm off-break

Tests
Test Career: 1949
Cap Number: 51
Tests Played: 1
Test Batting
Innings: 2
Highest Score: 15
No. 50s: 0
Runs: 15
Average: 7.50
No. 100s: 0

Test Bowling & Fielding

Wickets:	0	Runs:	0
Best Bowling:		Average:	0.00
5 WI:	0	10 WM:	0
Catches:	1	Stumpings:	0

An opening batsman who was selected for only one Test against West Indies, at Chennai in 1949, where he made 15 in the first innings and a duck in the second.

ROY, Ambar Khirid

Born:	June 5, 1945
Batting:	Left handed
Bowling:	Right arm fast

Tests

Test Career:	1969		
Cap Number:	121		
Tests Played:	4		

Test Batting

Innings:	7	Runs:	91
Highest Score:	48	Average:	13.00
No. 50s:	0	No. 100s:	0

Test Bowling & Fielding

Wickets:	0	Runs:	0
Best Bowling:		Average:	0.00
5 WI:	0	10 WM:	0
Catches:	0	Stumpings:	0

Nephew of Pankaj Roy, Ambar Khirid Roy was a left hander who played his four Tests against New Zealand and Australia in 1969. Originally from Kolkata.

ROY, Pankaj

Born:	May 31, 1928
Batting:	Right handed
Bowling:	Right arm medium

Tests

Test Career:	1951-60
Cap Number:	54
Tests Played:	43

Test Batting

Innings:	79	Runs:	2,442
Highest Score:	173	Average:	32.56
No. 50s:	9	No. 100s:	5

Test Bowling & Fielding

Wickets:	0	Runs:	0
Best Bowling:		Average:	0.00
5 WI:	0	10 WM:	0
Catches:	16	Stumpings:	0

A bespectacled opener who scored two of his five centuries in his maiden Test series against England in 1951-52. However he suffered a severe form slump a year later. Roy regained form and went on to play 43 Tests for his country and eventually captained India in one Test against England, in 1959. However he is best remembered for his 431 partnership with Vinoo Mankad against New Zealand, at Chennai in 1956, which to date remains an all-time Test record for the first wicket. It was during that marathon partnership that he made his highest score of 173. Roy retired with a Test average of 32. His son, Pranab, later played Test cricket for India.

ROY, Pranab

Born:	February 10, 1957
Batting:	Right handed

Tests

Test Career:	1982
Cap Number:	156
Tests Played:	2

Test Batting

Innings:	3	Runs:	71
Highest Score:	60*	Average:	35.50
No. 50s:	1	No. 100s:	0

Test Bowling & Fielding

Wickets:	0	Runs:	0
Best Bowling:		Average:	0.00
5 WI:	0	10 WM:	0
Catches:	1	Stumpings:	0

An opening batsman from Kolkata, Pranab Roy, the son of Pankaj Roy, made 60 not out on debut against England at Chennai. Played two Tests, both against England.

SALVI, Aavishkar Madhav

Born:	October 20, 1981
Batting:	Right handed
Bowling:	Right arm medium

One Day Internationals

ODI Career:	2003
ODIs Played:	4

ODI Batting

Innings:	3	Runs:	4
Highest Score:	4*	Average:	2.00
No. 50s:	0	No. 100s:	0

ODI Bowling & Fielding

Wickets:	4	Runs:	120
Best Bowling:	2/15	Average:	30.00
5 WM:	0	Catches:	2
Stumpings:	0		

A lanky right arm pace bowler from Mumbai, Salvi developed into a promising seamer which earned him a guernsey in the One Day side against Bangladesh at Dhaka in 2003. Has played just the three ODI matches but has not been ruled out of another call up.

SANDHU, Balwinder Singh

Born:	August 3, 1956
Batting:	Right handed
Bowling:	Right arm medium-fast

Tests

Test Career:	1983
Cap Number:	162
Tests Played:	8

Test Batting

Innings:	11	Runs:	214
Highest Score:	71	Average:	30.57
No. 50s:	2	No. 100s:	0

Test Bowling & Fielding

Wickets:	10	Runs:	557
Best Bowling:	3/87	Average:	55.70
5 WI:	0	10 WM:	0
Catches:	1	Stumpings:	0

One Day Internationals

ODI Career:	1982-84
ODIs Played:	22

ODI Batting

Innings:	7	Runs:	51
Highest Score:	16*	Average:	12.75
No. 50s:	0	No. 100s:	0

ODI Bowling & Fielding

Wickets:	16	Runs:	763
Best Bowling:	3/27	Average:	47.68
5 WM:	0	Catches:	5
Stumpings:	0		

A pace bowler from Bombay, Sandhu proved he was no bunny with the bat scoring 71, coming in at number nine, on debut against Pakistan at Hyderabad in 1982. A handy limited overs player, he took the vital wickets of Gordon Greenidge and Faoud Bacchus in India's 1983 World Cup win over the West Indies.

SANGHVI, Rahul Laxman

Born:	September 3, 1974
Batting:	Left handed
Bowling:	Left arm off-break

Tests

Test Career:	2000
Cap Number:	234
Tests Played:	1

Test Batting

Innings:	2	Runs:	2
Highest Score:	2	Average:	1.00
No. 50s:	0	No. 100s:	0

Test Bowling & Fielding

Wickets:	2	Runs:	78
Best Bowling:	2/67	Average:	39.00
5 WI:	0	10 WM:	0
Catches:	0	Stumpings:	0

One Day Internationals

ODI Career:	1998
ODIs Played:	10

ODI Batting

Innings:	2	Runs:	8
Highest Score:	8	Average:	4.00
No. 50s:	0	No. 100s:	0

ODI Bowling & Fielding

Wickets:	10	Runs:	399
Best Bowling:	3/29	Average:	39.89
5 WM:	0	Catches:	4
Stumpings:	0		

Mentored by Bishen Bedi, Sanghvi worked hard for his place in the Indian side and performed reasonably well in the ten One Day Internationals he participated in. He played the one Test against Australia, at Mumbai in 2000.

SARDESAI, Dilip Narayan

Born:	August 8, 1940
Batting:	Right handed
Bowling:	Right arm medium

Tests

Test Career:	1961-72
Cap Number:	103
Tests Played:	30

Test Batting

Innings:	55	Runs:	2,001
Highest Score:	212	Average:	39.23
No. 50s:	9	No. 100s:	5

Test Bowling & Fielding

Wickets:	0	Runs:	45
Best Bowling:	0	Average:	0.00
5 WI:	0	10 WM:	0
Catches:	0	Stumpings:	0

Although a good player of spin, Sardesai welcomed the mighty West Indian pace attack during the 1971 tour of the Carribean with two hundreds and a double century, amassing over 600 runs in the series. He played his best cricket during the twilight of his career.

SARWATE, Chandrasekhar Trimbak

Born:	July 22, 1920
Batting:	Right handed
Bowling:	Right arm medium

Tests

Test Career:	1946-51
Cap Number:	34
Tests Played:	9

Test Batting

Innings:	17	Runs:	208
Highest Score:	37	Average:	13.00
No. 50s:	0	No. 100s:	0

Test Bowling & Fielding

Wickets:	3	Runs:	374
Best Bowling:	1/16	Average:	124.66
5 WI:	0	10 WM:	0
Catches:	0	Stumpings:	0

He enjoyed a long and distinguished first class career but could only manage modest results when playing Tests. Sarwate became a national selector and was a fingerprint expert by trade.

SAXENA, Ramesh Chand

Born:	September 20, 1940
Batting:	Right handed
Bowling:	Right arm leg-break

Tests

Test Career:	1967
Cap Number:	115
Tests Played:	1

Test Batting

Innings:	2	Runs:	25
Highest Score:	16	Average:	12.50
No. 50s:	0	No. 100s:	0

Test Bowling & Fielding

Wickets:	0	Runs:	1
Best Bowling:	0/11	Average:	0.00
5 WI:	0	10 WM:	0
Catches:	0	Stumpings:	0

A right handed batsmen and part time leg spinner from Delhi who played his one and only Test against England at Headingley in 1967.

SEHWAG, Virender

Born:	October 20, 1978
Batting:	Right handed
Bowling:	Right arm off-break

Tests
Test Career: 2001-06
Cap Number: 239
Tests Played: 49

Test Batting

Innings:	81	Runs:	4,066
Highest Score:	309	Average:	52.12
No. 50s:	12	No. 100s:	12

Test Bowling & Fielding

Wickets:	12	Runs:	628
Best Bowling:	3/33	Average:	52.33
5 WI:	0	10 WM:	0
Catches:	38	Stumpings:	0

One Day Internationals
ODI Career: 1999-06
ODIs Played: 152

ODI Batting

Innings:	149	Runs:	4,608
Highest Score:	130	Average:	32.45
No. 50s:	23	No. 100s:	7

ODI Bowling & Fielding

Wickets:	69	Runs:	2,753
Best Bowling:	3/25	Average:	39.09
5 WM:	0	Catches:	64
Stumpings:	0		

A cracking 105 on debut against South Africa in November 2001 was a sign of things to come from this compact, but highly talented right hander. By the start of 2002, Virender Sehwag was elevated from the middle order to opener and became an overnight run machine to the point where he became universally considered the best Indian opener since Sunil Gavaskar. Sehwag also has the enviable ability to convert most starts into high scores, as statistically, every second fifty becomes a century. Of his 12 tons, Sehwag has scored two double centuries, 254 & 201 both against Pakistan. In April 2004, he became the first, and to date the only, Indian batsman to score a triple century when he smashed an amazing 309 again against arch rival Pakistan at Multan. In typical style, he notched up his 300 (from 364 balls) with a huge six. In December 2005, Virender Sehwag was appointed caretaker captain against Sri Lanka in the 3rd Test at Ahmedabad.

SEKHAR, Thirumalai Ananthanpillai
Born: March 28, 1956
Batting: Right handed
Bowling: Right arm medium-fast

Tests
Test Career: 1983
Cap Number: 163
Tests Played: 2

Test Batting

Innings:	1	Runs:	0
Highest Score:	0*	Average:	0.00
No. 50s:	0	No. 100s:	0

Test Bowling & Fielding

Wickets:	0	Runs:	129
Best Bowling:		Average:	0.00
5 WI:	0	10 WM:	0
Catches:	0	Stumpings:	0

One Day Internationals
ODI Career: 1983-85
ODIs Played: 4

ODI Batting

Innings:	0	Runs:	0
Highest Score:	0	Average:	0.00
No. 50s:	0	No. 100s:	0

ODI Bowling & Fielding

Wickets:	5	Runs:	128
Best Bowling:	3/23	Average:	25.60
5 WM:	0	Catches:	0
Stumpings:	0		

A pace bowler from Chennai who made his Test debut against Pakistan at Lahore in 1983. Played just the one more Test and a handful of One Day Internationals.

SEN, Probir Kumar
Born: May 31, 1926
Batting: Right handed
Wicket Keeper

Tests
Test Career: 1948-52
Cap Number: 43
Tests Played: 14

Test Batting

Innings:	18	Runs:	165
Highest Score:	25	Average:	11.78
No. 50s:	0	No. 100s:	0

Test Bowling & Fielding

Wickets:	0	Runs:	0
Best Bowling:		Average:	0.00
5 WI:	0	10 WM:	0
Catches:	20	Stumpings:	11

Took over the number one keeper's mantle from JK Irani during the 1947/48 tour and never looked back. Clean and agile behind the stumps, Sen became a master at stumpings and gave India exceptional service during his five years at Test level. A handy batsmen and some believe India's finest keeper alongside Syed Kirmani.

SENGUPTA, Apoorva Kumar
Born: August 3, 1939
Batting: Right handed
Bowling: Right arm leg-break

Tests
Test Career: 1958-59
Cap Number: 89
Tests Played: 1

Test Batting

Innings:	2	Runs:	9
Highest Score:	8	Average:	4.50
No. 50s:	0	No. 100s:	0

Test Bowling & Fielding

Wickets:	0	Runs:	0
Best Bowling:		Average:	0.00
5 WI:	0	10 WM:	0
Catches:	0	Stumpings:	0

A leg break, googly bowler from Lucknow who played just the one Test against West Indies at Chennai, in 1958.

SHARMA, Ajay Kumar

Born: April 3, 1964
Batting: Right handed
Bowling: Left arm off-break

Tests

Test Career:	1988		
Cap Number:	182		
Tests Played:	1		

Test Batting

Innings:	2	Runs:	53
Highest Score:	30	Average:	26.50
No. 50s:	0	No. 100s:	0

Test Bowling & Fielding

Wickets:	0	Runs:	9
Best Bowling:	0/9	Average:	0.00
5 WI:	0	10 WM:	0
Catches:	1	Stumpings:	0

One Day Internationals

ODI Career:	1988-93		
ODIs Played:	31		

ODI Batting

Innings:	27	Runs:	424
Highest Score:	59*	Average:	20.19
No. 50s:	3	No. 100s:	0

ODI Bowling & Fielding

Wickets:	15	Runs:	875
Best Bowling:	3/41	Average:	58.33
5 WM:	0	Catches:	6
Stumpings:	0		

Touted as an all rounder, Ajay Sharma made his Test debut against West Indies at Chennai in 1988 but this would be the only time that he would don the whites of Test cricket. He was a handy ODI player from 1988 to 1993 but in 2000 was embroiled in a match fixing controversy that saw him suspended for life.

SHARMA, Chetan

Born: January 3, 1966
Batting: Right handed
Bowling: Right arm medium-fast

Tests

Test Career:	1984-89		
Cap Number:	167		
Tests Played:	23		

Test Batting

Innings:	27	Runs:	396
Highest Score:	54	Average:	22.00
No. 50s:	1	No. 100s:	0

Test Bowling & Fielding

Wickets:	61	Runs:	2,163
Best Bowling:	6/58	Average:	35.45
5 WI:	4	10 WM:	1
Catches:	7	Stumpings:	0

One Day Internationals

ODI Career:	1983-94		
ODIs Played:	65		

ODI Batting

Innings:	35	Runs:	456
Highest Score:	101*	Average:	24.00
No. 50s:	0	No. 100s:	1

ODI Bowling & Fielding

Wickets:	67	Runs:	2,336
Best Bowling:	3/22	Average:	34.86
5 WM:	0	Catches:	7
Stumpings:	0		

Although considered short for a genuine pace bowler, Chetan Sharma's powerful physique and competitive nature made up for any lack of inches. He bowled in tandem with Kapil Dev for most of his Test career and took five wickets in an innings on four occasions and ten in a match (10/188) against England in 1986. That feat saw him become the first Indian to take ten wickets in a Test match on English soil. He was also the first bowler, from any nation, to take a hat-trick in World Cup competition. Handy with the bat at both Test and ODI's, he made his highest Test score of 54 against Australia in 1985 when he was sent in as night-watchman. His only century at limited overs competition was a dour 101 not out against England at Kanpur in 1989.

SHARMA, Gopal

Born: August 3, 1960
Batting: Right handed
Bowling: Right arm off-break

Tests

Test Career:	1985-90		
Cap Number:	170		
Tests Played:	5		

Test Batting

Innings:	4	Runs:	11
Highest Score:	10*	Average:	3.66
No. 50s:	0	No. 100s:	0

Test Bowling & Fielding

Wickets:	10	Runs:	418
Best Bowling:	4/88	Average:	41.79
5 WI:	0	10 WM:	0
Catches:	2	Stumpings:	0

One Day Internationals

ODI Career:	1985-87		
ODIs Played:	11		

ODI Batting

Innings:	2	Runs:	11
Highest Score:	7	Average:	5.50
No. 50s:	0	No. 100s:	0

ODI Bowling & Fielding

Wickets:	10	Runs:	361
Best Bowling:	3/29	Average:	36.10
5 WM:	0	Catches:	2
Stumpings:	0		

The first cricketer from Uttar Pradesh to represent India since the Maharajkumar of Vizianagaram in 1936, off-spinner Sharma made his Test debut against India at Kanpur in 1984 but struggled to hold a regular spot.

SHARMA, Joginder

Born: October 23, 1983
Batting: Right handed
Bowling: Right arm medium-fast

One Day Internationals

ODI Career:	2004		
ODIs Played:	3		

ODI Batting

Innings:	2	Runs:	34
Highest Score:	29*	Average:	34.00
No. 50s:	0	No. 100s:	0

ODI Bowling & Fielding

Wickets:	1	Runs:	99
Best Bowling:	1/28	Average:	99.00
5 WM:	0	Catches:	3
Stumpings:	0		

A right arm fast seam bowler who is also a capable batsman, Joginder Sharma has played three ODI's against Bangladesh in 2004.

SHARMA, Parthasarathy Harishchandra

Born:	January 5, 1948
Batting:	Right handed
Bowling:	Right arm medium

Tests

Test Career:	1974-77		
Cap Number:	134		
Tests Played:	5		

Test Batting

Innings:	10	Runs:	187
Highest Score:	54	Average:	18.69
No. 50s:	1	No. 100s:	0

Test Bowling & Fielding

Wickets:	0	Runs:	8
Best Bowling:	0/8	Average:	0.00
5 WI:	0	10 WM:	0
Catches:	1	Stumpings:	0

One Day Internationals

ODI Career:	1976		
ODIs Played:	2		

ODI Batting

Innings:	2	Runs:	20
Highest Score:	14	Average:	10.00
No. 50s:	0	No. 100s:	0

ODI Bowling & Fielding

Wickets:	0	Runs:	0
Best Bowling:		Average:	0.00
5 WM:	0	Catches:	0
Stumpings:	0		

A right-hand batsman from Rajasthan, Sharma made an impressive debut against the West Indies at New Delhi in 1974 scoring what would be a career high 54 followed by 49 in the second innings. He failed to emulate similar performances in his next four Tests thus leading to his permanent omission from the national squad.

SHARMA, Sanjeev Kumar

Born:	August 25, 1965
Batting:	Right handed
Bowling:	Right arm medium

Tests

Test Career:	1988-90		
Cap Number:	184		
Tests Played:	2		

Test Batting

Innings:	3	Runs:	56
Highest Score:	38	Average:	28.00
No. 50s:	0	No. 100s:	0

Test Bowling & Fielding

Wickets:	6	Runs:	247
Best Bowling:	3/37	Average:	41.16
5 WI:	0	10 WM:	0
Catches:	1	Stumpings:	0

One Day Internationals

ODI Career:	1988-90		
ODIs Played:	23		

ODI Batting

Innings:	12	Runs:	80
Highest Score:	28	Average:	10.00
No. 50s:	0	No. 100s:	0

ODI Bowling & Fielding

Wickets:	22	Runs:	813
Best Bowling:	5/26	Average:	36.95
5 WM:	1	Catches:	7
Stumpings:	0		

A right arm medium pacer from Delhi who made hist Test debut against New Zealand at Hyderabad in 1988/89.

SHARMA, Yashpal

Born:	August 11, 1954
Batting:	Right handed
Bowling:	Right arm medium

Tests

Test Career:	1979-83		
Cap Number:	145		
Tests Played:	37		

Test Batting

Innings:	59	Runs:	1,606
Highest Score:	140	Average:	33.45
No. 50s:	9	No. 100s:	2

Test Bowling & Fielding

Wickets:	1	Runs:	17
Best Bowling:	1/6	Average:	17.00
5 WI:	0	10 WM:	0
Catches:	16	Stumpings:	0

One Day Internationals

ODI Career:	1978-85		
ODIs Played:	42		

ODI Batting

Innings:	40	Runs:	883
Highest Score:	89	Average:	28.48
No. 50s:	4	No. 100s:	10

ODI Bowling & Fielding

Wickets:	1	Runs:	199
Best Bowling:	1/27	Average:	0.00
5 WM:	0	Catches:	10
Stumpings:	0		

A courageous middle order batsman from Punjab, Yashpal Sharma was servicable in both Tests and ODI's. He made his Test dedut against England in 1979 and his highest score of 140 was also against England in 1981/82 at Chennai. A part time wicket-keeper, Sharma was a member of India's 1983 victorious World Cup side.

SHASTRI, Ravishankar Jayadritha (Ravi)

Born:	May 27, 1962
Batting:	Right handed
Bowling:	Left arm off-break

Tests

Test Career:	1981-92
Cap Number:	151
Tests Played:	80

Test Batting

Innings:	121	Runs:	3,830
Highest Score:	206	Average:	35.79
No. 50s:	12	No. 100s:	11

Test Bowling & Fielding

Wickets:	151	Runs:	6,185
Best Bowling:	5/75	Average:	40.96
5 WI:	2	10 WM:	0
Catches:	36	Stumpings:	0

One Day Internationals

ODI Career:	1981-92
ODIs Played:	150

ODI Batting

Innings:	128	Runs:	3,108
Highest Score:	109	Average:	29.04
No. 50s:	18	No. 100s:	4

ODI Bowling & Fielding

Wickets:	129	Runs:	4,650
Best Bowling:	5/15	Average:	36.04
5 WM:	1	Catches:	40
Stumpings:	0		

Tall, handsome and athletic, Ravi Shastri was a consistent performer for India for just over a decade. Considered in many corners as a batsman who could bowl a bit there are those who would argue that Shastri would qualify as a genuine all-rounder. In Tests, he averaged just under 36 with the bat, scored 11 Test hundreds, with a highest score of 206 against Australia in Sydney in 1991. As a bowler, he captured 151 wickets with his best 5/75 against Pakistan in 1983/84. His One Day record just as impressive having a scored four centuries and a taken 129 wickets at 36.04. Admired for always giving 100%, the left arm off spinner captained India in one Test, against West Indies at Chennai, in 1987-88, where the home side was victorious. Shastri, who is still a popular figure in world cricket, is a highly respected TV commentator.

SHINDE, Sadu

Born:	August 18, 1923
Batting:	Right handed

Tests

Test Career:	1946-52
Cap Number:	33
Tests Played:	7

Test Batting

Innings:	11	Runs:	85
Highest Score:	14	Average:	14.16
No. 50s:	0	No. 100s:	0

Test Bowling & Fielding

Wickets:	12	Runs:	717
Best Bowling:	6/91	Average:	59.75
5 WI:	0	10 WM:	0
Catches:	0	Stumpings:	0

Apart from his 6/91 against Engand at New Delhi in 1951-52, the tallish leg spinner averaged just over one wicket per match in his 11 Tests.

SHODHAN, Roshan Harshadlal (Deepak)

Born:	October 18, 1928
Batting:	Left handed
Bowling:	Left arm medium

Tests

Test Career:	1952-53
Cap Number:	68
Tests Played:	3

Test Batting

Innings:	4	Runs:	181
Highest Score:	110	Average:	60.33
No. 50s:	0	No. 100s:	1

Test Bowling & Fielding

Wickets:	0	Runs:	26
Best Bowling:		Average:	0.00
5 WI:	0	10 WM:	0
Catches:	0	Stumpings:	0

Shodhan holds the unique, but impressive mantle of being the first Indian to score a ton in his first innings on debut. What makes this feat even more amazing is that Shodhan came in at number eight. He continued his good form during the early days of the West Indies tour but unforunately sustained an injury which kept him out of the following three Tests. At the end of the tour he held a Test average of just over 60 and for reasons unbeknown, was never again selected to play for his country.

SHUKLA, Laxmi Ratan (Bittu)

Born:	May 6, 1981
Batting:	Right handed
Bowling:	Right arm medium

One Day Internationals

ODI Career:	1999
ODIs Played:	3

ODI Batting

Innings:	2	Runs:	18
Highest Score:	13	Average:	9.00
No. 50s:	0	No. 100s:	0

ODI Bowling & Fielding

Wickets:	1	Runs:	94
Best Bowling:	1/25	Average:	94.00
5 WM:	0	Catches:	1
Stumpings:	0		

An all rounder who showed plenty of promise as a youngster. Made his ODI debut against Sri Lanka at Nagpur in 1999.

SHUKLA, Rakesh Chandra

Born:	February 4, 1948
Batting:	Right handed
Bowling:	Right arm leg-break

Tests

Test Career:	1982
Cap Number:	160
Tests Played:	1

Test Batting

Innings:	0	Runs:	0
Highest Score:	0	Average:	0.00
No. 50s:	0	No. 100s:	0

Test Bowling & Fielding			
Wickets:	2	Runs:	152
Best Bowling:	2/82	Average:	76.00
5 WI:	0	10 WM:	0
Catches:	0	Stumpings:	0

A leg break bowler from Kanpur, Uttar Pradesh, Shukla is another who played just the one Test. His opportunity came in 1982 against Sri Lanka at Chennai.

SIDDIQUI, Iqbal Rashid

Born:	December 26, 1974
Batting:	Right handed
Bowling:	Right arm medium-fast

Tests

Test Career:	2001		
Cap Number:	241		
Tests Played:	1		
Test Batting			
Innings:	2	Runs:	29
Highest Score:	24	Average:	29.00
No. 50s:	0	No. 100s:	0
Test Bowling & Fielding			
Wickets:	1	Runs:	48
Best Bowling:	1/32	Average:	48.00
5 WI:	0	10 WM:	0
Catches:	1	Stumpings:	0

Fiery right arm pace bowler from Maharashtra who is one of several to have played just the one Test. Siddiqui got his one and only opportunity in 2001 when he was selected to play against England at Chandigarh. His only wicket was that of Englishman Graham Thorpe.

SIDHU, Navjot Singh

Born:	October 20, 1963
Batting:	Right handed
Bowling:	Right arm medium

Tests

Test Career:	1983-99		
Cap Number:	166		
Tests Played:	51		
Test Batting			
Innings:	78	Runs:	3,202
Highest Score:	201	Average:	42.13
No. 50s:	15	No. 100s:	9
Test Bowling & Fielding			
Wickets:	0	Runs:	9
Best Bowling:	0/9	Average:	0.00
5 WI:	0	10 WM:	0
Catches:	9	Stumpings:	0

One Day Internationals

ODI Career:	1987-98		
ODIs Played:	136		
ODI Batting			
Innings:	127	Runs:	4,413
Highest Score:	134*	Average:	37.08
No. 50s:	33	No. 100s:	6
ODI Bowling & Fielding			
Wickets:	0	Runs:	3
Best Bowling:	0/3	Average:	0.00
5 WM:	0	Catches:	20
Stumpings:	0		

Shortly after his Test debut against West Indies at Ahmedabad in 1983, Navjot Sidhu was considered too conservative for limited overs cricket. In fact, he made his ODI debut some four years later and revolutionised his batting style. He was selected in the 1987 World Cup squad and instantly opened up the shoulders. He made four successive half centuries with scores of 73, 75, 51 & 55, but more importantly showed the cricketing world that he was more than making up the numbers when playing the shorter version of the game. His new found flair did not detract from his Test performances as his average of 42.13 would indicate. His finest hour, well hours for that matter, occurred during a patient and meticulous 201 against West Indies in 1996, which took over 10 hours to compile.

SINGH, Amar

Born:	December 4, 1910
Batting:	Right handed
Bowling:	Right arm medium-fast

Tests

Test Career:	1932-36		
Cap Number:	1		
Tests Played:	7		
Test Batting			
Innings:	14	Runs:	292
Highest Score:	51	Average:	22.46
No. 50s:	1	No. 100s:	0
Test Bowling & Fielding			
Wickets:	28	Runs:	858
Best Bowling:	7/86	Average:	30.64
5 WI:	2	10 WM:	0
Catches:	3	Stumpings:	0

Credited with India's 'number one Test cap', having played in India's inaugural Test against England at Lord's in 1932, today, Amar Singh, is still considered one of India's finest fast bowlers. Originally, from Gujarat, Singh could also handle himself with the willow hitting a swashbuckling 51 on debut after coming in at number nine. After playing all his seven Tests prior to World War 2, Singh died at the tender age of 29.

SINGH, Amritsar Govindsingh (Kripal)

Born:	August 6, 1933
Batting:	Right handed
Bowling:	Right arm off-break

Tests

Test Career:	1955-64		
Cap Number:	75		
Tests Played:	14		
Test Batting			
Innings:	20	Runs:	422
Highest Score:	100*	Average:	28.13
No. 50s:	2	No. 100s:	1
Test Bowling & Fielding			
Wickets:	10	Runs:	584
Best Bowling:	3/43	Average:	58.39
5 WI:	0	10 WM:	0
Catches:	4	Stumpings:	0

Got off to absolute flyer scoring 100 not out on debut against New Zaland at Hyderabad.

However 13 Tests, and nine years later that hundred still stands alone alongside Kripal Singh's final Test figures. He never really cemented a spot during his career, which may have led to his inconsistent performances. Another who excelled in Ranji Trophy competition.

SINGH, Bhupinder

Born: April 1, 1965
Batting: Right handed
Bowling: Right arm medium-fast

One Day Internationals

ODI Career: 1994
ODIs Played: 2

ODI Batting

Innings:	1	Runs:	6
Highest Score:	6	Average:	6.00
No. 50s:	0	No. 100s:	0

ODI Bowling & Fielding

Wickets:	3	Runs:	78
Best Bowling:	3/34	Average:	26.00
5 WM:	0	Catches:	0
Stumpings:	0		

A medium pacer from Hoshiarpur, Punjab, who played his two One Day Internationals during the Pepsi Austral-Asia Cup at Sharjah in 1994.

SINGH, Gursharan

Born: March 8, 1963
Batting: Right handed

Tests

Test Career: 1989
Cap Number: 191
Tests Played: 1

Test Batting

Innings:	1	Runs:	18
Highest Score:	18	Average:	18.00
No. 50s:	0	No. 100s:	0

Test Bowling & Fielding

Wickets:	0	Runs:	0
Best Bowling:		Average:	0.00
5 WI:	0	10 WM:	0
Catches:	2	Stumpings:	0

One Day Internationals

ODI Career: 1989/90
ODIs Played: 1

ODI Batting

Innings:	1	Runs:	4
Highest Score:	4	Average:	4.00
No. 50s:	0	No. 100s:	0

ODI Bowling & Fielding

Wickets:	0	Runs:	0
Best Bowling:		Average:	0.00
5 WM:	0	Catches:	1
Stumpings:	0		

A right arm batsman from Amritsar, Punjab, who played one Test against New Zealand at Auckland, in 1989.

SINGH, Hanumant

Born: March 29, 1939
Batting: Right handed
Bowling: Right arm leg-break

Tests

Test Career: 1964-69
Cap Number: 108
Tests Played: 14

Test Batting

Innings:	24	Runs:	686
Highest Score:	105	Average:	31.18
No. 50s:	5	No. 100s:	1

Test Bowling & Fielding

Wickets:	0	Runs:	51
Best Bowling:		Average:	0.00
5 WI:	0	10 WM:	0
Catches:	11	Stumpings:	0

A.K.A Maharajkumar of Banswara. He scored a century on debut against England at New Delhi in 1964, but did not reach triple figures in his 13 Tests thereafter, although fell six short against Australia in Chennai. He finished his career with a modest average of 31.18 then later became an ICC match referee. From a family of cricketers, his cousin Prince Indrajitsinhji played four Tests for India from 1964 to 1969 and his uncle, Kumar Shri Ranjitsinhji played Test cricket for England between 1896 to 1902.

SINGH, Harbhajan

Born: July 3, 1980
Batting: Right handed
Bowling: Right arm off-break

Tests

Test Career: 1998-06
Cap Number: 215
Tests Played: 57

Test Batting

Innings:	79	Runs:	986
Highest Score:	66	Average:	16.16
No. 50s:	2	No. 100s:	0

Test Bowling & Fielding

Wickets:	238	Runs:	7,108
Best Bowling:	8/84	Average:	29.86
5 WI:	19	10 WM:	4
Catches:	30	Stumpings:	0

One Day Internationals

ODI Career: 1998-06
ODIs Played: 129

ODI Batting

Innings:	65	Runs:	604
Highest Score:	46	Average:	13.13
No. 50s:	0	No. 100s:	0

ODI Bowling & Fielding

Wickets:	154	Runs:	4,804
Best Bowling:	5/31	Average:	31.19
5 WM:	2	Catches:	38
Stumpings:	0		

Affectionately dubbed The Turbanator, - a dual purpose nickname which combines the off-spinner's bowling prowess and the familiar black turban he dons each time he takes the field, Harbhajan Singh, is now duly recognised an one of India's all time great spin bowlers. After making his Test debut against Australia at Bangalore in 1998, Singh was pulled up early in his career for a suspect bowling action but immediately remedied his action. From then on, 'Bhajj', the handle bestowed on him by his teammates, went from strength to strength. Singh 'arrived' as a world class bowler in 2001 during the home series against the Australians. During the Second Test of the Border/Gavaskar series at Kolkata, Singh, after already dismissing Matthew Hayden and Mark Waugh, trapped future Aussie captain Ricky Ponting leg before. His next two deliveries were complete replicas capturing both Adam Gilchrist and Shane Warne dead in front. The three LBW's gave Harbhajan Singh the honour of being the first Indian to claim at hat-trick at Test level. Singh finished with the figures of 7/123 then followed up in the second innings with 6/73 thus helping India cruise to a 171 run victory. But Harbhajan wasn't quite done yet. In the third and final Test in Chennai he again ripped through the Australian batting to give him 7/133 and then in the second innings captured a career best 8/84 which set India on their way to a two wicket and series victory. With 32 wickets in three matches, Harbhajan Singh was the undisputed 'Player of the Series'. Singh, with 238 Test wickets, is currently fifth on India's all time leading wicket-taker list and headed by some of the finest bowlers India has ever produced in Chandrasekhar, Bedi, Dev and Kumble. And while only in his mid 20's, Harbhajan Singh has time, and more importantly, ability on his side which could see him become India's greatest ever wicket-taker by the time he hangs up his turban.

SINGH, Harvinder

Born: December 3, 1977
Batting: Right handed
Bowling: Right arm medium-fast

Tests

Test Career:	1998-01		
Cap Number:	214		
Tests Played:	3		

Test Batting

Innings:	4	Runs:	6
Highest Score:	6	Average:	2.00
No. 50s:	0	No. 100s:	0

Test Bowling & Fielding

Wickets:	4	Runs:	185
Best Bowling:	2/62	Average:	46.25
5 WI:	0	10 WM:	0
Catches:	0	Stumpings:	0

One Day Internationals

ODI Career:	1997-01		
ODIs Played:	16		

ODI Batting

Innings:	5	Runs:	6
Highest Score:	3*	Average:	1.50
No. 50s:	0	No. 100s:	0

ODI Bowling & Fielding

Wickets:	24	Runs:	609
Best Bowling:	3/44	Average:	25.37
5 WM:	0	Catches:	6
Stumpings:	0		

A fast-medium bowler from Amritsar Punjab, Singh played three Tests in all. He made his debut against Australia, at Chennai in 1998 but as he was often wayward, Singh's ODI career, just as his Test career, was short lived.

SINGH, Lall

Born: December 16, 1909
Batting: Right handed

Tests

Test Career:	1932		
Cap Number:	4		
Tests Played:	1		

Test Batting

Innings:	2	Runs:	44
Highest Score:	22	Average:	29.00
No. 50s:	0	No. 100s:	0

Test Bowling & Fielding

Wickets:	0	Runs:	0
Best Bowling:		Average:	0.00
5 WI:	0	10 WM:	0
Catches:	1	Stumpings:	0

Although only having played the one Test - India's inaugural against England in 1932 - Singh, who was athletic with incredible reflexes, was considered the premier fieldsman of his day.

SINGH, Maninder

Born: June 13, 1965
Batting: Right handed
Bowling: Left arm off-break

Tests

Test Career:	1982-93		
Cap Number:	161		
Tests Played:	35		

Test Batting

Innings:	38	Runs:	99
Highest Score:	15	Average:	3.80
No. 50s:	0	No. 100s:	0

Test Bowling & Fielding

Wickets:	88	Runs:	3,288
Best Bowling:	7/27	Average:	37.36
5 WI:	3	10 WM:	2
Catches:	9	Stumpings:	0

One Day Internationals

ODI Career:	1983-93		
ODIs Played:	59		

ODI Batting

Innings:	18	Runs:	49
Highest Score:	8*	Average:	12.25
No. 50s:	0	No. 100s:	0

ODI Bowling & Fielding

Wickets:	66	Runs:	2,066
Best Bowling:	4/22	Average:	31.30
5 WM:	0	Catches:	18
Stumpings:	0		

Like many off spinners in his era, Maninder Singh struggled to break into the Test side early in his career, mainly due to the presence of Bedi and Prasanna. He made his Test debut at age 27 and captured 7/27 against Pakistan at Bangalore in 1986/87. A favourite among the trivia buffs, Singh was the last man dismissed in the historic second Tied Test against Australia at Chennai in 1986.

SINGH, Rabindra Ramanarayan
Born: September 14, 1963
Batting: Left handed
Bowling: Right arm medium-fast

Tests
Test Career: 1998
Cap Number: 217
Tests Played: 1

Test Batting
Innings:	2	Runs:	27
Highest Score:	15	Average:	13.50
No. 50s:	0	No. 100s:	0

Test Bowling & Fielding
Wickets:	0	Runs:	32
Best Bowling:	0/32	Average:	0.00
5 WI:	0	10 WM:	0
Catches:	5	Stumpings:	0

One Day Internationals
ODI Career: 1989-01
ODIs Played: 136

ODI Batting
Innings:	113	Runs:	2,336
Highest Score:	100	Average:	25.95
No. 50s:	9	No. 100s:	1

ODI Bowling & Fielding
Wickets:	69	Runs:	2,985
Best Bowling:	5/22	Average:	43.26
5 WM:	0	Catches:	33
Stumpings:	0		

Trinidad born all rounder, Robin Singh, was a regular member of India's ODI side for the best part of the 1990's. He played his one and only Test against Zimbabwe at Harare in 1998, almost a decade after making his ODI debut. A brilliant cover fieldsman, Singh later became coach of India 'A'.

SINGH, Randhir
Born: August 16, 1957
Batting: Right handed
Bowling: Right arm medium-fast

One Day Internationals
ODI Career: 1981-83
ODIs Played: 2

ODI Batting
Innings:	0	Runs:	0
Highest Score:	0	Average:	0.00
No. 50s:	0	No. 100s:	0

ODI Bowling & Fielding
Wickets:	1	Runs:	48
Best Bowling:	1/30	Average:	48.00
5 WM:	0	Catches:	0
Stumpings:	0		

A pace bowler from Delhi who made his ODI debut against England at Ahmedabad in 1981.

SINGH, Robin
Born: January 1, 1970
Batting: Right handed
Bowling: Right arm medium-fast

Tests
Test Career: 1998-99
Cap Number: 218
Tests Played: 1

Test Batting
Innings:	1	Runs:	0
Highest Score:	0	Average:	0.00
No. 50s:	0	No. 100s:	0

Test Bowling & Fielding
Wickets:	3	Runs:	176
Best Bowling:	2/74	Average:	58.66
5 WI:	0	10 WM:	0
Catches:	1	Stumpings:	0

A fast-medium pacer from Delhi who showed alot of promise and was selected to tour New Zealand in 1998/99. He made his Test debut on the tour and picked up 2/74. Struggled to press for further selection due to the presence of Srinath and Prasad.

SINGH, Rudra Pratap
Born: December 6, 1985
Batting: Right handed
Bowling: Left arm medium-fast

Tests
Test Career: 2006
Cap Number: 252
Tests Played: 2

Test Batting
Innings:	3	Runs:	6
Highest Score:	6	Average:	6.00
No. 50s:	0	No. 100s:	0

Test Bowling & Fielding
Wickets:	9	Runs:	345
Best Bowling:	4/89	Average:	38.33
5 WI:	0	10 WM:	0
Catches:	0	Stumpings:	0

One Day Internationals
ODI Career: 2005-06
ODIs Played: 15

ODI Batting
Innings:	5	Runs:	20
Highest Score:	9*	Average:	20.00
No. 50s:	0	No. 100s:	0

ODI Bowling & Fielding
Wickets:	19	Runs:	561
Best Bowling:	4/35	Average:	29.52
5 WM:	0	Catches:	4
Stumpings:	0		

A left arm pace bowler who was awarded the 'Man of the Match' trophy on his Test debut when he took 4/89 in the first innings against Pakistan at Faisalabad.

SINGH, Rudra Pratap
Born: January 6, 1963
Batting: Right handed
Bowling: Left arm medium-fast

One Day Internationals
ODI Career: 1986
ODIs Played: 2

ODI Batting
Innings:	0	Runs:	0
Highest Score:	0	Average:	0.00
No. 50s:	0	No. 100s:	0

ODI Bowling & Fielding		
Wickets:	1	
Best Bowling:	1/58	
5 WM:	0	
Stumpings:	0	
Runs:	77	
Average:	77.00	
Catches:	0	

A seam bowler from Uttar Pradesh who played his only two ODI's against Australia in 1986. His only ODI wicket was that of one of world's finest limited overs players in Dean Jones.

SINGH, Sarandeep

Born:	October 21, 1979
Batting:	Right handed
Bowling:	Right arm off-break

Tests
Test Career:	2000-02
Cap Number:	233
Tests Played:	3

Test Batting
Innings:	2	Runs:	43
Highest Score:	39*	Average:	43.00
No. 50s:	0	No. 100s:	0

Test Bowling & Fielding
Wickets:	10	Runs:	340
Best Bowling:	4/136	Average:	34.00
5 WI:	0	10 WM:	0
Catches:	1	Stumpings:	0

One Day Internationals
ODI Career:	2002-03
ODIs Played:	5

ODI Batting
Innings:	4	Runs:	47
Highest Score:	19	Average:	15.66
No. 50s:	0	No. 100s:	0

ODI Bowling & Fielding
Wickets:	3	Runs:	180
Best Bowling:	2/34	Average:	60.00
5 WM:	0	Catches:	2
Stumpings:	0		

A right arm off break bowler from Amritsar, Punjab who donned the turban in much the same fashion as the great Bishen Bedi, but unfortunately, like many others, was not blessed with the same talent. He netted a respectable six wickets, 2/70 & 4/136, in his first Test against Zimbabwe at Nagpur.

SINGH, Vikram Raj Vir

Born:	September 17, 1984
Batting:	Right handed
Bowling:	Right arm medium-fast

Tests
Test Career:	2006
Cap Number:	256
Tests Played:	2

Test Batting
Innings:	1	Runs:	2
Highest Score:	2	Average:	2.00
No. 50s:	0	No. 100s:	0

Test Bowling & Fielding
Wickets:	2	Runs:	158
Best Bowling:	2/61	Average:	79.00
5 WI:	0	10 WM:	0
Catches:	0	Stumpings:	0

One Day Internationals
ODI Career:	2006
ODIs Played:	2

ODI Batting
Innings:	1	Runs:	8
Highest Score:	8	Average:	8.00
No. 50s:	0	No. 100s:	0

ODI Bowling & Fielding
Wickets:	0	Runs:	105
Best Bowling:		Average:	0.00
5 WM:	0	Catches:	3
Stumpings:	0		

A genuine 'quickie' who made his Test debut against West Indies at St.Johns, Antigua.

SINGH, Yajurvindra

Born:	August 1, 1952
Batting:	Right handed
Bowling:	Right arm medium

Tests
Test Career:	1977-79
Cap Number:	140
Tests Played:	4

Test Batting
Innings:	7	Runs:	109
Highest Score:	43*	Average:	18.16
No. 50s:	0	No. 100s:	0

Test Bowling & Fielding
Wickets:	0	Runs:	50
Best Bowling:	0/50	Average:	0.00
5 WI:	0	10 WM:	0
Catches:	11	Stumpings:	0

While his Test record is modest at best, Yajurvindra Singh managed to rewrite the record books during his short stint at the highest level. On debut, against England at Bangalore in 1977, Singh took five catches to equal the record (by a non-wicketkeeper) held by Australia's Victor Richardson and in the second innings he took another two catches, to equal the match record record held by Richardson's grandson, Greg Chappell.

SINGH, Yograj

Born:	March 25, 1958
Batting:	Right handed
Bowling:	Right arm medium-fast

Tests
Test Career:	1981
Cap Number:	152
Tests Played:	1

Test Batting
Innings:	2	Runs:	10
Highest Score:	6	Average:	5.00
No. 50s:	0	No. 100s:	0

Test Bowling & Fielding
Wickets:	1	Runs:	63
Best Bowling:	1/63	Average:	63.00
5 WI:	0	10 WM:	0
Catches:	0	Stumpings:	0

One Day Internationals
ODI Career:	1980-81
ODIs Played:	6

ODI Batting			
Innings:	4	Runs:	1
Highest Score:	1	Average:	0.50
No. 50s:	0	No. 100s:	0

ODI Bowling & Fielding			
Wickets:	4	Runs:	186
Best Bowling:	2/44	Average:	46.50
5 WM:	0	Catches:	2
Stumpings:	0		

A right arm medium-fast bowler from Chandigarh who took four wickets in his one Test against New Zealand at Wellington in 1981.

SINGH, Yuvraj

Born:	December 12, 1981
Batting:	Left handed
Bowling:	Left arm off-break

Tests

Test Career:	2003-06
Cap Number:	247
Tests Played:	19

Test Batting			
Innings:	29	Runs:	830
Highest Score:	122	Average:	33.20
No. 50s:	3	No. 100s:	2

Test Bowling & Fielding			
Wickets:	1	Runs:	90
Best Bowling:	1/25	Average:	90.00
5 WI:	0	10 WM:	0
Catches:	21	Stumpings:	0

One Day Internationals

ODI Career:	2000-06
ODIs Played:	154

ODI Batting			
Innings:	140	Runs:	4,232
Highest Score:	139	Average:	35.26
No. 50s:	25	No. 100s:	7

ODI Bowling & Fielding			
Wickets:	41	Runs:	1,558
Best Bowling:	4/6	Average:	38.00
5 WM:	0	Catches:	53
Stumpings:	0		

The son of Yograj Singh who played just the one Test in 1981, Yuvrag, like his father, made his Test debut against New Zealand. A talented middle order batsman who has been in and out of the One Day side, his 2006 form suggests Singh will now push for a more regular spot in both forms of the game.

SIVARAMAKRISHNAN, Laxman

Born:	December 31, 1965
Batting:	Right handed
Bowling:	Right arm leg-break

Tests

Test Career:	1983-86
Cap Number:	164
Tests Played:	9

Test Batting			
Innings:	9	Runs:	130
Highest Score:	25	Average:	16.25
No. 50s:	0	No. 100s:	0

Test Bowling & Fielding			
Wickets:	26	Runs:	1,145
Best Bowling:	6/64	Average:	44.03
5 WI:	3	10 WM:	1
Catches:	9	Stumpings:	0

One Day Internationals

ODI Career:	1985-87
ODIs Played:	16

ODI Batting			
Innings:	4	Runs:	5
Highest Score:	2*	Average:	2.50
No. 50s:	0	No. 100s:	0

ODI Bowling & Fielding			
Wickets:	15	Runs:	538
Best Bowling:	3/35	Average:	35.86
5 WM:	0	Catches:	7
Stumpings:	0		

After capturing 12/181 against England at Mumbai, in 1984 and named 'Player of the Series', tiny 19 year old Laxman Sivaramakrishnan was hailed as India's next great spin bowler. He crushed the myth about leg spinners not having a place in One Day Internationals when he helped steer India to victory in the World Championship of Cricket held in Australia in 1985. But on his return trip 'down under' just a few months later, he could do little to trouble the Australian batsmen and subsequently found himself out of the side. He was recalled for the 1987 World Cup squad but hardly made an impact. Within three years of making his debut, a once promising international career was all but over.

SODHI, Reetinder Singh

Born:	October 18, 1980
Batting:	Right handed
Bowling:	Right arm medium

One Day Internationals

ODI Career:	2000-02
ODIs Played:	18

ODI Batting			
Innings:	14	Runs:	280
Highest Score:	67	Average:	25.45
No. 50s:	2	No. 100s:	0

ODI Bowling & Fielding			
Wickets:	5	Runs:	365
Best Bowling:	2/31	Average:	73.00
5 WM:	0	Catches:	9
Stumpings:	0		

An enthusiastic all rounder who was vice-captain of Sri Lanka's under 19's just prior to making his ODI debut against Zimbabwe, at Cuttack in 2000. He is considered a chance to return to the One Day side if he continues to prosper in the domestic competition.

SOHONI, Sriranga Wasudev (Ranga)

Born:	March 5, 1918
Batting:	Right handed
Bowling:	Right arm medium-fast

Tests

Test Career:	1946-51
Cap Number:	35
Tests Played:	4

Test Batting			
Innings:	7	Runs:	83
Highest Score:	29*	Average:	16.60
No. 50s:	0	No. 100s:	0
Test Bowling & Fielding			
Wickets:	2	Runs:	202
Best Bowling:	1/16	Average:	101.00
5 WI:	0	10 WM:	0
Catches:	2	Stumpings:	0

An all-rounder, 'Ranga' was another who enjoyed success in the Ranji Trophy competition but struggled once on the Test scene.

SOLKAR, Eknath Dhondu
Born: March 18, 1948
Batting: Left handed
Bowling: Left arm medium

Tests
Test Career: 1969-77
Cap Number: 123
Tests Played: 27

Test Batting			
Innings:	48	Runs:	1,068
Highest Score:	102	Average:	25.42
No. 50s:	6	No. 100s:	1
Test Bowling & Fielding			
Wickets:	18	Runs:	1,070
Best Bowling:	3/28	Average:	59.44
5 WI:	0	10 WM:	0
Catches:	53	Stumpings:	0

One Day Internationals
ODI Career: 1974-76
ODIs Played: 7

ODI Batting			
Innings:	6	Runs:	27
Highest Score:	13	Average:	4.50
No. 50s:	0	No. 100s:	0
ODI Bowling & Fielding			
Wickets:	4	Runs:	169
Best Bowling:	2/31	Average:	42.25
5 WM:	0	Catches:	0
Stumpings:	0		

An all rounder in the true sense of the word, Ekki Solkar, was a regular feature of the powerful Indian sides of the mid 1970's. A handy middle order batsman and medium pace bowler, Sokar is best remembered as a fearlerss and highly skilled 'close to the wicket' fieldsman who at one stage held the record for most catches (by a non wicketkeeper) in a Test match - six.

SOMASUNDER, Sujith Bijjahali
Born: December 2, 1972
Batting: Right handed
Bowling: Right arm medium

One Day Internationals
ODI Career: 1996
ODIs Played: 2

ODI Batting			
Innings:	2	Runs:	16
Highest Score:	9	Average:	8.00
No. 50s:	0	No. 100s:	0

ODI Bowling & Fielding			
Wickets:	0	Runs:	0
Best Bowling:	0	Average:	0.00
5 WM:	0	Catches:	0
Stumpings:	0		

A gritty batsman whose dominance in the domestic competition earned him a call up to the ODI side to play South Africa, at Hyderabad in 1996. Many thought Somasunder may have gone on to bigger things but just added one further ODI to his career tally.

SOOD, Man Mohan
Born: July 6, 1939
Batting: Right handed

Tests
Test Career: 1959-60
Cap Number: 98
Tests Played: 1

Test Batting			
Innings:	2	Runs:	3
Highest Score:	3	Average:	1.50
No. 50s:	0	No. 100s:	0
Test Bowling & Fielding			
Wickets:	0	Runs:	0
Best Bowling:	0	Average:	0.00
5 WI:	0	10 WM:	0
Catches:	0	Stumpings:	0

Originally from Lahore, Sood played the one Test against the Richie Benaud led Australians at Chennai, in 1959. He later became a national selector.

SREESANTH, Shanthakumaran
Born: February 6, 1983
Batting: Right handed
Bowling: Right arm medium-fast

Tests
Test Career: 2006
Cap Number: 253
Tests Played: 5

Test Batting			
Innings:	7	Runs:	75
Highest Score:	29*	Average:	18.75
No. 50s:	0	No. 100s:	0
Test Bowling & Fielding			
Wickets:	19	Runs:	566
Best Bowling:	4/70	Average:	29.78
5 WI:	0	10 WM:	0
Catches:	1	Stumpings:	0

One Day Internationals
ODI Career: 2005-06
ODIs Played: 18

ODI Batting			
Innings:	5	Runs:	3
Highest Score:	2*	Average:	1.50
No. 50s:	0	No. 100s:	0
ODI Bowling & Fielding			
Wickets:	24	Runs:	869
Best Bowling:	6/55	Average:	36.20
5 WM:	1	Catches:	2
Stumpings:	0		

After consolidating a position in the One Day side, Sreesanth, a right arm fast-medium pacer, got his opportunity at Test level against England, at Nagpur in 2006. Later that year he was selected on the tour of the West Indies where he took a respectable 10 wickets in the series.

SRIKKANTH, Krishnamachari (Kris)
Born: December 21, 1959
Batting: Right handed
Bowling: Right arm medium

Tests
Test Career: 1981-92
Cap Number: 154
Tests Played: 43

Test Batting
Innings:	72	Runs:	2,062
Highest Score:	123	Average:	29.88
No. 50s:	12	No. 100s:	2

Test Bowling & Fielding
Wickets:	0	Runs:	114
Best Bowling:		Average:	0.00
5 WI:	0	10 WM:	0
Catches:	0	Stumpings:	0

One Day Internationals
ODI Career: 1981-92
ODIs Played: 146

ODI Batting
Innings:	145	Runs:	4,091
Highest Score:	123	Average:	29.01
No. 50s:	27	No. 100s:	4

ODI Bowling & Fielding
Wickets:	25	Runs:	641
Best Bowling:	5/27	Average:	25.64
5 WM:	2	Catches:	42
Stumpings:	0		

Arguably the most aggressive and entertaining batsman of his time, Kris Srikkanth threw away the text book when it came to opening the batting. From the very outset if the ball was there to be hit - hit it he would, much in the same vain as Sri Lanka's Sanath Jayasuria and later, Australia's Adam Gilchrist. It was observed from his very first Test that the highly religious batsmen had a few rituals. When walking out to bat he would look directly into the sun for a considerable amount of time, and then while at the crease there would be constant twitching of the facial area. But these tendencies did not hinder his ability. His first century in Test cricket, when he smashed 116 against Australia in Sydney was scintillating. Naturally, his style suited the shorter version of the game and he played over 140 games, including the 1983 World Cup final where he top scored with 38 in India's memorable win over the highly fancied West Indies. His uncompromising approach did come at a cost and eventually found himself in and out of the Test side. But by the late 80's he was back in favour and in 1989 was appointed captain for the tour of Pakistan where India drew all four Tests. He was replaced by Mohammed Azharuddin and continued to represent India at both Test and One Day level until his retirement in 1992.

SRINATH, Javagal
Born: August 31, 1969
Batting: Right handed
Bowling: Right arm fast

Tests
Test Career: 1991-02
Cap Number: 193
Tests Played: 67

Test Batting
Innings:	92	Runs:	1,009
Highest Score:	76	Average:	14.21
No. 50s:	4	No. 100s:	0

Test Bowling & Fielding
Wickets:	236	Runs:	7,196
Best Bowling:	8/86	Average:	30.49
5 WI:	10	10 WM:	1
Catches:	22	Stumpings:	0

One Day Internationals
ODI Career: 1991-03
ODIs Played: 229

ODI Batting
Innings:	121	Runs:	883
Highest Score:	53	Average:	10.63
No. 50s:	1	No. 100s:	0

ODI Bowling & Fielding
Wickets:	315	Runs:	8,847
Best Bowling:	5/23	Average:	28.08
5 WM:	3	Catches:	32
Stumpings:	0		

In an era where India was the dominant force in spin bowling, Javagal Srinath almost single-handedly put genuine pace bowling on the Indian map. Bowling mainly in-swingers, and then leg cutters later in his career, Srinath became India's fifth highest wicket taker, with 236, but as far as pace bowlers are concerned he was second only to the great Kepi Dev as the other three, Kumble, Bedi & Chandrasekhar are all spin bowlers. He took his best haul of 8/86 against Pakistan at Kolkata in 1998/99. From the moment he made his debut against Australia, in Brisbane, in 1991, Srinath gave his all when representing his country in both Tests and in ODI's, where he played over 200 matches.

SRINIVASAN, Tirumalai Echambadi
Born: October 26, 1950
Batting: Right handed
Bowling: Right arm leg-break

Tests
Test Career: 1981
Cap Number: 153
Tests Played: 1

Test Batting
Innings:	2	Runs:	48
Highest Score:	29	Average:	24.00
No. 50s:	0	No. 100s:	0

Test Bowling & Fielding
Wickets:	0	Runs:	0
Best Bowling:		Average:	0.00
5 WI:	0	10 WM:	0
Catches:	0	Stumpings:	0

One Day Internationals
ODI Career: 1980-81
ODIs Played: 2

ODI Batting			
Innings:	2	Runs:	10
Highest Score:	6	Average:	5.00
No. 50s:	0	No. 100s:	0
ODI Bowling & Fielding			
Wickets:	0	Runs:	0
Best Bowling:		Average:	0.00
5 WM:	0	Catches:	0
Stumpings:	0		

A right handed batsman and occasional leg break bowler from Chennai, Srinivasan played just the one Test against New Zealand, at Auckland in 1981.

SRIRAM, Sridharan

Born:	February 21, 1976
Batting:	Left handed
Bowling:	Left arm medium

One Day Internationals

ODI Career:	2000-04
ODIs Played:	8

ODI Batting			
Innings:	7	Runs:	81
Highest Score:	57	Average:	13.50
No. 50s:	1	No. 100s:	0
ODI Bowling & Fielding			
Wickets:	9	Runs:	274
Best Bowling:	3/43	Average:	30.44
5 WM:	0	Catches:	1
Stumpings:	0		

A capable all rounder who made his ODI debut against South Africa at Nagpur in 2000. He made his highest ODI score of 57 against Bangladesh in 2004. A few credible performances at domestic level saw him press for further international selection in mid 2006.

SUBRAMANYA, Venkataraman

Born:	July 16, 1936
Batting:	Right handed
Bowling:	Right arm leg-break

Tests

Test Career:	1965-68
Cap Number:	111
Tests Played:	9

Test Batting			
Innings:	15	Runs:	263
Highest Score:	75	Average:	18.78
No. 50s:	2	No. 100s:	0
Test Bowling & Fielding			
Wickets:	3	Runs:	201
Best Bowling:	2/32	Average:	67.00
5 WI:	0	10 WM:	0
Catches:	9	Stumpings:	0

A tall and athletic batsman who made his debut against New Zealand at Delhi in 1964/65. "Subbu" played in nine Tests, mainly as a middle order batsman. His 75 against Australia during the summer of 1967/68 was the closest he got to a Test century.

SUDHAKAR RAO, Ramchandra

Born:	August 8, 1952
Batting:	Right handed
Bowling:	Right arm medium
	Wicket Keeper

One Day Internationals

ODI Career:	1975-76
ODIs Played:	1

ODI Batting			
Innings:	1	Runs:	4
Highest Score:	4	Average:	4.00
No. 50s:	0	No. 100s:	0
ODI Bowling & Fielding			
Wickets:	0	Runs:	0
Best Bowling:		Average:	0.00
5 WM:	0	Catches:	1
Stumpings:	0		

A wicket-keeper from Karnataka who played his one and only ODI against New Zealand at Auckland in 1975.

SUNDERAM, Gundibail Rama

Born:	March 29, 1930
Batting:	Right handed
Bowling:	Right arm medium-fast

Tests

Test Career:	1955
Cap Number:	81
Tests Played:	2

Test Batting			
Innings:	1	Runs:	3
Highest Score:	3*	Average:	3.00
No. 50s:	0	No. 100s:	0
Test Bowling & Fielding			
Wickets:	3	Runs:	166
Best Bowling:	2/46	Average:	55.33
5 WI:	0	10 WM:	0
Catches:	0	Stumpings:	0

A right arm, fast-medium pacer who took three career wickets in his only two Tests against New Zealand in 1955.

SURENDRANATH, Raman

Born:	January 4, 1937
Batting:	Right handed
Bowling:	Right arm medium

Tests

Test Career:	1959-61
Cap Number:	88
Tests Played:	11

Test Batting			
Innings:	20	Runs:	136
Highest Score:	27	Average:	10.46
No. 50s:	0	No. 100s:	0
Test Bowling & Fielding			
Wickets:	26	Runs:	1,053
Best Bowling:	5/75	Average:	40.50
5 WI:	2	10 WM:	0
Catches:	4	Stumpings:	0

With the ability to swing the ball in both directions, Raman Surendranath was your typical workhorse medium pacer. He took five wickets in an innings on two ocassions, with a best effort 5/75 against England at The Oval in 1959. A proven performer, it was thought that he should have been selected for more than the 11 tests that stand alongside his name.

SURTI, Rusi Framroze

Born: May 25, 1936
Batting: Left handed
Bowling: Left arm medium

Tests
Test Career: 1960-69
Cap Number: 99
Tests Played: 26

Test Batting
Innings:	48	Runs:	1,263
Highest Score:	99	Average:	28.70
No. 50s:	9	No. 100s:	0

Test Bowling & Fielding
Wickets:	42	Runs:	1,962
Best Bowling:	5/74	Average:	46.71
5 WI:	1	10 WM:	0
Catches:	26	Stumpings:	0

Surti could not gain a regular spot until the 1966/67 series against West Indies. He was unlucky not to score a Test ton when he was caught on 99 against New Zealand, in the final Test at Auckland, in 1968. He later played for Queensland in the Sheffield Shield competition.

SWAMY, Venkatraman Narayan

Born: May 23, 1924
Batting: Right handed
Bowling: Right arm medium-fast

Tests
Test Career: 1955-56
Cap Number: 76
Tests Played: 1

Test Batting
Innings:	0	Runs:	0
Highest Score:	0	Average:	0.00
No. 50s:	0	No. 100s:	0

Test Bowling & Fielding
Wickets:	0	Runs:	45
Best Bowling:		Average:	0.00
5 WI:	0	10 WM:	0
Catches:	0	Stumpings:	0

A medium pacer who played just the one Test against New Zealand, at Hyderabad in 1955. He did not get the chance to bat and had little opportunity to impress with the ball. Originally from Kerala.

TAMHANE, Narendra Shankar

Born: August 4, 1931
Batting: Right handed
Wicket Keeper

Tests
Test Career: 1955-61
Cap Number: 72
Tests Played: 21

Test Batting
Innings:	27	Runs:	225
Highest Score:	54*	Average:	10.22
No. 50s:	1	No. 100s:	0

Test Bowling & Fielding
Wickets:	0	Runs:	0
Best Bowling:		Average:	0.00
5 WI:	0	10 WM:	0
Catches:	35	Stumpings:	16

Touted as the 'accidental keeper' as Tamhane initially donned the gloves when his team's regular keeper was unavailable during a Ranji Trophy match. After making his Test debut against Pakistan at Dhaka in 1955, Tamhane gained the reputation as a stumping specialist, claiming 16 victims in his six year career. His calling card was removing just the one bail when executing a stumping. Handy with the bat with 54 not out as his highest score.

TARAPORE, Keki Khurshedji

Born: December 17, 1910
Batting: Right handed
Bowling: Left arm off-break

Tests
Test Career: 1948-49
Cap Number: 46
Tests Played: 1

Test Batting
Innings:	1	Runs:	2
Highest Score:	2	Average:	2.00
No. 50s:	0	No. 100s:	0

Test Bowling & Fielding
Wickets:	0	Runs:	72
Best Bowling:		Average:	0.00
5 WI:	0	10 WM:	0
Catches:	0	Stumpings:	0

Tarapore was better known as highly influential administrator rather than a Test cricketer. He managed Indian teams to England and the West Indies in 1971 where India was victorious for the first time in the Caribbean.

TENDULKAR, Sachin Ramesh

Born: April 24, 1973
Batting: Right handed
Bowling: Right arm leg-break

Tests
Test Career: 1989-06
Cap Number: 187
Tests Played: 132

Test Batting
Innings:	211	Runs:	10,469
Highest Score:	248*	Average:	55.39
No. 50s:	41	No. 100s:	35

Test Bowling & Fielding
Wickets:	37	Runs:	1,893
Best Bowling:	3/10	Average:	51.16
5 WI:	0	10 WM:	0
Catches:	82	Stumpings:	0

One Day Internationals
ODI Career: 1989-06
ODIs Played: 362

ODI Batting
Innings:	353	Runs:	14,146
Highest Score:	186*	Average:	44.20
No. 50s:	72	No. 100s:	39

ODI Bowling & Fielding
Wickets: 142
Best Bowling: 5/32
5 WM: 2
Stumpings: 0
Runs: 6,194
Average: 43.61
Catches: 107

From his early days as schoolboy prodigy in Mumbai, the brilliant Tendulkar was earmarked for greatness. As a teenager he had been involved in a mammoth 664 run stand with another future Indian Test cricketer Vinod Kambli, and so impressive was Sachin that by the age of 16 he was playing Test cricket. His first Test series saw him thrown in at the deepest of deep ends, having to play arch rival Pakistan on foreign soil. To make matters worse it was one of the few times that the Pakistanis had the pace trio of Imran Khan, Wasim Akram and Waqar Younis fit and available. The baby faced teenager came through his initiation with flying colours, scoring two half centuries in four Tests and leaving Pakistan with a Test average of almost 40. He didn't have to wait long for his first Test century, it came in 1990 at Old Trafford with 119 not out in the second innings of the Second Test against the English. If that alerted the world to the arrival of a new star batsman then his tour to Australia during summer of 1991/92 confirmed it. He scored an unbeaten 148 at the SCG and then a 114 on the rock hard WACA wicket that he still regards as his best ever Test knock. Amazingly Tendulkar played just one Test on home soil in his first 21 outings, and that quirk in fixturing meant India's cricket mad public were at fever pitch when he finally played a full series at home in 1992/93. He didn't let the adoring throng down, plundering a faultless 165 off England at Chennai in the Second Test. The 'little master' was up and running and in the 15 years since he scored that maiden 'home' hundred he has gone on to score a record 35 Test centuries and over 10,000 Test runs. Befitting his standing as one of the greatest batsmen to ever play the game, he can play off both the front and back foot and has mastered every shot in the book. He caresses rather than thrashes the bowling, but when hit by Tendulkar the ball seems to speed to the boundary as if shot by a bazooka. His innings build like a summer's day in his native India, mild at first but with a creeping heat that turns to blistering at its zenith. When playing India, the world's best bowlers have always had one thing on their mind, get Tendulkar, and whilst he hasn't always come out on top he has had some stunning victories like his 116 against arch rival Glenn McGrath at the MCG in 1999. If he is only one of the best Test players of all time then he is surely the best one day cricketer the game has ever seen. That assessment seemed unlikely when it took him 77 matches to score his first ODI century but since scoring that 110 against Australia at Colombo in 1994 he has hit another 38 tons and become the highest scorer in the abbreviated version of the game with over 14,000 runs to his name. He occasionally rolls his arm over, bowling over the wrist straight breaks, and for a champion batsman fields only moderately, but it hardly matters when you are the player that Sir Donald Bradman anointed as the modern cricketer that most reminds him of himself.

UMRIGAR, Pahlan Ratanji (Polly)

Born: March 28, 1926
Batting: Right handed
Bowling: Right arm off-break

Tests

Test Career: 1948-62
Cap Number: 47
Tests Played: 59

Test Batting
Innings: 94
Highest Score: 223
No. 50s: 14
Runs: 3,631
Average: 42.22
No. 100s: 12

Test Bowling & Fielding
Wickets: 35
Best Bowling: 6/74
5 WI: 2
Catches: 33
Runs: 4,725
Average: 42.08
10 WM: 0
Stumpings: 0

Hailed as one of India's finest, the charismatic 'Polly' Umrigar enjoyed a distinguished Test career, spanning over three decades. With 12 centuries and over 3,500 runs, Umrigar held records for most runs and most centuries, as well as most Tests played by an Indian cricketer. He also holds the distinction of being the first Indian to score a Test double century, when he racked up a stunning 223 against New Zealand, at Hyderabad in 1955. In fact India had to wait until the arrival of its next favourite son, Sunil Gavaskar, before Polly's records could be threatened, and eventually broken. Unlike Gavaskar, Umrigar was big in stature and took on the bowling on just about every occasion. He was a handy bowler with a personal best of 6/74 against Pakistan in 1955. He later became Chairman of the selection committee.

UTHAPPA, Aiyudda Robin

Born: November 11, 1985
Batting: Right handed
Bowling: Right arm medium

One Day Internationals

ODI Career: 2006
ODIs Played: 3

ODI Batting
Innings: 3
Highest Score: 86
No. 50s: 1
Runs: 98
Average: 32.66
No. 100s: 0

ODI Bowling & Fielding
Wickets: 0
Best Bowling:
5 WM: 0
Stumpings: 0
Runs: 0
Average: 0.00
Catches: 1

A wicketkeeper-batsman by trade, Robin Uthappa hung up the gloves to focus solely on his batting. And if his first ODI, where he was run out for 86 against England, is anything to go by, then it looks as though Uthappa has made a wise decision. He was selected for the 2006 tour of the Caribbean.

VAIDYA, Prashant Sridhar

Born: September 23, 1967
Batting: Right handed
Bowling: Right arm medium-fast

One Day Internationals
ODI Career: 1995-96
ODIs Played: 4

ODI Batting
Innings:	2	Runs:	15
Highest Score:	12	Average:	7.50
No. 50s:	0	No. 100s:	0

ODI Bowling & Fielding
Wickets:	4	Runs:	174
Best Bowling:	2/41	Average:	43.50
5 WM:	0	Catches:	2
Stumpings:	0		

A medium pacer from Nagpur who played four ODI's between 1995/96. He made his ODI debut against Australia, at Dunedin in 1995.

VENGSARKAR, Dilip Balwant

Born: April 6, 1956
Batting: Right handed
Bowling: Right arm medium

Tests
Test Career: 1976-91
Cap Number: 139
Tests Played: 116

Test Batting
Innings:	185	Runs:	6,868
Highest Score:	166	Average:	42.13
No. 50s:	35	No. 100s:	17

Test Bowling & Fielding
Wickets:	0	Runs:	36
Best Bowling:	0/36	Average:	0.00
5 WI:	0	10 WM:	0
Catches:	78	Stumpings:	0

One Day Internationals
ODI Career: 1976-91
ODIs Played: 129

ODI Batting
Innings:	120	Runs:	3,508
Highest Score:	105	Average:	34.73
No. 50s:	23	No. 100s:	1

ODI Bowling & Fielding
Wickets:	0	Runs:	4
Best Bowling:	0/4	Average:	0.00
5 WM:	0	Catches:	37
Stumpings:	0		

A tall and classy right hand batsman, Vengsarkar, with almost 7,000 Test runs, is heralded as one of India's finest batsmen. He established himself in the late 1970's and 80's batting alongside captain Sunil Gavaskar, Mohinder Amarnath and the diminutive Gundappa Viswanath. He and Viswanath, an interesting combination considering their obvious height differences, held the Indian middle order together on many occasions, their most memorable partnership being their 210 third wicket stand against England at Lord's in 1979, which helped India avoid defeat. Vengsarkar captained India on ten occasions and played in 129 ODI's with a highest score of 105 against England in 1984.

VENKATARAGHAVAN (VENKAT), Srinivasaraghavan

Born: April 21, 1945
Batting: Right handed
Bowling: Right arm off-break

Tests
Test Career: 1965-83
Cap Number: 110
Tests Played: 57

Test Batting
Innings:	76	Runs:	748
Highest Score:	64	Average:	1.68
No. 50s:	2	No. 100s:	0

Test Bowling & Fielding
Wickets:	156	Runs:	5,634
Best Bowling:	8/72	Average:	36.11
5 WI:	3	10 WM:	1
Catches:	44	Stumpings:	0

One Day Internationals
ODI Career: 1974-83
ODIs Played: 15

ODI Batting
Innings:	9	Runs:	54
Highest Score:	26*	Average:	10.80
No. 50s:	0	No. 100s:	0

ODI Bowling & Fielding
Wickets:	5	Runs:	542
Best Bowling:	2/34	Average:	108.40
5 WM:	0	Catches:	4
Stumpings:	0		

A member of the 'fab four' spinners, which included Bishen Bedi, Bhagwat Chandrasekhar and Erapalli Prasanna. Between them they added a new dimension to the art of spin bowling as they worked in unison to torment batsmen throughout the late sixties and seventies. While Bedi & Chandrasekhar were the recognised "Lennon and McCartney" of the quartet, Venkat and Prasanna were constantly vying for a gig between themselves, thus seeing Venkat sidelined more often than not in the early days. It was only once the quartet had disbursed in the late 1970's that he could actually entrench himself in the starting eleven. Superbly fit and durable, Venkat played at the highest level throughout three decades. He captained India in the first two World Cup competitions. By 1980, and at age 35, he was dropped from the side and it looked as if he would join his former spin buddies in the stands. He did for awhile but then in 1983 was picked for the tour of the West Indies. Upon his second, and final, retirement he walked away with 156 wickets at 36.11. He also managed to squeeze in 15 One Day Internationals. He then took on various roles within the cricket fraternity such as manager of the Indian national side and then umpiring at Test and One Day level.

VENKATARAMANA, Margashayam

Born: April 26, 1966
Batting: Right handed
Bowling: Right arm off-break

Tests
Test Career: 1988-89
Cap Number: 185
Tests Played: 1

Test Batting
Innings:	2	Runs:	0
Highest Score:	0*	Average:	0.00
No. 50s:	0	No. 100s:	0

Test Bowling & Fielding
Wickets:	1	Runs:	58
Best Bowling:	1/10	Average:	58.00
5 WI:	0	10 WM:	0
Catches:	1	Stumpings:	0

One Day Internationals
ODI Career: 1988-89
ODIs Played: 1

ODI Batting
Innings:	1	Runs:	0
Highest Score:	0*	Average:	0.00
No. 50s:	0	No. 100s:	0

ODI Bowling & Fielding
Wickets:	2	Runs:	36
Best Bowling:	2/36	Average:	18.00
5 WM:	0	Catches:	0
Stumpings:	0		

An off spinner from Andhra Pradesh who played just the one Test against West Indies at Kingston, in 1988. He only wicket was that of champion opener Desmond Haynes.

VENUGOPAL RAO, Yalaka

Born: February 26, 1982
Batting: Right handed
Bowling: Right arm off-break

One Day Internationals
ODI Career: 2005-06
ODIs Played: 16

ODI Batting
Innings:	11	Runs:	218
Highest Score:	61*	Average:	24.22
No. 50s:	1	No. 100s:	0

ODI Bowling & Fielding
Wickets:	0	Runs:	0
Best Bowling:		Average:	0.00
5 WM:	0	Catches:	6
Stumpings:	0		

A regular for India in ODI's Venugopal Rao is a talented middle order batsman who has yet to realise his full potential. His best effort, a 61 not out against Pakistan, was a sample of his underlying talent.

VISWANATH, Gundappa Rangnath

Born: February 12, 1949
Batting: Right handed
Bowling: Right arm off-break

Tests
Test Career: 1969-83
Cap Number: 124
Tests Played: 91

Test Batting
Innings:	155	Runs:	6,080
Highest Score:	222	Average:	41.93
No. 50s:	35	No. 100s:	14

Test Bowling & Fielding
Wickets:	1	Runs:	46
Best Bowling:	1/11	Average:	46.00
5 WI:	0	10 WM:	0
Catches:	63	Stumpings:	0

One Day Internationals
ODI Career: 1974-82
ODIs Played: 25

ODI Batting
Innings:	23	Runs:	439
Highest Score:	75	Average:	19.95
No. 50s:	2	No. 100s:	0

ODI Bowling & Fielding
Wickets:	0	Runs:	0
Best Bowling:		Average:	0.00
5 WM:	0	Catches:	2
Stumpings:	0		

A diminutive right hand batsmen, standing at 5.4, Gundappa Viswanath was blessed with impeccable timing and footwork. 'Vishy' made his first of 14 centuries on debut against Australia at Kanpur, in 1969, when he scored 137 in the second innings as after a duck in the first. Together with Vengsarker and Amarnath, Viswanath provided the stability the Indian middle order so desperately longed for in the mid 70's to early 80's. He enjoyed a fruitful tour of Australia in 1977/78 where he netted 473 runs at 52.55. Shortly after he notched up centuries against Pakistan and the touring West Indies. However, it was not until the twilight of his career, against England at Chennai, in 1981, when he scored his maiden Test double century and highest score of 222. Brother-in-Law to Indian great Sunil Gavaskar, Viswanath became an ICC Referee in 1999.

VISWANATH, Sadanand

Born: November 29, 1962
Batting: Right handed
 Wicket Keeper

Tests
Test Career: 1985
Cap Number: 172
Tests Played: 3

Test Batting
Innings:	5	Runs:	31
Highest Score:	20	Average:	6.20
No. 50s:	0	No. 100s:	0

Test Bowling & Fielding

Wickets:	0	Runs:	0
Best Bowling:		Average:	0.00
5 WI:	0	10 WM:	0
Catches:	11	Stumpings:	0

One Day Internationals

ODI Career:	1985-88		
ODIs Played:	22		

ODI Batting

Innings:	12	Runs:	72
Highest Score:	23*	Average:	9.00
No. 50s:	0	No. 100s:	0

ODI Bowling & Fielding

Wickets:	0	Runs:	0
Best Bowling:		Average:	0.00
5 WM:	0	Catches:	17
Stumpings:	7		

A stylish wicket-keeper from Bangalore, Viswanath was chosen as first keeper in the World Championship of Cricket in Australia, in 1985 and represented India at ODI level for over three years. He broke into the Test team but was dropped after just three appearances.

WADEKAR, Ajit Laxman

Born:	April 1, 1941
Batting:	Left handed
Bowling:	Left arm off-break

Tests

Test Career:	1966-74		
Cap Number:	112		
Tests Played:	37		

Test Batting

Innings:	71	Runs:	2,113
Highest Score:	143	Average:	31.07
No. 50s:	14	No. 100s:	1

Test Bowling & Fielding

Wickets:	0	Runs:	55
Best Bowling:		Average:	0.00
5 WI:	0	10 WM:	0
Catches:	46	Stumpings:	0

One Day Internationals

ODI Career:	1974		
ODIs Played:	2		

ODI Batting

Innings:	2	Runs:	73
Highest Score:	67	Average:	36.50
No. 50s:	1	No. 100s:	0

ODI Bowling & Fielding

Wickets:	0	Runs:	0
Best Bowling:		Average:	0.00
5 WM:	0	Catches:	1
Stumpings:	0		

Regarded as one of India's best ever 'number three' batsman and slips fielder, Wadekar was appointed captain in 1971, taking over from the long standing Pataudi jnr. He enjoyed instant success as India defeated both the West Indies then England. However things turned sour after an unsuccessful tour of England in 1974 thus leading to a somewhat enforced 'retirement'. Scoring over 2000 runs in Tests, with a highest score of 143 against New Zealand, at The Basin in 1968, Wadekar was a loyal servant to his country both as a player and as a captain.

WASSAN, Atul Satish

Born:	March 23, 1968
Batting:	Right handed
Bowling:	Right arm medium-fast

Tests

Test Career:	1990		
Cap Number:	190		
Tests Played:	4		

Test Batting

Innings:	5	Runs:	94
Highest Score:	53	Average:	23.50
No. 50s:	1	No. 100s:	0

Test Bowling & Fielding

Wickets:	10	Runs:	504
Best Bowling:	4/108	Average:	50.39
5 WI:	0	10 WM:	0
Catches:	0	Stumpings:	0

One Day Internationals

ODI Career:	1990-91		
ODIs Played:	9		

ODI Batting

Innings:	6	Runs:	33
Highest Score:	16	Average:	8.25
No. 50s:	0	No. 100s:	0

ODI Bowling & Fielding

Wickets:	11	Runs:	283
Best Bowling:	3/28	Average:	25.72
5 WM:	0	Catches:	0
Stumpings:	2		

A pace bowler from Delhi, Atul Wassan made his Test debut against New Zealand at Christchurch in 1990. He captured his best figures of 4/108 while on that tour.

YADAV, Jai Prakash

Born:	August 7, 1974
Batting:	Right handed
Bowling:	Right arm medium

One Day Internationals

ODI Career:	2002-05		
ODIs Played:	12		

ODI Batting

Innings:	7	Runs:	81
Highest Score:	69	Average:	20.25
No. 50s:	1	No. 100s:	0

ODI Bowling & Fielding

Wickets:	6	Runs:	326
Best Bowling:	2/32	Average:	54.33
5 WM:	0	Catches:	3
Stumpings:	0		

An all rounder from Madhya Pradesh who was thought to be the answer to India's lower order batting problems. But with a highest score of just 69 in his 12 ODI's, the Indian selectors ran out of patience and sought alternative options.

YADAV, Nandlal (Shivlal)

Born:	January 26, 1957
Batting:	Right handed
Bowling:	Right arm off-break

Tests

Test Career:	1979-87		
Cap Number:	147		
Tests Played:	35		

YADAV (continued)

Test Batting

Innings:	40	Runs:	403
Highest Score:	43	Average:	14.39
No. 50s:	0	No. 100s:	0

Test Bowling & Fielding

Wickets:	102	Runs:	3,580
Best Bowling:	5/76	Average:	35.09
5 WI:	3	10 WM:	0
Catches:	10	Stumpings:	0

One Day Internationals

ODI Career:	1986-87		
ODIs Played:	7		

ODI Batting

Innings:	2	Runs:	1
Highest Score:	1*	Average:	1.00
No. 50s:	0	No. 100s:	0

ODI Bowling & Fielding

Wickets:	8	Runs:	228
Best Bowling:	2/18	Average:	28.50
5 WM:	0	Catches:	1
Stumpings:	0		

Tallish off-spinner from Hyderabad, Yadav bowled in tandem with Dilip Doshi during the 1980's. Not a huge turner, Yadav did well to reach 100 Test wickets, capturing his best figures of 5/76 against Sri Lanka at Nagpur in 1987, which was his final year at Test level.

YADAV, Vijay

Born:	March 14, 1967
Batting:	Right handed
	Wicket Keeper

Tests

Test Career:	1993		
Cap Number:	199		
Tests Played:	1		

Test Batting

Innings:	1	Runs:	30
Highest Score:	30	Average:	30.00
No. 50s:	0	No. 100s:	0

Test Bowling & Fielding

Wickets:	0	Runs:	0
Best Bowling:	0	Average:	0.00
5 WI:	0	10 WM:	0
Catches:	1	Stumpings:	2

One Day Internationals

ODI Career:	1992-94		
ODIs Played:	19		

ODI Batting

Innings:	12	Runs:	118
Highest Score:	34*	Average:	11.80
No. 50s:	0	No. 100s:	0

ODI Bowling & Fielding

Wickets:	0	Runs:	0
Best Bowling:	0	Average:	0.00
5 WM:	0	Catches:	12
Stumpings:	7		

Suited to the one day game, Vijay Yadev was considered the likely successor to Kiran More. He got the one chance at Test level against Zimbabwe at Delhi in 1993, but thereafter was overlooked for the number one keeping job.

YADAVENADRASINGH, Yuvraj of Patiala

Born:	January 17, 1913
Batting:	Right handed

Tests

Test Career:	1934		
Cap Number:	21		
Tests Played:	1		

Test Batting

Innings:	2	Runs:	84
Highest Score:	60	Average:	42.00
No. 50s:	1	No. 100s:	0

Test Bowling & Fielding

Wickets:	0	Runs:	0
Best Bowling:		Average:	0.00
5 WI:	0	10 WM:	0
Catches:	2	Stumpings:	0

Played the one Test and boasted a healthy average of 42. His father, the Maharaja of Patiala, donated the Ranji Trophy which is the title of India's domestic competition. He became India's ambassador to Holland from 1971 until his death in 1974.

YOHANNAN, Tinu

Born:	February 18, 1979
Batting:	Right handed
Bowling:	Right arm medium-fast

Tests

Test Career:	2001-02		
Cap Number:	242		
Tests Played:	3		

Test Batting

Innings:	4	Runs:	13
Highest Score:	8*	Average:	13.00
No. 50s:	0	No. 100s:	0

Test Bowling & Fielding

Wickets:	5	Runs:	256
Best Bowling:	2/56	Average:	51.20
5 WI:	0	10 WM:	0
Catches:	1	Stumpings:	0

One Day Internationals

ODI Career:	2002		
ODIs Played:	3		

ODI Batting

Innings:	2	Runs:	7
Highest Score:	5*	Average:	7.00
No. 50s:	0	No. 100s:	0

ODI Bowling & Fielding

Wickets:	5	Runs:	122
Best Bowling:	3/33	Average:	24.39
5 WM:	0	Catches:	0
Stumpings:	0		

A champion junior athlete who took up cricket later in life, Yohannan was mentored by the great Dennis Lillee. He was selected in the Test side to play England at Chandigarh in 2001 and was touted as a possible long term proposition but could only manage a further two Tests. Interestingly enough he has not been dismissed in any of the Tests or ODI's that he has participated in.

New Zealand

ADAMS, Andre Ryan
Born: July 17, 1975
Batting: Right handed
Bowling: Right arm medium-fast

Tests
Test Career: 2002
Cap Number: 219
Tests Played: 1

Test Batting
Innings:	2	Runs:	18
Highest Score:	11	Average:	9.00
No. 50s:	0	No. 100s:	0

Test Bowling & Fielding
Wickets:	6	Runs:	105
Best Bowling:	3/44	Average:	17.50
5 WI:	0	10 WM:	0
Catches:	1	Stumpings:	0

One Day Internationals
ODI Career: 2001-
ODIs Played: 39

ODI Batting
Innings:	31	Runs:	409
Highest Score:	45	Average:	19.47
No. 50s:	0	No. 100s:	0

ODI Bowling & Fielding
Wickets:	52	Runs:	1,494
Best Bowling:	5/22	Average:	28.73
5 WM:	1	Catches:	7
Stumpings:	0		

A medium fast bowler who is also a hard hitting tailender and excellent outfielder. Adams played a single Test against England in 2002 but he seems better suited to the shorter versions of the game, with 39 ODI's and a couple of twenty/20 matches to his name.

ALABASTER, John Chaloner
Born: July 11, 1930
Batting: Right handed
Bowling: Right arm leg-break

Tests
Test Career: 1955-72
Cap Number: 71
Tests Played: 21

Test Batting
Innings:	34	Runs:	272
Highest Score:	34	Average:	9.71
No. 50s:	0	No. 100s:	0

Test Bowling & Fielding
Wickets:	49	Runs:	1,863
Best Bowling:	4/46	Average:	38.02
5 WI:	0	10 WM:	0
Catches:	7	Stumpings:	0

A leg spinner from Otago who enjoyed a fine series against South Africa in 1961/62 when he took 22 wickets. He played his last Test at Port of Spain as a 41 year old.

ALLCOTT, Cyril Francis Walter
Born: October 7, 1896
Batting: Left handed
Bowling: Left arm off-break

Tests
Test Career: 1930-32
Cap Number: 15
Tests Played: 6

Test Batting
Innings:	7	Runs:	113
Highest Score:	33	Average:	22.60
No. 50s:	0	No. 100s:	0

Test Bowling & Fielding
Wickets:	6	Runs:	541
Best Bowling:	2/102	Average:	90.16
5 WI:	0	10 WM:	0
Catches:	3	Stumpings:	0

A left arm off spinner and middle order batsman who was one of his country's most experienced players in their early Tests against England and South Africa. He had previously toured England in 1927 with great success scoring a century against Warwickshire.

ALLOTT, Geoffrey Ian
Born: December 24, 1971
Batting: Right handed
Bowling: Left arm medium-fast

Tests
Test Career: 1996-99
Cap Number: 196
Tests Played: 10

Test Batting
Innings:	15	Runs:	27
Highest Score:	8*	Average:	3.37
No. 50s:	0	No. 100s:	0

Test Bowling & Fielding
Wickets:	19	Runs:	1,111
Best Bowling:	4/74	Average:	58.47
5 WI:	0	10 WM:	0
Catches:	2	Stumpings:	0

One Day Internationals
ODI Career: 1997-2000
ODIs Played: 31

ODI Batting
Innings:	11	Runs:	17
Highest Score:	7*	Average:	3.40
No. 50s:	0	No. 100s:	0

ODI Bowling & Fielding
Wickets:	52	Runs:	1,207
Best Bowling:	4/35	Average:	23.21
5 WM:	0	Catches:	5
Stumpings:	0		

The promising left arm medium pace bowler was struck down by injury in 2000 but not before he was able to score Test cricket's longest ever duck. Playing the South Africans at Eden Park in 1999 Allott took 101 minutes to make nought. Whilst he became famous for making nothing happen with the bat, he could bowl, and had an excellent World Cup in 1999 taking a then record 20 wickets for the tournament.

ANDERSON, Robert Wickham
Born: October 2, 1948
Batting: Right handed
Bowling: Right arm leg-break

Tests
Test Career: 1976-78
Cap Number: 134
Tests Played: 9

Test Batting
Innings:	18	Runs:	423
Highest Score:	92	Average:	23.50
No. 50s:	3	No. 100s:	0

Test Bowling & Fielding
Wickets:	0	Runs:	0
Best Bowling:		Average:	0.00
5 WI:	0	10 WM:	0
Catches:	1	Stumpings:	0

One Day Internationals
ODI Career: 1976-78
ODIs Played: 2

ODI Batting
Innings:	2	Runs:	16
Highest Score:	12	Average:	16.00
No. 50s:	0	No. 100s:	0

ODI Bowling & Fielding
Wickets:	0	Runs:	0
Best Bowling:		Average:	0.00
5 WM:	0	Catches:	1
Stumpings:	0		

A journeyman who played for four sides in Shell Shield. His best performance at Test level was a 92 at Lahore in 1976/77.

ANDERSON, William McDougall (Mac)
Born: October 8, 1919
Batting: Left handed
Bowling: Left arm leg-break

Tests
Test Career: 1946
Cap Number: 34
Tests Played: 1

Test Batting
Innings:	2	Runs:	5
Highest Score:	4	Average:	2.50
No. 50s:	0	No. 100s:	0

Test Bowling & Fielding
Wickets:	0	Runs:	0
Best Bowling:		Average:	0.00
5 WI:	0	10 WM:	0
Catches:	1	Stumpings:	0

The opening batsman played just one Test, the first meeting between New Zealand and Australia at Wellington in 1946.

ANDREWS, Bryan
Born: April 4, 1945
Batting: Right handed
Bowling: Right arm medium

Tests
Test Career: 1974
Cap Number: 127
Tests Played: 2

Test Batting
Innings:	3	Runs:	22
Highest Score:	17	Average:	22.00
No. 50s:	0	No. 100s:	0

Test Bowling & Fielding
Wickets:	2	Runs:	154
Best Bowling:	2/40	Average:	77.00
5 WI:	0	10 WM:	0
Catches:	1	Stumpings:	0

He played two Tests in Australia in 1973/74 but struggled and could mange only two wickets.

ASTLE, Nathan John
Born: September 15, 1971
Batting: Right handed
Bowling: Right arm medium

Tests
Test Career: 1996-
Cap Number: 197
Tests Played: 79

Test Batting
Innings:	133	Runs:	4,650
Highest Score:	222	Average:	37.80
No. 50s:	24	No. 100s:	11

Test Bowling & Fielding
Wickets:	51	Runs:	2,119
Best Bowling:	3/27	Average:	41.54
5 WI:	0	10 WM:	0
Catches:	69	Stumpings:	0

One Day Internationals
ODI Career: 1995-
ODIs Played: 212

ODI Batting
Innings:	207	Runs:	6,890
Highest Score:	145*	Average:	35.69
No. 50s:	40	No. 100s:	16

ODI Bowling & Fielding
Wickets:	99	Runs:	3,741
Best Bowling:	4/43	Average:	37.78
5 WM:	0	Catches:	80
Stumpings:	0		

When word spread around the world that Nathan Astle had scored the fastest double century in Test there were a few raised eyebrows, but for those who have followed his career closely it came as no surprise. He had always been a free scoring batsman, capable of working the ball though gaps or hitting hard over the top. Fifteen ODI centuries back up the claim, as do his eleven centuries in the Test side. His record breaking double century against England at Christchurch in 2001/02 took only 153 balls, demoting cricket's king of crunch, Adam Gilchrist to second on the all time list. Astle is also a canny bowler, and though his military mediums are better suited to one day cricket they have frustrated 51 batsmen into surrendering their wickets at Test level.

BADCOCK, Frederick Theodore
Born: August 9, 1897
Batting: Right handed
Bowling: Right arm medium-fast

Tests
Test Career: 1930-33
Cap Number: 1
Tests Played: 7

Test Batting
Innings:	9	Runs:	137
Highest Score:	64	Average:	19.57
No. 50s:	2	No. 100s:	0

Test Bowling & Fielding
Wickets:	16	Runs:	610
Best Bowling:	4/80	Average:	38.12
5 WI:	0	10 WM:	0
Catches:	1	Stumpings:	0

An all-rounder from Wellington who played in New Zealand's first ever Test side. Born in India, he took 2/29 against England in that famous first Test but had a game to forget with the bat scoring a pair.

BAILEY, Mark
Born: November 26, 1970
Batting: Right handed
Bowling: Right arm medium

One Day Internationals
ODI Career: 1998
ODIs Played: 1

ODI Batting
Innings:	0	Runs:	0
Highest Score:	0	Average:	0.00
No. 50s:	0	No. 100s:	0

ODI Bowling & Fielding
Wickets:	0	Runs:	0
Best Bowling:		Average:	0.00
5 WM:	0	Catches:	0
Stumpings:	0		

Originally from Hamilton who played one ODI against Zimbabwe, at Dhaka, 1998 but did not get a chance to bat.

BARBER, Richard Trevor
Born: June 23, 1925
Batting: Right handed

Tests
Test Career: 1956
Cap Number: 80
Tests Played: 1

Test Batting
Innings:	2	Runs:	17
Highest Score:	12	Average:	8.50
No. 50s:	0	No. 100s:	0

Test Bowling & Fielding
Wickets:	0	Runs:	0
Best Bowling:		Average:	0.00
5 WI:	0	10 WM:	0
Catches:	1	Stumpings:	0

A right handed batsman from Wellington who played a single Test against the West Indies in 1956.

BARTLETT, Gary Alex
Born: February 3, 1941
Batting: Right handed
Bowling: Right arm fast

Tests
Test Career: 1961-68
Cap Number: 88
Tests Played: 10

Test Batting
Innings:	18	Runs:	263
Highest Score:	40	Average:	15.47
No. 50s:	0	No. 100s:	0

Test Bowling & Fielding
Wickets:	24	Runs:	792
Best Bowling:	6/38	Average:	33.00
5 WI:	1	10 WM:	0
Catches:	8	Stumpings:	0

A genuine fast bowler who played for both Canterbury and Central Districts in Plunket Shield. He was part of the attack that thrashed India by six wickets at Christchurch in 1968, taking 6/38 in the second innings of what was to be his second last game for New Zealand.

BARTON, Paul Thomas
Born: October 9, 1935
Batting: Right handed

Tests
Test Career: 1961-63
Cap Number: 89
Tests Played: 7

Test Batting
Innings:	14	Runs:	285
Highest Score:	109	Average:	20.35
No. 50s:	1	No. 100s:	1

Test Bowling & Fielding
Wickets:	0	Runs:	0
Best Bowling:		Average:	0.00
5 WI:	0	10 WM:	0
Catches:	4	Stumpings:	0

He looked set for a healthy Test career when he scored a century on his maiden tour, but poor form against the touring English side the following summer saw him fade from the Test scene. That 109 against the South Africans at Port Elizabeth was highly unusual given it took 276 minutes to compile yet contained 20 boundaries.

BEARD, Donald Derek
Born: January 14, 1920
Batting: Right handed
Bowling: Right arm medium

Tests
Test Career: 1952-56
Cap Number: 54
Tests Played: 4

Test Batting
Innings:	7	Runs:	101
Highest Score:	31	Average:	20.20
No. 50s:	0	No. 100s:	0

Test Bowling & Fielding

Wickets:	9	Runs:	302
Best Bowling:	3/22	Average:	33.55
5 WI:	0	10 WM:	0
Catches:	2	Stumpings:	0

A medium pacer from Central Districts who played in his country's first winning Test side against the West Indies in 1956.

BECK, John Edward Francis

Born:	August 1, 1934
Batting:	Left handed
Bowling:	Left arm off-break

Tests

Test Career:	1953-56
Cap Number:	65
Tests Played:	8

Test Batting

Innings:	15	Runs:	394
Highest Score:	99	Average:	26.26
No. 50s:	3	No. 100s:	0

Test Bowling & Fielding

Wickets:	0	Runs:	0
Best Bowling:		Average:	0.00
5 WI:	0	10 WM:	0
Catches:	0	Stumpings:	0

Of those unfortunate Test payers whose highest score is 99, John Beck is one of the unluckiest. Playing in his second Test against the South Africans at Cape Town in 1953/54 he was run out by his partner who was attempting to give him the strike. Beck would play a handful more tests but never get close to scoring that elusive test hundred.

BELL, Matthew David

Born:	February 25, 1977
Batting:	Right handed
Bowling:	Right arm off-break

Tests

Test Career:	1998-2001
Cap Number:	206
Tests Played:	13

Test Batting

Innings:	23	Runs:	484
Highest Score:	105	Average:	22.00
No. 50s:	2	No. 100s:	1

Test Bowling & Fielding

Wickets:	0	Runs:	0
Best Bowling:		Average:	0.00
5 WI:	0	10 WM:	0
Catches:	10	Stumpings:	0

One Day Internationals

ODI Career:	1998-2001
ODIs Played:	7

ODI Batting

Innings:	7	Runs:	133
Highest Score:	66	Average:	19.00
No. 50s:	1	No. 100s:	0

ODI Bowling & Fielding

Wickets:	0	Runs:	0
Best Bowling:		Average:	0.00
5 WM:	0	Catches:	1
Stumpings:	0		

A top order batsman from Northern Districts, he had a torrid start to his Test career with only 56 runs in his first eight innings but he recovered to hit a maiden century against Pakistan at Hamilton in 2001. The promising youngster played 13 Tests in total but with an average of only 22 the chances eventually dried up.

BELL, William

Born:	September 5, 1931
Batting:	Right handed
Bowling:	Right arm leg-break

Tests

Test Career:	1954
Cap Number:	66
Tests Played:	2

Test Batting

Innings:	3	Runs:	21
Highest Score:	21*	Average:	0.00
No. 50s:	0	No. 100s:	0

Test Bowling & Fielding

Wickets:	2	Runs:	235
Best Bowling:	1/54	Average:	117.50
5 WI:	0	10 WM:	0
Catches:	1	Stumpings:	0

Selected to tour South Africa in 1953/54, the leg spinner played in two Tests but could snare only two wickets at more than 100 runs apiece.

BILBY, Grahame Paul

Born:	May 7, 1941
Batting:	Right handed

Tests

Test Career:	1966
Cap Number:	110
Tests Played:	2

Test Batting

Innings:	4	Runs:	55
Highest Score:	28	Average:	13.75
No. 50s:	0	No. 100s:	0

Test Bowling & Fielding

Wickets:	0	Runs:	0
Best Bowling:		Average:	0.00
5 WI:	0	10 WM:	0
Catches:	3	Stumpings:	0

A top order batsman from Wellington, he played two Tests against the touring English in 1966.

BLAIN, Tony Elston

Born:	February 17, 1962
Batting:	Right handed
Bowling:	Right arm leg-break
	Wicket Keeper

Tests

Test Career:	1986-94
Cap Number:	160
Tests Played:	11

Test Batting

Innings:	20	Runs:	456
Highest Score:	78	Average:	26.82
No. 50s:	2	No. 100s:	0

Test Bowling & Fielding			
Wickets:	0	Runs:	0
Best Bowling:		Average:	0.00
5 WI:	0	10 WM:	0
Catches:	19	Stumpings:	2

One Day Internationals
ODI Career: 1986-94
ODIs Played: 38

ODI Batting

Innings:	38	Runs:	442
Highest Score:	49*	Average:	16.37
No. 50s:	0	No. 100s:	0

ODI Bowling & Fielding

Wickets:	0	Runs:	0
Best Bowling:		Average:	0.00
5 WM:	0	Catches:	37
Stumpings:	1		

A smart wicketkeeper and number seven batsman who spent much of his career waiting in the wings as New Zealand's second choice keeper.

BLAIR, Bruce Robert
Born: December 27, 1957
Batting: Left handed
Bowling: Right arm medium

One Day Internationals
ODI Career: 1982-86
ODIs Played: 14

ODI Batting

Innings:	14	Runs:	174
Highest Score:	29*	Average:	14.50
No. 50s:	0	No. 100s:	0

ODI Bowling & Fielding

Wickets:	1	Runs:	34
Best Bowling:	1/7	Average:	34.00
5 WM:	0	Catches:	4
Stumpings:	0		

A left hand middle order batsman, Bruce Blair represented New Zealand in 14 ODI's between 1982-86. He struggled for consistency averaging just 14.50. A part time medium pacer, Blair's only wicket was that of Australian beanpole paceman Bruce Reid.

BLAIR, Robert William
Born: June 23, 1932
Batting: Right handed
Bowling: Right arm medium-fast

Tests
Test Career: 1953-64
Cap Number: 57
Tests Played: 19

Test Batting

Innings:	34	Runs:	189
Highest Score:	64*	Average:	6.75
No. 50s:	1	No. 100s:	0

Test Bowling & Fielding

Wickets:	43	Runs:	1,515
Best Bowling:	4/85	Average:	35.23
5 WI:	0	10 WM:	0
Catches:	5	Stumpings:	0

An opening bowler from Wellington who captured over 500 first class wickets in New Zealand. His best return in a Test was 7/143 against the touring South Africans in 1963/64.

BLUNT, Roger Charles
Born: November 3, 1900
Batting: Right handed
Bowling: Right arm leg-break

Tests
Test Career: 1930-32
Cap Number: 2
Tests Played: 9

Test Batting

Innings:	13	Runs:	330
Highest Score:	96	Average:	27.50
No. 50s:	1	No. 100s:	0

Test Bowling & Fielding

Wickets:	12	Runs:	472
Best Bowling:	3/17	Average:	39.33
5 WI:	0	10 WM:	0
Catches:	5	Stumpings:	0

A renowned first class cricketer prior to the war, his 338 not out for Otago against Canterbury in 1931/32 stood as the highest first class score by a New Zealander for over 20 years. He played in the famous first Test against England where he was clearly New Zealand's best performer with 45 out of 112 in the first innings and then captured 3/17 with his leg-spinners.

BOLTON, Bruce Alfred
Born: May 31, 1935
Batting: Right handed
Bowling: Right arm leg-break

Tests
Test Career: 1959
Cap Number: 85
Tests Played: 2

Test Batting

Innings:	3	Runs:	59
Highest Score:	33	Average:	19.66
No. 50s:	0	No. 100s:	0

Test Bowling & Fielding

Wickets:	0	Runs:	0
Best Bowling:		Average:	0.00
5 WI:	0	10 WM:	0
Catches:	1	Stumpings:	0

The top order batsman played his two Tests against England in 1959.

BOND, Shane Edward
Born: June 7, 1975
Batting: Right handed
Bowling: Right arm fast

Tests
Test Career: 2001-
Cap Number: 216
Tests Played: 14

Test Batting

Innings:	14	Runs:	123
Highest Score:	41*	Average:	17.57
No. 50s:	0	No. 100s:	0

Test Bowling & Fielding

Wickets:	64	Runs:	1,378
Best Bowling:	6/51	Average:	21.53
5 WI:	4	10 WM:	1
Catches:	5	Stumpings:	0

One Day Internationals

ODI Career:	2002-		
ODIs Played:	45		

ODI Batting

Innings:	19	Runs:	152
Highest Score:	31*	Average:	16.88
No. 50s:	0	No. 100s:	0

ODI Bowling & Fielding

Wickets:	87	Runs:	1,621
Best Bowling:	6/19	Average:	18.63
5 WM:	3	Catches:	9
Stumpings:	0		

With his long run and fluid action, a fit Shane Bond is one of the fastest bowlers in the world. Unfortunately for Bond that is a big 'if' with a recurring back injury hanging over his career like a big black could. At his best against an inexperienced Zimbabwe in 2005, he took ten wickets in the second Test at Bulawayo.

BOOCK, Stephen Lewis

Born:	September 20, 1951
Batting:	Right handed
Bowling:	Left arm off-break

Tests

Test Career:	1978-89		
Cap Number:	140		
Tests Played:	30		

Test Batting

Innings:	41	Runs:	207
Highest Score:	37	Average:	6.27
No. 50s:	0	No. 100s:	0

Test Bowling & Fielding

Wickets:	74	Runs:	2,564
Best Bowling:	7/87	Average:	34.64
5 WI:	4	10 WM:	0
Catches:	14	Stumpings:	0

One Day Internationals

ODI Career:	1978-87		
ODIs Played:	14		

ODI Batting

Innings:	7	Runs:	30
Highest Score:	12	Average:	10.00
No. 50s:	0	No. 100s:	0

ODI Bowling & Fielding

Wickets:	15	Runs:	513
Best Bowling:	3/28	Average:	34.20
5 WM:	0	Catches:	5
Stumpings:	0		

A tall and talented finger spinner, despite his often marathon spells at the bowling crease his accuracy never seemed to waiver. He took seven wickets in an innings at Hyderabad in 1984 off a characteristically tight 37 overs. In all his 30 tests yielded a more than respectable 74 wickets during which time he went for only 2.33 runs per over.

BRACEWELL, Brendon Paul

Born:	September 14, 1959
Batting:	Right handed
Bowling:	Right arm medium

Tests

Test Career:	1978-85		
Cap Number:	142		
Tests Played:	6		

Test Batting

Innings:	12	Runs:	24
Highest Score:	8	Average:	2.40
No. 50s:	0	No. 100s:	0

Test Bowling & Fielding

Wickets:	14	Runs:	585
Best Bowling:	3/110	Average:	41.78
5 WI:	0	10 WM:	0
Catches:	1	Stumpings:	0

One Day Internationals

ODI Career:	1978		
ODIs Played:	1		

ODI Batting

Innings:	1	Runs:	0
Highest Score:	0*	Average:	0.00
No. 50s:	0	No. 100s:	0

ODI Bowling & Fielding

Wickets:	1	Runs:	41
Best Bowling:	1/41	Average:	41.00
5 WM:	0	Catches:	0
Stumpings:	0		

The brother of John, he was a medium pace bowler who toured England as a teenager in 1978. His international career was severely restricted by injuries and after breaking down against Australia when attempting a comeback in the late 80's he announced his retirement.

BRACEWELL, John Garry

Born:	April 15, 1958
Batting:	Right handed
Bowling:	Right arm off-break

Tests

Test Career:	1980-90		
Cap Number:	147		
Tests Played:	41		

Test Batting

Innings:	60	Runs:	1,001
Highest Score:	110	Average:	20.42
No. 50s:	4	No. 100s:	1

Test Bowling & Fielding

Wickets:	102	Runs:	3,653
Best Bowling:	6/32	Average:	35.81
5 WI:	4	10 WM:	1
Catches:	31	Stumpings:	0

One Day Internationals

ODI Career:	1983-90		
ODIs Played:	53		

ODI Batting

Innings:	43	Runs:	512
Highest Score:	43	Average:	16.51
No. 50s:	0	No. 100s:	0

ODI Bowling & Fielding

Wickets:	33	Runs:	1,884
Best Bowling:	2/3	Average:	57.09
5 WM:	0	Catches:	19
Stumpings:	0		

He was a tall off spinner and lusty lower order batsman who bowled his slow turners with the attitude of a tearaway quick. Bracewell had a high action that imparted plenty of loop and when on song was a dangerous proposition. He took five or more wickets in an innings on four occasions with his best a match winning 6/32 against the Australians at Auckland in 1985/86. His batting was very much a case of chocolates or boiled lollies, with a Test century and 12 ducks to his name. He scored 110 at Trent Bridge in 1986 coming in at number eight. A year earlier he hit a smashing 83 not out against the Australians at the SCG that was part of an amazing 124 run tenth wicket partnership with fellow spinner Stephen Boock. He coached for many years in English county cricket before returning home to coach the national side in 2003.

BRADBURN, Grant Eric
Born: May 26, 1966
Batting: Right handed
Bowling: Right arm off-break

Tests
Test Career: 1990-2001
Cap Number: 172
Tests Played: 7

Test Batting
Innings:	10	Runs:	105
Highest Score:	30*	Average:	13.12
No. 50s:	0	No. 100s:	0

Test Bowling & Fielding
Wickets:	6	Runs:	460
Best Bowling:	3/134	Average:	76.66
5 WI:	0	10 WM:	0
Catches:	6	Stumpings:	0

One Day Internationals
ODI Career: 1990-2001
ODIs Played: 11

ODI Batting
Innings:	10	Runs:	60
Highest Score:	30	Average:	8.57
No. 50s:	0	No. 100s:	0

ODI Bowling & Fielding
Wickets:	6	Runs:	318
Best Bowling:	2/18	Average:	53.00
5 WM:	0	Catches:	2
Stumpings:	0		

An off spinner from Northern Districts whose modest Test career spanned eleven years. Bradburn hadn't played for his country for almost eight years when he earnt a surprise recall against Pakistan in 2001 but could only add a single wicket to the five he had taken previously.

BRADBURN, Wynne Pennell
Born: November 24, 1938
Batting: Right handed
Bowling: Right arm off-break

Tests
Test Career: 1964
Cap Number: 100
Tests Played: 2

Test Batting
Innings:	4	Runs:	62
Highest Score:	32	Average:	15.50
No. 50s:	0	No. 100s:	0

Test Bowling & Fielding
Wickets:	0	Runs:	0
Best Bowling:		Average:	0.00
5 WI:	0	10 WM:	0
Catches:	2	Stumpings:	0

He was a Northern Districts batsman who played two Tests against the touring South Africans in 1964.

BROWN, Vaughan Raymond
Born: November 3, 1959
Batting: Left handed
Bowling: Right arm off-break

Tests
Test Career: 1985
Cap Number: 156
Tests Played: 2

Test Batting
Innings:	3	Runs:	51
Highest Score:	36*	Average:	25.50
No. 50s:	0	No. 100s:	0

Test Bowling & Fielding
Wickets:	1	Runs:	176
Best Bowling:	1/17	Average:	176.00
5 WI:	0	10 WM:	0
Catches:	3	Stumpings:	0

One Day Internationals
ODI Career: 1988
ODIs Played: 3

ODI Batting
Innings:	3	Runs:	44
Highest Score:	32	Average:	14.66
No. 50s:	0	No. 100s:	0

ODI Bowling & Fielding
Wickets:	1	Runs:	75
Best Bowling:	1/24	Average:	75.00
5 WM:	0	Catches:	2
Stumpings:	0		

No-one would begrudge a Test bowler a single wicket but in Vaughan Brown's case his only Test scalp cost Richard Hadlee the chance of taking a historic 10 wickets in an innings. The Black Caps were playing Australia at the 'Gabba in 1985 and had the home team eight wickets down when Brown had Lawson caught in the deep by of all people, Hadlee. The fast bowler took the final wicket in that innings just missing out on becoming the only paceman in Test history to claim the magical ten.

BULFIN, Carl Edwin
Born: August 19, 1973
Batting: Right handed
Bowling: Right arm medium-fast

One Day Internationals
ODI Career: 1999
ODIs Played: 4

ODI Batting
Innings:	2	Runs:	9
Highest Score:	7*	Average:	9.00
No. 50s:	0	No. 100s:	0

ODI Bowling & Fielding			
Wickets:	0	Runs:	109
Best Bowling:		Average:	0.00
5 WM:	0	Catches:	1
Stumpings:	0		

A blonde-bombshell who was touted as the fastest bowler in New Zealand when he appeared in three ODI's against South Africa in 1999. Bulfin was selected in the World Cup squad later that year where he played the one match against Scotland. In total he played four ODI's for just one wicket and was overlooked for selection thereafter.

BURGESS, Mark Gordon

Born:	July 17, 1944
Batting:	Right handed
Bowling:	Right arm off-break

Tests

Test Career:	1968-80
Cap Number:	112
Tests Played:	50

Test Batting

Innings:	92	Runs:	2,684
Highest Score:	119*	Average:	31.20
No. 50s:	14	No. 100s:	5

Test Bowling & Fielding

Wickets:	6	Runs:	212
Best Bowling:	3/23	Average:	35.33
5 WI:	0	10 WM:	0
Catches:	34	Stumpings:	0

One Day Internationals

ODI Career:	1973-81
ODIs Played:	26

ODI Batting

Innings:	20	Runs:	336
Highest Score:	47	Average:	16.80
No. 50s:	0	No. 100s:	0

ODI Bowling & Fielding

Wickets:	1	Runs:	69
Best Bowling:	1/10	Average:	69.00
5 WM:	0	Catches:	8
Stumpings:	0		

An accomplished top order batsman from Auckland, he was handed the national captaincy at the age of 33 and responded by almost leading his side into the World Cup final two years later. The sound top order bat made five Test centuries but surprisingly his highest score was only an unbeaten 119 in Pakistan during the 1969/70 tour. He and Bev Congdon both scored centuries at Lord's in 1973 to guide the side to a then record first innings score in excess of 500.

BURKE, Cecil

Born:	March 27, 1914
Batting:	Right handed
Bowling:	Right arm leg-break

Tests

Test Career:	1946
Cap Number:	35
Tests Played:	1

Test Batting

Innings:	2	Runs:	4
Highest Score:	3	Average:	2.00
No. 50s:	0	No. 100s:	0

Test Bowling & Fielding

Wickets:	2	Runs:	30
Best Bowling:	2/30	Average:	15.00
5 WI:	0	10 WM:	0
Catches:	0	Stumpings:	0

The leg spinner from Auckland played a single test, the historic first Test meeting between New Zealand and Australia at Wellington in 1946.

BURTT, Thomas Browning

Born:	January 22, 1915
Batting:	Right handed
Bowling:	Left arm off-break

Tests

Test Career:	1947-53
Cap Number:	40
Tests Played:	10

Test Batting

Innings:	15	Runs:	252
Highest Score:	42	Average:	21.00
No. 50s:	0	No. 100s:	0

Test Bowling & Fielding

Wickets:	33	Runs:	1,170
Best Bowling:	6/162	Average:	35.45
5 WI:	3	10 WM:	0
Catches:	2	Stumpings:	0

A chunky left arm off spinner from Canterbury who reveled in long stints at the bowling crease. He was a key bowler in New Zealand's 1949 Test side that toured England when all four matches ended in a draw. He did the bulk of the bowling for his side, finishing with 17 wickets for the series. He also played hockey for New Zealand.

BUTLER, Ian Gareth

Born:	November 24, 1981
Batting:	Right handed
Bowling:	Right arm fast

Tests

Test Career:	2002-04
Cap Number:	218
Tests Played:	8

Test Batting

Innings:	10	Runs:	76
Highest Score:	26	Average:	9.50
No. 50s:	0	No. 100s:	0

Test Bowling & Fielding

Wickets:	24	Runs:	884
Best Bowling:	6/46	Average:	36.83
5 WI:	1	10 WM:	0
Catches:	4	Stumpings:	0

One Day Internationals

ODI Career:	2002-04
ODIs Played:	15

ODI Batting

Innings:	6	Runs:	6
Highest Score:	3	Average:	3.00
No. 50s:	0	No. 100s:	0

ODI Bowling & Fielding

Wickets:	14	Runs:	558
Best Bowling:	3/41	Average:	39.85
5 WM:	0	Catches:	6
Stumpings:	0		

A speedster from Northern Districts who got his chance due to the injury of Shane Bond and took full advantage of it with 24 wickets in his first eight Tests. His best performance in a single innings was 6/46 against Pakistan at Wellington in 2004.

BUTTERFIELD, Leonard Arthur

Born:	August 29, 1913
Batting:	Right handed
Bowling:	Right arm medium-fast

Tests

Test Career:	1946
Cap Number:	36
Tests Played:	1

Test Batting

Innings:	2	Runs:	0
Highest Score:	0	Average:	0.00
No. 50s:	0	No. 100s:	0

Test Bowling & Fielding

Wickets:	0	Runs:	24
Best Bowling:		Average:	0.00
5 WI:	0	10 WM:	0
Catches:	0	Stumpings:	0

The medium pace bowler and middle order batsman's only Test was the 1946 meeting with Australia that was not considered a Test at the time but later given Test status. He scored a pair, falling LBW to Bill O'Reilly in both innings.

CAIRNS, Bernard Lance

Born:	October 10, 1949
Batting:	Right handed
Bowling:	Right arm medium-fast

Tests

Test Career:	1974-85
Cap Number:	130
Tests Played:	43

Test Batting

Innings:	65	Runs:	928
Highest Score:	64	Average:	16.28
No. 50s:	2	No. 100s:	0

Test Bowling & Fielding

Wickets:	130	Runs:	4,280
Best Bowling:	7/74	Average:	32.92
5 WI:	6	10 WM:	1
Catches:	30	Stumpings:	0

One Day Internationals

ODI Career:	1974-85
ODIs Played:	78

ODI Batting

Innings:	65	Runs:	987
Highest Score:	60	Average:	16.72
No. 50s:	2	No. 100s:	0

ODI Bowling & Fielding

Wickets:	89	Runs:	2,717
Best Bowling:	5/28	Average:	30.52
5 WM:	1	Catches:	19
Stumpings:	0		

There was nothing conventional about Lance Cairns the cricketer. As a bowler he delivered his bending in-swingers off the wrong foot and as a lower order batsman he had the perfect technique for chopping wood. Whatever the method, the results were there for all to see. More a bowler than a batsman, he claimed 130 wickets in only 43 Tests, including a career best 7/74 at Headingly in 1983 that was part of ten wickets for the match. A crowd favourite, he even got the parochial Melbourne crowd onside in 1983 when he smashed 52 off 25 balls in a one day innings that included six 6's.

CAIRNS, Christopher Lance

Born:	June 13, 1970
Batting:	Right handed
Bowling:	Right arm medium-fast

Tests

Test Career:	1989-2004
Cap Number:	168
Tests Played:	62

Test Batting

Innings:	104	Runs:	3,320
Highest Score:	158	Average:	33.53
No. 50s:	22	No. 100s:	5

Test Bowling & Fielding

Wickets:	218	Runs:	6,410
Best Bowling:	7/27	Average:	29.40
5 WI:	13	10 WM:	1
Catches:	14	Stumpings:	0

One Day Internationals

ODI Career:	1991-
ODIs Played:	215

ODI Batting

Innings:	193	Runs:	4,950
Highest Score:	115	Average:	29.46
No. 50s:	26	No. 100s:	4

ODI Bowling & Fielding

Wickets:	201	Runs:	6,594
Best Bowling:	5/42	Average:	32.80
5 WM:	1	Catches:	66
Stumpings:	0		

The son of Test all-rounder Lance, he went in to the family business of taking wickets and clearing pickets at a young age when he made his Test debut as a 19 year old. Whilst his father was a great competitor and real crowd pleaser, Chris had the technique and talent to become one of the great all-rounders in the game. When fit, his bowling was a threatening fast medium pace that combined bounce and seam. His batting was just as dangerous, and whilst he was happy to hit the ball in the air he rarely went across the line. In Tests he made five hundreds and took five or more wickets in an innings on no less than 13 occasions. His biggest knock in Test cricket was a predictably high octane affair against South Africa at Eden Park in 2004; 158 off just 171 deliveries. Cairns smacked seven 6's in that innings and in total cleared the ropes a then record 87 times in his Test career. His game was perfectly suited to one day cricket where he had a number of standout performances. In total he won 11 'Man of the Match' awards in ODI's, including one at Pune in 1995, when he made 103 in only 87 minutes then followed it up with 3/37 off his ten overs. In the end it was injury that brought about his premature retirement from Test cricket in 2004. Respected New Zealand cricket writer Richard Boock speculated as to what might have been had his body not succumbed to the pressures of international cricket, "It's not a scientific measure of course, but if Cairns' body had held together long enough for him to have played 100 Tests, his figures extrapolate out to something like 5334 runs and 351 wickets - very similar to those of Botham." He went on to say "He was, and should be remembered as, one of the game's best all-rounders."

CAMERON, Francis James

Born: June 1, 1932
Batting: Right handed
Bowling: Right arm medium

Tests
Test Career: 1961-65
Cap Number: 90
Tests Played: 19

Test Batting
Innings:	30	Runs:	116
Highest Score:	27*	Average:	11.60
No. 50s:	0	No. 100s:	0

Test Bowling & Fielding
Wickets:	62	Runs:	1,849
Best Bowling:	5/34	Average:	29.82
5 WI:	3	10 WM:	0
Catches:	2	Stumpings:	0

He was a steady medium pace bowler who could swing the ball substantially under the right conditions. Cameron took 20 wickets on the tour of South Africa in 1961/62, including 5/48 in the first innings of the win at Cape Town. He later as served as New Zealand chairman of selectors and as an ICC match referee.

CANNING, Tamahau

Born: April 7, 1977
Batting: Right handed
Bowling: Right arm medium-fast

One Day Internationals
ODI Career: 2003-05
ODIs Played: 4

ODI Batting
Innings:	4	Runs:	52
Highest Score:	23*	Average:	17.33
No. 50s:	0	No. 100s:	0

ODI Bowling & Fielding
Wickets:	5	Runs:	203
Best Bowling:	2/30	Average:	40.60
5 WM:	0	Catches:	1
Stumpings:	0		

An all-rounder who made his ODI debut against Pakistan at Lahore, in 2003, Canning played his last ODI against Australia, at McLean Park, Napier, in 2005. He was born in South Australia.

CAVE, Henry Butler (Harry)

Born: October 10, 1922
Batting: Right handed
Bowling: Right arm medium

Tests
Test Career: 1949-58
Cap Number: 46
Tests Played: 19

Test Batting
Innings:	31	Runs:	229
Highest Score:	22*	Average:	8.80
No. 50s:	0	No. 100s:	0

Test Bowling & Fielding
Wickets:	34	Runs:	1,467
Best Bowling:	4/21	Average:	43.14
5 WI:	0	10 WM:	0
Catches:	8	Stumpings:	0

A medium pace bowler from Wellington, he was New Zealand's longest standing captain until his record was passed by John Reid in the late 50's. His bowling was just military medium but what he lacked in pace he made up for with accuracy and movement. He was particularly effective in the subcontinent where he played eight of his 19 Tests. In nine Tests as captain he lost five matches and won four.

CHAPPLE, Murray Ernest

Born: July 25, 1930
Batting: Right handed
Bowling: Left arm medium

Tests
Test Career: 1953-66
Cap Number: 61
Tests Played: 14

Test Batting
Innings:	27	Runs:	497
Highest Score:	76	Average:	19.11
No. 50s:	3	No. 100s:	0

Test Bowling & Fielding
Wickets:	1	Runs:	84
Best Bowling:	1/24	Average:	84.00
5 WI:	0	10 WM:	0
Catches:	10	Stumpings:	0

An opening batsman who played in 19 Tests even though he averaged less 20 in Test cricket. He was a well respected first class cricketer with Central Districts and Canterbury and was vice captain to John Reid in a number of Tests. In his final Test against England at Christchurch in 1966 he actually captained the side.

CHATFIELD, Ewen John

Born: July 3, 1950
Batting: Right handed
Bowling: Right arm medium-fast

Tests
Test Career: 1975-89
Cap Number: 131
Tests Played: 43

Test Batting					Test Batting				
Innings:	54	Runs:	180		Innings:	50	Runs:	533	
Highest Score:	21*	Average:	8.57		Highest Score:	68*	Average:	14.40	
No. 50s:	0	No. 100s:	0		No. 50s:	2	No. 100s:	0	

Test Bowling & Fielding					Test Bowling & Fielding				
Wickets:	123	Runs:	3,958		Wickets:	116	Runs:	3,393	
Best Bowling:	6/73	Average:	32.17		Best Bowling:	6/63	Average:	29.25	
5 WI:	3	10 WM:	1		5 WI:	3	10 WM:	0	
Catches:	7	Stumpings:	0		Catches:	10	Stumpings:	0	

One Day Internationals

ODI Career:	1979-89				ODI Career:	1973-78			
ODIs Played:	114				ODIs Played:	15			

ODI Batting					ODI Batting				
Innings:	48	Runs:	118		Innings:	9	Runs:	34	
Highest Score:	19*	Average:	10.72		Highest Score:	9	Average:	5.66	
No. 50s:	0	No. 100s:	0		No. 50s:	0	No. 100s:	0	

ODI Bowling & Fielding					ODI Bowling & Fielding				
Wickets:	140	Runs:	3,618		Wickets:	18	Runs:	479	
Best Bowling:	5/34	Average:	25.84		Best Bowling:	5/23	Average:	26.61	
5 WM:	1	Catches:	19		5 WM:	1	Catches:	1	
Stumpings:	0				Stumpings:	0			

A tall medium pace bowler from Wellington he was often working into the wind or uphill while Richard Hadlee was wreaking havoc at the other end. Ewen Chatfield's first Test was very nearly his last after he was struck by a bouncer from English paceman Peter Lever. Clinically dead, he was revived by the English physiotherapist and rushed to hospital where he made a full recovery. Chatfield went on to be a fine servant in the national side for almost a decade and a half.

CLEVERLEY, Donald Charles

Born:	December 23, 1909
Batting:	Left handed
Bowling:	Right arm medium-fast

Tests

Test Career:	1932-46
Cap Number:	21
Tests Played:	2

Test Batting			
Innings:	4	Runs:	19
Highest Score:	10*	Average:	19.00
No. 50s:	0	No. 100s:	0

Test Bowling & Fielding			
Wickets:	0	Runs:	130
Best Bowling:		Average:	0.00
5 WI:	0	10 WM:	0
Catches:	0	Stumpings:	0

An opening bowler whose only two Tests were 14 years apart because of the long break imposed on New Zealand cricket by the Second World War. The wait wasn't worth it, he took no wickets in either match.

COLLINGE, Richard Owen

Born:	April 2, 1946
Batting:	Right handed
Bowling:	Left arm medium-fast

Tests

Test Career:	1965-78
Cap Number:	102
Tests Played:	35

New Zealand's 'tall terror' of the 60's and 70's, he was a fine fast bowler who played in the first New Zealand side to beat England and Australia in Tests. The first of those historic wins was against Australia at Lancaster Park in 1974. Collinge team up with the Hadlee brothers to steer the Black Caps to victory, and whilst he took only five wickets for the match, they included the opening wicket in each innings when the Aussies had precious few runs on the board. He was also on hand for New Zealand's stunning first ever win over England when the tourists were routed for 64 as the chased 137 for victory at the Basin Reserve in Wellington. He took the first three wickets to fall in that calamitous English second innings before Richard Hadlee stepped in to claim the remainder. Collinge took his 100th wicket in that Test and also the 101st that at the time made him his country's all-time leading wicket taker in Test cricket. He was also a hard hitting late order batsman who put his name into the record books at Auckland in 1973 when teamed up with Brian Hastings to add a world record 151 for the final wicket against Pakistan.

COLQUHOUN, Ian Alexander

Born:	June 8, 1924
Batting:	Right handed
	Wicket Keeper

Tests

Test Career:	1955
Cap Number:	68
Tests Played:	2

Test Batting			
Innings:	4	Runs:	1
Highest Score:	1*	Average:	0.50
No. 50s:	0	No. 100s:	0

Test Bowling & Fielding			
Wickets:	0	Runs:	0
Best Bowling:		Average:	0.00
5 WI:	0	10 WM:	0
Catches:	4	Stumpings:	0

The wicketkeeper from Central Districts played two Tests against the touring Englishmen in 1955, one them being that fateful match that saw the Black Caps dismissed for Test cricket's all time low of 26. It wasn't a good game for Colquhoun either who scored a golden duck in either innings of the match.

COMAN, Peter George

Born: April 13, 1943
Batting: Right handed

One Day Internationals

ODI Career: 1973-74
ODIs Played: 3

ODI Batting

Innings:	3	Runs:	62
Highest Score:	38	Average:	20.66
No. 50s:	0	No. 100s:	0

ODI Bowling & Fielding

Wickets:	0	Runs:	0
Best Bowling:		Average:	0.00
5 WM:	0	Catches:	2
Stumpings:	0		

Peter Coman played in New Zealand's inaugural ODI against Pakistan at Christchurch, in 1973. A right hand opener, Coman has the honour of facing New Zealand's first ball in one-day cricket. He went on to make 24 in New Zealand's historic 22-run victory. He represented New Zealand in a further two ODI's.

CONEY, Jeremy Vernon

Born: June 21, 1952
Batting: Right handed
Bowling: Right arm medium

Tests

Test Career: 1974-87
Cap Number: 129
Tests Played: 52

Test Batting

Innings:	85	Runs:	2,668
Highest Score:	174*	Average:	37.57
No. 50s:	16	No. 100s:	3

Test Bowling & Fielding

Wickets:	27	Runs:	966
Best Bowling:	3/28	Average:	35.77
5 WI:	0	10 WM:	0
Catches:	64	Stumpings:	0

One Day Internationals

ODI Career: 1979-87
ODIs Played: 88

ODI Batting

Innings:	80	Runs:	1,874
Highest Score:	66*	Average:	30.72
No. 50s:	8	No. 100s:	0

ODI Bowling & Fielding

Wickets:	54	Runs:	2,039
Best Bowling:	4/46	Average:	37.75
5 WM:	0	Catches:	40
Stumpings:	0		

The hard working Coney was rewarded first with a regular spot in the national team and then with the captaincy in the mid 80's. He played a handful of Tests against the Australians in 1973/74 but lost his place in the side and wasn't seen at international level for another five years. He returned a better batsman and a useful medium pace trundler who would regularly make a valuable contribution when needed most. A tall man, he wasn't a forceful or elegant batsman, just effective. His first Test century was a long time coming. His 174 not out against England at Wellington in 1983/84 was in his 25th Test and took eight hours to compile. Whilst laborious, it was typically appropriate and denied the tourists victory. Coney was a popular team member and leader who captained his country in 15 Tests including a historic first ever series win over the English. In retirement he became a popular TV commentator.

CONGDON, Bevan Ernest

Born: February 11, 1938
Batting: Right handed
Bowling: Right arm medium

Tests

Test Career: 1965-78
Cap Number: 103
Tests Played: 61

Test Batting

Innings:	114	Runs:	3,448
Highest Score:	176	Average:	32.22
No. 50s:	19	No. 100s:	7

Test Bowling & Fielding

Wickets:	59	Runs:	2,154
Best Bowling:	5/65	Average:	36.50
5 WI:	1	10 WM:	0
Catches:	44	Stumpings:	0

One Day Internationals

ODI Career: 1973-78
ODIs Played: 11

ODI Batting

Innings:	9	Runs:	338
Highest Score:	101	Average:	56.33
No. 50s:	2	No. 100s:	1

ODI Bowling & Fielding

Wickets:	7	Runs:	287
Best Bowling:	2/17	Average:	41.00
5 WM:	0	Catches:	0
Stumpings:	0		

The man in charge of New Zealand cricket at the start of the 70's, he was a world class top order batsman and an underrated medium pace bowler. Congdon replaced Geoff Dowling as captain in 1971 and continued to mold the side into a respected Test playing nation. Under his leadership they only won a single Test in 17 matches but it was the historic first ever victory against the Australians. As a batsman he was the model number three, watchful yet capable of scoring with a full array of strokes. His two highest Test scores came in consecutive innings against England in 1973. The first was a fighting 176 in the second innings at Trent Bridge when the entire side had been dismissed for 97 in the first dig. He then scored 175 at Lord's in a match that New Zealand was unlucky not to win.

Congdon was also a handy swing bowler, but like many skippers tended to underbowl himself. He was a fine servant for New Zealand cricket and was rewarded in retirement with an OBE.

COWIE, John (Jack)

Born: March 30, 1912
Batting: Right handed
Bowling: Right arm medium-fast

Tests

Test Career: 1937-49
Cap Number: 27
Tests Played: 9

Test Batting

Innings:	13	Runs:	90
Highest Score:	45	Average:	10.00
No. 50s:	0	No. 100s:	0

Test Bowling & Fielding

Wickets:	45	Runs:	969
Best Bowling:	6/40	Average:	21.53
5 WI:	4	10 WM:	0
Catches:	3	Stumpings:	0

Powerfully built and nicknamed 'Bull', he was New Zealand's premier paceman just prior to, and immediately after the Second World War. Cowie toured England in 1937 and was clearly his side's best bowler with 19 wickets in three Tests. At Old Trafford he became the first New Zealander to take 10 wickets in a match when he returned figures of 4/63 and 6/67. The highlight of that match was bowling the great Walter Hammond out for a duck in the second innings. As prized a scalp as Hammond's was, possibly Cowie's greatest claim to fame was becoming the only New Zealander to dismiss Don Bradman. That happened in Adelaide in 1937 when the New Zealanders, returning from England, played South Australia in a one-off match in Adelaide. When Test cricket resumed after the war he could still make the ball move in the air and off the wicket as he had done so effectively almost ten years earlier. Now in his mid thirties, he took 6/40 against the Australians in a Test where NZ could only manage 42 and 54 in their two at bats. He grabbed a 'five for' against England at Lord's in 1949, where he did come in for some stick, but was able to add Len Hutton to his list of famous victims. Jack Cowie played his last Test at the age of 37 but far from being lost to the game turned to umpiring and stood in three Tests during the 50's.

CRESSWELL, George Fenwick (Fen)

Born: March 22, 1915
Batting: Left handed

Tests

Test Career: 1949-51
Cap Number: 50
Tests Played: 3

Test Batting

Innings:	5	Runs:	14
Highest Score:	12*	Average:	7.00
No. 50s:	0	No. 100s:	0

Test Bowling & Fielding

Wickets:	13	Runs:	292
Best Bowling:	6/168	Average:	22.46
5 WI:	1	10 WM:	0
Catches:	0	Stumpings:	0

The late bloomer with an unusual front on bowling style, he played only three Tests but on the tour of England in 1949 did manage to take six wickets in an innings at The Oval.

CROMB, Ian Burns

Born: June 25, 1905
Batting: Right handed
Bowling: Right arm medium-fast

Tests

Test Career: 1931-32
Cap Number: 18
Tests Played: 5

Test Batting

Innings:	8	Runs:	123
Highest Score:	51*	Average:	20.50
No. 50s:	1	No. 100s:	0

Test Bowling & Fielding

Wickets:	8	Runs:	442
Best Bowling:	3/113	Average:	55.25
5 WI:	0	10 WM:	0
Catches:	1	Stumpings:	0

A speedy swing bowler from Canterbury who was well suited to English conditions taking five wickets at Lord's in his first Test appearance. He was a more than useful lower order batsman and scored an unbeaten 51 against the touring South Africans in Wellington in 1932.

CROWE, Jeffrey John

Born: September 14, 1958
Batting: Right handed
Bowling: Right arm medium

Tests

Test Career: 1983-90
Cap Number: 151
Tests Played: 39

Test Batting

Innings:	65	Runs:	1,601
Highest Score:	128	Average:	26.24
No. 50s:	6	No. 100s:	3

Test Bowling & Fielding

Wickets:	0	Runs:	9
Best Bowling:		Average:	0.00
5 WI:	0	10 WM:	0
Catches:	41	Stumpings:	0

One Day Internationals

ODI Career: 1983-90
ODIs Played: 75

ODI Batting

Innings:	71	Runs:	1,518
Highest Score:	88*	Average:	25.72
No. 50s:	7	No. 100s:	0

ODI Bowling & Fielding

Wickets:	0	Runs:	1
Best Bowling:		Average:	0.00
5 WM:	0	Catches:	28
Stumpings:	0		

Four years older than Martin, he made his debut a year after his precocious brother, having played much of his first class cricket with South Australia. Jeff certainly didn't have the natural flair of his younger brother but he was a fighting batsman who played some fine innings for his country. His first Test century was 128 against the touring Englishmen in 1983/84 but his finest hour came at Sabina Park in 1985 when he stood up to the likes of Joel Garner, Malcolm Marshall and Courtney Walsh to score a brave 112. He currently works as an ICC match referee.

CROWE, Martin David

Born:	September 22, 1962
Batting:	Right handed
Bowling:	Right arm medium

Tests

Test Career:	1982-95		
Cap Number:	150		
Tests Played:	77		

Test Batting

Innings:	131	Runs:	5,444
Highest Score:	299	Average:	45.36
No. 50s:	18	No. 100s:	17

Test Bowling & Fielding

Wickets:	14	Runs:	676
Best Bowling:	2/25	Average:	48.28
5 WI:	0	10 WM:	0
Catches:	71	Stumpings:	0

One Day Internationals

ODI Career:	1982-95		
ODIs Played:	143		

ODI Batting

Innings:	140	Runs:	4,704
Highest Score:	107*	Average:	38.55
No. 50s:	34	No. 100s:	4

ODI Bowling & Fielding

Wickets:	29	Runs:	954
Best Bowling:	2/9	Average:	32.89
5 WM:	0	Catches:	66
Stumpings:	0		

With apologies to Glenn Turner, Martin Crowe is the only New Zealander who could claim at one point in time to have been the best batsman in the world. The year was 1991 and at the height of his powers Crowe scored 299 against Sri Lanka to go within an ace of becoming the first Kiwi to score a Test triple century. It wasn't his ability to make big scores (he scored 17 Test centuries including two scores of 188 and one of 174) rather the way he did it. He could play every shot both brutally and correctly, always getting his feet in the right position whilst keeping his head perfectly still. His total of 77 Tests would have been considerably higher had he not been subject to a succession of injuries. Through his career he suffered back, hamstring and knee injuries that brought about his premature retirement in 1995 at the age of only 33. He was less impressive as a captain, who like many naturally gifted sportspeople could not always relate to the battles of mere mortals. Crowe led New Zealand in 16 Tests for just two victories. Since retiring from Test cricket he was worked as both a broadcaster and coach.

CUMMING, Craig Derek

Born:	August 31, 1975
Batting:	Right handed

Tests

Test Career:	2005-		
Cap Number:	228		
Tests Played:	5		

Test Batting

Innings:	9	Runs:	208
Highest Score:	74	Average:	26.00
No. 50s:	1	No. 100s:	0

Test Bowling & Fielding

Wickets:	0	Runs:	0
Best Bowling:		Average:	0.00
5 WI:	0	10 WM:	0
Catches:	2	Stumpings:	0

One Day Internationals

ODI Career:	2003-		
ODIs Played:	12		

ODI Batting

Innings:	12	Runs:	161
Highest Score:	45*	Average:	14.63
No. 50s:	0	No. 100s:	0

ODI Bowling & Fielding

Wickets:	0	Runs:	17
Best Bowling:		Average:	0.00
5 WM:	0	Catches:	6
Stumpings:	0		

A batsman from Canterbury via Otago, he has had five Tests to secure a spot in the team but with only the one half century remains on the fringes.

CUNIS, Robert Smith

Born:	January 5, 1941
Batting:	Right handed
Bowling:	Right arm medium-fast

Tests

Test Career:	1964-72		
Cap Number:	101		
Tests Played:	20		

Test Batting

Innings:	31	Runs:	295
Highest Score:	51	Average:	12.82
No. 50s:	1	No. 100s:	0

Test Bowling & Fielding

Wickets:	51	Runs:	1,887
Best Bowling:	6/76	Average:	37.00
5 WI:	1	10 WM:	0
Catches:	1	Stumpings:	0

The medium pace bowler was a handy servant with his steady line and length and useful lower order batting. His best innings figures of 6/78 camem against England at Auckland in 1970/71.

Legendary commentator John Arlott was at his wittiest best when he once described his bowling as being like his name, "Neither one thing nor the other".

D'ARCY, John William
Born: April 23, 1936
Batting: Right handed

Tests
Test Career:	1958		
Cap Number:	81		
Tests Played:	5		

Test Batting
Innings:	10	Runs:	136
Highest Score:	33	Average:	13.60
No. 50s:	0	No. 100s:	0

Test Bowling & Fielding
Wickets:	0	Runs:	0
Best Bowling:		Average:	0.00
5 WI:	0	10 WM:	0
Catches:	0	Stumpings:	0

Times were tough for the Black Caps in the late 1950's, and whilst John D'Arcy was a good fighting opener with Canterbury, you wonder how a batsman with a first class average of 23 could play Test cricket. In ten Test innings he could only manage a top score of 33.

DAVIS, Heath Te-Ihi-O-Te-Rangi
Born: November 30, 1971
Batting: Right handed
Bowling: Right arm fast

Tests
Test Career:	1994-97		
Cap Number:	189		
Tests Played:	5		

Test Batting
Innings:	7	Runs:	20
Highest Score:	8*	Average:	6.66
No. 50s:	0	No. 100s:	0

Test Bowling & Fielding
Wickets:	17	Runs:	499
Best Bowling:	5/63	Average:	29.35
5 WI:	1	10 WM:	0
Catches:	4	Stumpings:	0

One Day Internationals
ODI Career:	1994-97		
ODIs Played:	11		

ODI Batting
Innings:	6	Runs:	13
Highest Score:	7*	Average:	6.50
No. 50s:	0	No. 100s:	0

ODI Bowling & Fielding
Wickets:	11	Runs:	436
Best Bowling:	4/35	Average:	39.63
5 WM:	0	Catches:	2
Stumpings:	0		

A speedster who had all the makings of a top class strike bowler but was constantly hampered by overstepping the bowling crease. He took 17 wickets in five Tests including 5/63 in the first innings against Sri Lanka at Hastings in 1996/97 but like so many New Zealand quicks at the time ended up succumbing to injury.

DE GROEN, Richard Paul
Born: August 5, 1962
Batting: Right handed
Bowling: Right arm medium-fast

Tests
Test Career:	1993-94		
Cap Number:	185		
Tests Played:	5		

Test Batting
Innings:	10	Runs:	45
Highest Score:	26	Average:	7.50
No. 50s:	0	No. 100s:	0

Test Bowling & Fielding
Wickets:	11	Runs:	505
Best Bowling:	3/40	Average:	45.90
5 WI:	0	10 WM:	0
Catches:	0	Stumpings:	0

One Day Internationals
ODI Career:	1993-94		
ODIs Played:	12		

ODI Batting
Innings:	8	Runs:	12
Highest Score:	7*	Average:	2.40
No. 50s:	0	No. 100s:	0

ODI Bowling & Fielding
Wickets:	8	Runs:	478
Best Bowling:	2/34	Average:	59.75
5 WM:	0	Catches:	2
Stumpings:	0		

A right arm quick who played in five Tests for 11 wickets. His best match was the first Test of the 1993/94 series against Pakistan played at Eden Park when he returned match figures of 5/88.

DEMPSTER, Charles Stewart
Born: November 15, 1903
Batting: Right handed

Tests
Test Career:	1930-33		
Cap Number:	3		
Tests Played:	10		

Test Batting
Innings:	15	Runs:	723
Highest Score:	136	Average:	65.72
No. 50s:	5	No. 100s:	2

Test Bowling & Fielding
Wickets:	0	Runs:	10
Best Bowling:		Average:	0.00
5 WI:	0	10 WM:	0
Catches:	2	Stumpings:	0

Stewie Dempster was New Zealand's first great batsman The chunky opener played in only ten Tests until business took him to England, but in that time scored his country's first Test century and the first hundred by a New Zealander in England. The historic first century was 136 against England at Wellington and was part of an opening stand of 276 with Jackie Mills that still stands as the highest opening partnership in Tests between the two countries. Other than Rodney Redmond who only played a single Test, Dempster's Test average of 65.72 is the highest of any NZ batsman. After moving to England he captained Leicestershire in the county cricket competition.

DEMPSTER, Eric William
Born:	January 25, 1925
Batting:	Left handed
Bowling:	Left arm off-break

Tests

Test Career:	1953-54
Cap Number:	62
Tests Played:	5

Test Batting

Innings:	8	Runs:	106
Highest Score:	47	Average:	17.66
No. 50s:	0	No. 100s:	0

Test Bowling & Fielding

Wickets:	2	Runs:	219
Best Bowling:	1/24	Average:	109.50
5 WI:	0	10 WM:	0
Catches:	1	Stumpings:	0

A left arm off spinner and more that useful lower order batsman who played against the South Africans both at home and away in the mid 50's. He later became an umpire and stood in three ODI's between 1974 and 1976.

DICK, Arthur Edward
Born:	October 10, 1936
Batting:	Right handed
	Wicket Keeper

Tests

Test Career:	1961-65
Cap Number:	91
Tests Played:	17

Test Batting

Innings:	30	Runs:	370
Highest Score:	50*	Average:	14.23
No. 50s:	1	No. 100s:	0

Test Bowling & Fielding

Wickets:	0	Runs:	0
Best Bowling:		Average:	0.00
5 WI:	0	10 WM:	0
Catches:	47	Stumpings:	4

On glovework alone he should be thought of as one of the finest wicket keepers to ever play for New Zealand. Equally at home standing back to the quicks or up the spinners he equaled the record for most dismissals by a New Zealand keeper in a Test with seven on debut at Durban in 1961. He was a brave lower order batsman with a Test high of 50 not out against South Africa at Cape Town that helped his country to a famous victory.

DICKINSON, George Ritchie
Born:	March 11, 1903
Batting:	Right handed
Bowling:	Right arm fast

Tests

Test Career:	1930-32
Cap Number:	4
Tests Played:	3

Test Batting

Innings:	5	Runs:	31
Highest Score:	11	Average:	6.20
No. 50s:	0	No. 100s:	0

Test Bowling & Fielding

Wickets:	8	Runs:	245
Best Bowling:	3/66	Average:	30.62
5 WI:	0	10 WM:	0
Catches:	3	Stumpings:	0

An opening bowler who played in the historic first Test against England in 1929/30 and also New Zealand's first Test against South Africa.

DONNELLY, Martin Paterson
Born:	October 17, 1917
Batting:	Left handed
Bowling:	Left arm off-break

Tests

Test Career:	1937-49
Cap Number:	28
Tests Played:	7

Test Batting

Innings:	12	Runs:	582
Highest Score:	206	Average:	52.90
No. 50s:	4	No. 100s:	1

Test Bowling & Fielding

Wickets:	0	Runs:	20
Best Bowling:		Average:	0.00
5 WI:	0	10 WM:	0
Catches:	7	Stumpings:	0

A brilliant left handed batsman, Martin Donnelly played relatively little cricket in New Zealand and all his seven tests were played in England. Standing little more than five and a half foot he was a punishing batsman with dazzling footwork. It was after World War II, when he was studying at Oxford, that Donnelly established his reputation. He is best remembered for his 206 at Lords in 1949 which was the first double century for New Zealand in Test cricket. In all he batted six times in that Test series and passed 50 in all bar one innings. Whilst in England he played for both Middlesex and Warwickshire earning the reputation as one of the best batsman in the game. Donnelly was also a first five-eighth or centre at rugby, and played for England against Ireland in 1947. He is one of 13 cricketers that have been inducted in to New Zealand's Sporting Hall of Fame.

DOUGLAS, Mark William
Born:	October 20, 1968
Batting:	Left handed
	Wicket Keeper

One Day Internationals

ODI Career:	1994-95
ODIs Played:	6

ODI Batting

Innings:	6	Runs:	55
Highest Score:	30	Average:	9.16
No. 50s:	0	No. 100s:	0

ODI Bowling & Fielding
Wickets: 0
Best Bowling:
5 WM: 0
Stumpings: 0
Runs: 0
Average: 0.00
Catches: 2

A wicket keeper from Nelson who made his debut against Australia at Sharjah, in 1994.

DOULL, Simon Blair
Born: August 6, 1969
Batting: Right handed
Bowling: Right arm medium

Tests
Test Career: 1992-2000
Cap Number: 178
Tests Played: 32

Test Batting
Innings: 50
Highest Score: 46
No. 50s: 0
Runs: 570
Average: 14.61
No. 100s: 0

Test Bowling & Fielding
Wickets: 98
Best Bowling: 7/65
5 WI: 6
Catches: 16
Runs: 2,872
Average: 29.30
10 WM: 0
Stumpings: 0

One Day Internationals
ODI Career: 1992-2000
ODIs Played: 42

ODI Batting
Innings: 27
Highest Score: 22
No. 50s: 0
Runs: 172
Average: 12.28
No. 100s: 0

ODI Bowling & Fielding
Wickets: 36
Best Bowling: 4/25
5 WM: 0
Stumpings: 0
Runs: 1,459
Average: 40.52
Catches: 10

One of many New Zealand paceman in recent years who was forced to retire prematurely because of injury. A strongly built quick who put his whole body into his bowling, he had an excellent record taking 98 wickets from 32 Tests. Doull took five or more wickets in an innings on six occasions including a career best 7/65 at Wellington in 1998. It was a performance to remember for Doull who took the first seven wickets to fall in the innings including Dravid, Ganguly and Tendulkar. Since bad knees forced him to give the game away in 2002 he has worked as a commentator.

DOWLING, Graham Thorne
Born: March 4, 1937
Batting: Right handed
Bowling: Right arm medium

Tests
Test Career: 1961-72
Cap Number: 93
Tests Played: 39

Test Batting
Innings: 77
Highest Score: 239
No. 50s: 11
Runs: 2,306
Average: 31.16
No. 100s: 3

Test Bowling & Fielding
Wickets: 1
Best Bowling: 1/19
5 WI: 0
Catches: 23
Runs: 19
Average: 19.00
10 WM: 0
Stumpings: 0

An accomplished opening batsman and intelligent captain, he lead the revival of New Zealand cricket in the 1960's. The national side had wallowed in the 50's and was in the process of rebuilding when they toured South Africa in 1961/62. The side contained talented youngsters such as Graham Dowling, Dick Motz and Frank Cameron and returned home with a meritorious series draw. Cowling made a huge impression on debut, scoring 74 and 58 at Johannesburg in the second Test. The right hander with a fine technique showed he had great powers of concentration in that first knock of 74, occupying the crease for over four hours. It was his ability to bat with patience that saw him hit three centuries against India later in his career, including a then national record 239 at Christchurch in 1968. That double century was in his first Test as captain and the much respected Dowling went on to lead the team in 19 Tests for four victories. Following his retirement he became an umpire, standing in nine Tests between 1995 and 2000.

DRUM, Christopher James
Born: July 10, 1974
Batting: Right handed
Bowling: Right arm medium-fast

Tests
Test Career: 2001-02
Cap Number: 215
Tests Played: 5

Test Batting
Innings: 5
Highest Score: 4
No. 50s: 0
Runs: 10
Average: 3.33
No. 100s: 0

Test Bowling & Fielding
Wickets: 16
Best Bowling: 3/36
5 WI: 0
Catches: 4
Runs: 482
Average: 30.12
10 WM: 0
Stumpings: 0

One Day Internationals
ODI Career: 1999
ODIs Played: 5

ODI Batting
Innings: 2
Highest Score: 7*
No. 50s: 0
Runs: 9
Average: 0.00
No. 100s: 0

ODI Bowling & Fielding
Wickets: 4
Best Bowling: 2/31
5 WM: 0
Stumpings: 0
Runs: 261
Average: 65.25
Catches: 1

A fast medium bowler from Auckland who took 16 wickets in his five Tests between 2001 and 2002.

DUNNING, John Angus
Born: February 6, 1903
Batting: Right handed

Tests
Test Career: 1933-37
Cap Number: 26
Tests Played: 4

Test Batting
Innings:	6	Runs:	38
Highest Score:	19	Average:	7.60
No. 50s:	0	No. 100s:	0

Test Bowling & Fielding
Wickets:	5	Runs:	493
Best Bowling:	2/35	Average:	98.60
5 WI:	0	10 WM:	0
Catches:	2	Stumpings:	0

A right arm seam bowler who had an excellent first class record but found wickets harder to come by in the Test arena with only five in four matches. He later moved to Australia where he was a highly respected cricket administrator.

EDGAR, Bruce Adrian
Born: November 23, 1956
Batting: Right handed

Tests
Test Career: 1978-86
Cap Number: 143
Tests Played: 39

Test Batting
Innings:	68	Runs:	1,958
Highest Score:	161	Average:	30.59
No. 50s:	12	No. 100s:	3

Test Bowling & Fielding
Wickets:	0	Runs:	3
Best Bowling:		Average:	0.00
5 WI:	0	10 WM:	0
Catches:	14	Stumpings:	0

One Day Internationals
ODI Career: 1978-86
ODIs Played: 64

ODI Batting
Innings:	64	Runs:	1,814
Highest Score:	102*	Average:	30.74
No. 50s:	10	No. 100s:	1

ODI Bowling & Fielding
Wickets:	0	Runs:	5
Best Bowling:		Average:	0.00
5 WM:	0	Catches:	12
Stumpings:	0		

One of two left handers who opened the New Zealand batting in the early 80's, he was a consistent rather than brilliant performer. Like John Wright he seemed unflappable at the top of the order and scored three hundreds including a career high 161 against Australia at Auckland in 1981. Edgar was the disbelieving batsman at the non-striker's end when Trevor Chappell bowled that infamous underarm delivery at Brian McKechnie to the MCG in 1981. He was 102 not out at the time.

EDWARDS, Graham Neil (Jock)
Born: May 27, 1955
Batting: Right handed
Wicket Keeper

Tests
Test Career: 1977-81
Cap Number: 139
Tests Played: 8

Test Batting
Innings:	15	Runs:	377
Highest Score:	55	Average:	25.13
No. 50s:	3	No. 100s:	0

Test Bowling & Fielding
Wickets:	0	Runs:	0
Best Bowling:		Average:	0.00
5 WI:	0	10 WM:	0
Catches:	7	Stumpings:	0

One Day Internationals
ODI Career: 1976-81
ODIs Played: 6

ODI Batting
Innings:	6	Runs:	138
Highest Score:	41	Average:	23.00
No. 50s:	0	No. 100s:	0

ODI Bowling & Fielding
Wickets:	1	Runs:	5
Best Bowling:	1/5	Average:	5.00
5 WM:	0	Catches:	5
Stumpings:	0		

A solidly built keeper, he was a surprise replacement for Warren Lees on the tour of England in 1978. The useful batsman scored three Test half centuries but completed only seven dismissals in his eight Test appearances.

EMERY, Raymond William George
Born: March 28, 1915
Batting: Right handed
Bowling: Right arm medium

Tests
Test Career: 1952
Cap Number: 55
Tests Played: 2

Test Batting
Innings:	4	Runs:	46
Highest Score:	28	Average:	11.50
No. 50s:	0	No. 100s:	0

Test Bowling & Fielding
Wickets:	2	Runs:	52
Best Bowling:	2/52	Average:	26.00
5 WI:	0	10 WM:	0
Catches:	0	Stumpings:	0

A medium pace bowler from Canterbury who played two Tests against the touring West Indians in 1952.

FISHER, Frederick Eric
Born: July 28, 1924
Batting: Right handed
Bowling: Left arm medium

Tests
Test Career: 1953
Cap Number: 58
Tests Played: 1

Test Batting

Innings:	2	Runs:	23
Highest Score:	14	Average:	11.50
No. 50s:	0	No. 100s:	0

Test Bowling & Fielding

Wickets:	1	Runs:	78
Best Bowling:	1/78	Average:	78.00
5 WI:	0	10 WM:	0
Catches:	0	Stumpings:	0

Eric Fisher's only Test was against the touring South Africans in 1953.

FLEMING, Stephen Paul

Born:	April 1, 1973
Batting:	Left handed

Tests

Test Career:	1994-		
Cap Number:	188		
Tests Played:	102		

Test Batting

Innings:	173	Runs:	6,545
Highest Score:	274*	Average:	40.15
No. 50s:	41	No. 100s:	9

Test Bowling & Fielding

Wickets:	0	Runs:	0
Best Bowling:		Average:	0.00
5 WI:	0	10 WM:	0
Catches:	152	Stumpings:	0

One Day Internationals

ODI Career:	1994-		
ODIs Played:	253		

ODI Batting

Innings:	243	Runs:	7,184
Highest Score:	134*	Average:	32.07
No. 50s:	43	No. 100s:	6

ODI Bowling & Fielding

Wickets:	1	Runs:	28
Best Bowling:	1/8	Average:	28.00
5 WM:	0	Catches:	116
Stumpings:	0		

From his debut as a 20 year old in 1994, Stephen Fleming has gone from talented youngster, to the man charged with the dual responsibility of being his side's premier batsman and captain. His first Test was against India at Hamilton, and in the second innings of that match he went tantalisingly close to scoring a first up century when he was caught by Kapil Dev for 92. That was to be the closest he would get to a Test hundred for almost three years. It was a frustrating period for Fleming, who came under close scrutiny for his inability to convert good starts into big scores. He finally got the monkey off his back with 129 against England at Eden Park early in 1997 and has since gone on to make a number of big knocks in Test cricket. As he became a more mature batsman he amassed three big double centuries, including a national record 274 not out against Sri Lanka at Saravanamuttu Stadium in 2003. Like many tall top order batsmen he looks best when attacking off the front foot and when in full flight there are few better drivers in the game. Given his natural talent, a Test average of 40.15 seems under the odds, with critics pointing out it would be considerably better if he didn't struggle against Australia against whom he averages only 25.18. Fleming has led his country into battle on 78 occasions, more than twice as many times as any other New Zealander. His record of 27 wins, 26 draws and 25 losses is full of merit given the number of players, particularly fast bowlers, that have been sidelined with injury during his tenure.

FOLEY, Henry

Born:	January 28, 1906
Batting:	Left handed

Tests

Test Career:	1930		
Cap Number:	5		
Tests Played:	1		

Test Batting

Innings:	2	Runs:	4
Highest Score:	2	Average:	2.00
No. 50s:	0	No. 100s:	0

Test Bowling & Fielding

Wickets:	0	Runs:	0
Best Bowling:		Average:	0.00
5 WI:	0	10 WM:	0
Catches:	0	Stumpings:	0

His only Test was his country's first against England in January, 1930. Foley opened the batting but could only manage two runs in his only two Test knocks.

FRANKLIN, James Edward Charles

Born:	November 7, 1980
Batting:	Left handed
Bowling:	Left arm medium-fast

Tests

Test Career:	2001-		
Cap Number:	214		
Tests Played:	19		

Test Batting

Innings:	25	Runs:	460
Highest Score:	122*	Average:	23.00
No. 50s:	1	No. 100s:	1

Test Bowling & Fielding

Wickets:	70	Runs:	1,970
Best Bowling:	6/119	Average:	28.14
5 WI:	3	10 WM:	0
Catches:	7	Stumpings:	0

One Day Internationals

ODI Career:	2001-		
ODIs Played:	41		

ODI Batting

Innings:	25	Runs:	221
Highest Score:	29*	Average:	11.63
No. 50s:	0	No. 100s:	0

ODI Bowling & Fielding

Wickets:	37	Runs:	1,468
Best Bowling:	5/42	Average:	39.67
5 WM:	1	Catches:	13
Stumpings:	0		

The left arm quick is just short of top pace, but with his ability to move the ball in the air and land it on the seam he is a tricky customer to face.

Franklin had a taste of Test cricket as a 20 year old with two Tests against the touring Pakistanis but when he re-emerged over three years later he took his opportunity with both hands taking six wickets for not many at Trent Bridge. Since then he has gone on to take four or more wickets in another seven innings with a career best 'six for' against the powerful Aussies at Eden Park in 2005. Almost an all-rounder he had three first class centuries to his name when he teamed up with Stephen Fleming to put on a record 256 for the eighth wicket against South Africa at Newlands in May, 2006. Frnaklin's contribution was an unbeaten 122.

FRANKLIN, Trevor John
Born: March 15, 1962
Batting: Right handed
Bowling: Right arm medium

Tests
Test Career: 1983-91
Cap Number: 153
Tests Played: 21

Test Batting
Innings:	37	Runs:	828
Highest Score:	101	Average:	23.00
No. 50s:	4	No. 100s:	1

Test Bowling & Fielding
Wickets:	0	Runs:	0
Best Bowling:		Average:	0.00
5 WI:	0	10 WM:	0
Catches:	8	Stumpings:	0

One Day Internationals
ODI Career: 1983-88
ODIs Played: 3

ODI Batting
Innings:	3	Runs:	27
Highest Score:	21	Average:	9.00
No. 50s:	0	No. 100s:	0

ODI Bowling & Fielding
Wickets:	0	Runs:	0
Best Bowling:		Average:	0.00
5 WM:	0	Catches:	0
Stumpings:	0		

One of the modern games most notorious plodders, the opening batsman from Auckland had a strike rate of only 26.44 in Test cricket. His highest score at the top level was a predictably laborious 101 at Lord's in 1991 that took 435 minutes to compile.

FREEMAN, Douglas Linford
Born: September 8, 1914
Batting: Right handed
Bowling: Right arm leg-break

Tests
Test Career: 1933
Cap Number: 23
Tests Played: 2

Test Batting
Innings:	2	Runs:	2
Highest Score:	1	Average:	1.00
No. 50s:	0	No. 100s:	0

Test Bowling & Fielding
Wickets:	1	Runs:	169
Best Bowling:	1/91	Average:	169.00
5 WI:	0	10 WM:	0
Catches:	0	Stumpings:	0

The Australian born leg spinner played two Tests against the touring Englishmen in 1933 but could manage only the single wicket.

FULTON, Peter Gordon
Born: February 1, 1979
Batting: Right handed
Bowling: Right arm medium

Tests
Test Career: 2006-
Cap Number: 231
Tests Played: 5

Test Batting
Innings:	7	Runs:	185
Highest Score:	75	Average:	26.42
No. 50s:	1	No. 100s:	0

Test Bowling & Fielding
Wickets:	0	Runs:	0
Best Bowling:		Average:	0.00
5 WI:	0	10 WM:	0
Catches:	3	Stumpings:	0

One Day Internationals
ODI Career: 2004-
ODIs Played: 10

ODI Batting
Innings:	10	Runs:	382
Highest Score:	112	Average:	47.75
No. 50s:	2	No. 100s:	1

ODI Bowling & Fielding
Wickets:	0	Runs:	0
Best Bowling:		Average:	0.00
5 WM:	0	Catches:	5
Stumpings:	0		

A tall middle order batsman with a first class triple century to his name for Canterbury. He has been inconsistent at Test level but his 75 against the touring West Indies early in 2006 suggests that he's worth persisting with.

GALLICHAN, Norman
Born: June 3, 1906
Batting: Right handed
Bowling: Left arm off-break

Tests
Test Career: 1937
Cap Number: 33
Tests Played: 1

Test Batting
Innings:	2	Runs:	32
Highest Score:	30	Average:	16.00
No. 50s:	0	No. 100s:	0

Test Bowling & Fielding
Wickets:	3	Runs:	113
Best Bowling:	3/99	Average:	37.66
5 WI:	0	10 WM:	0
Catches:	0	Stumpings:	0

He played a single Test at Old Trafford in 1937 and despite taking three wickets that included Walter Hammond and scoring 30 at number nine, never played another Test.

GEDYE, Sydney Graham

Born: May 2, 1929
Batting: Right handed

Tests
Test Career: 1964-65
Cap Number: 98
Tests Played: 4

Test Batting
Innings:	8	Runs:	193
Highest Score:	55	Average:	24.12
No. 50s:	2	No. 100s:	0

Test Bowling & Fielding
Wickets:	0	Runs:	0
Best Bowling:		Average:	0.00
5 WI:	0	10 WM:	0
Catches:	0	Stumpings:	0

A right hand batsman from Auckland who showed promise in his first series for New Zealand with two half centuries at home to South Africa in 1964. He played a single Test the following year against Pakistan but after scoring only 1 and 26 was dropped from the team.

GERMON, Lee Kenneth

Born: November 4, 1968
Batting: Right handed
Bowling: Right arm leg-break
Wicket Keeper

Tests
Test Career: 1995-97
Cap Number: 193
Tests Played: 12

Test Batting
Innings:	21	Runs:	382
Highest Score:	55	Average:	21.22
No. 50s:	1	No. 100s:	0

Test Bowling & Fielding
Wickets:	0	Runs:	0
Best Bowling:		Average:	0.00
5 WI:	0	10 WM:	0
Catches:	27	Stumpings:	2

One Day Internationals
ODI Career: 1994-97
ODIs Played: 37

ODI Batting
Innings:	31	Runs:	519
Highest Score:	89	Average:	19.96
No. 50s:	3	No. 100s:	0

ODI Bowling & Fielding
Wickets:	0	Runs:	0
Best Bowling:		Average:	0.00
5 WM:	0	Catches:	21
Stumpings:	9		

Cricket has seen few more controversial selection decisions than the choice of Lee Germon to replace Ken Rutherford as New Zealand skipper in 1995. Germon who had never played for New Zealand, was in fact been playing in Holland when plucked to lead his country. The selection highlighted the disharmony at the highest level of NZ cricket and whilst the keeper batsman performed admirably in 12 Tests, he was quickly replaced when a new national coach was appointed in 1997.

GILLESPIE, Stuart Ross

Born: March 2, 1957
Batting: Right handed
Bowling: Right arm medium-fast

Tests
Test Career: 1986
Cap Number: 157
Tests Played: 1

Test Batting
Innings:	1	Runs:	28
Highest Score:	28	Average:	28.00
No. 50s:	0	No. 100s:	0

Test Bowling & Fielding
Wickets:	1	Runs:	79
Best Bowling:	1/79	Average:	79.00
5 WI:	0	10 WM:	0
Catches:	0	Stumpings:	0

One Day Internationals
ODI Career: 1986-88
ODIs Played: 19

ODI Batting
Innings:	11	Runs:	70
Highest Score:	18	Average:	11.66
No. 50s:	0	No. 100s:	0

ODI Bowling & Fielding
Wickets:	23	Runs:	736
Best Bowling:	4/30	Average:	32.00
5 WM:	0	Catches:	7
Stumpings:	0		

A medium pace bowler who played a single Test against the Australians at Wellington in 1986. He also played in 19 ODI's for 23 wickets.

GRAY, Evan John

Born: November 18, 1954
Batting: Right handed
Bowling: Left arm off-break

Tests
Test Career: 1983-88
Cap Number: 152
Tests Played: 10

Test Batting
Innings:	16	Runs:	248
Highest Score:	50	Average:	15.50
No. 50s:	1	No. 100s:	0

Test Bowling & Fielding
Wickets:	17	Runs:	886
Best Bowling:	3/73	Average:	52.11
5 WI:	0	10 WM:	0
Catches:	6	Stumpings:	0

One Day Internationals
ODI Career: 1984-88
ODIs Played: 10

ODI Batting
Innings:	7	Runs:	98
Highest Score:	38	Average:	16.33
No. 50s:	0	No. 100s:	0

ODI Bowling & Fielding
Wickets:	8	Runs:	286
Best Bowling:	2/26	Average:	35.75
5 WM:	0	Catches:	3
Stumpings:	0		

A left arm spinner who played a handful of Tests in the 1980's. He was a more than handy batsman in the Shell Trophy where he scored six first class centuries but his only half century at Test level came at Trent Bridge in 1986.

GREATBATCH, Mark John

Born: December 11, 1963
Batting: Left handed
Bowling: Right arm medium
Wicket Keeper

Tests

Test Career: 1988-96
Cap Number: 165
Tests Played: 41

Test Batting

Innings:	71	Runs:	2,021
Highest Score:	146*	Average:	30.62
No. 50s:	10	No. 100s:	3

Test Bowling & Fielding

Wickets:	0	Runs:	0
Best Bowling:		Average:	0.00
5 WI:	0	10 WM:	0
Catches:	27	Stumpings:	0

One Day Internationals

ODI Career: 1988-96
ODIs Played: 84

ODI Batting

Innings:	83	Runs:	2,206
Highest Score:	111	Average:	28.28
No. 50s:	13	No. 100s:	2

ODI Bowling & Fielding

Wickets:	0	Runs:	5
Best Bowling:		Average:	0.00
5 WM:	0	Catches:	35
Stumpings:	0		

There were two very different versions of the cricketer, Mark Greatbatch. In Tests he was a watchful top order batsman who scored a painstaking century in his first Test that took almost seven hours to compile. Throughout his Test career he was a dogged batsman who only rarely opened his shoulders. He was however a different proposition in one day cricket where put his bulky frame to good use, belting the ball until he ran out of either steam or luck. Greatbatch had a brilliant 1992 World Cup where he opened the batting throughout the tournament scoring 313 at almost a run ball. He was also a brilliant fieldsman at first slip.

GUILLEN, Simpson Clairmonte (Sammy)

Born: September 24, 1924
Batting: Right handed
Wicket Keeper

Tests

Test Career: 1951-56
Cap Number: 78
Tests Played: 8

Test Batting

Innings:	12	Runs:	202
Highest Score:	54	Average:	20.20
No. 50s:	1	No. 100s:	0

Test Bowling & Fielding

Wickets:	0	Runs:	0
Best Bowling:		Average:	0.00
5 WI:	0	10 WM:	0
Catches:	13	Stumpings:	3

One of the most amazing stories involving a cricketer who played just a handful of Tests. Sammy Guillen was a wicketkeeper from Trinidad, who played his first Test against Australia, at the Adelaide Oval, in 1951. In all, he represented the West Indies in five Tests and then headed overseas to live in New Zealand. Three years later, he was selected in New Zealand's Test eleven, therefore becoming one of 14 cricketers to have played Test cricket for two nations. In an ironic twist. during his eighth and final Test against the West Indies, at Auckland in 1956. he stumped former teammate Alf Valentine for five, and in the process secured New Zealand's first ever Test win. Guillen was voted New Zealand Cricket Almanack 'Player of the Year' in 1956.

GUY, John William

Born: August 29, 1934
Batting: Left handed

Tests

Test Career: 1955-61
Cap Number: 76
Tests Played: 12

Test Batting

Innings:	23	Runs:	440
Highest Score:	102	Average:	20.95
No. 50s:	3	No. 100s:	1

Test Bowling & Fielding

Wickets:	0	Runs:	0
Best Bowling:		Average:	0.00
5 WI:	0	10 WM:	0
Catches:	2	Stumpings:	0

The left handed top order batsman played in a tough period for New Zealand cricket, but his only Test century, a seven hour effort against India at Hyerabad showed that in John Guy the Kiwis had a gritty customer.

HADLEE, Barry George

Born: December 14, 1941
Batting: Right handed

One Day Internationals

ODI Career: 1975
ODIs Played: 2

ODI Batting

Innings:	2	Runs:	26
Highest Score:	19	Average:	26.00
No. 50s:	0	No. 100s:	0

ODI Bowling & Fielding

Wickets:	0	Runs:	0
Best Bowling:		Average:	0.00
5 WM:	0	Catches:	0
Stumpings:	0		

A right hand opener, Barry Hadlee made his ODI debut against England at Dunedin, in 1975 where he played alongside younger brothers Dayle and Richard. He played in just two ODI's, his second coming on the tour of England later that year, where he made 19 before being bowled by future England captain, Tony Greig. Unlike his siblings, and father, former Test captain Walter, Barry did not get the opportunity to represent his country at Test level.

HADLEE, Dayle Robert
Born: January 6, 1948
Batting: Right handed
Bowling: Right arm medium-fast

Tests
Test Career: 1969-78
Cap Number: 119
Tests Played: 26

Test Batting
Innings:	42	Runs:	530
Highest Score:	56	Average:	14.32
No. 50s:	1	No. 100s:	0

Test Bowling & Fielding
Wickets:	71	Runs:	2,389
Best Bowling:	4/30	Average:	33.64
5 WI:	0	10 WM:	0
Catches:	8	Stumpings:	0

One Day Internationals
ODI Career: 1973-76
ODIs Played: 11

ODI Batting
Innings:	7	Runs:	40
Highest Score:	20	Average:	8.00
No. 50s:	0	No. 100s:	0

ODI Bowling & Fielding
Wickets:	20	Runs:	364
Best Bowling:	4/34	Average:	18.20
5 WM:	0	Catches:	2
Stumpings:	0		

It's not easy to carve a name for yourself when your father was a giant figure in the early days of New Zealand cricket and your brother is the greatest cricketer to ever represent his country, but Dayle Hadlee was a fine bowler in his own right, playing 26 Tests over a nine year period. Injuries prevented him from bowling as quickly as brother Richard but he was a dangerous swing bowler who teamed up successfully in the 70's with his brother and Richard Collinge. He took four wickets in Australia's second innings at Christchurch in 1974 to engineer his country's first win over their antipodean neighbours.

HADLEE, Sir Richard John
Born: July 3, 1951
Batting: Left handed
Bowling: Right arm fast

Tests
Test Career: 1973-90
Cap Number: 123
Tests Played: 86

Test Batting
Innings:	134	Runs:	3,124
Highest Score:	151*	Average:	27.16
No. 50s:	15	No. 100s:	2

Test Bowling & Fielding
Wickets:	431	Runs:	9,611
Best Bowling:	9/52	Average:	22.29
5 WI:	36	10 WM:	9
Catches:	39	Stumpings:	0

One Day Internationals
ODI Career: 1973-90
ODIs Played: 115

ODI Batting
Innings:	96	Runs:	1,751
Highest Score:	79	Average:	21.61
No. 50s:	4	No. 100s:	0

ODI Bowling & Fielding
Wickets:	158	Runs:	3,407
Best Bowling:	5/25	Average:	21.56
5 WM:	5	Catches:	27
Stumpings:	0		

In 1990 Richard Hadlee both retired from international cricket and received a knighthood for services to the game, confirmation from the highest quarter that the curtain had come down on the career of New Zealand's greatest ever cricketer. With a father who was a former New Zealand captain and a brother who was already in the Test side, much was expected of the 19 year old when he made his Test debut at home against Pakistan in 1973. He opened the bowling and batted at number eight in that first outing for his country, but after taking two wickets and scoring 46 was dropped. He was given time to develop over the next three years, and made good on that investment with a breakout performance against India at the Basin Reserve in Wellington in 1976. He captured 4/35 and 7/23 as the visitors crumbled to an innings defeat. From that point on there was no turning back forHadlee as he became first his country's main strike bowler, then one of the game's best quicks, and ultimately the premier paceman in the world. Like the best of his fast bowling contemporaries, Dennis Lillee and Michael Holding, he had a classical bowling action. In Hadlee's case it there was an easy long run up that culminated in a whipping delivery stride which took full advantage of his sinewy strength. Over the years the length of the run was reduced, but it didn't hamper his ability to bowl genuinely quick and to make the ball move. He could gain movement both in the air and off the seam, and like Lillee had a devilish leg cutter that found the outside edge of countless Test batsmen. There were many highlights, but none better than when he brought the Australians to their knees at the 'Gabba in 1985, capturing 15 wickets for the match including nine in the first innings. The speedster cost himself a place in the history books that innings when he caught tailender Geoff Lawson off the bowling of spinner Vaughan Brown. Hadlee captured a staggering 49 wickets in six Tests against the Australians that summer and was single handedly responsible for his country's rare domination over their trans-Transman neighbours. Right up until his last Test in 1990 the output never diminished. He claimed a five wicket haul in his last Test innings at Bridgetown to bring the number of times he captured five or more wickets in a Test innings to 36. On nine of those occasions it was as part of a match haul of at least ten wickets. That record confirms his status as one of the game's greatest ever bowlers, which brings up the question as to whether or not he was also one of cricket's greatest all-rounders? In the 1980's he was one of the game's four master bowler/batsmen along with Kapil Dev, Imran Khan and Ian Botham. Superior to the other three with the ball, he was the only one of the four with a Test batting average below 30. If the definition of an all-rounder is someone whose batting and bowling is of equal ability, than Hadlee is most definitely a bowler. If another definition is a player that could be selected in his side as either a batsman or a bowler, then once again Hadlee is a bowler. For all of that he was fine batsman who scored two Test centuries, including a career high 151 not out against Sri Lanka at Colombo in 1987. A hard hitter with a full array of strokes, he was also at ease just occupying the crease, as that near seven hour innings in Colombo proved. In retirement Sir Richard Hadlee remains New Zealand's most recognisable cricketing figure, via his work as a commentator and time spent as chairman of New Zealand's Test selection committee.

HADLEE, Walter Arnold

Born: June 4, 1915
Batting: Right handed
Bowling: Right arm medium

Tests

Test Career: 1937-51
Cap Number: 29
Tests Played: 11

Test Batting

Innings:	19	Runs:	543
Highest Score:	116	Average:	30.16
No. 50s:	2	No. 100s:	1

Test Bowling & Fielding

Wickets:	0	Runs:	0
Best Bowling:		Average:	0.00
5 WI:	0	10 WM:	0
Catches:	6	Stumpings:	0

With his glasses and fatherly demeanor Walter Hadlee looked more like a school principal than Test cricketer. He was however a talented and aggressive batsman who captained his country immediately after World War II. Whilst the side didn't win a Test under his captaincy they enjoyed a highly successful tour of England in 1949, drawing the Test series and losing just a single match. Walter Hadlee's only Test century was a 116 against the touring Englishmen at Christchurch in 1951. Following his playing career he became an administrator, serving as national selector, chairman and president. He was a father figure to New Zealand cricket and is also the father of the great Sir Richard Hadlee. His two other sons, Barry and Dayle, also played cricket for New Zealand.

HAMILTON, Lance

Born: April 5, 1973
Batting: Right handed
Bowling: Left arm medium-fast

One Day Internationals

ODI Career: 2005
ODIs Played: 2

ODI Batting

Innings:	2	Runs:	3
Highest Score:	2*	Average:	0.00
No. 50s:	0	No. 100s:	0

ODI Bowling & Fielding

Wickets:	1	Runs:	143
Best Bowling:	1/76	Average:	143.00
5 WM:	0	Catches:	0
Stumpings:	0		

A powerful left arm paceman who played two ODI's against Australia in 2005. Has taken one wicket to date, that of Simon Katich.

HARFORD, Noel Sherwin

Born: August 30, 1930
Batting: Right handed

Tests

Test Career: 1955-58
Cap Number: 74
Tests Played: 8

Test Batting

Innings:	15	Runs:	229
Highest Score:	93	Average:	15.26
No. 50s:	2	No. 100s:	0

Test Bowling & Fielding

Wickets:	0	Runs:	0
Best Bowling:		Average:	0.00
5 WI:	0	10 WM:	0
Catches:	0	Stumpings:	0

He made a bright start to his Test career scoring 93 and 64 on debut against Pakistan at Lahore in 1955. It was all downhill from there with only 72 runs in his next seven Tests.

HARFORD, Roy Ivan

Born: May 30, 1936
Batting: Left handed
Wicket Keeper

Tests

Test Career: 1968
Cap Number: 113
Tests Played: 3

Test Batting

Innings:	5	Runs:	7
Highest Score:	6	Average:	2.33
No. 50s:	0	No. 100s:	0

Test Bowling & Fielding

Wickets:	0	Runs:	0
Best Bowling:		Average:	0.00
5 WI:	0	10 WM:	0
Catches:	11	Stumpings:	0

An English born wicketkeeper who performed well with the gloves in his only three Test appearances. Unfortunately his batting was less impressive and it was the reason for his hasty omission from the side.

HARRIS, Chris Zinzan
Born: November 20, 1969
Batting: Left handed
Bowling: Right arm medium

Tests
Test Career: 1992-2002
Cap Number: 181
Tests Played: 23

Test Batting
Innings:	42	Runs:	777
Highest Score:	71	Average:	20.44
No. 50s:	5	No. 100s:	0

Test Bowling & Fielding
Wickets:	16	Runs:	1,170
Best Bowling:	2/16	Average:	73.12
5 WI:	0	10 WM:	0
Catches:	14	Stumpings:	0

One Day Internationals
ODI Career: 1990-
ODIs Played: 250

ODI Batting
Innings:	213	Runs:	4,379
Highest Score:	130	Average:	29.00
No. 50s:	16	No. 100s:	1

ODI Bowling & Fielding
Wickets:	203	Runs:	7,613
Best Bowling:	5/42	Average:	37.50
5 WM:	1	Catches:	96
Stumpings:	0		

The son of former Test player Zin Harris, he may have lacked the penetration to be a top class Test all rounder but there have been few more effective one day cricketers. His 250 ODI's is the most by a New Zealander as are his 203 one day wickets. His bowling may seem innocuous, but it requires the batsman to force the ball and is ideal for those overs in one day cricket when the field is out. Harris is equally effective as a limited over batsman with a top score of 130 and 16 scores above 50. He suffered a serious injury at the end of 2004 but is far from finished in international cricket and has his eyes firmly set on the 2007 World Cup.

HARRIS, Parke Gerald Zinzan
Born: July 18, 1927
Batting: Right handed
Bowling: Right arm medium

Tests
Test Career: 1955-65
Cap Number: 72
Tests Played: 9

Test Batting
Innings:	18	Runs:	378
Highest Score:	101	Average:	22.23
No. 50s:	1	No. 100s:	1

Test Bowling & Fielding
Wickets:	0	Runs:	14
Best Bowling:		Average:	0.00
5 WI:	0	10 WM:	0
Catches:	6	Stumpings:	0

Zinzan is a famous name in New Zealand, may it be with the Harris family in cricket or the great All-Black Zinzan Brooke. Zin Harris played in nine Tests scoring a century against the South Africans at Cape Town in 1961/62.

HARRIS, Roger Meredith
Born: July 27, 1933
Batting: Right handed
Bowling: Right arm medium

Tests
Test Career: 1959
Cap Number: 86
Tests Played: 2

Test Batting
Innings:	3	Runs:	31
Highest Score:	13	Average:	10.33
No. 50s:	0	No. 100s:	0

Test Bowling & Fielding
Wickets:	0	Runs:	0
Best Bowling:		Average:	0.00
5 WI:	0	10 WM:	0
Catches:	0	Stumpings:	0

He had a long and successful career with Auckland in Plunket Shield but did little in two Tests against England in 1959.

HART, Matthew Norman
Born: May 16, 1972
Batting: Left handed
Bowling: Left arm off-break

Tests
Test Career: 1994-95
Cap Number: 187
Tests Played: 14

Test Batting
Innings:	24	Runs:	353
Highest Score:	45	Average:	17.65
No. 50s:	0	No. 100s:	0

Test Bowling & Fielding
Wickets:	29	Runs:	1,438
Best Bowling:	5/77	Average:	49.58
5 WI:	1	10 WM:	0
Catches:	9	Stumpings:	0

One Day Internationals
ODI Career: 1994-2002
ODIs Played: 13

ODI Batting
Innings:	8	Runs:	61
Highest Score:	16	Average:	7.62
No. 50s:	0	No. 100s:	0

ODI Bowling & Fielding
Wickets:	13	Runs:	373
Best Bowling:	5/22	Average:	28.69
5 WM:	1	Catches:	7
Stumpings:	0		

A left arm finger spinner who played 14 Tests prior to the emergence of Daniel Vettori. In that period he captured 29 wickets including a five wicket haul against South Africa in 1994/95.

After losing his spot in the Test side Hart concentrated on his batting and was rewarded with a first class double century for Northern Districts.

HART, Robert Gary

Born:	December 2, 1974
Batting:	Right handed
	Wicket Keeper

Tests

Test Career:	2002-03		
Cap Number:	220		
Tests Played:	11		

Test Batting

Innings:	19	Runs:	260
Highest Score:	57*	Average:	16.25
No. 50s:	1	No. 100s:	0

Test Bowling & Fielding

Wickets:	0	Runs:	0
Best Bowling:		Average:	0.00
5 WI:	0	10 WM:	0
Catches:	29	Stumpings:	1

One Day Internationals

ODI Career:	2002		
ODIs Played:	2		

ODI Batting

Innings:	1	Runs:	0
Highest Score:	0	Average:	0.00
No. 50s:	0	No. 100s:	0

ODI Bowling & Fielding

Wickets:	0	Runs:	0
Best Bowling:		Average:	0.00
5 WM:	0	Catches:	1
Stumpings:	0		

The younger brother of Matthew, he replaced Adam Parore as national keeper and played a handful of Tests before in turn being replaced by Brendon McCullum. In 2004 he announced his retirement at the age of only 29.

HART, Ronald Terence

Born:	November 7, 1961
Batting:	Right handed
Bowling:	Right arm off-break
	Wicket Keeper

One Day Internationals

ODI Career:	1985		
ODIs Played:	1		

ODI Batting

Innings:	1	Runs:	3
Highest Score:	3	Average:	3.00
No. 50s:	0	No. 100s:	0

ODI Bowling & Fielding

Wickets:	0	Runs:	0
Best Bowling:		Average:	0.00
5 WM:	0	Catches:	0
Stumpings:	0		

Opened the batting with veteran John Wright in his only ODI appearance against West Indies, at St John's in 1985.

HARTLAND, Blair Robert

Born:	October 22, 1966
Batting:	Right handed

Tests

Test Career:	1992-94		
Cap Number:	175		
Tests Played:	9		

Test Batting

Innings:	18	Runs:	303
Highest Score:	52	Average:	16.83
No. 50s:	1	No. 100s:	0

Test Bowling & Fielding

Wickets:	0	Runs:	0
Best Bowling:		Average:	0.00
5 WI:	0	10 WM:	0
Catches:	5	Stumpings:	0

One Day Internationals

ODI Career:	1992-94		
ODIs Played:	16		

ODI Batting

Innings:	16	Runs:	311
Highest Score:	68*	Average:	20.73
No. 50s:	2	No. 100s:	0

ODI Bowling & Fielding

Wickets:	0	Runs:	0
Best Bowling:		Average:	0.00
5 WM:	0	Catches:	5
Stumpings:	0		

An opening batsman from Canterbury who made his debut against England at Christchurch in 1992 in a game dominated by England's Phil Tufnell. He fell twice to the off spinner but still earnt a spot in New Zealand touring sides over the next two years.

HASLAM, Mark James

Born:	September 26, 1972
Batting:	Left handed
Bowling:	Left arm off-break

Tests

Test Career:	1992-95		
Cap Number:	179		
Tests Played:	4		

Test Batting

Innings:	2	Runs:	4
Highest Score:	3	Average:	4.00
No. 50s:	0	No. 100s:	0

Test Bowling & Fielding

Wickets:	2	Runs:	245
Best Bowling:	1/33	Average:	122.50
5 WI:	0	10 WM:	0
Catches:	2	Stumpings:	0

One Day Internationals

ODI Career:	1992		
ODIs Played:	1		

ODI Batting

Innings:	1	Runs:	9
Highest Score:	9	Average:	9.00
No. 50s:	0	No. 100s:	0

ODI Bowling & Fielding

Wickets:	1	Runs:	28
Best Bowling:	1/28	Average:	28.00
5 WM:	0	Catches:	0
Stumpings:	0		

An English born finger spinner who toured Zimbabwe in 1992 and India in 1995 but could mange only two Test wickets.

HASTINGS, Brian Frederick
Born: March 23, 1940
Batting: Right handed
Bowling: Right arm leg-break

Tests
Test Career: 1969-76
Cap Number: 116
Tests Played: 31

Test Batting
Innings:	56	Runs:	1,510
Highest Score:	117*	Average:	30.20
No. 50s:	7	No. 100s:	4

Test Bowling & Fielding
Wickets:	0	Runs:	9
Best Bowling:		Average:	0.00
5 WI:	0	10 WM:	0
Catches:	23	Stumpings:	0

One Day Internationals
ODI Career: 1973-75
ODIs Played: 11

ODI Batting
Innings:	9	Runs:	151
Highest Score:	37	Average:	18.87
No. 50s:	0	No. 100s:	0

ODI Bowling & Fielding
Wickets:	0	Runs:	0
Best Bowling:		Average:	0.00
5 WM:	0	Catches:	4
Stumpings:	0		

The balding Hastings played a number of important innings for his country as a fast scoring middle order batsman. He scored four Test centuries with the most memorable clearly being his 110 against Pakistan at Auckland in 1973. New Zealand were battling at 9/251 when fast bowler Richard Collinge joined Hastings at the crease. When Hastings was finally dismissed the score had reached 402 and the two had broken the record for the highest 10th wicket partnership in Test history. He was also part of the team that beat Australia for the first time in Tests at Christchurch in 1973/74.

HAYES, John Arthur
Born: January 11, 1927
Batting: Right handed
Bowling: Right arm fast

Tests
Test Career: 1951-58
Cap Number: 51
Tests Played: 15

Test Batting
Innings:	22	Runs:	73
Highest Score:	19	Average:	4.86
No. 50s:	0	No. 100s:	0

Test Bowling & Fielding
Wickets:	30	Runs:	1,217
Best Bowling:	4/36	Average:	40.56
5 WI:	0	10 WM:	0
Catches:	3	Stumpings:	0

An opening bowler who enjoyed a fine career with Canterbury and Auckland in the Plunket Shield. Tall and quick he was a consistent bowler at Test level without ever tearing through an opposition line-up.

HAYES, Roydon Leslie
Born: May 9, 1971
Batting: Right handed
Bowling: Right arm fast

One Day Internationals
ODI Career: 1995
ODIs Played: 1

ODI Batting
Innings:	1	Runs:	13
Highest Score:	13	Average:	13.00
No. 50s:	0	No. 100s:	0

ODI Bowling & Fielding
Wickets:	0	Runs:	31
Best Bowling:		Average:	0.00
5 WM:	0	Catches:	0
Stumpings:	0		

While he may not have taken a wicket in his one and only ODI against West Indies at Christchurch, Hayes made a handy 13 runs batting at number eleven.

HENDERSON, Matthew
Born: August 2, 1895
Batting: Left handed
Bowling: Left arm medium-fast

Tests
Test Career: 1930
Cap Number: 6
Tests Played: 1

Test Batting
Innings:	2	Runs:	8
Highest Score:	6	Average:	8.00
No. 50s:	0	No. 100s:	0

Test Bowling & Fielding
Wickets:	2	Runs:	64
Best Bowling:	2/38	Average:	32.00
5 WI:	0	10 WM:	0
Catches:	1	Stumpings:	0

A left arm medium pace bowler who played in New Zealand's inaugural Test match. He captured the first ever wicket taken by a Kiwi in Tests when he had Edward Dawson caught for seven.

HITCHCOCK, Paul Anthony
Born: January 23, 1975
Batting: Right handed
Bowling: Right arm medium

One Day Internationals
ODI Career: 2002-03
ODIs Played: 13

ODI Batting
Innings:	6	Runs:	30
Highest Score:	10	Average:	7.50
No. 50s:	0	No. 100s:	0

ODI Bowling & Fielding
Wickets:	12	Runs:	412
Best Bowling:	3/30	Average:	34.33
5 WM:	0	Catches:	4
Stumpings:	0		

A medium pacer who played in 13 ODI's in 2002/03. Took a career best 3/30 against India, at Christchurch.

HOPKINS, Gareth

Born:	November 24, 1976
Batting:	Right handed
	Wicket Keeper

One Day Internationals

ODI Career:	2004		
ODIs Played:	5		
ODI Batting			
Innings:	1	Runs:	0
Highest Score:	0	Average:	0.00
No. 50s:	0	No. 100s:	0
ODI Bowling & Fielding			
Wickets:	0	Runs:	0
Best Bowling:		Average:	0.00
5 WM:	0	Catches:	8
Stumpings:	0		

Selected for the 2004 tour of England as a stand-in for regular keeper Brendon McCullum, Gareth Hopkins played five ODI's in the triangular series against England and the West Indies. But he only got the opportunity to bat in his last ODI where he was run out for zero.

HORNE, Matthew Jeffery

Born:	December 5, 1970
Batting:	Right handed
Bowling:	Right arm medium

Tests

Test Career:	1997-2003		
Cap Number:	201		
Tests Played:	35		
Test Batting			
Innings:	65	Runs:	1,788
Highest Score:	157	Average:	28.38
No. 50s:	5	No. 100s:	4
Test Bowling & Fielding			
Wickets:	0	Runs:	26
Best Bowling:		Average:	0.00
5 WI:	0	10 WM:	0
Catches:	17	Stumpings:	0

One Day Internationals

ODI Career:	1997-2002		
ODIs Played:	50		
ODI Batting			
Innings:	48	Runs:	980
Highest Score:	74	Average:	20.41
No. 50s:	5	No. 100s:	0
ODI Bowling & Fielding			
Wickets:	0	Runs:	0
Best Bowling:		Average:	0.00
5 WM:	0	Catches:	12
Stumpings:	0		

A hard hitting opener with a less than perfect technique, he scored 133 against Australia in 1998 and an uncharacteristically circumspect century against England at Lord's in 1999. That century, an even 100 took over six hours to compile and guided his side to victory. From that point on there more downs than ups in Horne's Test career and by 2003 he was out of the Test side for good.

HORNE, Philip Andrew

Born:	January 21, 1960
Batting:	Left handed

Tests

Test Career:	1987-90		
Cap Number:	162		
Tests Played:	4		
Test Batting			
Innings:	7	Runs:	71
Highest Score:	27	Average:	10.14
No. 50s:	0	No. 100s:	0
Test Bowling & Fielding			
Wickets:	0	Runs:	0
Best Bowling:		Average:	0.00
5 WI:	0	10 WM:	0
Catches:	3	Stumpings:	0

One Day Internationals

ODI Career:	1987		
ODIs Played:	4		
ODI Batting			
Innings:	4	Runs:	50
Highest Score:	18	Average:	12.50
No. 50s:	0	No. 100s:	0
ODI Bowling & Fielding			
Wickets:	0	Runs:	0
Best Bowling:		Average:	0.00
5 WM:	0	Catches:	0
Stumpings:	0		

A left handed opener from Auckland who was disappointing in his short Test career with a top score of only 27 in seven innings.

HOUGH, Kenneth William

Born:	October 24, 1928
Batting:	Right handed
Bowling:	Right arm medium-fast

Tests

Test Career:	1959		
Cap Number:	87		
Tests Played:	2		
Test Batting			
Innings:	3	Runs:	62
Highest Score:	31*	Average:	62.00
No. 50s:	0	No. 100s:	0
Test Bowling & Fielding			
Wickets:	6	Runs:	175
Best Bowling:	3/79	Average:	29.16
5 WI:	0	10 WM:	0
Catches:	1	Stumpings:	0

The Australian born paceman played against the touring English in 1959 and performed well with bat and ball taking six wickets in total and scoring a quick fire 31 not out at Christchurch.

HOW, Jamie Michael

Born:	May 19, 1981
Batting:	Right handed
Bowling:	Right arm medium

Tests

Test Career:	2006-
Cap Number:	232
Tests Played:	4

Test Batting

Innings:	6	Runs:	61
Highest Score:	37	Average:	12.20
No. 50s:	0	No. 100s:	0

Test Bowling & Fielding

Wickets:	0	Runs:	0
Best Bowling:		Average:	0.00
5 WI:	0	10 WM:	0
Catches:	6	Stumpings:	0

One Day Internationals

ODI Career:	2005-
ODIs Played:	6

ODI Batting

Innings:	5	Runs:	141
Highest Score:	66	Average:	28.20
No. 50s:	2	No. 100s:	0

ODI Bowling & Fielding

Wickets:	0	Runs:	0
Best Bowling:		Average:	0.00
5 WM:	0	Catches:	2
Stumpings:	0		

A top order batsman from Central Districts who has struggled at Test level but played a couple of promising innings in the one day side.

HOWARTH, Geoffrey Philip

Born:	March 29, 1951
Batting:	Right handed
Bowling:	Right arm off-break

Tests

Test Career:	1975-85
Cap Number:	132
Tests Played:	47

Test Batting

Innings:	83	Runs:	2,531
Highest Score:	147	Average:	32.44
No. 50s:	11	No. 100s:	6

Test Bowling & Fielding

Wickets:	3	Runs:	271
Best Bowling:	1/13	Average:	90.33
5 WI:	0	10 WM:	0
Catches:	29	Stumpings:	0

One Day Internationals

ODI Career:	1975-85
ODIs Played:	70

ODI Batting

Innings:	65	Runs:	1,384
Highest Score:	76	Average:	23.06
No. 50s:	6	No. 100s:	0

ODI Bowling & Fielding

Wickets:	3	Runs:	68
Best Bowling:	1/4	Average:	22.66
5 WM:	0	Catches:	16
Stumpings:	0		

One of New Zealand's most successful captains, he was an ebullient character who imparted his positive outlook on most of the cricketers who played under him. Before taking over the reins in the late 70's he had to secure his place in the side which he did with a century in either innings against England at Eden Park in 1977/78. From that point on the classy front foot batsman was the mainstay of the NZ middle order, scoring big hundreds against Pakistan, the West Indies and India. Under Howarth's captaincy New Zealand won more Tests in six years than they had in the previous fifty.

HOWARTH, Hedley John

Born:	December 25, 1943
Batting:	Left handed
Bowling:	Left arm off-break

Tests

Test Career:	1969-77
Cap Number:	120
Tests Played:	30

Test Batting

Innings:	42	Runs:	291
Highest Score:	61	Average:	12.12
No. 50s:	1	No. 100s:	0

Test Bowling & Fielding

Wickets:	86	Runs:	3,178
Best Bowling:	5/34	Average:	36.95
5 WI:	2	10 WM:	0
Catches:	33	Stumpings:	0

One Day Internationals

ODI Career:	1973-75
ODIs Played:	9

ODI Batting

Innings:	5	Runs:	18
Highest Score:	11	Average:	6.00
No. 50s:	0	No. 100s:	0

ODI Bowling & Fielding

Wickets:	11	Runs:	280
Best Bowling:	3/29	Average:	25.45
5 WM:	0	Catches:	3
Stumpings:	0		

The older brother of Geoff, he was a left arm off spinner who relied on flight and changes in pace. He enjoyed bowling in the subcontinent and on the Test tour of India and Pakistan in 1969/70 captured 28 wickets, including match figures of 9/100 at Nagpur.

HOWELL, Llorne

Born:	July 8, 1972
Batting:	Right handed
Bowling:	Right arm medium

One Day Internationals

ODI Career:	1998
ODIs Played:	12

ODI Batting

Innings:	12	Runs:	287
Highest Score:	68	Average:	23.91
No. 50s:	4	No. 100s:	0

ODI Bowling & Fielding

Wickets:	0	Runs:	0
Best Bowling:		Average:	0.00
5 WM:	0	Catches:	2
Stumpings:	0		

An opening batsman who partnered with Nathan Astle in the majority of his 12 matches throughout 1998.

JAMES, Kenneth Cecil

Born:	March 12, 1904
Batting:	Right handed
	Wicket Keeper

Tests

Test Career:	1930-33		
Cap Number:	7		
Tests Played:	11		

Test Batting

Innings:	13	Runs:	52
Highest Score:	14	Average:	4.72
No. 50s:	0	No. 100s:	0

Test Bowling & Fielding

Wickets:	0	Runs:	0
Best Bowling:		Average:	0.00
5 WI:	0	10 WM:	0
Catches:	11	Stumpings:	5

New Zealand's first ever Test keeper, he was a fine gloveman from Wellington. Even though his Test record suggests he was an ordinary batsman he performed far better in domestic cricket and later for Northamptonshire in England where he had a total of seven first class centuries.

JARVIS, Terrence Wayne

Born:	July 29, 1944
Batting:	Right handed
Bowling:	Right arm medium

Tests

Test Career:	1965-73		
Cap Number:	106		
Tests Played:	13		

Test Batting

Innings:	22	Runs:	625
Highest Score:	182	Average:	29.76
No. 50s:	2	No. 100s:	1

Test Bowling & Fielding

Wickets:	0	Runs:	3
Best Bowling:		Average:	0.00
5 WI:	0	10 WM:	0
Catches:	3	Stumpings:	0

After a haltering start to his Test career in the mid 60's he was recalled to the side that toured the West Indies in 1971/72. He enjoyed a fine series averaging 46.16 with the highlight clearly his 182 at Guyana. He was joined at the top of the order by Glenn Turner in that Test with the pair adding a record 387 for the first wicket. Poor form against the touring Pakistani side the following summer saw him on the outer once again. A successful businessman in his post cricket days he has become a well known figure in the NZ thoroughbred industry.

JONES, Andrew Howard

Born:	May 9, 1959
Batting:	Right handed
Bowling:	Right arm off-break

Tests

Test Career:	1987-95		
Cap Number:	163		
Tests Played:	39		

Test Batting

Innings:	74	Runs:	2,922
Highest Score:	186	Average:	44.27
No. 50s:	11	No. 100s:	7

Test Bowling & Fielding

Wickets:	1	Runs:	194
Best Bowling:	1/40	Average:	194.00
5 WI:	0	10 WM:	0
Catches:	25	Stumpings:	0

One Day Internationals

ODI Career:	1987-95		
ODIs Played:	87		

ODI Batting

Innings:	87	Runs:	2,784
Highest Score:	93	Average:	35.69
No. 50s:	25	No. 100s:	0

ODI Bowling & Fielding

Wickets:	4	Runs:	216
Best Bowling:	2/42	Average:	54.00
5 WM:	0	Catches:	23
Stumpings:	0		

He was a cautious top order batsman who worked within his limitations to become an excellent Test player. Whilst he wasn't able to flay the bat he was capable of big scores and struck seven centuries including three in consecutive innings against Sri Lanka in 1990/91. The first of those three centuries, 186 at Wellington was part the then highest ever partnership in Test cricket when he teamed with Martin Crowe to put on 467 for the third wicket of the second innings.

JONES, Richard Andrew

Born:	October 22, 1973
Batting:	Right handed

Tests

Test Career:	2003		
Cap Number:	223		
Tests Played:	1		

Test Batting

Innings:	2	Runs:	23
Highest Score:	16	Average:	11.50
No. 50s:	0	No. 100s:	0

Test Bowling & Fielding

Wickets:	0	Runs:	0
Best Bowling:		Average:	0.00
5 WI:	0	10 WM:	0
Catches:	0	Stumpings:	0

One Day Internationals

ODI Career:	2003		
ODIs Played:	5		

ODI Batting

Innings:	5	Runs:	168
Highest Score:	63	Average:	33.60
No. 50s:	1	No. 100s:	0

ODI Bowling & Fielding

Wickets:	0	Runs:	0
Best Bowling:		Average:	0.00
5 WM:	0	Catches:	0
Stumpings:	0		

A right handed batsman from Wellington via Auckland who played a single Test against Pakistan in 2003.

KENNEDY, Robert John

Born:	June 3, 1972
Batting:	Right handed
Bowling:	Right arm medium

Tests
Test Career:	1996		
Cap Number:	198		
Tests Played:	4		

Test Batting
Innings:	5	Runs:	28
Highest Score:	22	Average:	7.00
No. 50s:	0	No. 100s:	0

Test Bowling & Fielding
Wickets:	6	Runs:	380
Best Bowling:	3/28	Average:	63.33
5 WI:	0	10 WM:	0
Catches:	2	Stumpings:	0

One Day Internationals
ODI Career:	1996		
ODIs Played:	7		

ODI Batting
Innings:	4	Runs:	17
Highest Score:	8*	Average:	17.00
No. 50s:	0	No. 100s:	0

ODI Bowling & Fielding
Wickets:	5	Runs:	283
Best Bowling:	2/36	Average:	56.60
5 WM:	0	Catches:	1
Stumpings:	0		

A tall medium pace bowler from Otago who was considered a promising one day bowler but played only a handful of games in 1996.

KERR, John Lambert (Jack)
Born:	December 28, 1910
Batting:	Right handed
Bowling:	Right arm medium

Tests
Test Career:	1931-37		
Cap Number:	19		
Tests Played:	7		

Test Batting
Innings:	12	Runs:	212
Highest Score:	59	Average:	19.27
No. 50s:	1	No. 100s:	0

Test Bowling & Fielding
Wickets:	0	Runs:	0
Best Bowling:		Average:	0.00
5 WI:	0	10 WM:	0
Catches:	4	Stumpings:	0

A fine top order batsman from Canterbury who scored almost 5,000 first class runs but failed to realise that form in his seven Test appearances. In 2006 the 95 year old was New Zealand's oldest living Test cricketer.

KUGGELEIJN, Christopher Mary
Born:	May 10, 1956
Batting:	Right handed
Bowling:	Right arm off-break

Tests
Test Career:	1988		
Cap Number:	167		
Tests Played:	2		

Test Batting
Innings:	4	Runs:	7
Highest Score:	7	Average:	1.75
No. 50s:	0	No. 100s:	0

Test Bowling & Fielding
Wickets:	1	Runs:	67
Best Bowling:	1/50	Average:	67.00
5 WI:	0	10 WM:	0
Catches:	1	Stumpings:	0

One Day Internationals
ODI Career:	1988-89		
ODIs Played:	16		

ODI Batting
Innings:	11	Runs:	142
Highest Score:	40	Average:	15.77
No. 50s:	0	No. 100s:	0

ODI Bowling & Fielding
Wickets:	12	Runs:	604
Best Bowling:	2/31	Average:	50.33
5 WM:	0	Catches:	9
Stumpings:	0		

An off spinner from Auckland who played two Tests in India in 1988. Surely the only Test cricketer with the middle name Mary.

LARSEN, Gavin Rolf
Born:	September 27, 1962
Batting:	Right handed
Bowling:	Right arm medium

Tests
Test Career:	1994-96		
Cap Number:	190		
Tests Played:	8		

Test Batting
Innings:	13	Runs:	127
Highest Score:	26*	Average:	14.11
No. 50s:	0	No. 100s:	0

Test Bowling & Fielding
Wickets:	24	Runs:	689
Best Bowling:	3/57	Average:	28.70
5 WI:	0	10 WM:	0
Catches:	5	Stumpings:	0

One Day Internationals
ODI Career:	1990-99		
ODIs Played:	121		

ODI Batting
Innings:	70	Runs:	629
Highest Score:	37	Average:	14.62
No. 50s:	0	No. 100s:	0

ODI Bowling & Fielding
Wickets:	113	Runs:	4,000
Best Bowling:	4/24	Average:	35.39
5 WM:	0	Catches:	23
Stumpings:	0		

Gavin Larsen was the archetypal one day cricketer. He was a nagging medium pacer who could hit the same spot every time, an urgent late order batsman skilled at turning over the strike and a busy fieldsman. The key to Larsen over his 121 ODI's was an economy rate of 3.76 which made him one of the game's most miserly bowlers.

LATHAM, Rodney Terry
Born:	June 12, 1961
Batting:	Right handed
Bowling:	Right arm medium

Tests
Test Career:	1992-93		
Cap Number:	177		
Tests Played:	4		

Test Batting
Innings:	7	Runs:	219
Highest Score:	119	Average:	31.28
No. 50s:	0	No. 100s:	1

Test Bowling & Fielding
Wickets:	0	Runs:	6
Best Bowling:		Average:	0.00
5 WI:	0	10 WM:	0
Catches:	5	Stumpings:	0

One Day Internationals
ODI Career:	1990-94		
ODIs Played:	33		

ODI Batting
Innings:	33	Runs:	583
Highest Score:	60	Average:	20.10
No. 50s:	1	No. 100s:	0

ODI Bowling & Fielding
Wickets:	11	Runs:	386
Best Bowling:	5/32	Average:	35.09
5 WM:	1	Catches:	11
Stumpings:	0		

An opening batsman and dinky medium pacer who seemed pigeon-holed as a one day cricketer despite scoring a century in only four Test appearances. He scored 119 at Bulawayo in 1992/93 but was out of the side only two Tests later.

LEES, Warren Kenneth
Born:	March 19, 1952
Batting:	Right handed
Bowling:	Right arm medium
	Wicket Keeper

Tests
Test Career:	1976-83		
Cap Number:	135		
Tests Played:	21		

Test Batting
Innings:	37	Runs:	778
Highest Score:	152	Average:	23.57
No. 50s:	1	No. 100s:	1

Test Bowling & Fielding
Wickets:	0	Runs:	4
Best Bowling:		Average:	0.00
5 WI:	0	10 WM:	0
Catches:	52	Stumpings:	7

One Day Internationals
ODI Career:	1979-83		
ODIs Played:	31		

ODI Batting
Innings:	24	Runs:	215
Highest Score:	26	Average:	11.31
No. 50s:	0	No. 100s:	0

ODI Bowling & Fielding
Wickets:	0	Runs:	0
Best Bowling:		Average:	0.00
5 WI:	0	Catches:	28
Stumpings:	2		

He had the difficult task of replacing the late Ken Wadsworth, but the smart gloveman performed admirably both behind the sumps and with the bat. In only his third Test he hit a fighting 152 at Karachi to save his side from certain defeat.

LEGGAT, Ian Bruce
Born:	June 7, 1930
Batting:	Right handed
Bowling:	Right arm medium

Tests
Test Career:	1954		
Cap Number:	67		
Tests Played:	1		

Test Batting
Innings:	1	Runs:	0
Highest Score:	0	Average:	0.00
No. 50s:	0	No. 100s:	0

Test Bowling & Fielding
Wickets:	0	Runs:	6
Best Bowling:		Average:	0.00
5 WI:	0	10 WM:	0
Catches:	2	Stumpings:	0

A cousin of John Leggat, he played just the one Test against South Africa at Cape Town in 1954.

LEGGAT, John Gordon
Born:	May 27, 1926
Batting:	Right handed

Tests
Test Career:	1952-56		
Cap Number:	56		
Tests Played:	9		

Test Batting
Innings:	18	Runs:	351
Highest Score:	61	Average:	21.93
No. 50s:	2	No. 100s:	0

Test Bowling & Fielding
Wickets:	0	Runs:	0
Best Bowling:		Average:	0.00
5 WI:	0	10 WM:	0
Catches:	0	Stumpings:	0

The right handed batsman was part of the New Zealand side that was dismissed for 26 in 1955 by the English, the lowest score by any side in the history of Test cricket. A barrister, he became a Test selector and was serving as the Chairman of the New Zealand Cricket board when he died suddenly in 1973 aged only 46.

LISSETTE, Allen Fisher
Born:	November 6, 1919
Batting:	Right handed
Bowling:	Left arm off-break

Tests
Test Career:	1956		
Cap Number:	77		
Tests Played:	2		

Test Batting
Innings:	4	Runs:	2
Highest Score:	1*	Average:	1.00
No. 50s:	0	No. 100s:	0

Test Bowling & Fielding
Wickets:	3	Runs:	124
Best Bowling:	2/73	Average:	41.33
5 WI:	0	10 WM:	0
Catches:	1	Stumpings:	0

A left arm off spinner from Northern Districts who played in two Tests against the touring West Indians in 1955/56.

LOVERIDGE, Greg Riaka
Born: January 15, 1975
Batting: Right handed
Bowling: Right arm leg-break

Tests
Test Career: 1996
Cap Number: 199
Tests Played: 1

Test Batting
Innings:	1	Runs:	4
Highest Score:	4*	Average:	0.00
No. 50s:	0	No. 100s:	0

Test Bowling & Fielding
Wickets:	0	Runs:	0
Best Bowling:		Average:	0.00
5 WI:	0	10 WM:	0
Catches:	0	Stumpings:	0

A legspinner, his Test career consisted of a single ill-fated match against Zimbabwe. He was struck on the hand whilst batting and the subsequent break meant he wasn't able to bowl or field for the rest of the game.

LOWRY, Thomas Coleman
Born: February 17, 1898
Batting: Right handed
         Wicket Keeper

Tests
Test Career: 1930-31
Cap Number: 8
Tests Played: 7

Test Batting
Innings:	8	Runs:	223
Highest Score:	80	Average:	27.87
No. 50s:	2	No. 100s:	0

Test Bowling & Fielding
Wickets:	0	Runs:	5
Best Bowling:		Average:	0.00
5 WI:	0	10 WM:	0
Catches:	8	Stumpings:	0

A wicketkeeper and batsman from Wellington who captained New Zealand's first Test side. He top scored with 40 for NZ in the second innings of that first Test and also hit a fine 80 later in the series. He also played county cricket in England for Surrey.

MACGIBBON, Anthony Roy
Born: August 28, 1924
Batting: Right handed
Bowling: Right arm medium-fast

Tests
Test Career: 1951-58
Cap Number: 52
Tests Played: 26

Test Batting
Innings:	46	Runs:	814
Highest Score:	66	Average:	19.85
No. 50s:	3	No. 100s:	0

Test Bowling & Fielding
Wickets:	70	Runs:	2,160
Best Bowling:	5/64	Average:	30.85
5 WI:	1	10 WM:	0
Catches:	13	Stumpings:	0

A towering opening bowler from Canterbury who shouldered the new ball responsibility for the Black Caps during the 1950's. He had a fine tour of South Africa in 1953/54 taking 22 wickets in five Tests and was part of his country's first successful Test side that beat the West Indies in 1956. The lower order batsman scored 35 in that match to help his side to that historic victory.

MARSHALL, Hamish John Hamilton
Born: February 15, 1979
Batting: Right handed
Bowling: Right arm medium

Tests
Test Career: 2000-
Cap Number: 213
Tests Played: 13

Test Batting
Innings:	19	Runs:	652
Highest Score:	160	Average:	38.35
No. 50s:	2	No. 100s:	2

Test Bowling & Fielding
Wickets:	0	Runs:	4
Best Bowling:		Average:	0.00
5 WI:	0	10 WM:	0
Catches:	1	Stumpings:	0

One Day Internationals
ODI Career: 2003-
ODIs Played: 55

ODI Batting
Innings:	51	Runs:	1,310
Highest Score:	101*	Average:	30.46
No. 50s:	11	No. 100s:	1

ODI Bowling & Fielding
Wickets:	0	Runs:	0
Best Bowling:		Average:	0.00
5 WM:	0	Catches:	15
Stumpings:	0		

Half of New Zealand's first Test cricketing twins, he is an accomplished middle order batsman who was in and out of the Test side until cementing his place with a glorious maiden Test hundred against Australia in 2004. He followed that 146 with 160 a year later against Sri Lanka and now looks set for a sustained period in the New Zealand side. He was the star performer when the New Zealand side went retro for a one day game against Australia in 2005. The side was dressed in beige and wearing the old-style floppy hats to evoke the memories of the 1980s with Hamish getting into the sprit of the event by growing his hair into an outrageous afro and then setting it off with a terry-towelling headband.

MARSHALL, James Andrew Hamilton
Born: February 15, 1979
Batting: Right handed
Bowling: Right arm medium

Tests
Test Career: 2005-
Cap Number: 230
Tests Played: 5

Test Batting
Innings:	7	Runs:	166
Highest Score:	52	Average:	23.71
No. 50s:	1	No. 100s:	0

Test Bowling & Fielding
Wickets:	0	Runs:	0
Best Bowling:		Average:	0.00
5 WI:	0	10 WM:	0
Catches:	3	Stumpings:	0

One Day Internationals
ODI Career: 2005-
ODIs Played: 5

ODI Batting
Innings:	5	Runs:	30
Highest Score:	14	Average:	6.00
No. 50s:	0	No. 100s:	0

ODI Bowling & Fielding
Wickets:	0	Runs:	0
Best Bowling:		Average:	0.00
5 WM:	0	Catches:	0
Stumpings:	0		

The brother of Hamish, he has found the going tougher than his identical twin with only 30 runs in five ODI's and an average of 23.71 in Tests.

MARTIN, Christopher Stewart
Born: December 10, 1974
Batting: Right handed
Bowling: Right arm medium-fast

Tests
Test Career: 2000-
Cap Number: 211
Tests Played: 31

Test Batting
Innings:	41	Runs:	48
Highest Score:	7	Average:	2.08
No. 50s:	0	No. 100s:	0

Test Bowling & Fielding
Wickets:	99	Runs:	3,413
Best Bowling:	6/54	Average:	34.47
5 WI:	7	10 WM:	1
Catches:	9	Stumpings:	0

One Day Internationals
ODI Career: 2001-
ODIs Played: 9

ODI Batting
Innings:	6	Runs:	6
Highest Score:	3	Average:	1.20
No. 50s:	0	No. 100s:	0

ODI Bowling & Fielding
Wickets:	11	Runs:	397
Best Bowling:	3/62	Average:	36.09
5 WM:	0	Catches:	3
Stumpings:	0		

A speedster from Canterbury who seemed to have missed his chance at Test level when dropped after playing Pakistan early in 2002. Recalled to the side to play South Africa at Auckland in March 2004, he signaled his return by taking 6/76 and 5/104. Since then Martin has been a regular in the side and in his next Test should become only the 11th New Zealander to take 100 Test wickets.

MASON, Michael James
Born: August 27, 1974
Batting: Right handed
Bowling: Right arm medium-fast

Tests
Test Career: 2004
Cap Number: 226
Tests Played: 1

Test Batting
Innings:	2	Runs:	3
Highest Score:	3	Average:	1.50
No. 50s:	0	No. 100s:	0

Test Bowling & Fielding
Wickets:	0	Runs:	105
Best Bowling:		Average:	0.00
5 WI:	0	10 WM:	0
Catches:	0	Stumpings:	0

One Day Internationals
ODI Career: 2003-
ODIs Played: 8

ODI Batting
Innings:	1	Runs:	13
Highest Score:	13*	Average:	0.00
No. 50s:	0	No. 100s:	0

ODI Bowling & Fielding
Wickets:	10	Runs:	391
Best Bowling:	2/32	Average:	39.10
5 WM:	0	Catches:	0
Stumpings:	0		

A fast medium pace bowler who played a single Test against South Africa at Wellington in 2004 but failed to take a wicket.

MATHESON, Alexander Malcolm
Born: February 27, 1906
Batting: Right handed
Bowling: Right arm medium

Tests
Test Career: 1930-31
Cap Number: 17
Tests Played: 2

Test Batting
Innings:	1	Runs:	7
Highest Score:	7	Average:	7.00
No. 50s:	0	No. 100s:	0

Test Bowling & Fielding
Wickets:	2	Runs:	136
Best Bowling:	2/7	Average:	68.00
5 WI:	0	10 WM:	0
Catches:	2	Stumpings:	0

A swing bowler from Wellington who took 2/7 in an innings in his first Test. He toured England in 1931 playing at Old Trafford but failed to add to his total of Test wickets.

McCULLUM, Brendon Barrie
Born: September 27, 1981
Batting: Right handed
Wicket Keeper

Tests
Test Career:	2004-		
Cap Number:	224		
Tests Played:	23		

Test Batting
Innings:	35	Runs:	1,083
Highest Score:	143	Average:	32.81
No. 50s:	6	No. 100s:	4

Test Bowling & Fielding
Wickets:	0	Runs:	0
Best Bowling:		Average:	0.00
5 WI:	0	10 WM:	0
Catches:	56	Stumpings:	5

One Day Internationals
ODI Career:	2002-		
ODIs Played:	84		

ODI Batting
Innings:	65	Runs:	1,120
Highest Score:	56*	Average:	21.96
No. 50s:	4	No. 100s:	0

ODI Bowling & Fielding
Wickets:	0	Runs:	0
Best Bowling:		Average:	0.00
5 WM:	0	Catches:	104
Stumpings:	8		

Modern cricket dictates that wicket keepers need to be more than good glovemen and in Brendon McCullum New Zealand have also got a fine attacking batsman. Originally overlooked for Robbie Hart who was thought to be the better keeper, he fought his way into the side on the back of his good form in the one day team. McCullum has scored two centuries in 23 Tests and with his attacking hard hitting and neat work behind the stumps looks set for a long international career.

McEWAN, Paul Ernest
Born:	December 19, 1953
Batting:	Right handed
Bowling:	Right arm medium

Tests
Test Career:	1980-84		
Cap Number:	146		
Tests Played:	4		

Test Batting
Innings:	7	Runs:	96
Highest Score:	40*	Average:	16.00
No. 50s:	0	No. 100s:	0

Test Bowling & Fielding
Wickets:	0	Runs:	13
Best Bowling:		Average:	0.00
5 WI:	0	10 WM:	0
Catches:	5	Stumpings:	0

One Day Internationals
ODI Career:	1980-85		
ODIs Played:	17		

ODI Batting
Innings:	15	Runs:	204
Highest Score:	41	Average:	13.60
No. 50s:	0	No. 100s:	0

ODI Bowling & Fielding
Wickets:	6	Runs:	353
Best Bowling:	2/29	Average:	58.83
5 WM:	0	Catches:	1
Stumpings:	0		

An all rounder from Canterbury who was better suited to one day cricket than the longer version of the game.

McGIRR, Herbert Mendelson
Born:	November 5, 1891
Batting:	Right handed
Bowling:	Right arm medium

Tests
Test Career:	1930		
Cap Number:	16		
Tests Played:	2		

Test Batting
Innings:	1	Runs:	51
Highest Score:	51	Average:	51.00
No. 50s:	1	No. 100s:	0

Test Bowling & Fielding
Wickets:	1	Runs:	115
Best Bowling:	1/65	Average:	115.00
5 WI:	0	10 WM:	0
Catches:	0	Stumpings:	0

He was a medium pace bowler from Wellington who played two Tests against England in 1930. Whilst he was selected in the side as a bowler, his finest moment came at Eden Park in Auckland when the number eight batsman scored 51 in his only Test innings.

McGREGOR, Spencer Noel
Born:	December 18, 1931
Batting:	Right handed

Tests
Test Career:	1955-65		
Cap Number:	69		
Tests Played:	25		

Test Batting
Innings:	47	Runs:	892
Highest Score:	111	Average:	19.82
No. 50s:	3	No. 100s:	1

Test Bowling & Fielding
Wickets:	0	Runs:	0
Best Bowling:		Average:	0.00
5 WI:	0	10 WM:	0
Catches:	9	Stumpings:	0

An opening batsman from Otago who held the New Zealand top order together as they struggled in the late 1950's. He scored a single Test century against Pakistan at Lahore in 1955/56, but the fact he played 25 Tests and had an average of under 20 says a great deal about the state of cricket in New Zealand at the time.

McKECHNIE, Brian John
Born:	November 6, 1953
Batting:	Right handed
Bowling:	Right arm medium-fast

One Day Internationals
ODI Career:	1975-81		
ODIs Played:	14		

ODI Batting
Innings:	8	Runs:	54
Highest Score:	27	Average:	13.50
No. 50s:	0	No. 100s:	0

ODI Bowling & Fielding
Wickets:	19	Runs:	495
Best Bowling:	3/23	Average:	26.05
5 WM:	0	Catches:	2
Stumpings:	0		

The subject of cricket's favourite trivia question, Brian McKechnie was the innocent victim of cricket's infamous the 'under-arm affair'. In what has been touted as the most controversial incident in international cricket, McKechnie role was to face the final delivery in the third One Day final between Australia and New Zealand at the MCG in 1981. With New Zealand requiring six runs to draw the game, it would have taken the most optimistic of Kiwi fans to think that tail-ender McKechnie could clear any of the long MCG boundaries off the last ball, but Greg Chappell obviously had an inflated opinion of McKechnie and hatched a plan that would deny him the opportunity of saving the game. He spoke to his younger brother Trevor, who was bowling at the time, and instructed him to bowl the ball underarm. Sensing what was about to occur, Rod Marsh voiced his protest but skipper Chappell was defiant. As the ball rolled along the wicket the parochial Australian crowd let there feelings be known by jeering and booing. McKechnie, begrudgingly blocked the delivery and threw his bat on the ground before walking off in disgust The incident cut deep with the New Zealanders and soured relations between the sporting rivals for many years to come. It also created unwanted notoriety for both McKechnie and Trevor Chappell as McKechnie would explain in an interview in 2004, "Everywhere I go in New Zealand you can bet your life someone will ask me a question about it". Thankfully, the under-arm law was amended shortly after the incident, eliminating any chance of history repeating itself. For the record, McKechnie a was strongly built medium pace bowler who played in 14 ODI's but never managed to crack it for a single Test.

McLEOD, Edwin George
Born:	October 14, 1900
Batting:	Left handed
Bowling:	Left arm leg-break

Tests
Test Career:	1930		
Cap Number:	12		
Tests Played:	1		

Test Batting
Innings:	2	Runs:	18
Highest Score:	16	Average:	18.00
No. 50s:	0	No. 100s:	0

Test Bowling & Fielding
Wickets:	0	Runs:	5
Best Bowling:		Average:	0.00
5 WI:	0	10 WM:	0
Catches:	0	Stumpings:	0

A left handed batsman from Wellington who played a single Test in the first series played by the national side in 1930.

McMAHON, Trevor George
Born:	November 0, 1929
Batting:	Right handed

Tests
Test Career:	1955-56		
Cap Number:	73		
Tests Played:	5		

Test Batting
Innings:	7	Runs:	7
Highest Score:	4*	Average:	2.33
No. 50s:	0	No. 100s:	0

Test Bowling & Fielding
Wickets:	0	Runs:	0
Best Bowling:		Average:	0.00
5 WI:	0	10 WM:	0
Catches:	7	Stumpings:	1

A wicketkeeper from Wellington, he would never have made the Test side in the modern era because his batting was so poor. A more than capable gloveman, McMahon averaged less than three in Tests and less than ten in all first class cricket.

McMILLAN, Craig Douglas
Born:	September 13, 1976
Batting:	Right handed
Bowling:	Right arm medium

Tests
Test Career:	1997-		
Cap Number:	204		
Tests Played:	55		

Test Batting
Innings:	91	Runs:	3,116
Highest Score:	142	Average:	38.46
No. 50s:	19	No. 100s:	6

Test Bowling & Fielding
Wickets:	28	Runs:	1,257
Best Bowling:	3/48	Average:	44.89
5 WI:	0	10 WM:	0
Catches:	22	Stumpings:	0

One Day Internationals
ODI Career:	1997-		
ODIs Played:	175		

ODI Batting
Innings:	164	Runs:	4,148
Highest Score:	105	Average:	27.47
No. 50s:	25	No. 100s:	2

ODI Bowling & Fielding
Wickets:	39	Runs:	1,399
Best Bowling:	3/20	Average:	35.87
5 WM:	0	Catches:	43
Stumpings:	0		

The keenly competitive McMillan made his debut in 1997 against Australia at the 'Gabba with a brave 54 and from that point on has been a consistent performer at international level. A quick scoring middle order batsman and feisty medium pacer, he has six Test centuries to his name in Test cricket and another two in ODI's. His record against the powerful Australians however is not up to his overall Test record with no centuries and a batting average of just 28. McMillan was controversially overlooked for the 2003 World Cup and looks to be on the outer heading into the 2007 tournament having been left out of a 30 man squad for the Champion's Trophy at the end of 2006.

McRAE, Donald Alexander Noel

Born: December 25, 1912
Batting: Left handed
Bowling: Left arm medium

Tests

Test Career: 1946
Cap Number: 37
Tests Played: 1

Test Batting
Innings:	2	Runs:	8
Highest Score:	8	Average:	4.00
No. 50s:	0	No. 100s:	0

Test Bowling & Fielding
Wickets:	0	Runs:	44
Best Bowling:		Average:	0.00
5 WI:	0	10 WM:	0
Catches:	0	Stumpings:	0

One of five New Zealanders who played their only Test against Australia at Wellington in 1947.

McSWEENEY, Ervin Bruce

Born: March 8, 1957
Batting: Right handed
           Wicket Keeper

One Day Internationals

ODI Career: 1986-87
ODIs Played: 16

ODI Batting
Innings:	14	Runs:	73
Highest Score:	18*	Average:	8.11
No. 50s:	0	No. 100s:	0

ODI Bowling & Fielding
Wickets:	0	Runs:	0
Best Bowling:		Average:	0.00
5 WM:	0	Catches:	14
Stumpings:	3		

Wicket-keeper Ervin McSweeney was selected on the 1985/86 tour of Australia where he played in the triangular ODI competition against the host nation and India. Averaging just 4.33 with the bat, he played in a further six ODI's.

MEALE, Trevor

Born: November 11, 1928
Batting: Left handed
Bowling: Right arm medium

Tests

Test Career: 1958
Cap Number: 82
Tests Played: 2

Test Batting
Innings:	4	Runs:	21
Highest Score:	10	Average:	5.25
No. 50s:	0	No. 100s:	0

Test Bowling & Fielding
Wickets:	0	Runs:	0
Best Bowling:		Average:	0.00
5 WI:	0	10 WM:	0
Catches:	0	Stumpings:	0

He was part of a weak New Zealand side that toured England in 1958 but in two Tests could manage only 21 runs.

MERRIT, William Edward

Born: August 18, 1908
Batting: Right handed
Bowling: Right arm leg-break

Tests

Test Career: 1930-31
Cap Number: 9
Tests Played: 6

Test Batting
Innings:	8	Runs:	73
Highest Score:	19	Average:	10.42
No. 50s:	0	No. 100s:	0

Test Bowling & Fielding
Wickets:	12	Runs:	617
Best Bowling:	4/104	Average:	51.41
5 WI:	0	10 WM:	0
Catches:	2	Stumpings:	0

An orthodox leg spinner from Canterbury, he played in his country's early Test cricket with moderate success but had a long a successful first class career both at home and with Northamptonshire in England.

MEULI, Edgar Milton (Ted)

Born: February 20, 1926
Batting: Right handed
Bowling: Right arm leg-break

Tests

Test Career: 1953
Cap Number: 59
Tests Played: 1

Test Batting
Innings:	2	Runs:	38
Highest Score:	23	Average:	19.00
No. 50s:	0	No. 100s:	0

Test Bowling & Fielding
Wickets:	0	Runs:	0
Best Bowling:		Average:	0.00
5 WI:	0	10 WM:	0
Catches:	0	Stumpings:	0

An opening batsman from Central Districts, he played a single Test against the touring South Africans at Wellington in 1953.

MILBURN, Barry Douglas

Born: November 24, 1943
Batting: Right handed
         Wicket Keeper

Tests

Test Career: 1969
Cap Number: 117
Tests Played: 3

Test Batting
Innings:	3	Runs:	8
Highest Score:	4*	Average:	8.00
No. 50s:	0	No. 100s:	0

Test Bowling & Fielding			
Wickets:	0	Runs:	0
Best Bowling:		Average:	0.00
5 WI:	0	10 WM:	0
Catches:	6	Stumpings:	2

A wicket keeper from Otago who played all of his three Tests against the touring West Indians in 1969.

MILLER, Lawrence Somerville Martin

Born: March 31, 1923
Batting: Left handed

Tests
Test Career: 1953-58
Cap Number: 60
Tests Played: 13

Test Batting
Innings:	25	Runs:	346
Highest Score:	47	Average:	13.84
No. 50s:	0	No. 100s:	0

Test Bowling & Fielding
Wickets:	0	Runs:	1
Best Bowling:		Average:	0.00
5 WI:	0	10 WM:	0
Catches:	1	Stumpings:	0

An opening batsman from Wellington who played in 13 Tests but never scored a half century. He played during a period when New Zealand cricket was struggling, but his highest score of 47 came in his country's historic first Test victory.

MILLMOW, Jonathan Paul

Born: September 22, 1967
Batting: Right handed
Bowling: Right arm medium-fast

One Day Internationals
ODI Career: 1990
ODIs Played: 5

ODI Batting
Innings:	1	Runs:	0
Highest Score:	0	Average:	0.00
No. 50s:	0	No. 100s:	0

ODI Bowling & Fielding
Wickets:	4	Runs:	232
Best Bowling:	2/22	Average:	58.00
5 WM:	0	Catches:	1
Stumpings:	0		

A right arm paceman who was plagued with injury early in his career, Millmow played in five ODI's after making his debut against Australia at Sharjah. He later became a sports journalist.

MILLS, John Ernest (Jackie)

Born: September 3, 1905
Batting: Left handed

Tests
Test Career: 1930
Cap Number: 13
Tests Played: 7

Test Batting
Innings:	10	Runs:	241
Highest Score:	117	Average:	26.77
No. 50s:	0	No. 100s:	1

Test Bowling & Fielding
Wickets:	0	Runs:	0
Best Bowling:		Average:	0.00
5 WI:	0	10 WM:	0
Catches:	1	Stumpings:	0

An elegant left handed opening batsman whose first Test innings was a famous century. Playing in the second Test of New Zealand's historic first series against England at Wellington he scored 117 with Stewart Dempster as part of an opening partnership of 276 that stills stands as a record against England. He toured England later that year but was never able to recapture the form of that sparkling debut.

MILLS, Kyle David

Born: March 15, 1979
Batting: Right handed
Bowling: Right arm medium-fast

Tests
Test Career: 2004-
Cap Number: 227
Tests Played: 7

Test Batting
Innings:	12	Runs:	120
Highest Score:	31	Average:	13.33
No. 50s:	0	No. 100s:	0

Test Bowling & Fielding
Wickets:	17	Runs:	534
Best Bowling:	4/43	Average:	31.41
5 WI:	0	10 WM:	0
Catches:	2	Stumpings:	0

One Day Internationals
ODI Career: 2001-
ODIs Played: 60

ODI Batting
Innings:	34	Runs:	230
Highest Score:	44*	Average:	13.52
No. 50s:	0	No. 100s:	0

ODI Bowling & Fielding
Wickets:	78	Runs:	2,321
Best Bowling:	4/14	Average:	29.75
5 WM:	0	Catches:	19
Stumpings:	0		

The swing bowler from Auckland was one of many New Zealand pacemen who had their international careers interrupted by injury in the past decade. He was a member of New Zealand's 2003 World Cup squad but had to wait until the tour of England over a year later to make his Test debut. In seven Tests he has taken 17 wickets with a best performance of 4/43 in the first innings of the Test at Centurion in 2006.

MOIR, Alexander McKenzie

Born: July 17, 1919
Batting: Right handed
Bowling: Right arm leg-break

Tests
Test Career: 1951-59
Cap Number: 53
Tests Played: 17

Test Batting			
Innings:	30	Runs:	327
Highest Score:	41*	Average:	14.86
No. 50s:	0	No. 100s:	0
Test Bowling & Fielding			
Wickets:	28	Runs:	1,418
Best Bowling:	6/155	Average:	50.64
5 WI:	2	10 WM:	0
Catches:	2	Stumpings:	0

A leg spinner from Otago who made a fine debut, taking six wickets in an innings at Christchurch in 1950/51. He was involved in a controversial incident during that series when he mistakenly bowled two overs in succession, one immediately before and after tea.

MOLONEY, Denis Andrew Robert
Born: August 11, 1910
Batting: Right handed
Bowling: Right arm leg-break

Tests
Test Career:	1937		
Cap Number:	30		
Tests Played:	3		
Test Batting			
Innings:	6	Runs:	156
Highest Score:	64	Average:	26.00
No. 50s:	1	No. 100s:	0
Test Bowling & Fielding			
Wickets:	0	Runs:	9
Best Bowling:		Average:	0.00
5 WI:	0	10 WM:	0
Catches:	3	Stumpings:	0

The promising right hand batsman played three Tests on the tour of England in 1937 with a high score of 64 in the first Test at Lord's. 'Sonny' Williams was a prisoner of war and died at El Alamien in Egypt in 1942. He was only 31.

MOONEY, Francis Leonard Hugh
Born: May 26, 1921
Batting: Right handed
Bowling: Right arm medium
Wicket Keeper

Tests
Test Career:	1949-54		
Cap Number:	47		
Tests Played:	14		
Test Batting			
Innings:	22	Runs:	343
Highest Score:	46	Average:	17.15
No. 50s:	0	No. 100s:	0
Test Bowling & Fielding			
Wickets:	0	Runs:	0
Best Bowling:		Average:	0.00
5 WI:	0	10 WM:	0
Catches:	22	Stumpings:	8

A wicket keeper and lower order batsman from Wellington whose colourful exploits off the field earnt him notoriety throughout New Zealand. He would play cricket during the day and spend all night at clubs and bars earning him the soubriquet, 'Starlight'. Despite a fondness for late nights and gambling he was a nimble wicket keeper who had a high percentage of stumpings in his 30 Test dismissals.

MORGAN, Ross Winston
Born: February 12, 1941
Batting: Right handed
Bowling: Right arm off-break

Tests
Test Career:	1965-72		
Cap Number:	104		
Tests Played:	20		
Test Batting			
Innings:	34	Runs:	734
Highest Score:	97	Average:	22.24
No. 50s:	5	No. 100s:	0
Test Bowling & Fielding			
Wickets:	5	Runs:	609
Best Bowling:	1/16	Average:	121.80
5 WI:	0	10 WM:	0
Catches:	12	Stumpings:	0

A top order batsman from Auckland who favoured playing the ball through the on-side. He made an auspicious start to Test cricket scoring 66 on debut against Pakistan at Auckland then following it up with 97 in the very next Test.

MORRISON, Bruce Donald
Born: December 17, 1933
Batting: Left handed
Bowling: Right arm medium

Tests
Test Career:	1963		
Cap Number:	96		
Tests Played:	1		
Test Batting			
Innings:	2	Runs:	10
Highest Score:	10	Average:	5.00
No. 50s:	0	No. 100s:	0
Test Bowling & Fielding			
Wickets:	2	Runs:	129
Best Bowling:	2/129	Average:	64.50
5 WI:	0	10 WM:	0
Catches:	1	Stumpings:	0

A medium pacer from Wellington who played a single Test against England at the Basin Reserve in 1963.

MORRISON, Daniel Kyle
Born: February 3, 1966
Batting: Right handed
Bowling: Right arm medium-fast

Tests
Test Career:	1987-97		
Cap Number:	164		
Tests Played:	48		
Test Batting			
Innings:	71	Runs:	379
Highest Score:	42	Average:	8.42
No. 50s:	0	No. 100s:	0
Test Bowling & Fielding			
Wickets:	160	Runs:	5,549
Best Bowling:	7/89	Average:	34.68
5 WI:	10	10 WM:	0
Catches:	14	Stumpings:	0

MOTZ, Richard Charles

Born:	January 12, 1940
Batting:	Right handed
Bowling:	Right arm fast

Tests

Test Career:	1961-69
Cap Number:	92
Tests Played:	32

Test Batting

Innings:	56	Runs:	612
Highest Score:	60	Average:	11.54
No. 50s:	3	No. 100s:	0

Test Bowling & Fielding

Wickets:	100	Runs:	3,148
Best Bowling:	6/63	Average:	31.48
5 WI:	5	10 WM:	0
Catches:	9	Stumpings:	0

He was tall, powerful and quick, a combination that made him New Zealand's first genuine strike bowler. A genuinely fast bowler, Dick Motz first played for New Zealand when he spearheaded the Test attack in South Africa in 1961-62 taking 19 wickets as his side drew the series two all. He was named one of the five players of the year by Wisden for his efforts on the 1965 tour of England and though troubled by a recurring back injury on the following tour in 1969, he was still able to become the first New Zealander to take 100 Test wickets. That back injury was diagnosed as a displaced vertebrae and he retired immediately. Motz was also a damaging lower order batsman who put his considerable power to good use. He scored three Test half centuries, all of which were liberally laced with 6's.

MURRAY, Bruce Alexander Grefell

Born:	September 18, 1940
Batting:	Right handed
Bowling:	Right arm leg-break

Tests

Test Career:	1968-71
Cap Number:	114
Tests Played:	13

Test Batting

Innings:	26	Runs:	598
Highest Score:	90	Average:	23.92
No. 50s:	5	No. 100s:	0

Test Bowling & Fielding

Wickets:	1	Runs:	0
Best Bowling:	1/0	Average:	0.00
5 WI:	0	10 WM:	0
Catches:	21	Stumpings:	0

The tall opening batsman from Wellington was somewhat of a stonewaller as his 54 on debut against India proved. It took almost three hours to compile but provided much need backbone to a brittle batting line up.

MURRAY, Darrin James

Born:	September 4, 1967
Batting:	Right handed
Bowling:	Right arm medium

One Day Internationals

ODI Career:	1987-96
ODIs Played:	96

ODI Batting

Innings:	43	Runs:	171
Highest Score:	20*	Average:	9.00
No. 50s:	0	No. 100s:	0

ODI Bowling & Fielding

Wickets:	126	Runs:	3,470
Best Bowling:	5/34	Average:	27.53
5 WM:	2	Catches:	19
Stumpings:	0		

New Zealand's front line bowler for a decade between 1987 and 1997, he was stymied by injury throughout his career. Morrison had a classical fast bowing action that almost forced him to send down outswingers. He used his pace and swing to capture 160 Test wickets in only 48 Tests with his best efforts a match winning 6/37 against Australia in 1992/93 and 7/89 against the Aussies in the same series. A batting bunny of the highest order, he held the record for most Test ducks with 24 until that number was passed by West Indian paceman Courtney Walsh.

MORRISON, John Francis Maclean

Born:	August 27, 1947
Batting:	Right handed
Bowling:	Left arm off-break

Tests

Test Career:	1974-82
Cap Number:	128
Tests Played:	17

Test Batting

Innings:	29	Runs:	656
Highest Score:	117	Average:	22.62
No. 50s:	3	No. 100s:	1

Test Bowling & Fielding

Wickets:	2	Runs:	71
Best Bowling:	2/52	Average:	35.50
5 WI:	0	10 WM:	0
Catches:	9	Stumpings:	0

One Day Internationals

ODI Career:	1975-83
ODIs Played:	18

ODI Batting

Innings:	15	Runs:	252
Highest Score:	55	Average:	21.00
No. 50s:	1	No. 100s:	0

ODI Bowling & Fielding

Wickets:	8	Runs:	199
Best Bowling:	3/24	Average:	24.87
5 WM:	0	Catches:	6
Stumpings:	0		

A top order batsman who looked set for a long Test career when he made a fine century in his second Test. The 26 year old opened the batting at the SCG in the second Test of the 1973/74 series and his fighting 117 saved New Zealand from defeat. He was dropped from the Test side in 1976 but earnt a recall five years later against Australia. Morrison struggled in his comeback series scoring 46 runs in five innings.

Tests
Test Career:	1994-95		
Cap Number:	191		
Tests Played:	8		

Test Batting
Innings:	16	Runs:	303
Highest Score:	52	Average:	20.20
No. 50s:	1	No. 100s:	0

Test Bowling & Fielding
Wickets:	0	Runs:	0
Best Bowling:		Average:	0.00
5 WI:	0	10 WM:	0
Catches:	6	Stumpings:	0

One Day Internationals
ODI Career:	1994		
ODIs Played:	1		

ODI Batting
Innings:	1	Runs:	3
Highest Score:	3	Average:	3.00
No. 50s:	0	No. 100s:	0

ODI Bowling & Fielding
Wickets:	0	Runs:	0
Best Bowling:		Average:	0.00
5 WM:	0	Catches:	0
Stumpings:	0		

A batsman from Canterbury who played in eight Tests but could manage only the one half century. He also played in Holland for VRA Amsterdam.

NASH, Dion Joseph
Born:	November 20, 1971
Batting:	Right handed
Bowling:	Right arm medium-fast

Tests
Test Career:	1992-2001		
Cap Number:	180		
Tests Played:	32		

Test Batting
Innings:	45	Runs:	729
Highest Score:	89*	Average:	23.51
No. 50s:	4	No. 100s:	0

Test Bowling & Fielding
Wickets:	93	Runs:	2,649
Best Bowling:	6/27	Average:	28.48
5 WI:	3	10 WM:	1
Catches:	13	Stumpings:	0

One Day Internationals
ODI Career:	1992-2002		
ODIs Played:	81		

ODI Batting
Innings:	53	Runs:	624
Highest Score:	42	Average:	15.60
No. 50s:	0	No. 100s:	0

ODI Bowling & Fielding
Wickets:	64	Runs:	2,622
Best Bowling:	4/38	Average:	40.96
5 WM:	0	Catches:	25
Stumpings:	0		

A solidly built left hander, he made an impression as a hard hitting batsman and menacing bowler. Nash made a quiet start in Test ranks against Zimbabwe in 1992, but was considered a player of promise and was given a spot in the squad that toured England in 1994. He took 17 wickets in three Tests, including 11 at Lord's in a Man of the Match performance. Hampered by a recurring back injury throughout his Test and one day career, the hard nosed competitor was always selected when fit. When Stephen Fleming missed three Tests in 1998 and 1999 through injury, Nash was elevated to the top job. He played his final series against the Australians in 2001/02 before his back forced him to retire. Respected for his forthright attitude and keen cricket brain, he is now a national selector.

NEVIN, Christopher John
Born:	August 3, 1975
Batting:	Right handed
	Wicket Keeper

One Day Internationals
ODI Career:	2000-03		
ODIs Played:	37		

ODI Batting
Innings:	36	Runs:	732
Highest Score:	74	Average:	20.33
No. 50s:	4	No. 100s:	0

ODI Bowling & Fielding
Wickets:	0	Runs:	0
Best Bowling:		Average:	0.00
5 WM:	0	Catches:	16
Stumpings:	3		

A talented wicket-keeper and attacking ODI batsman, Chris Nevin made a superb 74 to take out the 'Man of the Match' award, in only his second ODI against Australia, at Eden Park in 2000. Nevin made four 50's in his 37 ODI appearances and could be considered unlucky not to have been tried at Test level.

NEWMAN, Jack
Born:	July 3, 1902
Batting:	Right handed
Bowling:	Left arm medium

Tests
Test Career:	1932-33		
Cap Number:	22		
Tests Played:	3		

Test Batting
Innings:	4	Runs:	33
Highest Score:	19	Average:	8.25
No. 50s:	0	No. 100s:	0

Test Bowling & Fielding
Wickets:	2	Runs:	254
Best Bowling:	2/76	Average:	127.00
5 WI:	0	10 WM:	0
Catches:	0	Stumpings:	0

A medium pace bowler from Wellington who played three Tests in the 30's. He was a long standing cricket administrator and leading figure in his country's airline industry. Jack Newman received a knighthood in 1978.

O'BRIEN, Iain Edward
Born:	July 10, 1976
Batting:	Right handed
Bowling:	Right arm medium

Tests
Test Career:	2005-		
Cap Number:	229		
Tests Played:	2		

Test Batting
Innings:	3	Runs:	10
Highest Score:	5	Average:	3.33
No. 50s:	0	No. 100s:	0

Test Bowling & Fielding
Wickets:	2	Runs:	197
Best Bowling:	1/73	Average:	98.50
5 WI:	0	10 WM:	0
Catches:	1	Stumpings:	0

A medium pacer from Wellington he played a pair of Tests against the touring Australians in 2005. His only Test wickets were the Australian duo of Matthew Hayden and Damien Martyn.

O'CONNOR, Shayne Barry
Born:	November 15, 1973
Batting:	Left handed
Bowling:	Left arm medium-fast

Tests
Test Career:	1997-2001		
Cap Number:	202		
Tests Played:	19		

Test Batting
Innings:	27	Runs:	103
Highest Score:	20	Average:	5.72
No. 50s:	0	No. 100s:	0

Test Bowling & Fielding
Wickets:	53	Runs:	1,724
Best Bowling:	5/51	Average:	32.52
5 WI:	1	10 WM:	0
Catches:	6	Stumpings:	0

One Day Internationals
ODI Career:	1997-2000		
ODIs Played:	38		

ODI Batting
Innings:	13	Runs:	24
Highest Score:	8	Average:	3.42
No. 50s:	0	No. 100s:	0

ODI Bowling & Fielding
Wickets:	46	Runs:	1,396
Best Bowling:	5/39	Average:	30.34
5 WM:	2	Catches:	11
Stumpings:	0		

Tall and angular, he was a left arm speedy swing bowler who was struck down in his prime by a serious injury. O'Connor had a promising start to his career but truly came to the fore against Australia at Hamilton in 2000 when his new ball spell had Australia teetering at 4/25. New Zealand seemed to have unearthed a new strike bowler, but less than 12 months later he was on the sidelines with a knee injury that ultimately forced him to retire in 2003.

O'SULLIVAN, David Robert
Born:	November 16, 1944
Batting:	Right handed
Bowling:	Left arm off-break

Tests
Test Career:	1973-76		
Cap Number:	125		
Tests Played:	11		

Test Batting
Innings:	21	Runs:	158
Highest Score:	23*	Average:	9.29
No. 50s:	0	No. 100s:	0

Test Bowling & Fielding
Wickets:	18	Runs:	1,224
Best Bowling:	5/148	Average:	68.00
5 WI:	1	10 WM:	0
Catches:	2	Stumpings:	0

One Day Internationals
ODI Career:	1974-76		
ODIs Played:	3		

ODI Batting
Innings:	2	Runs:	2
Highest Score:	1*	Average:	2.00
No. 50s:	0	No. 100s:	0

ODI Bowling & Fielding
Wickets:	2	Runs:	123
Best Bowling:	1/38	Average:	61.50
5 WM:	0	Catches:	0
Stumpings:	0		

A left arm off spinner who played 11 Tests for 18 rather expensive wickets. He did take five wickets in an innings against Australia at Adelaide in 1974 but they cost 148 runs.

ORAM, Jacob David Phillip
Born:	July 28, 1978
Batting:	Left handed
Bowling:	Right arm medium-fast

Tests
Test Career:	2002-		
Cap Number:	222		
Tests Played:	20		

Test Batting
Innings:	35	Runs:	1,203
Highest Score:	133	Average:	42.96
No. 50s:	4	No. 100s:	3

Test Bowling & Fielding
Wickets:	38	Runs:	1,384
Best Bowling:	4/41	Average:	36.42
5 WI:	0	10 WM:	0
Catches:	12	Stumpings:	0

One Day Internationals
ODI Career:	2001-		
ODIs Played:	83		

ODI Batting
Innings:	62	Runs:	1,034
Highest Score:	81	Average:	18.46
No. 50s:	3	No. 100s:	0

ODI Bowling & Fielding
Wickets:	94	Runs:	2,812
Best Bowling:	5/26	Average:	29.91
5 WM:	2	Catches:	21
Stumpings:	0		

The towering all-rounder is New Zealand's answer to Freddie Flintoff, and with three Test hundreds and 38 wickets in his first 20 Tests, he has the chance to even outstrip the more famous Englishman. In his early Tests he showed more promise with the ball than bat, capturing 11 wickets in his first two appearances. His batting came to the fore with an unbeaten century against South Africa in Hamilton in 2003/04 and a spanking 126 not out against Australia in Brisbane in 2004/05. Whilst he caught the Australia public's attention with his batting, his bowling was less impressive and he failed to take a wicket in the two Tests he has played. Oram scored 133 in the first Test of the Black Caps' last Test series, away to South Africa, and will be looking to have a big say when his country heads to the Caribbean for the 2007 World Cup.

OVERTON, Guy William Fitzroy

Born: June 8, 1919
Batting: Left handed
Bowling: Right arm fast

Tests
Test Career: 1953-54
Cap Number: 64
Tests Played: 3
Test Batting
Innings:	6	Runs:	8
Highest Score:	3*	Average:	1.60
No. 50s:	0	No. 100s:	0

Test Bowling & Fielding
Wickets:	9	Runs:	258
Best Bowling:	3/65	Average:	28.66
5 WI:	0	10 WM:	0
Catches:	1	Stumpings:	0

A medium pace bowler who played three Tests on the tour of South Africa in 1953/54.

OWENS, Michael Barry

Born: November 11, 1969
Batting: Right handed
Bowling: Right arm medium-fast

Tests
Test Career: 1992-94
Cap Number: 182
Tests Played: 8
Test Batting
Innings:	12	Runs:	16
Highest Score:	8*	Average:	2.66
No. 50s:	0	No. 100s:	0

Test Bowling & Fielding
Wickets:	17	Runs:	585
Best Bowling:	4/99	Average:	34.41
5 WI:	0	10 WM:	0
Catches:	3	Stumpings:	0

One Day Internationals
ODI Career: 1992
ODIs Played: 1
ODI Batting
Innings:	1	Runs:	0
Highest Score:	0	Average:	0.00
No. 50s:	0	No. 100s:	0

ODI Bowling & Fielding
Wickets:	0	Runs:	37
Best Bowling:		Average:	0.00
5 WM:	0	Catches:	0
Stumpings:	0		

A medium pace bowler from Canterbury who played eight Tests in the early 90's. He twice took four wickets in an innings, once against Sri Lanka and in his final Test against England at Old Trafford.

PAGE, Milford Laurenson

Born: May 8, 1902
Batting: Right handed
Bowling: Right arm slow

Tests
Test Career: 1930-37
Cap Number: 10
Tests Played: 14
Test Batting
Innings:	20	Runs:	492
Highest Score:	104	Average:	24.60
No. 50s:	2	No. 100s:	1

Test Bowling & Fielding
Wickets:	5	Runs:	231
Best Bowling:	2/21	Average:	46.20
5 WI:	0	10 WM:	0
Catches:	6	Stumpings:	0

A top order batsman and slow change bowler who scored his country's first Test century on foreign soil with 104 at Lord's in 1931. 'Curly' Page replaced Tom Lowry as captain of New Zealand after that tour to England, but like his predecessor couldn't lead his side to that historic first Test win.

PAPPS, Michael Hugh William

Born: July 2, 1979
Batting: Right handed
Wicket Keeper

Tests
Test Career: 1979-07-02
Cap Number: 225
Tests Played: 6
Test Batting
Innings:	12	Runs:	229
Highest Score:	86	Average:	20.81
No. 50s:	2	No. 100s:	0

Test Bowling & Fielding
Wickets:	0	Runs:	0
Best Bowling:		Average:	0.00
5 WI:	0	10 WM:	0
Catches:	7	Stumpings:	0

One Day Internationals
ODI Career: 2004-
ODIs Played: 6
ODI Batting
Innings:	6	Runs:	207
Highest Score:	92*	Average:	51.75
No. 50s:	2	No. 100s:	0

ODI Bowling & Fielding
Wickets:	0	Runs:	0
Best Bowling:		Average:	0.00
5 WM:	0	Catches:	1
Stumpings:	0		

A useful top order batsman and occasional wicket keeper, he made 59 on debut at home against South Africa and was equally impressive in his first Test on English soil with 86 at Leeds. He broke his finger in that Test and when he returned to the side for the tour of South Africa later in 2004 was unable to recapture his earlier good form

PARKER, John Morton

Born: February 21, 1951
Batting: Right handed
Bowling: Right arm leg-break
Wicket Keeper

Tests
Test Career: 1973-80
Cap Number: 124
Tests Played: 36

Test Batting
Innings:	63	Runs:	1,498
Highest Score:	121	Average:	24.55
No. 50s:	5	No. 100s:	3

Test Bowling & Fielding
Wickets:	1	Runs:	24
Best Bowling:	1/24	Average:	24.00
5 WI:	0	10 WM:	0
Catches:	30	Stumpings:	0

One Day Internationals
ODI Career: 1974-81
ODIs Played: 24

ODI Batting
Innings:	20	Runs:	248
Highest Score:	66	Average:	12.40
No. 50s:	1	No. 100s:	0

ODI Bowling & Fielding
Wickets:	1	Runs:	10
Best Bowling:	1/10	Average:	10.00
5 WM:	0	Catches:	11
Stumpings:	0		

The right hander from Northern Districts was tried first as an opener and later as a middle order batsman but apart from three Test centuries against Australia, England and India was generally disappointing.

PARKER, Norman Murray

Born: August 28, 1948
Batting: Right handed

Tests
Test Career: 1976
Cap Number: 137
Tests Played: 3

Test Batting
Innings:	6	Runs:	89
Highest Score:	40	Average:	14.83
No. 50s:	0	No. 100s:	0

Test Bowling & Fielding
Wickets:	0	Runs:	0
Best Bowling:		Average:	0.00
5 WI:	0	10 WM:	0
Catches:	2	Stumpings:	0

One Day Internationals
ODI Career: 1976
ODIs Played: 1

ODI Batting
Innings:	1	Runs:	0
Highest Score:	0	Average:	0.00
No. 50s:	0	No. 100s:	0

ODI Bowling & Fielding
Wickets:	0	Runs:	0
Best Bowling:		Average:	0.00
5 WM:	0	Catches:	1
Stumpings:	0		

The brother of John, he played three Tests on the tour of Pakistan in 1976.

PARORE, Adam Craig

Born: January 23, 1971
Batting: Right handed
Wicket Keeper

Tests
Test Career: 1990-2002
Cap Number: 171
Tests Played: 78

Test Batting
Innings:	128	Runs:	2,865
Highest Score:	110	Average:	26.28
No. 50s:	14	No. 100s:	2

Test Bowling & Fielding
Wickets:	0	Runs:	0
Best Bowling:		Average:	0.00
5 WI:	0	10 WM:	0
Catches:	197	Stumpings:	7

One Day Internationals
ODI Career: 1992-2002
ODIs Played: 179

ODI Batting
Innings:	161	Runs:	3,314
Highest Score:	108	Average:	25.68
No. 50s:	14	No. 100s:	1

ODI Bowling & Fielding
Wickets:	0	Runs:	0
Best Bowling:		Average:	0.00
5 WM:	0	Catches:	116
Stumpings:	25		

No wicketkeeper has stood in more Tests for New Zealand than the athletic Adam Parore. At his best he was as good as any keeper playing Test cricket, with his energetic leaps and dives and as a batsman he was considered good enough to retain his spot in the side as a batsman when keeper Lee Germon was appointed captain. His two Test centuries were an even 100 at Christchurch when facing the West Indies and 110 against Australia at the WACA in 2001/02. Popular amongst his teammates and supporters, he was less so with opposition batsman who had to put up with his constant chattering behind the stumps.

PATEL, Dipak Narshibhai

Born: October 25, 1958
Batting: Right handed
Bowling: Right arm off-break

Tests
Test Career: 1987-97
Cap Number: 161
Tests Played: 37

Test Batting
Innings:	66	Runs:	1,200
Highest Score:	99	Average:	20.68
No. 50s:	5	No. 100s:	0

Test Bowling & Fielding			
Wickets:	75	Runs:	3,154
Best Bowling:	6/50	Average:	42.05
5 WI:	3	10 WM:	0
Catches:	15	Stumpings:	0

One Day Internationals

ODI Career:	1987-97		
ODIs Played:	75		
ODI Batting			
Innings:	63	Runs:	623
Highest Score:	71	Average:	11.75
No. 50s:	1	No. 100s:	0
ODI Bowling & Fielding			
Wickets:	45	Runs:	2,261
Best Bowling:	3/22	Average:	50.24
5 WM:	0	Catches:	23
Stumpings:	0		

The Kenyan born Patel was a tight off spinner and useful batsman who famously opened the bowling for New Zealand in their 1992 World Cup campaign. His quick finger spin was well suited to the shorter version of the game, though he did have his moments in Test cricket with three bags of five or more wickets in an innings. He is one of those unfortunate Test cricketers whose highest Test score is 99 having been run out against England at Christchurch on that score in 1992.

PATEL, Jeetan Shashi

Born:	May 7, 1980
Batting:	Right handed
Bowling:	Right arm off-break

Tests

Test Career:	2006-		
Cap Number:	233		
Tests Played:	1		
Test Batting			
Innings:	1	Runs:	27
Highest Score:	27*	Average:	0.00
No. 50s:	0	No. 100s:	0
Test Bowling & Fielding			
Wickets:	3	Runs:	117
Best Bowling:	3/117	Average:	39.00
5 WI:	0	10 WM:	0
Catches:	1	Stumpings:	0

One Day Internationals

ODI Career:	2005-		
ODIs Played:	9		
ODI Batting			
Innings:	0	Runs:	0
Highest Score:	0	Average:	0.00
No. 50s:	0	No. 100s:	0
ODI Bowling & Fielding			
Wickets:	13	Runs:	392
Best Bowling:	3/42	Average:	30.15
5 WM:	0	Catches:	4
Stumpings:	0		

The right arm off spinner was selected to tour South Africa in 2006 and in his only Test took three wickets. He had already played a handful of ODI's for the national side and impressed with his control and flight.

PENN, Andrew Jonathan

Born:	July 27, 1974
Batting:	Right handed
Bowling:	Right arm medium-fast

One Day Internationals

ODI Career:	1997-01		
ODIs Played:	5		
ODI Batting			
Innings:	3	Runs:	23
Highest Score:	15	Average:	11.50
No. 50s:	0	No. 100s:	0
ODI Bowling & Fielding			
Wickets:	1	Runs:	201
Best Bowling:	1/50	Average:	201.00
5 WM:	0	Catches:	1
Stumpings:	0		

A swing bowler who played five ODI's from 1997 to 2001. His only wicket was that of Pakistani opener Saeed Anwar.

PETHERICK, Peter James

Born:	September 25, 1942
Batting:	Right handed
Bowling:	Right arm off-break

Tests

Test Career:	1976-77		
Cap Number:	136		
Tests Played:	6		
Test Batting			
Innings:	11	Runs:	34
Highest Score:	13	Average:	4.85
No. 50s:	0	No. 100s:	0
Test Bowling & Fielding			
Wickets:	16	Runs:	681
Best Bowling:	3/90	Average:	42.56
5 WI:	0	10 WM:	0
Catches:	4	Stumpings:	0

At thirty Peter Petherick had never played first class cricket, by the time he was 34 he had taken a Test hat trick. He played in only six Tests, but in his first, the right arm off spinner claimed the wickets of Javed Miandad, Wasim Raja and Intikhab Alam in successive balls.

PETRIE, Eric Charlton

Born:	May 22, 1927
Batting:	Right handed
Bowling:	Right arm leg-break
	Wicket Keeper

Tests

Test Career:	1955-66		
Cap Number:	75		
Tests Played:	14		
Test Batting			
Innings:	25	Runs:	258
Highest Score:	55	Average:	12.90
No. 50s:	1	No. 100s:	0
Test Bowling & Fielding			
Wickets:	0	Runs:	0
Best Bowling:		Average:	0.00
5 WI:	0	10 WM:	0
Catches:	25	Stumpings:	0

He was a much respected first class cricketer in New Zealand whose career spanned 16 seasons.

In fourteen Tests for New Zealand he proved a reliable gloveman but showed little with the bat scoring only the one half century.

PETRIE, Richard George
Born: August 23, 1967
Batting: Right handed
Bowling: Right arm medium-fast

One Day Internationals
ODI Career: 1990-91
ODIs Played: 12

ODI Batting
Innings:	8	Runs:	65
Highest Score:	21	Average:	13.00
No. 50s:	0	No. 100s:	0

ODI Bowling & Fielding
Wickets:	12	Runs:	449
Best Bowling:	2/25	Average:	37.41
5 WM:	0	Catches:	2
Stumpings:	0		

An exciting pace bowler who played his first of 12 ODI's against Australia at the SCG. However injuries shortened what could have been a long and fruitful career.

PLAYLE, William Rodger
Born: December 1, 1938
Batting: Right handed
Bowling: Right arm off-break

Tests
Test Career: 1958-63
Cap Number: 83
Tests Played: 8

Test Batting
Innings:	15	Runs:	151
Highest Score:	65	Average:	10.06
No. 50s:	1	No. 100s:	0

Test Bowling & Fielding
Wickets:	0	Runs:	0
Best Bowling:		Average:	0.00
5 WI:	0	10 WM:	0
Catches:	4	Stumpings:	0

An opening batsman from Auckland who toured England in 1958 and then appeared in the Test side more than four years later to face the visiting Englishmen. His highest Test score was a 65 against the English at Wellington in 1963. Playle later moved to Western Australia where he played for the WA state side.

POCOCK, Blair Andrew
Born: June 18, 1971
Batting: Right handed
Bowling: Right arm slow

Tests
Test Career: 1993-97
Cap Number: 184
Tests Played: 15

Test Batting
Innings:	29	Runs:	665
Highest Score:	85	Average:	22.93
No. 50s:	6	No. 100s:	0

Test Bowling & Fielding
Wickets:	0	Runs:	20
Best Bowling:		Average:	0.00
5 WI:	0	10 WM:	0
Catches:	5	Stumpings:	0

The Auckland batsman had a taste of Test cricket in the 90's when he played 15 Tests, but a shoulder injury saw him make way for Brian Young and he never regained his spot.

POLLARD, Victor
Born: September 7, 1945
Batting: Right handed
Bowling: Right arm off-break

Tests
Test Career: 1965-73
Cap Number: 107
Tests Played: 32

Test Batting
Innings:	59	Runs:	1,266
Highest Score:	116	Average:	24.34
No. 50s:	7	No. 100s:	2

Test Bowling & Fielding
Wickets:	40	Runs:	1,853
Best Bowling:	3/3	Average:	46.32
5 WI:	0	10 WM:	0
Catches:	19	Stumpings:	0

One Day Internationals
ODI Career: 1973-74
ODIs Played: 3

ODI Batting
Innings:	2	Runs:	67
Highest Score:	55	Average:	33.50
No. 50s:	1	No. 100s:	0

ODI Bowling & Fielding
Wickets:	0	Runs:	0
Best Bowling:		Average:	0.00
5 WM:	0	Catches:	1
Stumpings:	0		

The English born Pollard was a reliable contributor for the New Zealand side with both the bat and ball. A powerfully built man, he put his strong forearms to good use on a number of occasions and was particularly effective in England in 1973 where he scored centuries in consecutive Tests. He was not a big spinner of the ball but knew how to land it on a nagging length and it was in fact his bowling that originally got him a spot in the Test side.

POORE, Matt Beresford
Born: June 1, 1930
Batting: Right handed
Bowling: Right arm off-break

Tests
Test Career: 1953-56
Cap Number: 63
Tests Played: 14

Test Batting
Innings:	24	Runs:	355
Highest Score:	45	Average:	15.43
No. 50s:	0	No. 100s:	0

Test Bowling & Fielding

Wickets:	9	Runs:	367
Best Bowling:	2/28	Average:	40.77
5 WI:	0	10 WM:	0
Catches:	1	Stumpings:	0

A right arm off spinner and handy lower batsman who played in 14 Tests but could only manage nine wickets.

PRIEST, Mark Wellings

Born: August 12, 1961
Batting: Left handed
Bowling: Left arm off-break

Tests

Test Career: 1990-98
Cap Number: 170
Tests Played: 3

Test Batting

Innings:	4	Runs:	56
Highest Score:	26	Average:	14.00
No. 50s:	0	No. 100s:	0

Test Bowling & Fielding

Wickets:	3	Runs:	158
Best Bowling:	2/42	Average:	52.66
5 WI:	0	10 WM:	0
Catches:	0	Stumpings:	0

One Day Internationals

ODI Career: 1990-98
ODIs Played: 18

ODI Batting

Innings:	14	Runs:	103
Highest Score:	24	Average:	10.30
No. 50s:	0	No. 100s:	0

ODI Bowling & Fielding

Wickets:	8	Runs:	590
Best Bowling:	2/27	Average:	72.75
5 WM:	0	Catches:	2
Stumpings:	0		

Nicknamed 'Popeye', he had a long and successful career with Canterbury as a finger spinner but played just three Tests over an eight year period.

PRINGLE, Christopher

Born: January 26, 1968
Batting: Right handed
Bowling: Right arm medium-fast

Tests

Test Career: 1990-95
Cap Number: 173
Tests Played: 14

Test Batting

Innings:	21	Runs:	175
Highest Score:	30	Average:	10.29
No. 50s:	0	No. 100s:	0

Test Bowling & Fielding

Wickets:	30	Runs:	1,389
Best Bowling:	7/52	Average:	46.30
5 WI:	1	10 WM:	1
Catches:	3	Stumpings:	0

One Day Internationals

ODI Career: 1990-95
ODIs Played: 64

ODI Batting

Innings:	41	Runs:	193
Highest Score:	34*	Average:	8.77
No. 50s:	0	No. 100s:	0

ODI Bowling & Fielding

Wickets:	103	Runs:	2,459
Best Bowling:	5/45	Average:	23.87
5 WM:	1	Catches:	7
Stumpings:	0		

Any young cricketer who has exhausted the normal avenues to represent his country might try Chris Pringle's method. He was playing minor county cricket in England in 1990 when he visited a New Zealand net session looking for tickets for the upcoming one day series. The youngster was recognised by some of the squad members and asked to provide some bowling back-up at training. Within days the Black Caps had lost a bowler to injury and Pringle was representing his country. He was selected to tour Pakistan later that year and in only his third Test took 11 wickets at Faisalabad. From that point on he was steady rather than brilliant and was used predominately in the one day side.

PUNA, Narotam (Tom)

Born: October 28, 1929
Batting: Right handed
Bowling: Right arm off-break

Tests

Test Career: 1966
Cap Number: 111
Tests Played: 3

Test Batting

Innings:	5	Runs:	31
Highest Score:	18*	Average:	15.50
No. 50s:	0	No. 100s:	0

Test Bowling & Fielding

Wickets:	4	Runs:	240
Best Bowling:	2/40	Average:	60.00
5 WI:	0	10 WM:	0
Catches:	1	Stumpings:	0

Born in India, the right arm off spinner played all of his three Tests against the touring English in 1966.

RABONE, Geoffrey Osbourne

Born: November 6, 1921
Batting: Right handed
Bowling: Right arm off-break

Tests

Test Career: 1949-55
Cap Number: 48
Tests Played: 12

Test Batting

Innings:	20	Runs:	562
Highest Score:	107	Average:	31.22
No. 50s:	2	No. 100s:	1

Test Bowling & Fielding

Wickets:	16	Runs:	635
Best Bowling:	6/68	Average:	39.68
5 WI:	1	10 WM:	0
Catches:	5	Stumpings:	0

A versatile cricketer, he was not only a fine top order batsman but a canny change bowler who could bowl off spin, leggies or medium pace. Rabone led the side to South Africa in 1953/54 and before breaking his foot scored 254 runs in three Tests, including a 107 at Cape Town. He also returned his best Test bowling figures of 6/68 during that series.

REDMOND, Rodney Ernest

Born: December 29, 1944
Batting: Left handed
Bowling: Left arm off-break

Tests

Test Career: 1973
Cap Number: 126
Tests Played: 1

Test Batting

Innings:	2	Runs:	163
Highest Score:	107	Average:	81.50
No. 50s:	1	No. 100s:	1

Test Bowling & Fielding

Wickets:	0	Runs:	0
Best Bowling:		Average:	0.00
5 WI:	0	10 WM:	0
Catches:	0	Stumpings:	0

One Day Internationals

ODI Career: 1973
ODIs Played: 2

ODI Batting

Innings:	1	Runs:	3
Highest Score:	3	Average:	3.00
No. 50s:	0	No. 100s:	0

ODI Bowling & Fielding

Wickets:	0	Runs:	0
Best Bowling:		Average:	0.00
5 WM:	0	Catches:	0
Stumpings:	0		

There are few more curious Tests careers than that of Rodney Redmond. His only Test was against Pakistan at Auckland in 1973 where the powerfully built opener scored 107 and 56. He was selected to tour England later that year but indifferent form in the warm up matches saw him miss a Test berth and he never played for his country again

REID, John Fulton

Born: March 3, 1956
Batting: Left handed
Bowling: Left arm leg-break

Tests

Test Career: 1979-86
Cap Number: 144
Tests Played: 19

Test Batting

Innings:	31	Runs:	1,296
Highest Score:	180	Average:	46.28
No. 50s:	2	No. 100s:	6

Test Bowling & Fielding

Wickets:	0	Runs:	7
Best Bowling:		Average:	0.00
5 WI:	0	10 WM:	0
Catches:	9	Stumpings:	0

One Day Internationals

ODI Career: 1980-86
ODIs Played: 25

ODI Batting

Innings:	24	Runs:	633
Highest Score:	88	Average:	27.52
No. 50s:	4	No. 100s:	0

ODI Bowling & Fielding

Wickets:	0	Runs:	0
Best Bowling:		Average:	0.00
5 WM:	0	Catches:	5
Stumpings:	0		

Very few Test batsmen can boast more hundreds than fifties and certainly not at a ration of 3:1, but that is exactly what John Reid did in his 19 Tests. He scored six Test tons that included successive hundreds against the touring Pakistanis in 1984/85 and an excellent 108 a year later against an Australian side spearheaded by Geoff Lawson and Craig McDermott. Unfortunately that six Test series in Australia and at home was to be Reid's undoing, with only 111 runs in the final five Tests.

REID, John Richard

Born: June 3, 1928
Batting: Right handed
Wicket Keeper

Tests

Test Career: 1949-65
Cap Number: 49
Tests Played: 58

Test Batting

Innings:	108	Runs:	3,428
Highest Score:	142	Average:	33.28
No. 50s:	22	No. 100s:	6

Test Bowling & Fielding

Wickets:	85	Runs:	2,835
Best Bowling:	6/60	Average:	33.35
5 WI:	1	10 WM:	0
Catches:	43	Stumpings:	1

John Reid was not only New Zealand's first successful Test captain, he was also his country's first world class all-rounder. The robust Reid played in 58 Tests for New Zealand for a total of 3428 runs at an average of 33.28. He scored six centuries, with his best a typically hard hitting 142 against South Africa. He was also a useful all rounder who bowled vigorous medium pace and captured 85 wickets with a best of 6-60, against South Africa in 1964. So complete an all-rounder was Reid that he even kept wickets for his country.

REID, Richard Bruce

Born: December 3, 1958
Batting: Right handed

One Day Internationals

ODI Career: 1988-91
ODIs Played: 9

ODI Batting

Innings:	9	Runs:	248
Highest Score:	64	Average:	27.55
No. 50s:	2	No. 100s:	0

ODI Bowling & Fielding

Wickets:	1	Runs:	13
Best Bowling:	1/13	Average:	13.00
5 WM:	0	Catches:	3
Stumpings:	0		

An opening batsman who partnered with stalwart John Wright, Reid made his ODI debut against England at Dunedin in 1988. He performed reasonably well in his nine appearances averaging 27.55.

RICHARDSON, Mark Hunter

Born: June 11, 1971
Batting: Left handed
Bowling: Left arm off-break

Tests

Test Career:	2000-04
Cap Number:	210
Tests Played:	38

Test Batting

Innings:	65	Runs:	2,776
Highest Score:	145	Average:	44.77
No. 50s:	19	No. 100s:	4

Test Bowling & Fielding

Wickets:	1	Runs:	21
Best Bowling:	1/16	Average:	21.00
5 WI:	0	10 WM:	0
Catches:	26	Stumpings:	0

One Day Internationals

ODI Career:	2002
ODIs Played:	4

ODI Batting

Innings:	4	Runs:	42
Highest Score:	26	Average:	10.50
No. 50s:	0	No. 100s:	0

ODI Bowling & Fielding

Wickets:	0	Runs:	0
Best Bowling:		Average:	0.00
5 WM:	0	Catches:	1
Stumpings:	0		

Big Mark Richardson made a name for himself for a being slow and steady, both with the bat and in his famous post Test races against slow-coaches from the opposition. As a Test opener he batted within his limitations to carve out a fine career after making his debut as a 29 year old. Richardson had been an off spinner in domestic cricket but concentrated on his batting to win a Test spot. He scored in excess of 50 twenty three times in Tests with a top score of 145 against India in 2003. When he hung up his whites, Richardson left behind a very satisfying Test career with a batting average of almost 55.

ROBERTS, Albert William

Born: August 20, 1909
Batting: Right handed
Bowling: Right arm medium

Tests

Test Career:	1930-37
Cap Number:	11
Tests Played:	5

Test Batting

Innings:	10	Runs:	248
Highest Score:	66*	Average:	27.55
No. 50s:	3	No. 100s:	0

Test Bowling & Fielding

Wickets:	7	Runs:	209
Best Bowling:	4/101	Average:	29.85
5 WI:	0	10 WM:	0
Catches:	4	Stumpings:	0

A medium pace bowler and top order batsman who played in New Zealand's first Test ever and in their first Test against South Africa. He was a star all-rounder for both Canterbury and Otago.

ROBERTS, Andrew Duncan Glenn

Born: May 6, 1947
Batting: Right handed
Bowling: Right arm medium

Tests

Test Career:	1976
Cap Number:	133
Tests Played:	7

Test Batting

Innings:	12	Runs:	254
Highest Score:	84*	Average:	23.09
No. 50s:	1	No. 100s:	0

Test Bowling & Fielding

Wickets:	4	Runs:	182
Best Bowling:	1/12	Average:	45.50
5 WI:	0	10 WM:	0
Catches:	4	Stumpings:	0

One Day Internationals

ODI Career:	1976
ODIs Played:	1

ODI Batting

Innings:	1	Runs:	16
Highest Score:	16	Average:	16.00
No. 50s:	0	No. 100s:	0

ODI Bowling & Fielding

Wickets:	1	Runs:	30
Best Bowling:	1/30	Average:	30.00
5 WM:	0	Catches:	1
Stumpings:	0		

Cricket's other Andy Roberts, he was a middle order batsman and handy change bowler. His best innings for New Zealand was an unbeaten 84 against India at Kanpur in 1976/77.

ROBERTS, Stuart

Born: March 22, 1965
Batting: Right handed
Bowling: Right arm medium-fast

One Day Internationals

ODI Career:	1990
ODIs Played:	2

ODI Batting

Innings:	1	Runs:	1
Highest Score:	1*	Average:	0.00
No. 50s:	0	No. 100s:	0

ODI Bowling & Fielding

Wickets:	0	Runs:	47
Best Bowling:		Average:	0.00
5 WM:	0	Catches:	0
Stumpings:	0		

A medium pacer who made his debut against India at Dunedin in 1990.

ROBERTSON, Gary Keith

Born: July 15, 1960
Batting: Right handed
Bowling: Right arm medium-fast

Tests

Test Career:	1986		
Cap Number:	158		
Tests Played:	1		

Test Batting

Innings:	1	Runs:	12
Highest Score:	12	Average:	12.00
No. 50s:	0	No. 100s:	0

Test Bowling & Fielding

Wickets:	1	Runs:	91
Best Bowling:	1/91	Average:	91.00
5 WI:	0	10 WM:	0
Catches:	0	Stumpings:	0

One Day Internationals

ODI Career:	1981-89		
ODIs Played:	10		

ODI Batting

Innings:	6	Runs:	49
Highest Score:	17	Average:	8.16
No. 50s:	0	No. 100s:	0

ODI Bowling & Fielding

Wickets:	6	Runs:	321
Best Bowling:	2/29	Average:	53.50
5 WM:	0	Catches:	2
Stumpings:	0		

A pace bowler from Central Districts who played his only Test against the touring Aussies in 1986.

ROWE, Charles Gordon

Born: June 30, 1915
Batting: Right handed

Tests

Test Career:	1946		
Cap Number:	38		
Tests Played:	1		

Test Batting

Innings:	2	Runs:	0
Highest Score:	0	Average:	0.00
No. 50s:	0	No. 100s:	0

Test Bowling & Fielding

Wickets:	0	Runs:	0
Best Bowling:		Average:	0.00
5 WI:	0	10 WM:	0
Catches:	1	Stumpings:	0

His only Test was the one off match with Australia in 1946. He was one of two New Zealanders to fall to Bill O'Reilly for a pair.

RUTHERFORD, Kenneth Robert

Born: October 26, 1965
Batting: Right handed
Bowling: Right arm medium

Tests

Test Career:	1985-95		
Cap Number:	155		
Tests Played:	56		

Test Batting

Innings:	99	Runs:	2,465
Highest Score:	107*	Average:	27.08
No. 50s:	18	No. 100s:	3

Test Bowling & Fielding

Wickets:	1	Runs:	161
Best Bowling:	1/38	Average:	161.00
5 WI:	0	10 WM:	0
Catches:	32	Stumpings:	0

One Day Internationals

ODI Career:	1985-95		
ODIs Played:	121		

ODI Batting

Innings:	115	Runs:	3,143
Highest Score:	108	Average:	29.65
No. 50s:	18	No. 100s:	2

ODI Bowling & Fielding

Wickets:	10	Runs:	323
Best Bowling:	2/39	Average:	32.30
5 WM:	0	Catches:	41
Stumpings:	0		

When your Test career starts with scores of 0,0,4,0,2,1 and 5 you either better be a very good bowler or prepared to look for another career. In Ken Rutherford's case he fought back to be a regular Test batsman who provided his country with solid service for a decade. That horror start in the West Indies was halted with a fine 65 not out against the Australians the next summer and finally a century against England at Wellington in 1987/88. Throughout his career he did enough to either be in the Test team or earn a recall and in 1992 led the Test side while Martin Crowe was unavailable through injury.

SCOTT, Roy Hamilton

Born: May 6, 1917
Batting: Right handed
Bowling: Right arm medium

Tests

Test Career:	1947		
Cap Number:	41		
Tests Played:	1		

Test Batting

Innings:	1	Runs:	18
Highest Score:	18	Average:	18.00
No. 50s:	0	No. 100s:	0

Test Bowling & Fielding

Wickets:	1	Runs:	74
Best Bowling:	1/74	Average:	74.00
5 WI:	0	10 WM:	0
Catches:	0	Stumpings:	0

A medium pace bowler from Canterbury who played his only Test against the touring English in 1947. He was no relation to Verdun Scott who played for New Zealand at the same time.

SCOTT, Verdun John

Born: July 31, 1916
Batting: Right handed
Bowling: Right arm medium

Tests

Test Career: 1946-52
Cap Number: 39
Tests Played: 10

Test Batting

Innings:	17	Runs:	458
Highest Score:	84	Average:	28.62
No. 50s:	3	No. 100s:	0

Test Bowling & Fielding

Wickets:	0	Runs:	14
Best Bowling:		Average:	0.00
5 WI:	0	10 WM:	0
Catches:	7	Stumpings:	0

A solidly batsman from Auckland who was described as being effective rather than elegant. His first Test was against Australia in 1946 and whilst his debut knock of 14 might not sound like much of an achievement it was the side's top score in their paltry total of 26. He played nine more Tests over the next six years with his career ending like it started when he top scored for the side with an 84 against the West Indies at Auckland in 1952.

SEWELL, David Graham

Born: October 20, 1977
Batting: Right handed
Bowling: Left arm medium-fast

Tests

Test Career: 1997
Cap Number: 203
Tests Played: 1

Test Batting

Innings:	1	Runs:	1
Highest Score:	1*	Average:	0.00
No. 50s:	0	No. 100s:	0

Test Bowling & Fielding

Wickets:	0	Runs:	90
Best Bowling:		Average:	0.00
5 WI:	0	10 WM:	0
Catches:	0	Stumpings:	0

The medium pace bowler played his only Test against Zimbabwe at Bulawayo in 1997 but failed to take a wicket.

SHRIMPTON, Michael John Froud

Born: June 23, 1940
Batting: Right handed
Bowling: Right arm leg-break

Tests

Test Career: 1963-74
Cap Number: 97
Tests Played: 10

Test Batting

Innings:	19	Runs:	265
Highest Score:	46	Average:	13.94
No. 50s:	0	No. 100s:	0

Test Bowling & Fielding

Wickets:	5	Runs:	158
Best Bowling:	3/35	Average:	31.60
5 WI:	0	10 WM:	0
Catches:	2	Stumpings:	0

A top order batsman and occasional leg spinner, Shrimpton had a long and successful first class career in New Zealand but disappointed in the Test team where he could only average 13.94 in a Test career that spanned 11 years. He has enjoyed great success in recent years as coach of the New Zealand women's side, winning the World Cup in 2000.

SINCLAIR, Barry Whitley

Born: October 23, 1936
Batting: Right handed
Bowling: Right arm medium

Tests

Test Career: 1963-68
Cap Number: 94
Tests Played: 21

Test Batting

Innings:	40	Runs:	1,148
Highest Score:	138	Average:	29.43
No. 50s:	3	No. 100s:	3

Test Bowling & Fielding

Wickets:	2	Runs:	32
Best Bowling:	2/32	Average:	16.00
5 WI:	0	10 WM:	0
Catches:	8	Stumpings:	0

A pint-sized top order batsman who could flay the bowling despite his lack of inches. The right hander from Wellington played in 21 Tests and when on song was the equal of any player in the side. He scored three fine Test centuries against South Africa, Pakistan and England and was also a brilliant cover fieldsman. Sinclair captained New Zealand in three Tests against the touring English in 1965/66 for a draw and two losses.

SINCLAIR, Ian McKay

Born: June 1, 1933
Batting: Left handed
Bowling: Right arm off-break

Tests

Test Career: 1956
Cap Number: 79
Tests Played: 2

Test Batting

Innings:	4	Runs:	25
Highest Score:	18*	Average:	8.33
No. 50s:	0	No. 100s:	0

Test Bowling & Fielding

Wickets:	1	Runs:	120
Best Bowling:	1/79	Average:	120.00
5 WI:	0	10 WM:	0
Catches:	1	Stumpings:	0

A right arm off spinner from New Zealand whose only Test wicket didn't come cheap.

SINCLAIR, Matthew Stuart

Born: November 9, 1975
Batting: Right handed
Bowling: Right arm medium
Wicket Keeper

Tests

Test Career: 1999-2004
Cap Number: 208
Tests Played: 25

Test Batting

Innings:	42	Runs:	1,365
Highest Score:	214	Average:	36.89
No. 50s:	4	No. 100s:	3

Test Bowling & Fielding

Wickets:	0	Runs:	13
Best Bowling:		Average:	0.00
5 WI:	0	10 WM:	0
Catches:	22	Stumpings:	0

One Day Internationals

ODI Career: 2000-
ODIs Played: 45

ODI Batting

Innings:	44	Runs:	1,180
Highest Score:	118*	Average:	28.09
No. 50s:	7	No. 100s:	2

ODI Bowling & Fielding

Wickets:	0	Runs:	0
Best Bowling:		Average:	0.00
5 WM:	0	Catches:	15
Stumpings:	0		

He made cricket headlines around the globe when he scored 214 on debut against the West Indies in 1999. A prolific scorer with Central Districts where he had a number of big scores, Sinclair proved that debut double ton was no fluke with an unbeaten 204 against Pakistan a year later. Since then the going has been more difficult and at present he isn't part of the Test or one day squads.

SMITH, Frank Brunton

Born: March 13, 1922
Batting: Right handed
Bowling: Right arm off-break

Tests

Test Career: 1947-52
Cap Number: 42
Tests Played: 4

Test Batting

Innings:	6	Runs:	237
Highest Score:	96	Average:	47.40
No. 50s:	2	No. 100s:	0

Test Bowling & Fielding

Wickets:	0	Runs:	0
Best Bowling:		Average:	0.00
5 WI:	0	10 WM:	0
Catches:	1	Stumpings:	0

The pint sized Brun Smith had the rather unflattering nickname 'Runty' but he was an accomplished batsman from Canterbury who was part of the side that toured England with great success in 1949. The 'Forty-niners' didn't lose a Test on that tour and Smith played a key role at Headingly where he scored 96 and 54 not out.

SMITH, Horace Dennis

Born: January 8, 1913
Batting: Right handed
Bowling: Right arm fast

Tests

Test Career: 1933
Cap Number: 24
Tests Played: 1

Test Batting

Innings:	1	Runs:	4
Highest Score:	4	Average:	4.00
No. 50s:	0	No. 100s:	0

Test Bowling & Fielding

Wickets:	1	Runs:	113
Best Bowling:	1/113	Average:	113.00
5 WI:	0	10 WM:	0
Catches:	0	Stumpings:	0

The Australian born fast bowler played a single Test against England in 1933 but in his only innings with the ball came up against a rampaging Walter Hammond who scored 227.

SMITH, Ian David Stockley

Born: February 28, 1957
Batting: Right handed
Bowling: Right arm medium
Wicket Keeper

Tests

Test Career: 1980-92
Cap Number: 148
Tests Played: 63

Test Batting

Innings:	88	Runs:	1,815
Highest Score:	173	Average:	25.56
No. 50s:	6	No. 100s:	2

Test Bowling & Fielding

Wickets:	0	Runs:	5
Best Bowling:		Average:	0.00
5 WI:	0	10 WM:	0
Catches:	168	Stumpings:	8

One Day Internationals

ODI Career: 1980-92
ODIs Played: 98

ODI Batting

Innings:	77	Runs:	1,055
Highest Score:	62*	Average:	17.29
No. 50s:	3	No. 100s:	0

ODI Bowling & Fielding

Wickets:	0	Runs:	0
Best Bowling:		Average:	0.00
5 WM:	0	Catches:	81
Stumpings:	5		

An excellent wicket keeper and fighting lower order batsman who was his country's longest standing keeper until his record was passed by Adam Parore. More than capable behind the stumps, he was an effective if not stylish batsman who scored a marvelous century against India at Auckland in 1991. New Zealand were teetering at 7/131 when Smith came into bat but the keeper smashed 173 with twenty three 4's and three 6's to see his side to a far more respectable all out for 391. Happy to have his say behind the stumps, Smith has kept talking about cricket in retirement as one of the game's leading television commentators.

SNEDDEN, Colin Alexander

Born:	January 7, 1918
Batting:	Right handed
Bowling:	Right arm off-break

Tests

Test Career:	1947
Cap Number:	43
Tests Played:	1

Test Batting

Innings:	0	Runs:	0
Highest Score:	0	Average:	0.00
No. 50s:	0	No. 100s:	0

Test Bowling & Fielding

Wickets:	0	Runs:	46
Best Bowling:		Average:	0.00
5 WI:	0	10 WM:	0
Catches:	0	Stumpings:	0

An off spinner from Auckland who played one Test against England at Christchurch in 1947. He is the uncle of Test cricketer Martin Snedden.

SNEDDEN, Martin Colin

Born:	November 23, 1958
Batting:	Left handed
Bowling:	Right arm medium-fast

Tests

Test Career:	1981-90
Cap Number:	149
Tests Played:	25

Test Batting

Innings:	30	Runs:	327
Highest Score:	33*	Average:	14.86
No. 50s:	0	No. 100s:	0

Test Bowling & Fielding

Wickets:	58	Runs:	2,199
Best Bowling:	5/68	Average:	37.91
5 WI:	1	10 WM:	0
Catches:	7	Stumpings:	0

One Day Internationals

ODI Career:	1980-90
ODIs Played:	93

ODI Batting

Innings:	54	Runs:	535
Highest Score:	64	Average:	15.28
No. 50s:	1	No. 100s:	0

ODI Bowling & Fielding

Wickets:	114	Runs:	3,237
Best Bowling:	4/34	Average:	28.39
5 WM:	0	Catches:	19
Stumpings:	0		

A seam bowler with an attractive rhythmic action, he battled hard for New Zealand in both their one day and Test sides. Snedden was involved in a controversial incident on the day of the famous underarm incident at the MCG in 1981. He took a spectacular low outfield catch off the batting of Greg Chappell but it was disallowed by the umpires, although TV replays clearly showed it was a clean catch. A lawyer by profession, Snedden is currently serving as chief executive of New Zealand Cricket.

SPARLING, John Trevor

Born:	July 24, 1938
Batting:	Right handed
Bowling:	Right arm off-break

Tests

Test Career:	1958-64
Cap Number:	84
Tests Played:	11

Test Batting

Innings:	20	Runs:	229
Highest Score:	50	Average:	12.72
No. 50s:	1	No. 100s:	0

Test Bowling & Fielding

Wickets:	5	Runs:	327
Best Bowling:	1/9	Average:	65.40
5 WI:	0	10 WM:	0
Catches:	3	Stumpings:	0

A right arm off spinner and useful lower order batsman from Auckland. The promising teenager made his debut as a 19 year old, but other than a fifty at Old Trafford in 1958 failed to flatter at Test level.

SPEARMAN, Craig Murray

Born:	July 4, 1972
Batting:	Right handed

Tests

Test Career:	1995-2000
Cap Number:	195
Tests Played:	19

Test Batting

Innings:	37	Runs:	922
Highest Score:	112	Average:	26.34
No. 50s:	3	No. 100s:	1

Test Bowling & Fielding

Wickets:	0	Runs:	0
Best Bowling:		Average:	0.00
5 WI:	0	10 WM:	0
Catches:	21	Stumpings:	0

One Day Internationals

ODI Career:	1995-2001
ODIs Played:	51

ODI Batting

Innings:	50	Runs:	936
Highest Score:	86	Average:	18.72
No. 50s:	5	No. 100s:	0

ODI Bowling & Fielding

Wickets:	0	Runs:	6
Best Bowling:		Average:	0.00
5 WM:	0	Catches:	15
Stumpings:	0		

An opening batsman from Auckland who was tipped for great things when he made his Test debut as a 23 year old. He only averaged 26.44 in his 19 Tests with a solitary century against Zimbabwe in 1995/96. Spearman has had a much better time of it with Gloucestershire in English county cricket and in 2004 scored a record 341 against Middlesex.

STEAD, Gary Raymond

Born:	January 9, 1972
Batting:	Right handed
Bowling:	Right arm leg-break

Tests

Test Career:	1999
Cap Number:	207
Tests Played:	5

Test Batting

Innings:	8	Runs:	278
Highest Score:	78	Average:	34.75
No. 50s:	2	No. 100s:	0

Test Bowling & Fielding

Wickets:	0	Runs:	1
Best Bowling:		Average:	0.00
5 WI:	0	10 WM:	0
Catches:	2	Stumpings:	0

An honest number four or five, the Canterbury batsman played his entire Test cricket in 1999 and with a top score of 78 against India and an average of 34.75 seemed unlucky to have been discarded so quickly.

STIRLING, Derek Alexander

Born:	October 5, 1961
Batting:	Right handed
Bowling:	Right arm medium-fast

Tests

Test Career:	1984-86
Cap Number:	154
Tests Played:	6

Test Batting

Innings:	9	Runs:	108
Highest Score:	26	Average:	15.42
No. 50s:	0	No. 100s:	0

Test Bowling & Fielding

Wickets:	13	Runs:	601
Best Bowling:	4/88	Average:	46.23
5 WI:	0	10 WM:	0
Catches:	1	Stumpings:	0

One Day Internationals

ODI Career:	1984
ODIs Played:	6

ODI Batting

Innings:	5	Runs:	21
Highest Score:	13*	Average:	7.00
No. 50s:	0	No. 100s:	0

ODI Bowling & Fielding

Wickets:	6	Runs:	207
Best Bowling:	2/29	Average:	34.50
5 WM:	0	Catches:	3
Stumpings:	0		

A speedster from Northern Districts who played six Tests before being literally hit out of international cricket by Ian Botham. In his final Test at The Oval in 1986, 'Beefy' belted him for 24 off one over and Stirling was never sighted at Test level again.

STOTT, Leslie Warren

Born:	December 8, 1946
Batting:	Right handed
Bowling:	Right arm medium

One Day Internationals

ODI Career:	1979
ODIs Played:	1

ODI Batting

Innings:	0	Runs:	0
Highest Score:	0	Average:	0.00
No. 50s:	0	No. 100s:	0

ODI Bowling & Fielding

Wickets:	3	Runs:	48
Best Bowling:	3/48	Average:	16.00
5 WM:	0	Catches:	1
Stumpings:	0		

An English born medium pacer, Warren Stott returned to his homeland to take three wickets in his only ODI against Sri Lanka, at Trent Bridge, during the 1979 World Cup.

STYRIS, Scott Bernard

Born:	July 10, 1975
Batting:	Right handed
Bowling:	Right arm medium

Tests

Test Career:	2002-
Cap Number:	221
Tests Played:	27

Test Batting

Innings:	44	Runs:	1,527
Highest Score:	170	Average:	38.17
No. 50s:	6	No. 100s:	5

Test Bowling & Fielding

Wickets:	20	Runs:	981
Best Bowling:	3/28	Average:	49.05
5 WI:	0	10 WM:	0
Catches:	23	Stumpings:	0

One Day Internationals

ODI Career:	1999-
ODIs Played:	116

ODI Batting

Innings:	99	Runs:	2,503
Highest Score:	141	Average:	28.77
No. 50s:	14	No. 100s:	3

ODI Bowling & Fielding

Wickets:	106	Runs:	3,365
Best Bowling:	6/25	Average:	31.74
5 WM:	1	Catches:	45
Stumpings:	0		

The solidly built Styris seemed destined to be just a one day player with three years in the ODI side before finally being called up for Test duty. When he finally got his chance on the tour of the Caribbean in 2002 he made the most of it with 107 and 69 not out on debut at St. George's. Since then he has gone on to score four more hundreds and also made a contribution with his useful medium pace bowling.

SU'A, Murphy Logo

Born:	November 7, 1966
Batting:	Left handed
Bowling:	Left arm medium-fast

Tests

Test Career:	1992-95
Cap Number:	176
Tests Played:	13

Test Batting
Innings:	18	Runs:	165
Highest Score:	44	Average:	12.69
No. 50s:	0	No. 100s:	0

Test Bowling & Fielding
Wickets:	36	Runs:	1,377
Best Bowling:	5/73	Average:	38.25
5 WI:	2	10 WM:	0
Catches:	8	Stumpings:	0

One Day Internationals
ODI Career:	1992-95
ODIs Played:	12

ODI Batting
Innings:	7	Runs:	24
Highest Score:	12*	Average:	4.80
No. 50s:	0	No. 100s:	0

ODI Bowling & Fielding
Wickets:	9	Runs:	367
Best Bowling:	4/59	Average:	40.77
5 WM:	0	Catches:	1
Stumpings:	0		

A whole hearted bowler from Northern Districts who had a promising start to his Test career with 27 wickets in his first seven Tests. The left armer found the going much tougher against Australia in 1993/94 and after playing two more Tests against the West Indies and Sri Lanka a year later permanently lost his place in the side.

SULZBERGER, Glen Paul
Born:	March 14, 1973
Batting:	Left handed
Bowling:	Right arm off-break

One Day Internationals
ODI Career:	2000
ODIs Played:	3

ODI Batting
Innings:	2	Runs:	9
Highest Score:	6*	Average:	9.00
No. 50s:	0	No. 100s:	0

ODI Bowling & Fielding
Wickets:	3	Runs:	102
Best Bowling:	1/28	Average:	34.00
5 WM:	0	Catches:	0
Stumpings:	0		

An off-spinning all-rounder who was selected on the tour of Zimbabwe in 2000 where he played in three ODI's.

SUTCLIFFE, Bert
Born:	November 17, 1923
Batting:	Left handed
Bowling:	Left arm off-break

Tests
Test Career:	1947-65
Cap Number:	44
Tests Played:	42

Test Batting
Innings:	76	Runs:	2,727
Highest Score:	230*	Average:	40.10
No. 50s:	15	No. 100s:	5

Test Bowling & Fielding
Wickets:	4	Runs:	344
Best Bowling:	2/38	Average:	86.00
5 WI:	0	10 WM:	0
Catches:	20	Stumpings:	0

The left handed batsman from Otago was one of New Zealand's greatest ever cricketers. He came to attention in the summer of 1946-47 when he scored 197 and 128 for his district against MCC and was rewarded with a spot in the side for the one off Test against England at Lancaster Park in Christchurch. He scored a 58 in that rain shortened match and would go on to play in the Test side until 1965. Sutcliffe was an opener or middle-order batsman who played in 42 test matches for 2727 runs at an average of 40.10. His highest Test score was a then national record 230 not out against India at Delhi in 1955/56 and his 385 for Otago against Canterbury in 1952-53 remains the highest ever first class score by a New Zealander. He became a national hero in South Africa in 1954 when he resumed batting after being struck on the side of the head by a bouncer from Neil Adcock. Sutcliffe returned from hospital to score 80 not out in his country's total of 187. He captained New Zealand in four Tests for three losses and a draw and despite many fine individual performances for his country, incredibly never played in a winning Test team.

TAIT, Alex Ross
Born:	June 13, 1972
Batting:	Right handed
Bowling:	Right arm medium

One Day Internationals
ODI Career:	1998-99
ODIs Played:	5

ODI Batting
Innings:	5	Runs:	35
Highest Score:	13*	Average:	11.66
No. 50s:	0	No. 100s:	0

ODI Bowling & Fielding
Wickets:	3	Runs:	88
Best Bowling:	2/37	Average:	29.33
5 WM:	0	Catches:	0
Stumpings:	0		

A right arm medium pacer who took 2/37 on his ODI debut against Zimbabwe at Dhaka, in 1998. Played five ODI's between 1998-99.

TAYLOR, Bruce Richard
Born:	July 12, 1943
Batting:	Left handed
Bowling:	Right arm medium-fast

Tests
Test Career:	1965-73
Cap Number:	108
Tests Played:	30

Test Batting
Innings:	50	Runs:	898
Highest Score:	124	Average:	20.40
No. 50s:	2	No. 100s:	2

Test Bowling & Fielding			
Wickets:	111	Runs:	2,953
Best Bowling:	7/74	Average:	26.60
5 WI:	4	10 WM:	0
Catches:	10	Stumpings:	0

One Day Internationals
ODI Career:	1973		
ODIs Played:	2		

ODI Batting
Innings:	1	Runs:	22
Highest Score:	22	Average:	22.00
No. 50s:	0	No. 100s:	0

ODI Bowling & Fielding
Wickets:	4	Runs:	62
Best Bowling:	3/25	Average:	15.50
5 WM:	0	Catches:	1
Stumpings:	0		

One of New Zealand's best ever all rounders, he was a penetrating right arm quick and equally effective left hand middle order batsman. Big Bruce made a dashing start to his test career with a century on debut against India at Calcutta in 1965. He followed his heroics with the bat with a five wicket haul when New Zealand was in the field. In doing so he became the first Test cricketer to do the double on debut. He followed it up in the next Test at Bombay with 5/26 and went from unknown to a key figure in the New Zealand side. Things didn't come as easily over the next few years, but the balding tyro could be relied upon for a full hearted effort whenever he pulled on the black cap. He scored a career high 124 against the West Indies in 1968/69 and recorded his best ever bowling figures of 7/74 in an innings when the two teams met at Bridgetown in 1971/72.

TAYLOR, Donald Dougald
Born:	March 2, 1923
Batting:	Right handed
Bowling:	Right arm off-break

Tests
Test Career:	1947-56		
Cap Number:	45		
Tests Played:	3		

Test Batting
Innings:	5	Runs:	159
Highest Score:	77	Average:	31.80
No. 50s:	1	No. 100s:	0

Test Bowling & Fielding
Wickets:	0	Runs:	0
Best Bowling:		Average:	0.00
5 WI:	0	10 WM:	0
Catches:	2	Stumpings:	0

He played in only three Tests, but the top order batsman from Auckland was a member of the side that beat the West Indies in 1956 to claim New Zealand's first win in Test cricket.

TAYLOR, Ross Luteru
Born:	March 8, 1984
Batting:	Right handed
Bowling:	Right arm off-break

One Day Internationals
ODI Career:	2006		
ODIs Played:	2		

ODI Batting
Innings:	2	Runs:	46
Highest Score:	31	Average:	23.00
No. 50s:	0	No. 100s:	0

ODI Bowling & Fielding
Wickets:	0	Runs:	0
Best Bowling:		Average:	0.00
5 WM:	0	Catches:	0
Stumpings:	0		

An exciting young batsman who impressed in two ODI's against the West Indies in 2006.

THOMSON, Keith
Born:	February 26, 1941
Batting:	Right handed
Bowling:	Right arm medium

Tests
Test Career:	1968		
Cap Number:	115		
Tests Played:	2		

Test Batting
Innings:	4	Runs:	94
Highest Score:	69	Average:	31.33
No. 50s:	1	No. 100s:	0

Test Bowling & Fielding
Wickets:	1	Runs:	9
Best Bowling:	1/9	Average:	9.00
5 WI:	0	10 WM:	0
Catches:	0	Stumpings:	0

A right handed batsman from Canterbury who played two Tests against India in 1968. He was unlucky to have not played more given he scored 69 on debut. Also represented New Zealand at hockey.

THOMSON, Shane Alexander
Born:	January 27, 1969
Batting:	Right handed

Tests
Test Career:	1990-95		
Cap Number:	169		
Tests Played:	19		

Test Batting
Innings:	35	Runs:	958
Highest Score:	120*	Average:	30.90
No. 50s:	5	No. 100s:	1

Test Bowling & Fielding
Wickets:	19	Runs:	953
Best Bowling:	3/63	Average:	50.15
5 WI:	0	10 WM:	0
Catches:	7	Stumpings:	0

One Day Internationals
ODI Career:	1990-96		
ODIs Played:	56		

ODI Batting
Innings:	52	Runs:	964
Highest Score:	83	Average:	22.95
No. 50s:	5	No. 100s:	0

ODI Bowling & Fielding
Wickets:	42	Runs:	1,602
Best Bowling:	3/14	Average:	38.14
5 WM:	0	Catches:	18
Stumpings:	0		

A right arm off spinner and talented batsman, he initially made the Test side on the strength of his bowling but retained his spot as a batsman. He scored one Test century, an unbeaten 120 against Pakistan at Christchurch in 1993/94 that saw New Zealand secure an unlikely victory.

TINDILL, Eric William Thomas
Born: December 18, 1910
Batting: Left handed
Wicket Keeper

Tests
Test Career: 1937-47
Cap Number: 31
Tests Played: 5

Test Batting
Innings:	9	Runs:	73
Highest Score:	37*	Average:	9.12
No. 50s:	0	No. 100s:	0

Test Bowling & Fielding
Wickets:	0	Runs:	0
Best Bowling:		Average:	0.00
5 WI:	0	10 WM:	0
Catches:	6	Stumpings:	1

A wicketkeeper and opening batsman, his five Tests straddled the Second World War. Tindill was better known as a brilliant footballer who played 17 times for the All Blacks between 1935 and 1938.

TROUP, Gary Bertram
Born: October 3, 1952
Batting: Right handed
Bowling: Left arm medium-fast

Tests
Test Career: 1976-86
Cap Number: 138
Tests Played: 15

Test Batting
Innings:	18	Runs:	55
Highest Score:	13*	Average:	4.58
No. 50s:	0	No. 100s:	0

Test Bowling & Fielding
Wickets:	39	Runs:	1,454
Best Bowling:	10/166	Average:	37.28
5 WI:	1	10 WM:	1
Catches:	2	Stumpings:	0

One Day Internationals
ODI Career: 1976-85
ODIs Played: 22

ODI Batting
Innings:	12	Runs:	101
Highest Score:	39	Average:	25.25
No. 50s:	0	No. 100s:	0

ODI Bowling & Fielding
Wickets:	32	Runs:	791
Best Bowling:	4/19	Average:	24.71
5 WM:	0	Catches:	2
Stumpings:	0		

A left arm speedster from Auckland who was in the Test side over an 11 year period and was unlucky not to play more than his 16 Tests. Troup played a key role in the surprise series win over the West Indies in 1979/80 with 18 wickets in three matches including ten in the third and final Test at Eden Park. Hardly a recognized batsman, he hung around with Lance Cairns and Stephen Boock to secure a victory in what would be the deciding first Test of that series.

TRUSCOTT, Peter Bennetts
Born: August 14, 1941
Batting: Right handed

Tests
Test Career: 1965
Cap Number: 105
Tests Played: 1

Test Batting
Innings:	2	Runs:	29
Highest Score:	26	Average:	14.50
No. 50s:	0	No. 100s:	0

Test Bowling & Fielding
Wickets:	0	Runs:	0
Best Bowling:		Average:	0.00
5 WI:	0	10 WM:	0
Catches:	1	Stumpings:	0

He played his only test against Pakistan at Christchurch in 1965.

TUFFEY, Daryl Raymond
Born: June 11, 1978
Batting: Right handed
Bowling: Right arm medium-fast

Tests
Test Career: 2000-04
Cap Number: 209
Tests Played: 22

Test Batting
Innings:	30	Runs:	263
Highest Score:	35	Average:	11.43
No. 50s:	0	No. 100s:	0

Test Bowling & Fielding
Wickets:	66	Runs:	2,057
Best Bowling:	6/54	Average:	31.16
5 WI:	2	10 WM:	0
Catches:	12	Stumpings:	0

One Day Internationals
ODI Career: 2000-
ODIs Played: 76

ODI Batting
Innings:	40	Runs:	146
Highest Score:	20*	Average:	7.30
No. 50s:	0	No. 100s:	0

ODI Bowling & Fielding
Wickets:	90	Runs:	2,693
Best Bowling:	4/24	Average:	29.92
5 WM:	0	Catches:	19
Stumpings:	0		

An energetic opening bowler who had been a key member of the side until he ran foul of coach John Bracewell in 2004. Tuffey provided good support for the likes of Shane Bond and was often his side's chief destroyer with six Test bags of four or more wickets in an innings. His best match haul was 9/116 in a 'Man of the Match' performance against England at Eden Park in 2002.

TURNER, Glenn Maitland

Born:	May 26, 1947
Batting:	Right handed
Bowling:	Right arm off-break

Tests

Test Career:	1969-83
Cap Number:	118
Tests Played:	41

Test Batting

Innings:	73	Runs:	2,991
Highest Score:	259	Average:	44.64
No. 50s:	14	No. 100s:	7

Test Bowling & Fielding

Wickets:	0	Runs:	5
Best Bowling:		Average:	0.00
5 WI:	0	10 WM:	0
Catches:	42	Stumpings:	0

One Day Internationals

ODI Career:	1973-83
ODIs Played:	41

ODI Batting

Innings:	40	Runs:	1,598
Highest Score:	171*	Average:	47.00
No. 50s:	9	No. 100s:	3

ODI Bowling & Fielding

Wickets:	0	Runs:	0
Best Bowling:		Average:	0.00
5 WM:	0	Catches:	13
Stumpings:	0		

His country's master batsman of the 70's, Glenn Turner was an integral part of the first New Zealand side to be feared by the cricket world. He was an opening batsman of the highest calibre with a technique that was honed on the playing fields of Dunedin and perfected on the county grounds of England. Turner was a 12 month a year cricketer, playing at home in the southern hemisphere summer and then heading to Worcestershire for the county season. He played 41 tests for 2991 runs, with his most famous period the tour of the West Indies in 1972, when he scored two double centuries. First came an unbeaten 223 in Jamaica and then a national record 259 at Georgetown. He left the Caribbean not only at the top of his game, but in the eyes of most people, the best opening batsman in the world. It was the first time a New Zealand batsman was held in such high esteem and the added pressure seemed to affect Turner. He was below his best, first at home to Pakistan in 1972/73 then in England in 1973, but he bounced back in style to brilliantly lead the New Zealanders to their first ever Test win over Australia with a century in each innings at Christchurch in 1974. Among his feats, he is the only New Zealander to have scored more than 100 first class centuries and he was the first player to score a century against every other county in English cricket. The strong willed Turner captained the side in ten Tests but stood down after a run in with administrators. His brother Greg was one of New Zealand's greatest ever golfers.

TWOSE, Roger Graham

Born:	April 17, 1968
Batting:	Left handed
Bowling:	Right arm medium

Tests

Test Career:	1995-99
Cap Number:	194
Tests Played:	16

Test Batting

Innings:	27	Runs:	628
Highest Score:	94	Average:	25.12
No. 50s:	6	No. 100s:	0

Test Bowling & Fielding

Wickets:	3	Runs:	130
Best Bowling:	2/36	Average:	43.33
5 WI:	0	10 WM:	0
Catches:	5	Stumpings:	0

One Day Internationals

ODI Career:	1995-2001
ODIs Played:	87

ODI Batting

Innings:	81	Runs:	2,717
Highest Score:	103	Average:	38.81
No. 50s:	20	No. 100s:	1

ODI Bowling & Fielding

Wickets:	4	Runs:	235
Best Bowling:	2/31	Average:	58.75
5 WM:	0	Catches:	37
Stumpings:	0		

Warwickshire's Roger Twose moved to New Zealand on the promise of playing Test cricket and was given a place in the Test side almost automatically. An industrious top order batsman and handy medium pace bowler, he was better suited to one day cricket and represented his adopted country in 87 ODI's. His only hundred came in a one day game at Cape Town in 2000. Twose was the nephew of English wicketkeeper Roger Tolchard.

VANCE, Robert Howard (Bert)

Born:	March 31, 1955
Batting:	Right handed
Bowling:	Right arm off-break

Tests

Test Career:	1988-89
Cap Number:	166
Tests Played:	4

Test Batting

Innings:	7	Runs:	207
Highest Score:	68	Average:	29.57
No. 50s:	1	No. 100s:	0

Test Bowling & Fielding

Wickets:	0	Runs:	0
Best Bowling:		Average:	0.00
5 WI:	0	10 WM:	0
Catches:	0	Stumpings:	0

One Day Internationals

ODI Career:	1988-89
ODIs Played:	8

ODI Batting

Innings:	8	Runs:	248
Highest Score:	96	Average:	31.00
No. 50s:	1	No. 100s:	0

ODI Bowling & Fielding			
Wickets:	0	Runs:	0
Best Bowling:		Average:	0.00
5 WM:	0	Catches:	4
Stumpings:	0		

A capable batsman from Wellington who played a handful of Tests and ODI's in the late 1980's. Vance holds a record that will most likely never be beaten, conceding the most runs off a single over in first class cricket. In an attempt to cajole his opponents to risk going for a victory he intentionally conceded 77 runs in an over by bowling a succession of no-balls against Canterbury in 1990.

VAUGHAN, Justin Thomas Caldwell

Born:	August 30, 1967
Batting:	Left handed
Bowling:	Right arm medium

Tests

Test Career:	1992-97
Cap Number:	183
Tests Played:	6

Test Batting

Innings:	12	Runs:	201
Highest Score:	44	Average:	18.27
No. 50s:	0	No. 100s:	0

Test Bowling & Fielding

Wickets:	11	Runs:	450
Best Bowling:	4/27	Average:	40.90
5 WI:	0	10 WM:	0
Catches:	4	Stumpings:	0

One Day Internationals

ODI Career:	1992-96
ODIs Played:	18

ODI Batting

Innings:	16	Runs:	162
Highest Score:	33	Average:	18.00
No. 50s:	0	No. 100s:	0

ODI Bowling & Fielding

Wickets:	15	Runs:	524
Best Bowling:	4/33	Average:	34.93
5 WM:	0	Catches:	4
Stumpings:	0		

A left handed batsman who did little with the bat for New Zealand, but proved somewhat of a surprise with the ball when he captured 4/27 with his dipping medium pace at Lahore in 1996.

VETTORI, Daniel Luca

Born:	January 27, 1979
Batting:	Left handed
Bowling:	Left arm off-break

Tests

Test Career:	1997-
Cap Number:	200
Tests Played:	71

Test Batting

Innings:	102	Runs:	2,136
Highest Score:	137*	Average:	24.83
No. 50s:	11	No. 100s:	2

Test Bowling & Fielding

Wickets:	219	Runs:	7,658
Best Bowling:	7/87	Average:	34.96
5 WI:	12	10 WM:	2
Catches:	35	Stumpings:	0

One Day Internationals

ODI Career:	1997-
ODIs Played:	173

ODI Batting

Innings:	108	Runs:	1,043
Highest Score:	83	Average:	14.09
No. 50s:	2	No. 100s:	0

ODI Bowling & Fielding

Wickets:	167	Runs:	5,608
Best Bowling:	5/30	Average:	33.58
5 WM:	1	Catches:	43
Stumpings:	0		

Tall and immensely talented, Daniel Vettori is arguably the best figure spinner in the game today, with the only question being whether one would describe Murali and Harbhajan Singh as finger spinners. He made his debut as an 18 year old against the touring English side in 1997 and impressed almost immediately with a four wicket in an innings haul in only his second Test. The youngster was unafraid to flight the ball and more importantly had the ability to make it dip and turn. His first Test against arch rival Australia on home soil was outstanding. The bespectacled Vettori claimed 5/62 and 7/87 against the best batting line-up in the world in a 'Man of the Match' performance at Auckland in 1999/2000. His record against Australia is eerily similar to his total Test record, with 3.7 wickets per Test at 34.94 compared to an overall record of 3.1 wickets per Test at 34.96. As a batsman he has developed from a stubborn lower order batler to a genuine all-rounder. He has two Test centuries to his name with his 137 not out against Pakistan at Hamilton in 2003/04 his highest ever first class score. Vettori has had some serious injuries in recent years, but seems to have recovered from fractures of the back to once again be his country's leading Test and one day bowler.

VINCENT, Lou

Born:	November 11, 1978
Batting:	Right handed
Bowling:	Right arm medium

Tests

Test Career:	2001-
Cap Number:	217
Tests Played:	22

Test Batting

Innings:	38	Runs:	1,295
Highest Score:	224	Average:	35.00
No. 50s:	9	No. 100s:	3

Test Bowling & Fielding

Wickets:	0	Runs:	2
Best Bowling:		Average:	0.00
5 WI:	0	10 WM:	0
Catches:	19	Stumpings:	0

One Day Internationals

ODI Career:	2001-
ODIs Played:	83

ODI Batting

Innings:	80	Runs:	1,867
Highest Score:	172	Average:	26.29
No. 50s:	7	No. 100s:	2

ODI Bowling & Fielding

Wickets:	0	Runs:	3
Best Bowling:		Average:	0.00
5 WM:	0	Catches:	33
Stumpings:	0		

The right handed batsman from Auckland is a genuine fighter who shot to prominence when he scored a 104 and 54 on debut against Australia at the WACA in 2001. It was an outstanding performance, made all the better by the fact that he was opening the batting against McGrath, Lee and Gillespie on the bounciest track in Test cricket. Since that sparkling debut Vincent has had his ups downs. The ups have included a century against India at Chandigarh in 2003/04 and 224 against Sri Lanka at Wellington in 2005. The downs have been frequent changes in his spot in the batting line-up, a number of scores under ten and no Tests in 2006. He has retained his spot in the 30 man squad for the Champion's Trophy in October 2006, and those same fighting qualities that were on display at the WACA in 2001 will surely see him back in the Test side before too long as well.

VIVIAN, Graham Ellery

Born:	February 28, 1946
Batting:	Left handed
Bowling:	Left arm leg-break

Tests

Test Career:	1965-72
Cap Number:	109
Tests Played:	5

Test Batting

Innings:	6	Runs:	110
Highest Score:	43	Average:	18.33
No. 50s:	0	No. 100s:	0

Test Bowling & Fielding

Wickets:	1	Runs:	107
Best Bowling:	1/14	Average:	107.00
5 WI:	0	10 WM:	0
Catches:	3	Stumpings:	0

One Day Internationals

ODI Career:	1973
ODIs Played:	1

ODI Batting

Innings:	1	Runs:	14
Highest Score:	14	Average:	14.00
No. 50s:	0	No. 100s:	0

ODI Bowling & Fielding

Wickets:	0	Runs:	0
Best Bowling:		Average:	0.00
5 WM:	0	Catches:	0
Stumpings:	0		

The son of Test player Giff, he was given a handful of chances in the Test side but failed to make a lasting impression with either his batting or his leg spin bowling.

VIVIAN, Henry Gifford (Giff)

Born:	November 4, 1912
Batting:	Left handed
Bowling:	Left arm off-break

Tests

Test Career:	1931-37
Cap Number:	20
Tests Played:	7

Test Batting

Innings:	10	Runs:	421
Highest Score:	100	Average:	42.10
No. 50s:	5	No. 100s:	1

Test Bowling & Fielding

Wickets:	17	Runs:	633
Best Bowling:	4/58	Average:	37.23
5 WI:	0	10 WM:	0
Catches:	4	Stumpings:	0

A left arm off spinner and middle order batsman who was only 18 years old when he made his Test debut at The Oval in 1931. He played a single Test against the touring South Africans in 1932, scoring 100 and 73 and taking four wickets in a side that was beaten comfortably. He was said to have been a wonderful striker of the ball and would surely have played much more Test cricket had the Second World War not intervened.

WADSWORTH, Kenneth John

Born:	November 30, 1946
Batting:	Right handed
	Wicket Keeper

Tests

Test Career:	1969-76
Cap Number:	121
Tests Played:	33

Test Batting

Innings:	51	Runs:	1,010
Highest Score:	80	Average:	21.48
No. 50s:	5	No. 100s:	0

Test Bowling & Fielding

Wickets:	0	Runs:	0
Best Bowling:		Average:	0.00
5 WI:	0	10 WM:	0
Catches:	92	Stumpings:	4

One Day Internationals

ODI Career:	1973-76
ODIs Played:	13

ODI Batting

Innings:	10	Runs:	258
Highest Score:	104	Average:	28.66
No. 50s:	0	No. 100s:	1

ODI Bowling & Fielding

Wickets:	0	Runs:	0
Best Bowling:		Average:	0.00
5 WM:	0	Catches:	13
Stumpings:	2		

He was an integral part of the New Zealand Test side that emerged form cricket's margins in the 1970's. A spectacular keeper, industrious batsman and aggressive competitor, he played in 33 Tests before putting his career on hold to fight cancer in 1976. Sadly the 29 year old lost his brave battle only nine months after playing his last Test.

WALKER, Brooke Graeme Keith

Born: March 25, 1977
Batting: Right handed
Bowling: Right arm leg-break

Tests
Test Career: 2000-02
Cap Number: 212
Tests Played: 5

Test Batting
Innings: 8 Runs: 118
Highest Score: 27* Average: 19.66
No. 50s: 0 No. 100s: 0

Test Bowling & Fielding
Wickets: 5 Runs: 399
Best Bowling: 2/92 Average: 79.80
5 WI: 0 10 WM: 0
Catches: 0 Stumpings: 0

One Day Internationals
ODI Career: 2000-02
ODIs Played: 11

ODI Batting
Innings: 7 Runs: 47
Highest Score: 16* Average: 15.66
No. 50s: 0 No. 100s: 0

ODI Bowling & Fielding
Wickets: 8 Runs: 417
Best Bowling: 2/43 Average: 52.12
5 WM: 0 Catches: 5
Stumpings: 0

A leg spinner from Auckland who was tried in five Tests but discarded when selectors chose to partner Daniel Vettori with another finger spinner in Paul Wiseman.

WALKER, Matthew David John

Born: January 17, 1977
Batting: Right handed
Bowling: Right arm medium

One Day Internationals
ODI Career: 2003
ODIs Played: 3

ODI Batting
Innings: 1 Runs: 10
Highest Score: 10 Average: 10.00
No. 50s: 0 No. 100s: 0

ODI Bowling & Fielding
Wickets: 4 Runs: 119
Best Bowling: 4/49 Average: 29.75
5 WM: 0 Catches: 2
Stumpings: 0

A medium pacer who played three ODI's against Pakistan in 2003. His best effort was at Faisalabad where he took 4/49.

WALLACE, Walter Mervyn

Born: December 19, 1916
Batting: Right handed
Bowling: Right arm off-break

Tests
Test Career: 1937-53
Cap Number: 32
Tests Played: 13

Test Batting
Innings: 21 Runs: 439
Highest Score: 66 Average: 20.90
No. 50s: 5 No. 100s: 0

Test Bowling & Fielding
Wickets: 0 Runs: 5
Best Bowling: Average: 0.00
5 WI: 0 10 WM: 0
Catches: 5 Stumpings: 0

The compact top order batsman had a Test career that spanned 16 years, but other than two standout Tests in England, he struggled to show the form that made him one of Auckland's finest. Those two Tests were his first and last on English soil in which he scored half centuries in both innings. He scored 52 and 56 as a 20 year old at Lord's and 12 years later said goodbye to England with 55 and 58 at The Oval.

WALMSLEY, Kerry Peter

Born: August 23, 1973
Batting: Right handed
Bowling: Right arm medium-fast

Tests
Test Career: 1995-2000
Cap Number: 192
Tests Played: 3

Test Batting
Innings: 5 Runs: 13
Highest Score: 5 Average: 2.60
No. 50s: 0 No. 100s: 0

Test Bowling & Fielding
Wickets: 9 Runs: 391
Best Bowling: 3/70 Average: 43.44
5 WI: 0 10 WM: 0
Catches: 0 Stumpings: 0

One Day Internationals
ODI Career: 2003
ODIs Played: 2

ODI Batting
Innings: 0 Runs: 0
Highest Score: 0 Average: 0.00
No. 50s: 0 No. 100s: 0

ODI Bowling & Fielding
Wickets: 2 Runs: 117
Best Bowling: 1/53 Average: 58.50
5 WM: 0 Catches: 0
Stumpings: 0

He played his first two Tests against Sri Lanka in 1995 then received a surprise call up to the national side as a replacement on the South African tour in 2000. The medium pacer returned his best figures of 3/70 in his very first outing at Napier back in March, 1995.

WARD, John Thomas

Born: March 11, 1937
Batting: Right handed
  Wicket Keeper

Tests
Test Career:	1964-68		
Cap Number:	99		
Tests Played:	8		

Test Batting
Innings:	12	Runs:	75
Highest Score:	35*	Average:	12.50
No. 50s:	0	No. 100s:	0

Test Bowling & Fielding
Wickets:	0	Runs:	0
Best Bowling:		Average:	0.00
5 WI:	0	10 WM:	0
Catches:	16	Stumpings:	1

A capable wicketkeeper from Caterbury who would have played more than eight Tests had his batting been of a higher standard. His son Barry also kept wickets for Canterbury in the 80's.

WATSON, William
Born: August 31, 1965
Batting: Right handed
Bowling: Right arm medium-fast

Tests
Test Career:	1986-93		
Cap Number:	159		
Tests Played:	15		

Test Batting
Innings:	18	Runs:	60
Highest Score:	11	Average:	5.00
No. 50s:	0	No. 100s:	0

Test Bowling & Fielding
Wickets:	40	Runs:	1,387
Best Bowling:	6/78	Average:	34.67
5 WI:	1	10 WM:	0
Catches:	4	Stumpings:	0

One Day Internationals
ODI Career:	1986-94		
ODIs Played:	61		

ODI Batting
Innings:	24	Runs:	86
Highest Score:	21	Average:	7.81
No. 50s:	0	No. 100s:	0

ODI Bowling & Fielding
Wickets:	74	Runs:	2,247
Best Bowling:	4/27	Average:	30.36
5 WM:	0	Catches:	9
Stumpings:	0		

A medium pace bowler who was in his thirties when he made his debut against England at Lord's in 1986. He led the charge when New Zealand scored a surprise victory over the powerful Australian side in 1993 with three valuable first innings wickets. The trio of David Boon, Damien Martyn and Steve Waugh all fell cheaply to the hard worker from Auckland.

WATT, Leslie
Born: September 17, 1924
Batting: Right handed

Tests
Test Career:	1955		
Cap Number:	70		
Tests Played:	1		

Test Batting
Innings:	2	Runs:	2
Highest Score:	2	Average:	1.00
No. 50s:	0	No. 100s:	0

Test Bowling & Fielding
Wickets:	0	Runs:	0
Best Bowling:		Average:	0.00
5 WI:	0	10 WM:	0
Catches:	0	Stumpings:	0

An opening batsman from Otago, he had the honour of playing in the first Test at Dunedin, but failed scoring a duck and two.

WEBB, Murray George
Born: June 22, 1947
Batting: Right handed
Bowling: Right arm fast

Tests
Test Career:	1971-74		
Cap Number:	122		
Tests Played:	3		

Test Batting
Innings:	2	Runs:	12
Highest Score:	12	Average:	6.00
No. 50s:	0	No. 100s:	0

Test Bowling & Fielding
Wickets:	4	Runs:	471
Best Bowling:	2/114	Average:	117.75
5 WI:	0	10 WM:	0
Catches:	0	Stumpings:	0

A right arm fast bowler from Otago who played three Tests over a three year period.

WEBB, Peter Neil
Born: July 14, 1957
Batting: Right handed

Tests
Test Career:	1980		
Cap Number:	145		
Tests Played:	2		

Test Batting
Innings:	3	Runs:	11
Highest Score:	5	Average:	3.66
No. 50s:	0	No. 100s:	0

Test Bowling & Fielding
Wickets:	0	Runs:	0
Best Bowling:		Average:	0.00
5 WI:	0	10 WM:	0
Catches:	2	Stumpings:	0

One Day Internationals
ODI Career:	1983-84		
ODIs Played:	5		

ODI Batting
Innings:	5	Runs:	38
Highest Score:	10*	Average:	9.50
No. 50s:	0	No. 100s:	0

ODI Bowling & Fielding
Wickets:	0	Runs:	0
Best Bowling:		Average:	0.00
5 WM:	0	Catches:	3
Stumpings:	0		

A right hand batsman from Auckland, he played two Tests against the touring West Indians in 1979/80 but could only manage 11 runs in three innings.

WEBB, Richard John
Born: September 15, 1952
Batting: Right handed
Bowling: Right arm medium-fast

One Day Internationals
ODI Career: 1983
ODIs Played: 3

ODI Batting
Innings:	1	Runs:	6
Highest Score:	6*	Average:	0.00
No. 50s:	0	No. 100s:	0

ODI Bowling & Fielding
Wickets:	4	Runs:	105
Best Bowling:	2/28	Average:	26.25
5 WM:	0	Catches:	0
Stumpings:	0		

A pace bowler who played three ODI's on the 1983 tour of Australia.

WEIR, Gordon Lindsay
Born: June 2, 1908
Batting: Right handed
Bowling: Right arm medium

Tests
Test Career: 1930-37
Cap Number: 14
Tests Played: 11

Test Batting
Innings:	16	Runs:	416
Highest Score:	74*	Average:	29.71
No. 50s:	3	No. 100s:	0

Test Bowling & Fielding
Wickets:	7	Runs:	209
Best Bowling:	3/38	Average:	29.85
5 WI:	0	10 WM:	0
Catches:	3	Stumpings:	0

The balding Weir was nicknamed 'Dad' and looked older than his 21 years when he made his debut against England in 1930. The all-rounder played 11 Tests in total with a career high score of 74 not out against the South Africans at Christchurch in 1932.

WHITE, David John
Born: June 26, 1961
Batting: Right handed
Bowling: Right arm off-break

Tests
Test Career: 1990
Cap Number: 174
Tests Played: 2

Test Batting
Innings:	4	Runs:	31
Highest Score:	18	Average:	7.75
No. 50s:	0	No. 100s:	0

Test Bowling & Fielding
Wickets:	0	Runs:	5
Best Bowling:		Average:	0.00
5 WI:	0	10 WM:	0
Catches:	0	Stumpings:	0

One Day Internationals
ODI Career: 1990
ODIs Played: 3

ODI Batting
Innings:	3	Runs:	37
Highest Score:	15	Average:	12.33
No. 50s:	0	No. 100s:	0

ODI Bowling & Fielding
Wickets:	0	Runs:	0
Best Bowling:		Average:	0.00
5 WM:	0	Catches:	1
Stumpings:	0		

An off-spinner from Northern Districts who toured Pakistan in 1990.

WHITELAW, Paul Erskine
Born: February 10, 1910
Batting: Right handed

Tests
Test Career: 1933
Cap Number: 25
Tests Played: 2

Test Batting
Innings:	4	Runs:	64
Highest Score:	30	Average:	32.00
No. 50s:	0	No. 100s:	0

Test Bowling & Fielding
Wickets:	0	Runs:	0
Best Bowling:		Average:	0.00
5 WI:	0	10 WM:	0
Catches:	0	Stumpings:	0

A batsman from Auckland who played two Tests against the touring English side in 1933. In 1937 he was involved in a then world record third wicket stand of 445 in a Plunket Shield game against Otago.

WILSON, Jeffrey William
Born: October 24, 1973
Batting: Right handed
Bowling: Right arm medium-fast

One Day Internationals
ODI Career: 1993-05
ODIs Played: 6

ODI Batting
Innings:	6	Runs:	103
Highest Score:	44*	Average:	20.60
No. 50s:	0	No. 100s:	0

ODI Bowling & Fielding
Wickets:	4	Runs:	260
Best Bowling:	2/21	Average:	65.00
5 WM:	0	Catches:	4
Stumpings:	0		

One of the most gifted sportsmen to come out of New Zealand, Jeffrey Wilson played his first ODI against Australia at Dunedin in 1993, but after four matches he embarked on a highly successful rugby union career where he played 60 internationals for the All Blacks. At 29, he made a return to international cricket playing a further two ODI's in 2004/05. Interestingly, all of his six ODI's were against Australia.

WISEMAN, Paul John
Born: May 4, 1970
Batting: Right handed
Bowling: Right arm off-break

Tests
Test Career:	1998-		
Cap Number:	205		
Tests Played:	25		

Test Batting
Innings:	34	Runs:	366
Highest Score:	36	Average:	14.07
No. 50s:	0	No. 100s:	0

Test Bowling & Fielding
Wickets:	61	Runs:	2,903
Best Bowling:	5/82	Average:	47.59
5 WI:	2	10 WM:	0
Catches:	11	Stumpings:	0

One Day Internationals
ODI Career:	1998-2003		
ODIs Played:	15		

ODI Batting
Innings:	7	Runs:	45
Highest Score:	16	Average:	22.50
No. 50s:	0	No. 100s:	0

ODI Bowling & Fielding
Wickets:	12	Runs:	368
Best Bowling:	4/45	Average:	30.66
5 WM:	0	Catches:	2
Stumpings:	0		

New Zealand's other off spinner is played in tandem with Daniel Vettori when the conditions either favour spin or batting. More than just a foil for his better credentialed partner, he has twice taken five wickets in a Test innings, including a career best 5/82 in the second innings of his Test debut against Sri Lanka at Colombo in 1998.

WISNESKI, Warren
Born:	February 19, 1969
Batting:	Right handed
Bowling:	Right arm medium

One Day Internationals
ODI Career:	2000		
ODIs Played:	3		

ODI Batting
Innings:	2	Runs:	10
Highest Score:	6	Average:	10.00
No. 50s:	0	No. 100s:	0

ODI Bowling & Fielding
Wickets:	0	Runs:	123
Best Bowling:		Average:	0.00
5 WM:	0	Catches:	1
Stumpings:	0		

A hard working medium pacer who failed to capture a wicket when opening the bowling with Chris Cairns in three ODI's against Australia.

WRIGHT, John Geoffrey
Born:	July 5, 1954
Batting:	Left handed
Bowling:	Right arm medium

Tests
Test Career:	1978-93		
Cap Number:	141		
Tests Played:	82		

Test Batting
Innings:	148	Runs:	5,334
Highest Score:	185	Average:	37.82
No. 50s:	23	No. 100s:	12

Test Bowling & Fielding
Wickets:	0	Runs:	5
Best Bowling:		Average:	0.00
5 WI:	0	10 WM:	0
Catches:	38	Stumpings:	0

One Day Internationals
ODI Career:	1978-92		
ODIs Played:	149		

ODI Batting
Innings:	148	Runs:	3,891
Highest Score:	101	Average:	26.46
No. 50s:	24	No. 100s:	1

ODI Bowling & Fielding
Wickets:	0	Runs:	8
Best Bowling:		Average:	0.00
5 WM:	0	Catches:	51
Stumpings:	0		

A left handed opener, he gave his country reliable service at the top of the order for 15 years. He was a sound technician who was never ruffled, making him the ideal opening batsman. Wright made a half century on debut against the touring English at Wellington as a 23 year old and was never out of the side from that time on. He was the first New Zealander to pass 4,000 Test runs, finishing with 5334 at an average of 37.82. The wavy haired Wright made 12 Test centuries with a high score of 185 against India at Christchurch in 1989/90. Wright followed that fine innings with another hundred at Napier ending the three Test series with an average of 125. In 1987 he was appointed captain of the Test team and was in charge for three years until replaced by Martin Crowe. The transition from player to coach seemed natural for the intelligent Wright who held the position of Indian national coach for a number of seasons.

YOUNG, Bryan Andrew
Born:	November 3, 1964
Batting:	Right handed
	Wicket Keeper

Tests
Test Career:	1993-99		
Cap Number:	186		
Tests Played:	35		

Test Batting
Innings:	68	Runs:	2,034
Highest Score:	267*	Average:	31.78
No. 50s:	12	No. 100s:	2

Test Bowling & Fielding
Wickets:	0	Runs:	0
Best Bowling:		Average:	0.00
5 WI:	0	10 WM:	0
Catches:	54	Stumpings:	0

One Day Internationals
ODI Career:	1990-99		
ODIs Played:	74		

ODI Batting
Innings:	73	Runs:	1,668
Highest Score:	74	Average:	24.52
No. 50s:	9	No. 100s:	0

ODI Bowling & Fielding
Wickets:	0	Runs:	0
Best Bowling:		Average:	0.00
5 WM:	0	Catches:	28
Stumpings:	0		

As a Northern Districts wicketkeeper the chances were slim that Bryan Young would ever see Test action so he put away the keeping gloves, moved up the order, and went on to hit the third highest score ever by a New Zealand batsman in Test cricket. That 267 not out against Sri Lanka at Dunedin in 1996/97 may have been the knock by which he is remembered but the gritty opener played many stout innings in a Test career that didn't start until he was almost 30.

YUILE, Bryan William

Born:	October 29, 1941
Batting:	Right handed
Bowling:	Left arm off-break

Tests

Test Career:	1963-69
Cap Number:	95
Tests Played:	17

Test Batting
Innings:	33	Runs:	481
Highest Score:	64	Average:	17.81
No. 50s:	1	No. 100s:	0

Test Bowling & Fielding
Wickets:	34	Runs:	1,213
Best Bowling:	4/43	Average:	35.67
5 WI:	0	10 WM:	0
Catches:	12	Stumpings:	0

A left arm spinner and more than handy lower order batsman from Central Districts. He hit a career high 64 against the English at Auckland in 1962/63 in his very first Test and though not a big turner of ball averaged exactly two wickets in each of his 17 Test matches.

Pakistan

ABBAS, Ghulam
Born: May 1, 1947
Batting: Left handed
Bowling: Left arm off-break

Tests
Test Career: 1967
Cap Number: 56
Tests Played: 1

Test Batting
Innings:	2	Runs:	12
Highest Score:	12	Average:	6.00
No. 50s:	0	No. 100s:	0

Test Bowling & Fielding
Wickets:	0	Runs:	0
Best Bowling:		Average:	0.00
5 WI:	0	10 WM:	0
Catches:	0	Stumpings:	0

A left hand middle order batsman who played the one Test against England at The Oval in 1967.

ABBAS, Imran
Born: March 25, 1978
Batting: Right handed

One Day Internationals
ODI Career: 2000
ODIs Played: 2

ODI Batting
Innings:	2	Runs:	29
Highest Score:	28	Average:	14.50
No. 50s:	0	No. 100s:	0

ODI Bowling & Fielding
Wickets:	0	Runs:	0
Best Bowling:		Average:	0.00
5 WM:	0	Catches:	1
Stumpings:	0		

Bearing the name Imran Abbas would imply that a prosperous fate beckons the aspiring cricketer holding such a prestigious mantle. However, there was no such omen for the young batsman from Gujranwala as Abbas played just the two ODI's - both against Sri Lanka in 2000.

ABBAS, Qaiser
Born: May 7, 1982
Batting: Left handed
Bowling: Left arm off-break

Tests
Test Career: 2000
Cap Number: 162
Tests Played: 1

Test Batting
Innings:	1	Runs:	2
Highest Score:	2	Average:	2.00
No. 50s:	0	No. 100s:	0

Test Bowling & Fielding
Wickets:	0	Runs:	35
Best Bowling:		Average:	0.00
5 WI:	0	10 WM:	0
Catches:	0	Stumpings:	0

Left handed all-rounder who played one Test against England at Lahore, in 2000.

ABBAS, Zaheer
Born: July 24, 1947
Batting: Right handed
Bowling: Right arm off-break

Tests
Test Career: 1969-85
Cap Number: 63
Tests Played: 78

Test Batting
Innings:	124	Runs:	5,062
Highest Score:	274	Average:	44.79
No. 50s:	20	No. 100s:	12

Test Bowling & Fielding
Wickets:	3	Runs:	132
Best Bowling:	2/21	Average:	44.00
5 WI:	0	10 WM:	0
Catches:	34	Stumpings:	0

One Day Internationals
ODI Career: 1974-85
ODIs Played: 62

ODI Batting
Innings:	60	Runs:	2,572
Highest Score:	123	Average:	47.62
No. 50s:	13	No. 100s:	7

ODI Bowling & Fielding
Wickets:	7	Runs:	223
Best Bowling:	2/26	Average:	31.85
5 WM:	0	Catches:	16
Stumpings:	0		

A classical right hand batsman with impeccable timing, Zaheer Abbas was a purist's dream. The bespectacled Zaheer made his Test debut against New Zealand at Karachi in 1969 and in his next test reached triple figures in the most stylish fashion with 274 against England, at Edgbaston. It was to remain his highest score over a distinguished career spanning some 17 years and is the fourth highest score in Pakistan's history. Not content with having one double century alongside his name so early in his career, Zaheer punished the Poms again by scoring 240 at The Oval, in 1974. It was 'two from two' for Zaheer as it was the second time he had reached triple figures and the second time he had registered a double ton. Zaheer finally proved that he was human after all when he was dismissed for 101 against Australia in Adelaide, in 1976. But his thirst for big scores had not been quenched as a year later he notched up his third double century with a stunning 235 not out against India at Lahore. As he did against England, he repeated the dose on the Indians scoring 215 at the same venue three years later in 1982. Dubbed the 'Asian Bradman', Zaheer with 5,062 runs is the fifth highest runs scorer for Pakistan, however he did miss quite a few Tests while at his peak when he decided to join Kerry Packer's World Series Cricket for two seasons between 1977 to 79. In 1983, Zaheer took over the Pakistani captaincy from the injured Imran Khan until his retirement in 1985. Zaheer Abbas was named Wisden 'Cricketer of the Year' for 1972, and is undoubtedly one of the most elegant batsmen of his era.

ABBASI, Nadeem Ahmed

Born: April 15, 1964
Batting: Right handed
Wicket Keeper

Tests

Test Career: 1989
Cap Number: 112
Tests Played: 3

Test Batting
Innings:	2	Runs:	46
Highest Score:	36	Average:	23.00
No. 50s:	0	No. 100s:	0

Test Bowling & Fielding
Wickets:	0	Runs:	0
Best Bowling:		Average:	0.00
5 WI:	0	10 WM:	0
Catches:	6	Stumpings:	0

One of several glovemen who auditioned for the number one post after Wasim Bari's retirement, Abbasi made 36 on debut against India at Faisalabad in 1989 but could only manage another two Tests thereafter.

ADIL, Farhan

Born: September 25, 1977
Batting: Right handed
Bowling: Right arm off-break

Tests

Test Career: 2003
Cap Number: 177
Tests Played: 1

Test Batting
Innings:	2	Runs:	33
Highest Score:	25	Average:	16.50
No. 50s:	0	No. 100s:	0

Test Bowling & Fielding
Wickets:	0	Runs:	0
Best Bowling:		Average:	0.00
5 WI:	0	10 WM:	0
Catches:	0	Stumpings:	0

A middle order batsman from Karachi who has been since overlooked after playing his only Test against Bangladesh, at Multan, in 2003.

AFRIDI, Riaz

Born: January 21, 1985
Batting: Right handed
Bowling: Right arm medium-fast

Tests

Test Career: 2004
Cap Number: 182
Tests Played: 1

Test Batting
Innings:	1	Runs:	9
Highest Score:	9	Average:	9.00
No. 50s:	0	No. 100s:	0

Test Bowling & Fielding
Wickets:	2	Runs:	87
Best Bowling:	2/42	Average:	43.50
5 WI:	0	10 WM:	0
Catches:	0	Stumpings:	0

Took the wickets of Sangakkara and Jayawardene in his first Test at Karachi in 2004, but the young, right arm paceman has not been selected since.

AFRIDI, Shahid Khan

Born: March 1, 1980
Batting: Right handed
Bowling: Right arm leg-break

Tests

Test Career: 1998-06
Cap Number: 153
Tests Played: 26

Test Batting
Innings:	46	Runs:	1,683
Highest Score:	156	Average:	37.40
No. 50s:	8	No. 100s:	5

Test Bowling & Fielding
Wickets:	47	Runs:	1,640
Best Bowling:	5/53	Average:	34.89
5 WI:	1	10 WM:	0
Catches:	10	Stumpings:	0

One Day Internationals

ODI Career: 1996-06
ODIs Played: 225

ODI Batting
Innings:	215	Runs:	4,835
Highest Score:	109	Average:	23.47
No. 50s:	26	No. 100s:	4

ODI Bowling & Fielding
Wickets:	187	Runs:	6,761
Best Bowling:	5/11	Average:	36.15
5 WM:	2	Catches:	82
Stumpings:	0		

In October 1996, sixteen year old Shahid Afridi became the most exciting prospect in world cricket when he smashed his way to his maiden ODI century of just 37 balls against Sri Lanka at Nairobi. In an innings comprising of 11 sixes and six fours, Afridi was prematurely hailed as a future Pakistan great. When 'on song', he rivals the likes of Sanath Jayasuriya and Adam Gilchrist as the most entertaining player to watch. While he boasts the best strike rate (108.16) of any player in ODI history, his career in both forms of the game have been littered with inconsistent performances, as his average of 23.47 in ODI's and

37.06 in Tests suggest. Afridi has made five Test centuries but only scored his last three in 2005/06. After almost a three year drought, Afridi brought up his third Test century against West Indies at Bridgetown off just 78 balls. He repeated the effort nine months later against India at Lahore in January 2006, when he again reached his ton off exactly 78 balls. In the following Test against the Indians, at Faisalabad, he registered his highest score of 156. Surprisingly he has reached triple figures in ODI's on only four occasions. In April 2005, Afridi almost broke his own 'fastest ODI record' when he scored a century off 45 balls against India at Kanpur. Afridi now holds both top, and shares the second highest position with Brain Lara. He has also scored an ODI 50 off 18 balls on two occasions thus missing out on equaling Sanath Jayasuriya's record by one ball. In November 2005, Afridi made headlines yet again but this time for the wrong reasons. He was banned for one Test and two ODI's for deliberately damaging the pitch against England when TV cameras caught him scraping his boots on the pitch while play was interrupted due to a gas canister explosion behind the sidescreen. Now a senior member of the Pakistan squad, Afridi, under coach Bob Woolmer, has started to regain some confidence, which has translated into consistency in form. And being only in his mid 20's, the exciting all-rounder has enough years ahead to fulfill the unlimited potential that made him an overnight success over a decade ago.

AHMED, Ashfaq

Born: June 6, 1973
Batting: Right handed
Bowling: Right arm medium-fast

Tests
Test Career: 1993
Cap Number: 130
Tests Played: 1

Test Batting
Innings:	2	Runs:	1
Highest Score:	1*	Average:	1.00
No. 50s:	0	No. 100s:	0

Test Bowling & Fielding
Wickets:	2	Runs:	53
Best Bowling:	2/31	Average:	26.50
5 WI:	0	10 WM:	0
Catches:	0	Stumpings:	0

One Day Internationals
ODI Career: 1994
ODIs Played: 3

ODI Batting
Innings:	0	Runs:	0
Highest Score:	0	Average:	0.00
No. 50s:	0	No. 100s:	0

ODI Bowling & Fielding
Wickets:	0	Runs:	84
Best Bowling:		Average:	0.00
5 WM:	0	Catches:	0
Stumpings:	0		

A pace bowler from Lahore who played the one Test against Zimbabwe at Rawalpindi in 1993.

AHMED, Ijaz

Born: September 20, 1968
Batting: Right handed
Bowling: Left arm medium

Tests
Test Career: 1987-01
Cap Number: 107
Tests Played: 60

Test Batting
Innings:	92	Runs:	3,315
Highest Score:	211	Average:	37.67
No. 50s:	12	No. 100s:	12

Test Bowling & Fielding
Wickets:	2	Runs:	77
Best Bowling:	1/9	Average:	38.50
5 WI:	0	10 WM:	0
Catches:	45	Stumpings:	0

One Day Internationals
ODI Career: 1986-00
ODIs Played: 250

ODI Batting
Innings:	232	Runs:	6,564
Highest Score:	139*	Average:	32.33
No. 50s:	37	No. 100s:	10

ODI Bowling & Fielding
Wickets:	5	Runs:	476
Best Bowling:	2/31	Average:	95.20
5 WM:	0	Catches:	0
Stumpings:	0		

A stalwart of Pakistan cricket, Ijaz Ahmed was a regular top order batsman since making his debut against India at Chennai in 1986. He enjoyed batting against Australia as six of his 12 Test centuries were scored against the Aussies. He made his only double century and highest score of 211 against Sri Lanka in 1999. A member of the victorious 1992 World Cup team that defeated England in the final at the MCG.

AHMED, Imtiaz

Born: January 5, 1928
Batting: Right handed
Bowling: Right arm off-break
Wicket Keeper

Tests
Test Career: 1952-62
Cap Number: 5
Tests Played: 41

Test Batting
Innings:	72	Runs:	2,079
Highest Score:	209	Average:	29.28
No. 50s:	11	No. 100s:	3

Test Bowling & Fielding
Wickets:	0	Runs:	0
Best Bowling:		Average:	0.00
5 WI:	0	10 WM:	0
Catches:	0	Stumpings:	0

A member of Pakistan's inaugural Test side that played India at Delhi in 1952, Imtiaz Ahmed became Pakistan's regular wicket-keeper taking over the gloves from the great Hanif

Mohammad. Like Hanif, Ahmed was also a well accomplished batsman scoring three centuries including Pakistan's first ever double-century when he compiled a magnificent 209 against New Zealand at Lahore in 1955. This effort also made him the first Test wicket-keeper to score a double century. Ahmed captained Pakistan in four Tests from 1959 to 1962.

AHMED, Maqsood

Born:	March 26, 1925
Batting:	Right handed
Bowling:	Right arm medium

Tests

Test Career:	1952-55
Cap Number:	9
Tests Played:	16

Test Batting

Innings:	27	Runs:	507
Highest Score:	99	Average:	19.50
No. 50s:	2	No. 100s:	0

Test Bowling & Fielding

Wickets:	3	Runs:	191
Best Bowling:	2/12	Average:	63.66
5 WI:	0	10 WM:	0
Catches:	13	Stumpings:	0

A right arm medium pacer who opened the bowling with Khan Mohammad in Pakistan's inaugural Test against India at Delhi in 1952. Ahmed took just three wickets in 16 consecutive Tests and just missed out on his maiden Test century when in 1954 at Lahore, against India, he was stumped on 99.

AHMED, Mohammad Shakeel

Born:	November 12, 1971
Batting:	Right handed
Bowling:	Right arm off-break
	Wicket Keeper

Tests

Test Career:	1993-95
Cap Number:	129
Tests Played:	3

Test Batting

Innings:	5	Runs:	74
Highest Score:	33	Average:	14.80
No. 50s:	0	No. 100s:	0

Test Bowling & Fielding

Wickets:	0	Runs:	0
Best Bowling:		Average:	0.00
5 WI:	0	10 WM:	0
Catches:	4	Stumpings:	0

One Day Internationals

ODI Career:	1995
ODIs Played:	2

ODI Batting

Innings:	2	Runs:	61
Highest Score:	36	Average:	30.50
No. 50s:	0	No. 100s:	0

ODI Bowling & Fielding

Wickets:	0	Runs:	0
Best Bowling:		Average:	0.00
5 WM:	0	Catches:	0
Stumpings:	0		

A wicket-keeper who was selected as an opener with little success in his three Tests between 1993-95.

AHMED, Mushtaq

Born:	June 28, 1970
Batting:	Right handed
Bowling:	Right arm leg-break

Tests

Test Career:	1990-03
Cap Number:	116
Tests Played:	52

Test Batting

Innings:	72	Runs:	659
Highest Score:	59	Average:	11.71
No. 50s:	2	No. 100s:	0

Test Bowling & Fielding

Wickets:	185	Runs:	6,100
Best Bowling:	7/56	Average:	32.97
5 WI:	10	10 WM:	3
Catches:	23	Stumpings:	0

One Day Internationals

ODI Career:	1989-03
ODIs Played:	144

ODI Batting

Innings:	76	Runs:	399
Highest Score:	34*	Average:	9.50
No. 50s:	0	No. 100s:	0

ODI Bowling & Fielding

Wickets:	161	Runs:	5,361
Best Bowling:	5/36	Average:	33.29
5 WM:	1	Catches:	30
Stumpings:	0		

An underrated leg break bowler, outside Pakistan, Mushtaq Ahmed sits sixth in Pakistan's list of all time Test wicket-takers. An imaginative bowler, Mushtaq made his Test debut against Australia, at the Adelaide Oval in 1990 and was a solid contributor throughout his 52 Test appearances. His best haul was a match winning 7/56 against New Zealand at Christchurch in 1995. Mushtaq was also a valuable contributor in Pakistan's victorious World Cup squad in 1992, taking three vital wickets in the final against England at the MCG. He was named Wisden 'Cricketer of the Year' in 1997.

AHMED, Saeed

Born:	October 1, 1937
Batting:	Right handed
Bowling:	Right arm off-break

Tests

Test Career:	1958-73
Cap Number:	27
Tests Played:	41

Test Batting

Innings:	78	Runs:	2,991
Highest Score:	172	Average:	40.41
No. 50s:	16	No. 100s:	5

Test Bowling & Fielding

Wickets:	22	Runs:	802
Best Bowling:	4/64	Average:	36.45
5 WI:	0	10 WM:	0
Catches:	13	Stumpings:	0

A classical right hand batsman who had a much publicised altercation with Australian legendary fast bowler, Dennis Lillee in Melbourne, Saeed Ahmed became one of Pakistan's premier batsman in the 60's and early 70's. He scored five brilliant hundreds, his first a dazzling 150 at Georgetown, in 1958, during his first tour of the West Indies and then registered his highest score with his last - 172 against New Zealand at Karachi in 1965. Saeed was appointed captain in 1968 taking over from the Hanif Mohammad. He captained his country in just three Tests before being succeeded by Intikhab Alam a year later.

AHMED, Shabbir

Born:	April 21, 1976
Batting:	Right handed
Bowling:	Right arm medium-fast

Tests

Test Career:	1993-05
Cap Number:	174
Tests Played:	10

Test Batting

Innings:	15	Runs:	88
Highest Score:	24*	Average:	8.80
No. 50s:	0	No. 100s:	0

Test Bowling & Fielding

Wickets:	51	Runs:	1,175
Best Bowling:	5/48	Average:	23.03
5 WI:	2	10 WM:	0
Catches:	3	Stumpings:	0

One Day Internationals

ODI Career:	1999-05
ODIs Played:	32

ODI Batting

Innings:	11	Runs:	10
Highest Score:	2	Average:	1.60
No. 50s:	0	No. 100s:	0

ODI Bowling & Fielding

Wickets:	33	Runs:	1,192
Best Bowling:	3/32	Average:	36.12
5 WM:	0	Catches:	10
Stumpings:	0		

A tallish pace bowler from Khanewal, who took eight wickets, including a career best 5/48, on debut against Bangladesh at Karachi. A questionable bowling action saw him banned for a year.

AHMED, Shafiq

Born:	March 28, 1949
Batting:	Right handed
Bowling:	Right arm medium

Tests

Test Career:	1974-81
Cap Number:	68
Tests Played:	6

Test Batting

Innings:	10	Runs:	99
Highest Score:	27*	Average:	11.00
No. 50s:	0	No. 100s:	0

Test Bowling & Fielding

Wickets:	0	Runs:	1
Best Bowling:	0/1	Average:	0.00
5 WI:	0	10 WM:	0
Catches:	0	Stumpings:	0

One Day Internationals

ODI Career:	1977-78
ODIs Played:	3

ODI Batting

Innings:	3	Runs:	41
Highest Score:	29	Average:	13.66
No. 50s:	0	No. 100s:	0

ODI Bowling & Fielding

Wickets:	0	Runs:	0
Best Bowling:		Average:	0.00
5 WM:	0	Catches:	1
Stumpings:	0		

Shafiq Ahmed, a right hand opener from Lahore who debuted against England at Headingley in 1974, was yet another who dominated in the domestic competition but found the going tough at Test level.

AHMED, Syed Zahid

Born:	November 15, 1961
Batting:	Left handed

One Day Internationals

ODI Career:	1987
ODIs Played:	2

ODI Batting

Innings:	2	Runs:	3
Highest Score:	3*	Average:	3.00
No. 50s:	0	No. 100s:	0

ODI Bowling & Fielding

Wickets:	3	Runs:	61
Best Bowling:	2/24	Average:	20.33
5 WM:	0	Catches:	0
Stumpings:	0		

A left arm off-break bowler, Zahid Ahmed played two ODI's against England in 1987. He took the wickets of Embeurey and Fairbrother on debut to give him 2/24 for the match.

AHMED, Tauseef

Born:	May 10, 1958
Batting:	Right handed
Bowling:	Right arm off-break

Tests

Test Career:	1980-83
Cap Number:	83
Tests Played:	34

Test Batting

Innings:	38	Runs:	318
Highest Score:	35*	Average:	17.66
No. 50s:	0	No. 100s:	0

Test Bowling & Fielding

Wickets:	93	Runs:	2,950
Best Bowling:	6/45	Average:	31.72
5 WI:	3	10 WM:	0
Catches:	9	Stumpings:	0

One Day Internationals

ODI Career:	1982-90
ODIs Played:	70

ODI Batting
Innings:	25	Runs:	116
Highest Score:	27*	Average:	10.54
No. 50s:	0	No. 100s:	0

ODI Bowling & Fielding
Wickets:	55	Runs:	2,247
Best Bowling:	4/38	Average:	40.85
5 WM:	0	Catches:	10
Stumpings:	0		

A talented off-spinner from Karachi, who on debut, ripped through the Australian batting with fellow spinner Iqbal Qasim. Ironically, it would be Qasim, along with Abdul Qadir that would limit Tauseef's regular selection at Test level even though he did manage to play in 34. Tauseef took 93 wickets at a respectable 31.72 with a best haul of 6/45 against Sri Lanka at Kandy in 1985.

AHMED, Younis
Born:	October 20, 1947
Batting:	Left handed
Bowling:	Left arm medium

Tests

Test Batting
Test Career:	1969-87		
Cap Number:	62		
Tests Played:	4		
Innings:	7	Runs:	177
Highest Score:	62	Average:	29.50
No. 50s:	1	No. 100s:	0

Test Bowling & Fielding
Wickets:	0	Runs:	6
Best Bowling:	0/6	Average:	0.00
5 WI:	0	10 WM:	0
Catches:	0	Stumpings:	0

One Day Internationals
ODI Career:	1987
ODIs Played:	2

ODI Batting
Innings:	2	Runs:	84
Highest Score:	58	Average:	42.00
No. 50s:	1	No. 100s:	0

ODI Bowling & Fielding
Wickets:	0	Runs:	0
Best Bowling:		Average:	0.00
5 WM:	0	Catches:	1
Stumpings:	0		

Younis Ahmed made his Test debut against New Zealand at Karachi in 1969 alongside three other debutants in Mohammad Nazir jnr, Sadiq Mohammad, and eventual batting sensation, Zaheer Abbas. A left hand, middle order batsman, Younis scored 62 in the second innings whcih was to be his highest Test score in his short career. He is also known as Mohammad Younis.

AHMED, Zulfiqar
Born:	November 22, 1926
Batting:	Right handed
Bowling:	Right arm off-break

Tests
Test Career:	1952-56
Cap Number:	13
Tests Played:	9

Test Batting
Innings:	10	Runs:	200
Highest Score:	63*	Average:	33.33
No. 50s:	1	No. 100s:	0

Test Bowling & Fielding
Wickets:	20	Runs:	366
Best Bowling:	6/42	Average:	18.50
5 WI:	2	10 WM:	1
Catches:	5	Stumpings:	0

A right arm off-spinner who made his Test debut against India at Lucknow in 1952, where he bowled just five overs for the match. Ahmed played just the nine Tests in four years but in 1955, against New Zealand in Karachi, had one of the most memorable purple patches when he took 5/37 in the first innings followed by a career best 6/42 in the second giving him 11 wickets for the match and leading his country to a memorable innings and one run victory.

AHMED (JNR), Ijaz
Born:	February 2, 1969
Batting:	Right handed
Bowling:	Right arm off-break

Tests
Test Career:	1995
Cap Number:	133
Tests Played:	2

Test Batting
Innings:	3	Runs:	29
Highest Score:	16	Average:	9.66
No. 50s:	0	No. 100s:	0

Test Bowling & Fielding
Wickets:	0	Runs:	6
Best Bowling:	0/6	Average:	0.00
5 WI:	0	10 WM:	0
Catches:	3	Stumpings:	0

One Day Internationals
ODI Career:	1997
ODIs Played:	2

ODI Batting
Innings:	1	Runs:	3
Highest Score:	3*	Average:	3.00
No. 50s:	0	No. 100s:	0

ODI Bowling & Fielding
Wickets:	1	Runs:	25
Best Bowling:	1/9	Average:	25.00
5 WM:	0	Catches:	1
Stumpings:	0		

A middle order batsman from Faisalabad who made his Test debut against Sri Lanka at Peshawar in 1995.

AHMED KHAN, Naeem
Born:	September 20, 1952
Batting:	Right handed
Bowling:	Left arm off-break

One Day Internationals
ODI Career:	1978
ODIs Played:	1

455

ODI Batting

Innings:	1	Runs:	0
Highest Score:	0*	Average:	0.00
No. 50s:	0	No. 100s:	0

ODI Bowling & Fielding

Wickets:	0	Runs:	0
Best Bowling:		Average:	0.00
5 WM:	0	Catches:	1
Stumpings:	0		

Naeem Ahmed played just the solitary ODI against England at The Oval in 1978. Unfortunately, he didn't trouble the scorers when either bowling or batting.

AHMED SIDDIQI, Niaz

Born:	November 11, 1945
Batting:	Right handed
Bowling:	Right arm medium-fast

Tests

Test Career:	1967-69
Cap Number:	55
Tests Played:	2

Test Batting

Innings:	3	Runs:	17
Highest Score:	16*	Average:	17.00
No. 50s:	0	No. 100s:	0

Test Bowling & Fielding

Wickets:	3	Runs:	94
Best Bowling:	2/72	Average:	31.33
5 WI:	0	10 WM:	0
Catches:	1	Stumpings:	0

Niaz Ahmed played his first Test for Pakistan against England at Trent Bridge in 1967. His second and last Test was also against England but on what was home soil at Dhaka in 1969.

AHMED SNR, Shakeel

Born:	February 12, 1966
Batting:	Left handed
Bowling:	Left arm off-break

Tests

Test Career:	1998
Cap Number:	154
Tests Played:	1

Test Batting

Innings:	1	Runs:	1
Highest Score:	1	Average:	1.00
No. 50s:	0	No. 100s:	0

Test Bowling & Fielding

Wickets:	4	Runs:	139
Best Bowling:	4/91	Average:	34.75
5 WI:	0	10 WM:	0
Catches:	1	Stumpings:	0

Shakeel Ahmed snr made his Test debut against Australia at Karachi in 1998, aged 32. And although he bowled reasonably well to take 4/91 in the second innings, including the wickets of the Waugh twins, Shakeel was not asked back after his debut.

AHSAN, Haseeb

Born:	July 15, 1939
Batting:	Right handed
Bowling:	Right arm off-break

Tests

Test Career:	1958-62
Cap Number:	25
Tests Played:	12

Test Batting

Innings:	16	Runs:	61
Highest Score:	14	Average:	6.77
No. 50s:	0	No. 100s:	0

Test Bowling & Fielding

Wickets:	27	Runs:	1,330
Best Bowling:	6/202	Average:	49.25
5 WI:	2	10 WM:	0
Catches:	1	Stumpings:	0

A right arm offspinner who made his Test debut against West Indies at Bridgetown, Haseeb Ahsan was probably the first Pakistan bowler to be 'called' for throwing when his action was questioned against India in Mumbai in 1960. His best figures of 6/202 typified his less than economical wicket to run ratio of 49.25.

AKBAR, Sajjad

Born:	March 1, 1961
Batting:	Right handed
Bowling:	Right arm off-break

One Day Internationals

ODI Career:	1990
ODIs Played:	2

ODI Batting

Innings:	1	Runs:	5
Highest Score:	5	Average:	5.00
No. 50s:	0	No. 100s:	0

ODI Bowling & Fielding

Wickets:	2	Runs:	45
Best Bowling:	2/45	Average:	22.50
5 WM:	0	Catches:	0
Stumpings:	0		

An off-spinner from Lahore, Sajjad Akbar, on debut, took the important wickets of Srikkanth and Manjrakar in Pakistan's 26 run win over India. Akbar played just the one more ODI against New Zealand a few days later.

AKHTAR, Javed

Born:	November 21, 1940
Batting:	Right handed
Bowling:	Right arm off-break

Tests

Test Career:	1962
Cap Number:	39
Tests Played:	1

Test Batting

Innings:	2	Runs:	4
Highest Score:	2	Average:	4.00
No. 50s:	0	No. 100s:	0

Test Bowling & Fielding

Wickets:	0	Runs:	52
Best Bowling:		Average:	0.00
5 WI:	0	10 WM:	0
Catches:	0	Stumpings:	0

A tall off-spinner who played just the one Test against England at Headingley in 1962. Upon retirement Akhtar became an international umpire.

AKHTAR, Mansoor

Born: December 25, 1957
Batting: Right handed
Bowling: Right arm medium

Tests
Test Career:	1980-90		
Cap Number:	86		
Tests Played:	19		

Test Batting
Innings:	29	Runs:	655
Highest Score:	111	Average:	25.19
No. 50s:	3	No. 100s:	1

Test Bowling & Fielding
Wickets:	0	Runs:	0
Best Bowling:		Average:	0.00
5 WI:	0	10 WM:	0
Catches:	9	Stumpings:	0

One Day Internationals
ODI Career:	1980-90		
ODIs Played:	41		

ODI Batting
Innings:	35	Runs:	593
Highest Score:	47	Average:	17.44
No. 50s:	0	No. 100s:	0

ODI Bowling & Fielding
Wickets:	2	Runs:	110
Best Bowling:	1/7	Average:	55.00
5 WM:	0	Catches:	14
Stumpings:	0		

At times Mansoor Akhtar showed that he had the ability to become a permanent fixture in the Pakistan Test eleven but the gulf between his best and his worst was far too great. Akhtar made his Test debut against West Indies at Lahore in 1980 and over a ten year career, scored the just the one century, 111 against Australia at Faisalabad in 1983.

AKHTAR, Manzoor

Born: April 16, 1968
Batting: Right handed
Bowling: Right arm leg-break

One Day Internationals
ODI Career:	1997-98		
ODIs Played:	7		

ODI Batting
Innings:	4	Runs:	97
Highest Score:	44	Average:	24.25
No. 50s:	0	No. 100s:	0

ODI Bowling & Fielding
Wickets:	5	Runs:	184
Best Bowling:	4/50	Average:	36.80
5 WM:	0	Catches:	1
Stumpings:	0		

An all-rounder from Karachi who made his ODI debut against India at Sharjah in 1997. Akhtar's form with both bat and ball suggests that he should have been given more opportunities at the elite level.

AKHTAR, Shoaib

Born: August 13, 1975
Batting: Right handed
Bowling: Right arm fast

Tests
Test Career:	1997-06		
Cap Number:	150		
Tests Played:	42		

Test Batting
Innings:	62	Runs:	537
Highest Score:	47	Average:	10.74
No. 50s:	0	No. 100s:	0

Test Bowling & Fielding
Wickets:	165	Runs:	4,240
Best Bowling:	6/11	Average:	25.69
5 WI:	12	10 WM:	2
Catches:	11	Stumpings:	0

One Day Internationals
ODI Career:	1998-05		
ODIs Played:	129		

ODI Batting
Innings:	63	Runs:	332
Highest Score:	43	Average:	10.06
No. 50s:	0	No. 100s:	0

ODI Bowling & Fielding
Wickets:	199	Runs:	4,686
Best Bowling:	6/16	Average:	23.54
5 WM:	4	Catches:	16
Stumpings:	0		

Dubbed the "Rawalpindi Express", Shoaib Akhtar is the undisputed fastest bowler in world cricket having recorded the fastest ball (ever measured) with a lightning quick 161.4 kmh. Akhtar has clocked over the 100mph mark on two occasions but in doing so has had to endure his fair share of controversy. His action was questioned by the authorities, and as a result was sidelined while investigations were taking place. He was subsequently cleared and from 2005 has regained some much needed consistency. Apart from his unprecedented pace, Akhtar also has the ability to swing the ball both ways and like most Pakistani paceman, Akhtar is also a proficient exponent of the reverse swing delivery. He has taken five wickets in an innings on a dozen occasions with a career best 6/11 of 8.2 overs when he single-handedly tore through the New Zealand line up at Lahore in 2002.

AKMAL, Kamran

Born: January 13, 1982
Batting: Right handed
Wicket Keeper

Tests
Test Career:	2002-06		
Cap Number:	172		
Tests Played:	25		

Test Batting
Innings:	42	Runs:	1,218
Highest Score:	154	Average:	30.45
No. 50s:	3	No. 100s:	4

Test Bowling & Fielding
Wickets:	0	Runs:	0
Best Bowling:		Average:	0.00
5 WI:	0	10 WM:	0
Catches:	82	Stumpings:	16

One Day Internationals
ODI Career:	2002-06		
ODIs Played:	45		

ODI Batting

Innings:	38	Runs:	913
Highest Score:	124	Average:	30.43
No. 50s:	0	No. 100s:	3

ODI Bowling & Fielding

Wickets:	0	Runs:	0
Best Bowling:		Average:	0.00
5 WM:	0	Catches:	38
Stumpings:	6		

Since making a duck in his Test debut against Zimbabwe, at Harare, in 2002, Kamran has developed an appetite for big scores, making four Test centuries (three against India) including a highest score of 154 against England at Lahore in 2006. He has also scored three centuries at ODI level where he opens the batting. Lived in the shadow of Moin Khan and Rashid Latif for a short while but has now clearly established himself as the premier wicket-keeper.

AKRAM, Wasim

Born:	June 3, 1966
Batting:	Left handed
Bowling:	Left arm fast

Tests

Test Career:	1985-02
Cap Number:	102
Tests Played:	104

Test Batting

Innings:	147	Runs:	2,898
Highest Score:	257*	Average:	22.64
No. 50s:	7	No. 100s:	3

Test Bowling & Fielding

Wickets:	414	Runs:	9,779
Best Bowling:	7/119	Average:	23.62
5 WI:	25	10 WM:	5
Catches:	44	Stumpings:	0

One Day Internationals

ODI Career:	1984-03
ODIs Played:	356

ODI Batting

Innings:	280	Runs:	3,717
Highest Score:	86	Average:	16.52
No. 50s:	6	No. 100s:	0

ODI Bowling & Fielding

Wickets:	502	Runs:	11,812
Best Bowling:	5/15	Average:	23.52
5 WM:	6	Catches:	88
Stumpings:	0		

Just as Imran Khan was heading into the twilight of his illustrious career and Pakistan cricket was coming to terms with eventually losing a 'once in a lifetime' all rounder of such exceptional class, along comes a protege in the form of Wasim Akram. Almost a left handed version of Imran, Wasim Akram was a fast bowler who could also club the ball with enormous power while maintaining a fine sense of control. He made his Test debut against New Zealand in 1985 and 'arrived' on the international arena with a ten wicket haul in his second Test. A fierce competitor, Akram partnered with fellow pace man Waqar Younis and for a while were hailed as the most potent pace attack in world cricket. In 1992, Akram was a valuable member of Pakistan's triumphant World Cup squad, scoring 33 and taking three wickets in the final against England at the MCG. Later that year he took over the captaincy from his mentor Imran and led his country in 25 Tests for a respectable win/loss ratio of 12 wins, eight losses and five draws. Akram has taken five wickets in an innings on 25 occasions with a career best 7/119 against New Zealand at The Basin in 1994. Within a space of week in March 1999, Akram took two Test hat-tricks; both against Sri Lanka. The first at Lahore where he cleaned up the tail (though one being Kaluwitharana who had made a century) and the second at Dhaka taking the early wickets of Gunawardene, Vaas, and Jayawardene. He, along with current day Pakistani paceman, Mohammad Sami, are the only two bowlers to have taken hat-tricks in both Tests and ODI's. Akram is Pakistan's highest wicket-taker in both forms of the game having taken 414 at Test level and 502 in ODI's. He and Sri Lanka's Muttiah Muralitharan are the only bowlers to have claimed 400 wickets in both Test Matches and ODI's. The list of records continue as Akram has also taken more wickets in World Cup competition than any other bowler and holds the record for most World Cup appearances - 38 in all. While he may have surpassed Imran's feats with the ball, as a batsman, Imran does however take the honours. But Akram's record with the bat is more than respectable. He has scored three Test centuries, his first a valuable 123 against Australia in Adelaide in 1989 and racked up his highest score of 257 not out against Zimbabwe at Sheikhupura in 1996. Along with Imran, Akram is one of the finest bowlers in the history of the game.

AKRAM AWAN, Mohammad

Born:	September 10, 1974
Batting:	Right handed
Bowling:	Right arm medium-fast

Tests

Test Career:	1995-01
Cap Number:	135
Tests Played:	9

Test Batting

Innings:	15	Runs:	24
Highest Score:	10*	Average:	2.66
No. 50s:	0	No. 100s:	0

Test Bowling & Fielding

Wickets:	17	Runs:	859
Best Bowling:	5/138	Average:	50.52
5 WI:	1	10 WM:	0
Catches:	4	Stumpings:	0

One Day Internationals

ODI Career:	1995-00
ODIs Played:	23

ODI Batting

Innings:	9	Runs:	14
Highest Score:	7*	Average:	7.00
No. 50s:	0	No. 100s:	0

ODI Bowling & Fielding

Wickets:	19	Runs:	790
Best Bowling:	2/28	Average:	41.57
5 WM:	0	Catches:	8
Stumpings:	0		

Ironically it was his name-sake Wasim Akram, along with Waqar Younis who made it difficult for the tall seamer to hold down a permanent place in either the Test or One Day sides. Akram made his Test debut against Sri Lanka at Faisalabad.

ALAM (KHAN), Intikhab

Born:	December 28, 1941
Batting:	Right handed
Bowling:	Right arm leg-break

Tests

Test Career:	1959-77		
Cap Number:	34		
Tests Played:	47		

Test Batting

Innings:	77	Runs:	1,493
Highest Score:	138	Average:	22.28
No. 50s:	8	No. 100s:	1

Test Bowling & Fielding

Wickets:	125	Runs:	4,494
Best Bowling:	7/52	Average:	35.95
5 WI:	5	10 WM:	2
Catches:	20	Stumpings:	0

One Day Internationals

ODI Career:	1973-76		
ODIs Played:	4		

ODI Batting

Innings:	2	Runs:	17
Highest Score:	10	Average:	8.50
No. 50s:	0	No. 100s:	0

ODI Bowling & Fielding

Wickets:	4	Runs:	118
Best Bowling:	2/36	Average:	29.50
5 WM:	0	Catches:	0
Stumpings:	0		

One of Pakistan's finest servants, all-rounder Intikhab Alam played his first Test against Wally Grout's Australians in 1959. After being run out for a duck in the first innings, Alam scored just six in the second. But he did manage to create history with the ball when he became the first - and to date the only - Pakistan bowler to take a wicket with his first delivery in Test cricket. The hard working, yet bulky leg spinner, went about improving his game and thus became a regular fixture in Pakistan's Test 11. He was appointed captain in 1969, ten years after his debut, when he took over from Saeed Ahmed who held the post for just 12 months. He captained his country in 17 Tests over a seven year period for the just the one victory, which was against New Zealand at Dunedin in 1973. Alam was the main catalyst in the win, where he took career best 7/52 and 11 wickets for the match. His 'purple patch' against the Kiwis continued into the next Test where he took 6/127. It was also during the twilight of his career when he finally registered his first Test ton, scoring a hard hitting 138 against England at Hyderabad in 1973.

ALI, Agha Saadat

Born:	June 21, 1929
Batting:	Right handed
Bowling:	Right arm medium

Tests

Test Career:	1955
Cap Number:	22
Tests Played:	1

Test Batting

Innings:	1	Runs:	8
Highest Score:	8*	Average:	8.00
No. 50s:	0	No. 100s:	0

Test Bowling & Fielding

Wickets:	0	Runs:	0
Best Bowling:		Average:	0.00
5 WI:	0	10 WM:	0
Catches:	3	Stumpings:	0

Agha Saadat Ali batted at number eleven but did not get the opportunity to bowl during his solitary Test against New Zealand at Dhaka in 1955. He did however manage to take three catches.

ALI, Ashraf

Born:	April 22, 1958
Batting:	Right handed
	Wicket Keeper

Tests

Test Career:	1982-87
Cap Number:	93
Tests Played:	8

Test Batting

Innings:	8	Runs:	229
Highest Score:	65	Average:	45.80
No. 50s:	2	No. 100s:	0

Test Bowling & Fielding

Wickets:	0	Runs:	0
Best Bowling:		Average:	0.00
5 WI:	0	10 WM:	0
Catches:	17	Stumpings:	5

One Day Internationals

ODI Career:	1980-85
ODIs Played:	16

ODI Batting

Innings:	9	Runs:	69
Highest Score:	19*	Average:	17.25
No. 50s:	0	No. 100s:	0

ODI Bowling & Fielding

Wickets:	0	Runs:	0
Best Bowling:		Average:	0.00
5 WM:	0	Catches:	17
Stumpings:	3		

A wicket-keeper and competent batsman, Ashraf Ali was destined to be the bridesmaid and never the bride. He made his Test debut against Sri Lanka in 1982 and scored an impressive 58 in the first innings and an unbeaten 29 in the second while filling in for stalwart Wasim Bari. However, even after Bari hung up the gloves, Ali played second-fiddle to Saleem Yousuf and hence managed just the eight Tests in six years.

ALI, Basit
Born: December 3, 1970
Batting: Right handed
Bowling: Right arm off-break

Tests
Test Career: 1993-95
Cap Number: 126
Tests Played: 19

Test Batting
Innings:	33	Runs:	858
Highest Score:	103	Average:	26.81
No. 50s:	5	No. 100s:	1

Test Bowling & Fielding
Wickets:	0	Runs:	6
Best Bowling:	0/6	Average:	0.00
5 WI:	0	10 WM:	0
Catches:	6	Stumpings:	0

One Day Internationals
ODI Career: 1993-96
ODIs Played: 50

ODI Batting
Innings:	43	Runs:	1,265
Highest Score:	127*	Average:	34.18
No. 50s:	9	No. 100s:	1

ODI Bowling & Fielding
Wickets:	1	Runs:	21
Best Bowling:	1/17	Average:	21.00
5 WM:	0	Catches:	15
Stumpings:	0		

An aggressive right hand batsman who scored a century against New Zealand, at Christchurch, in 1994.

ALI, Israr
Born: May 1, 1927
Batting: Left handed
Bowling: Left arm medium-fast

Tests
Test Career: 1952-59
Cap Number: 6
Tests Played: 4

Test Batting
Innings:	8	Runs:	33
Highest Score:	10	Average:	4.71
No. 50s:	0	No. 100s:	0

Test Bowling & Fielding
Wickets:	0	Runs:	0
Best Bowling:		Average:	0.00
5 WI:	0	10 WM:	0
Catches:	1	Stumpings:	0

An all-rounder who batted at number three in Pakistan's inaugural Test against India at Delhi in 1952, Israr Ali was also a useful left arm fast-medium pacer. Israr played four Tests between 1952-59.

ALI, Saadat
Born: February 6, 1955
Batting: Right handed
Bowling: Right arm off-break

One Day Internationals
ODI Career: 1984
ODIs Played: 8

ODI Batting
Innings:	7	Runs:	184
Highest Score:	78*	Average:	30.66
No. 50s:	1	No. 100s:	0

ODI Bowling & Fielding
Wickets:	2	Runs:	29
Best Bowling:	2/24	Average:	14.50
5 WM:	0	Catches:	1
Stumpings:	0		

The brother of wicket keeper Ashraf Ali, opener Saadat Ali played in eight ODIs after making his international debut against the England in 1984. He became the first Pakistan batsman to carry his bat in a one day international, making 78 not out.

ALI, Sajid
Born: July 1, 1963
Batting: Right handed
Bowling: Right arm medium

One Day Internationals
ODI Career: 1984-97
ODIs Played: 13

ODI Batting
Innings:	12	Runs:	130
Highest Score:	28	Average:	10.83
No. 50s:	0	No. 100s:	0

ODI Bowling & Fielding
Wickets:	0	Runs:	0
Best Bowling:		Average:	0.00
5 WM:	0	Catches:	1
Stumpings:	0		

Sajid Ali was a right hand opener from Karachi who made his ODI debut against India at Sialkot in 1984. While he represented his country at ODI level over 13 years he averaged just one appearance per year.

ALI, Yasir
Born: October 15, 1985
Batting: Right handed
Bowling: Right arm medium-fast

Tests
Test Career: 2003
Cap Number: 179
Tests Played: 1

Test Batting
Innings:	2	Runs:	1
Highest Score:	1*	Average:	1.00
No. 50s:	0	No. 100s:	0

Test Bowling & Fielding
Wickets:	2	Runs:	55
Best Bowling:	1/12	Average:	27.50
5 WI:	0	10 WM:	0
Catches:	0	Stumpings:	0

A young pace bowler from Hazro who many believe may have huge potential, but Ali has not played a Test match since his debut against Bangladesh in 2003.

ALI ANSARI, Ghulam

Born: September 8, 1966
Batting: Right handed
Bowling: Right arm medium

One Day Internationals
ODI Career: 1993-95
ODIs Played: 3

ODI Batting
Innings:	3	Runs:	53
Highest Score:	38	Average:	17.66
No. 50s:	0	No. 100s:	0

ODI Bowling & Fielding
Wickets:	0	Runs:	0
Best Bowling:		Average:	0.00
5 WM:	0	Catches:	0
Stumpings:	0		

An opening batsman from Karachi who made his debut against the West Indies at Cape Town, Ali struggled to string together any consistent performances averaging just over 17. He played his last ODI against Bangladesh at Sharjah in 1995.

ALI KHAN, Liaqat

Born: May 21, 1955
Batting: Right handed
Bowling: Left arm medium-fast

Tests
Test Career: 1975-78
Cap Number: 70
Tests Played: 5

Test Batting
Innings:	7	Runs:	28
Highest Score:	12	Average:	7.00
No. 50s:	0	No. 100s:	0

Test Bowling & Fielding
Wickets:	6	Runs:	359
Best Bowling:	3/80	Average:	59.83
5 WI:	0	10 WM:	0
Catches:	1	Stumpings:	0

One Day Internationals
ODI Career: 1977-78
ODIs Played: 3

ODI Batting
Innings:	1	Runs:	7
Highest Score:	7	Average:	7.00
No. 50s:	0	No. 100s:	0

ODI Bowling & Fielding
Wickets:	2	Runs:	111
Best Bowling:	1/41	Average:	55.50
5 WM:	0	Catches:	0
Stumpings:	0		

A sharp, left arm pace bowler from Karachi who played the first of his five Tests against the West Indies in front of his home crowd in 1975.

ALI MALIK, Talat

Born: May 29, 1950
Batting: Right handed
Bowling: Right arm medium

Tests
Test Career: 1972-79
Cap Number: 66
Tests Played: 10

Test Batting
Innings:	18	Runs:	370
Highest Score:	61	Average:	23.12
No. 50s:	2	No. 100s:	0

Test Bowling & Fielding
Wickets:	0	Runs:	7
Best Bowling:	0/7	Average:	0.00
5 WI:	0	10 WM:	0
Catches:	4	Stumpings:	0

A right hand opener from Lahore whose introduction to Test cricket was facing Australian great Dennis Lillee at his fiery best in Adelaide in 1972. Ali retired hurt for seven after fracturing his thumb while trying to fend off a brytal Lillee delivery. He played just the ten Tests and became an ICC Match referee upon retirement.

ALI RIZVI, Naushad

Born: October 1, 1943
Batting: Right handed
Wicket Keeper

Tests
Test Career: 1965
Cap Number: 50
Tests Played: 6

Test Batting
Innings:	11	Runs:	156
Highest Score:	39	Average:	14.18
No. 50s:	0	No. 100s:	0

Test Bowling & Fielding
Wickets:	0	Runs:	0
Best Bowling:		Average:	0.00
5 WI:	0	10 WM:	0
Catches:	9	Stumpings:	0

Naushad Ali made his Test debut as a wicket-keeper and opening batsman against New Zealand at Wellington in 1965. He played the just six Tests, mainly as a stand-in keeper. Ali became an ICC referee in 2000.

ALIMUDDIN, Alimuddin

Born: December 15, 1930
Batting: Right handed
Bowling: Right arm leg-break

Tests
Test Career: 1954-62
Cap Number: 15
Tests Played: 25

Test Batting
Innings:	45	Runs:	1,091
Highest Score:	109	Average:	25.37
No. 50s:	7	No. 100s:	2

Test Bowling & Fielding
Wickets:	1	Runs:	75
Best Bowling:	1/17	Average:	75.00
5 WI:	0	10 WM:	0
Catches:	8	Stumpings:	0

A dour opener, Alimuddin's career had an English flavour about it the moment it began. He debuted against England at Lords in 1954, scored his two centuries, 103 not out and 109, against England, both at Karachi and upon retirement moved to England.

ALTAF BOKHARI, Saleem

Born: April 19, 1944
Batting: Right handed
Bowling: Right arm medium-fast

Tests

Test Career: 1967-78
Cap Number: 53
Tests Played: 21

Test Batting

Innings:	31	Runs:	276
Highest Score:	53*	Average:	14.52
No. 50s:	1	No. 100s:	0

Test Bowling & Fielding

Wickets:	46	Runs:	1,710
Best Bowling:	4/11	Average:	37.17
5 WI:	0	10 WM:	0
Catches:	3	Stumpings:	0

One Day Internationals

ODI Career: 1973-78
ODIs Played: 6

ODI Batting

Innings:	2	Runs:	25
Highest Score:	21	Average:	25.00
No. 50s:	0	No. 100s:	0

ODI Bowling & Fielding

Wickets:	5	Runs:	151
Best Bowling:	2/7	Average:	30.20
5 WM:	0	Catches:	1
Stumpings:	0		

A genuine pace bowler who could also swing the ball, Saleem Altaf opened the bowling in his first Test against England at Lord's in 1967 where he took four wickets for the match. He played in 21 Tests over an eleven year, injury riddled career.

ANJUM, Naved

Born: July 27, 1963
Batting: Right handed
Bowling: Right arm medium-fast

Tests

Test Career: 1989-90
Cap Number: 113
Tests Played: 2

Test Batting

Innings:	3	Runs:	44
Highest Score:	22	Average:	14.66
No. 50s:	0	No. 100s:	0

Test Bowling & Fielding

Wickets:	4	Runs:	162
Best Bowling:	2/57	Average:	40.50
5 WI:	0	10 WM:	0
Catches:	0	Stumpings:	0

One Day Internationals

ODI Career: 1984-92
ODIs Played: 13

ODI Batting

Innings:	12	Runs:	113
Highest Score:	30	Average:	12.55
No. 50s:	0	No. 100s:	0

ODI Bowling & Fielding

Wickets:	8	Runs:	344
Best Bowling:	2/27	Average:	43.00
5 WM:	0	Catches:	0
Stumpings:	0		

A pace bowler from Lahore who struggled for a regular place due to the emergence of Waqar Younis and Aaqib Javed.

ANJUM, Rao Iftikhar

Born: December 1, 1980
Batting: Right handed
Bowling: Right arm medium

Tests

Test Career: 2006
Cap Number: 186
Tests Played: 1

Test Batting

Innings:	1	Runs:	9
Highest Score:	9*	Average:	9.00
No. 50s:	0	No. 100s:	0

Test Bowling & Fielding

Wickets:	0	Runs:	62
Best Bowling:		Average:	0.00
5 WI:	0	10 WM:	0
Catches:	0	Stumpings:	0

One Day Internationals

ODI Career: 2004-06
ODIs Played: 18

ODI Batting

Innings:	9	Runs:	59
Highest Score:	19*	Average:	59.00
No. 50s:	0	No. 100s:	0

ODI Bowling & Fielding

Wickets:	12	Runs:	644
Best Bowling:	2/13	Average:	53.66
5 WM:	0	Catches:	5
Stumpings:	0		

Although wicket-less on debut against Sri Lanka at Kandy, Anjum's excellent form at Domestic level and reverse swing ability should ensure that he adds to his solitary Test tally within the near future.

ANWAR, Masood

Born: December 12, 1967
Batting: Left handed
Bowling: Left arm fast

Tests

Test Career: 1990
Cap Number: 121
Tests Played: 1

Test Batting

Innings:	2	Runs:	39
Highest Score:	37	Average:	19.50
No. 50s:	0	No. 100s:	0

Test Bowling & Fielding

Wickets:	3	Runs:	102
Best Bowling:	2/59	Average:	34.00
5 WI:	0	10 WM:	0
Catches:	0	Stumpings:	0

A left arm off-spinner whose 37, in the second innings of his only Test, helped secure a draw against the West Indies at Lahore in 1990.

ANWAR, Saeed

Born: September 6, 1968
Batting: Left handed
Bowling: Left arm off-break

Tests
Test Career:	1990-01		
Cap Number:	120		
Tests Played:	55		

Test Batting
Innings:	91	Runs:	4,052
Highest Score:	188*	Average:	45.52
No. 50s:	25	No. 100s:	11

Test Bowling & Fielding
Wickets:	0	Runs:	23
Best Bowling:		Average:	0.00
5 WI:	0	10 WM:	0
Catches:	18	Stumpings:	0

One Day Internationals
ODI Career:	1989-03		
ODIs Played:	247		

ODI Batting
Innings:	244	Runs:	8,823
Highest Score:	194	Average:	39.21
No. 50s:	43	No. 100s:	20

ODI Bowling & Fielding
Wickets:	6	Runs:	191
Best Bowling:	2/9	Average:	31.83
5 WM:	0	Catches:	0
Stumpings:	0		

When Saeed Anwar made a pair on debut against the West Indies at Faisalabad in 1990, even the most ardent Pakistan follower could not have predicted that the elegant left hand opener would at one stage be ranked in the same class as Sachin Tendular and Brian Lara. Forming one half of a long standing partnership with fellow left hand opener Aamer Sohail, by the mid 90's Anwar had clocked up five centuries and was named as one of Wisden's Cricketers of the Year in 1997. In all he scored 11 Tests centuries, with a highest score of 188 not out against India at Kolkata in 1998 and boasted a Test average of 45.52 - the fifth highest by a Pakistan batsman. One of the finest One Day batsman of his era, Anwar was Pakistan's highest run scorer in both 1996 and 1999 World Cup campaigns. In 1997 scored an amazing 194 against India at Chennai which overtook Viv Richards long-standing record of 189 not out as the highest score in One Day Internationals. Anwar's record still stands today.

ANWAR, Shahid
Born:	July 5, 1968
Batting:	Right handed
Bowling:	Right arm medium-fast

One Day Internationals
ODI Career:	1996		
ODIs Played:	1		

ODI Batting
Innings:	1	Runs:	37
Highest Score:	37	Average:	37.00
No. 50s:	0	No. 100s:	0

ODI Bowling & Fielding
Wickets:	0	Runs:	0
Best Bowling:		Average:	0.00
5 WM:	0	Catches:	0
Stumpings:	0		

A right hand batsman who on debut, opened the innings against England at Trent Bridge with namesake Saeed Anwar. Shahid scored an impressive 37 but surprisingly this was not enough to earn him another cap at international level.

ARIF, Taslim
Born:	May 1, 1954
Batting:	Right handed
Bowling:	Right arm medium
	Wicket Keeper

Tests
Test Career:	1980		
Cap Number:	82		
Tests Played:	6		

Test Batting
Innings:	10	Runs:	501
Highest Score:	210*	Average:	62.62
No. 50s:	2	No. 100s:	1

Test Bowling & Fielding
Wickets:	1	Runs:	28
Best Bowling:	1/28	Average:	28.00
5 WI:	0	10 WM:	0
Catches:	6	Stumpings:	3

One Day Internationals
ODI Career:	1980		
ODIs Played:	2		

ODI Batting
Innings:	2	Runs:	28
Highest Score:	24	Average:	14.00
No. 50s:	0	No. 100s:	0

ODI Bowling & Fielding
Wickets:	0	Runs:	0
Best Bowling:		Average:	0.00
5 WM:	0	Catches:	1
Stumpings:	1		

It was clear from the very outset that Karachi born, Taslim Arif was much more than just a fill-in wicket-keeper. Selected as an opener in his very first Test appearance against India at Kolkata in 1980, Taslim carved out a magnificent 90 and then followed up in the second innings with a dour 46. While many may have been forgiven for not being totally convinced of his batting ability after one outing, they only had to wait until his third Test, against Australia at Faisalabad, to make up their minds. On this occasion, Taslim, who was also assigned keeping duties, scored a massive 210 not out when opening the batting with Haroon Rashid. It was the highest Test score by a wicket-keeper until Zimbabwean Andy Flower scored his 232 not out in 2000. Amazingly, Taslim played only six Tests and his career lasted just under a year mainly because of Wasim Bari's superiority and experience as number one keeper. But you would have to wonder why any batsmen averaging over 62 wouldn't be persevered with as a specialist batsman for just a little longer.

ASHRAF, Naeem

Born: November 10, 1972
Batting: Left handed
Bowling: Left arm medium-fast

One Day Internationals
ODI Career: 1995
ODIs Played: 2

ODI Batting
Innings:	2	Runs:	24
Highest Score:	16	Average:	24.00
No. 50s:	0	No. 100s:	0

ODI Bowling & Fielding
Wickets:	0	Runs:	52
Best Bowling:		Average:	0.00
5 WM:	0	Catches:	0
Stumpings:	0		

A left arm medium pace bowler from Lahore who made his ODI debut against India at Sharjah in 1995 but did not capture a wicket in his two ODI's.

ASHRAF QURESHI, Naved

Born: September 4, 1974
Batting: Right handed
Bowling: Right arm medium

Tests
Test Career: 1998-00
Cap Number: 155
Tests Played: 2

Test Batting
Innings:	3	Runs:	64
Highest Score:	32	Average:	21.33
No. 50s:	0	No. 100s:	0

Test Bowling & Fielding
Wickets:	0	Runs:	0
Best Bowling:		Average:	0.00
5 WI:	0	10 WM:	0
Catches:	0	Stumpings:	0

Opened with Saeed Anwar in his first Test against Zimbabwe at Lahore in 1998. Played his second Test almost two years later against Sri Lanka at Karachi.

ASIF, Mohammad

Born: December 20, 1982
Batting: Left handed
Bowling: Right arm medium-fast

Tests
Test Career: 2005-06
Cap Number: 184
Tests Played: 5

Test Batting
Innings:	7	Runs:	18
Highest Score:	12*	Average:	4.50
No. 50s:	0	No. 100s:	0

Test Bowling & Fielding
Wickets:	25	Runs:	500
Best Bowling:	6/44	Average:	20.00
5 WI:	2	10 WM:	0
Catches:	2	Stumpings:	0

One Day Internationals
ODI Career: 2005-06
ODIs Played: 12

ODI Batting
Innings:	3	Runs:	99
Highest Score:	6	Average:	4.50
No. 50s:	0	No. 100s:	0

ODI Bowling & Fielding
Wickets:	11	Runs:	382
Best Bowling:	3/30	Average:	34.75
5 WM:	0	Catches:	2
Stumpings:	0		

Although he was wicket-less on debut against Australia in Sydney in 2005, Asif looms as one of Pakistan's most exciting pace bowling prospects. Tall and athletically built, Asif took an impressive 6/44 against Sri Lanka at Kandy in 2006.

ASLAM, Mohammad

Born: January 5, 1920
Batting: Right handed
Bowling: Right arm leg-break

Tests
Test Career: 1954
Cap Number: 20
Tests Played: 1

Test Batting
Innings:	2	Runs:	34
Highest Score:	18	Average:	17.00
No. 50s:	0	No. 100s:	0

Test Bowling & Fielding
Wickets:	0	Runs:	0
Best Bowling:		Average:	0.00
5 WI:	0	10 WM:	0
Catches:	0	Stumpings:	0

A fine fieldsman and leg break bowler from Lahore, Aslam didn't get an opportunity to bowl in his one and only Test appearance against England at Trent Bridge in 1954.

ATA-UR-REHMAN,

Born: March 28, 1975
Batting: Right handed
Bowling: Right arm medium-fast

Tests
Test Career: 1992-96
Cap Number: 123
Tests Played: 13

Test Batting
Innings:	15	Runs:	76
Highest Score:	19	Average:	8.44
No. 50s:	0	No. 100s:	0

Test Bowling & Fielding
Wickets:	31	Runs:	1,071
Best Bowling:	4/50	Average:	34.54
5 WI:	0	10 WM:	0
Catches:	2	Stumpings:	0

One Day Internationals
ODI Career: 1992-96
ODIs Played: 30

ODI Batting
Innings:	13	Runs:	34
Highest Score:	11*	Average:	4.85
No. 50s:	0	No. 100s:	0

ODI Bowling & Fielding
Wickets:	27	Runs:	1,186
Best Bowling:	3/27	Average:	43.92
5 WM:	0	Catches:	0
Stumpings:	0		

A tall right arm paceman who, in his Test debut against England at Edgbaston as a 17 year old, showed that he had enough raw ability to become a permanent member of Pakistan's already lethal pace attack. However, after 13 Tests in four years Ata-ur-Rehman was embroiled in a match-fixing controversy, which consequently saw him become the fifth player, alongside Salim Malik, India's Mohammad Azharuddin and Ajay Sharma, and Hansie Cronje to be banned for life.

ATHAR, Faisal

Born: October 15, 1975
Batting: Right handed

One Day Internationals
ODI Career: 2003
ODIs Played: 1

ODI Batting
Innings:	1	Runs:	9
Highest Score:	9	Average:	9.00
No. 50s:	0	No. 100s:	0

ODI Bowling & Fielding
Wickets:	0	Runs:	0
Best Bowling:		Average:	0.00
5 WM:	0	Catches:	0
Stumpings:	0		

Another member of the unofficial 'one match club', Faisal Athar, an opener from Hyderabad, played his maiden ODI against New Zealand at Dambulla, in 2003.

ATIQ-UZ-ZAMAN,

Born: July 20, 1975
Batting: Right handed
Wicket Keeper

Tests
Test Career: 2000
Cap Number: 160
Tests Played: 1

Test Batting
Innings:	2	Runs:	26
Highest Score:	25	Average:	13.00
No. 50s:	0	No. 100s:	0

Test Bowling & Fielding
Wickets:	0	Runs:	0
Best Bowling:		Average:	0.00
5 WI:	0	10 WM:	0
Catches:	5	Stumpings:	0

One Day Internationals
ODI Career: 2000
ODIs Played: 3

ODI Batting
Innings:	3	Runs:	34
Highest Score:	18	Average:	17.00
No. 50s:	0	No. 100s:	0

ODI Bowling & Fielding
Wickets:	0	Runs:	0
Best Bowling:		Average:	0.00
5 WM:	0	Catches:	3
Stumpings:	1		

A wicket-keeper from Karachi who took five catches in his only Test against Sri Lanka at Peshawar in 2000.

AZAD, Mohammad Saeed

Born: August 14, 1964
Batting: Right handed
Bowling: Right arm medium

One Day Internationals
ODI Career: 1995-96
ODIs Played: 4

ODI Batting
Innings:	4	Runs:	65
Highest Score:	31	Average:	16.25
No. 50s:	0	No. 100s:	0

ODI Bowling & Fielding
Wickets:	0	Runs:	0
Best Bowling:		Average:	0.00
5 WM:	0	Catches:	2
Stumpings:	0		

A middle order batsman from Karachi, Saeed Azad struggled to consolidate on any of his starts in his four ODI's between 1995-96.

BAKHT, Sikander

Born: August 25, 1957
Batting: Right handed
Bowling: Right arm medium-fast

Tests
Test Career: 1976-83
Cap Number: 74
Tests Played: 26

Test Batting
Innings:	35	Runs:	146
Highest Score:	22*	Average:	6.34
No. 50s:	0	No. 100s:	0

Test Bowling & Fielding
Wickets:	6	Runs:	2,412
Best Bowling:	8/69	Average:	36.80
5 WI:	3	10 WM:	1
Catches:	7	Stumpings:	0

One Day Internationals
ODI Career: 1977-89
ODIs Played: 27

ODI Batting
Innings:	11	Runs:	31
Highest Score:	16*	Average:	7.35
No. 50s:	0	No. 100s:	0

ODI Bowling & Fielding
Wickets:	33	Runs:	860
Best Bowling:	4/34	Average:	26.06
5 WM:	0	Catches:	4
Stumpings:	0		

Almost stick-figure in appearance, Sikander Bakht made his Test debut against New Zealand at Karachi in 1976. He soon became a regular member of Pakistan's pace attack of the mid 70's and early 80's providing more than serviceable back up to Imran Khan and Sarfraz Nawaz. His day in the sun arrived in 1979 when he tore through the cream of India's batting in Delhi, taking a career best 8/69.

BALOCH, Aftab

Born: April 1, 1953
Batting: Right handed
Bowling: Right arm off-break

Tests
Test Career:	1969-75		
Cap Number:	64		
Tests Played:	2		

Test Batting
Innings:	3	Runs:	97
Highest Score:	60*	Average:	48.50
No. 50s:	1	No. 100s:	0

Test Bowling & Fielding
Wickets:	0	Runs:	17
Best Bowling:		Average:	0.00
5 WI:	0	10 WM:	0
Catches:	0	Stumpings:	0

Aftab Baloch from Karachi made his Test debut just a few months shy of his 17th birthday when he was selected to play against New Zealand at Dhaka in 1969. However the youngster was made to wait six years before he got his next chance which finally arrived in 1975 against the West Indies at Lahore. The now mature Baloch seized his opportunity with an unbeaten 60 in the second innings and hoped that there wouldn't be as much of a wait until he was called up for his third Test appearance. But that day never arrived as Baloch's Test match appearances still stand at two.

BARI, Wasim
Born:	March 23, 1948
Batting:	Right handed
Bowling:	Right arm slow
	Wicket Keeper

Tests
Test Career:	1967-84
Cap Number:	54
Tests Played:	81

Test Batting
Innings:	112	Runs:	1,366
Highest Score:	85	Average:	15.88
No. 50s:	6	No. 100s:	0

Test Bowling & Fielding
Wickets:	0	Runs:	2
Best Bowling:	0/2	Average:	0.00
5 WI:	0	10 WM:	0
Catches:	201	Stumpings:	27

One Day Internationals
ODI Career:	1973-84
ODIs Played:	51

ODI Batting
Innings:	26	Runs:	221
Highest Score:	34	Average:	17.00
No. 50s:	0	No. 100s:	0

ODI Bowling & Fielding
Wickets:	0	Runs:	0
Best Bowling:		Average:	0.00
5 WI:	0	Catches:	52
Stumpings:	10		

By far Pakistan's finest wicket-keeper, Wasim Bari was also one of Pakistan's most loyal servants. The Karachi born 'keeper made his Test debut against England at Lords in 1967 and his position was rarely threatened during his seventeen year career. Bari played at a time when international cricket was blessed with outstanding gloveman. Amongst his contemporaries were Australia's Rod Marsh, England's Alan Knott, India's Farokh Engineer and Syed Kirmani and in the latter part of his career, West Indian dynamo, Jeffrey Dujon. Bari wasn't as flamboyant or athletic as some of the aforementioned but as far as Pakistan cricket was concerned, he was flawless and a model of stability. Keeping to the spinners on the sub-continent wickets became his specialty and along with Syed Kiramani, he was regarded as a 'stumping specialist', having taken 27 victims in Tests. In 1978 Bari was asked to step in as captain when regular skipper Mushtaq Mohammad, along with high profile players such as Imran and Majid Khan, Asif Iqbal and Zaheer Abbas signed with the Kerry Packer led World Series Cricket tournament in Australia. He captained his country in six Tests and in much the same manner as he played - with a great deal of caution. His reign yielded four draws and two losses and within a year, Mushtaq Mohammad returned to the helm and Bari continued behind the stumps with a minimum of fuss until his retirement in 1994. Three years later Bari was fittingly awarded with the Life Achievement Award by the Pakistan Cricket Board.

BHATTI, Irfan Ahsan Kaleem
Born:	September 28, 1964
Batting:	Right handed
Bowling:	Right arm medium-fast

One Day Internationals
ODI Career:	1993
ODIs Played:	1

ODI Batting
Innings:	0	Runs:	0
Highest Score:	0	Average:	0.00
No. 50s:	0	No. 100s:	0

ODI Bowling & Fielding
Wickets:	2	Runs:	22
Best Bowling:	2/22	Average:	11.00
5 WI:	0	Catches:	1
Stumpings:	0		

A right arm medium pacer, Irfan Bhatti took the wickets of Zimbabwean openers Andy Flower and Mark Dekker in his only ODI appearance at Lahore in 1993.

BURKI, Javed
Born:	May 8, 1938
Batting:	Right handed
Bowling:	Right arm medium

Tests
Test Career:	1960-69
Cap Number:	36
Tests Played:	25

Test Batting
Innings:	48	Runs:	1,341
Highest Score:	140	Average:	30.47
No. 50s:	4	No. 100s:	3

Test Bowling & Fielding			
Wickets:	0	Runs:	23
Best Bowling:		Average:	0.00
5 WI:	0	10 WM:	0
Catches:	7	Stumpings:	0

The cousin of Imran and Majid Khan, Javed Burki made his Test debut against India, at Mumbai in 1960. A fine middle order batsman, Burki was appointed captain in 1962, which was a surprise selection to some, and led the side in just five Tests before being succeeded by Hanif Mohammad in 1964. Burki scored three Test hundreds - all against England, two on home soil in the 1961/62 series and the other at Lords in 1962. He retired at the end of 1969 and became an ICC official in 1993.

BUTT, Arif

Born:	May 17, 1944
Batting:	Right handed
Bowling:	Right arm medium-fast

Tests

Test Career:	1964-65
Cap Number:	47
Tests Played:	3

Test Batting

Innings:	5	Runs:	59
Highest Score:	20	Average:	11.30
No. 50s:	0	No. 100s:	0

Test Bowling & Fielding

Wickets:	14	Runs:	288
Best Bowling:	6/89	Average:	20.57
5 WI:	1	10 WM:	0
Catches:	0	Stumpings:	0

It was nothing short of a 'dream debut' for 20 year old Lahore pace bowler Arif Butt when he captured an amazing 6/89 against the Australians at the MCG in 1964. Included in his bag of half dozen scalps were both openers - skipper Bob Simpson and Bill Lawry. Butt became the first Pakistan bowler to take five wickets in an innings on debut and although rated as a handy lower order batsman, he was surprisingly elevated to open the batting in Pakistan's second innings. And just as he was elevated to open with the bat, he was promptly given the new ball in Australia's second innings after being first change bowler in the first. Butt's form didn't desert him as he dismissed the Australian captain for the second time in the match, this time for just one run. Butt was Pakistan's only wicket taker of the innings, giving him the more than impressive match figures of 7/118, as the game petered out to a draw. While many pundits were hailing the emergence of a new bowling sensation, Butt was to play just the two more Tests for his country as his Test career lasted a few days short of two months.

BUTT, Mohammed Ijaz

Born:	March 10, 1938
Batting:	Right handed
	Wicket Keeper

Tests

Test Career:	1959-62
Cap Number:	30
Tests Played:	8

Test Batting

Innings:	16	Runs:	279
Highest Score:	58	Average:	19.92
No. 50s:	1	No. 100s:	0

Test Bowling & Fielding

Wickets:	0	Runs:	0
Best Bowling:		Average:	0.00
5 WI:	0	10 WM:	0
Catches:	5	Stumpings:	0

An opening right hand batsman and part time wicket-keeper, Ijaz Butt made his Test debut in Pakistan's memorable 10 wicket win against West Indies at Karachi in 1958. Although he didn't get the chance to don the 'keepers gloves due to the presence of Imtiaz Ahmed, he made an impressive 41 not out when he opened the second innings and followed up with his only half-century against the Australians at Karachi a year later. Many believe Ijaz should have played more than the eight Tests he was granted. Upon his retirement he served as the secretary of the then Board of Control for Cricket in Pakistan between 1984 and 1988. He became President of Lahore City Cricket Association and in 1982-83 managed the Pakistan cricket team and headed the national selection committee.

BUTT, Salman

Born:	October 7, 1984
Batting:	Left handed
Bowling:	Right arm off-break

Tests

Test Career:	2003-06
Cap Number:	178
Tests Played:	13

Test Batting

Innings:	24	Runs:	741
Highest Score:	122	Average:	30.87
No. 50s:	4	No. 100s:	2

Test Bowling & Fielding

Wickets:	0	Runs:	0
Best Bowling:		Average:	0.00
5 WI:	0	10 WM:	0
Catches:	6	Stumpings:	0

One Day Internationals

ODI Career:	2004-06
ODIs Played:	33

ODI Batting

Innings:	33	Runs:	962
Highest Score:	108*	Average:	30.06
No. 50s:	3	No. 100s:	3

ODI Bowling & Fielding

Wickets:	0	Runs:	42
Best Bowling:		Average:	0.00
5 WM:	0	Catches:	9
Stumpings:	0		

Since the retirements of Saeed Anwar and Aamer Sohail, Pakistan has been searching frantically for a openers of similar calibre. Salman Butt may have provided the solution to half the problem. After making his debut against Bangladesh at Multan in 2003, Butt, a left hander like his aforementioned predecessors, at one stage consolidated himself as the country's number one opener, rated higher than the slightly more experienced Imran Farhat. In early 2006, the two formed a relatively solid partnership and could become, like Anwar and Sohail, long term partners at the top of the batting order. With two centuries alongside his name, (108 v Australia and 122 v England) Butt has the natural talent, poise and maturity to become a batsman of world class standard but after a mediocre performance on the 2006 tour of England the jury has yet to reach its verdict.

BUTT, Shujauddin

Born:	April 10, 1930
Batting:	Right handed
Bowling:	Left arm off-break

Tests

Test Career:	1954-62
Cap Number:	17
Tests Played:	19

Test Batting

Innings:	32	Runs:	395
Highest Score:	47	Average:	15.19
No. 50s:	0	No. 100s:	0

Test Bowling & Fielding

Wickets:	20	Runs:	801
Best Bowling:	3/18	Average:	40.15
5 WI:	0	10 WM:	0
Catches:	8	Stumpings:	0

A left arm off-break bowler and right hand batsman from Lahore, Shujauddin was a member of the inaugural tour of England of 1954. A former prisoner of war during the Indo-Pakistan War, he was a consistent performer over his 19 Test career taking a personal best 3/18 against the West Indies at Karachi in 1958. After his career ended in 1962 he later became a national selector.

BUX, Malik Miran

Born:	April 20, 1907
Batting:	Right handed
Bowling:	Right arm off-break

Tests

Test Career:	1955
Cap Number:	21
Tests Played:	2

Test Batting

Innings:	3	Runs:	1
Highest Score:	1*	Average:	1.00
No. 50s:	0	No. 100s:	0

Test Bowling & Fielding

Wickets:	2	Runs:	115
Best Bowling:	2/82	Average:	57.50
5 WI:	0	10 WM:	0
Catches:	0	Stumpings:	0

At 47 years of age, Miran Bux, an off-spinner from Rawalpindi, became the second oldest Test debutant in history when he was selected against India at Lahore in 1955. Although Miran played just the two Tests he performed admirably during his short time at the elite level.

D'SOUZA, Antao

Born:	January 17, 1939
Batting:	Right handed
Bowling:	Right arm medium

Tests

Test Career:	1959-62
Cap Number:	29
Tests Played:	6

Test Batting

Innings:	10	Runs:	76
Highest Score:	23*	Average:	38.00
No. 50s:	0	No. 100s:	0

Test Bowling & Fielding

Wickets:	17	Runs:	745
Best Bowling:	5/122	Average:	43.82
5 WI:	1	10 WM:	0
Catches:	3	Stumpings:	0

A right arm medium pacer and occasional off spinner, Antao D'Souza captured a career best 5/122 against England at Karachi in 1962. A handy lower order batsman, he was not out in eight of his ten innings thus providing him with the healthy average of 38 with the bat.

DALPAT SONAVARIA, Anil

Born:	September 20, 1963
Batting:	Right handed
	Wicket Keeper

Tests

Test Career:	1984-85
Cap Number:	98
Tests Played:	9

Test Batting

Innings:	12	Runs:	167
Highest Score:	52	Average:	15.18
No. 50s:	1	No. 100s:	0

Test Bowling & Fielding

Wickets:	0	Runs:	0
Best Bowling:		Average:	0.00
5 WI:	0	10 WM:	0
Catches:	22	Stumpings:	3

One Day Internationals

ODI Career:	1984-86
ODIs Played:	15

ODI Batting

Innings:	10	Runs:	87
Highest Score:	37	Average:	12.42
No. 50s:	0	No. 100s:	0

ODI Bowling & Fielding

Wickets:	0	Runs:	0
Best Bowling:		Average:	0.00
5 WM:	0	Catches:	13
Stumpings:	2		

The cousin of leg-spinner Danish Kaneria, Anil Dalpat was the first Hindu to play Test cricket for Pakistan when he made his debut against England at Karachi in 1984. An adept keeper to spin, Dalpat was one of many keepers that were given an opportunity to fill the void left by stalwart Wasim Bari. And although he hardly put a foot wrong during his audition, the selectors finally settled on Saleem Yousuf as Bari's long term successor.

DURRANI, Fazl-e-Akbar
Born: October 20, 1980
Batting: Right handed
Bowling: Right arm medium-fast

Tests
Test Career:	1998-04		
Cap Number:	151		
Tests Played:	5		

Test Batting
Innings:	8	Runs:	52
Highest Score:	25	Average:	13.50
No. 50s:	0	No. 100s:	0

Test Bowling & Fielding
Wickets:	11	Runs:	511
Best Bowling:	3/85	Average:	46.45
5 WI:	0	10 WM:	0
Catches:	2	Stumpings:	0

One Day Internationals
ODI Career:	1998-01		
ODIs Played:	2		

ODI Batting
Innings:	1	Runs:	7
Highest Score:	7	Average:	7.00
No. 50s:	0	No. 100s:	0

ODI Bowling & Fielding
Wickets:	0	Runs:	48
Best Bowling:		Average:	0.00
5 WM:	0	Catches:	0
Stumpings:	0		

A right arm seam bowler, Fazl-e-Akbar performed reasonably well on debut against South Africa at Durban in 1998. He captured the wickets of openers Kirsten and Bacher, giving him 2/16 in the first innings and followed up with 1/16 in the second innings, again taking Bacher's wicket. However, like many young pacemen, Fazl-e-Akbar found it tough to maintain consistency at the highest level and has beenn overlooked since his fifth Test.

EHTESHAMUDDIN,
Born: September 4, 1950
Batting: Right handed
Bowling: Right arm medium-fast

Tests
Test Career:	1979-82		
Cap Number:	81		
Tests Played:	5		

Test Batting
Innings:	3	Runs:	2
Highest Score:	2	Average:	1.00
No. 50s:	0	No. 100s:	0

Test Bowling & Fielding
Wickets:	16	Runs:	375
Best Bowling:	5/47	Average:	23.43
5 WI:	0	10 WM:	0
Catches:	2	Stumpings:	0

A right arm fast-medium pacer who played the first of his five Tests against India at Bangalore in 1979. It was in the Fourth Test of that series, at Kanpur where Ehteshamuddin took his best haul of 5/47. Originally from Lahore.

ELAHI, Amir
Born: September 1, 1908
Batting: Right handed
Bowling: Right arm medium

Tests
Test Career:	1947-52		
Cap Number:	1		
Tests Played:	6		

Test Batting
Innings:	9	Runs:	82
Highest Score:	47	Average:	10.25
No. 50s:	0	No. 100s:	0

Test Bowling & Fielding
Wickets:	7	Runs:	248
Best Bowling:	4/134	Average:	35.42
5 WI:	0	10 WM:	0
Catches:	0	Stumpings:	0

One of a handful of players who played Test cricket for both India and Pakistan. He represented India against Australia in 1947, and then his remaining five Tests for Pakistan, were all against India in 1952-53 including Pakistan's inaugural Test at Delhi whee he is credited with the Pakistan's 'number one' Test cap.

ELAHI, Manzoor
Born: April 15, 1963
Batting: Right handed
Bowling: Right arm medium-fast

Tests
Test Career:	1984-95		
Cap Number:	101		
Tests Played:	6		

Test Batting
Innings:	10	Runs:	123
Highest Score:	52	Average:	15.37
No. 50s:	1	No. 100s:	0

Test Bowling & Fielding
Wickets:	7	Runs:	194
Best Bowling:	2/38	Average:	27.71
5 WI:	0	10 WM:	0
Catches:	7	Stumpings:	0

One Day Internationals
ODI Career:	1984-95		
ODIs Played:	54		

ODI Batting
Innings:	46	Runs:	741
Highest Score:	50*	Average:	22.45
No. 50s:	1	No. 100s:	0

ODI Bowling & Fielding
Wickets:	29	Runs:	1,262
Best Bowling:	3/22	Average:	43.51
5 WM:	0	Catches:	21
Stumpings:	0		

The eldest of three brothers to play Test cricket for Pakistan, Manzoor Elahi was a right arm pace bowler who made his Test debut against India at Faisalabad in 1985. He was better suited to the shorter version of the game where he played over 50 ODI's.

ELAHI, Saleem

Born:	November 21, 1976
Batting:	Right handed
Bowling:	Right arm off-break
	Wicket Keeper

Tests
Test Career:	1995-03
Cap Number:	136
Tests Played:	13

Test Batting
Innings:	24	Runs:	436
Highest Score:	72	Average:	18.95
No. 50s:	1	No. 100s:	0

Test Bowling & Fielding
Wickets:	0	Runs:	0
Best Bowling:		Average:	0.00
5 WI:	0	10 WM:	0
Catches:	10	Stumpings:	1

One Day Internationals
ODI Career:	1995-04
ODIs Played:	48

ODI Batting
Innings:	47	Runs:	1,579
Highest Score:	135	Average:	36.72
No. 50s:	9	No. 100s:	4

ODI Bowling & Fielding
Wickets:	0	Runs:	10
Best Bowling:		Average:	0.00
5 WM:	0	Catches:	10
Stumpings:	0		

The youngest, but arguably the most talented of the three brothers to represent Pakistan at both Test and ODI level, Saleem Elahi made his Test debut against Australia at Brisbane in 1995. Just like middle sibling Zahoor, Saleem was also a right hand opening batsman but got his opportunity at Test level a year earlier. Another familiar trait between the siblings (Manzoor was the eldest brother) was that all three were better suited to Limited Overs competition with Saleem scoring a remarkable 102 not out on his ODI debut against Sri Lanka in 1995.

ELAHI, Zahoor

Born:	March 1, 1971
Batting:	Right handed
Bowling:	Right arm medium

Tests
Test Career:	1996
Cap Number:	143
Tests Played:	2

Test Batting
Innings:	3	Runs:	30
Highest Score:	22	Average:	10.00
No. 50s:	0	No. 100s:	0

Test Bowling & Fielding
Wickets:	0	Runs:	0
Best Bowling:		Average:	0.00
5 WI:	0	10 WM:	0
Catches:	1	Stumpings:	0

One Day Internationals
ODI Career:	1996-97
ODIs Played:	14

ODI Batting
Innings:	14	Runs:	297
Highest Score:	86	Average:	22.84
No. 50s:	3	No. 100s:	0

ODI Bowling & Fielding
Wickets:	0	Runs:	0
Best Bowling:		Average:	0.00
5 WM:	0	Catches:	0
Stumpings:	0		

A right hand opener and the third of three brothers to play Test cricket for Pakistan. Zahoor Elahi made his Test debut against New Zealand at Lahore in 1996. Although he was the last of the brothers to be selected at Test Level, Zahoor was the 'middle child', as Manzoor the pace bowler was the eldest and Saleem, who was also an opener, was the youngest.

FAQIH, Ijaz

Born:	March 24, 1956
Batting:	Right handed
Bowling:	Right arm off-break

Tests
Test Career:	1980-88
Cap Number:	87
Tests Played:	5

Test Batting
Innings:	8	Runs:	183
Highest Score:	105	Average:	26.14
No. 50s:	0	No. 100s:	1

Test Bowling & Fielding
Wickets:	4	Runs:	299
Best Bowling:	1/38	Average:	74.75
5 WI:	0	10 WM:	0
Catches:	0	Stumpings:	0

One Day Internationals
ODI Career:	1980-88
ODIs Played:	27

ODI Batting
Innings:	19	Runs:	197
Highest Score:	42*	Average:	12.31
No. 50s:	0	No. 100s:	0

ODI Bowling & Fielding
Wickets:	13	Runs:	819
Best Bowling:	4/43	Average:	63.00
5 WM:	0	Catches:	2
Stumpings:	0		

An off-break bowler from Karachi, Ijaz Faqih worked hard at Test level but rarely troubled competent batsmen and was probably suited more to the shorter version of the game. Although a bowler by trade, Faqui does have a Test century alongside his name when he scored a match saving 105 against India at Ahmedabad in 1987 to earn 'Man of the Match' honours. Faqui played his first and last Tests against the West Indies.

FARHAT, Humayun

Born: January 24, 1981
Batting: Right handed
Wicket Keeper

Tests
Test Career: 2001
Cap Number: 168
Tests Played: 1

Test Batting
Innings:	2	Runs:	54
Highest Score:	28	Average:	27.00
No. 50s:	0	No. 100s:	0

Test Bowling & Fielding
Wickets:	0	Runs:	0
Best Bowling:		Average:	0.00
5 WI:	0	10 WM:	0
Catches:	0	Stumpings:	0

One Day Internationals
ODI Career: 2001
ODIs Played: 5

ODI Batting
Innings:	3	Runs:	60
Highest Score:	39	Average:	20.00
No. 50s:	0	No. 100s:	0

ODI Bowling & Fielding
Wickets:	0	Runs:	0
Best Bowling:		Average:	0.00
5 WM:	0	Catches:	4
Stumpings:	3		

A wicket-keeper from Lahore and brother of Imran Farhat, Humayun became yet another wicket-keeper to get just the one chance at Test level. His opportunity came in 2001 when selected in the Third Test against New Zealand at Hamilton where Pakistan was defeated by an innings and 185 runs.

FARHAT, Imran

Born: May 20, 1982
Batting: Left handed
Bowling: Right arm off-break

Tests
Test Career: 2001-06
Cap Number: 165
Tests Played: 20

Test Batting
Innings:	38	Runs:	1,196
Highest Score:	128	Average:	31.47
No. 50s:	7	No. 100s:	2

Test Bowling & Fielding
Wickets:	3	Runs:	192
Best Bowling:	2/69	Average:	64.00
5 WI:	0	10 WM:	0
Catches:	26	Stumpings:	0

One Day Internationals
ODI Career: 2001-06
ODIs Played: 26

ODI Batting
Innings:	26	Runs:	808
Highest Score:	107	Average:	32.32
No. 50s:	4	No. 100s:	1

ODI Bowling & Fielding
Wickets:	5	Runs:	89
Best Bowling:	3/10	Average:	17.80
5 WM:	0	Catches:	8
Stumpings:	0		

A left handed opener who made 63 on his Test debut against New Zealand at Auckland in 2001, Imran Farhat has played 20 Tests and scored two centuries in six seasons. After being in and out of the side in his early days, these days Farhat, together with fellow left hander Salman Butt, are looking to establish themselves as the most solid opening combination since Saeed Anwar and Aamer Sohail. While they were both selected on the controversial tour of England in mid 2006, their form was patchy.

FAROOQ, Mohammad

Born: April 8, 1938
Batting: Right handed
Bowling: Right arm medium-fast

Tests
Test Career: 1960-65
Cap Number: 37
Tests Played: 7

Test Batting
Innings:	9	Runs:	85
Highest Score:	47	Average:	17.00
No. 50s:	0	No. 100s:	0

Test Bowling & Fielding
Wickets:	21	Runs:	682
Best Bowling:	4/70	Average:	32.47
5 WI:	0	10 WM:	0
Catches:	1	Stumpings:	0

A right arm, hard working pace bowler Mohammad Farooq took four wickets on debut against India at Mumbai in 1960. While enjoying the 1962 tour of England, taking 4 for 70 in the Second Test at Lord's, injury struck and he was forced him to miss the remainder of the series.

FAZAL, Sohail

Born: November 11, 1967
Batting: Right handed
Bowling: Right arm medium-fast

One Day Internationals
ODI Career: 1989
ODIs Played: 2

ODI Batting
Innings:	2	Runs:	56
Highest Score:	32	Average:	28.00
No. 50s:	0	No. 100s:	0

ODI Bowling & Fielding
Wickets:	0	Runs:	4
Best Bowling:	0/4	Average:	0.00
5 WM:	0	Catches:	1
Stumpings:	0		

An all-rounder from Lahore, Sohail Fazal was serviceable in his two ODI's against West Indies and India at Sharjah in 1989.

FAZAL, Zahid

Born: November 10, 1973
Batting: Right handed
Bowling: Right arm off-break

Tests
Test Career:	1990-95		
Cap Number:	118		
Tests Played:	9		

Test Batting
Innings:	16	Runs:	288
Highest Score:	78	Average:	18.00
No. 50s:	1	No. 100s:	0

Test Bowling & Fielding
Wickets:	0	Runs:	0
Best Bowling:		Average:	0.00
5 WI:	0	10 WM:	0
Catches:	5	Stumpings:	0

One Day Internationals
ODI Career:	1990-94		
ODIs Played:	19		

ODI Batting
Innings:	18	Runs:	348
Highest Score:	98*	Average:	23.20
No. 50s:	2	No. 100s:	0

ODI Bowling & Fielding
Wickets:	0	Runs:	0
Best Bowling:		Average:	0.00
5 WM:	0	Catches:	2
Stumpings:	0		

A right hand batsman who made his debut against West Indies at Karachi in 1990. Played just the nine Tests.

FAZAL-UR-REHMAN, Sheikh
Born: June 11, 1935
Batting: Right handed
Bowling: Right arm leg-break

Tests
Test Career:	1958		
Cap Number:	28		
Tests Played:	1		

Test Batting
Innings:	2	Runs:	10
Highest Score:	8	Average:	5.00
No. 50s:	0	No. 100s:	0

Test Bowling & Fielding
Wickets:	1	Runs:	99
Best Bowling:	1/43	Average:	99.00
5 WI:	0	10 WM:	0
Catches:	0	Stumpings:	0

A right arm leg spinner who got his Test call up at age 33, Rehman took one wicket - that of opener Conrad Hunte - in his solitary Test against the West Indies at Georgetown in 1958.

FAZIL, Irfan
Born: November 2, 1981
Batting: Right handed
Bowling: Right arm medium-fast

Tests
Test Career:	2000		
Cap Number:	161		
Tests Played:	1		

Test Batting
Innings:	2	Runs:	4
Highest Score:	3	Average:	4.00
No. 50s:	0	No. 100s:	0

Test Bowling & Fielding
Wickets:	2	Runs:	65
Best Bowling:	1/30	Average:	32.50
5 WI:	0	10 WM:	0
Catches:	2	Stumpings:	0

One Day Internationals
ODI Career:	2000		
ODIs Played:	1		

ODI Batting
Innings:	1	Runs:	15
Highest Score:	15	Average:	15.00
No. 50s:	0	No. 100s:	0

ODI Bowling & Fielding
Wickets:	0	Runs:	46
Best Bowling:	0/46	Average:	0.00
5 WM:	0	Catches:	0
Stumpings:	0		

A pace bowler from Lahore who made one appearance at both Test and One Day level.

GHAURI, Mohammad Nadeem
Born: October 12, 1962
Batting: Right handed
Bowling: Left arm off-break

Tests
Test Career:	1990		
Cap Number:	117		
Tests Played:	1		

Test Batting
Innings:	1	Runs:	0
Highest Score:	0	Average:	0.00
No. 50s:	0	No. 100s:	0

Test Bowling & Fielding
Wickets:	0	Runs:	20
Best Bowling:		Average:	0.00
5 WI:	0	10 WM:	0
Catches:	0	Stumpings:	0

One Day Internationals
ODI Career:	1990		
ODIs Played:	6		

ODI Batting
Innings:	3	Runs:	14
Highest Score:	7	Average:	14.00
No. 50s:	0	No. 100s:	0

ODI Bowling & Fielding
Wickets:	5	Runs:	230
Best Bowling:	2/51	Average:	46.00
5 WM:	0	Catches:	0
Stumpings:	0		

Left arm off-spinner Nadeem Ghauri's didn't get much of chance to show his wares in his first and only Test against Australia in Sydney, in 1990, as apart from two days, the match was riddled with showers.

GHAZALI, Mohammad Ebrahim Zainuddin (Ebbu)
Born: June 15, 1924
Batting: Right handed
Bowling: Right arm off-break

Tests
Test Career:	1954	
Cap Number:	18	
Tests Played:	2	

Test Batting
Innings:	4	Runs:	32
Highest Score:	18	Average:	8.00
No. 50s:	0	No. 100s:	0

Test Bowling & Fielding
Wickets:	0	Runs:	18
Best Bowling:		Average:	0.00
5 WI:	0	10 WM:	0
Catches:	0	Stumpings:	0

An all-rounder "Ebbu" Ghazali played two Tests on Pakistan's tour of England in 1954. He holds the unenviable record of scoring the fastest 'pair' in Test cricket - when he was dismissed for two ducks within a two hour period at Trent Bridge in his last Test.

GUL, Aftab
Born:	March 31, 1946
Batting:	Right handed
Bowling:	Left arm leg-break

Tests
Test Career:	1969-71
Cap Number:	57
Tests Played:	6

Test Batting
Innings:	8	Runs:	182
Highest Score:	33	Average:	22.75
No. 50s:	0	No. 100s:	0

Test Bowling & Fielding
Wickets:	0	Runs:	4
Best Bowling:		Average:	0.00
5 WI:	0	10 WM:	0
Catches:	3	Stumpings:	0

A diminutive opener who made his Test debut against England at Lahore in 1969. He played just six Tests.

GUL, Umar
Born:	April 14, 1984
Batting:	Right handed
Bowling:	Right arm medium-fast

Tests
Test Career:	2003-06
Cap Number:	175
Tests Played:	9

Test Batting
Innings:	11	Runs:	47
Highest Score:	14	Average:	4.70
No. 50s:	0	No. 100s:	0

Test Bowling & Fielding
Wickets:	33	Runs:	1,125
Best Bowling:	5/31	Average:	34.04
5 WI:	1	10 WM:	0
Catches:	3	Stumpings:	0

One Day Internationals
ODI Career:	2003-06
ODIs Played:	19

ODI Batting
Innings:	2	Runs:	19
Highest Score:	17*	Average:	19.00
No. 50s:	0	No. 100s:	0

ODI Bowling & Fielding
Wickets:	22	Runs:	664
Best Bowling:	5/17	Average:	30.18
5 WM:	1	Catches:	1
Stumpings:	0		

It took just over half a dozen Test appearances for Pakistan to settle on Umar Gul as the new ball partner to Mohammed Sami. A hard-working medium-fast seamer, Gul made his Test debut against Bangladesh in 2003, but it was his five wicket haul against India at Lahore in 2003, where he captured the wickets of Sehwag, Dravid and Tendulkar that put him on the map as a potential long term prospect. Plagued with back injuries early in his career, Gul was selected on the tour of England in 2006.

HAFEEZ, Azeem
Born:	July 29, 1963
Batting:	Left handed
Bowling:	Left arm medium-fast

Tests
Test Career:	1983-85
Cap Number:	95
Tests Played:	18

Test Batting
Innings:	21	Runs:	134
Highest Score:	24	Average:	8.37
No. 50s:	0	No. 100s:	0

Test Bowling & Fielding
Wickets:	63	Runs:	2,204
Best Bowling:	6/46	Average:	34.98
5 WI:	4	10 WM:	0
Catches:	1	Stumpings:	0

One Day Internationals
ODI Career:	1983-85
ODIs Played:	15

ODI Batting
Innings:	10	Runs:	45
Highest Score:	15	Average:	15.00
No. 50s:	0	No. 100s:	0

ODI Bowling & Fielding
Wickets:	15	Runs:	586
Best Bowling:	4/22	Average:	39.06
5 WM:	0	Catches:	3
Stumpings:	0		

A tall left-arm pace bowler, Azeem Hafeez made his Test debut against India at Bangalore in 1983. He was selected for the Australian tour later that year as a replacement for injured captain Imran Khan and bowled tirelessly throughout the series taking five wickets in an innings on two occasions. Although born with two fingers missing on his right hand, Azeem's determination and work ethic never let his disability hinder him. He took 63 wickets at 34.98 with a career best 6/46 against India at Lahore.

HAFEEZ, Mohammad
Born:	October 17, 1980
Batting:	Right handed
Bowling:	Right arm off-break

Tests
Test Career:	2003
Cap Number:	173
Tests Played:	4

Test Batting			
Innings:	7	Runs:	309
Highest Score:	102*	Average:	51.50
No. 50s:	2	No. 100s:	1
Test Bowling & Fielding			
Wickets:	1	Runs:	74
Best Bowling:	1/14	Average:	74.00
5 WI:	0	10 WM:	0
Catches:	1	Stumpings:	0

One Day Internationals

ODI Career:	2003-05		
ODIs Played:	30		
ODI Batting			
Innings:	30	Runs:	543
Highest Score:	69	Average:	18.10
No. 50s:	3	No. 100s:	0
ODI Bowling & Fielding			
Wickets:	27	Runs:	841
Best Bowling:	3/17	Average:	31.14
5 WM:	0	Catches:	13
Stumpings:	0		

A right hand opener who doubles as a handy off-break bowler, Mohammad Hafeez showed a lot of promise in the early part of his career. Many thought his 102 not out against Bangladesh would be a sign of things to come but for quite awhile the selectors deemed his performances to be too hot and cold for their liking. However, he was selected for the 2006 tour of England where he made 95 opening the batting in the controversial 'abandoned match' at The Oval.

HAIDER, Wasim

Born:	June 6, 1967
Batting:	Right handed
Bowling:	Right arm medium-fast

One Day Internationals

ODI Career:	1992		
ODIs Played:	3		
ODI Batting			
Innings:	2	Runs:	26
Highest Score:	13	Average:	13.00
No. 50s:	0	No. 100s:	0
ODI Bowling & Fielding			
Wickets:	1	Runs:	79
Best Bowling:	1/36	Average:	79.00
5 WM:	0	Catches:	0
Stumpings:	0		

A strong, pace bowler from Faisalabad who played his three ODI's in Australia during the triangular series between the host nation, Pakistan and India.

HAMEED, Aamer

Born:	October 18, 1954
Batting:	Right handed
Bowling:	Right arm medium-fast

One Day Internationals

ODI Career:	1977-78		
ODIs Played:	2		
ODI Batting			
Innings:	0	Runs:	0
Highest Score:	0	Average:	0.00
No. 50s:	0	No. 100s:	0
ODI Bowling & Fielding			
Wickets:	1	Runs:	38
Best Bowling:	1/32	Average:	38.00
5 WM:	0	Catches:	1
Stumpings:	0		

Aamer Hameed was a right arm pace bowler from Lahore who did't get to bat in his two ODI appearances. His sole wicket was that of English captain Mike Brearley.

HAMEED, Yasir

Born:	February 28, 1978
Batting:	Right handed
Bowling:	Right arm off-break
	Wicket Keeper

Tests

Test Career:	2003-05		
Cap Number:	176		
Tests Played:	17		
Test Batting			
Innings:	33	Runs:	1,168
Highest Score:	170	Average:	38.93
No. 50s:	7	No. 100s:	2
Test Bowling & Fielding			
Wickets:	0	Runs:	5
Best Bowling:		Average:	0.00
5 WI:	0	10 WM:	0
Catches:	13	Stumpings:	0

One Day Internationals

ODI Career:	2003-05		
ODIs Played:	48		
ODI Batting			
Innings:	48	Runs:	1,805
Highest Score:	127*	Average:	38.40
No. 50s:	10	No. 100s:	3
ODI Bowling & Fielding			
Wickets:	0	Runs:	26
Best Bowling:		Average:	0.00
5 WM:	0	Catches:	11
Stumpings:	0		

He became the second player in Test history - after West Indian Lawrence Rowe - to score a century in both innings on debut. A part time wicket-keeper, Hameed was selected at number three in his first Test against Bangladesh at Karachi in 2003. His amazing 170 eclipsed the previous best by a Pakistan debutant - 166 by Khalid Ibadulla in 1964/65. He followed up in the second innings with 109 to take home the 'Man of the Match' award. He was later elevated to open the innings with Imran Farhat but will need to improve on his Test average of just under 39, to be considered a permanent member of the current day Test eleven. A solid performer in limited overs competition.

HAMID, Farooq

Born:	March 3, 1945
Batting:	Right handed
Bowling:	Right arm medium-fast

Tests

Test Career:	1964
Cap Number:	48
Tests Played:	1

Test Batting				
Innings:	2	Runs:	3
Highest Score:	3	Average:	1.50
No. 50s:	0	No. 100s:	0

Test Bowling & Fielding				
Wickets:	1	Runs:	107
Best Bowling:	1/107	Average:	107.00
5 WI:	0	10 WM:	0
Catches:	0	Stumpings:	0

Another 'One-Test-Wonder' Farooq Hamid, a pace bowler from Lahore, got his chance at Test level in a one off Test against the Australians at the MCG in 1964. He sole wicket was that of fellow debutant and future Australian captain, Ian Chappell.

HAMID, Mahmood

Born: January 19, 1969
Batting: Right handed
Bowling: Right arm medium

One Day Internationals

ODI Career:	1995
ODIs Played:	1

ODI Batting				
Innings:	1	Runs:	1
Highest Score:	1	Average:	1.00
No. 50s:	0	No. 100s:	0

ODI Bowling & Fielding				
Wickets:	0	Runs:	0
Best Bowling:		Average:	0.00
5 WM:	0	Catches:	0
Stumpings:	0		

A promising right hand batsman from Karachi who was run out for one in his only ODI against Sri Lanka at Sharjah in 1995.

HANIF, Aamer

Born: October 4, 1967
Batting: Right handed
Bowling: Right arm medium

One Day Internationals

ODI Career:	1993-95
ODIs Played:	5

ODI Batting				
Innings:	4	Runs:	89
Highest Score:	36*	Average:	44.50
No. 50s:	0	No. 100s:	0

ODI Bowling & Fielding				
Wickets:	4	Runs:	122
Best Bowling:	3/66	Average:	30.50
5 WM:	0	Catches:	0
Stumpings:	0		

A right arm medium pacer, Aamer Hanif hit the winning runs against Sri Lanka on his ODI debut in 1993. He went on to play in another four ODI's with reasonable success.

HASAN, Khalid

Born: July 14, 1937
Batting: Right handed
Bowling: Right arm leg-break

Tests

Test Career:	1954
Cap Number:	19
Tests Played:	1

Test Batting				
Innings:	2	Runs:	17
Highest Score:	10	Average:	17.00
No. 50s:	0	No. 100s:	0

Test Bowling & Fielding				
Wickets:	2	Runs:	116
Best Bowling:	2/116	Average:	58.00
5 WI:	0	10 WM:	0
Catches:	0	Stumpings:	0

At 13 days shy of his 17th birthday, leg spinner Khalid Hassan became the youngest Pakistan Test cricketer when he made his debut against England, at Trent Bridge in 1954. Unfortunately, for the promising youngster, he was not given the opportunity to fulfill his potential and therefore became yet another reluctant member of the unofficial 'One Test' club.

HASAN, Waqar

Born: September 12, 1932
Batting: Right handed
Bowling: Right arm medium

Tests

Test Career:	1952-59
Cap Number:	11
Tests Played:	21

Test Batting				
Innings:	35	Runs:	1,071
Highest Score:	189	Average:	31.50
No. 50s:	6	No. 100s:	1

Test Bowling & Fielding				
Wickets:	0	Runs:	10
Best Bowling:	0/10	Average:	0.00
5 WI:	0	10 WM:	0
Catches:	10	Stumpings:	0

Although recognised as an accomplished batsman, Waqar Hasan batted at number eight in Pakistan's first Test against India at Dehli in 1952. An excellent fielder, Hasan made six fifties and a memorable 189 against New Zealand at Lahore in 1956.

HUSSAIN, Afaq

Born: December 31, 1939
Batting: Right handed
Bowling: Right arm off-break

Tests

Test Career:	1961-64
Cap Number:	38
Tests Played:	2

Test Batting				
Innings:	4	Runs:	66
Highest Score:	35*	Average:	66.00
No. 50s:	0	No. 100s:	0

Test Bowling & Fielding				
Wickets:	1	Runs:	106
Best Bowling:	1/40	Average:	35.00
5 WI:	0	10 WM:	0
Catches:	0	Stumpings:	0

A right arm off break bowler from Lucknow, Afaq Hussain took just the one wicket in his two Tests but was never dismissed in his four innings.

HUSSAIN, Mahmood

Born:	April 2, 1932
Batting:	Right handed
Bowling:	Right arm medium-fast

Tests

Test Career:	1952-62
Cap Number:	12
Tests Played:	27

Test Batting

Innings:	39	Runs:	336
Highest Score:	35	Average:	10.18
No. 50s:	0	No. 100s:	0

Test Bowling & Fielding

Wickets:	68	Runs:	2,628
Best Bowling:	6/67	Average:	38.64
5 WI:	2	10 WM:	0
Catches:	5	Stumpings:	0

A right arm fast bowler from Lahore, Mahmood Hussain made his Test debut against India at Lucknow in 1952, when he was brought into the side to replace the injured Khan Mohammad. He took 3/35 in the first innings and ended with a respectable four wickets for the match. From then on he partnered with Fazal Mahmood and Khan Mohammed in what became a highly respected pace attack over almost a decade. He took a career best 6/67 against India at Dhaka in 1955.

HUSSAIN, Mohammad

Born:	October 8, 1976
Batting:	Left handed
Bowling:	Left arm off-break

Tests

Test Career:	1996-98
Cap Number:	141
Tests Played:	2

Test Batting

Innings:	3	Runs:	18
Highest Score:	17	Average:	6.00
No. 50s:	0	No. 100s:	0

Test Bowling & Fielding

Wickets:	3	Runs:	87
Best Bowling:	2/66	Average:	29.00
5 WI:	0	10 WM:	0
Catches:	1	Stumpings:	0

One Day Internationals

ODI Career:	1997-98
ODIs Played:	14

ODI Batting

Innings:	12	Runs:	154
Highest Score:	31*	Average:	30.80
No. 50s:	0	No. 100s:	0

ODI Bowling & Fielding

Wickets:	13	Runs:	547
Best Bowling:	4/33	Average:	42.07
5 WM:	0	Catches:	5
Stumpings:	0		

His two Test appearances against Zimbabwe and Australia yielded him three wickets from limited opportunities.

HUSSAIN KHOKHAR, Anwar

Born:	July 16, 1920
Batting:	Right handed
Bowling:	Right arm medium-fast

Tests

Test Career:	1952
Cap Number:	2
Tests Played:	4

Test Batting

Innings:	6	Runs:	42
Highest Score:	17	Average:	7.00
No. 50s:	0	No. 100s:	0

Test Bowling & Fielding

Wickets:	1	Runs:	29
Best Bowling:	1/25	Average:	29.00
5 WI:	0	10 WM:	0
Catches:	0	Stumpings:	0

A right arm pace bowler and capable batsman, Anwar Hussain was vice captain in Pakistan's inaugural Test against India, at Delhi, in 1952.

IBADULLA, Khalid (Billy)

Born:	December 20, 1935
Batting:	Right handed
Bowling:	Right arm medium

Tests

Test Career:	1964-67
Cap Number:	43
Tests Played:	4

Test Batting

Innings:	8	Runs:	253
Highest Score:	166	Average:	31.62
No. 50s:	0	No. 100s:	1

Test Bowling & Fielding

Wickets:	1	Runs:	99
Best Bowling:	1/42	Average:	99.00
5 WI:	0	10 WM:	0
Catches:	3	Stumpings:	0

One of six Pakistan players to make their debut in a one off Test against Australia at Karachi in 1964, 'Billy' Ibadulla made an immediate impact when he smashed 166 while opening the batting with fellow debutant Abdul Kadir. It was to remain the highest score on debut, by a Pakistani, for almost 40 years until Yasir Hameed scored 170 on debut in 2003. Ibadulla and Kadir put on 249 and looked destined to reach 300 and beyond if not for Kadir being run out on 95. But it was a hard act to follow and after four Tests 'Billy' was no longer considered a 'hero'.

ILYAS MAHMOOD, Mohammad

Born:	March 19, 1946
Batting:	Right handed
Bowling:	Right arm leg-break

Tests

Test Career:	1964-69
Cap Number:	49
Tests Played:	10

Test Batting

Innings:	19	Runs:	441
Highest Score:	126	Average:	23.31
No. 50s:	2	No. 100s:	1

Test Bowling & Fielding

Wickets:	0	Runs:	63
Best Bowling:		Average:	0.00
5 WI:	0	10 WM:	0
Catches:	6	Stumpings:	0

A right hand opener from Lahore, Mohammad Ilyas made his Test debut, along with Arif Butt and Farooq Hamid, in a 'one off' Test against Bob Simpson's Australians at the MCG in 1964. Like his fellow debutants Ilyas' Test career was not a long one but he did manage to sneak in a Test century with a fine 126 against New Zealand at Karachi in 1965.

INZAMAM-UL-HAQ,

Born:	March 3, 1970
Batting:	Right handed
Bowling:	Left arm slow

Tests

Test Career:	1992-06
Cap Number:	124
Tests Played:	111

Test Batting

Innings:	184	Runs:	8,404
Highest Score:	329	Average:	51.24
No. 50s:	44	No. 100s:	25

Test Bowling & Fielding

Wickets:	0	Runs:	8
Best Bowling:		Average:	0.00
5 WI:	0	10 WM:	0
Catches:	79	Stumpings:	0

One Day Internationals

ODI Career:	1991-06
ODIs Played:	362

ODI Batting

Innings:	337	Runs:	11,414
Highest Score:	137*	Average:	39.63
No. 50s:	83	No. 100s:	10

ODI Bowling & Fielding

Wickets:	3	Runs:	64
Best Bowling:	1/0	Average:	21.33
5 WM:	0	Catches:	105
Stumpings:	0		

While he has been often maligned because of his supposedly laconic attitude, Inzamam-ul-Haq's record speaks for itself. 'Inzi', who was plucked from obscurity by then captain Imran Khan, is narrowly closing on Javed Miandad as Pakistan's highest run scorer and has made more hundreds at Test level than any batsman in Pakistan's history. Of his 25 centuries, he scored a superb 200 not out against Sri Lanka in 1999 and then in 2002 became only the second Pakistani to score a triple century when he belted the Kiwis all over the Lahore stadium on his way to a massive 329 - falling just eight runs short of Hanif Mohammad's record highest score of 337. He is also only the third player in Pakistan's history to average over 50 in Tests. Arguably, the finest player of pace in the world today, Inzamam's classical yet seemingly effortless strokes are complimented with a sound, resolute defence. When settled in his innings he looks unflappable and some have described the experience as bowling to a brick wall. Big in stature, the only flaw in his game would be his lack of pace and running between wickets at times. But this hasn't compromised his ability to perform at ODI level, having scored over 11,000 runs at an average of just under 40. The current day Pakistan captain, Inzamam has led his country in 25 Tests and although heading into his late 30's, he is still playing some of the best cricket of his career. However, on the 2006 tour of England he was embroiled in the infamous ball-tampering affair, during the last Test at The Oval. The situation heightened when on the fourth day, controversial umpire Darrel Hair awarded five runs to England after alleging that Pakistan had tampered with the match ball. In protest, Inzamam delayed his team's return to the field after a tea break. This action led to Umpires Hair and Doctrove awarding the match to England stipulating that Pakistan had forfeited the match. It was the first time in Test history that a win was awarded by match officials.

IQBAL, Asif

Born:	June 6, 1943
Batting:	Right handed
Bowling:	Right arm medium

Tests

Test Career:	1964-80
Cap Number:	42
Tests Played:	58

Test Batting

Innings:	99	Runs:	3,575
Highest Score:	175	Average:	38.85
No. 50s:	12	No. 100s:	11

Test Bowling & Fielding

Wickets:	53	Runs:	1,502
Best Bowling:	5/48	Average:	28.33
5 WI:	2	10 WM:	0
Catches:	36	Stumpings:	0

One Day Internationals

ODI Career:	1973-79
ODIs Played:	10

ODI Batting

Innings:	8	Runs:	330
Highest Score:	62	Average:	55.00
No. 50s:	5	No. 100s:	0

ODI Bowling & Fielding

Wickets:	16	Runs:	378
Best Bowling:	4/56	Average:	23.62
5 WM:	0	Catches:	7
Stumpings:	0		

When the dapper 21 year old all-rounder from Hyderabad made his Test debut against Australia, at Karachi in 1964, he found himself batting way down the order at number ten. But the talented youngster defied his ranking by compiling an impressive 41. And by the time the second innings came around, Asif was elevated to first drop and scored 36. However, Asif's debut performance with the bat didn't convince the selectors to etch his name higher in the order as they continued to juggle his batting position throughout the early stages of his career. Although a gentle medium pacer, Asif surprisingly started out as an opening bowler, together with fellow debutant, and another unlikely new ball candidate, Majid Khan. The pair performed admirably as they took two wickets each. On the tour of New Zealand in 1965, Asif snared, what would become his career best bowling figures of 5/48 in the first Test at Wellington, and then followed up with an almost identical performance in the second Test in Auckland with 5/52. But as history would indicate, Asif's role as a front line bowler would be short lived as he went on to establish himself as a world class and one of Pakistan's finest batsmen. Asif's first Test century came in 1967 against England at the Oval, where he again demonstrated his batting prowess from the lower order, when batting at number nine, he top scored with 146 out of Pakistan's second innings total of 255. He took the only two wickets in England's second innings who otherwise would have secured an innings victory if not for Asif's effort with the bat. He followed up with his second Test century in 1971, again against England on English soil when he scored 104 not out - batting from his more customary number six position. Now playing arguably the best cricket of his career and focusing more on his batting, Asif registered his highest score on the tour of New Zealand with a dashing 175 in the second Test at Dunedin, helping Pakistan secure an innings and 166 run victory. During the Australian tour of 1976/77, Asif, who was now entrenched in the middle order, scored two centuries down under. The first an undefeated 152 in Adelaide followed by 120 in the third Test at Sydney. But it wouldn't be his performances with the bat that would capture the headlines as shortly after the tour, Asif, along with 50 of the world's best cricketers, including team mates Imran Khan, Zaheer Abbas, Majid Khan and captain Mushtaq Mohammad, joined Kerry Packer's World Series Cricket for the upcoming Australian summer. Asif was part of the 'World Eleven' squad, which led by Tony Greig, included players from South Africa, England, and of course Pakistan. Considered 'rebels' by the Pakistan board, it was suggested that Asif and co would be suspended, and maybe even expelled, from playing Test cricket for their country. However upon their return home, the Pakistan board conceded that they could not afford to lose such a plethora of talent in the one hit and thus all 'rebels' were recalled to the Test side shortly afterwards. In fact Asif was not only forgiven, but was appointed captain only a year later (taking over from Wasim Bari) while Imran and Zaheer were both handed the reins shortly afterwards. Although he retired amidst some controversy regarding match fixing during his reign as captain, Asif Iqbal is still regarded as one of Pakistan's finest cricketers.

IQBAL, Faisal

Born: December 30, 1981
Batting: Right handed
Bowling: Right arm medium

Tests

Test Career: 2001-06
Cap Number: 164
Tests Played: 15

Test Batting

Innings:	27	Runs:	694
Highest Score:	139	Average:	26.69
No. 50s:	4	No. 100s:	1

Test Bowling & Fielding

Wickets:	0	Runs:	7
Best Bowling:		Average:	0.00
5 WI:	0	10 WM:	0
Catches:	9	Stumpings:	0

One Day Internationals

ODI Career: 2000-03
ODIs Played: 17

ODI Batting

Innings:	15	Runs:	284
Highest Score:	100*	Average:	21.84
No. 50s:	0	No. 100s:	1

ODI Bowling & Fielding

Wickets:	0	Runs:	33
Best Bowling:		Average:	0.00
5 WM:	0	Catches:	2
Stumpings:	0		

The nephew of one of Pakistan's finest and highest run scorer - Javed Miandad, Faisal Iqbal was under immense pressure to perform from the outset. His 42 and 52 on Test debut against New Zealand at Auckland, in 2001, silenced the cynics for a short while but in his six years, Iqbal has not been able to maintain enough consistency to consolidate a permanent position in the middle order. An undoubted talent, he finally scored his maiden Test century against India at Karachi in 2006 and was subsequently selected for the tour of England later that year.

IQBAL CHAUDHRY, Zafar

Born: March 6, 1969
Batting: Right handed
Bowling: Right arm medium-fast

One Day Internationals

ODI Career: 1995
ODIs Played: 8

ODI Batting

Innings:	6	Runs:	48
Highest Score:	18	Average:	8.00
No. 50s:	0	No. 100s:	0

ODI Bowling & Fielding
Wickets:	3	Runs:	137
Best Bowling:	2/37	Average:	45.60
5 WM:	0	Catches:	1
Stumpings:	0		

A right arm pace bowler from Karachi who was rather expensive in his eight ODI's.

IQBAL QURESHI, Masood
Born:	April 17, 1952
Batting:	Right handed
	Wicket Keeper

One Day Internationals
ODI Career:	1984
ODIs Played:	1

ODI Batting
Innings:	1	Runs:	2
Highest Score:	2	Average:	2.00
No. 50s:	0	No. 100s:	0

ODI Bowling & Fielding
Wickets:	0	Runs:	0
Best Bowling:		Average:	0.00
5 WM:	0	Catches:	0
Stumpings:	0		

A wicket-keeper from Lahore who was called up to play just the one ODI against New Zealand at Multan where he was run out for two.

ISRAR, Shahid
Born:	March 1, 1950
Batting:	Right handed
	Wicket Keeper

Tests
Test Career:	1976
Cap Number:	73
Tests Played:	1

Test Batting
Innings:	1	Runs:	7
Highest Score:	7*	Average:	7.00
No. 50s:	0	No. 100s:	0

Test Bowling & Fielding
Wickets:	0	Runs:	0
Best Bowling:		Average:	0.00
5 WI:	0	10 WM:	0
Catches:	0	Stumpings:	0

A stand in wicket-keeper from Karachi, Shahid was not given another chance at Test level after an uneventful debut against New Zealand at Karachi in 1976.

JAFFAR, Saleem
Born:	November 19, 1962
Batting:	Right handed
Bowling:	Left arm medium-fast

Tests
Test Career:	1986-92
Cap Number:	106
Tests Played:	14

Test Batting
Innings:	14	Runs:	42
Highest Score:	10*	Average:	5.25
No. 50s:	0	No. 100s:	0

Test Bowling & Fielding
Wickets:	36	Runs:	1,139
Best Bowling:	5/40	Average:	31.63
5 WI:	1	10 WM:	0
Catches:	2	Stumpings:	0

One Day Internationals
ODI Career:	1986-90
ODIs Played:	39

ODI Batting
Innings:	13	Runs:	36
Highest Score:	10*	Average:	18.00
No. 50s:	0	No. 100s:	0

ODI Bowling & Fielding
Wickets:	40	Runs:	1,382
Best Bowling:	3/25	Average:	34.55
5 WM:	0	Catches:	3
Stumpings:	0		

A left arm pace bowler from Karachi who took a career best 5/40 against New Zealand at The Basin in 1989. Surprisingly, Jaffar played just 14 Tests considering he was initially hailed as a likely long term prospect.

JALAL-UD-DIN,
Born:	June 12, 1959
Batting:	Right handed
Bowling:	Right arm medium-fast

Tests
Test Career:	1982-85
Cap Number:	94
Tests Played:	6

Test Batting
Innings:	3	Runs:	3
Highest Score:	2	Average:	3.00
No. 50s:	0	No. 100s:	0

Test Bowling & Fielding
Wickets:	11	Runs:	537
Best Bowling:	3/77	Average:	48.81
5 WI:	0	10 WM:	0
Catches:	0	Stumpings:	0

One Day Internationals
ODI Career:	1982-83
ODIs Played:	8

ODI Batting
Innings:	2	Runs:	5
Highest Score:	5	Average:	2.50
No. 50s:	0	No. 100s:	0

ODI Bowling & Fielding
Wickets:	14	Runs:	211
Best Bowling:	4/32	Average:	15.07
5 WM:	0	Catches:	1
Stumpings:	0		

A bespectacled right arm pace bowler from Karachi who took his best figures of 3/77 on debut against Australia at Lahore, in 1982. A few weeks earlier, Jalal-ud-Din became the first player to take a hat-trick in One Day Internationals when he dismissed Aussies Rod Marsh, Bruce Yardley and Geoff Lawson in successive balls.

JAMIL ALVI, Hasan
Born:	July 25, 1952
Batting:	Left handed
Bowling:	Left arm medium-fast

One Day Internationals

ODI Career:	1977-78		
ODIs Played:	6		
ODI Batting			
Innings:	5	**Runs:**	111
Highest Score:	28	**Average:**	22.20
No. 50s:	0	**No. 100s:**	0
ODI Bowling & Fielding			
Wickets:	8	**Runs:**	154
Best Bowling:	3/18	**Average:**	19.25
5 WM:	0	**Catches:**	1
Stumpings:	0		

A left arm all rounder who made his ODI debut against England at Sahiwal in 1977. Jamil played in six ODI's taking a career best 3/18 but was not considered for Test selection.

JAMSHED, Mujahid

Born:	December 1, 1971
Batting:	Right handed
Bowling:	Right arm medium

One Day Internationals

ODI Career:	1997		
ODIs Played:	4		
ODI Batting			
Innings:	3	**Runs:**	27
Highest Score:	23	**Average:**	13.50
No. 50s:	0	**No. 100s:**	0
ODI Bowling & Fielding			
Wickets:	1	**Runs:**	6
Best Bowling:	1/6	**Average:**	6.00
5 WM:	0	**Catches:**	0
Stumpings:	0		

Mujahid Jamshed played all four ODI's on Australian soil. He made his debut against the Aussies at Hobart where he took his only wicket that of Queenslander Stuart Law.

JAVED, Aaqib

Born:	August 5, 1972
Batting:	Right handed
Bowling:	Right arm medium-fast

Tests

Test Career:	1989-98		
Cap Number:	109		
Tests Played:	22		
Test Batting			
Innings:	27	**Runs:**	101
Highest Score:	28*	**Average:**	5.05
No. 50s:	0	**No. 100s:**	0
Test Bowling & Fielding			
Wickets:	54	**Runs:**	1,874
Best Bowling:	5/84	**Average:**	34.70
5 WI:	1	**10 WM:**	0
Catches:	2	**Stumpings:**	0

One Day Internationals

ODI Career:	1988-98		
ODIs Played:	163		
ODI Batting			
Innings:	51	**Runs:**	267
Highest Score:	45*	**Average:**	10.68
No. 50s:	0	**No. 100s:**	0
ODI Bowling & Fielding			
Wickets:	182	**Runs:**	5,721
Best Bowling:	7/37	**Average:**	31.43
5 WM:	4	**Catches:**	24
Stumpings:	0		

An exciting right arm paceman, Aaqib Javed made his Test debut against New Zealand at Wellington a few months shy of his 17th birthday. Like several Pakistan paceman of that era, Javed too learnt the art of reverse swing and used it with great effect. Javed played a supporting role to Wasim Akram and Waqar Younis and the trio was considered the most feared pace attack during the early 90's. Arguably more suited to the shorter version of the game, Javed was a valuable member of Pakistan's victorious World Cup squad of 1992.

KABIR SIDDIQI, Mohammad Shadab

Born:	November 12, 1977
Batting:	Left handed
Bowling:	Right arm off-break

Tests

Test Career:	1996-02		
Cap Number:	137		
Tests Played:	5		
Test Batting			
Innings:	7	**Runs:**	148
Highest Score:	55	**Average:**	21.14
No. 50s:	1	**No. 100s:**	0
Test Bowling & Fielding			
Wickets:	0	**Runs:**	9
Best Bowling:		**Average:**	0.00
5 WI:	0	**10 WM:**	0
Catches:	11	**Stumpings:**	0

One Day Internationals

ODI Career:	1996		
ODIs Played:	3		
ODI Batting			
Innings:	3	**Runs:**	0
Highest Score:	0	**Average:**	0.00
No. 50s:	0	**No. 100s:**	0
ODI Bowling & Fielding			
Wickets:	0	**Runs:**	0
Best Bowling:		**Average:**	0.00
5 WM:	0	**Catches:**	1
Stumpings:	0		

A opener from Karachi who played just five Tests in six years after making his debut against England at Lords.

KADIR, Abdul

Born:	May 10, 1944
Batting:	Right handed
	Wicket Keeper

Tests

Test Career:	1964-65		
Cap Number:	41		
Tests Played:	4		
Test Batting			
Innings:	8	**Runs:**	272
Highest Score:	95	**Average:**	34.00
No. 50s:	2	**No. 100s:**	0

Test Bowling & Fielding			
Wickets:	0	Runs:	0
Best Bowling:		Average:	0.00
5 WI:	0	10 WM:	0
Catches:	0	Stumpings:	1

Abdul Kadir was selected as a wicket-keeper and opening batsman in his Test debut against Australia at Karachi in 1964. While opening the batting with fellow debutant, Khalid Ibadulla, the pair put on an incredible 249 for the first wicket with Kadir run out on 95. A thumb injury put pay to future chances behind the stumps thus leading to Kadir playing just the four Tests. His finished his career with a respectable average of 34.00.

KAMAL, Asim

Born: May 31, 1976
Batting: Left handed

Tests

Test Career: 2003-05
Cap Number: 180
Tests Played: 12

Test Batting

Innings:	20	Runs:	717
Highest Score:	99	Average:	37.73
No. 50s:	8	No. 100s:	0

Test Bowling & Fielding

Wickets:	0	Runs:	0
Best Bowling:		Average:	0.00
5 WI:	0	10 WM:	0
Catches:	10	Stumpings:	0

A solid left hand, middle order batsman who came within one run of making a century on debut but was bowled by South African paceman Andre Nel. With eight fifties alongside his name, Asim came close again in 2004 when he scored a dour 91 against India at Chandigarh. At 30 years of age his is now finding it difficult to break into the current line up.

KAMAL, Mohsin

Born: June 16, 1963
Batting: Right handed
Bowling: Right arm fast

Tests

Test Career: 1984-94
Cap Number: 100
Tests Played: 9

Test Batting

Innings:	11	Runs:	37
Highest Score:	13*	Average:	9.25
No. 50s:	0	No. 100s:	0

Test Bowling & Fielding

Wickets:	24	Runs:	822
Best Bowling:	4/116	Average:	34.25
5 WI:	0	10 WM:	0
Catches:	4	Stumpings:	0

One Day Internationals

ODI Career: 1984-94
ODIs Played: 19

ODI Batting

Innings:	6	Runs:	27
Highest Score:	11*	Average:	9.00
No. 50s:	0	No. 100s:	0

ODI Bowling & Fielding

Wickets:	27	Runs:	760
Best Bowling:	4/47	Average:	36.49
5 WM:	0	Catches:	4
Stumpings:	0		

A right arm fast bowler from Faisalabad who became Pakistan's 100th Test Player when he debuted against England at Lahore in 1984.

KANERIA, Danish

Born: December 16, 1980
Batting: Right handed
Bowling: Right arm leg-break

Tests

Test Career: 2000-06
Cap Number: 163
Tests Played: 38

Test Batting

Innings:	51	Runs:	131
Highest Score:	15	Average:	5.24
No. 50s:	0	No. 100s:	0

Test Bowling & Fielding

Wickets:	163	Runs:	5,216
Best Bowling:	7/77	Average:	32.00
5 WI:	11	10 WM:	2
Catches:	11	Stumpings:	0

One Day Internationals

ODI Career: 2001-06
ODIs Played: 16

ODI Batting

Innings:	8	Runs:	6
Highest Score:	3*	Average:	3.00
No. 50s:	0	No. 100s:	0

ODI Bowling & Fielding

Wickets:	12	Runs:	590
Best Bowling:	3/31	Average:	49.16
5 WM:	0	Catches:	2
Stumpings:	0		

Probably Pakistan's most exciting leg-spinning prospect since Abdul Qadir, Danish Kaneria has been an automatic selection at Test level since making his debut against England at Faisalabad in 2000. His 163 wickets from just 38 Tests has him on track to challenge records held by Murali and Warne should he last the distance. Armed with an uncompromising googly and well disguised flipper, Kaneria has taken seven wickets in a match on three occasions, with a career best 7/77 against Bangladesh at Dhaka in 2001. Originally from Karachi, Kaneria and cousin Anil Dalpat are the only two Hindus to have represented Pakistan at international level.

KARDAR, Abdul Hafeez

Born: January 17, 1925
Batting: Left handed
Bowling: Left arm off-break

Tests
Test Career:	1946-58		
Cap Number:	7		
Tests Played:	26		

Test Batting
Innings:	42	Runs:	927
Highest Score:	93	Average:	23.76
No. 50s:	5	No. 100s:	0

Test Bowling & Fielding
Wickets:	0	Runs:	0
Best Bowling:		Average:	0.00
5 WI:	0	10 WM:	0
Catches:	10	Stumpings:	0

Abdul Kardar played his first of three Tests for India, at Lords in 1946 but finished his career donning the green cap of Pakistan in 1958. Kardar played in Pakistan's inaugural Test against India, at Delhi in 1952, and was Pakistan's first captain. He went on to play in 23 Tests for Pakistan and his highest score of 93 was, ironically, made against India at Karachi, in 1955. A pioneer of Pakistan cricket, Kardar, (who in earlier days played under the name Hafeez) became chairman of selectors, and President of Pakistan's Board of Control from 1972 to 1977. Originally from Lahore, he was an outspoken advocate about introducing neutral umpires in Test cricket. (In the early part of his career he played under the name Abdul Hafeez)

KHALIL, Mohammad
Born:	November 11, 1982
Batting:	Left handed
Bowling:	Left arm medium

Tests
Test Career:	2004-05		
Cap Number:	183		
Tests Played:	2		

Test Batting
Innings:	4	Runs:	9
Highest Score:	5	Average:	3.00
No. 50s:	0	No. 100s:	0

Test Bowling & Fielding
Wickets:	0	Runs:	200
Best Bowling:		Average:	0.00
5 WI:	0	10 WM:	0
Catches:	0	Stumpings:	0

One Day Internationals
ODI Career:	2005		
ODIs Played:	3		

ODI Batting
Innings:	1	Runs:	0
Highest Score:	0*	Average:	0.00
No. 50s:	0	No. 100s:	0

ODI Bowling & Fielding
Wickets:	5	Runs:	144
Best Bowling:	2/55	Average:	28.80
5 WM:	0	Catches:	2
Stumpings:	0		

A left arm medium pacer who remains wicket-less after two Tests against Australia and India in 2004/05. But as Khalil is still in his early 20's, time is on his side to seriously push for future selection.

KHAN, Anwar
Born:	December 24, 1955
Batting:	Right handed
Bowling:	Right arm medium-fast

Tests
Test Career:	1979		
Cap Number:	80		
Tests Played:	1		

Test Batting
Innings:	2	Runs:	15
Highest Score:	12	Average:	15.00
No. 50s:	0	No. 100s:	0

Test Bowling & Fielding
Wickets:	0	Runs:	12
Best Bowling:	0/12	Average:	0.00
5 WI:	0	10 WM:	0
Catches:	0	Stumpings:	0

It was a case of 'one Khan for another' when Anwar Khan was selected to replace the injured Imran Khan against New Zealand at Christchurch in 1979. The chance selection was to be Anwar's only international appearance.

KHAN, Arshad
Born:	March 22, 1971
Batting:	Right handed
Bowling:	Right arm off-break

Tests
Test Career:	1997-05		
Cap Number:	149		
Tests Played:	9		

Test Batting
Innings:	8	Runs:	31
Highest Score:	9*	Average:	5.16
No. 50s:	0	No. 100s:	0

Test Bowling & Fielding
Wickets:	32	Runs:	960
Best Bowling:	5/38	Average:	30.00
5 WI:	1	10 WM:	0
Catches:	0	Stumpings:	0

One Day Internationals
ODI Career:	1993-06		
ODIs Played:	58		

ODI Batting
Innings:	29	Runs:	133
Highest Score:	20	Average:	12.09
No. 50s:	0	No. 100s:	0

ODI Bowling & Fielding
Wickets:	56	Runs:	1,948
Best Bowling:	4/33	Average:	34.78
5 WM:	0	Catches:	10
Stumpings:	0		

A tallish off-spinner from Peshawar, who made his Test debut against West Indies in front of his home crowd. The selectors have felt that Arshad's bowling is better suited to limited overs competition.

KHAN, Azam
Born:	March 1, 1969
Batting:	Right handed

Tests
Test Career:	1996		
Cap Number:	138		
Tests Played:	1		

Test Batting
Innings:	1	Runs:	14
Highest Score:	14	Average:	14.00
No. 50s:	0	No. 100s:	0

Test Bowling & Fielding
Wickets:	0	Runs:	0
Best Bowling:		Average:	0.00
5 WI:	0	10 WM:	0
Catches:	0	Stumpings:	0

One Day Internationals
ODI Career: 1996-98
ODIs Played: 6

ODI Batting
Innings:	5	Runs:	116
Highest Score:	72	Average:	23.20
No. 50s:	1	No. 100s:	0

ODI Bowling & Fielding
Wickets:	0	Runs:	0
Best Bowling:		Average:	0.00
5 WM:	0	Catches:	2
Stumpings:	0		

A serviceable player in limited overs competition, Azam Khan was a right hand batsman from Karachi who played just the one Test against Zimbabwe at Sheikhupura in 1996.

KHAN, Azhar

Born:	September 7, 1955
Batting:	Right handed
Bowling:	Right arm off-break

Tests
Test Career: 1980
Cap Number: 84
Tests Played: 1

Test Batting
Innings:	1	Runs:	14
Highest Score:	14	Average:	14.00
No. 50s:	0	No. 100s:	0

Test Bowling & Fielding
Wickets:	1	Runs:	2
Best Bowling:	1/1	Average:	2.00
5 WI:	0	10 WM:	0
Catches:	0	Stumpings:	0

An all-rounder, Azhar Khan played just the one Test against Australia at Lahore in 1980. Bowling right arm off-breaks, he took the wicket of future Australian captain Allan Border in Australia's second innings.

KHAN, Bazid

Born:	March 25, 1981
Batting:	Right handed
Bowling:	Right arm off-break

Tests
Test Career: 2005
Cap Number: 185
Tests Played: 1

Test Batting
Innings:	2	Runs:	32
Highest Score:	23	Average:	16.00
No. 50s:	0	No. 100s:	0

Test Bowling & Fielding
Wickets:	0	Runs:	0
Best Bowling:		Average:	0.00
5 WI:	0	10 WM:	0
Catches:	2	Stumpings:	0

One Day Internationals
ODI Career: 2004/05
ODIs Played: 3

ODI Batting
Innings:	3	Runs:	78
Highest Score:	66	Average:	26.00
No. 50s:	1	No. 100s:	0

ODI Bowling & Fielding
Wickets:	0	Runs:	1
Best Bowling:		Average:	0.00
5 WM:	0	Catches:	1
Stumpings:	0		

From the finest cricketing stock, Bazid Khan is the son of Majid, grandson of India's Jahangir and nephew of Pakistan's greatest ever player, Imran. He made his Test debut against West Indies at Bridgetown in 2005 and although it is his only Test appearance to date, Bazid has enough talent and potential to warrant future selection.

KHAN, Imran

Born:	November 25, 1952
Batting:	Right handed
Bowling:	Right arm fast

Tests
Test Career: 1971-92
Cap Number: 65
Tests Played: 88

Test Batting
Innings:	126	Runs:	3,807
Highest Score:	136	Average:	37.69
No. 50s:	18	No. 100s:	6

Test Bowling & Fielding
Wickets:	362	Runs:	8,258
Best Bowling:	8/58	Average:	22.81
5 WI:	23	10 WM:	6
Catches:	28	Stumpings:	0

One Day Internationals
ODI Career: 1974-92
ODIs Played: 175

ODI Batting
Innings:	151	Runs:	3,709
Highest Score:	102*	Average:	33.41
No. 50s:	19	No. 100s:	1

ODI Bowling & Fielding
Wickets:	182	Runs:	4,844
Best Bowling:	6/14	Average:	26.61
5 WM:	1	Catches:	36
Stumpings:	0		

Without doubt Pakistan's favourite son and the most high profile player in their history, Imran Khan hails from proud cricketing blood lines as his uncle Dr Jahingir Khan played in India's inaugural Test match and cousins Javed Burki and Majid Khan both captained Pakistan. Like his older cousins, Imran was to also lead his country but also went on to become Pakistan's greatest player. At age 19, he made his Test debut against England, at Edgbaston in 1971, and was a member of Pakistan's inaugural World Cup squad of 1975. He played in an era where cricket was blessed with some of the greatest all-rounders of all time, such as Ian Botham, Kapil Dev and Richard Hadlee. The ongoing question as to who of the quartet was the finest is still an argument the purists continue to debate today. Statistically, the case for Imran is a solid one. With the bat, he clearly leads the pack with a Test average of 37.69 ahead of Botham on 33.54 followed by Dev 31.05 and Hadlee 27.16. He again reigns supreme in ODI's with a batting average of 33.41 almost ten runs ahead of his nearest rival, Kapil Dev with 23.79. With the ball, in Tests he is marginally pipped by Hadlee (22.29 to 22.81) while Botham and Dev average in the high 20's. And again in ODI's he is second only to Hadlee. Clearly, from a statistical perspective at least, Imran comes out in front overall. In 1977 Imran, along with fellow high profile team mates such as Mushtaq Mohammad, Zaheer Abbas, Asif Iqbal and cousin Majid Khan joined Kerry Packer's World Series Cricket held in Australia over two seasons. Imran and his Pakistan team mates formed part of the World Eleven team, which competed in a triangular series against Australia and the West Indies. It was during his time at WSC that Imran was duly recognised as a genuine pace bowler when he finished second to Jeff Thomson during a fastest ball competition that was held during the series. Although it was murmured that Imran and his fellow 'rebels' would be suspended from competing in Tests due to their defection to the Packer led competition, all was forgiven upon their return to Pakistan's shores. Imran was eventually appointed captain in 1982 and led his country in 48 Tests which superseded the previous record held by Javed Miandad by some 14 matches. He openly states that he is the only Pakistan captain to stand down from the job on two occasions, citing a lack of authority in team selection as the main reason. With an exceptional eye for talent, Imran appointed scouts to scour the country to ensure that every talented youngster would be captured on his radar. After closely watching a discarded grade player practising in the nets, he invited the unsuspecting batsman to train with the squad. That same player, Inzamam-ul-Haq, is the current day captain and is edging closer to eclipsing Javed Miandad's record as Pakistan's leading run scorer in Tests. Pace bowler, Waqar Younis was also plucked out of obscurity when Imran was watching a low grade match on T.V while suffering from a stomach complaint. He led Pakistan to their first ever series win in England in 1987 and he had the honour of leading his side to World Cup glory in 1992 where he smashed 72 against England in the final, at the MCG, while batting at the unfamiliar number three position. In his 88 Tests he took five wickets in an innings on 23 occasions and ten in a match on six. His best hauls were two bags of eight in 1982. His career best 8/58 against Sri Lanka at Lahore was followed up with 8/60 against India at Karachi shortly afterwards. Imran is the third highest wicket-taker in Pakistan's history behind Wasim Akram and Waqar Younis. And if not for his time at World Series Cricket and a horrific run with injury in the early 80's it is safe to assume that Imran would have had a considerably higher tally that the 362 Test scalps that sit alongside his name. Upon his retirement, Imran continued to make headlines with his brief encounter in the political arena and his highly publicised marriage, and eventual split, with popular English figure Jemima Goldsmith. However, his tireless work with charitable organisations is what has made Pakistan's most admired sportsman a respected humanitarian. He established the Shaukat-Khanum Memorial Hospital, in honour of his mother, which specialises in the treatment and care of cancer patients throughout Pakistan. He was quoted as saying that seeing the hospital doors open for the first time was far more rewarding than winning the World Cup. To the cricket world, Imran Khan is regarded as one of the finest all-rounders to have ever played the game and for many of the female contingent, the biggest heart-throb the game has produced. However for most, Imran Khan is an exceptional ambassador for both his sport and country.

KHAN, Majid Jahangir

Born: September 28, 1946
Batting: Right handed
Bowling: Right arm off-break

Tests
Test Career: 1964-83
Cap Number: 44
Tests Played: 63

Test Batting
Innings:	106	Runs:	3,931
Highest Score:	167	Average:	38.92
No. 50s:	19	No. 100s:	8

Test Bowling & Fielding
Wickets:	27	Runs:	1,456
Best Bowling:	4/45	Average:	53.92
5 WI:	0	10 WM:	0
Catches:	70	Stumpings:	0

One Day Internationals
ODI Career: 1973-82
ODIs Played: 23

ODI Batting
Innings:	22	Runs:	786
Highest Score:	109	Average:	37.42
No. 50s:	0	No. 100s:	1

ODI Bowling & Fielding
Wickets:	13	Runs:	374
Best Bowling:	3/27	Average:	28.76
5 WM:	0	Catches:	3
Stumpings:	0		

Hailing from a highly respected cricketing family, being the older cousin of Imran, younger cousin of former captain Javed Burki and son of Jahangir Khan, who played in India's inaugural Test against England in 1932, Majid Khan was a quality cricketer in his own right. While he did not reach the international stardom of his younger cousin, Majid was an elegant opening batsman and is rated by legendary Australian pace bowler, Dennis Lillee, as one of the best of his era. Ironically it was his bowling that initially caught the eye of the Pakistan selectors. On his debut against Australia at Karachi in 1964, Majid and fellow debutant, Asif Iqbal, were given the new ball. But a back injury and questions about his action led to Majid's cricket career taking a completely new direction. A consistent performer in his formative years, Majid captained his country in three Tests between 1972 and '73. It was also in 1973 that Majid registered his first Test century with 158 against Australia at the MCG. This was followed by a gritty 110 against the Kiwis. In 1974 he became the first Pakistan batsman to score an ODI century and was an outstanding performer in the inaugural World Cup of 1975 where he scored three fifties (65, 60 and 84) while opening the batting. In 1977, Majid along with team mates Zaheer Abbas, Asif Iqbal, Mushtaq Mohammed and cousin Imran signed on with Kerry Packer's World Series Cricket. The Pakistan contingent, along with players from South Africa and England made up a World Eleven team that would play in a triangular series against host nation Australia and the West Indies over a two year period. While the World Series Australians were, at the time, deemed ineligible to play Test cricket for their country, there was talk of Pakistan also threatening to suspend their 'rebels'. however, Majid, along with the others was invited to represent Pakistan shortly after their return. As the man who made the floppy, wide brimmed hat a fashion statement, Majid Khan departed the game with just under 4,000 runs alongside his name and heralded as one of Pakistan's finest openers. And while it has been some two decades since he played at international level, the Khan dynasty continued into the new millennium when son Bazid made his Test debut in 2005.

KHAN, Mohammad Kabir
Born: April 12, 1974
Batting: Right handed
Bowling: Left arm medium-fast

Tests
Test Career: 1994-95
Cap Number: 132
Tests Played: 4
Test Batting
Innings:	5	Runs:	24
Highest Score:	10	Average:	8.00
No. 50s:	0	No. 100s:	0

Test Bowling & Fielding
Wickets:	9	Runs:	370
Best Bowling:	3/26	Average:	41.11
5 WI:	0	10 WM:	0
Catches:	1	Stumpings:	0

One Day Internationals
ODI Career: 1994-00
ODIs Played: 10
ODI Batting
Innings:	5	Runs:	10
Highest Score:	5	Average:	10.00
No. 50s:	0	No. 100s:	0

ODI Bowling & Fielding
Wickets:	12	Runs:	303
Best Bowling:	2/23	Average:	25.25
5 WM:	0	Catches:	1
Stumpings:	0		

A quickish left arm seamer who made his Test debut against Sri Lanka at Kandy, in 1994. Kabir rarely troubled the better batsmen and as he was rather expensive at Test level, he was discarded after four Tests.

KHAN, Mohsin Hasan
Born: March 15, 1955
Batting: Right handed
Bowling: Right arm medium

Tests
Test Career: 1978-86
Cap Number: 79
Tests Played: 48
Test Batting
Innings:	79	Runs:	2,709
Highest Score:	200	Average:	37.10
No. 50s:	9	No. 100s:	7

Test Bowling & Fielding
Wickets:	0	Runs:	30
Best Bowling:		Average:	0.00
5 WI:	0	10 WM:	0
Catches:	34	Stumpings:	0

One Day Internationals
ODI Career: 1977-86
ODIs Played: 75
ODI Batting
Innings:	75	Runs:	1,877
Highest Score:	117*	Average:	26.81
No. 50s:	8	No. 100s:	2

ODI Bowling & Fielding
Wickets:	1	Runs:	5
Best Bowling:	1/2	Average:	5.00
5 WM:	0	Catches:	13
Stumpings:	0		

Although he came as first drop in his first Test against England at Karachi in 1977, Mohsin Khan was soon rated as Pakistan's most talented opener and hence formed a long-standing partnership with the durable Mudassar Nazar. It took Mohsin four years to score his first Test century,129 against Sri Lanka at Lahore in 1982, but followed up with a remarkable double-century against England at Lord's later that year. Over the next two years, Mohsin peaked as a batsman, scoring his remaining five centuries, including two on Australian soil, in a two-year period.

KHAN, Moin
Born: September 23, 1971
Batting: Right handed
Wicket Keeper

Tests
Test Career:	1990-04		
Cap Number:	119		
Tests Played:	69		

Test Batting
Innings:	104	Runs:	2,741
Highest Score:	137	Average:	28.55
No. 50s:	15	No. 100s:	4

Test Bowling & Fielding
Wickets:	0	Runs:	0
Best Bowling:		Average:	0.00
5 WI:	0	10 WM:	0
Catches:	128	Stumpings:	20

One Day Internationals
ODI Career:	1990-04		
ODIs Played:	219		

ODI Batting
Innings:	183	Runs:	3,266
Highest Score:	72*	Average:	23.00
No. 50s:	12	No. 100s:	0

ODI Bowling & Fielding
Wickets:	0	Runs:	0
Best Bowling:		Average:	0.00
5 WM:	0	Catches:	214
Stumpings:	73		

Second only to Wasim Bari for most dismissals by a keeper, Moin Khan played musical chairs with fellow gloveman Rashid Latif as to who would hold down the country's number one keeping job. Overall Moin played almost double the amount of Tests than his counterpart and around 60 more ODI's, mainly because of his superior batting skills. A talkative and sometimes annoying figure behind the stumps, Moin made four Test centuries, his first three within a 12-month period between 1995 & 96. He had to wait a further seven years before knocking up his fourth ton and highest score of 137 against New Zealand at Hamilton in 2003. A member of Pakistan's victorious World Cup side of 1992, Moin captained his country in 13 Tests from 1998 to 2001.

KHAN, Nadeem
Born:	December 10, 1969
Batting:	Right handed
Bowling:	Left arm off-break

Tests
Test Career:	1993-99		
Cap Number:	128		
Tests Played:	2		

Test Batting
Innings:	3	Runs:	34
Highest Score:	25	Average:	17.00
No. 50s:	0	No. 100s:	0

Test Bowling & Fielding
Wickets:	2	Runs:	230
Best Bowling:	2/147	Average:	115.00
5 WI:	0	10 WM:	0
Catches:	0	Stumpings:	0

One Day Internationals
ODI Career:	1993-95		
ODIs Played:	2		

ODI Batting
Innings:	1	Runs:	2
Highest Score:	2	Average:	2.00
No. 50s:	0	No. 100s:	0

ODI Bowling & Fielding
Wickets:	0	Runs:	81
Best Bowling:		Average:	0.00
5 WM:	0	Catches:	0
Stumpings:	0		

A left arm off-spinner Nadeem Kahan was aged 24 when he played his first Test against West Indies at St.John's and 30 when he made his second Test appearance against Pakistan at Chennai in 1999.

KHAN, Rashid
Born:	December 15, 1959
Batting:	Right handed
Bowling:	Right arm medium-fast

Tests
Test Career:	1982-85		
Cap Number:	89		
Tests Played:	4		

Test Batting
Innings:	6	Runs:	155
Highest Score:	59	Average:	51.66
No. 50s:	1	No. 100s:	0

Test Bowling & Fielding
Wickets:	8	Runs:	360
Best Bowling:	3/129	Average:	45.00
5 WI:	0	10 WM:	0
Catches:	2	Stumpings:	0

One Day Internationals
ODI Career:	1980-85		
ODIs Played:	29		

ODI Batting
Innings:	15	Runs:	110
Highest Score:	17	Average:	13.75
No. 50s:	0	No. 100s:	0

ODI Bowling & Fielding
Wickets:	20	Runs:	923
Best Bowling:	3/47	Average:	46.15
5 WM:	0	Catches:	3
Stumpings:	0		

Even though no relation, Rashid Khan lived up to the 'Khan' name when he made a stellar Test debut against Sri Lanka at Karachi in 1982. Coming in at number ten, Khan, with Haroon Rashid added 127 for the ninth wicket until he was caught on 59. Selected primarily for his pace bowling, he captured three wickets for the match as Pakistan cruised to a 204 run victory. Khan played just three more Tests but enjoyed greater success as a member of the ODI team.

KHAN, Shakeel Ahmed
Born:	May 28, 1968
Batting:	Right handed
Bowling:	Right arm medium-fast

One Day Internationals
ODI Career:	1987		
ODIs Played:	1		

ODI Batting
Innings:	1	Runs:	0
Highest Score:	0	Average:	0.00
No. 50s:	0	No. 100s:	0

ODI Bowling & Fielding
Wickets:	1	Runs:	50
Best Bowling:	1/50	Average:	50.00
5 WM:	0	Catches:	0
Stumpings:	0		

He may have arguably the most recognised surname in Pakistani cricket, but Shakeel Khan, a tallish pace bowler from Lahore, never reached the dizzy heights of his more famous namesakes. Khan got his one and only chance at international level when he was selected to replace the injured Wasim Akram, against England in 1987. He took just the one wicket, that of opener Chris Broad.

KHAN, Younis

Born:	November 29, 1977
Batting:	Right handed
Bowling:	Right arm slow

Tests

Test Career:	2000-06
Cap Number:	159
Tests Played:	45

Test Batting
Innings:	80	Runs:	3,661
Highest Score:	267	Average:	48.17
No. 50s:	15	No. 100s:	11

Test Bowling & Fielding
Wickets:	2	Runs:	169
Best Bowling:	1/24	Average:	84.50
5 WI:	0	10 WM:	0
Catches:	47	Stumpings:	0

One Day Internationals

ODI Career:	2000-06
ODIs Played:	134

ODI Batting
Innings:	129	Runs:	3,541
Highest Score:	144	Average:	31.61
No. 50s:	24	No. 100s:	1

ODI Bowling & Fielding
Wickets:	1	Runs:	101
Best Bowling:	1/24	Average:	101.00
5 WM:	0	Catches:	70
Stumpings:	0		

Regarded as one of the best players of spin in the world, Younis Khan is the current vice-captain of Pakistan and one of the more experienced 'heads' in a team full of emerging youngsters. He is touted as a possible future captain and has filled in as skipper in two Tests between 2004 & '05. Against Sri Lanka at Rawalpindi in 2000, Younis became the seventh Pakistan batsman to register a Test century on debut when he knocked up a valuable 107 in the second innings. He has gone on to record 11 centuries with a highest score of 267 against India at Bangalore in 2005. It was his first double-century but came close again in 2006 with 199 at Lahore, also against the Indians. His Test average of 48.17 is the fourth highest in Pakistan's history.

KHAN, Zakirullah

Born:	April 3, 1963
Batting:	Right handed
Bowling:	Right arm medium-fast

Tests

Test Career:	1986-89
Cap Number:	104
Tests Played:	2

Test Batting
Innings:	2	Runs:	9
Highest Score:	9*	Average:	9.00
No. 50s:	0	No. 100s:	0

Test Bowling & Fielding
Wickets:	5	Runs:	259
Best Bowling:	3/80	Average:	51.80
5 WI:	0	10 WM:	0
Catches:	1	Stumpings:	0

One Day Internationals

ODI Career:	1984-90
ODIs Played:	17

ODI Batting
Innings:	5	Runs:	27
Highest Score:	11*	Average:	27.00
No. 50s:	0	No. 100s:	0

ODI Bowling & Fielding
Wickets:	16	Runs:	494
Best Bowling:	4/19	Average:	30.87
5 WM:	0	Catches:	0
Stumpings:	0		

Zakir Khan was a tall right arm bowler who took 3/80 on debut against Sri Lanka at Colombo in 1986.

KHAN NIAZI, Misbah-ul-Haq

Born:	May 28, 1974
Batting:	Right handed
Bowling:	Right arm leg-break

Tests

Test Career:	2001-03
Cap Number:	166
Tests Played:	5

Test Batting
Innings:	9	Runs:	120
Highest Score:	28	Average:	13.33
No. 50s:	0	No. 100s:	0

Test Bowling & Fielding
Wickets:	0	Runs:	0
Best Bowling:		Average:	0.00
5 WI:	0	10 WM:	0
Catches:	1	Stumpings:	0

One Day Internationals

ODI Career:	2002-04
ODIs Played:	12

ODI Batting
Innings:	11	Runs:	305
Highest Score:	50*	Average:	33.88
No. 50s:	2	No. 100s:	0

ODI Bowling & Fielding
Wickets:	0	Runs:	0
Best Bowling:		Average:	0.00
5 WM:	0	Catches:	5
Stumpings:	0		

A top order batsman who didn't make the most of his opportunities at the elite level. Made his Test debut on the tour of New Zealand in 2001.

LATIF, Naved

Born: February 21, 1976
Batting: Right handed
Bowling: Right arm medium

Tests
Test Career: 2002
Cap Number: 171
Tests Played: 1

Test Batting
Innings:	2	Runs:	20
Highest Score:	20	Average:	10.00
No. 50s:	0	No. 100s:	0

Test Bowling & Fielding
Wickets:	0	Runs:	0
Best Bowling:		Average:	0.00
5 WI:	0	10 WM:	0
Catches:	0	Stumpings:	0

One Day Internationals
ODI Career: 2001-03
ODIs Played: 11

ODI Batting
Innings:	11	Runs:	262
Highest Score:	113	Average:	23.81
No. 50s:	0	No. 100s:	1

ODI Bowling & Fielding
Wickets:	0	Runs:	51
Best Bowling:		Average:	0.00
5 WM:	0	Catches:	2
Stumpings:	0		

An opener who played just the one Test against West Indies at Sharjah where he was dismissed for a duck in the first innings.

LATIF, Rashid

Born: October 14, 1968
Batting: Right handed
Bowling: Right arm leg-break
        Wicket Keeper

Tests
Test Career: 1992-03
Cap Number: 125
Tests Played: 37

Test Batting
Innings:	57	Runs:	1,381
Highest Score:	150	Average:	2,877.00
No. 50s:	7	No. 100s:	1

Test Bowling & Fielding
Wickets:	0	Runs:	10
Best Bowling:		Average:	0.00
5 WI:	0	10 WM:	0
Catches:	119	Stumpings:	11

One Day Internationals
ODI Career: 1992-03
ODIs Played: 166

ODI Batting
Innings:	117	Runs:	1,709
Highest Score:	79	Average:	19.42
No. 50s:	3	No. 100s:	0

ODI Bowling & Fielding
Wickets:	0	Runs:	0
Best Bowling:		Average:	0.00
5 WM:	0	Catches:	182
Stumpings:	38		

An impressive 50 on debut against England at The Oval in 1992 and proven competency with the gloves was not enough for Rashid Latif to permanently secure the number one keeping job. He and fellow gloveman Moin Khan competed for main gig for around a decade and in the end, it was Moin who was to play the more Tests and ODI's. The fact that Latif was often at the centre of controversy didn't help his cause. A roller-coaster career to say the least, Latif announced his retirement during 1994-95 tour of Zimbabwe because of differences between he and a few senior players. He was touted a 'whistle blower' during the match fixing scandals but returned to the Test arena and was appointed captain in 1997. He was dropped shortly afterwards and replaced by, who else, Moin Khan. Four years later, in 2001, the wheels had turned as he replaced Moin and produced the best batting of his career scoring his only Test century - 150 against West Indies at Sharjah. After the 2003 World Cup he was appointed captain for a second time. A vocal campaigner against match-fixing, Latif 'rocked the boat' on one too many occasions and was subsequently replaced as skipper by current day captain Inzamam-ul-Haq.

MAHBOOB, Shahid

Born: August 25, 1962
Batting: Right handed
Bowling: Right arm medium-fast

Tests
Test Career: 1989
Cap Number: 115
Tests Played: 1

Test Batting
Innings:	0	Runs:	0
Highest Score:	0	Average:	0.00
No. 50s:	0	No. 100s:	0

Test Bowling & Fielding
Wickets:	2	Runs:	131
Best Bowling:	2/131	Average:	65.50
5 WI:	0	10 WM:	0
Catches:	0	Stumpings:	0

One Day Internationals
ODI Career: 1982-84
ODIs Played: 10

ODI Batting
Innings:	6	Runs:	119
Highest Score:	77	Average:	23.80
No. 50s:	1	No. 100s:	0

ODI Bowling & Fielding
Wickets:	7	Runs:	382
Best Bowling:	1/23	Average:	54.57
5 WM:	0	Catches:	1
Stumpings:	0		

An all rounder who played his solitary Test against India at Lahore in 1989 some five years after playing his last ODI. Mahboob was a member of Pakistan's 1983 World Cup squad and it was during this tournament where he scored a career best 77, batting at number seven.

MAHMOOD, Azhar

Born: February 28, 1975
Batting: Right handed
Bowling: Right arm medium-fast

Tests
Test Career: 1997-01
Cap Number: 146
Tests Played: 21

Test Batting
Innings:	34	Runs:	900
Highest Score:	136	Average:	30.00
No. 50s:	1	No. 100s:	3

Test Bowling & Fielding
Wickets:	39	Runs:	1,402
Best Bowling:	4/50	Average:	35.94
5 WI:	0	10 WM:	0
Catches:	14	Stumpings:	0

One Day Internationals
ODI Career: 1996-05
ODIs Played: 139

ODI Batting
Innings:	107	Runs:	1,492
Highest Score:	67	Average:	18.19
No. 50s:	3	No. 100s:	0

ODI Bowling & Fielding
Wickets:	122	Runs:	4,741
Best Bowling:	6/18	Average:	38.86
5 WM:	5	Catches:	37
Stumpings:	0		

An all-rounder from Rawalpindi, Azhar Mahmood treated his home crowd to a feast with unbeaten knocks of 128 and 50 on debut against South Africa in 1997. He became the sixth Pakistani to score a century on debut and liked the Proteas so much that he followed up with two more centuries (136 & 132) during the tour of South Africa later that year. A fine ODI player, Mahmood captured a career best 6/18 against the West Indies at Sharjah in 1999.

MAHMOOD, Fazal

Born: February 18, 1927
Batting: Right handed
Bowling: Right arm medium-fast

Tests
Test Career: 1952-62
Cap Number: 3
Tests Played: 34

Test Batting
Innings:	50	Runs:	620
Highest Score:	60	Average:	14.09
No. 50s:	1	No. 100s:	0

Test Bowling & Fielding
Wickets:	139	Runs:	3,434
Best Bowling:	7/42	Average:	24.70
5 WI:	13	10 WM:	4
Catches:	11	Stumpings:	0

A member of Pakistan's inaugural Test side that played India at Delhi in 1952, Fazal Mahmood was a quality pace/swing bowler who is heralded as one of Pakistan's finest. He was the undisputed match winner in Pakistan's second Test against India - Pakistan's first Test victory - taking 5/52 in their first innings and 7/42 in the second and thus becoming the first Pakistan bowler to take ten wickets in a match. He went on to take ten wickets (or more) in a match on another three occasions in his career against quality opposition in England, Australia and the West Indies and became the first Pakistan bowler to reach 100 Test wickets. A highly respected figure throughout Pakistan, Fazal captained his country in ten Tests from 1958 to 1961. He retired with an impressive bowling average of 24.70.

MAHMOOD, Raja Asif

Born: December 18, 1975
Batting: Right handed
Bowling: Right arm off-break

One Day Internationals
ODI Career: 1998
ODIs Played: 2

ODI Batting
Innings:	2	Runs:	14
Highest Score:	14	Average:	7.00
No. 50s:	0	No. 100s:	0

ODI Bowling & Fielding
Wickets:	0	Runs:	0
Best Bowling:		Average:	0.00
5 WM:	0	Catches:	0
Stumpings:	0		

An opening batsman originally from Rawalpindi, opener Asif Mahmood played both his ODI's against Australia, on home soil, in 1998.

MAHMOOD, Shahid

Born: March 17, 1939
Batting: Left handed
Bowling: Left arm medium

Tests
Test Career: 1962
Cap Number: 40
Tests Played: 1

Test Batting
Innings:	2	Runs:	25
Highest Score:	16	Average:	12.50
No. 50s:	0	No. 100s:	0

Test Bowling & Fielding
Wickets:	0	Runs:	23
Best Bowling:		Average:	0.00
5 WI:	0	10 WM:	0
Catches:	0	Stumpings:	0

A left hand opening batsman who was selected for the 1962 tour of England where he played just the one Test at Trent Bridge scoring just 16 and nine.

MALIK, Aamer

Born: January 3, 1963
Batting: Right handed
Bowling: Right arm medium-fast
Wicket Keeper

Tests
Test Career: 1987-94
Cap Number: 108
Tests Played: 14

Test Batting
Innings:	19	Runs:	565
Highest Score:	117	Average:	35.31
No. 50s:	3	No. 100s:	2

Test Bowling & Fielding
Wickets:	1	Runs:	89
Best Bowling:	1/0	Average:	89.00
5 WI:	0	10 WM:	0
Catches:	15	Stumpings:	1

One Day Internationals
ODI Career: 1988-94
ODIs Played: 24

ODI Batting
Innings:	23	Runs:	556
Highest Score:	90	Average:	25.27
No. 50s:	5	No. 100s:	0

ODI Bowling & Fielding
Wickets:	3	Runs:	86
Best Bowling:	2/35	Average:	28.66
5 WM:	0	Catches:	13
Stumpings:	3		

A 'jack-of-all-trades' keeper, Aamer Malik scored his two Test centuries in successive Tests against India in 1990 and was a handy right arm medium pacer. However, Malik could not cement a permanent place in the side and played just 14 Tests over eight years.

MALIK, Munir

Born: July 10, 1934
Batting: Right handed
Bowling: Right arm medium-fast

Tests
Test Career: 1959-62
Cap Number: 35
Tests Played: 3

Test Batting
Innings:	4	Runs:	7
Highest Score:	4	Average:	2.33
No. 50s:	0	No. 100s:	0

Test Bowling & Fielding
Wickets:	9	Runs:	358
Best Bowling:	5/128	Average:	39.77
5 WI:	1	10 WM:	0
Catches:	1	Stumpings:	0

A tireless right arm pace bowler who made his Test debut against Australia at Karachi in 1959. He was selected on the 1962 tour of England where he played in a further two Tests, taking a career best 5/128 at Headingley. Munir bowled marathon spells during his three Tests and his determination arguably warrented further Test selection.

MALIK, Naseer Ahmed

Born: February 1, 1950
Batting: Right handed
Bowling: Right arm medium-fast

One Day Internationals
ODI Career: 1975
ODIs Played: 3

ODI Batting
Innings:	1	Runs:	0
Highest Score:	0	Average:	0.00
No. 50s:	0	No. 100s:	0

ODI Bowling & Fielding
Wickets:	5	Runs:	98
Best Bowling:	2/97	Average:	19.60
5 WM:	0	Catches:	0
Stumpings:	0		

A right arm medium pace bowler from Faisalabad who took the wickets of Rick McCosker and Doug Walters in his first ODI against Australia during the 1975 World Cup.

MALIK, Saleem

Born: April 16, 1963
Batting: Right handed
Bowling: Right arm medium

Tests
Test Career: 1982-99
Cap Number: 90
Tests Played: 103

Test Batting
Innings:	154	Runs:	5,768
Highest Score:	237	Average:	43.69
No. 50s:	29	No. 100s:	15

Test Bowling & Fielding
Wickets:	5	Runs:	414
Best Bowling:	1/3	Average:	82.80
5 WI:	0	10 WM:	0
Catches:	65	Stumpings:	0

One Day Internationals
ODI Career: 1982-99
ODIs Played: 284

ODI Batting
Innings:	257	Runs:	7,193
Highest Score:	102	Average:	32.84
No. 50s:	47	No. 100s:	5

ODI Bowling & Fielding
Wickets:	89	Runs:	2,978
Best Bowling:	5/35	Average:	33.40
5 WM:	0	Catches:	82
Stumpings:	0		

There was never a doubt about Saleem Malik's talent from the moment he scored 100 not out on debut against Sri Lanka at Karachi in 1982. Over a 17 year career, the stylish right hand batsman amassed 5,768 runs to become Pakistan's third highest run scorer. Named 'Wisden Cricketer of the Year' for 1988, Malik made 15 centuries, with a highest score of 237 against Australia at Rawalpindi in 1994, captained his nation in 12 Tests and was second only to Javed Miandad as the most 'capped' Pakistan Test player. With these credentials, Saleem Malik should have been heralded as a legend of Pakistani cricket. However, sadly for Malik, his name will be forever linked with scandal and controversy as the once admired figure became the first player to receive a life ban, from all forms of the game, for match fixing.

MALIK, Shoaib

Born:	February 1, 1982
Batting:	Right handed
Bowling:	Right arm off-break

Tests

Test Career:	2001-06
Cap Number:	169
Tests Played:	15

Test Batting

Innings:	24	Runs:	798
Highest Score:	148*	Average:	39.90
No. 50s:	4	No. 100s:	1

Test Bowling & Fielding

Wickets:	13	Runs:	748
Best Bowling:	4/42	Average:	57.53
5 WI:	0	10 WM:	0
Catches:	5	Stumpings:	0

One Day Internationals

ODI Career:	1999-06
ODIs Played:	118

ODI Batting

Innings:	103	Runs:	3,102
Highest Score:	143	Average:	33.71
No. 50s:	18	No. 100s:	5

ODI Bowling & Fielding

Wickets:	98	Runs:	3,310
Best Bowling:	4/19	Average:	33.77
5 WM:	0	Catches:	39
Stumpings:	0		

Pakistan's most versatile current day player, Shoaib Malik has been used as an opener, middle order batsman and tail-ender in both forms of the game. He made his Test debut against Bangladesh at Multan in 2001 as an off-spinner but with the vast improvement in his batting, Malik is now recognised as a genuine all-rounder. With a healthy batting average of 39.90, Malik has scored one Test century - a match saving 148 not out against Sri Lanka where he batted out the entire last day. Upon the death of his father in January 2006, Malik had to pull out of the Third Test against India but came back to play in the ODI series, where he scored 90, 95, and 108. He was an automatic selection for the 2006 tour of England but had to be sent home due to a reoccurring elbow injury. Blessed with an abundance of natural ability and leadership qualities, Malik is seen as a potential future captain.

MASOOD SHAH, Asif

Born:	January 23, 1946
Batting:	Right handed
Bowling:	Right arm medium-fast

Tests

Test Career:	1969-77
Cap Number:	58
Tests Played:	16

Test Batting

Innings:	19	Runs:	93
Highest Score:	30*	Average:	10.33
No. 50s:	0	No. 100s:	0

Test Bowling & Fielding

Wickets:	38	Runs:	1,568
Best Bowling:	5/111	Average:	41.26
5 WI:	1	10 WM:	0
Catches:	5	Stumpings:	0

One Day Internationals

ODI Career:	1973-77
ODIs Played:	7

ODI Batting

Innings:	3	Runs:	10
Highest Score:	6	Average:	5.00
No. 50s:	0	No. 100s:	0

ODI Bowling & Fielding

Wickets:	5	Runs:	234
Best Bowling:	2/9	Average:	46.80
5 WM:	0	Catches:	1
Stumpings:	0		

A tall and strongly built right arm pace bowler Asif Masood was a consistent performer in his 16 Tests. He made his debut against England in front of his home crowd at Lahore in 1969 and took his career best figures of 5/111 also against England in 1971 at Edgbaston.

MATHIAS, Wallis

Born:	February 4, 1935
Batting:	Right handed
Bowling:	Right arm medium

Tests

Test Career:	1955-62
Cap Number:	23
Tests Played:	36

Test Batting

Innings:	21	Runs:	783
Highest Score:	77	Average:	23.72
No. 50s:	3	No. 100s:	0

Test Bowling & Fielding

Wickets:	0	Runs:	20
Best Bowling:		Average:	0.00
5 WI:	0	10 WM:	0
Catches:	0	Stumpings:	0

One of the finest fieldsmen of his era, Wallis Mathias grasped 22 catches in 21 matches. His soft hands, much in a same vain as Australia's Mark Waugh, made tough slip catches look relatively simple. A right handed middle order batsman, Mathias made his Test debut against New Zealand at Dhaka in 1955. And while he didn't score a Test century he played some very important cameo roles, especially against the West Indies. Mathias, the first non Muslim to represent Pakistan at Test level, was a popular and respected member of the side.

MEHDI, Tanvir

Born:	November 7, 1972
Batting:	Right handed
Bowling:	Right arm medium-fast

One Day Internationals

ODI Career:	1992		
ODIs Played:	1		

ODI Batting

Innings:	1	Runs:	0
Highest Score:	0	Average:	0.00
No. 50s:	0	No. 100s:	0

ODI Bowling & Fielding

Wickets:	1	Runs:	72
Best Bowling:	1/72	Average:	72.00
5 WM:	0	Catches:	0
Stumpings:	0		

A pace bowler from Lahore, Mehdi took one wicket - that of Nick Fairbrother at a cost of 72 runs in his first and only ODI against England at The Oval in 1992.

MIANDAD, Mohammed Javed

Born:	June 12, 1957
Batting:	Right handed
Bowling:	Right arm leg-break

Tests

Test Career:	1976-93		
Cap Number:	71		
Tests Played:	124		

Test Batting

Innings:	189	Runs:	8,832
Highest Score:	280*	Average:	52.57
No. 50s:	43	No. 100s:	23

Test Bowling & Fielding

Wickets:	17	Runs:	682
Best Bowling:	3/74	Average:	40.11
5 WI:	0	10 WM:	0
Catches:	93	Stumpings:	1

One Day Internationals

ODI Career:	1975-96		
ODIs Played:	233		

ODI Batting

Innings:	218	Runs:	7,381
Highest Score:	119*	Average:	41.70
No. 50s:	50	No. 100s:	8

ODI Bowling & Fielding

Wickets:	7	Runs:	297
Best Bowling:	2/22	Average:	42.42
5 WM:	0	Catches:	71
Stumpings:	2		

Pakistan's greatest ever scorer at Test level, the fiery middle order batsman may have had his detractors but his ability with the bat cannot be questioned. A cricketer of immense concentration, he made sure the scoreboard was always ticking over with his faultless timing and placement. Miandad's Test debut, against New Zealand in Lahore, was spectacular. With his side reeling at 4/55 and Richard Hadlee in full flight, the debutant made 163 in a 281 run partnership with Asif Iqbal. A double century in the same series cemented his spot in the powerful Pakistani batting line-up and the youngster who originally was selected in the national one day side as a bowling all rounder was on the way to a long and fruitful Test career. In 1978/79 he showed that he could handle all pitches with 160 not out against New Zealand in Christchurch and an unbeaten century on the bouncy Perth pitch later that summer. His highest Test score, 280 not out was struck against the Indians at Hyderabad in 1982/83. Of his 23 Test centuries he converted six of them into double tons and boasts the incredible record of having hit over 200 in a Test innings against five separate nations. Equally effective as a one day cricketer, he played in the first six World Cup tournaments and was a member of Pakistan's victorious World Cup squad of 1992 where he scored a valuable 58 in the final against England at the MCG. His 139 run partnership with skipper Imran Khan set Pakistan on their way to a historic, and in many ways, an unexpected victory. Overall, he represented his country in over 200 ODI's. Possibly his most famous moment came against India in the final of the 1986 Australasian Cup when he guided Pakistan to victory with a last ball six off Chetan Sharma. A sharp cover fieldsman, but an intense individual, Miandad had the knack of rubbing opponents and occasionally teammates the wrong way. In 1981 he famously clashed with Australian fast bowler Dennis Lillee at the WACA. The images of Miandad raising his bat after contact was made between the two remains one of the game's most infamous images. Javed Miandad captained his country in 34 Tests between 1979 and 1993 and was named Wisden 'Cricketer of the Year' for 1982. Post retirement he has held the coaching position in Pakistan on various occasions but run-ins with players and officials meant that he was never fully accepted in the position. His nephew, Faisal Iqbal, is a middle order batsman with the current day side.

MIR, Pervez Jamil

Born:	September 24, 1953
Batting:	Right handed
Bowling:	Right arm medium-fast

One Day Internationals

ODI Career:	1975-77		
ODIs Played:	3		

ODI Batting

Innings:	3	Runs:	26
Highest Score:	18	Average:	13.00
No. 50s:	0	No. 100s:	0

ODI Bowling & Fielding

Wickets:	3	Runs:	77
Best Bowling:	1/17	Average:	25.66
5 WM:	0	Catches:	2
Stumpings:	0		

Pervez Mir was a member of Pakistan's 1975 World Cup squad. A medium pace bowler, Mir's first international wicket was that of West Indian great Viv Richards. He played three ODI's over a three year period.

MOHAMMAD, Gul

Born:	February 10, 2019
Batting:	Left handed
Bowling:	Left arm medium

Tests
Test Career:	1946-56		
Cap Number:	24		
Tests Played:	9		

Test Batting
Innings:	17	Runs:	205
Highest Score:	34	Average:	12.81
No. 50s:	0	No. 100s:	0

Test Bowling & Fielding
Wickets:	2	Runs:	24
Best Bowling:	2/21	Average:	12.00
5 WI:	0	10 WM:	0
Catches:	3	Stumpings:	0

An elegant left handed batsmen and outstanding fielder in his day, Gul Mohammad made his debut against England at Lords in 1946 and played a further seven Tests for India. He finished his career playing one Test for Pakistan in 1956-57 against Australia. One of a handful of players to have represented two countries at Test level.

MOHAMMAD, Hanif
Born:	December 21, 1934
Batting:	Right handed
Bowling:	Right arm off-break
	Wicket Keeper

Tests
Test Career:	1952-69		
Cap Number:	4		
Tests Played:	55		

Test Batting
Innings:	97	Runs:	3,915
Highest Score:	337	Average:	43.98
No. 50s:	15	No. 100s:	12

Test Bowling & Fielding
Wickets:	1	Runs:	95
Best Bowling:	1/1	Average:	95.00
5 WI:	0	10 WM:	0
Catches:	40	Stumpings:	0

One of the greats of Pakistani cricket, Hanif Mohammed became the first man to 'keep wickets' for Pakistan when he played in their inaugural Test against India at Delhi, in 1952. Apart from being the premier gloveman, Hanif doubled as an opener and scored his country's first half century with 51 in the first innings. In a stellar career spanning almost two decades Hanif scored 12 centuries including a patient 337 against West Indies in Bridgetown in 1958 which, at 970 minutes, is still the longest century in Test history. It is also remains the highest Test score by a Pakistan batsman. Hanif Mohammed was appointed captain of his country in 1964 and led the side in 11 Tests until he was succeeded by Saeed Ahmed in 1968. His younger brother Mushtaq also captainedPakistan while older brother Wazir and youngest sibling Sadiq also represented their country at Test level.

MOHAMMAD, Khan
Born:	January 1, 1928
Batting:	Right handed
Bowling:	Right arm medium-fast

Tests
Test Career:	1952-58		
Cap Number:	8		
Tests Played:	13		

Test Batting
Innings:	17	Runs:	100
Highest Score:	26	Average:	10.00
No. 50s:	0	No. 100s:	0

Test Bowling & Fielding
Wickets:	54	Runs:	1,292
Best Bowling:	6/21	Average:	23.92
5 WI:	4	10 WM:	0
Catches:	4	Stumpings:	0

A right arm fast-medium pacer who was given the new ball in Pakistan's first ever Test against India at Delhi in 1952. Khan Mohammed took a career best 6/21 from 16 overs against New Zealand at Dhaka in 1952.

MOHAMMAD, Mushtaq
Born:	November 22, 1943
Batting:	Right handed
Bowling:	Right arm leg-break

Tests
Test Career:	1959-79		
Cap Number:	31		
Tests Played:	57		

Test Batting
Innings:	100	Runs:	3,643
Highest Score:	201	Average:	39.17
No. 50s:	19	No. 100s:	10

Test Bowling & Fielding
Wickets:	79	Runs:	2,309
Best Bowling:	5/28	Average:	29.28
5 WI:	3	10 WM:	0
Catches:	42	Stumpings:	0

One Day Internationals
ODI Career:	1973-78
ODIs Played:	10

ODI Batting
Innings:	9	Runs:	209
Highest Score:	55	Average:	34.83
No. 50s:	1	No. 100s:	0

ODI Bowling & Fielding
Wickets:	0	Runs:	0
Best Bowling:		Average:	0.00
5 WM:	0	Catches:	3
Stumpings:	0		

One of four brothers to represent Pakistan at Test level, Mushtaq Mohammad, at 15 years and 124 days became the youngest Test cricketer when he made his debut against West Indies at Lahore in 1959. While there has been some conjecture about his correct age over the years, the record stood until 1996 when fellow countryman Hasan Raza was selected to play against Zimbabwe at Faisalabad aged 14 and 227 days. And as in Mushtaq's case there have also been some questions raised about Raza's official age. An accomplished middle order batsman and occasional leg spinner, Mushtaq scored the first of his ten Test centuries - 101 against India at Delhi, in 1961, aged 17 years and 78 days, thus etching his name into the record books for a second time as the youngest player in history to score a Test century. The record stood for 40 years until Bangladesh's Mohammad Ashraful, aged 17 years and 61 days, notched up his first century against Sri Lanka in 2001. The younger brother of the legendary Hanif and Wazir, and older brother of Sadiq, Mushtaq became the second sibling (after Hanif) to lead his country when he was appointed captain in 1976, taking over from Majid Khan. A dynamic leader, Mushtaq, captained Pakistan in 19 Tests, for eight wins, seven draws and four losses - the best win/loss ratio by any Pakistan captain up until that point in time. But during the Australian summer of 1977/78, Mushtaq surrendered his tenure to Wasim Bari when he and fellow high profile countrymen, Imran Khan, Majid Khan, Asif Iqbal and Zaheer Abbas decided to join the Kerry Packer led World Series Cricket in its inaugural year. It was almost certain that the so called 'rebels' would be suspended if not expelled indefinitely from the Test side. But almost immediately upon their return, the temptation to play cricketers of this calibre proved too great for the match committee. A consistent performer over two decades, Mushtaq, a master of the sweep shot, averaged just under 40 in Tests and scored a sensational double century against New Zealand in Dunedin in 1972/73. As a bowler he took five wickets in an innings on three occasions, his best a memorable 5/28 against the West Indies at Trinidad, in 1977. Mushtaq was also a member of Pakistan's inaugural World Cup squad of 1975 and played ten One Day Internationals for his country.

MOHAMMAD, Nazar

Born: March 5, 1921
Batting: Right handed
Bowling: Right arm medium

Tests
Test Career: 1952
Cap Number: 10
Tests Played: 5

Test Batting
Innings:	8	Runs:	277
Highest Score:	124*	Average:	39.57
No. 50s:	1	No. 100s:	1

Test Bowling & Fielding
Wickets:	0	Runs:	4
Best Bowling:	0/4	Average:	0.00
5 WI:	0	10 WM:	0
Catches:	7	Stumpings:	0

One of three unrelated 'Mohammads' to play in Pakistan's inaugural Test against India in 1952, Nazar Mohammad opened the batting on this historic occasion with namesake Hanif Mohammad. The pair put on 64 in an impressive first up performance. The father of the popular Mudassar Nazar, Mohammad was not only the first Pakistan batsman to make a Test century but also the first to 'carry his bat' in Test cricket when he scored 124 not out against India at Lucknow in 1952.

MOHAMMAD, Sadiq

Born: May 3, 1945
Batting: Left handed
Bowling: Left arm leg-break

Tests
Test Career: 1969-81
Cap Number: 61
Tests Played: 41

Test Batting
Innings:	74	Runs:	2,579
Highest Score:	166	Average:	35.81
No. 50s:	10	No. 100s:	5

Test Bowling & Fielding
Wickets:	0	Runs:	98
Best Bowling:		Average:	0.00
5 WI:	0	10 WM:	0
Catches:	28	Stumpings:	0

One Day Internationals
ODI Career: 1973-80
ODIs Played: 19

ODI Batting
Innings:	19	Runs:	383
Highest Score:	74	Average:	21.27
No. 50s:	2	No. 100s:	0

ODI Bowling & Fielding
Wickets:	2	Runs:	26
Best Bowling:	2/20	Average:	13.00
5 WM:	0	Catches:	5
Stumpings:	0		

A member of the legendary Mohammad brethren, Sadiq Mohammad became the fourth brother to play Test cricket. He was also the youngest and only left-hander. Sadiq made his debut against New Zealand, at Karachi in 1969, in familiar surrounds when he opened the batting with brother Hanif and later put on a 33 run partnership with Mushtaq. After making 69 in the first innings, Sadiq looked to set to score consecutive half centuries until he was unfortunately run out for 37. Although he didn't reach the heights of Hanif and Mushtaq, who both captained Pakistan at various stages, Sadiq's record was quite respectable in it's own right. He scored five centuries and ten fifties from 41 Tests in his 12 year career. He came of age in the 1972/73 season when he scored three centuries in three months. His first was a solid 137 against Australia at the MCG, followed by his highest career score of 166, against New Zealand at Wellington and then registered his first century on home soil with 119 against England at Lahore. Sadiq played in 19 ODI's and opened the batting in Pakistan's World Cup sides of 1975 and '79.

MOHAMMAD, Shoaib

Born: January 8, 1961
Batting: Right handed
Bowling: Right arm off-break

Tests
Test Career:	1983-95		
Cap Number:	97		
Tests Played:	45		

Test Batting
Innings:	68	Runs:	2,705
Highest Score:	203*	Average:	44.34
No. 50s:	13	No. 100s:	7

Test Bowling & Fielding
Wickets:	5	Runs:	170
Best Bowling:	2/8	Average:	34.00
5 WI:	0	10 WM:	0
Catches:	22	Stumpings:	0

One Day Internationals
ODI Career:	1984-93
ODIs Played:	63

ODI Batting
Innings:	58	Runs:	1,269
Highest Score:	126*	Average:	24.40
No. 50s:	8	No. 100s:	1

ODI Bowling & Fielding
Wickets:	20	Runs:	725
Best Bowling:	3/20	Average:	36.25
5 WM:	0	Catches:	13
Stumpings:	0		

The son of the legendary Hanif Mohammad, Shoaib was a dour and honest opening batsman who played 45 serviceable Tests for his country between 1983 to 1995. He scored seven centuries, including two double centuries of 203 not out - both in 1990. The first against India at Lahore and the second against New Zealand at Karachi.

MOHAMMAD, Wazir
Born:	December 22, 1929
Batting:	Right handed
Bowling:	Right arm medium

Tests
Test Career:	1952-59
Cap Number:	14
Tests Played:	20

Test Batting
Innings:	33	Runs:	801
Highest Score:	189	Average:	27.62
No. 50s:	3	No. 100s:	2

Test Bowling & Fielding
Wickets:	0	Runs:	15
Best Bowling:		Average:	0.00
5 WI:	0	10 WM:	0
Catches:	5	Stumpings:	0

While he was the eldest of four brothers who played Test cricket for Pakistan, Wazir was arguably the lesser known. Hanif and Mushtaq both captained Pakistan while the youngest Sadiq played double the amount of Tests. Nevertheless, Wazir was a talented right hand middle order batsman who made his Test debut against India at Mumbai in 1952. He scored both his Test centuries (106 & 189) against the West Indies during the 1957/58 tour of the Caribbean.

MOIN-UL-ATIQ,
Born:	August 5, 1964
Batting:	Right handed
Bowling:	Right arm leg-break

One Day Internationals
ODI Career:	1988-89
ODIs Played:	5

ODI Batting
Innings:	5	Runs:	199
Highest Score:	105	Average:	39.80
No. 50s:	0	No. 100s:	1

ODI Bowling & Fielding
Wickets:	0	Runs:	0
Best Bowling:		Average:	0.00
5 WM:	0	Catches:	0
Stumpings:	0		

A right hand opener from Karachi, Moin-ul-Atiq made an impressive 46 on debut against West Indies at Trinidad in 1988. An accomplished batsman, he was named 'Man of the Match' when he scored his only ODI century against Bangladesh at Chitagong later that year. But even with an average of just under 40, he struggled to cement a regular place in Pakistan's ODI side.

MUFASIR-UL-HAQ,
Born:	August 16, 1944
Batting:	Right handed
Bowling:	Left arm medium-fast

Tests
Test Career:	1965
Cap Number:	51
Tests Played:	1

Test Batting
Innings:	1	Runs:	8
Highest Score:	8*	Average:	8.00
No. 50s:	0	No. 100s:	0

Test Bowling & Fielding
Wickets:	3	Runs:	84
Best Bowling:	2/50	Average:	28.00
5 WI:	0	10 WM:	0
Catches:	0	Stumpings:	0

A left arm pace bowler who performed admirably in his only Test against New Zealand at Christchurch where he took three wickets for the match. Mufasir-ul-Haq became an umpire after retiring but sadly passed away at age 38.

MUJTABA, Mohammad Asif
Born:	November 4, 1967
Batting:	Left handed
Bowling:	Left arm off-break

Tests
Test Career:	1986-97
Cap Number:	105
Tests Played:	25

Test Batting
Innings:	41	Runs:	928
Highest Score:	65*	Average:	24.42
No. 50s:	8	No. 100s:	0

Test Bowling & Fielding
Wickets:	4	Runs:	303
Best Bowling:	1/0	Average:	75.75
5 WI:	0	10 WM:	0
Catches:	19	Stumpings:	0

One Day Internationals
ODI Career:	1986-96
ODIs Played:	66

ODI Batting
Innings:	55	Runs:	1,068
Highest Score:	113*	Average:	26.04
No. 50s:	6	No. 100s:	1

ODI Bowling & Fielding
Wickets:	7	Runs:	658
Best Bowling:	2/38	Average:	94.00
5 WM:	0	Catches:	18
Stumpings:	0		

A left handed middle order batsman who is best remembered for taking 16 off Steve Waugh's final over at Bellerive in 1992 to force a tie.

MULLA, Salahuddin
Born:	February 14, 1947
Batting:	Right handed
Bowling:	Right arm off-break

Tests
Test Career:	1965-69
Cap Number:	52
Tests Played:	5

Test Batting
Innings:	8	Runs:	117
Highest Score:	34*	Average:	19.50
No. 50s:	0	No. 100s:	0

Test Bowling & Fielding
Wickets:	7	Runs:	187
Best Bowling:	2/36	Average:	26.71
5 WI:	0	10 WM:	0
Catches:	0	Stumpings:	0

An off-spinner from Karachi who made a gallant 34 not out on debut against New Zealand at Rawalpindi in 1965. A fringe player, he managed five Tests over four years.

MUNAF, Mohammad
Born:	November 2, 1935
Batting:	Right handed
Bowling:	Right arm medium-fast

Tests
Test Career:	1959-62
Cap Number:	33
Tests Played:	4

Test Batting
Innings:	7	Runs:	63
Highest Score:	19	Average:	12.60
No. 50s:	0	No. 100s:	0

Test Bowling & Fielding
Wickets:	11	Runs:	341
Best Bowling:	4/42	Average:	31.00
5 WI:	0	10 WM:	0
Catches:	0	Stumpings:	0

A right arm pace bowler who moved the ball off the seam, Munaf made his Test debut against Australia at Lahore in 1959. Although he showed early promise he played just four Tests in three years taking a personal best 4/42 against England at Lahore in 1961.

MUSHTAQ, Saqlain
Born:	December 29, 1976
Batting:	Right handed
Bowling:	Right arm off-break

Tests
Test Career:	1995-04
Cap Number:	134
Tests Played:	49

Test Batting
Innings:	78	Runs:	927
Highest Score:	101*	Average:	14.48
No. 50s:	2	No. 100s:	1

Test Bowling & Fielding
Wickets:	208	Runs:	6,206
Best Bowling:	8/164	Average:	29.83
5 WI:	13	10 WM:	3
Catches:	15	Stumpings:	0

One Day Internationals
ODI Career:	1995-03
ODIs Played:	169

ODI Batting
Innings:	98	Runs:	711
Highest Score:	37*	Average:	11.85
No. 50s:	0	No. 100s:	0

ODI Bowling & Fielding
Wickets:	288	Runs:	6,275
Best Bowling:	5/20	Average:	21.78
5 WM:	6	Catches:	40
Stumpings:	0		

The fifth highest Test wicket-taker for Pakistan, Saqlain is only headed by four of the greats in Wasim Akram, Waquar Younis, Imran Khan and Abdul Qadir. Always trying to out think the batsman, Saqlain was an energetic, yet at times an overworked performer for his country in 49 Tests. His best haul of 8/164 was against England at Lahore, in 2000. He is credited, in some corners, as having invented the 'doosra' and became the first off-spinner to take a hat-trick at ODI level - a feat he performed on two occasions. The first, against Zimbabwe, in 1996 at Peshawar and again against the Zimbabweans, this time at The Oval during the 1999 World Cup. He became the second player, after Chetan Sharma, to take a hat-trick in World Cup Competition. Saqlain fell out favour with the selectors after the 2004 series against India.

NAQQASH, Tahir
Born:	June 6, 1959
Batting:	Right handed
Bowling:	Right arm medium-fast

Tests
Test Career:	1982-85
Cap Number:	92
Tests Played:	15

Test Batting
Innings:	19	Runs:	300
Highest Score:	57	Average:	21.42
No. 50s:	1	No. 100s:	0

Test Bowling & Fielding

Wickets:	34	Runs:	1,398
Best Bowling:	5/40	Average:	41.11
5 WI:	2	10 WM:	0
Catches:	3	Stumpings:	0

One Day Internationals

ODI Career:	1980-85		
ODIs Played:	40		

ODI Batting

Innings:	23	Runs:	210
Highest Score:	61	Average:	15.00
No. 50s:	1	No. 100s:	0

ODI Bowling & Fielding

Wickets:	34	Runs:	1,240
Best Bowling:	3/23	Average:	36.47
5 WM:	0	Catches:	11
Stumpings:	0		

An explosive pace bowler who made his Test debut against Sri Lanka at Karachi in 1982. Took a career best 5/40 against England at Edgbaston but was more suited to One Day competition.

NAQVI, Syed Ali Urooj

Born:	March 19, 1977
Batting:	Right handed
Bowling:	Right arm off-break

Tests

Test Career:	1997-98		
Cap Number:	145		
Tests Played:	5		

Test Batting

Innings:	9	Runs:	242
Highest Score:	115	Average:	30.25
No. 50s:	0	No. 100s:	1

Test Bowling & Fielding

Wickets:	0	Runs:	11
Best Bowling:		Average:	0.00
5 WI:	0	10 WM:	0
Catches:	1	Stumpings:	0

An opener who came from nowhere to score a century on debut against South Africa at Rawalpindi in 1997. Unfortunately for Naqvi his debut proved a hard act to follow and subsequently disappeared from the international arena after five Tests.

NASIM-UL-GHANI,

Born:	May 14, 1941
Batting:	Left handed
Bowling:	Left arm off-break

Tests

Test Career:	1958-73		
Cap Number:	26		
Tests Played:	29		

Test Batting

Innings:	50	Runs:	747
Highest Score:	101	Average:	16.50
No. 50s:	2	No. 100s:	1

Test Bowling & Fielding

Wickets:	52	Runs:	1,959
Best Bowling:	6/67	Average:	37.67
5 WI:	2	10 WM:	0
Catches:	0	Stumpings:	0

One Day Internationals

ODI Career:	1973		
ODIs Played:	1		

ODI Batting

Innings:	1	Runs:	1
Highest Score:	1	Average:	1.00
No. 50s:	0	No. 100s:	0

ODI Bowling & Fielding

Wickets:	0	Runs:	0
Best Bowling:		Average:	0.00
5 WM:	0	Catches:	0
Stumpings:	0		

A jack of all trades cricketer who batted as opener and tail-ender, bowled off spin and medium pace, Nasim-ul-Ghani seemed to have the world at his feet when he made his Test debut against West Indies at age 16. His maiden Test century against England at Lords, in 1962, was made as a night watchman and there was no doubting the youngster's talent. But the 29 Tests and solitary ODI alongside his name suggest that the young man's potential was somewhat unfulfilled. After retiring in 1973 he later became a national selector and then match referee.

NAVED-UL-HASAN, Rana

Born:	February 28, 1978
Batting:	Right handed
Bowling:	Right arm medium-fast

Tests

Test Career:	2004-06		
Cap Number:	181		
Tests Played:	8		

Test Batting

Innings:	13	Runs:	176
Highest Score:	42*	Average:	17.60
No. 50s:	0	No. 100s:	0

Test Bowling & Fielding

Wickets:	16	Runs:	931
Best Bowling:	3/30	Average:	58.18
5 WI:	0	10 WM:	0
Catches:	3	Stumpings:	0

One Day Internationals

ODI Career:	2003-06		
ODIs Played:	45		

ODI Batting

Innings:	30	Runs:	278
Highest Score:	29	Average:	15.44
No. 50s:	0	No. 100s:	0

ODI Bowling & Fielding

Wickets:	77	Runs:	1,962
Best Bowling:	6/27	Average:	25.48
5 WM:	1	Catches:	9
Stumpings:	0		

Used predominantly as a back up bowler, Naved-ul-Hasanhas performed moderately at Test level and is finding it difficult to break into a side comprising the likes of Sami, Gul and Shoaib Akhtar. He made his Test debut against Sri Lanka at Karachi in 2005 and has been a solid performer at ODI level where captured a career best 6/27 against India in 2005.

NAWAZ, Sarfraz

Born: December 1, 1948
Batting: Right handed
Bowling: Right arm medium-fast

Tests
Test Career: 1969-84
Cap Number: 59
Tests Played: 55

Test Batting
Innings:	72	Runs:	1,045
Highest Score:	90	Average:	17.71
No. 50s:	4	No. 100s:	0

Test Bowling & Fielding
Wickets:	177	Runs:	5,798
Best Bowling:	9/86	Average:	32.75
5 WI:	4	10 WM:	1
Catches:	26	Stumpings:	0

One Day Internationals
ODI Career: 1973-84
ODIs Played: 45

ODI Batting
Innings:	31	Runs:	221
Highest Score:	34*	Average:	9.60
No. 50s:	0	No. 100s:	0

ODI Bowling & Fielding
Wickets:	63	Runs:	1,463
Best Bowling:	4/27	Average:	23.22
5 WM:	0	Catches:	8
Stumpings:	0		

Sarfraz Nazaz (full name Sarfraz Nawaz Malik) was one of the true characters of not only Pakistan, but also international cricket. While his style and physique did not mirror that of a primed athlete, Sarfraz's competitive nature combined with an uncanny ability to swing the ball either way made him one of cricket's toughest bowlers to negotiate. In various circles, Sarfraz is considered the inventor of reverse swing, which has become a regulation 'tool of trade' for Pakistani pacemen ever since. After making his Test debut in an eventually abandoned match against England at Karachi in 1969, Sarfraz became a permanent fixture in the Pakistan eleven. But it was the 1979 series in Australia, which produced both Sarfraz's best and most controversial performances. In a see-sawing First Test at the MCG, the Australians, at 3/305, looked comfortable chasing the target of 381 set by the visitors. Enter Sarfraz and unbeknownst to the parochial Melbourne crowd, and more importantly, the Australian eleven, one of the most incredible spells of seam bowling was about to unfold. After clean bowling the promising Allan Border for 105, opener Graeme Wood returned to the crease after having retired hurt in the first innings. But Wood's stay at the crease was shorter than his brave walk from the pavilion. With the score now at 5/305, the Aussies were still in the box seat as vice captain Kim Hughes was in the 80's and heading towards a certain hundred. And with just under 80 runs to get with five wickets in hand a draw was thought to be the worse possible scenario. However, Sarfraz wasn't quite done yet and in almost a blink of an eye, took the wickets of debutant Peter Sleep, Hughes, Wayne Clark and Rodney Hogg to have the Aussies reeling at 9/310. Young wicket-keeper Kevin Wright, stuck on one run at the non-strikers end, watched on helplessly as number eleven batsman and local hero, Allan Hurst, edged another superb inswinger to wicket-keeper Wasim Bari. The Australians fell 71 runs short and Sarfraz had taken a career best 9/86, including a devastating 33 ball spell of 7/1. It was the first time a Pakistani had taken nine wickets in an innings and was by far the best figures by a Pakistan bowler in Test cricket. If Sarfraz wasn't considered the 'villain' by the Aussie faithful for his heroics in the first Test in Melbourne, he was definitely 'lynch mob' material after the second and final Test in Perth. With the Australians again looking comfortable in their second innings chase at 0/87, opener Andrew Hilditch, at the non strikers end, picked up the 'dead' ball in his vicinity and politely returned it to the Pakistan fielders. Suddenly there was a huge shout from Sarfraz and the umpire had no choice but to adjudge Hilditch out 'handling the ball'. Hilditch became only the second man in Test history to be given out in this unusual and rather unsporting manner. While there may have been feelings of deja vu, a Sarfraz inspired revival was not on the agenda as the Australians coasted to a seven wicket victory. It is now almost impossible not to associate the incident anytime the name Hilditch is raised in conversation. Sarfraz played 55 Tests and 45 ODI's in all and was a member of Pakistan's 1975, '79 and '83 World Cup squads. Aside from the odd on-field controversy, Sarfraz's has left an invaluable legacy to world cricket, especially with regards to the art of swing bowling.

NAZAR, Mudassar

Born: April 6, 1956
Batting: Right handed
Bowling: Right arm medium

Tests
Test Career: 1976-89
Cap Number: 76
Tests Played: 76

Test Batting
Innings:	116	Runs:	4,114
Highest Score:	231	Average:	38.04
No. 50s:	17	No. 100s:	10

Test Bowling & Fielding
Wickets:	66	Runs:	2,532
Best Bowling:	6/32	Average:	38.36
5 WI:	1	10 WM:	0
Catches:	48	Stumpings:	0

One Day Internationals
ODI Career: 1977-89
ODIs Played: 123

ODI Batting

Innings:	116	Runs:	2,655
Highest Score:	95	Average:	25.04
No. 50s:	16	No. 100s:	0

ODI Bowling & Fielding

Wickets:	112	Runs:	3,481
Best Bowling:	5/28	Average:	31.08
5 WM:	1	Catches:	21
Stumpings:	0		

The son of Nazar Mohammad who played in Pakistan's inaugural Test against India in 1952, the somewhat under-rated Mudassar Nazar did not attract the limelight as his more famous contemporaries such as Javed, Imran, Zaheer and Sarfraz but was admired throughout the cricket world for the manner in which he played the game. Sixth on the list for the most runs scored in Tests for Pakistan, Mudassar, an opener like his father, made his Test debut against Australia, in Adelaide, in 1976 and over the years forged a long-standing partnership with Mohsin Khan. Mudassar scored the first of his ten centuries (114) against England at Lahore in 1977. His next six were all against India, including his highest score of 231 at Hyderabad in 1983. He came close to reaching another double century the following year but was caught by Syed Kirmani of the bowling of Yadav for 199 at Faisalabad. An all-rounder of some description, Mudassar bowled medium pace swing quite effectively and possessed a fluent and almost graceful style, which is best described as a side-on, sliding action. Before long he was widely regarded as the specialist 'partnership breaker' as the part time seamer would invariably change the course of an innings when given the ball after all else had failed. As a third change bowler against England at Lords in 1982, Mudassar ripped through the English batting taking six of the first seven wickets giving him a career best 6/32 and thus steered his country to a rare ten-wicket victory on English soil. Equally adept at both forms of the game, Mudassar, a member of Pakistan's World Cup squads of 1979, '86 and '87, was a fine one-day player, some say better suited at the shorter version, and represented Pakistan on 123 occasions. In 2005, Mudassar became head coach of Kenya.

NAZIR, Aamer

Born:	January 2, 1971
Batting:	Right handed
Bowling:	Right arm medium-fast

Tests

Test Career:	1993-95
Cap Number:	127
Tests Played:	6

Test Batting

Innings:	11	Runs:	31
Highest Score:	11	Average:	6.20
No. 50s:	0	No. 100s:	0

Test Bowling & Fielding

Wickets:	20	Runs:	597
Best Bowling:	5/46	Average:	29.85
5 WI:	1	10 WM:	0
Catches:	2	Stumpings:	0

One Day Internationals

ODI Career:	1993-95
ODIs Played:	9

ODI Batting

Innings:	3	Runs:	13
Highest Score:	9*	Average:	13.00
No. 50s:	0	No. 100s:	0

ODI Bowling & Fielding

Wickets:	11	Runs:	346
Best Bowling:	3/43	Average:	31.45
5 WM:	0	Catches:	0
Stumpings:	0		

Played just the six Tests and took a career best 5/46 against Zimbabwe at Harare in 1995.

NAZIR, Imran

Born:	December 16, 1981
Batting:	Right handed
Bowling:	Right arm leg-break

Tests

Test Career:	1999-02
Cap Number:	157
Tests Played:	8

Test Batting

Innings:	13	Runs:	427
Highest Score:	131	Average:	32.84
No. 50s:	1	No. 100s:	2

Test Bowling & Fielding

Wickets:	0	Runs:	0
Best Bowling:		Average:	0.00
5 WI:	0	10 WM:	0
Catches:	4	Stumpings:	0

One Day Internationals

ODI Career:	1999-04
ODIs Played:	61

ODI Batting

Innings:	61	Runs:	1,392
Highest Score:	105*	Average:	23.59
No. 50s:	8	No. 100s:	1

ODI Bowling & Fielding

Wickets:	1	Runs:	48
Best Bowling:	1/3	Average:	48.00
5 WM:	0	Catches:	19
Stumpings:	0		

An aggressive right hand opener who made 64 on debut against Sri Lanka at Lahore. Showed plenty of promise with his two Test centuries against West Indies at Barbados and New Zealand at Lahore but struggled to hold a permanent Test spot. A valuable One Day contributor where he has made 61 appearances.

NAZIR, Shahid

Born:	December 4, 1977
Batting:	Right handed
Bowling:	Right arm medium-fast

Tests

Test Career:	1996-99
Cap Number:	139
Tests Played:	8

Test Batting
Innings:	9	Runs:	55
Highest Score:	18	Average:	7.85
No. 50s:	0	No. 100s:	0

Test Bowling & Fielding
Wickets:	17	Runs:	566
Best Bowling:	5/33	Average:	33.29
5 WI:	1	10 WM:	0
Catches:	3	Stumpings:	0

One Day Internationals
ODI Career:	1996-00
ODIs Played:	17

ODI Batting
Innings:	8	Runs:	25
Highest Score:	8	Average:	25.00
No. 50s:	0	No. 100s:	0

ODI Bowling & Fielding
Wickets:	19	Runs:	649
Best Bowling:	3/14	Average:	34.15
5 WM:	0	Catches:	4
Stumpings:	0		

An energetic paceman from Faisalabad who, on debut, took 5/33 against Zimbabwe at Sheikhupura in 1996.

NAZIR (JNR), Mohammad

Born:	March 8, 1946
Batting:	Right handed
Bowling:	Right arm off-break

Tests
Test Career:	1969-83
Cap Number:	60
Tests Played:	14

Test Batting
Innings:	18	Runs:	144
Highest Score:	29*	Average:	18.00
No. 50s:	0	No. 100s:	0

Test Bowling & Fielding
Wickets:	34	Runs:	1,124
Best Bowling:	7/99	Average:	33.05
5 WI:	3	10 WM:	0
Catches:	4	Stumpings:	0

One Day Internationals
ODI Career:	1980-84
ODIs Played:	4

ODI Batting
Innings:	3	Runs:	4
Highest Score:	2*	Average:	4.00
No. 50s:	0	No. 100s:	0

ODI Bowling & Fielding
Wickets:	3	Runs:	156
Best Bowling:	2/37	Average:	52.00
5 WM:	0	Catches:	0
Stumpings:	0		

A slow right arm off-spinner, Mohammad Nazir jnr made his Test debut against New Zealand at Karachi in 1969 alongside youngsters Sadiq Mohammad and Zaheer Abbas. While his fellow debutants went on to enjoy highly distinguished careers, it was the stocky and unassuming Nazir who initially stole the limelight. Batting at number nine, Nazir compiled an unbeaten 29, which added some respectability to Pakistan's first innings score of 220 when at one stage reaching 200 looked ambitious. It was to remain Nazir's highest Test score in his 14 year career but he wasn't in the side for his batting. When given his opportunity with the ball, Nazir all but destroyed the New Zealand batting taking an unprecedented 7/99. But like his performance with the bat, Nazir's inaugural bowling figures were never surpassed.

OMAR (UMAR), Qasim Ali

Born:	February 9, 1957
Batting:	Right handed
Bowling:	Right arm medium

Tests
Test Career:	1983-86
Cap Number:	96
Tests Played:	26

Test Batting
Innings:	43	Runs:	1,502
Highest Score:	210	Average:	36.63
No. 50s:	5	No. 100s:	3

Test Bowling & Fielding
Wickets:	0	Runs:	0
Best Bowling:		Average:	0.00
5 WI:	0	10 WM:	0
Catches:	15	Stumpings:	0

One Day Internationals
ODI Career:	1983-87
ODIs Played:	31

ODI Batting
Innings:	31	Runs:	642
Highest Score:	69	Average:	22.92
No. 50s:	4	No. 100s:	0

ODI Bowling & Fielding
Wickets:	0	Runs:	0
Best Bowling:		Average:	0.00
5 WM:	0	Catches:	4
Stumpings:	0		

A short but athletically built cricketer, Qasim Omar became a crowd favourite, world wide, with his buoyant enthusiasm and happy-go-lucky nature. Born in Kenya, Omar played his first Test against India at Jalandhar in 1983. A brilliant fielder, Omar scored two double centuries, including a highest score of 210 against India at Faisalabad in 1984, but unfortunately his career lasted just four years - at a time when international cricket was craving for some new characters. He became one of the first cricketers to raise concerns about corruption at international level.

PERVEZ, Arshad

Born:	October 1, 1953
Batting:	Right handed
Bowling:	Right arm medium

One Day Internationals
ODI Career:	1978
ODIs Played:	2

ODI Batting
Innings:	2	Runs:	11
Highest Score:	8	Average:	5.50
No. 50s:	0	No. 100s:	0

ODI Bowling & Fielding
Wickets:	0	Runs:	0
Best Bowling:		Average:	0.00
5 WM:	0	Catches:	0
Stumpings:	0		

A right hand opener who made his ODI debut against England at Lahore in 1977.

PERVEZ, Saleem
Born:	September 9, 1947
Batting:	Right handed
Bowling:	Right arm medium-fast

One Day Internationals
ODI Career:	1980		
ODIs Played:	1		

ODI Batting
Innings:	1	Runs:	18
Highest Score:	18	Average:	18.00
No. 50s:	0	No. 100s:	0

ODI Bowling & Fielding
Wickets:	0	Runs:	0
Best Bowling:		Average:	0.00
5 WM:	0	Catches:	0
Stumpings:	0		

An opening batsman from Lahore who played his one and only ODI against West Indies in front of his home crowd.

QADEER, Javed
Born:	August 25, 1976
Batting:	Right handed
	Wicket Keeper

One Day Internationals
ODI Career:	1995		
ODIs Played:	1		

ODI Batting
Innings:	1	Runs:	12
Highest Score:	12	Average:	12.00
No. 50s:	0	No. 100s:	0

ODI Bowling & Fielding
Wickets:	0	Runs:	0
Best Bowling:		Average:	0.00
5 WM:	0	Catches:	1
Stumpings:	0		

A wicket-keeper from Karachi who took one catch in his only ODI against Sri Lanka at Sharjah in 1995.

QADIR, Abdul
Born:	September 15, 1955
Batting:	Right handed
Bowling:	Right arm leg-break

Tests
Test Career:	1977-90		
Cap Number:	78		
Tests Played:	67		

Test Batting
Innings:	77	Runs:	1,029
Highest Score:	61	Average:	15.59
No. 50s:	3	No. 100s:	0

Test Bowling & Fielding
Wickets:	236	Runs:	7,742
Best Bowling:	9/56	Average:	32.80
5 WI:	15	10 WM:	5
Catches:	15	Stumpings:	0

One Day Internationals
ODI Career:	1983-93		
ODIs Played:	104		

ODI Batting
Innings:	68	Runs:	641
Highest Score:	41*	Average:	15.26
No. 50s:	0	No. 100s:	0

ODI Bowling & Fielding
Wickets:	132	Runs:	3,454
Best Bowling:	5/44	Average:	26.16
5 WM:	5	Catches:	21
Stumpings:	0		

A lively leg spinner whose bouncy run up was complimented with a whippy wrist action, Abdul Qadir (Khan) stands fourth on Pakistan's all time Test wicket takers. And if not for the emergence of Shane Warne a few years later, Qadir could well have been rated as the greatest leggie the game had ever seen. After making an uneventful debut against England on his home patch, Lahore, in 1977, Qadir soon became a regular in the Pakistan spin attack teaming up with the experienced Iqbal Qasim. Rated by opposition batsman as 'unplayable' when in the zone, Qadir took five wickets in an innings on 15 occasions and ten in a match five times. His best haul of 9/56 in 1987, overtook Sarfraz Nawaz's 9/86 (v Australia at the MCG, '78) as the best figures by a Pakistan bowler. Qadir's effort occurred at the same venue and against the same opposition as per his debut - v England at Lahore. A handy late order batsman whose defiant nature would frustrate pace bowlers who were trying to quickly clean up the tail, Qadir also performed admirably at ODI level. He was a member of Pakistan's World Cup squads of 1983 & 1987 and helped dismiss the notion that leg-spinners did not have a place in the shorter version of the game.

QASIM, Iqbal
Born:	August 6, 1953
Batting:	Left handed
Bowling:	Left arm off-break

Tests
Test Career:	1976-78		
Cap Number:	75		
Tests Played:	50		

Test Batting
Innings:	57	Runs:	549
Highest Score:	56	Average:	13.07
No. 50s:	1	No. 100s:	0

Test Bowling & Fielding
Wickets:	171	Runs:	4,807
Best Bowling:	7/49	Average:	28.11
5 WI:	8	10 WM:	2
Catches:	42	Stumpings:	0

One Day Internationals
ODI Career:	1977-88		
ODIs Played:	15		

ODI Batting
Innings:	7	Runs:	39
Highest Score:	13	Average:	6.50
No. 50s:	0	No. 100s:	0

ODI Bowling & Fielding

Wickets:	12	Runs:	500
Best Bowling:	3/13	Average:	41.66
5 WM:	0	Catches:	3
Stumpings:	0		

A dour, left arm off spinner who may not have had the flair of an Abdul Qadir but was highly respected for his craft and consistent enough to hold a regular place in the Test side throughout the mid 70's and 80's. An excellent close to the wicket fielder, the diminutive Iqbal Qasim played in exactly fifty Tests and captured five wickets in an innings on eight occasions - his best haul, a frugal, yet destructive 7/49 from 42 overs, against Australia at Karachi in 1980. With his four wickets in the first innings, this effort gave Qasim his best match figures of 11/118. Although he rarely gave opposition bowlers much to worry about, Qasim did score the one Test fifty.

RAJA, Rameez Hasan

Born:	August 14, 1962
Batting:	Right handed
Bowling:	Right arm leg-break

Tests

Test Career:	1984-97		
Cap Number:	99		
Tests Played:	57		

Test Batting

Innings:	94	Runs:	2,833
Highest Score:	122	Average:	31.83
No. 50s:	22	No. 100s:	2

Test Bowling & Fielding

Wickets:	0	Runs:	0
Best Bowling:		Average:	0.00
5 WI:	0	10 WM:	0
Catches:	34	Stumpings:	0

One Day Internationals

ODI Career:	1985-97		
ODIs Played:	198		

ODI Batting

Innings:	197	Runs:	5,841
Highest Score:	119*	Average:	32.09
No. 50s:	31	No. 100s:	9

ODI Bowling & Fielding

Wickets:	0	Runs:	10
Best Bowling:	0/10	Average:	0.00
5 WM:	0	Catches:	33
Stumpings:	0		

Although he scored a pair of 'ones' on debut against England at Karachi in 1983, many pundits believed that there was an abundance of talent waiting to be unearthed from the younger brother of Wasim Raja. But in 57 Tests, Rameez could only manage just the two centuries with a modest average of 31.83. Highly rated by the match committee, Rameez was appointed captain of Pakistan when Salim Malik was implicated in match fixing scandals. He captained his country in five Tests for just the one win. In retirement, Raja works as a television commentator and is a respected authority on Pakistan cricket.

RAJA, Wasim Hasan

Born:	July 3, 1952
Batting:	Left handed
Bowling:	Left arm leg-break

Tests

Test Career:	1973-85		
Cap Number:	67		
Tests Played:	57		

Test Batting

Innings:	92	Runs:	2,821
Highest Score:	125	Average:	36.16
No. 50s:	18	No. 100s:	4

Test Bowling & Fielding

Wickets:	51	Runs:	1,826
Best Bowling:	4/50	Average:	35.80
5 WI:	0	10 WM:	0
Catches:	0	Stumpings:	0

One Day Internationals

ODI Career:	1973-85		
ODIs Played:	54		

ODI Batting

Innings:	45	Runs:	782
Highest Score:	60	Average:	22.34
No. 50s:	0	No. 100s:	0

ODI Bowling & Fielding

Wickets:	21	Runs:	687
Best Bowling:	4/25	Average:	32.71
5 WM:	0	Catches:	24
Stumpings:	0		

The older brother of former captain Rameez, Wasim Raja was a serviceable all-rounder in his 57 Tests for Pakistan. Like Rameez, Wasim too was a leg break bowler, but unlike his younger sibling, Wasim was totally left sided. He made his Test debut against New Zealand at Wellington in 1973 on the same day as Sir Richard Hadlee and scored a respectable 41 batting at number six. In all, Wasim scored 18 fifties and four centuries with a highest score of 125 against India at Jullundur in 1984. In August 2006, Wasim sadly died of a heart-attack while playing in a social game of cricket. He was aged 54.

RAMZAN, Mohammad

Born:	December 25, 1970
Batting:	Right handed
Bowling:	Right arm medium

Tests

Test Career:	1997		
Cap Number:	147		
Tests Played:	1		

Test Batting

Innings:	2	Runs:	36
Highest Score:	29	Average:	18.00
No. 50s:	0	No. 100s:	0

Test Bowling & Fielding

Wickets:	0	Runs:	0
Best Bowling:		Average:	0.00
5 WI:	0	10 WM:	0
Catches:	1	Stumpings:	0

Another inductee to the 'One Test Club', Ramzan, a right hand batsman from Faisalabad, played his solitary Test against South Africa at Rawalpindi, in 1997.

RANA, Azmat

Born:	November 3, 1951
Batting:	Left handed
Bowling:	Right arm off-break

Tests

Test Career:	1980
Cap Number:	85
Tests Played:	1

Test Batting

Innings:	1	Runs:	49
Highest Score:	49	Average:	49.00
No. 50s:	0	No. 100s:	0

Test Bowling & Fielding

Wickets:	0	Runs:	0
Best Bowling:	0	Average:	0.00
5 WI:	0	10 WM:	0
Catches:	0	Stumpings:	0

One Day Internationals

ODI Career:	1978
ODIs Played:	2

ODI Batting

Innings:	2	Runs:	42
Highest Score:	22*	Average:	42.00
No. 50s:	0	No. 100s:	0

ODI Bowling & Fielding

Wickets:	0	Runs:	0
Best Bowling:		Average:	0.00
5 WM:	0	Catches:	0
Stumpings:	0		

A right hand batsman from Lahore who made an impressive 49, batting at number four against Australia in front of his home crowd. Azmat Rana is the younger brother of Shafqat Rana.

RANA, Mansoor

Born:	December 27, 1962
Batting:	Right handed
Bowling:	Right arm off-break

One Day Internationals

ODI Career:	1990
ODIs Played:	2

ODI Batting

Innings:	2	Runs:	15
Highest Score:	10	Average:	7.50
No. 50s:	0	No. 100s:	0

ODI Bowling & Fielding

Wickets:	0	Runs:	7
Best Bowling:		Average:	0.00
5 WM:	0	Catches:	0
Stumpings:	0		

From Lahore, off-spinner Rana played two ODI's (against Sri Lanka and Australia) in the Austral-Asia Cup competition held in Sharjah in 1990.

RANA, Maqsood

Born:	August 1, 1972
Batting:	Right handed
Bowling:	Right arm medium-fast

One Day Internationals

ODI Career:	1990
ODIs Played:	1

ODI Batting

Innings:	1	Runs:	5
Highest Score:	5	Average:	5.00
No. 50s:	0	No. 100s:	0

ODI Bowling & Fielding

Wickets:	0	Runs:	11
Best Bowling:	0/11	Average:	0.00
5 WM:	0	Catches:	0
Stumpings:	0		

A right arm pace bowler from Lahore who was run out for five in his only ODI against Australia, at the MCG in 1990.

RANA, Shafqat

Born:	October 10, 1943
Batting:	Right handed
Bowling:	Right arm medium

Tests

Test Career:	1964-69
Cap Number:	46
Tests Played:	5

Test Batting

Innings:	7	Runs:	221
Highest Score:	95	Average:	31.57
No. 50s:	2	No. 100s:	0

Test Bowling & Fielding

Wickets:	1	Runs:	9
Best Bowling:	1/2	Average:	9.00
5 WI:	0	10 WM:	0
Catches:	5	Stumpings:	0

A right-hand middle order batsman who played just the five Tests, Shafqat Rana fell five runs short of a Test century against New Zealand at Lahore in 1969. He was on track again in his last Test against the Kiwis at Dhaka before being run out for 65.

RASHID, Haroon

Born:	March 25, 1953
Batting:	Right handed
Bowling:	Right arm medium

Tests

Test Career:	1977-83
Cap Number:	77
Tests Played:	23

Test Batting

Innings:	36	Runs:	1,217
Highest Score:	153	Average:	34.77
No. 50s:	5	No. 100s:	3

Test Bowling & Fielding

Wickets:	0	Runs:	3
Best Bowling:	0/3	Average:	0.00
5 WI:	0	10 WM:	0
Catches:	16	Stumpings:	0

One Day Internationals

ODI Career:	1977-82
ODIs Played:	12

ODI Batting

Innings:	10	Runs:	166
Highest Score:	63*	Average:	20.75
No. 50s:	1	No. 100s:	0

ODI Bowling & Fielding
Wickets:	0	Runs:	0
Best Bowling:		Average:	0.00
5 WM:	0	Catches:	3
Stumpings:	0		

Although described as a volatile batsman, Haroon Rashid certainly kept the turnstiles clicking. He made his debut against Australia in 1977 where he scored a valuable 57 in Pakistan's memorable eight wicket win at the Sydney Cricket Ground. Rashid along with regulars Wasim Bari, Sarfraz Nawaz and Sikander Bakht basically held the Pakistani 'fort' together shortly after the Australian tour as key players such as Zaheer Abbas, Imran and Majid Khan, Mushtaq Mohammad and Asif Iqbal signed on to play in World Series Cricket's inaugural year. Rashid took the opportunity to consolidate his position by scoring successive centuries against England that year. Ironically, Rashid and Sarfraz were lured to World Series Cricket a year later. But like his 'rebel' predecessors, Rashid was welcomed back to the Test side and scored his third century and highest score of 153 against new Test cricket entrants, Sri Lanka, at Karachi in 1981.

RAUF, Atif

Born:	March 3, 1964
Batting:	Right handed
Bowling:	Right arm off-break

Tests

Test Career:	1994
Cap Number:	131
Tests Played:	1

Test Batting
Innings:	2	Runs:	25
Highest Score:	16	Average:	12.50
No. 50s:	0	No. 100s:	0

Test Bowling & Fielding
Wickets:	0	Runs:	0
Best Bowling:		Average:	0.00
5 WI:	0	10 WM:	0
Catches:	0	Stumpings:	0

A right hand batsman from Lahore who came in at 'first drop' in his solitary Test against New Zealand at Christchurch in 1994.

RAZA, Akram

Born:	November 22, 1964
Batting:	Right handed
Bowling:	Right arm off-break

Tests

Test Career:	1989-95
Cap Number:	114
Tests Played:	9

Test Batting
Innings:	12	Runs:	153
Highest Score:	32	Average:	15.30
No. 50s:	0	No. 100s:	0

Test Bowling & Fielding
Wickets:	13	Runs:	732
Best Bowling:	3/46	Average:	56.30
5 WI:	0	10 WM:	0
Catches:	8	Stumpings:	0

One Day Internationals

ODI Career:	1989-95
ODIs Played:	49

ODI Batting
Innings:	25	Runs:	193
Highest Score:	33*	Average:	17.54
No. 50s:	0	No. 100s:	0

ODI Bowling & Fielding
Wickets:	38	Runs:	1,611
Best Bowling:	3/18	Average:	42.39
5 WM:	0	Catches:	19
Stumpings:	0		

An off-break bowler who made his Test debut against India at Lahore in 1989. Enjoyed greater success at ODI level taking a career best 3/18 against New Zealand a Dunedin.

RAZA, Hasan

Born:	March 11, 1982
Batting:	Right handed
Bowling:	Right arm off-break

Tests

Test Career:	1996-05
Cap Number:	140
Tests Played:	7

Test Batting
Innings:	10	Runs:	235
Highest Score:	68	Average:	26.11
No. 50s:	2	No. 100s:	0

Test Bowling & Fielding
Wickets:	0	Runs:	0
Best Bowling:		Average:	0.00
5 WI:	0	10 WM:	0
Catches:	5	Stumpings:	0

One Day Internationals

ODI Career:	1996-99
ODIs Played:	16

ODI Batting
Innings:	13	Runs:	242
Highest Score:	77	Average:	18.61
No. 50s:	1	No. 100s:	0

ODI Bowling & Fielding
Wickets:	0	Runs:	0
Best Bowling:		Average:	0.00
5 WM:	0	Catches:	1
Stumpings:	0		

Hasan Raza is credited as being the youngest ever Test player when, in 1996, he made his debut against Zimbabwe at Faisalabad, aged 14 years and 227 days. However, there have been considerable doubts placed upon the authenticity of his reported age.

RAZA, Kashif

Born:	December 26, 1979
Batting:	Right handed
Bowling:	Right arm medium

One Day Internationals

ODI Career:	2001
ODIs Played:	1

ODI Batting

Innings:	1	Runs:	2
Highest Score:	2*	Average:	2.00
No. 50s:	0	No. 100s:	0

ODI Bowling & Fielding

Wickets:	1	Runs:	36
Best Bowling:	1/36	Average:	36.00
5 WM:	0	Catches:	0
Stumpings:	0		

A right arm medium pacer who played his maiden ODI against Sri Lanka, at Sharjah, in 2001 where he took the wicket of Romesh Kaluwitharana.

RAZZAQ, Abdul

Born:	December 2, 1979
Batting:	Right handed
Bowling:	Right arm medium-fast

Tests

Test Career:	1999-06		
Cap Number:	158		
Tests Played:	43		

Test Batting

Innings:	72	Runs:	1,828
Highest Score:	134	Average:	28.56
No. 50s:	6	No. 100s:	3

Test Bowling & Fielding

Wickets:	95	Runs:	3,521
Best Bowling:	5/35	Average:	37.06
5 WI:	1	10 WM:	0
Catches:	12	Stumpings:	0

One Day Internationals

ODI Career:	1999-06		
ODIs Played:	212		

ODI Batting

Innings:	184	Runs:	4,201
Highest Score:	112	Average:	30.44
No. 50s:	21	No. 100s:	2

ODI Bowling & Fielding

Wickets:	230	Runs:	7,054
Best Bowling:	6/35	Average:	30.66
5 WM:	0	Catches:	3
Stumpings:	0		

A hard hitting all-rounder who many believe the best is yet to come. Such is his talent that Abdul Razzaq can turn it on with the bat in One Day competition one minute, and then bat with resilience and control, at Test level, the next. He has scored three centuries in Tests, his first against England at Faisalabad and his next two against Bangladesh in 2001/02. With the ball, he has taken 95 wickets with a career best 5/35. In June 2000, and just six month shy of his 21st birthday, Razzaq captured the wickets of Sri Lankans Kaluwitharana, Herath, and Pushpakumara in successive balls to make him the youngest player in history take a Test hat-trick.

RIZVI, Ali Hussain

Born:	January 6, 1974
Batting:	Right handed
Bowling:	Right arm leg-break

Tests

Test Career:	1997		
Cap Number:	148		
Tests Played:	1		

Test Batting

Innings:	0	Runs:	0
Highest Score:	0	Average:	0.00
No. 50s:	0	No. 100s:	0

Test Bowling & Fielding

Wickets:	2	Runs:	72
Best Bowling:	2/72	Average:	36.00
5 WI:	0	10 WM:	0
Catches:	0	Stumpings:	0

A leg spinner who took two wickets on debut against South Africa, at Sheikhupura, in a rain effected Test match.

RIZWAN-UZ-ZAMAN,

Born:	September 4, 1961
Batting:	Right handed
Bowling:	Right arm leg-break

Tests

Test Career:	1981-89		
Cap Number:	88		
Tests Played:	11		

Test Batting

Innings:	19	Runs:	345
Highest Score:	60	Average:	19.16
No. 50s:	3	No. 100s:	0

Test Bowling & Fielding

Wickets:	4	Runs:	46
Best Bowling:	3/26	Average:	11.50
5 WI:	0	10 WM:	0
Catches:	4	Stumpings:	0

One Day Internationals

ODI Career:	1981		
ODIs Played:	3		

ODI Batting

Innings:	3	Runs:	20
Highest Score:	14	Average:	6.65
No. 50s:	0	No. 100s:	0

ODI Bowling & Fielding

Wickets:	0	Runs:	0
Best Bowling:		Average:	0.00
5 WM:	0	Catches:	2
Stumpings:	0		

Rizwan-uz-Zaman was selected for the tour of Australia in 1981/82 and made his debut on the fast WACA wicket at Perth. Shortly after opening the innings with Mudassar Nazar, Rizwan was dismissed for a duck, somewhat fittingly by local hero Terry Alderman. But the debutant wasn't alone as Pakistan crumbled to be all out for 62. He went on to play in another ten Tests managing a highest score of 60.

SAEED, Shahid

Born:	January 6, 1966
Batting:	Right handed
Bowling:	Right arm medium

Tests

Test Career:	1989
Cap Number:	110
Tests Played:	1

Test Batting
Innings:	1	Runs:	12
Highest Score:	12	Average:	12.00
No. 50s:	0	No. 100s:	0

Test Bowling & Fielding
Wickets:	0	Runs:	43
Best Bowling:		Average:	0.00
5 WI:	0	10 WM:	0
Catches:	0	Stumpings:	0

One Day Internationals
ODI Career:	1989-93		
ODIs Played:	10		

ODI Batting
Innings:	10	Runs:	141
Highest Score:	50	Average:	14.10
No. 50s:	1	No. 100s:	0

ODI Bowling & Fielding
Wickets:	3	Runs:	159
Best Bowling:	2/20	Average:	53.00
5 WM:	0	Catches:	2
Stumpings:	0		

A right hand batsman from Lahore who played one Test against India at Karachi in 1989.

SAJJAD HASAN, Pervez
Born: August 30, 1942
Batting: Right handed
Bowling: Left arm leg-break

Tests
Test Career:	1964-73		
Cap Number:	45		
Tests Played:	19		

Test Batting
Innings:	20	Runs:	123
Highest Score:	24	Average:	13.66
No. 50s:	0	No. 100s:	0

Test Bowling & Fielding
Wickets:	59	Runs:	1,410
Best Bowling:	7/74	Average:	23.89
5 WI:	3	10 WM:	0
Catches:	9	Stumpings:	0

A left arm leg-spinner from Lahore, Pervez Sajjad seemed to save his best for the Kiwis as his three hauls of five wickets in an innings all occurred against New Zealand. His best effort was an amazing 7/74 at Lahore. In all, Pervez played just 19 Tests over a nine year period after making his debut against Australia at Karachi in 1964.

SAMI, Mohammad
Born: February 24, 1981
Batting: Right handed
Bowling: Right arm fast

Tests
Test Career:	2001-06		
Cap Number:	167		
Tests Played:	27		

Test Batting
Innings:	41	Runs:	318
Highest Score:	49	Average:	10.60
No. 50s:	0	No. 100s:	0

Test Bowling & Fielding
Wickets:	68	Runs:	3,296
Best Bowling:	5/36	Average:	48.47
5 WI:	2	10 WM:	0
Catches:	4	Stumpings:	0

One Day Internationals
ODI Career:	2001-06		
ODIs Played:	76		

ODI Batting
Innings:	41	Runs:	227
Highest Score:	23	Average:	10.31
No. 50s:	0	No. 100s:	0

ODI Bowling & Fielding
Wickets:	109	Runs:	3,093
Best Bowling:	5/10	Average:	28.37
5 WM:	1	Catches:	18
Stumpings:	0		

The spearhead of the current day Pakistan bowling attack, and one of the quickest bowlers in the world, Mohammad Sami made an impressive start to his Test career taking eight wickets for the match against New Zealand at Auckland in 2001. Just as adept at the shorter version of the game, he took his best ODI figures of 5/10 from 7.5 overs against the Kiwis, in 2003. Sami is one of only two bowlers to have taken a hat-trick in both Test cricket and ODIs, (Wasim Akram is the other). His ODI hat-trick occurred in 2001 against the West Indies at Sharjah, and completed the double a year later when he wrapped up the Sri Lankan tail at Lahore. Although his figures suggest he is not the most economical of bowlers, Sami, for the moment, remains Pakistan's most viable option with the new ball. He was selected with Umar Gul as the frontline bowlers for the 2006 tour of England.

SARFRAZ, Akhtar
Born: February 20, 1976
Batting: Left handed
Bowling: Right arm off-break

One Day Internationals
ODI Career:	1997-98		
ODIs Played:	4		

ODI Batting
Innings:	4	Runs:	66
Highest Score:	25	Average:	16.50
No. 50s:	0	No. 100s:	0

ODI Bowling & Fielding
Wickets:	0	Runs:	0
Best Bowling:		Average:	0.00
5 WM:	0	Catches:	0
Stumpings:	0		

A left hand middle order batsman who made his international debut against West Indies at Sharjah in 1997.

SATTI, Yasir Arafat
Born: March 12, 1982
Batting: Right handed
Bowling: Right arm medium

One Day Internationals
ODI Career:	2000-06		
ODIs Played:	6		

ODI Batting
Innings:	4	Runs:	21
Highest Score:	10	Average:	7.00
No. 50s:	0	No. 100s:	0

ODI Bowling & Fielding
Wickets:	3	Runs:	200
Best Bowling:	1/28	Average:	66.66
5 WM:	0	Catches:	1
Stumpings:	0		

A right arm medium pacer, Yasir Arafat's ODI record over his six year career to date is modest at best. But he does have time on his side if he is to give himself every opportunity to cement a spot in the ODI squad.

SHAHID YAQOOB, Haafiz
Born: May 10, 1963
Batting: Right handed
Bowling: Right arm medium-fast

One Day Internationals
ODI Career: 1988
ODIs Played: 3

ODI Batting
Innings:	3	Runs:	11
Highest Score:	7*	Average:	11.00
No. 50s:	0	No. 100s:	0

ODI Bowling & Fielding
Wickets:	3	Runs:	112
Best Bowling:	2/56	Average:	37.33
5 WM:	0	Catches:	0
Stumpings:	0		

A right arm pace bowler from Lahore who took the wicket of West Indian great Gordon Greenidge on debut at St Johns, Antigua, in 1988.

SHARPE, Duncan Albert
Born: August 3, 1937
Batting: Right handed
Bowling: Right arm off-break
Wicket Keeper

Tests
Test Career: 1959
Cap Number: 32
Tests Played: 3

Test Batting
Innings:	6	Runs:	134
Highest Score:	56	Average:	22.33
No. 50s:	1	No. 100s:	0

Test Bowling & Fielding
Wickets:	0	Runs:	0
Best Bowling:		Average:	0.00
5 WI:	0	10 WM:	0
Catches:	2	Stumpings:	0

Duncan Sharpe enjoyed a memorable Test debut when he top scored in both innings against Australia at Dhaka in 1959. A confident stroke player and capable wicketkeeper, all three of Sharpe's Tests were against Australia. Ironically he immigrated to Australia in 1960 and played Sheffield Shield cricket for South Australia.

SIKANDER, Mohammad Iqbal
Born: December 19, 1958
Batting: Right handed
Bowling: Right arm leg-break

One Day Internationals
ODI Career: 1992
ODIs Played: 4

ODI Batting
Innings:	1	Runs:	1
Highest Score:	1*	Average:	1.00
No. 50s:	0	No. 100s:	0

ODI Bowling & Fielding
Wickets:	3	Runs:	147
Best Bowling:	1/30	Average:	49.00
5 WM:	0	Catches:	0
Stumpings:	0		

A leg spinner from Karachi, Sikander made his international debut against the West Indies at the Melbourne Cricket Ground during the ODI tri-angular series held in the Australian summer of 1991/92.

SOHAIL, Mohammad Aamer
Born: September 14, 1966
Batting: Left handed

Tests
Test Career: 1992-00
Cap Number: 122
Tests Played: 47

Test Batting
Innings:	83	Runs:	2,823
Highest Score:	205	Average:	35.28
No. 50s:	13	No. 100s:	5

Test Bowling & Fielding
Wickets:	25	Runs:	1,049
Best Bowling:	4/54	Average:	41.96
5 WI:	0	10 WM:	0
Catches:	36	Stumpings:	0

One Day Internationals
ODI Career: 1990-00
ODIs Played: 156

ODI Batting
Innings:	155	Runs:	4,780
Highest Score:	134	Average:	31.86
No. 50s:	31	No. 100s:	5

ODI Bowling & Fielding
Wickets:	85	Runs:	3,703
Best Bowling:	4/22	Average:	43.56
5 WM:	0	Catches:	49
Stumpings:	0		

An attacking left hand opening batsman who was a member of Pakistan's victorious World Cup side of 1992, Aamer Sohail became a permanent fixture in Pakistan's Test and One Day sides for just under a decade. After making his Test debut against England at Edgbaston, he formed a solid partnership with fellow left hander Saeed Anwar. The pair provided the foundations for many a Pakistani innings over the years but it was Sohail's 298 run stand with Ijaz Ahmed, against the West Indies at Karachi in 1997, which remains a Pakistan 'first wicket' record. Sohail scored 160 of the record partnership and remarkably was the second time that year that he had scored exactly that number against the West Indies. In all Sohail scored five Test centuries, his first was a career best 205 against England, at Old Trafford, in 1992. Sohail captained Pakistan in six Tests in 1998 and became first captain to lead Pakistan to victory over South Africa. He voiced his concerns during the time of the match fixing scandal which many believe may have compromised his career as a result.

UMAR, Taufeeq
Born: June 20, 1981
Batting: Left handed
Bowling: Right arm off-break

Tests
Test Career: 2001-05
Cap Number: 170
Tests Played: 24
Test Batting
Innings:	44	Runs:	1,711
Highest Score:	135	Average:	40.73
No. 50s:	9	No. 100s:	4

Test Bowling & Fielding
Wickets:	0	Runs:	36
Best Bowling:		Average:	0.00
5 WI:	0	10 WM:	0
Catches:	32	Stumpings:	0

One Day Internationals
ODI Career: 2001-05
ODIs Played: 19
ODI Batting
Innings:	19	Runs:	447
Highest Score:	81*	Average:	24.83
No. 50s:	3	No. 100s:	0

ODI Bowling & Fielding
Wickets:	1	Runs:	85
Best Bowling:	1/49	Average:	85.00
5 WM:	0	Catches:	9
Stumpings:	0		

Taufeeq Umar became the eighth Pakistan batsman to score a century on debut when he and fellow left hand opener, Saeed Anwar, both scored tons to put on 168 for the first wicket, against Bangladesh at Multan in 2001. But it was somewhat of a 'free for all' as Inzamam, Yousuf Youhana and Abdul Razzaq also reached triple figures in the first innings as Pakistan clobbered their way to 3-546 and an eventual innings and 264 run victory. Added to the 2006 tour squad of England, Umar has scored four Test centuries in his career to date and with a healthy average of just over 40, will no doubt be considered in Pakistan's long term plans.

WASIM, Mohammad
Born: August 8, 1977
Batting: Right handed
Wicket Keeper

Tests
Test Career: 1996-00
Cap Number: 142
Tests Played: 18
Test Batting
Innings:	28	Runs:	783
Highest Score:	192	Average:	30.11
No. 50s:	2	No. 100s:	2

Test Bowling & Fielding
Wickets:	0	Runs:	0
Best Bowling:		Average:	0.00
5 WI:	0	10 WM:	0
Catches:	22	Stumpings:	2

One Day Internationals
ODI Career: 1996-00
ODIs Played: 25
ODI Batting
Innings:	25	Runs:	543
Highest Score:	76	Average:	23.60
No. 50s:	3	No. 100s:	0

ODI Bowling & Fielding
Wickets:	0	Runs:	0
Best Bowling:		Average:	0.00
5 WM:	0	Catches:	9
Stumpings:	0		

A player who experienced the ultimate roller-coaster debut against New Zealand at Lahore in 1996. Wasim's first innings duck was followed by an unbeaten 109 in the second making him the fourth Pakistani to score a century on debut. A part time keeper, he scored his second century and highest score of 192 against Zimbabwe in 1997 but like his debut form, Wasim's career was inconsistent averaging just over 30 in 18 Tests.

WASTI, Wajahatullah
Born: November 11, 1974
Batting: Right handed
Bowling: Right arm off-break

Tests
Test Career: 1999-00
Cap Number: 156
Tests Played: 6
Test Batting
Innings:	10	Runs:	329
Highest Score:	133	Average:	36.55
No. 50s:	0	No. 100s:	2

Test Bowling & Fielding
Wickets:	0	Runs:	8
Best Bowling:		Average:	0.00
5 WI:	0	10 WM:	0
Catches:	7	Stumpings:	0

One Day Internationals
ODI Career: 1999-00
ODIs Played: 15
ODI Batting
Innings:	15	Runs:	349
Highest Score:	84	Average:	23.26
No. 50s:	1	No. 100s:	0

ODI Bowling & Fielding
Wickets:	3	Runs:	69
Best Bowling:	3/36	Average:	23.00
5 WM:	0	Catches:	5
Stumpings:	0		

An opening batsman who impressed in just six Test matches. He scored both centuries in the one Test against Sri Lanka at Lahore in 1999. He was run out in the first innings for 133 and was looking to 'carry his bat' in the second when, on 121, skipper Wasim Akram declared the innings closed at 8/314.

WAZIR, Syed Khalid

Born:	April 27, 1936
Batting:	Right handed
Bowling:	Right arm medium-fast

Tests

Test Career:	1954
Cap Number:	16
Tests Played:	2

Test Batting

Innings:	3	Runs:	14
Highest Score:	9*	Average:	7.00
No. 50s:	0	No. 100s:	0

Test Bowling & Fielding

Wickets:	0	Runs:	0
Best Bowling:		Average:	0.00
5 WI:	0	10 WM:	0
Catches:	0	Stumpings:	0

An all-rounder who was selected for the 1954 tour of England, Wazir played just the two Tests - both against England.

YOUHANA, Yousuf

Born:	August 27, 1974
Batting:	Right handed
Bowling:	Right arm medium

See Mohammad Yousuf.

YOUNIS, Waqar

Born:	November 16, 1971
Batting:	Right handed
Bowling:	Right arm fast

Tests

Test Career:	1989-03
Cap Number:	111
Tests Played:	87

Test Batting

Innings:	120	Runs:	1,010
Highest Score:	45	Average:	10.20
No. 50s:	0	No. 100s:	0

Test Bowling & Fielding

Wickets:	373	Runs:	8,788
Best Bowling:	7/76	Average:	23.56
5 WI:	22	10 WM:	5
Catches:	18	Stumpings:	0

One Day Internationals

ODI Career:	1989-03
ODIs Played:	262

ODI Batting

Innings:	139	Runs:	969
Highest Score:	37	Average:	10.30
No. 50s:	0	No. 100s:	0

ODI Bowling & Fielding

Wickets:	416	Runs:	9,919
Best Bowling:	7/36	Average:	23.84
5 WM:	13	Catches:	35
Stumpings:	0		

Renowned for mastering the art of reverse swing, Waqar Younis formed part of the most fearsome bowling double act in Pakistan's history when he partnered Wasim Akram during the 90's. The left/right arm combination terrorised batsmen world wide and not since Lillee and Thomson had world cricket seen such a genuine pace attack working as cohesively. The pair took nearly 800 wickets between and are the only bowlers to have overtaken Pakistan's greatest ever cricketer Imran Khan for most career Test wickets (Akram, 414 and Younis 373). Waqar's swinging yorkers became his trademark ball and because of his consistent accuracy, his average of 43.4 deliveries per wicket is the best strike rate of any Test bowler. Nicknamed the "Burewala Express", Waqar made his Test debut against India at Karachi in 1989, the same day as Sachin Tendulkar. Waqar impressed from the outset taking four wickets in the first innings including the wicket of the 'little master' who he comprehensively clean bowled. It was a sign of things to come as Waqar went on to take five wickets in an innings on 22 occasions and ten in a match, five times. His took a career best 7/86 against New Zealand, in the second Test at Lahore in 1990 but by the time the ink had dried, he again destroyed the Kiwi batting line-up with 7/76 in the following Test at Faisalabad. Not surprisingly, he was named 'Man of the Match' in both Tests and shared the 'Player of the Series' award with Martin Crowe and Shoaib Mohammad. Waqar's fiery pace combined with his deadly accuracy meant that he was just as suited to limited overs cricket as he was at Test. His 7/36 against England at Lords in 2001, where he took the first seven wickets of the innings, is a Pakistan record and again he is only second to Akram for most wickets in ODI's. Waqar captained his country in 17 Tests at various intervals between 1993 and 2003. Upon his retirement, Waqar became a television commentator.

YOUSUF, Mohammad

Born:	August 27, 1974
Batting:	Right handed
Bowling:	Right arm fast

Tests

Test Career:	1998-06
Cap Number:	152
Tests Played:	68

Test Batting

Innings:	114	Runs:	5,409
Highest Score:	223	Average:	51.51
No. 50s:	25	No. 100s:	18

Test Bowling & Fielding

Wickets:	0	Runs:	3
Best Bowling:	0/3	Average:	0.00
5 WI:	0	10 WM:	0
Catches:	58	Stumpings:	0

One Day Internationals

ODI Career:	1998-06
ODIs Played:	218

ODI Batting

Innings:	207	Runs:	7,306
Highest Score:	141*	Average:	41.04
No. 50s:	0	No. 100s:	0

ODI Bowling & Fielding

Wickets:	0	Runs:	1
Best Bowling:	0/1	Average:	0.00
5 WM:	0	Catches:	50
Stumpings:	0		

(Previously known as Yousuf Youhana). Upon his conversion to Islam in 2005, Mohammad Yousuf was known as Yousuf Youhana. Since his rather modest debut against South Africa at Durban in 1998, Yousuf has well established himself in Pakistani middle order and currently sits fourth, behind Javed Miandad, teammate Inzamam and Saleem Malik as the highest Test run scorer for Pakistan and holds the third highest average with 51.51. Of his 18 Test centuries, one of his most memorable was his 111 against Australia at the MCG when he was captained the side in Inzamam's absence. He followed up with his fourth double-century and career best 223 against England at Lahore in 2006. A delight to watch Yousuf is just as adept at the one-day game scoring over 7,000 runs at 41.00. Although in his early 30's, Yousuf has plenty of cricket left in him and barring any unforeseen injuries, should continue to pile on the runs for a few more years to come.

YOUSUF, Saleem

Born:	December 7, 1959
Batting:	Right handed
	Wicket Keeper

Tests

Test Career:	1982-90		
Cap Number:	91		
Tests Played:	32		

Test Batting

Innings:	44	Runs:	1,055
Highest Score:	91*	Average:	27.05
No. 50s:	5	No. 100s:	0

Test Bowling & Fielding

Wickets:	0	Runs:	0
Best Bowling:		Average:	0.00
5 WI:	0	10 WM:	0
Catches:	91	Stumpings:	13

One Day Internationals

ODI Career:	1982-90
ODIs Played:	86

ODI Batting

Innings:	62	Runs:	768
Highest Score:	62	Average:	17.86
No. 50s:	4	No. 100s:	0

ODI Bowling & Fielding

Wickets:	0	Runs:	0
Best Bowling:		Average:	0.00
5 WM:	0	Catches:	81
Stumpings:	22		

After a nation-wide search, the Pakistani selectors finally settled on Karachi born Saleem Yousuf as the eventual successor to long standing gloveman Wasim Bari. A superb keeper to spin bowling, Yousuf made his Test debut against Sri Lanka at Karachi in 1982 and amassed 13 stumpings in Tests and 22 at ODI level. Adept with the bat at both forms of the game, Yousef scored five fifties at Test level and fell nine runs short of a maiden Test century.

ZAHID, Agha

Born:	January 7, 1953
Batting:	Right handed
Bowling:	Right arm medium

Tests

Test Career:	1975		
Cap Number:	69		
Tests Played:	1		

Test Batting

Innings:	2	Runs:	15
Highest Score:	14	Average:	7.50
No. 50s:	0	No. 100s:	0

Test Bowling & Fielding

Wickets:	0	Runs:	0
Best Bowling:		Average:	0.00
5 WI:	0	10 WM:	0
Catches:	0	Stumpings:	0

From Lahore, Agha Zahid was another highly decorated Domestic player who managed just the one Test appearance, against West Indies at Lahore in 1975.

ZAHID, Mohammad

Born:	August 2, 1976
Batting:	Right handed
Bowling:	Right arm medium-fast

Tests

Test Career:	1996-03		
Cap Number:	144		
Tests Played:	5		

Test Batting

Innings:	6	Runs:	7
Highest Score:	6*	Average:	1.40
No. 50s:	0	No. 100s:	0

Test Bowling & Fielding

Wickets:	15	Runs:	502
Best Bowling:	7/66	Average:	33.46
5 WI:	1	10 WM:	1
Catches:	0	Stumpings:	0

One Day Internationals

ODI Career:	1996-02
ODIs Played:	11

ODI Batting

Innings:	4	Runs:	15
Highest Score:	7*	Average:	7.50
No. 50s:	0	No. 100s:	0

ODI Bowling & Fielding

Wickets:	10	Runs:	391
Best Bowling:	2/20	Average:	39.10
5 WM:	0	Catches:	1
Stumpings:	0		

Against New Zealand at Rawalpindi, Mohammad Zahid followed up his four wickets in the first innings with a match-winning 7/66 in the second, thus not only securing the 'Man of the Match' award but bestowing him with the honour of being the first Pakistan bowler to take

10 wickets on debut. A severe back injury limited his opportunities at international level.

ZAMAN, Farrukh
Born: April 2, 1956
Batting: Right handed
Bowling: Left arm off-break

Tests
Test Career: 1976
Cap Number: 72
Tests Played: 1

Test Batting
Innings:	0	Runs:	0
Highest Score:	0	Average:	0.00
No. 50s:	0	No. 100s:	0

Test Bowling & Fielding
Wickets:	0	Runs:	15
Best Bowling:		Average:	0.00
5 WI:	0	10 WM:	0
Catches:	0	Stumpings:	0

Farrukh Zaman was a left arm off-spinner who was given just ten overs to impress in his one and only Test match against New Zealand at Hyderabad in 1976.

ZIA, Junaid
Born: November 11, 1983
Batting: Right handed
Bowling: Right arm medium-fast

One Day Internationals
ODI Career: 2003
ODIs Played: 4

ODI Batting
Innings:	2	Runs:	2
Highest Score:	2*	Average:	2.00
No. 50s:	0	No. 100s:	0

ODI Bowling & Fielding
Wickets:	3	Runs:	127
Best Bowling:	3/21	Average:	42.33
5 WM:	0	Catches:	0
Stumpings:	0		

A super fit cricketer from Lahore who arguably deserved more chances than he got at the highest level. Zia made his ODI debut against Bangladesh at Multan in 2003.

ZULQARNAIN,
Born: May 25, 1962
Batting: Right handed
Wicket Keeper

Tests
Test Career: 1986
Cap Number: 103
Tests Played: 3

Test Batting
Innings:	4	Runs:	24
Highest Score:	13	Average:	6.00
No. 50s:	0	No. 100s:	0

Test Bowling & Fielding
Wickets:	0	Runs:	0
Best Bowling:		Average:	0.00
5 WI:	0	10 WM:	0
Catches:	8	Stumpings:	2

One Day Internationals
ODI Career: 1985-89
ODIs Played: 16

ODI Batting
Innings:	6	Runs:	18
Highest Score:	11*	Average:	6.00
No. 50s:	0	No. 100s:	0

ODI Bowling & Fielding
Wickets:	0	Runs:	0
Best Bowling:		Average:	0.00
5 WM:	0	Catches:	18
Stumpings:	5		

A fill-in wicket-keeper who took two stumpings on debut against Sri Lanka at Kandy in 1986.

South Africa

ABRAHAMS, Shafiek
Born: March 4, 1968
Batting: Right handed
Bowling: Right arm off-break

One Day Internationals
ODI Career: 2000
ODIs Played: 1

ODI Batting
Innings:	1	Runs:	16
Highest Score:	16*	Average:	0.00
No. 50s:	0	No. 100s:	0

ODI Bowling & Fielding
Wickets:	0	Runs:	40
Best Bowling:		Average:	0.00
5 WM:	0	Catches:	1
Stumpings:	0		

An off-break bowler from Port Elizabeth, Abrahams played one ODI against New Zealand, at Cape Town, in 2000.

ACKERMAN, Hylton Deon (HD)
Born: February 14, 1973
Batting: Right handed
Bowling: Right arm medium

Tests
Test Career: 1998
Cap Number: 268
Tests Played: 4

Test Batting
Innings:	8	Runs:	161
Highest Score:	57	Average:	20.12
No. 50s:	1	No. 100s:	0

Test Bowling & Fielding
Wickets:	0	Runs:	0
Best Bowling:		Average:	0.00
5 WI:	0	10 WM:	0
Catches:	1	Stumpings:	0

A top order batsman from Cape Town who played four Tests in 1998 but averaged just a tick over 20. He also plays for Leicestershire in England.

ADAMS, Paul Regan
Born: January 20, 1977
Batting: Right handed
Bowling: Left arm leg-break

Tests
Test Career: 1995-2004
Cap Number: 263
Tests Played: 45

Test Batting
Innings:	55	Runs:	360
Highest Score:	35	Average:	9.00
No. 50s:	0	No. 100s:	0

Test Bowling & Fielding
Wickets:	134	Runs:	4,405
Best Bowling:	7/128	Average:	32.87
5 WI:	4	10 WM:	1
Catches:	29	Stumpings:	0

One Day Internationals
ODI Career: 1996-2003
ODIs Played: 24

ODI Batting
Innings:	9	Runs:	66
Highest Score:	33*	Average:	16.50
No. 50s:	0	No. 100s:	0

ODI Bowling & Fielding
Wickets:	29	Runs:	815
Best Bowling:	3/26	Average:	28.10
5 WM:	0	Catches:	7
Stumpings:	0		

With arms and legs flaying in four different directions, Paul Adams bowling action has been described as a frog in a blender or less commonly as someone trying to steal the hubcaps off a moving car. Whatever the style, it was good enough to earn 45 Test caps and 134 wickets including ten in a single Test against Bangladesh at Chittagong in 2003. He recent years he has lost his spot in the side to the more economical finger spin of Nicky Boje, but Adams is still young enough to work his way back into the national side.

ADCOCK, Neil Amwin Treharne
Born: March 8, 1931
Batting: Right handed
Bowling: Right arm fast

Tests
Test Career: 1953-62
Cap Number: 189
Tests Played: 26

Test Batting
Innings:	39	Runs:	146
Highest Score:	24	Average:	5.40
No. 50s:	0	No. 100s:	0

Test Bowling & Fielding
Wickets:	104	Runs:	2,195
Best Bowling:	6/43	Average:	21.10
5 WI:	5	10 WM:	0
Catches:	4	Stumpings:	0

A tall right arm opening bowler from Transvaal and Natal who was his country's first paceman to take 100 Test wickets. He starred in his first Test series, taking 24 wickets in total, including eight in only his second Test. In 1958 he routed a strong Australian side to claim 6/43 in the first innings of the Test at Durban, with Neil Harvey and Richie Benaud falling cheaply to his aggressive bowling. In all his 104 wickets at 21.10 sees Adcock ranked twelfth overall in the Test averages for players who have taken 100 or more wickets.

AMLA, Hashim Mahomed

Born: March 31, 1983
Batting: Right handed
Bowling: Right arm medium

Tests
Test Career: 2004-
Cap Number: 295
Tests Played: 7

Test Batting
Innings:	13	Runs:	364
Highest Score:	149	Average:	28.00
No. 50s:	1	No. 100s:	1

Test Bowling & Fielding
Wickets:	0	Runs:	4
Best Bowling:		Average:	0.00
5 WI:	0	10 WM:	0
Catches:	6	Stumpings:	0

The talented stroke player from Natal has impressed in his short time at Test level after a stuttering start in which he scored only 62 from his first six innings. After countless appearances as 12th man, Amla returned the faith shown in him by selectors with a breakout innings against New Zealand at Newlands in 2006. His guarded 149 took almost seven hours to compile and secured his spot in the top order for the tour of Sri Lanka later that year. A devout Muslim of Indian descent, he was thrust into the public limelight on that tour of Sri Lanka when commentator Dean Jones was overheard calling him a terrorist.

ANDERSON, James Henry

Born: April 26, 1874
Batting: Right handed

Tests
Test Career: 1902
Cap Number: 55
Tests Played: 1

Test Batting
Innings:	2	Runs:	43
Highest Score:	32	Average:	21.50
No. 50s:	0	No. 100s:	0

Test Bowling & Fielding
Wickets:	0	Runs:	0
Best Bowling:		Average:	0.00
5 WI:	0	10 WM:	0
Catches:	1	Stumpings:	0

A batsman from Western Province who performed well in his only Test, scoring 32 and 11 against The Australians at Johannesburg in 1902.

ASHLEY, William Hare

Born: February 10, 1862
Batting: Right handed
Bowling: Left arm medium

Tests
Test Career: 1889
Cap Number: 12
Tests Played: 1

Test Batting
Innings:	2	Runs:	1
Highest Score:	1	Average:	0.50
No. 50s:	0	No. 100s:	0

Test Bowling & Fielding
Wickets:	7	Runs:	95
Best Bowling:	7/95	Average:	13.57
5 WI:	1	10 WM:	0
Catches:	0	Stumpings:	0

A slow left arm bowler, he captured seven wickets in his only spell for South Africa. Known as 'Gobo', he took 7/95 in the second Test against England at Cape Town in 1888/89.

BACHER, Adam Marc

Born: October 29, 1973
Batting: Right handed
Bowling: Right arm medium

Tests
Test Career: 1996-99
Cap Number: 266
Tests Played: 19

Test Batting
Innings:	33	Runs:	833
Highest Score:	96	Average:	26.03
No. 50s:	5	No. 100s:	0

Test Bowling & Fielding
Wickets:	0	Runs:	4
Best Bowling:		Average:	0.00
5 WI:	0	10 WM:	0
Catches:	11	Stumpings:	0

One Day Internationals
ODI Career: 1997-
ODIs Played: 13

ODI Batting
Innings:	13	Runs:	270
Highest Score:	56	Average:	20.76
No. 50s:	1	No. 100s:	0

ODI Bowling & Fielding
Wickets:	3	Runs:	64
Best Bowling:	2/36	Average:	21.33
5 WM:	0	Catches:	4
Stumpings:	0		

The nephew of former South African skipper Dr. Ali Bacher, he was a promising young opener when elevated to the national side in 1996. Adam Bacher seemed set for a long stay in the national side when he scored a fighting 96 against the strong Australian attack at Centurion in 1997 and another 96 later that year in Pakistan. From that point on he struggled and after failing to score a half century in his last eight Tests was permanently dropped form the side in 1999.

BACHER, Aron (Ali)

Born: May 24, 1942
Batting: Right handed
Bowling: Right arm leg-break

BACHER, Aron (Ali)

Tests
Test Career:	1965-70
Cap Number:	225
Tests Played:	12

Test Batting
Innings:	22	Runs:	679
Highest Score:	73	Average:	32.33
No. 50s:	6	No. 100s:	0

Test Bowling & Fielding
Wickets:	0	Runs:	0
Best Bowling:		Average:	0.00
5 WI:	0	10 WM:	0
Catches:	10	Stumpings:	0

Ali Bacher will always be better known as a leader than a player, first in his role as South African captain, and then as the administrator who promoted cricket as a multi-cultural sport in the new South Africa. The top order batsman had played just eight Tests when elevated to the captaincy for political reasons in 1969. It was already a difficult time for the game in South Africa with the cancellation of the 1968/69 tour by England, and increased calls for a blanket sporting boycott of the country by the international community. At the time a Jewish doctor with liberal views was considered a better choice to lead the Test side than an Afrikaner or Englishman. Whatever the reason, Bacher led South Africa's strongest ever side to a 4-0 whitewash of the touring Australians.

BALASKAS, Xenophon Constantine

Born:	October 15, 1910
Batting:	Right handed
Bowling:	Right arm leg-break

Tests
Test Career:	1930-39
Cap Number:	132
Tests Played:	9

Test Batting
Innings:	13	Runs:	174
Highest Score:	122*	Average:	14.50
No. 50s:	0	No. 100s:	1

Test Bowling & Fielding
Wickets:	22	Runs:	806
Best Bowling:	5/49	Average:	36.63
5 WI:	1	10 WM:	0
Catches:	5	Stumpings:	0

The chunky leg spinner had a short but spectacular Test career. In one of his Tests he single handedly bowler England to their first victory at Lord's with match figures of 9/103 in 1935. In his other standout performance he held his side's innings together against New Zealand at Wellington to score 122 not out and help South Africa avoid an embarrassing defeat at the hands of New Zealand. As his name suggests he was one of the few Test cricketers of Greek heritage.

BARLOW, Edgar John

Born:	August 12, 1940
Batting:	Right handed
Bowling:	Right arm medium

Tests
Test Career:	1961-70
Cap Number:	205
Tests Played:	30

Test Batting
Innings:	57	Runs:	2,516
Highest Score:	201	Average:	45.74
No. 50s:	15	No. 100s:	6

Test Bowling & Fielding
Wickets:	40	Runs:	1,362
Best Bowling:	5/85	Average:	34.05
5 WI:	1	10 WM:	0
Catches:	35	Stumpings:	0

Whilst no reasonable person would suggest that the ban placed on South African sporting sides in the 70's and 80's was inappropriate, it did deny cricket fans the chance to see many fine cricketers in the prime of their career. One such player was Pretorian born pig farmer Eddie Barlow. Nicknamed 'Bunter' because of his likeness to the fictional character Billy Bunter, he may not have looked liked an elite athlete but he was a batsman/bowler of the highest order. As good as blind without his spectacles, he certainly had no trouble with them on, scoring six Test centuries including a career high 201 against Australia at Adelaide in 1963/64. He was typical of South African openers in that his first goal was to occupy the crease, but the powerfully built Barlow could put away the loose ball as well as anyone, particularly if it was short. As a bowler he was a bustling medium pacer with a short run who could make the ball bend at right angles given the right conditions. Barlow was at the peak of his powers in what was to be his final Test series when South Africa routed the visiting Australians four Tests to nil in 1970. He scored two centuries and took eleven wickets to play a major role in the whitewash. 'Bunter' Barlow had been forgotten by most international cricket fans when he turned up in Australia to be part of the World Series Cricket revolution in the late 1970's. Far from a spent force, he moved down the order and thrilled crowds with his lusty late order batting and canny bowling. In 2000 the highly respected Barlow suffered a serious stroke and moved to Wales where he passed away in 2005.

BAUMGARTNER, Harold Vane

Born:	November 17, 1883
Batting:	Right handed
Bowling:	Left arm off-break

Tests
Test Career:	1913
Cap Number:	80
Tests Played:	1

Test Batting
Innings:	2	Runs:	19
Highest Score:	16	Average:	9.50
No. 50s:	0	No. 100s:	0

Test Bowling & Fielding
Wickets:	2	Runs:	99
Best Bowling:	2/99	Average:	49.50
5 WI:	0	10 WM:	0
Catches:	1	Stumpings:	0

The little left arm off spinner played one Test against England at Durban in 1913.

BEAUMONT, Rolland
Born:	February 4, 1884
Batting:	Right handed
Bowling:	Right arm medium

Tests
Test Career:	1912-14
Cap Number:	74
Tests Played:	5

Test Batting
Innings:	9	Runs:	70
Highest Score:	31	Average:	7.77
No. 50s:	0	No. 100s:	0

Test Bowling & Fielding
Wickets:	0	Runs:	0
Best Bowling:		Average:	0.00
5 WI:	0	10 WM:	0
Catches:	2	Stumpings:	0

A top order batsman from Transvaal who did little in his five Tests after a promising debut against Australia at Old Trafford in the triangular series in 1912 when he scored 37 and 12.

BEGBIE, Denis Warburton
Born:	December 12, 1914
Batting:	Right handed

Tests
Test Career:	1948-50
Cap Number:	166
Tests Played:	5

Test Batting
Innings:	7	Runs:	138
Highest Score:	48	Average:	19.71
No. 50s:	0	No. 100s:	0

Test Bowling & Fielding
Wickets:	1	Runs:	130
Best Bowling:	1/38	Average:	130.00
5 WI:	0	10 WM:	0
Catches:	2	Stumpings:	0

A right handed middle order batsman and occasional leg-spinner from Transvaal. The hard hitter once scored an unbeaten double century in Currie Cup but couldn't find that form when in the Test side.

BELL, Alexander John (Sandy)
Born:	April 15, 1906
Batting:	Right handed
Bowling:	Right arm medium-fast

Tests
Test Career:	1929-35
Cap Number:	128
Tests Played:	16

Test Batting
Innings:	23	Runs:	69
Highest Score:	26*	Average:	6.27
No. 50s:	0	No. 100s:	0

Test Bowling & Fielding
Wickets:	48	Runs:	1,567
Best Bowling:	6/99	Average:	32.64
5 WI:	4	10 WM:	0
Catches:	6	Stumpings:	0

An accomplished medium pace bowler who used his considerable height to good advantage. Bell was clearly South Africa's leading bowler on the tour to Australia in 1931/32 when he captured 23 Test wickets, ten more than any other member of his side.

BENKENSTEIN, Dale
Born:	June 9, 1974
Batting:	Right handed
Bowling:	Right arm medium

One Day Internationals
ODI Career:	1998-2002
ODIs Played:	23

ODI Batting
Innings:	20	Runs:	305
Highest Score:	69	Average:	17.94
No. 50s:	1	No. 100s:	0

ODI Bowling & Fielding
Wickets:	4	Runs:	44
Best Bowling:	3/5	Average:	11.00
5 WM:	0	Catches:	3
Stumpings:	0		

An all-rounder with quality leadership skills, the Zimbabwean born Benkenstein was pigeon-holed as a one day specialist which probably hindered his chances of playing Test cricket.

BISSET, Murray
Born:	April 14, 1876
Batting:	Right handed
Bowling:	Left arm off-break
	Wicket Keeper

Tests
Test Career:	1899-1910
Cap Number:	39
Tests Played:	3

Test Batting
Innings:	6	Runs:	103
Highest Score:	35	Average:	25.75
No. 50s:	0	No. 100s:	0

Test Bowling & Fielding
Wickets:	0	Runs:	0
Best Bowling:		Average:	0.00
5 WI:	0	10 WM:	0
Catches:	2	Stumpings:	1

A long standing captain with Western Province, in two of the three Tests he played for his country Sir Murray Bissett both kept wickets and led the side.

BLANCKENBERG, James Manuel
Born:	December 31, 1892
Batting:	Right handed
Bowling:	Right arm medium

Tests
Test Career:	1913-24
Cap Number:	81
Tests Played:	18

Test Batting

Innings:	30	Runs:	455
Highest Score:	59	Average:	19.78
No. 50s:	2	No. 100s:	0

Test Bowling & Fielding

Wickets:	60	Runs:	1,817
Best Bowling:	6/76	Average:	30.28
5 WI:	4	10 WM:	0
Catches:	9	Stumpings:	0

Well suited to the mats in South Africa, the medium pace bowler took 60 wickets in his 18 Tests. His best period came in the years immediately after the First World War when he took 25 wickets against the touring English.

BLAND, Kenneth Colin (Colin)

Born: April 5, 1938
Batting: Right handed
Bowling: Right arm medium

Tests

Test Career:	1961-66
Cap Number:	206
Tests Played:	21

Test Batting

Innings:	39	Runs:	1,669
Highest Score:	144*	Average:	49.08
No. 50s:	9	No. 100s:	3

Test Bowling & Fielding

Wickets:	2	Runs:	125
Best Bowling:	2/16	Average:	62.50
5 WI:	0	10 WM:	0
Catches:	10	Stumpings:	0

Colin Bland was the 'Bradman' of fieldsmen, a brilliant athlete who patrolled the covers with speed, balance and a throwing arm that was both accurate and ferocious. It was said that he saved his side 50 runs per Test with his exceptional fielding, but given the number of batsman he ran out the figure is probably much higher. The one negative of being considered the best fieldsman in the world is that few people talk about Colin Bland the batsman, which is unfortunate given that he averaged 49.08 in Tests. He was a patient batsman who was happy to loft the ball in search of runs, and enjoyed nothing more than a smote back over the bowler's head. Bland scored three Test centuries; 126 at the SCG in 1963/64, 144 not out against England at Johannesburg in 19645/65 and another century against the English at The Oval in 1965. His Test career came to a premature halt in 1966 when he suffered a severe knee injury. Unsurprisingly the injury occurred when he crashed into a boundary fence trying to stop a four.

BOCK, Ernest George

Born: September 17, 1908
Batting: Right handed
Bowling: Right arm medium

Tests

Test Career:	1935
Cap Number:	146
Tests Played:	1

Test Batting

Innings:	2	Runs:	11
Highest Score:	9*	Average:	0.00
No. 50s:	0	No. 100s:	0

Test Bowling & Fielding

Wickets:	0	Runs:	91
Best Bowling:	0	Average:	0.00
5 WI:	0	10 WM:	0
Catches:	0	Stumpings:	0

A medium pace bowler who failed to take a wicket in his only Test in 1935 against the touring Australians.

BOJE, Nico (Nicky)

Born: March 20, 1973
Batting: Left handed
Bowling: Left arm off-break

Tests

Test Career:	2000-
Cap Number:	276
Tests Played:	43

Test Batting

Innings:	62	Runs:	1,312
Highest Score:	85	Average:	25.23
No. 50s:	4	No. 100s:	0

Test Bowling & Fielding

Wickets:	100	Runs:	4,265
Best Bowling:	5/62	Average:	42.65
5 WI:	3	10 WM:	0
Catches:	18	Stumpings:	0

One Day Internationals

ODI Career:	1995-
ODIs Played:	115

ODI Batting

Innings:	71	Runs:	1,414
Highest Score:	129	Average:	26.67
No. 50s:	4	No. 100s:	2

ODI Bowling & Fielding

Wickets:	96	Runs:	3,415
Best Bowling:	5/21	Average:	35.57
5 WM:	1	Catches:	33
Stumpings:	0		

The left arm off spinner worked his way into the Test side during the disgraced tour of India in 2000 under Hansie Cronje. Whilst he was able to maintain a tight line, wickets were hard to come by, and for the next four years he found it difficult to hold down a regular spot in the side. In the end it was his energetic fielding and smart batting that saw him elevated above the likes of Paul Adams and Robin Peterson. Boje has four Test half centuries to his name, including three scores in excess of 70. His 76 and 4/71 against the English at Newlands in 2004/05 went a long way to winning the Test for South Africa and to finally securing his place in the side. Boje is not afraid of hard work and he earnt his pay when Sri Lanka scored an amazing win at Colombo in July 2006, taking 0/221 off a grueling 65 overs.

BOND, Gerald Edward

Born: April 5, 1909
Batting: Right handed
Bowling: Right arm medium

Tests

Test Career: 1938
Cap Number: 150
Tests Played: 1

Test Batting

Innings:	1	Runs:	0
Highest Score:	0	Average:	0.00
No. 50s:	0	No. 100s:	0

Test Bowling & Fielding

Wickets:	0	Runs:	16
Best Bowling:		Average:	0.00
5 WI:	0	10 WM:	0
Catches:	0	Stumpings:	0

A top order batsman from Western Province who would have rather forgot his only Test innings, a golden duck against England at Johannesburg in 1938.

BOSCH, Tertius

Born: March 14, 1966
Batting: Right handed
Bowling: Right arm fast

Tests

Test Career: 1992
Cap Number: 236
Tests Played: 1

Test Batting

Innings:	2	Runs:	5
Highest Score:	5*	Average:	0.00
No. 50s:	0	No. 100s:	0

Test Bowling & Fielding

Wickets:	3	Runs:	104
Best Bowling:	2/61	Average:	34.66
5 WI:	0	10 WM:	0
Catches:	0	Stumpings:	0

One Day Internationals

ODI Career: 1992
ODIs Played: 2

ODI Batting

Innings:	0	Runs:	0
Highest Score:	0	Average:	0.00
No. 50s:	0	No. 100s:	0

ODI Bowling & Fielding

Wickets:	0	Runs:	66
Best Bowling:		Average:	0.00
5 WI:	0	Catches:	0
Stumpings:	0		

It's a sad fact that there were only nine survivors of the historic South African side that played the West Indies at Bridgetown in 1992. That was the first Test played in over 20 years by South Africa, and sadly Hansie Cronje and Tertius Bosch have both since died. Whilst Cronje's case has been well documented, the facts that surround the passing of Bosch are less well known. The opening bowler from Natal was thought to have died from Guillain Bare syndrome in 2000, but when the police became aware of problems in his marriage his body was exhumed and tested for poison. The results were inconclusive, but police were so convinced that he met with foul play that they exhumed the body on a second occasion in 2004. Whilst that second post mortem examination found traces of poison in Bosch's body, no-one has ever been charged with his murder.

BOTHA, Johan

Born: May 2, 1982
Batting: Right handed
Bowling: Right arm off-break

Tests

Test Career: 2006-
Cap Number: 299
Tests Played: 1

Test Batting

Innings:	1	Runs:	20
Highest Score:	20*	Average:	0.00
No. 50s:	0	No. 100s:	0

Test Bowling & Fielding

Wickets:	2	Runs:	103
Best Bowling:	1/26	Average:	51.50
5 WI:	0	10 WM:	0
Catches:	0	Stumpings:	0

One Day Internationals

ODI Career: 2005-
ODIs Played: 11

ODI Batting

Innings:	6	Runs:	98
Highest Score:	46	Average:	32.66
No. 50s:	0	No. 100s:	0

ODI Bowling & Fielding

Wickets:	7	Runs:	361
Best Bowling:	2/49	Average:	51.57
5 WM:	0	Catches:	6
Stumpings:	0		

Johan Botha's only Test was against Australia at the SCG in 2006 and unfortunately for the young off spinner it may well be his last. He claimed the prized scalps of Mike Hussey and Matthew Hayden but was cited by the ICC for a suspect action and was subsequently banned.

BOTTEN, James Thomas (Jackie)

Born: June 21, 1938
Batting: Right handed
Bowling: Right arm medium-fast

Tests

Test Career: 1965
Cap Number: 226
Tests Played: 3

Test Batting

Innings:	6	Runs:	65
Highest Score:	33	Average:	10.83
No. 50s:	0	No. 100s:	0

Test Bowling & Fielding

Wickets:	8	Runs:	337
Best Bowling:	2/56	Average:	42.12
5 WI:	0	10 WM:	0
Catches:	1	Stumpings:	0

An outswing bowler form the Transvaal who toured England in 1965 and played three tests.

BOUCHER, Mark Verdon

Born: December 3, 1976
Batting: Right handed
Wicket Keeper

Tests
Test Career: 1997-
Cap Number: 267
Tests Played: 96

Test Batting
Innings:	136	Runs:	3,582
Highest Score:	125	Average:	30.10
No. 50s:	23	No. 100s:	4

Test Bowling & Fielding
Wickets:	1	Runs:	6
Best Bowling:	1/6	Average:	6.00
5 WI:	0	10 WM:	0
Catches:	350	Stumpings:	14

One Day Internationals
ODI Career: 1998-
ODIs Played: 217

ODI Batting
Innings:	158	Runs:	3,175
Highest Score:	76	Average:	26.68
No. 50s:	19	No. 100s:	0

ODI Bowling & Fielding
Wickets:	0	Runs:	0
Best Bowling:		Average:	0.00
5 WM:	0	Catches:	303
Stumpings:	17		

Statistics say he is the best gloveman to have played for South Africa, and in the case of Mark Boucher the numbers don't lie. As a keeper he is enthusiastic and as safe as houses. A neat mover behind the stumps, his record of close to four dismissals per match over almost 100 Tests, rates him the equal of the game's elite. His batting is just as important to the team, and in recent years has he has been required to shore up many an innings after the top order has come up short. In only his second Test, at the Wanderers in 1998, he made 78 and in doing so put on a record 195 for the ninth wicket with Pat Symcox. It was to be a typical Boucher performance, coming in at 8/166 and saving the day. The keeper from provincial side Border has scored four Tests hundreds including a career high 125 against Zimbabwe and a fighting 108 not out against England at Durban in 1999 that saved the Test after South Africa trailed by over 200 runs on the first innings. His leadership qualities have also been recognised by selectors who made him vice-captain when Shaun Pollock took over the captaincy from Hansie Cronje.

BRANN, William Henry

Born: April 4, 1899
Batting: Right handed

Tests
Test Career: 1922-23
Cap Number: 101
Tests Played: 3

Test Batting
Innings:	5	Runs:	71
Highest Score:	50	Average:	14.20
No. 50s:	1	No. 100s:	0

Test Bowling & Fielding
Wickets:	0	Runs:	0
Best Bowling:		Average:	0.00
5 WI:	0	10 WM:	0
Catches:	2	Stumpings:	0

An Eastern Province batsman who played three Tests against the touring English in 1922/23. He scored a half century on debut at Johannesburg.

BRISCOE, Arthur Wellesley

Born: February 6, 1911
Batting: Right handed

Tests
Test Career: 1935-39
Cap Number: 147
Tests Played: 2

Test Batting
Innings:	3	Runs:	33
Highest Score:	16	Average:	11.00
No. 50s:	0	No. 100s:	0

Test Bowling & Fielding
Wickets:	0	Runs:	0
Best Bowling:		Average:	0.00
5 WI:	0	10 WM:	0
Catches:	1	Stumpings:	0

Nicknamed 'Dooley', he was a batsman from Transvaal who failed to flatter in his only two Tests but had an impressive first class average in excess of 40. Briscoe was killed during the Second World War whilst serving in Ethiopia.

BROMFIELD, Harry Dudley

Born: June 26, 1932
Batting: Right handed
Bowling: Right arm off-break

Tests
Test Career: 1961-65
Cap Number: 207
Tests Played: 9

Test Batting
Innings:	12	Runs:	59
Highest Score:	21	Average:	11.80
No. 50s:	0	No. 100s:	0

Test Bowling & Fielding
Wickets:	17	Runs:	599
Best Bowling:	5/88	Average:	35.23
5 WI:	1	10 WM:	0
Catches:	13	Stumpings:	0

An economical off-spinner from Western Province who played nine Tests following the retirement of Hugh Tayfield. His best effort was 5/88 in a side that lost to the English at Newlands in 1965.

BROWN, Lennox Sydney

Born: November 24, 1910
Batting: Right handed
Bowling: Right arm medium-fast

	Tests		
Test Career:	1931-32		
Cap Number:	137		
Tests Played:	2		
Test Batting			
Innings:	3	Runs:	17
Highest Score:	8	Average:	5.66
No. 50s:	0	No. 100s:	0
Test Bowling & Fielding			
Wickets:	3	Runs:	189
Best Bowling:	1/30	Average:	63.00
5 WI:	0	10 WM:	0
Catches:	0	Stumpings:	0

A leg spinner who played two Tests on the tour of Australia and New Zealand in 1931/32.

BRYSON, Rudi

Born: July 25, 1968
Batting: Right handed
Bowling: Right arm medium-fast

	One Day Internationals		
ODI Career:	1997		
ODIs Played:	7		
ODI Batting			
Innings:	4	Runs:	32
Highest Score:	17*	Average:	32.00
No. 50s:	0	No. 100s:	0
ODI Bowling & Fielding			
Wickets:	7	Runs:	323
Best Bowling:	2/34	Average:	46.14
5 WM:	0	Catches:	1
Stumpings:	0		

A right arm pace bowler who opened the bowling on his ODI debut against Zimbabwe, at Cape Town. Played seven ODI's in 1997.

BURGER, Christopher George de Villiers

Born: July 12, 1935
Batting: Right handed
Bowling: Right arm medium

	Tests		
Test Career:	1958		
Cap Number:	197		
Tests Played:	2		
Test Batting			
Innings:	4	Runs:	62
Highest Score:	37*	Average:	20.66
No. 50s:	0	No. 100s:	0
Test Bowling & Fielding			
Wickets:	0	Runs:	0
Best Bowling:		Average:	0.00
5 WI:	0	10 WM:	0
Catches:	1	Stumpings:	0

A right handed batsman from Natal who played two Tests against the visiting Australians in 1958.

BURKE, Sydney Frank

Born: March 11, 1934
Batting: Right handed
Bowling: Right arm medium-fast

	Tests		
Test Career:	1962-65		
Cap Number:	212		
Tests Played:	2		
Test Batting			
Innings:	4	Runs:	42
Highest Score:	20	Average:	14.00
No. 50s:	0	No. 100s:	0
Test Bowling & Fielding			
Wickets:	11	Runs:	257
Best Bowling:	6/128	Average:	23.36
5 WI:	2	10 WM:	1
Catches:	0	Stumpings:	0

Sydney Burke may well be the unluckiest Test cricketer to have been dropped after just one Test. The right arm medium-fast bowler from Transvaal took 11 wickets in his first Test, albeit against a relatively weak New Zealand side at Cape Town in 1962. He was demoted to twelfth man for the very next Test and soon fell out of favour. Burke must have thought that would be his only Test, but three years to the day after his made his debut, he was recalled to face the English at the same ground. This time there were no wickets and he was dropped for a second and final time.

BUYS, Isaac Daniel

Born: February 4, 1895
Batting: Right handed
Bowling: Left arm medium-fast

	Tests		
Test Career:	1922		
Cap Number:	102		
Tests Played:	1		
Test Batting			
Innings:	2	Runs:	4
Highest Score:	4*	Average:	4.00
No. 50s:	0	No. 100s:	0
Test Bowling & Fielding			
Wickets:	0	Runs:	52
Best Bowling:		Average:	0.00
5 WI:	0	10 WM:	0
Catches:	0	Stumpings:	0

A slow bowler from Western Province who did little in his only Test against England.

CALLAGHAN, David

Born: February 1, 1965
Batting: Right handed
Bowling: Right arm medium

	One Day Internationals		
ODI Career:	1992-00		
ODIs Played:	29		
ODI Batting			
Innings:	25	Runs:	493
Highest Score:	169*	Average:	25.94
No. 50s:	0	No. 100s:	1
ODI Bowling & Fielding			
Wickets:	10	Runs:	365
Best Bowling:	3/32	Average:	36.50
5 WM:	0	Catches:	6
Stumpings:	0		

An attacking opener who could bat anywhere in the order, Dave Callaghan played 29 ODI's over an eight year period. He scored a massive 169 against New Zealand, at Centurion Park in 1994, but unfortunately never received a Test call up.

CAMERON, Horace Brakenridge
Born: July 5, 1905
Batting: Right handed
Wicket Keeper

Tests
Test Career: 1927-35
Cap Number: 113
Tests Played: 26

Test Batting
Innings:	45	Runs:	1,239
Highest Score:	90	Average:	30.21
No. 50s:	10	No. 100s:	0

Test Bowling & Fielding
Wickets:	0	Runs:	0
Best Bowling:		Average:	0.00
5 WI:	0	10 WM:	0
Catches:	39	Stumpings:	12

The nimble wicket keeper from Johannesburg was at the height of his powers when he contracted enteric fever and passed away at the age of just 30. He had just toured England as the side's number one wicket keeper where his hard hitting batting was at it's best. He swatted a career high 90 at Lord's and competed for more scores in excess of 40. As a keeper he had gazelle like reflexes and was considered one of the best glovemen of his time. Jock Cameron skippered the side in nine Tests between 1930 and 1932 for two wins and two draws.

CAMPBELL, Thomas
Born: February 9, 1882
Batting: Right handed
Wicket Keeper

Tests
Test Career: 1910-12
Cap Number: 65
Tests Played: 5

Test Batting
Innings:	9	Runs:	90
Highest Score:	48	Average:	15.00
No. 50s:	0	No. 100s:	0

Test Bowling & Fielding
Wickets:	0	Runs:	0
Best Bowling:		Average:	0.00
5 WI:	0	10 WM:	0
Catches:	7	Stumpings:	1

A wicket keeper from Transvaal who played all of his Test cricket in England. He was not a renowned batsman so he did well to score 48 at Durban in 1909/10. He was killed in the 1924 Natal mail train accident at the age of 42.

CARLSTEIN, Peter Rudolph
Born: October 28, 1938
Batting: Right handed
Bowling: Right arm leg-break
Wicket Keeper

Tests
Test Career: 1958-64
Cap Number: 198
Tests Played: 8

Test Batting
Innings:	14	Runs:	190
Highest Score:	42	Average:	14.61
No. 50s:	0	No. 100s:	0

Test Bowling & Fielding
Wickets:	0	Runs:	0
Best Bowling:		Average:	0.00
5 WI:	0	10 WM:	0
Catches:	3	Stumpings:	0

Big things were expected of the slightly built Carlstein when he made his first class debut for Orange Free State at the age of 16. He was in the Test side by 19, but in eight Tests could only manage 190 runs with a top score of just 42 against England at The Oval in 1960.

CARTER, Claude Pagdett
Born: April 23, 1881
Batting: Right handed
Bowling: Left arm off-break

Tests
Test Career: 1912-24
Cap Number: 79
Tests Played: 10

Test Batting
Innings:	15	Runs:	181
Highest Score:	45	Average:	18.10
No. 50s:	0	No. 100s:	0

Test Bowling & Fielding
Wickets:	28	Runs:	694
Best Bowling:	6/50	Average:	24.78
5 WI:	2	10 WM:	0
Catches:	2	Stumpings:	0

A left arm off spinner who came to notice when he made his first class debut at the age of 16. His ten Tests straddled the First World War as did his two six wickets in an innings hauls. He took 6/50 against England at Durban in 1913/14 and then 6/91 playing Australia at Johannesburg in 1921/22.

CATTERALL, Robert Hector
Born: July 10, 1900
Batting: Right handed
Bowling: Right arm medium

Tests
Test Career: 1922-31
Cap Number: 103
Tests Played: 24

Test Batting
Innings:	43	Runs:	1,555
Highest Score:	120	Average:	37.92
No. 50s:	11	No. 100s:	3

Test Bowling & Fielding			
Wickets:	7	Runs:	162
Best Bowling:	3/15	Average:	23.14
5 WI:	0	10 WM:	0
Catches:	12	Stumpings:	0

A key member of the South African top order in the 1920's, he enjoyed immense success on his first tour of England. Catterall was the standout batsman in 1924 scoring 471 runs in Tests at an average of 67.28. He was part of the side at Edgbaston that scored what was then the lowest innings score in Test cricket of 30, but led the charge in the second dig scoring a brave 120. He scored another century at Lord's to confirm his standing as South Africa's best batsman. Catterall was a nagging medium pace bowler who was used at the end of his Test career, and in 1930/31 took seven wickets against the touring English. Interestingly he didn't play a single Test against Australia.

CHAPMAN, Horace William

Born:	June 30, 1890
Batting:	Right handed
Bowling:	Right arm leg-break

Tests

Test Career:	1914-21
Cap Number:	90
Tests Played:	2

Test Batting

Innings:	4	Runs:	39
Highest Score:	17	Average:	13.00
No. 50s:	0	No. 100s:	0

Test Bowling & Fielding

Wickets:	1	Runs:	104
Best Bowling:	1/51	Average:	104.00
5 WI:	0	10 WM:	0
Catches:	1	Stumpings:	0

A leg spinner from Natal who laboured in his two Tests taking just the solitary wicket for 104 runs.

CHEETHAM, John Erskine (Jack)

Born:	May 26, 1920
Batting:	Right handed
Bowling:	Right arm leg-break

Tests

Test Career:	1949-55
Cap Number:	171
Tests Played:	24

Test Batting

Innings:	43	Runs:	883
Highest Score:	89	Average:	23.86
No. 50s:	5	No. 100s:	0

Test Bowling & Fielding

Wickets:	0	Runs:	2
Best Bowling:		Average:	0.00
5 WI:	0	10 WM:	0
Catches:	13	Stumpings:	0

When Jack Cheetham was selected in the South African side in 1949 at the age 28, it was with thought that the Western Province man would one day take over the captaincy from Dudley Nourse. That's exactly what happened in 1952 and Cheetham became the first South African captain since 'Tip' Snooke in 1910 to leave the game with a winning record. His finest hour came on the tour of Australasia in 1952/53 when the underdogs drew the series with Australia 2-2 and then trounced the New Zealanders 4-0. In all he won seven Tests out of 15 and lost only three. As a cricketer he was a careful top order batsman, who whilst never scoring a Test century played many valuable innings.

CHEVALIER, Grahame Anton

Born:	March 9, 1937
Batting:	Left handed
Bowling:	Left arm off-break

Tests

Test Career:	1970
Cap Number:	231
Tests Played:	1

Test Batting

Innings:	2	Runs:	0
Highest Score:	0	Average:	0.00
No. 50s:	0	No. 100s:	0

Test Bowling & Fielding

Wickets:	5	Runs:	100
Best Bowling:	3/68	Average:	20.00
5 WI:	0	10 WM:	0
Catches:	1	Stumpings:	0

He was a genuine left arm off spinner who took five wickets in the only Test he ever played. That useful cameo was in the first Test of the 1969/70 series against Australia, and whilst it was to be the last series South Africa would play in over 20 years, it's doubtful that the 33 year old would have forced his way back into the team anyway. Chevalier was the type of number eleven batsman that captains declare on, with only 84 runs in his 47 first class innings.

CHRISTY, James Alexander Joseph

Born:	December 12, 1904
Batting:	Right handed
Bowling:	Right arm medium

Tests

Test Career:	1929-32
Cap Number:	124
Tests Played:	10

Test Batting

Innings:	18	Runs:	618
Highest Score:	103	Average:	34.33
No. 50s:	5	No. 100s:	1

Test Bowling & Fielding

Wickets:	2	Runs:	92
Best Bowling:	1/15	Average:	46.00
5 WI:	0	10 WM:	0
Catches:	3	Stumpings:	0

A top order batsman who would have been pleased when a tour match against New Zealand in 1932 was ultimately recognised as a Test match. Christy made his highest score and only Test century in that game in Wellington with 102 in the first innings. He played a season of first class cricket in Australia with Queensland in 1934/35.

CHUBB, Geoffrey Walter Ashton

Born: April 12, 1911
Batting: Right handed
Bowling: Right arm medium-fast

Tests
Test Career: 1951
Cap Number: 175
Tests Played: 5

Test Batting
Innings:	9	Runs:	63
Highest Score:	15*	Average:	10.50
No. 50s:	0	No. 100s:	0

Test Bowling & Fielding
Wickets:	21	Runs:	577
Best Bowling:	6/51	Average:	27.47
5 WI:	2	10 WM:	0
Catches:	0	Stumpings:	0

South Africa's oldest Test debutant at the age of 40, he played his first Test at Trent Bridge in 1952. The bespectacled medium paceman may have lacked a yard, but with his late swing he was well suited to English conditions and he captured a more than respectable 21 wickets over that English summer. He later served as President of the South African Cricket Association.

COCHRAN, John Alexander Kennedy

Born: July 15, 1909
Batting: Right handed
Bowling: Right arm medium-fast

Tests
Test Career: 1931
Cap Number: 136
Tests Played: 1

Test Batting
Innings:	1	Runs:	4
Highest Score:	4	Average:	4.00
No. 50s:	0	No. 100s:	0

Test Bowling & Fielding
Wickets:	0	Runs:	47
Best Bowling:		Average:	0.00
5 WI:	0	10 WM:	0
Catches:	0	Stumpings:	0

A fast bowler who was brought into the side to play at Durban in 1931. It was only the second Test played on turf in South Africa but Cochran failed to take a wicket and never played Test cricket again.

COEN, Stanley Keppel

Born: October 14, 1902
Batting: Right handed
Bowling: Right arm medium

Tests
Test Career: 1927-28
Cap Number: 114
Tests Played: 2

Test Batting
Innings:	4	Runs:	101
Highest Score:	41*	Average:	50.50
No. 50s:	0	No. 100s:	0

Test Bowling & Fielding
Wickets:	0	Runs:	7
Best Bowling:		Average:	0.00
5 WI:	0	10 WM:	0
Catches:	1	Stumpings:	0

Nicknamed 'Shunter', he played two Tests in 1927/28 against the touring English. Coen played for no less than four provinces in South African first class cricket.

COMMAILLE, John McIllwaine Moore

Born: February 21, 1883
Batting: Right handed

Tests
Test Career: 1910-28
Cap Number: 66
Tests Played: 12

Test Batting
Innings:	22	Runs:	355
Highest Score:	47	Average:	16.90
No. 50s:	0	No. 100s:	0

Test Bowling & Fielding
Wickets:	0	Runs:	0
Best Bowling:		Average:	0.00
5 WI:	0	10 WM:	0
Catches:	1	Stumpings:	0

An opening batsman who scored over 5,000 first class runs, he enjoyed little success in his 12 Tests failing to reach 50 in any innings. He also represented South Africa in soccer.

COMMINS, John Brian

Born: February 19, 1965
Batting: Right handed
Bowling: Right arm medium

Tests
Test Career: 1994-95
Cap Number: 258
Tests Played: 3

Test Batting
Innings:	6	Runs:	125
Highest Score:	45	Average:	25.00
No. 50s:	0	No. 100s:	0

Test Bowling & Fielding
Wickets:	0	Runs:	0
Best Bowling:		Average:	0.00
5 WI:	0	10 WM:	0
Catches:	2	Stumpings:	0

A batsman from Boland and Western Province who played three Tests in 1994/95 against the touring New Zealanders and Pakistanis.

CONYNGHAM, Dalton Parry

Born: May 10, 1897
Batting: Right handed
Bowling: Right arm medium

Tests
Test Career: 1923
Cap Number: 109
Tests Played: 1

Test Batting
Innings:	2	Runs:	6
Highest Score:	3*	Average:	0.00
No. 50s:	0	No. 100s:	0

Test Bowling & Fielding			
Wickets:	2	Runs:	103
Best Bowling:	1/40	Average:	51.50
5 WI:	0	10 WM:	0
Catches:	1	Stumpings:	0

A Currie Cup journeyman who played with Natal, Transvaal and Western Province. The popular medium pace bowler was known to all and sundry as 'Conky'.

COOK, Frederick James
Born:	May 0, 1870
Batting:	Right handed

Tests
Test Career:	1896
Cap Number:	24
Tests Played:	1

Test Batting
Innings:	2	Runs:	7
Highest Score:	7	Average:	3.50
No. 50s:	0	No. 100s:	0

Test Bowling & Fielding
Wickets:	0	Runs:	0
Best Bowling:		Average:	0.00
5 WI:	0	10 WM:	0
Catches:	0	Stumpings:	0

A batsman from Eastern Province who played a single Test in 1892. He was killed at Gallipoli in the First World War.

COOK, Stephen James (Jimmy)
Born:	July 31, 1953
Batting:	Right handed
Bowling:	Right arm off-break

Tests
Test Career:	1992-93
Cap Number:	247
Tests Played:	3

Test Batting
Innings:	6	Runs:	107
Highest Score:	43	Average:	17.83
No. 50s:	0	No. 100s:	0

Test Bowling & Fielding
Wickets:	0	Runs:	0
Best Bowling:		Average:	0.00
5 WI:	0	10 WM:	0
Catches:	0	Stumpings:	0

One Day Internationals
ODI Career:	1991-93
ODIs Played:	4

ODI Batting
Innings:	4	Runs:	67
Highest Score:	35	Average:	16.75
No. 50s:	0	No. 100s:	0

ODI Bowling & Fielding
Wickets:	0	Runs:	0
Best Bowling:		Average:	0.00
5 WM:	0	Catches:	1
Stumpings:	0		

South Africa's return to Test cricket came too late for Jimmy Cook. He had been a leading light for both Transvaal and Somerset, scoring over 20,000 first class runs at an average of more than fifty during his country's exile from international cricket. Cook did play three Tests for South Africa upon their re-admission but was past his best and failed to hit a single half century.

COOPER, Alfred Henry Cecil
Born:	September 2, 1893
Batting:	Right handed
Bowling:	Right arm medium

Tests
Test Career:	1913
Cap Number:	82
Tests Played:	1

Test Batting
Innings:	2	Runs:	6
Highest Score:	6	Average:	3.00
No. 50s:	0	No. 100s:	0

Test Bowling & Fielding
Wickets:	0	Runs:	0
Best Bowling:		Average:	0.00
5 WI:	0	10 WM:	0
Catches:	1	Stumpings:	0

He played a single Test just prior to the First World War at Durban against the English. In 1921/22 he scored an unbeaten 171 for Transvaal.

COX, Joseph Lovell
Born:	June 28, 1886
Batting:	Right handed
Bowling:	Right arm medium

Tests
Test Career:	1913-14
Cap Number:	83
Tests Played:	3

Test Batting
Innings:	6	Runs:	17
Highest Score:	12*	Average:	3.40
No. 50s:	0	No. 100s:	0

Test Bowling & Fielding
Wickets:	4	Runs:	245
Best Bowling:	2/74	Average:	61.25
5 WI:	0	10 WM:	0
Catches:	1	Stumpings:	0

A medium pace bowler from Natal who did little in his three Tests against the touring English in 1913/14.

CRIPPS, Godfrey
Born:	October 19, 1865
Batting:	Right handed
Bowling:	Right arm medium

Tests
Test Career:	1892
Cap Number:	15
Tests Played:	1

Test Batting
Innings:	2	Runs:	21
Highest Score:	18	Average:	10.50
No. 50s:	0	No. 100s:	0

Test Bowling & Fielding
Wickets:	0	Runs:	23
Best Bowling:		Average:	0.00
5 WI:	0	10 WM:	0
Catches:	0	Stumpings:	0

A fine top order batsman, he enjoyed little success in his only Test match but led South Africa on a tour of England in 1894. Cripps died in Australia in the 1940's.

CRISP, Robert James

Born:	May 28, 1911
Batting:	Right handed
Bowling:	Right arm fast

Tests

Test Career:	1935-36
Cap Number:	138
Tests Played:	9

Test Batting

Innings:	13	Runs:	123
Highest Score:	35	Average:	10.25
No. 50s:	0	No. 100s:	0

Test Bowling & Fielding

Wickets:	20	Runs:	747
Best Bowling:	5/99	Average:	37.35
5 WI:	1	10 WM:	0
Catches:	3	Stumpings:	0

Bob Crisp was an adventurer, war-hero, newspaper reporter and when he had time an excellent Test paceman. Crisp the cricketer played nine Tests, with a career best return of 5/99 at Old Trafford in 1935 when his quick swing claimed English skipper Wyatt and Walter Hammond in rapid succession. As an adventurer he climbed Mt. Kilimanjaro twice and fought as a tank commander in World War II. He was injured in battle a number of times and on one occasion had an audience with the King of England. The monarch asked if his bowling would be affected with the inimitable Crisp supposedly replying "No Sire, I was hit in the head"!

CRONJE, Wessel Johannes (Hansie)

Born:	September 25, 1969
Batting:	Right handed
Bowling:	Right arm medium

Tests

Test Career:	1992-2000
Cap Number:	237
Tests Played:	68

Test Batting

Innings:	111	Runs:	3,714
Highest Score:	135	Average:	36.41
No. 50s:	23	No. 100s:	6

Test Bowling & Fielding

Wickets:	43	Runs:	1,288
Best Bowling:	3/14	Average:	29.95
5 WI:	0	10 WM:	0
Catches:	33	Stumpings:	0

One Day Internationals

ODI Career:	1992-2000
ODIs Played:	188

ODI Batting

Innings:	175	Runs:	5,565
Highest Score:	112	Average:	38.64
No. 50s:	39	No. 100s:	2

ODI Bowling & Fielding

Wickets:	114	Runs:	3,966
Best Bowling:	5/32	Average:	34.78
5 WM:	1	Catches:	73
Stumpings:	0		

The word tragedy is overused in sport, but it is an apt description of both Hansie Cronje's fall from grace as a Test captain and his untimely death at the age of only 32. It all started so promisingly for the young batsman from Orange Free State who was captaining his province at 21 and playing Test cricket a year later. He was selected in the South African side that played a historic Test at Bridgetown after over twenty years of Test match isolation, and whilst he failed in both innings, success wasn't far away. In only his third Test he scored a masterful 135 at Port Elizabeth against India that took over eight hours and saw his side to their first Test win in the modern era. An intense individual, his introduction to the captaincy was an auspicious one. As Kepler Wessels' vice captain he took over when his skipper was forced from the field with a broken finger at the SCG in 1993/94. He was in charge on the final day of that Test and lead the side to a momentous victory when Australia stumbled chasing only 117. Cronje was made permanent captain in 1994 and after losing his first Test against New Zealand won the next five Tests in a row. He was an aggressive captain who seemed keen to mould the side in the image of the all-conquering Australians. South African captains had been traditionally conservative, preferring to make a Test safe before pressing for victory, but under Cronje the side played adventurous cricket as his record of 26 wins in 53 Tests would suggest. It was as captain that the handsome Cronje became involved with some of the shady figures that make their living betting on the results of international cricket matches. He was on a tour to India in 1996 when he was introduced to a gambler by the name of M.K. Gupta. Gupta paid the South African skipper for information relating to pitch conditions and team selection, and whilst there was initially no suggestion of throwing any matches, Cronje was on the slippery slope to self destruction. Exactly how much he received, and what he did for that money over the next four years is unclear, but what is certain is that by the time he returned to India in 2000 he was in no position to reject the advances of the Indian match fixers. Prior to the final one day game of that tour he approached two young cricketers under his charge, and offered them a bribe to under perform. Hansie Cronje had picked his marks with callous disregard for the sensitive political situation in South African cricket at the time, as both Herschell Gibbs and Henry Williams were non-whites and particularly vulnerable. With so many people now involved it was inevitable that Cronje would get caught, and after an investigation by Indian police that involved a phone tap he was charged with match fixing. The disgraced skipper faced a commission in South Africa chaired by Justice King during which he admitted to accepting a number of bribes. The man given the responsibility of leading an integrated cricket side in the new South Africa was banned for life. An at times tearful Cronje offered little explanation for his actions other than claiming to have an "unfortunate love of money". He had not only sullied his own name, but had also done irreparable damage to the game of cricket. Following his lifetime ban, Cronje turned to God and spoke of his fervent wish to one day return to the game he loved as a coach and a commentator. Those wishes were dashed on the first day of June in 2002, when the light plane on which he was traveling crashed into a mountainside. In recent years there has been talk of a plot to silence Cronje that suggests the crash was not on accident, but in 2006 South African police announced that there was no evidence of foul play. When he passed away, his team mates and supporters remembered Cronje as a fiercely competitive cricketer and accomplished Test captain, but for most people he will always be the player who threw it all away for a sack full of cash.

CROOKES, Derek Norman

Born: March 5, 1969
Batting: Right handed
Bowling: Right arm off-break

One Day Internationals

ODI Career: 1994-2000
ODIs Played: 32

ODI Batting

Innings:	23	Runs:	296
Highest Score:	54	Average:	14.80
No. 50s:	1	No. 100s:	0

ODI Bowling & Fielding

Wickets:	25	Runs:	1,011
Best Bowling:	3/30	Average:	40.44
5 WM:	0	Catches:	20
Stumpings:	0		

An all-rounder and brilliant fielder, Crookes took a career best 3/30 against India at Nairobi, in 1999. Probably unlucky not to gain a Test cap.

CULLINAN, Daryll John

Born: March 4, 1967
Batting: Right handed
Bowling: Right arm off-break

Tests

Test Career: 1993-2001
Cap Number: 253
Tests Played: 70

Test Batting

Innings:	115	Runs:	4,554
Highest Score:	275*	Average:	44.21
No. 50s:	20	No. 100s:	14

Test Bowling & Fielding

Wickets:	2	Runs:	71
Best Bowling:	1/10	Average:	35.50
5 WI:	0	10 WM:	0
Catches:	67	Stumpings:	0

One Day Internationals

ODI Career: 1993-2000
ODIs Played: 138

ODI Batting

Innings:	133	Runs:	3,860
Highest Score:	124	Average:	32.99
No. 50s:	23	No. 100s:	3

ODI Bowling & Fielding

Wickets:	5	Runs:	124
Best Bowling:	2/30	Average:	24.80
5 WM:	0	Catches:	62
Stumpings:	0		

To Australian fans he is little more than Shane Warne's bunny, but whilst he may have lost the battle to the world's best spinner, his record suggests that he had a good time of it against everyone else. In a 70 Test career that spanned eight years, he averaged over 44 with 14 Test centuries. At one stage he held the highest score by a South African in Test and first class cricket. He scored 337 not out for Transvaal against Northern Transvaal in 1993/94 and 275 not out against New Zealand at Auckland in 1998/99. He was a perfect timer of the ball, who despite his difficulties with Shane Warne, was comfortable against both pace and spin. Had he not averaged only 12.75 against the Australian 'leggie' in seven Tests he would have been rated as one of his country's best batsmen in Test cricket.

CURNOW, Sydney Harry

Born: December 16, 1907
Batting: Right handed

Tests

Test Career: 1930-32
Cap Number: 133
Tests Played: 7

Test Batting

Innings:	14	Runs:	168
Highest Score:	47	Average:	12.00
No. 50s:	0	No. 100s:	0

Test Bowling & Fielding

Wickets:	0	Runs:	0
Best Bowling:		Average:	0.00
5 WI:	0	10 WM:	0
Catches:	5	Stumpings:	0

A prolific scorer with Transvaal in Currie Cup, he was disappointing when he played for his country averaging only 12 in his seven Tests.

DALTON, Eric Londesbrough

Born: December 2, 1906
Batting: Right handed

Tests
Test Career:	1929-39		
Cap Number:	129		
Tests Played:	15		

Test Batting
Innings:	24	Runs:	698
Highest Score:	117	Average:	31.72
No. 50s:	3	No. 100s:	2

Test Bowling & Fielding
Wickets:	12	Runs:	490
Best Bowling:	4/59	Average:	40.83
5 WI:	0	10 WM:	0
Catches:	5	Stumpings:	0

The selection of a young Eric Dalton as part of the squad to tour England in 1929 came as quite a surprise. He had played only nine first class games, and whilst his piano playing and wonderful baritone voice were ideal for the cruise ship sing-a-longs, his value to the Test side was less certain. He played only one Test on that tour for little success but the experience was invaluable, and over the next decade he proved to be a fine player, making two Test tons and averaging 31.72. His talent didn't only extend to cricket and music, Dalton was also an outstanding golfer who won the South African Amateur title in 1950.

DAVIES, Eric Quail
Born:	August 26, 1909
Batting:	Left handed
Bowling:	Right arm fast

Tests
Test Career:	1936-39		
Cap Number:	148		
Tests Played:	5		

Test Batting
Innings:	8	Runs:	9
Highest Score:	3	Average:	1.80
No. 50s:	0	No. 100s:	0

Test Bowling & Fielding
Wickets:	7	Runs:	481
Best Bowling:	4/75	Average:	68.71
5 WI:	0	10 WM:	0
Catches:	0	Stumpings:	0

A pace bowler who had a fine Test debut, capturing four wickets against the strong Australian side in 1936 at Johannesburg. His scalps included no less a trio than Jack Fingleton, Stan McCabe and Victor Richardson.

DAWSON, Alan Charles
Born:	November 27, 1969
Batting:	Right handed
Bowling:	Right arm medium-fast

Tests
Test Career:	2003		
Cap Number:	288		
Tests Played:	2		

Test Batting
Innings:	1	Runs:	10
Highest Score:	10	Average:	10.00
No. 50s:	0	No. 100s:	0

Test Bowling & Fielding
Wickets:	5	Runs:	117
Best Bowling:	2/20	Average:	23.40
5 WI:	0	10 WM:	0
Catches:	0	Stumpings:	0

One Day Internationals
ODI Career:	1998-2004		
ODIs Played:	19		

ODI Batting
Innings:	7	Runs:	69
Highest Score:	23*	Average:	23.00
No. 50s:	0	No. 100s:	0

ODI Bowling & Fielding
Wickets:	21	Runs:	715
Best Bowling:	4/49	Average:	34.04
5 WM:	0	Catches:	2
Stumpings:	0		

One of many quicks tried by South Africa in recent years, he played two Tests against Bangladesh in 2002 but could manage only five wickets against the relatively weak opposition.

DAWSON, Oswald Charles
Born:	September 1, 1919
Batting:	Right handed
Bowling:	Right arm medium

Tests
Test Career:	1947-49		
Cap Number:	156		
Tests Played:	9		

Test Batting
Innings:	15	Runs:	293
Highest Score:	55	Average:	20.92
No. 50s:	1	No. 100s:	0

Test Bowling & Fielding
Wickets:	10	Runs:	578
Best Bowling:	2/57	Average:	57.80
5 WI:	0	10 WM:	0
Catches:	10	Stumpings:	0

He was an all-rounder from Natal who toured England in 1947. Dawson's best effort was 55 in the fifth Test at The Oval.

DE BRUYN, Zander
Born:	July 5, 1975
Batting:	Right handed
Bowling:	Right arm medium-fast

Tests
Test Career:	2004		
Cap Number:	293		
Tests Played:	3		

Test Batting
Innings:	5	Runs:	155
Highest Score:	83	Average:	38.75
No. 50s:	1	No. 100s:	0

Test Bowling & Fielding
Wickets:	3	Runs:	92
Best Bowling:	2/32	Average:	30.66
5 WI:	0	10 WM:	0
Catches:	0	Stumpings:	0

An all-rounder from Transvaal who played three Tests in 2004, performing well with both bat and ball. His best efforts were his 83 on debut against India at Kanpur and 2/32 in the next Test at Kolkata.

DE VILLERS, Abraham Benjamin (AB)

Born:	February 17, 1984
Batting:	Right handed
Bowling:	Right arm medium
	Wicket Keeper

Tests

Test Career:	2004-
Cap Number:	296
Tests Played:	22

Test Batting

Innings:	40	Runs:	1,607
Highest Score:	178	Average:	41.20
No. 50s:	10	No. 100s:	3

Test Bowling & Fielding

Wickets:	2	Runs:	99
Best Bowling:	2/49	Average:	49.50
5 WI:	0	10 WM:	0
Catches:	29	Stumpings:	1

One Day Internationals

ODI Career:	2005-
ODIs Played:	19

ODI Batting

Innings:	19	Runs:	402
Highest Score:	68	Average:	21.15
No. 50s:	1	No. 100s:	0

ODI Bowling & Fielding

Wickets:	0	Runs:	0
Best Bowling:		Average:	0.00
5 WM:	0	Catches:	7
Stumpings:	0		

A brilliant young sportsman, de Villiers could have played golf or tennis professionally but chose to concentrate on cricket. He made his debut against England at the age of 20 as a batsman, but by the next Test was filling in as wicket keeper for the injured Mark Boucher. When the number one keeper returned, de Villiers was retained in the side, enjoying a wonderful tour of the Caribbean in 2004/05 where he scored 460 runs at 65.71 including a high score of 178 at Bridgetown. Runs were harder to come by against the Australians the following summer but a return to form against Sri Lanka in 2006 should see the youngster as a permanent figure in the Test side for many years to come.

DE VILLIERS, Petrus Stephanus (Fanie)

Born:	October 13, 1964
Batting:	Right handed
Bowling:	Right arm medium-fast

Tests

Test Career:	1993-98
Cap Number:	256
Tests Played:	18

Test Batting

Innings:	26	Runs:	359
Highest Score:	67*	Average:	18.89
No. 50s:	2	No. 100s:	0

Test Bowling & Fielding

Wickets:	85	Runs:	2,063
Best Bowling:	6/23	Average:	24.27
5 WI:	5	10 WM:	2
Catches:	11	Stumpings:	0

One Day Internationals

ODI Career:	1992-97
ODIs Played:	83

ODI Batting

Innings:	36	Runs:	170
Highest Score:	20*	Average:	8.09
No. 50s:	0	No. 100s:	0

ODI Bowling & Fielding

Wickets:	95	Runs:	2,636
Best Bowling:	4/27	Average:	27.74
5 WM:	0	Catches:	15
Stumpings:	0		

Tall and ultra competitive, Fanie de Villiers rocked Australia in 1994 when he tore through their powerful batting line-up at the SCG to secure an unlikely victory for his country. It was only the Northern Transvaal bowler's second Test, but he matched speed and late swing to take ten wickets and claim the man of the match award. In the years that followed injury meant he was in and out of the Test side, but as his record of 85 wickets at only 24.27 suggests, he was a world class bowler when fit. De Villiers was a renowned joker who once sent a remote control car that he was operating from the pavilion on to the field during a Test.

DEANE, Hubert Gouvaine

Born:	July 21, 1895
Batting:	Right handed

Tests

Test Career:	1924-31
Cap Number:	110
Tests Played:	17

Test Batting

Innings:	27	Runs:	628
Highest Score:	93	Average:	25.12
No. 50s:	3	No. 100s:	0

Test Bowling & Fielding

Wickets:	0	Runs:	0
Best Bowling:		Average:	0.00
5 WI:	0	10 WM:	0
Catches:	8	Stumpings:	0

'Nummy' Deane captained South Africa in 12 of his 17 Tests and despite playing against some of England's most powerful sides had a more than respectable record of two wins and six losses. He was a free flowing batsman whose highest Test score was an uncharacteristically watchful 93 against England at The Oval in 1929. Deane was talked into leading the side against England in South Africa in 1930/31 but after struggling in two Tests announced his retirement from all forms of cricket. He served as a selector and administrator before passing away from a heart attack at the age of only 44.

DIPPENAAR, Hendrik Human (Boeta)

Born:	June 14, 1977
Batting:	Right handed
Bowling:	Right arm off-break

Tests

Test Career:	1999-		
Cap Number:	273		
Tests Played:	37		

Test Batting

Innings:	60	Runs:	1,715
Highest Score:	177*	Average:	31.18
No. 50s:	7	No. 100s:	3

Test Bowling & Fielding

Wickets:	0	Runs:	1
Best Bowling:		Average:	0.00
5 WI:	0	10 WM:	0
Catches:	27	Stumpings:	0

One Day Internationals

ODI Career:	1999-		
ODIs Played:	99		

ODI Batting

Innings:	87	Runs:	3,234
Highest Score:	125*	Average:	43.70
No. 50s:	24	No. 100s:	4

ODI Bowling & Fielding

Wickets:	0	Runs:	0
Best Bowling:		Average:	0.00
5 WM:	0	Catches:	33
Stumpings:	0		

Like many of the current South African batsmen, Dippenaar's batting is like the girl with the curl. When he's good, he's very, very good but when he's bad he's terrible. He has three Test hundreds to his name including an unbeaten 177 against Bangladesh at Chittagong in 2003, but too many scores under 30 means that he has yet to make a spot in the top order his own.

DIXON, Cecil Donovan

Born:	February 12, 1891
Batting:	Right handed
Bowling:	Right arm medium

Tests

Test Career:	1914		
Cap Number:	88		
Tests Played:	1		

Test Batting

Innings:	2	Runs:	0
Highest Score:	0	Average:	0.00
No. 50s:	0	No. 100s:	0

Test Bowling & Fielding

Wickets:	3	Runs:	118
Best Bowling:	2/62	Average:	39.33
5 WI:	0	10 WM:	0
Catches:	1	Stumpings:	0

A quickish off spinner from Transvaal, he took three wickets in his only Test.

DONALD, Allan Anthony

Born:	October 20, 1966
Batting:	Right handed
Bowling:	Right arm fast

Tests

Test Career:	1992-2002		
Cap Number:	238		
Tests Played:	72		

Test Batting

Innings:	94	Runs:	652
Highest Score:	37	Average:	10.68
No. 50s:	0	No. 100s:	0

Test Bowling & Fielding

Wickets:	330	Runs:	7,344
Best Bowling:	8/71	Average:	22.25
5 WI:	20	10 WM:	3
Catches:	18	Stumpings:	0

One Day Internationals

ODI Career:	1991-2003		
ODIs Played:	164		

ODI Batting

Innings:	40	Runs:	95
Highest Score:	13	Average:	4.31
No. 50s:	0	No. 100s:	0

ODI Bowling & Fielding

Wickets:	272	Runs:	5,926
Best Bowling:	6/23	Average:	21.78
5 WM:	2	Catches:	28
Stumpings:	0		

He was a tireless opening bowler who was able to maintain top pace over both longs spells and a long and successful career. He was the first South African to take 300 wickets in Tests, no mean feat given he was already in his mid twenties when he played his first Test. Allan Donald had to wait until his country was readmitted to Test cricket in 1992, but from that very first Test at Bridgetown when he took six wickets it was clear that he was a world class opening bowler. Neither overly tall nor muscular, he derived his pace from a long, rhythmical run up and energetic ball release. For over a decade he shouldered the load in the South African side, taking five or more wickets in an innings on 20 occasions. In only his fourth Test he engineered the historic victory over India at Port Elizabeth in 1992. It was South Africa's first Test victory since 1970 and Donald received the 'Man of the Match' award for his 12 wicket return. In all he claimed 20 wickets in four Tests for the series to stamp himself as his country's primary spearhead. He claimed 11 wickets in a Test on two occasions, once in his country's first meeting with Zimbabwe in 1995/96 and then again when England toured in 1999/2000. The latter was during the first Test at Johannesburg when he had the tourists reeling in their first innings at four wickets for only two runs. Donald was still opening the bowling in the Test side at the age of 35, but the years of toil had taken its toll and whilst the mind was willing the body no longer allowed him to bowl as fast as he once did. Whilst the record books show he has been passed by Shaun Pollock as his country's leading wicket taker, he is still clearly the best fast bowler to have played for South Africa.

DOWER, Robert Reid

Born:	June 4, 1876
Batting:	Right handed

Tests
Test Career:	1899
Cap Number:	40
Tests Played:	1

Test Batting
Innings:	2	Runs:	9
Highest Score:	9	Average:	4.50
No. 50s:	0	No. 100s:	0

Test Bowling & Fielding
Wickets:	0	Runs:	0
Best Bowling:		Average:	0.00
5 WI:	0	10 WM:	0
Catches:	2	Stumpings:	0

A batsman from Eastern Province who had a rough time of it in his only Test scoring 0 and 9.

DRAPER, Ronald George
Born:	December 24, 1926
Batting:	Right handed Wicket Keeper

Tests
Test Career:	1950
Cap Number:	175
Tests Played:	2

Test Batting
Innings:	3	Runs:	25
Highest Score:	15	Average:	8.33
No. 50s:	0	No. 100s:	0

Test Bowling & Fielding
Wickets:	0	Runs:	0
Best Bowling:		Average:	0.00
5 WI:	0	10 WM:	0
Catches:	0	Stumpings:	0

A wicket keeper from Griqualand West who played two Tests against Australia as a batsman in 1950.

DU PREEZ, John Harcourt (Jackie)
Born:	November 14, 1942
Batting:	Right handed
Bowling:	Right arm leg-break

Tests
Test Career:	1967
Cap Number:	230
Tests Played:	2

Test Batting
Innings:	2	Runs:	0
Highest Score:	0	Average:	0.00
No. 50s:	0	No. 100s:	0

Test Bowling & Fielding
Wickets:	3	Runs:	51
Best Bowling:	2/22	Average:	17.00
5 WI:	0	10 WM:	0
Catches:	2	Stumpings:	0

A capable leg-spinner from Rhodesia who played two Tests against the touring Australians in 1967.

DU TOIT, Jacobus Francois (Flooi)
Born:	April 2, 1869
Batting:	Right handed
Bowling:	Right arm leg-break

Tests
Test Career:	1892
Cap Number:	16
Tests Played:	1

Test Batting
Innings:	2	Runs:	2
Highest Score:	2*	Average:	0.00
No. 50s:	0	No. 100s:	0

Test Bowling & Fielding
Wickets:	1	Runs:	47
Best Bowling:	1/47	Average:	47.00
5 WI:	0	10 WM:	0
Catches:	1	Stumpings:	0

A leg spinner who played in the South African side that met W.W. Read's Englishmen in 1892. He took a single wicket for the match.

DUCKWORTH, Christopher Anthony Russell
Born:	March 22, 1933
Batting:	Right handed Wicket Keeper

Tests
Test Career:	1957
Cap Number:	196
Tests Played:	2

Test Batting
Innings:	4	Runs:	28
Highest Score:	13	Average:	7.00
No. 50s:	0	No. 100s:	0

Test Bowling & Fielding
Wickets:	0	Runs:	0
Best Bowling:		Average:	0.00
5 WI:	0	10 WM:	0
Catches:	3	Stumpings:	0

South Africa's reserve keeper for almost a decade, his patience was rewarded in 1957 when he was chosen for two Tests against England as a batsman. Unfortunately for Duckworth he scored only 28 runs in his four at bats.

DUMBRILL, Richard
Born:	November 19, 1938
Batting:	Right handed
Bowling:	Right arm medium

Tests
Test Career:	1965-67
Cap Number:	227
Tests Played:	5

Test Batting
Innings:	10	Runs:	153
Highest Score:	36	Average:	15.30
No. 50s:	0	No. 100s:	0

Test Bowling & Fielding
Wickets:	9	Runs:	336
Best Bowling:	4/30	Average:	37.33
5 WI:	0	10 WM:	0
Catches:	3	Stumpings:	0

The English born all-rounder had limited chances in a strong South African side, but impressed on debut against England at Lord's in 1965 taking seven wickets.

DUMINY, Jacobus Petrus

Born: December 16, 1897
Batting: Left handed
Bowling: Left arm off-break

Tests
Test Career: 1927-29
Cap Number: 115
Tests Played: 3

Test Batting
Innings:	6	Runs:	30
Highest Score:	12	Average:	5.00
No. 50s:	0	No. 100s:	0

Test Bowling & Fielding
Wickets:	1	Runs:	39
Best Bowling:	1/17	Average:	39.00
5 WI:	0	10 WM:	0
Catches:	2	Stumpings:	0

A fine batsman for Transvaal, he showed little in two Tests against the touring English side in 1927/28 and was subsequently dropped. Whilst holidaying in Europe in 1929 he was called up to play a Test in Leeds but made only 12 and 2 and was again dropped for a second and final time.

DUMINY, Jean-Paul

Born: April 14, 1984
Batting: Left handed
Bowling: Right arm off-break

One Day Internationals
ODI Career: 2004
ODIs Played: 5

ODI Batting
Innings:	5	Runs:	29
Highest Score:	22	Average:	5.80
No. 50s:	0	No. 100s:	0

ODI Bowling & Fielding
Wickets:	1	Runs:	62
Best Bowling:	1/28	Average:	62.00
5 WM:	0	Catches:	2
Stumpings:	0		

A left hand batsman who played five ODI's on the 2004 tour of Sri Lanka. Still young enough to push for further international selection.

DUNELL, Owen Robert

Born: July 15, 1856
Batting: Right handed

Tests
Test Career: 1889
Cap Number: 1
Tests Played: 2

Test Batting
Innings:	4	Runs:	42
Highest Score:	26*	Average:	14.00
No. 50s:	0	No. 100s:	0

Test Bowling & Fielding
Wickets:	0	Runs:	0
Best Bowling:		Average:	0.00
5 WI:	0	10 WM:	0
Catches:	1	Stumpings:	0

South Africa's first Test side had precious little first class experience and despite the fact that Dunnell had attended Eton and Oxford but failed to make their first XI, he was made his country's first Test captain. He was one of only two batsmen to reach double figures in South Africa's first innings, scoring 26 not out.

DYER, Dennis Victor

Born: May 2, 1914
Batting: Right handed
Bowling: Left arm off-break

Tests
Test Career: 1947
Cap Number: 163
Tests Played: 3

Test Batting
Innings:	6	Runs:	96
Highest Score:	62	Average:	16.00
No. 50s:	1	No. 100s:	0

Test Bowling & Fielding
Wickets:	0	Runs:	0
Best Bowling:		Average:	0.00
5 WI:	0	10 WM:	0
Catches:	0	Stumpings:	0

A steady opening batsman from Natal who played three Tests on South Africa's tour of England in 1947.

EKSTEEN, Clive Edward

Born: December 2, 1966
Batting: Right handed
Bowling: Left arm off-break

Tests
Test Career: 1993-2000
Cap Number: 254
Tests Played: 7

Test Batting
Innings:	11	Runs:	91
Highest Score:	22	Average:	10.11
No. 50s:	0	No. 100s:	0

Test Bowling & Fielding
Wickets:	8	Runs:	494
Best Bowling:	3/12	Average:	61.75
5 WI:	0	10 WM:	0
Catches:	5	Stumpings:	0

One Day Internationals
ODI Career: 1991-94
ODIs Played: 6

ODI Batting
Innings:	2	Runs:	6
Highest Score:	6*	Average:	0.00
No. 50s:	0	No. 100s:	0

ODI Bowling & Fielding
Wickets:	2	Runs:	181
Best Bowling:	1/26	Average:	90.50
5 WM:	0	Catches:	3
Stumpings:	0		

A left arm orthodox spinner from Transvaal who played seven Tests over a seven year period, but could manage only eight wickets. In later years he was restricted by patellar tendonitis.

ELGIE, Michael Kelsey (Kim)

Born: March 6, 1933
Batting: Right handed
Bowling: Left arm off-break

Tests
Test Career:	1961-62		
Cap Number:	208		
Tests Played:	3		

Test Batting
Innings:	6	Runs:	75
Highest Score:	56	Average:	12.50
No. 50s:	1	No. 100s:	0

Test Bowling & Fielding
Wickets:	0	Runs:	46
Best Bowling:		Average:	0.00
5 WI:	0	10 WM:	0
Catches:	4	Stumpings:	0

A top order batsman from Natal who played all of his three Tests against the touring New Zealanders in 1961/62. Elgie was an excellent rugby player who represented Scotland in internationals.

ELWORTHY, Steven
Born: February 23, 1965
Batting: Right handed
Bowling: Right arm medium-fast

Tests
Test Career:	1998-2002		
Cap Number:	271		
Tests Played:	4		

Test Batting
Innings:	5	Runs:	72
Highest Score:	48	Average:	18.00
No. 50s:	0	No. 100s:	0

Test Bowling & Fielding
Wickets:	13	Runs:	444
Best Bowling:	4/66	Average:	34.15
5 WI:	0	10 WM:	0
Catches:	1	Stumpings:	0

One Day Internationals
ODI Career:	1998-2002		
ODIs Played:	39		

ODI Batting
Innings:	16	Runs:	100
Highest Score:	23	Average:	12.50
No. 50s:	0	No. 100s:	0

ODI Bowling & Fielding
Wickets:	44	Runs:	1,235
Best Bowling:	3/17	Average:	28.06
5 WM:	0	Catches:	9
Stumpings:	0		

A lean speedster who had played extensively in South Africa and England prior to being given his chance at Test level. His best effort was eight wickets in his only Test against New Zealand, at Wellington in 1998/99.

ENDEAN, William Russell (Russell)
Born: May 31, 1924
Batting: Right handed
Wicket Keeper

Tests
Test Career:	1951-58		
Cap Number:	184		
Tests Played:	28		

Test Batting
Innings:	52	Runs:	1,630
Highest Score:	162*	Average:	33.95
No. 50s:	8	No. 100s:	3

Test Bowling & Fielding
Wickets:	0	Runs:	0
Best Bowling:		Average:	0.00
5 WI:	0	10 WM:	0
Catches:	41	Stumpings:	0

Originally selected in the side as a keeper, he had to re-invent himself when shouldered out of that position by John Waite. Endean toured Australia as a batsman in 1952/53 scoring 438 in five Tests to clearly be South Africa's leading run scorer. He amassed a career high 162 not out at the MCG in an innings that took 452 minutes and earnt him the nickname 'endless Endean'. He scored two more Test hundreds, one against New Zealand and the other against England and coincidentally they were both scores of 116 that took just over four hours to compile. After discarding the gloves, Endean moved into the outfield where he joined the list of brilliant South African fieldsmen. An all-round athlete, he was also a member of the South African hockey side.

FARRER, William Stephen
Born: December 8, 1936
Batting: Right handed
Bowling: Right arm off-break

Tests
Test Career:	1962-64		
Cap Number:	213		
Tests Played:	6		

Test Batting
Innings:	10	Runs:	221
Highest Score:	40	Average:	27.62
No. 50s:	0	No. 100s:	0

Test Bowling & Fielding
Wickets:	0	Runs:	0
Best Bowling:		Average:	0.00
5 WI:	0	10 WM:	0
Catches:	2	Stumpings:	0

Nicknamed 'Buster', he was a fine all-round sportsman who was also a member of the South African hockey side. Farrer played in six Tests but could not find the form that made him a star with Border in the Currie Cup.

FAULKNER, George Aubrey
Born: December 17, 1881
Batting: Right handed
Bowling: Right arm leg-break

Tests
Test Career:	1906-24		
Cap Number:	58		
Tests Played:	25		

Test Batting
Innings:	47	Runs:	1,754
Highest Score:	204	Average:	40.79
No. 50s:	8	No. 100s:	4

Test Bowling & Fielding			
Wickets:	82	Runs:	2,180
Best Bowling:	7/84	Average:	26.58
5 WI:	4	10 WM:	0
Catches:	20	Stumpings:	0

Aubrey Faulkner was an all-rounder of the highest calibre, whose figures were not only outstanding for the era in which he played but still measure up today. He was a leg spinner with a range of deliveries that relied more on variations in pace rather directions of spin. His first Test was a triumph, as his four wickets in England's second innings played a major role in South Africa recording their first ever Test victory. Over the years he would have many triumphs with the ball, including 6/17 in a Test at Leeds in 1907 and 29 wickets during the Test series in England in 1909/10. He claimed 17 wickets during the triangular Test series held again in England in 1912 including career best figures of 7/84 in England's first innings at The Oval. As a batsman he may have had an unorthodox grip on the bat, but he was the ideal number three at once both difficult to remove yet capable of scoring quickly. He was the first South African to score a Test double century when he made 204 at the MCG in 1910/11. He was facing a strong Australian attack that included renowned paceman Tibby Cottter and the great slow bowler Warwick Armstrong yet was able to bring up his 200 in just over 300 balls. He played nearly all of his Test cricket prior to the First World War, where he served as a Major in the Middle East and Greece, but he did play a single unsuccessful Test as 42 year old in 1924. Following his retirement he became a distinguished coach, creating and running the Faulkner School of Cricket in Fulham, England. Sadly he suffered from depression, which was little understood at the time, and took his own life at his famous cricket academy in 1930.

FELLOWS-SMITH, Jonathan Payn

Born:	February 3, 1932		
Batting:	Right handed		
Bowling:	Right arm medium		
Tests			
Test Career:	1960		
Cap Number:	199		
Tests Played:	4		
Test Batting			
Innings:	8	Runs:	166
Highest Score:	35	Average:	27.66
No. 50s:	0	No. 100s:	0
Test Bowling & Fielding			
Wickets:	0	Runs:	61
Best Bowling:		Average:	0.00
5 WI:	0	10 WM:	0
Catches:	2	Stumpings:	0

Nicknamed Pom-Pom, he was an all-rounder who played the bulk of his first class cricket in England. He was chosen for the side that toured England in 1960, but in four Tests failed to take a wicket never scored more than 35 in an innings.

FICHARDT, Charles Gustav

Born:	March 20, 1870		
Batting:	Right handed		
Tests			
Test Career:	1892-96		
Cap Number:	17		
Tests Played:	2		
Test Batting			
Innings:	4	Runs:	15
Highest Score:	10	Average:	3.75
No. 50s:	0	No. 100s:	0
Test Bowling & Fielding			
Wickets:	0	Runs:	0
Best Bowling:		Average:	0.00
5 WI:	0	10 WM:	0
Catches:	2	Stumpings:	0

A well performed club cricketer in South Africa, he also played first class cricket for Orange Free State where he was an upper order batsman and slow underarm lob bowler.

FINLASON, Charles Edward

Born:	February 19, 1860		
Batting:	Right handed		
Bowling:	Right arm fast		
Tests			
Test Career:	1889		
Cap Number:	2		
Tests Played:	1		
Test Batting			
Innings:	2	Runs:	6
Highest Score:	6	Average:	3.00
No. 50s:	0	No. 100s:	0
Test Bowling & Fielding			
Wickets:	0	Runs:	7
Best Bowling:		Average:	0.00
5 WI:	0	10 WM:	0
Catches:	0	Stumpings:	0

A journalist who went on to become editor of the Johannesburg Star, he played in South Africa's first Test side.

FINLAY-BISSETT, George

Born:	November 5, 1905		
Batting:	Right handed		
Bowling:	Right arm fast		
Tests			
Test Career:	1928		
Cap Number:	119		
Tests Played:	4		
Test Batting			
Innings:	4	Runs:	38
Highest Score:	23	Average:	19.00
No. 50s:	0	No. 100s:	0
Test Bowling & Fielding			
Wickets:	25	Runs:	469
Best Bowling:	7/29	Average:	18.76
5 WI:	2	10 WM:	0
Catches:	0	Stumpings:	0

The lanky opening bowler saved the series against England in 1927/28 when he bowled his side to victory in the final Test at Durban. He tore though the Englishmen taking 7/29 claiming the likes of Walter Hammond along the way. Even though he continued on in the Currie Cup for another two seasons, that outstanding spell was to be his last act in Test cricket.

FLOQUET, Claude Eugene

Born:	November 3, 1884
Batting:	Right handed
Bowling:	Right arm medium

Tests

Test Career:	1910
Cap Number:	69
Tests Played:	1

Test Batting

Innings:	2	Runs:	12
Highest Score:	11*	Average:	12.00
No. 50s:	0	No. 100s:	0

Test Bowling & Fielding

Wickets:	0	Runs:	24
Best Bowling:		Average:	0.00
5 WI:	0	10 WM:	0
Catches:	0	Stumpings:	0

An opening batsman from Transvaal, he played in only six first class matches one of which was a Test against England at Johannesburg in 1910.

FRANCIS, Howard Henry

Born:	May 26, 1868
Batting:	Right handed
	Wicket Keeper

Tests

Test Career:	1899
Cap Number:	41
Tests Played:	2

Test Batting

Innings:	4	Runs:	39
Highest Score:	29	Average:	9.75
No. 50s:	0	No. 100s:	0

Test Bowling & Fielding

Wickets:	0	Runs:	0
Best Bowling:		Average:	0.00
5 WI:	0	10 WM:	0
Catches:	1	Stumpings:	0

A wicket keeper who studied in England and played a handful of games with Gloucesterhire. He played two Tests against Lord Hawke's English side in 1899.

FRANCOIS, Cyril Matthew

Born:	June 20, 1897
Batting:	Right handed
Bowling:	Right arm medium-fast

Tests

Test Career:	1922-23
Cap Number:	104
Tests Played:	5

Test Batting

Innings:	9	Runs:	252
Highest Score:	72	Average:	31.50
No. 50s:	1	No. 100s:	0

Test Bowling & Fielding

Wickets:	6	Runs:	225
Best Bowling:	3/23	Average:	37.50
5 WI:	0	10 WM:	0
Catches:	5	Stumpings:	0

The English born all rounder played in all five Tests against the touring Englishmen in 1922/23. Batting down the order, the strongly built Francois put plenty of gusto into his work, hitting 252 runs including a quickfire 72 at Kingsmead in the Third Test.

FRANK, Charles Newton

| Born: | January 27, 1891 |
| Batting: | Right handed |

Tests

Test Career:	1921
Cap Number:	95
Tests Played:	3

Test Batting

Innings:	6	Runs:	236
Highest Score:	152	Average:	39.33
No. 50s:	0	No. 100s:	1

Test Bowling & Fielding

Wickets:	0	Runs:	0
Best Bowling:		Average:	0.00
5 WI:	0	10 WM:	0
Catches:	0	Stumpings:	0

Charlie Frank had survived the horrors of the First World War to return home and earn a spot against the Australian side that toured in 1921/22. He played one of cricket's most stubborn innings in the second Test at Johannesburg, when his 152 took a grueling 512 minutes and denied the powerful Australians a victory they were expecting.

FRANK, William Hughes Bowker

Born:	November 23, 1872
Batting:	Right handed
Bowling:	Right arm medium

Tests

Test Career:	1896
Cap Number:	31
Tests Played:	1

Test Batting

Innings:	2	Runs:	7
Highest Score:	5	Average:	3.50
No. 50s:	0	No. 100s:	0

Test Bowling & Fielding

Wickets:	1	Runs:	52
Best Bowling:	1/52	Average:	52.00
5 WI:	0	10 WM:	0
Catches:	0	Stumpings:	0

A medium pace bowler who played a single Test against England at Johannesburg in 1896.

FULLER, Edward Russell Henry

Born:	August 2, 1931
Batting:	Right handed
Bowling:	Right arm medium-fast

Tests
Test Career:	1953-58
Cap Number:	187
Tests Played:	7

Test Batting
Innings:	9	Runs:	64
Highest Score:	17	Average:	8.00
No. 50s:	0	No. 100s:	0

Test Bowling & Fielding
Wickets:	22	Runs:	668
Best Bowling:	5/66	Average:	30.36
5 WI:	1	10 WM:	0
Catches:	3	Stumpings:	0

A right arm medium fast bowler from Western Province who played a key role on the tour to Australia in 1952/53. In only his second Test he took 3/74 and 5/66 at the MCG. It proved to be the series decider as South Africa won the Test and leveled the series. Fuller would play a handful more Tests but never enjoy the same success as he did at the MCG in February of 1953.

FULLERTON, George Murray
Born:	December 8, 1922
Batting:	Right handed
Bowling:	Right arm medium
	Wicket Keeper

Tests
Test Career:	1947-51
Cap Number:	165
Tests Played:	7

Test Batting
Innings:	13	Runs:	325
Highest Score:	88	Average:	25.00
No. 50s:	3	No. 100s:	0

Test Bowling & Fielding
Wickets:	0	Runs:	0
Best Bowling:		Average:	0.00
5 WI:	0	10 WM:	0
Catches:	10	Stumpings:	2

A more than useful cricketer from Transvaal who played in the Test side both as a keeper and as a stand alone batsman. His best effort with the bat was against Australia in 1949/50 when he scored 88 at Johannesburg in the fourth Test. Fullerton was playing as a wicket keeper at the time.

FUNSTON, Kenneth James
Born:	December 3, 1925
Batting:	Right handed

Tests
Test Career:	1952-58
Cap Number:	185
Tests Played:	18

Test Batting
Innings:	33	Runs:	824
Highest Score:	92	Average:	25.75
No. 50s:	5	No. 100s:	0

Test Bowling & Fielding
Wickets:	0	Runs:	0
Best Bowling:		Average:	0.00
5 WI:	0	10 WM:	0
Catches:	7	Stumpings:	0

He was a good striker of the ball who had a fine debut at Brisbane in 1952/53 scoring 33 and 65 against a strong Australian attack. He scored 92 in that same series at Adelaide but was disappointing thereafter and departed Test cricket with an average in the mid twenties.

GAMSY, Dennis
Born:	February 17, 1940
Batting:	Right handed
	Wicket Keeper

Tests
Test Career:	1970
Cap Number:	232
Tests Played:	2

Test Batting
Innings:	3	Runs:	39
Highest Score:	30*	Average:	19.50
No. 50s:	0	No. 100s:	0

Test Bowling & Fielding
Wickets:	0	Runs:	0
Best Bowling:		Average:	0.00
5 WI:	0	10 WM:	0
Catches:	5	Stumpings:	0

The bespectacled keeper made the Test side in 1970, but after only two Tests was faced with the prospect of no longer having a country to play for when South Africa was isolated because of its apartheid policy.

GIBBS, Herschelle Herman
Born:	February 23, 1974
Batting:	Right handed
Bowling:	Right arm medium

Tests
Test Career:	1996-
Cap Number:	264
Tests Played:	79

Test Batting
Innings:	135	Runs:	5,728
Highest Score:	228	Average:	44.40
No. 50s:	22	No. 100s:	14

Test Bowling & Fielding
Wickets:	0	Runs:	4
Best Bowling:		Average:	0.00
5 WI:	0	10 WM:	0
Catches:	72	Stumpings:	0

One Day Internationals
ODI Career:	1996-
ODIs Played:	185

ODI Batting
Innings:	184	Runs:	6,117
Highest Score:	175	Average:	35.77
No. 50s:	25	No. 100s:	16

ODI Bowling & Fielding
Wickets:	0	Runs:	0
Best Bowling:		Average:	0.00
5 WM:	0	Catches:	77
Stumpings:	0		

When he made his debut for Western Province at the age of only 16, Gibbs was seen as a batsman with the talent to lead his country back to the top of the cricket tree. Whilst he has since carved out a fine international career, and is the third highest scorer in the history of South African Test cricket, he hasn't quite lived up to those early expectations. He was unfortunately involved in the match fixing scandal with Hansie Cronje who offered him $15,000 to score "less than 20" in a one day international. He tearfully told the King Commission of inquiry into corruption in South African cricket that he couldn't bring himself to throwing his wicket, and ultimately made 74. He was banned for six months, and even though he has served his sentence he still refuses to tour India for fear of being arrested over the incident. Possibly even more damaging than his involvement in the scandal was his portrayal as a naive pawn. It did little for the image of a man described by those who know him as a decent and caring person. Gibbs fought back after his suspension to play many fine innings for South Africa, including his pulsating 175 off 111 balls in a One Day International against Australia in 2006, that saw the Proteas chase down a total of over 400. He has many monumental Test scores to his credit, including a high of 228 against Pakistan at Cape Town in 2002/03. Poor form saw him dropped during the series against New Zealand early in 2006 but he was recalled to the side to play Sri Lanka, and made 92 in his last knock at Colombo.

GLEESON, Robert Anthony

Born: December 6, 1873
Batting: Right handed
Bowling: Right arm medium

Tests

Test Career: 1896
Cap Number: 25
Tests Played: 1

Test Batting
Innings:	2	Runs:	4
Highest Score:	3	Average:	4.00
No. 50s:	0	No. 100s:	0

Test Bowling & Fielding
Wickets:	0	Runs:	0
Best Bowling:		Average:	0.00
5 WI:	0	10 WM:	0
Catches:	2	Stumpings:	0

A batsman from Eastern Province who played a single Test against Lord Hawke's touring Englishmen in 1896.

GLOVER, George Keyworth

Born: May 13, 1870
Batting: Right handed
Bowling: Right arm off-break

Tests

Test Career: 1896
Cap Number: 36
Tests Played: 1

Test Batting
Innings:	2	Runs:	21
Highest Score:	18*	Average:	21.00
No. 50s:	0	No. 100s:	0

Test Bowling & Fielding
Wickets:	1	Runs:	28
Best Bowling:	1/28	Average:	28.00
5 WI:	0	10 WM:	0
Catches:	0	Stumpings:	0

An English educated all-rounder who did little in his two Tests but did score a century for Transvaal in Currie Cup competition.

GODDARD, Trevor Leslie

Born: August 1, 1931
Batting: Left handed
Bowling: Left arm medium

Tests

Test Career: 1955-70
Cap Number: 192
Tests Played: 41

Test Batting
Innings:	78	Runs:	2,516
Highest Score:	112	Average:	34.46
No. 50s:	18	No. 100s:	1

Test Bowling & Fielding
Wickets:	123	Runs:	3,226
Best Bowling:	6/53	Average:	26.22
5 WI:	5	10 WM:	0
Catches:	48	Stumpings:	0

One of South Africa's most respected Test captains, he was a fine technician both with bat and ball. Goddard made his Test debut in 1955 on the tour of England and whilst he scored two elegant half centuries, it was his bowling that caught the eye. A left hander who relied on movement in the air rather than sheer pace, he captured 25 wickets in five Tests on that debut tour for a cost of only 21.12, securing his spot in the national side in the process. He was a guarded opening batsman whose only Test hundred was against the touring English side in 1964/65, and as captain he was just as circumspect. Under his leadership the side drew ten out of thirteen Tests, but he did return home from Australia with a series draw in 1963/64 when most pundits expected them to suffer a heavy defeat. As a 38 year old Goddard was still a member of the Test team when South Africa was banned from all international matches in 1970. In retirement he became an evangelist preacher.

GORDON, Norman

Born: August 6, 1911
Batting: Right handed
Bowling: Right arm fast

Tests

Test Career: 1938-39
Cap Number: 151
Tests Played: 5

Test Batting
Innings:	6	Runs:	8
Highest Score:	7*	Average:	2.00
No. 50s:	0	No. 100s:	0

Test Bowling & Fielding

Wickets:	20	Runs:	807
Best Bowling:	5/103	Average:	40.35
5 WI:	2	10 WM:	0
Catches:	1	Stumpings:	0

A more than capable fast bowler from Transvaal, he played five Tests before World War II brought a premature curtain down on his career. He played all of his Tests in the series against England at home in 1938/39 and was the leading wicket taker for either side with 20. Unlike a number a batsman who were able to resume after the war, the ten year break was too long for a genuine paceman and he never played for South Africa again. In 2006 the 95 year old was his country's oldest living Test cricketer.

GRAHAM, Robert

Born:	September 16, 1877
Batting:	Right handed
Bowling:	Right arm medium

Tests

Test Career:	1899		
Cap Number:	42		
Tests Played:	2		

Test Batting

Innings:	4	Runs:	6
Highest Score:	4	Average:	1.50
No. 50s:	0	No. 100s:	0

Test Bowling & Fielding

Wickets:	3	Runs:	127
Best Bowling:	2/22	Average:	42.33
5 WI:	0	10 WM:	0
Catches:	2	Stumpings:	0

A bowler from Cape Colony and later Western Province who played two Tests in 1899. He enjoyed a successful tour of England in 1901.

GRIEVESON, Ronald Eustace

Born:	August 24, 1909
Batting:	Right handed
	Wicket Keeper

Tests

Test Career:	1939		
Cap Number:	155		
Tests Played:	2		

Test Batting

Innings:	2	Runs:	114
Highest Score:	75	Average:	57.00
No. 50s:	1	No. 100s:	0

Test Bowling & Fielding

Wickets:	0	Runs:	0
Best Bowling:		Average:	0.00
5 WI:	0	10 WM:	0
Catches:	7	Stumpings:	3

A wicket keeper who stood in two Tests against England in 1939. He scored a 75 in the 'timeless' Test at Durban and completed ten dismissals behind the stumps. Unfortunately due to the war he would be denied the chance of furthering his Test career.

GRIFFIN, Geoffrey Merton

Born:	June 12, 1939
Batting:	Right handed
Bowling:	Right arm fast

Tests

Test Career:	1960		
Cap Number:	200		
Tests Played:	2		

Test Batting

Innings:	4	Runs:	25
Highest Score:	14	Average:	6.25
No. 50s:	0	No. 100s:	0

Test Bowling & Fielding

Wickets:	8	Runs:	192
Best Bowling:	4/87	Average:	24.00
5 WI:	0	10 WM:	0
Catches:	0	Stumpings:	0

Long before the controversy that surrounded Murali and his perennially bent arm, came George Griffin. He had suffered an accident in childhood, and like Murali couldn't fully extend his arm. A tall and robust paceman, he burst on to the scene at Lord's in only his second Test when he became the first South African to take a Test hat-trick. In the very next match on that tour, the crooked-armed quick was no-balled eleven times, bringing his Test career to an untimely end.

HALL, Alfred Ewart

Born:	January 23, 1896
Batting:	Left handed
Bowling:	Left arm medium-fast

Tests

Test Career:	1923-31		
Cap Number:	106		
Tests Played:	7		

Test Batting

Innings:	8	Runs:	11
Highest Score:	5	Average:	1.83
No. 50s:	0	No. 100s:	0

Test Bowling & Fielding

Wickets:	40	Runs:	886
Best Bowling:	7/63	Average:	22.15
5 WI:	3	10 WM:	1
Catches:	4	Stumpings:	0

The English born Hall opened the bowling for Transvaal and represented South Africa in Tests on seven occasions. He made his debut on the mats at Cape Town in 1923 and duly won the match for his adopted country taking 7/63 and 4/49 to snatch victory by only one wicket. He later returned to England to play for Lancashire in county cricket.

HALL, Andrew James

Born:	July 31, 1975
Batting:	Right handed
Bowling:	Right arm medium-fast

Tests

Test Career:	2002-
Cap Number:	284
Tests Played:	19

Test Batting

Innings:	30	Runs:	735
Highest Score:	163	Average:	28.26
No. 50s:	3	No. 100s:	1

Test Bowling & Fielding

Wickets:	39	Runs:	1,511
Best Bowling:	3/1	Average:	38.74
5 WI:	0	10 WM:	0
Catches:	15	Stumpings:	0

One Day Internationals

ODI Career:	1999-
ODIs Played:	68

ODI Batting

Innings:	46	Runs:	761
Highest Score:	81	Average:	21.74
No. 50s:	2	No. 100s:	0

ODI Bowling & Fielding

Wickets:	65	Runs:	1,848
Best Bowling:	4/23	Average:	28.34
5 WM:	0	Catches:	23
Stumpings:	0		

Fortunate to survive a shooting in 1998, Andrew Hall not only lived to tell the tale but has gone on to be a fine Test all rounder. He made 70 on debut against Australia at Cape Town in 2002, a performance good enough to win him a spot in the side that toured England a year later. Hall had been performing well as the fourth paceman but was struggling with the bat when he made a telling contribution in the fourth Test at Headingly. South Africa was labouring at 7/232, but his 99 not out was enough to get the score to 365 and ensure victory for the tourists. The disappointment of missing out on a Test century in England was put to bed at Kanpur in 2004, when he took to the Indians and made a career high 163. The all rounder is also an energetic fieldsman and looks set to play a key role in South Africa's bid to win the 2007 World Cup.

HALL, Glen Gordon

Born:	May 24, 1938
Batting:	Right handed
Bowling:	Right arm leg-break

Tests

Test Career:	1965
Cap Number:	223
Tests Played:	1

Test Batting

Innings:	1	Runs:	0
Highest Score:	0	Average:	0.00
No. 50s:	0	No. 100s:	0

Test Bowling & Fielding

Wickets:	1	Runs:	94
Best Bowling:	1/94	Average:	94.00
5 WI:	0	10 WM:	0
Catches:	0	Stumpings:	0

A leg spinner who was given one Test against England at Cape Town in 1965.

HALLIWELL, Ernest Austin (Baberton)

Born:	September 7, 1864
Batting:	Right handed
	Wicket Keeper

Tests

Test Career:	1892-1902
Cap Number:	18
Tests Played:	8

Test Batting

Innings:	15	Runs:	188
Highest Score:	57	Average:	12.53
No. 50s:	1	No. 100s:	0

Test Bowling & Fielding

Wickets:	0	Runs:	0
Best Bowling:	0	Average:	0.00
5 WI:	0	10 WM:	0
Catches:	9	Stumpings:	2

South Africa's third captain, he was an excellent wicket keeper batsman who played first class cricket in South Africa and county cricket in England with Middlesex. He scored 41 against England at Johannesburg in 1895/96 and in his country's first Test against Australia in 1902/03 scored 57 coming in at number nine. As a keeper he was considered world class, standing up to the stumps when South Africa's fastest bowler Johannes Kotze was bowling.

HALSE, Clive Grey

Born:	February 28, 1935
Batting:	Right handed
Bowling:	Right arm fast

Tests

Test Career:	1964
Cap Number:	221
Tests Played:	3

Test Batting

Innings:	3	Runs:	30
Highest Score:	19*	Average:	0.00
No. 50s:	0	No. 100s:	0

Test Bowling & Fielding

Wickets:	6	Runs:	260
Best Bowling:	3/50	Average:	43.33
5 WI:	0	10 WM:	0
Catches:	1	Stumpings:	0

A speedster from Natal who toured Australia in 1963/64 and played three Tests.

HANDS, Philip Albert Myburgh

Born:	March 18, 1890
Batting:	Right handed
Bowling:	Right arm medium

Tests

Test Career:	1913-24
Cap Number:	84
Tests Played:	7

Test Batting

Innings:	12	Runs:	300
Highest Score:	83	Average:	25.00
No. 50s:	2	No. 100s:	0

Test Bowling & Fielding

Wickets:	0	Runs:	18
Best Bowling:		Average:	0.00
5 WI:	0	10 WM:	0
Catches:	3	Stumpings:	0

Phillip Hands played his early Tests against England in 1913/14 but then had to wait almost eight years for his next chance because of World War I. He didn't remain idle during those war years serving his country with distinction and receiving medals for bravery.

HANDS, Reginald Harry Myburgh
Born: June 26, 1888
Batting: Right handed

Tests
Test Career:	1914
Cap Number:	93
Tests Played:	1

Test Batting
Innings:	2	Runs:	7
Highest Score:	7	Average:	3.50
No. 50s:	0	No. 100s:	0

Test Bowling & Fielding
Wickets:	0	Runs:	0
Best Bowling:		Average:	0.00
5 WI:	0	10 WM:	0
Catches:	0	Stumpings:	0

The brother of Philip, he made no impact in his only Test against England at Port Elizabeth in 1914. Like his brother he served with distinction in the First World War but tragically never returned home.

HANLEY, Martin Andrew
Born: November 10, 1918
Batting: Right handed
Bowling: Right arm off-break

Tests
Test Career:	1949
Cap Number:	169
Tests Played:	1

Test Batting
Innings:	1	Runs:	0
Highest Score:	0	Average:	0.00
No. 50s:	0	No. 100s:	0

Test Bowling & Fielding
Wickets:	1	Runs:	88
Best Bowling:	1/57	Average:	88.00
5 WI:	0	10 WM:	0
Catches:	0	Stumpings:	0

A more than handy off spinner with Western Province, he played in just the one Test against England at Newlands in 1949.

HARRIS, Terence Anthony (Tony)
Born: August 27, 1916
Batting: Right handed

Tests
Test Career:	1947-49
Cap Number:	157
Tests Played:	3

Test Batting
Innings:	5	Runs:	100
Highest Score:	60	Average:	25.00
No. 50s:	1	No. 100s:	0

Test Bowling & Fielding
Wickets:	0	Runs:	0
Best Bowling:		Average:	0.00
5 WI:	0	10 WM:	0
Catches:	1	Stumpings:	0

A diminutive right handed batsman from Cape Province who toured the UK in 1947. He scored 60 on debut at Trent Bridge but showed little in his next two Tests.

HARTIGAN, Gerald Patrick Desmond
Born: December 30, 1884
Batting: Right handed
Bowling: Right arm medium-fast

Tests
Test Career:	1912-14
Cap Number:	75
Tests Played:	5

Test Batting
Innings:	10	Runs:	114
Highest Score:	51	Average:	11.40
No. 50s:	1	No. 100s:	0

Test Bowling & Fielding
Wickets:	1	Runs:	141
Best Bowling:	1/72	Average:	141.00
5 WI:	0	10 WM:	0
Catches:	0	Stumpings:	0

He was an accomplished sportsman who played both association football and cricket for South Africa. His cricket career amounted to little with only the single half century against England at Johannesburg in 1913/14 of any note, though the intervention of World War I restricted his opportunities.

HARVEY, Robert Lyon
Born: September 14, 1911
Batting: Right handed
Bowling: Right arm medium

Tests
Test Career:	1936
Cap Number:	149
Tests Played:	2

Test Batting
Innings:	4	Runs:	51
Highest Score:	28	Average:	12.75
No. 50s:	0	No. 100s:	0

Test Bowling & Fielding
Wickets:	0	Runs:	0
Best Bowling:		Average:	0.00
5 WI:	0	10 WM:	0
Catches:	0	Stumpings:	0

An accomplished right handed batsman from Natal who achieved little in his two Tests with a top score of only 28 against Australia at Kingsmead in 1936.

HATHORN, Christopher Maitland Howard
Born: April 7, 1878
Batting: Right handed

Tests
Test Career:	1902-11		
Cap Number:	49		
Tests Played:	12		

Test Batting
Innings:	20	Runs:	325
Highest Score:	102	Average:	17.10
No. 50s:	0	No. 100s:	1

Test Bowling & Fielding
Wickets:	0	Runs:	0
Best Bowling:		Average:	0.00
5 WI:	0	10 WM:	0
Catches:	5	Stumpings:	0

A number three batsman of note, he scored a century at Johannesburg in 1906 to guide South Africa to victory over England.

HAYWARD, Mornantau (Nantie)
Born:	March 6, 1977
Batting:	Right handed
Bowling:	Right arm fast

Tests
Test Career:	1999-2004		
Cap Number:	274		
Tests Played:	16		

Test Batting
Innings:	17	Runs:	66
Highest Score:	14	Average:	7.33
No. 50s:	0	No. 100s:	0

Test Bowling & Fielding
Wickets:	54	Runs:	1,609
Best Bowling:	5/56	Average:	29.79
5 WI:	1	10 WM:	0
Catches:	4	Stumpings:	0

One Day Internationals
ODI Career:	1998-2002		
ODIs Played:	21		

ODI Batting
Innings:	5	Runs:	12
Highest Score:	4	Average:	3.00
No. 50s:	0	No. 100s:	0

ODI Bowling & Fielding
Wickets:	21	Runs:	858
Best Bowling:	4/31	Average:	40.85
5 WM:	0	Catches:	4
Stumpings:	0		

The ghostly speedster from Cape Province was seen as Allan Donald's successor when he played his first Test in 1999/2000. The paceman showed promise with four wickets in his first Test against England, but apart from a seven wicket effort against Pakistan three years later, he hasn't proved to be the consistent strike bowler that selectors had hoped for.

HEARNE, Frank
Born:	November 23, 1858
Batting:	Right handed
Bowling:	Right arm medium-fast

Tests
Test Career:	1889-96
Cap Number:	19
Tests Played:	6

Test Batting
Innings:	10	Runs:	168
Highest Score:	30	Average:	16.80
No. 50s:	0	No. 100s:	0

Test Bowling & Fielding
Wickets:	2	Runs:	40
Best Bowling:	2/40	Average:	20.00
5 WI:	0	10 WM:	0
Catches:	3	Stumpings:	0

Only a shade taller than the stumps, Hearne was a fine top order batsman and useful slow bowler who played Test cricket for both England and South Africa. He toured South Africa in 1888/89, and so enjoyed his time there that he emigrated and played in four Tests for his adopted country when England returned in 1891/92.

HEARNE, George Alfred Lawrence
Born:	March 27, 1888
Batting:	Right handed
	Wicket Keeper

Tests
Test Career:	1922-24
Cap Number:	105
Tests Played:	3

Test Batting
Innings:	5	Runs:	59
Highest Score:	28	Average:	11.80
No. 50s:	0	No. 100s:	0

Test Bowling & Fielding
Wickets:	0	Runs:	0
Best Bowling:		Average:	0.00
5 WI:	0	10 WM:	0
Catches:	3	Stumpings:	0

The son of Frank Hearne who played for England and South Africa, and related to numerous other Hearnes who played in England, he lined up in three Tests for his adopted country but could manage no more than 28 in any one innings.

HEINE, Peter Samuel
Born:	June 28, 1928
Batting:	Right handed
Bowling:	Right arm fast

Tests
Test Career:	1955-62
Cap Number:	193
Tests Played:	14

Test Batting
Innings:	24	Runs:	209
Highest Score:	31	Average:	9.95
No. 50s:	0	No. 100s:	0

Test Bowling & Fielding
Wickets:	58	Runs:	1,455
Best Bowling:	6/58	Average:	25.08
5 WI:	4	10 WM:	0
Catches:	8	Stumpings:	0

A strapping fireman from Orange Free State, he opened the bowling with Neil Adcock in most of his fourteen Tests and like his new ball partner generated plenty of pace and bounce. Heine in fact outbowled his more illustrious teammate in

Australia in 1957/58 when he led the aggregates and averages with 17 wickets at a cost of 18.88. In a short but sharp Test career he took five or more wickets in an innings on four separate occasions including an eye-catching 5/60 on debut at Lord's in 1955.

HENDERSON, Claude William

Born: June 14, 1972
Batting: Right handed
Bowling: Left arm off-break

Tests
Test Career: 2001-02
Cap Number: 280
Tests Played: 75

Test Batting
Innings:	74	Runs:	65
Highest Score:	30	Average:	9.28
No. 50s:	0	No. 100s:	0

Test Bowling & Fielding
Wickets:	22	Runs:	928
Best Bowling:	4/116	Average:	42.18
5 WI:	0	10 WM:	0
Catches:	2	Stumpings:	0

One Day Internationals
ODI Career: 2001
ODIs Played: 4

ODI Batting
Innings:	0	Runs:	0
Highest Score:	0	Average:	0.00
No. 50s:	0	No. 100s:	0

ODI Bowling & Fielding
Wickets:	7	Runs:	132
Best Bowling:	4/17	Average:	18.85
5 WM:	0	Catches:	0
Stumpings:	0		

A left arm off spinner from Boland who was 29 when he made his debut against Zimbabwe in 2001. He had won a spot in the side after Nicky Boje became unavailable because of injury, but after taking 22 wickets in seven Tests, Henderson was replaced by a then fully recovered Boje.

HENRY, Omar

Born: January 23, 1952
Batting: Right handed
Bowling: Left arm off-break

Tests
Test Career: 1992-93
Cap Number: 248
Tests Played: 3

Test Batting
Innings:	3	Runs:	53
Highest Score:	34	Average:	17.66
No. 50s:	0	No. 100s:	0

Test Bowling & Fielding
Wickets:	3	Runs:	189
Best Bowling:	2/56	Average:	63.00
5 WI:	0	10 WM:	0
Catches:	2	Stumpings:	0

One Day Internationals
ODI Career: 1992
ODIs Played: 3

ODI Batting
Innings:	3	Runs:	20
Highest Score:	11	Average:	10.00
No. 50s:	0	No. 100s:	0

ODI Bowling & Fielding
Wickets:	2	Runs:	125
Best Bowling:	1/31	Average:	62.50
5 WM:	0	Catches:	1
Stumpings:	0		

Henry was already 40 when he played the first of his three Tests against the touring Indians in 1992. Whilst the slightly built left arm off spinner did little, it was a historic moment for South African cricket as he was first non-white to ever play in the Test side.

HIME, Charles Frederick William

Born: October 24, 1869
Batting: Right handed
Bowling: Right arm medium

Tests
Test Career: 1896
Cap Number: 26
Tests Played: 1

Test Batting
Innings:	2	Runs:	8
Highest Score:	8	Average:	4.00
No. 50s:	0	No. 100s:	0

Test Bowling & Fielding
Wickets:	1	Runs:	31
Best Bowling:	1/20	Average:	31.00
5 WI:	0	10 WM:	0
Catches:	0	Stumpings:	0

An all rounder who came to prominence when he took six wickets for Pietermaritzburg against England in 1888/89. He was rewarded with a Test many years later but achieved little and was not called upon again.

HUDSON, Andrew Charles

Born: March 17, 1965
Batting: Right handed
Bowling: Right arm medium

Tests
Test Career: 1992-98
Cap Number: 239
Tests Played: 35

Test Batting
Innings:	63	Runs:	2,007
Highest Score:	163	Average:	33.45
No. 50s:	13	No. 100s:	4

Test Bowling & Fielding
Wickets:	0	Runs:	0
Best Bowling:		Average:	0.00
5 WI:	0	10 WM:	0
Catches:	36	Stumpings:	0

One Day Internationals
ODI Career: 1991-97
ODIs Played: 89

ODI Batting
Innings:	88	Runs:	2,559
Highest Score:	161	Average:	29.41
No. 50s:	18	No. 100s:	2

ODI Bowling & Fielding
Wickets:	0	Runs:	3
Best Bowling:		Average:	0.00
5 WM:	0	Catches:	18
Stumpings:	0		

South Africa was given a stern test on their return to Test cricket in 1992. A one-off match against the West Indies in Bridgetown was no easy task given their opponents boasted an attack that included Curtly Ambrose, Courtney Walsh and Patrick Patterson. It was a tight fought encounter with South Africa almost pulling off a surprise victory thanks to the batting heroics of Andrew Hudson. The opener defied the West Indian paceman for 519 minutes, making 163 and holding the innings together. That was to be the Natal opener's highest Test score and was at the time the highest score on debut by any South African. He would go on to offer stout resistance at the top of the order for another six years, but Andrew Hudson will be best remembered for the role he played in his country's first Test for over two decades.

HUTCHINSON, Philip
Born:	January 25, 1862
Batting:	Right handed

Tests
Test Career:	1889
Cap Number:	3
Tests Played:	2

Test Batting
Innings:	4	Runs:	14
Highest Score:	11	Average:	3.50
No. 50s:	0	No. 100s:	0

Test Bowling & Fielding
Wickets:	0	Runs:	0
Best Bowling:		Average:	0.00
5 WI:	0	10 WM:	0
Catches:	3	Stumpings:	0

An English born batsman who played in his country's first two Tests.

IRONSIDE, David Ernest James
Born:	May 2, 1925
Batting:	Right handed
Bowling:	Right arm medium-fast

Tests
Test Career:	1953-54
Cap Number:	190
Tests Played:	3

Test Batting
Innings:	4	Runs:	37
Highest Score:	13	Average:	18.50
No. 50s:	0	No. 100s:	0

Test Bowling & Fielding
Wickets:	15	Runs:	275
Best Bowling:	5/51	Average:	18.33
5 WI:	1	10 WM:	0
Catches:	1	Stumpings:	0

The Mozambique born swing bowler performed well in his only three Tests, taking 15 wickets in total including eight on debut at Johannesburg.

IRVINE, Brian Lee (Lee)
Born:	March 9, 1944
Batting:	Left handed
Bowling:	Right arm medium Wicket Keeper

Tests
Test Career:	1970
Cap Number:	233
Tests Played:	4

Test Batting
Innings:	7	Runs:	353
Highest Score:	102	Average:	50.42
No. 50s:	2	No. 100s:	1

Test Bowling & Fielding
Wickets:	0	Runs:	0
Best Bowling:		Average:	0.00
5 WI:	0	10 WM:	0
Catches:	2	Stumpings:	0

The hard hitting left hander was involved in the last four Tests South Africa played prior to their isolation. He scored a century in his final Test against Australia at Port Elizabeth in March of 1970.

JACK, Steven Douglas
Born:	August 4, 1970
Batting:	Right handed
Bowling:	Right arm fast

Tests
Test Career:	1994-95
Cap Number:	259
Tests Played:	2

Test Batting
Innings:	2	Runs:	7
Highest Score:	7	Average:	3.50
No. 50s:	0	No. 100s:	0

Test Bowling & Fielding
Wickets:	8	Runs:	196
Best Bowling:	4/69	Average:	24.50
5 WI:	0	10 WM:	0
Catches:	1	Stumpings:	0

One Day Internationals
ODI Career:	1994-95
ODIs Played:	2

ODI Batting
Innings:	2	Runs:	7
Highest Score:	6	Average:	3.50
No. 50s:	0	No. 100s:	0

ODI Bowling & Fielding
Wickets:	3	Runs:	86
Best Bowling:	2/41	Average:	28.66
5 WM:	0	Catches:	3
Stumpings:	0		

A right arm pace bowler from Transvaal who was given an opportunity when Allan Donald was injured in 1994. He played two Tests against the touring New Zealanders but was dropped when Donald returned to the fold.

JOHNSON, Clement Lecky
Born:	March 31, 1871
Batting:	Right handed
Bowling:	Right arm medium-fast

Tests

Test Career:	1896		
Cap Number:	32		
Tests Played:	1		

Test Batting

Innings:	2	Runs:	10
Highest Score:	7	Average:	5.00
No. 50s:	0	No. 100s:	0

Test Bowling & Fielding

Wickets:	0	Runs:	57
Best Bowling:		Average:	0.00
5 WI:	0	10 WM:	0
Catches:	1	Stumpings:	0

The Irish born Johnson played just one Test in 1896, but was member of a team from Dublin that toured the United States in the 1890's.

KALLIS, Jacques Henry

Born:	October 16, 1975
Batting:	Right handed
Bowling:	Right arm medium-fast

Tests

Test Career:	1995-		
Cap Number:	262		
Tests Played:	102		

Test Batting

Innings:	172	Runs:	8,033
Highest Score:	189*	Average:	55.78
No. 50s:	40	No. 100s:	24

Test Bowling & Fielding

Wickets:	200	Runs:	6,342
Best Bowling:	6/54	Average:	31.71
5 WI:	4	10 WM:	0
Catches:	98	Stumpings:	0

One Day Internationals

ODI Career:	1996-		
ODIs Played:	231		

ODI Batting

Innings:	221	Runs:	7,995
Highest Score:	139	Average:	43.92
No. 50s:	56	No. 100s:	13

ODI Bowling & Fielding

Wickets:	203	Runs:	6,564
Best Bowling:	5/30	Average:	32.33
5 WM:	2	Catches:	90
Stumpings:	0		

On appearances Jacques Kallis looks like your standard issue Test all-rounder. With his broad shoulders and strong forearms, you can imagine a bustling medium pace bowler and hard hitting middle order batsman who likes nothing more that giving the ball a whack. Whilst that may be an apt description of his bowling, Kallis the batsman is a grinder of the highest order who long ago deferred to the age old South African tradition of occupying the crease in Test matches. It may not always be pretty but he has become his country's most prolific scorer in Tests, having compiled 24 Test hundreds. At present he has an average of 55.78 that sees him rated among the top five batsmen in the world. His batting is an exercise in self control, waiting for the loose delivery to present itself rather than pressuring the bowler into making mistakes. When he does latch on to an errant delivery he can take full advantage, particularly when it's pitched short outside off stump. In one day cricket Kallis bats with greater urgency, and has an enviable record of 13 hundreds and 7995 runs at an average of 43.92. His bowling has been hampered in recent times by an elbow injury, but when fit he has an action that cries outswinger. He mixes up his movement away from the bat with the occasional in cutter, and has taken 200 Test wickets to prove that the combination is highly effective. At times he has been accused of batting for himself and not pressing on when victory is in sight, but today there is no better all-rounder in the game and certainly no player more important to his side than Jacques Kallis.

KEITH, Headley James

Born:	October 25, 1927
Batting:	Left handed
Bowling:	Left arm off-break

Tests

Test Career:	1953-57		
Cap Number:	188		
Tests Played:	8		

Test Batting

Innings:	16	Runs:	318
Highest Score:	73	Average:	21.20
No. 50s:	2	No. 100s:	0

Test Bowling & Fielding

Wickets:	0	Runs:	63
Best Bowling:		Average:	0.00
5 WI:	0	10 WM:	0
Catches:	9	Stumpings:	0

He played a single Test at the MCG in 1952/53 and then had to wait over two years for another chance in the national side. Keith toured England in 1955 and performed adequately, scoring two half centuries, but was still unable to nail down a permanent place in the team.

KEMP, Justin Miles

Born:	October 2, 1977
Batting:	Right handed
Bowling:	Right arm medium-fast

Tests

Test Career:	2001-		
Cap Number:	279		
Tests Played:	4		

Test Batting

Innings:	6	Runs:	80
Highest Score:	55	Average:	13.33
No. 50s:	1	No. 100s:	0

Test Bowling & Fielding

Wickets:	9	Runs:	222
Best Bowling:	3/33	Average:	24.66
5 WI:	0	10 WM:	0
Catches:	3	Stumpings:	0

One Day Internationals

ODI Career:	2001-		
ODIs Played:	54		

ODI Batting

Innings:	42	Runs:	938
Highest Score:	80	Average:	31.26
No. 50s:	7	No. 100s:	0

ODI Bowling & Fielding

Wickets:	22	Runs:	726
Best Bowling:	3/20	Average:	33.90
5 WM:	0	Catches:	24
Stumpings:	0		

A good spare parts man, Kemp is ideally suited to one day cricket bowling off pace mediums and batting lustily in the middle order. His best performances for the Proteas thus far have been a quick fire 80 off 50 balls against England at Port Elizabeth in 2004/05 and a 73 against New Zealand at Bloemfontein that won him the 'Man of the Match' award.

KEMPIS, Gustav Adolph

Born:	August 4, 1865
Batting:	Right handed
Bowling:	Left arm medium

Tests

Test Career:	1889
Cap Number:	4
Tests Played:	1

Test Batting

Innings:	2	Runs:	0
Highest Score:	0	Average:	0.00
No. 50s:	0	No. 100s:	0

Test Bowling & Fielding

Wickets:	4	Runs:	76
Best Bowling:	3/53	Average:	19.00
5 WI:	0	10 WM:	0
Catches:	0	Stumpings:	0

A medium pace bowler who opened the bowling in his country's first Test and in fact took the first wicket taken by a South African in Test cricket. He went on to take 3/53 in the innings and four wickets for the match. He contracted a fatal bout fever in what is now Mozambique in 1890 at the age of 24.

KENT, Jon

Born:	May 7, 1979
Batting:	Right handed
Bowling:	Right arm medium-fast

One Day Internationals

ODI Career:	2002
ODIs Played:	2

ODI Batting

Innings:	0	Runs:	0
Highest Score:	0	Average:	0.00
No. 50s:	0	No. 100s:	0

ODI Bowling & Fielding

Wickets:	0	Runs:	57
Best Bowling:		Average:	0.00
5 WM:	0	Catches:	1
Stumpings:	0		

A medium pacer from Cape Town, Kent played in two ODI's against Australia in 2002.

KIRSTEN, Gary

Born:	November 23, 1967
Batting:	Left handed
Bowling:	Right arm off-break

Tests

Test Career:	1993-2004
Cap Number:	257
Tests Played:	101

Test Batting

Innings:	176	Runs:	7,289
Highest Score:	275	Average:	45.27
No. 50s:	34	No. 100s:	21

Test Bowling & Fielding

Wickets:	2	Runs:	142
Best Bowling:	1/0	Average:	71.00
5 WI:	0	10 WM:	0
Catches:	83	Stumpings:	0

One Day Internationals

ODI Career:	1993-2003
ODIs Played:	185

ODI Batting

Innings:	185	Runs:	6,798
Highest Score:	188*	Average:	40.95
No. 50s:	45	No. 100s:	13

ODI Bowling & Fielding

Wickets:	0	Runs:	23
Best Bowling:		Average:	0.00
5 WM:	0	Catches:	61
Stumpings:	1		

A prolific run scorer, the top order batsman defied his critics to become his country's highest scorer in Tests until being passed recently by Jacques Kallis. Gary Kirsten was hardly a classical batsman; rather he was a patient opener who understood his limitations and concentrated on his strengths. He would lean on his front foot shots rather than stroking them whilst on the back foot he was most comfortable outside off where he almost never let a loose ball go unpunished. His 7289 Test runs included 21 hundreds, and Kirsten had the will and patience to turn many of them into big scores. He scored three double centuries, including a record breaking 275 against England at Kingsmead in 1999/2000 that equaled Darryl Cullinan's score for highest innings by a South African in Test cricket. He remained a relevant Test batsman to the end scoring 137 in his final series against New Zealand as a 36 year old.

KIRSTEN, Peter Noel

Born:	May 14, 1955
Batting:	Right handed
Bowling:	Right arm off-break

Tests

Test Career:	1992-94
Cap Number:	240
Tests Played:	12

Test Batting

Innings:	22	Runs:	626
Highest Score:	104	Average:	31.30
No. 50s:	4	No. 100s:	1

Test Bowling & Fielding

Wickets:	0	Runs:	30
Best Bowling:		Average:	0.00
5 WI:	0	10 WM:	0
Catches:	8	Stumpings:	0

One Day Internationals

ODI Career: 1991-94
ODIs Played: 40

ODI Batting

Innings:	40	Runs:	1,293
Highest Score:	97	Average:	38.02
No. 50s:	9	No. 100s:	0

ODI Bowling & Fielding

Wickets:	6	Runs:	152
Best Bowling:	3/31	Average:	25.33
5 WM:	0	Catches:	11
Stumpings:	0		

The half brother of Gary, he had already carved out of a fine career in England and at home when South Africa returned to Test cricket in 1992. He made one Test century in his 12 Tests, 104 against at Headingly in 1994.

KLUSENER, Lance

Born: September 4, 1971
Batting: Left handed
Bowling: Right arm medium-fast

Tests

Test Career: 1996-2004
Cap Number: 265
Tests Played: 49

Test Batting

Innings:	69	Runs:	1,906
Highest Score:	174	Average:	32.86
No. 50s:	8	No. 100s:	4

Test Bowling & Fielding

Wickets:	80	Runs:	3,033
Best Bowling:	8/64	Average:	37.91
5 WI:	1	10 WM:	0
Catches:	34	Stumpings:	0

One Day Internationals

ODI Career: 1996-2004
ODIs Played: 171

ODI Batting

Innings:	137	Runs:	3,576
Highest Score:	103*	Average:	41.10
No. 50s:	19	No. 100s:	2

ODI Bowling & Fielding

Wickets:	192	Runs:	5,751
Best Bowling:	6/49	Average:	29.95
5 WM:	6	Catches:	35
Stumpings:	0		

Lance Klusener's arrival onto the international scene was as loud and brash as his cricket. He took eight wickets in his first match and scored his maiden century within his first completed series, against the Indians in 1996/97. Tall and lean, his bowling was pure aggression and his batting likewise. It was that all out assault with bat and ball that saw him thought of as primarily an ODI cricketer and in the end even cost him his spot in the one day side. At his best he was as damaging as any batsman in the world. He destroyed the English at Port Elizabeth in 1999, belting a 174 off only 221 deliveries and was even more brutal against the Indians at Bloemfontein in 2001 when his century came at just over a run a ball and included 70 runs in boundaries. Unfortunately the failures began to outweigh the successes, and when injury reduced his bowling to gentle off spin his days representing South Africa appeared over.

KOEN, Louis Johannes

Born: March 28, 1967
Batting: Right handed

One Day Internationals

ODI Career: 1997-00
ODIs Played: 5

ODI Batting

Innings:	5	Runs:	82
Highest Score:	28	Average:	16.40
No. 50s:	0	No. 100s:	0

ODI Bowling & Fielding

Wickets:	0	Runs:	0
Best Bowling:		Average:	0.00
5 WM:	0	Catches:	3
Stumpings:	0		

An opener from Cape Province who made his ODI debut against Australia, at Port Elizabeth. Koen played five ODI's between 1997 and 2000, averaging 16.40.

KOTZE, Johannes Jacobus

Born: August 7, 1879
Batting: Right handed
Bowling: Right arm fast

Tests

Test Career: 1902-07
Cap Number: 56
Tests Played: 3

Test Batting

Innings:	5	Runs:	2
Highest Score:	2	Average:	0.40
No. 50s:	0	No. 100s:	0

Test Bowling & Fielding

Wickets:	6	Runs:	243
Best Bowling:	3/64	Average:	40.50
5 WI:	0	10 WM:	0
Catches:	3	Stumpings:	0

Nicknamed 'Kodgee', he had little interest in Test cricket and played only three times for South Africa for a total of six wickets. He was however regarded by all who saw him as the fastest bowler in the world and old-timers rated him the equal of latter day greats such as Frank Tyson and Wes Hall. Kotze was a devastating cricketer in the Currie Cup where he averaged almost five wickets a match and famously made keepers line their gloves with beefsteak so they could take his thunderbolts without breaking their hands.

KRUGER, Garnett

Born: January 5, 1977
Batting: Right handed
Bowling: Right arm medium-fast

544

One Day Internationals
ODI Career:	2006		
ODIs Played:	3		

ODI Batting
Innings:	2	Runs:	0
Highest Score:	0	Average:	0.00
No. 50s:	0	No. 100s:	0

ODI Bowling & Fielding
Wickets:	2	Runs:	139
Best Bowling:	1/43	Average:	69.50
5 WM:	0	Catches:	1
Stumpings:	0		

Originally from Port Elizabeth, pace bowler Garnett Kruger was selected on the 2006 tour of Australia, where he played in three ODI's.

KUIPER, Adrian Paul
Born:	August 24, 1959
Batting:	Right handed
Bowling:	Right arm medium

Tests
Test Career:	1992		
Cap Number:	241		
Tests Played:	1		

Test Batting
Innings:	2	Runs:	34
Highest Score:	34	Average:	17.00
No. 50s:	0	No. 100s:	0

Test Bowling & Fielding
Wickets:	0	Runs:	0
Best Bowling:		Average:	0.00
5 WI:	0	10 WM:	0
Catches:	1	Stumpings:	0

One Day Internationals
ODI Career:	1991-96		
ODIs Played:	25		

ODI Batting
Innings:	23	Runs:	539
Highest Score:	63*	Average:	33.68
No. 50s:	3	No. 100s:	0

ODI Bowling & Fielding
Wickets:	18	Runs:	518
Best Bowling:	3/33	Average:	28.77
5 WM:	0	Catches:	3
Stumpings:	0		

A middle order batsman and useful medium pace bowler who played the bulk of his international cricket in the one day side. Kuiper's only Test was the historic meeting between South Africa and West Indies in 1992 that marked his country's return to the Test scene.

KUYS, Frederick
Born:	March 21, 1870
Batting:	Right handed
Bowling:	Right arm medium

Tests
Test Career:	1899		
Cap Number:	45		
Tests Played:	1		

Test Batting
Innings:	2	Runs:	26
Highest Score:	26	Average:	13.00
No. 50s:	0	No. 100s:	0

Test Bowling & Fielding
Wickets:	2	Runs:	31
Best Bowling:	2/31	Average:	15.50
5 WI:	0	10 WM:	0
Catches:	0	Stumpings:	0

A bowler and handy batsman from Western Province whose only Test was against England at Cape Town in 1899.

LANCE, Herbert Roy
Born:	June 6, 1940
Batting:	Right handed
Bowling:	Right arm medium

Tests
Test Career:	1962-70		
Cap Number:	214		
Tests Played:	13		

Test Batting
Innings:	22	Runs:	591
Highest Score:	70	Average:	28.14
No. 50s:	5	No. 100s:	0

Test Bowling & Fielding
Wickets:	12	Runs:	479
Best Bowling:	3/30	Average:	39.91
5 WI:	0	10 WM:	0
Catches:	7	Stumpings:	0

Tiger Lance was a good spare parts man who was unfortunate that his career pre-dated one day cricket. He was an industrious middle order batsman and steady medium pace bowler, making five Test half centuries and taking 12 wickets in his 13 Tests.

LANGEVELDT, Charl Kenneth
Born:	December 17, 1974
Batting:	Right handed
Bowling:	Right arm medium-fast

Tests
Test Career:	2005-		
Cap Number:	298		
Tests Played:	6		

Test Batting
Innings:	4	Runs:	16
Highest Score:	10	Average:	8.00
No. 50s:	0	No. 100s:	0

Test Bowling & Fielding
Wickets:	16	Runs:	593
Best Bowling:	5/46	Average:	37.06
5 WI:	1	10 WM:	0
Catches:	2	Stumpings:	0

One Day Internationals
ODI Career:	2001-		
ODIs Played:	29		

ODI Batting
Innings:	5	Runs:	7
Highest Score:	3	Average:	1.75
No. 50s:	0	No. 100s:	0

ODI Bowling & Fielding
Wickets:	38	Runs:	1,102
Best Bowling:	5/62	Average:	29.00
5 WI:	1	Catches:	1
Stumpings:	0		

Squat and strong, the one time prison warder has been mainly a one day bowler but has also had some success in Test cricket. He impressed on debut against England at Cape Town in 2005 with five wickets in an innings, and took seven wickets in two Tests against Australia later that year. Those Australian wickets didn't come cheap though, and in one innings at Perth his 1/100 came off only 17 overs. He's a smart one day bowler with 38 wickets in 29 matches that includes one five wicket return against the West Indies in Barbados in 2005.

LANGTON, Arthur Chudleigh Beaumont

Born: March 2, 1912
Batting: Right handed
Bowling: Right arm medium-fast

Tests

Test Career: 1935-39
Cap Number: 139
Tests Played: 15

Test Batting
Innings:	23	Runs:	298
Highest Score:	73*	Average:	15.68
No. 50s:	2	No. 100s:	0

Test Bowling & Fielding
Wickets:	40	Runs:	1,827
Best Bowling:	5/58	Average:	45.67
5 WI:	1	10 WM:	0
Catches:	8	Stumpings:	0

Nicknamed 'Chud' from his middle name Chudleigh, the lanky Langton was an excellent all-rounder from Transvaal who played a key role in South Africa's historic victory over England at Lord's in 1935. He took six wickets for the match and was involved in a century partnership with Bruce Mitchell.

LAWRENCE, Godfrey Bernard

Born: March 31, 1932
Batting: Right handed
Bowling: Right arm medium-fast

Tests

Test Career: 1961-62
Cap Number: 209
Tests Played: 5

Test Batting
Innings:	8	Runs:	141
Highest Score:	43	Average:	17.62
No. 50s:	0	No. 100s:	0

Test Bowling & Fielding
Wickets:	28	Runs:	512
Best Bowling:	8/53	Average:	18.28
5 WI:	2	10 WM:	0
Catches:	2	Stumpings:	0

The towering fast bowler played of all his Test cricket against New Zealand at home in 1961/62. Big 'Goofy' Lawrence had an excellent series, capturing 28 wickets including 8/53 in the first innings of the second Test at Johannesburg. Selectors preferred Neil Adcock and Peter Heine which meant the unfortunate Lawrence never played another Test after that series.

LE ROUX, Frederick Louis

Born: February 5, 1882
Batting: Right handed
Bowling: Right arm medium

Tests

Test Career: 1914
Cap Number: 91
Tests Played: 1

Test Batting
Innings:	2	Runs:	1
Highest Score:	1	Average:	0.50
No. 50s:	0	No. 100s:	0

Test Bowling & Fielding
Wickets:	0	Runs:	24
Best Bowling:		Average:	0.00
5 WI:	0	10 WM:	0
Catches:	0	Stumpings:	0

A medium pace bowler who did next to nothing in his only Test at Lord's cricket ground in Durban in 1914.

LEWIS, Percy Tyson

Born: October 2, 1884
Batting: Right handed

Tests

Test Career: 1913
Cap Number: 85
Tests Played: 1

Test Batting
Innings:	2	Runs:	0
Highest Score:	0	Average:	0.00
No. 50s:	0	No. 100s:	0

Test Bowling & Fielding
Wickets:	0	Runs:	0
Best Bowling:		Average:	0.00
5 WI:	0	10 WM:	0
Catches:	0	Stumpings:	0

'Plum' Lewis was a high respected batsman who played a single Test just prior to World War I. He served in France during the Great War but received a severe leg wound and never played cricket again.

LIEBENBERG, Gerhardus Frederick Johannes

Born: April 7, 1972
Batting: Right handed
Bowling: Right arm medium-fast
Wicket Keeper

Tests

Test Career: 1998
Cap Number: 270
Tests Played: 5

Test Batting
Innings:	8	Runs:	104
Highest Score:	45	Average:	13.00
No. 50s:	0	No. 100s:	0

Test Bowling & Fielding
Wickets:	0	Runs:	0
Best Bowling:		Average:	0.00
5 WI:	0	10 WM:	0
Catches:	1	Stumpings:	0

One Day Internationals

ODI Career: 1995-98
ODIs Played: 4

ODI Batting
Innings:	4	Runs:	94
Highest Score:	39	Average:	23.50
No. 50s:	0	No. 100s:	0

ODI Bowling & Fielding
Wickets:	0	Runs:	0
Best Bowling:		Average:	0.00
5 WM:	0	Catches:	0
Stumpings:	0		

Much was expected of the tall right handed batsman when selected to play Sri Lanka in 1998, but as his Test average of only 13.00 shows, he failed to meet those expectations.

LINDSAY, Denis Thomson

Born:	September 4, 1939
Batting:	Right handed
	Wicket Keeper

Tests
Test Career:	1963-70
Cap Number:	215
Tests Played:	19

Test Batting
Innings:	31	Runs:	1,130
Highest Score:	182	Average:	37.66
No. 50s:	5	No. 100s:	3

Test Bowling & Fielding
Wickets:	0	Runs:	0
Best Bowling:		Average:	0.00
5 WI:	0	10 WM:	0
Catches:	57	Stumpings:	2

A majestic wicket keeper/batsman, he was lost to international cricket when his country was isolated because of their abhorrent racial policies. In only 19 Tests Lindsay proved himself to be a spectacular yet safe keeper and a world class batsman. He was at his best when clearly the player of the series in South Africa's 3-1 defeat of Australia at home in 1966/67. Lindsay completed 24 dismissals against the Aussies and led the aggregates for either side with 606 runs. His 182 at Johannesburg was his highest Test score, with all of his three Test tons coming in that series. He served as an ICC Match referee between 2001 and 2003.

LINDSAY, John Dixon

Born:	September 8, 1908
Batting:	Right handed
	Wicket Keeper

Tests
Test Career:	1947
Cap Number:	158
Tests Played:	3

Test Batting
Innings:	51	Runs:	21
Highest Score:	91*	Average:	7.00
No. 50s:	0	No. 100s:	0

Test Bowling & Fielding
Wickets:	0	Runs:	0
Best Bowling:		Average:	0.00
5 WI:	0	10 WM:	0
Catches:	4	Stumpings:	1

War cost Johnny Lindsay the chance to play more Test cricket, but in only three Tests he showed enough to suggest he would have been a fine keeper at Test level. He was the father of Dennis, who also kept wickets for South Africa.

LINDSAY, Nevil Vernon

Born:	July 30, 1886
Batting:	Right handed

Tests
Test Career:	1921
Cap Number:	99
Tests Played:	1

Test Batting
Innings:	2	Runs:	35
Highest Score:	29	Average:	17.50
No. 50s:	0	No. 100s:	0

Test Bowling & Fielding
Wickets:	0	Runs:	0
Best Bowling:		Average:	0.00
5 WI:	0	10 WM:	0
Catches:	1	Stumpings:	0

A top order batsman from Transvaal and later Orange Free State who played a single Test against the Australians in 1921. He was related to Test keepers John and Dennis Lindsay.

LING, William Victor Stone

Born:	October 3, 1891
Batting:	Right handed
Bowling:	Right arm leg-break

Tests
Test Career:	1921-23
Cap Number:	96
Tests Played:	6

Test Batting
Innings:	10	Runs:	168
Highest Score:	38	Average:	16.80
No. 50s:	0	No. 100s:	0

Test Bowling & Fielding
Wickets:	0	Runs:	20
Best Bowling:		Average:	0.00
5 WI:	0	10 WM:	0
Catches:	1	Stumpings:	0

A batsman and useful leg spinner from the Cape who seemed under utilized in his six Tests. After making an impressive 33 on debut against the Australians he was shunted down the order and throughout his short Test career only bowled three overs.

LLEWELLYN, Charles Bennett

Born:	September 26, 1876
Batting:	Left handed

Tests
Test Career:	1896-1912
Cap Number:	33
Tests Played:	15

Test Batting
Innings:	28	Runs:	544
Highest Score:	90	Average:	20.14
No. 50s:	4	No. 100s:	0

Test Bowling & Fielding

Wickets:	48	Runs:	1,421
Best Bowling:	6/92	Average:	29.60
5 WI:	4	10 WM:	1
Catches:	7	Stumpings:	0

He was a brilliant all-rounder in the formative years of international cricket and the first South African to claim ten wickets in a Test. He achieved that feat against the touring Australians at Johannesburg in 1902/03. The accomplished batsman scored 90 against the Aussies in the same series and whilst he never scored a Test century he had a fine first class record with 18 centuries. Llewellyn played the bulk of his first class cricket with Hampshire in England and was named as one of Wisden's five Cricketers of the Year in 1911. He spent much of his life in England was went within an ace of representing them in Tests in the early part of the 20th century.

LUNDIE, Eric Balfour

Born:	March 15, 1888
Batting:	Right handed
Bowling:	Right arm fast

Tests

Test Career:	1914
Cap Number:	94
Tests Played:	1

Test Batting

Innings:	2	Runs:	1
Highest Score:	1	Average:	1.00
No. 50s:	0	No. 100s:	0

Test Bowling & Fielding

Wickets:	4	Runs:	107
Best Bowling:	4/101	Average:	26.75
5 WI:	0	10 WM:	0
Catches:	0	Stumpings:	0

A fast bowler, he was said to have toiled manfully in his only Test bowling 46 overs and taking four wickets. Like many young South African cricketers he went to fight in the Great War and never returned. Lundie fell at Passchendaele in Belgium at the age of 29.

MACAULAY, Michael John

Born:	April 19, 1939
Batting:	Right handed

Tests

Test Career:	1965
Cap Number:	224
Tests Played:	1

Test Batting

Innings:	2	Runs:	33
Highest Score:	21	Average:	16.50
No. 50s:	0	No. 100s:	0

Test Bowling & Fielding

Wickets:	2	Runs:	73
Best Bowling:	1/10	Average:	36.50
5 WI:	0	10 WM:	0
Catches:	0	Stumpings:	0

He lined up for no less than five provinces in the Currie Cup, and added South Africa to the list of teams he played for when he was selected for a single Test against England in 1965.

MANN, Norman Bertram Fleetwood

Born:	December 28, 1920
Batting:	Right handed
Bowling:	Left arm off-break

Tests

Test Career:	1947-51
Cap Number:	159
Tests Played:	19

Test Batting

Innings:	31	Runs:	400
Highest Score:	52	Average:	13.33
No. 50s:	1	No. 100s:	0

Test Bowling & Fielding

Wickets:	58	Runs:	1,920
Best Bowling:	6/59	Average:	33.10
5 WI:	1	10 WM:	0
Catches:	3	Stumpings:	0

A left arm off spinner, he looked more like a tax inspector than Test cricketer with his slight build and spectacles. 'Tufty' as he was known, relied on unerring accuracy to frustrate batsmen, often avoiding the punishment that his fellow bowlers were receiving. Mann took 58 wickets in his 19 Tests going for less than two runs per over in each of his 966 Test overs.

MANSELL, Percy Neville Frank

Born:	March 16, 1920
Batting:	Right handed
Bowling:	Right arm leg-break

Tests

Test Career:	1951-55
Cap Number:	183
Tests Played:	13

Test Batting

Innings:	22	Runs:	355
Highest Score:	90	Average:	17.75
No. 50s:	2	No. 100s:	0

Test Bowling & Fielding

Wickets:	11	Runs:	736
Best Bowling:	3/58	Average:	66.90
5 WI:	0	10 WM:	0
Catches:	15	Stumpings:	0

Born in England, raised in Rhodesia and selected for South Africa, he was a leg spinner and middle order batsman who provided fine service for the Test team, predominately abroad. Mansell's highest Test score of 90 was scored on debut against England in Leeds in 1951, and whilst he never reached those heights again he remained a useful contributor. On the tour of Australia in 1952/53 he showed enough to play in all five Tests and proved his worth by taking nine wickets and averaging 21.50 with the bat.

MARKHAM, Lawrence Anderson

Born:	September 12, 1924
Batting:	Right handed
Bowling:	Right arm leg-break

548

Tests

Test Career:	1949		
Cap Number:	170		
Tests Played:	1		

Test Batting

Innings:	1	Runs:	20
Highest Score:	20	Average:	20.00
No. 50s:	0	No. 100s:	0

Test Bowling & Fielding

Wickets:	1	Runs:	72
Best Bowling:	1/34	Average:	72.00
5 WI:	0	10 WM:	0
Catches:	0	Stumpings:	0

A looping leg spinner and entertaining batsman, 'Fish' Markham played his only Test against England at Johannesburg in 1949.

MARX, Waldemar Frederick Eric (Eric)

Born:	July 4, 1895
Batting:	Left handed
Bowling:	Right arm medium

Tests

Test Career:	1921		
Cap Number:	97		
Tests Played:	3		

Test Batting

Innings:	6	Runs:	125
Highest Score:	36	Average:	20.83
No. 50s:	0	No. 100s:	0

Test Bowling & Fielding

Wickets:	4	Runs:	144
Best Bowling:	3/85	Average:	36.00
5 WI:	0	10 WM:	0
Catches:	0	Stumpings:	0

He played all his first class cricket in the space of just two years between 1920 and 1922, including three Tests against the touring Australians in 1921. Marx was very much a Mr. Fixit in those matches for his country, opening the bowling and batting anywhere from number three to number nine. His best effort was at the Old Wanderers Stadium in the second Test when he scored 36 and 34.

MATTHEWS, Craig Russell

Born:	February 15, 1965
Batting:	Right handed
Bowling:	Right arm medium-fast

Tests

Test Career:	1992-95		
Cap Number:	252		
Tests Played:	18		

Test Batting

Innings:	25	Runs:	348
Highest Score:	62*	Average:	18.31
No. 50s:	1	No. 100s:	0

Test Bowling & Fielding

Wickets:	52	Runs:	1,502
Best Bowling:	5/42	Average:	28.88
5 WI:	2	10 WM:	0
Catches:	4	Stumpings:	0

One Day Internationals

ODI Career:	1991-97
ODIs Played:	56

ODI Batting

Innings:	22	Runs:	141
Highest Score:	26	Average:	10.84
No. 50s:	0	No. 100s:	0

ODI Bowling & Fielding

Wickets:	79	Runs:	1,975
Best Bowling:	4/10	Average:	25.00
5 WM:	0	Catches:	10
Stumpings:	0		

He was a hard working bowler and handy lower order batsman who gave South Africa sturdy service upon their return to international cricket. He rarely went wicketless, and when Australia toured in early 1994 for a three Test series, Matthews was his country's leading bowler with 13 wickets. He was also nuisance value at the bottom of the order, occasionally providing resolute support and at other times hitting out, like he did at Leeds in 1994 when he made 62 not out. He was a key player with Western Province for almost 15 years, and after retiring worked for them as an administrator.

McCARTHY, Cuan Neil

Born:	March 24, 1929
Batting:	Right handed
Bowling:	Right arm fast

Tests

Test Career:	1948-51		
Cap Number:	167		
Tests Played:	15		

Test Batting

Innings:	24	Runs:	28
Highest Score:	5	Average:	3.11
No. 50s:	0	No. 100s:	0

Test Bowling & Fielding

Wickets:	36	Runs:	1,510
Best Bowling:	6/43	Average:	41.94
5 WI:	2	10 WM:	0
Catches:	6	Stumpings:	0

The blonde bombshell from Natal was South Africa's fastest bowler after the war but whatever he had in pace he lacked in accuracy. At his best devastating, McCarthy tore through a strong English batting line-up in his very first Test taking six second innings wickets. From then on he was selected more on promise than form and when selectors finally tired he had taken only 36 Test wickets in 15 Tests at more than 40 runs apiece. He was a notoriously shabby number eleven batsman who never scored more than five in 24 Test innings.

McGLEW, Derrick John (Jackie)

Born:	March 11, 1929
Batting:	Right handed
Bowling:	Right arm leg-break

Tests

Test Career:	1951-62
Cap Number:	179
Tests Played:	34

Test Batting

Innings:	64	Runs:	2,440
Highest Score:	255*	Average:	42.06
No. 50s:	10	No. 100s:	7

Test Bowling & Fielding

Wickets:	0	Runs:	23
Best Bowling:		Average:	0.00
5 WI:	0	10 WM:	0
Catches:	18	Stumpings:	0

In Test cricket through the 1950's there was nothing harder to get than Jackie McGlew's wicket. He was a dogged opening batsman with immense powers of concentration as his 105 against Australia in 1957/58 at Kingsmead proved. With South Africa batting second and in early trouble he occupied the crease for nine and a half hours to deny the tourists. Much of that time was spent with fellow plodder John Waite and together they put on a record 231 run partnership. It wasn't always slow going when little Jackie was batting, though to be fair the pace was never electric. He took just less than nine hours to bring up his highest score in Test cricket, an unbeaten 255 at Wellington in 1953 that was at the time the highest score by a South African in a Test. On that occasion he was involved in another famous partnership, 246 with Anton Murray which still stands as the South African record for the 7th wicket in a Test match. McGlew was also a brilliant cover fieldsman and respected captain with a record of four wins and four losses in his 14 Tests at the helm.

McKENZIE, Neil Douglas

Born:	November 24, 1975
Batting:	Right handed
Bowling:	Right arm medium

Tests

Test Career:	2000-04
Cap Number:	277
Tests Played:	41

Test Batting

Innings:	65	Runs:	2,028
Highest Score:	120	Average:	33.24
No. 50s:	13	No. 100s:	2

Test Bowling & Fielding

Wickets:	0	Runs:	63
Best Bowling:		Average:	0.00
5 WI:	0	10 WM:	0
Catches:	37	Stumpings:	0

One Day Internationals

ODI Career:	2000-03
ODIs Played:	59

ODI Batting

Innings:	51	Runs:	1,580
Highest Score:	131*	Average:	38.53
No. 50s:	9	No. 100s:	2

ODI Bowling & Fielding

Wickets:	0	Runs:	27
Best Bowling:		Average:	0.00
5 WM:	0	Catches:	19
Stumpings:	0		

He is a middle order batsman whose father Kevin represented South Africa against rebel sides in the 1980's. He struggled in his first tour with the national side, scoring only 54 runs in five innings against Sri Lanka in 2000. He was able to save his Test career with a fighting 120 against New Zealand at Port Elizabeth later that year, but a perceived weakness against top class spinners saw him play his last Test by the start of 2004. In 2006 he was recalled to the national side for a twenty/20 international rekindling hopes of another chance at Test level.

McKINNON, Atholl Henry

Born:	August 20, 1932
Batting:	Right handed
Bowling:	Left arm off-break

Tests

Test Career:	1960-66
Cap Number:	204
Tests Played:	8

Test Batting

Innings:	13	Runs:	107
Highest Score:	27	Average:	17.83
No. 50s:	0	No. 100s:	0

Test Bowling & Fielding

Wickets:	26	Runs:	925
Best Bowling:	4/128	Average:	35.57
5 WI:	0	10 WM:	0
Catches:	1	Stumpings:	0

Atholl McKinnon was a solidly built left arm off spinner who was in and out of the side over a seven year period for a total of eight Tests. Whilst he never played more than two Tests in any one series, he was a steady contributor who took at least one wicket in each of his Test innings. McKinnon was also an excellent provincial rugby player who earnt the nickname 'The Boot' because of his ability to kick the ball phenomenal distances.

McLEAN, Roy Alastair

Born:	July 9, 1930
Batting:	Right handed

Tests

Test Career:	1951-64
Cap Number:	182
Tests Played:	40

Test Batting

Innings:	73	Runs:	2,120
Highest Score:	142	Average:	30.28
No. 50s:	10	No. 100s:	5

Test Bowling & Fielding

Wickets:	0	Runs:	1
Best Bowling:		Average:	0.00
5 WI:	0	10 WM:	0
Catches:	23	Stumpings:	0

He was one of the most elegant stroke makers to play Test cricket, and whilst his overall average suggests that he may have been disappointing, there were times that seeing him bat was worth the price of admission. McLean came to notice in Australia in 1952/53 when his heroics with the bat in the fifth and final Test earnt his side an unlikely win. McLean scored 81 in the first innings and an unbeaten 76 in the second as South Africa were able to snatch victory and draw the series 2-2. He led the charge on the tour of England in 1955 when he scored 145 at Lord's and a match winning half century at Old Trafford. Five years later he was one of the few South African's to prosper as he side floundered on the tour of England. In a wet summer he led the aggregates with 269 runs and scored a rare Test century Manchester. When Roy McLean came in to bat it was feast or famine, to which his five Test centuries and eleven Test ducks lay testament.

McMILLAN, Brian Mervin

Born: December 22, 1963
Batting: Right handed
Bowling: Right arm medium-fast

Tests

Test Career: 1992-98
Cap Number: 249
Tests Played: 38

Test Batting

Innings:	62	Runs:	1,968
Highest Score:	113	Average:	39.36
No. 50s:	13	No. 100s:	3

Test Bowling & Fielding

Wickets:	75	Runs:	2,537
Best Bowling:	4/65	Average:	33.82
5 WI:	0	10 WM:	0
Catches:	49	Stumpings:	0

One Day Internationals

ODI Career: 1991-98
ODIs Played: 78

ODI Batting

Innings:	52	Runs:	841
Highest Score:	127	Average:	23.36
No. 50s:	0	No. 100s:	1

ODI Bowling & Fielding

Wickets:	70	Runs:	2,589
Best Bowling:	4/32	Average:	36.98
5 WM:	0	Catches:	42
Stumpings:	0		

The burly all-rounder was a fine performer for his country in a career that spanned six years. 'Big Mac' was almost 29 years old when he made his Test debut, yet he still managed to score almost 2,000 Test runs and claim 75 wickets. He scored 98 in his second Test against India at Johannesburg in 1992 and another score in the 90's when South Africa toured England in 1994. That illusive first Test century came against Pakistan in a one-off Test at Johannesburg in 1993/94, with a well struck 113. There would be two more Test centuries and countless valuable innings where he occupied the crease with his side's top order batsmen. Whilst he never took five wickets in an innings, he was an able contributor with the ball, where his height and pace made him a fine foil for the likes of Allan Donald and Fanie de Villiers.

McMILLAN, Quintin

Born: June 23, 1904
Batting: Right handed
Bowling: Right arm leg-break

Tests

Test Career: 1929-32
Cap Number: 130
Tests Played: 13

Test Batting

Innings:	21	Runs:	306
Highest Score:	50*	Average:	18.00
No. 50s:	1	No. 100s:	0

Test Bowling & Fielding

Wickets:	36	Runs:	1,243
Best Bowling:	5/66	Average:	34.52
5 WI:	2	10 WM:	0
Catches:	8	Stumpings:	0

A leg spinner who dominated New Zealand in the first Tests between the two countries. He took 16 wickets in two Tests against the fledgling Test playing nation including career best match figures of 9/127 at Christchurch in 1932. McMillan retired after that two Test series to concentrate on business.

MEINTJES, Douglas James

Born: June 9, 1890
Batting: Right handed
Bowling: Right arm medium-fast

Tests

Test Career: 1923
Cap Number: 107
Tests Played: 2

Test Batting

Innings:	3	Runs:	43
Highest Score:	21	Average:	14.33
No. 50s:	0	No. 100s:	0

Test Bowling & Fielding

Wickets:	6	Runs:	115
Best Bowling:	3/38	Average:	19.16
5 WI:	0	10 WM:	0
Catches:	3	Stumpings:	0

An opening bowler and accomplished lower order batsman from Transvaal. Meintjes played both of his Tests against England in February 1923.

MELLE, Michael George

Born: June 3, 1930
Batting: Right handed
Bowling: Right arm fast

Tests

Test Career: 1950-53
Cap Number: 176
Tests Played: 7

Test Batting

Innings:	12	Runs:	68
Highest Score:	17	Average:	8.50
No. 50s:	0	No. 100s:	0

Test Bowling & Fielding

Wickets:	26	Runs:	851
Best Bowling:	6/71	Average:	32.73
5 WI:	2	10 WM:	0
Catches:	4	Stumpings:	0

A right arm paceman from Western Province who was described as being as quick as any bowler in South Africa in the early 1950's. He had a number of fiery spells for his country including a five wicket haul on debut against the Australians at Johannesburg in 1950 and four wickets for not many at The Oval a year later.

MELVILLE, Alan

Born:	May 19, 1910
Batting:	Right handed

Tests

Test Career:	1938-49
Cap Number:	152
Tests Played:	11

Test Batting

Innings:	19	Runs:	894
Highest Score:	189	Average:	52.58
No. 50s:	3	No. 100s:	4

Test Bowling & Fielding

Wickets:	0	Runs:	0
Best Bowling:		Average:	0.00
5 WI:	0	10 WM:	0
Catches:	8	Stumpings:	0

A gifted batsman and respected leader who captained his country in ten of his eleven Tests. Melville had his career cruelly curtailed by the war but was still able to make three fine Test centuries in consecutive innings. In 1947 he scored 189 and 104 not out at Trent Bridge and then followed the double with 117 at Lord's in the very next Test. Under Melville's leadership South Africa failed to win a match but it was no fault of their skipper who retired from Test cricket with an average of 52.58.

MIDDLETON, James (Bonnor)

Born:	September 30, 1865
Batting:	Right handed

Tests

Test Career:	1896-1902
Cap Number:	27
Tests Played:	6

Test Batting

Innings:	12	Runs:	52
Highest Score:	22	Average:	7.42
No. 50s:	0	No. 100s:	0

Test Bowling & Fielding

Wickets:	24	Runs:	442
Best Bowling:	5/51	Average:	18.41
5 WI:	2	10 WM:	0
Catches:	1	Stumpings:	0

Nicknamed 'Bonnor' after the towering early Australian batsman George Bonner, he was an accomplished seam bowler who took nine wickets in his first ever Test match. In all he took 24 wickets in six Tests, to be South Africa's leading bowler prior to the turn of last century. He was less impressive with the bat in those six Tests averaging only 7.42.

MILLS, Charles Henry

Born:	November 26, 1867
Batting:	Right handed
Bowling:	Right arm medium

Tests

Test Career:	1892
Cap Number:	20
Tests Played:	1

Test Batting

Innings:	2	Runs:	25
Highest Score:	21	Average:	12.50
No. 50s:	0	No. 100s:	0

Test Bowling & Fielding

Wickets:	2	Runs:	83
Best Bowling:	2/83	Average:	41.50
5 WI:	0	10 WM:	0
Catches:	2	Stumpings:	0

The English all-rounder performed well in his only Test for his adopted country, taking two wickets and scoring 21 in the second innings of the one-off Test at Cape Town in 1892. He also played county cricket for Surrey.

MILTON, Wiliam Henry

Born:	December 3, 1854
Batting:	Right handed
Bowling:	Right arm medium

Tests

Test Career:	1889-92
Cap Number:	5
Tests Played:	3

Test Batting

Innings:	6	Runs:	68
Highest Score:	21	Average:	11.33
No. 50s:	0	No. 100s:	0

Test Bowling & Fielding

Wickets:	2	Runs:	48
Best Bowling:	1/5	Average:	24.00
5 WI:	0	10 WM:	0
Catches:	1	Stumpings:	0

A batsman from Western Province who played in South Africa's inaugural Test side. He played in three Tests in total captaining the side in two of them.

MITCHELL, Bruce

Born:	January 8, 1909
Batting:	Right handed
Bowling:	Right arm leg-break

Tests

Test Career:	1929-49
Cap Number:	125
Tests Played:	42

Test Batting

Innings:	80	Runs:	3,471
Highest Score:	189*	Average:	48.88
No. 50s:	21	No. 100s:	8

Test Bowling & Fielding

Wickets:	27	Runs:	1,380
Best Bowling:	5/87	Average:	51.11
5 WI:	1	10 WM:	0
Catches:	56	Stumpings:	0

South African cricket may not have had an abundance of top class batsman in the years prior to the Second World War but in Bruce Mitchell they had at least one. The right handed top order batsman from Transvaal was always rock solid in defense and a fine driver and cutter of the ball when given the opportunity. He made his Test debut in 1929 at Edgbaston and showed maturity beyond his 20 years scoring 88 in the first innings and an unbeaten 61 in the second that denied England any chance of victory. His first century was 123 on the mats at Cape Town when he opened the batting with Jack Siedle. The put on a record first wicket stand of 260 in exactly five hours against the touring English as part of a team score in excess of 500. He scored a hundred in the first Test played by South Africa against New Zealand and whilst he never scored a century against Australia he led the batting averages on the 1931/32 to that country with a top score of 95 at Adelaide. He ranks as one of South Africa's greatest ever batsmen, an argument that would be backed up by the English who saw the very best of Mitchell as he scored seven Test hundreds and averaged in excess of 54 against them in Tests.

MITCHELL, Frank

Born: August 13, 1972
Batting: Right handed
Bowling: Right arm medium
Wicket Keeper

Tests
Test Career: 1899-12
Cap Number: 76
Tests Played: 5

Test Batting
Innings:	10	Runs:	16
Highest Score:	41	Average:	11.60
No. 50s:	0	No. 100s:	0

Test Bowling & Fielding
Wickets:	0	Runs:	0
Best Bowling:		Average:	0.00
5 WI:	0	10 WM:	0
Catches:	2	Stumpings:	0

One of the few who represented two countries at Test level. An England cap in cricket and rugby, Mitchell visited South Africa as part of Lord Hawke's touring party in 1899. He served in South Africa during the Boer War and then returned there to captain their cricket side. He led the South African side that toured England in both 1904 and 1912.

MORKEL, Denijs Paul Beck

Born: January 25, 1906
Batting: Right handed

Tests
Test Career: 1927-32
Cap Number: 116
Tests Played: 16

Test Batting
Innings:	28	Runs:	663
Highest Score:	88	Average:	24.55
No. 50s:	4	No. 100s:	0

Test Bowling & Fielding
Wickets:	18	Runs:	821
Best Bowling:	4/93	Average:	45.61
5 WI:	0	10 WM:	0
Catches:	13	Stumpings:	0

A right handed middle order batsman and medium fast bowler form Western Province who performed well on the tour of England in 1929. He had a fine match at Lord's where he made 88 in the first innings and returned match figures of 7/156. His final Test was the historic first meeting between New Zealand and South Africa in which he scored 51.

MORKEL, Johannes Albertus (Albie)

Born: June 10, 1981
Batting: Left handed
Bowling: Right arm medium-fast

One Day Internationals
ODI Career: 2004-05
ODIs Played: 8

ODI Batting
Innings:	6	Runs:	63
Highest Score:	23*	Average:	12.60
No. 50s:	0	No. 100s:	0

ODI Bowling & Fielding
Wickets:	7	Runs:	212
Best Bowling:	2/23	Average:	30.28
5 WM:	0	Catches:	1
Stumpings:	0		

A promising all-rounder, Albie Morkel made his ODI debut against New Zealand, at Wellington in 2004. He has performed reasonably well in his eight ODI's to date.

MPITSANG, Victor

Born: March 28, 1980
Batting: Right handed
Bowling: Right arm medium-fast

One Day Internationals
ODI Career: 1999
ODIs Played: 2

ODI Batting
Innings:	1	Runs:	1
Highest Score:	1*	Average:	0.00
No. 50s:	0	No. 100s:	0

ODI Bowling & Fielding
Wickets:	2	Runs:	63
Best Bowling:	2/49	Average:	31.50
5 WM:	0	Catches:	0
Stumpings:	0		

Victor Mpitsang became the youngest person to represent South Africa at international level when, at age 18 years and 314 days, he made his ODI debut against West Indies at Bloemfontein in 1999.

MURRAY, Anton Ronald Andrew

Born: April 30, 1922
Batting: Right handed

Tests
Test Career: 1952-54
Cap Number: 186
Tests Played: 10

Test Batting

Innings:	14	Runs:	289
Highest Score:	109	Average:	22.23
No. 50s:	1	No. 100s:	1

Test Bowling & Fielding

Wickets:	18	Runs:	710
Best Bowling:	4/169	Average:	39.44
5 WI:	0	10 WM:	0
Catches:	3	Stumpings:	0

A steady medium pace bowler and reliable lower order batsman who was involved in a famous partnership with Jackie McGlew at Wellington in 1953. He scored his only Test century as the pair put on what was a then world record 246 runs for the seventh wicket.

NEL, Andre

Born:	July 15, 1977
Batting:	Right handed
Bowling:	Right arm medium-fast

Tests

Test Career:	2001-
Cap Number:	281
Tests Played:	23

Test Batting

Innings:	25	Runs:	135
Highest Score:	18*	Average:	7.10
No. 50s:	0	No. 100s:	0

Test Bowling & Fielding

Wickets:	84	Runs:	2,503
Best Bowling:	6/32	Average:	29.79
5 WI:	3	10 WM:	1
Catches:	9	Stumpings:	0

One Day Internationals

ODI Career:	2001-
ODIs Played:	45

ODI Batting

Innings:	7	Runs:	12
Highest Score:	4*	Average:	6.00
No. 50s:	0	No. 100s:	0

ODI Bowling & Fielding

Wickets:	58	Runs:	1,716
Best Bowling:	4/39	Average:	29.58
5 WM:	0	Catches:	12
Stumpings:	0		

If it's true that a good fast bowler needs to be a little mad then Andre Nel is bound for greatness. He's tall and powerful and loves nothing more than to work himself into a frenzy when he's at the bowling crease. He came to prominence against the Australians in 2005, when he not only took 14 wickets but also became the man that the Australian players and fans loved to hate. He was less successful when Australia visited early in 2006, but with his boundless energy and determination, Andre Nel remains a key to South Africa's hopes both at the 2007 World Cup and beyond.

NEL, John Desmond (Jack)

Born:	July 10, 1928
Batting:	Right handed

Tests

Test Career:	1949-57
Cap Number:	172
Tests Played:	6

Test Batting

Innings:	11	Runs:	150
Highest Score:	38	Average:	13.63
No. 50s:	0	No. 100s:	0

Test Bowling & Fielding

Wickets:	0	Runs:	0
Best Bowling:		Average:	0.00
5 WI:	0	10 WM:	0
Catches:	1	Stumpings:	0

An opening batsman who was tried in the home series against the touring Australians in 1949/50 but struggled with 139 runs in nine innings.

NEWBERRY, Claude

Born:	July 0, 1889
Batting:	Right handed
Bowling:	Right arm fast

Tests

Test Career:	1913-14
Cap Number:	87
Tests Played:	4

Test Batting

Innings:	8	Runs:	62
Highest Score:	16	Average:	7.75
No. 50s:	0	No. 100s:	0

Test Bowling & Fielding

Wickets:	11	Runs:	268
Best Bowling:	4/72	Average:	24.36
5 WI:	0	10 WM:	0
Catches:	3	Stumpings:	0

An all-rounder from Transvaal, he played four Tests against the touring English in 1913/14 with his best effort 4/72 in the third Test at Johannesburg.

NEWSON, Edward Serrurier (Bob)

Born:	December 2, 1910
Batting:	Right handed
Bowling:	Right arm fast

Tests

Test Career:	1930-39
Cap Number:	134
Tests Played:	3

Test Batting

Innings:	5	Runs:	30
Highest Score:	16	Average:	7.50
No. 50s:	0	No. 100s:	0

Test Bowling & Fielding

Wickets:	4	Runs:	265
Best Bowling:	2/58	Average:	66.25
5 WI:	0	10 WM:	0
Catches:	3	Stumpings:	0

An opening bowler from Transvaal whose Test career was interrupted by studies, with his three Tests spaced out over a nine year period. After the Second World War he moved to Rhodesia where he continued to play first class cricket until 1950.

NGAM, Mfuneko
Born: January 29, 1979
Batting: Right handed
Bowling: Right arm fast

Tests
Test Career: 2000-01
Cap Number: 278
Tests Played: 3

Test Batting
Innings:	1	Runs:	0
Highest Score:	0*	Average:	0.00
No. 50s:	0	No. 100s:	0

Test Bowling & Fielding
Wickets:	11	Runs:	189
Best Bowling:	3/26	Average:	17.18
5 WI:	0	10 WM:	0
Catches:	1	Stumpings:	0

A genuinely fast bowler who took 11 wickets in three Tests over the 2000/01 South African summer. He hasn't played for South Africa since that promising start because of a series of injuries that have been blamed on a genetic bone disorder.

NICHOLSON, Frank
Born: September 17, 1909
Batting: Right handed
Wicket Keeper

Tests
Test Career: 1935-36
Cap Number: 144
Tests Played: 4

Test Batting
Innings:	8	Runs:	76
Highest Score:	29	Average:	10.85
No. 50s:	0	No. 100s:	0

Test Bowling & Fielding
Wickets:	0	Runs:	0
Best Bowling:		Average:	0.00
5 WI:	0	10 WM:	0
Catches:	3	Stumpings:	0

A wicket keeper who played for Orange Free State, he replaced Jock Cameron after he passed away from enteric fever on the return trip from England in 1935.

NICOLSON, John Fairless William
Born: July 19, 1899
Batting: Left handed
Bowling: Right arm medium

Tests
Test Career: 1928
Cap Number: 121
Tests Played: 3

Test Batting
Innings:	5	Runs:	179
Highest Score:	78	Average:	35.80
No. 50s:	1	No. 100s:	0

Test Bowling & Fielding
Wickets:	0	Runs:	17
Best Bowling:		Average:	0.00
5 WI:	0	10 WM:	0
Catches:	0	Stumpings:	0

Nicholson came to notice with an unbeaten 252 for Natal against Orange Free State in 1926. The left hander made a fine start to his Test career scoring 39 and 78 on debut against England at Kingsmead Oval in 1928 but struggled in this next two Tests and was subsequently dropped.

NORTON, Norman Ogilvie
Born: May 11, 1881
Batting: Right handed
Bowling: Right arm medium

Tests
Test Career: 1910
Cap Number: 71
Tests Played: 1

Test Batting
Innings:	2	Runs:	9
Highest Score:	7	Average:	4.50
No. 50s:	0	No. 100s:	0

Test Bowling & Fielding
Wickets:	4	Runs:	47
Best Bowling:	4/47	Average:	11.75
5 WI:	0	10 WM:	0
Catches:	0	Stumpings:	0

He was far from disgraced in his only Test, taking 4/47 against England in 1910 with his medium pace bowling. Norton captained the Border side in Currie Cup competition.

NOURSE, Arthur Dudley
Born: November 12, 1910
Batting: Right handed
Bowling: Right arm medium

Tests
Test Career: 1935-51
Cap Number: 140
Tests Played: 34

Test Batting
Innings:	62	Runs:	2,960
Highest Score:	231	Average:	53.81
No. 50s:	14	No. 100s:	9

Test Bowling & Fielding
Wickets:	0	Runs:	9
Best Bowling:		Average:	0.00
5 WI:	0	10 WM:	0
Catches:	12	Stumpings:	0

The son of Dave, he was and still is regarded as one of the finest batsmen South Africa has ever produced. He was tall and powerful batsman who gave the ball an almighty 'thwack' if the chance arose. Dudley made his debut as part of the side that toured England in 1935 and even though he struggled was retained to face the touring Australians later that year. The selectors saw more in him than just a famous surname and he repaid their faith with a momentous 231 at the Old Wanderers Stadium in the second Test. Nourse ended that series as the highest scorer on either side, and in doing so established himself alongside Bruce Mitchell as his country's star batsman. He scored two centuries against England in 1938/39 but wouldn't play any more Test cricket for close to a decade because of the

Second World War. The star batsman almost didn't survive the war, coming perilously close to losing his life whilst serving in the Western Desert, but when Tests resumed so did Nourse with 149 against the English at Trent Bridge. The runs and the centuries kept coming, amongst them his famous innings at Trent Bridge in 1948, when as skipper he batted with a broken thumb to score 208 and lead his side to a rare win. A Test average of 53.81 is achievement enough, but in a side where the opposition's focus was always on getting him out, it makes Nourse one of the game's less obvious champions.

NOURSE, Arthur William (Dave)

Born:	January 25, 1879
Batting:	Left handed
Bowling:	Left arm medium

Tests

Test Career:	1902-24
Cap Number:	50
Tests Played:	45

Test Batting

Innings:	83	Runs:	2,234
Highest Score:	111	Average:	29.78
No. 50s:	15	No. 100s:	1

Test Bowling & Fielding

Wickets:	41	Runs:	1,553
Best Bowling:	4/25	Average:	37.87
5 WI:	0	10 WM:	0
Catches:	43	Stumpings:	0

As W.G. Grace was to English cricket so Dave Nourse was to the game in South Africa. He was a prolific batsman at first class level, scoring well over 10,000 runs for Transvaal and Western Province and in Tests was the first South African to score over 2,000 runs. He scored only the one Test century, 111 against Australia at the Old Wanderers Stadium in 1921/22 at the age of 42 but his most famous innings came many years earlier at the same ground. South Africa had gone eleven Tests without a victory, and were facing another defeat when they found themselves at 6/105 chasing 287 to win. Dave Nourse joined Gordon White at the crease and the pair saw the score to 226 before White fell. Nourse 'nursed' the batting from that point on, seeing his side home for a historic win with just one wicket to spare. He was also a wily medium pace bowler and brilliant slip fieldsman who claimed almost a catch a Test over a career that spanned more than two decades.

NTINI, Makhaya

Born:	July 6, 1977
Batting:	Right handed
Bowling:	Right arm fast

Tests

Test Career:	1998-
Cap Number:	269
Tests Played:	69

Test Batting

Innings:	78	Runs:	572
Highest Score:	32*	Average:	10.40
No. 50s:	0	No. 100s:	0

Test Bowling & Fielding

Wickets:	274	Runs:	7,751
Best Bowling:	7/37	Average:	28.28
5 WI:	14	10 WM:	4
Catches:	18	Stumpings:	0

One Day Internationals

ODI Career:	1998-
ODIs Played:	129

ODI Batting

Innings:	31	Runs:	147
Highest Score:	42*	Average:	10.50
No. 50s:	0	No. 100s:	0

ODI Bowling & Fielding

Wickets:	206	Runs:	4,772
Best Bowling:	6/22	Average:	23.16
5 WM:	3	Catches:	25
Stumpings:	0		

As the first black cricketer to play for South Africa, the spotlight was always going to be on pace bowler Makhaya Ntini, and as if those pressures were not enough, he had to battle rape charges in 1999. The youngster strenuously voiced his innocence, and after initially being convicted had the decision reversed on appeal. When Ntini was finally able to concentrate on his cricket he quickly went from project player to South Africa's main strike bowler. In 69 Tests he has taken 274 wickets and in doing so overcome a tendency to let the ball slide down leg slide. He now makes a concerted effort to bowl stump to stump, and in recent years has been rewarded with big hauls, such as his 19 wickets in three Tests against the Australia in 2005/06. In the third of those Tests at Johannesburg, he claimed ten wickets and followed that up with another ten wicket haul in his very next Test against New Zealand at Centurion. Energetic and genuinely quick, the cheerful Ntini has blossomed into a wonderful ambassador for cricket in the new South Africa.

NUPEN, Eiulf Peter (Buster)

Born:	January 1, 1902
Batting:	Right handed
Bowling:	Right arm medium-fast

Tests

Test Career:	1921-36
Cap Number:	98
Tests Played:	17

Test Batting

Innings:	31	Runs:	348
Highest Score:	69	Average:	14.50
No. 50s:	2	No. 100s:	0

Test Bowling & Fielding

Wickets:	50	Runs:	1,788
Best Bowling:	6/46	Average:	35.76
5 WI:	5	10 WM:	1
Catches:	9	Stumpings:	0

Prior to 1931 all South African Test cricket was played on the mats and as a result there were a handful of bowlers who became specialists on that particular surface. One such player was 'Buster' Nupen who was so good on matting and so poor on turf that during the 1930/31 series in South Africa he was dropped for the 3rd and 5th Tests in Durban because they were being played on turf for the first time. On the mats the seaming medium pacer was near unplayable, capturing five or more wickets in a Test innings on six occasions. He captained South Africa in one Test, against England at Johannesburg in 1930/31. South Africa won the match and Nupen returned career best match figures of 11/150. The match was played on mats.

O'LINN, Sidney

Born:	May 5, 1927
Batting:	Left handed

Tests

Test Career:	1960-61
Cap Number:	201
Tests Played:	7

Test Batting

Innings:	12	Runs:	297
Highest Score:	98	Average:	27.00
No. 50s:	2	No. 100s:	0

Test Bowling & Fielding

Wickets:	0	Runs:	0
Best Bowling:		Average:	0.00
5 WI:	0	10 WM:	0
Catches:	4	Stumpings:	0

Like many of his compatriots at the time, O'Linn was a top order batsman with a defensive mindset. He made his debut at Birmingham in 1960 with an encouraging 42 and followed it up two Tests later with a 98 at Trent Bridge that took five and a half hours to compile. Whilst he never kept wickets for South Africa, he played county cricket for Kent where he was second wicket keeper behind the great Godfrey Evans. A fine footballer, he played for Charlton Athletic in the English FA and also represented South Africa in a full international.

OCHSE, Arthur Edward

Born:	March 11, 1870
Batting:	Right handed

Tests

Test Career:	1889
Cap Number:	6
Tests Played:	2

Test Batting

Innings:	4	Runs:	16
Highest Score:	8	Average:	4.00
No. 50s:	0	No. 100s:	0

Test Bowling & Fielding

Wickets:	0	Runs:	0
Best Bowling:		Average:	0.00
5 WI:	0	10 WM:	0
Catches:	0	Stumpings:	0

The 19 year old batsman from Transvaal was the youngest member of South Africa's first Test side. He was killed in France during World War I.

OCHSE, Arthur Lennox

Born:	October 11, 1899
Batting:	Right handed
Bowling:	Right arm fast

Tests

Test Career:	1928-29
Cap Number:	122
Tests Played:	3

Test Batting

Innings:	4	Runs:	11
Highest Score:	4	Average:	3.66
No. 50s:	0	No. 100s:	0

Test Bowling & Fielding

Wickets:	10	Runs:	362
Best Bowling:	4/79	Average:	36.20
5 WI:	0	10 WM:	0
Catches:	1	Stumpings:	0

A speedster from Eastern Province who showed little in his first Test having opened the bowling without success against England at Durban in 1927. He was nevertheless chosen to tour England in 1929 and fared much better taking ten wickets in two Tests.

ONTONG, Justin Lee

Born:	January 4, 1980
Batting:	Right handed
Bowling:	Right arm off-break

Tests

Test Career:	2002-04
Cap Number:	282
Tests Played:	2

Test Batting

Innings:	4	Runs:	57
Highest Score:	32	Average:	19.00
No. 50s:	0	No. 100s:	0

Test Bowling & Fielding

Wickets:	1	Runs:	133
Best Bowling:	1/79	Average:	133.00
5 WI:	0	10 WM:	0
Catches:	1	Stumpings:	0

One Day Internationals

ODI Career:	2001-
ODIs Played:	21

ODI Batting

Innings:	12	Runs:	98
Highest Score:	32	Average:	8.90
No. 50s:	0	No. 100s:	0

ODI Bowling & Fielding

Wickets:	9	Runs:	396
Best Bowling:	3/30	Average:	44.00
5 WM:	0	Catches:	11
Stumpings:	0		

Like Australia's Ashley Mallet, he's a right arm off spinner who is so unassuming that he's earnt the nickname 'Rowdy'. In his only two Tests Ontong claimed just the one wicket, and at present would be considered as more of a one day player than Test prospect.

OWEN-SMITH, Harold Geoffrey

Born: February 18, 1909
Batting: Right handed
Bowling: Right arm leg-break

Tests

Test Career: 1929
Cap Number: 126
Tests Played: 5

Test Batting

Innings:	8	Runs:	252
Highest Score:	129	Average:	42.00
No. 50s:	1	No. 100s:	1

Test Bowling & Fielding

Wickets:	0	Runs:	113
Best Bowling:		Average:	0.00
5 WI:	0	10 WM:	0
Catches:	4	Stumpings:	0

A brilliant all-round sportsman who excelled in rugby and boxing, 'Tuppy' Owen-Smith had made runs against the touring MCC side as a teenager was subsequently selected to tour England in 1929. He performed as well as any batsman in that series averaging 42 and scoring a 129 at Headingly when coming in at number seven. Owen-Smith was also regarded as the finest out fieldsman South Africa had seen up to that point. In 1930 he returned to England to study medicine and never played Test cricket again.

PALFRAMAN, Steven

Born: May 12, 1970
Batting: Right handed
Bowling: Right arm off-break
Wicket Keeper

One Day Internationals

ODI Career: 1996
ODIs Played: 7

ODI Batting

Innings:	4	Runs:	55
Highest Score:	28	Average:	13.75
No. 50s:	0	No. 100s:	0

ODI Bowling & Fielding

Wickets:	0	Runs:	0
Best Bowling:		Average:	0.00
5 WM:	0	Catches:	9
Stumpings:	0		

Wicket-keeper Steve Palframan got a surprise call to fill in during the 1996 World Cup torunament when regular keeper Dave Richardson fractured a finger. He struggled to hold his place once Richardson returned.

PALM, Archibald William

Born: June 8, 1901
Batting: Right handed

Tests

Test Career: 1928
Cap Number: 120
Tests Played: 1

Test Batting

Innings:	2	Runs:	15
Highest Score:	13	Average:	7.50
No. 50s:	0	No. 100s:	0

Test Bowling & Fielding

Wickets:	0	Runs:	0
Best Bowling:		Average:	0.00
5 WI:	0	10 WM:	0
Catches:	1	Stumpings:	0

A batsman from Western Province who played just the one Test against England at Cape Town in 1927.

PARKER, George Macdonald

Born: May 27, 1899
Batting: Right handed
Bowling: Right arm fast

Tests

Test Career: 1924
Cap Number: 111
Tests Played: 2

Test Batting

Innings:	4	Runs:	3
Highest Score:	2*	Average:	1.50
No. 50s:	0	No. 100s:	0

Test Bowling & Fielding

Wickets:	8	Runs:	273
Best Bowling:	6/152	Average:	34.12
5 WI:	1	10 WM:	0
Catches:	0	Stumpings:	0

He was playing cricket in England for the minor counties when called up to represent his country in 1924. The paceman bowled with great heart in both of his Test appearances, taking six wickets on debut at Edgbaston. His entire first class career would consist of those two Tests and another tour match for the South Africans.

PARKIN, Durant Clifford (Dante)

Born: February 20, 1873
Batting: Right handed
Bowling: Right arm medium

Tests

Test Career: 1892
Cap Number: 21
Tests Played: 1

Test Batting

Innings:	2	Runs:	6
Highest Score:	6	Average:	3.00
No. 50s:	0	No. 100s:	0

Test Bowling & Fielding

Wickets:	3	Runs:	82
Best Bowling:	3/82	Average:	27.33
5 WI:	0	10 WM:	0
Catches:	1	Stumpings:	0

A paceman who played a single Test against W.W. Read's Englishmen in 1892. He also toured England in 1894 in a side that played no official tests.

PARTRIDGE, Joseph Titus

Born: December 9, 1932
Batting: Right handed
Bowling: Right arm medium-fast

Tests

Test Career: 1963-65
Cap Number: 216
Tests Played: 11

Test Batting

Innings:	12	Runs:	73
Highest Score:	13*	Average:	10.42
No. 50s:	0	No. 100s:	0

Test Bowling & Fielding

Wickets:	44	Runs:	1,373
Best Bowling:	7/91	Average:	31.20
5 WI:	3	10 WM:	0
Catches:	6	Stumpings:	0

He was an acclaimed seamer from Rhodesia who had an outstanding bowling average in all first class matches of just over 20. Partridge played 11 Tests between 1963 and 1965, claiming 44 scalps, including seven wickets in an innings at the SCG in 1963/64. There are few more tragic tales in cricket than the story of what happened to Joe Partridge after he retired. The former bank clerk became an alcoholic, and was living on the streets, when arrested for not paying a hotel bill. The shamed former Test cricketer was taken to a police station where he produced a gun and shot himself in the head.

PEARSE, Charles Ormerod Cato

Born:	October 10, 1884
Batting:	Right handed
Bowling:	Right arm medium

Tests

Test Career:	1910-11
Cap Number:	73
Tests Played:	3

Test Batting

Innings:	6	Runs:	55
Highest Score:	31	Average:	9.16
No. 50s:	0	No. 100s:	0

Test Bowling & Fielding

Wickets:	3	Runs:	106
Best Bowling:	3/56	Average:	35.33
5 WI:	0	10 WM:	0
Catches:	1	Stumpings:	0

Ormy Pearse toured Australia in 1910/11, playing in three Tests and taking three wickets with his gentle medium pace. Unfortunately for him and his side he had been selected as a batsman and only averaged 9.17 for the series.

PEGLER, Sidney James

Born:	July 28, 1888
Batting:	Right handed

Tests

Test Career:	1910-24
Cap Number:	70
Tests Played:	16

Test Batting

Innings:	28	Runs:	356
Highest Score:	35*	Average:	15.47
No. 50s:	0	No. 100s:	0

Test Bowling & Fielding

Wickets:	47	Runs:	1,572
Best Bowling:	7/65	Average:	33.44
5 WI:	2	10 WM:	0
Catches:	5	Stumpings:	0

One of many South Africa wrist spinners in the early part of last century, he bowled with enough pace that he could hardly be regarded as a slow bowler. He enjoyed his finest hour in the ill-conceived triangular tournament in England in 1912 when playing against sub standard sides from Australia and England. Pegler captured 29 wickets in that series to be South Africa's leading wicket taker.

PETERSON, Robin John

Born:	August 4, 1979
Batting:	Left handed
Bowling:	Left arm off-break

Tests

Test Career:	2003-04
Cap Number:	291
Tests Played:	5

Test Batting

Innings:	6	Runs:	159
Highest Score:	61	Average:	31.80
No. 50s:	1	No. 100s:	0

Test Bowling & Fielding

Wickets:	8	Runs:	403
Best Bowling:	3/46	Average:	50.37
5 WI:	0	10 WM:	0
Catches:	4	Stumpings:	0

One Day Internationals

ODI Career:	2002-
ODIs Played:	26

ODI Batting

Innings:	10	Runs:	98
Highest Score:	36	Average:	10.88
No. 50s:	0	No. 100s:	0

ODI Bowling & Fielding

Wickets:	10	Runs:	717
Best Bowling:	2/26	Average:	71.70
5 WM:	0	Catches:	4
Stumpings:	0		

A left arm off spinner who has been given a handful of chances in the South African Test and one day sides, but remains at best second in line to Nicky Boje. His best effort in a single Test was his match figures of 5/68 on debut against Bangladesh at Dhaka in 2003. Peterson also scored 61 in that match; hardly surprising given that he is a recognised all-rounder in domestic cricket with four first class centuries to his name.

PITHEY, Anthony John

Born:	July 17, 1933
Batting:	Right handed
Bowling:	Right arm off-break

Tests

Test Career:	1957-65
Cap Number:	195
Tests Played:	17

Test Batting

Innings:	27	Runs:	819
Highest Score:	154	Average:	31.50
No. 50s:	4	No. 100s:	1

Test Bowling & Fielding

Wickets:	0	Runs:	5
Best Bowling:		Average:	0.00
5 WI:	0	10 WM:	0
Catches:	3	Stumpings:	0

Like many South African batsman in the 1950's he was a grinder who liked nothing more than to occupy the crease. He was generally an opening batsman but as the opening spot was held down by Jackie McGlew and Trevor Goddard he moved down the order. It was at number three that he made his highest Test score, 154 in 440 minutes against England at Newlands in 1965 that was anything but pithy.

PITHEY, David Bartlett

Born:	October 4, 1936
Batting:	Right handed
Bowling:	Right arm off-break

Tests

Test Career:	1963-67
Cap Number:	217
Tests Played:	8

Test Batting

Innings:	12	Runs:	138
Highest Score:	55	Average:	12.54
No. 50s:	1	No. 100s:	0

Test Bowling & Fielding

Wickets:	12	Runs:	577
Best Bowling:	6/58	Average:	48.08
5 WI:	1	10 WM:	0
Catches:	6	Stumpings:	0

The younger brother of Tony, he was an off spinner who played a handful of Tests in the mid 60's. He took all 12 of his Test wickets in three Tests against New Zealand in 1963/64, meaning that he went wicketless in his other five Test appearances.

PLIMSOLL, John Bruce (Jack)

Born:	October 27, 1917
Batting:	Right handed
Bowling:	Left arm medium-fast

Tests

Test Career:	1947
Cap Number:	164
Tests Played:	1

Test Batting

Innings:	2	Runs:	16
Highest Score:	8	Average:	16.00
No. 50s:	0	No. 100s:	0

Test Bowling & Fielding

Wickets:	3	Runs:	143
Best Bowling:	3/128	Average:	47.66
5 WI:	0	10 WM:	0
Catches:	0	Stumpings:	0

A medium pace bowler who came in for plenty of attention in his only Test at Old Trafford in 1947. He took three wickets in the first innings at a cost of 128 runs.

POLLOCK, Peter Maclean

Born:	June 30, 1941
Batting:	Right handed
Bowling:	Right arm fast

Tests

Test Career:	1961-70
Cap Number:	210
Tests Played:	28

Test Batting

Innings:	41	Runs:	607
Highest Score:	75*	Average:	21.67
No. 50s:	2	No. 100s:	0

Test Bowling & Fielding

Wickets:	116	Runs:	2,806
Best Bowling:	6/38	Average:	24.18
5 WI:	9	10 WM:	1
Catches:	9	Stumpings:	0

The older brother of Graeme and father of Shaun, he could have got lost in the crush had he not been a brilliant Test cricketer himself. The opening bowler burst onto the first class scene in South Africa with Eastern Province as a teenager and was in the Test side by the age of 20. He took nine wickets in his first Test against the touring New Zealanders in 1961 and never looked back. By the time South Africa was banned from Test cricket in 1970, Peter Pollock had taken 116 wickets in only 28 Tests. In his final series he claimed 15 wickets in a 4-0 thrashing of Australia. He was also a good lower order batsman who once scored an unbeaten 75 against the Aussies in a Test at Cape Town. Pollock served as national convener of selectors in the era that immediately followed the country's re-admittance to Test cricket.

POLLOCK, Robert Graeme

Born:	February 27, 1944
Batting:	Left handed
Bowling:	Left arm leg-break

Tests

Test Career:	1963-70
Cap Number:	218
Tests Played:	23

Test Batting

Innings:	41	Runs:	2,256
Highest Score:	274	Average:	60.97
No. 50s:	11	No. 100s:	7

Test Bowling & Fielding

Wickets:	4	Runs:	204
Best Bowling:	2/50	Average:	51.00
5 WI:	0	10 WM:	0
Catches:	17	Stumpings:	0

Circumstances beyond his control meant that Graeme Pollock played only 23 Tests, but that was enough for most good judges to claim he was the best left handed batsman to ever play the game. Tall and powerful, he was an exquisite timer of the ball who never needed to use brute force to reach the boundary. Pollock made his debut as a 19 year old on the tour of Australia in 1963/64, and after going out cheaply three times in the first two Tests, finally found form at the SCG. His 122 in Sydney included 19 four's and a six, and he maintained that form in the next Test at Adelaide where he scored 175. Lindsay Hassett described the second hundred as an innings of "unusual brilliance" and likened the wunderkind to West Indian legend Garfield Sobers. Expectations were high when Pollock returned home and initially he was below his best against the touring English. It wasn't until the fifth Test at Port Elizabeth that he finally threw off the shackles with 137 in the first innings and an unbeaten 77 in the second. Pollock would play in only twelve more Tests but that was enough to score two famous double centuries against Australia. The first of them was a 209 at Cape Town in 1967 when his side was soundly beaten. It was the only time in that series that Australia got the better of South Africa, but they still couldn't suppress Pollock who scored more than half of his side's first innings total. When Australia toured in 1969/70 the South African Test side was reputed to be the best in the world, and Graeme Pollock its premier player. Both side and player lived up to their star billing with the Springboks winning all four Tests in the series and Graeme Pollock leading the aggregates and averages for both sides with 517 runs at 73.86. His crowning moment came at Durban in the second Test when he made 274, as the home team thrashed the Aussies by a record margin of an innings and 129 runs. And then, with the 26 year old on top of the world, it all came to a screeching halt as South Africa paid the price for its apartheid policy. Graeme Pollock never played another Test, and as a result will always be remembered as the young batting genius who dominating the game in the 1960's.

POLLOCK, Shaun Maclean

Born:	July 16, 1973
Batting:	Right handed
Bowling:	Right arm medium-fast

Tests

Test Career:	1995-		
Cap Number:	261		
Tests Played:	102		
Test Batting			
Innings:	147	Runs:	3,515
Highest Score:	111	Average:	31.95
No. 50s:	15	No. 100s:	2
Test Bowling & Fielding			
Wickets:	395	Runs:	9,253
Best Bowling:	7/87	Average:	23.42
5 WI:	16	10 WM:	1
Catches:	68	Stumpings:	0

One Day Internationals

ODI Career:	1996-		
ODIs Played:	259		
ODI Batting			
Innings:	171	Runs:	2,805
Highest Score:	75	Average:	25.04
No. 50s:	11	No. 100s:	0
ODI Bowling & Fielding			
Wickets:	348	Runs:	8,456
Best Bowling:	6/35	Average:	24.29
5 WM:	4	Catches:	96
Stumpings:	0		

With the surname Pollock he was always going to be the focus of attention, but the red headed all rounder has very much created a name of his own. A young Shaun was first selected to play against the touring Englishmen in 1995, and made an immediate impression taking 16 wickets in the five Test series. His bowling may have been just fast medium, but he had an immaculate line and the ability to move the ball in the air and off the wicket. His batting took longer to come to the fore, taking him over 50 Tests to score his first Test century, 111 against Sri Lanka at Centurion in 2000/01. In 102 Tests he has averaged over 30 with the bat, taken a record 395 wickets, and at his peak was ranked the number one Test bowler in the world. Pollock also proved to be a fine Test captain who was given the onerous task of taking over from the disgraced Hansie Cronje. He not only won 14 Tests from 26 games in charge, but also helped to reinstall the faith of a shattered South African sporting public. Pollock is in the twilight of his career but he remains in the side and will deservedly become the first South African to take 400 Test wickets before the curtain is finally drawn on his Test career.

POORE, Robert Montagu

Born:	March 20, 1866
Batting:	Right handed

Tests

Test Career:	1896		
Cap Number:	28		
Tests Played:	3		
Test Batting			
Innings:	6	Runs:	76
Highest Score:	20	Average:	12.66
No. 50s:	0	No. 100s:	0
Test Bowling & Fielding			
Wickets:	1	Runs:	4
Best Bowling:	1/4	Average:	4.00
5 WI:	0	10 WM:	0
Catches:	3	Stumpings:	0

Tall and athletic, he was a late bloomer who only played cricket after being introduced to it in India by the Englishman Lord Harris. He played three Tests for South Africa without great distinction but was a brilliant batsman with Hampshire in county cricket, where he scored seven first class centuries, including 301 at Somerset in 1899.

POTHAS, Nic

Born:	November 18, 1973
Batting:	Right handed
	Wicket Keeper

One Day Internationals

ODI Career:	2000		
ODIs Played:	3		
ODI Batting			
Innings:	1	Runs:	24
Highest Score:	24	Average:	24.00
No. 50s:	0	No. 100s:	0

ODI Bowling & Fielding

Wickets:	0	Runs:	0
Best Bowling:		Average:	0.00
5 WM:	0	Catches:	4
Stumpings:	1		

A wicket-keeper from Transvaal who played all his three ODI's against Pakistan in Singapore, during the 2000 Godrej Singapore Challenge.

POTHECARY, James Edward

Born:	December 6, 1933
Batting:	Right handed
Bowling:	Right arm medium

Tests

Test Career:	1960		
Cap Number:	203		
Tests Played:	3		

Test Batting

Innings:	4	Runs:	26
Highest Score:	12	Average:	6.50
No. 50s:	0	No. 100s:	0

Test Bowling & Fielding

Wickets:	9	Runs:	354
Best Bowling:	4/58	Average:	39.33
5 WI:	0	10 WM:	0
Catches:	2	Stumpings:	0

An opening bowler from Western Province who played three Tests in the series in England during 1960. Pothecary saved his best till last, taking 4/58 in the first innings of his final Test at The Oval.

POWELL, Albert William

Born:	July 18, 1873
Batting:	Right handed
Bowling:	Right arm medium

Tests

Test Career:	1899		
Cap Number:	46		
Tests Played:	1		

Test Batting

Innings:	2	Runs:	16
Highest Score:	11	Average:	8.00
No. 50s:	0	No. 100s:	0

Test Bowling & Fielding

Wickets:	1	Runs:	10
Best Bowling:	1/10	Average:	10.00
5 WI:	0	10 WM:	0
Catches:	2	Stumpings:	0

An all-rounder from Griqualand West who played just the one Test in 1899.

PRETORIUS, Dewald

Born:	December 6, 1977
Batting:	Right handed
Bowling:	Right arm fast

Tests

Test Career:	2002-03		
Cap Number:	285		
Tests Played:	4		

Test Batting

Innings:	4	Runs:	22
Highest Score:	9	Average:	7.33
No. 50s:	0	No. 100s:	0

Test Bowling & Fielding

Wickets:	6	Runs:	430
Best Bowling:	4/115	Average:	71.66
5 WI:	0	10 WM:	0
Catches:	0	Stumpings:	0

A powerfully built opening bowler who took four of his six Test wickets in one innings against England in Birmingham in 2003.

PRINCE, Ashwell Gavin

Born:	May 28, 1977
Batting:	Left handed
Bowling:	Left arm slow

Tests

Test Career:	2002-		
Cap Number:	283		
Tests Played:	23		

Test Batting

Innings:	36	Runs:	1,254
Highest Score:	139*	Average:	38.00
No. 50s:	3	No. 100s:	4

Test Bowling & Fielding

Wickets:	1	Runs:	31
Best Bowling:	1/2	Average:	31.00
5 WI:	0	10 WM:	0
Catches:	9	Stumpings:	0

One Day Internationals

ODI Career:	2002-
ODIs Played:	37

ODI Batting

Innings:	33	Runs:	870
Highest Score:	89*	Average:	39.54
No. 50s:	3	No. 100s:	0

ODI Bowling & Fielding

Wickets:	0	Runs:	0
Best Bowling:		Average:	0.00
5 WM:	0	Catches:	20
Stumpings:	0		

When injury meant that both Graeme Smith and Jacques Kallis were unavailable for the tour of Sri Lanka in 2006, Ashwell Prince was handed the captaincy of the side. It marked another milestone for a fully integrated South Africa, with Prince the first black captain to lead the national cricket side. As a Test batsman Prince has had his battles, but he continues to fight hard for a regular place. He has scored four Test centuries including a career high 139 not out against Zimbabwe and a character filled 119 against Australia at the SCG in 2005/06. That hundred came after a particularly difficult tour in which he had been targeted by Shane Warne, who declared that Prince was his new Darryl Cullinan. Whilst the side lost both Tests to Sri Lanka under his captaincy, Prince performed admirably scoring 61 and 86 in either Test.

PRINCE, Charles Frederick Henry

Born:	September 11, 1874
Batting:	Right handed
	Wicket Keeper

Tests
Test Career:	1899		
Cap Number:	47		
Tests Played:	1		

Test Batting
Innings:	2	Runs:	6
Highest Score:	5	Average:	3.00
No. 50s:	0	No. 100s:	0

Test Bowling & Fielding
Wickets:	0	Runs:	0
Best Bowling:		Average:	0.00
5 WI:	0	10 WM:	0
Catches:	0	Stumpings:	0

A batsman/wicket keeper who struggled in his only Test scoring 5 and 1 against England at Cape Town in 1899.

PRINGLE, Meyrick Wayne
Born: June 22, 1966
Batting: Right handed
Bowling: Right arm medium-fast

Tests
Test Career:	1992-95		
Cap Number:	242		
Tests Played:	4		

Test Batting
Innings:	6	Runs:	67
Highest Score:	33	Average:	16.75
No. 50s:	0	No. 100s:	0

Test Bowling & Fielding
Wickets:	5	Runs:	270
Best Bowling:	2/62	Average:	54.00
5 WI:	0	10 WM:	0
Catches:	0	Stumpings:	0

One Day Internationals
ODI Career:	1992-94		
ODIs Played:	17		

ODI Batting
Innings:	8	Runs:	48
Highest Score:	13*	Average:	9.60
No. 50s:	0	No. 100s:	0

ODI Bowling & Fielding
Wickets:	22	Runs:	604
Best Bowling:	4/11	Average:	27.45
5 WM:	0	Catches:	2
Stumpings:	0		

In the 90's South Africa, England and New Zealand all had a fast medium bowler by the name of Pringle. None of them were related with South Africa's Meyrick probably the least well known. He played in four Tests when his country was re-admitted to international cricket but never took more than two wickets in a single innings.

PROCTOR, Michael John
Born: September 15, 1946
Batting: Right handed

Tests
Test Career:	1967-70		
Cap Number:	228		
Tests Played:	7		

Test Batting
Innings:	10	Runs:	226
Highest Score:	48	Average:	25.11
No. 50s:	0	No. 100s:	0

Test Bowling & Fielding
Wickets:	41	Runs:	616
Best Bowling:	6/73	Average:	15.02
5 WI:	1	10 WM:	0
Catches:	4	Stumpings:	0

One of the great cricketing tragedies of South Africa's years of isolation was that Mike Procter only played seven Tests. A brilliant all-rounder who was built like a Sherman tank, he put his abundant strength to good use, either opening the bowling or as a middle order batsman. As a bowler he had a bustling run-up and was generally on to the batsman quicker than expected. In only seven Tests he captured 41 wickets, including a series defining 25 in four Tests against the touring Australians in 1969/70. His never did anything startling with the bat in his short Test career, but the man who scored over 20,000 first class would have made his mark given the opportunity. Cricket fans around the world got a taste of how talented he was courtesy of the time he spent in the World XI with World Series Cricket.

PROMNITZ, Henry Louis Ernest
Born: February 23, 1904
Batting: Right handed
Bowling: Right arm slow

Tests
Test Career:	1927-28		
Cap Number:	117		
Tests Played:	2		

Test Batting
Innings:	4	Runs:	14
Highest Score:	5	Average:	3.50
No. 50s:	0	No. 100s:	0

Test Bowling & Fielding
Wickets:	8	Runs:	161
Best Bowling:	5/58	Average:	20.12
5 WI:	1	10 WM:	0
Catches:	2	Stumpings:	0

A bowler of considerable guile who bowled both wrist and finger spin. He took eight wickets in only two Tests but was thereafter overlooked because of his sub-standard batting and fielding.

PUTTICK, Andrew
Born: December 11, 1980
Batting: Left handed
Bowling: Right arm medium

One Day Internationals
ODI Career:	2005		
ODIs Played:	1		

ODI Batting
Innings:	1	Runs:	0
Highest Score:	0	Average:	0.00
No. 50s:	0	No. 100s:	0

ODI Bowling & Fielding
Wickets:	0	Runs:	0
Best Bowling:		Average:	0.00
5 WM:	0	Catches:	1
Stumpings:	0		

A left hand opener who unfortunately made a duck when filling in for Herschelle Gibbs against New Zealand, at Cape Town, 2005.

QUINN, Neville Anthony

Born: February 21, 1908
Batting: Left handed
Bowling: Left arm medium-fast

Tests
Test Career: 1929-32
Cap Number: 127
Tests Played: 12

Test Batting
Innings:	18	Runs:	90
Highest Score:	28	Average:	6.00
No. 50s:	0	No. 100s:	0

Test Bowling & Fielding
Wickets:	35	Runs:	1,145
Best Bowling:	6/92	Average:	32.71
5 WI:	1	10 WM:	0
Catches:	1	Stumpings:	0

A swing bowler from Griqualand West who performed well in his 12 Tests taking 35 wickets including three hauls of four or more wickets in an innings. He captured 13 wickets against Australia in 1931/32 including an excellent 4/42 at the MCG in the third Test when Australia was surprisingly dismissed for only 198. He was only 26 when he died suddenly at Kimberley.

REID, Norman

Born: December 26, 1890
Batting: Right handed
Bowling: Right arm medium

Tests
Test Career: 1921
Cap Number: 100
Tests Played: 1

Test Batting
Innings:	2	Runs:	17
Highest Score:	11	Average:	8.50
No. 50s:	0	No. 100s:	0

Test Bowling & Fielding
Wickets:	2	Runs:	63
Best Bowling:	2/63	Average:	31.50
5 WI:	0	10 WM:	0
Catches:	0	Stumpings:	0

An all-rounder from the Cape who played his only Test against Australia in 1921.

RHODES, Jonathan Neil (Jonty)

Born: July 27, 1969
Batting: Right handed
Bowling: Right arm medium

Tests
Test Career: 1992-2000
Cap Number: 250
Tests Played: 52

Test Batting
Innings:	80	Runs:	2,532
Highest Score:	117	Average:	35.66
No. 50s:	17	No. 100s:	3

Test Bowling & Fielding
Wickets:	0	Runs:	5
Best Bowling:		Average:	0.00
5 WI:	0	10 WM:	0
Catches:	34	Stumpings:	0

One Day Internationals
ODI Career: 1992-2003
ODIs Played: 245

ODI Batting
Innings:	220	Runs:	5,935
Highest Score:	121	Average:	35.11
No. 50s:	33	No. 100s:	2

ODI Bowling & Fielding
Wickets:	0	Runs:	4
Best Bowling:		Average:	0.00
5 WM:	0	Catches:	105
Stumpings:	0		

Like Colin Bland before him, Jonty Rhodes may be best known as the pre-eminent fieldsman of his time, but in recognising his abilities in the field, one should not overlook the fact that he was a fine Test and one day batsman. A multi-talented young athlete from Natal, Rhodes was also a brilliant hockey player who could have represented his country at the Olympics had he not been forced to choose between that sport and cricket. He scored three Test hundreds, with his best effort being 117 at Lord's in 1998. Whilst he seemed best suited to one day cricket where his athletic fielding was of greater use, it came as a shock when he retired from Test cricket in 2000 to concentrate on the shorter version of the game. Rhodes played his last representative match for South Africa against Kenya in 2003, and even though he was approaching 34 he was still was still recognised as the best outfielder in the sport.

RICE, Clive

Born: July 23, 1949
Batting: Right handed
Bowling: Right arm medium-fast

One Day Internationals
ODI Career: 1991
ODIs Played: 3

ODI Batting
Innings:	2	Runs:	26
Highest Score:	14	Average:	13.00
No. 50s:	0	No. 100s:	0

ODI Bowling & Fielding
Wickets:	2	Runs:	114
Best Bowling:	1/46	Average:	57.00
5 WM:	0	Catches:	0
Stumpings:	0		

Clive Rice burst onto the international arena, during the second season of Kerry Packer's World Series Cricket, in 1978/79, when he, along with fellow countryman, Garth Le Roux, were the exciting new additions to the World XI side. He was the quintessential all-rounder, as he could bat anywhere in the order and as a medium fast bowler could either defend or attack depending on the circumstances. Even though he never played in any official Tests because of South

Africa's ban from international sport, Rice, at the prime of his career, was considered by many experts as one of the best all-rounders of his era. He captained South Africa in his three official ODI's when South Africa was welcomed back to international cricket in 1991.

RICHARDS, Alfred Renfrew

Born:	December 14, 1867
Batting:	Right handed
	Wicket Keeper

Tests

Test Career:	1896
Cap Number:	37
Tests Played:	1

Test Batting

Innings:	2	Runs:	6
Highest Score:	6	Average:	3.00
No. 50s:	0	No. 100s:	0

Test Bowling & Fielding

Wickets:	0	Runs:	0
Best Bowling:		Average:	0.00
5 WI:	0	10 WM:	0
Catches:	0	Stumpings:	0

The Western Province keeper did little in his only Test but the fact he led the side makes him one of South Africa's 31 Test captains.

RICHARDS, Barry Anderson

Born:	July 21, 1945
Batting:	Right handed
Bowling:	Right arm off-break

Tests

Test Career:	1970
Cap Number:	234
Tests Played:	4

Test Batting

Innings:	7	Runs:	508
Highest Score:	140	Average:	72.57
No. 50s:	2	No. 100s:	2

Test Bowling & Fielding

Wickets:	1	Runs:	26
Best Bowling:	1/12	Average:	26.00
5 WI:	0	10 WM:	0
Catches:	3	Stumpings:	0

Because of the political situation in South Africa Barry Richards only played in four Tests, but even in that short time it was clear that here was a batsman of enormous talent. His only series was the four nil thrashing of Australia in 1969/70, in a team many believe to be the best South African side of all time. He opened the batting in every Test, scoring 508 at an average of 72.57 with a high score of 140 at Durban. It was hard to believe Richards made that century in only his second Test, as he played with the assured ease of a seasoned campaigner. By the end of the series he was being talked of as not only one of the best batsman of his day, but of all time. Sadly circumstances robbed him of what surely would have been a glorious Test career, but he played first class cricket around the globe and was a dominant force in South Africa, Australia and England. Even though there was precious little Test cricket, there was short period in World series Cricket when he had the chance to bat alongside the likes of Viv Richards, Gordon Greenidge and Clive Lloyd. He made 207 in a Supertest in Perth in 1978, combining with first Greenidge then Viv Richards to score over for 400 runs in a single day.

RICHARDS, William Henry Matthews (Dicky)

Born:	March 26, 1862
Batting:	Right handed

Tests

Test Career:	1889
Cap Number:	13
Tests Played:	1

Test Batting

Innings:	2	Runs:	4
Highest Score:	4	Average:	2.00
No. 50s:	0	No. 100s:	0

Test Bowling & Fielding

Wickets:	0	Runs:	0
Best Bowling:		Average:	0.00
5 WI:	0	10 WM:	0
Catches:	0	Stumpings:	0

A club cricketer from Western Province who played a single Test against the touring English in 1888/89.

RICHARDSON, David John

Born:	September 16, 1959
Batting:	Right handed
	Wicket Keeper

Tests

Test Career:	1992-98
Cap Number:	243
Tests Played:	42

Test Batting

Innings:	64	Runs:	1,359
Highest Score:	109	Average:	24.26
No. 50s:	8	No. 100s:	1

Test Bowling & Fielding

Wickets:	0	Runs:	0
Best Bowling:		Average:	0.00
5 WI:	0	10 WM:	0
Catches:	150	Stumpings:	2

One Day Internationals

ODI Career:	1991-98
ODIs Played:	122

ODI Batting

Innings:	77	Runs:	868
Highest Score:	53	Average:	19.72
No. 50s:	1	No. 100s:	0

ODI Bowling & Fielding

Wickets:	0	Runs:	0
Best Bowling:		Average:	0.00
5 WM:	0	Catches:	148
Stumpings:	17		

South Africa's first keeper upon their re-introduction to international cricket, he was a nimble gloveman and gritty lower order batsman. Richardson was a worker of the ball who hit his only

Test century against New Zealand at Cape Town in 1994/95.

RINDEL, Michael
Born:	February 9, 1963
Batting:	Left handed

One Day Internationals
ODI Career:	1994-99
ODIs Played:	22

ODI Batting
Innings:	22	Runs:	575
Highest Score:	106	Average:	27.38
No. 50s:	2	No. 100s:	1

ODI Bowling & Fielding
Wickets:	6	Runs:	242
Best Bowling:	2/15	Average:	40.33
5 WM:	0	Catches:	8
Stumpings:	0		

A dashing left hand opener who was run out for 106 against Pakistan, at Johannesburg in 1995. He was presented with the 'Man of the Match' award after South Africa cruised to a 157 run victory to take out the Mandela Trophy. A solid contributor throughout his 22 ODI's.

ROBERTSON, John Benjamin (Jack)
Born:	June 5, 1906
Batting:	Right handed
Bowling:	Right arm slow

Tests
Test Career:	1935-36
Cap Number:	145
Tests Played:	3

Test Batting
Innings:	6	Runs:	51
Highest Score:	17	Average:	10.20
No. 50s:	0	No. 100s:	0

Test Bowling & Fielding
Wickets:	6	Runs:	321
Best Bowling:	3/143	Average:	53.50
5 WI:	0	10 WM:	0
Catches:	2	Stumpings:	0

A right arm off spinner who played three Tests against the touring Australians in 1935/36.

ROSE-INNES, Albert
Born:	February 16, 1868
Batting:	Right handed
Bowling:	Left arm off-break

Tests
Test Career:	1889
Cap Number:	7
Tests Played:	2

Test Batting
Innings:	4	Runs:	14
Highest Score:	13	Average:	3.50
No. 50s:	0	No. 100s:	0

Test Bowling & Fielding
Wickets:	5	Runs:	89
Best Bowling:	5/43	Average:	17.80
5 WI:	1	10 WM:	0
Catches:	2	Stumpings:	0

A medium pace bowler from the Cape who was a key figure in the formation of the South African Cricket Association. He was also a key figure in South Africa's first Test taking five wickets in England's first innings and opening the batting.

ROUTLEDGE, Thomas William
Born:	April 18, 1867
Batting:	Right handed
Bowling:	Right arm medium

Tests
Test Career:	1892-96
Cap Number:	22
Tests Played:	4

Test Batting
Innings:	8	Runs:	72
Highest Score:	24	Average:	9.00
No. 50s:	0	No. 100s:	0

Test Bowling & Fielding
Wickets:	0	Runs:	0
Best Bowling:	0	Average:	0.00
5 WI:	0	10 WM:	0
Catches:	2	Stumpings:	0

Born in England, he was a noted hard hitter who played in four Tests against England in 1892 and 1896. Routledge was also a member of the South African squad that toured England in 1894.

ROWAN, Athol Matthew Burchell
Born:	February 7, 1921
Batting:	Right handed
Bowling:	Right arm off-break

Tests
Test Career:	1947-51
Cap Number:	160
Tests Played:	15

Test Batting
Innings:	23	Runs:	290
Highest Score:	41	Average:	17.05
No. 50s:	0	No. 100s:	0

Test Bowling & Fielding
Wickets:	54	Runs:	2,084
Best Bowling:	5/68	Average:	38.59
5 WI:	4	10 WM:	0
Catches:	7	Stumpings:	0

He was a right arm finger spinner who had many an interesting tussle with the great Len Hutton. Whilst on the end of some of Hutton's finest innings he also dismissed the great Englishman 11 times in Tests. Not scared of long spells he took 5/167 off 60 arduous overs at the Crusaders Ground in 1949. He was the younger brother of Eric, playing a number of Tests alongside the renowned opening batsman.

ROWAN, Eric Alfred Burchell
Born:	July 20, 1909
Batting:	Right handed
Bowling:	Right arm leg-break

Tests
Test Career:	1935-51
Cap Number:	141
Tests Played:	26

Test Batting
Innings:	50	Runs:	1,965
Highest Score:	236	Average:	43.66
No. 50s:	12	No. 100s:	3

Test Bowling & Fielding
Wickets:	0	Runs:	7
Best Bowling:		Average:	0.00
5 WI:	0	10 WM:	0
Catches:	14	Stumpings:	0

Like a good wine, Eric Rowan got better as he matured. He was a high scoring, free flowing batsman who performed well prior to the Second World War and brilliantly after it. When Test cricket resumed in 1948 Rowan was almost 40 years old, but he played three famous innings in the years that followed. He was playing in the second Test against England at Johannesburg in 1948/49 when selectors announced that he had been dropped for the upcoming third Test at Cape Town. The opener responded by scoring his first Test century, an unbeaten 156. Dropped but recalled for the fourth Test he again highlighted the selectors' folly by scoring an unbeaten 83. His next masterful innings was 143 at Kingsmead in 1950 against an Australian attack that consisted of Ray Lindwall, Bill Johnston and Keith Miller. Rowan's final act of middle aged belligerence was as a 42 year old when hit 236 at Headingly in 1951. In all he averaged 43.66 in Tests, but if life actually did begin at 40 he would have had a Test average of 51.05.

ROWE, George Alexander
Born:	June 15, 1874
Batting:	Right handed
Bowling:	Left arm off-break

Tests
Test Career:	1896-1902
Cap Number:	34
Tests Played:	5

Test Batting
Innings:	9	Runs:	26
Highest Score:	13*	Average:	4.33
No. 50s:	0	No. 100s:	0

Test Bowling & Fielding
Wickets:	15	Runs:	456
Best Bowling:	5/115	Average:	30.40
5 WI:	1	10 WM:	0
Catches:	4	Stumpings:	0

A left arm off spinner who played a handful of Tests at the turn of last century with a career best 5/115 on debut against England at Johannesburg in 1896.

RUDOLPH, Jacobus Andries (Jacques)
Born:	May 4, 1981
Batting:	Left handed
Bowling:	Left arm leg-break

Tests
Test Career:	2003-
Cap Number:	289
Tests Played:	35

Test Batting
Innings:	63	Runs:	2,028
Highest Score:	222*	Average:	36.21
No. 50s:	8	No. 100s:	5

Test Bowling & Fielding
Wickets:	4	Runs:	432
Best Bowling:	1/1	Average:	108.00
5 WI:	0	10 WM:	0
Catches:	22	Stumpings:	0

One Day Internationals
ODI Career:	2003-
ODIs Played:	45

ODI Batting
Innings:	39	Runs:	1,174
Highest Score:	81	Average:	35.57
No. 50s:	7	No. 100s:	0

ODI Bowling & Fielding
Wickets:	0	Runs:	26
Best Bowling:		Average:	0.00
5 WM:	0	Catches:	11
Stumpings:	0		

The left-hander had to bide his time before making his Test debut, a victim of South Africa's controversial quota system that required a specified number of non-whites play in the Test side. When Rudolph finally stepped out against Bangladesh at Chittagong in 2003 he made good on the promise he had show in domestic competition with a record score of 222 not out. That was the highest score by any South African on debut, and whilst the runs haven't been as forthcoming since then, there have still been a number of important innings including four more centuries.

RUNDLE, David
Born:	September 25, 1965
Batting:	Right handed
Bowling:	Right arm off-break

One Day Internationals
ODI Career:	1994
ODIs Played:	2

ODI Batting
Innings:	2	Runs:	6
Highest Score:	6	Average:	3.00
No. 50s:	0	No. 100s:	0

ODI Bowling & Fielding
Wickets:	5	Runs:	95
Best Bowling:	4/42	Average:	19.00
5 WM:	0	Catches:	3
Stumpings:	0		

A right arm off-spinner who played two ODI's - at the SCG & the Gabba - during the 1994 tour of Australia.

RUSHMERE, Mark Weir
Born:	January 7, 1965
Batting:	Right handed
Bowling:	Right arm medium

Tests
Test Career:	1992
Cap Number:	244
Tests Played:	1

Test Batting			
Innings:	2	Runs:	6
Highest Score:	3	Average:	3.00
No. 50s:	0	No. 100s:	0

Test Bowling & Fielding			
Wickets:	0	Runs:	0
Best Bowling:		Average:	0.00
5 WI:	0	10 WM:	0
Catches:	0	Stumpings:	0

One Day Internationals

ODI Career: 1992
ODIs Played: 4

ODI Batting			
Innings:	4	Runs:	78
Highest Score:	35	Average:	19.50
No. 50s:	0	No. 100s:	0

ODI Bowling & Fielding			
Wickets:	0	Runs:	0
Best Bowling:		Average:	0.00
5 WM:	0	Catches:	1
Stumpings:	0		

An opening batsman from Eastern Province who played in his country's first Test back after 22 years in exile. He made three in both innings of that game and despite a fine career in domestic cricket never played for South Africa again.

SAMUELSON, Sivert Vause

Born: November 21, 1883
Batting: Right handed

Tests

Test Career: 1910
Cap Number: 72
Tests Played: 1

Test Batting			
Innings:	2	Runs:	22
Highest Score:	15	Average:	11.00
No. 50s:	0	No. 100s:	0

Test Bowling & Fielding			
Wickets:	0	Runs:	64
Best Bowling:		Average:	0.00
5 WI:	0	10 WM:	0
Catches:	1	Stumpings:	0

A slow bowler from Natal who failed to capture a wicket in his only Test.

SCHULTZ, Brett Nolan

Born: August 26, 1970
Batting: Left handed
Bowling: Left arm fast

Tests

Test Career: 1992-97
Cap Number: 251
Tests Played: 9

Test Batting			
Innings:	8	Runs:	9
Highest Score:	6	Average:	1.50
No. 50s:	0	No. 100s:	0

Test Bowling & Fielding			
Wickets:	37	Runs:	749
Best Bowling:	5/48	Average:	20.24
5 WI:	2	10 WM:	0
Catches:	2	Stumpings:	0

One Day Internationals

ODI Career: 1992
ODIs Played: 1

ODI Batting			
Innings:	0	Runs:	0
Highest Score:	0	Average:	0.00
No. 50s:	0	No. 100s:	0

ODI Bowling & Fielding			
Wickets:	1	Runs:	35
Best Bowling:	1/35	Average:	35.00
5 WM:	0	Catches:	0
Stumpings:	0		

He was a powerful left arm pace bowler who was restricted to only nine Tests because of injury. Schultz took 20 wickets in only three Tests against Sri Lanka in 1993, including a career best of nine wickets in the second Test at Colombo. He was a truly awful number 11 batsman who averaged just 1.50 in Test cricket.

SCHWARZ, Reginald Oscar

Born: May 4, 1875
Batting: Right handed

Tests

Test Career: 1906-12
Cap Number: 59
Tests Played: 20

Test Batting			
Innings:	35	Runs:	374
Highest Score:	61	Average:	13.85
No. 50s:	1	No. 100s:	0

Test Bowling & Fielding			
Wickets:	55	Runs:	1,417
Best Bowling:	6/47	Average:	25.76
5 WI:	2	10 WM:	0
Catches:	18	Stumpings:	0

In the early 1900's, the South African Test team went from easy beats to world class, on the back of, or should it be said in the fingers of, three excellent leg spinners. Faulkner, Volger and Reggie Schwarz had observed the like of England's Bosanquet and applied what they learnt first on the mats in their own country, then on the turf pitches abroad. Schwarz was a particularly good exponent of leg spin who dominated the Australians away in 1910/11, taking 25 wickets in five Tests, including career best figures of 6/47 in the fifth Test at the SCG. He played his final Test in the triangular series in England in 1912 before going off to serve in the First World War. He survived the hostilities, but was claimed by influenza just days after war's end in 1918.

SECCULL, Arthur William

Born: September 14, 1868
Batting: Right handed
Bowling: Right arm medium

Tests

Test Career: 1896
Cap Number: 38
Tests Played: 1

Test Batting			
Innings:	2	Runs:	23
Highest Score:	17*	Average:	23.00
No. 50s:	0	No. 100s:	0

Test Bowling & Fielding			
Wickets:	2	Runs:	37
Best Bowling:	2/37	Average:	18.50
5 WI:	0	10 WM:	0
Catches:	1	Stumpings:	0

A medium pacer and useful middle order batsman from Transvaal who played a single Test against Lord Hawke's Englishmen in 1896.

SEYMOUR, Michael Arthur (Kelly)

Born: June 5, 1936
Batting: Right handed
Bowling: Right arm off-break

Tests

Test Career:	1963-70		
Cap Number:	219		
Tests Played:	7		

Test Batting
Innings:	10	Runs:	84
Highest Score:	36	Average:	12.00
No. 50s:	0	No. 100s:	0

Test Bowling & Fielding
Wickets:	9	Runs:	588
Best Bowling:	3/80	Average:	65.33
5 WI:	0	10 WM:	0
Catches:	2	Stumpings:	0

An off-spinner who was given a number a chances in the Test side over a seven year period but could manage no more than three wickets in any one Test.

SHALDERS, William Alfred

Born: February 12, 1880
Batting: Right handed
Bowling: Right arm medium

Tests

Test Career:	1899-1907		
Cap Number:	48		
Tests Played:	12		

Test Batting
Innings:	23	Runs:	355
Highest Score:	42	Average:	16.13
No. 50s:	0	No. 100s:	0

Test Bowling & Fielding
Wickets:	1	Runs:	6
Best Bowling:	1/6	Average:	6.00
5 WI:	0	10 WM:	0
Catches:	3	Stumpings:	0

An opening batsman and occasional bowler who whilst not being a star cricketer was member of the first great South African side. He was part of the team that defeated England at Johannesburg in 1905/06 to secure South Africa's first Test win scoring a valuable 38 in the second innings.

SHAW, Timothy

Born: July 5, 1959
Batting: Left handed
Bowling: Left arm off-break

One Day Internationals

ODI Career:	1991-94
ODIs Played:	9

ODI Batting
Innings:	6	Runs:	26
Highest Score:	17*	Average:	13.00
No. 50s:	0	No. 100s:	0

ODI Bowling & Fielding
Wickets:	9	Runs:	298
Best Bowling:	2/19	Average:	33.11
5 WM:	0	Catches:	2
Stumpings:	0		

A left arm off-spinner, Tim Shaw played in South Africa's first official, post apartheid, ODI, against India at Kolkata, in 1991. He took the wicket of Indian skipper Mohammad Azharuddin and then went on to play in a further eight ODI's, but was never considered for Test duties.

SHEPSTONE, George Harold

Born: April 9, 1876
Batting: Right handed
Bowling: Right arm fast

Tests

Test Career:	1896-99		
Cap Number:	35		
Tests Played:	2		

Test Batting
Innings:	4	Runs:	38
Highest Score:	21	Average:	9.50
No. 50s:	0	No. 100s:	0

Test Bowling & Fielding
Wickets:	0	Runs:	47
Best Bowling:		Average:	0.00
5 WI:	0	10 WM:	0
Catches:	2	Stumpings:	0

An English educated all-rounder who did little in his two Tests, but did score a century for Transvaal in Currie Cup competition.

SHERWELL, Percy William

Born: August 17, 1880
Batting: Right handed
         Wicket Keeper

Tests

Test Career:	1906-11		
Cap Number:	60		
Tests Played:	13		

Test Batting
Innings:	22	Runs:	427
Highest Score:	115	Average:	23.72
No. 50s:	1	No. 100s:	1

Test Bowling & Fielding
Wickets:	0	Runs:	0
Best Bowling:		Average:	0.00
5 WI:	0	10 WM:	0
Catches:	20	Stumpings:	16

He was South Africa's first successful Test captain, leading his side to a one wicket victory over England in the very first Test he played in 1906. Sherwell was a wicket keeper batsman who made a century at Lord's in 1907. He was also an outstanding tennis player who won the South African men's singles title in 1904.

SIEDLE, Ivan Julian

Born: January 11, 1903
Batting: Right handed
Bowling: Right arm medium

Tests

Test Career: 1928-36
Cap Number: 123
Tests Played: 18

Test Batting

Innings:	34	Runs:	977
Highest Score:	141	Average:	28.73
No. 50s:	5	No. 100s:	1

Test Bowling & Fielding

Wickets:	1	Runs:	7
Best Bowling:	1/7	Average:	7.00
5 WI:	0	10 WM:	0
Catches:	7	Stumpings:	0

He was an opening batsman, who despite scoring heavily for Natal in the Currie Cup, struggled in his early Tests and looked destined to remain an unfulfilled talent. All of that turned around in a single innings against England at Cape Town in 1930/31, when his 141 was top score in a masterful display by the South Africans that saw them record a first innings score of 8/513. Siedle batted for exactly five hours to anchor the innings and cement his place in the side. He was a consistent performer thereafter, but another big score eluded him as he made 15 scores between 30 and 62 in his next 12 Tests.

SIMONS, Eric

Born: March 9, 1962
Batting: Right handed
Bowling: Right arm medium-fast

One Day Internationals

ODI Career: 1994-95
ODIs Played: 23

ODI Batting

Innings:	18	Runs:	217
Highest Score:	24	Average:	15.50
No. 50s:	0	No. 100s:	0

ODI Bowling & Fielding

Wickets:	33	Runs:	810
Best Bowling:	4/42	Average:	24.54
5 WM:	0	Catches:	6
Stumpings:	0		

A talented and hard-hitting all-rounder from Western Province, Simons made his ODI debut against Australia, at Johannesburg in 1994 at age 32. He was a serviceable contributor in 23 ODI's.

SINCLAIR, James Hugh

Born: October 16, 1876
Batting: Right handed
Bowling: Right arm medium-fast

Tests

Test Career: 1896-1911
Cap Number: 29
Tests Played: 25

Test Batting

Innings:	47	Runs:	1,069
Highest Score:	106	Average:	23.23
No. 50s:	3	No. 100s:	3

Test Bowling & Fielding

Wickets:	63	Runs:	1,996
Best Bowling:	6/26	Average:	31.68
5 WI:	1	10 WM:	0
Catches:	9	Stumpings:	0

The first champion South African cricketer, Jimmy Sinclair not only scored his country's first Test century, but it's second and third as well. Quite aside from being a great batsman he was also a prominent medium pace bowler who took 63 wickets in only 25 Tests. He made his Test debut in 1896 against the powerful English side and impressed in his second Test at Johannesburg with scores of 40 and 26 as well as four wickets when given the ball. He was devastating when the English returned in 1898/99, and at Cape Town in April he claimed match figures of 9/89 and struck his first hundred. Sinclair scored two more Test hundreds when Australia visited for the first time in 1902 to confirm his reputation as one of the finest cricketers not only in South Africa, but the world. From that point on his Test batting tended to be a disappointment, as the lusty hitting that had brought him so many runs early in his career often caused his downfall. He continued to be a sturdy contributor with the ball, playing his final Test on his country's first tour of Australia in 1911/12. Sinclair passed away in 1913 at the age of only 36.

SMITH, Charles James Edward

Born: December 25, 1872
Batting: Right handed

Tests

Test Career: 1902
Cap Number: 51
Tests Played: 3

Test Batting

Innings:	6	Runs:	106
Highest Score:	45	Average:	21.20
No. 50s:	0	No. 100s:	0

Test Bowling & Fielding

Wickets:	0	Runs:	0
Best Bowling:	0	Average:	0.00
5 WI:	0	10 WM:	0
Catches:	2	Stumpings:	0

A batsman from Transvaal, he played all of his three Tests against the touring Australians in 1902. His best effort was 45 in the final Test at Cape Town.

SMITH, Frederick W

Born: March 31, 1861
Batting: Right handed
Wicket Keeper

Tests

Test Career: 1889-96
Cap Number: 8
Tests Played: 3

Test Batting
Innings:	6	Runs:	45
Highest Score:	12	Average:	9.00
No. 50s:	0	No. 100s:	0

Test Bowling & Fielding
Wickets:	0	Runs:	0
Best Bowling:		Average:	0.00
5 WI:	0	10 WM:	0
Catches:	2	Stumpings:	0

South Africa's first wicket keeper, he completed two catches in his first innings behind the stumps for his country. Smith also played a Test against the English when they toured in 1896.

SMITH, Graeme Craig
Born: February 1, 1981
Batting: Left handed
Bowling: Right arm off-break

Tests
Test Career:	2002-		
Cap Number:	286		
Tests Played:	48		

Test Batting
Innings:	84	Runs:	3,891
Highest Score:	277	Average:	49.25
No. 50s:	14	No. 100s:	11

Test Bowling & Fielding
Wickets:	8	Runs:	724
Best Bowling:	2/145	Average:	90.50
5 WI:	0	10 WM:	0
Catches:	59	Stumpings:	0

One Day Internationals
ODI Career:	2002-		
ODIs Played:	91		

ODI Batting
Innings:	90	Runs:	3,389
Highest Score:	134*	Average:	39.87
No. 50s:	19	No. 100s:	6

ODI Bowling & Fielding
Wickets:	10	Runs:	655
Best Bowling:	3/30	Average:	65.50
5 WM:	0	Catches:	36
Stumpings:	0		

Big things have been expected from the big man since he made his Test debut as a precocious 21 year old. He started out against the all conquering Australians, making 68 in his first Test and showing that he had the confidence to take on world class opposition. Two Tests later Smith was playing Bangladesh, and even though it was a clear drop in class, the fact he made a double century so early in his career was a notable achievement. His efforts did not go unnoticed, and when selectors were looking to re-invigorate the side in 2003, he was chosen to replace Shaun Pollock as captain. Smith's form in England in 2003 was nothing short of staggering. He scored back to back double centuries in the first two Tests that included a South African record 277 at Edgbaston. The runs have kept coming for Smith, with 11 Test centuries in total, and an average of just below 50 in Tests. His form did wane against Australia over 2005/06, when he failed to reach a half century in any innings and as he struggled with the bat his captaincy also came into question. Smith took time off in 2006 to overcome an ankle injury, and following the break will regain the captaincy and spearhead his country's assault on the 2007 World Cup

SMITH, Vivian Ian (Ian)
Born: February 23, 1925
Batting: Right handed
Bowling: Right arm leg-break

Tests
Test Career:	1947-57		
Cap Number:	161		
Tests Played:	9		

Test Batting
Innings:	16	Runs:	39
Highest Score:	11*	Average:	3.90
No. 50s:	0	No. 100s:	0

Test Bowling & Fielding
Wickets:	12	Runs:	769
Best Bowling:	4/143	Average:	64.08
5 WI:	0	10 WM:	0
Catches:	3	Stumpings:	0

A leg spinner from Natal who took seven wickets on debut at Trent Bridge in 1947. That was to be his best effort in a Test by a fair margin with only five more wickets in his next eight appearances for South Africa.

SNELL, Richard Peter
Born: September 12, 1968
Batting: Right handed
Bowling: Right arm medium-fast

Tests
Test Career:	1992-94		
Cap Number:	245		
Tests Played:	5		

Test Batting
Innings:	8	Runs:	95
Highest Score:	48	Average:	13.57
No. 50s:	0	No. 100s:	0

Test Bowling & Fielding
Wickets:	19	Runs:	538
Best Bowling:	4/74	Average:	28.31
5 WI:	0	10 WM:	0
Catches:	1	Stumpings:	0

One Day Internationals
ODI Career:	1991-96		
ODIs Played:	42		

ODI Batting
Innings:	28	Runs:	322
Highest Score:	63	Average:	16.10
No. 50s:	2	No. 100s:	0

ODI Bowling & Fielding
Wickets:	44	Runs:	1,574
Best Bowling:	5/40	Average:	35.77
5 WM:	1	Catches:	7
Stumpings:	0		

A fast medium bowler from Transvaal who took the first wicket to be taken by a South African in Tests for over 22 years, when he had PV Simmons caught by Peter Kirsten. Snell claimed eight wickets in his country's return to Test cricket at Bridgetown in 1992 to be his side's leading bowler. The handy bowler and useful lower order batsman would play four more Tests and 42 ODI's.

SNOOKE, Sibley John (Tip)
Born: February 1, 1881
Batting: Right handed
Bowling: Right arm medium-fast

Tests
Test Career:	1906-23		
Cap Number:	61		
Tests Played:	26		

Test Batting
Innings:	46	Runs:	1,008
Highest Score:	103	Average:	22.40
No. 50s:	5	No. 100s:	1

Test Bowling & Fielding
Wickets:	35	Runs:	702
Best Bowling:	8/70	Average:	20.05
5 WI:	1	10 WM:	1
Catches:	24	Stumpings:	0

A leading figure in early Currie Cup competition, 'Tip' Snooke made his first class debut for Border at the age of only 17. He was an accomplished top order batsman and lively opening bowler who scored a century in Adelaide in 1911 that helped his country to their first ever win over Australia. That win was an extraordinary result for the South Africans who were thrashed in the four other Tests of that series. His bowling was said to be menacing, with career best figures of 12/127 against England in 1906. Snooke led South Africa in five Tests for three wins and two losses.

SNOOKE, Stanley de la Courtte
Born: November 11, 1878
Batting: Right handed

Tests
Test Career:	1907		
Cap Number:	64		
Tests Played:	1		

Test Batting
Innings:	1	Runs:	0
Highest Score:	0	Average:	0.00
No. 50s:	0	No. 100s:	0

Test Bowling & Fielding
Wickets:	0	Runs:	0
Best Bowling:		Average:	0.00
5 WI:	0	10 WM:	0
Catches:	2	Stumpings:	0

The brother of 'Tip' Snooke, he played a single Test against England at The Oval in 1907.

SOLOMON, William Rodger Thomson
Born: April 23, 1872
Batting: Right handed
Bowling: Right arm medium

Tests
Test Career:	1899
Cap Number:	43
Tests Played:	1

Test Batting
Innings:	2	Runs:	4
Highest Score:	2	Average:	2.00
No. 50s:	0	No. 100s:	0

Test Bowling & Fielding
Wickets:	0	Runs:	0
Best Bowling:		Average:	0.00
5 WI:	0	10 WM:	0
Catches:	1	Stumpings:	0

Whilst he had a non-descript Test career with four runs in his only Test, he was the oldest living Test cricketer just prior to his death in 1964 at the age of 92.

STEWART, Errol
Born: July 30, 1969
Batting: Right handed
Bowling: Right arm medium
         Wicket Keeper

One Day Internationals
ODI Career:	1993-02
ODIs Played:	6

ODI Batting
Innings:	6	Runs:	61
Highest Score:	23*	Average:	15.25
No. 50s:	0	No. 100s:	0

ODI Bowling & Fielding
Wickets:	0	Runs:	0
Best Bowling:		Average:	0.00
5 WM:	0	Catches:	5
Stumpings:	0		

A reserve wicket-keeper from Natal who made his ODI debut against Pakistan, at Buffalo Park in 1993. Stewart played in six ODI's over an eight year period.

STEWART, Robert Bernard
Born: September 3, 1856
Batting: Right handed

Tests
Test Career:	1889
Cap Number:	9
Tests Played:	1

Test Batting
Innings:	2	Runs:	13
Highest Score:	9	Average:	6.50
No. 50s:	0	No. 100s:	0

Test Bowling & Fielding
Wickets:	0	Runs:	0
Best Bowling:		Average:	0.00
5 WI:	0	10 WM:	0
Catches:	2	Stumpings:	0

A leading cricketer in the formative years of South African cricket, he was an all-rounder who appeared in his country's first Test side.

STEYN, Dale Williem
Born: June 27, 1983
Batting: Right handed
Bowling: Right arm fast

Tests
Test Career:	2004-
Cap Number:	297
Tests Played:	8

Test Batting

Innings:	13	Runs:	70
Highest Score:	13	Average:	7.77
No. 50s:	0	No. 100s:	0

Test Bowling & Fielding

Wickets:	32	Runs:	1,124
Best Bowling:	5/47	Average:	35.12
5 WI:	2	10 WM:	0
Catches:	2	Stumpings:	0

One Day Internationals

ODI Career: 2005-
ODIs Played: 4

ODI Batting

Innings:	2	Runs:	4
Highest Score:	3	Average:	2.00
No. 50s:	0	No. 100s:	0

ODI Bowling & Fielding

Wickets:	3	Runs:	132
Best Bowling:	1/2	Average:	44.00
5 WM:	0	Catches:	0
Stumpings:	0		

South African selectors have persisted with the raw boned paceman and were rewarded in 2006 with good performances against New Zealand and Sri Lanka. He took 16 wickets in the three Test series against the Black Caps, and followed that up with eight wickets in two Tests on the tour of Sri Lanka, including five wickets in an innings in his last Test at Colombo. It was a fine effort in difficult conditions, as the South Africans were soundly thrashed and Steyn had to toil for long spells. He's quick and can bowl genuine outswing, making him a good long term Test prospect for the Proteas.

STEYN, Philippus Jeremia Rudolf (Rudi)

Born:	June 30, 1967
Batting:	Right handed
Bowling:	Right arm medium
	Wicket Keeper

Tests

Test Career: 1995
Cap Number: 260
Tests Played: 3

Test Batting

Innings:	6	Runs:	127
Highest Score:	46	Average:	21.16
No. 50s:	0	No. 100s:	0

Test Bowling & Fielding

Wickets:	0	Runs:	0
Best Bowling:		Average:	0.00
5 WI:	0	10 WM:	0
Catches:	0	Stumpings:	0

One Day Internationals

ODI Career: 1995
ODIs Played: 1

ODI Batting

Innings:	1	Runs:	4
Highest Score:	4	Average:	4.00
No. 50s:	0	No. 100s:	0

ODI Bowling & Fielding

Wickets:	0	Runs:	0
Best Bowling:		Average:	0.00
5 WM:	0	Catches:	0
Stumpings:	0		

An opening batsman and occasional wicket keeper, he played three Tests against New Zealand in 1995. His highest Test score was a laborious 46 in 220 minutes at Auckland.

STRICKER, Louis Anthony

Born:	May 26, 1884
Batting:	Right handed
Bowling:	Right arm medium
	Wicket Keeper

Tests

Test Career: 1910-12
Cap Number: 67
Tests Played: 13

Test Batting

Innings:	24	Runs:	342
Highest Score:	48	Average:	14.25
No. 50s:	0	No. 100s:	0

Test Bowling & Fielding

Wickets:	1	Runs:	105
Best Bowling:	1/36	Average:	105.00
5 WI:	0	10 WM:	0
Catches:	3	Stumpings:	0

He was an opening batsman with Transvaal for many seasons but failed to make much of an impression in the national side. In thirteen Tests he averaged only 14.25 and failed to make a single half century.

STRYDOM, Pieter Coenraad

Born:	June 10, 1969
Batting:	Right handed
Bowling:	Left arm off-break

Tests

Test Career: 2000
Cap Number: 275
Tests Played: 2

Test Batting

Innings:	3	Runs:	35
Highest Score:	30	Average:	11.66
No. 50s:	0	No. 100s:	0

Test Bowling & Fielding

Wickets:	0	Runs:	27
Best Bowling:		Average:	0.00
5 WI:	0	10 WM:	0
Catches:	1	Stumpings:	0

One Day Internationals

ODI Career: 2000
ODIs Played: 10

ODI Batting

Innings:	8	Runs:	48
Highest Score:	34	Average:	9.60
No. 50s:	0	No. 100s:	0

ODI Bowling & Fielding

Wickets:	2	Runs:	206
Best Bowling:	1/18	Average:	103.00
5 WM:	0	Catches:	3
Stumpings:	0		

A left arm off spinner and competent middle order batsman from Border, who played two Tests early in 2000, but with limited opportunities did little and was quickly dropped back to his provincial side. He was part of Hansie Croje's side that toured India in 2000 and even though accused of placing bets on the results of certain matches was never found guilty and ultimately exonerated.

SUSSKIND, Manfred John

Born: June 8, 1891
Batting: Right handed
Wicket Keeper

Tests

Test Career: 1924
Cap Number: 112
Tests Played: 5

Test Batting

Innings:	8	Runs:	268
Highest Score:	65	Average:	33.50
No. 50s:	4	No. 100s:	0

Test Bowling & Fielding

Wickets:	0	Runs:	0
Best Bowling:		Average:	0.00
5 WI:	0	10 WM:	0
Catches:	1	Stumpings:	0

An occasional wicket keeper, he was used to great effect as a number three batsman on the tour of England in 1924. Whilst most of the side struggled, he scored four half centuries and returned an average of 33.50 in eight innings. Even though he continued to be a regular in the strong Transvaal side, he was never called up to play for South Africa again.

SYMCOX, Patrick Leonard

Born: April 14, 1960
Batting: Right handed
Bowling: Right arm off-break

Tests

Test Career: 1993-98
Cap Number: 255
Tests Played: 20

Test Batting

Innings:	27	Runs:	741
Highest Score:	108	Average:	28.50
No. 50s:	4	No. 100s:	1

Test Bowling & Fielding

Wickets:	37	Runs:	1,603
Best Bowling:	4/69	Average:	43.32
5 WI:	0	10 WM:	0
Catches:	5	Stumpings:	0

One Day Internationals

ODI Career: 1993-99
ODIs Played: 80

ODI Batting

Innings:	54	Runs:	694
Highest Score:	61	Average:	16.92
No. 50s:	3	No. 100s:	0

ODI Bowling & Fielding

Wickets:	72	Runs:	2,762
Best Bowling:	4/28	Average:	38.36
5 WM:	0	Catches:	23
Stumpings:	0		

One of the game's real characters, Symcox was a crafty off spinner and belligerent lower order batsman who made it to the Test arena on a little talent and a lot of determination. Whilst he wasn't a big spinner of the ball, his main weapon was his height and he would almost stand on his toes at delivery point to accentuate it. He never took five wickets in a Test innings, and though he was clearly selected for his bowling, his finest moment came with the bat in 1999. The Proteas were playing Pakistan in Johannesburg, and coming in at number ten, Symcox scored an unlikely Test hundred. The late bloomer played international cricket until he was 38 and today continues to entertain fans around the world from behind the microphone.

TABERER, Henry Melville

Born: October 7, 1870
Batting: Right handed
Bowling: Right arm fast

Tests

Test Career: 1902
Cap Number: 52
Tests Played: 1

Test Batting

Innings:	1	Runs:	2
Highest Score:	2	Average:	2.00
No. 50s:	0	No. 100s:	0

Test Bowling & Fielding

Wickets:	1	Runs:	48
Best Bowling:	1/25	Average:	48.00
5 WI:	0	10 WM:	0
Catches:	0	Stumpings:	0

He captained the side in his only Test and has the honour of being the first South African skipper to avoid losing a Test.

TANCRED, Augustus Bernard

Born: August 20, 1865
Batting: Right handed
Bowling: Right arm medium

Tests

Test Career: 1889
Cap Number: 10
Tests Played: 2

Test Batting

Innings:	4	Runs:	87
Highest Score:	29	Average:	29.00
No. 50s:	0	No. 100s:	0

Test Bowling & Fielding

Wickets:	0	Runs:	0
Best Bowling:		Average:	0.00
5 WI:	0	10 WM:	0
Catches:	2	Stumpings:	0

A well known figure in South Africa club cricket in the 19th century, he played in the South African side that met England for two Tests in 1888/89. The opener top scored on the mats at Port Elizabeth in his country's first ever innings with 29 and was thankfully on hand in the second Test at Cape Town when he carried his bat to score 26 not out in a team score of 47.

TANCRED, Louis Joseph

Born:	October 7, 1876
Batting:	Right handed

Tests

Test Career:	1902-13
Cap Number:	53
Tests Played:	14

Test Batting

Innings:	26	Runs:	530
Highest Score:	97	Average:	21.20
No. 50s:	2	No. 100s:	0

Test Bowling & Fielding

Wickets:	0	Runs:	0
Best Bowling:		Average:	0.00
5 WI:	0	10 WM:	0
Catches:	3	Stumpings:	0

One of three Tancred brothers to play for South Africa, he was an opening batsman who made it his job to wear down the opening bowlers. He scored 97 on debut against the Australians at Johannesburg in 1902, adding a record 173 for the second innings with Charlie Llewellyn. His patient knock went a long way to securing a draw for the home side, the first time they had avoided defeat in Test cricket.

TANCRED, Vincent Maximillian

Born:	July 7, 1875
Batting:	Right handed

Tests

Test Career:	1899
Cap Number:	44
Tests Played:	1

Test Batting

Innings:	2	Runs:	25
Highest Score:	18	Average:	12.50
No. 50s:	0	No. 100s:	0

Test Bowling & Fielding

Wickets:	0	Runs:	0
Best Bowling:		Average:	0.00
5 WI:	0	10 WM:	0
Catches:	0	Stumpings:	0

The brother of Augustus and Louis who also played for South Africa, he lined up against the English at Johannesburg in 1899. He tragically took his own life only five years later at the age of 28.

TAPSCOTT, George Lancelot

Born:	November 7, 1889
Batting:	Right handed
Bowling:	Right arm medium

Tests

Test Career:	1913
Cap Number:	86
Tests Played:	1

Test Batting

Innings:	2	Runs:	5
Highest Score:	4	Average:	2.50
No. 50s:	0	No. 100s:	0

Test Bowling & Fielding

Wickets:	0	Runs:	0
Best Bowling:		Average:	0.00
5 WI:	0	10 WM:	0
Catches:	1	Stumpings:	0

He failed in his only Test, scoring 4 and 1 against England at Durban in 1913.

TAPSCOTT, Lionel Eric

Born:	March 18, 1894
Batting:	Right handed
Bowling:	Right arm medium

Tests

Test Career:	1923
Cap Number:	108
Tests Played:	2

Test Batting

Innings:	3	Runs:	58
Highest Score:	50*	Average:	29.00
No. 50s:	1	No. 100s:	0

Test Bowling & Fielding

Wickets:	0	Runs:	2
Best Bowling:		Average:	0.00
5 WI:	0	10 WM:	0
Catches:	0	Stumpings:	0

The brother of George who also played for South Africa, he scored an unbeaten 50 in his Test debut against England at Johannesburg. The Tapscott brothers were known as 'Dusty' and 'Doodles' with Lionel the 'Doodles'. A third brother, Norman, also played first class cricket with Griqualand West.

TAYFIELD, Hugh Joseph

Born:	January 30, 1929
Batting:	Right handed
Bowling:	Right arm off-break

Tests

Test Career:	1949-60
Cap Number:	173
Tests Played:	37

Test Batting

Innings:	60	Runs:	862
Highest Score:	75	Average:	16.90
No. 50s:	2	No. 100s:	0

Test Bowling & Fielding

Wickets:	170	Runs:	4,405
Best Bowling:	9/113	Average:	25.91
5 WI:	14	10 WM:	2
Catches:	26	Stumpings:	0

A right arm off spinner of the highest order, he is still considered to be the best finger spinner South Africa has ever produced. Hugh Tayfield famously kissed his cap for luck prior to bowling an over, but with his unerring accuracy and ability to spin the ball back into the right hander, he hardly needed much luck. He made his debut against the touring Australians in 1949/50 and in only his third Test tore through their highly regarded line-up on a soft track at Durban to claim 7/23. Tayfield was no less effective when he toured Australia in 1952/53, claiming 30 wickets in the five Test series to clearly be his side's leading bowler. He simply destroyed the Australians at the MCG, claiming 13 wickets for the match and leading his side to a surprise 82 run victory. He was also a useful lower order batsman and his scores of 23 and 22 batting at number ten in that game were almost as important as his wickets. Statistically his most successful series was his 37 wickets against England when they toured in 1956/57. It was a record for most wickets in a series by a South African and included nine wickets in a single innings at Johannesburg in the fourth Test. By the time he played his last Test, Tayfield had claimed 170 wickets in only 37 outings, a record that places him amongst the all time bowling elite.

TAYLOR, Alistair Innes

Born: July 25, 1925
Batting: Right handed
Bowling: Right arm leg-break

Tests

Test Career: 1956
Cap Number: 194
Tests Played: 1

Test Batting

Innings:	2	Runs:	18
Highest Score:	12	Average:	9.00
No. 50s:	0	No. 100s:	0

Test Bowling & Fielding

Wickets:	0	Runs:	0
Best Bowling:		Average:	0.00
5 WI:	0	10 WM:	0
Catches:	0	Stumpings:	0

An opening batsman from Transvaal who played just the one Test against the touring English in 1956.

TAYLOR, Daniel

Born: January 9, 1887
Batting: Left handed
Bowling: Right arm medium

Tests

Test Career: 1914
Cap Number: 92
Tests Played: 24

Test Batting

Innings:	45	Runs:	85
Highest Score:	36	Average:	21.25
No. 50s:	0	No. 100s:	0

Test Bowling & Fielding

Wickets:	0	Runs:	0
Best Bowling:		Average:	0.00
5 WI:	0	10 WM:	0
Catches:	0	Stumpings:	0

The brother of South African great Herbie Taylor, he played a brace of Tests against the touring English in 1913/14.

TAYLOR, Herbert Wilfred

Born: May 5, 1889
Batting: Right handed
Bowling: Right arm medium

Tests

Test Career: 1912-32
Cap Number: 77
Tests Played: 42

Test Batting

Innings:	76	Runs:	2,936
Highest Score:	176	Average:	40.77
No. 50s:	17	No. 100s:	7

Test Bowling & Fielding

Wickets:	5	Runs:	156
Best Bowling:	3/15	Average:	31.20
5 WI:	0	10 WM:	0
Catches:	19	Stumpings:	0

When he played his final Test at the age of 42, no South African had captained his country in more Tests or played more first class cricket. He had a wonderful record both at home and abroad, with seven Test centuries and another 17 scores that surpassed 50. Taylor was hardly an imposing looking cricketer, being of slight build, but he had the finest technique of any batsman that had previously come out of South Africa. He put his nimble feet and good eye to work against the touring English in 1913/14 with 508 runs at over 50 apiece. In that series he made a century in the first Test at Durban against the English tyro Sydney Barnes, establishing himself as the man the English had to get out. Taylor captained the side in 1913/14 and even though the South Africans were soundly beaten he lost no admirers as a leader. That series would be the last Test cricket he would see for seven years as war gripped Europe and Africa, but when Test cricket resumed Taylor's powers were undiminished. He continued to lead his country both as captain and as their leading batsman, playing in the Test side for another decade. Herbie Taylor was over 40 when he visited Australia in 1931/32, but facing Clarrie Grimmet and Bill O'Reilly at the Adelaide Oval he scored 78 and 84 to show the world that whilst greying his was still a world class batsman.

TELEMACHUS, Roger

Born: March 27, 1973
Batting: Right handed
Bowling: Right arm medium-fast

One Day Internationals

ODI Career: 1998-
ODIs Played: 36

ODI Batting

Innings:	15	Runs:	73
Highest Score:	29	Average:	6.08
No. 50s:	0	No. 100s:	0

ODI Bowling & Fielding

Wickets:	54	Runs:	1,532
Best Bowling:	4/43	Average:	28.37
5 WM:	0	Catches:	4
Stumpings:	0		

A genuine fast bowler from Stellenbosch, Roger Telemachus had his fair share of injury woes which limited his chances of a Test call up. He took a career best 4/43 in only his second ODI against Sri Lanka at Johannesburg in 1998. Still in his early 30's, he has time to add to his tally of 36 international appearances.

TERBRUGGE, David John

Born: January 31, 1977
Batting: Right handed
Bowling: Right arm medium-fast

Tests
Test Career: 1998-2004
Cap Number: 272
Tests Played: 7

Test Batting
Innings:	8	Runs:	16
Highest Score:	4*	Average:	5.33
No. 50s:	0	No. 100s:	0

Test Bowling & Fielding
Wickets:	20	Runs:	517
Best Bowling:	5/46	Average:	25.85
5 WI:	1	10 WM:	0
Catches:	4	Stumpings:	0

One Day Internationals
ODI Career: 2000
ODIs Played: 4

ODI Batting
Innings:	2	Runs:	5
Highest Score:	5	Average:	5.00
No. 50s:	0	No. 100s:	0

ODI Bowling & Fielding
Wickets:	4	Runs:	105
Best Bowling:	4/20	Average:	26.25
5 WM:	0	Catches:	0
Stumpings:	0		

The red headed Tebrugge enjoyed a promising debut series against the West Indies but after injuring an ankle was off the international scene for five years. His best effort in a Test was seven wickets against Bangladesh at East London in 2003/04.

THEUNISSEN, Nicolaas Hendrik Christiaan de Jong

Born: May 4, 1867
Batting: Right handed
Bowling: Right arm fast

Tests
Test Career: 1889
Cap Number: 14
Tests Played: 1

Test Batting
Innings:	2	Runs:	2
Highest Score:	2*	Average:	2.00
No. 50s:	0	No. 100s:	0

Test Bowling & Fielding
Wickets:	0	Runs:	51
Best Bowling:		Average:	0.00
5 WI:	0	10 WM:	0
Catches:	0	Stumpings:	0

A seam bowler from Cape Town who performed well against the English on their tour in 1888/89, but when called up for the second Test failed to take a wicket.

THORNTON, George

Born: December 24, 1867
Batting: Left handed
Bowling: Left arm off-break

Tests
Test Career: 1902
Cap Number: 54
Tests Played: 1

Test Batting
Innings:	1	Runs:	1
Highest Score:	1*	Average:	0.00
No. 50s:	0	No. 100s:	0

Test Bowling & Fielding
Wickets:	1	Runs:	20
Best Bowling:	1/20	Average:	20.00
5 WI:	0	10 WM:	0
Catches:	1	Stumpings:	0

An English born off spinner who played a single Test against Australia at the Old Wanderers Stadium in 1902.

TOMLINSON, Denis Stanley

Born: September 4, 1910
Batting: Right handed
Bowling: Right arm leg-break

Tests
Test Career: 1935
Cap Number: 142
Tests Played: 1

Test Batting
Innings:	1	Runs:	9
Highest Score:	9	Average:	9.00
No. 50s:	0	No. 100s:	0

Test Bowling & Fielding
Wickets:	0	Runs:	38
Best Bowling:		Average:	0.00
5 WI:	0	10 WM:	0
Catches:	0	Stumpings:	0

A leg spinner who played a single Test against England at Trent Bridge in 1935.

TRAICOS, Athanasios John

Born: May 17, 1947
Batting: Right handed
Bowling: Right arm off-break

Tests
Test Career: 1970-93
Cap Number: 235
Tests Played: 7

Test Batting
Innings:	10	Runs:	19
Highest Score:	5*	Average:	3.16
No. 50s:	0	No. 100s:	0

Test Bowling & Fielding
Wickets:	18	Runs:	769
Best Bowling:	5/86	Average:	42.72
5 WI:	1	10 WM:	0
Catches:	8	Stumpings:	0

One Day Internationals
ODI Career: 1983-93
ODIs Played: 27

ODI Batting
Innings:	17	Runs:	88
Highest Score:	19	Average:	11.00
No. 50s:	0	No. 100s:	0

ODI Bowling & Fielding

Wickets:	19	Runs:	987
Best Bowling:	3/35	Average:	51.94
5 WM:	0	Catches:	3
Stumpings:	0		

A player with an unusual history. John Traicos was born in Egypt, raised in South Africa, and played his first Test for that nation in 1969/70 - South Africa's final series before they were banned from participating in international cricket. Traicos, a clever off-spinner returned to the international arena almost 23 years later, this time representing neighboring Zimbabwe in their inaugural Test against India at Harare. Traicos, who was 45 years of age, showed that he had got better with age when he took 5/86 in his first outing. He went on to play in another three Tests for Zimbabwe, taking his overall tally to seven.

TRIMBORN, Patrick Henry Joseph

Born:	May 18, 1940
Batting:	Right handed
Bowling:	Right arm medium-fast

Tests

Test Career:	1967-70		
Cap Number:	229		
Tests Played:	4		

Test Batting

Innings:	4	Runs:	13
Highest Score:	11*	Average:	6.50
No. 50s:	0	No. 100s:	0

Test Bowling & Fielding

Wickets:	11	Runs:	257
Best Bowling:	3/12	Average:	23.36
5 WI:	0	10 WM:	0
Catches:	7	Stumpings:	0

A medium pacer who may have played more than four Tests had South Africa not been banished from the Test scene in 1970.

TSOLEKILE, Thami Lungisa

Born:	October 9, 1980
Batting:	Right handed
Bowling:	Right arm off-break

Tests

Test Career:	2004		
Cap Number:	294		
Tests Played:	3		

Test Batting

Innings:	5	Runs:	47
Highest Score:	22	Average:	9.40
No. 50s:	0	No. 100s:	0

Test Bowling & Fielding

Wickets:	0	Runs:	0
Best Bowling:		Average:	0.00
5 WI:	0	10 WM:	0
Catches:	6	Stumpings:	0

A young wicket keeper who played two Tests against India in 2004, and another in the same year on home soil against the touring English.

TUCKETT, Lindsay

Born:	February 6, 1919
Batting:	Right handed
Bowling:	Right arm medium-fast

Tests

Test Career:	1947-49		
Cap Number:	162		
Tests Played:	9		

Test Batting

Innings:	14	Runs:	131
Highest Score:	40*	Average:	11.90
No. 50s:	0	No. 100s:	0

Test Bowling & Fielding

Wickets:	19	Runs:	980
Best Bowling:	5/68	Average:	51.57
5 WI:	2	10 WM:	0
Catches:	9	Stumpings:	0

The son of Len who played a single Test in 1913/14, he was a tall speedster from Orange Free State who appeared in nine Tests during the late 1940's. Tuckett twice took five or more wickets in an innings, once on debut against England at Trent Bridge and then in his next Test at Lord's.

TUCKETT, Lindsay Richard (Len)

Born:	April 19, 1885
Batting:	Right handed
Bowling:	Right arm medium-fast

Tests

Test Career:	1914		
Cap Number:	89		
Tests Played:	1		

Test Batting

Innings:	2	Runs:	0
Highest Score:	0	Average:	0.00
No. 50s:	0	No. 100s:	0

Test Bowling & Fielding

Wickets:	0	Runs:	69
Best Bowling:		Average:	0.00
5 WI:	0	10 WM:	0
Catches:	2	Stumpings:	0

He played just the one Test in 1914 against England at the Old Wanderers Stadium in Johannesburg. He later became a Test selector.

TWENTYMAN-JONES, Percy Sydney

Born:	September 13, 1876
Batting:	Right handed

Tests

Test Career:	1902		
Cap Number:	57		
Tests Played:	1		

Test Batting

Innings:	2	Runs:	0
Highest Score:	0	Average:	0.00
No. 50s:	0	No. 100s:	0

Test Bowling & Fielding

Wickets:	0	Runs:	0
Best Bowling:		Average:	0.00
5 WI:	0	10 WM:	0
Catches:	0	Stumpings:	0

He was a talented all round sportsman who not only played a Test against Australia in 1902 but also represented the country at rugby.

VAN DER BIJL, Pieter Gerhard Vintcent

Born: October 21, 1907
Batting: Right handed

Tests
Test Career:	1938-39		
Cap Number:	153		
Tests Played:	5		

Test Batting
Innings:	9	Runs:	460
Highest Score:	125	Average:	51.11
No. 50s:	2	No. 100s:	1

Test Bowling & Fielding
Wickets:	0	Runs:	0
Best Bowling:		Average:	0.00
5 WI:	0	10 WM:	0
Catches:	1	Stumpings:	0

There was plenty of Pieter van der Bijl, which is hardly surprising given he was not only a Test cricketer but a champion shot-putter and heavyweight boxer as well. Despite his size, he was a watchful opening batsman who played a key role in cricket's most famous timeless Test. It was played at Durban between the 3rd and 14th of March in 1939 and was finally called a draw because the visitors had to catch their boat back to England. Whilst van der Bijl wasn't solely to blame, his 125 in over seven hours certainly didn't help achieve a result.

VAN DER MERWE, Edward Alexander

Born: November 9, 1903
Batting: Right handed
Wicket Keeper

Tests
Test Career:	1929-36		
Cap Number:	131		
Tests Played:	2		

Test Batting
Innings:	4	Runs:	27
Highest Score:	19	Average:	9.00
No. 50s:	0	No. 100s:	0

Test Bowling & Fielding
Wickets:	0	Runs:	0
Best Bowling:		Average:	0.00
5 WI:	0	10 WM:	0
Catches:	3	Stumpings:	0

A fine all round athlete who played both cricket and rugby for Transvaal, he was a reserve wicket keeper whose two Tests were separated by a gap of seven years. Van der Merwe was described as an excellent gloveman but inferior batsman to Jock Cameron, the keeper to which he was understudy.

VAN DER MERWE, Peter Laurence

Born: March 14, 1937
Batting: Right handed
Bowling: Left arm off-break

Tests
Test Career:	1963-67		
Cap Number:	220		
Tests Played:	15		

Test Batting
Innings:	23	Runs:	533
Highest Score:	76	Average:	25.38
No. 50s:	3	No. 100s:	0

Test Bowling & Fielding
Wickets:	1	Runs:	22
Best Bowling:	1/6	Average:	22.00
5 WI:	0	10 WM:	0
Catches:	11	Stumpings:	0

On Test match performances alone he was a surprise choice to replace Trevor Goddard as captain in 1965, but the chunky all-rounder proved to be a more than capable skipper with four wins and three draws from eight Tests in charge. He originally made the side as an off spinner, but a distinct lack of success saw him switch to middle order batsman. He was hardly a huge hit there either, with a top score of 76 and an average of just 25.38. It was as captain that Peter van der Merwe made a name for himself in South African cricket.

VAN DER WATH, Johan

Born: January 10, 1978
Batting: Right handed
Bowling: Right arm fast

One Day Internationals
ODI Career:	2006		
ODIs Played:	7		

ODI Batting
Innings:	6	Runs:	80
Highest Score:	37*	Average:	20.00
No. 50s:	0	No. 100s:	0

ODI Bowling & Fielding
Wickets:	10	Runs:	399
Best Bowling:	2/21	Average:	39.90
5 WM:	0	Catches:	2
Stumpings:	0		

An all-rounder orginally from Natal, Johan van der Wath made his ODI debut against Australia, at Docklands in 2006, when he was flown in to replace the injured Jacques Kallis.

VAN JAARSVELD, Martin

Born: June 18, 1974
Batting: Right handed
Bowling: Right arm medium

Tests
Test Career:	2002-04		
Cap Number:	287		
Tests Played:	9		

Test Batting
Innings:	15	Runs:	397
Highest Score:	73	Average:	30.53
No. 50s:	3	No. 100s:	0

Test Bowling & Fielding
Wickets:	0	Runs:	28
Best Bowling:		Average:	0.00
5 WI:	0	10 WM:	0
Catches:	11	Stumpings:	0

One Day Internationals
ODI Career:	2002-04
ODIs Played:	11

ODI Batting
Innings:	7	Runs:	124
Highest Score:	45	Average:	20.66
No. 50s:	0	No. 100s:	0

ODI Bowling & Fielding
Wickets:	2	Runs:	18
Best Bowling:	1/0	Average:	9.00
5 WM:	0	Catches:	4
Stumpings:	0		

A middle order batsman from Northerns who has been in and out of the Test side since making his debut against Bangladesh in 2002. He scored 73 against the touring West Indians in 2003/04 and followed that up with a half century against New Zealand, but since then has found runs harder to come by at Test level.

VAN RYNEVELD, Clive Berrange
Born:	March 19, 1928
Batting:	Right handed
Bowling:	Right arm leg-break

Tests
Test Career:	1951-58
Cap Number:	180
Tests Played:	19

Test Batting
Innings:	33	Runs:	724
Highest Score:	83	Average:	26.81
No. 50s:	3	No. 100s:	0

Test Bowling & Fielding
Wickets:	17	Runs:	671
Best Bowling:	4/67	Average:	39.47
5 WI:	0	10 WM:	0
Catches:	14	Stumpings:	0

An all rounder of the highest order, he not only played Test cricket for South Africa he also played Rugby for England. As a cricketer he was an accomplished middle order batsman and leg spinner. Business commitments prevented him from traveling away from home, but he captained South Africa against the touring English in 1956/57 and against the Australians a year later for two wins and four losses in eight Tests. Van Ryneveld later became a member of the South African Parliament.

VAN WYK, Morne
Born:	March 20, 1979
Batting:	Right handed
Bowling:	Left arm slow
	Wicket Keeper

One Day Internationals
ODI Career:	2003
ODIs Played:	1

ODI Batting
Innings:	1	Runs:	17
Highest Score:	17	Average:	17.00
No. 50s:	0	No. 100s:	0

ODI Bowling & Fielding
Wickets:	0	Runs:	0
Best Bowling:		Average:	0.00
5 WM:	0	Catches:	0
Stumpings:	0		

A promising wicket-keeper from Bloemfontein, Morne van Wyk played his only ODI to date against England at Lord's, in 2003.

VAN ZYL, Cornelius
Born:	October 1, 1961
Batting:	Right handed
Bowling:	Right arm medium-fast

One Day Internationals
ODI Career:	1992
ODIs Played:	2

ODI Batting
Innings:	2	Runs:	3
Highest Score:	3*	Average:	3.00
No. 50s:	0	No. 100s:	0

ODI Bowling & Fielding
Wickets:	0	Runs:	93
Best Bowling:		Average:	0.00
5 WM:	0	Catches:	0
Stumpings:	0		

A right arm medium-pacer who played two ODI's against the West Indies when he toured the Carribean in 1992.

VARNALS, George Derek
Born:	July 24, 1935
Batting:	Right handed
Bowling:	Right arm medium

Tests
Test Career:	1964-65
Cap Number:	222
Tests Played:	3

Test Batting
Innings:	6	Runs:	97
Highest Score:	23	Average:	16.16
No. 50s:	0	No. 100s:	0

Test Bowling & Fielding
Wickets:	0	Runs:	2
Best Bowling:		Average:	0.00
5 WI:	0	10 WM:	0
Catches:	0	Stumpings:	0

A journeyman in the Currie Cup competition, Varnals played for Eastern Province, Natal and Transvaal. The top order batsman was given a chance in the Test side in 1964/65 but failed dismally, scoring just 97 runs in six innings against the touring Englishmen.

VILJOEN, Kenneth George
Born:	May 14, 1910
Batting:	Right handed
Bowling:	Right arm medium

	Tests		
Test Career:	1930-49		
Cap Number:	135		
Tests Played:	27		
Test Batting			
Innings:	50	Runs:	1,365
Highest Score:	124	Average:	28.43
No. 50s:	9	No. 100s:	2
Test Bowling & Fielding			
Wickets:	0	Runs:	23
Best Bowling:		Average:	0.00
5 WI:	0	10 WM:	0
Catches:	5	Stumpings:	0

He was a right hand batsman of note whose Test career was interrupted by World War II. Viljoen was a promising youngster who made his first class debut at 19 and Test debut at 20. On the 1932/33 tour to Australia he was the only South African to score a century in Tests, with 111 at the MCG. Later that series South Africa was humiliated at the same ground, being dismissed for 36 and 45, with Viljoen and Curnow the only players to reach double figures in either innings. His other Test century was a knock of 124 out of 318 at Old Trafford in 1935 that denied England the chance to press for a win. When cricket resumed after the war Viljoen was in his mid thirties, but he continued to be a presence in the side, playing seven more Tests and scoring three more valuable innings in excess of 50. In retirement he became a leading cricket administrator in South Africa.

VINCENT, Cyril Leverton

Born:	February 16, 1902		
Batting:	Left handed		
Bowling:	Left arm off-break		
	Tests		
Test Career:	1927-35		
Cap Number:	118		
Tests Played:	25		
Test Batting			
Innings:	38	Runs:	526
Highest Score:	60	Average:	20.23
No. 50s:	2	No. 100s:	0
Test Bowling & Fielding			
Wickets:	84	Runs:	2,631
Best Bowling:	6/51	Average:	31.32
5 WI:	3	10 WM:	0
Catches:	27	Stumpings:	0

A left arm finger spinner who could be as effective as the more highly regarded English turners on the right wicket. He took five or more wickets in a Test innings on three occasions, with the victim and venue twice being England in Durban. Vincent was a capable lower order batsman who once scored a 60 at Headingly.

VINTCENT, Charles Henry

Born:	September 2, 1866
Batting:	Left handed
Bowling:	Left arm medium-fast

	Tests		
Test Career:	1889-92		
Cap Number:	11		
Tests Played:	3		
Test Batting			
Innings:	6	Runs:	26
Highest Score:	9	Average:	4.33
No. 50s:	0	No. 100s:	0
Test Bowling & Fielding			
Wickets:	4	Runs:	193
Best Bowling:	3/88	Average:	48.25
5 WI:	0	10 WM:	0
Catches:	1	Stumpings:	0

A left arm medium pace bowler who claimed three wickets in his country's match against England at Cape Town in 1888/89. He had played in the first South African Test team a fortnight earlier.

VOGLER, Albert Edward Ernest

Born:	November 28, 1876
Batting:	Right handed

	Tests		
Test Career:	1906-11		
Cap Number:	62		
Tests Played:	15		
Test Batting			
Innings:	26	Runs:	340
Highest Score:	65	Average:	17.00
No. 50s:	2	No. 100s:	0
Test Bowling & Fielding			
Wickets:	64	Runs:	1,455
Best Bowling:	7/94	Average:	22.73
5 WI:	5	10 WM:	1
Catches:	20	Stumpings:	0

One of four masterful leg-spinners that played for South Africa in the early part of the 20th century, he was considered the best of the quartet by England captain 'Tip' Foster. In 1909/10 he broke the record for most wickets in a Test series by a South African with 36 in five Tests against the English, including his career best figures of 12/181 in the first Test at Johannesburg. He was also a thumping lower batsman with two Test half-tons to his name.

WADE, Herbert Frederick

Born:	September 14, 1905
Batting:	Right handed

	Tests		
Test Career:	1935-36		
Cap Number:	143		
Tests Played:	10		
Test Batting			
Innings:	18	Runs:	327
Highest Score:	40*	Average:	20.43
No. 50s:	0	No. 100s:	0
Test Bowling & Fielding			
Wickets:	0	Runs:	0
Best Bowling:		Average:	0.00
5 WI:	0	10 WM:	0
Catches:	4	Stumpings:	0

The Natal skipper was elevated to the national captaincy in 1935 and lead South Africa in their historic first ever victory at Lord's in 1935. That win was enough to secure a famous series victory and in all Herby Wade captained the side in ten Tests for that one won and five draws.

WADE, Walter Wareham (Billy)

Born:	June 18, 1914
Batting:	Right handed
	Wicket Keeper

Tests

Test Career:	1938-50		
Cap Number:	154		
Tests Played:	11		
Test Batting			
Innings:	19	Runs:	511
Highest Score:	125	Average:	28.38
No. 50s:	3	No. 100s:	1
Test Bowling & Fielding			
Wickets:	0	Runs:	0
Best Bowling:		Average:	0.00
5 WI:	0	10 WM:	0
Catches:	15	Stumpings:	2

The brother of South African skipper Herby, he was a wicket keeper batsman who played in Tests both before and after the Second World War. He scored a single Test century against the English at Port Elizabeth in 1948/49. Billy Wade became an umpire after he hung up his gloves, standing in a Test between South Africa and Australia in 1970.

WAITE, John Henry Bickford

Born:	January 19, 1930
Batting:	Right handed
	Wicket Keeper

Tests

Test Career:	1951-65		
Cap Number:	181		
Tests Played:	50		
Test Batting			
Innings:	86	Runs:	2,405
Highest Score:	134	Average:	30.44
No. 50s:	16	No. 100s:	4
Test Bowling & Fielding			
Wickets:	0	Runs:	0
Best Bowling:		Average:	0.00
5 WI:	0	10 WM:	0
Catches:	124	Stumpings:	17

Tall for a keeper, Waite was the first South African to play 50 Tests and to this day remains one of his country's finest wicket keeper batsmen. He made his debut against England at Trent Bridge in 1951 with the dual responsibility of standing behind the stumps and opening the batting. His innings of 76 in 275 minutes was to become typical of his approach to the game. He was a fighter of the highest order and whilst capable of playing almost any stroke, was most comfortable in defense. He made four Test centuries which included an infamous 134 against the Australians at Durban in 1957/58 that took 510 minutes. The infamy arose from the fact the Jackie McGlew was stonewalling at the other end and together they brought the Test to a grinding halt as they added 231 in well over a days play. As a keeper he was as efficient as he was with the bat, taking the ball to the spinners and pacemen without fanfare or flourish.

WALTER, Kenneth Alexander

Born:	November 5, 1939
Batting:	Right handed
Bowling:	Right arm fast

Tests

Test Career:	1961		
Cap Number:	211		
Tests Played:	2		
Test Batting			
Innings:	3	Runs:	11
Highest Score:	10	Average:	3.66
No. 50s:	0	No. 100s:	0
Test Bowling & Fielding			
Wickets:	6	Runs:	197
Best Bowling:	4/63	Average:	32.83
5 WI:	0	10 WM:	0
Catches:	3	Stumpings:	0

An opening bowler from Transvaal who played a couple of Tests against New Zealand at home in 1961.

WARD, Thomas Alfred

Born:	August 2, 1887
Batting:	Right handed
	Wicket Keeper

Tests

Test Career:	1912-24		
Cap Number:	78		
Tests Played:	23		
Test Batting			
Innings:	42	Runs:	459
Highest Score:	64	Average:	13.90
No. 50s:	2	No. 100s:	0
Test Bowling & Fielding			
Wickets:	0	Runs:	0
Best Bowling:		Average:	0.00
5 WI:	0	10 WM:	0
Catches:	19	Stumpings:	13

If the question is which cricketer had the worst ever Test debut then the answer must surely be Tommy Ward. A fine wicket keeper from Transvaal he was selected for the triangular series against Australia and England 1912. In his first Test at Manchester he scored a golden pair, and if that wasn't bad enough he was dismissed on the third ball of a hat trick on both occasions. To Ward's credit he fought back to play 22 more Tests scoring two half centuries along the way.

WATKINS, John Cecil

Born:	April 10, 1923
Batting:	Right handed
Bowling:	Right arm medium

Tests

Test Career:	1949-57
Cap Number:	174
Tests Played:	15

Test Batting

Innings:	27	Runs:	612
Highest Score:	92	Average:	23.53
No. 50s:	3	No. 100s:	0

Test Bowling & Fielding

Wickets:	29	Runs:	816
Best Bowling:	4/22	Average:	28.13
5 WI:	0	10 WM:	0
Catches:	12	Stumpings:	0

A rangy all-rounder from Natal who was a free scoring batsman and economical medium pace bowler. He was particularly effective on the tour of Australia in 1952/53 scoring 352 runs at 35.20 and taking eight wickets. His scored 76 in the fourth Test at Adelaide and followed it up with a career high 92 at the MCG that went immeasurably to helping South Africa secure a surprise 2-2 series result.

WESLEY, Colin

Born:	September 5, 1937
Batting:	Left handed
Bowling:	Left arm off-break

Tests

Test Career:	1960
Cap Number:	202
Tests Played:	3

Test Batting

Innings:	5	Runs:	49
Highest Score:	35	Average:	9.80
No. 50s:	0	No. 100s:	0

Test Bowling & Fielding

Wickets:	0	Runs:	0
Best Bowling:		Average:	0.00
5 WI:	0	10 WM:	0
Catches:	1	Stumpings:	0

The Natal batsman didn't fare well in his three Tests, averaging only 9.80 and suffering the ignominy of going out for two golden ducks in the one Test at Trent Bridge in 1960.

WESSELS, Kepler Christoffel

Born:	September 14, 1957
Batting:	Left handed
Bowling:	Left arm off-break

Tests

Test Career:	1982-94
Cap Number:	246
Tests Played:	40

Test Batting

Innings:	71	Runs:	2,788
Highest Score:	179	Average:	41.00
No. 50s:	15	No. 100s:	6

Test Bowling & Fielding

Wickets:	0	Runs:	42
Best Bowling:		Average:	0.00
5 WI:	0	10 WM:	0
Catches:	30	Stumpings:	0

One Day Internationals

ODI Career:	1983-94
ODIs Played:	109

ODI Batting

Innings:	105	Runs:	3,367
Highest Score:	107	Average:	34.55
No. 50s:	26	No. 100s:	1

ODI Bowling & Fielding

Wickets:	18	Runs:	666
Best Bowling:	2/16	Average:	37.00
5 WM:	0	Catches:	49
Stumpings:	0		

The expression 'have bat will travel' may well have been coined for Kepler Wessels. Frustrated at the lack of opportunity at Test level brought about by an international ban that had been placed on his native South Africa, he first went to England where he played county cricket for Sussex and then on to Australia. The talented left handed opener was introduced to the Australian public during the second season of World Series Cricket in 1978/79. He then fulfilled the requirements to play for Australia whilst playing for Queensland in the Sheffield Shield competition. He celebrated his selection for his adopted country by scoring 162 on debut against England at Brisbane in the 1982/83 Ashes series. His style was hardly textbook, with a stance that had his bat facing point, but he was always butal on any loose delivery, be they short or overpitched. Kepler returned home to South Africa when they were re-admitted to international cricket and was their first captain after the hiatus.

WESTCOTT, Richard John

Born:	September 19, 1927
Batting:	Right handed
Bowling:	Right arm medium

Tests

Test Career:	1954-58
Cap Number:	191
Tests Played:	5

Test Batting

Innings:	9	Runs:	166
Highest Score:	62	Average:	18.44
No. 50s:	1	No. 100s:	0

Test Bowling & Fielding

Wickets:	0	Runs:	22
Best Bowling:		Average:	0.00
5 WI:	0	10 WM:	0
Catches:	0	Stumpings:	0

The fact Westcott played any Test cricket at all was a great achievement given that he had been seriously injured in a car accident early in his career. The opening batsman played a handful of Tests against New Zealand in 1954 but apart from 62 on debut showed little. He was given another chance against the touring Australians in 1957/58 but could only manage 18 runs in three innings.

WHITE, Gordon Charles

Born:	February 5, 1882
Batting:	Right handed
Bowling:	Right arm leg-break

Tests

Test Career:	1906-12
Cap Number:	63
Tests Played:	17

Test Batting			
Innings:	31	Runs:	872
Highest Score:	147	Average:	30.06
No. 50s:	4	No. 100s:	2

Test Bowling & Fielding			
Wickets:	9	Runs:	301
Best Bowling:	4/47	Average:	33.44
5 WI:	0	10 WM:	0
Catches:	10	Stumpings:	0

An accomplished batsman and leg spin bower from Transvaal, he was his country's standout batsman in their first successful Test series against England in 1905/06, scoring 437 runs at just under 55. Hopes were high when he toured England in 1907, but he could mange only 15 runs in three Tests. He died of wounds suffered on the Western Front in France in 1918.

WILLIAMS, Henry

Born:	June 11, 1967
Batting:	Right handed
Bowling:	Right arm medium-fast

One Day Internationals

ODI Career:	1999-00
ODIs Played:	7

ODI Batting			
Innings:	2	Runs:	8
Highest Score:	7	Average:	8.00
No. 50s:	0	No. 100s:	0

ODI Bowling & Fielding			
Wickets:	9	Runs:	228
Best Bowling:	3/38	Average:	25.33
5 WM:	0	Catches:	2
Stumpings:	0		

A right arm medium pacer who made his ODI debut against West Indies, at Buffalo Park in 1999, Henry Williams played just the seven ODI's but is unfortunately remembered for his involvement in the highly publicised Hansie Cronje match-fixing scandal which resulted in he and Herschelle Gibbs receiving six month bans for under-performing.

WILLOUGHBY, Charl Myles

Born:	December 3, 1974
Batting:	Left handed
Bowling:	Left arm medium-fast

Tests

Test Career:	2003
Cap Number:	290
Tests Played:	2

Test Batting			
Innings:	0	Runs:	0
Highest Score:	0	Average:	0.00
No. 50s:	0	No. 100s:	0

Test Bowling & Fielding			
Wickets:	1	Runs:	125
Best Bowling:	1/47	Average:	125.00
5 WI:	0	10 WM:	0
Catches:	0	Stumpings:	0

One Day Internationals

ODI Career:	2000-03
ODIs Played:	3

ODI Batting			
Innings:	2	Runs:	0
Highest Score:	0	Average:	0.00
No. 50s:	0	No. 100s:	0

ODI Bowling & Fielding			
Wickets:	2	Runs:	148
Best Bowling:	2/39	Average:	74.00
5 WM:	0	Catches:	0
Stumpings:	0		

He is a left arm swing bowler who has played extensively in England. Willoughby has played in two Tests and three ODI's for just the three wickets in total.

WILLOUGHBY, Joseph Thomas

Born:	November 7, 1874
Batting:	Right handed
Bowling:	Right arm fast

Tests

Test Career:	1896
Cap Number:	30
Tests Played:	2

Test Batting			
Innings:	4	Runs:	8
Highest Score:	5	Average:	2.00
No. 50s:	0	No. 100s:	0

Test Bowling & Fielding			
Wickets:	6	Runs:	159
Best Bowling:	2/37	Average:	26.50
5 WI:	0	10 WM:	0
Catches:	0	Stumpings:	0

A quick bowler whose only first class matches were a pair of Tests against England in 1896.

WIMBLE, Clarence Skelton

Born:	April 22, 1861
Batting:	Right handed

Tests

Test Career:	1892
Cap Number:	23
Tests Played:	1

Test Batting			
Innings:	2	Runs:	0
Highest Score:	0	Average:	0.00
No. 50s:	0	No. 100s:	0

Test Bowling & Fielding			
Wickets:	0	Runs:	0
Best Bowling:		Average:	0.00
5 WI:	0	10 WM:	0
Catches:	0	Stumpings:	0

A batsman who fared poorly in his only Test, making a pair against England at Cape Town in 1892.

WINSLOW, Paul Lyndhurst

Born:	May 21, 1929
Batting:	Right handed
Bowling:	Right arm leg-break

Tests

Test Career:	1950-55
Cap Number:	177
Tests Played:	5

Test Batting

Innings:	9	**Runs:**	186
Highest Score:	108	**Average:**	20.66
No. 50s:	0	**No. 100s:**	1

Test Bowling & Fielding

Wickets:	0	**Runs:**	0
Best Bowling:		**Average:**	0.00
5 WI:	0	**10 WM:**	0
Catches:	1	**Stumpings:**	0

A top order batsman who originally played with Sussex in the hope of becoming eligible to play in the English Test side. When that proved unsuccessful he returned to South Africa and gained selection in the team that faced Australia at home in 1950. He was a hard hitter who generally failed in Tests, apart from one famous innings at Old Trafford in 1955 when he rescued the side with a well compiled century. His only Test ton was brought up with a straight six that sailed into the grandstand.

WYNNE, Owen Edgar

Born: June 1, 1919
Batting: Right handed

Tests

Test Career: 1948-50
Cap Number: 168
Tests Played: 6

Test Batting

Innings:	12	**Runs:**	219
Highest Score:	50	**Average:**	18.25
No. 50s:	1	**No. 100s:**	0

Test Bowling & Fielding

Wickets:	0	**Runs:**	0
Best Bowling:		**Average:**	0.00
5 WI:	0	**10 WM:**	0
Catches:	3	**Stumpings:**	0

A hard to remove opening batsman who was selected in the Test side on the strength of a double century in the Currie Cup. He battled at Test level, averaging only 18, with just the one half century.

YACHAD, Mandy

Born: November 17, 1960
Batting: Right handed
Bowling: Right arm leg-break

One Day Internationals

ODI Career: 1991
ODIs Played: 1

ODI Batting

Innings:	1	**Runs:**	31
Highest Score:	31	**Average:**	31.00
No. 50s:	0	**No. 100s:**	0

ODI Bowling & Fielding

Wickets:	0	**Runs:**	0
Best Bowling:		**Average:**	0.00
5 WM:	0	**Catches:**	1
Stumpings:	0		

Mandy Yachad was a right hand opener who, at age 31, made 31 in his only ODI against India at Gwalior, in 1991.

ZONDEKI, Monde

Born: July 25, 1982
Batting: Right handed
Bowling: Right arm fast

Tests

Test Career: 2003-
Cap Number: 292
Tests Played: 5

Test Batting

Innings:	4	**Runs:**	82
Highest Score:	59	**Average:**	20.50
No. 50s:	1	**No. 100s:**	0

Test Bowling & Fielding

Wickets:	16	**Runs:**	438
Best Bowling:	6/39	**Average:**	27.37
5 WI:	1	**10 WM:**	0
Catches:	1	**Stumpings:**	0

One Day Internationals

ODI Career: 2002-
ODIs Played: 11

ODI Batting

Innings:	3	**Runs:**	4
Highest Score:	3*	**Average:**	4.00
No. 50s:	0	**No. 100s:**	0

ODI Bowling & Fielding

Wickets:	8	**Runs:**	414
Best Bowling:	2/46	**Average:**	51.75
5 WM:	0	**Catches:**	3
Stumpings:	0		

A young speedster from Cape Cobras who has shown enough in his early Test cricket to suggest that he may yet open the bowling with Makhaya Ntini. Zondeki made his Test debut in England at the age of 21, playing just the one Test at Headingly. Whilst there were no wickets, the number nine batsman did confound the experts by scoring 59 as part of a 150 run partnership with Gary Kirsten. His next Test was over 12 months later against Zimbabwe, and the youngster impressed again with nine wickets and a 'Man of the Match' award. Since then there have been three Tests on a tour of the Caribbean and a smattering of one day cricket, and whilst he is yet to cement a place in the national side, at 24 he still has time on his side.

ZULCH, Johan Wilhelm (Billy)

Born: February 2, 1886
Batting: Right handed
Bowling: Right arm medium

Tests

Test Career: 1910-21
Cap Number: 68
Tests Played: 16

Test Batting

Innings:	32	**Runs:**	985
Highest Score:	150	**Average:**	32.83
No. 50s:	4	**No. 100s:**	2

Test Bowling & Fielding

Wickets:	0	**Runs:**	28
Best Bowling:		**Average:**	0.00
5 WI:	0	**10 WM:**	0
Catches:	4	**Stumpings:**	0

A fine top order batsman and superb fieldsman, he enjoyed an excellent tour of Australia in 1910/11 where he scored two Test centuries. His 150 at the SCG may have been his highest Test score but his most important was his 105 at the Adelaide Oval that helped his side to a shock victory over the powerful Aussies.

Sri Lanka

AHANGAMA, Franklyn Saliya
Born: September 14, 1959
Batting: Left handed
Bowling: Right arm medium

Tests
Test Career: 1985
Cap Number: 28
Tests Played: 3

Test Batting
Innings:	3	Runs:	11
Highest Score:	11	Average:	5.50
No. 50s:	0	No. 100s:	0

Test Bowling & Fielding
Wickets:	18	Runs:	348
Best Bowling:	5/52	Average:	19.33
5 WI:	1	10 WM:	0
Catches:	1	Stumpings:	0

One Day Internationals
ODI Career: 1985
ODIs Played: 1

ODI Batting
Innings:	0	Runs:	0
Highest Score:	0	Average:	0.00
No. 50s:	0	No. 100s:	0

ODI Bowling & Fielding
Wickets:	0	Runs:	23
Best Bowling:	0/23	Average:	0.00
5 WM:	0	Catches:	0
Stumpings:	0		

A right arm medium-pacer. His respectable average of 19.33 with the ball suggests that he would have been considered for a few more than the three Tests alongside his name if not for constant injury.

AMALEAN, Kaushik Naginda
Born: April 7, 1965
Batting: Right handed
Bowling: Right arm medium-fast

Tests
Test Career: 1986-88
Cap Number: 37
Tests Played: 2

Test Batting
Innings:	3	Runs:	9
Highest Score:	7*	Average:	9.00
No. 50s:	0	No. 100s:	0

Test Bowling & Fielding
Wickets:	7	Runs:	156
Best Bowling:	4/97	Average:	22.28
5 WI:	0	10 WM:	0
Catches:	1	Stumpings:	0

One Day Internationals
ODI Career: 1986-88
ODIs Played: 8

ODI Batting
Innings:	3	Runs:	15
Highest Score:	9	Average:	7.50
No. 50s:	0	No. 100s:	0

ODI Bowling & Fielding
Wickets:	9	Runs:	207
Best Bowling:	4/46	Average:	23.00
5 WM:	0	Catches:	0
Stumpings:	0		

A fast bowler from Colombo who made his debut against Pakistan at Colombo in 1986. Took his career best of 4/97 in his second and final Test against Australia at the WACA ground in Perth, in 1987/88.

AMERASINGHE, Jayantha Gamini
Born: February 2, 1954
Batting: Right handed
Bowling: Left arm slow

Tests
Test Career: 1984
Cap Number: 25
Tests Played: 2

Test Batting
Innings:	4	Runs:	54
Highest Score:	34	Average:	18.00
No. 50s:	0	No. 100s:	0

Test Bowling & Fielding
Wickets:	3	Runs:	150
Best Bowling:	2/73	Average:	50.00
5 WI:	0	10 WM:	0
Catches:	3	Stumpings:	0

A left arm off spinner who top scored with 34 on debut, coming in at number ten against New Zealand at Kandy in 1984. He played just the one more Test which was also against New Zealand in that same series.

ANURASIRI, Sangarange (Don)
Born: February 25, 1966
Batting: Right handed
Bowling: Left arm off-break

Tests
Test Career: 1986-98
Cap Number: 34
Tests Played: 18

Test Batting
Innings:	22	Runs:	91
Highest Score:	24	Average:	5.35
No. 50s:	0	No. 100s:	0

Test Bowling & Fielding
Wickets:	41	Runs:	1,548
Best Bowling:	4/71	Average:	37.35
5 WI:	0	10 WM:	0
Catches:	4	Stumpings:	0

One Day Internationals

ODI Career:	1986-94		
ODIs Played:	45		

ODI Batting

Innings:	18	Runs:	62
Highest Score:	11	Average:	10.33
No. 50s:	0	No. 100s:	0

ODI Bowling & Fielding

Wickets:	32	Runs:	1,464
Best Bowling:	3/40	Average:	45.75
5 WM:	0	Catches:	10
Stumpings:	0		

A tireless left-arm off spinner, Don Anurasiri had a stop-start career after making his Test debut against Pakistan at Colombo in 1986. It seemed that his Test career was over after being dropped in 1994 but surprisingly was called back in the final Test against Zimbabwe in 1997/98.

ARNOLD, Russel Premakumaran

Born:	October 25, 1973
Batting:	Left handed
Bowling:	Right arm off-break

Tests

Test Career:	1997-04		
Cap Number:	68		
Tests Played:	44		

Test Batting

Innings:	69	Runs:	1,821
Highest Score:	123	Average:	28.01
No. 50s:	10	No. 100s:	3

Test Bowling & Fielding

Wickets:	11	Runs:	598
Best Bowling:	3/76	Average:	54.36
5 WI:	0	10 WM:	0
Catches:	0	Stumpings:	0

One Day Internationals

ODI Career:	1997-06		
ODIs Played:	160		

ODI Batting

Innings:	139	Runs:	3,676
Highest Score:	103	Average:	36.03
No. 50s:	26	No. 100s:	1

ODI Bowling & Fielding

Wickets:	37	Runs:	1,683
Best Bowling:	3/47	Average:	45.48
5 WM:	0	Catches:	45
Stumpings:	0		

A left-handed opener who made his Test debut against Pakistan at Colombo in 1997. Ordinary form early in his career saw Arnold moved further down the batting order when the selectors decided to run with the Jayasuria/Atapattu combination. But Arnold proved that his best batting was done when opening and eventually was returned to the the top of the order. He scored three Test centuries - all while opening. His maiden Test century, 123 - and highest score - was made against Pakistan at Lahore in 1999. Later that year he made 104 while carrying his bat after opening the innings with Atapattu, who scored a duck. His third century, 109 against England at Old Trafford was made when he was reunited with his original opening partner Sanath Jayasuria. From 2002 onwards Arnold was once again in and out of the Test eleven but continued to be a permanent fixture in the One Day side where he bats in the middle order, averages just over 36 and bowls some handy off-spin.

ATAPATTU, Marvan Samson

Born:	November 22, 1970
Batting:	Right handed
Bowling:	Right arm leg-break

Tests

Test Career:	1990-05		
Cap Number:	46		
Tests Played:	88		

Test Batting

Innings:	152	Runs:	5,330
Highest Score:	249	Average:	38.90
No. 50s:	15	No. 100s:	16

Test Bowling & Fielding

Wickets:	1	Runs:	24
Best Bowling:	1/9	Average:	24.00
5 WI:	0	10 WM:	0
Catches:	0	Stumpings:	57

One Day Internationals

ODI Career:	1990-06		
ODIs Played:	253		

ODI Batting

Innings:	246	Runs:	8,233
Highest Score:	132*	Average:	37.76
No. 50s:	59	No. 100s:	11

ODI Bowling & Fielding

Wickets:	0	Runs:	41
Best Bowling:		Average:	0.00
5 WM:	0	Catches:	70
Stumpings:	0		

A strong willed opening batsman, Marvan Atapattu was the perfect foil for his fellow opening partner Sanath Jayasuriya. For many years the pair provided the perfect balance of compusure and aggression. Even thought it took almost seven years for Atapattu to register his maiden Test century, his conversion of 50's into hundreds was as good as anyone going around having made 16 tons from 31 scores over 50. A player who once settled was destined to hang around having scored six double centuries, with a highest score of 249 against Zimbabwe, at Bulawayo in 2004. However, it wasn't all smooth sailing for the tenacious opener as he was embroiled in a match-fixing investigation in 2003 which muddied his reputation even though he was later cleared of anything untoward and subsequently appointed capatin just over 12 months later replacing the out of favour Tillakaratne. A fine limited overs player, having represented his country in over 250 ODI's, a back injury forced Atapattu to miss the 2006 tour of England.

BANDARA, Charitha Malinga

Born: December 31, 1979
Batting: Right handed
Bowling: Right arm slow

Tests
Test Career: 1998-06
Cap Number: 71
Tests Played: 8

Test Batting
Innings:	11	Runs:	124
Highest Score:	43	Average:	15.50
No. 50s:	0	No. 100s:	0

Test Bowling & Fielding
Wickets:	16	Runs:	633
Best Bowling:	3/84	Average:	39.56
5 WI:	0	10 WM:	0
Catches:	4	Stumpings:	0

One Day Internationals
ODI Career: 2006
ODIs Played: 17

ODI Batting
Innings:	7	Runs:	72
Highest Score:	28*	Average:	14.40
No. 50s:	0	No. 100s:	0

ODI Bowling & Fielding
Wickets:	20	Runs:	613
Best Bowling:	4/31	Average:	30.15
5 WM:	0	Catches:	0
Stumpings:	0		

A right arm leg spinner who continues to press for Test selection even though he has played just eight Tests in nine years. A useful lower order batsman, Bandara finally made his ODI debut when Sri Lanka took on New Zealand at Wellington, in early 2006.

BANDARATILLEKE, Niroshan

Born: May 16, 1975
Batting: Right handed
Bowling: Left arm off-break
Wicket Keeper

Tests
Test Career: 1998-01
Cap Number: 72
Tests Played: 7

Test Batting
Innings:	9	Runs:	93
Highest Score:	25	Average:	11.62
No. 50s:	0	No. 100s:	0

Test Bowling & Fielding
Wickets:	23	Runs:	698
Best Bowling:	5/36	Average:	30.34
5 WI:	1	10 WM:	0
Catches:	0	Stumpings:	0

One Day Internationals
ODI Career: 1998
ODIs Played: 3

ODI Batting
Innings:	1	Runs:	0
Highest Score:	0	Average:	0.00
No. 50s:	0	No. 100s:	0

ODI Bowling & Fielding
Wickets:	2	Runs:	111
Best Bowling:	2/34	Average:	55.50
5 WM:	0	Catches:	0
Stumpings:	0		

A left arm slow off-break bowler who made his debut against New Zealand at Colombo in 1998. In his second Test, against New Zealand at Galle, he captured 5/36 in the second innings giving him nine wickets for the match. His form tapered off a little thereafter and never got another opportunity after a wicket-less yield in his seventh Test against West Indies at Colombo, but in fairness, he was rarely utilised during what would be his final Test match.

BOTEJU, Hemantha Devapriya

Born: November 3, 1977
Batting: Right handed
Bowling: Right arm medium

One Day Internationals
ODI Career: 1999
ODIs Played: 2

ODI Batting
Innings:	2	Runs:	3
Highest Score:	2	Average:	3.00
No. 50s:	0	No. 100s:	0

ODI Bowling & Fielding
Wickets:	0	Runs:	113
Best Bowling:		Average:	0.00
5 WM:	0	Catches:	1
Stumpings:	0		

A promising all rounder who made his ODI debut against India at Nagpur but was unable to fulfill his potential.

CHANDANA, Umagiliya Durage (Upul)

Born: May 7, 1972
Batting: Right handed
Bowling: Right arm slow

Tests
Test Career: 1999-05
Cap Number: 77
Tests Played: 16

Test Batting
Innings:	24	Runs:	616
Highest Score:	92	Average:	26.78
No. 50s:	2	No. 100s:	0

Test Bowling & Fielding
Wickets:	37	Runs:	1,535
Best Bowling:	6/179	Average:	41.48
5 WI:	3	10 WM:	1
Catches:	7	Stumpings:	0

One Day Internationals
ODI Career: 1994-05
ODIs Played: 146

ODI Batting
Innings:	110	Runs:	1,626
Highest Score:	89	Average:	17.48
No. 50s:	5	No. 100s:	0

ODI Bowling & Fielding
Wickets:	151	Runs:	4,790
Best Bowling:	5/61	Average:	31.72
5 WM:	1	Catches:	77
Stumpings:	0		

Unlike most leg spinners, Upul Chandana is rated a better option at One Day Level than at Tests but this is mainly due to his hard hitting ability as a middle order batsman. Having played almost 150 ODI's in comparison to his 16 Tests, Chandana's chances of further Test selection look slim.

DASSANAYAKE, Pubudu Bathiya
Born: July 11, 1970
Batting: Right handed
Wicket Keeper

Tests
Test Career:	1993-94		
Cap Number:	57		
Tests Played:	11		

Test Batting
Innings:	17	Runs:	196
Highest Score:	36	Average:	13.06
No. 50s:	0	No. 100s:	0

Test Bowling & Fielding
Wickets:	0	Runs:	0
Best Bowling:		Average:	0.00
5 WI:	0	10 WM:	0
Catches:	19	Stumpings:	5

One Day Internationals
ODI Career:	1993-94		
ODIs Played:	16		

ODI Batting
Innings:	10	Runs:	85
Highest Score:	20*	Average:	10.62
No. 50s:	0	No. 100s:	0

ODI Bowling & Fielding
Wickets:	0	Runs:	0
Best Bowling:		Average:	0.00
5 WM:	0	Catches:	9
Stumpings:	2		

A wicket-keeper from Kandy who broke into the Test side in 1993 when he was selected in the First Test against South Africa at Moratuwa. Like many keepers before him, it was his batting that came under heavier scrutiny than his ability with the gloves. After only 11 Tests, he was succeeded by Chamara Dunusinghe.

DE ALWIS, Ronald Guy
Born: February 15, 1959
Batting: Right handed
Wicket Keeper

Tests
Test Career:	1983-88		
Cap Number:	16		
Tests Played:	11		

Test Batting
Innings:	19	Runs:	152
Highest Score:	28	Average:	8.00
No. 50s:	0	No. 100s:	0

Test Bowling & Fielding
Wickets:	0	Runs:	0
Best Bowling:		Average:	0.00
5 WI:	0	10 WM:	0
Catches:	21	Stumpings:	2

One Day Internationals
ODI Career:	1983-88		
ODIs Played:	31		

ODI Batting
Innings:	27	Runs:	401
Highest Score:	59*	Average:	21.10
No. 50s:	2	No. 100s:	0

ODI Bowling & Fielding
Wickets:	0	Runs:	0
Best Bowling:		Average:	0.00
5 WM:	0	Catches:	27
Stumpings:	3		

A tallish keeper who made his Test debut against New Zealand in Christchurch in 1983 but couldn't consolidate a regular place as he was continually playing second fiddle to Amal Silva. A handy ODI player having scored two 50's.

DE MEL, Ashantha Lakdasa Francis
Born: May 9, 1959
Batting: Right handed
Bowling: Right arm medium-fast

Tests
Test Career:	1982-86		
Cap Number:	1		
Tests Played:	17		

Test Batting
Innings:	28	Runs:	326
Highest Score:	34	Average:	14.17
No. 50s:	0	No. 100s:	0

Test Bowling & Fielding
Wickets:	59	Runs:	2,180
Best Bowling:	6/109	Average:	36.94
5 WI:	3	10 WM:	0
Catches:	9	Stumpings:	0

One Day Internationals
ODI Career:	1982-87		
ODIs Played:	57		

ODI Batting
Innings:	41	Runs:	466
Highest Score:	36	Average:	14.56
No. 50s:	0	No. 100s:	0

ODI Bowling & Fielding
Wickets:	59	Runs:	2,237
Best Bowling:	5/32	Average:	37.91
5 WM:	2	Catches:	13
Stumpings:	0		

Credited with Sri Lanka's 'number one' Test Cap, Ashantha de Mel was a member of Sri Lanka's inaugural Test side of 1982 which played against England. He took five wickets for the match including 4/70 in the first innings. His 5/68 against India in 1982/83 gave him the honour as the first Sri Lankan to take a five wickets in an innings. A handy One Day player, de Mel was a member of the 1987 World Cup squad but sustained a crippling knee injury which saw his career come to a premature end.

DE SARAM, Indika
Born: September 2, 1973
Batting: Right handed
Bowling: Right arm off-break
Wicket Keeper

Tests
Test Career:	1999-00
Cap Number:	79
Tests Played:	4

Test Batting

Innings:	5	Runs:	117
Highest Score:	39	Average:	23.39
No. 50s:	0	No. 100s:	0

Test Bowling & Fielding

Wickets:	0	Runs:	0
Best Bowling:		Average:	0.00
5 WI:	0	10 WM:	0
Catches:	1	Stumpings:	0

One Day Internationals

ODI Career:	1999-01
ODIs Played:	15

ODI Batting

Innings:	13	Runs:	183
Highest Score:	38	Average:	16.63
No. 50s:	0	No. 100s:	0

ODI Bowling & Fielding

Wickets:	0	Runs:	0
Best Bowling:		Average:	0.00
5 WM:	0	Catches:	9
Stumpings:	0		

A clever keeper from Matara who was selected for the tour of Zimbabwe in 1999/2000. De Saram debuted in the First Test of that series where he was selected as a lower order batsman while Kaluwitharana kept wickets. Nevertheless he made a respectable 39 coming in at number seven but his chances were few and far between thereafter.

DE SILVA, Ajit

Born:	December 12, 1952
Batting:	Left handed
Bowling:	Left arm slow

Tests

Test Career:	1982
Cap Number:	3
Tests Played:	4

Test Batting

Innings:	7	Runs:	41
Highest Score:	14	Average:	8.19
No. 50s:	0	No. 100s:	0

Test Bowling & Fielding

Wickets:	7	Runs:	385
Best Bowling:	2/38	Average:	55.00
5 WI:	0	10 WM:	0
Catches:	0	Stumpings:	0

One Day Internationals

ODI Career:	1975-82
ODIs Played:	6

ODI Batting

Innings:	4	Runs:	9
Highest Score:	6*	Average:	4.50
No. 50s:	0	No. 100s:	0

ODI Bowling & Fielding

Wickets:	9	Runs:	262
Best Bowling:	3/41	Average:	29.11
5 WM:	0	Catches:	2
Stumpings:	0		

A left arm leggie who made his International debut in the 1975 World Cup against Pakistan at Trent Bridge and later a member of Sri Lanka's inaugural Test team in 1981 at Colombo. Played just a handful of Tests and ODI's.

DE SILVA, Ashley Matthew

Born:	December 3, 1963
Batting:	Right handed
	Wicket Keeper

Tests

Test Career:	1993
Cap Number:	55
Tests Played:	3

Test Batting

Innings:	3	Runs:	10
Highest Score:	9	Average:	3.33
No. 50s:	0	No. 100s:	0

Test Bowling & Fielding

Wickets:	0	Runs:	0
Best Bowling:		Average:	0.00
5 WI:	0	10 WM:	0
Catches:	4	Stumpings:	1

One Day Internationals

ODI Career:	1986-93
ODIs Played:	4

ODI Batting

Innings:	2	Runs:	12
Highest Score:	8	Average:	6.00
No. 50s:	0	No. 100s:	0

ODI Bowling & Fielding

Wickets:	0	Runs:	0
Best Bowling:		Average:	0.00
5 WM:	0	Catches:	4
Stumpings:	2		

A wicket-keeper from Colombo who played his first ODI some seven years prior to making his Test debut in 1993. Unfortunately de Silva didn't do enough with the bat to convince the Sri Lankan selectors that he could be considered a long term proposition.

DE SILVA, Asoka Ranjit

Born:	March 28, 1956
Batting:	Left handed
Bowling:	Left arm slow

Tests

Test Career:	1985-91
Cap Number:	29
Tests Played:	10

Test Batting

Innings:	16	Runs:	185
Highest Score:	50	Average:	15.41
No. 50s:	1	No. 100s:	0

Test Bowling & Fielding

Wickets:	8	Runs:	1,032
Best Bowling:	2/67	Average:	129.00
5 WI:	0	10 WM:	0
Catches:	4	Stumpings:	0

One Day Internationals

ODI Career:	1986-92
ODIs Played:	28

ODI Batting

Innings:	20	Runs:	138
Highest Score:	19*	Average:	9.85
No. 50s:	0	No. 100s:	0

ODI Bowling & Fielding

Wickets:	17	Runs:	967
Best Bowling:	3/38	Average:	56.88
5 WM:	0	Catches:	6
Stumpings:	0		

A left arm leggie from Kalutara who played ten Tests between 195 to 1991. He has earned a fine reputation as an International Umpire.

DE SILVA, Dandeniyage Somachandra

Born: June 11, 1942
Batting: Right handed
Bowling: Right arm slow

Tests
Test Career: 1982-4
Cap Number: 2
Tests Played: 12

Test Batting
Innings:	22	Runs:	406
Highest Score:	61	Average:	21.36
No. 50s:	2	No. 100s:	0

Test Bowling & Fielding
Wickets:	37	Runs:	1,347
Best Bowling:	5/59	Average:	36.40
5 WI:	1	10 WM:	0
Catches:	5	Stumpings:	0

One Day Internationals
ODI Career: 1975-85
ODIs Played: 41

ODI Batting
Innings:	29	Runs:	371
Highest Score:	37*	Average:	19.52
No. 50s:	0	No. 100s:	0

ODI Bowling & Fielding
Wickets:	32	Runs:	1,557
Best Bowling:	3/29	Average:	48.65
5 WM:	0	Catches:	5
Stumpings:	0		

A gifted legspinner, Somachandra De Silva represented his country in World Cup competition and was a member of Sri Lanka's inaugural Test team against England even though he was pushing forty years of age at the time. During the Test series against New Zealand in 1982/83, he was appointed caretaker captain while Duleep Mendis recovered from injury. Hailed as one of his countries finest leg spinners, De Silva later went on to coach the national side.

DE SILVA, Deva Lokesh Stanley

Born: November 17, 1956
Batting: Right handed
Bowling: Right arm medium-fast

One Day Internationals
ODI Career: 1979
ODIs Played: 2

ODI Batting
Innings:	1	Runs:	10
Highest Score:	10	Average:	10.00
No. 50s:	0	No. 100s:	0

ODI Bowling & Fielding
Wickets:	2	Runs:	54
Best Bowling:	2/36	Average:	27.00
5 WM:	0	Catches:	1
Stumpings:	0		

A right arm pace bowler from Ambalangodawho opened the bowling for Sri Lanka during the 1979 World Cup. Sadly, Stanley de Silva died a year later aged 23.

DE SILVA, Granville Nissanka

Born: March 12, 1955
Batting: Right handed
Bowling: Right arm medium-fast

One Day Internationals
ODI Career: 1983-85
ODIs Played: 4

ODI Batting
Innings:	2	Runs:	9
Highest Score:	7	Average:	9.00
No. 50s:	0	No. 100s:	0

ODI Bowling & Fielding
Wickets:	0	Runs:	169
Best Bowling:		Average:	0.00
5 WM:	0	Catches:	0
Stumpings:	0		

A right arm fast bowler who made his International debut against Australia at Colombo in 1983. He was unlucky not to capture a wicket in his four ODI appearances.

DE SILVA, Pinnaduwage (Aravinda)

Born: October 17, 1965
Batting: Right handed
Bowling: Right arm off-break

Tests
Test Career: 1984-02
Cap Number: 27
Tests Played: 93

Test Batting
Innings:	159	Runs:	6,361
Highest Score:	267	Average:	42.97
No. 50s:	22	No. 100s:	20

Test Bowling & Fielding
Wickets:	29	Runs:	1,208
Best Bowling:	3/30	Average:	41.65
5 WI:	0	10 WM:	0
Catches:	43	Stumpings:	0

One Day Internationals
ODI Career: 1984-03
ODIs Played: 308

ODI Batting
Innings:	296	Runs:	9,284
Highest Score:	145	Average:	34.90
No. 50s:	64	No. 100s:	11

ODI Bowling & Fielding
Wickets:	106	Runs:	4,177
Best Bowling:	4/30	Average:	39.40
5 WM:	0	Catches:	95
Stumpings:	0		

A diminutive super-star of Sri Lankan cricket, de Silva was blessed with natural talent and had all the shots in the book. He had an incredible ability to convert his starts into high scores as every second fifty became a hundred. He loved to attack the bowling, regardless of form, and along with Sanath Jayasuriya, is arguably Sri Lanka's most entertaining batsman in their short history to date. With 22 Test hundreds alongside his name, his highest score of 267, against New Zealand at Wellington in 1991, surprisingly did not earn him the Man of the Match award. The prize went to Martin Crowe for his 299. Just as good at the shorter version of the game, de Silva represented his country at ODI level on over 300 occassions. His most memorable and most valuable knock was his unbeaten 107, against Australia in the 1996 World Cup final - which was without doubt Sri Lanka's greatest moment in International Cricket.

DE SILVA, S K Lanka

Born: July 29, 1975
Batting: Right handed
Bowling: Right arm off-break
 Wicket Keeper

Tests
Test Career: 1997
Cap Number: 70
Tests Played: 3

Test Batting
Innings:	4	Runs:	36
Highest Score:	20*	Average:	18.00
No. 50s:	0	No. 100s:	0

Test Bowling & Fielding
Wickets:	0	Runs:	0
Best Bowling:		Average:	0.00
5 WI:	0	10 WM:	0
Catches:	1	Stumpings:	0

One Day Internationals
ODI Career: 1997
ODIs Played: 11

ODI Batting
Innings:	6	Runs:	161
Highest Score:	57	Average:	53.66
No. 50s:	2	No. 100s:	0

ODI Bowling & Fielding
Wickets:	0	Runs:	0
Best Bowling:		Average:	0.00
5 WM:	0	Catches:	9
Stumpings:	6		

Wicket-keeper Lanka De Silva made his Test debut against India at Chandigarh when he replaced ageing favourite Kaluwitharana. But before he could even get warm in his seat, the selectors had a change of heart and recalled 'Kalu'. An agile keeper and competant with the bat, De Silva enjoyed success at One Day level where he scored two fifties and averaged a healthy 53.66.

DE SILVA, Sajeewa Chanaka

Born: January 11, 1971
Batting: Left handed
Bowling: Left arm medium-fast

Tests
Test Career: 1997-99
Cap Number: 67
Tests Played: 8

Test Batting
Innings:	12	Runs:	65
Highest Score:	27	Average:	9.28
No. 50s:	0	No. 100s:	0

Test Bowling & Fielding
Wickets:	16	Runs:	889
Best Bowling:	5/85	Average:	55.56
5 WI:	1	10 WM:	0
Catches:	5	Stumpings:	0

One Day Internationals
ODI Career: 1996-00
ODIs Played: 38

ODI Batting
Innings:	19	Runs:	39
Highest Score:	13*	Average:	6.50
No. 50s:	0	No. 100s:	0

ODI Bowling & Fielding
Wickets:	52	Runs:	1,323
Best Bowling:	3/18	Average:	25.44
5 WM:	0	Catches:	12
Stumpings:	0		

A swing bowler from Kalutara who made his Test debut against New Zealand at Hamilton in 1997. While he was a tireless contributor in Tests, he was quite expensive and was clearly more suited to the one day version of the game where his bowling average was more than halved.

DE SILVA, Sujeewa

Born: October 7, 1979
Batting: Right handed
Bowling: Left arm medium-fast

Tests
Test Career: 2002
Cap Number: 89
Tests Played: 2

Test Batting
Innings:	2	Runs:	10
Highest Score:	5*	Average:	10.00
No. 50s:	0	No. 100s:	0

Test Bowling & Fielding
Wickets:	7	Runs:	146
Best Bowling:	4/35	Average:	20.85
5 WI:	0	10 WM:	0
Catches:	0	Stumpings:	0

A left arm fast medium pacer who played his only two career Tests against Bangladesh in 2002. Took his best figures of 4/35 in the second innings of his second, and last Test.

DHARMASENA, Kumar

Born: April 24, 1971
Batting: Right handed
Bowling: Right arm off-break

Tests
Test Career: 1993-04
Cap Number: 59
Tests Played: 31

Test Batting
Innings:	51	Runs:	868
Highest Score:	62*	Average:	19.72
No. 50s:	3	No. 100s:	0

Test Bowling & Fielding
Wickets:	69	Runs:	2,920
Best Bowling:	6/72	Average:	42.31
5 WI:	3	10 WM:	0
Catches:	14	Stumpings:	0

One Day Internationals
ODI Career: 1994-04
ODIs Played: 141

ODI Batting
Innings:	87	Runs:	1,222
Highest Score:	69*	Average:	22.62
No. 50s:	4	No. 100s:	0

ODI Bowling & Fielding

Wickets:	138	Runs:	4,998
Best Bowling:	4/37	Average:	36.21
5 WM:	0	Catches:	34
Stumpings:	0		

A talented off-spinner who made his Test debut against South Africa at Colombo in 1993. His zippy bowling action was questioned by the ICC in 1998 but was later cleared. Although Dharmasena was considered a limited overs specialist he did provide a few outstanding efforts in the Test arena - most notably his 6/99 against Pakistan in 1994, his 5/57 against India in '97 and his 6/72 at Galle in '98 where he cleaned up the New Zealand middle order and tail. Also quite capable with the bat, Dharmasena scored three fifties at Test level and four in One Day Internationals.

DIAS, Roy Luke

Born:	October 18, 1952
Batting:	Right handed
Bowling:	Right arm off-break

Tests

Test Career:	1982-87
Cap Number:	4
Tests Played:	20

Test Batting

Innings:	36	Runs:	1,285
Highest Score:	109	Average:	36.71
No. 50s:	8	No. 100s:	3

Test Bowling & Fielding

Wickets:	0	Runs:	17
Best Bowling:		Average:	0.00
5 WI:	0	10 WM:	0
Catches:	6	Stumpings:	0

One Day Internationals

ODI Career:	1979-87
ODIs Played:	58

ODI Batting

Innings:	55	Runs:	1,573
Highest Score:	121	Average:	31.46
No. 50s:	11	No. 100s:	2

ODI Bowling & Fielding

Wickets:	3	Runs:	70
Best Bowling:	3/25	Average:	23.33
5 WM:	0	Catches:	16
Stumpings:	0		

A member of Sri Lanka's inaugural Test side against England at Colombo in 1981, Roy Dias was a classical batsman and solid performer in Sri Lanka's early days as a Test cricketing nation. Scoring three career Test centuries, including an impressive 109 against Pakistan at Lahore, Dias provided Sri Lankan cricket with a touch of credibility that was desperately required during their days as the new 'kids on the block'. He was a valuable contibutor in Sri Lanka's maiden Test victory against India, on home soil in 1985/86, which was also their first ever Test series win.

DILSHAN, Tillakaratne Mudiyanselage

Born:	October 14, 1976
Batting:	Right handed
Bowling:	Right arm off-break
	Wicket Keeper

Tests

Test Career:	1999-06
Cap Number:	80
Tests Played:	37

Test Batting

Innings:	60	Runs:	1,989
Highest Score:	168	Average:	37.52
No. 50s:	9	No. 100s:	4

Test Bowling & Fielding

Wickets:	6	Runs:	261
Best Bowling:	2/4	Average:	43.50
5 WI:	0	10 WM:	0
Catches:	41	Stumpings:	0

One Day Internationals

ODI Career:	1999-06
ODIs Played:	96

ODI Batting

Innings:	82	Runs:	1,869
Highest Score:	117*	Average:	29.20
No. 50s:	7	No. 100s:	1

ODI Bowling & Fielding

Wickets:	35	Runs:	1,406
Best Bowling:	4/29	Average:	40.17
5 WM:	0	Catches:	48
Stumpings:	1		

A sound middle order batsman and part time keeper, Tillakaratne Dilshan has established himself as a regular in both Tests and ODI's for Sri Lanka. Although pushing 30 years of age, Dilshan has room for improvement, as many believe we are yet to see the best of his batting talents. Dilshan has scored 1,686 runs with a highest score of 168 against Bangladesh at Colombo in 2005. That performance helped Dilshan clinch the 'Player of the Series' award. In July 2006 he registered his maiden ODI century with an unbeaten 117 against Holland at Amstelveen

DUNUSINGHE, Chamara Iroshan

Born:	October 19, 1970
Batting:	Right handed
	Wicket Keeper

Tests

Test Career:	1995
Cap Number:	64
Tests Played:	5

Test Batting

Innings:	10	Runs:	160
Highest Score:	91	Average:	16.00
No. 50s:	1	No. 100s:	0

Test Bowling & Fielding

Wickets:	0	Runs:	0
Best Bowling:		Average:	0.00
5 WI:	0	10 WM:	0
Catches:	13	Stumpings:	2

One Day Internationals

ODI Career:	1995
ODIs Played:	1

ODI Batting
Innings:	1	Runs:	1
Highest Score:	1	Average:	1.00
No. 50s:	0	No. 100s:	0

ODI Bowling & Fielding
Wickets:	0	Runs:	0
Best Bowling:		Average:	0.00
5 WM:	0	Catches:	1
Stumpings:	1		

As part of the ongoing search for Sri Lanka's next long term wicket-keeper, Dunusinghe was selected on the tour of New Zealand in 1994/95 and vindicated the selectors' decision when he debuted with a match winning 91 in the second innings at Napier. He had also captured seven dismissals and a long career behind the stumps was what many were envisaging. However, Dunusinghe struggled with the bat on the following tour of Pakistan and by the time the tour of Australia came around, Romesh Kaluwitharana was back in favour with the selectors.

FERNANDO, Charitha Buddhika
Born: August 22, 1980
Batting: Right handed
Bowling: Right arm medium-fast

Tests
Test Career:	2001-02
Cap Number:	88
Tests Played:	9

Test Batting
Innings:	8	Runs:	132
Highest Score:	45	Average:	26.40
No. 50s:	0	No. 100s:	0

Test Bowling & Fielding
Wickets:	18	Runs:	792
Best Bowling:	4/27	Average:	44.00
5 WI:	0	10 WM:	0
Catches:	4	Stumpings:	0

One Day Internationals
ODI Career:	2001-03
ODIs Played:	17

ODI Batting
Innings:	10	Runs:	29
Highest Score:	14*	Average:	7.25
No. 50s:	0	No. 100s:	0

ODI Bowling & Fielding
Wickets:	15	Runs:	586
Best Bowling:	5/67	Average:	39.06
5 WM:	1	Catches:	3
Stumpings:	0		

A right arm fast bowler from Panadura whose style was better suited to limited overs cricket. Made an impression in his first ODI against Zimbabwe at Sharjah in 2001 where he took a wicket with his first ball and finished with 5/67 and the 'Man of the Match' award. But his amazing debut proved a hard act to follow as he struggled to find consistency thereafter.

FERNANDO, Dilhara
Born: July 19, 1979
Batting: Right handed
Bowling: Right arm medium-fast

Tests
Test Career:	2000-06
Cap Number:	82
Tests Played:	23

Test Batting
Innings:	31	Runs:	124
Highest Score:	16	Average:	5.90
No. 50s:	0	No. 100s:	0

Test Bowling & Fielding
Wickets:	63	Runs:	2,084
Best Bowling:	5/42	Average:	33.07
5 WI:	3	10 WM:	0
Catches:	8	Stumpings:	0

One Day Internationals
ODI Career:	2001-06
ODIs Played:	91

ODI Batting
Innings:	33	Runs:	120
Highest Score:	13*	Average:	9.23
No. 50s:	0	No. 100s:	0

ODI Bowling & Fielding
Wickets:	110	Runs:	3,507
Best Bowling:	4/48	Average:	31.88
5 WM:	0	Catches:	12
Stumpings:	0		

A lightning quick but somewhat erratic right arm bowler who has endured ongoing injuries since making his Test debut against Pakistan at Colombo in 2000.

FERNANDO, Dinusha Manoj
Born: August 10, 1979
Batting: Right handed
Bowling: Right arm medium-fast

Tests
Test Career:	2003
Cap Number:	97
Tests Played:	2

Test Batting
Innings:	3	Runs:	56
Highest Score:	51*	Average:	28.00
No. 50s:	1	No. 100s:	0

Test Bowling & Fielding
Wickets:	1	Runs:	107
Best Bowling:	1/29	Average:	107.00
5 WI:	0	10 WM:	0
Catches:	0	Stumpings:	0

One Day Internationals
ODI Career:	2003
ODIs Played:	1

ODI Batting
Innings:	0	Runs:	0
Highest Score:	0	Average:	0.00
No. 50s:	0	No. 100s:	0

ODI Bowling & Fielding
Wickets:	2	Runs:	13
Best Bowling:	2/13	Average:	6.50
5 WM:	0	Catches:	1
Stumpings:	0		

A pace bowler from Panadura who played just the two Tests, both against England in 2003. His only scalp at Test level was that of English captain Michael Vaughan.

FERNANDO, Edward Ranjit
Born: February 22, 1944
Batting: Right handed
Wicket Keeper

One Day Internationals
ODI Career: 1975
ODIs Played: 3

ODI Batting

Innings:	3	Runs:	47
Highest Score:	22	Average:	15.66
No. 50s:	0	No. 100s:	0

ODI Bowling & Fielding

Wickets:	0	Runs:	0
Best Bowling:		Average:	0.00
5 WM:	0	Catches:	0
Stumpings:	0		

Sri Lanka's first International wicket-keeper when he was selected for the 1975 World Cup in England. In addition to keeping wickets he also opened the batting where he made respectable scores of 21 & 22.

FERNANDO, Ellekutige Rufus N.S.
Born: December 19, 1955
Batting: Right handed

Tests
Test Career: 1983-84
Cap Number: 17
Tests Played: 5

Test Batting

Innings:	10	Runs:	112
Highest Score:	46	Average:	11.19
No. 50s:	0	No. 100s:	0

Test Bowling & Fielding

Wickets:	0	Runs:	0
Best Bowling:		Average:	0.00
5 WI:	0	10 WM:	0
Catches:	0	Stumpings:	0

One Day Internationals
ODI Career: 1983
ODIs Played: 7

ODI Batting

Innings:	5	Runs:	101
Highest Score:	36	Average:	20.19
No. 50s:	0	No. 100s:	0

ODI Bowling & Fielding

Wickets:	0	Runs:	0
Best Bowling:		Average:	0.00
5 WM:	0	Catches:	0
Stumpings:	0		

A right hand batsman from Colombo who made an impressive 46 on debut against New Zealand at Christchurch in 1983.

FERNANDO, Hasantha
Born: October 14, 1979
Batting: Right handed
Bowling: Right arm medium-fast

Tests
Test Career: 2002
Cap Number: 93
Tests Played: 2

Test Batting

Innings:	4	Runs:	38
Highest Score:	24	Average:	9.50
No. 50s:	0	No. 100s:	0

Test Bowling & Fielding

Wickets:	4	Runs:	108
Best Bowling:	3/63	Average:	27.00
5 WI:	0	10 WM:	0
Catches:	1	Stumpings:	0

One Day Internationals
ODI Career: 2002-06
ODIs Played: 7

ODI Batting

Innings:	5	Runs:	43
Highest Score:	23*	Average:	21.50
No. 50s:	0	No. 100s:	0

ODI Bowling & Fielding

Wickets:	6	Runs:	159
Best Bowling:	3/12	Average:	26.50
5 WM:	0	Catches:	2
Stumpings:	0		

An all rounder who played in 2003 World Cup, Hasantha Fernando unfortunately clocked up a 'pair' on Test debut against South Africa at Johannesburg in 2002. He was considered for just one more Test thereafter and when it looked as if his international career was over, Fernando was recalled to the One Day side in early 2006.

FERNANDO, Lalithamana
Born: December 27, 1962
Batting: Right handed
Bowling: Right arm medium

One Day Internationals
ODI Career: 1989
ODIs Played: 1

ODI Batting

Innings:	1	Runs:	8
Highest Score:	8	Average:	8.00
No. 50s:	0	No. 100s:	0

ODI Bowling & Fielding

Wickets:	1	Runs:	16
Best Bowling:	1/16	Average:	16.00
5 WM:	0	Catches:	0
Stumpings:	0		

A medium pacer who took the wicket of David Boon in his only ODI against Australia at Kandy in 1989.

FERNANDO, Nisal Kumudusiri
Born: March 10, 1970
Batting: Right handed
Wicket Keeper

One Day Internationals
ODI Career: 1994
ODIs Played: 2

ODI Batting

Innings:	2	Runs:	22
Highest Score:	20*	Average:	22.00
No. 50s:	0	No. 100s:	0

ODI Bowling & Fielding

Wickets:	0	Runs:	0
Best Bowling:		Average:	0.00
5 WM:	0	Catches:	0
Stumpings:	0		

An agile wicket-keeper who donned the gloves for the first time against India at Rajkot, in 1994. He played just one more ODI also against India at Hyderabad.

GALLAGE, Indika Sanjeewa
Born: November 22, 1975
Batting: Right handed
Bowling: Right arm medium-fast

Tests
Test Career: 1999
Cap Number: 81
Tests Played: 1
Test Batting
Innings:	1	Runs:	3
Highest Score:	3	Average:	3.00
No. 50s:	0	No. 100s:	0

Test Bowling & Fielding
Wickets:	0	Runs:	77
Best Bowling:		Average:	0.00
5 WI:	0	10 WM:	0
Catches:	0	Stumpings:	0

One Day Internationals
ODI Career: 2001
ODIs Played: 3
ODI Batting
Innings:	2	Runs:	17
Highest Score:	14	Average:	17.00
No. 50s:	0	No. 100s:	0

ODI Bowling & Fielding
Wickets:	3	Runs:	115
Best Bowling:	2/42	Average:	38.33
5 WM:	0	Catches:	0
Stumpings:	0		

A tall right arm fast bowler who showed huge potential leading up to his maiden Test appearance against Zimbabwe at Bulawayo in 1999.

GAMAGE, Dharshana
Born: March 2, 1979
Batting: Right handed
Bowling: Right arm medium-fast

One Day Internationals
ODI Career: 2003
ODIs Played: 3
ODI Batting
Innings:	2	Runs:	3
Highest Score:	2*	Average:	3.00
No. 50s:	0	No. 100s:	0

ODI Bowling & Fielding
Wickets:	2	Runs:	83
Best Bowling:	1/26	Average:	41.50
5 WM:	0	Catches:	2
Stumpings:	0		

Also known as HGD Nayanakantha, Gamage, a tall seamer, got his ODI opportunity against New Zealand at Dambulla in 2003, where he claimed the prize wicket of Chris Cairns.

GAMAGE, Janak Champika
Born: April 17, 1964
Batting: Right handed
Bowling: Right arm medium-fast

One Day Internationals
ODI Career: 1995
ODIs Played: 4
ODI Batting
Innings:	2	Runs:	8
Highest Score:	7*	Average:	8.00
No. 50s:	0	No. 100s:	0

ODI Bowling & Fielding
Wickets:	3	Runs:	104
Best Bowling:	2/17	Average:	34.66
5 WM:	0	Catches:	2
Stumpings:	0		

A paper thin right-arm pace bowler who had to wait for his chance at international level when he was selected to tour New Zealand at age 30. Gamage made his ODI debut against the Kiwis at Hamilton but it was his last ODI against Bangladesh, where he racked up his best bowling figures of 2/17. Played all of his four ODI's in 1995.

GAMAGE (LAKSHITHA), Chamila Premanath
Born: January 4, 1979
Batting: Right handed
Bowling: Right arm medium-fast

Tests
Test Career: 2002
Cap Number: 90
Tests Played: 2
Test Batting
Innings:	3	Runs:	42
Highest Score:	40	Average:	14.00
No. 50s:	0	No. 100s:	0

Test Bowling & Fielding
Wickets:	5	Runs:	158
Best Bowling:	2/33	Average:	31.60
5 WI:	0	10 WM:	0
Catches:	1	Stumpings:	0

One Day Internationals
ODI Career: 2002-03
ODIs Played: 7
ODI Batting
Innings:	2	Runs:	7
Highest Score:	4	Average:	7.00
No. 50s:	0	No. 100s:	0

ODI Bowling & Fielding
Wickets:	8	Runs:	254
Best Bowling:	2/34	Average:	31.75
5 WM:	0	Catches:	0
Stumpings:	0		

Chamila Gamage had a dream start to his Test career when the pace bowler scored 40 from 46 balls when batting at number eleven against Bangladesh, at Colombo in 2002. If that wasn't impressive enough, he then took the wicket of Bangladesh premier batsman Mohammad Ashraful with his first delivery in Test cricket. Gamage finished with 2/33 and 1/48 for the match but surprisingly could only manage just one more Test appearance after experiencing such a memorable debut.

GANEGAMA, Akalanka

Born: March 29, 1981
Batting: Right handed
Bowling: Right arm medium-fast

One Day Internationals

ODI Career: 2001-06
ODIs Played: 4

ODI Batting
Innings:	2	Runs:	7
Highest Score:	7	Average:	3.50
No. 50s:	0	No. 100s:	0

ODI Bowling & Fielding
Wickets:	2	Runs:	88
Best Bowling:	2/27	Average:	44.00
5 WM:	0	Catches:	1
Stumpings:	0		

A medium fast bowler who made his ODI debut against Pakistan at Sharjah in 2000 where he picked up the early wickets of Shahid Afridi and Imran Farhat. And just when it seemed that things would only get better for the youngster, fate dealt him a bitter blow as he would play just two more ODI's over the next four years. In early 2006, Ganegama was a surprise replacement for Farveez Maharoof, who was ruled out of the tri nations series in Australia due to a groin injury. But he was only utilised as a super sub and hence didn't add to his personal wicket tally.

GOONASEKERA, Yohan

Born: November 8, 1957
Batting: Left handed
Bowling: Left arm medium

Tests

Test Career: 1983
Cap Number: 18
Tests Played: 2

Test Batting
Innings:	4	Runs:	48
Highest Score:	23	Average:	12.00
No. 50s:	0	No. 100s:	0

Test Bowling & Fielding
Wickets:	0	Runs:	0
Best Bowling:		Average:	0.00
5 WI:	0	10 WM:	0
Catches:	0	Stumpings:	0

One Day Internationals

ODI Career: 1983
ODIs Played: 3

ODI Batting
Innings:	3	Runs:	69
Highest Score:	35	Average:	23.00
No. 50s:	0	No. 100s:	0

ODI Bowling & Fielding
Wickets:	1	Runs:	35
Best Bowling:	1/24	Average:	35.00
5 WM:	0	Catches:	0
Stumpings:	0		

A left hand batsman from Colombo who made his Test debut on the tour of New Zealand. He could only manage one Test thereafter.

GOONATILLEKE, Hettiarachige Mahes

Born: August 16, 1952
Batting: Right handed
Wicket Keeper

Tests

Test Career: 1982
Cap Number: 5
Tests Played: 5

Test Batting
Innings:	10	Runs:	177
Highest Score:	56	Average:	22.12
No. 50s:	1	No. 100s:	0

Test Bowling & Fielding
Wickets:	0	Runs:	0
Best Bowling:		Average:	0.00
5 WI:	0	10 WM:	0
Catches:	10	Stumpings:	3

One Day Internationals

ODI Career: 1982
ODIs Played: 6

ODI Batting
Innings:	4	Runs:	31
Highest Score:	14*	Average:	31.00
No. 50s:	0	No. 100s:	0

ODI Bowling & Fielding
Wickets:	0	Runs:	0
Best Bowling:		Average:	0.00
5 WM:	0	Catches:	0
Stumpings:	4		

Sri Lanka's first Test wicket-keeper, Goonatilleke was not just a fine gloveman but also a very handy batsman having scored a 50 at Test level with a respectable average of 22. A later order batsman who was difficult to dismiss, he was just as suited to the shorter version of the game averaging 31 in ODI's. Could have played more Tests if not for his decision to tour South Africa in 1982/83.

GUNARATNE, Pulasthi Waruna

Born: September 27, 1973
Batting: Right handed
Bowling: Right arm medium-fast

One Day Internationals

ODI Career: 2002-03
ODIs Played: 23

ODI Batting
Innings:	8	Runs:	36
Highest Score:	15*	Average:	7.20
No. 50s:	0	No. 100s:	0

ODI Bowling & Fielding
Wickets:	27	Runs:	908
Best Bowling:	4/44	Average:	33.62
5 WM:	0	Catches:	3
Stumpings:	0		

A right arm pace bowler who had the ability to move the ball off the seam, Gunaratne made his ODI debut against Bangladesh at Colombo in 2002 where he opened the bowling and took a respectable 2/39. Unable to break into the Test side, Gunaratne was also in and out of the One Day side over his short career.

GUNATILLEKE, Frederick Ranjan Manilal de Silva

Born: August 15, 1951
Batting: Right handed
Bowling: Right arm medium

One Day Internationals
ODI Career: 1979
ODIs Played: 1

ODI Batting
Innings:	0	Runs:	0
Highest Score:	0	Average:	0.00
No. 50s:	0	No. 100s:	0

ODI Bowling & Fielding
Wickets:	0	Runs:	34
Best Bowling:	0/34	Average:	0.00
5 WM:	0	Catches:	0
Stumpings:	0		

Opened the bowling in his one and only ODI against India at Old Trafford during the 1979 World Cup but failed to take a wicket.

GUNAWARDENE, Aruna Alwis Wijesiri

Born: March 31, 1969
Batting: Right handed
Bowling: Right arm medium

One Day Internationals
ODI Career: 1994
ODIs Played: 1

ODI Batting
Innings:	1	Runs:	2
Highest Score:	2	Average:	2.00
No. 50s:	0	No. 100s:	0

ODI Bowling & Fielding
Wickets:	0	Runs:	0
Best Bowling:		Average:	0.00
5 WM:	0	Catches:	0
Stumpings:	0		

Another member of the 'one match club', Gunawardene opened the batting in his one and only ODI against India at Hyderabad in 1994, but his international career was over just as quick as it began when he was dismissed for two.

GUNAWARDENE, Avishka

Born: May 26, 1977
Batting: Left handed

Tests
Test Career: 1999-05
Cap Number: 76
Tests Played: 6

Test Batting
Innings:	11	Runs:	181
Highest Score:	43	Average:	16.45
No. 50s:	0	No. 100s:	0

Test Bowling & Fielding
Wickets:	0	Runs:	0
Best Bowling:		Average:	0.00
5 WI:	0	10 WM:	0
Catches:	2	Stumpings:	0

One Day Internationals
ODI Career: 1998-06
ODIs Played: 61

ODI Batting
Innings:	61	Runs:	1,708
Highest Score:	132	Average:	28.46
No. 50s:	12	No. 100s:	1

ODI Bowling & Fielding
Wickets:	0	Runs:	0
Best Bowling:		Average:	0.00
5 WM:	0	Catches:	13
Stumpings:	0		

An exciting left-hand opener who takes on the bowling at every opportunity. Played six Tests after making his debut against Pakistan at Lahore in 1999, but was clearly suited to the shorter version of the game where he scored a memorable 132 against West Indies in 2000.

GUNERATNE, Roshan Punyajith Wijesinghe

Born: January 26, 1962
Batting: Right handed
Bowling: Right arm slow

Tests
Test Career: 1983
Cap Number: 24
Tests Played: 1

Test Batting
Innings:	2	Runs:	0
Highest Score:	0*	Average:	0.00
No. 50s:	0	No. 100s:	0

Test Bowling & Fielding
Wickets:	0	Runs:	84
Best Bowling:		Average:	0.00
5 WI:	0	10 WM:	0
Catches:	0	Stumpings:	0

A leg spinner from Colombo who played just the one Test against Australia, at Kandy, in 1983. Passed away at age 43.

GURUSINHA, Asanka Pradeep

Born: September 16, 1966
Batting: Left handed
Bowling: Right arm medium
Wicket Keeper

Tests
Test Career: 1985-96
Cap Number: 32
Tests Played: 41

Test Batting
Innings:	70	Runs:	2,452
Highest Score:	143	Average:	38.92
No. 50s:	8	No. 100s:	7

Test Bowling & Fielding
Wickets:	20	Runs:	681
Best Bowling:	2/7	Average:	34.04
5 WI:	0	10 WM:	0
Catches:	33	Stumpings:	0

One Day Internationals
ODI Career: 1985-96
ODIs Played: 147

ODI Batting
Innings:	143	Runs:	3,902
Highest Score:	117*	Average:	28.27
No. 50s:	22	No. 100s:	2

ODI Bowling & Fielding
Wickets:	26	Runs:	1,354
Best Bowling:	2/25	Average:	52.07
5 WM:	0	Catches:	49
Stumpings:	0		

Asanka Gurusinha started his career as a wicket-keeper but pretty soon his gutsy and technically correct batting style earned him the number three spot. He provided the steel and consistency that the Sri Lankan top order so desperately required. He scored seven Test hundreds with a highest score of 143 against Australia during the Boxing Day Test at the MCG in 1995. However that Test is best remembered for the controversial 'calling' of Muralitharan by Daryl Hair rather than Gurusinha's outstanding batting display or for much else for that matter. Gurusinha was just as comfortable in the one day game were he scored 22 fifties and two centuries. But his most important knock occured in 1996 when he scored a valuable 65 in Sri Lanka's shock World Cup win against Australia. He retired shortly afterwards, prematurely in most people's minds, and now resides in Melbourne.

HATHURUSINGHA, Chandika

Born:	September 13, 1968
Batting:	Right handed
Bowling:	Right arm medium-fast

Tests
Test Career:	1991-99		
Cap Number:	48		
Tests Played:	26		

Test Batting
Innings:	44	Runs:	1,274
Highest Score:	83	Average:	29.62
No. 50s:	8	No. 100s:	0

Test Bowling & Fielding
Wickets:	17	Runs:	789
Best Bowling:	4/66	Average:	46.41
5 WI:	0	10 WM:	0
Catches:	0	Stumpings:	0

One Day Internationals
ODI Career:	1992-99		
ODIs Played:	35		

ODI Batting
Innings:	33	Runs:	669
Highest Score:	66	Average:	20.90
No. 50s:	4	No. 100s:	0

ODI Bowling & Fielding
Wickets:	14	Runs:	709
Best Bowling:	4/57	Average:	50.64
5 WM:	0	Catches:	6
Stumpings:	0		

An right hand opening batsman who partnered with Roshan Mahanama in the early 90's. Unlike traditional openers, Hathurusingha had another string to his bow being a capable medium-fast bowler taking a career best 4/66. Having made three early fifties, Hathurusingha had hardly put a foot wrong but the temptation to play arguably the most exciting prospect Sri Lanakan cricket had set eyes upon in Sanath Jayasuriya, was too great and thus the ever improving Hathurusingha had to make way. Hathurusingha finished his career with servicable if not modest statistics but would definately have had more matches alongside his name if not for a bit of luck.

HERATH, Mudiyanselage Rangana Keerthi Bandara

Born:	March 19, 1978
Batting:	Left handed
Bowling:	Left arm off-break

Tests
Test Career:	1999-05		
Cap Number:	78		
Tests Played:	12		

Test Batting
Innings:	16	Runs:	123
Highest Score:	33*	Average:	8.78
No. 50s:	0	No. 100s:	0

Test Bowling & Fielding
Wickets:	35	Runs:	1,204
Best Bowling:	4/38	Average:	34.40
5 WI:	0	10 WM:	0
Catches:	2	Stumpings:	0

One Day Internationals
ODI Career:	2004		
ODIs Played:	6		

ODI Batting
Innings:	1	Runs:	0
Highest Score:	0*	Average:	0.00
No. 50s:	0	No. 100s:	0

ODI Bowling & Fielding
Wickets:	5	Runs:	149
Best Bowling:	3/28	Average:	29.80
5 WM:	0	Catches:	3
Stumpings:	0		

A talented left arm off-spinner who took an impressive 4/97 on his Test debut against Australia at Galle in 1999. Although he has not played in a Test since late 2005, Herath has the opportunity to consolidate his position as a regular spinner alongside Murali.

HETTIARACHCHI, Dinuka

Born:	July 15, 1976
Batting:	Right handed
Bowling:	Left arm off-break

Tests
Test Career:	2001		
Cap Number:	85		
Tests Played:	1		

Test Batting
Innings:	2	Runs:	0
Highest Score:	0	Average:	0.00
No. 50s:	0	No. 100s:	0

Test Bowling & Fielding
Wickets:	2	Runs:	41
Best Bowling:	2/36	Average:	20.50
5 WI:	0	10 WM:	0
Catches:	0	Stumpings:	0

A left arm off spinner who played just the one Test against England at Colombo in 2001 where he captured the wickets of Marcus Trescothick and Nasser Hussain.

HEYN, Peter David
Born: June 26, 1945
Batting: Left handed
Bowling: Right arm medium

One Day Internationals
ODI Career: 1975
ODIs Played: 2
ODI Batting
Innings:	2	Runs:	3
Highest Score:	2	Average:	1.50
No. 50s:	0	No. 100s:	0

ODI Bowling & Fielding
Wickets:	0	Runs:	0
Best Bowling:		Average:	0.00
5 WM:	0	Catches:	1
Stumpings:	0		

A middle order batsman who played his two ODI's for Sri Lanka during the 1975 World Cup in England.

JAYANTHA, Saman
Born: January 26, 1974
Batting: Right handed
Bowling: Right arm off-break

One Day Internationals
ODI Career: 2004
ODIs Played: 17
ODI Batting
Innings:	17	Runs:	400
Highest Score:	74*	Average:	26.66
No. 50s:	2	No. 100s:	0

ODI Bowling & Fielding
Wickets:	0	Runs:	46
Best Bowling:		Average:	0.00
5 WM:	0	Catches:	5
Stumpings:	0		

A stylish and confident right hand opener from Ambalangoda who showed alot of promise and became a regular of the ODI side in 2004. Did not do much wrong during his time on the international arena, scoring two fifties with a top score of 74 not out against Zimbabwe and averaging just over 26. He struggled to hold his place later on due to the depth in Sri Lanka's batting.

JAYAPRAKASHDARAN, Pradeep Sri
Born: January 13, 1984
Batting: Right handed
Bowling: Right arm medium-fast

One Day Internationals
ODI Career: 2005
ODIs Played: 1
ODI Batting
Innings:	0	Runs:	0
Highest Score:	0	Average:	0.00
No. 50s:	0	No. 100s:	0

ODI Bowling & Fielding
Wickets:	1	Runs:	21
Best Bowling:	1/21	Average:	21.00
5 WM:	0	Catches:	0
Stumpings:	0		

A talented youngster who made his ODI debut against India at Dambulla in 2005 where he picked up the prize wicket of highly accomplished opener Virender Sehwag.

JAYASEKERA, Rohan Stanley Amarasiriwardene
Born: December 7, 1957
Batting: Right handed
 Wicket Keeper

Tests
Test Career: 1982
Cap Number: 14
Tests Played: 1
Test Batting
Innings:	2	Runs:	2
Highest Score:	2	Average:	1.00
No. 50s:	0	No. 100s:	0

Test Bowling & Fielding
Wickets:	0	Runs:	0
Best Bowling:		Average:	0.00
5 WI:	0	10 WM:	0
Catches:	0	Stumpings:	0

One Day Internationals
ODI Career: 1982
ODIs Played: 2
ODI Batting
Innings:	1	Runs:	17
Highest Score:	17	Average:	17.00
No. 50s:	0	No. 100s:	0

ODI Bowling & Fielding
Wickets:	0	Runs:	0
Best Bowling:		Average:	0.00
5 WM:	0	Catches:	0
Stumpings:	0		

A reserve wicket-keeper who played just the one Test against Pakistan at Lahore in 1982. He made his ODI debut in Sri Lanka's inaugural one-day international on home soil.

JAYASINGHE, Sunil Asoka
Born: July 15, 1955
Batting: Right handed
 Wicket Keeper

One Day Internationals
ODI Career: 1979
ODIs Played: 2
ODI Batting
Innings:	1	Runs:	1
Highest Score:	1	Average:	1.00
No. 50s:	0	No. 100s:	0

ODI Bowling & Fielding
Wickets:	0	Runs:	0
Best Bowling:		Average:	0.00
5 WM:	0	Catches:	1
Stumpings:	0		

Jayasinghe was the prefered keeper during Sri Lanka's 1979 World Cup campaign. He was run out in his only innings.

JAYASURIYA, Sanath Teran
Born: June 30, 1969
Batting: Left handed
Bowling: Left arm off-break

Tests
Test Career:	1991-06		
Cap Number:	49		
Tests Played:	103		

Test Batting
Innings:	175	Runs:	6,621
Highest Score:	340	Average:	41.12
No. 50s:	29	No. 100s:	14

Test Bowling & Fielding
Wickets:	95	Runs:	3,126
Best Bowling:	5/34	Average:	32.90
5 WI:	2	10 WM:	0
Catches:	74	Stumpings:	0

One Day Internationals
ODI Career:	1989-06		
ODIs Played:	363		

ODI Batting
Innings:	354	Runs:	11
Highest Score:	189	Average:	32.75
No. 50s:	60	No. 100s:	22

ODI Bowling & Fielding
Wickets:	278	Runs:	10
Best Bowling:	6/29	Average:	36.82
5 WM:	4	Catches:	107
Stumpings:	0		

Apart from being one of Sri Lanka's most decorated players, Sanath Jayasuriya is just one of a handful of batsmen, in the history of the game that has been able to provide optimum entertainment value by simply playing his natural game. Together with fellow 'pocket dynamo' Romesh Kaluwitharana, the pair revolutionised the very way limited overs cricket was played and thought about thereafter. Their seemingly straight forward, but effective tactic of attacking from the opening ball during the first fifteen overs made cricket brain trusts world wide, reassess the traditional role of the opener. After making a rather innocuous Test debut against New Zealand at Hamilton in 1991, the stylish left hander came to prominence during the 1996 World Cup where he racked up scores of 79, 44 and 82, which helped steer Sri Lanka, the then 'minnows' of world cricket, to a fairytale seven wicket win over the much fancied Australians in the final. It was a metaphorical 'line in the sand' for Sri Lanka as they had now gained the much belated respect they had sought since their induction as a Test nation almost 15 years earlier. Jayasuriya continued to wreak havoc with the bat thereafter and it is no surprise that when one scrolls through Sri Lanka's records for highest scores in limited overs cricket they will find his name occupying the top spot with the 189 he made against India at Sharjah in 2001. Jayasuriya's scores of 157, 152 & 151 occupy the next three positions and, in fact, the aggressive, but modest opener holds seven of the top ten ODI scores. He has also scored more runs at One-Day level (over 11,000) than any other Sri Lankan with an amazing strike rate of 89.88. While his One-Day resume reeks of overwhelming success, many distant observers would be forgiven for pigeon-holing Jayasuriya as a limited overs specialist. A specialist maybe, but by no means one dimensional as Jayasuria's record at Test level is just as impressive. He is second only to Murali as having played the most Tests for his country and heads Sri Lanka's list of 'Most Test Runs' with 6,621 (at 41.12). Up until July 2006, when Mahela Jayawardene smashed 374 against South Africa at Colombo, he held the highest Test score by a Sri Lankan, with his masterful 340 against India at Colombo, in 1997. In that same match, he along with Roshan Mahanama, captured the record for highest partnership in Test history when they hammered 576 for the second wicket. And while the Jayawardene/Sangakkara partnership of 624 in July 2006, saw Jayasuria and Mahanama's record slip to second place, it still remains a Test record for the second wicket. Of his 14 triple figure efforts, Jayasuriya has reached a double century on two occasions and just missed out on a third when he racked up 199 against India at Colombo in 1998. As a part time bowler he has made various cameo appearances as a partnership breaker with his well-flighted left arm off-spinners. His best haul, a match winning 5/34 against South Africa at Colombo in 2004. Appointed captain for the 1999/2000 tour of Australia, Jayasuriya led his country in 38 Tests for 18 victories and eight draws. He resigned after the 2003 World Cup handing over the reigns to Marvan Atapattu. With retirement on the agenda on at least two occasions in the past three years, Jayasuria is still a popular choice amongst the national selectors as he had just turned 37 when he was named in the squad to take on South Africa in August 2006. Hopefully for the purists, and novices for that matter, 'Father Time' continues to bypass the little champion with the warm smile, for just a few more years.

JAYAWARDENE, Hewasandatchige Asiri Prasanna Wishvanath

Born:	October 9, 1979
Batting:	Right handed
	Wicket Keeper

Tests
Test Career:	2000-04		
Cap Number:	83		
Tests Played:	7		

Test Batting
Innings:	5	Runs:	81
Highest Score:	42	Average:	16.20
No. 50s:	0	No. 100s:	0

Test Bowling & Fielding
Wickets:	0	Runs:	0
Best Bowling:		Average:	0.00
5 WI:	0	10 WM:	0
Catches:	15	Stumpings:	3

Unlike his namesake, wicket-keeper Prasanna Jayawardene struggled early on to become a permanent member of the Test side mainly because of the presence of stalwart Romesh Kaluwitharana and then due to the emergence of his eventual successor Kumar Sangakkara. However, when the selectors decided to allow Sangakkara to concentrate solely on his batting, Jayawardene was given a reprieve and was hence recalled to the Test side to take on South Africa in mid 2006 after a two year hiatus. He seized his opportunity scoring 42 & 30 in his only two innings of the series and also impressed with some polished work with the gloves. As he is only in his mid 20's, Jayawardene now has the opportunity to consolidate a permanent place in the Test side.

JAYAWARDENE, Mahela de Silva

Born:	May 27, 1977
Batting:	Right handed
Bowling:	Right arm medium

Tests

Test Career:	1997-06		
Cap Number:	69		
Tests Played:	83		

Test Batting

Innings:	136	Runs:	6,250
Highest Score:	374	Average:	49.60
No. 50s:	29	No. 100s:	16

Test Bowling & Fielding

Wickets:	4	Runs:	228
Best Bowling:	2/32	Average:	57.00
5 WI:	0	10 WM:	0
Catches:	111	Stumpings:	0

One Day Internationals

ODI Career:	1998-00		
ODIs Played:	221		

ODI Batting

Innings:	205	Runs:	5,917
Highest Score:	128	Average:	32.33
No. 50s:	34	No. 100s:	8

ODI Bowling & Fielding

Wickets:	7	Runs:	539
Best Bowling:	2/56	Average:	77.00
5 WM:	0	Catches:	109
Stumpings:	0		

It was evident very early in his career that Mahela Jayawardene would become a regular fixture in Sri Lanka's middle order. Jayawardene's impressive batting record tended to 'repeat itself' in the early days when examined closely. After his maiden Test century - 167 against New Zealand in his fourth Test - the talented middle order batsman again scored 167 when Sri Lanka met South Africa at Galle in 2000. Four years later, he scored his second Test double century with a superb 237 against South Africa and again at Galle. In 1999, Jayawardene registered his then highest Test score of 242, against India at Colombo and is currently the third highest run scorer in Sri Lanka's history, closing in on former great Aravinda de Silva. Just as proficient at the shorter version of the game, Jayawardene has scored over 5,000 runs at ODI level to be in Sri Lanka's top five run scorers. Highly respected amongst his peers Jayawardene has captained his country in nine Tests to date, including the 2006 tour of England while relieving for Marvan Atapattu. In July 2006, during the Second Test against South Africa, at Colombo, Jayawardene, while still captaining the side, rewrote the record books in a big way. His 624 run partnership with Kumar Sangakkara is not only a Test record for the third wicket, but the highest partnership of any kind in Test history, eclipsing the previous record of 576 set by fellow countrymen Sanath Jayasuria and Roshan Mahanama in 1997/98. Jayawardene's contribution of 374, overtook Jayasuria's 340 as the highest score made by a Sri Lankan in Tests. It was also the fourth highest score of all time behind Brain Lara's pair of 400 not out & 375 and Matthew Hayden's 380.

JEGANATHAN, Sridharan

Born:	July 11, 1957
Batting:	Right handed
Bowling:	Left arm off-break

Tests

Test Career:	1983		
Cap Number:	19		
Tests Played:	2		

Test Batting

Innings:	4	Runs:	19
Highest Score:	8	Average:	4.75
No. 50s:	0	No. 100s:	0

Test Bowling & Fielding

Wickets:	0	Runs:	12
Best Bowling:	0/12	Average:	0.00
5 WI:	0	10 WM:	0
Catches:	0	Stumpings:	0

One Day Internationals

ODI Career:	1983-88		
ODIs Played:	5		

ODI Batting

Innings:	4	Runs:	25
Highest Score:	20*	Average:	8.33
No. 50s:	0	No. 100s:	0

ODI Bowling & Fielding

Wickets:	5	Runs:	208
Best Bowling:	2/45	Average:	41.60
5 WM:	0	Catches:	1
Stumpings:	0		

A left arm off spinner with a modest Test record, Jeganathan represented India in the 1987 World

Cup. He was later appointed National Coach of Malaysia.

JOHN, Vinothen Bede

Born:	May 27, 1960
Batting:	Right handed
Bowling:	Right arm medium-fast

Tests

Test Career:	1983-84
Cap Number:	20
Tests Played:	6

Test Batting

Innings:	10	Runs:	53
Highest Score:	27*	Average:	10.59
No. 50s:	0	No. 100s:	0

Test Bowling & Fielding

Wickets:	28	Runs:	614
Best Bowling:	5/60	Average:	21.92
5 WI:	2	10 WM:	0
Catches:	2	Stumpings:	0

One Day Internationals

ODI Career:	1982-87
ODIs Played:	45

ODI Batting

Innings:	19	Runs:	84
Highest Score:	15	Average:	9.33
No. 50s:	0	No. 100s:	0

ODI Bowling & Fielding

Wickets:	34	Runs:	1,655
Best Bowling:	3/28	Average:	48.67
5 WM:	0	Catches:	5
Stumpings:	0		

His full name was Vinothen John Bede Jeyarajasingham but better known just as Vinothen John. A strong bodied medium fast bowler who gave his all during Sri Lanka's early days as a Test playing nation. He made his debut against New Zealand at Christchurch in 1982 where he captured a career best 5/60 in the Second Test. A handy limited overs player as well.

JURANGPATHY, Roshan

Born:	June 25, 1967
Batting:	Right handed
Bowling:	Right arm off-break

Tests

Test Career:	1985-86
Cap Number:	31
Tests Played:	2

Test Batting

Innings:	4	Runs:	1
Highest Score:	1	Average:	0.25
No. 50s:	0	No. 100s:	0

Test Bowling & Fielding

Wickets:	1	Runs:	93
Best Bowling:	1/69	Average:	93.00
5 WI:	0	10 WM:	0
Catches:	2	Stumpings:	0

Rated as a promising all rounder, Jurangpathy failed to trouble the scorers in three of his four innings and thus was overlooked after just two Tests.

KALAVITIGODA, Shantha

Born:	December 23, 1977
Batting:	Right handed
Bowling:	Right arm off-break

Tests

Test Career:	2005
Cap Number:	101
Tests Played:	1

Test Batting

Innings:	2	Runs:	8
Highest Score:	7	Average:	4.00
No. 50s:	0	No. 100s:	0

Test Bowling & Fielding

Wickets:	0	Runs:	0
Best Bowling:	0	Average:	0.00
5 WI:	0	10 WM:	0
Catches:	2	Stumpings:	0

Another member of the 'One Test Club', Kalavitigoda got his chance at Test level when he was selected on the tour of New Zealand in 2005. He made his debut against the Kiwis in the 2nd Test at Wellington.

KALPAGE, Ruwan Senani

Born:	February 19, 1970
Batting:	Left handed
Bowling:	Right arm off-break

Tests

Test Career:	1993-99
Cap Number:	56
Tests Played:	11

Test Batting

Innings:	18	Runs:	2,964
Highest Score:	63	Average:	18.37
No. 50s:	2	No. 100s:	0

Test Bowling & Fielding

Wickets:	12	Runs:	774
Best Bowling:	2/27	Average:	64.50
5 WI:	0	10 WM:	0
Catches:	10	Stumpings:	0

One Day Internationals

ODI Career:	1993-99
ODIs Played:	86

ODI Batting

Innings:	69	Runs:	844
Highest Score:	51	Average:	20.58
No. 50s:	1	No. 100s:	0

ODI Bowling & Fielding

Wickets:	73	Runs:	2,975
Best Bowling:	4/36	Average:	40.75
5 WM:	0	Catches:	33
Stumpings:	0		

An all-rounder who made his Test debut against India at Colombo in 1993. Kalpage was suited more to the one day game than Test cricket as reflected in his record. Although he played some servicable cricket at ODI level, Kalpage was considered more of a fringe player than a regular.

KALUPERUMA, Lalith Wasantha Silva

Born:	June 25, 1949
Batting:	Right handed
Bowling:	Right arm off-break

Tests
Test Career:	1982
Cap Number:	6
Tests Played:	2

Test Batting
Innings:	4	Runs:	12
Highest Score:	11*	Average:	4.00
No. 50s:	0	No. 100s:	0

Test Bowling & Fielding
Wickets:	0	Runs:	93
Best Bowling:		Average:	0.00
5 WI:	0	10 WM:	0
Catches:	2	Stumpings:	0

One Day Internationals
ODI Career:	1975-82
ODIs Played:	4

ODI Batting
Innings:	3	Runs:	33
Highest Score:	14*	Average:	33.00
No. 50s:	0	No. 100s:	0

ODI Bowling & Fielding
Wickets:	2	Runs:	137
Best Bowling:	1/35	Average:	68.50
5 WM:	0	Catches:	0
Stumpings:	0		

An off spinner from Colombo, Kaluperuma made his Test debut in front of his home crowd when he was selected in Sri Lanka's inaugural Test side against England in 1982. As he didn't get too many bowling opportunities in his two Tests he decided to join the rebel tour to South Africa in 1982/83.

KALUPERUMA, Sanath Mohan Silva
Born:	October 22, 1961
Batting:	Right handed
Bowling:	Right arm off-break

Tests
Test Career:	1984-88
Cap Number:	26
Tests Played:	4

Test Batting
Innings:	8	Runs:	88
Highest Score:	23	Average:	11.00
No. 50s:	0	No. 100s:	0

Test Bowling & Fielding
Wickets:	2	Runs:	124
Best Bowling:	2/17	Average:	62.00
5 WI:	0	10 WM:	0
Catches:	6	Stumpings:	0

One Day Internationals
ODI Career:	1988
ODIs Played:	2

ODI Batting
Innings:	2	Runs:	11
Highest Score:	7	Average:	5.50
No. 50s:	0	No. 100s:	0

ODI Bowling & Fielding
Wickets:	0	Runs:	3
Best Bowling:	0/3	Average:	0.00
5 WM:	0	Catches:	2
Stumpings:	0		

An all rounder of some sorts, Kaluperuma could bat high in the order and bowl quality off spin. He struggled to hold a regular place after making his debut against New Zealand at Kandy in 1984, averaging just 11 and five in Tests and ODI's respectively.

KALUWITHARANA, Romesh Shantha
Born:	November 24, 1969
Batting:	Right handed
	Wicket Keeper

Tests
Test Career:	1992-04
Cap Number:	52
Tests Played:	49

Test Batting
Innings:	78	Runs:	1,933
Highest Score:	132*	Average:	26.12
No. 50s:	9	No. 100s:	3

Test Bowling & Fielding
Wickets:	0	Runs:	0
Best Bowling:		Average:	0.00
5 WI:	0	10 WM:	0
Catches:	93	Stumpings:	26

One Day Internationals
ODI Career:	1990-04
ODIs Played:	189

ODI Batting
Innings:	181	Runs:	3,711
Highest Score:	102*	Average:	22.22
No. 50s:	23	No. 100s:	2

ODI Bowling & Fielding
Wickets:	0	Runs:	0
Best Bowling:		Average:	0.00
5 WM:	0	Catches:	132
Stumpings:	75		

Although he became an international favourite because of his explosive nature while opening the batting with Sanath Jayasuria in one day internationals, Romesh Kaluwitharana was also fine Test cricketer. He commenced his Test career in a blaze of glory, scoring 132 not out on debut against Australia, at Colombo in 1992/93, batting at number seven. The diminutive keeper was to score two more centuries and nine fifties in a Test career spanning 49 games. Although Kaluwitharana was a keeper first and foremost, his form with the gloves was haphazard at times and was subsequently dropped early in his career. He was recalled for the tour of Australia in 1995/96 and that's where he and Jayasuriya went about changing the conservative image of opening batsmen. Their philosophy was simple - attack any loose, or playable ball for that matter, in the first fifteen overs while the field was in. While it could be argued that at times the strategy didn't pay off, more often than not, it did - and with damaging effect. Later that year Kaluwitharana and Jayasuria took their ideaology and form to the 1996 World Cup and were both instrumental in Sri Lanka's campaign which saw the once minnows of International cricket, defy the odds by winning the Championship. Due to the emergence of Sangakkara, 'Kalu's opportunities became rare shortly after returning from the World Cup. He retired from the international scene in early 2004 but his revolutionary and entertaining batting style will continue to live in the memories of those who were fortunate enough to witness the dynamic opener in full flight.

KANDAMBY, Thilina

Born:	June 4, 1982
Batting:	Left handed
Bowling:	Left arm off-break

One Day Internationals

ODI Career:	2004		
ODIs Played:	4		
ODI Batting			
Innings:	4	Runs:	23
Highest Score:	13	Average:	5.75
No. 50s:	0	No. 100s:	0
ODI Bowling & Fielding			
Wickets:	0	Runs:	0
Best Bowling:		Average:	0.00
5 WM:	0	Catches:	0
Stumpings:	0		

A powerful yet technically correct middle order batsman who toured Zimbabwe in 2004. A duck on debut was not the start he was looking for and struggled to impress in his further three ODI appearances.

KAPUGEDERA, Chamara Kantha

Born:	February 24, 1987
Batting:	Right handed
Bowling:	Right arm medium

Tests

Test Career:	2006		
Cap Number:	104		
Tests Played:	2		
Test Batting			
Innings:	4	Runs:	74
Highest Score:	50	Average:	18.50
No. 50s:	1	No. 100s:	0
Test Bowling & Fielding			
Wickets:	0	Runs:	0
Best Bowling:		Average:	0.00
5 WI:	0	10 WM:	0
Catches:	0	Stumpings:	0

One Day Internationals

ODI Career:	2006		
ODIs Played:	12		
ODI Batting			
Innings:	11	Runs:	154
Highest Score:	50	Average:	14.00
No. 50s:	1	No. 100s:	0
ODI Bowling & Fielding			
Wickets:	0	Runs:	0
Best Bowling:		Average:	0.00
5 WM:	0	Catches:	3
Stumpings:	0		

An opener by trade, Chamara Kapugedera batted in the middle order in both Test appearances during the 2006 tour of England. The youngster made a duck on debut but in his last innings of the tour, he struck back with a well made 50. A brilliant fielder and capable medium pacer, many are touting Kapugedera as a potential all-rounder.

KARNAIN, Shaul Hameed Uvais

Born:	August 11, 1962
Batting:	Right handed
Bowling:	Right arm medium

One Day Internationals

ODI Career:	1984-90		
ODIs Played:	19		
ODI Batting			
Innings:	17	Runs:	229
Highest Score:	41*	Average:	19.08
No. 50s:	0	No. 100s:	0
ODI Bowling & Fielding			
Wickets:	16	Runs:	505
Best Bowling:	5/26	Average:	31.56
5 WM:	1	Catches:	1
Stumpings:	0		

An all rounder who took a career best haul of 5/26 on debut against New Zealand at Moratuwa. He represented Sri Lanka in 19 ODI's over a seven year period but was unable to make in-roads into the Test arena.

KULASEKARA, Nuwan

Born:	July 22, 1982
Batting:	Right handed
Bowling:	Right arm medium-fast

Tests

Test Career:	2005-06		
Cap Number:	100		
Tests Played:	4		
Test Batting			
Innings:	7	Runs:	15
Highest Score:	64	Average:	16.42
No. 50s:	1	No. 100s:	0
Test Bowling & Fielding			
Wickets:	4	Runs:	302
Best Bowling:	2/45	Average:	75.50
5 WI:	0	10 WM:	0
Catches:	1	Stumpings:	0

One Day Internationals

ODI Career:	2003-06		
ODIs Played:	15		
ODI Batting			
Innings:	8	Runs:	19
Highest Score:	11	Average:	4.75
No. 50s:	0	No. 100s:	0
ODI Bowling & Fielding			
Wickets:	9	Runs:	459
Best Bowling:	2/19	Average:	51.00
5 WM:	0	Catches:	3
Stumpings:	0		

After impressive performances in limited overs competition, Nuwan Kulasekara got his chance at Test level when Sri Lanka faced New Zealand at Napier in 2005. He again played just the one Test during the series against Pakistan and was subsequently 'punted on' for the tour of England. But his two Test appearances on English soil did not yield any wickets.

KURUPPU, Don Sardha (Brendon)

Born: January 5, 1962
Batting: Right handed
Wicket Keeper

Tests
Test Career:	1987-91		
Cap Number:	39		
Tests Played:	4		

Test Batting
Innings:	7	Runs:	320
Highest Score:	201*	Average:	53.33
No. 50s:	0	No. 100s:	1

Test Bowling & Fielding
Wickets:	0	Runs:	0
Best Bowling:		Average:	0.00
5 WI:	0	10 WM:	0
Catches:	1	Stumpings:	0

One Day Internationals
ODI Career:	1983-90		
ODIs Played:	54		

ODI Batting
Innings:	52	Runs:	1,022
Highest Score:	72	Average:	20.03
No. 50s:	4	No. 100s:	0

ODI Bowling & Fielding
Wickets:	0	Runs:	0
Best Bowling:		Average:	0.00
5 WM:	0	Catches:	30
Stumpings:	8		

Surprised the cricketing world when he became only the third player in Test history to score a double-century on debut when he made 201 not out against New Zealand at Colombo, in 1987. It was highly likely that Kuruppu would have 'carried his bat' if not for skipper Dulip Mendis declaring the first innings closed at 9/397. With no time to rest, he donned the gloves and kept wickets as the match slowly fizzled out to a draw. Remarkably, the agile Kuruppu was to play just the four Tests as he was preferred for the shorter version of the game where he went on to play in 54 ODI's.

KURUPPUARACHCHI, Ajith Kosala

Born: November 1, 1964
Batting: Right handed
Bowling: Left arm medium-fast

Tests
Test Career:	1986-87		
Cap Number:	35		
Tests Played:	2		

Test Batting
Innings:	2	Runs:	0
Highest Score:	0*	Average:	0.00
No. 50s:	0	No. 100s:	0

Test Bowling & Fielding
Wickets:	8	Runs:	149
Best Bowling:	5/44	Average:	18.62
5 WI:	1	10 WM:	0
Catches:	0	Stumpings:	0

A left arm swing bowler who captured an impressive 5/44 on debut in 1985, and helped his country secure their first ever victory against Pakistan in Test cricket. Struck down by injury early in his career, Kuruppuarachchi was unlucky not to have played more Tests.

LABROOY, Graeme Fredrick

Born: June 7, 1964
Batting: Right handed
Bowling: Right arm medium-fast

Tests
Test Career:	1986-91		
Cap Number:	38		
Tests Played:	9		

Test Batting
Innings:	14	Runs:	158
Highest Score:	70*	Average:	14.36
No. 50s:	1	No. 100s:	0

Test Bowling & Fielding
Wickets:	27	Runs:	1,194
Best Bowling:	5/133	Average:	44.22
5 WI:	1	10 WM:	0
Catches:	3	Stumpings:	0

One Day Internationals
ODI Career:	1986-92		
ODIs Played:	44		

ODI Batting
Innings:	36	Runs:	249
Highest Score:	33	Average:	8.58
No. 50s:	0	No. 100s:	0

ODI Bowling & Fielding
Wickets:	45	Runs:	1,876
Best Bowling:	5/57	Average:	41.68
5 WM:	1	Catches:	8
Stumpings:	0		

A determined medium-fast swing bowler. He made his Test debut against India at Kanpur in 1986/87 and remarkably played all of his nine Tests outside of Sri Lanka.

LIYANAGE, Dulip Kapila

Born: June 6, 1972
Batting: Left handed
Bowling: Right arm medium-fast

Tests
Test Career:	1992-01		
Cap Number:	53		
Tests Played:	9		

Test Batting
Innings:	9	Runs:	69
Highest Score:	23	Average:	7.66
No. 50s:	0	No. 100s:	0

Test Bowling & Fielding
Wickets:	17	Runs:	666
Best Bowling:	4/56	Average:	39.17
5 WI:	0	10 WM:	0
Catches:	0	Stumpings:	0

One Day Internationals
ODI Career:	1992-01		
ODIs Played:	16		

ODI Batting
Innings:	11	Runs:	144
Highest Score:	43	Average:	16.00
No. 50s:	0	No. 100s:	0

ODI Bowling & Fielding
Wickets:	10	Runs:	510
Best Bowling:	3/49	Average:	51.00
5 WM:	0	Catches:	6
Stumpings:	0		

A right arm fast-medium pacer who opened the bowling on debut against Australia at Colombo in 1992. Liyanage was immediately in the spotlight taking a wicket with his third ball and finishing with 3/66 from 30 overs. But injuries took their toll shortly afterwards as the promising youngster did not reach double figures in Test appearances.

LOKUARACHCHI, Kaushal Samaraweera

Born: May 20, 1982
Batting: Right handed
Bowling: Right arm leg-break

Tests
Test Career: 2003-04
Cap Number: 94
Tests Played: 4

Test Batting
Innings:	5	Runs:	94
Highest Score:	28*	Average:	23.50
No. 50s:	0	No. 100s:	0

Test Bowling & Fielding
Wickets:	5	Runs:	295
Best Bowling:	2/47	Average:	59.00
5 WI:	0	10 WM:	0
Catches:	1	Stumpings:	0

One Day Internationals
ODI Career: 2003-06
ODIs Played: 16

ODI Batting
Innings:	13	Runs:	174
Highest Score:	69	Average:	15.81
No. 50s:	0	No. 100s:	0

ODI Bowling & Fielding
Wickets:	21	Runs:	539
Best Bowling:	3/37	Average:	25.66
5 WM:	0	Catches:	3
Stumpings:	0		

A right arm leg-spinner who was also a competant lower order batsman, Lokuarachchi played just four Tests between 2003/04 but is still in regular consideration for ODI selection.

LOKUHETTIGE, Dilhara

Born: July 3, 1980
Batting: Right handed
Bowling: Right arm medium-fast

One Day Internationals
ODI Career: 2005
ODIs Played: 8

ODI Batting
Innings:	8	Runs:	77
Highest Score:	29	Average:	9.60
No. 50s:	0	No. 100s:	0

ODI Bowling & Fielding
Wickets:	6	Runs:	221
Best Bowling:	2/30	Average:	36.83
5 WM:	0	Catches:	3
Stumpings:	0		

A dashing all rounder who can swing the ball either way, Dilhara Lokuhettige was a surprise selection in his ODI debut against India at Dambulla in 2005. He was a major contributor in Sri Lanka's three wicket victory by capturing two early wickets and scoring a handy 21 coming in at number seven. His form tapered off slightly thereafter and now in his mid 20's, he has shown enough to still press for future selection.

MADUGALLE, Ranjan Senerath

Born: April 22, 1959
Batting: Right handed
Bowling: Right arm off-break

Tests
Test Career: 1982-88
Cap Number: 7
Tests Played: 21

Test Batting
Innings:	39	Runs:	1,029
Highest Score:	103	Average:	29.39
No. 50s:	7	No. 100s:	1

Test Bowling & Fielding
Wickets:	0	Runs:	38
Best Bowling:		Average:	0.00
5 WI:	0	10 WM:	0
Catches:	9	Stumpings:	0

One Day Internationals
ODI Career: 1979-88
ODIs Played: 63

ODI Batting
Innings:	56	Runs:	950
Highest Score:	73	Average:	18.62
No. 50s:	3	No. 100s:	0

ODI Bowling & Fielding
Wickets:	0	Runs:	1
Best Bowling:	0/1	Average:	0.00
5 WM:	0	Catches:	18
Stumpings:	0		

An elegant right-hand batsman from Kandy, he made his international debut against India, during the 1979 World Cup in England and then made his Test debut in Sri Lanka's inaugural Test against England in 1982, where he top scored with a patient 65. Scored seven 50's and made his sole Test century against India in 1985/86. Since retiring he headed of ICC's panel of match referees.

MADURASINGHE, Ranjith

Born: January 30, 1961
Batting: Left handed
Bowling: Right arm off-break

Tests
Test Career: 1988-92
Cap Number: 41
Tests Played: 3

Test Batting
Innings:	6	Runs:	24
Highest Score:	11	Average:	4.79
No. 50s:	0	No. 100s:	0

Test Bowling & Fielding
Wickets:	3	Runs:	172
Best Bowling:	3/60	Average:	57.33
5 WI:	0	10 WM:	0
Catches:	0	Stumpings:	0

One Day Internationals
ODI Career: 1988-92
ODIs Played: 12

A tallish off-spinner from Kurunegala, Madurasinghe made an uneventful debut against England at Lord's in 1988. He took his best figures of 3/60 in his second Test against India but managed just the one further Test, against Australia at Colombo, some four years later.

MAHANAMA, Roshan Siriwardene

Born: May 31, 1966
Batting: Right handed

Tests
Test Career: 1986-98
Cap Number: 36
Tests Played: 52

Test Batting
Innings:	89	Runs:	2,576
Highest Score:	225	Average:	29.27
No. 50s:	11	No. 100s:	4

Test Bowling & Fielding
Wickets:	0	Runs:	30
Best Bowling:	0/30	Average:	0.00
5 WI:	0	10 WM:	0
Catches:	56	Stumpings:	0

One Day Internationals
ODI Career: 1986-99
ODIs Played: 213

ODI Batting
Innings:	198	Runs:	5,162
Highest Score:	119*	Average:	29.49
No. 50s:	35	No. 100s:	4

ODI Bowling & Fielding
Wickets:	0	Runs:	7
Best Bowling:	0/7	Average:	0.00
5 WM:	0	Catches:	109
Stumpings:	0		

A quality fielder and stylish batsman who performed solidly over his 12 year career. His highest score of 225 was made in remarkable circumstances when, in 1997, he and dashing opener Sanath Jayasuriya put on 576 for the second wicket - thus setting a new record for the highest partnership in Test history. Mahanama also played over 200 ODI's for his country and was a member of the World Cup-winning squad in 1996.

MAHAROOF, Mohamed Farveez

Born: September 7, 1984
Batting: Right handed
Bowling: Right arm medium-fast

Tests
Test Career: 2004-06
Cap Number: 98
Tests Played: 13

Test Batting
Innings:	21	Runs:	364
Highest Score:	72	Average:	20.22
No. 50s:	2	No. 100s:	0

Test Bowling & Fielding
Wickets:	16	Runs:	910
Best Bowling:	4/52	Average:	56.87
5 WI:	0	10 WM:	0
Catches:	4	Stumpings:	0

One Day Internationals
ODI Career: 2004-06
ODIs Played: 45

ODI Batting
Innings:	29	Runs:	404
Highest Score:	58*	Average:	20.20
No. 50s:	1	No. 100s:	0

ODI Bowling & Fielding
Wickets:	52	Runs:	1,438
Best Bowling:	4/20	Average:	27.65
5 WM:	0	Catches:	9
Stumpings:	0		

An exciting all-rounder who made his Test debut against Sri Lanka at Harare in 2004, Maharoof, who bowls at a rapid pace, performed solidly during the 2005/06 series against Pakistan and hence was selected for the 2006 tour of England. But in his three appearances, Maharoof could only capture the one wicket, which again will have the selectors contemplating his future. A competent One Day player and blessed with raw talent it would not be at all surprising if the Sri Lankan brains trust continue to persevere with Maharoof for just a little longer.

MALINGA, Separamadu Lasith

Born: August 28, 1983
Batting: Right handed
Bowling: Right arm medium-fast

Tests
Test Career: 2004-06
Cap Number: 99
Tests Played: 17

Test Batting
Innings:	22	Runs:	116
Highest Score:	26	Average:	8.28
No. 50s:	0	No. 100s:	0

Test Bowling & Fielding
Wickets:	58	Runs:	1,775
Best Bowling:	5/80	Average:	30.60
5 WI:	1	10 WM:	0
Catches:	7	Stumpings:	0

One Day Internationals
ODI Career: 2004-06
ODIs Played: 14

ODI Batting
Innings:	8	Runs:	30
Highest Score:	15	Average:	10.00
No. 50s:	0	No. 100s:	0

ODI Bowling & Fielding
Wickets:	20	Runs:	573
Best Bowling:	4/44	Average:	28.65
5 WM:	0	Catches:	1
Stumpings:	0		

Lasith Malinga made his Test debut in what could be considered non traditional circumstances. Firstly, Sri Lanka was playing Australia in June, (Winter) and secondly the match took place in Darwin's Marrara Stadium. However, despite the seemingly 'exhibition style' environment, Malinga took to the world stage like a duck to water debut by taking two wickets in the first innings - including the prize wicket of Adam Gilchrist - and then four in the second. Later that year, Malinga captured a career best 5/80 when he cleaned up the New Zealand batting line up in Napier. Considered Sri Lanka quickest bowler, Malinga was selected for 2006 tour of England and should there be moderate improvement in his line and length, Malinga should become a regular and exciting member of the Sri Lankan pace attack for many years to come.

MENDIS, Chaminda

Born: December 28, 1968
Batting: Right handed
Bowling: Right arm off-break

One Day Internationals

ODI Career: 1995
ODIs Played: 1

ODI Batting

Innings:	1	Runs:	3
Highest Score:	3*	Average:	3.00
No. 50s:	0	No. 100s:	0

ODI Bowling & Fielding

Wickets:	0	Runs:	0
Best Bowling:		Average:	0.00
5 WM:	0	Catches:	2
Stumpings:	0		

A highly respected batsman at domestic level who many thought would go on to play Test cricket. But in his sole ODI against New Zealand at Auckland in 1995 he was selected low in the order and thus didn't get much of a chance to demonstrate his true talent.

MENDIS, Louis Rohan (Duleep)

Born: August 25, 1952
Batting: Right handed
Bowling: Right arm medium
 Wicket Keeper

Tests

Test Career: 1982-88
Cap Number: 8
Tests Played: 24

Test Batting

Innings:	43	Runs:	1,329
Highest Score:	124	Average:	31.64
No. 50s:	8	No. 100s:	4

Test Bowling & Fielding

Wickets:	0	Runs:	0
Best Bowling:		Average:	0.00
5 WI:	0	10 WM:	0
Catches:	9	Stumpings:	0

One Day Internationals

ODI Career: 1975-89
ODIs Played: 79

ODI Batting

Innings:	74	Runs:	1,527
Highest Score:	80	Average:	23.49
No. 50s:	7	No. 100s:	0

ODI Bowling & Fielding

Wickets:	0	Runs:	0
Best Bowling:		Average:	0.00
5 WM:	0	Catches:	14
Stumpings:	0		

One of the true pioneers of Sri Lankan International cricket, Mendis was a solidly built and classy middle order batsman. He made his International debut in the 1975 World Cup series against the powerful West Indies at Old Trafford. When Sri Lanka were finally admitted into the Test arena, Mendis, at age 30, was part of the inaugural Test side who took on England in a one off Test series at Colombo in 1982 where he made a respectable 17 & 27. As Mendis was seen by many as the face of Sri Lankan cricket, it is often thought today that he was in fact Sri Lanka's inaugural captain. This mantle, however, belongs to Bandula Warnapura but Mendis did take over the reigns shortly afterwards when Warnapura decided to tour South Africa. Mendis went from strength to strength scoring two lots of 105 in both innings against India at Chennai in 1982/83. He had the honour of leading Sri Lanka to its first ever Test and eventually series victory against India in 1985/86. His highest score of 124 at Kandy was made during this series. In 1988 he was relieved of the captaincy when the Sri Lankan selectors decided to hand the reins to Ranjan Madugalle. A respected elder of Sri Lankan cricket, Mendis later became manager of the national team and enjoyed his country's fairy tale World Cup success while at the helm.

MIRANDO, Thilan Thushara

Born: March 1, 1981
Batting: Left handed
Bowling: Left arm medium-fast

Tests

Test Career: 2003
Cap Number: 96
Tests Played: 1

Test Batting

Innings:	2	Runs:	24
Highest Score:	13	Average:	12.00
No. 50s:	0	No. 100s:	0

Test Bowling & Fielding

Wickets:	0	Runs:	59
Best Bowling:		Average:	0.00
5 WI:	0	10 WM:	0
Catches:	0	Stumpings:	0

Thilan Mirando played his one and only Test against the West Indies at Kingston in 2003. While the left arm pace bowler was given the new ball with Chaminda Vaas, he failed to take a wicket in both innings.

MUBARAK, Jehan

Born:	January 10, 1981
Batting:	Left handed
Bowling:	Right arm off-break

Tests

Test Career:	2002-06
Cap Number:	91
Tests Played:	8

Test Batting

Innings:	14	Runs:	236
Highest Score:	48	Average:	18.15
No. 50s:	0	No. 100s:	0

Test Bowling & Fielding

Wickets:	0	Runs:	42
Best Bowling:		Average:	0.00
5 WI:	0	10 WM:	0
Catches:	10	Stumpings:	0

One Day Internationals

ODI Career:	2002-06
ODIs Played:	20

ODI Batting

Innings:	19	Runs:	315
Highest Score:	61	Average:	16.57
No. 50s:	2	No. 100s:	0

ODI Bowling & Fielding

Wickets:	1	Runs:	49
Best Bowling:	1/10	Average:	49.00
5 WM:	0	Catches:	6
Stumpings:	0		

The U.S born Mubarak made his Test debut against Bangladesh in Colombo in 2002. As an opener he has averaged just 18 in Tests and 16 in ODI's which may limit further opportunities at international level.

MUNASINGHE, Manjula Nishantha

Born:	December 10, 1971
Batting:	Right handed
Bowling:	Right arm medium-fast

One Day Internationals

ODI Career:	1994-96
ODIs Played:	5

ODI Batting

Innings:	4	Runs:	13
Highest Score:	8	Average:	4.33
No. 50s:	0	No. 100s:	0

ODI Bowling & Fielding

Wickets:	4	Runs:	146
Best Bowling:	3/30	Average:	36.50
5 WM:	0	Catches:	0
Stumpings:	0		

A medium pace bowler from Colombo, Munasinghe made his ODI debut against Australia at Sharjah in 1993/94. Took his best figures of 3/30 against the Aussies at the MCG when Sri Lanka toured 'down under' a year later.

MURALITHARAN, Muttiah

Born:	April 17, 1972
Batting:	Right handed
Bowling:	Right arm off-break

Tests

Test Career:	1992-98
Cap Number:	54
Tests Played:	106

Test Batting

Innings:	138	Runs:	1,093
Highest Score:	67	Average:	12.28
No. 50s:	1	No. 100s:	0

Test Bowling & Fielding

Wickets:	635	Runs:	14,035
Best Bowling:	9/51	Average:	22.10
5 WI:	53	10 WM:	16
Catches:	57	Stumpings:	0

One Day Internationals

ODI Career:	1993-
ODIs Played:	275

ODI Batting

Innings:	128	Runs:	456
Highest Score:	27	Average:	5.77
No. 50s:	0	No. 100s:	0

ODI Bowling & Fielding

Wickets:	416	Runs:	9,685
Best Bowling:	7/30	Average:	23.28
5 WM:	8	Catches:	111
Stumpings:	0		

The wide-eyed maestro from Sri Lanka lies second on the list of all-time Test wicket takers behind Shane Warne and given that he is younger than the sheik of tweak, who is to say the he will not one day reclaim the number one position? The deadly spinner also holds the mantle as one of the most controversial figures in the modern game with an action that has been scrutinised by fans, commentators, umpires and even scientists. In the end he has prevailed and sits as one of the games all time great bowlers. A front of the hand finger spinner who extracts devilish spin with a final flick of the wrist, controversy stems from the amount of purchase he gains when straightening his arm at delivery point. He employs a range of deliveries included a standard off spinner that turns in to the right handed batsman, another ball that straightens, and a famous 'doosra' that goes the other way. On a conducive pitch he can make the ball turn viciously, the result being a record 16 hauls of ten or more wickets in Test matches. His bowling prowess was well known when he visited England for a one-off Test in 1998 but no one could predict the manner in which he would devastate the opposition. He took seven first innings wickets to restrict England to 445 and then with the wicket deteriorating, tore through the home side with nine more second innings wickets for career best figures of 16/220. Murali the master had arrived. In 2001 he took ten wickets in four consecutive Tests and on the tour of England in 2006 led his side to an unlikely victory with two more wonderful performances at Edgbaston and Trent Bridge. The affable spinner is no less impressive in one day cricket where he goes for less than four runs an over and has taken over 400 wickets at a cost of only 23.28. He, along with former Pakistan fast bowler, Wasim Akram, are the only two bowlers to have taken over 400 wickets at both Test and ODI Level. He was a key member of the

Sri Lankan side that shocked the cricket world by winning the 1996 World Cup. The greatest challenge to Murali's career came on the tour of Australia in 1995 when he was called for throwing on seven occasions, in three overs, by local umpire Darrel Hair during the traditional Boxing Day Test at the MCG. Interestingly enough, Murali bowled a further 32 overs from umpire Steve Dunne's end without raising an eyebrow. Subsequently cleared by the ICC, he has had to live with the innuendo regarding his action ever since, but his sincere nature and openness has seen him weather the storm and earn the respect of the cricketing world. While his action may continue to be disputed, his record speaks for itself.

NAWAZ, Naveed

Born: September 20, 1973
Batting: Left handed
Bowling: Left arm leg-break

Tests

Test Career: 2002
Cap Number: 92
Tests Played: 1

Test Batting
Innings:	2	Runs:	99
Highest Score:	78*	Average:	99.00
No. 50s:	1	No. 100s:	0

Test Bowling & Fielding
Wickets:	0	Runs:	0
Best Bowling:		Average:	0.00
5 WI:	0	10 WM:	0
Catches:	0	Stumpings:	0

One Day Internationals

ODI Career: 1998-02
ODIs Played: 3

ODI Batting
Innings:	3	Runs:	31
Highest Score:	15*	Average:	15.50
No. 50s:	0	No. 100s:	0

ODI Bowling & Fielding
Wickets:	0	Runs:	0
Best Bowling:		Average:	0.00
5 WM:	0	Catches:	0
Stumpings:	0		

A right hand batsman from Colombo who played just the one Test against Bangladesh in his home town in 2002. Nawaz scored 78 not out in the second innings to give him an impressive average of 99 but it was not enough to gain another Test cap.

NISSANKA, Prabath

Born: October 25, 1980
Batting: Right handed
Bowling: Right arm medium-fast

Tests

Test Career: 2003
Cap Number: 95
Tests Played: 4

Test Batting
Innings:	5	Runs:	18
Highest Score:	12*	Average:	6.00
No. 50s:	0	No. 100s:	0

Test Bowling & Fielding
Wickets:	10	Runs:	366
Best Bowling:	5/64	Average:	36.60
5 WI:	1	10 WM:	0
Catches:	0	Stumpings:	0

One Day Internationals

ODI Career: 2001-03
ODIs Played: 23

ODI Batting
Innings:	13	Runs:	53
Highest Score:	11	Average:	6.62
No. 50s:	0	No. 100s:	0

ODI Bowling & Fielding
Wickets:	27	Runs:	857
Best Bowling:	4/12	Average:	31.74
5 WM:	0	Catches:	3
Stumpings:	0		

A right arm pace bowler from Ambalantota who made his Test debut against New Zealand at Colombo in 2003. Nissanka captured his best figures of 5/64 in his last Test appearance against the West Indies at Kingston later that year.

OPATHA, Antony Ralph Marinon (Tony)

Born: August 5, 1947
Batting: Right handed
Bowling: Right arm medium

One Day Internationals

ODI Career: 1975-79
ODIs Played: 5

ODI Batting
Innings:	3	Runs:	29
Highest Score:	18	Average:	9.66
No. 50s:	0	No. 100s:	0

ODI Bowling & Fielding
Wickets:	5	Runs:	180
Best Bowling:	3/31	Average:	36.00
5 WM:	0	Catches:	3
Stumpings:	0		

A medium pacer who made his International debut against the West Indies, at Old Trafford, during the 1975 World Cup. Played his last ODI four years later against India at the same venue.

PASQUAL, Sudath Prajiv

Born: October 15, 1961
Batting: Left handed
Bowling: Right arm medium

One Day Internationals

ODI Career: 1979
ODIs Played: 2

ODI Batting
Innings:	2	Runs:	24
Highest Score:	23*	Average:	24.00
No. 50s:	0	No. 100s:	0

ODI Bowling & Fielding
Wickets:	0	Runs:	20
Best Bowling:	0/20	Average:	0.00
5 WM:	0	Catches:	0
Stumpings:	0		

An all rounder who played two matches in India's 1979 World Cup campaign. Scored a brave 23 not out in Sri Lanka's win over India which was the first by an associate ICC member against a full ICC member which again provided further argument for Sri Lanka's push for full Test status.

PERERA, Kahawalage Gamini

Born: May 22, 1964
Batting: Right handed
Bowling: Left arm off-break

One Day Internationals
ODI Career: 1986
ODIs Played: 1
ODI Batting
Innings:	0	Runs:	0
Highest Score:	0	Average:	0.00
No. 50s:	0	No. 100s:	0

ODI Bowling & Fielding
Wickets:	0	Runs:	15
Best Bowling:		Average:	0.00
5 WM:	0	Catches:	0
Stumpings:	0		

A left arm off break bowler who played just the one ODI against Pakistan at Kandy in 1986.

PERERA, Ruchira Laksiri

Born: April 6, 1977
Batting: Left handed
Bowling: Left arm medium-fast

Tests
Test Career: 1999-02
Cap Number: 74
Tests Played: 8
Test Batting
Innings:	9	Runs:	33
Highest Score:	11*	Average:	11.00
No. 50s:	0	No. 100s:	0

Test Bowling & Fielding
Wickets:	17	Runs:	661
Best Bowling:	3/40	Average:	38.88
5 WI:	0	10 WM:	0
Catches:	2	Stumpings:	0

One Day Internationals
ODI Career: 1999-06
ODIs Played: 14
ODI Batting
Innings:	5	Runs:	8
Highest Score:	4*	Average:	2.66
No. 50s:	0	No. 100s:	0

ODI Bowling & Fielding
Wickets:	16	Runs:	613
Best Bowling:	3/23	Average:	38.31
5 WM:	0	Catches:	2
Stumpings:	0		

A left-arm fast, swing bowler who debuted against India at Colombo in 1999 where he opened the bowling with Chaminda Vaas and took just the one wicket in a rain interrupted match. But like a few of his compatriots Perera too was questioned over a suspect action. He modified his lower arm action after consulting with bio mechanics and was cleared shortly afterwards. Played just the eight Tests but was a regular in the One Day side until sustaining a shoulder injury in early 2006.

PERERA, Suresh Asanka

Born: February 16, 1978
Batting: Right handed
Bowling: Right arm medium-fast

Tests
Test Career: 1998-01
Cap Number: 73
Tests Played: 3
Test Batting
Innings:	4	Runs:	77
Highest Score:	43*	Average:	25.66
No. 50s:	0	No. 100s:	0

Test Bowling & Fielding
Wickets:	1	Runs:	180
Best Bowling:	1/104	Average:	180.00
5 WI:	0	10 WM:	0
Catches:	1	Stumpings:	0

One Day Internationals
ODI Career: 1998-01
ODIs Played: 20
ODI Batting
Innings:	13	Runs:	195
Highest Score:	56*	Average:	17.72
No. 50s:	1	No. 100s:	0

ODI Bowling & Fielding
Wickets:	13	Runs:	522
Best Bowling:	2/25	Average:	40.15
5 WM:	0	Catches:	4
Stumpings:	0		

An exciting all rounder, Suresh Perera made his Test debut against England at The Oval in 1998 where he opened the bowling with Wickramasinghe and scored a swashbuckling 43 not out. But unfortunately for the promising youngster a back injury saw him sidelined for a year just as his career was about to take off. He returned in 2001 and as he was aiming to get his career back on track, he was reported for having a suspect action. Although eventually cleared by the ICC he did not play at either Test or ODI level after 2001.

PIERIS, Hemal Sri Mevan

Born: February 16, 1946
Batting: Left handed
Bowling: Right arm medium-fast

One Day Internationals
ODI Career: 1975
ODIs Played: 3
ODI Batting
Innings:	3	Runs:	19
Highest Score:	16	Average:	9.50
No. 50s:	0	No. 100s:	0

ODI Bowling & Fielding
Wickets:	2	Runs:	135
Best Bowling:	2/68	Average:	67.50
5 WM:	0	Catches:	0
Stumpings:	0		

PRASAD, Dammika

Born:	May 30, 1983
Batting:	Right handed
Bowling:	Right arm medium-fast

One Day Internationals

ODI Career:	2006		
ODIs Played:	3		

ODI Batting

Innings:	1	Runs:	8
Highest Score:	8	Average:	8.00
No. 50s:	0	No. 100s:	0

ODI Bowling & Fielding

Wickets:	3	Runs:	116
Best Bowling:	2/29	Average:	38.66
5 WM:	0	Catches:	0
Stumpings:	0		

A plethora of wickets at domestic level earnt the 22 year old Dammika Prasad a place on the 2005/06 tour of Bangladesh. He was the only new face in the squad and made his ODI debut at Chittagong where he captured 2/29 off six overs. However he was selected for only two more ODI's. At 23, age is on his side and depending on first class form, another chance at the international level may beckon.

PUSHPAKUMARA, Ravindra

Born:	July 21, 1975
Batting:	Right handed
Bowling:	Right arm medium-fast

Tests

Test Career:	1994-01		
Cap Number:	61		
Tests Played:	23		

Test Batting

Innings:	31	Runs:	166
Highest Score:	44	Average:	8.73
No. 50s:	0	No. 100s:	0

Test Bowling & Fielding

Wickets:	58	Runs:	2,242
Best Bowling:	7/116	Average:	38.65
5 WI:	4	10 WM:	0
Catches:	10	Stumpings:	0

One Day Internationals

ODI Career:	1994-99		
ODIs Played:	31		

ODI Batting

Innings:	9	Runs:	36
Highest Score:	14*	Average:	9.00
No. 50s:	0	No. 100s:	0

ODI Bowling & Fielding

Wickets:	24	Runs:	1,181
Best Bowling:	3/25	Average:	49.20
5 WM:	0	Catches:	8
Stumpings:	0		

A pace bowler from Panadura, Ravindra Pushpakumara made his Test debut against Pakistan at Kandy, in 1994, where he took four wickets in the first innings. He teamed with Chaminda Vaas, who was also new on the scene, and arguably, for the first time in Sri Lanka's history, they had two genuine pace bowlers operating from either end. In his first year, Pushpakumara took an impressive 7/116 against Zimbabwe at Harare and seemed destined for a long and distinguished Test career. However, as has happened to other pace hopefuls on the sub continent, pitch conditions rarely suit the quicks hence Pushpakumara struggled with consistency and played 23 Tests.

RAMANAYAKE, Champaka Priyadarshana Hewage

Born:	January 8, 1965
Batting:	Right handed
Bowling:	Right arm medium-fast

Tests

Test Career:	1988-93		
Cap Number:	40		
Tests Played:	18		

Test Batting

Innings:	24	Runs:	143
Highest Score:	34*	Average:	9.53
No. 50s:	0	No. 100s:	0

Test Bowling & Fielding

Wickets:	44	Runs:	1,880
Best Bowling:	5/82	Average:	42.72
5 WI:	1	10 WM:	0
Catches:	6	Stumpings:	0

One Day Internationals

ODI Career:	1986-95		
ODIs Played:	62		

ODI Batting

Innings:	35	Runs:	210
Highest Score:	26	Average:	10.00
No. 50s:	0	No. 100s:	0

ODI Bowling & Fielding

Wickets:	68	Runs:	2,049
Best Bowling:	4/17	Average:	30.13
5 WM:	0	Catches:	11
Stumpings:	0		

A hard working medium pacer who served Sri Lanka admirably at both Test and ODI level. Not overly blessed with talent but always toiled hard and made batsmen earn every run. Captured his persnal best of 5/82 against Australia at Moratuwa.

RANASINGHE, Anura Nandana

Born:	October 13, 1956
Batting:	Right handed
Bowling:	Left arm medium

Tests

Test Career:	1982		
Cap Number:	13		
Tests Played:	2		

Test Batting

Innings:	4	Runs:	88
Highest Score:	77	Average:	22.00
No. 50s:	1	No. 100s:	0

Test Bowling & Fielding

Wickets:	1	Runs:	69
Best Bowling:	1/23	Average:	69.00
5 WI:	0	10 WM:	0
Catches:	0	Stumpings:	0

One Day Internationals

ODI Career:	1975-82		
ODIs Played:	9		

ODI Batting

Innings:	8	Runs:	153
Highest Score:	51	Average:	21.85
No. 50s:	1	No. 100s:	0

ODI Bowling & Fielding

Wickets:	2	Runs:	281
Best Bowling:	1/21	Average:	140.50
5 WM:	0	Catches:	0
Stumpings:	0		

A member of the 1975 World Cup squad who played two Tests then decided to join the rebel tour of South Africa.

RANASINGHE, Sirimewan Keerthi

Born:	July 4, 1962
Batting:	Left handed
Bowling:	Right arm medium

One Day Internationals

ODI Career:	1986		
ODIs Played:	4		

ODI Batting

Innings:	3	Runs:	55
Highest Score:	41	Average:	18.33
No. 50s:	0	No. 100s:	0

ODI Bowling & Fielding

Wickets:	3	Runs:	96
Best Bowling:	1/28	Average:	32.00
5 WM:	0	Catches:	1
Stumpings:	0		

A left handed opener who made his highest ODI score of 41 on debut against Pakistan at Kandy in 1986.

RANATUNGA, Arjuna

Born:	December 1, 1963
Batting:	Left handed
Bowling:	Right arm medium

Tests

Test Career:	1982-00		
Cap Number:	9		
Tests Played:	93		

Test Batting

Innings:	155	Runs:	5,105
Highest Score:	135*	Average:	35.69
No. 50s:	38	No. 100s:	4

Test Bowling & Fielding

Wickets:	16	Runs:	1,040
Best Bowling:	2/17	Average:	65.00
5 WI:	0	10 WM:	0
Catches:	47	Stumpings:	0

One Day Internationals

ODI Career:	1982-99		
ODIs Played:	269		

ODI Batting

Innings:	255	Runs:	7,456
Highest Score:	131*	Average:	35.84
No. 50s:	49	No. 100s:	4

ODI Bowling & Fielding

Wickets:	79	Runs:	3,757
Best Bowling:	4/14	Average:	47.55
5 WM:	0	Catches:	63
Stumpings:	0		

One of the most recognisable names and figures in Sri Lankan cricket, Arjuna Ranatunga, although controversial at times, is best remembered as the man who led Sri Lanka to their fairy-tale World Cup win against the much fancied Australians in 1996 - and to date still considered as Sri Lanka's greatest cricketing achievement. It was fitting that the lateral thinking and often 'misunderstood' captain was there at end as his unbeaten 47, together with De Silva's century saw the underdogs home. A stocky left handed batsman and clever medium pace bowler, Ranatunga burst on the scene as an 18 year old when he made his debut in Sri Lanka's inaugural Test against England at Colombo in 1982, where he scored 50 in the first innings batting at number six. Over the two decades that followed, he provided Sri Lanka with impeccable service scoring 38 fifties and four centuries at Test level and averaging just over 35 in ODI's. An icon of Sri Lankan cricket.

RANATUNGA, Dammika

Born:	October 12, 1962
Batting:	Right handed
Bowling:	Right arm off-break

Tests

Test Career:	1989		
Cap Number:	43		
Tests Played:	2		

Test Batting

Innings:	3	Runs:	87
Highest Score:	45	Average:	29.00
No. 50s:	0	No. 100s:	0

Test Bowling & Fielding

Wickets:	0	Runs:	0
Best Bowling:		Average:	0.00
5 WI:	0	10 WM:	0
Catches:	0	Stumpings:	0

One Day Internationals

ODI Career:	1990		
ODIs Played:	4		

ODI Batting

Innings:	4	Runs:	49
Highest Score:	25	Average:	12.25
No. 50s:	0	No. 100s:	0

ODI Bowling & Fielding

Wickets:	0	Runs:	0
Best Bowling:		Average:	0.00
5 WM:	0	Catches:	1
Stumpings:	0		

Part of the Ranatunga dynasty. In total, there were four brothers who played international cricket for their country - Dammika, Sanjeeva and Arjuna at Test & ODI level while Nishantha represented Sri Lanka at limited overs cricket only. The eldest brother, Dammika Ranatunga's career was short lived and somewhat modestly uneventful when compared to his much heralded brother, Arjuna. He made his Test debut against Australia at the 'Gabba in 1989 where he scored a respectable 40 when opening the innings but was overlooked after his second Test in Hobart.

RANATUNGA, Nishantha

Born:	January 22, 1966
Batting:	Right handed
Bowling:	Right arm medium-fast

One Day Internationals

ODI Career:	1993
ODIs Played:	2

ODI Batting

Innings:	1	Runs:	0
Highest Score:	0	Average:	0.00
No. 50s:	0	No. 100s:	0

ODI Bowling & Fielding

Wickets:	1	Runs:	82
Best Bowling:	1/33	Average:	82.00
5 WM:	0	Catches:	0
Stumpings:	0		

A more than capable pace bowler and younger brother of former captain and Sri Lankan batsman Arjuna, Nishantha was the only of the four brothers not to play at Test level.

RANATUNGA, Sanjeeva

Born:	April 25, 1969
Batting:	Left handed
Bowling:	Right arm off-break

Tests

Test Career:	1994-97
Cap Number:	62
Tests Played:	9

Test Batting

Innings:	17	Runs:	531
Highest Score:	118	Average:	33.18
No. 50s:	2	No. 100s:	2

Test Bowling & Fielding

Wickets:	0	Runs:	0
Best Bowling:		Average:	0.00
5 WI:	0	10 WM:	0
Catches:	2	Stumpings:	0

One Day Internationals

ODI Career:	1994-96
ODIs Played:	13

ODI Batting

Innings:	11	Runs:	253
Highest Score:	70	Average:	23.00
No. 50s:	2	No. 100s:	0

ODI Bowling & Fielding

Wickets:	0	Runs:	0
Best Bowling:		Average:	0.00
5 WM:	0	Catches:	2
Stumpings:	0		

The youngest of four brothers to represent Sri Lanka at International level, Sanjeeva Ranatunga's introduction to Test Cricket was a baptism of fire in many respects. He failed to reach double figures in both innings (against Pakistan at Kandy, 1994) but when you consider that Sri Lanka recorded their lowest ever score - 71 in the first innings, it's fair to say that Sanjeeva had quite a few mates on the day as well. But things did get better for young Sanjeeva as he went on to score two test hundreds in succesive Tests against Zimbabwe in 1994. His maiden century in the First Test at Harare, where he scored 118 (highest score) and then 100 not out at Bulawayo in the second innings of the 2nd Test. But like his two brothers, Dammika and Nishantha, Sanjeeva did not reach the dizzy heights of brother Arjuna and within three years of making his debut, his international career was over.

RATNAYAKE, Nilantha Lakshitha Kithsiri

Born:	November 22, 1968
Batting:	Left handed
Bowling:	Right arm medium-fast

One Day Internationals

ODI Career:	1989-90
ODIs Played:	2

ODI Batting

Innings:	0	Runs:	0
Highest Score:	0	Average:	0.00
No. 50s:	0	No. 100s:	0

ODI Bowling & Fielding

Wickets:	2	Runs:	98
Best Bowling:	1/39	Average:	49.00
5 WM:	0	Catches:	0
Stumpings:	0		

A pace bowler from Colombo who made his International debut against Pakistan at Sharjah in 1989.

RATNAYAKE, Rumesh Joseph

Born:	January 2, 1964
Batting:	Right handed
Bowling:	Right arm medium-fast

Tests

Test Career:	1983-92
Cap Number:	21
Tests Played:	23

Test Batting

Innings:	36	Runs:	433
Highest Score:	56	Average:	14.43
No. 50s:	2	No. 100s:	0

Test Bowling & Fielding

Wickets:	73	Runs:	2,563
Best Bowling:	6/66	Average:	35.10
5 WI:	5	10 WM:	0
Catches:	9	Stumpings:	0

One Day Internationals

ODI Career:	1982-93
ODIs Played:	70

ODI Batting

Innings:	55	Runs:	612
Highest Score:	33*	Average:	16.54
No. 50s:	0	No. 100s:	0

ODI Bowling & Fielding

Wickets:	76	Runs:	2,712
Best Bowling:	5/32	Average:	35.68
5 WM:	1	Catches:	11
Stumpings:	0		

An energetic pace bowler who made his Test debut as an 18 year old against New Zealand at Christchurch in 1983. Took a career best 6/66 against Australia at Hobart in 1990/91. A fine competitor who also played an exciting brand of limited overs cricket.

RATNAYEKE, Joseph Ravindran (Ravi)

Born: May 2, 1960
Batting: Left handed
Bowling: Right arm medium-fast

Tests
Test Career: 1982-89
Cap Number: 12
Tests Played: 22

Test Batting
Innings:	38	Runs:	807
Highest Score:	93	Average:	25.21
No. 50s:	5	No. 100s:	0

Test Bowling & Fielding
Wickets:	56	Runs:	1,972
Best Bowling:	8/83	Average:	35.21
5 WI:	4	10 WM:	0
Catches:	1	Stumpings:	0

One Day Internationals
ODI Career: 1982-90
ODIs Played: 78

ODI Batting
Innings:	69	Runs:	824
Highest Score:	50	Average:	14.98
No. 50s:	1	No. 100s:	0

ODI Bowling & Fielding
Wickets:	85	Runs:	2,866
Best Bowling:	4/23	Average:	33.71
5 WM:	0	Catches:	14
Stumpings:	0		

Sri Lanka's first recognised all-rounder, Ravi Ratnayeke was the excitement tonic that Sri Lankan cricket needed in their formative years. A wonderful swing bowler who, as a left hand batsman, could score quick runs with his aggressive and hard hitting approach. Such was his versatility and natural talent that he opened the batting at Test level. His highest score of 93 was made as an opener against India in 1985/86. However arguably his greatest moment was his 8/83, haul in 1985 when he single-handedly tore apart the cream of Pakistan batting.

SAMARASEKERA, Athula Rohitha

Born: August 5, 1961
Batting: Right handed
Bowling: Right arm medium

Tests
Test Career: 1988-91
Cap Number: 42
Tests Played: 4

Test Batting
Innings:	7	Runs:	118
Highest Score:	57	Average:	16.85
No. 50s:	1	No. 100s:	0

Test Bowling & Fielding
Wickets:	3	Runs:	104
Best Bowling:	2/38	Average:	34.66
5 WI:	0	10 WM:	0
Catches:	3	Stumpings:	0

One Day Internationals
ODI Career: 1983-94
ODIs Played: 39

ODI Batting
Innings:	39	Runs:	844
Highest Score:	76	Average:	22.81
No. 50s:	4	No. 100s:	0

ODI Bowling & Fielding
Wickets:	0	Runs:	291
Best Bowling:		Average:	0.00
5 WM:	0	Catches:	5
Stumpings:	0		

An aggressive batsman, Samarasekera was highly rated by the Sri Lankan selectors and was asked to bat at number three on his Test debut against England at Lords, in 1988. Thats where the fairy-tale ended as he was caught behind for a duck. He played just the four Tests but his natural flair earned him a spot as a regular in the one day squad. Lightning did strike twice though for Samarasekera as he was run out for a duck in his first ODI.

SAMARAWEERA, Dulip Prasanna

Born: February 12, 1972
Batting: Right handed
Bowling: Right arm off-break

Tests
Test Career: 1993-95
Cap Number: 60
Tests Played: 7

Test Batting
Innings:	14	Runs:	211
Highest Score:	42	Average:	15.07
No. 50s:	0	No. 100s:	0

Test Bowling & Fielding
Wickets:	0	Runs:	0
Best Bowling:		Average:	0.00
5 WI:	0	10 WM:	0
Catches:	5	Stumpings:	0

One Day Internationals
ODI Career: 1993-94
ODIs Played: 5

ODI Batting
Innings:	4	Runs:	91
Highest Score:	49	Average:	22.75
No. 50s:	0	No. 100s:	0

ODI Bowling & Fielding
Wickets:	0	Runs:	0
Best Bowling:		Average:	0.00
5 WM:	0	Catches:	3
Stumpings:	0		

A dour opener who made his Test debut in Sri Lanka's inaugural Test against the West Indies, at Morattuwa in 1993. The match was subsequently drawn and Samaraweera, who was a replacement, was given another chance but failed to impress in his seven Test matches.

SAMARAWEERA, Thilan Thusara

Born: September 22, 1976
Batting: Right handed
Bowling: Right arm off-break

Tests
Test Career: 2001-06
Cap Number: 86
Tests Played: 39

Test Batting			
Innings:	58	Runs:	2,089
Highest Score:	142	Average:	41.78
No. 50s:	13	No. 100s:	5
Test Bowling & Fielding			
Wickets:	14	Runs:	671
Best Bowling:	4/49	Average:	47.92
5 WI:	0	10 WM:	0
Catches:	30	Stumpings:	0

One Day Internationals

ODI Career:	1998-05		
ODIs Played:	17		
ODI Batting			
Innings:	13	Runs:	199
Highest Score:	33	Average:	16.58
No. 50s:	0	No. 100s:	0
ODI Bowling & Fielding			
Wickets:	10	Runs:	509
Best Bowling:	3/34	Average:	50.90
5 WM:	0	Catches:	3
Stumpings:	0		

The younger brother of Dulip Samaraweera, Thilan Samaraweera, like many off-spinners of his era, desperately vied for bridesmaid honours in partnering the great Murali. However a vast improvement in his batting carved Samaraweera a handy niche as a regular middle order batsman. Although he failed to impress during the 2006 tour of England, Samaraweera enjoys a healthy average of 41.78, which should be enough for the Test selectors to persevere with him for awhile longer.

SANGAKKARA, Kumar Chokshanada

Born:	October 27, 1977
Batting:	Left handed
Bowling:	Right arm off-break
	Wicket Keeper

Tests

Test Career:	2000-06		
Cap Number:	84		
Tests Played:	62		
Test Batting			
Innings:	103	Runs:	4,796
Highest Score:	287	Average:	48.93
No. 50s:	22	No. 100s:	10
Test Bowling & Fielding			
Wickets:	0	Runs:	4
Best Bowling:	0/4	Average:	0.00
5 WI:	0	10 WM:	0
Catches:	142	Stumpings:	20

One Day Internationals

ODI Career:	2000-06		
ODIs Played:	174		
ODI Batting			
Innings:	160	Runs:	4,974
Highest Score:	138*	Average:	35.78
No. 50s:	33	No. 100s:	5
ODI Bowling & Fielding			
Wickets:	0	Runs:	0
Best Bowling:		Average:	0.00
5 WM:	0	Catches:	146
Stumpings:	45		

Just when it looked like stalwart wicket-keeper Romesh Kaluwitharana would never be superseded, out of nowhere arrives an almost 'replica' in the form of Kumar Sangakkara. Soon after making his debut against South Africa at Galle in 2000, it became quite apparent that Sri Lanka would continue to enjoy the luxury of having a wicket-keeper who could bat solidly in the top order. The talented left hander clocked up four centuries in his first two years including a sensational 230 against Pakistan at Lahore in early 2002. And just to prove that it was no fluke, Sangakkara's next two triple figure efforts were also double centuries. His first, a massive 270 against Zimbabwe at Bulawayo in 2004, was followed up with 232 against South Africa at Colombo in the same year. After a trifecta of double tons, Sangakkara settled down and scored a mere 157 not out against West Indies at Kandy, in 2005. But his best was yet to come. In March 2006, he amassed 185 against Pakistan at Kandy but it was his effort with captain Mahela Jayawardene, against South Africa at Colombo that would rewrite the record books. In the 1st Test, the pair put on 624 for the second wicket, which eclipsed the previous record of 576 set by Sanath Jayasuria and Roshan Mahanama as the highest partnership in not only Sri Lankan, but Test history. During the marathon partnership, Sangakkara registered his highest score of 287 - his fourth double century.

SENANAYAKE, Charith Panduka

Born:	December 19, 1962
Batting:	Left handed
Bowling:	Right arm medium

Tests

Test Career:	1991		
Cap Number:	47		
Tests Played:	3		
Test Batting			
Innings:	5	Runs:	97
Highest Score:	64	Average:	19.39
No. 50s:	1	No. 100s:	0
Test Bowling & Fielding			
Wickets:	0	Runs:	0
Best Bowling:		Average:	0.00
5 WI:	0	10 WM:	0
Catches:	2	Stumpings:	0

One Day Internationals

ODI Career:	1990-91		
ODIs Played:	7		
ODI Batting			
Innings:	7	Runs:	120
Highest Score:	27	Average:	18.00
No. 50s:	0	No. 100s:	0
ODI Bowling & Fielding			
Wickets:	0	Runs:	0
Best Bowling:		Average:	0.00
5 WM:	0	Catches:	2
Stumpings:	0		

A left-handed opener who made his Test debut against New Zealand at Wellington in 1991. He was starved of opportunities due to Sri Lanka's plethora of talented openers at the time.

SILVA, Chamara

Born:	December 14, 1979
Batting:	Right handed
Bowling:	Right arm leg-break

One Day Internationals

ODI Career:	1999-02		
ODIs Played:	10		

ODI Batting

Innings:	8	Runs:	134
Highest Score:	55	Average:	16.75
No. 50s:	0	No. 100s:	0

ODI Bowling & Fielding

Wickets:	0	Runs:	0
Best Bowling:		Average:	0.00
5 WM:	0	Catches:	2
Stumpings:	0		

An excellent fielder and hard working right hand batsman, Silva after making his debut against Australia at Colombo in 1999, showed at various times that he had what it took to make at the elite level but could not earn a regular spot in the ODI side

SILVA, Jayantha

Born:	June 2, 1973
Batting:	Right handed
Bowling:	Left arm off-break

Tests

Test Career:	1995-98		
Cap Number:	65		
Tests Played:	7		

Test Batting

Innings:	4	Runs:	6
Highest Score:	6*	Average:	2.00
No. 50s:	0	No. 100s:	0

Test Bowling & Fielding

Wickets:	20	Runs:	647
Best Bowling:	4/16	Average:	32.35
5 WI:	0	10 WM:	0
Catches:	1	Stumpings:	0

One Day Internationals

ODI Career:	1995		
ODIs Played:	1		

ODI Batting

Innings:	1	Runs:	1
Highest Score:	1	Average:	1.00
No. 50s:	0	No. 100s:	0

ODI Bowling & Fielding

Wickets:	0	Runs:	55
Best Bowling:	0/55	Average:	0.00
5 WM:	0	Catches:	0
Stumpings:	0		

A left arm off break bowler from Kalutara who struggled against the better batsmen. Played just the seven Tests and the solitary ODI.

SILVA, Sampathwaduge Amal Rohitha (Amal)

Born:	December 12, 1960
Batting:	Left handed
Bowling:	Right arm off-break
	Wicket Keeper

Tests

Test Career:	1983-88		
Cap Number:	23		
Tests Played:	9		

Test Batting

Innings:	16	Runs:	353
Highest Score:	111	Average:	25.21
No. 50s:	0	No. 100s:	2

Test Bowling & Fielding

Wickets:	0	Runs:	0
Best Bowling:		Average:	0.00
5 WI:	0	10 WM:	0
Catches:	33	Stumpings:	1

One Day Internationals

ODI Career:	1984-85		
ODIs Played:	20		

ODI Batting

Innings:	20	Runs:	441
Highest Score:	85	Average:	22.05
No. 50s:	3	No. 100s:	0

ODI Bowling & Fielding

Wickets:	0	Runs:	0
Best Bowling:		Average:	0.00
5 WM:	0	Catches:	17
Stumpings:	3		

The preferred keeper in his day because of his ability with the bat, Amal Silva did, like many dual purpose keepers, struggle to juggle the roles. He was asked to open the batting and was eventually was replaced by de Alwis in the three Tests against New Zealand. He reclaimed his spot in 1984 against England, after De Alwis became injured. His batting continued to flourish scoring two Test centuries including a highest score of 111 against India which was a major contribution towards Sri Lanka's inaugural Test match victory.

TENNEKOON, Anura Punchi Banda

Born:	October 29, 1946
Batting:	Right handed
Bowling:	Left arm off-break

One Day Internationals

ODI Career:	1975-79		
ODIs Played:	4		

ODI Batting

Innings:	4	Runs:	137
Highest Score:	59	Average:	34.25
No. 50s:	0	No. 100s:	0

ODI Bowling & Fielding

Wickets:	0	Runs:	0
Best Bowling:		Average:	0.00
5 WM:	0	Catches:	3
Stumpings:	0		

A classy right hand batsman who captained Sri Lanka during their inaugural World Cup campaign in 1975 and then again in 1979, but was injured for Sri Lanka's last match of the tournament. He was one of the very few in the early days who showed some form of resistance to the world's best bowlers. He is rated by many as Sri Lanka's best ever batsman to have never played Test cricket. Tennekoon became CEO of the Sri Lankan cricket board.

THARANGA, Warushavithana Upul
Born: February 2, 1985
Batting: Left handed
Wicket Keeper

Tests
Test Career:	2005-06		
Cap Number:	103		
Tests Played:	8		

Test Batting
Innings:	16	Runs:	582
Highest Score:	165	Average:	38.80
No. 50s:	3	No. 100s:	1

Test Bowling & Fielding
Wickets:	0	Runs:	0
Best Bowling:		Average:	0.00
5 WI:	0	10 WM:	0
Catches:	9	Stumpings:	0

One Day Internationals
ODI Career:	2005-06		
ODIs Played:	28		

ODI Batting
Innings:	27	Runs:	946
Highest Score:	120	Average:	35.03
No. 50s:	3	No. 100s:	4

ODI Bowling & Fielding
Wickets:	0	Runs:	0
Best Bowling:		Average:	0.00
5 WM:	0	Catches:	6
Stumpings:	0		

A wicket-keeper/batsman from Balapitiya who made his Test debut as an opener against India at Ahmedabad in 2005. After a stellar series against Bangladesh where he averaged 99, Tharanga struggled in the following home series against Pakistan, in early 2006, and also on the tour of England where he averaged in the low 20's. He has not had a chance to show his wares with the gloves due to Sangkkarra's presence.

TILLAKARATNE, Hashan Prasantha
Born: July 14, 1967
Batting: Left handed
Bowling: Right arm off-break
Wicket Keeper

Tests
Test Career:	1989-04		
Cap Number:	45		
Tests Played:	83		

Test Batting
Innings:	131	Runs:	4,545
Highest Score:	204*	Average:	42.87
No. 50s:	20	No. 100s:	11

Test Bowling & Fielding
Wickets:	0	Runs:	25
Best Bowling:	0/25	Average:	0.00
5 WI:	0	10 WM:	0
Catches:	122	Stumpings:	2

One Day Internationals
ODI Career:	1986-03		
ODIs Played:	200		

ODI Batting
Innings:	168	Runs:	3,789
Highest Score:	104	Average:	29.60
No. 50s:	13	No. 100s:	2

ODI Bowling & Fielding
Wickets:	6	Runs:	141
Best Bowling:	1/3	Average:	23.50
5 WM:	0	Catches:	89
Stumpings:	6		

A run machine in both Tests and Limited Over cricket, Hashan Tillakaratne got his chance at Test level when he replaced the injured Gamini Wickremasinghe in the Second Test against Australia, at Hobart, in 1989. He took five catches and became the preferred keeper because of his, supposedly, superior batting - which seemed a bit ironic at the time considering he made a duck and six on debut. He eventually vindicated the selectors decision and became a key component of the Sri Lankan batting line up for years to come scoring 11 centuries, including a highest score of 204 not out against West Indies at Colombo in 1991, 20 fifties and boasting a Test average just under 43. In 1994, he was asked to hand over the gloves and concentrate solely on his batting, which he did for around five years until being dropped in 1999. He returned to the national side shortly afterwards and was eventually named captain in 2003. However, Tillakaratne struggled with the captaincy and resigned from the post after ten matches but continued to serve his country with some fine batting displays for the remaining 12 months of his career.

TISSERA, Michael Hugh
Born: March 23, 1939
Batting: Right handed
Bowling: Right arm leg-break

One Day Internationals
ODI Career:	1975		
ODIs Played:	3		

ODI Batting
Innings:	3	Runs:	78
Highest Score:	52	Average:	26.00
No. 50s:	1	No. 100s:	0

ODI Bowling & Fielding
Wickets:	0	Runs:	0
Best Bowling:		Average:	0.00
5 WM:	0	Catches:	0
Stumpings:	0		

A member of Sri Lanka's inaugural World Cup squad of 1975. Bating at number six, Tissera scored 52 (his highest score) against Ian Chappell's Australians.

UPASHANTHA, Eric Amila
Born: June 10, 1972
Batting: Right handed
Bowling: Right arm medium-fast

Tests
Test Career:	1999-02		
Cap Number:	75		
Tests Played:	2		

Test Batting			
Innings:	3	Runs:	10
Highest Score:	63	Average:	3.33
No. 50s:	0	No. 100s:	0
Test Bowling & Fielding			
Wickets:	4	Runs:	200
Best Bowling:	2/41	Average:	50.00
5 WI:	0	10 WM:	0
Catches:	0	Stumpings:	0
One Day Internationals			
ODI Career:	1995-01		
ODIs Played:	12		
ODI Batting			
Innings:	8	Runs:	49
Highest Score:	15	Average:	7.00
No. 50s:	0	No. 100s:	0
ODI Bowling & Fielding			
Wickets:	12	Runs:	481
Best Bowling:	4/37	Average:	40.08
5 WM:	0	Catches:	2
Stumpings:	0		

A right arm fast bowler from Kurunegala who played his first ODI some four years prior to breaking into the Test side against India at Colombo in 1999. But he could rarely string together enough solid performances to become a Test regular.

VAAS, Chaminda

Born: January 27, 1974
Batting: Left handed
Bowling: Left arm medium-fast

Tests

Test Career:	1994-06		
Cap Number:	63		
Tests Played:	93		
Test Batting			
Innings:	134	Runs:	2,435
Highest Score:	74*	Average:	22.54
No. 50s:	10	No. 100s:	0
Test Bowling & Fielding			
Wickets:	306	Runs:	8,938
Best Bowling:	7/71	Average:	29.20
5 WI:	11	10 WM:	2
Catches:	28	Stumpings:	0
One Day Internationals			
ODI Career:	1994-06		
ODIs Played:	280		
ODI Batting			
Innings:	194	Runs:	1,814
Highest Score:	50*	Average:	13.74
No. 50s:	1	No. 100s:	0
ODI Bowling & Fielding			
Wickets:	354	Runs:	9,694
Best Bowling:	8/19	Average:	27.38
5 WM:	4	Catches:	55
Stumpings:	0		

Although he didn't set the world alight on debut when he returned figures of 0/80 against Pakistan at Kandy, in 1994, Chaminda Vaas has gone on to become Sri Lanka's premier pace bowler in their short history to date. A lion hearted performer, Vaas continually leads from the front, as far as determination and work ethic is concerned, and is only headed by Muralitharan as Sri Lanka's chief Test wicket taker. A 'thinking' swing bowler and only the second Sri Lankan bowler to reach triple figures, Vaas has taken five wickets in an innings on eleven occasions with his most memorable performance occurring in 2001, at Colombo, where he single-handedly bowled Sri Lanka to victory against the West Indies. In what was described as the best bowling performance by a Sri Lankan pace bowler, Vaas took a career best 7/120 in the first innings, but beat his own 'p.b' with 7/71 in the second and thus finished with 14/191 for the match. While his match-winning feat is unprecedented in Sri Lankan cricket, it took a double century and century from Brian Lara to convince the judges to split the 'Man of the Match' award between the pair. Just as in Tests, Vaas is also Sri Lanka's second highest wicket taker at ODI level - again sitting behind Murali. His 8/19, against Zimbabwe at Colombo in 2001 - which included a hat-trick with his first three balls - is the best bowling performance by a Sri Lankan in One Day competition. A more than capable late order batsman, Vass has chimed in with some important cameos when the side has been on the ropes. To date Vaas has ten Test 50's.

VANDORT, Michael Graydon

Born: January 19, 1980
Batting: Left handed
Bowling: Right arm medium

Tests

Test Career:	2001-06		
Cap Number:	87		
Tests Played:	6		
Test Batting			
Innings:	11	Runs:	461
Highest Score:	140	Average:	51.22
No. 50s:	2	No. 100s:	2
Test Bowling & Fielding			
Wickets:	0	Runs:	0
Best Bowling:		Average:	0.00
5 WI:	0	10 WM:	0
Catches:	0	Stumpings:	0
One Day Internationals			
ODI Career:	2006		
ODIs Played:	1		
ODI Batting			
Innings:	1	Runs:	48
Highest Score:	48	Average:	48.00
No. 50s:	0	No. 100s:	0
ODI Bowling & Fielding			
Wickets:	0	Runs:	0
Best Bowling:		Average:	0.00
5 WM:	0	Catches:	0
Stumpings:	0		

Michael Vandort made a respectable 36 on debut against Bangladesh at Colombo in 2001 and then followed up with a century in his second Test. From then on the tall, left handed opener batsman struggled for regular Test selection but has reemerged as a possible candidate due to the pending retirement of Sanath Jayasuriya.

VONHAGT, Dudley Marlon
Born: March 31, 1965
Batting: Right handed
Bowling: Right arm medium

One Day Internationals
ODI Career: 1985
ODIs Played: 1

ODI Batting
Innings:	1	Runs:	8
Highest Score:	8	Average:	8.00
No. 50s:	0	No. 100s:	0

ODI Bowling & Fielding
Wickets:	0	Runs:	0
Best Bowling:		Average:	0.00
5 WM:	0	Catches:	0
Stumpings:	0		

A right-hand opener who played just the one ODI against Australia at the WACA, Perth, in 1985.

WARNAPURA, Bandula
Born: March 1, 1953
Batting: Right handed
Bowling: Right arm medium

Tests
Test Career: 1982
Cap Number: 10
Tests Played: 4

Test Batting
Innings:	8	Runs:	96
Highest Score:	38	Average:	12.00
No. 50s:	0	No. 100s:	0

Test Bowling & Fielding
Wickets:	0	Runs:	46
Best Bowling:		Average:	0.00
5 WI:	0	10 WM:	0
Catches:	2	Stumpings:	0

One Day Internationals
ODI Career: 1975-82
ODIs Played: 12

ODI Batting
Innings:	12	Runs:	180
Highest Score:	77	Average:	15.00
No. 50s:	1	No. 100s:	0

ODI Bowling & Fielding
Wickets:	8	Runs:	316
Best Bowling:	3/42	Average:	39.50
5 WM:	0	Catches:	5
Stumpings:	0		

Sri Lanka's inaugural Test captain, Warnapura opened the batting for his country in their maiden Test against England, at Colombo in 1982. Although he didn't reach double figures in the first innings, he followed up with a gutsy 38 in the second. This was to remain his highest score in the four Tests he was to play. Although he had performed admirably as captain in trying conditions, he decided to join the rebel tour of South Africa in 1982-83, and thus was suspended from playing for his country ever again.

WARNAWEERA, Jayananda
Born: November 23, 1960
Batting: Left handed
Bowling: Right arm off-break

Tests
Test Career: 1986-94
Cap Number: 33
Tests Played: 10

Test Batting
Innings:	12	Runs:	39
Highest Score:	20	Average:	4.33
No. 50s:	0	No. 100s:	0

Test Bowling & Fielding
Wickets:	32	Runs:	1,021
Best Bowling:	4/25	Average:	31.90
5 WI:	0	10 WM:	0
Catches:	0	Stumpings:	0

One Day Internationals
ODI Career: 1990-93
ODIs Played: 6

ODI Batting
Innings:	3	Runs:	1
Highest Score:	1*	Average:	1.00
No. 50s:	0	No. 100s:	0

ODI Bowling & Fielding
Wickets:	6	Runs:	200
Best Bowling:	2/24	Average:	33.33
5 WM:	0	Catches:	2
Stumpings:	0		

An quickish off-spinner whose suspect action eventually saw him sanctioned from international cricket. Warnaweera made his Test debut against Pakistan, at Kandy in 1986.

WEERAKKODY, Ajith Priyantha
Born: October 1, 1970
Batting: Right handed
Bowling: Right arm medium-fast

One Day Internationals
ODI Career: 1994
ODIs Played: 1

ODI Batting
Innings:	1	Runs:	2
Highest Score:	2	Average:	2.00
No. 50s:	0	No. 100s:	0

ODI Bowling & Fielding
Wickets:	0	Runs:	41
Best Bowling:	0/41	Average:	0.00
5 WM:	0	Catches:	0
Stumpings:	0		

A fast bowler who was used for just 6 overs in his only ODI against New Zealand at Sharjah.

WEERARATNE, Kaushalya
Born: January 29, 1981
Batting: Left handed
Bowling: Right arm medium-fast

One Day Internationals
ODI Career: 2000-03
ODIs Played: 11

ODI Batting
Innings:	5	Runs:	41
Highest Score:	14*	Average:	10.25
No. 50s:	0	No. 100s:	0

ODI Bowling & Fielding			
Wickets:	6	Runs:	302
Best Bowling:	3/46	Average:	50.33
5 WM:	0	Catches:	1
Stumpings:	0		

Heavily touted as a great all rounder in the making, Weeraratne failed to make the impact that many were looking for once on the international arena, even though he took a personal best of 3/46. A pace bowler and clean hitting batsman, Weeraratne made headlines in late 2005 when playing for domestic side Ragama, he scored the fastest fifty in first class cricket notching up his half century in just 12 balls. He beat the previous record held by Adam Holioake by three balls, thus sending a clear message to selectors that he hadn't given up hope of breaking back into the national side.

WEERASINGHE, Colombage Don Udesh Sanjeewa

Born:	March 1, 1968
Batting:	Right handed
Bowling:	Right arm slow

Tests

Test Career:	1985		
Cap Number:	30		
Tests Played:	1		

Test Batting

Innings:	1	Runs:	3
Highest Score:	3	Average:	3.00
No. 50s:	0	No. 100s:	0

Test Bowling & Fielding

Wickets:	0	Runs:	36
Best Bowling:	0/36	Average:	0.00
5 WI:	0	10 WM:	0
Catches:	0	Stumpings:	0

A leg spiner from Colombo who took 0/36 in his one Test against India, in 1985.

WETTIMUNY, Mithra de Silva

Born:	June 11, 1951
Batting:	Right handed

Tests

Test Career:	1983
Cap Number:	22
Tests Played:	2

Test Batting

Innings:	4	Runs:	28
Highest Score:	17	Average:	7.00
No. 50s:	0	No. 100s:	0

Test Bowling & Fielding

Wickets:	0	Runs:	0
Best Bowling:		Average:	0.00
5 WI:	0	10 WM:	0
Catches:	2	Stumpings:	0

One Day Internationals

ODI Career:	1983
ODIs Played:	1

ODI Batting

Innings:	1	Runs:	2
Highest Score:	2	Average:	2.00
No. 50s:	0	No. 100s:	0

ODI Bowling & Fielding			
Wickets:	0	Runs:	0
Best Bowling:		Average:	0.00
5 WM:	0	Catches:	0
Stumpings:	0		

A right-handed batsman who opened the innings with younger brother Sidath, against New Zealand in 1983. It was only the third time in history that such an event occured.

WETTIMUNY, Sidath

Born:	August 12, 1956
Batting:	Right handed
Bowling:	Right arm medium

Tests

Test Career:	1982-87
Cap Number:	11
Tests Played:	23

Test Batting

Innings:	43	Runs:	1,221
Highest Score:	190	Average:	29.07
No. 50s:	6	No. 100s:	2

Test Bowling & Fielding

Wickets:	0	Runs:	37
Best Bowling:	0/37	Average:	0.00
5 WI:	0	10 WM:	0
Catches:	10	Stumpings:	0

One Day Internationals

ODI Career:	1982-87
ODIs Played:	35

ODI Batting

Innings:	33	Runs:	786
Highest Score:	86*	Average:	24.56
No. 50s:	4	No. 100s:	0

ODI Bowling & Fielding

Wickets:	1	Runs:	70
Best Bowling:	1/13	Average:	70.00
5 WM:	0	Catches:	3
Stumpings:	0		

Sidath Wettimuny opened the batting with captain Bandula Warnapura in Sri Lanka's inaugural Test, against England at Colombo, in 1982. Although he didn't reach double figures in either innings, he went on to establish himself as a dour and respected batsman throughout his career. His first Test century was memorable for reasons other than just the personal milestone. His 157 against Pakistan at Faisalabad, on Sri Lanka's maiden tour, was the first century, at Test level, by a Sri Lankan player. His highest score of 190 was made against England at Lord's in 1984. Wettimuny was also responsible for another 'first' in Sri Lankan cricket when he carried his bat, 63 not out, against New Zealand at Christchurch in 1982/83. And for the trivia minded he was also the first Sri Lankan to open the batting with his brother, Mithra, in two Tests in 1983.

WICKRAMARATNE, Hemantha

Born:	February 21, 1971
Batting:	Left handed
Bowling:	Left arm leg-break
	Wicket Keeper

One Day Internationals

ODI Career:	1993		
ODIs Played:	3		

ODI Batting

Innings:	2	Runs:	4
Highest Score:	3	Average:	2.00
No. 50s:	0	No. 100s:	0

ODI Bowling & Fielding

Wickets:	0	Runs:	0
Best Bowling:		Average:	0.00
5 WM:	0	Catches:	0
Stumpings:	0		

Although a keeper by trade, Wickramaratne never got much of a chance to show off his wares during his short ODI career.

WICKRAMASINGHE, Pramodya

Born:	August 14, 1971
Batting:	Right handed
Bowling:	Right arm fast

Tests

Test Career:	1991-01		
Cap Number:	51		
Tests Played:	40		

Test Batting

Innings:	64	Runs:	555
Highest Score:	51	Average:	9.40
No. 50s:	1	No. 100s:	0

Test Bowling & Fielding

Wickets:	85	Runs:	3,559
Best Bowling:	6/60	Average:	41.87
5 WI:	3	10 WM:	0
Catches:	18	Stumpings:	0

One Day Internationals

ODI Career:	1990-02		
ODIs Played:	134		

ODI Batting

Innings:	64	Runs:	344
Highest Score:	32	Average:	8.59
No. 50s:	0	No. 100s:	0

ODI Bowling & Fielding

Wickets:	109	Runs:	4,321
Best Bowling:	4/48	Average:	39.64
5 WM:	0	Catches:	26
Stumpings:	0		

A medium pacer who bowled with a great deal of accuracy, Wickramasinghe was a consistant performer for Sri Lanka in both Tests and ODI for just over a decade. Captured five wickets in an innings on three occasions at Test level, twice against Pakistan and his best haul of 6/60 was against Zimbabwe at Bulawayo, in 1999.

WICKREMASINGHE, Gamini Dayantha

Born:	December 27, 1965
Batting:	Right handed
Bowling:	Right arm fast
	Wicket Keeper

Tests

Test Career:	1989-92		
Cap Number:	44		
Tests Played:	3		

Test Batting

Innings:	3	Runs:	17
Highest Score:	13*	Average:	8.50
No. 50s:	0	No. 100s:	0

Test Bowling & Fielding

Wickets:	0	Runs:	0
Best Bowling:		Average:	0.00
5 WI:	0	10 WM:	0
Catches:	9	Stumpings:	1

One Day Internationals

ODI Career:	1992-93		
ODIs Played:	4		

ODI Batting

Innings:	1	Runs:	2
Highest Score:	2	Average:	2.00
No. 50s:	0	No. 100s:	0

ODI Bowling & Fielding

Wickets:	0	Runs:	0
Best Bowling:		Average:	0.00
5 WM:	0	Catches:	2
Stumpings:	4		

Gamini Wickremasinghe's record of three Tests and four ODI's does not accurately reflect his true talent. After making his debut against Australia, at the 'Gabba, in 1989, the talented keeper was injured for the Second Test and subsequently replaced by Tillekeratne. From then on the selectors favoured Tilekeratne who went from 'caretaker' to first choice almost overnight, mainly because of his superior batting. It was almost four years later when Wickremasinghe was called for international duties when Sri Lanka took on New Zealand in 1992/93. During the series, he provided a polished display behind the stumps but it was not enough for him to regain the number one mantle - even though he was rated by many as the best gloveman in the country at the time.

WIJEGUNAWARDENE, Kapila

Born:	November 23, 1964
Batting:	Right handed
Bowling:	Right arm medium-fast

Tests

Test Career:	1991-92		
Cap Number:	50		
Tests Played:	2		

Test Batting

Innings:	4	Runs:	14
Highest Score:	6*	Average:	4.66
No. 50s:	0	No. 100s:	0

Test Bowling & Fielding

Wickets:	7	Runs:	147
Best Bowling:	4/51	Average:	21.00
5 WI:	0	10 WM:	0
Catches:	0	Stumpings:	0

One Day Internationals

ODI Career:	1988-92		
ODIs Played:	26		

ODI Batting

Innings:	12	Runs:	20
Highest Score:	8*	Average:	2.85
No. 50s:	0	No. 100s:	0

ODI Bowling & Fielding

Wickets:	25	Runs:	896
Best Bowling:	4/49	Average:	39.44
5 WM:	0	Catches:	3
Stumpings:	0		

A medium pace bowler who made his Test debut against England at Lord's and captured a career best of 4/51 against Pakistan at Faisalabad in 1991. Wijegunawardene fared better in the shorter version of the game than in Tests and was probably pigeon holed as an ODI specialist by the Sri Lankan selectors.

WIJEKOON, Gayan

Born:	December 21, 1976
Batting:	Left handed
Bowling:	Left arm medium

Tests

Test Career:	2005
Cap Number:	102
Tests Played:	2

Test Batting

Innings:	3	Runs:	38
Highest Score:	14	Average:	12.66
No. 50s:	0	No. 100s:	0

Test Bowling & Fielding

Wickets:	2	Runs:	66
Best Bowling:	2/49	Average:	33.00
5 WI:	0	10 WM:	0
Catches:	0	Stumpings:	0

A left arm medium pacer who played two Tests against West Indies in 2005.

WIJESURIYA, Roger Gerard Christopher

Born:	February 18, 1960
Batting:	Right handed
Bowling:	Left arm leg-break

Tests

Test Career:	1982
Cap Number:	15
Tests Played:	4

Test Batting

Innings:	7	Runs:	22
Highest Score:	8	Average:	4.40
No. 50s:	0	No. 100s:	0

Test Bowling & Fielding

Wickets:	1	Runs:	294
Best Bowling:	1/68	Average:	294.00
5 WI:	0	10 WM:	0
Catches:	1	Stumpings:	0

One Day Internationals

ODI Career:	1982
ODIs Played:	8

ODI Batting

Innings:	3	Runs:	18
Highest Score:	12*	Average:	18.00
No. 50s:	0	No. 100s:	0

ODI Bowling & Fielding

Wickets:	8	Runs:	287
Best Bowling:	2/25	Average:	35.87
5 WM:	0	Catches:	2
Stumpings:	0		

A left arm leg break bowler from Moratuwa who made very little impact in his four Tests. Made his debut against Pakistan at Lahore in 1982.

WIJETUNGE, Piyal Kashyapa

Born:	August 6, 1971
Batting:	Right handed
Bowling:	Left arm off-break

Tests

Test Career:	1993
Cap Number:	58
Tests Played:	1

Test Batting

Innings:	2	Runs:	10
Highest Score:	10	Average:	5.00
No. 50s:	0	No. 100s:	0

Test Bowling & Fielding

Wickets:	2	Runs:	118
Best Bowling:	1/58	Average:	59.00
5 WI:	0	10 WM:	0
Catches:	0	Stumpings:	0

A left arm orthodox bowler from Kandy who played his one and only Test against South Africa at Moratuwa in 1993.

ZOYSA, Demuni Nuwan Tharanga

Born:	May 13, 1978
Batting:	Left handed
Bowling:	Left arm medium-fast

Tests

Test Career:	1997-04
Cap Number:	66
Tests Played:	30

Test Batting

Innings:	40	Runs:	288
Highest Score:	28*	Average:	8.47
No. 50s:	0	No. 100s:	0

Test Bowling & Fielding

Wickets:	64	Runs:	2,157
Best Bowling:	5/20	Average:	33.70
5 WI:	1	10 WM:	0
Catches:	4	Stumpings:	0

One Day Internationals

ODI Career:	1997-05
ODIs Played:	94

ODI Batting

Innings:	47	Runs:	343
Highest Score:	47*	Average:	13.19
No. 50s:	0	No. 100s:	0

ODI Bowling & Fielding

Wickets:	108	Runs:	3,213
Best Bowling:	5/26	Average:	29.75
5 WM:	1	Catches:	13
Stumpings:	0		

A promising left arm seamer, Nuwan Zoysa was riddled with injuries for the best part of his career. Zoysa took a hat-trick against Zimbabwe at Harare in 1999 and five years later took a career best 5/20 also against Zimbabwe at the same venue. He was also an accomplished one day player and a serviceable late order batsman.

West Indies

ACHONG, Ellis Edgar (Puss)
Born: February 16, 1904
Origin: Trinidad
Batting: Left handed
Bowling: Left arm slow

Tests
Test Career: 1930-35
Cap Number: 22
Tests Played: 6

Test Batting
Innings:	11	Runs:	81
Highest Score:	22	Average:	8.10
No. 50s:	0	No. 100s:	0

Test Bowling & Fielding
Wickets:	8	Runs:	378
Best Bowling:	2/64	Average:	47.25
5 WI:	0	10 WM:	0
Catches:	6	Stumpings:	0

A ball bowled by a left-arm slow bowler that turns into the right-hand batsman, (in other words a left-arm leg-spinner) is referred to as a 'chinaman'. It is reported that the term left arm "chinaman" originated after Achong, a left arm leg break bowler, had dismissed England's Walter Robbins at Old Trafford in 1933. It is rumoured that as Robbins walked back to pavilion he said to umpire Joe Hardstaff Snr, "Fancy being done by a bloody chinaman". Achong was of Chinese extraction. He became a Test umpire after retiring form Test cricket.

ADAMS, James Clive (Jimmy)
Born: January 9, 1968
Origin: Jamaica
Batting: Left handed
Bowling: Left arm slow
Wicket Keeper

Tests
Test Career: 1992-01
Cap Number: 199
Tests Played: 54

Test Batting
Innings:	90	Runs:	3,012
Highest Score:	208*	Average:	41.26
No. 50s:	14	No. 100s:	6

Test Bowling & Fielding
Wickets:	27	Runs:	1,336
Best Bowling:	5/17	Average:	49.48
5 WI:	1	10 WM:	0
Catches:	48	Stumpings:	0

One Day Internationals
ODI Career: 1992-01
ODIs Played: 127

ODI Batting
Innings:	105	Runs:	2,204
Highest Score:	82	Average:	28.62
No. 50s:	14	No. 100s:	0

ODI Bowling & Fielding
Wickets:	43	Runs:	1,499
Best Bowling:	5/37	Average:	34.86
5 WM:	1	Catches:	68
Stumpings:	5		

A technically adept and dashing left handed batsman, Jimmy Adams had a dream start in Test cricket. His average of 87, after only 12 Tests, was second only to the great Don Bradman. He scored three centuries in 94/95 and after a bit of a drought, he brought up his highest score of 208 not out against New Zealand, at St.Johns in 1996. In the previous Test at Bridgetown, he took his best figures of 5/17 and was later named 'Player of the Series'. In 2000 he took over the captaincy from Brian Lara and led the West Indies in 15 Tests for four wins and three draws. He was subsequently replaced as skipper by Carl Hooper and almost immediately lost his overall place in the side.

ALEXANDER, Franz Copeland Murray (Gerry)
Born: November 2, 1928
Origin: Jamaica
Batting: Right handed
Wicket Keeper

Tests
Test Career: 1957-61
Cap Number: 96
Tests Played: 25

Test Batting
Innings:	38	Runs:	961
Highest Score:	108	Average:	30.03
No. 50s:	7	No. 100s:	1

Test Bowling & Fielding
Wickets:	0	Runs:	0
Best Bowling:		Average:	0.00
5 WI:	0	10 WM:	0
Catches:	85	Stumpings:	5

A wicket-keeper and handy batsman, Gerry Alexander was made captain shortly after his debut against England at Headingley in 1957. He captained the West Indies in 18 matches until 1960 when he was replaced by the great Sir Frank Worrell. He made one Test century - 108 against Australia, at the SCG in his final year, 1961.

ALI, Imitaz
Born: July 28, 1954
Origin: Trinidad
Batting: Right handed
Bowling: Right arm leg-break

Tests
Test Career: 1976
Cap Number: 154
Tests Played: 1

Test Batting
Innings:	1	Runs:	1
Highest Score:	1*	Average:	0.00
No. 50s:	0	No. 100s:	0

Test Bowling & Fielding
Wickets:	2	Runs:	89
Best Bowling:	2/37	Average:	44.50
5 WI:	0	10 WM:	0
Catches:	0	Stumpings:	0

A leg spinner who took the wickets of Viswanath and Venkat in his only Test appearance against India, at Port of Spain, in 1976.

ALI, Inshan
Born: September 25, 1949
Origin: Trinidad
Batting: Left handed
Bowling: Left arm leg-break

Tests
Test Career: 1971-77
Cap Number: 139
Tests Played: 12

Test Batting
Innings:	18	Runs:	172
Highest Score:	25	Average:	10.75
No. 50s:	0	No. 100s:	0

Test Bowling & Fielding
Wickets:	34	Runs:	1,621
Best Bowling:	5/59	Average:	47.67
5 WI:	1	10 WM:	0
Catches:	7	Stumpings:	0

A left arm 'chinaman' who made his debut against India, at Bridgetown, in 1971. Struggled to hold a regular place in a side blessed with quality pace bowlers.

ALLAN, David Walter
Born: November 5, 1937
Origin: Barbados
Batting: Right handed
Wicket Keeper

Tests
Test Career: 1962-66
Cap Number: 118
Tests Played: 5

Test Batting
Innings:	7	Runs:	75
Highest Score:	40*	Average:	12.50
No. 50s:	0	No. 100s:	0

Test Bowling & Fielding
Wickets:	0	Runs:	0
Best Bowling:		Average:	0.00
5 WI:	0	10 WM:	0
Catches:	15	Stumpings:	3

A wicket-keeper from Barbados who made his debut against India at Bridgetown in 1962. Although considered a talented gloveman, Allan could only manage two Tests due to the emergence of Deryck Murray.

ALLEN, Ian Basil
Born: October 6, 1965
Origin: St Vincent
Batting: Right handed
Bowling: Right arm medium-fast

Tests
Test Career: 1991
Cap Number: 197
Tests Played: 2

Test Batting
Innings:	2	Runs:	5
Highest Score:	4*	Average:	0.00
No. 50s:	0	No. 100s:	0

Test Bowling & Fielding
Wickets:	5	Runs:	180
Best Bowling:	2/69	Average:	36.00
5 WI:	0	10 WM:	0
Catches:	1	Stumpings:	0

A pace bowler from St.Vincent who played two Tests on the 1991 tour of England.

AMBROSE, Curtly Elconn Lynwall
Born: September 21, 1963
Origin: Antigua
Batting: Left handed
Bowling: Right arm fast

Tests
Test Career: 1988-00
Cap Number: 192
Tests Played: 98

Test Batting
Innings:	145	Runs:	1,439
Highest Score:	53	Average:	12.40
No. 50s:	1	No. 100s:	0

Test Bowling & Fielding
Wickets:	405	Runs:	8,501
Best Bowling:	8/45	Average:	20.99
5 WI:	22	10 WM:	3
Catches:	18	Stumpings:	0

One Day Internationals
ODI Career: 1988-00
ODIs Played: 176

ODI Batting
Innings:	96	Runs:	639
Highest Score:	31*	Average:	10.65
No. 50s:	0	No. 100s:	0

ODI Bowling & Fielding
Wickets:	225	Runs:	5,429
Best Bowling:	5/17	Average:	24.12
5 WM:	4	Catches:	45
Stumpings:	0		

With Michael Holding and Joel Garner having eased into retirement only a year earlier and Malcolm Marshall well and truly in the twilight of his career, the West Indian pace attack needed an injection of new blood. Preferably someone who could bowl with the same venom and accuracy of his predecessors as well as being able to intimidate the world's finest batsmen. Enter 6.7, Antiguan Curtly Ambrose. He had the height of Garner, and could extract similar bounce, the pace and accuracy of Holding and the competitive temperament of Andy Roberts. He opened the bowling with Patrick Patterson in his first Test against Pakistan, at Georgetown in 1988, but was to form a long and formidable partnership with his eventual skipper and one time leading Test wicket taker, Courtney Walsh. In fact, by the time the pair ended their respective careers, they had become the only two West Indian bowlers to break the 400 Test wicket barrier with Walsh finishing with 519 and Ambrose in second place with 405. Ambrose was ultra competitive in his 98 Tests and often provided the spark that a lack lustre match needed. He took five wickets in an innings on 22 occasions, with a career best 8/45 against England, at Bridgetown in 1990. His most memorable performance occurred in 1993, during the 5th Test at the WACA ground in Perth, when a brilliant spell of 7/1, sent the home side reeling to be all out for 119. Ambrose finished with the figures of 7/25 and was aptly named 'Man of the Match' as well as taking out the 'Player of the Series' award. A hard-hitting left-handed batsman, Ambrose wasn't one to prod and block. He played some important cameos in both Test and ODI's and scored his one Test 50 against Australia, at Port of Spain in 1991. A refreshing character of the game who instilled genuine passion every time he took to the field.

ANTHONY, Hamish

Born: January 16, 1971
Origin: Antigua
Batting: Right handed
Bowling: Right arm medium-fast

One Day Internationals

ODI Career: 1995
ODIs Played: 3

ODI Batting
Innings:	3	Runs:	23
Highest Score:	21	Average:	7.66
No. 50s:	0	No. 100s:	0

ODI Bowling & Fielding
Wickets:	3	Runs:	143
Best Bowling:	2/47	Average:	47.66
5 WM:	0	Catches:	0
Stumpings:	0		

An all-rounder an all-rounder from Antigua who made his ODI debut against Sri Lanka at Sharjah in 1995.

ARTHURTON, Keith Lloyd Thomas

Born: February 21, 1965
Origin: Nevis
Batting: Left handed
Bowling: Left arm off-break

Tests

Test Career: 1988-95
Cap Number: 193
Tests Played: 33

Test Batting
Innings:	50	Runs:	1,382
Highest Score:	157*	Average:	30.71
No. 50s:	8	No. 100s:	2

Test Bowling & Fielding
Wickets:	1	Runs:	183
Best Bowling:	1/17	Average:	183.00
5 WI:	0	10 WM:	0
Catches:	22	Stumpings:	0

One Day Internationals

ODI Career: 1988-99
ODIs Played: 105

ODI Batting
Innings:	93	Runs:	1,904
Highest Score:	84	Average:	26.08
No. 50s:	9	No. 100s:	0

ODI Bowling & Fielding
Wickets:	42	Runs:	1,159
Best Bowling:	4/31	Average:	27.59
5 WM:	0	Catches:	27
Stumpings:	0		

From the tiny island of Nevis, the left handed Keith Arthurton was looked upon as one of the shining lights as the West Indies looked to rebuild after their most successful era had come to an end. But since making his Test debut against England at Headingley, in 1988, Arthurton struggled for consistency. His performance in the First Test against Australia, at the 'Gabba in 1992, was an indication of his haphazard form, as his highest score of 157 not out in the first innings was followed up with a duck in the second.

ASGARALI, Nyron

Born: December 28, 1920
Origin: Trinidad
Batting: Right handed
Bowling: Right arm medium

Tests

Test Career: 1957
Cap Number: 95
Tests Played: 2

Test Batting
Innings:	4	Runs:	62
Highest Score:	29	Average:	15.50
No. 50s:	0	No. 100s:	0

Test Bowling & Fielding
Wickets:	0	Runs:	0
Best Bowling:		Average:	0.00
5 WI:	0	10 WM:	0
Catches:	0	Stumpings:	0

An opener from Trinidad who played two Tests on the 1937 tour of England.

ATKINSON, Denis

Born: August 9, 1926
Origin: Barbados
Batting: Right handed
Bowling: Right arm medium

Tests

Test Career: 1948-58
Cap Number: 67
Tests Played: 22

Test Batting

Innings:	35	Runs:	922
Highest Score:	219	Average:	31.79
No. 50s:	5	No. 100s:	1

Test Bowling & Fielding

Wickets:	47	Runs:	1,647
Best Bowling:	7/53	Average:	35.04
5 WI:	3	10 WM:	0
Catches:	11	Stumpings:	0

An all-rounder, Denis Atkinson made his Test debut against India, at Delhi in 1948 and immediately impressed by scoring 45, coming in at number ten. He captained West Indies in seven Tests while filling in for Jeff Stollmeyer. His 347 run partnership with Clairmonte Depeiaza, for the seventh wicket, against Australia in 1955, remains a Test record.

ATKINSON, Eric St Eval

Born:	November 6, 1927
Origin:	Barbados
Batting:	Right handed
Bowling:	Right arm medium-fast

Tests

Test Career:	1958-59
Cap Number:	97
Tests Played:	8

Test Batting

Innings:	9	Runs:	126
Highest Score:	37	Average:	15.75
No. 50s:	0	No. 100s:	0

Test Bowling & Fielding

Wickets:	25	Runs:	589
Best Bowling:	5/42	Average:	23.56
5 WI:	1	10 WM:	0
Catches:	2	Stumpings:	0

A pace bowler from Barbados and younger brother of Denis, Eric Atkinson played eight Tests in all. He made his debut against Pakistan, at Bridgetown in 1958.

AUSTIN, Richard Arkwright

Born:	September 5, 1954
Origin:	Jamaica
Batting:	Right handed
Bowling:	Right arm medium

Tests

Test Career:	1978
Cap Number:	162
Tests Played:	2

Test Batting

Innings:	2	Runs:	22
Highest Score:	20	Average:	11.00
No. 50s:	0	No. 100s:	0

Test Bowling & Fielding

Wickets:	0	Runs:	5
Best Bowling:		Average:	0.00
5 WI:	0	10 WM:	0
Catches:	2	Stumpings:	0

One Day Internationals

ODI Career:	1978
ODIs Played:	1

ODI Batting

Innings:	1	Runs:	8
Highest Score:	8	Average:	8.00
No. 50s:	0	No. 100s:	0

ODI Bowling & Fielding

Wickets:	0	Runs:	13
Best Bowling:		Average:	0.00
5 WM:	0	Catches:	0
Stumpings:	0		

An all-rounder with a bit of flair, Richard Austin played the first two Tests against Australia in 1978. He then signed a contract to play World Series Cricket but as the officials got hold of this news, he was subsequently dropped for the third Test at Georgetown, causing fellow WSC players to withdraw from the side. After World Series Cricket, Austin joined the rebel tour of South Africa and was banned from playing international cricket for the West Indies.

BACCHUS, Sheik Faoud Ahamul Fasiel

Born:	January 31, 1954
Origin:	Guyana
Batting:	Right handed
Bowling:	Right arm medium

Tests

Test Career:	1978-82
Cap Number:	171
Tests Played:	19

Test Batting

Innings:	30	Runs:	782
Highest Score:	250	Average:	26.06
No. 50s:	3	No. 100s:	1

Test Bowling & Fielding

Wickets:	0	Runs:	3
Best Bowling:		Average:	0.00
5 WI:	0	10 WM:	0
Catches:	17	Stumpings:	0

One Day Internationals

ODI Career:	1978-83
ODIs Played:	29

ODI Batting

Innings:	26	Runs:	612
Highest Score:	80*	Average:	26.60
No. 50s:	3	No. 100s:	0

ODI Bowling & Fielding

Wickets:	0	Runs:	0
Best Bowling:		Average:	0.00
5 WM:	0	Catches:	10
Stumpings:	0		

A middle order batsman, who sometimes opened, Faoud Bacchus got his chance at Test level due to the temporary exodus of premier batsmen to World Series Cricket. He made his debut against Australia, at Port of Spain, in 1978 and played 19 Tests over a four year period, which could be aptly described as a career of extremities. His highest score of 250 was made against India, at Kanpur, in 1978 and if not for slipping on his stumps while attempting to sweep, he could have joined the likes of Sobers and Rowe as the only West Indians (at the time) to have scored a triple century. Apart from his 'moment in the sun' at Kanpur, he has been dismissed for a duck seven times and failed to reach double figures on another seven occasions. A fine cover fieldsman, Bacchus was more suited to One Day competition and was a member of 1983 World Cup side that lost to India in the final.

BAICHAN, Len

Born:	May 12, 1946
Origin:	Guyana
Batting:	Left handed
Bowling:	Right arm medium

Tests

Test Career:	1975-76
Cap Number:	152
Tests Played:	3

Test Batting

Innings:	6	Runs:	184
Highest Score:	105*	Average:	46.00
No. 50s:	0	No. 100s:	1

Test Bowling & Fielding

Wickets:	0	Runs:	0
Best Bowling:		Average:	0.00
5 WI:	0	10 WM:	0
Catches:	2	Stumpings:	0

A promising left hand opener who scored 105 not out on debut against Pakistan, at Lahore in 1975. If not for the emergence of Gordon Greenidge, there is no doubt Baichan would have played more than three Tests.

BANKS, Omari

Born:	July 17, 1982
Origin:	Anguilla
Batting:	Right handed
Bowling:	Right arm off-break

Tests

Test Career:	2003-05
Cap Number:	250
Tests Played:	10

Test Batting

Innings:	16	Runs:	318
Highest Score:	50*	Average:	26.50
No. 50s:	1	No. 100s:	0

Test Bowling & Fielding

Wickets:	28	Runs:	1,367
Best Bowling:	4/87	Average:	48.82
5 WI:	0	10 WM:	0
Catches:	6	Stumpings:	0

One Day Internationals

ODI Career:	2003-05
ODIs Played:	5

ODI Batting

Innings:	5	Runs:	83
Highest Score:	33	Average:	16.60
No. 50s:	0	No. 100s:	0

ODI Bowling & Fielding

Wickets:	7	Runs:	189
Best Bowling:	2/24	Average:	27.00
5 WM:	0	Catches:	0
Stumpings:	0		

When Omari Banks made his debut against Australia, at Bridgetown, in 2003, he became the first player from the Leeward island of Anguilla to play Test cricket for the West Indies. A promising all-rounder, Banks has performed admirably in his ten Tests to date and with any luck should consolidate his place over the long term.

BAPTISTE, Eldine

Born:	March 12, 1960
Origin:	Antigua
Batting:	Right handed
Bowling:	Right arm medium-fast

Tests

Test Career:	1983-90
Cap Number:	179
Tests Played:	10

Test Batting

Innings:	11	Runs:	233
Highest Score:	87*	Average:	23.30
No. 50s:	1	No. 100s:	0

Test Bowling & Fielding

Wickets:	16	Runs:	563
Best Bowling:	3/31	Average:	35.18
5 WI:	0	10 WM:	0
Catches:	2	Stumpings:	0

One Day Internationals

ODI Career:	1983-90
ODIs Played:	43

ODI Batting

Innings:	16	Runs:	184
Highest Score:	31	Average:	15.33
No. 50s:	0	No. 100s:	0

ODI Bowling & Fielding

Wickets:	36	Runs:	1,511
Best Bowling:	2/10	Average:	41.97
5 WM:	0	Catches:	14
Stumpings:	0		

An all-rounder who made his Test debut against India, at Kanpur, in 1983. Although not in the bowling class of his peers such as Marshall, Holding and Ambrose, Baptsite was some form of a 'good luck charm' as he played in ten victorious Test sides from 1983 to 1990. A regular member of the ODI team.

BARRETT, Arthur George

Born:	April 4, 1944
Origin:	Jamaica
Batting:	Right handed
Bowling:	Right arm leg-break

Tests

Test Career:	1971-75
Cap Number:	135
Tests Played:	6

Test Batting

Innings:	7	Runs:	40
Highest Score:	19	Average:	6.66
No. 50s:	0	No. 100s:	0

Test Bowling & Fielding

Wickets:	13	Runs:	603
Best Bowling:	3/43	Average:	46.38
5 WI:	0	10 WM:	0
Catches:	0	Stumpings:	0

A leg-spinner from Jamaica who made his Test debut against India, at Kingston, in 1971. He was called up for Test duties on an ad-hoc basis where he managed just six appearances in four years.

BARROW, Ivan
Born: January 16, 1911
Origin: Jamaica
Batting: Right handed
Wicket Keeper

Tests
Test Career: 1930-39
Cap Number: 26
Tests Played: 11

Test Batting
Innings:	19	Runs:	276
Highest Score:	105	Average:	16.23
No. 50s:	0	No. 100s:	1

Test Bowling & Fielding
Wickets:	0	Runs:	0
Best Bowling:		Average:	0.00
5 WI:	0	10 WM:	0
Catches:	17	Stumpings:	5

A wicket-keeper from Jamaica who was the first West Indian to score a hundred on English soil - 105 at Old Trafford in 1933.

BARTLETT, Edward Lawson
Born: March 10, 1906
Origin: Barbados
Batting: Right handed

Tests
Test Career: 1928-31
Cap Number: 14
Tests Played: 5

Test Batting
Innings:	8	Runs:	131
Highest Score:	84	Average:	18.71
No. 50s:	1	No. 100s:	0

Test Bowling & Fielding
Wickets:	0	Runs:	0
Best Bowling:		Average:	0.00
5 WI:	0	10 WM:	0
Catches:	2	Stumpings:	0

He made his Test debut against England at The Oval in 1928 and scored an impressive 84 against Australia on the 1930 tour down under.

BAUGH, Carlton Seymour
Born: June 23, 1982
Origin: Jamaica
Batting: Right handed
Bowling: Right arm leg-break
Wicket Keeper

Tests
Test Career: 2003-04
Cap Number: 248
Tests Played: 5

Test Batting
Innings:	10	Runs:	196
Highest Score:	68	Average:	19.60
No. 50s:	1	No. 100s:	0

Test Bowling & Fielding
Wickets:	0	Runs:	0
Best Bowling:		Average:	0.00
5 WI:	0	10 WM:	0
Catches:	4	Stumpings:	1

One Day Internationals
ODI Career: 2003-06
ODIs Played: 12

ODI Batting
Innings:	11	Runs:	146
Highest Score:	29	Average:	24.33
No. 50s:	0	No. 100s:	0

ODI Bowling & Fielding
Wickets:	0	Runs:	0
Best Bowling:		Average:	0.00
5 WM:	0	Catches:	6
Stumpings:	0		

An up and coming wicket-keeper from Jamaica who made his Test debut against Australia, at Port of Spain, in 2003.

BENJAMIN, Kenneth Charlie Griffith
Born: April 8, 1967
Origin: Antigua
Batting: Right handed
Bowling: Right arm fast

Tests
Test Career: 1992-98
Cap Number: 200
Tests Played: 26

Test Batting
Innings:	36	Runs:	222
Highest Score:	43*	Average:	7.92
No. 50s:	0	No. 100s:	0

Test Bowling & Fielding
Wickets:	92	Runs:	2,785
Best Bowling:	6/66	Average:	30.27
5 WI:	4	10 WM:	1
Catches:	2	Stumpings:	0

One Day Internationals
ODI Career: 1992-96
ODIs Played: 26

ODI Batting
Innings:	13	Runs:	65
Highest Score:	17	Average:	10.83
No. 50s:	0	No. 100s:	0

ODI Bowling & Fielding
Wickets:	33	Runs:	923
Best Bowling:	3/34	Average:	27.96
5 WM:	0	Catches:	4
Stumpings:	0		

No relation to fellow Antiguan paceman Winston, Kenny Benjamin was a sharp, pace bowler who also had the ability to swing the ball with great effect. He made his debut in the inaugural Test between the West Indies and South Africa, at Georgetown, in 1991. His best haul was his 6/66 against England at Kingston in 1993.

BENJAMIN, Winston
Born: December 31, 1964
Origin: Antigua
Batting: Right handed
Bowling: Right arm fast

Tests
Test Career: 1987-95
Cap Number: 189
Tests Played: 21

Test Batting
Innings:	26	Runs:	470
Highest Score:	85	Average:	18.80
No. 50s:	2	No. 100s:	0

BENJAMIN, Winston Keithroy Matthew (cont.)

Test Bowling & Fielding			
Wickets:	61	Runs:	1,648
Best Bowling:	4/46	Average:	27.01
5 WI:	0	10 WM:	0
Catches:	12	Stumpings:	0

One Day Internationals
ODI Career: 1986-95
ODIs Played: 85

ODI Batting			
Innings:	52	Runs:	298
Highest Score:	31	Average:	7.45
No. 50s:	0	No. 100s:	0

ODI Bowling & Fielding			
Wickets:	100	Runs:	3,079
Best Bowling:	5/22	Average:	30.79
5 WM:	1	Catches:	16
Stumpings:	0		

After making an impressive Test debut against India, at Delhi, in 1987, Winston Benjamin looked like he would fit perfectly into the already potent West Indian pace attack. But the Antiguan made just 21 Test appearances in nine years. A member of West Indies World Cup squads of 1987 and 1992.

BERNARD, David Eddison
Born: July 19, 1981
Origin: Jamaica
Batting: Right handed
Bowling: Right arm medium-fast

Tests
Test Career: 2003
Cap Number: 249
Tests Played: 1

Test Batting			
Innings:	2	Runs:	11
Highest Score:	7	Average:	5.50
No. 50s:	0	No. 100s:	0

Test Bowling & Fielding			
Wickets:	0	Runs:	61
Best Bowling:		Average:	0.00
5 WI:	0	10 WM:	0
Catches:	0	Stumpings:	0

One Day Internationals
ODI Career: 2003
ODIs Played: 4

ODI Batting			
Innings:	2	Runs:	7
Highest Score:	7	Average:	3.50
No. 50s:	0	No. 100s:	0

ODI Bowling & Fielding			
Wickets:	1	Runs:	28
Best Bowling:	1/11	Average:	28.00
5 WM:	0	Catches:	1
Stumpings:	0		

A Jamaican all-rounder who has played just the one Test against Australia, at Port of Spain, in 2003.

BEST, Carlisle Alonza
Born: May 14, 1959
Origin: Barbados
Batting: Right handed
Bowling: Right arm medium

Tests
Test Career: 1986-90
Cap Number: 185
Tests Played: 8

Test Batting			
Innings:	13	Runs:	342
Highest Score:	164	Average:	28.50
No. 50s:	1	No. 100s:	1

Test Bowling & Fielding			
Wickets:	0	Runs:	21
Best Bowling:		Average:	0.00
5 WI:	0	10 WM:	0
Catches:	8	Stumpings:	0

One Day Internationals
ODI Career: 1986-92
ODIs Played: 24

ODI Batting			
Innings:	23	Runs:	473
Highest Score:	100	Average:	24.89
No. 50s:	2	No. 100s:	1

ODI Bowling & Fielding			
Wickets:	0	Runs:	12
Best Bowling:		Average:	0.00
5 WM:	0	Catches:	5
Stumpings:	0		

A middle order batsman who scored struggled for consistency in his eight Tests. Scored 164 against England at Kingston in 1986.

BEST, Tino la Bertram
Born: August 26, 1981
Origin: Barbados
Batting: Right handed
Bowling: Right arm fast

Tests
Test Career: 2003-05
Cap Number: 251
Tests Played: 12

Test Batting			
Innings:	19	Runs:	174
Highest Score:	27	Average:	10.23
No. 50s:	0	No. 100s:	0

Test Bowling & Fielding			
Wickets:	26	Runs:	1,171
Best Bowling:	4/46	Average:	45.03
5 WI:	0	10 WM:	0
Catches:	1	Stumpings:	0

One Day Internationals
ODI Career: 2004-06
ODIs Played: 11

ODI Batting			
Innings:	7	Runs:	44
Highest Score:	24	Average:	11.00
No. 50s:	0	No. 100s:	0

ODI Bowling & Fielding			
Wickets:	13	Runs:	427
Best Bowling:	4/35	Average:	32.84
5 WM:	0	Catches:	3
Stumpings:	0		

While he may stand at just 5.8', make no mistake, Tino Best is genuine pace. Upon making his debut against Australia, at Bridgetown, in 2003, Best has injected some long, overdue passion into the West Indian bowling attack. Although his Test figures to date are merely reasonable, Best, at 25, does have enough time on his side, and the right work ethic, to become a class bowler.

BETANCOURT, Nelson
Born: June 4, 1887
Origin: Trinidad
Batting: Right handed
Wicket Keeper

Tests
Test Career: 1930
Cap Number: 23
Tests Played: 1

Test Batting
Innings:	2	Runs:	52
Highest Score:	39	Average:	26.00
No. 50s:	0	No. 100s:	0

Test Bowling & Fielding
Wickets:	0	Runs:	0
Best Bowling:		Average:	0.00
5 WI:	0	10 WM:	0
Catches:	0	Stumpings:	0

Nelson Betancourt captained the West Indies in his only Test appearance against England at Port of Spain, in 1930.

BINNS, Alfred
Born: July 24, 1929
Origin: Jamaica
Batting: Right handed
Wicket Keeper

Tests
Test Career: 1953
Cap Number: 74
Tests Played: 5

Test Batting
Innings:	8	Runs:	64
Highest Score:	27	Average:	9.14
No. 50s:	0	No. 100s:	0

Test Bowling & Fielding
Wickets:	0	Runs:	0
Best Bowling:		Average:	0.00
5 WI:	0	10 WM:	0
Catches:	14	Stumpings:	3

A wicket-keeper who played just five Tests after making his debut against India at Port of Spain in 1953.

BIRKETT, Lionel
Born: April 14, 1905
Origin: Barbados
Batting: Right handed
Bowling: Right arm medium

Tests
Test Career: 1930-31
Cap Number: 30
Tests Played: 4

Test Batting
Innings:	8	Runs:	136
Highest Score:	64	Average:	17.00
No. 50s:	1	No. 100s:	0

Test Bowling & Fielding
Wickets:	1	Runs:	71
Best Bowling:	1/16	Average:	71.00
5 WI:	0	10 WM:	0
Catches:	4	Stumpings:	0

An opening batsman whose highest score of 64 was made on debut against Australia at the Adelaide Oval in 1930.

BISHOP, Ian Raphael
Born: October 24, 1967
Origin: Trinidad
Batting: Right handed
Bowling: Right arm fast

Tests
Test Career: 1989-98
Cap Number: 194
Tests Played: 43

Test Batting
Innings:	63	Runs:	632
Highest Score:	48	Average:	12.15
No. 50s:	0	No. 100s:	0

Test Bowling & Fielding
Wickets:	161	Runs:	3,909
Best Bowling:	6/40	Average:	24.27
5 WI:	6	10 WM:	0
Catches:	8	Stumpings:	0

One Day Internationals
ODI Career: 1988-97
ODIs Played: 84

ODI Batting
Innings:	44	Runs:	405
Highest Score:	33*	Average:	16.20
No. 50s:	0	No. 100s:	0

ODI Bowling & Fielding
Wickets:	118	Runs:	3,127
Best Bowling:	5/25	Average:	26.50
5 WM:	2	Catches:	12
Stumpings:	0		

Ian Bishop, along with Curtly Ambrose, were seen as the genuine successors to former champions Marshall, Holding and Garner. He impressed early taking 6/87 in his second Test against India at Bridgetown. However, soon afterwards Bishop was plagued with chronic back problems and although he finished with a respectable 161 wickets at 24.27, he was never really at his best for long periods. He took five wickets in an innings on six occasions with a career best 6/40 against Australia at the WACA, in 1993. These days Bishop is a successful TV commentator.

BLACK, Marlon Ian
Born: June 7, 1975
Origin: Trinidad
Batting: Right handed
Bowling: Right arm medium-fast

Tests
Test Career: 2000-02
Cap Number: 236
Tests Played: 6

Test Batting
Innings:	11	Runs:	21
Highest Score:	6	Average:	2.62
No. 50s:	0	No. 100s:	0

Test Bowling & Fielding
Wickets:	12	Runs:	597
Best Bowling:	4/83	Average:	49.75
5 WI:	0	10 WM:	0
Catches:	0	Stumpings:	0

One Day Internationals
ODI Career: 2001
ODIs Played: 5

ODI Batting
Innings:	2	Runs:	4
Highest Score:	4	Average:	2.00
No. 50s:	0	No. 100s:	0

ODI Bowling & Fielding
Wickets:	0	Runs:	196
Best Bowling:		Average:	0.00
5 WM:	0	Catches:	0
Stumpings:	0		

Marlon Black took 4/83 on debut against Australia, at the 'Gabba in 2000, when he opened the bowling with veteran Courtney Walsh. Although he seemed a likely prospect, he played just the four Tests in two years. Black struggled at One-Day level, failing to take a wicket in five matches.

BOYCE, Keith David
Born: October 11, 1943
Origin: Barbados
Batting: Right handed
Bowling: Right arm medium-fast

Tests
Test Career: 1971-76
Cap Number: 137
Tests Played: 21

Test Batting
Innings:	30	Runs:	657
Highest Score:	95*	Average:	24.33
No. 50s:	4	No. 100s:	0

Test Bowling & Fielding
Wickets:	60	Runs:	1,801
Best Bowling:	6/77	Average:	30.01
5 WI:	2	10 WM:	1
Catches:	5	Stumpings:	0

One Day Internationals
ODI Career: 1973-75
ODIs Played: 8

ODI Batting
Innings:	4	Runs:	57
Highest Score:	34	Average:	14.25
No. 50s:	0	No. 100s:	0

ODI Bowling & Fielding
Wickets:	13	Runs:	313
Best Bowling:	4/50	Average:	24.07
5 WM:	0	Catches:	0
Stumpings:	0		

An all-rounder who could not only bowl fast but could hit the ball as hard as anyone, 'Stingray' Boyce was an integral component of the West Indian side that took out the inaugural World Cup title, against Australia, in 1975. Taking on Jeff Thomson, who was rated as the fastest bowler in the world at the time, Boyce scored a valuable 34, and then followed up with a match-winning 4/50 from 12 overs. Although the One Day game had only just become part of the international format, Boyce was immediately heralded as a 'specialist' after just eight appearances. As a Test player, Boyce's performances with both bat and ball were more than serviceable. He took 60 wickets at 30.01 with a best haul of 6/77 against England, at the Oval, in 1973, and while he never scored a Test hundred, Boyce contributed many a fine innings as a late order batsman, including a magnificent 95 against Australia, at Adelaide, in his final year at Test level.

BRADSHAW, Ian David Russell
Born: July 9, 1974
Origin: Barbados
Batting: Left handed
Bowling: Left arm medium-fast

Tests
Test Career: 2006
Cap Number: 265
Tests Played: 5

Test Batting
Innings:	8	Runs:	93
Highest Score:	33	Average:	13.71
No. 50s:	0	No. 100s:	0

Test Bowling & Fielding
Wickets:	9	Runs:	540
Best Bowling:	3/73	Average:	60.00
5 WI:	0	10 WM:	0
Catches:	3	Stumpings:	0

One Day Internationals
ODI Career: 2004-06
ODIs Played: 43

ODI Batting
Innings:	24	Runs:	235
Highest Score:	37	Average:	14.68
No. 50s:	0	No. 100s:	0

ODI Bowling & Fielding
Wickets:	58	Runs:	1,548
Best Bowling:	3/15	Average:	26.68
5 WM:	0	Catches:	6
Stumpings:	0		

Two years after making his ODI debut against England in 2004, Ian Bradshaw, a regular member of the ODI side, received his first call up for Test duties at age 32, against New Zealand, at Auckland. A left arm pace bowler and versatile batsman he played five Tests in 2006.

BRAVO, Dwayne
Born: October 7, 1983
Origin: Trinidad
Batting: Right handed
Bowling: Right arm medium-fast

Tests
Test Career: 2004-06
Cap Number: 256
Tests Played: 16

Test Batting
Innings:	30	Runs:	956
Highest Score:	113	Average:	32.96
No. 50s:	5	No. 100s:	2

Test Bowling & Fielding

Wickets:	36	Runs:	1,295
Best Bowling:	6/55	Average:	35.97
5 WI:	2	10 WM:	0
Catches:	13	Stumpings:	0

One Day Internationals

ODI Career:	2004-06		
ODIs Played:	43		

ODI Batting

Innings:	33	Runs:	513
Highest Score:	62*	Average:	22.30
No. 50s:	2	No. 100s:	0

ODI Bowling & Fielding

Wickets:	45	Runs:	1,415
Best Bowling:	3/24	Average:	31.44
5 WM:	0	Catches:	15
Stumpings:	0		

A quality all-rounder Dwayne Bravo, at 23 years of age, is without doubt the most exciting prospect in West Indian cricket today. A right-arm medium-fast bowler and accomplished middle order batsman, Bravo made an impressive Test debut against England, at Lords, in 2004, scoring 44 and taking three wickets. He went on to take 16 wickets for the series. He scored his maiden Test century, while batting at number seven against South Africa, at St Johns, in May 2005. However, for some reason was dropped for the first Test against Australia at the 'Gabba. After the Windies were easily trounced, he was recalled for the Second Test at Hobart and immediately made a statement by scoring 113. In the next Test at Adelaide, Bravo showed what he could do with the ball taking a career best 6/64. With 16 Tests and over 40 ODI's alongside his name, the faithful are now looking towards the youngster to help bring West Indian cricket back to the pinnacle status it enjoyed some 25 years ago.

BREESE, Gareth Rohan

Born:	January 9, 1976
Origin:	Jamaica
Batting:	Right handed
Bowling:	Right arm off-break

Tests

Test Career:	2002
Cap Number:	244
Tests Played:	1

Test Batting

Innings:	2	Runs:	5
Highest Score:	5	Average:	2.50
No. 50s:	0	No. 100s:	0

Test Bowling & Fielding

Wickets:	2	Runs:	135
Best Bowling:	2/108	Average:	67.50
5 WI:	0	10 WM:	0
Catches:	1	Stumpings:	0

An off-spinner who took two wickets against India, at Chennai, in 2002, in what was his only Test appearance.

BROWN, Darryl

Born:	December 18, 1973
Origin:	Trinidad
Batting:	Right handed
Bowling:	Right arm medium

One Day Internationals

ODI Career:	2001-02
ODIs Played:	3

ODI Batting

Innings:	2	Runs:	10
Highest Score:	9	Average:	10.00
No. 50s:	0	No. 100s:	0

ODI Bowling & Fielding

Wickets:	5	Runs:	124
Best Bowling:	3/21	Average:	24.80
5 WM:	0	Catches:	0
Stumpings:	0		

A right arm medium pacer who played just three ODI's after making his debut against Zimbabwe at Kandy in 2001.

BROWNE, Barrington

Born:	September 16, 1967
Origin:	Guyana
Batting:	Right handed
Bowling:	Right arm fast

One Day Internationals

ODI Career:	1994
ODIs Played:	4

ODI Batting

Innings:	3	Runs:	8
Highest Score:	8*	Average:	8.00
No. 50s:	0	No. 100s:	0

ODI Bowling & Fielding

Wickets:	2	Runs:	156
Best Bowling:	2/50	Average:	78.00
5 WM:	0	Catches:	0
Stumpings:	0		

Right arm quick from Guyana who made his ODI debut against India at Mumbai in 1994. Played just the four ODI's.

BROWNE, Courtney Oswald

Born:	December 7, 1970
Origin:	Barbados
Batting:	Right handed
	Wicket Keeper

Tests

Test Career:	1995-05
Cap Number:	209
Tests Played:	20

Test Batting

Innings:	30	Runs:	387
Highest Score:	68	Average:	16.12
No. 50s:	1	No. 100s:	0

Test Bowling & Fielding

Wickets:	0	Runs:	0
Best Bowling:		Average:	0.00
5 WI:	0	10 WM:	0
Catches:	79	Stumpings:	2

One Day Internationals

ODI Career:	1995-05
ODIs Played:	46

BROWNE, Cyril 'Snuffy'

Born:	October 8, 1890
Origin:	Barbados
Batting:	Right handed
Bowling:	Right arm medium

Tests

Test Career:	1928-30
Cap Number:	1
Tests Played:	4

Test Batting

Innings:	8	Runs:	176
Highest Score:	70*	Average:	25.14
No. 50s:	1	No. 100s:	0

Test Bowling & Fielding

Wickets:	6	Runs:	288
Best Bowling:	2/72	Average:	48.00
5 WI:	0	10 WM:	0
Catches:	1	Stumpings:	0

ODI Batting

Innings:	32	Runs:	415
Highest Score:	46*	Average:	17.29
No. 50s:	0	No. 100s:	0

ODI Bowling & Fielding

Wickets:	0	Runs:	0
Best Bowling:		Average:	0.00
5 WM:	0	Catches:	59
Stumpings:	9		

The English born Courtney Browne was selected as the number one keeper for the 1996 World Cup. He had a roller-coaster career playing 20 Tests over a ten-year period. He was eventually succeeded by Ridley Jacobs.

BROWNE, Cyril 'Snuffy'

Born:	October 8, 1890
Origin:	Barbados
Batting:	Right handed
Bowling:	Right arm medium

Tests

Test Career:	1928-30
Cap Number:	1
Tests Played:	4

Test Batting

Innings:	8	Runs:	176
Highest Score:	70*	Average:	25.14
No. 50s:	1	No. 100s:	0

Test Bowling & Fielding

Wickets:	6	Runs:	288
Best Bowling:	2/72	Average:	48.00
5 WI:	0	10 WM:	0
Catches:	1	Stumpings:	0

A medium pace bowler who played in West Indies inaugural Test against England at Lord's in 1928. Browne was the first West Indian to become an honorary life member of MCC.

BRYAN, Hendy

Born:	March 17, 1970
Origin:	Barbados
Batting:	Right handed
Bowling:	Right arm medium-fast

One Day Internationals

ODI Career:	1999
ODIs Played:	15

ODI Batting

Innings:	8	Runs:	43
Highest Score:	11	Average:	7.16
No. 50s:	0	No. 100s:	0

ODI Bowling & Fielding

Wickets:	12	Runs:	518
Best Bowling:	4/24	Average:	43.16
5 WM:	0	Catches:	4
Stumpings:	0		

A paceman from Barbados, Hendy Bryan collected four wickets and the 'Man of the Match' award on his ODI debut against Australia in Kingston, in 1999. He played 15 ODI's in his first year but was overlooked thereafter.

BUTCHER, Basil

Born:	September 3, 1933
Origin:	Guyana
Batting:	Right handed
Bowling:	Right arm leg-break

Tests

Test Career:	1958-69
Cap Number:	103
Tests Played:	44

Test Batting

Innings:	78	Runs:	3,104
Highest Score:	209*	Average:	43.11
No. 50s:	16	No. 100s:	7

Test Bowling & Fielding

Wickets:	5	Runs:	90
Best Bowling:	5/34	Average:	18.00
5 WI:	1	10 WM:	0
Catches:	15	Stumpings:	0

Superb timing and elegant stroke-play complimented with great powers of concentration were the key features of Basil Butcher's batting. A middle order batsman from Guyana, Butcher's Test average of 43.11 clearly indicates genuine consistency throughout his eleven year career. Butcher made seven centuries in all, his finest knock a solid 209 not out against England at Trent Bridge, in 1966.

BUTLER, Deighton

Born:	July 14, 1974
Origin:	St Vincent
Batting:	Left handed
Bowling:	Left arm medium-fast

One Day Internationals

ODI Career:	2005-06
ODIs Played:	5

ODI Batting

Innings:	4	Runs:	25
Highest Score:	13*	Average:	25.00
No. 50s:	0	No. 100s:	0

ODI Bowling & Fielding

Wickets:	3	Runs:	188
Best Bowling:	1/25	Average:	62.66
5 WM:	0	Catches:	0
Stumpings:	0		

A left arm swing bowler Deighton Butler made his ODI debut against Sri Lanka at Dambulla in 2005 but will need to produce more consistent performances if he is to become a regular member of the One Day side.

BUTLER, Lennox Stephen (Bunny)

Born:	February 9, 1929
Origin:	Trinidad
Batting:	Right handed
Bowling:	Right arm medium-fast

Tests

Test Career:	1955
Cap Number:	87
Tests Played:	1

Test Batting

Innings:	1	Runs:	16
Highest Score:	16	Average:	16.00
No. 50s:	0	No. 100s:	0

Test Bowling & Fielding		
Wickets:	2	Runs: 151
Best Bowling:	2/151	Average: 75.50
5 WI:	0	10 WM: 0
Catches:	0	Stumpings: 0

A medium pacer who played just the one Test against Australia at Port of Spain in 1955.

BUTTS, Clyde Godfrey
Born: July 8, 1957
Origin: Guyana
Batting: Right handed
Bowling: Right arm off-break

Tests

Test Career: 1985-88
Cap Number: 184
Tests Played: 7

Test Batting
Innings:	8	Runs:	108
Highest Score:	38	Average:	15.42
No. 50s:	0	No. 100s:	0

Test Bowling & Fielding
Wickets:	10	Runs:	595
Best Bowling:	4/73	Average:	59.50
5 WI:	0	10 WM:	0
Catches:	2	Stumpings:	0

An off-spinner from Guyana who made his debut against New Zealand, at Georgetown, in 1985. Played seven Tests in three years taking a career best 4/73 against Pakistan at Karachi, in 1986.

BYNOE, Michael Robin
Born: February 23, 1941
Origin: Barbados
Batting: Right handed
Bowling: Left arm medium

Tests

Test Career: 1959-67
Cap Number: 106
Tests Played: 4

Test Batting
Innings:	6	Runs:	111
Highest Score:	48	Average:	18.50
No. 50s:	0	No. 100s:	0

Test Bowling & Fielding
Wickets:	1	Runs:	5
Best Bowling:	1/5	Average:	5.00
5 WI:	0	10 WM:	0
Catches:	4	Stumpings:	0

A right hand opening batsman who made his debut against Pakistan, at Lahore in 1959, but never really got used to the sub continent wickets during his maiden tour.

CAMACHO, George Stephen
Born: October 15, 1945
Origin: Guyana
Batting: Right handed
Bowling: Right arm leg-break

Tests

Test Career: 1968-71
Cap Number: 126
Tests Played: 11

Test Batting
Innings:	22	Runs:	640
Highest Score:	87	Average:	29.09
No. 50s:	4	No. 100s:	0

Test Bowling & Fielding
Wickets:	0	Runs:	12
Best Bowling:		Average:	0.00
5 WI:	0	10 WM:	0
Catches:	4	Stumpings:	0

A right hand opener who made his Test debut against England, at Port of Spain, in 1968. Played 11 Tests over three years making four 50's with a highest score of 87 against England, at Port of Spain, Trinidad, in 1968.

CAMERON, Francis James (Jimmy)
Born: June 22, 1923
Origin: Jamaica
Batting: Right handed
Bowling: Right arm off-break

Tests

Test Career: 1948-49
Cap Number: 68
Tests Played: 5

Test Batting
Innings:	7	Runs:	151
Highest Score:	75*	Average:	25.16
No. 50s:	1	No. 100s:	0

Test Bowling & Fielding
Wickets:	3	Runs:	278
Best Bowling:	2/74	Average:	92.66
5 WI:	0	10 WM:	0
Catches:	0	Stumpings:	0

A right arm off-spinner who made his debut against India at Delhi in 1948. His brother John also played Test cricket for West Indies.

CAMERON, John
Born: April 8, 1914
Origin: Jamaica
Batting: Right handed
Bowling: Right arm slow

Tests

Test Career: 1939
Cap Number: 45
Tests Played: 2

Test Batting
Innings:	3	Runs:	6
Highest Score:	5	Average:	2.00
No. 50s:	0	No. 100s:	0

Test Bowling & Fielding
Wickets:	3	Runs:	88
Best Bowling:	3/66	Average:	29.33
5 WI:	0	10 WM:	0
Catches:	0	Stumpings:	0

A right arm leg-spinner who played just the two Tests during the 1939 tour of England. His younger brother Jimmy played five Tests in 1948/49.

CAMPBELL, Sherwin Legay
Born: November 1, 1970
Origin: Barbados
Batting: Right handed
Bowling: Right arm medium

Tests
Test Career:	1995-02		
Cap Number:	208		
Tests Played:	52		

Test Batting
Innings:	93	Runs:	2,882
Highest Score:	208	Average:	32.38
No. 50s:	18	No. 100s:	4

Test Bowling & Fielding
Wickets:	0	Runs:	0
Best Bowling:		Average:	0.00
5 WI:	0	10 WM:	0
Catches:	47	Stumpings:	0

One Day Internationals
ODI Career:	1994-01		
ODIs Played:	90		

ODI Batting
Innings:	87	Runs:	2,283
Highest Score:	105	Average:	26.24
No. 50s:	14	No. 100s:	2

ODI Bowling & Fielding
Wickets:	8	Runs:	170
Best Bowling:	4/30	Average:	21.25
5 WM:	0	Catches:	23
Stumpings:	0		

Although he made 50 on debut against New Zealand, at Christchurch, and then followed up with 88 in his second Test, Sherwin Campbell is best described as a 'hot and cold' opening batsman. Four Test centuries, his first a superb 208 against New Zealand in 1995, and 18 fifties are fine credentials on face value but are unfortunately accompanied by numerous single figure performances. Campbell played in 52 Tests and was a member of the 1996 World Cup squad.

CAREW, George
Born:	June 4, 1910
Origin:	Barbados
Batting:	Right handed
Bowling:	Left arm off-break

Tests
Test Career:	1935-49		
Cap Number:	37		
Tests Played:	4		

Test Batting
Innings:	7	Runs:	170
Highest Score:	107	Average:	28.33
No. 50s:	0	No. 100s:	1

Test Bowling & Fielding
Wickets:	0	Runs:	2
Best Bowling:		Average:	0.00
5 WI:	0	10 WM:	0
Catches:	1	Stumpings:	0

A right hand opener who played four Tests over a 14 year, war interrupted, career. Carew made a duck on debut against England at Bridgetown in 1935, but became the sixth West Indian to score a Test century when he scored a dashing 107 against England at Port of Spain during the twilight of his career in 1947.

CAREW, Michael Conrad (Joey)
Born:	September 15, 1937
Origin:	Trinidad
Batting:	Left handed
Bowling:	Left arm fast

Tests
Test Career:	1963-72		
Cap Number:	120		
Tests Played:	19		

Test Batting
Innings:	36	Runs:	1,127
Highest Score:	109	Average:	34.15
No. 50s:	5	No. 100s:	1

Test Bowling & Fielding
Wickets:	8	Runs:	437
Best Bowling:	1/11	Average:	54.62
5 WI:	0	10 WM:	0
Catches:	13	Stumpings:	0

An early mentor to Brian Lara, Carew was an elegant left-hand opener who made his debut against England, at Old Trafford, in 1963. Scored his only Test century, 109 against New Zealand at Christchurch in 1969.

CHALLENOR, George
Born:	June 28, 1888
Origin:	Barbados
Batting:	Right handed
Bowling:	Right arm medium

Tests
Test Career:	1928		
Cap Number:	2		
Tests Played:	3		

Test Batting
Innings:	6	Runs:	101
Highest Score:	46	Average:	16.83
No. 50s:	0	No. 100s:	0

Test Bowling & Fielding
Wickets:	0	Runs:	0
Best Bowling:		Average:	0.00
5 WI:	0	10 WM:	0
Catches:	0	Stumpings:	0

Opened the batting with Frank 'Freddie' Martin in West Indies' inaugural Test against England at Lord's in 1928. The pair put on 86 for the first wicket out of a total of 177.

CHANDERPAUL, Shivnarine
Born:	August 16, 1974
Origin:	Guyana
Batting:	Left handed
Bowling:	Right arm leg-break

Tests
Test Career:	1994-06		
Cap Number:	204		
Tests Played:	98		

Test Batting
Innings:	168	Runs:	6,531
Highest Score:	203*	Average:	44.73
No. 50s:	38	No. 100s:	14

Test Bowling & Fielding
Wickets:	8	Runs:	786
Best Bowling:	1/2	Average:	98.25
5 WI:	0	10 WM:	0
Catches:	41	Stumpings:	0

One Day Internationals

ODI Career:	1994-06		
ODIs Played:	191		

ODI Batting

Innings:	179	Runs:	5,715
Highest Score:	150	Average:	36.40
No. 50s:	38	No. 100s:	3

ODI Bowling & Fielding

Wickets:	14	Runs:	617
Best Bowling:	3/18	Average:	44.07
5 WM:	0	Catches:	58
Stumpings:	0		

A left hand, middle order batsman and member of the current side, Shivnarine Chanderpaul was appointed captain in 2005 as a result of Brian Lara, along with six other senior players, being dropped due to the Cable and Wireless sponsorship row. Chanderpaul's 203 not out in the First Test against South Africa, at Georgetown, was his highest Test score and saw him become only the second player to score a double century on debut as captain. He led the side in 14 Tests for just the one win and three draws and as his appointment was always going to be a short term solution, he handed the reins back to Lara in early 2006. Although not the most technically gifted batsman, Chanderpaul has been a loyal servant of West Indian cricket over the past 12 years, scoring over six and half thousand runs at a healthy 44.73.

CHANG, Herbert

Born:	July 2, 1952
Origin:	Jamaica
Batting:	Left handed
Bowling:	Right arm medium

Tests

Test Career:	1979			
Cap Number:	173			
Tests Played:	1			

Test Batting

Innings:	2	Runs:	8
Highest Score:	6	Average:	4.00
No. 50s:	0	No. 100s:	0

Test Bowling & Fielding

Wickets:	0	Runs:	0
Best Bowling:		Average:	0.00
5 WI:	0	10 WM:	0
Catches:	0	Stumpings:	0

A left handed middle order batsman who played just the one Test against India, at Chennai, in 1979 without much success. Chang later joined the rebel tour of South Africa in 1983.

CHATTERGOON, Sewnarine

Born:	April 3, 1981
Origin:	Guyana
Batting:	Left handed
Bowling:	Right arm leg-break

One Day Internationals

ODI Career:	2006
ODIs Played:	3

ODI Batting

Innings:	3	Runs:	63
Highest Score:	54*	Average:	31.50
No. 50s:	1	No. 100s:	0

ODI Bowling & Fielding

Wickets:	0	Runs:	6
Best Bowling:		Average:	0.00
5 WM:	0	Catches:	1
Stumpings:	0		

A left hand opening batsman who has impressed in his three ODI appearances. From Guyana, Chattergoon made his debut against Zimbabwe, in Georgetown in 2006.

CHRISTIANI, Cyril

Born:	October 28, 1913
Origin:	Guyana
Batting:	Right handed
	Wicket Keeper

Tests

Test Career:	1935			
Cap Number:	38			
Tests Played:	4			

Test Batting

Innings:	7	Runs:	98
Highest Score:	32*	Average:	19.60
No. 50s:	0	No. 100s:	0

Test Bowling & Fielding

Wickets:	0	Runs:	0
Best Bowling:		Average:	0.00
5 WI:	0	10 WM:	0
Catches:	6	Stumpings:	1

A wicket-keeper who played just four Tests in 1935 after making his debut against England at Bridgetown. His younger brother Robert also kept wickets in Tests for the West Indies.

CHRISTIANI, Robert

Born:	July 19, 1920
Origin:	Guyana
Batting:	Right handed
Bowling:	Right arm off-break
	Wicket Keeper

Tests

Test Career:	1948-54			
Cap Number:	53			
Tests Played:	22			

Test Batting

Innings:	37	Runs:	896
Highest Score:	107	Average:	26.35
No. 50s:	4	No. 100s:	1

Test Bowling & Fielding

Wickets:	3	Runs:	108
Best Bowling:	3/52	Average:	36.00
5 WI:	0	10 WM:	0
Catches:	19	Stumpings:	2

Like older brother Cyril, Robert Christiani was also a talented wicket-keeper but was selected as a batsman in his first Test, against England at Bridgetown. An all-round cricketer, Robert bowled useful off-spinners and took a career best 3/52. He scored 107 against India at Delhi in 1948, batting at number eight.

CLARKE, Carlos Bertram (Bertie)

Born: April 7, 1918
Origin: Barbados
Batting: Right handed
Bowling: Right arm slow

Tests
Test Career: 1939
Cap Number: 46
Tests Played: 3

Test Batting
Innings:	4	Runs:	3
Highest Score:	2	Average:	1.00
No. 50s:	0	No. 100s:	0

Test Bowling & Fielding
Wickets:	6	Runs:	261
Best Bowling:	3/59	Average:	43.50
5 WI:	0	10 WM:	0
Catches:	0	Stumpings:	0

A leg break bowler who made his debut against England at Old Trafford in 1939. Studying medicine during his playing days, Bertie later became a doctor and was awarded an OBE.

CLARKE, Sylvester Theophilus

Born: December 11, 1954
Origin: Barbados
Batting: Right handed
Bowling: Right arm fast

Tests
Test Career: 1978-82
Cap Number: 165
Tests Played: 11

Test Batting
Innings:	16	Runs:	172
Highest Score:	35*	Average:	15.63
No. 50s:	0	No. 100s:	0

Test Bowling & Fielding
Wickets:	42	Runs:	1,170
Best Bowling:	5/126	Average:	27.85
5 WI:	1	10 WM:	0
Catches:	2	Stumpings:	0

One Day Internationals
ODI Career: 1978-82
ODIs Played: 10

ODI Batting
Innings:	8	Runs:	60
Highest Score:	20	Average:	10.00
No. 50s:	0	No. 100s:	0

ODI Bowling & Fielding
Wickets:	13	Runs:	245
Best Bowling:	3/22	Average:	18.84
5 WM:	0	Catches:	4
Stumpings:	0		

Sylvester Clarke was a heavily built paceman from Barbados who thrived in putting the fear of God in batsmen. Clarke got his chance at Test level when the likes of regular pacemen in Garner, Roberts and Holding were competing in the non recognised World Series Cricket competition in Australia. He made his Test debut against a patchwork Australian side, at Georgetown in 1978, and performed admirably taking three wickets in each innings. A passionate individual, Clarke was involved in a spiteful incident during a Test against Pakistan, at Multan in 1981. After being pelted by oranges and missiles from the partisan crowd, Clarke retaliated by hurling a nearby brick. The brick struck and seriously injured a spectator. Clarke was subsequently suspended for two matches. Upon the return of the WSC players, such as Holding, Garner and Roberts, Clarke found it difficult to compete for a regular spot and thus played only eleven Tests in all. In 1983, he joined the rebel West Indian side that toured South Africa. In a rather sad footnote, on December 4, 1999, exactly a month after bidding farewell to former team mate Malcolm Marshall, who has lost his battle with cancer, Sylvester Clarke died from a heart attack. He was just seven days away from his 45th birthday.

COLLINS, Pedro Tyrone

Born: August 12, 1976
Origin: Barbados
Batting: Right handed
Bowling: Left arm medium-fast

Tests
Test Career: 1999-06
Cap Number: 225
Tests Played: 32

Test Batting
Innings:	47	Runs:	235
Highest Score:	24	Average:	5.87
No. 50s:	0	No. 100s:	0

Test Bowling & Fielding
Wickets:	106	Runs:	3,671
Best Bowling:	6/53	Average:	34.63
5 WI:	3	10 WM:	0
Catches:	7	Stumpings:	0

One Day Internationals
ODI Career: 1999-05
ODIs Played: 30

ODI Batting
Innings:	12	Runs:	30
Highest Score:	10*	Average:	4.28
No. 50s:	0	No. 100s:	0

ODI Bowling & Fielding
Wickets:	39	Runs:	1,212
Best Bowling:	5/43	Average:	31.07
5 WM:	1	Catches:	8
Stumpings:	0		

A left arm, swing bowler Pedro Collins together with Jerome Taylor, leads the current day West Indian pace attack. The half brother of fellow paceman Fidel Edwards, Pedro Collins made his Test debut against Australia at Port of Spain, in 1999. An injury interrupted career to date, Collins has taken five wickets in an innings on three occasions, his best 6/53 against Bangladesh, at Kingston, in 2004.

COLLYMORE, Corey

Born: December 21, 1977
Origin: Barbados
Batting: Right handed
Bowling: Right arm medium-fast

Tests
Test Career:	1999-06		
Cap Number:	230		
Tests Played:	23		

Test Batting
Innings:	40	Runs:	149
Highest Score:	16*	Average:	7.84
No. 50s:	0	No. 100s:	0

Test Bowling & Fielding
Wickets:	75	Runs:	2,219
Best Bowling:	7/57	Average:	29.58
5 WI:	4	10 WM:	1
Catches:	5	Stumpings:	0

One Day Internationals
ODI Career:	1999-06		
ODIs Played:	69		

ODI Batting
Innings:	26	Runs:	149
Highest Score:	13*	Average:	5.21
No. 50s:	0	No. 100s:	0

ODI Bowling & Fielding
Wickets:	69	Runs:	2,410
Best Bowling:	5/51	Average:	34.92
5 WM:	1	Catches:	12
Stumpings:	0		

Part of the current day West Indian pace attack, Corey Collymore made his Test debut against Australia, at Antigua in 1999, where he took just one wicket, that of opener Greg Blewett. Not express by any means, Collymore's strength is his line and length and has been a consistent performer over the years as the West Indies continually try to rebuild a pace attack that one day may resemble the potent ensemble of the late 1970's and 80's. Although hampered by injuries at various stages, Collymore has taken seven wickets in an innings on two occasions, the first, a career best 7/57 against Sri Lanka at Kingston, in 2003, and then at the same venue in 2005, he captured 7/78 against Pakistan.

CONSTANTINE, Learie
Born:	September 21, 1901
Origin:	Trinidad
Batting:	Right handed

Tests
Test Career:	1928-39		
Cap Number:	3		
Tests Played:	18		

Test Batting
Innings:	33	Runs:	635
Highest Score:	90	Average:	19.24
No. 50s:	4	No. 100s:	0

Test Bowling & Fielding
Wickets:	58	Runs:	1,746
Best Bowling:	5/75	Average:	30.10
5 WI:	2	10 WM:	0
Catches:	28	Stumpings:	0

A talented all-rounder who played in West Indies' inaugural Test against England, at Lord's in 1928. Constantine took the very first wicket in West Indian cricket - that of English opener, Charles Hallows for 26, and finished with his team's best figures of 4/82. A hard working campaigner against racism, Constantine was knighted in 1962.

CROFT, Colin Everton Hunte
Born:	March 15, 1953
Origin:	Guyana
Batting:	Right handed
Bowling:	Right arm fast

Tests
Test Career:	1977-82		
Cap Number:	159		
Tests Played:	27		

Test Batting
Innings:	37	Runs:	158
Highest Score:	33	Average:	10.53
No. 50s:	0	No. 100s:	0

Test Bowling & Fielding
Wickets:	125	Runs:	2,913
Best Bowling:	8/29	Average:	23.30
5 WI:	3	10 WM:	0
Catches:	8	Stumpings:	0

One Day Internationals
ODI Career:	1977-81		
ODIs Played:	19		

ODI Batting
Innings:	6	Runs:	18
Highest Score:	8	Average:	9.00
No. 50s:	0	No. 100s:	0

ODI Bowling & Fielding
Wickets:	30	Runs:	620
Best Bowling:	6/15	Average:	20.66
5 WM:	1	Catches:	1
Stumpings:	0		

There were far more pleasant sights for unsuspecting batsmen than the image of Colin Croft's 6.6, solidly built frame steaming in off a long run. Croft's bowling style was one of the most unique seen in international cricket. Once in delivery stride, he would suddenly veer wide of the bowling crease, and sharply angle the ball across the batsman. While Croft's shorter pitched deliveries were no doubt tough to negotiate, his action made it difficult for umpires to give him a favourable nod when adjudicating on leg before decisions. His Test career got off to a flying start with 3/85 and 4/47 on debut against Pakistan, at Bridgetown, and then followed up with what is still to date, the best figures by a West Indian paceman of 8/29 in the second Test at Port of Spain. Jack Noreiga who holds the West Indian record of 9/95, in 1970 was an off-spinner. After establishing himself as part of the potent West Indian pace attack in his rookie season, surprisingly Croft opted to sign on for the second season of World Series Cricket, in 1978. He returned to the Test scene immediately after the World Series Cricket competition folded and took three crucial wickets in the 1979 World Cup Final against England in 1979, where the West Indies made it back-to-back titles. After his retirement in 1981, he embarked on the rebel tour of South Africa in 1982. These days Croft is a respected commentator.

CUFFY, Cameron

Born:	February 8, 1970
Origin:	St Vincent
Batting:	Right handed
Bowling:	Right arm fast

Tests

Test Career:	1994-02
Cap Number:	206
Tests Played:	15

Test Batting

Innings:	23	Runs:	58
Highest Score:	15	Average:	4.14
No. 50s:	0	No. 100s:	0

Test Bowling & Fielding

Wickets:	43	Runs:	1,455
Best Bowling:	4/82	Average:	33.83
5 WI:	0	10 WM:	0
Catches:	5	Stumpings:	0

One Day Internationals

ODI Career:	1994-02
ODIs Played:	41

ODI Batting

Innings:	22	Runs:	62
Highest Score:	17*	Average:	4.42
No. 50s:	0	No. 100s:	0

ODI Bowling & Fielding

Wickets:	41	Runs:	1,436
Best Bowling:	4/24	Average:	35.02
5 WM:	0	Catches:	5
Stumpings:	0		

A tall and strong pace bowler from St. Vincent, who looked like being the next 'batsman's nightmare' after making his debut against India, at Mumbai, in 1994. However, Cuffy struggled for consistency playing just 15 Tests. A member of the 1996 World Cup squad, Cuffy was a valuable contributor in the One-Day side over a nine year period.

CUMMINS, Anderson Cleophas

Born:	May 7, 1966
Origin:	Barbados
Batting:	Right handed
Bowling:	Right arm medium-fast

Tests

Test Career:	1993-94
Cap Number:	203
Tests Played:	5

Test Batting

Innings:	6	Runs:	98
Highest Score:	50	Average:	19.60
No. 50s:	1	No. 100s:	0

Test Bowling & Fielding

Wickets:	8	Runs:	342
Best Bowling:	4/54	Average:	42.75
5 WI:	0	10 WM:	0
Catches:	1	Stumpings:	0

One Day Internationals

ODI Career:	1991-95
ODIs Played:	63

ODI Batting

Innings:	41	Runs:	459
Highest Score:	44*	Average:	15.30
No. 50s:	0	No. 100s:	0

ODI Bowling & Fielding

Wickets:	78	Runs:	2,246
Best Bowling:	5/31	Average:	28.79
5 WM:	1	Catches:	11
Stumpings:	0		

An excellent One Day bowler who was a member of the 1992 World Cup squad. Played the first of his five Tests against Australia, at Perth, in 1993.

DA COSTA, Oscar

Born:	September 11, 1907
Origin:	Jamaica
Batting:	Right handed
Bowling:	Right arm medium

Tests

Test Career:	1930-35
Cap Number:	27
Tests Played:	5

Test Batting

Innings:	9	Runs:	153
Highest Score:	39	Average:	19.12
No. 50s:	0	No. 100s:	0

Test Bowling & Fielding

Wickets:	3	Runs:	175
Best Bowling:	1/14	Average:	58.33
5 WI:	0	10 WM:	0
Catches:	5	Stumpings:	0

An all-rounder who made his debut against England at Kingston in 1930.

DANIEL, Wayne

Born:	January 16, 1956
Origin:	Barbados
Batting:	Right handed
Bowling:	Right arm fast

Tests

Test Career:	1976-84
Cap Number:	156
Tests Played:	10

Test Batting

Innings:	11	Runs:	46
Highest Score:	11	Average:	6.57
No. 50s:	0	No. 100s:	0

Test Bowling & Fielding

Wickets:	36	Runs:	910
Best Bowling:	5/39	Average:	25.27
5 WI:	1	10 WM:	0
Catches:	4	Stumpings:	0

One Day Internationals

ODI Career:	1978-84
ODIs Played:	18

ODI Batting

Innings:	5	Runs:	49
Highest Score:	16*	Average:	49.00
No. 50s:	0	No. 100s:	0

ODI Bowling & Fielding

Wickets:	23	Runs:	595
Best Bowling:	3/27	Average:	25.86
5 WM:	0	Catches:	5
Stumpings:	0		

A solidly built pace bowler with a powerful action, Wayne Daniel was part of a much feared pace quartet, comprising of Michael Holding, Andy Roberts and Joel Garner. Ironically, Daniel is best remembered for his spectacular, match winning six during a World Series Cricket, one day final, against Australia in 1978/79. With two balls remaining, the Australians were content to concede a run, which would see the hard-hitting Joel Garner stuck at the non-strikers end. This meant that the number eleven 'bunny', Daniel, would face the frugal medium pace bowling of Mick Malone. A seemingly unplayable ball pitched at Daniel's feet, at first glance, seemed an appropriate option. But the lateral thinking tail-ender had other ideas. With a quick shift to the left, he clubbed the ball over square leg for one of the most massive, and amazing, sixes ever witnessed in international cricket. With the focus primarily on Garner, Daniel became the quintessential accidental hero.

DAVIS, Bryan

Born:	May 2, 1940
Origin:	Trinidad
Batting:	Right handed
Bowling:	Right arm off-break

Tests

Test Career:	1965		
Cap Number:	123		
Tests Played:	4		
Test Batting			
Innings:	8	Runs:	245
Highest Score:	68	Average:	30.62
No. 50s:	3	No. 100s:	0
Test Bowling & Fielding			
Wickets:	0	Runs:	0
Best Bowling:		Average:	0.00
5 WI:	0	10 WM:	0
Catches:	1	Stumpings:	0

An highly rated opening batsman who scored two fifties on debut against Australia, at Port of Spain, in 1965.

DAVIS, Charles Allan

Born:	January 1, 1944
Origin:	Trinidad
Batting:	Right handed
Bowling:	Right arm medium

Tests

Test Career:	1968-73		
Cap Number:	127		
Tests Played:	15		
Test Batting			
Innings:	29	Runs:	1,301
Highest Score:	183	Average:	54.20
No. 50s:	4	No. 100s:	4
Test Bowling & Fielding			
Wickets:	2	Runs:	330
Best Bowling:	1/27	Average:	165.00
5 WI:	0	10 WM:	0
Catches:	4	Stumpings:	0

A middle order batsman who scored four Test centuries. His first was a solid 103 against England, at Lords in 1969, and his last, a career best 183 against New Zealand at Bridgetown in 1972.

DAVIS, Winston Walter

Born:	September 18, 1958
Origin:	St Vincent
Batting:	Right handed
Bowling:	Right arm fast

Tests

Test Career:	1983-88		
Cap Number:	178		
Tests Played:	15		
Test Batting			
Innings:	17	Runs:	202
Highest Score:	77	Average:	15.53
No. 50s:	1	No. 100s:	0
Test Bowling & Fielding			
Wickets:	45	Runs:	1,472
Best Bowling:	4/19	Average:	32.71
5 WI:	0	10 WM:	0
Catches:	10	Stumpings:	0

One Day Internationals

ODI Career:	1983-88		
ODIs Played:	35		
ODI Batting			
Innings:	5	Runs:	28
Highest Score:	10	Average:	14.00
No. 50s:	0	No. 100s:	0
ODI Bowling & Fielding			
Wickets:	39	Runs:	1,302
Best Bowling:	7/51	Average:	33.38
5 WM:	1	Catches:	1
Stumpings:	0		

Winston Davis' finest hour arrived when he took a record 7/51 against Australia at Headingley, during the 1983 World Cup. But as the tournament continued, the young bowler couldn't emulate the feat, or come anywhere near it for that matter. Talent wise, Winston Davis could have walked into just about any Test side of that era. But he, like several aspiring pacemen of his day, found it too difficult to break into a side containing the likes of Garner, Holding, Roberts and Marshall. Davis played in 15 Tests and 35 ODI's until his retirement in 1988. He unfortunately suffered horrific spinal injuries when he fell from a great height while clearing trees on a farm back home.

DE CAIRES, Frank

Born:	May 12, 1909
Origin:	Guyana
Batting:	Right handed
Bowling:	Right arm fast

Tests

Test Career:	1930		
Cap Number:	16		
Tests Played:	3		
Test Batting			
Innings:	6	Runs:	232
Highest Score:	80	Average:	38.66
No. 50s:	2	No. 100s:	0
Test Bowling & Fielding			
Wickets:	0	Runs:	9
Best Bowling:		Average:	0.00
5 WI:	0	10 WM:	0
Catches:	1	Stumpings:	0

A middle order batsman who made 80 and 70 on debut against England, at Bridgetown in 1930.

DEONARINE, Narsingh

Born:	August 16, 1983
Origin:	Guyana
Batting:	Left handed
Bowling:	Right arm off-break

Tests
Test Career:	2005
Cap Number:	258
Tests Played:	4

Test Batting
Innings:	6	Runs:	107
Highest Score:	40	Average:	21.40
No. 50s:	0	No. 100s:	0

Test Bowling & Fielding
Wickets:	2	Runs:	151
Best Bowling:	1/5	Average:	75.50
5 WI:	0	10 WM:	0
Catches:	2	Stumpings:	0

One Day Internationals
ODI Career:	2005
ODIs Played:	4

ODI Batting
Innings:	4	Runs:	91
Highest Score:	41	Average:	22.75
No. 50s:	0	No. 100s:	0

ODI Bowling & Fielding
Wickets:	5	Runs:	142
Best Bowling:	2/18	Average:	28.40
5 WM:	0	Catches:	0
Stumpings:	0		

A right arm off-spinner, Deonarine was another who was asked to 'cover the fort' while seven senior players were sorting out a sponsorship dispute with the board. He performed well in his four Tests, against South Africa and Sri Lanka, but it was always going to be difficult to hold a place once the regular players had sorted out their differences and were once again available for selection.

DEPEIAZA, Clairmonte

Born:	October 10, 1928
Origin:	Barbados
Batting:	Right handed
Bowling:	Right arm fast
	Wicket Keeper

Tests
Test Career:	1955-56
Cap Number:	88
Tests Played:	5

Test Batting
Innings:	8	Runs:	187
Highest Score:	122	Average:	31.16
No. 50s:	0	No. 100s:	1

Test Bowling & Fielding
Wickets:	0	Runs:	15
Best Bowling:		Average:	0.00
5 WI:	0	10 WM:	0
Catches:	7	Stumpings:	4

A dour but talented wicket-keeper/batsman from Barbados, Clairmonte Depeiaza, scored his maiden Test century in his second Test, against Australia at Bridgetown in 1955. In that same innings, he and captain Denis Atkinson added 347 for the seventh wicket - a Test record which still stands today.

DEWDNEY, Tom

Born:	October 23, 1933
Origin:	Jamaica
Batting:	Right handed
Bowling:	Right arm fast

Tests
Test Career:	1955-58
Cap Number:	90
Tests Played:	9

Test Batting
Innings:	12	Runs:	17
Highest Score:	5*	Average:	2.42
No. 50s:	0	No. 100s:	0

Test Bowling & Fielding
Wickets:	21	Runs:	807
Best Bowling:	5/21	Average:	38.42
5 WI:	1	10 WM:	0
Catches:	0	Stumpings:	0

Opened the bowling with Frank Worrell and took 4/125 on debut against Australia, at Bridgetown, in 1955.

DHANRAJ, Rajindra

Born:	February 6, 1969
Origin:	Trinidad
Batting:	Right handed
Bowling:	Right arm leg-break

Tests
Test Career:	1994-96
Cap Number:	207
Tests Played:	4

Test Batting
Innings:	4	Runs:	17
Highest Score:	9	Average:	4.25
No. 50s:	0	No. 100s:	0

Test Bowling & Fielding
Wickets:	8	Runs:	595
Best Bowling:	2/49	Average:	74.37
5 WI:	0	10 WM:	0
Catches:	1	Stumpings:	0

One Day Internationals
ODI Career:	1994-95
ODIs Played:	6

ODI Batting
Innings:	2	Runs:	8
Highest Score:	8	Average:	8.00
No. 50s:	0	No. 100s:	0

ODI Bowling & Fielding
Wickets:	10	Runs:	170
Best Bowling:	4/26	Average:	17.00
5 WM:	0	Catches:	1
Stumpings:	0		

One of the very few leg-spinners coming out of the Caribbean, Dhanraj was selected on the 1994 tour of India but played only four Tests.

DILLON, Mervyn

Born: June 5, 1974
Origin: Trinidad
Batting: Right handed
Bowling: Right arm medium-fast

Tests
Test Career: 1997-04
Cap Number: 216
Tests Played: 38

Test Batting
Innings:	68	Runs:	549
Highest Score:	43	Average:	8.44
No. 50s:	0	No. 100s:	0

Test Bowling & Fielding
Wickets:	131	Runs:	4,398
Best Bowling:	5/71	Average:	33.57
5 WI:	2	10 WM:	0
Catches:	16	Stumpings:	0

One Day Internationals
ODI Career: 1997-05
ODIs Played: 108

ODI Batting
Innings:	51	Runs:	227
Highest Score:	21*	Average:	7.32
No. 50s:	0	No. 100s:	0

ODI Bowling & Fielding
Wickets:	130	Runs:	4,218
Best Bowling:	5/29	Average:	32.44
5 WM:	3	Catches:	20
Stumpings:	0		

A valiant competitor, Dillon spearheaded the bowling attack after the retirements of Courtney Walsh and Curtly Ambrose but, by no fault of his own, was simply not in their class. In his 38 Tests, he took a career best 5/71 against India, at Kingston in 2002. Dillon was a solid performer during the 1999 World Cup tournament.

DOWE, Uton George

Born: March 29, 1949
Origin: Jamaica
Batting: Right handed
Bowling: Right arm fast

Tests
Test Career: 1971-73
Cap Number: 140
Tests Played: 4

Test Batting
Innings:	3	Runs:	8
Highest Score:	5*	Average:	8.00
No. 50s:	0	No. 100s:	0

Test Bowling & Fielding
Wickets:	12	Runs:	534
Best Bowling:	4/69	Average:	44.50
5 WI:	0	10 WM:	0
Catches:	3	Stumpings:	0

A pace bowler from Jamaica who took his best haul of 4/69 against India, at Bridgetown, in 1971.

DRAKES, Vasbert Conniel

Born: August 5, 1969
Origin: Barbados
Batting: Right handed
Bowling: Right arm fast

Tests
Test Career: 2002-04
Cap Number: 246
Tests Played: 12

Test Batting
Innings:	20	Runs:	386
Highest Score:	67	Average:	21.44
No. 50s:	1	No. 100s:	0

Test Bowling & Fielding
Wickets:	33	Runs:	1,362
Best Bowling:	5/93	Average:	41.27
5 WI:	1	10 WM:	0
Catches:	2	Stumpings:	0

One Day Internationals
ODI Career: 1995-04
ODIs Played: 34

ODI Batting
Innings:	17	Runs:	94
Highest Score:	25	Average:	7.83
No. 50s:	0	No. 100s:	0

ODI Bowling & Fielding
Wickets:	51	Runs:	1,293
Best Bowling:	5/33	Average:	25.35
5 WM:	2	Catches:	5
Stumpings:	0		

A right arm quick and competant middle/lower order batsman, Drakes took four wickets on debut against Bangladesh, at Dhaka, in 2002. He went on to take a career best 5/93 against Australia but has struggled to claim a Test cap since 2004. A member of the 2003 World Cup squad.

DUJON, Peter Jeffrey Leroy

Born: May 28, 1956
Origin: Jamaica
Batting: Right handed
Bowling: Right arm medium
Wicket Keeper

Tests
Test Career: 1981-91
Cap Number: 176
Tests Played: 81

Test Batting
Innings:	115	Runs:	3,322
Highest Score:	139	Average:	31.94
No. 50s:	16	No. 100s:	5

Test Bowling & Fielding
Wickets:	0	Runs:	0
Best Bowling:		Average:	0.00
5 WI:	0	10 WM:	0
Catches:	267	Stumpings:	5

One Day Internationals
ODI Career: 1981-91
ODIs Played: 169

ODI Batting
Innings:	120	Runs:	1,945
Highest Score:	82*	Average:	23.15
No. 50s:	6	No. 100s:	0

ODI Bowling & Fielding
Wickets:	0	Runs:	0
Best Bowling:		Average:	0.00
5 WM:	0	Catches:	183
Stumpings:	21		

Scoring a Test hundred on debut or taking a hat-trick to wrap up a match is every budding cricketer's dream. A catch behind the stumps or flicking off the bails in a close run out has never really had the same romance as per the aforementioned deeds with bat and ball. But that was until Jeffrey Dujon entered the international arena. His agility, athleticism, and decision making while keeping to arguably the fastest pace attack ever, single-handedly revolutionised the image of the crouching gloveman. Dujon made his debut in the 1981 Boxing Day Test against Australia, at the MCG. His 41 in the first innings and 43 in the second was a sample of what was to come from Dujon the batsman. Such was his ability, Dujon was often played as a middle order batsman thus providing the West Indies with the luxury of playing a fifth bowler when and if the need arose. Dujon made five Test hundreds and scored 3,322 runs, which is the most by a West Indian wicket-keeper. While his average of 31.94 is the also the best by a West Indian keeper, he was most valuable when called upon to rescue the side from a batting collapse. In fact, his highest score of 139 against Australia at Perth, in 1984, was made in such circumstances. When Dujon joined Larry Gomes at the crease, the West Indies were reeling at 6/186. The pair put on 149 for the 7th wicket and the change in momentum enabled the Windies cruise to a comfortable innings and 112 run win. This was typical of his fighting, yet cool in a crisis character. While Dujon's gymnastic-like wizardry clearly demonstrated his competence when keeping to the sheer pace of the likes of Marshall, Holding, Garner, Ambrose, it was often murmured that he was never really tested with spin. Apart from Roger Harper and part time spinners, Viv Richards and Larry Gomes, there wasn't that many opportunities for Dujon to stand close to the stumps and demonstrate his glovemanship towards the slower bowlers. An inadvertent entertainer during his decade at the elite level, Dujon retired in 1991 and his 272 dismissals (267 catches & 5 stumpings) remains as West Indian, wicket-keeping record.

EDWARDS, Fidel Henderson

Born: February 6, 1982
Origin: Barbados
Batting: Right handed
Bowling: Right arm fast

Tests
Test Career: 2003-06
Cap Number: 253
Tests Played: 24

Test Batting
Innings:	39	Runs:	119
Highest Score:	20	Average:	4.25
No. 50s:	0	No. 100s:	0

Test Bowling & Fielding
Wickets:	62	Runs:	2,675
Best Bowling:	5/36	Average:	43.14
5 WI:	4	10 WM:	0
Catches:	4	Stumpings:	0

One Day Internationals
ODI Career: 2003-06
ODIs Played: 19

ODI Batting
Innings:	6	Runs:	12
Highest Score:	4*	Average:	6.00
No. 50s:	0	No. 100s:	0

ODI Bowling & Fielding
Wickets:	24	Runs:	684
Best Bowling:	6/22	Average:	28.50
5 WM:	1	Catches:	2
Stumpings:	0		

The half brother of paceman Pedro Collins, Fidel Edwards, although a quick bowler, concentrates on swing rather than out and out speed. While his 5/36 on debut against Sri Lanka at Kingston, in 2003, remains his best haul to date, Edwards has performed reasonably well at both Test and ODI level. At 25, Edwards has the opportunity to establish himself as a permanent fixture in the West Indies pace attack alongside the likes of Taylor and Collins.

EDWARDS, Richard Martin

Born: June 3, 1940
Origin: Barbados
Batting: Right handed
Bowling: Right arm fast

Tests
Test Career: 1968-69
Cap Number: 128
Tests Played: 5

Test Batting
Innings:	8	Runs:	65
Highest Score:	22	Average:	9.28
No. 50s:	0	No. 100s:	0

Test Bowling & Fielding
Wickets:	18	Runs:	626
Best Bowling:	5/84	Average:	34.77
5 WI:	1	10 WM:	0
Catches:	0	Stumpings:	0

A pace bowler from Barbados who made his debut against Australia, at the MCG in 1968. Took a career best 5/84 against New Zealand a year later.

FERGUSON, Wilfred

Born: December 14, 1917
Origin: Trinidad
Batting: Right handed
Bowling: Right arm leg-break

Tests
Test Career: 1948-54
Cap Number: 54
Tests Played: 8

Test Batting
Innings:	10	Runs:	200
Highest Score:	75	Average:	28.57
No. 50s:	2	No. 100s:	0

Test Bowling & Fielding
Wickets:	34	Runs:	1,165
Best Bowling:	6/92	Average:	34.26
5 WI:	3	10 WM:	1
Catches:	11	Stumpings:	0

A leg spinner who was also very competant batsman. Batting at number nine on debut against England at Bridgetown, Ferguson scored 56 not out and went on to open the batting at various times during his career. With the ball he claimed a career best 6/92 against England, at Port of Spain, in just his second Test. He captured 11 wickets for the match.

FERNANDES, Maurius (Maurice)
Born: August 12, 1897
Origin: Guyana
Batting: Right handed

Tests
Test Career: 1928-30
Cap Number: 4
Tests Played: 2
Test Batting
Innings: 4 Runs: 49
Highest Score: 22 Average: 12.25
No. 50s: 0 No. 100s: 0
Test Bowling & Fielding
Wickets: 0 Runs: 0
Best Bowling: Average: 0.00
5 WI: 0 10 WM: 0
Catches: 0 Stumpings: 0

Batted at first drop in West Indies' inaugural Test against England, at Lord's in 1928. He later captained the Windies in one Test in 1930.

FINDLAY, Thaddeus Michael
Born: October 19, 1943
Origin: St Vincent
Batting: Right handed
Wicket Keeper

Tests
Test Career: 1969-73
Cap Number: 133
Tests Played: 10
Test Batting
Innings: 16 Runs: 212
Highest Score: 44* Average: 16.30
No. 50s: 0 No. 100s: 0
Test Bowling & Fielding
Wickets: 0 Runs: 0
Best Bowling: Average: 0.00
5 WI: 0 10 WM: 0
Catches: 19 Stumpings: 2

A wicket-keeper from St.Vincent who played in ten Tests between 1969-73 after making his debut against England, at Lord's, in 1969.

FOSTER, Maurice Linton
Born: May 9, 1943
Origin: Jamaica
Batting: Right handed
Bowling: Right arm off-break

Tests
Test Career: 1969-78
Cap Number: 130
Tests Played: 14
Test Batting
Innings: 24 Runs: 580
Highest Score: 125 Average: 30.52
No. 50s: 1 No. 100s: 1

Test Bowling & Fielding
Wickets: 9 Runs: 600
Best Bowling: 2/41 Average: 66.66
5 WI: 0 10 WM: 0
Catches: 3 Stumpings: 0

One Day Internationals
ODI Career: 1973
ODIs Played: 2
ODI Batting
Innings: 1 Runs: 25
Highest Score: 25 Average: 25.00
No. 50s: 0 No. 100s: 0
ODI Bowling & Fielding
Wickets: 2 Runs: 22
Best Bowling: 2/22 Average: 11.00
5 WM: 0 Catches: 0
Stumpings: 0

A middle order batsman from Jamaica who scored the one Test century - 125 against Australia, at Kingston in 1973.

FRANCIS, George
Born: December 11, 1897
Origin: Barbados
Batting: Right handed
Bowling: Right arm fast

Tests
Test Career: 1928-33
Cap Number: 5
Tests Played: 10
Test Batting
Innings: 18 Runs: 81
Highest Score: 19* Average: 5.78
No. 50s: 0 No. 100s: 0
Test Bowling & Fielding
Wickets: 23 Runs: 763
Best Bowling: 4/40 Average: 33.17
5 WI: 0 10 WM: 0
Catches: 7 Stumpings: 0

He opened the bowling and took 2/72 in West Indies inaugural Test against England at Lord's, in 1928.

FREDERICK, Michael Campbell
Born: May 6, 1927
Origin: Barbados
Batting: Right handed
Bowling: Right arm medium

Tests
Test Career: 1954
Cap Number: 81
Tests Played: 1
Test Batting
Innings: 2 Runs: 30
Highest Score: 30 Average: 15.00
No. 50s: 0 No. 100s: 0
Test Bowling & Fielding
Wickets: 0 Runs: 0
Best Bowling: Average: 0.00
5 WI: 0 10 WM: 0
Catches: 0 Stumpings: 0

A right hand opener who scored a duck in the first innings on debut against England at Kingston. He followed up with 30 in the second innings but it was not enough to earn another Test cap.

FREDERICKS, Roy Clifton

Born: November 11, 1942
Origin: Guyana
Batting: Left handed
Bowling: Left arm leg-break

Tests

Test Career: 1968-77
Cap Number: 129
Tests Played: 59

Test Batting

Innings:	109	Runs:	4,334
Highest Score:	169	Average:	42.49
No. 50s:	26	No. 100s:	8

Test Bowling & Fielding

Wickets:	7	Runs:	548
Best Bowling:	1/12	Average:	78.28
5 WI:	0	10 WM:	0
Catches:	62	Stumpings:	0

One Day Internationals

ODI Career: 1973-77
ODIs Played: 12

ODI Batting

Innings:	12	Runs:	311
Highest Score:	105	Average:	25.91
No. 50s:	1	No. 100s:	1

ODI Bowling & Fielding

Wickets:	2	Runs:	10
Best Bowling:	2/10	Average:	5.00
5 WM:	0	Catches:	4
Stumpings:	0		

Although standing at just 5.6, Roy Fredericks was one of toughest openers of all time. His 76 and 47 on debut against Australia, at the MCG in 1968, typified the consistency that was to follow. An excellent exponent of the late cut, the stylish left-hander was also an aggressive hooker and rarely intimidated by fast bowling. In fact, his greatest innings occurred when he took on Aussie speed demons, Lillee and Thomson, at the WACA ground in Perth, in 1975. With the West Indies batting first, Fredericks hooked, cut and pulled the Australian pace attack all over the park, reaching his century before lunch, off just 71 balls. The onslaught continued after the interval and he was eventually out for a career best 169. Partnering with Gordon Greenidge throughout the mid 1970's, the pair was soon recognised as the most potent opening combination of their era as they averaged just under 55 every time they welcomed the new ball. In the twilight of his career, he along with Greenidge, Viv Richards, Clive Lloyd and several other key West Indian cricketers joined Kerry Packer's World Series Cricket competition in 1977.

FULLER, Dickie

Born: January 30, 1913
Origin: Jamaica
Batting: Right handed
Bowling: Right arm medium-fast

Tests

Test Career: 1935
Cap Number: 43
Tests Played: 1

Test Batting

Innings:	1	Runs:	1
Highest Score:	1	Average:	1.00
No. 50s:	0	No. 100s:	0

Test Bowling & Fielding

Wickets:	0	Runs:	12
Best Bowling:		Average:	0.00
5 WI:	0	10 WM:	0
Catches:	0	Stumpings:	0

An all-rounder from Jamaica who played just one Test against England, at Kingston in 1935.

FURLONGE, Hammond Allan

Born: June 19, 1934
Origin: Trinidad
Batting: Right handed

Tests

Test Career: 1955-56
Cap Number: 91
Tests Played: 3

Test Batting

Innings:	5	Runs:	99
Highest Score:	64	Average:	19.80
No. 50s:	1	No. 100s:	0

Test Bowling & Fielding

Wickets:	0	Runs:	0
Best Bowling:		Average:	0.00
5 WI:	0	10 WM:	0
Catches:	0	Stumpings:	0

A right hand opener, Furlonge made his Test debut against Australia, at Kingston, in 1955. He scored 64 in his third and final Test against New Zealand, at Eden Park, Auckland.

GABRIEL, Richard

Born: June 5, 1952
Origin: Trinidad
Batting: Right handed
Bowling: Right arm off-break

One Day Internationals

ODI Career: 1984
ODIs Played: 11

ODI Batting

Innings:	11	Runs:	167
Highest Score:	41	Average:	15.18
No. 50s:	0	No. 100s:	0

ODI Bowling & Fielding

Wickets:	0	Runs:	0
Best Bowling:		Average:	0.00
5 WM:	0	Catches:	1
Stumpings:	0		

A right hand opening batsman who partnered Desmond Haynes in the Australian tour of 1984. Gabriel made his ODI debut at the MCG and played 11 ODI's in the triangular series.

GANGA, Daren
Born: January 14, 1979
Origin: Trinidad
Batting: Right handed
Bowling: Right arm off-break

Tests
Test Career: 1998-06
Cap Number: 223
Tests Played: 38

Test Batting
Innings:	67	Runs:	1,765
Highest Score:	135	Average:	26.74
No. 50s:	7	No. 100s:	3

Test Bowling & Fielding
Wickets:	0	Runs:	86
Best Bowling:		Average:	0.00
5 WI:	0	10 WM:	0
Catches:	25	Stumpings:	0

One Day Internationals
ODI Career: 1999-06
ODIs Played: 33

ODI Batting
Innings:	32	Runs:	802
Highest Score:	71	Average:	25.87
No. 50s:	9	No. 100s:	0

ODI Bowling & Fielding
Wickets:	0	Runs:	4
Best Bowling:		Average:	0.00
5 WM:	0	Catches:	11
Stumpings:	0		

An opener who started off his career as a middle order batsman, Daren Ganga has overcome a period of inconsistency to become a permanent member of the Test team. In early 2006, he was one of six candidates short listed for the captaincy. To date, Ganga has hit three Test centuries, his most recent a career best 135 against India at Basseterre in 2006.

GANTEAUME, Andrew Gordon
Born: January 22, 1921
Origin: Trinidad
Batting: Right handed
Wicket Keeper

Tests
Test Career: 1948
Cap Number: 60
Tests Played: 1

Test Batting
Innings:	1	Runs:	112
Highest Score:	112	Average:	112.00
No. 50s:	0	No. 100s:	1

Test Bowling & Fielding
Wickets:	0	Runs:	0
Best Bowling:		Average:	0.00
5 WI:	0	10 WM:	0
Catches:	0	Stumpings:	0

A wicket-keeper from Trinidad who scored 112 while opening the batting with George Carew against England, at Port of Spain in 1948. The pair put on 173 for the first wicket but Ganteaume was heavily criticized for being too cautious when he neared triple figures. As a result, he was dropped for the next Test and never recalled.

GARNER, Joel
Born: December 16, 1952
Origin: Barbados
Batting: Right handed
Bowling: Right arm medium-fast

Tests
Test Career: 1977-87
Cap Number: 160
Tests Played: 58

Test Batting
Innings:	68	Runs:	672
Highest Score:	60	Average:	12.44
No. 50s:	1	No. 100s:	0

Test Bowling & Fielding
Wickets:	259	Runs:	5,433
Best Bowling:	6/56	Average:	20.97
5 WI:	7	10 WM:	0
Catches:	42	Stumpings:	0

One Day Internationals
ODI Career: 1977-87
ODIs Played: 98

ODI Batting
Innings:	41	Runs:	239
Highest Score:	37	Average:	9.19
No. 50s:	0	No. 100s:	0

ODI Bowling & Fielding
Wickets:	146	Runs:	2,752
Best Bowling:	5/31	Average:	18.84
5 WM:	3	Catches:	30
Stumpings:	0		

Affectionately known as 'Big Bird', the 6.8 Garner became a popular figure during the first season of World Series Cricket in the Australian summer of 1977/78. Taking full advantage of his excess height, his ability to gain extra bounce, especially against shorter batsman, was one distinct string to his bow but this trademark stock ball was his dipping yorker, which was virtually unplayable even for the elite batsmen. It was during his WSC days that his uncanny ability as a gully fieldsman was uncovered. Just when a batsman thought his meatish square cut was well on its way to crashing into the fence, suddenly the outstretched, bucket-like hands of Garner would appear from nowhere. Garner made his Test debut, alongside fellow giant paceman Colin Croft, a few months prior to joining Kerry Packer's WSC when the pair were selected for the 1st Test against Pakistan at Bridgetown. When Croft neatly caught opener Sadiq Mohammad, the twin towers had combined to give Garner his first Test wicket. Part of what experts consider to be the most formidable pace attack in history, comprising of Michael Holding, Andy Roberts, Croft and then later Malcolm Marshall, Garner may not have been the quickest of the bunch but was probably the most frugal. He took 259 wickets at 20.97 and is currently the fifth highest West Indian wicket-taker behind Walsh, Ambrose, Marshall and Gibbs. A superb limited overs bowler, where he averaged a wicket every 18.84 runs, his most memorable feat was his 5/38 in the 1979 World Cup Final against England, which all but secured consecutive titles for the West Indies who had taken out the inaugural trophy in 1975.

GARRICK, Leon Vivian

Born:	November 11, 1976
Origin:	Jamaica
Batting:	Right handed
Bowling:	Right arm medium
	Wicket Keeper

Tests

Test Career:	2001
Cap Number:	240
Tests Played:	1

Test Batting

Innings:	2	Runs:	27
Highest Score:	27	Average:	13.50
No. 50s:	0	No. 100s:	0

Test Bowling & Fielding

Wickets:	0	Runs:	0
Best Bowling:		Average:	0.00
5 WI:	0	10 WM:	0
Catches:	2	Stumpings:	0

One Day Internationals

ODI Career:	2001
ODIs Played:	3

ODI Batting

Innings:	3	Runs:	99
Highest Score:	76	Average:	33.00
No. 50s:	1	No. 100s:	0

ODI Bowling & Fielding

Wickets:	0	Runs:	0
Best Bowling:		Average:	0.00
5 WM:	0	Catches:	0
Stumpings:	0		

An opener who made a duck then 27 in his only Test against South Africa, at Kingston, in 2001.

GASKIN, Berkeley

Born:	March 21, 1908
Origin:	Guyana
Batting:	Right handed
Bowling:	Right arm medium

Tests

Test Career:	1948
Cap Number:	55
Tests Played:	2

Test Batting

Innings:	3	Runs:	17
Highest Score:	10	Average:	5.66
No. 50s:	0	No. 100s:	0

Test Bowling & Fielding

Wickets:	2	Runs:	158
Best Bowling:	1/15	Average:	79.00
5 WI:	0	10 WM:	0
Catches:	1	Stumpings:	0

A medium pace bowler from Guyana who made his Test debut against England at Bridgetown in 1948, just a few months shy of his 40th birthday.

GAYLE, Christopher

Born:	September 21, 1979
Origin:	Jamaica
Batting:	Left handed
Bowling:	Right arm off-break

Tests

Test Career:	2000-06
Cap Number:	232
Tests Played:	61

Test Batting

Innings:	108	Runs:	4,079
Highest Score:	317	Average:	38.84
No. 50s:	25	No. 100s:	7

Test Bowling & Fielding

Wickets:	49	Runs:	1,825
Best Bowling:	5/34	Average:	37.24
5 WI:	2	10 WM:	0
Catches:	65	Stumpings:	0

One Day Internationals

ODI Career:	1999-06
ODIs Played:	138

ODI Batting

Innings:	135	Runs:	4,919
Highest Score:	153*	Average:	38.42
No. 50s:	26	No. 100s:	12

ODI Bowling & Fielding

Wickets:	114	Runs:	3,651
Best Bowling:	5/46	Average:	32.02
5 WI:	1	Catches:	63
Stumpings:	0		

An attacking left hand opening batsman, Chris Gayle had a slow start to his Test career after failing against Zimbabwe on debut and averaging under 15 in his first three Test series. However, Gayle was given a lifeline and was selected for the 2000/01 series against South Africa. Showing obvious improvement over the five Tests, Gayle was selected on the tour of Zimbabwe and this time didn't let the undermanned Zimbabweans off the hook, scoring his maiden Test century - 175 in the First Test at Bulawayo. Unfortunately, Gayle's immune system could not repel the inconsistency virus as shortly afterwards he suffered another dose of the yips, registering three successive ducks on the tour of Sri Lanka. But the selectors continued to show faith in the young Jamaican and his double century against New Zealand at Grenada, in 2002, seemed to provide the much-needed tonic that would eventually help resurrect his career. Since the double ton, Gayle has reached triple figures on another five occasions, including a massive 317 against South Africa at St John's, Antigua, in 2005. Gayle's effort has him sitting alongside West Indian royalty as it is the fourth highest score behind Brian Lara's quinella of 400 not out & 375, and Sir Garfield Sobers 365 not out against Pakistan. Even though Gayle's form in mid 2006 has again been patchy, the West Indian selectors have again persevered with the Gayle as Daren Ganga's opening partner, ahead of Wavell Hinds.

GIBBS, Glendon Lionel

Born: December 27, 1925
Origin: Guyana
Batting: Left handed
Bowling: Left arm slow

Tests
Test Career: 1955
Cap Number: 85
Tests Played: 1

Test Batting
Innings:	2	Runs:	12
Highest Score:	12	Average:	6.00
No. 50s:	0	No. 100s:	0

Test Bowling & Fielding
Wickets:	0	Runs:	7
Best Bowling:		Average:	0.00
5 WI:	0	10 WM:	0
Catches:	1	Stumpings:	0

A left opener who did not go on to become a household name like his namesake Lance, who made his debut a couple of years later. Glendon played just the one Test against Australia, at Kingston in 1955.

GIBBS, Lancelot Richard

Born: September 29, 1934
Origin: Guyana
Batting: Right handed
Bowling: Right arm off-break

Tests
Test Career: 1958-76
Cap Number: 99
Tests Played: 79

Test Batting
Innings:	109	Runs:	488
Highest Score:	25	Average:	6.97
No. 50s:	0	No. 100s:	0

Test Bowling & Fielding
Wickets:	309	Runs:	8,989
Best Bowling:	8/38	Average:	29.09
5 WI:	18	10 WM:	2
Catches:	52	Stumpings:	0

One Day Internationals
ODI Career: 1973-75
ODIs Played: 3

ODI Batting
Innings:	1	Runs:	0
Highest Score:	0*	Average:	0.00
No. 50s:	0	No. 100s:	0

ODI Bowling & Fielding
Wickets:	2	Runs:	59
Best Bowling:	1/12	Average:	29.50
5 WM:	0	Catches:	0
Stumpings:	0		

At one stage the highest wicket-taker in Test History, Lance Gibbs was one of the finest off-spinners the game had seen. His long fingers enabled him to extract extra spin and bounce, and his deceptive flight together with a variation in pace, made him one of the toughest bowler to score from, as his economy rate of 1.99 will testify. A cousin to fellow West Indian great, and former team mate, Clive Lloyd, Gibbs made his Test debut against Pakistan at Queen's Park Oval, Port of Spain, in 1958. He performed admirably taking four wickets and earned selection on the tour of India and Pakistan. However, it was during the 1960/61 tour of Australia that Gibbs made his mark on the international scene, taking 19 wickets at 20.78, including at hat-trick at the Adelaide Oval. He followed up with an even finer performance against India at home, capturing 24 wickets and taking a career best 8/38 in what can only be described as one of the finest spells in Test history, where he took 8/6 from 15 overs, with 14 of them being maidens. By the time he retired in 1976, Gibbs had become the first spinner, from any nation, to reach the 300 Test wicket milestone and only the second bowler overall, alongside Fred Truman, whose record he broke shortly afterwards. His 309 wickets remained a Test record until December 1981 when Australian bowling great, Dennis Lillee claimed the wicket of West Indian Larry Gomes at the MCG. Ironically, it was the same venue where Gibbs had claimed the record from Truman. To date, Gibbs has taken more wickets than any other West Indian spinner and sits in overall fourth position behind pacemen Courtney Walsh, Curtly Ambrose and the late Malcolm Marshall.

GIBSON, Ottis Delroy

Born: March 16, 1969
Origin: Barbados
Batting: Right handed
Bowling: Right arm fast

Tests
Test Career: 1995-99
Cap Number: 210
Tests Played: 2

Test Batting
Innings:	4	Runs:	93
Highest Score:	37	Average:	23.25
No. 50s:	0	No. 100s:	0

Test Bowling & Fielding
Wickets:	3	Runs:	275
Best Bowling:	2/81	Average:	91.66
5 WI:	0	10 WM:	0
Catches:	0	Stumpings:	0

One Day Internationals
ODI Career: 1995-97
ODIs Played: 15

ODI Batting
Innings:	11	Runs:	141
Highest Score:	52	Average:	14.10
No. 50s:	1	No. 100s:	0

ODI Bowling & Fielding
Wickets:	34	Runs:	621
Best Bowling:	5/40	Average:	18.26
5 WM:	0	Catches:	3
Stumpings:	0		

A strong and robust pace bowler who made an uneventful Test debut against England, at Lord's, in 1995. He followed up with just one more appearance some four years later against South Africa, at Capetown, in 1999.

GILCHRIST, Roy

Born:	June 28, 1934
Origin:	Jamaica
Batting:	Right handed
Bowling:	Right arm fast

Tests

Test Career:	1957-59
Cap Number:	93
Tests Played:	13

Test Batting

Innings:	14	Runs:	60
Highest Score:	12	Average:	5.45
No. 50s:	0	No. 100s:	0

Test Bowling & Fielding

Wickets:	57	Runs:	1,521
Best Bowling:	6/55	Average:	26.68
5 WI:	1	10 WM:	0
Catches:	4	Stumpings:	0

A fiery individual both on and off the field, Gilchrist made his Test debut against England at Edgbaston in 1957. Took a career best 6/55 against India at Kolkata.

GLADSTONE, George

Born:	January 14, 1901
Origin:	Jamaica
Batting:	Left handed
Bowling:	Left arm slow

Tests

Test Career:	1930
Cap Number:	28
Tests Played:	1

Test Batting

Innings:	1	Runs:	12
Highest Score:	12*	Average:	0.00
No. 50s:	0	No. 100s:	0

Test Bowling & Fielding

Wickets:	1	Runs:	189
Best Bowling:	1/139	Average:	189.00
5 WI:	0	10 WM:	0
Catches:	0	Stumpings:	0

A left hander from Jamaica who played just the one Test against England, at Kingston in 1930.

GODDARD, John

Born:	April 21, 1919
Origin:	Barbados
Batting:	Left handed
Bowling:	Right arm off-break

Tests

Test Career:	1948-57
Cap Number:	56
Tests Played:	27

Test Batting

Innings:	39	Runs:	859
Highest Score:	83*	Average:	30.67
No. 50s:	4	No. 100s:	0

Test Bowling & Fielding

Wickets:	33	Runs:	1,050
Best Bowling:	5/31	Average:	31.81
5 WI:	1	10 WM:	0
Catches:	22	Stumpings:	0

The first long term captain of the West Indies, John Goddard was appointed skipper shortly after his debut against England at Bridgetown in early 1948, and led the side during their most successful era since their inclusion as a Test nation in 1928. Although he wasn't without his detractors late in his career, Goddard was universally considered a fine leader of men. An all-rounder, he took a career best 5/31 against England, at Georgetown in 1947. He could bat anywhere from opener to low in the order, scoring four fifties with a highest score of 83 not out against New Zealand, at Christchurch in 1956.

GOMES, Hilary Angelo (Larry)

Born:	July 13, 1953
Origin:	Trinidad
Batting:	Left handed
Bowling:	Right arm off-break

Tests

Test Career:	1976-87
Cap Number:	157
Tests Played:	60

Test Batting

Innings:	91	Runs:	3,171
Highest Score:	143	Average:	39.63
No. 50s:	13	No. 100s:	9

Test Bowling & Fielding

Wickets:	15	Runs:	930
Best Bowling:	2/20	Average:	62.00
5 WI:	0	10 WM:	0
Catches:	18	Stumpings:	0

One Day Internationals

ODI Career:	1978-87
ODIs Played:	83

ODI Batting

Innings:	64	Runs:	1,415
Highest Score:	101	Average:	28.87
No. 50s:	6	No. 100s:	1

ODI Bowling & Fielding

Wickets:	41	Runs:	1,045
Best Bowling:	4/31	Average:	25.48
5 WM:	0	Catches:	14
Stumpings:	0		

A fluent left-handed batsman whose calm demeanour was mirrored in his batting, Larry Gomes' introduction to Test cricket had the scribes pondering his future when he was dismissed for two ducks from his first three starts. However, upon the defection of the core batting line-up to World Series Cricket in 1977, Gomes seized the opportunity to cement a permanent spot in the middle order. In his next Test, at Georgetown, he scored his maiden Test century against Bob Simpson's Australians, and then followed up with 115 in the 5th Test at Kingston. A handy left arm off-spinner, Gomes often moonlighted as a partnership breaker in both ODI's and Tests. Later in his career, opposition pacemen started honing in on his off-stump as it was perceived that he had developed a weakness in that area. And it would be his flirtation with a delivery outside off stump that would induct Gomes into the annals of cricket history. During the 1981 Boxing Day Test at the MCG, his outside edge found its way into the soft hands of

Greg Chappell, thus giving Dennis Lillee his 310th Test wicket and crowning the Australian paceman as the highest wicket taker in Test cricket history, over taking legendary West Indian off-spinner, Lance Gibbs. A modest individual, Gomes retired from International cricket in 1987 with a Test average of just under 40.

GOMEZ, Gerry

Born: October 10, 1919
Origin: Trinidad
Batting: Right handed
Bowling: Right arm medium

Tests
Test Career: 1939-54
Cap Number: 49
Tests Played: 29

Test Batting
Innings:	46	Runs:	1,243
Highest Score:	101	Average:	30.31
No. 50s:	8	No. 100s:	1

Test Bowling & Fielding
Wickets:	58	Runs:	1,590
Best Bowling:	7/55	Average:	27.41
5 WI:	1	10 WM:	1
Catches:	18	Stumpings:	0

A tireless servant of West Indian cricket, both on and off the field, Gerry Gomez made a duck on his Test debut against England at Old Trafford but went on to average over 27 in his 29 Tests. He scored a century against India, at Delhi in 1948-49, and took a career best 7/55 against the Australians at the SCG in 1951/52. Gomez captained the West Indies in one Test in 1947/48 and shortly after his retirement became team manager then board member.

GRANT, George Copeland (Jackie)

Born: May 9, 1907
Origin: Trinidad
Batting: Right handed
Bowling: Right arm medium-fast

Tests
Test Career: 1930-35
Cap Number: 31
Tests Played: 12

Test Batting
Innings:	22	Runs:	413
Highest Score:	71*	Average:	25.81
No. 50s:	3	No. 100s:	0

Test Bowling & Fielding
Wickets:	0	Runs:	18
Best Bowling:		Average:	0.00
5 WI:	0	10 WM:	0
Catches:	10	Stumpings:	0

George Grant was appointed captain of the inaugural tour of Australia in 1930, where the West Indies recorded their first ever Test win on Australian soil. Grant captained the West Indies in all of his 12 Test matches.

GRANT, Rolph

Born: December 15, 1909
Origin: Trinidad
Batting: Right handed
Bowling: Right arm off-break

Tests
Test Career: 1935-39
Cap Number: 39
Tests Played: 7

Test Batting
Innings:	11	Runs:	220
Highest Score:	77	Average:	22.00
No. 50s:	1	No. 100s:	0

Test Bowling & Fielding
Wickets:	11	Runs:	353
Best Bowling:	3/68	Average:	32.09
5 WI:	0	10 WM:	0
Catches:	13	Stumpings:	0

An all-rounder of sorts who made his debut against England at Bridgetown in 1935. He was appointed captain of the West Indian side that toured England in 1939 and also took on the responsibility of opening the batting during that series.

GRAY, Anthony Hollis

Born: May 23, 1963
Origin: Trinidad
Batting: Right handed
Bowling: Right arm fast

Tests
Test Career: 1986-87
Cap Number: 188
Tests Played: 5

Test Batting
Innings:	8	Runs:	48
Highest Score:	12*	Average:	8.00
No. 50s:	0	No. 100s:	0

Test Bowling & Fielding
Wickets:	22	Runs:	377
Best Bowling:	4/39	Average:	17.13
5 WI:	0	10 WM:	0
Catches:	6	Stumpings:	0

One Day Internationals
ODI Career: 1985-91
ODIs Played: 25

ODI Batting
Innings:	11	Runs:	51
Highest Score:	10*	Average:	8.50
No. 50s:	0	No. 100s:	0

ODI Bowling & Fielding
Wickets:	44	Runs:	835
Best Bowling:	6/50	Average:	18.97
5 WM:	1	Catches:	3
Stumpings:	0		

A tall paceman from Trinidad who took six match wickets on debut against Pakistan, at Faisalabad, in 1986. Gray's day in the sun occurred in 1991, at Trinidad, when during an ODI he ripped through the Australian batting line-up taking 6/50.

GREENIDGE, Alvin Ethelbert

Born:	August 20, 1956
Origin:	Barbados
Batting:	Right handed
Bowling:	Right arm medium

Tests

Test Career:	1978-79
Cap Number:	166
Tests Played:	6

Test Batting

Innings:	10	Runs:	222
Highest Score:	69	Average:	22.20
No. 50s:	2	No. 100s:	0

Test Bowling & Fielding

Wickets:	0	Runs:	0
Best Bowling:		Average:	0.00
5 WI:	0	10 WM:	0
Catches:	5	Stumpings:	0

One Day Internationals

ODI Career:	1978
ODIs Played:	1

ODI Batting

Innings:	1	Runs:	23
Highest Score:	23	Average:	23.00
No. 50s:	0	No. 100s:	0

ODI Bowling & Fielding

Wickets:	0	Runs:	0
Best Bowling:		Average:	0.00
5 WM:	0	Catches:	0
Stumpings:	0		

The third Greenidge to play Test cricket for West Indies. All three were openers - and from Barbados - but amazingly not related in any way. Alvin made his debut against Australia, at Georgetown, in 1978 and played just six Tests in 1978/79.

GREENIDGE, Cuthbert Gordon

Born:	May 1, 1951
Origin:	Barbados
Batting:	Right handed
Bowling:	Right arm slow

Tests

Test Career:	1974-91
Cap Number:	150
Tests Played:	108

Test Batting

Innings:	185	Runs:	7,558
Highest Score:	226	Average:	44.72
No. 50s:	34	No. 100s:	19

Test Bowling & Fielding

Wickets:	0	Runs:	4
Best Bowling:		Average:	0.00
5 WI:	0	10 WM:	0
Catches:	96	Stumpings:	0

One Day Internationals

ODI Career:	1975-91
ODIs Played:	128

ODI Batting

Innings:	127	Runs:	5,134
Highest Score:	226	Average:	45.03
No. 50s:	31	No. 100s:	11

ODI Bowling & Fielding

Wickets:	1	Runs:	45
Best Bowling:	1/21	Average:	45.00
5 WM:	0	Catches:	45
Stumpings:	0		

Expansive drives, flashing cuts and more famously hammering hooks and pulls were all trademarks of the great West Indian opener. From Barbados, he joined the Test side in the mid 1970's just as the West Indies were beginning to assemble one of the great cricket sides of all time. Initially an opening partner with Roy Fredericks, where the pair averaged almost 55 every time they opened, he would soon be joined at the top of the order by Desmond Haynes and together they would form one of the cricket's great opening combinations, reaching 100 without loss on a record 16 occasions. Greenidge made his Test debut in late 1974 and took no time in establishing himself. He missed out on a century in his first Test innings by only seven runs but quickly made up for it by scoring 107 in the second innings of the same game. Possibly even more damaging as an opener in the one-day side, Greenidge played in the West Indian team that won the inaugural World Cup in 1975, in only his fourth One Day International, and then followed up as opener in the back-to back win of 1979. A member of media magnate Kerry Packer's World Series Cricket, Greenidge represented West Indian and World Eleven teams during the tournament from 1977 to '79. And although World Series Cricket comprised of the creme de la creme of international cricketers, the competition was never officially recognised by the ICC and hence any scores, with either bat or ball, would not be credited to the players' career records. However, the cricket was first class and revitalised the public's interest in the game. Greenidge's 140 in his 369 run opening stand with South Africa's Barry Richards was just one of the amazing highlights that revolutionised the way cricket would be played thereafter. Unlike their Australian counterparts, Greenidge and his 'rebel' teammates continued to represent the West Indies at Test level during the WSC off-season. He reached the height of his powers in 1984 when the touring West Indians thrashed the English. He scored a masterful unbeaten 214 at Lord's and followed it up with a first innings 223 at Old Trafford. With a dominant batting order behind him, he felt free to bat with little caution at the top of the order and belted that double ton at Lord's in only 242 deliveries. Throughout his career, the opener continued to thrill and he departed the game on a high note scoring a career high 226 in his penultimate Test. With just over 7,500 Test runs alongside his name and thus being the fourth highest run scorer in West Indian history, it is testament to his ability that he is headed only by arguably West Indies' greatest trio in Lara, Richards and Sobers.

GREENIDGE, Geoff Alan

Born: May 26, 1948
Origin: Barbados
Batting: Right handed
Bowling: Right arm leg-break

Tests
Test Career: 1972-73
Cap Number: 142
Tests Played: 5

Test Batting
Innings:	9	Runs:	209
Highest Score:	50	Average:	29.85
No. 50s:	1	No. 100s:	0

Test Bowling & Fielding
Wickets:	0	Runs:	75
Best Bowling:		Average:	0.00
5 WI:	0	10 WM:	0
Catches:	3	Stumpings:	0

A right hand opening batsman who made fifty on debut against New Zealand, at Georgetown, in 1972, Geoff Greenidge, (no relation to the great Gordon) is one of the few Caucasians to play international cricket for the West Indies.

GRELL, Mervyn

Born: December 18, 1899
Origin: Trinidad
Batting: Right handed
Bowling: Right arm medium

Tests
Test Career: 1930
Cap Number: 24
Tests Played: 1

Test Batting
Innings:	2	Runs:	34
Highest Score:	21	Average:	17.00
No. 50s:	0	No. 100s:	0

Test Bowling & Fielding
Wickets:	0	Runs:	17
Best Bowling:		Average:	0.00
5 WI:	0	10 WM:	0
Catches:	1	Stumpings:	0

Played the one Test against England at Port of Spain, in 1930.

GRIFFITH, Adrian

Born: November 19, 1971
Origin: Barbados
Batting: Left handed
Bowling: Right arm medium

Tests
Test Career: 1997-00
Cap Number: 213
Tests Played: 14

Test Batting
Innings:	27	Runs:	638
Highest Score:	114	Average:	14.14
No. 50s:	4	No. 100s:	1

Test Bowling & Fielding
Wickets:	0	Runs:	0
Best Bowling:		Average:	0.00
5 WI:	0	10 WM:	0
Catches:	5	Stumpings:	0

One Day Internationals
ODI Career: 1996-00
ODIs Played: 9

ODI Batting
Innings:	8	Runs:	99
Highest Score:	47	Average:	14.14
No. 50s:	0	No. 100s:	0

ODI Bowling & Fielding
Wickets:	0	Runs:	0
Best Bowling:		Average:	0.00
5 WM:	0	Catches:	5
Stumpings:	0		

A left hand opener, who apart from his 114 against New Zealand at Hamilton, in 1999, did not do enough to consolidate a regular place in either the Test or One Day side.

GRIFFITH, Charles Christopher

Born: December 14, 1938
Origin: Barbados
Batting: Right handed
Bowling: Right arm fast

Tests
Test Career: 1960-69
Cap Number: 111
Tests Played: 28

Test Batting
Innings:	42	Runs:	530
Highest Score:	54	Average:	16.56
No. 50s:	1	No. 100s:	0

Test Bowling & Fielding
Wickets:	94	Runs:	2,683
Best Bowling:	6/36	Average:	28.54
5 WI:	5	10 WM:	0
Catches:	16	Stumpings:	0

Originally a right arm spinner, Charlie Griffith was one of, if not the, fastest bowler of his era. He made his Test debut against England, at Port of Spain in 1960, and formed a formidable partnership with the great Wes Hall over many years. In many quarters, Griffith's bowling was considered a potential 'lethal weapon' as demonstrated during a 1961 Test in Barbados, where he fractured the skull of Indian captain Nari Contractor. In that same match he was called for 'throwing', and hence the debate surrounding his action continued for the remainder of his career. Griffith played 28 Tests in all, taking 94 wickets at 28.54. He took six wickets in an innings on three occasions with a career best 6/36, against England, at Headingley in 1963.

GRIFFITH, Herman

Born: December 1, 1893
Origin: Trinidad
Batting: Right handed
Bowling: Right arm fast

655

Tests
Test Career:	1928-33		
Cap Number:	6		
Tests Played:	13		

Test Batting
Innings:	23	Runs:	91
Highest Score:	18	Average:	5.05
No. 50s:	0	No. 100s:	0

Test Bowling & Fielding
Wickets:	44	Runs:	1,243
Best Bowling:	6/103	Average:	28.25
5 WI:	2	10 WM:	0
Catches:	4	Stumpings:	0

Played in the inaugural Test against England at Lord's, 1928, where he took 2/78. His first wicket was that of Douglas Jardine whom he trapped lbw.

GUILLEN, Simpson Clairmonte (Sammy)

Born:	September 24, 1924
Origin:	Trinidad
Batting:	Right handed
	Wicket Keeper

Tests
Test Career:	1951-56		
Cap Number:	73		
Tests Played:	8		

Test Batting
Innings:	12	Runs:	202
Highest Score:	54	Average:	20.20
No. 50s:	1	No. 100s:	0

Test Bowling & Fielding
Wickets:	0	Runs:	0
Best Bowling:	0	Average:	0.00
5 WI:	0	10 WM:	0
Catches:	13	Stumpings:	3

One of the most amazing stories involving a cricketer who played just a handful of Tests. Sammy Guillen was a wicketkeeper from Trinidad, who played his first Test against Australia, at the Adelaide Oval, in 1951. In all, he represented the West Indies in five Tests and then headed overseas to live in New Zealand. Three years later, he was selected in New Zealand's Test eleven, therefore becoming one of 14 cricketers to have played Test cricket for two nations. In an ironic twist, during his eighth and final Test against the West Indies, at Auckland in 1956, he stumped former teammate Alf Valentine for five, and in the process secured New Zealand's first ever Test win.

HALL, Wesley Winfield

Born:	September 12, 1937
Origin:	Barbados
Batting:	Right handed
Bowling:	Right arm fast

Tests
Test Career:	1958-69
Cap Number:	104
Tests Played:	48

Test Batting
Innings:	66	Runs:	818
Highest Score:	50*	Average:	15.73
No. 50s:	2	No. 100s:	0

Test Bowling & Fielding
Wickets:	192	Runs:	5,066
Best Bowling:	7/69	Average:	26.38
5 WI:	9	10 WM:	1
Catches:	11	Stumpings:	0

It is hard to imagine that one of the greatest West Indian bowlers started out as a wicket-keeper/batsman. Even a year prior to his Test debut in 1958, Hall had never taken a wicket in first class cricket but that was all about to change. In his second Test, against India at Kanpur, Hall ripped through the Indian batting taking 6/50 in the first innings and 5/76 in the second, giving him eleven for the match. He went on to take 30 wickets for the series at 17.66. The destruction continued during the series in Pakistan, taking 16 wickets with his average again hovering around the 17 mark. And when he claimed the wickets of first gamer, Mushtaq Mohammad - the then youngest ever Test player on debut - Fazal Mahmood and Nasim-ul-Ghani in successive balls, during the Third Test at Lahore, Hall became the first West Indian to take a Test match hat-trick. After a successful maiden tour of the subcontinent, he returned home to take on the English. In the second Test at Port of Spain, Hall was at his devastating best taking a career best 7/69 in the first innings. In the fifth and final Test, which was also at Port of Spain, Hall shared the new ball with debutant Charlie Griffith. Although Griffith's debut was rather innocuous, their partnership would soon become one of the most feared and formidable pace attacks the game had seen as the pair would terrorise batsmen, in tandem, for just under a decade. A muscular individual with tremendous stamina, Hall rarely played a poor match during his stellar career. He was a key figure in the 1960 tied Test at the 'Gabba. After scoring a career high 50 not out in the first innings, when coming in at number ten, Hall went on to take nine wickets for the match. He showed his class and professionalism during the drama packed final over as the Australians needed just six runs to win. He took the crucial wicket of captain Richie Benaud and after the run outs of wicketkeeper Grout and Ian Meckiff off the last ball, the match was tied - it was first in Test history.

HARPER, Roger Andrew

Born:	March 17, 1963
Origin:	British Guiana
Batting:	Right handed
Bowling:	Right arm off-break

Tests
Test Career:	1983-93
Cap Number:	181
Tests Played:	25

Test Batting
Innings:	32	Runs:	535
Highest Score:	74	Average:	18.44
No. 50s:	3	No. 100s:	0

Test Bowling & Fielding
Wickets:	46	Runs:	1,291
Best Bowling:	6/57	Average:	28.06
5 WI:	1	10 WM:	0
Catches:	36	Stumpings:	0

One Day Internationals
ODI Career:	1983-96
ODIs Played:	105

ODI Batting
Innings:	73	Runs:	855
Highest Score:	45*	Average:	16.13
No. 50s:	0	No. 100s:	0

ODI Bowling & Fielding
Wickets:	100	Runs:	3,431
Best Bowling:	4/40	Average:	34.31
5 WM:	0	Catches:	55
Stumpings:	0		

Hardly a household name but rated by many of the former greats as the finest fielder the game has seen. Classed as an all-rounder, Harper who had the height and athleticism of an express bowler, was an off-spin bowler. He made his Test debut against India at Kolkata in 1983, but as he was playing during West Indies' greatest era, it was difficult to consolidate a regular place in a side comprising the most potent pace attack in history. In all, Harper played in 25 Tests over a ten year period, and took a career best 6/57 against England at Old Trafford in 1984. His best effort with the bat was 74, which was also against England at the same venue, but four years later. While his Test record with bat and ball is serviceable at best, Roger Harper's ability to grasp the 'uncatchable' catch out of nowhere and instigate a run-out from virtually nothing, has earned him a regular (hypothetical) spot as '12th man' in many of the 'greatest ever' sides compiled by various authorities on the game.

HAYNES, Desmond Leo
Born:	February 15, 1956
Origin:	Barbados
Batting:	Right handed
Bowling:	Right arm off-break

Tests
Test Career:	1978-94
Cap Number:	163
Tests Played:	116

Test Batting
Innings:	202	Runs:	7,487
Highest Score:	184	Average:	42.29
No. 50s:	39	No. 100s:	18

Test Bowling & Fielding
Wickets:	1	Runs:	8
Best Bowling:	1/2	Average:	8.00
5 WI:	0	10 WM:	0
Catches:	65	Stumpings:	0

One Day Internationals
ODI Career:	1978-94
ODIs Played:	238

ODI Batting
Innings:	237	Runs:	8,648
Highest Score:	152*	Average:	41.37
No. 50s:	57	No. 100s:	17

ODI Bowling & Fielding
Wickets:	0	Runs:	24
Best Bowling:		Average:	0.00
5 WM:	0	Catches:	59
Stumpings:	0		

When left hand opener Roy Fredericks retired from Test cricket in 1976, he extended his association with long time partner Gordon Greenidge in the first season of World Series Cricket in 1977/78. By 1978 the Fredericks/Greenidge combination was well and truly over and most would be forgiven for thinking that it would be considerable time before West Indian cricket would be blessed with another opening pair of such calibre. Desmond Haynes first joined his Barbados team mate at the crease during the First Test against Australia at Port of Spain, in 1978. Being the new kid on the block, Haynes was keen to impress and that he did by scoring three successive fifties including 61 on debut. By his third Test, he was averaging 60. Later that year, Haynes, along with paceman Colin Croft and Richard Austin joined the second season of World Series Cricket in the Australian summer of 1978/79. By the time the competition concluded, Haynes had proven to be just as capable at the shorter version of the game as he was at Tests, and together with Greenidge, helped secure back to back titles for the West Indies in the 1979 World Cup. The Greenidge/Haynes combination was now in full swing and ready to take the shine off any new ball the opposition Test nations had to offer. In 1980, Haynes brought up his maiden Test century against New Zealand, at Dunedin, and followed up with 122 in the next Test at Christchurch where he and Greenidge put on 225 for the first wicket. In that same year, he scored a career best 184 against England at Lord's, and although he continued to produce quality scores it took three years before he notched up his next ton, which was 136 against India at St.Johns. But from then on it was runs a plenty for the energetic Haynes who unlike he more reserved partner, liked to wear his heart on his sleeve. In 1990, against England at St.Johns, the pair eclipsed their effort from a decade ago at Christchurch, when they amassed an amazing 298 for the first wicket - a West Indian record that still stands today. Haynes captained the West Indies in four Tests between 1989 and 1991 and took just the one wicket at Test Level - that of Pakistan swing bowler, Sarfraz Nawaz. When Haynes retired in 1984, he walked away with 7,487 runs and a Test average of 42 - fifth behind the biggest names to ever take guard for the West Indies, in Lloyd, Greenidge, Sobers, Richards and Lara. And although Haynes' individual record speaks for itself, his long standing partnership with Greenidge is rated as one of the finest opening combinations the game has seen. The pair opened the batting on a record 148 occasions, averaging 47.31 and together made sixteen, 100 run partnerships, which also remains a Test record.

HAYNES, Robert

Born:	November 2, 1964
Origin:	Jamaica
Batting:	Left handed
Bowling:	Right arm leg-break

One Day Internationals

ODI Career:	1989-91
ODIs Played:	8

ODI Batting

Innings:	6	Runs:	26
Highest Score:	18	Average:	5.20
No. 50s:	0	No. 100s:	0

ODI Bowling & Fielding

Wickets:	5	Runs:	224
Best Bowling:	2/36	Average:	44.80
5 WI:	0	Catches:	5
Stumpings:	0		

A leg spinner from Jamaica who made his ODI debut against Pakistan at Sharjah in 1989.

HEADLEY, George

Born:	May 30, 1909
Origin:	Jamaica
Batting:	Right handed
Bowling:	Right arm leg-break

Tests

Test Career:	1930-54
Cap Number:	17
Tests Played:	22

Test Batting

Innings:	40	Runs:	2,190
Highest Score:	270*	Average:	60.83
No. 50s:	5	No. 100s:	10

Test Bowling & Fielding

Wickets:	0	Runs:	230
Best Bowling:		Average:	0.00
5 WI:	0	10 WM:	0
Catches:	14	Stumpings:	0

Born in Panama and raised in Jamaica, George Headley made a stunning 176 on debut against England at Bridgetown, in 1930. Clearly, the premier West Indian batsman of his era, Headley scored an amazing ten centuries in 22 matches, including two double centuries. His career best 270 not out against England at Kingston, in 1935, remained the highest score by a West Indian for 23 years. It was fitting that it took a player of Sir Garfield Sobers' calibre to eclipse his record. Hailed as the West Indian equivalent to Bradman, Headley captained the West Indies in one Test against England in 1947/48. The first true legend of West Indian cricket, Headley's Test average of 60.83 still remains the highest by any West Indian batsman - a remarkable feat considering the chain of undisputed champions such as Sobers, Richards, Lloyd and Lara that followed. Apart from the record books, the Headley name has lived on through the eras as his son Ron represented West Indies at Test level while grandson Dean represented England.

HEADLEY, Ronald George

Born:	June 29, 1939
Origin:	Jamaica
Batting:	Left handed
Bowling:	Left arm slow

Tests

Test Career:	1973
Cap Number:	147
Tests Played:	2

Test Batting

Innings:	4	Runs:	62
Highest Score:	42	Average:	15.50
No. 50s:	0	No. 100s:	0

Test Bowling & Fielding

Wickets:	0	Runs:	0
Best Bowling:		Average:	0.00
5 WI:	0	10 WM:	0
Catches:	2	Stumpings:	0

One Day Internationals

ODI Career:	1973
ODIs Played:	1

ODI Batting

Innings:	1	Runs:	19
Highest Score:	19	Average:	19.00
No. 50s:	0	No. 100s:	0

ODI Bowling & Fielding

Wickets:	0	Runs:	0
Best Bowling:		Average:	0.00
5 WM:	0	Catches:	0
Stumpings:	0		

The son of the legendary George Headley, Ron was also a leg spinner, but unlike his father, he was a left hander with both bat and ball. He played just the two Tests in 1973. His son Dean made it three generations of Headleys to play Test cricket when he made his debut for England in 1997.

HENDRIKS, John Leslie (Jackie)

Born:	December 21, 1933
Origin:	Jamaica
Batting:	Right handed
	Wicket Keeper

Tests

Test Career:	1962-69
Cap Number:	114
Tests Played:	20

Test Batting

Innings:	32	Runs:	447
Highest Score:	64	Average:	18.62
No. 50s:	2	No. 100s:	0

Test Bowling & Fielding

Wickets:	0	Runs:	0
Best Bowling:		Average:	0.00
5 WI:	0	10 WM:	0
Catches:	42	Stumpings:	5

A tallish wicket-keeper who top scored with 64 on debut against India, at Port of Spain, in 1962.

HINDS, Ryan

Born:	February 17, 1981
Origin:	Barbados
Batting:	Left handed
Bowling:	Left arm slow

Tests

Test Career:	2002-05
Cap Number:	241
Tests Played:	9

Test Batting

Innings:	16	Runs:	363
Highest Score:	84	Average:	24.20
No. 50s:	2	No. 100s:	0

Test Bowling & Fielding

Wickets:	5	Runs:	390
Best Bowling:	2/83	Average:	78.00
5 WI:	0	10 WM:	0
Catches:	4	Stumpings:	0

One Day Internationals

ODI Career:	2001-04
ODIs Played:	14

ODI Batting

Innings:	9	Runs:	101
Highest Score:	18*	Average:	16.83
No. 50s:	0	No. 100s:	0

ODI Bowling & Fielding

Wickets:	6	Runs:	350
Best Bowling:	2/19	Average:	58.33
5 WM:	0	Catches:	2
Stumpings:	0		

A promising all-rounder who made 62 on debut against Pakistan, at Sharjah, in 2002. However, Hinds will need to improve as a bowler if he is to eventually cement a regular place.

HINDS, Wavell Wayne

Born:	September 7, 1976
Origin:	Jamaica
Batting:	Left handed
Bowling:	Right arm medium

Tests

Test Career:	2000-05
Cap Number:	233
Tests Played:	45

Test Batting

Innings:	80	Runs:	2,608
Highest Score:	213	Average:	33.01
No. 50s:	14	No. 100s:	5

Test Bowling & Fielding

Wickets:	16	Runs:	590
Best Bowling:	3/79	Average:	36.87
5 WI:	0	10 WM:	0
Catches:	32	Stumpings:	0

One Day Internationals

ODI Career:	1999-06
ODIs Played:	105

ODI Batting

Innings:	101	Runs:	2,795
Highest Score:	127*	Average:	30.38
No. 50s:	14	No. 100s:	5

ODI Bowling & Fielding

Wickets:	28	Runs:	796
Best Bowling:	3/24	Average:	28.42
5 WM:	0	Catches:	28
Stumpings:	0		

An aggressive left hand batsman from Jamaica, Wavell Hinds started his career as a middle order batsman and then after four matches was promoted to first drop. This was met with instantaneous success as he smashed his way to 165 against Pakistan, at Bridgetown in 2000. Hinds though, struggled to emulate his stellar performance, as his form thereafter was patchy. In order to regain form, he was elevated to opener and again the change was as good as a holiday as he scored 70 and 46 against the Australians, at Sydney in 2001. Although at times he was rotated throughout the order, his four centuries that followed were all made while opening the batting, including a career best 213 against South Africa at Guyana in 2004. However, since the double century, runs have been scarce and Hinds has been overlooked since late 2005 with the selectors opting for the Ganga/Gayle opening combination.

HOAD, Edward Lisle Goldsworthy (Teddy)

Born:	January 29, 1896
Origin:	Barbados
Batting:	Right handed
Bowling:	Right arm leg-break

Tests

Test Career:	1928-33
Cap Number:	12
Tests Played:	4

Test Batting

Innings:	8	Runs:	98
Highest Score:	36	Average:	12.25
No. 50s:	0	No. 100s:	0

Test Bowling & Fielding

Wickets:	0	Runs:	0
Best Bowling:		Average:	0.00
5 WI:	0	10 WM:	0
Catches:	1	Stumpings:	0

Teddy Hoad made his debut against England at Old Trafford in 1928. He was West Indies' second ever Test captain but first to captain the side on home soil.

HOLDER, Roland Irwin Christopher

Born:	December 22, 1967
Origin:	Trinidad
Batting:	Right handed
Bowling:	Right arm medium

Tests

Test Career:	1997-99
Cap Number:	214
Tests Played:	11

Test Batting

Innings:	17	Runs:	380
Highest Score:	91	Average:	25.33
No. 50s:	2	No. 100s:	0

Test Bowling & Fielding

Wickets:	0	Runs:	0
Best Bowling:		Average:	0.00
5 WI:	0	10 WM:	0
Catches:	9	Stumpings:	0

One Day Internationals

ODI Career:	1993-97		
ODIs Played:	37		

ODI Batting

Innings:	31	Runs:	599
Highest Score:	65	Average:	23.96
No. 50s:	2	No. 100s:	0

ODI Bowling & Fielding

Wickets:	0	Runs:	0
Best Bowling:		Average:	0.00
5 WM:	0	Catches:	8
Stumpings:	0		

A middle order batsman who made his debut against India, at Kingston, in 1997. He came within nine runs of scoring his maiden Test century, in his second Test which was also against India. Ironically, he was to score nine runs in the second innings.

HOLDER, Vanburn

Born:	October 10, 1945
Origin:	Barbados
Batting:	Right handed
Bowling:	Right arm medium-fast

Tests

Test Career:	1969-79		
Cap Number:	131		
Tests Played:	40		

Test Batting

Innings:	59	Runs:	682
Highest Score:	42	Average:	14.20
No. 50s:	0	No. 100s:	0

Test Bowling & Fielding

Wickets:	109	Runs:	3,627
Best Bowling:	6/28	Average:	33.27
5 WI:	3	10 WM:	0
Catches:	16	Stumpings:	0

One Day Internationals

ODI Career:	1973-78		
ODIs Played:	12		

ODI Batting

Innings:	6	Runs:	64
Highest Score:	30	Average:	12.80
No. 50s:	0	No. 100s:	0

ODI Bowling & Fielding

Wickets:	19	Runs:	454
Best Bowling:	5/50	Average:	23.89
5 WM:	1	Catches:	6
Stumpings:	0		

A pace bowler from Barbados who played in West Indies triumphant World Cup side in 1975. Took a career best 6/28 against Australia, at Trinidad in 1977.

HOLDING, Michael Anthony

Born:	February 16, 1954
Origin:	Jamaica
Batting:	Right handed
Bowling:	Right arm fast

Tests

Test Career:	1975-87
Cap Number:	153
Tests Played:	60

Test Batting

Innings:	76	Runs:	910
Highest Score:	73	Average:	13.78
No. 50s:	6	No. 100s:	0

Test Bowling & Fielding

Wickets:	249	Runs:	5,898
Best Bowling:	8/92	Average:	23.68
5 WI:	13	10 WM:	2
Catches:	22	Stumpings:	0

One Day Internationals

ODI Career:	1976-87		
ODIs Played:	102		

ODI Batting

Innings:	42	Runs:	282
Highest Score:	64	Average:	9.09
No. 50s:	2	No. 100s:	0

ODI Bowling & Fielding

Wickets:	142	Runs:	3,034
Best Bowling:	5/26	Average:	21.36
5 WM:	1	Catches:	30
Stumpings:	0		

Michael Holding's graceful style made the physically taxing craft of fast bowling seem like an effortless pastime. Dubbed 'Whispering Death' because of his almost silent approach to the bowling crease, Holding was a key figure in one of the most potent pace attacks that terrorised batsmen between the mid 1970's and 80's. A former 400-metre athletics champion, Holding made his Test debut in November 1975 where he opened the bowling with Andy Roberts, against Australia at the 'Gabba. Improving with each match, Holding came to prominence during the 1976 tour of England where he was at his absolute fastest. He collected 28 wickets for the series, at an incredible 12.71, his most memorable efforts being his 5/17 from 14 overs at Old Trafford and his career best 8/92 in the Fifth Test at The Oval, where he finished with 14 wickets for match. His 14/149 remains the best match figures by a West Indian to date. At 22 and with Test records waiting to be broken, Holding, in 1977 agreed to sign with Kerry Packer's World Series Cricket competition. He joined skipper Clive Lloyd, vice captain Deryck Murray, Viv Richards, Gordon Greenidge and bowling partner Andy Roberts amongst several others who will represent a West Indian eleven in a non-recognised triangular series in Australia later that year. Holding, together with Roberts, Wayne Daniel and Joel Garner became the recognised pace quartet of World Series Cricket during its first season. Colin Croft joined the party in the second season and by the time World Series Cricket concluded after the 1978/79 season, Holding was just reaching his prime. In 1979, he opened the bowling with Andy Roberts in the second World Cup final against England, at Lords. He captured the vital wickets of openers Boycott and Brearley, who had put on 129 without loss, to have England at 2/135 and hence swing the momentum back in favour of the West

Indies. Holding and his team mates celebrated back to back titles as the West Indies ran out comfortable 92 run winners. He also represented West Indies in their 1983 World Cup campaign but couldn't make it a 'three peat'. Upon entering into the twilight of his career, Holding was off a shorter run and handed the new ball to speed sensation Malcolm Marshall. Upon his retirement in 1987, Holding had collected 249 Test wickets at 23.68. He is currently the sixth highest wicket-taker in West Indian history and works as a Television commentator.

HOLFORD, David

Born:	April 16, 1940
Origin:	Barbados
Batting:	Right handed
Bowling:	Right arm leg-break

Tests

Test Career:	1966-77
Cap Number:	124
Tests Played:	24

Test Batting

Innings:	39	Runs:	768
Highest Score:	105*	Average:	22.58
No. 50s:	3	No. 100s:	1

Test Bowling & Fielding

Wickets:	51	Runs:	2,009
Best Bowling:	5/23	Average:	39.39
5 WI:	1	10 WM:	0
Catches:	18	Stumpings:	0

The cousin of the greatest West Indian cricketer, Sir Garfield Sobers, David Holford was a middle order batsman and a handy leg spin bowler. He made his debut against England, at Old Trafford in 1966, and in his second Test, at Lord's, he scored his only Test century, 105 not out, and together with cousin Gary, put on 274 for the sixth wicket to save the match. While Holford did not reach the heights of his more high profile team mates, let alone his legendary relative, he was part of the inaugural West Indian World Series Cricket squad of 1977/78.

HOLT, John Kenneth

Born:	August 12, 1923
Origin:	Jamaica
Batting:	Right handed
Bowling:	Right arm off-break

Tests

Test Career:	1954-59
Cap Number:	82
Tests Played:	17

Test Batting

Innings:	31	Runs:	1,066
Highest Score:	166	Average:	36.75
No. 50s:	5	No. 100s:	2

Test Bowling & Fielding

Wickets:	1	Runs:	20
Best Bowling:	1/20	Average:	20.00
5 WI:	0	10 WM:	0
Catches:	8	Stumpings:	0

An elegant opening or number three batsman, John Holt was well on his way to becoming the fourth West Indian batsman to score a century on debut. However, a dubious lbw decision left the Jamaican stranded on 94 and in turn sent the parochial Kingston crowd into a frenzy. Holt did not have to wait long to secure what many believed was what was owing to him - a maiden Test century. In just the next Test, Holt belted the English bowlers all over Kensington Oval, Bridgetown, to score, what would be a career best 166. While the fans waited anxiously for more of the same, it would be almost five years later, and on foreign soil, when Holt would next reach triple figures.

HOOPER, Carl Llewellyn

Born:	December 15, 1966
Origin:	Guyana
Batting:	Right handed
Bowling:	Right arm off-break

Tests

Test Career:	1987-02
Cap Number:	190
Tests Played:	102

Test Batting

Innings:	173	Runs:	5,762
Highest Score:	233	Average:	36.46
No. 50s:	27	No. 100s:	13

Test Bowling & Fielding

Wickets:	114	Runs:	5,635
Best Bowling:	5/26	Average:	49.42
5 WI:	4	10 WM:	0
Catches:	115	Stumpings:	0

One Day Internationals

ODI Career:	1987-03
ODIs Played:	227

ODI Batting

Innings:	206	Runs:	5,761
Highest Score:	113*	Average:	35.34
No. 50s:	29	No. 100s:	7

ODI Bowling & Fielding

Wickets:	193	Runs:	6,958
Best Bowling:	4/34	Average:	36.05
5 WM:	0	Catches:	120
Stumpings:	0		

A veteran of 102 Tests over a 16-year career, Carl Hooper, was a middle order batsman who possessed undoubted natural ability, but his casual style gave many the impression that a great deal of his talent remained virtually untapped. Hooper made his Test debut against India at Mumbai in 1987, and scored his maiden Test century, 100 not out, in his second Test at Kolkata. However, he didn't notch up his next triple figure score until three years later against Pakistan at Lahore. He scored 13 centuries with a highest score of 233 against India in front of his crowd at Georgetown. But overall his form did waver throughout his career, as his average of 36.46 would testify. A handy cameo off-spinner in both Tests and ODI's, Hooper was appointed captain in 2000 as the West Indies were undergoing a major rebuilding phase. He led the side in 22 matches for just four wins. He was eventually succeeded by wicket-keeper Ridley Jacobs.

HOWARD, Anthony Bourne
Born:	August 27, 1946
Origin:	Barbados
Batting:	Left handed
Bowling:	Right arm off-break

Tests

Test Career:	1972
Cap Number:	143
Tests Played:	1

Test Batting

Innings:	0	Runs:	0
Highest Score:	0	Average:	0.00
No. 50s:	0	No. 100s:	0

Test Bowling & Fielding

Wickets:	2	Runs:	140
Best Bowling:	2/140	Average:	70.00
5 WI:	0	10 WM:	0
Catches:	0	Stumpings:	0

An off-break bowler from Barbados who took two of the three New Zealand wickets to fall in the Fourth Test at Georgetown in 1972.

HUNTE, Conrad Cleophas
Born:	May 9, 1932
Origin:	Barbados
Batting:	Right handed
Bowling:	Right arm medium

Tests

Test Career:	1958-67
Cap Number:	98
Tests Played:	44

Test Batting

Innings:	78	Runs:	3,245
Highest Score:	260	Average:	45.06
No. 50s:	13	No. 100s:	8

Test Bowling & Fielding

Wickets:	2	Runs:	110
Best Bowling:	1/17	Average:	55.00
5 WI:	0	10 WM:	0
Catches:	16	Stumpings:	0

An aggressive, but reliable opener who scored plenty of runs with his trademark leg glance, Conrad Hunte, in 1958, became the fifth West Indian batsman to score a century on debut. His 142 against Pakistan at Bridgetown, was the first of three for the series. In the Third Test at Kingston, Hunte was in total control of the Pakistan bowling. It would take an unfortunate run out that would see him fall ten runs short from equalling George Headley's record score of 270. He followed up with his third century in the next Test, at Georgetown, and by the end of the series, Hunte had accrued an amazing 622 runs at a whopping 77.75. However, on his maiden tour of the sub continent, Hunte struggled to recapture his early form averaging just 27.00 in India and a meagre 10.50 in Pakistan. While he didn't reach the stellar heights of his debut series, Hunte was a consistent performer throughout his ten year career, scoring over 3,000 runs, including eight centuries, at 45.06. A dour competitor, Hunte was appointed vice-captain in the 1966 tour of England.

HUNTE, Errol
Born:	October 3, 1905
Origin:	Trinidad
Batting:	Right handed
	Wicket Keeper

Tests

Test Career:	1930
Cap Number:	18
Tests Played:	3

Test Batting

Innings:	6	Runs:	166
Highest Score:	58	Average:	33.20
No. 50s:	2	No. 100s:	0

Test Bowling & Fielding

Wickets:	0	Runs:	0
Best Bowling:	0	Average:	0.00
5 WI:	0	10 WM:	0
Catches:	5	Stumpings:	0

A wicket-keeper/opening batsman who made his debut against England at Bridgetown in 1930. Played just three Tests.

HURLEY, Ryan
Born:	September 13, 1975
Origin:	Barbados
Batting:	Right handed
Bowling:	Right arm off-break

One Day Internationals

ODI Career:	2003-04
ODIs Played:	9

ODI Batting

Innings:	4	Runs:	13
Highest Score:	6	Average:	3.25
No. 50s:	0	No. 100s:	0

ODI Bowling & Fielding

Wickets:	5	Runs:	313
Best Bowling:	1/25	Average:	62.60
5 WM:	0	Catches:	5
Stumpings:	0		

A promising all rounder from Barbados who didn't quite live up to expectations. Made his ODI debut against Australia at Port of Spain in 2003.

HYLTON, Leslie
Born:	March 29, 1905
Origin:	Jamaica
Batting:	Right handed
Bowling:	Right arm fast

Tests

Test Career:	1935-39
Cap Number:	40
Tests Played:	6

Test Batting

Innings:	8	Runs:	70
Highest Score:	19	Average:	11.66
No. 50s:	0	No. 100s:	0

Test Bowling & Fielding			
Wickets:	16	Runs:	418
Best Bowling:	4/27	Average:	26.12
5 WI:	0	10 WM:	0
Catches:	1	Stumpings:	0

A right arm fast bowler from Kingston, Jamaica, Hylton played his first of six Tests against England at Bridgetown in 1935. His best haul was 4/27 against England, at Georgetown, that same year.

JACOBS, Ridley Detamore

Born:	November 26, 1967
Origin:	Antigua
Batting:	Left handed
	Wicket Keeper

Tests

Test Career:	1998-04		
Cap Number:	222		
Tests Played:	65		

Test Batting

Innings:	112	Runs:	2,577
Highest Score:	118	Average:	28.31
No. 50s:	14	No. 100s:	3

Test Bowling & Fielding

Wickets:	0	Runs:	0
Best Bowling:		Average:	0.00
5 WI:	0	10 WM:	0
Catches:	207	Stumpings:	12

One Day Internationals

ODI Career:	1996-04		
ODIs Played:	147		

ODI Batting

Innings:	112	Runs:	1,865
Highest Score:	80*	Average:	23.31
No. 50s:	9	No. 100s:	0

ODI Bowling & Fielding

Wickets:	0	Runs:	0
Best Bowling:		Average:	0.00
5 WM:	0	Catches:	160
Stumpings:	29		

Like the prince in the Cinderella fable, the West Indies selectors tried to make various prospective keepers hands fit into the gloves left behind by Jeffrey Dujon. After a seven year search, it would be the 31 year old hands of Antiguan, Ridley Jacobs, that would 'fit like a glove'. Jacobs held the number one keeping job for just under a decade and with 219 dismissals in 65 Tests, he is only headed by the great Dujon as West Indies most successful wicket-keeper. Jacobs also performed admirably with the bat averaging 28.31 in Tests, with a highest score of 118 against India at St.Johns, in 2002.

JEREMY, Kerry

Born:	February 6, 1980
Origin:	Antigua
Batting:	Right handed
Bowling:	Right arm medium-fast

One Day Internationals

ODI Career:	2000-01		
ODIs Played:	6		

ODI Batting

Innings:	4	Runs:	17
Highest Score:	8*	Average:	8.50
No. 50s:	0	No. 100s:	0

ODI Bowling & Fielding

Wickets:	4	Runs:	163
Best Bowling:	2/42	Average:	40.75
5 WM:	0	Catches:	0
Stumpings:	0		

Blessed with raw pace, West Indian cricket never got to see the best of Kerry Jeremy as he was plagued with injury during his short stint at the elite level. Made his ODI debut against Sri Lanka at Nairobi in 2000.

JOHNSON, Hophnie Hobah Hines

Born:	July 13, 1910
Origin:	Jamaica
Batting:	Right handed
Bowling:	Right arm fast

Tests

Test Career:	1948-50		
Cap Number:	64		
Tests Played:	3		

Test Batting

Innings:	4	Runs:	38
Highest Score:	22	Average:	9.50
No. 50s:	0	No. 100s:	0

Test Bowling & Fielding

Wickets:	13	Runs:	238
Best Bowling:	5/41	Average:	18.30
5 WI:	2	10 WM:	1
Catches:	0	Stumpings:	0

Johnson took 13 wickets from just three Tests, with an impressive average of 18.30. He made his debut against England, at Kingston, in 1948.

JOHNSON, Tyrell

Born:	January 10, 1917
Origin:	Trinidad
Batting:	Left handed
Bowling:	Left arm fast

Tests

Test Career:	1939		
Cap Number:	51		
Tests Played:	1		

Test Batting

Innings:	1	Runs:	9
Highest Score:	9*	Average:	0.00
No. 50s:	0	No. 100s:	0

Test Bowling & Fielding

Wickets:	3	Runs:	129
Best Bowling:	2/53	Average:	43.00
5 WI:	0	10 WM:	0
Catches:	1	Stumpings:	0

A pace bowler from Trinidad who played just the one Test against England, at the Oval, in 1939.

JONES, Charles

Born:	November 3, 1902
Origin:	Guyana
Batting:	Left handed
Bowling:	Left arm slow

JONES, Charles Morris

Tests
Test Career: 1930-35
Cap Number: 25
Tests Played: 4

Test Batting
Innings:	7	Runs:	63
Highest Score:	19	Average:	9.00
No. 50s:	0	No. 100s:	0

Test Bowling & Fielding
Wickets:	0	Runs:	11
Best Bowling:		Average:	0.00
5 WI:	0	10 WM:	0
Catches:	3	Stumpings:	0

From Guyana, Charles Jones played just three more Tests after making his debut against England at Georgetown in 1930.

JONES, Prior Erskine Waverley

Born: June 6, 1917
Origin: Trinidad
Batting: Right handed
Bowling: Right arm fast

Tests
Test Career: 1948-51
Cap Number: 57
Tests Played: 9

Test Batting
Innings:	11	Runs:	47
Highest Score:	10*	Average:	5.22
No. 50s:	0	No. 100s:	0

Test Bowling & Fielding
Wickets:	25	Runs:	751
Best Bowling:	5/85	Average:	30.04
5 WI:	1	10 WM:	0
Catches:	4	Stumpings:	0

A medium pacer and excellent fieldsman from Trinidad, Prior Jones took four wickets on debut against England at Bridgetown in 1948. He took a career best 5/85 against India at Mumbai in 1949.

JOSEPH, David Rolston Emmanuel

Born: November 15, 1969
Origin: Antigua
Batting: Right handed
Bowling: Right arm medium-fast

Tests
Test Career: 1999
Cap Number: 226
Tests Played: 4

Test Batting
Innings:	7	Runs:	141
Highest Score:	50	Average:	20.14
No. 50s:	1	No. 100s:	0

Test Bowling & Fielding
Wickets:	0	Runs:	0
Best Bowling:		Average:	0.00
5 WI:	0	10 WM:	0
Catches:	10	Stumpings:	0

Joseph made 50 on debut against the Australians at Port of Spain, in 1999, but his form deserted him shortly afterwards.

JOSEPH, Sylvester Cleofoster

Born: June 5, 1978
Origin: Antigua
Batting: Right handed
Bowling: Right arm off-break

Tests
Test Career: 2004-05
Cap Number: 257
Tests Played: 4

Test Batting
Innings:	8	Runs:	133
Highest Score:	45	Average:	16.62
No. 50s:	0	No. 100s:	0

Test Bowling & Fielding
Wickets:	0	Runs:	8
Best Bowling:		Average:	0.00
5 WI:	0	10 WM:	0
Catches:	4	Stumpings:	0

One Day Internationals
ODI Career: 2000-05
ODIs Played: 13

ODI Batting
Innings:	11	Runs:	161
Highest Score:	58	Average:	16.10
No. 50s:	1	No. 100s:	0

ODI Bowling & Fielding
Wickets:	0	Runs:	0
Best Bowling:		Average:	0.00
5 WI:	0	Catches:	4
Stumpings:	0		

His highest score of 45 was scored on debut against England, at Old Trafford, in 2004, when opening the batting with Chris Gayle. Joseph has played just the four Tests.

JULIEN, Bernard Denis

Born: March 13, 1950
Origin: Trinidad
Batting: Right handed
Bowling: Left arm medium-fast

Tests
Test Career: 1973-77
Cap Number: 148
Tests Played: 24

Test Batting
Innings:	34	Runs:	866
Highest Score:	121	Average:	30.92
No. 50s:	3	No. 100s:	2

Test Bowling & Fielding
Wickets:	50	Runs:	1,868
Best Bowling:	5/57	Average:	37.36
5 WI:	1	10 WM:	0
Catches:	14	Stumpings:	0

One Day Internationals
ODI Career: 1973-77
ODIs Played: 12

ODI Batting
Innings:	8	Runs:	86
Highest Score:	26*	Average:	14.33
No. 50s:	0	No. 100s:	0

ODI Bowling & Fielding
Wickets:	18	Runs:	463
Best Bowling:	4/20	Average:	25.72
5 WI:	0	Catches:	4
Stumpings:	0		

A left arm swing bowler and an adventurous right arm batsman, all-rounder Bernard Julien may not have reached the heights of his famous contemporaries of the 1970's, but his fielding ability was second to none. Possessing one of the most powerful and accurate throwing arms, Julien's trademark bail height returns to wicket-keeper Deryck Murray were constantly followed with the expression 'beautiful return' from doyen West Indian commentator Tony Cozier. He played his first of 24 Tests against England, at The Oval in 1973, taking the wickets of Fletcher and Boycott in the first innings. In the Third Test at Lord's he scored his maiden Test century and highest score of 121. He was to score one more century, 101 against Pakistan at Karachi in 1974, and in the following year played in the inaugural World Cup final where he made 26 not out in West Indies' 17 run win over Australia. In 1977 he joined World Series Cricket where he became a crowd favourite mainly because of his unparalleled fielding ability.

JUMADEEN, Raphick

Born: April 12, 1948
Origin: Trinidad
Batting: Right handed
Bowling: Left arm leg-break

Tests
Test Career: 1972-79
Cap Number: 145
Tests Played: 12

Test Batting
Innings:	14	Runs:	84
Highest Score:	56	Average:	21.00
No. 50s:	1	No. 100s:	0

Test Bowling & Fielding
Wickets:	29	Runs:	1,141
Best Bowling:	4/72	Average:	39.34
5 WI:	0	10 WM:	0
Catches:	4	Stumpings:	0

A left arm off-spinner who made his Test debut against New Zealand, at Port of Spain, in 1972. Struggled to hold a regular place in the star studded pace attack of the 1970's. Played 12 Tests in seven years.

KALLICHARRAN, Alvin Isaac

Born: March 21, 1949
Origin: Guyana
Batting: Left handed
Bowling: Right arm off-break

Tests
Test Career: 1972-80
Cap Number: 144
Tests Played: 66

Test Batting
Innings:	109	Runs:	4,399
Highest Score:	187	Average:	44.43
No. 50s:	21	No. 100s:	12

Test Bowling & Fielding
Wickets:	4	Runs:	158
Best Bowling:	2/16	Average:	39.50
5 WI:	0	10 WM:	0
Catches:	51	Stumpings:	0

One Day Internationals
ODI Career: 1973-81
ODIs Played: 31

ODI Batting
Innings:	28	Runs:	826
Highest Score:	78	Average:	34.41
No. 50s:	6	No. 100s:	0

ODI Bowling & Fielding
Wickets:	3	Runs:	64
Best Bowling:	2/10	Average:	21.33
5 WM:	0	Catches:	8
Stumpings:	0		

An elegant left hand batsman, Alvin Kallicharran proved that good things do come in small packages. In 1972, he became the seventh West Indian to score a hundred on debut when he remained exactly 100 not out, in the first innings against New Zealand, in front of his home crowd at Georgetown. Kallicharran made it 'two from two' when he went one run better scoring 101 in the next Test, at Port of Spain. He continued to pile on the runs throughout 1972/73 and then in 1974, against England at Port of Spain, he complied a brilliant 158 but not without controversy. After all-rounder Bernard Julien had played the last ball of the day to England's Tony Greig, Kallicharran continued to walk towards the pavilion and was technically out of his crease. Greig threw down the stumps and subsequently Kallicharran was given out. After some heated discussions, umpire Sang Hue reinstated Kallicharran and he went in at stumps on 142 'not out'. He reached triple figures on another five occasions within the next two years and in 1977 decided that he too would join the World Series Cricket competition that was going to be held in Australia later that year. However, a bureaucratic blunder ensured that his defection would never eventuate. Ironically, Kallicharran was appointed captain of a depleted West Indian Test side as the then current skipper Clive Lloyd, along with several senior players such as wicket-keeper Deryck Murray, Viv Richards and Lawrence Rowe had all signed contracts to play World Series Cricket. Kallicharran captained the side in nine Tests from 1977 to 1979 for just the one win and six draws. Although he made a duck on debut as skipper, Kallicharran was a fine example for the young and up and coming players who many would not have got a chance if not for the temporary exodus of talent. During his reign, he scored two centuries including his highest score of 187 against India at Mumbai. An excellent fielder and talented player in both forms of the game, Kallicharran was a member of the victorious 1975 and 1979 World Cup sides.

KANHAI, Rohan

Born:	December 26, 1935
Origin:	Guyana
Batting:	Right handed
Bowling:	Right arm medium Wicket Keeper

Tests

Test Career:	1957-74		
Cap Number:	94		
Tests Played:	79		

Test Batting

Innings:	137	Runs:	6,227
Highest Score:	256	Average:	47.53
No. 50s:	28	No. 100s:	15

Test Bowling & Fielding

Wickets:	0	Runs:	85
Best Bowling:		Average:	0.00
5 WI:	0	10 WM:	0
Catches:	50	Stumpings:	0

One Day Internationals

ODI Career:	1973-75		
ODIs Played:	7		

ODI Batting

Innings:	5	Runs:	164
Highest Score:	55	Average:	54.66
No. 50s:	2	No. 100s:	0

ODI Bowling & Fielding

Wickets:	0	Runs:	0
Best Bowling:		Average:	0.00
5 WM:	0	Catches:	4
Stumpings:	0		

An innovative batsman and a wonderful timer of the ball, Rohan Kanhai is truly on the 'A list' as far as great West Indian batsmen are concerned. In a career spanning 17 years, Kanhai was renowned for his consistency and level-headedness, scoring 6,227 runs at an impressive 47.53. He made his Test debut against England, at Edgbaston in 1957 as an opener, doubling as a wicket-keeper. He relinquished the responsibility with the gloves after his third Test and thereafter only dabbled in the trade on occasions when covering for regular keeper Deryck Murray. As an opener, Kanhai's early performances were solid without being spectacular and after his tenth Test he was moved lower down the order, predominantly batting at number three for the remainder of his career. It was batting at 'first drop', just a few Tests later, when Kanhai brought up his maiden Test century - a career best 256 against India, at Kolkata. And it would have been back-to-back tons if not for being run out on 99 in the next Test at Chennai. However, Kanhai had plenty of runs left in him, and on the subsequent tour of Pakistan, reached triple figures for the second time. Kanhai again was not satisfied with a regular hundred as he posted an invaluable 217 at Lahore which set the West Indies on their way to their first ever win in Pakistan. Kanhai went on to record a further 13 centuries and eventually captain the West Indies in 13 Tests from 1972-74. One of the early pioneers of the One Day Game, Kanhai was a member of the victorious World Cup side of 1975 where he scored 55 in the final against Australia. He is the uncle of Mahendra Nagamootoo who played five Tests for the West Indies between 2000-02.

KENTISH, Esmond

Born:	November 21, 1916
Origin:	Jamaica
Batting:	Right handed
Bowling:	Right arm medium-fast

Tests

Test Career:	1948-54		
Cap Number:	65		
Tests Played:	2		

Test Batting

Innings:	2	Runs:	1
Highest Score:	1*	Average:	1.00
No. 50s:	0	No. 100s:	0

Test Bowling & Fielding

Wickets:	8	Runs:	178
Best Bowling:	5/49	Average:	22.25
5 WI:	1	10 WM:	0
Catches:	1	Stumpings:	0

A right arm pace bowler from Jamaica who in 1948, on debut, was given the new ball against England in front of his home crowd. Due to the Second World War, he played his second and final Test again at Kingston and against England. He bowed out with an impressive 5/49.

KING, Collis Llewellyn

Born:	June 11, 1951
Origin:	Barbados
Batting:	Right handed
Bowling:	Right arm medium

Tests

Test Career:	1976-80		
Cap Number:	158		
Tests Played:	9		

Test Batting

Innings:	16	Runs:	418
Highest Score:	100*	Average:	32.15
No. 50s:	2	No. 100s:	1

Test Bowling & Fielding

Wickets:	3	Runs:	282
Best Bowling:	1/30	Average:	94.00
5 WI:	0	10 WM:	0
Catches:	5	Stumpings:	0

One Day Internationals

ODI Career:	1976-80		
ODIs Played:	18		

ODI Batting

Innings:	14	Runs:	280
Highest Score:	86	Average:	23.33
No. 50s:	1	No. 100s:	0

ODI Bowling & Fielding

Wickets:	11	Runs:	529
Best Bowling:	4/23	Average:	48.09
5 WM:	0	Catches:	6
Stumpings:	0		

A passionate all-rounder who, along with Viv Richards, was the hero in West Indies 1979 World Cup victory over England at Lords. King and Richards put on 139 for the fifth wicket, with King smashing 86 from 67 balls. King played nine Tests in total after making his debut against England, at Old Trafford in 1976 but was clearly better suited to the one day game. A year later he, along with seven of his World Cup team mates, including Richards & Lloyd, joined Kerry Packer's World Series Cricket. Upon his return to Test cricket in 1979, King scored his maiden Test century against New Zealand at Christchurch.

KING, Frank McDonald

Born: December 14, 1926
Origin: Barbados
Batting: Right handed
Bowling: Right arm fast

Tests
Test Career: 1953-56
Cap Number: 75
Tests Played: 14

Test Batting
Innings:	17	Runs:	116
Highest Score:	21	Average:	8.28
No. 50s:	0	No. 100s:	0

Test Bowling & Fielding
Wickets:	29	Runs:	1,159
Best Bowling:	5/74	Average:	39.96
5 WI:	1	10 WM:	0
Catches:	5	Stumpings:	0

Opened the bowling on debut, and took three wickets for the match against India, at Port of Spain in 1953.

KING, Lester Anthony

Born: February 27, 1939
Origin: Jamaica
Batting: Right handed
Bowling: Right arm fast

Tests
Test Career: 1962-68
Cap Number: 119
Tests Played: 2

Test Batting
Innings:	4	Runs:	41
Highest Score:	20	Average:	10.25
No. 50s:	0	No. 100s:	0

Test Bowling & Fielding
Wickets:	9	Runs:	154
Best Bowling:	5/46	Average:	17.11
5 WI:	1	10 WM:	0
Catches:	2	Stumpings:	0

A fast bowler who took five wickets when he opened the bowling with Wes Hall on debut against India at Kingston, in 1962. He sustained various injuries throughout his career and hence played his second, and final Test, six years after his debut.

KING, Reon Dane

Born: October 6, 1975
Origin: Guyana
Batting: Right handed
Bowling: Right arm medium-fast

Tests
Test Career: 1999-05
Cap Number: 224
Tests Played: 19

Test Batting
Innings:	27	Runs:	66
Highest Score:	12*	Average:	3.47
No. 50s:	0	No. 100s:	0

Test Bowling & Fielding
Wickets:	53	Runs:	1,733
Best Bowling:	5/51	Average:	32.69
5 WI:	1	10 WM:	0
Catches:	2	Stumpings:	0

One Day Internationals
ODI Career: 1998-05
ODIs Played: 50

ODI Batting
Innings:	23	Runs:	65
Highest Score:	12*	Average:	7.22
No. 50s:	0	No. 100s:	0

ODI Bowling & Fielding
Wickets:	76	Runs:	1,807
Best Bowling:	4/25	Average:	23.77
5 WM:	0	Catches:	4
Stumpings:	0		

A genuine express bowler from Guyana who made his Test debut against South Africa, at Centurion, in 1999. At one stage, King was considered West Indies' quickest bowler and seemed to have a long and prosperous career ahead of him when he took 5/51 against Zimbabwe in 2000. However, he was to be hampered by niggling injuries and spent some time in the wilderness before being recalled to the Test arena in 2005.

LAMBERT, Clayton Benjamin

Born: February 10, 1962
Origin: Guyana
Batting: Left handed
Bowling: Right arm off-break

Tests
Test Career: 1991-98
Cap Number: 198
Tests Played: 5

Test Batting
Innings:	9	Runs:	284
Highest Score:	104	Average:	31.55
No. 50s:	1	No. 100s:	1

Test Bowling & Fielding
Wickets:	1	Runs:	5
Best Bowling:	1/4	Average:	5.00
5 WI:	0	10 WM:	0
Catches:	8	Stumpings:	0

One Day Internationals
ODI Career: 1990-04
ODIs Played: 12

ODI Batting
Innings:	12	Runs:	407
Highest Score:	119	Average:	33.91
No. 50s:	2	No. 100s:	1

ODI Bowling & Fielding
Wickets:	0	Runs:	74
Best Bowling:		Average:	0.00
5 WM:	0	Catches:	0
Stumpings:	0		

He made his Test debut against England, at The Oval, in 1991 but did not play his next Test until 1997 where he went on to record his maiden Test century against England at St.Johns. Clayton Lambert later represented the USA in limited overs competition.

LARA, Brian Charles

Born:	May 2, 1969
Origin:	Trinidad & Tobago
Batting:	Left handed
Bowling:	Left arm leg-break

Tests

Test Career:	1990-06
Cap Number:	196
Tests Played:	128

Test Batting

Innings:	227	Runs:	11,505
Highest Score:	400*	Average:	52.05
No. 50s:	47	No. 100s:	32

Test Bowling & Fielding

Wickets:	0	Runs:	28
Best Bowling:		Average:	0.00
5 WI:	0	10 WM:	0
Catches:	161	Stumpings:	0

One Day Internationals

ODI Career:	1990-06
ODIs Played:	270

ODI Batting

Innings:	262	Runs:	9,661
Highest Score:	169	Average:	41.11
No. 50s:	59	No. 100s:	19

ODI Bowling & Fielding

Wickets:	4	Runs:	61
Best Bowling:	2/5	Average:	15.25
5 WM:	0	Catches:	111
Stumpings:	0		

Cricket may have seen more consistent batsmen, but there has never been anyone who could match the brilliant West Indian's ability to plunder giant scores. In Test ranks Brian Lara broke, then re-broke, the record for the highest score in a single Test innings and in first class cricket he broke Hanif Mohammed's long standing highest ever score. With over 11,000 Test runs, Lara is the highest run scorer in West Indian history. He joined the West Indian side in 1990 and after a consistent if not spectacular start to his Test career caught the world's attention with a glorious double century in only his fifth Test. Playing Australia at the SCG he showed all his wares to smash 277 off an attack that included Shane Warne, Merv Hughes and Craig McDermott. With his wristy drives, punches and pulls, the innings flew along and announced the arrival of a new batting sensation. Lara himself recognised the importance of his first Test century by naming his daughter Sydney after the city in which it was scored. The spectacular turned into the amazing the following season when he broke the records for highest first class score then highest Test score. The former - an unbeaten 501 was struck for Warwickshire when playing Durham and the latter - a monstrous 375 in a Test against the English at St. John's in the Caribbean. Lara was now a cricket immortal but as the strength of the West Indian cricket side waned the pressures of leadership seemed to rest heavily on his shoulders. He went through sustained periods of poor form including a run of five consecutive Test scores under 10 against the Australians in 1996/97. Ultimately though the man with the million-dollar smile was always able to work his way out of form troughs with a characteristic innings of unthinkable magnitude. He plundered the Sri Lankans on foreign soil in 2001/02 scoring 178 in the first Test then 221 and 130 in the third. In 2003/04 the West Indians were hosting England and Lara once again found himself out of sorts, with exactly 100 runs from six innings through the first three Tests. It was hardly a portent for what was to follow, the highest innings in Test history. Skipper Lara may have been accused of batting on for too long and the wicket may have been benign but it should be noted that he hit an incredible 400 not out against the much vaunted English attack of Harmison, Flintoff, Hoggard and Jones. Now well into his 30's, he continues to amaze. He farewelled the Australian public on his last Test tour of that nation with a trademark double century in Adelaide and in 2006 added a 32nd Test century with a ton against the touring Indians. Records are made to be broken but in the case of Brian Lara's that day may be a long time coming.

LASHLEY, Peter

Born:	February 11, 1937
Origin:	Barbados
Batting:	Left handed
Bowling:	Right arm medium

Tests

Test Career:	1960-66
Cap Number:	112
Tests Played:	4

Test Batting

Innings:	7	Runs:	159
Highest Score:	49	Average:	22.71
No. 50s:	0	No. 100s:	0

Test Bowling & Fielding

Wickets:	1	Runs:	1
Best Bowling:	1/1	Average:	1.00
5 WI:	0	10 WM:	0
Catches:	4	Stumpings:	0

A versatile left handed batsman who made his debut against Australia at the 'Gabba in 1960. Played four Tests in six years.

LAWSON, Jermaine

Born:	January 13, 1982
Origin:	Jamaica
Batting:	Right handed
Bowling:	Right arm medium-fast

Tests

Test Career:	2002-05		
Cap Number:	245		
Tests Played:	13		

Test Batting

Innings:	21	Runs:	52
Highest Score:	14	Average:	3.46
No. 50s:	0	No. 100s:	0

Test Bowling & Fielding

Wickets:	51	Runs:	1,512
Best Bowling:	7/78	Average:	29.64
5 WI:	2	10 WM:	0
Catches:	3	Stumpings:	0

One Day Internationals

ODI Career:	2001-05		
ODIs Played:	13		

ODI Batting

Innings:	5	Runs:	18
Highest Score:	8	Average:	6.00
No. 50s:	0	No. 100s:	0

ODI Bowling & Fielding

Wickets:	17	Runs:	498
Best Bowling:	4/57	Average:	29.29
5 WM:	0	Catches:	0
Stumpings:	0		

Rated by the local media as a bowler of exceptional talent, Jermaine Lawson didn't let the scribes down early on in his career. In only his third Test, against Bangladesh at Dhaka, in December 2002, Lawson took the cricket world by storm when he produced one of the most amazing bowling spells, taking an unprecedented 6/3 in 6.5 overs. While many a bowler would have gladly accepted these figures as their 'career best', better was to come for Lawson. Five months later against the all-conquering Australians, at Bridgetown, Lawson made headlines yet again. After clean bowling tail-enders Brett Lee and Stuart MacGill to wrap up the Australian first innings, Lawson, with his opening delivery in the second innings, captured opener Justin Langer plumb in front, thus making him the first West Indian bowler to claim a Test hat-trick since Courtney Walsh's effort at the 'Gabba in 1989. In the next Test against the Australians, at St Johns, he eclipsed his previous best bowling with a superb 7/78. And just as Lawson's feats had captured the attention of the cricket world, so had his suspect bowling action. In May 2003, he was reported for an illegal action by the ICC but it was immediately remedied. Upon his return to the Test side in 2004, he sustained stress fractures of the back and in mid 2005, his action, was again questioned by the authorities. Although he was subsequently cleared for a second time, Lawson's career remained at the cross roads in mid 2006.

LEGALL, Ralph Archibald

Born:	December 1, 1925
Origin:	Barbados
Batting:	Right handed
	Wicket Keeper

Tests

Test Career:	1953		
Cap Number:	77		
Tests Played:	4		

Test Batting

Innings:	5	Runs:	50
Highest Score:	23	Average:	10.00
No. 50s:	0	No. 100s:	0

Test Bowling & Fielding

Wickets:	0	Runs:	0
Best Bowling:		Average:	0.00
5 WI:	0	10 WM:	0
Catches:	8	Stumpings:	1

A wicket-keeper from Barbados who made his debut against India, at Bridgetown, in 1953. Played just four Tests.

LEWIS, Desmond Michael

Born:	February 21, 1946
Origin:	Jamaica
Batting:	Right handed
	Wicket Keeper

Tests

Test Career:	1971		
Cap Number:	138		
Tests Played:	3		

Test Batting

Innings:	5	Runs:	259
Highest Score:	88	Average:	86.33
No. 50s:	3	No. 100s:	0

Test Bowling & Fielding

Wickets:	0	Runs:	0
Best Bowling:		Average:	0.00
5 WI:	0	10 WM:	0
Catches:	8	Stumpings:	0

A wicket-keeper who made 81 not out on debut against India, at Georgetown, in 1971.

LEWIS, Rawl

Born:	September 5, 1974
Origin:	Grenada
Batting:	Right handed
Bowling:	Right arm leg-break

Tests

Test Career:	1997-06		
Cap Number:	218		
Tests Played:	4		

Test Batting

Innings:	8	Runs:	88
Highest Score:	40	Average:	11.00
No. 50s:	0	No. 100s:	0

Test Bowling & Fielding

Wickets:	1	Runs:	388
Best Bowling:	1/67	Average:	388.00
5 WI:	0	10 WM:	0
Catches:	0	Stumpings:	0

One Day Internationals

ODI Career:	1997-06		
ODIs Played:	20		

ODI Batting

Innings:	15	Runs:	172
Highest Score:	49	Average:	15.63
No. 50s:	0	No. 100s:	0

ODI Bowling & Fielding			
Wickets:	14	Runs:	676
Best Bowling:	2/40	Average:	48.28
5 WM:	0	Catches:	6
Stumpings:	0		

A leg-spinner from Grenada who played his first Test against Pakistan, at Peshawar, in 1997. Since then Lewis has played four Tests in nine years taking just the one wicket, that of South African, Mark Boucher.

LLOYD, Clive Hubert

Born:	August 31, 1944
Origin:	Guyana
Batting:	Left handed
Bowling:	Right arm medium

Tests

Test Career:	1966-84
Cap Number:	125
Tests Played:	110

Test Batting

Innings:	175	Runs:	7,515
Highest Score:	242*	Average:	46.67
No. 50s:	39	No. 100s:	19

Test Bowling & Fielding

Wickets:	10	Runs:	622
Best Bowling:	2/13	Average:	62.20
5 WI:	0	10 WM:	0
Catches:	90	Stumpings:	0

One Day Internationals

ODI Career:	1973-85
ODIs Played:	87

ODI Batting

Innings:	69	Runs:	1,977
Highest Score:	102	Average:	39.54
No. 50s:	11	No. 100s:	1

ODI Bowling & Fielding

Wickets:	0	Runs:	0
Best Bowling:		Average:	0.00
5 WM:	0	Catches:	0
Stumpings:	0		

Great cricket sides invariably have great leaders and Clive Lloyd is the perfect case in point. He made his Test debut as a 22 year old in 1966 and made an immediate impression with 82 in his first Test knock against the Indians on a turning pitch in Mumbai. Tall and bespectacled, his first home series, against the English the following season, saw him score a maiden Test century in Trinidad and confirm him as a long term Test prospect. He was handed the reins of the West Indian side in 1974 and like no captain before or after was able to marshall men from the different Caribbean nations into a unified team of the highest order. His first series as captain was a series win in India with his unbeaten 242 in the final Test in Mumbai thus securing victory. The triumphant Lloyd then took Calypso cricket to the world with victory in the inaugural World Cup staged in England in 1975. By the time his side landed in Australia later that year the world champions were in full gear. An expected tight battle with the Aussies never eventuated, the West Indies trouncing their hosts 5-1. All the while Lloyd continued to flourish, scoring 469 for the series at an average of 46.90. A brilliant slips fielder and nicknamed 'Big Cat' for his panther like patrolling of the covers, the West Indies were unbeatable while he was at the helm. He rotated a battery of brilliant fast bowlers and thought nothing of unleashing his quickest and meanest on even the frailest of tail-enders. After relinquishing the Test captaincy during the World Series Cricket years, he took over the reins again in 1979 and led his country to their second World Cup title. In the early 80's and it was back to business as usual with crushing series wins over India, England and Australia. When a series of knee injuries saw him stand down he had skippered West Indies in a record 74 matches, including 26 successive games without defeat. He led them to a record 36 victories and in doing so presided over West Indian cricket's golden era. A true gentleman and leader, Lloyd was considered a 'father figure' by many of the younger players who he mentored during his time at the helm. Today the highly respected Lloyd acts as an international match referee.

LOGIE, Augustine Lawrence (Gus)

Born:	September 28, 1960
Origin:	Trinidad
Batting:	Right handed
Bowling:	Right arm off-break

Tests

Test Career:	1983-91
Cap Number:	177
Tests Played:	52

Test Batting

Innings:	78	Runs:	2,470
Highest Score:	130	Average:	35.79
No. 50s:	16	No. 100s:	2

Test Bowling & Fielding

Wickets:	0	Runs:	4
Best Bowling:		Average:	0.00
5 WI:	0	10 WM:	0
Catches:	57	Stumpings:	0

One Day Internationals

ODI Career:	1981-93
ODIs Played:	158

ODI Batting

Innings:	133	Runs:	2,809
Highest Score:	109*	Average:	28.95
No. 50s:	14	No. 100s:	1

ODI Bowling & Fielding

Wickets:	0	Runs:	18
Best Bowling:		Average:	0.00
5 WM:	0	Catches:	61
Stumpings:	0		

A lightning quick, pocket dynamo, Gus Logie was an accomplished fielder much in the same vain as South Africa's Jonty Rhodes. His fielding was the main feature of his game and what he is best remembered for during his eight years at the elite level. As a middle order batsman, Logie participated in several match saving partnerships with Jeffery Dujon, just when it seemed that he powerful West Indies batting line up would capitulate. After a slow start to his Test career, Logie scored a superb 130 in his fourth Test against India, at Bridgetown, in 1983. He came close again against Australia, at Port of Spain in 1984 but missed out by just three runs after being adjudged lbw to spinner Tom Hogan. He finally brought up his second, and last Test ton in 1987, when he made 101 in trying conditions at Kolkata. But along the way was unfortunate not to have at least five centuries alongside his name as he was dismissed a total of four times in the 90's. After retiring in 1991, Logie has coached Canada, the West Indies and in 2007 will lead Bermuda in their first World Cup campaign.

MADRAY, Ivan Samuel

Born:	July 2, 1934
Origin:	Guyana
Batting:	Right handed
Bowling:	Right arm leg-break

Tests

Test Career:	1958
Cap Number:	101
Tests Played:	2

Test Batting

Innings:	3	Runs:	3
Highest Score:	2	Average:	1.00
No. 50s:	0	No. 100s:	0

Test Bowling & Fielding

Wickets:	0	Runs:	108
Best Bowling:		Average:	0.00
5 WI:	0	10 WM:	0
Catches:	2	Stumpings:	0

A middle order batsman who played two Tests against Pakistan, in Port of Spain and Georgetown, in 1958

MARSHALL, Malcolm Denzil

Born:	April 18, 1958
Origin:	Barbados
Batting:	Right handed
Bowling:	Right arm fast

Tests

Test Career:	1978-91
Cap Number:	172
Tests Played:	81

Test Batting

Innings:	107	Runs:	1,810
Highest Score:	92	Average:	18.85
No. 50s:	10	No. 100s:	0

Test Bowling & Fielding

Wickets:	376	Runs:	7,876
Best Bowling:	7/22	Average:	20.94
5 WI:	22	10 WM:	4
Catches:	25	Stumpings:	0

One Day Internationals

ODI Career:	1980-92
ODIs Played:	136

ODI Batting

Innings:	83	Runs:	955
Highest Score:	66	Average:	14.92
No. 50s:	2	No. 100s:	0

ODI Bowling & Fielding

Wickets:	157	Runs:	4,233
Best Bowling:	4/18	Average:	26.96
5 WM:	0	Catches:	15
Stumpings:	0		

In an era where the West Indian pace attack comprised of towering paceman such as Holding, Garner, Croft, Walsh and Ambrose, ironically it would be a man who stood at just 5.10 that would prove to be, not only the most feared of them all, but also in many opinion, the best. Malcolm Marshall's incredible upper body strength and a panther like approach to the wicket made him the fastest bowler of his era and unlike some who are blessed with genuine raw pace, he also had the nous to use his weapon to its fullest potential. His deliveries were not only missile-like but also could swing either way. Because of his size, at times his deliveries would skid through making him virtually impossible to play. It was the exodus of West Indies premier bowlers such as Garner, Holding, Roberts and later Croft that would give the young unobtrusive Marshall his chance at Test level. He made his debut against India at Bangalore, in 1978, under the leadership of stalwart Alvin Kallicharran who had been put in charge of a rather depleted side. Although he didn't set the world alight, Marshall was selected on the 1980 tour of England and managed to hold his place despite the return of the World Series Cricket pacemen. His 15 wickets for the series was an admirable effort considering he was playing a support role to Holding, Roberts and Croft. His form continued to improve throughout the 1980/81 tour of Pakistan as well as the following home series against England. However, it was during the 1983/84 tour of India where Marshall made his mark as an elite bowler. Now sharing the new ball either Holding or Roberts, Marshall collected 33 wickets at an impressive 18.81. His stock value as an all-rounder increased when he scored a career best 92 during the 1st Test at Kanpur. After averaging in the teens throughout his career, Marshall sailed home with a more than respectable series average of 34.85. Now in full flight, Marshall continued to wreak havoc taking seven wickets in an innings twice in a calendar year. The first, a match winning 7/53 in the second innings against England at Headingley. What made the effort even more spectacular was that Marshall was sporting a double fracture in his thumb. Then in April 1985, he captured 7/80 - and 11 wickets for the match- against New Zealand at Bridgetown. But there is something about bowling in England that made Marshall 'grow another leg'. His 1988 tour of England was clearly his finest taking 35 wickets at an amazing 12.65. He also eclipsed his previous best bowling effort taking 7/22, in the Third Test, at Old Trafford. By the time he retired from international cricket in 1991, Marshall, with 376 Test wickets had well passed Lance Gibbs as West Indies' highest wicket taker. He currently sits in third position having been only overtaken by former team mates Courtney Walsh and Curtly Ambrose. However, his average of 20.94 is the best by any West Indian bowler and his ten wickets in a match on four occasions is also a West Indian record. On November 4, 1999, the cricket world was saddened to hear the passing of Malcolm Denzil Marshall after losing his battle with colon cancer. Marshall was just a few months shy of his 42nd birthday. Since his passing, the Malcolm Marshall Memorial Trophy was inaugurated, and is awarded to the leading wicket-taker in each England v West Indies Test series.

MARSHALL, Norman

Born: February 27, 1924
Origin: Barbados
Batting: Right handed
Bowling: Right arm off-break

Tests
Test Career:	1955
Cap Number:	89
Tests Played:	1

Test Batting
Innings:	2	Runs:	8
Highest Score:	8	Average:	4.00
No. 50s:	0	No. 100s:	0

Test Bowling & Fielding
Wickets:	2	Runs:	62
Best Bowling:	1/22	Average:	31.00
5 WI:	0	10 WM:	0
Catches:	0	Stumpings:	0

Older brother of Roy Marshall, Norman played his only Test against Australia, at Georgetown, in 1955.

MARSHALL, Roy Edwin

Born: April 25, 1930
Origin: Barbados
Batting: Right handed
Bowling: Right arm off-break

Tests
Test Career:	1951-52
Cap Number:	72
Tests Played:	4

Test Batting
Innings:	7	Runs:	143
Highest Score:	30	Average:	20.42
No. 50s:	0	No. 100s:	0

Test Bowling & Fielding
Wickets:	0	Runs:	15
Best Bowling:		Average:	0.00
5 WI:	0	10 WM:	0
Catches:	1	Stumpings:	0

Roy Marshall was an elegant and entertaining stroke-player who many felt should have played many more Tests than just the four alongside his name. His older brother Norman made his debut two years after Roy had played his last Test.

MARSHALL, Xavier Melbourne

Born: March 27, 1986
Origin: Jamaica
Batting: Right handed
Bowling: Right arm off-break

Tests
Test Career:	2005
Cap Number:	261
Tests Played:	2

Test Batting
Innings:	4	Runs:	17
Highest Score:	10	Average:	4.25
No. 50s:	0	No. 100s:	0

Test Bowling & Fielding
Wickets:	0	Runs:	0
Best Bowling:		Average:	0.00
5 WI:	0	10 WM:	0
Catches:	1	Stumpings:	0

One Day Internationals
ODI Career:	2005
ODIs Played:	10

ODI Batting
Innings:	10	Runs:	98
Highest Score:	26	Average:	9.80
No. 50s:	0	No. 100s:	0

ODI Bowling & Fielding
Wickets:	0	Runs:	0
Best Bowling:		Average:	0.00
5 WM:	0	Catches:	6
Stumpings:	0		

Although his natural ability is undisputed, Xavier Marshall's fiery temperament has no doubt hindered his progress as an international cricketer. An opening batsman, Marshall has played just the two Tests, both against Sri Lanka in 2005. He made his ODI debut in the city bearing his middle name.

MARTIN, Freddie

Born: October 12, 1893
Origin: Jamaica
Batting: Left handed
Bowling: Left arm slow

Tests
Test Career:	1928-31
Cap Number:	7
Tests Played:	9

Test Batting
Innings:	18	Runs:	486
Highest Score:	123*	Average:	28.58
No. 50s:	0	No. 100s:	1

Test Bowling & Fielding
Wickets:	8	Runs:	619
Best Bowling:	3/91	Average:	77.37
5 WI:	0	10 WM:	0
Catches:	2	Stumpings:	0

Opened the batting with George Challenor in West Indies' inaugural Test against England at Lord's in 1928. The left handed Martin top scored in the first innings with 44 and scored his only Test century against Australia in Sydney in 1931.

MARTINDALE, Manny

Born:	November 25, 1909
Origin:	Barbados
Batting:	Right handed
Bowling:	Right arm fast

Tests
Test Career:	1933-39		
Cap Number:	32		
Tests Played:	10		

Test Batting
Innings:	14	Runs:	58
Highest Score:	22	Average:	5.27
No. 50s:	0	No. 100s:	0

Test Bowling & Fielding
Wickets:	37	Runs:	804
Best Bowling:	5/22	Average:	21.72
5 WI:	3	10 WM:	0
Catches:	5	Stumpings:	0

A genuine quick bowler from Barbados who took 4/85 on debut against England at Lord's in 1933.

MATTIS, Everton

Born:	April 11, 1957
Origin:	Jamaica
Batting:	Right handed
Bowling:	Right arm off-break

Tests
Test Career:	1981		
Cap Number:	175		
Tests Played:	4		

Test Batting
Innings:	5	Runs:	145
Highest Score:	71	Average:	29.00
No. 50s:	1	No. 100s:	0

Test Bowling & Fielding
Wickets:	0	Runs:	14
Best Bowling:		Average:	0.00
5 WI:	0	10 WM:	0
Catches:	3	Stumpings:	0

One Day Internationals
ODI Career:	1981		
ODIs Played:	2		

ODI Batting
Innings:	2	Runs:	86
Highest Score:	62	Average:	43.00
No. 50s:	1	No. 100s:	0

ODI Bowling & Fielding
Wickets:	0	Runs:	0
Best Bowling:		Average:	0.00
5 WM:	0	Catches:	0
Stumpings:	0		

An impressive 62 in his first ODI against England, at Kingstown in 1981, saw Mattis given his chance at Test level at Port of Spain two weeks later. A duck on debut wasn't the dream start and he played just three more Tests.

McGARRELL, Neil Christopher

Born:	July 12, 1972
Origin:	Guyana
Batting:	Right handed
Bowling:	Left arm off-break

Tests
Test Career:	2001		
Cap Number:	239		
Tests Played:	4		

Test Batting
Innings:	6	Runs:	61
Highest Score:	33	Average:	15.25
No. 50s:	0	No. 100s:	0

Test Bowling & Fielding
Wickets:	17	Runs:	453
Best Bowling:	4/23	Average:	26.64
5 WI:	0	10 WM:	0
Catches:	2	Stumpings:	0

One Day Internationals
ODI Career:	1998-01		
ODIs Played:	17		

ODI Batting
Innings:	10	Runs:	60
Highest Score:	19	Average:	7.50
No. 50s:	0	No. 100s:	0

ODI Bowling & Fielding
Wickets:	15	Runs:	681
Best Bowling:	3/32	Average:	45.40
5 WM:	0	Catches:	9
Stumpings:	0		

A left arm orthodox bowler who made his Test debut against South Africa, at St John's in 2001. He took 4/23 against Zimbabwe at Harare and was unlucky not to have played more than four Tests.

McLEAN, Nixon

Born:	July 20, 1973
Origin:	St Vincent
Batting:	Left handed
Bowling:	Right arm fast

Tests
Test Career:	1998-01		
Cap Number:	220		
Tests Played:	19		

Test Batting
Innings:	32	Runs:	368
Highest Score:	46	Average:	12.26
No. 50s:	0	No. 100s:	0

Test Bowling & Fielding
Wickets:	44	Runs:	1,873
Best Bowling:	3/53	Average:	42.56
5 WI:	0	10 WM:	0
Catches:	5	Stumpings:	0

One Day Internationals
ODI Career:	1996-03		
ODIs Played:	45		

ODI Batting
Innings:	34	Runs:	314
Highest Score:	50*	Average:	12.07
No. 50s:	1	No. 100s:	0

ODI Bowling & Fielding
Wickets:	46	Runs:	1,729
Best Bowling:	3/21	Average:	37.58
5 WM:	0	Catches:	8
Stumpings:	0		

An athletic paceman, Nixon McLean made his Test debut against England, at Kingston in 1998. While he is blessed with good rhythm and style, his bowling lacks the necessary penetration to worry class batsmen. A member of the 2003 World Cup squad, McLean is probably another who is more suited to Limited Overs competition than Tests.

McMORRIS, Easton Dudley Ashton St John

Born: April 4, 1935
Origin: Jamaica
Batting: Right handed
Bowling: Right arm off-break

Tests

Test Career: 1958-66
Cap Number: 100
Tests Played: 13

Test Batting

Innings:	21	Runs:	564
Highest Score:	125	Average:	26.85
No. 50s:	3	No. 100s:	1

Test Bowling & Fielding

Wickets:	0	Runs:	0
Best Bowling:		Average:	0.00
5 WI:	0	10 WM:	0
Catches:	5	Stumpings:	0

An opening batsman, McMorris became the 100th West Indian Test player when he made his debut against Pakistan, at Port of Spain in 1958. In a topsy-turvy career spanning eight years, McMorris' finest moment occured when he scored his only Test century, 125 against India, in front of his home crowd in 1961/62.

McWATT, Clifford

Born: February 1, 1922
Origin: Guyana
Batting: Left handed
Bowling: Right arm fast
Wicket Keeper

Tests

Test Career: 1954-55
Cap Number: 83
Tests Played: 6

Test Batting

Innings:	9	Runs:	202
Highest Score:	54	Average:	28.85
No. 50s:	2	No. 100s:	0

Test Bowling & Fielding

Wickets:	1	Runs:	16
Best Bowling:	1/16	Average:	16.00
5 WI:	0	10 WM:	0
Catches:	9	Stumpings:	1

A wicket-keeper from Guyana who impressed with the bat on debut against England, at Kingston, when he scored 54 in the first innings and 36 not out in the second. His form waned thereafter and was selected in just six Tests in total.

MENDONCA, Ivor Leon

Born: July 13, 1934
Origin: Guyana
Batting: Right handed
Wicket Keeper

Tests

Test Career: 1962
Cap Number: 116
Tests Played: 2

Test Batting

Innings:	2	Runs:	81
Highest Score:	78	Average:	40.50
No. 50s:	1	No. 100s:	0

Test Bowling & Fielding

Wickets:	0	Runs:	0
Best Bowling:		Average:	0.00
5 WI:	0	10 WM:	0
Catches:	8	Stumpings:	2

A wicket-keeper who performed well in his two Tests while filling for Jackie Hendriks in 1962.

MERRY, Cyril Arthur

Born: January 20, 1911
Origin: Tobago
Batting: Right handed

Tests

Test Career: 1933
Cap Number: 33
Tests Played: 2

Test Batting

Innings:	4	Runs:	34
Highest Score:	13	Average:	8.50
No. 50s:	0	No. 100s:	0

Test Bowling & Fielding

Wickets:	0	Runs:	0
Best Bowling:		Average:	0.00
5 WI:	0	10 WM:	0
Catches:	1	Stumpings:	0

He made his debut against England at Lord's in 1933. Played just the two Tests and in 1951-52 and was appointed manager of the West Indian side that toured Australia and New Zealand.

MILLER, Roy

Born: December 24, 1924
Origin: Jamaica
Batting: Right handed
Bowling: Right arm medium-fast

Tests

Test Career: 1953
Cap Number: 78
Tests Played: 1

Test Batting

Innings:	1	Runs:	23
Highest Score:	23	Average:	23.00
No. 50s:	0	No. 100s:	0

Test Bowling & Fielding

Wickets:	0	Runs:	28
Best Bowling:		Average:	0.00
5 WI:	0	10 WM:	0
Catches:	0	Stumpings:	0

A Jamaican all-rounder who played just one Test against India, at Georgetown in 1953.

MOHAMMED, Dave

Born: October 8, 1979
Origin: Trinidad
Batting: Left handed
Bowling: Left arm slow

Tests
Test Career: 2004-06
Cap Number: 254
Tests Played: 3

Test Batting
Innings:	5	Runs:	139
Highest Score:	52	Average:	34.75
No. 50s:	1	No. 100s:	0

Test Bowling & Fielding
Wickets:	7	Runs:	430
Best Bowling:	3/112	Average:	61.42
5 WI:	0	10 WM:	0
Catches:	0	Stumpings:	0

One Day Internationals
ODI Career: 2006
ODIs Played: 3

ODI Batting
Innings:	0	Runs:	0
Highest Score:	0	Average:	0.00
No. 50s:	0	No. 100s:	0

ODI Bowling & Fielding
Wickets:	6	Runs:	76
Best Bowling:	3/37	Average:	12.66
5 WM:	0	Catches:	0
Stumpings:	0		

A left arm 'chinaman' who got his first chance at Test level on the tour of South Africa in 2004. Mohammed has played in three Tests, his last against India at St.Johns, in mid 2006, where he made his first Test 50 batting at number nine. Mohammed is considered a useful late order batsman and should get more opportunities, especially on sub continent tours.

MORTON, Runako Shakur

Born: July 22, 1978
Origin: Nevis
Batting: Right handed
Bowling: Right arm off-break

Tests
Test Career: 2005-06
Cap Number: 262
Tests Played: 4

Test Batting
Innings:	7	Runs:	193
Highest Score:	70*	Average:	32.16
No. 50s:	2	No. 100s:	0

Test Bowling & Fielding
Wickets:	0	Runs:	22
Best Bowling:		Average:	0.00
5 WI:	0	10 WM:	0
Catches:	6	Stumpings:	0

One Day Internationals
ODI Career: 2002-06
ODIs Played: 20

ODI Batting
Innings:	19	Runs:	656
Highest Score:	110*	Average:	36.44
No. 50s:	4	No. 100s:	0

ODI Bowling & Fielding
Wickets:	0	Runs:	2
Best Bowling:		Average:	0.00
5 WM:	0	Catches:	8
Stumpings:	0		

Morton got his chance when he replaced the injured Marlon Samuels against Sri Lanka, at Colombo, in 2005. His career got off to a respectable start by scoring 43 in the first innings. However, incidents off the field have been a major distraction for Morton hence he has played just the four Tests to date.

MOSELEY, Ezra

Born: January 5, 1958
Origin: Barbados
Batting: Right handed
Bowling: Right arm medium-fast

Tests
Test Career: 1990
Cap Number: 195
Tests Played: 2

Test Batting
Innings:	4	Runs:	35
Highest Score:	26	Average:	8.75
No. 50s:	0	No. 100s:	0

Test Bowling & Fielding
Wickets:	6	Runs:	261
Best Bowling:	2/70	Average:	43.50
5 WI:	0	10 WM:	0
Catches:	1	Stumpings:	0

One Day Internationals
ODI Career: 1990-91
ODIs Played: 9

ODI Batting
Innings:	6	Runs:	7
Highest Score:	2*	Average:	1.75
No. 50s:	0	No. 100s:	0

ODI Bowling & Fielding
Wickets:	7	Runs:	278
Best Bowling:	2/52	Average:	39.71
5 WM:	0	Catches:	0
Stumpings:	0		

A fast-medium pacer from Barbados who played two Tests against England in 1990.

MUDIE, George

Born: November 26, 1915
Origin: Jamaica
Batting: Right handed
Bowling: Left arm slow

Tests
Test Career: 1935
Cap Number: 44
Tests Played: 1

Test Batting
Innings:	1	Runs:	5
Highest Score:	5	Average:	5.00
No. 50s:	0	No. 100s:	0

Test Bowling & Fielding
Wickets:	3	Runs:	40
Best Bowling:	2/23	Average:	13.33
5 WI:	0	10 WM:	0
Catches:	0	Stumpings:	0

Like Dickie Fuller, Geroge Mudie was the other Jamaican to play his one Test match against England, in the Kingston Test of 1935.

MURRAY, David Anthony
Born: May 29, 1950
Origin: Barbados
Batting: Right handed
Wicket Keeper

Tests
Test Career: 1978-82
Cap Number: 167
Tests Played: 19
Test Batting
Innings: 31 Runs: 601
Highest Score: 84 Average: 21.46
No. 50s: 3 No. 100s: 0
Test Bowling & Fielding
Wickets: 0 Runs: 0
Best Bowling: Average: 0.00
5 WI: 0 10 WM: 0
Catches: 57 Stumpings: 5

One Day Internationals
ODI Career: 1973—81
ODIs Played: 10
ODI Batting
Innings: 7 Runs: 45
Highest Score: 35 Average: 9.00
No. 50s: 0 No. 100s: 0
ODI Bowling & Fielding
Wickets: 0 Runs: 0
Best Bowling: Average: 0.00
5 WM: 0 Catches: 16
Stumpings: 0

One of three unrelated 'Murrays' to have kept wickets for West Indies at Test level, David's career was wedged between his two namesakes, Deryck and Junior. After waiting in the wings for Deryck Murray's long and respectable career to come to a close, Murray finally got the number one 'gig'. But it was to be a short-lived tenure when one Jeffrey Dujon entered the scene. Devoid of further opportunities, Murray joined the rebel tour of South Africa.

MURRAY, Deryck Lance
Born: May 20, 1943
Origin: Trinidad
Batting: Right handed
Bowling: Right arm leg-break
Wicket Keeper

Tests
Test Career: 1963-80
Cap Number: 121
Tests Played: 62
Test Batting
Innings: 96 Runs: 1,993
Highest Score: 91 Average: 22.90
No. 50s: 11 No. 100s: 0
Test Bowling & Fielding
Wickets: 0 Runs: 0
Best Bowling: Average: 0.00
5 WI: 0 10 WM: 0
Catches: 181 Stumpings: 8

One Day Internationals
ODI Career: 1973-80
ODIs Played: 26
ODI Batting
Innings: 17 Runs: 294
Highest Score: 61* Average: 24.50
No. 50s: 2 No. 100s: 0
ODI Bowling & Fielding
Wickets: 0 Runs: 0
Best Bowling: Average: 0.00
5 WM: 0 Catches: 37
Stumpings: 1

Until the dynamic Jeffrey Dujon stamped his authority on the game in the 1980's, Deryck Murray was regarded as the finest West Indian wicket-keeper of all time. Gnome-like in stature, the diminutive Murray played his first Test against England, at Old Trafford, in 1963, under the watchful eye of the legendary Frank Worrell. He donned the gloves for 17 years, with his position rarely threatened, and became the first West Indian keeper to claim 100 Test victims. A handy batsman at both ODI and Test level, Murray kept wickets in the inaugural World Cup final of 1975, where the 'Windies' defeated Australia by 17 runs. Two years later, Murray joined fellow high profile teammates, such as skipper Clive Lloyd, Viv Richards, Gordon Greenidge and Michael Holding as part of the West Indian team that competed in the Kerry Packer led World Series Cricket competition in Australia. Murray and his teammates returned to the Test arena shortly afterwards and after deputising for Clive Lloyd for a number of years, Murray got the one opportunity to captain the West Indies when injury forced Lloyd out of the 1979 Test against Australia, at the 'Gabba. Without doubt, the pick of the three non-related Murrays to keep wickets for the West Indies, and second only to Jeffrey Dujon as far as reputations are concerned.

MURRAY, Junior Randalph
Born: January 20, 1968
Origin: Grenada
Batting: Right handed
Wicket Keeper

Tests
Test Career: 1993-00
Cap Number: 202
Tests Played: 33
Test Batting
Innings: 45 Runs: 918
Highest Score: 101* Average: 22.39
No. 50s: 3 No. 100s: 1
Test Bowling & Fielding
Wickets: 0 Runs: 0
Best Bowling: Average: 0.00
5 WI: 0 10 WM: 0
Catches: 99 Stumpings: 3

One Day Internationals
ODI Career: 1992-99
ODIs Played: 55

ODI Batting				
Innings:	36	Runs:		678
Highest Score:	86	Average:		22.60
No. 50s:	5	No. 100s:		0
ODI Bowling & Fielding				
Wickets:	0	Runs:		0
Best Bowling:		Average:		0.00
5 WM:	0	Catches:		46
Stumpings:	7			

Junior Murray was the third in a trilogy of 'Murrays' to have held the number one wicket-keeping post for the West Indies. Junior made his Test debut against Australia at the SCG, in 1993, and eventually wrestled the mantle from Jeffrey Dujon's immediate successor, David Williams. Serviceable in his 33 Tests, Junior scored the one Test century, 101 not out against New Zealand, at Wellington in 1995, but like Williams, Murray too struggled to fill the gaping void left by Dujon.

NAGAMOOTO, Mahendra

Born:	October 9, 1975
Origin:	Guyana
Batting:	Left handed
Bowling:	Right arm leg-break

Tests
Test Career:	2000-02			
Cap Number:	235			
Tests Played:	5			
Test Batting				
Innings:	8	Runs:		185
Highest Score:	68	Average:		26.42
No. 50s:	1	No. 100s:		0
Test Bowling & Fielding				
Wickets:	12	Runs:		637
Best Bowling:	3/119	Average:		53.08
5 WI:	0	10 WM:		0
Catches:	2	Stumpings:		0

One Day Internationals
ODI Career:	2000-02			
ODIs Played:	24			
ODI Batting				
Innings:	18	Runs:		162
Highest Score:	33	Average:		13.50
No. 50s:	0	No. 100s:		0
ODI Bowling & Fielding				
Wickets:	18	Runs:		998
Best Bowling:	4/32	Average:		55.44
5 WM:	0	Catches:		6
Stumpings:	0			

An all-rounder from sound pedigree, Mahendra Nagamootoo is the nephew of past greats Rohan Kanhai and Alvin Kallicharran. But as often happens in these situations, expectations are hard to fulfill as Nagamootoo played just five Tests in two years after making his debut against England, at The Oval in 2000.

NANAN, Rangy

Born:	May 29, 1953
Origin:	Trinidad
Batting:	Right handed
Bowling:	Right arm off-break

Tests
Test Career:	1980			
Cap Number:	174			
Tests Played:	1			
Test Batting				
Innings:	2	Runs:		16
Highest Score:	8	Average:		8.00
No. 50s:	0	No. 100s:		0
Test Bowling & Fielding				
Wickets:	4	Runs:		91
Best Bowling:	2/37	Average:		22.75
5 WI:	0	10 WM:		0
Catches:	2	Stumpings:		0

An off-spinner from Trinidad who took four wickets in his only Test, against Pakistan at Faisalabad, in 1980.

NEBLETT, James

Born:	November 13, 1901
Origin:	Barbados
Batting:	Right handed
Bowling:	Right arm leg-break

Tests
Test Career:	1935			
Cap Number:	41			
Tests Played:	1			
Test Batting				
Innings:	2	Runs:		16
Highest Score:	11*	Average:		16.00
No. 50s:	0	No. 100s:		0
Test Bowling & Fielding				
Wickets:	1	Runs:		75
Best Bowling:	1/44	Average:		75.00
5 WI:	0	10 WM:		0
Catches:	0	Stumpings:		0

Neblett was on the inaugural tour of England in 1928 but was overlooked for Test selection. He finally got his chance against England at Georgetown in 1935.

NOREIGA, Jack Mollinson

Born:	April 15, 1936
Origin:	Trinidad
Batting:	Right handed
Bowling:	Right arm off-break

Tests
Test Career:	1971			
Cap Number:	136			
Tests Played:	4			
Test Batting				
Innings:	5	Runs:		11
Highest Score:	9	Average:		3.66
No. 50s:	0	No. 100s:		0
Test Bowling & Fielding				
Wickets:	17	Runs:		493
Best Bowling:	9/95	Average:		29.00
5 WI:	2	10 WM:		0
Catches:	2	Stumpings:		0

Although relatively unknown outside the Caribbean, off-spinner Jack Noreiga's 9/95, in only his second Test, which was against India in front of his home crowd at Queen's Park Oval, in 1971, remains the best bowling figures by a West Indian bowler. A remarkable effort considering that the Caribbean has produced some of the finest bowlers in the history of the game. Noreiga played just four Tests - all in 1971, and all against India. His record-breaking effort would have to rate as one of the most notable cameo performances in the history of the game.

NUNES, Karl

Born: June 7, 1894
Origin: Jamaica
Batting: Left handed
Wicket Keeper

Tests
Test Career: 1928-30
Cap Number: 8
Tests Played: 4

Test Batting
Innings:	8	Runs:	245
Highest Score:	92	Average:	30.62
No. 50s:	2	No. 100s:	0

Test Bowling & Fielding
Wickets:	0	Runs:	0
Best Bowling:		Average:	0.00
5 WI:	0	10 WM:	0
Catches:	2	Stumpings:	0

West Indies' first ever Test captain and wicket-keeper who played in their inaugural Test against England at Lord's in 1928. A fine left handed batsman, Nunes scored a respectable 37 in the first innings when batting at number four. But he was more suited to opening the innings and in his last Test against England scored 66 and 92 as an opener. Nunes captained the West Indies in the four Test matches he participated in.

NURSE, Seymour MacDonald

Born: November 10, 1933
Origin: Barbados
Batting: Right handed
Bowling: Right arm off-break

Tests
Test Career: 1960-69
Cap Number: 110
Tests Played: 29

Test Batting
Innings:	54	Runs:	2,523
Highest Score:	258	Average:	47.60
No. 50s:	10	No. 100s:	6

Test Bowling & Fielding
Wickets:	0	Runs:	7
Best Bowling:		Average:	0.00
5 WI:	0	10 WM:	0
Catches:	21	Stumpings:	0

A superb fieldsman, Seymour Nurse was a well accomplished middle-order batsman who scored 70 on debut against England, at Kingston, in 1960. The tall, yet strongly built Nurse reached triple figures on six occasions, with two double-centuries as bookends. His first, a magnificent 201 against Australia, at Bridgetown, in 1965 and then capping off a wonderful career with a personal best 258 against the Kiwis, at Christchurch, in 1969.

PADMORE, Albert

Born: December 17, 1946
Origin: Barbados
Batting: Right handed
Bowling: Right arm off-break

Tests
Test Career: 1976
Cap Number: 155
Tests Played: 2

Test Batting
Innings:	2	Runs:	8
Highest Score:	8*	Average:	8.00
No. 50s:	0	No. 100s:	0

Test Bowling & Fielding
Wickets:	1	Runs:	135
Best Bowling:	1/36	Average:	135.00
5 WI:	0	10 WM:	0
Catches:	0	Stumpings:	0

A leg-spinner from Barbados who played just two Tests against India and England, in 1976, Padmore is best remembered as a member of the West Indian World Series Cricket squad of 1977/78. He later joined the rebel tour of South Africa in 1983.

PAGON, Donovan

Born: September 13, 1982
Origin: Jamaica
Batting: Right handed

Tests
Test Career: 2005
Cap Number: 259
Tests Played: 2

Test Batting
Innings:	3	Runs:	37
Highest Score:	35	Average:	12.33
No. 50s:	0	No. 100s:	0

Test Bowling & Fielding
Wickets:	0	Runs:	0
Best Bowling:		Average:	0.00
5 WI:	0	10 WM:	0
Catches:	0	Stumpings:	0

A Jamaican middle order batsman who in 2005, received his debut call up against South Africa, at Georgetown, due to leading players boycotting matches after a sponsorship dispute with the board. Pagon did enough on debut to be selected in the Second Test at Port of Spain but has not played another Test since.

PAIRAUDEAU, Bruce Hamilton

Born: April 14, 1931
Origin: Guyana
Batting: Right handed
Bowling: Right arm leg-break

Tests
Test Career: 1953-57
Cap Number: 76
Tests Played: 13

Test Batting
Innings:	21	Runs:	454
Highest Score:	115	Average:	21.61
No. 50s:	3	No. 100s:	1

Test Bowling & Fielding		
Wickets:	0	
Best Bowling:		
5 WI:	0	
Catches:	6	
Runs:	3	
Average:	0.00	
10 WM:	0	
Stumpings:	0	

Before Clive Lloyd, Bruce Pairaudeau held the unofficial record of most Tests played by a West Indian with glasses. Pairaudeau's career got off to a dream start, becoming only the third West Indian to score a century on debut with his 115 in the first innings against India at Port of Spain in 1953. Unfortunately, it was to become yet another case of the 'one hit wonders' as Pairaudeau's debut heroics proved a hard act to follow. The selectors' patience ran out after his 13th Test appearance.

PARRY, Derick Recaldo

Born:	December 22, 1954
Origin:	Nevis
Batting:	Right handed
Bowling:	Right arm off-break

Tests
Test Career:	1978-80
Cap Number:	164
Tests Played:	12

Test Batting
Innings:	20	Runs:	381
Highest Score:	65	Average:	22.41
No. 50s:	3	No. 100s:	0

Test Bowling & Fielding
Wickets:	23	Runs:	936
Best Bowling:	5/15	Average:	40.69
5 WI:	1	10 WM:	0
Catches:	4	Stumpings:	0

One Day Internationals
ODI Career:	1978-80
ODIs Played:	6

ODI Batting
Innings:	5	Runs:	61
Highest Score:	32	Average:	15.25
No. 50s:	0	No. 100s:	0

ODI Bowling & Fielding
Wickets:	11	Runs:	259
Best Bowling:	3/47	Average:	23.54
5 WM:	0	Catches:	8
Stumpings:	0		

An off-spinner, who in the fourth Test against Australia at Trinidad, in 1978, bowled the West Indies to victory by taking the wicket of Graham Yallop and then cleaning up the tail. Parry finished with the incredible figures of 5/15. Struggling for a regular Test spot, he later went on the rebel tour of South Africa.

PASSAILAIGUE, Charles

Born:	August 4, 1901
Origin:	Jamaica
Batting:	Right handed

Tests
Test Career:	1930
Cap Number:	29
Tests Played:	1

Test Batting
Innings:	2	Runs:	46
Highest Score:	44	Average:	46.00
No. 50s:	0	No. 100s:	0

Test Bowling & Fielding
Wickets:	0	Runs:	15
Best Bowling:		Average:	0.00
5 WI:	0	10 WM:	0
Catches:	3	Stumpings:	0

A middle-order batsman who is considered unlucky not to have played more than just the one Test against England at Kingston in 1930, where he scored 44 in the first innings.

PATTERSON, Balfour (Patrick)

Born:	September 15, 1961
Origin:	Jamaica
Batting:	Right handed
Bowling:	Right arm fast

Tests
Test Career:	1986-92
Cap Number:	186
Tests Played:	28

Test Batting
Innings:	38	Runs:	145
Highest Score:	21*	Average:	6.59
No. 50s:	0	No. 100s:	0

Test Bowling & Fielding
Wickets:	93	Runs:	2,874
Best Bowling:	5/24	Average:	30.90
5 WI:	5	10 WM:	0
Catches:	5	Stumpings:	0

One Day Internationals
ODI Career:	1986-93
ODIs Played:	59

ODI Batting
Innings:	20	Runs:	44
Highest Score:	13*	Average:	8.80
No. 50s:	0	No. 100s:	0

ODI Bowling & Fielding
Wickets:	90	Runs:	2,206
Best Bowling:	6/29	Average:	24.51
5 WM:	1	Catches:	9
Stumpings:	0		

A ferocious paceman from Jamaica who took seven English wickets on debut in front of his home crowd. Patrick Patterson was not in the class of a Marshall, Holding or an Ambrose but his passion could never be questioned. Took a career best 6/29 in ODI's and was a member of West Indies 1987 World Cup squad. Later played Shield Cricket for Tasmania.

PAYNE, Thelston

Born:	February 13, 1957
Origin:	Barbados
Batting:	Left handed
	Wicket Keeper

Tests
Test Career:	1986
Cap Number:	187
Tests Played:	1

Test Batting
Innings:	1	Runs:	5
Highest Score:	5	Average:	5.00
No. 50s:	0	No. 100s:	0

Test Bowling & Fielding
Wickets:	0	Runs:	0
Best Bowling:		Average:	0.00
5 WI:	0	10 WM:	0
Catches:	5	Stumpings:	0

One Day Internationals
ODI Career: 1984-87
ODIs Played: 7

ODI Batting
Innings:	4	Runs:	126
Highest Score:	60	Average:	31.50
No. 50s:	1	No. 100s:	0

ODI Bowling & Fielding
Wickets:	0	Runs:	0
Best Bowling:		Average:	0.00
5 WM:	0	Catches:	6
Stumpings:	0		

A reserve wicket-keeper, Payne played his only Test match against England at Port-of-Spain in 1986, when filling in for the injured Jeffrey Dujon.

PERRY, Nehemiah Odolphus
Born: June 16, 1968
Origin: Jamaica
Batting: Right handed
Bowling: Right arm off-break

Tests
Test Career: 1999
Cap Number: 228
Tests Played: 4

Test Batting
Innings:	7	Runs:	74
Highest Score:	26	Average:	12.33
No. 50s:	0	No. 100s:	0

Test Bowling & Fielding
Wickets:	10	Runs:	446
Best Bowling:	5/70	Average:	44.60
5 WI:	1	10 WM:	0
Catches:	1	Stumpings:	0

One Day Internationals
ODI Career: 1999-00
ODIs Played: 21

ODI Batting
Innings:	16	Runs:	212
Highest Score:	52*	Average:	26.50
No. 50s:	1	No. 100s:	0

ODI Bowling & Fielding
Wickets:	20	Runs:	783
Best Bowling:	3/45	Average:	39.15
5 WM:	0	Catches:	4
Stumpings:	0		

An off-spinner from Jamaica who on debut against Australia at Kingston, steered his side to victory by taking the prize wicket of captain Steve Waugh amongst his bag of 5/70 in the second innings

PHILLIP, Norbert
Born: June 12, 1948
Origin: Dominica
Batting: Right handed
Bowling: Right arm medium-fast

Tests
Test Career: 1978-79
Cap Number: 168
Tests Played: 9

Test Batting
Innings:	15	Runs:	297
Highest Score:	47	Average:	29.70
No. 50s:	0	No. 100s:	0

Test Bowling & Fielding
Wickets:	28	Runs:	1,041
Best Bowling:	4/48	Average:	37.17
5 WI:	0	10 WM:	0
Catches:	5	Stumpings:	0

One Day Internationals
ODI Career: 1978
ODIs Played: 1

ODI Batting
Innings:	1	Runs:	0
Highest Score:	0	Average:	0.00
No. 50s:	0	No. 100s:	0

ODI Bowling & Fielding
Wickets:	1	Runs:	22
Best Bowling:	1/22	Average:	22.00
5 WM:	0	Catches:	0
Stumpings:	0		

An all-rounder who played his first Test against Australia, at Georgetown, in 1978. Phillip, like a few of his team mates at that time, got an opportunity at Test level due to exodus of players to World Series Cricket.

PIERRE, Lancelot Richard
Born: June 5, 1921
Origin: Trinidad
Batting: Right handed
Bowling: Right arm medium-fast

Tests
Test Career: 1948
Cap Number: 62
Tests Played: 1

Test Batting
Innings:	0	Runs:	0
Highest Score:	0	Average:	0.00
No. 50s:	0	No. 100s:	0

Test Bowling & Fielding
Wickets:	0	Runs:	28
Best Bowling:		Average:	0.00
5 WI:	0	10 WM:	0
Catches:	0	Stumpings:	0

Played just the one Test - a rain interrupted match against England, at Georgetown, in 1948.

POWELL, Daren Brentlyle
Born: April 15, 1978
Origin: Jamaica
Batting: Right handed
Bowling: Right arm medium-fast

Tests

Test Career:	2002-06		
Cap Number:	243		
Tests Played:	17		

Test Batting

Innings:	26	Runs:	157
Highest Score:	16	Average:	6.03
No. 50s:	0	No. 100s:	0

Test Bowling & Fielding

Wickets:	43	Runs:	1,756
Best Bowling:	5/25	Average:	40.83
5 WI:	1	10 WM:	0
Catches:	1	Stumpings:	0

One Day Internationals

ODI Career:	2002-05		
ODIs Played:	9		

ODI Batting

Innings:	5	Runs:	14
Highest Score:	6	Average:	3.50
No. 50s:	0	No. 100s:	0

ODI Bowling & Fielding

Wickets:	5	Runs:	337
Best Bowling:	2/28	Average:	67.40
5 WM:	0	Catches:	1
Stumpings:	0		

A medium pacer who made his Test debut against New Zealand, at Bridgetown, in 2002. In and out of the side over the past four years, Powell's best effort to date was his 5/25 against Sri Lanka, at Kandy, in 2005.

POWELL, Ricardo Lloyd

Born:	December 16, 1978
Origin:	Jamaica
Batting:	Right handed
Bowling:	Right arm off-break

Tests

Test Career:	1999-04		
Cap Number:	231		
Tests Played:	2		

Test Batting

Innings:	3	Runs:	53
Highest Score:	30	Average:	17.66
No. 50s:	0	No. 100s:	0

Test Bowling & Fielding

Wickets:	0	Runs:	49
Best Bowling:		Average:	0.00
5 WI:	0	10 WM:	0
Catches:	1	Stumpings:	0

One Day Internationals

ODI Career:	1999-05		
ODIs Played:	109		

ODI Batting

Innings:	100	Runs:	2,085
Highest Score:	124	Average:	24.82
No. 50s:	8	No. 100s:	1

ODI Bowling & Fielding

Wickets:	11	Runs:	491
Best Bowling:	2/5	Average:	44.63
5 WM:	0	Catches:	43
Stumpings:	0		

An explosive middle order batsman, Ricardo Powell has established himself as a one day specialist having played over 100 ODI's after making his debut against Pakistan in the 1999 World Cup. Later that year he scored his only ODI century, 124 against India at Singapore. Powell has played two Tests, though five years apart. His debut against New Zealand at Hamilton in 1999 and his second, and more than likely his last, against England at St John's in 2004.

PYDANNA, Milton

Born:	January 27, 1950
Origin:	Guyana
Batting:	Right handed
	Wicket Keeper

One Day Internationals

ODI Career:	1980		
ODIs Played:	3		

ODI Batting

Innings:	1	Runs:	2
Highest Score:	2*	Average:	0.00
No. 50s:	0	No. 100s:	0

ODI Bowling & Fielding

Wickets:	0	Runs:	0
Best Bowling:		Average:	0.00
5 WM:	0	Catches:	2
Stumpings:	1		

A wicket-keeper from Guyana who made his ODI debut against Pakistan at Karachi in 1980.

RAE, Allan Fitzroy

Born:	September 30, 1922
Origin:	Jamaica
Batting:	Left handed

Tests

Test Career:	1948-53		
Cap Number:	69		
Tests Played:	15		

Test Batting

Innings:	24	Runs:	1,016
Highest Score:	109	Average:	46.18
No. 50s:	4	No. 100s:	4

Test Bowling & Fielding

Wickets:	0	Runs:	0
Best Bowling:		Average:	0.00
5 WI:	0	10 WM:	0
Catches:	10	Stumpings:	0

The President of the West Indies Cricket Board between 1981 and 1988, Allan Rae was one of West Indies finest openers. A left handed batsman, it only took until Rae's second time at the crease - Second Test against India at Mumbai, as he batted only once on debut - to notch up his first Test ton of 104. He followed up with 109 two Test matches later, at Chennai, then equaled his personal best with another 109 against England at The Oval in 1950. In all he scored four centuries averaging a healthy 46.18. Rae opened the batting with captain Jeffrey Stollmeyer on 21 occasions and the pairs' career average of 71 for the first wicket, is second only to English pair Jack Hobbs & Herbert Sutcliffe who averaged 87.

RAGOONATH, Suruj

Born: March 22, 1968
Origin: Trinidad
Batting: Right handed
Bowling: Right arm off-break

Tests

Test Career:	1999		
Cap Number:	227		
Tests Played:	2		

Test Batting

Innings:	4	Runs:	13
Highest Score:	9	Average:	4.33
No. 50s:	0	No. 100s:	0

Test Bowling & Fielding

Wickets:	0	Runs:	0
Best Bowling:		Average:	0.00
5 WI:	0	10 WM:	0
Catches:	0	Stumpings:	0

An aggressive opener from Trinidad who played two Tests against Australia in 1999 but on both occasions hardly troubled the scorers.

RAMADHIN, Sonny

Born: May 1, 1929
Origin: Trinidad
Batting: Right handed
Bowling: Right arm off-break

Tests

Test Career:	1950-60		
Cap Number:	70		
Tests Played:	43		

Test Batting

Innings:	58	Runs:	361
Highest Score:	44	Average:	8.20
No. 50s:	0	No. 100s:	0

Test Bowling & Fielding

Wickets:	158	Runs:	4,579
Best Bowling:	7/49	Average:	29.98
5 WI:	10	10 WM:	1
Catches:	9	Stumpings:	0

Standing at just 5.4, Sonny Ramadhin became the first East Indian to represent West Indies when he made his Test debut against England at Old Trafford in 1950, with fellow spinner, Alf Valentine. The pair, who were to become forever linked because of their tandem marathon spells, conquered the English batting, taking 59 wickets between them and thus steering the West Indies to their first ever series win on English soil. Ramadhin could bowl leg breaks just as well as he could off-spin thus confusing batsmen and keepers alike. He took five wickets in an innings on ten occasions with a career best 7/49 against England, at Edgbaston in 1957.

RAMDASS, Ryan Rakesh

Born: July 3, 1983
Origin: Guyana
Batting: Right handed
Bowling: Right arm off-break
 Wicket Keeper

Tests

Test Career:	2005		
Cap Number:	264		
Tests Played:	1		

Test Batting

Innings:	2	Runs:	26
Highest Score:	23	Average:	13.00
No. 50s:	0	No. 100s:	0

Test Bowling & Fielding

Wickets:	0	Runs:	0
Best Bowling:		Average:	0.00
5 WI:	0	10 WM:	0
Catches:	2	Stumpings:	0

One Day Internationals

ODI Career:	2005		
ODIs Played:	1		

ODI Batting

Innings:	1	Runs:	1
Highest Score:	1	Average:	1.00
No. 50s:	0	No. 100s:	0

ODI Bowling & Fielding

Wickets:	0	Runs:	0
Best Bowling:		Average:	0.00
5 WM:	0	Catches:	0
Stumpings:	0		

A batsman who can also keep wickets, Ryan Ramdass opened the batting with Xavier Marshall in his only Test appearance against Sri Lanka at Kandy, in 2005. Ramdass was run out for three in the first innings and scored 23 in the second but to date has yet to earn a Test recall. His only ODI was also against Sri Lanka in the same series.

RAMDIN, Denesh

Born: March 13, 1985
Origin: Trinidad
Batting: Right handed
 Wicket Keeper

Tests

Test Career:	2005-06		
Cap Number:	263		
Tests Played:	12		

Test Batting

Innings:	22	Runs:	478
Highest Score:	71	Average:	26.55
No. 50s:	3	No. 100s:	0

Test Bowling & Fielding

Wickets:	0	Runs:	0
Best Bowling:		Average:	0.00
5 WI:	0	10 WM:	0
Catches:	29	Stumpings:	0

One Day Internationals

ODI Career:	2005-06		
ODIs Played:	14		

ODI Batting

Innings:	12	Runs:	264
Highest Score:	74*	Average:	33.00
No. 50s:	1	No. 100s:	0

ODI Bowling & Fielding

Wickets:	0	Runs:	0
Best Bowling:		Average:	0.00
5 WM:	0	Catches:	16
Stumpings:	1		

Since the retirement of Jeffrey Dujon, the jury has definitely been out on every wicket-keeper who has attempted to fill the void since. Apart from his patented agility as a keeper, Dujon's batting prowess makes him a tough, if not an impossible, act to follow. Ridley Jacobs was an admirable performer during his 65 Tests, and is without doubt the best of the successors post Dujon. The net was cast yet again once Jacob's retired and since making his debut against Sri Lanka, at Colombo, in 2005, the West Indies brains trust believe that, after 15 years, they may have found their man in Trinidad's Denesh Ramdin. Not only competent with the gloves, Ramdin has impressed with the bat having scored 56 on debut and then in late 2005, compiled a dour 71 against the Australians at Hobart. His 62 not out against India at Kingston, in mid 2006, was his third half century and currently has an average of 26 in Tests and 33 in ODI's. Ramdin has shown all the signs of possibly emulating Jacobs' achievements but whether he is a clone of the great Dujon only time will tell.

RAMNARINE, Dinanath

Born:	June 4, 1975
Origin:	Trinidad
Batting:	Left handed
Bowling:	Right arm leg-break

Tests
Test Career:	1998-02
Cap Number:	221
Tests Played:	12

Test Batting
Innings:	21	Runs:	106
Highest Score:	35*	Average:	6.23
No. 50s:	0	No. 100s:	0

Test Bowling & Fielding
Wickets:	45	Runs:	1,383
Best Bowling:	5/78	Average:	30.73
5 WI:	1	10 WM:	0
Catches:	8	Stumpings:	0

One Day Internationals
ODI Career:	1997-01
ODIs Played:	4

ODI Batting
Innings:	3	Runs:	5
Highest Score:	2	Average:	1.66
No. 50s:	0	No. 100s:	0

ODI Bowling & Fielding
Wickets:	3	Runs:	164
Best Bowling:	2/52	Average:	54.66
5 WM:	0	Catches:	0
Stumpings:	0		

A leg-spinner from Trinidad who took a career best 5/78 against South Africa at Bridgetown in 2001. Played 12 Tests in four years and is the current President of the West Indies Players' Association.

RAMPAUL, Ravi

Born:	October 15, 1984
Origin:	Trinidad
Batting:	Left handed
Bowling:	Right arm medium-fast

One Day Internationals
ODI Career:	2003-04
ODIs Played:	17

ODI Batting
Innings:	4	Runs:	35
Highest Score:	24	Average:	11.66
No. 50s:	0	No. 100s:	0

ODI Bowling & Fielding
Wickets:	11	Runs:	544
Best Bowling:	2/34	Average:	49.45
5 WM:	0	Catches:	2
Stumpings:	0		

A lightly built paceman, but an exciting prospect, Ravi Rampaul made his ODI debut against Zimbabwe at Bulawayo in 2003 and has since played in 17 ODI's. He earned a scholarship to Cricket Australia's Commonwealth Bank Centre of Excellence in Brisbane, in June 2006.

REIFER, Floyd

Born:	July 23, 1972
Origin:	Barbados
Batting:	Left handed
Bowling:	Right arm medium
	Wicket Keeper

Tests
Test Career:	1997-99
Cap Number:	217
Tests Played:	4

Test Batting
Innings:	8	Runs:	63
Highest Score:	29	Average:	7.87
No. 50s:	0	No. 100s:	0

Test Bowling & Fielding
Wickets:	0	Runs:	0
Best Bowling:		Average:	0.00
5 WI:	0	10 WM:	0
Catches:	4	Stumpings:	0

One Day Internationals
ODI Career:	1997-99
ODIs Played:	2

ODI Batting
Innings:	2	Runs:	31
Highest Score:	22	Average:	15.50
No. 50s:	0	No. 100s:	0

ODI Bowling & Fielding
Wickets:	0	Runs:	0
Best Bowling:		Average:	0.00
5 WM:	0	Catches:	1
Stumpings:	0		

A wicket-keeper who, due to the presence of Junior Murray and Courtney Browne, was selected as a specialist batsman in both Test and One Day sides. The emergence of Ridley Jacobs didn't help his cause either.

RICHARDS, Sir Isaac Vivian Alexander (Viv)

Born: April 7, 1952
Origin: Antigua
Batting: Right handed
Bowling: Right arm off-break

Tests
Test Career: 1974-91
Cap Number: 151
Tests Played: 121

Test Batting
Innings:	182	Runs:	8,540
Highest Score:	291	Average:	50.23
No. 50s:	45	No. 100s:	24

Test Bowling & Fielding
Wickets:	32	Runs:	1,964
Best Bowling:	2/17	Average:	61.37
5 WI:	0	10 WM:	0
Catches:	122	Stumpings:	0

One Day Internationals
ODI Career: 1974-91
ODIs Played: 187

ODI Batting
Innings:	197	Runs:	6,721
Highest Score:	189*	Average:	47.00
No. 50s:	45	No. 100s:	11

ODI Bowling & Fielding
Wickets:	118	Runs:	4,228
Best Bowling:	6/41	Average:	35.83
5 WM:	2	Catches:	100
Stumpings:	0		

While there may have been cricketers with better statistical records, there have been none to match the aura that surrounded the great I.V.A Richards. With a boxer's swagger that earnt him the nickname 'Smokin Joe', Viv Richards tormented opposition bowlers for over 15 years. A talented sportsman who represented his native Antigua in football, Viv had to choose between the two sports at a young age. Choosing cricket, he made his debut on the tour of India in 1974/75 playing his first Test alongside another debutant, Gordon Greenidge. While his first Test outing yielded only scores of three and four, success was just around the corner, and in the Second Test in New Delhi he bludgeoned an unbeaten 192. His batting genius was there for all to see in that innings with perfectly timed drives and ferocious pulls and hooks that would later become his trademark. That knock was enough to earn him a spot in the West Indian World Cup squad and although he had an unspectacular tournament, he was part of the side that lifted the inaugural World Cup trophy in 1975. In 1975/76 he toured Australia but failed to capitalise on a number of good starts. It was later that year that Richards blossomed into the batsman that earnt him a spot in Wisden's five greatest cricketers of the 20th century. Three consecutive big hundreds against India in the Caribbean was followed up by a double century on debut in England. That 214 at Trent Bridge included 31 fours and four sixes but if the English public thought they had seen the 'Master Blaster' at his best they had another thing coming. In the final Test of that series at The Oval he hit a career best 291 to confirm him as a genuine superstar. In 1977 Richards, along with other notable West Indians such as Clive LLoyd, Gordon Greenidge and Andy Roberts joined the Kerry Packer led World Series Cricket held in Australia over two consecutive summers. And although records from the 'rebel' tournament are not officially recognised, the perennial gum chewer enthralled the Aussie crowd with his brilliant fielding and explosive batting, averaging 88.20, in 'Super Tests' in the opening season. Almost single-handedly Viv turned what was becoming a fledgling pastime, into a fashionable and exciting spectator sport for all ages - and sexes for that matter. Viv was just as devastating in the one-day arena. Of all his great ODI knocks arguably his most memorable performance was against Australia at the MCG in 1979. Facing the speed trio of Dennis Lillee, Jeff Thomson and Rodney Hogg, he clubbed 153 not out in 130 balls to the thunderous applause of the partisan Melbourne crowd. In that same year, Viv and his West Indian teammates again tasted World Cup success and this time his presence was far more prominent than in '75. His 138 not out in the final against England was not only a match-winning effort, but also a sheer delight to watch. In typical fashion, he played classical yet brutal shots to all sections of the ground. His last ball six off the bowling of frugal seamer Mike Hendricks, where he smashed a straight full toss over square leg, was 'Vintage Viv'. In 1984, he again tormented the English with a breath-taking 189 not out at Old Trafford. This remains the highest score by a West Indian in ODI's and second overall, behind Pakistan's Saeed Anwar's 194 against India in 1997. In 1985 he took over the captaincy from patriarch Clive Lloyd whom he had deputised for over so many years. He captained the West Indies in 50 Test matches thus making him the second longest serving captain behind Lloyd. The Antiguan would continue to thrill fans until the early 90's and by the time he declared his illustrious career closed in 1991, he had just managed to pass the great Sir Garfield Sobers as West Indies' leading Test run scorer. Admired by cricket followers world wide, Viv Richards was the pre-eminent batsman of his era. With only his maroon cap for protection, he faced up to and plundered the quickest and the best. In 1999 the Antiguan government knighted Viv Richards for services to cricket, a just reward for a true giant of the game.

RICHARDSON, Richard Benjamin

Born: January 12, 1962
Origin: Antigua
Batting: Right handed
Bowling: Right arm medium

Tests

Test Career: 1983-95
Cap Number: 180
Tests Played: 86

Test Batting

Innings:	146	Runs:	5,949
Highest Score:	194	Average:	44.39
No. 50s:	27	No. 100s:	16

Test Bowling & Fielding

Wickets:	0	Runs:	18
Best Bowling:		Average:	0.00
5 WI:	0	10 WM:	0
Catches:	90	Stumpings:	0

One Day Internationals

ODI Career: 1983-96
ODIs Played: 224

ODI Batting

Innings:	217	Runs:	6,248
Highest Score:	122	Average:	33.41
No. 50s:	44	No. 100s:	5

ODI Bowling & Fielding

Wickets:	1	Runs:	46
Best Bowling:	1/4	Average:	46.00
5 WM:	0	Catches:	75
Stumpings:	0		

When the world first set eyes on Richie Richardson back in late 1983, it seemed that the 'Cricket Gods' had created something of a batting specimen from the mould of the great Viv Richards. Apart from the fact that both were from Antigua and shared similar surnames, the physical similarities were remarkable. The athleticism, the stance, and the preference for the maroon cap rather than helmet had many a naive punter looking twice when Richardson took guard. However, maybe in order to seek some individuality, Richardson later discarded his cap for the wide brimmed hat, which became an unofficial trademark. The timing of his arrival couldn't have been scripted better as the legendary Richards was heading in the twilight of his career and the baton needed to passed on to a worthy recipient. Blessed with impeccable timing, Richardson was a purist's delight when in full flight and his cover drives were something to behold. As if almost on cue, he took over the captaincy from Viv Richards in 1991. The greats of West Indian cricket, such as Lloyd, Greenidge, Haynes, Holding and of course Richards, that were there to greet him upon his debut, were now retired and an important rebuilding phase for West Indian cricket lay ahead. Alongside the developing Courtney Walsh and Carl Hooper and new kids on the block Curtly Ambrose, Jimmy Adams and a potential superstar named Brian Lara, Richardson led his side to eleven wins and seven draws from 24 Tests over a five-year period. He also captained the West Indies in their two World Cup campaigns of 1992 and 1996. Upon his retirement, Richardson had scored just under 6,000 runs at 44.39 and to date is the ninth highest West Indian Test run scorer.

RICKARDS, Kenneth

Born: August 22, 1923
Origin: Jamaica
Batting: Right handed
Bowling: Right arm leg-break

Tests

Test Career: 1948-52
Cap Number: 66
Tests Played: 2

Test Batting

Innings:	3	Runs:	104
Highest Score:	67	Average:	34.66
No. 50s:	1	No. 100s:	0

Test Bowling & Fielding

Wickets:	0	Runs:	0
Best Bowling:		Average:	0.00
5 WI:	0	10 WM:	0
Catches:	0	Stumpings:	0

A middle order batsman who made 67 on debut against England, at Kingston, in 1948, but like many batsmen of his era, he too couldn't consolidate a regular place in the side due to the presence of the famous 'Three W's' - Worrell, Weekes and Walcott.

ROACH, Clifford

Born: March 13, 1904
Origin: Trinidad
Batting: Right handed
Bowling: Right arm slow

Tests

Test Career: 1928-35
Cap Number: 9
Tests Played: 16

Test Batting

Innings:	32	Runs:	952
Highest Score:	209	Average:	30.70
No. 50s:	6	No. 100s:	2

Test Bowling & Fielding

Wickets:	2	Runs:	103
Best Bowling:	1/18	Average:	51.50
5 WI:	0	10 WM:	0
Catches:	5	Stumpings:	0

Clifford Roach made his debut in West Indies inaugural Test against England at Lord's in 1928. He was run out for a duck in the first innings but went on to become an accomplished opener and the first West Indian to score a Test century with a fine 122 against England at Bridgetown in 1929. He was also the first West Indian to score a double century with 209 against England at Georgetown in 1930.

ROBERTS, Alphonso

Born: September 18, 1937
Origin: St Vincent
Batting: Right handed

Tests
Test Career:	1956		
Cap Number:	92		
Tests Played:	1		
Test Batting			
Innings:	2	Runs:	28
Highest Score:	28	Average:	14.00
No. 50s:	0	No. 100s:	0
Test Bowling & Fielding			
Wickets:	0	Runs:	0
Best Bowling:		Average:	0.00
5 WI:	0	10 WM:	0
Catches:	0	Stumpings:	0

A middle order batsman whose only Test appearance was against New Zealand at Auckland, in 1956, which was to be New Zealand's first ever Test win.

ROBERTS, Anderson Montgomery Everton (Andy)

Born:	January 29, 1951
Origin:	Antigua
Batting:	Right handed
Bowling:	Right arm fast

Tests
Test Career:	1974-83		
Cap Number:	149		
Tests Played:	47		
Test Batting			
Innings:	62	Runs:	762
Highest Score:	68	Average:	14.94
No. 50s:	3	No. 100s:	0
Test Bowling & Fielding			
Wickets:	202	Runs:	5,174
Best Bowling:	7/54	Average:	25.61
5 WI:	11	10 WM:	2
Catches:	9	Stumpings:	0

One Day Internationals
ODI Career:	1975-83		
ODIs Played:	56		
ODI Batting			
Innings:	32	Runs:	231
Highest Score:	37*	Average:	10.04
No. 50s:	0	No. 100s:	0
ODI Bowling & Fielding			
Wickets:	87	Runs:	1,771
Best Bowling:	5/22	Average:	20.35
5 WM:	1	Catches:	6
Stumpings:	0		

Although he was one of the most feared bowlers throughout the 1970's and early 80's, Andy Roberts did not rely solely on intimidation when attempting to remove the world's best batsmen. His physicality was matched with an astute mind as he plotted tirelessly while honing in on his opponent's weaknesses. The first Antiguan to play Test cricket for the West Indies, after making his Test debut against England at Bridgetown in 1974, Roberts was surprisingly dropped after one Test. However, the selectors saw enough potential to select him for the tour of India later that year. Their decision was vindicated as Roberts took 32 wickets in the series, including a crushing 7/64 in the Fourth Test at Chennai. He emulated the feat with a career best 7/54 when he tore through the Australian batting in the 2nd Test at Perth, during the 1975/76 tour. Within two years, he reached the 100-wicket milestone in just 19 Tests, equaling off-spinner Alf Valentine's record set in the 50's. In 1977, Roberts joined World Series Cricket along with the cream of the West Indian Test Eleven, which included the likes of Lloyd, Richards, Murray, Holding and Rowe. Although many back home believed Roberts to be at the cross-roads of his career, he showed that he hadn't lost any of his spark during the first season of the 'unofficial competition'. He led the averages for the West Indian eleven in both the WSC Super-Test and International Cup (limited over) competition. He also, inadvertently, lived up to his reputation of being one of the most hostile pace bowlers in the world when his trademark bouncer fractured the jaw of young Australian idol, David Hookes. Roberts continued his Test career after World Series Cricket and together with Michael Holding, Joel Garner, Colin Croft and later Malcolm Marshall, was part of the most potent and arguably most successful pace attack in history. Upon his retirement at the end of 1983, he finished with 202 Test victims alongside his name. Just as competitive at ODI competition, Roberts opened the bowling with all-rounder Bernard Julien in the inaugural World Cup final against Australia, in 1975, where the Windies were victorious by 17 runs. Four years later, he shared the new ball with Michael Holding in the 1979 final against England and helped steer the team to consecutive titles. Although not quite an all-rounder, Roberts proved a difficult customer to dismiss as his intense concentration was just as apparent when batting as it was when he had the new ball in his hand. He scored three 50's with a highest score of 68 that he compiled during a (West Indian) record ninth wicket partnership stand of 161 with skipper Clive Lloyd, against India at Kolkata in 1983.

ROBERTS, Lincoln Abraham

Born:	September 4, 1974
Origin:	Tobago
Batting:	Right handed
Bowling:	Right arm medium

Tests
Test Career:	1999		
Cap Number:	229		
Tests Played:	1		
Test Batting			
Innings:	1	Runs:	0
Highest Score:	0	Average:	0.00
No. 50s:	0	No. 100s:	0

Test Bowling & Fielding

Wickets:	0	Runs:	0
Best Bowling:		Average:	0.00
5 WI:	0	10 WM:	0
Catches:	0	Stumpings:	0

Although his given names may have a presidential ring, Lincoln Abraham Roberts hardly asserted any authority in his one and only Test appearance against Australia at Kingston, where he was dismissed for a duck in the first innings and didn't get a chance to bat in the second. Roberts is one of the very few from Tobago to make it to Test level, and while his Test record was modest, he was considered a run machine in the domestic competition.

RODRIGUEZ, William Vicente

Born:	June 25, 1934
Origin:	Trinidad
Batting:	Right handed
Bowling:	Right arm leg-break

Tests

Test Career:	1962-68		
Cap Number:	117		
Tests Played:	5		

Test Batting

Innings:	7	Runs:	96
Highest Score:	50	Average:	13.71
No. 50s:	1	No. 100s:	0

Test Bowling & Fielding

Wickets:	7	Runs:	374
Best Bowling:	3/51	Average:	53.42
5 WI:	0	10 WM:	0
Catches:	3	Stumpings:	0

An all-rounder who scored fifty on debut against India at Port-of-Spain in 1962. Played five Tests between 1962-68.

ROSE, Franklyn Albert

Born:	February 1, 1972
Origin:	Jamaica
Batting:	Right handed
Bowling:	Right arm fast

Tests

Test Career:	1997-00		
Cap Number:	215		
Tests Played:	19		

Test Batting

Innings:	28	Runs:	344
Highest Score:	69	Average:	13.23
No. 50s:	1	No. 100s:	0

Test Bowling & Fielding

Wickets:	53	Runs:	1,637
Best Bowling:	7/84	Average:	30.88
5 WI:	2	10 WM:	0
Catches:	4	Stumpings:	0

One Day Internationals

ODI Career:	1997-00		
ODIs Played:	27		

ODI Batting

Innings:	23	Runs:	217
Highest Score:	30	Average:	12.05
No. 50s:	0	No. 100s:	0

ODI Bowling & Fielding

Wickets:	29	Runs:	1,046
Best Bowling:	5/23	Average:	36.06
5 WM:	1	Catches:	6
Stumpings:	0		

A fiery, Jamaican pace bowler, who on debut in front of his crowd, claimed the scalps of India's batting elite in VVS Laxman, Rahul Dravid, Sourav Ganguly, Sachin Tendulkar and Mohammad Azharuddin, in what was to be a career best 6/100.

ROWE, Lawrence George

Born:	January 8, 1949
Origin:	Jamaica
Batting:	Right handed
Bowling:	Left arm medium

Tests

Test Career:	1972-80		
Cap Number:	141		
Tests Played:	30		

Test Batting

Innings:	49	Runs:	2,047
Highest Score:	302	Average:	43.55
No. 50s:	7	No. 100s:	7

Test Bowling & Fielding

Wickets:	0	Runs:	44
Best Bowling:		Average:	0.00
5 WI:	0	10 WM:	0
Catches:	17	Stumpings:	0

One Day Internationals

ODI Career:	1975-80		
ODIs Played:	11		

ODI Batting

Innings:	8	Runs:	136
Highest Score:	60	Average:	17.00
No. 50s:	1	No. 100s:	0

ODI Bowling & Fielding

Wickets:	0	Runs:	0
Best Bowling:		Average:	0.00
5 WM:	0	Catches:	2
Stumpings:	0		

You would be hard pressed to find a more impressive Test debut than that of Jamaican Lawrence Rowe. Playing against New Zealand, in front of his home crowd at Kingston in 1972, Rowe made 214 in the first innings, after coming in at first drop. He and opener Roy Fredericks added 269 for the second wicket and if that wasn't enough, Rowe followed up with 100 not out in the second. While his 214 wasn't the highest individual score on debut, as that honour goes to Englishman, Reginald 'Tip' Foster, who scored a mammoth 287 against Australia way back in 1903, his effort, none the less, earned him the distinction of being the first Test cricketer to score a double and single century on debut. An impeccable timer of the ball, Rowe, who apparently liked to whistle while he batted - whether it was to calm his nerves or annoy the bowler, or a bit of both, no one knows for sure - was partial to big scores in his early years. He became the second West Indian to score a triple century when he scored a marathon 302 against England, at Bridgetown in 1974. It seemed that Rowe would go on to compile a cavalcade of triple figure scores and eventually become West Indies' most prolific run scorer. However, continual problems with his eyesight and various other injuries took their toll and limited his career to just 30 Tests. In 1977, Rowe along with other high profile West Indians such as Clive Lloyd, Viv Richards, Michael Holding and Andy Roberts joined the newly formed World Series Cricket competition held in Australia. After two years, the Kerry Packer led competition was dissolved and Rowe together with his West Indian teammates returned to the Test scene where he played until 1980. In 1982, and nearing the end of his career, Rowe led the rebel 'West Indies' tour to South Africa.

SAMMY, Darren Julius Garvey

Born:	December 20, 1983
Origin:	St Lucia
Batting:	Right handed
Bowling:	Right arm medium-fast

One Day Internationals

ODI Career:	2004		
ODIs Played:	2		
ODI Batting			
Innings:	0	Runs:	0
Highest Score:	0	Average:	0.00
No. 50s:	0	No. 100s:	0
ODI Bowling & Fielding			
Wickets:	1	Runs:	19
Best Bowling:	1/19	Average:	19.00
5 WM:	0	Catches:	3
Stumpings:	0		

A right arm pace bowler and the first player from St.Lucia to represent the West Indies at international level. Sammy's only ODI wicket to date is that of Bangladesh's Mushfiqur Rahman.

SAMUELS, Marlon Nathaniel

Born:	January 5, 1981
Origin:	Jamaica
Batting:	Right handed
Bowling:	Right arm off-break

Tests

Test Career:	2000-06		
Cap Number:	237		
Tests Played:	23		
Test Batting			
Innings:	41	Runs:	1,044
Highest Score:	104	Average:	28.21
No. 50s:	7	No. 100s:	1
Test Bowling & Fielding			
Wickets:	5	Runs:	703
Best Bowling:	2/49	Average:	140.60
5 WI:	0	10 WM:	0
Catches:	9	Stumpings:	0

One Day Internationals

ODI Career:	2000-06		
ODIs Played:	65		
ODI Batting			
Innings:	61	Runs:	1,512
Highest Score:	108*	Average:	28.52
No. 50s:	10	No. 100s:	1
ODI Bowling & Fielding			
Wickets:	42	Runs:	1,667
Best Bowling:	3/25	Average:	39.69
5 WM:	0	Catches:	20
Stumpings:	0		

Classified in some corners as an all rounder, because of his ability to bowl off-spin, but a more accurate description of Marlon Samuels would be that of a competent middle order batsman, as his bowling record at Test level is fair, at best. He scored his only Test century, 104 against India at Kolkata in 2002, batting at number seven and averages 28 in both Tests and ODI's. Still in his mid 20's, Samuels has time on side if he is to become a regular member of the Test side. His older brother Robert played in six Tests between 1996-97.

SAMUELS, Robert George

Born:	March 13, 1971
Origin:	Jamaica
Batting:	Left handed

Tests

Test Career:	1996-97		
Cap Number:	211		
Tests Played:	6		
Test Batting			
Innings:	12	Runs:	372
Highest Score:	125	Average:	37.20
No. 50s:	1	No. 100s:	1
Test Bowling & Fielding			
Wickets:	0	Runs:	0
Best Bowling:	0	Average:	0.00
5 WI:	0	10 WM:	0
Catches:	8	Stumpings:	0

One Day Internationals

ODI Career:	1996-97		
ODIs Played:	8		
ODI Batting			
Innings:	5	Runs:	54
Highest Score:	36*	Average:	18.00
No. 50s:	0	No. 100s:	0
ODI Bowling & Fielding			
Wickets:	0	Runs:	0
Best Bowling:	0	Average:	0.00
5 WM:	0	Catches:	1
Stumpings:	0		

The older brother of Marlon Samuels, Robert was a left hand opening batsman who scored the one Test century against New Zealand, at St Johns, in 1996.

SANFORD, Adam

Born:	July 12, 1975
Origin:	Dominica
Batting:	Right handed
Bowling:	Right arm medium-fast

Tests

Test Career:	2002-04
Cap Number:	242
Tests Played:	11

Test Batting

Innings:	17	Runs:	72
Highest Score:	18*	Average:	4.80
No. 50s:	0	No. 100s:	0

Test Bowling & Fielding

Wickets:	30	Runs:	1,316
Best Bowling:	4/132	Average:	43.86
5 WI:	0	10 WM:	0
Catches:	4	Stumpings:	0

When medium pacer Adam Sanford made his debut against India, at Georgetown, 2002 he became the first indigenous Carib to represent the West Indies at international level. His best effort with the ball was his 4/132 against South Africa at Cape Town in 2004.

SARWAN, Ramnaresh

Born:	June 23, 1980
Origin:	Guyana
Batting:	Right handed
Bowling:	Right arm leg-break

Tests

Test Career:	2000-06
Cap Number:	234
Tests Played:	63

Test Batting

Innings:	114	Runs:	4,207
Highest Score:	261*	Average:	39.31
No. 50s:	26	No. 100s:	9

Test Bowling & Fielding

Wickets:	21	Runs:	970
Best Bowling:	4/37	Average:	46.19
5 WI:	0	10 WM:	0
Catches:	45	Stumpings:	0

One Day Internationals

ODI Career:	2000-06
ODIs Played:	102

ODI Batting

Innings:	96	Runs:	3,465
Highest Score:	115*	Average:	46.82
No. 50s:	23	No. 100s:	3

ODI Bowling & Fielding

Wickets:	8	Runs:	357
Best Bowling:	3/31	Average:	44.62
5 WM:	0	Catches:	29
Stumpings:	0		

Appointed as Brian Lara's deputy in 2003, Ramnaresh Sarwan has been a regular member of the West Indies Test eleven since making 84 on debut against Pakistan at Bridgetown, in 2002. While it may have taken him almost 50 innings to notch up his maiden Test century, Sarwan has scored a further eight in just the over the same amount of time. His highest score of 261 not out against Bangladesh, at Jamaica in 2004, is the ninth highest score by a West Indian and placed him alongside the great Sir Frank Worrell, who made the same score against England back in 1930. In June 2006, during the Third Test against India at St.Kitts, Sarwan smashed six fours in an over by paceman Munaf Patel while on the way to 116. He became the third batsman to achieve this unique feat, along with team mate Chris Gayle and India's Sandeep Patil.

SCARLETT, Reginald Osmond

Born:	August 15, 1934
Origin:	Jamaica
Batting:	Right handed
Bowling:	Right arm off-break

Tests

Test Career:	1960
Cap Number:	107
Tests Played:	3

Test Batting

Innings:	4	Runs:	54
Highest Score:	29*	Average:	18.00
No. 50s:	0	No. 100s:	0

Test Bowling & Fielding

Wickets:	2	Runs:	209
Best Bowling:	1/46	Average:	104.50
5 WI:	0	10 WM:	0
Catches:	2	Stumpings:	0

A powerful all-rounder from Jamaica who made his debut against England, at Bridgetown, in 1960. Played three Tests in 1960.

SCOTT, Alfred Homer Patrick

Born:	July 29, 1934
Origin:	Jamaica
Batting:	Right handed
Bowling:	Right arm slow

Tests

Test Career:	1953
Cap Number:	80
Tests Played:	1

Test Batting

Innings:	1	Runs:	5
Highest Score:	5	Average:	5.00
No. 50s:	0	No. 100s:	0

Test Bowling & Fielding

Wickets:	0	Runs:	140
Best Bowling:		Average:	0.00
5 WI:	0	10 WM:	0
Catches:	0	Stumpings:	0

A leg spinner from Jamaica who made his home town debut against India, at Kingston, in 1953.

SCOTT, Oscar Charles (Tommy)

Born:	August 14, 1892
Origin:	Jamaica
Batting:	Right handed
Bowling:	Right arm slow

Tests

Test Career:	1928-31
Cap Number:	13
Tests Played:	8

Test Batting

Innings:	13	Runs:	171
Highest Score:	35	Average:	17.10
No. 50s:	0	No. 100s:	0

Test Bowling & Fielding

Wickets:	22	Runs:	925
Best Bowling:	5/266	Average:	42.04
5 WI:	1	10 WM:	0
Catches:	0	Stumpings:	0

A slow leg-spinner who made his debut against England at Old Trafford in 1928.

SEALEY, Benjamin James

Born:	August 12, 1899
Origin:	Trinidad
Batting:	Right handed
Bowling:	Right arm medium

Tests

Test Career:	1933
Cap Number:	36
Tests Played:	1

Test Batting

Innings:	2	Runs:	41
Highest Score:	29	Average:	20.50
No. 50s:	0	No. 100s:	0

Test Bowling & Fielding

Wickets:	1	Runs:	10
Best Bowling:	1/10	Average:	10.00
5 WI:	0	10 WM:	0
Catches:	0	Stumpings:	0

Top scored with 29 in the first innings of his one and only Test against England at The Oval, in 1933. Could be considered a little unlucky not to have been chosen in more Tests.

SEALY, James Edward (Derek)

Born:	September 11, 1912
Origin:	Barbados
Batting:	Right handed
Bowling:	Right arm medium
	Wicket Keeper

Tests

Test Career:	1930-39
Cap Number:	20
Tests Played:	11

Test Batting

Innings:	19	Runs:	478
Highest Score:	92	Average:	28.11
No. 50s:	3	No. 100s:	0

Test Bowling & Fielding

Wickets:	3	Runs:	94
Best Bowling:	2/7	Average:	31.33
5 WI:	0	10 WM:	0
Catches:	6	Stumpings:	1

Talented with bat, ball and gloves, when Derek Sealy made 58 on debut against England at Bridgetown, aged 17 years and 122 days, he became the youngest Test cricketer in the history of the game. To date he still remains West Indies' youngest ever Test player.

SEMPLE, Keith

Born:	August 21, 1970
Origin:	Guyana
Batting:	Right handed
Bowling:	Right arm medium

One Day Internationals

ODI Career:	1999
ODIs Played:	7

ODI Batting

Innings:	6	Runs:	64
Highest Score:	23	Average:	10.66
No. 50s:	0	No. 100s:	0

ODI Bowling & Fielding

Wickets:	3	Runs:	121
Best Bowling:	2/35	Average:	40.33
5 WM:	0	Catches:	2
Stumpings:	0		

A capable middle-order batsman who struggled to make the transition from domestic to international cricket. Semple made his ODI debut against South Africa, at Johannesburg in 1999.

SHEPHERD, John

Born:	November 9, 1943
Origin:	Barbados
Batting:	Right handed
Bowling:	Right arm medium

Tests

Test Career:	1969-71
Cap Number:	132
Tests Played:	5

Test Batting

Innings:	8	Runs:	77
Highest Score:	32	Average:	9.62
No. 50s:	0	No. 100s:	0

Test Bowling & Fielding

Wickets:	19	Runs:	479
Best Bowling:	5/104	Average:	25.21
5 WI:	1	10 WM:	0
Catches:	4	Stumpings:	0

A seasoned swing bowler who played at Domestic level in five countries. Took his career best 5/104 on his Test debut against England, at Old Trafford in 1969.

SHILLINGFORD, Grayson Cleophas

Born:	September 25, 1944
Origin:	Dominica
Batting:	Left handed
Bowling:	Right arm medium-fast

Tests

Test Career:	1969-72
Cap Number:	134
Tests Played:	7

Test Batting

Innings:	8	Runs:	57
Highest Score:	25	Average:	8.14
No. 50s:	0	No. 100s:	0

Test Bowling & Fielding

Wickets:	15	Runs:	537
Best Bowling:	3/63	Average:	35.80
5 WI:	0	10 WM:	0
Catches:	2	Stumpings:	0

A fast bowler who took four wickets on debut against England, at Lord's in 1969 but found it difficult to cement a place in a team crammed with quality pacemen.

SHILLINGFORD, Irvine Theodore

Born:	April 18, 1944
Origin:	Dominica
Batting:	Right handed
Bowling:	Right arm off-break

Tests

Test Career:	1977-78
Cap Number:	161
Tests Played:	4

Test Batting

Innings:	7	Runs:	218
Highest Score:	120	Average:	31.14
No. 50s:	0	No. 100s:	1

Test Bowling & Fielding

Wickets:	0	Runs:	0
Best Bowling:		Average:	0.00
5 WI:	0	10 WM:	0
Catches:	1	Stumpings:	0

One Day Internationals

ODI Career:	1978
ODIs Played:	2

ODI Batting

Innings:	2	Runs:	30
Highest Score:	24	Average:	15.00
No. 50s:	0	No. 100s:	0

ODI Bowling & Fielding

Wickets:	0	Runs:	0
Best Bowling:		Average:	0.00
5 WM:	0	Catches:	2
Stumpings:	0		

A talented middle order batsman who made his debut, at age 32, against Pakistan at Port of Spain, in 1977. In his second Test at Georgetown, he scored 120 but played just two more Tests after that.

SHIVNARINE, Sewdatt

Born:	May 13, 1952
Origin:	Guyana
Batting:	Right handed
Bowling:	Left arm off-break

Tests

Test Career:	1978-79
Cap Number:	169
Tests Played:	8

Test Batting

Innings:	14	Runs:	379
Highest Score:	63	Average:	29.15
No. 50s:	4	No. 100s:	0

Test Bowling & Fielding

Wickets:	1	Runs:	167
Best Bowling:	1/13	Average:	167.00
5 WI:	0	10 WM:	0
Catches:	6	Stumpings:	0

One Day Internationals

ODI Career:	1979
ODIs Played:	1

ODI Batting

Innings:	1	Runs:	20
Highest Score:	20*	Average:	0.00
No. 50s:	0	No. 100s:	0

ODI Bowling & Fielding

Wickets:	0	Runs:	16
Best Bowling:		Average:	0.00
5 WM:	0	Catches:	0
Stumpings:	0		

An all-rounder from Guyana who made 53 & 63 on debut against Australia, at Georgetown. The return of the elite players from World Series Cricket made it difficult for Shivnarine to cement a regular spot in the side.

SIMMONS, Philip Verant

Born:	April 18, 1963
Origin:	Trinidad
Batting:	Right handed
Bowling:	Right arm medium

Tests

Test Career:	1988-97
Cap Number:	191
Tests Played:	26

Test Batting

Innings:	47	Runs:	1,002
Highest Score:	110	Average:	22.26
No. 50s:	4	No. 100s:	1

Test Bowling & Fielding

Wickets:	4	Runs:	257
Best Bowling:	2/34	Average:	64.25
5 WI:	0	10 WM:	0
Catches:	26	Stumpings:	0

One Day Internationals

ODI Career:	1987-99
ODIs Played:	143

ODI Batting

Innings:	138	Runs:	3,675
Highest Score:	122	Average:	28.93
No. 50s:	18	No. 100s:	5

ODI Bowling & Fielding

Wickets:	83	Runs:	2,876
Best Bowling:	4/3	Average:	34.65
5 WM:	0	Catches:	55
Stumpings:	0		

An all-rounder who could open the batting and bowl useful medium pace, Phil Simmons looked like he could provide the versatility the West Indian's so desperately needed in their rebuilding phase of the late 80's. However, Simmons did not develop into the 'wild card' the West Indian selectors had hoped for and was therefore pigeon-holed as a One Day specialist.

SINGH, Charran Kamkaran

Born:	November 27, 1935
Origin:	Trinidad
Batting:	Left handed
Bowling:	Left arm off-break

Tests

Test Career:	1960
Cap Number:	109
Tests Played:	2

Test Batting

Innings:	3	Runs:	11
Highest Score:	11	Average:	3.66
No. 50s:	0	No. 100s:	0

Test Bowling & Fielding

Wickets:	5	Runs:	166
Best Bowling:	2/28	Average:	33.20
5 WI:	0	10 WM:	0
Catches:	2	Stumpings:	0

A left arm off-break bowler who played two Tests against England in 1960.

SMALL, Joseph (Joe)

Born:	November 3, 1892
Origin:	Trinidad
Batting:	Right handed
Bowling:	Right arm medium-fast

Tests
Test Career:	1928-30
Cap Number:	11
Tests Played:	3

Test Batting
Innings:	6	Runs:	79
Highest Score:	52	Average:	13.16
No. 50s:	1	No. 100s:	0

Test Bowling & Fielding
Wickets:	3	Runs:	184
Best Bowling:	2/67	Average:	61.33
5 WI:	0	10 WM:	0
Catches:	3	Stumpings:	0

A talented all-rounder who top scored with 52 in West Indies' inaugural Test against England, at Lord's in 1928.

SMALL, Milton Aster

Born:	February 12, 1964
Origin:	Barbados
Batting:	Right handed
Bowling:	Right arm medium-fast

Tests
Test Career:	1984
Cap Number:	182
Tests Played:	2

Test Batting
Innings:	1	Runs:	3
Highest Score:	3*	Average:	0.00
No. 50s:	0	No. 100s:	0

Test Bowling & Fielding
Wickets:	4	Runs:	153
Best Bowling:	3/40	Average:	38.25
5 WI:	0	10 WM:	0
Catches:	0	Stumpings:	0

One Day Internationals
ODI Career:	1984
ODIs Played:	2

ODI Batting
Innings:	0	Runs:	0
Highest Score:	0	Average:	0.00
No. 50s:	0	No. 100s:	0

ODI Bowling & Fielding
Wickets:	1	Runs:	54
Best Bowling:	1/40	Average:	54.00
5 WM:	0	Catches:	1
Stumpings:	0		

Milton Small was selected for his first Test against Australia, at Port of Spain in 1984, when he replaced Winston Davis. He toured England later that year and played in the Lord's Test, this time filling in for the injured Michael Holding. Ironically, on that tour, Small suffered a severe knee injury, which sadly ended his international career.

SMITH, Cameron Wilberforce (Cammie)

Born:	July 29, 1933
Origin:	Barbados
Batting:	Right handed
	Wicket Keeper

Tests
Test Career:	1960-62
Cap Number:	113
Tests Played:	5

Test Batting
Innings:	10	Runs:	222
Highest Score:	55	Average:	24.66
No. 50s:	1	No. 100s:	0

Test Bowling & Fielding
Wickets:	0	Runs:	0
Best Bowling:		Average:	0.00
5 WI:	0	10 WM:	0
Catches:	4	Stumpings:	1

A wicket-keeper from Barbados who opened the batting on debut against Australia at the 'Gabba in 1960. 'Cammie' made his highest score of 55 against Australia at the SCG in 1961.

SMITH, Devon Sheldon

Born:	October 21, 1981
Origin:	Grenada
Batting:	Left handed
Bowling:	Right arm off-break

Tests
Test Career:	2003-05
Cap Number:	247
Tests Played:	16

Test Batting
Innings:	30	Runs:	735
Highest Score:	108	Average:	25.34
No. 50s:	3	No. 100s:	1

Test Bowling & Fielding
Wickets:	0	Runs:	0
Best Bowling:		Average:	0.00
5 WI:	0	10 WM:	0
Catches:	14	Stumpings:	0

One Day Internationals
ODI Career:	2003-04
ODIs Played:	7

ODI Batting
Innings:	6	Runs:	129
Highest Score:	44	Average:	25.80
No. 50s:	0	No. 100s:	0

ODI Bowling & Fielding
Wickets:	0	Runs:	0
Best Bowling:		Average:	0.00
5 WM:	0	Catches:	3
Stumpings:	0		

A left hand opener who made his Test debut against Australia, at Georgetown, in 2003. He has scored just the one Test century to date - 108 against England, at Jamaica in 2003.

SMITH, Dwayne Romel

Born:	April 12, 1983
Origin:	Barbados
Batting:	Right handed
Bowling:	Right arm medium

Tests
Test Career:	2004-06
Cap Number:	255
Tests Played:	10

Test Batting
Innings:	14	Runs:	320
Highest Score:	105*	Average:	24.61
No. 50s:	0	No. 100s:	1

Test Bowling & Fielding

Wickets:	7	Runs:	344
Best Bowling:	3/71	Average:	49.14
5 WI:	0	10 WM:	0
Catches:	9	Stumpings:	0

One Day Internationals
ODI Career: 2004-06
ODIs Played: 42

ODI Batting

Innings:	35	Runs:	611
Highest Score:	68	Average:	18.51
No. 50s:	2	No. 100s:	0

ODI Bowling & Fielding

Wickets:	27	Runs:	937
Best Bowling:	5/45	Average:	34.70
5 WM:	1	Catches:	15
Stumpings:	0		

When Dwayne Smith was flown in to replace the injured Marlon Samuels in the Third Test against South Africa at Cape Town, in January 2004, hardly anyone would have expected the relatively unknown batsman from Barbados to become the eleventh West Indian to score a century on debut. Smith's cavalier 105 in even time, surprisingly was the first debut ton by a West Indian in almost 26 years. The previous 'debutant centurion' was opener Basil Williams who scored exactly 100 against Australia at Georgetown, back in 1978. A powerful hitter, Smith's flying start has been a hard act to follow as he averages just 24 in Tests. But at age 24, time is on his side should he wish to take the next step in what could be an exciting career in both forms of the game.

SMITH, O'Neil Gordon (Collie)

Born: May 5, 1933
Origin: Jamaica
Batting: Right handed
Bowling: Right arm off-break

Tests
Test Career: 1955-59
Cap Number: 86
Tests Played: 26

Test Batting

Innings:	42	Runs:	1,331
Highest Score:	168	Average:	31.69
No. 50s:	6	No. 100s:	4

Test Bowling & Fielding

Wickets:	48	Runs:	1,625
Best Bowling:	5/90	Average:	33.85
5 WI:	1	10 WM:	0
Catches:	9	Stumpings:	0

When 'Collie' Smith brought up his maiden Test century against Australia in 1955, in front of his home crowd at Kingston, he became just the fourth West Indian to score a century on debut. It was a long awaited tonic for the parochial locals as only a year earlier, another local hero, John Holt, was given out to a dubious lbw decision while on his way to a debut century. Smith, by nature, was an adventurous batsman, and like many who fit this profile, consistency is usually an issue. It took almost two years for him register his second Test ton which was a solid 161 against England at Edgbaston. However, as unpredictable as he was, Smith only had to wait two Tests before his Edgbaston innings was superseded by his 168 at Trent Bridge. Also handy as a part time off-spinner, Smith took a career best 5/90 against India, at Delhi, in 1959.

SOBERS, Sir Garfield St Auburn

Born: July 28, 1936
Origin: Barbados
Batting: Left handed
Bowling: Left arm medium-fast

Tests
Test Career: 1954-74
Cap Number: 84
Tests Played: 93

Test Batting

Innings:	160	Runs:	8,032
Highest Score:	365*	Average:	57.78
No. 50s:	30	No. 100s:	26

Test Bowling & Fielding

Wickets:	235	Runs:	7,999
Best Bowling:	6/73	Average:	34.03
5 WI:	6	10 WM:	0
Catches:	109	Stumpings:	0

One Day Internationals
ODI Career: 1973
ODIs Played: 1

ODI Batting

Innings:	1	Runs:	0
Highest Score:	0	Average:	0.00
No. 50s:	0	No. 100s:	0

ODI Bowling & Fielding

Wickets:	1	Runs:	31
Best Bowling:	1/31	Average:	31.00
5 WM:	0	Catches:	1
Stumpings:	0		

If Don Bradman is the first player picked in the greatest cricket side of all time then Garfield Sobers must surely be the second. A peerless all-rounder, his record says he could have stood alone as either a great batsman or bowler in the Test arena. The brilliant young sportsman from Barbados chose cricket ahead of football and basketball, making his Test debut as a 17 year old against the powerful English side of the early 1950's. He started out as a medium pace bowler and whilst performing consistently in his first two years at Test level gave no indication that he was to become a legend of the game. All that was to change when the West Indies took on Pakistan at Port of Spain, in 1958. Batting at number three, he combined with Conrad Hunte to add 446 for the second wicket which remains a West Indian record. He went on to score his first Test century and the then highest score in Test history. His unbeaten 365 surprised no-one in the West Indies, but the rest of the cricket world asked if the amazing innings was going to be a one-off. They didn't have to wait long for their answer, in the very next Test Sobers hit a century in each innings and on the tour of India later that year scored three more. From that point on the centuries flowed, 26 at Test level in total, including a dazzling 226 against the visiting English at Bridgetown in 1959/60, where he and the great Sir Frank Worrell put on 399 for the fourth wicket - again another West Indian record that still stands today. The world was watching when he led the Rest of the World XI in Australia in 1971. His 254 at the MCG has long been described as one of the great cricket innings of all time show-casing his hitting power against a powerful Australian bowling attack. Sobers was also a brilliant bowler either as a paceman or a canny spinner. In 1968 he bowled his side to victory against the Australians in Brisbane, opening the bowling and taking career best figures of 6/73 along the way. It almost goes without saying that he was also a wonderful fieldsman, either close in or patrolling the outfield. With over 28,000 runs and 1,000 wickets in first class cricket it is questionable if we will ever see the likes of Sir Garry Sobers again. The black and white footage of him helping himself to six sixes in an over of county cricket in 1968 is the perfect way of remembering a man who was born to dominate the sport.

SOLOMAN, Joseph Stanislaus (Joe)

Born: August 26, 1930
Origin: Guyana
Batting: Right handed
Bowling: Right arm leg-break

Tests

Test Career: 1958-65
Cap Number: 105
Tests Played: 27

Test Batting

Innings:	46	Runs:	1,326
Highest Score:	100*	Average:	34.00
No. 50s:	9	No. 100s:	1

Test Bowling & Fielding

Wickets:	4	Runs:	268
Best Bowling:	1/20	Average:	67.00
5 WI:	0	10 WM:	0
Catches:	13	Stumpings:	0

An all rounder who made an impressive start to his Test career scoring 45 and 86 on debut, while batting at number seven against India, at Kanpur. While it looked like Solomon might go on to have a stellar career as a batsman, he was to score just the one century - exactly 100 not out against India at Delhi in 1959. But rightly or wrongly, Solomon is a favourite amongst trivia buffs as he is best remembered for his long-range throw which hit the stumps to run out Australian tail-ender Ian Meckiff in the famous 1960 'Tied Test', at the 'Gabba, between Australia and West Indies.

ST HILL, Edwin

Born: March 9, 1904
Origin: Trinidad
Batting: Right handed
Bowling: Right arm medium

Tests

Test Career: 1930
Cap Number: 19
Tests Played: 2

Test Batting

Innings:	4	Runs:	18
Highest Score:	12	Average:	4.50
No. 50s:	0	No. 100s:	0

Test Bowling & Fielding

Wickets:	3	Runs:	221
Best Bowling:	2/110	Average:	73.66
5 WI:	0	10 WM:	0
Catches:	0	Stumpings:	0

An all-rounder and younger brother of Wilton St.Hill, Edwin made his debut against England at Bridgetown in 1930.

ST HILL, Wilton

Born: July 6, 1893
Origin: Trinidad
Batting: Right handed
Bowling: Right arm medium

Tests

Test Career: 1928-30
Cap Number: 10
Tests Played: 3

Test Batting

Innings:	6	Runs:	117
Highest Score:	38	Average:	19.50
No. 50s:	0	No. 100s:	0

Test Bowling & Fielding

Wickets:	0	Runs:	9
Best Bowling:		Average:	0.00
5 WI:	0	10 WM:	0
Catches:	1	Stumpings:	0

Tall and athletically built, St Hill played in West Indies inaugural Test against England at Lord's in 1928. His brother Edwin played two Tests for West Indies.

STAYERS, Sven Conrad (Charlie)

Born: June 9, 1937
Origin: Guyana
Batting: Right handed
Bowling: Right arm medium-fast

Tests

Test Career: 1962
Cap Number: 115
Tests Played: 4

Test Batting

Innings:	4	Runs:	58
Highest Score:	35*	Average:	19.33
No. 50s:	0	No. 100s:	0

Test Bowling & Fielding

Wickets:	9	Runs:	364
Best Bowling:	3/65	Average:	40.44
5 WI:	0	10 WM:	0
Catches:	0	Stumpings:	0

A pace bowler from Guyana, Charlie Stayers played four Tests in 1962. He made his debut against India, at Port of Spain, in 1962.

STOLLMEYER, Jeffrey Baxter

Born: March 11, 1921
Origin: Trinidad
Batting: Right handed
Bowling: Right arm slow

Tests
Test Career: 1939-55
Cap Number: 47
Tests Played: 32

Test Batting
Innings:	56	Runs:	2,159
Highest Score:	160	Average:	42.33
No. 50s:	12	No. 100s:	4

Test Bowling & Fielding
Wickets:	13	Runs:	507
Best Bowling:	3/32	Average:	39.00
5 WI:	0	10 WM:	0
Catches:	20	Stumpings:	0

An inspirational leader who was vice-captain for a number of years then captained the West Indies in 13 Tests from 1951 to 1955. Jeffrey Stollmeyer was a solid opening batsman who made 59 on debut at Lord's and averaged 42.33 over a Test career lasting just short of two decades. He scored four centuries including a magnificent 160 against India at Chennai in 1949 where he and Allan Rae put on 239 for the first wicket. Their effort set the West Indies on their way to memorable innings and 193 run victory. Stollmeyer and Rae's opening combination is held in as high esteem as the Fredericks/Greenidge and Greenidge/Haynes combinations of the recent era. Over their career, the pair averaged 71 for the first wicket, which is the highest by any West Indian opening pair and second overall to England's Jack Hobbs & Herbert Sutcliffe who averaged 87 during the 1920 and '30's. He became a respected administrator for many years after his playing days were over and in 1989 died in tragic circumstances after being attacked in his home. Stollmeyer's brother, Victor, played the one Test cricket for West Indies in 1939.

STOLLMEYER, Victor Humphrey

Born: January 24, 1916
Origin: Trinidad
Batting: Right handed
Bowling: Right arm slow

Tests
Test Career: 1939
Cap Number: 52
Tests Played: 1

Test Batting
Innings:	1	Runs:	96
Highest Score:	96	Average:	96.00
No. 50s:	1	No. 100s:	0

Test Bowling & Fielding
Wickets:	0	Runs:	0
Best Bowling:		Average:	0.00
5 WI:	0	10 WM:	0
Catches:	0	Stumpings:	0

The older brother of Test captain Jeff, Vic Stollmeyer was a late minute inclusion against England at The Oval, in 1939, and missed out on a debut Test century by just four runs when he was stumped on 96. He didn't get the chance to bat in the second innings as the match petered out to a draw and remarkably never played another Test.

STUART, Colin Ellsworth

Born: September 28, 1973
Origin: Guyana
Batting: Right handed
Bowling: Right arm medium-fast

Tests
Test Career: 2000-01
Cap Number: 238
Tests Played: 6

Test Batting
Innings:	9	Runs:	24
Highest Score:	12*	Average:	3.42
No. 50s:	0	No. 100s:	0

Test Bowling & Fielding
Wickets:	20	Runs:	628
Best Bowling:	3/33	Average:	31.40
5 WI:	0	10 WM:	0
Catches:	2	Stumpings:	0

One Day Internationals
ODI Career: 2001
ODIs Played: 5

ODI Batting
Innings:	1	Runs:	3
Highest Score:	3*	Average:	0.00
No. 50s:	0	No. 100s:	0

ODI Bowling & Fielding
Wickets:	8	Runs:	205
Best Bowling:	5/44	Average:	25.62
5 WM:	1	Catches:	1
Stumpings:	0		

A pace bowler from Guyana who made his Test debut against Australia, at the MCG in 2000. Played six Tests in two years with a best haul of 3/33 against Zimbabwe at Harare.

TAYLOR, Jaswick

Born: January 3, 1932
Origin: Trinidad
Batting: Right handed
Bowling: Right arm medium-fast

Tests
Test Career: 1958-59
Cap Number: 102
Tests Played: 3

Test Batting
Innings:	5	Runs:	4
Highest Score:	4*	Average:	2.00
No. 50s:	0	No. 100s:	0

Test Bowling & Fielding

Wickets:	10	Runs:	273
Best Bowling:	5/109	Average:	27.30
5 WI:	1	10 WM:	0
Catches:	0	Stumpings:	0

A pace bowler who took a career best 5/109 against Pakistan at Queen's Park.

TAYLOR, Jerome Everton

Born:	June 22, 1984
Origin:	Jamaica
Batting:	Right handed
Bowling:	Right arm fast

Tests

Test Career:	2003-06
Cap Number:	252
Tests Played:	7

Test Batting

Innings:	11	Runs:	90
Highest Score:	23	Average:	11.25
No. 50s:	0	No. 100s:	0

Test Bowling & Fielding

Wickets:	18	Runs:	612
Best Bowling:	5/50	Average:	34.00
5 WI:	1	10 WM:	0
Catches:	0	Stumpings:	0

One Day Internationals

ODI Career:	2003-06
ODIs Played:	12

ODI Batting

Innings:	3	Runs:	19
Highest Score:	9	Average:	9.50
No. 50s:	0	No. 100s:	0

ODI Bowling & Fielding

Wickets:	17	Runs:	429
Best Bowling:	4/24	Average:	25.23
5 WM:	0	Catches:	3
Stumpings:	0		

Together with Pedro Collins, Jerome Taylor heads the current West Indies pace attack after an impressive series against India in mid 2006. In the final Test at Kingston, Taylor captured a career best 5/50 in the first innings and finished with 9/95 for the match. At 22, Taylor is an exciting talent and has the opportunity to become the premier bowler of the Caribbean for many years to come.

THOMPSON, Patterson Ian

Born:	September 26, 1971
Origin:	Barbados
Batting:	Right handed
Bowling:	Right arm medium-fast

Tests

Test Career:	1996-97
Cap Number:	212
Tests Played:	2

Test Batting

Innings:	3	Runs:	17
Highest Score:	10*	Average:	8.50
No. 50s:	0	No. 100s:	0

Test Bowling & Fielding

Wickets:	5	Runs:	215
Best Bowling:	2/58	Average:	43.00
5 WI:	0	10 WM:	0
Catches:	0	Stumpings:	0

One Day Internationals

ODI Career:	1997
ODIs Played:	2

ODI Batting

Innings:	1	Runs:	2
Highest Score:	2	Average:	2.00
No. 50s:	0	No. 100s:	0

ODI Bowling & Fielding

Wickets:	2	Runs:	110
Best Bowling:	1/46	Average:	55.00
5 WM:	0	Catches:	0
Stumpings:	0		

A pace bowler from Barbados, who played just two Tests (against Australia in 1996 and New Zealand in 1997) with little success.

TRIM, John

Born:	January 25, 1915
Origin:	Guyana
Batting:	Right handed
Bowling:	Right arm medium-fast

Tests

Test Career:	1948-52
Cap Number:	63
Tests Played:	4

Test Batting

Innings:	5	Runs:	21
Highest Score:	12	Average:	5.25
No. 50s:	0	No. 100s:	0

Test Bowling & Fielding

Wickets:	18	Runs:	291
Best Bowling:	5/34	Average:	16.16
5 WI:	1	10 WM:	0
Catches:	2	Stumpings:	0

A right arm pace bowler from Guyana who on debut, took 2/6 with the new ball against England at Georgetown, in 1948. Trim took his best haul of 5/34 against Australia in his fourth and last Test, at the MCG in 1952.

TUCKETT, Carl

Born:	May 18, 1970
Origin:	Leeward Islands (Nevis)
Batting:	Right handed
Bowling:	Right arm medium-fast

One Day Internationals

ODI Career:	1998
ODIs Played:	1

ODI Batting

Innings:	0	Runs:	0
Highest Score:	0	Average:	0.00
No. 50s:	0	No. 100s:	0

ODI Bowling & Fielding

Wickets:	2	Runs:	41
Best Bowling:	2/41	Average:	20.50
5 WM:	0	Catches:	0
Stumpings:	0		

A pace bowler from Nevis who took the wickets of Alec Stewart and Graeme Hick in his only ODI against England, at Port of Spain, in 1998.

VALENTINE, Alfred Louis

Born: April 28, 1930
Origin: Jamaica
Batting: Right handed
Bowling: Left arm off-break

Tests
Test Career: 1950-62
Cap Number: 71
Tests Played: 36

Test Batting
Innings:	51	Runs:	141
Highest Score:	14	Average:	4.70
No. 50s:	0	No. 100s:	0

Test Bowling & Fielding
Wickets:	139	Runs:	4,215
Best Bowling:	8/104	Average:	30.32
5 WI:	8	10 WM:	2
Catches:	13	Stumpings:	0

Alf Valentine became the first bowler, of any Test nation, to take eight wickets in their first innings of a Test match when he opened with 8/104 against England, at Old Trafford in 1950. Naturally, it also remains the best bowling figures by a West Indian on debut. The left arm orthodox spinner made his debut with fellow spinner Sonny Ramadhin and it was only fitting that Ramadhin would capture the two remaining wickets of England's first innings. The pair continued to cause heartache for their hosts as they collected 59 wickets between them and spearhead the West Indies to their first ever series win in England. Valentine and Ramadhin went on to become West Indies most formidable 'spin duo' and were renowned for their marathon spells. Again, almost fittingly, as they were spoken in the same breath on the field, they were to remain alongside each other in the record books as they hold positions 11th (Ramadhin) and 12th on the West Indian all time wicket takers list.

VALENTINE, Vincent

Born: April 4, 1908
Origin: Jamaica
Batting: Right handed
Bowling: Right arm medium-fast

Tests
Test Career: 1933
Cap Number: 34
Tests Played: 2

Test Batting
Innings:	4	Runs:	35
Highest Score:	19*	Average:	11.66
No. 50s:	0	No. 100s:	0

Test Bowling & Fielding
Wickets:	1	Runs:	104
Best Bowling:	1/55	Average:	104.00
5 WI:	0	10 WM:	0
Catches:	0	Stumpings:	0

A Jamaican pace bowler who bowled with exceptional line and length, Valentine made his Test debut against England at Old Trafford in 1933, taking just the one wicket. An excellent fielder and handy lower order batsman, Valentine played only two Tests and based on talent alone, should have been persevered with for a little while longer.

WALCOTT, Leslie

Born: January 18, 1894
Origin: Barbados
Batting: Right handed
Bowling: Right arm off-break

Tests
Test Career: 1930
Cap Number: 21
Tests Played: 1

Test Batting
Innings:	2	Runs:	40
Highest Score:	24	Average:	40.00
No. 50s:	0	No. 100s:	0

Test Bowling & Fielding
Wickets:	1	Runs:	32
Best Bowling:	1/17	Average:	32.00
5 WI:	0	10 WM:	0
Catches:	0	Stumpings:	0

An all-rounder from Barbados, Leslie Walcott played the one Test against England at Bridgetown in 1930 where he took 1/17 and scored 24 and 16 not out.

WALCOTT, Sir Clyde Leopold

Born: January 17, 1926
Origin: Barbados
Batting: Right handed
Bowling: Right arm medium-fast
Wicket Keeper

Tests
Test Career: 1948-60
Cap Number: 58
Tests Played: 44

Test Batting
Innings:	74	Runs:	3,798
Highest Score:	220	Average:	56.68
No. 50s:	14	No. 100s:	15

Test Bowling & Fielding
Wickets:	11	Runs:	408
Best Bowling:	3/50	Average:	37.09
5 WI:	0	10 WM:	0
Catches:	53	Stumpings:	11

A powerful all-round cricketer who opened the batting and kept wickets on his Test debut against England at Bridgetown in 1948. Part of the legendary 'W Trio' of Walcott, Weekes and Worrell, Clyde Walcott made an incredible 15 centuries against all comers - five against Australia, four against England & India and one against Pakistan and New Zealand. His first four centuries and remaining eleven on home soil. No doubt, his most memorable innings was his 220 against England at Bridgetown in 1954. A handy medium pacer, Walcott took 11 wickets with a career best 3/50 against Australia at Kingston, in 1954. Upon his retirement, he became president of the West Indian Board and then Chairman of ICC. He was knighted for services to cricket in

1994 and was awarded an OBE in 1966. On 26th August 2006, Clyde Walcott passed away aged 80, leaving Everton Weekes as the surviving member of the unofficial 'Three W' club.

WALLACE, Philo Alphonso

Born: August 2, 1970
Origin: Barbados
Batting: Right handed
Bowling: Right arm medium

Tests
Test Career: 1997-99
Cap Number: 219
Tests Played: 7

Test Batting
Innings:	13	Runs:	279
Highest Score:	92	Average:	21.46
No. 50s:	2	No. 100s:	0

Test Bowling & Fielding
Wickets:	0	Runs:	0
Best Bowling:		Average:	0.00
5 WI:	0	10 WM:	0
Catches:	9	Stumpings:	0

One Day Internationals
ODI Career: 1991-00
ODIs Played: 33

ODI Batting
Innings:	33	Runs:	701
Highest Score:	103	Average:	21.24
No. 50s:	2	No. 100s:	1

ODI Bowling & Fielding
Wickets:	0	Runs:	0
Best Bowling:		Average:	0.00
5 WM:	0	Catches:	11
Stumpings:	0		

A hard hitting opener from Barbados who made his Test debut against Pakistan, at Rawalpindi, in 1997. Wallace was more suited to the shorter version of the game where he scored 103 of 102 balls against South Africa at Dhaka in 1999.

WALSH, Courtney Andrew

Born: October 30, 1962
Origin: Jamaica
Batting: Right handed
Bowling: Right arm fast

Tests
Test Career: 1984-01
Cap Number: 183
Tests Played: 132

Test Batting
Innings:	185	Runs:	936
Highest Score:	30*	Average:	7.54
No. 50s:	0	No. 100s:	0

Test Bowling & Fielding
Wickets:	519	Runs:	12,688
Best Bowling:	7/37	Average:	24.44
5 WI:	22	10 WM:	3
Catches:	29	Stumpings:	0

One Day Internationals
ODI Career: 1985-00
ODIs Played: 205

ODI Batting
Innings:	79	Runs:	321
Highest Score:	30	Average:	6.97
No. 50s:	0	No. 100s:	0

ODI Bowling & Fielding
Wickets:	227	Runs:	6,918
Best Bowling:	5/1	Average:	30.47
5 WM:	1	Catches:	27
Stumpings:	0		

The former leading Test wicket taker, Courtney Walsh once lived in the shadows of his higher profile counterparts in Holding, Garner and Marshall. They formed a formidable quartet for the best part of four years but as the senior trio slowly eased into retirement, it was left to Walsh to marshall the new wave of pace bowlers. In 1988, he was joined by the enigmatic Curtly Ambrose, and for over a decade, the two spearheaded what was considered the most potent tandem attack in international cricket. Such was the success of their partnership that Ambrose sits in second place behind Walsh as West Indies leading wicket taker. Apart from his career best 7/37 against New Zealand, at The Basin in 1995, Walsh rarely experienced the peaks and troughs that most pace bowlers endure as he relied more on consistency than big hauls. However, he did collect an unexpected hat-trick in 1988 against Australia, at the 'Gabba, when in the second innings he dismissed Veletta and Wood in consecutive balls which followed on from his wicket of Tony Dodemaide in the 1st innings. In March 2000, during the 2nd Test against Zimbabwe, and in front of his home crowd at Kingston, Walsh passed Kapil Dev's record of 434 Test wickets when Wavell Hinds held on to a catch at short leg to dismiss Zimbabwean tail ender Henry Olonga. To add to the excitement, it was last wicket of the match and the Jamaican crowd celebrated in style. Walsh went on to become the first player to reach the 500 wicket milestone and upon his retirement finished with 519 Test wickets. His record was overtaken by Sri Lanka's spin king, Muttiah Muralitharan in 2004 and now sits in fifth place behind Shane Warne, Murali, Glenn McGrath and India's Anil Kumble. Walsh's economical bowling style was just as efficient in limited overs competition as it was in Tests. He played in over 200 ODI's and took 227 wickets with an amazing best haul of 5/1 from 4.3 overs against Sri Lanka in 1986. And speaking of records, while Walsh may not have been the most competent tail-ender batsman going around, - as he holds the record for the most ducks in Test cricket with 43 - he, with Carl Hooper hold the record for the highest tenth wicket partnership in West Indian history. The pair put on 106 against Pakistan at St.Johns, Antigua in 1993, where Walsh scored a career best 30. Courtney Walsh is neither the quickest, or most potent bowler the world, or for that matter, West Indian cricket has seen, but his durability in being able to bowl consistent pace at the elite level, over so many years, remains unprecedented.

WASHINGTON, Dwight Marlon

Born:	March 5, 1983
Origin:	Jamaica
Batting:	Right handed
Bowling:	Right arm fast

Tests

Test Career:	2005
Cap Number:	260
Tests Played:	1

Test Batting

Innings:	1	Runs:	7
Highest Score:	7*	Average:	0.00
No. 50s:	0	No. 100s:	0

Test Bowling & Fielding

Wickets:	0	Runs:	93
Best Bowling:	0	Average:	0.00
5 WI:	0	10 WM:	0
Catches:	3	Stumpings:	0

As a pace bowler, Washington's debut against South Africa, at St John's in 2005 was an understated baptism of fire. On a wicket which yielded over 1300 runs, the yongster's figures of 0/93, from 22 overs, doesn't really seem that bad.

WATSON, Chester Donald

Born:	July 1, 1938
Origin:	Jamaica
Batting:	Right handed
Bowling:	Right arm fast

Tests

Test Career:	1960-62
Cap Number:	108
Tests Played:	7

Test Batting

Innings:	6	Runs:	12
Highest Score:	5	Average:	2.40
No. 50s:	0	No. 100s:	0

Test Bowling & Fielding

Wickets:	19	Runs:	724
Best Bowling:	4/62	Average:	38.10
5 WI:	0	10 WM:	0
Catches:	1	Stumpings:	0

Chester Watson shared the new ball with the great Wes Hall on debut, against England at Bridgetown, in 1960. Taking three wickets in the first innings, he temporarily outshone Hall but could only manage a further six Tests.

WEEKES, Kenneth Hunnell (Bam Bam)

Born:	January 24, 1912
Origin:	Jamaica
Batting:	Left handed
Bowling:	Left arm fast
	Wicket Keeper

Tests

Test Career:	1939
Cap Number:	48
Tests Played:	2

Test Batting

Innings:	3	Runs:	173
Highest Score:	137	Average:	57.66
No. 50s:	0	No. 100s:	1

Test Bowling & Fielding

Wickets:	0	Runs:	0
Best Bowling:	0	Average:	0.00
5 WI:	0	10 WM:	0
Catches:	0	Stumpings:	0

Born in the USA, and no known relation to the great Everton Weekes, Ken Weekes was a talented wicket-keeper who was selected as a batsman in his first Test against England at Lord's in 1939. In his second and last Test innings he became the fifth West Indian to score a century when he made 137 at The Oval.

WEEKES, Sir Everton de Courcy

Born:	February 26, 1925
Origin:	Barbados
Batting:	Right handed
Bowling:	Right arm leg-break

Tests

Test Career:	1948-58
Cap Number:	59
Tests Played:	48

Test Batting

Innings:	81	Runs:	4,455
Highest Score:	207	Average:	58.61
No. 50s:	19	No. 100s:	15

Test Bowling & Fielding

Wickets:	1	Runs:	77
Best Bowling:	1/8	Average:	77.00
5 WI:	0	10 WM:	0
Catches:	49	Stumpings:	0

One of the first true batting greats of the Caribbean, Everton Weekes formed 1/3rd of the legendary 'Three W's', - the other two being Clyde Walcott and Frank Worrell, who, like Weekes, were both knighted in later life, with Weekes completing the treble when he received his honour in 1995. Shortly after making his debut against England in 1948, Weekes went on to create his own piece of history. He scored a record five centuries in consecutive innings and if not for being run out for 90 against India at Chennai in 1949, it would have been six centuries on the trot. Of recent times only India's Rahul Dravid has come close to emulating Weekes long standing record when he scored four tons in succession between in 2002 and '03. In all, Weekes scored 15 Test centuries including two double centuries of 206 and 207. His highest score of 207 was made against India at Queens Park Oval, Port of Spain, in 1953 and his 206 was made at the same venue a year later. His innings was part of a West Indian record partnership for the third wicket where he and Frank Worrell put on 338 against England. The record has stood the test of time and after 53 years, remains in tact. His Test average of 58.61 (by a West Indian batsman) is headed only by former teammate, George Headley. The passing of Clyde Walcott in late August 2006, sees Weekes become the last surviving member of the legendary 'Three W's'.

WHITE, Anthony Wilbur
Born: November 20, 1938
Origin: Barbados
Batting: Right handed
Bowling: Right arm medium

Tests
Test Career: 1965
Cap Number: 122
Tests Played: 2

Test Batting
Innings:	4	Runs:	71
Highest Score:	57*	Average:	23.66
No. 50s:	1	No. 100s:	0

Test Bowling & Fielding
Wickets:	3	Runs:	152
Best Bowling:	2/34	Average:	50.66
5 WI:	0	10 WM:	0
Catches:	1	Stumpings:	0

An all-rounder, Tony White came in at number eight on debut against Australia, at Kingston, in 1965, and top scored with 57 not out. Played just the one more Test, against Australia at Port of Spain.

WIGHT, Claude Vibart
Born: July 28, 1902
Origin: Guyana
Batting: Right handed
Bowling: Right arm fast

Tests
Test Career: 1928-30
Cap Number: 15
Tests Played: 2

Test Batting
Innings:	4	Runs:	67
Highest Score:	23	Average:	22.33
No. 50s:	0	No. 100s:	0

Test Bowling & Fielding
Wickets:	0	Runs:	6
Best Bowling:		Average:	0.00
5 WI:	0	10 WM:	0
Catches:	0	Stumpings:	0

From Guyana, Vibart Wight made his debut against England at The Oval, in 1928. He averaged 22.33 in his two Tests.

WIGHT, George Leslie
Born: May 28, 1929
Origin: Guyana
Batting: Right handed

Tests
Test Career: 1953
Cap Number: 79
Tests Played: 1

Test Batting
Innings:	1	Runs:	21
Highest Score:	21	Average:	21.00
No. 50s:	0	No. 100s:	0

Test Bowling & Fielding
Wickets:	0	Runs:	0
Best Bowling:		Average:	0.00
5 WI:	0	10 WM:	0
Catches:	0	Stumpings:	0

An excellent domestic cricketer who played the one Test, against India, at Georgetown in 1953.

WILES, Charles Archibald (Archie)
Born: August 11, 1892
Origin: Barbados
Batting: Right handed

Tests
Test Career: 1933
Cap Number: 35
Tests Played: 1

Test Batting
Innings:	2	Runs:	2
Highest Score:	2	Average:	1.00
No. 50s:	0	No. 100s:	0

Test Bowling & Fielding
Wickets:	0	Runs:	0
Best Bowling:		Average:	0.00
5 WI:	0	10 WM:	0
Catches:	0	Stumpings:	0

A highly regarded middle order batsman originally from Barbados then Trinidad, Archie Wiles who played the one Test against England at Old Trafford in 1933 just a month prior to his 41st birthday.

WILLETT, Elquemedo Tonito
Born: May 1, 1953
Origin: Leeward Islands
Batting: Left handed
Bowling: Left arm leg-break

Tests
Test Career: 1973-75
Cap Number: 146
Tests Played: 5

Test Batting
Innings:	8	Runs:	74
Highest Score:	26	Average:	14.80
No. 50s:	0	No. 100s:	0

Test Bowling & Fielding
Wickets:	11	Runs:	482
Best Bowling:	3/33	Average:	43.81
5 WI:	0	10 WM:	0
Catches:	0	Stumpings:	0

Left arm off-spinner Elquemedo Willett became the first player from the Leeward Islands to play Test cricket for West Indies when he debuted against Australia at Bridgetown, in 1973. Taking the wickets of wicket-keeper Rod Marsh and spinner Kerry O'Keefe, he finished with a credible 2/79 on debut. He took his career best 3/33 in his next Test where he captured the valuable scalps of skipper Ian Chappell for 97, opener Ian Redpath and the flamboyant Doug Walters. Willett played just three more Tests thereafter.

WILLIAMS, Alvadon Basil

Born: November 21, 1949
Origin: Jamaica
Batting: Right handed

Tests
Test Career: 1978-79
Cap Number: 170
Tests Played: 7

Test Batting
Innings:	12	Runs:	469
Highest Score:	111	Average:	39.08
No. 50s:	1	No. 100s:	2

Test Bowling & Fielding
Wickets:	0	Runs:	0
Best Bowling:		Average:	0.00
5 WI:	0	10 WM:	0
Catches:	5	Stumpings:	0

An opener from Jamaica, Basil Williams was yet another who got an opportunity at the elite level due to the defection of a number of established players to World Series Cricket. He grasped his chance with both hands scoring 100 on debut against Australia, at Georgetown in 1978 and then a year later against India at Kolkata, made a career best 111. Upon his return home for the tour of India, the likes of Richards, Lloyd, Greenidge and Rowe had returned to Test cricket and subsequently Williams found himself on the outer.

WILLIAMS, David

Born: November 4, 1963
Origin: Trinidad
Batting: Right handed
Bowling: Right arm leg-break
Wicket Keeper

Tests
Test Career: 1992-98
Cap Number: 201
Tests Played: 11

Test Batting
Innings:	19	Runs:	242
Highest Score:	65	Average:	13.44
No. 50s:	1	No. 100s:	0

Test Bowling & Fielding
Wickets:	0	Runs:	0
Best Bowling:		Average:	0.00
5 WI:	0	10 WM:	0
Catches:	40	Stumpings:	2

One Day Internationals
ODI Career: 1988-97
ODIs Played: 36

ODI Batting
Innings:	23	Runs:	147
Highest Score:	32*	Average:	9.18
No. 50s:	0	No. 100s:	0

ODI Bowling & Fielding
Wickets:	0	Runs:	0
Best Bowling:		Average:	0.00
5 WM:	0	Catches:	35
Stumpings:	10		

Taking over the gloves from Jeffrey Dujon was always going to be a hard act to follow. And even though he did not do much wrong, David Williams was never going to reach the heights of his predecessor and after eleven Tests was replaced by Junior Murray. A member of the 1992 World Cup squad.

WILLIAMS, Ernest Albert Vivian (Foffie)

Born: April 10, 1914
Origin: Barbados
Batting: Right handed
Bowling: Right arm medium-fast

Tests
Test Career: 1939-48
Cap Number: 50
Tests Played: 4

Test Batting
Innings:	6	Runs:	113
Highest Score:	72	Average:	18.83
No. 50s:	1	No. 100s:	0

Test Bowling & Fielding
Wickets:	9	Runs:	241
Best Bowling:	3/51	Average:	26.77
5 WI:	0	10 WM:	0
Catches:	2	Stumpings:	0

'Foffie' Williams made his Test debut against England at Old Trafford in 1939 but his finest hour came during the 1948 Test against England in Barbados when he clobbered his way to the then fastest Test 50. His was eventually out for a career best 72 and then with the ball took his best figures of 3/51.

WILLIAMS, Laurie Rohan

Born: December 12, 1968
Origin: Jamaica
Batting: Right handed
Bowling: Right arm medium

One Day Internationals
ODI Career: 1996-01
ODIs Played: 15

ODI Batting
Innings:	13	Runs:	124
Highest Score:	41	Average:	11.27
No. 50s:	0	No. 100s:	0

ODI Bowling & Fielding
Wickets:	18	Runs:	556
Best Bowling:	3/16	Average:	30.88
5 WM:	0	Catches:	8
Stumpings:	0		

A handy seamer who could also swing the ball with great effect. After making his ODI debut against New Zealand, at Port of Spain in 1996, Laurie Williams went on to play in a further 14 ODI's until his untimely death in 2002.

WILLIAMS, Stuart Clayton

Born: August 12, 1969
Origin: Nevis
Batting: Right handed
Bowling: Right arm medium

Tests
Test Career: 1994-02
Cap Number: 205
Tests Played: 31

Test Batting			
Innings:	52	Runs:	1,183
Highest Score:	128	Average:	24.14
No. 50s:	3	No. 100s:	1
Test Bowling & Fielding			
Wickets:	0	Runs:	19
Best Bowling:		Average:	0.00
5 WI:	0	10 WM:	0
Catches:	27	Stumpings:	0

One Day Internationals

ODI Career:	1994-99		
ODIs Played:	57		
ODI Batting			
Innings:	55	Runs:	1,586
Highest Score:	105*	Average:	32.36
No. 50s:	12	No. 100s:	1
ODI Bowling & Fielding			
Wickets:	1	Runs:	30
Best Bowling:	1/30	Average:	30.00
5 WM:	0	Catches:	18
Stumpings:	0		

An opening batsman who made his Test debut against England, at St Johns in 1994. Scored the one Test century, 128 against India on home soil. A regular member of the ODI side throughout the 1990's, Williams is the nephew of former Test spinner Elquemedo Willett.

WISHART, Kenneth Leslie

Born:	November 28, 1908
Origin:	Guyana
Batting:	Left handed

Tests

Test Career:	1935
Cap Number:	42
Tests Played:	1

Test Batting			
Innings:	2	Runs:	52
Highest Score:	52	Average:	26.00
No. 50s:	1	No. 100s:	0
Test Bowling & Fielding			
Wickets:	0	Runs:	0
Best Bowling:		Average:	0.00
5 WI:	0	10 WM:	0
Catches:	0	Stumpings:	0

A left handed opener who, on debut against England at Georgetown in 1935, was run out for 52 in the first innings and made a duck in the second. His luck had certainly 'run out' as Wishart did not make another Test appearance thereafter.

WORRELL, Sir Frank Mortimer Maglinne

Born:	August 1, 1924
Origin:	Barbados
Batting:	Right handed
Bowling:	Left arm medium-fast

Tests

Test Career:	1948-63
Cap Number:	61
Tests Played:	51

Test Batting			
Innings:	87	Runs:	3,860
Highest Score:	261	Average:	49.48
No. 50s:	22	No. 100s:	9
Test Bowling & Fielding			
Wickets:	69	Runs:	2,672
Best Bowling:	7/70	Average:	38.72
5 WI:	2	10 WM:	0
Catches:	43	Stumpings:	0

Part of the legendary Barbados born 'Three W's' - Worrell, Walcott and Weekes, Sir Frank Worrell was the first complete cricketer of his generation. An elegant right hand batsman, with sublime timing, Worrell possessed every stroke in the book. He was also a fine medium pace bowler and accomplished cover fieldsman. He made his debut against England, at Queens Park Oval, Port of Spain, in 1948, after breaking numerous batting records with Barbados in the domestic competition. Batting at number four, fittingly wedged between Everton Weekes at three and skipper Clyde Walcott at five, Worrell fell three runs short of becoming the third batsman in West Indian to history to score a century on debut. But Worrell and the cricket world didn't have to wait long as in the next Test at Georgetown, he scored a stunning 131 not out to set the West Indies on their way to a comfortable seven wicket victory. His coming of age, as an elite batsman, occurred during the 1950 tour of England. He clocked the second highest score by a West Indian, with a marathon 261 at Trent Bridge, which formed part of a 283 run stand with Everton Weekes. In his next innings at The Oval, he followed up with 138 after temporarily retiring hurt on 116. Worrell went on to score another seven hundreds including a second double century - 237 against India at Sabina Park, Kingston, in 1953 - an innings where all 'Three Ws' made centuries. A few months later in March 1954, Worrell, Weekes and Walcott repeated the feat when they all scored centuries against England in the Fourth Test at Port of Spain. Worrell's 167 was part of a record 338 run partnership with Weekes for the third wicket. In 1957, he became the first West Indian to 'carry his bat' with a magnificent 191 not out against England a Trent Bridge and then in 1959, against England, at Bridgetown, he and Sir Garfield Sobers put on 399 to claim the record for the fourth wicket. With the ball, Worrell was just as impressive. In 1957 at Headingley, he captured a career best 7/70, eclipsing his previous best 6/38 against Australia, at Adelaide in 1953. In 1960 Worrell was appointed captain and managed to galvanise a side that was traditionally segmented because of the various island groups that made up the West Indies as players tended to 'stick with their own'. He led the West Indies to nine victories and just three losses in his 15 games at the helm. He announced his retirement after the 1963 tour of England and was knighted a year later. In 1967, Sir Frank Worrell sadly passed away after losing his battle with leukemia. He was 42 years of age. A respected icon of the game and an exemplary ambassador for West Indian cricket, a perpetual trophy was created in his honour, featuring the ball used in the 1960 Tied Test. Since 1961, The Frank Worrell Trophy has been awarded to the Test series winner between West Indies and Australia.

Zimbabwe

ARNOTT, Kevin John

Born: March 8, 1961
Batting: Right handed

Tests
Test Career: 1992-93
Cap Number: 1
Tests Played: 4

Test Batting
Innings:	8	Runs:	302
Highest Score:	101*	Average:	43.14
No. 50s:	1	No. 100s:	1

Test Bowling & Fielding
Wickets:	0	Runs:	0
Best Bowling:		Average:	0.00
5 WI:	0	10 WM:	0
Catches:	4	Stumpings:	0

One Day Internationals
ODI Career: 1987-93
ODIs Played: 13

ODI Batting
Innings:	12	Runs:	238
Highest Score:	60	Average:	23.80
No. 50s:	3	No. 100s:	0

ODI Bowling & Fielding
Wickets:	0	Runs:	0
Best Bowling:		Average:	0.00
5 WM:	0	Catches:	3
Stumpings:	0		

A member of Zimbabwe's World Cup squad of 1987, Kevin Arnott went on to play in Zimbabwe's inaugural Test match against India in 1992. And for the trivia buffs Arnott was the first man to face a ball for Zimbabwe in Test cricket and is credited with the official 'number one' Test cap. A technically correct but cautious batsman, Arnott scored 40 on debut and in his next Test, scored 101 not out against New Zealand at Bulawayo. Arnott would have played a lot more Test cricket for his country had Zimbabwe's entry into the Test arena had not occured during the twilight of his career.

BLIGNAUT, Arnoldus Mauritius (Andy)

Born: August 1, 1978
Batting: Left handed
Bowling: Right arm medium-fast

Tests
Test Career: 2001-05
Cap Number: 48
Tests Played: 19

Test Batting
Innings:	36	Runs:	886
Highest Score:	92	Average:	26.84
No. 50s:	6	No. 100s:	0

Test Bowling & Fielding
Wickets:	53	Runs:	1,964
Best Bowling:	5/73	Average:	37.05
5 WI:	3	10 WM:	0
Catches:	13	Stumpings:	0

One Day Internationals
ODI Career: 1999-05
ODIs Played: 51

ODI Batting
Innings:	40	Runs:	625
Highest Score:	63*	Average:	19.53
No. 50s:	5	No. 100s:	0

ODI Bowling & Fielding
Wickets:	49	Runs:	2,021
Best Bowling:	4/43	Average:	41.24
5 WM:	0	Catches:	11
Stumpings:	0		

A strong and athletically built right arm pace bowler who was likened to New Zealand's Chris Cairns in his early days, Andy Blignaut etched his name in the record books when on debut he collected the impressive figures of 5/73 against Bangladesh, at Bulawayo, in 2001. It was the best bowling figures by a Zimbabwean on debut. And while it would look like that Blignaut would surely become the much needed glamour boy of Zimbabwean cricket, he, like a few others, became disillusioned with the ongoing internal problems at board level and thus sat out the 2001/02 season. In mid 2002, Blignaut returned to international cricket and almost replicated his personal best when he took 5/79 against Pakistan, in his first game back. He was selected for the 2003 World Cup and again showed why he was considered such a talent at both forms of the game. But the roller-coaster ride continued and upon his return from the World Cup, Blignaut was one of the 15 rebel players who were eventually sacked by the Zimbabwean board. He returned in 2005 and played in both Tests and ODI's for his country but again, in 2006 severed his ties with the Zimbabwean Cricket Union over a pay dispute and headed to neighboring South Africa to play domestic cricket in that country. But Blignaut has always stated that his loyalty is, and always will be to Zimbabwe and therefore there may be another chapter to add in what has been an unfortunate saga in Zimbabwean cricket.

BRAIN, David Hayden

Born: October 4, 1964
Batting: Right handed
Bowling: Left arm medium-fast

Tests

Test Career: 1992-95
Cap Number: 13
Tests Played: 9

Test Batting

Innings:	13	Runs:	115
Highest Score:	28	Average:	10.45
No. 50s:	0	No. 100s:	0

Test Bowling & Fielding

Wickets:	30	Runs:	915
Best Bowling:	5/42	Average:	30.50
5 WI:	1	10 WM:	0
Catches:	1	Stumpings:	0

One Day Internationals

ODI Career: 1992-95
ODIs Played: 23

ODI Batting

Innings:	18	Runs:	117
Highest Score:	27	Average:	8.35
No. 50s:	0	No. 100s:	0

ODI Bowling & Fielding

Wickets:	21	Runs:	849
Best Bowling:	3/51	Average:	40.42
5 WM:	0	Catches:	5
Stumpings:	0		

A red-headed left arm seam bowler, David Brain made his Test debut against New Zealand at Harare, in 1992. Before long he became a regular member of both the Test & One Day sides and was selected on the 1993/94 tour of Pakistan, where he led the Zimbabwe attack with aplomb taking a career best 5/42 at Lahore.

BRANDES, Eddo Andr

Born: March 5, 1963
Batting: Right handed
Bowling: Right arm medium-fast

Tests

Test Career: 1992-99
Cap Number: 2
Tests Played: 10

Test Batting

Innings:	15	Runs:	121
Highest Score:	39	Average:	10.08
No. 50s:	0	No. 100s:	0

Test Bowling & Fielding

Wickets:	26	Runs:	951
Best Bowling:	3/45	Average:	36.57
5 WI:	0	10 WM:	0
Catches:	4	Stumpings:	0

One Day Internationals

ODI Career: 1987-99
ODIs Played: 59

ODI Batting

Innings:	41	Runs:	404
Highest Score:	55	Average:	13.03
No. 50s:	2	No. 100s:	0

ODI Bowling & Fielding

Wickets:	70	Runs:	2,266
Best Bowling:	5/28	Average:	32.37
5 WM:	2	Catches:	11
Stumpings:	0		

A member of Zimbabwe's inaugural Test team of 1992, South African born Eddo Brandes made cricket history in 1996/97 when he became the first Zimbabwean to take a hat-trick at ODI level. In what was described as an inspirational spell of bowling, the ever competitive Brandes took the wickets of Knight, Crawley and Hussain and then two others which would help secure a rare victory on English soil. Brandes also enjoyed his time with the bat and quite often welcomed the opportunity to play handy cameo roles late in the order. He led the Zimbabwe pace attack for just under a decade and was a genuine stalwart in Zimbabwe's development as a Test playing nation.

BRENT, Gary Bazil

Born: January 13, 1976
Batting: Right handed
Bowling: Right arm medium-fast

Tests

Test Career: 1999-01
Cap Number: 42
Tests Played: 4

Test Batting

Innings:	6	Runs:	35
Highest Score:	25	Average:	5.83
No. 50s:	0	No. 100s:	0

Test Bowling & Fielding

Wickets:	7	Runs:	314
Best Bowling:	3/21	Average:	44.85
5 WI:	0	10 WM:	0
Catches:	1	Stumpings:	0

One Day Internationals

ODI Career: 1996-04
ODIs Played: 48

ODI Batting

Innings:	33	Runs:	202
Highest Score:	24	Average:	10.63
No. 50s:	0	No. 100s:	0

ODI Bowling & Fielding

Wickets:	50	Runs:	1,914
Best Bowling:	4/53	Average:	38.28
5 WM:	0	Catches:	10
Stumpings:	0		

A right arm seam bowler who made his ODI debut in 1996. It took another three years before he was given his chance at Test level - against Sri Lanka, at Bulawayo in 1999 - but failed to make an impact. Brent was one of the several players caught up in the dispute with the Zimbabwe Cricket Union in 2004 and thus played his last international that year.

BRIANT, Gavin Aubrey

Born: April 11, 1969
Batting: Right handed
Bowling: Right arm off-break
Wicket Keeper

Tests

Test Career: 1993
Cap Number: 14
Tests Played: 1

Test Batting
Innings:	2	Runs:	17
Highest Score:	16	Average:	8.50
No. 50s:	0	No. 100s:	0

Test Bowling & Fielding
Wickets:	0	Runs:	0
Best Bowling:		Average:	0.00
5 WI:	0	10 WM:	0
Catches:	0	Stumpings:	0

One Day Internationals

ODI Career:	1993		
ODIs Played:	5		

ODI Batting
Innings:	5	Runs:	39
Highest Score:	16	Average:	13.00
No. 50s:	0	No. 100s:	0

ODI Bowling & Fielding
Wickets:	0	Runs:	0
Best Bowling:		Average:	0.00
5 WM:	0	Catches:	0
Stumpings:	0		

A wicket-keeper who played just the one Test against India at Delhi in 1993, without having the opportunity to show his wares with the gloves. Has a highest score of 16 for both Tests and ODI's.

BROWN, Robin David

Born:	March 11, 1951
Batting:	Right handed
Bowling:	Right arm medium
	Wicket Keeper

One Day Internationals

ODI Career:	1983-87
ODIs Played:	7

ODI Batting
Innings:	7	Runs:	110
Highest Score:	38	Average:	15.71
No. 50s:	0	No. 100s:	0

ODI Bowling & Fielding
Wickets:	0	Runs:	0
Best Bowling:		Average:	0.00
5 WM:	0	Catches:	5
Stumpings:	0		

A talented right hand batsman and part time wicket-keeper who made his ODI debut against India during the 1983 World Cup in England. He was selected for the 1987 World Cup where he opened the batting on various occasions but could not produce consistent enough performances and played just the seven ODI's in total.

BRUK-JACKSON, Glen Keith

Born:	April 25, 1969
Batting:	Right handed
Bowling:	Right arm off-break

Tests

Test Career:	1993
Cap Number:	16
Tests Played:	2

Test Batting
Innings:	4	Runs:	39
Highest Score:	31	Average:	9.75
No. 50s:	0	No. 100s:	0

Test Bowling & Fielding
Wickets:	0	Runs:	0
Best Bowling:		Average:	0.00
5 WI:	0	10 WM:	0
Catches:	0	Stumpings:	0

One Day Internationals

ODI Career:	1993
ODIs Played:	1

ODI Batting
Innings:	1	Runs:	12
Highest Score:	12	Average:	12.00
No. 50s:	0	No. 100s:	0

ODI Bowling & Fielding
Wickets:	0	Runs:	0
Best Bowling:		Average:	0.00
5 WM:	0	Catches:	0
Stumpings:	0		

A right hand middle order batsman who scored 31 on his Test debut against Pakistan, coming in at number seven. He played two Tests and one ODI in 1993.

BURMESTER, Mark Greville

Born:	January 24, 1968
Batting:	Right handed
Bowling:	Right arm medium-fast

Tests

Test Career:	1992
Cap Number:	3
Tests Played:	3

Test Batting
Innings:	4	Runs:	54
Highest Score:	30*	Average:	27.00
No. 50s:	0	No. 100s:	0

Test Bowling & Fielding
Wickets:	3	Runs:	227
Best Bowling:	3/78	Average:	73.66
5 WI:	0	10 WM:	0
Catches:	1	Stumpings:	0

One Day Internationals

ODI Career:	1992-95
ODIs Played:	8

ODI Batting
Innings:	7	Runs:	109
Highest Score:	39	Average:	18.16
No. 50s:	0	No. 100s:	0

ODI Bowling & Fielding
Wickets:	5	Runs:	213
Best Bowling:	3/36	Average:	42.60
5 WM:	0	Catches:	2
Stumpings:	0		

A pioneer of Zimbabwean cricket, right arm medium pacer Mark Burmester made his international debut during the 1992 World Cup and later that year was selected in Zimbabwe's inaugural Test against India at Harare. After opening the bowling with Eddo Brandes, Burmester became the first Zimbabwean Test wicket taker when he had Indian opener Ravi Shastri caught by Andrew Pycroft for 11. Plagued by a back injury, Burmester played just the three Tests.

BUTCHART, Iain Peter

Born: May 9, 1960
Batting: Right handed
Bowling: Right arm medium

Tests

Test Career: 1995
Cap Number: 27
Tests Played: 1

Test Batting

Innings:	2	Runs:	23
Highest Score:	15	Average:	11.50
No. 50s:	0	No. 100s:	0

Test Bowling & Fielding

Wickets:	0	Runs:	11
Best Bowling:	0/11	Average:	0.00
5 WI:	0	10 WM:	0
Catches:	1	Stumpings:	0

One Day Internationals

ODI Career: 1983-95
ODIs Played: 20

ODI Batting

Innings:	16	Runs:	252
Highest Score:	54	Average:	18.00
No. 50s:	1	No. 100s:	0

ODI Bowling & Fielding

Wickets:	12	Runs:	640
Best Bowling:	3/57	Average:	53.33
5 WM:	0	Catches:	4
Stumpings:	0		

An all rounder who was a valuable contributor in Zimbabwe's shock win over Australia in the 1983 World Cup where he made 34 not out coming in at number eight and took 1/39. It was some 12 years later when Butchart played his one and only Test for his country - against Pakistan at Harare in 1995.

CAMPBELL, Alistair Douglas Ross

Born: September 23, 1972
Batting: Left handed
Bowling: Right arm off-break

Tests

Test Career: 1992-02
Cap Number: 4
Tests Played: 60

Test Batting

Innings:	109	Runs:	2,838
Highest Score:	103	Average:	27.21
No. 50s:	18	No. 100s:	2

Test Bowling & Fielding

Wickets:	0	Runs:	28
Best Bowling:		Average:	0.00
5 WI:	0	10 WM:	0
Catches:	0	Stumpings:	0

One Day Internationals

ODI Career: 1992-03
ODIs Played: 188

ODI Batting

Innings:	184	Runs:	5,185
Highest Score:	131*	Average:	30.50
No. 50s:	30	No. 100s:	7

ODI Bowling & Fielding

Wickets:	12	Runs:	434
Best Bowling:	2/20	Average:	36.16
5 WM:	0	Catches:	76
Stumpings:	0		

Alistair Campbell was just 19 years of age when he made his international debut against the West Indies during the 1992 World Cup in Australia. After a nervous start the youngster showed enough promise and thus was selected for Zimbabwe's inaugural Test against India later on in that year. The classical left hander made an impressive 45 coming in at first drop and became a permanent fixture in the both forms of the game thereafter. His aggressive nature was suited to the One Day game and scored over 5,000 runs at 30.50. A leader by nature, Campbell was awarded the captaincy in 1996 and led Zimbabwe to a memorable series victory in Pakistan in 1998/99. Although a consistent performer at Test level it took just on eight years for Campbell to register his maiden Test century (v India at Nagpur, 2000/01) and then registered his highest score of 103 against the West Indies a year later. An entertaining and powerful competitor, Campbell was an excellent fielder and possessed just about every shot in the book.

CARLISLE, Stuart Vance

Born: May 10, 1972
Batting: Right handed
Bowling: Right arm medium

Tests

Test Career: 1995-05
Cap Number: 24
Tests Played: 37

Test Batting

Innings:	66	Runs:	1,615
Highest Score:	118	Average:	26.91
No. 50s:	8	No. 100s:	2

Test Bowling & Fielding

Wickets:	0	Runs:	0
Best Bowling:		Average:	0.00
5 WI:	0	10 WM:	0
Catches:	34	Stumpings:	0

One Day Internationals

ODI Career: 1995-05
ODIs Played: 111

ODI Batting

Innings:	107	Runs:	2,740
Highest Score:	121*	Average:	27.67
No. 50s:	9	No. 100s:	3

ODI Bowling & Fielding

Wickets:	0	Runs:	0
Best Bowling:		Average:	0.00
5 WM:	0	Catches:	39
Stumpings:	0		

Stuart Carlisle made his Test debut in Zimbabwe's first ever Test win - against Pakistan at Harare in 1995. Amazingly Carlisle didn't to get the opportunity to either bat or bowl in this historic match but nevertheless became a regular in the Zimbabwe eleven over a ten year period. Depending on the situation, the versatile Carlisle could bat in any position. He scored centuries at both versions of the game and was also a magnificent fielder. In 2002, during the much publicised turmoil surrounding Zimbabwean cricket,

Carlisle was awarded the captaincy. But like his recent predecessors his tenure was short lived. Like several of his peers at the time, Carlisle's career was negatively impacted due to off field influences beyond his control.

CHIBHABHA, Cham Justice

Born: September 6, 1986
Batting: Right handed
Bowling: Right arm medium-fast

One Day Internationals

ODI Career: 2005-06
ODIs Played: 7

ODI Batting
Innings:	7	Runs:	260
Highest Score:	67	Average:	37.14
No. 50s:	0	No. 100s:	0

ODI Bowling & Fielding
Wickets:	3	Runs:	134
Best Bowling:	2/39	Average:	44.66
5 WM:	0	Catches:	4
Stumpings:	0		

An all rounder who got his opportunity at the elite level a little earlier than expected due to the player revolt in 2004. Chibhabha was a member of the victorious team that won the Tri Nations tournament (against Bermuda and Canada) which was held in the West Indies in 2006

CHIGUMBURA, Elton

Born: March 14, 1986
Batting: Right handed
Bowling: Right arm medium

Tests

Test Career: 2004-05
Cap Number: 61
Tests Played: 6

Test Batting
Innings:	12	Runs:	187
Highest Score:	71	Average:	15.58
No. 50s:	1	No. 100s:	0

Test Bowling & Fielding
Wickets:	9	Runs:	498
Best Bowling:	5/54	Average:	55.33
5 WI:	1	10 WM:	0
Catches:	2	Stumpings:	0

One Day Internationals

ODI Career: 2004-06
ODIs Played: 33

ODI Batting
Innings:	30	Runs:	592
Highest Score:	77	Average:	21.14
No. 50s:	4	No. 100s:	0

ODI Bowling & Fielding
Wickets:	10	Runs:	551
Best Bowling:	3/37	Average:	55.10
5 WM:	0	Catches:	14
Stumpings:	0		

A young all rounder, Elton Chigumbura, was another who got his chance at international level due to the exodus of the 'rebel' players. Chigumbura played his first Test against Sri Lanka at Harare in 2004, but many felt that he, and others at the time, were thrust into the elite level without being properly prepared. Now developing into a competant ODI player, Chigumbura was a member of the victorious side that defeated Bermuda in the Tri-Nation Tournament held in the West Indies in 2006.

COVENTRY, Charles Kevin

Born: March 8, 1983
Batting: Right handed
Bowling: Right arm leg-break
         Wicket Keeper

Tests

Test Career: 2005
Cap Number: 72
Tests Played: 2

Test Batting
Innings:	4	Runs:	88
Highest Score:	37	Average:	22.00
No. 50s:	0	No. 100s:	0

Test Bowling & Fielding
Wickets:	0	Runs:	0
Best Bowling:	0	Average:	0.00
5 WI:	0	10 WM:	0
Catches:	3	Stumpings:	0

One Day Internationals

ODI Career: 2003-06
ODIs Played: 11

ODI Batting
Innings:	10	Runs:	199
Highest Score:	74	Average:	19.90
No. 50s:	1	No. 100s:	0

ODI Bowling & Fielding
Wickets:	0	Runs:	0
Best Bowling:	0	Average:	0.00
5 WM:	0	Catches:	5
Stumpings:	0		

A bespectacled middle order batsman and wicket-keeper who made his Test debut against India at Bulawayo in 2005. Coventry hasn't had much of an opportunity to 'keep' at Test level having played just the two Tests, and seems more comfortable in the shorter version of the game.

CREMER, Alexander Graeme

Born: September 19, 1986
Batting: Right handed
Bowling: Right arm leg-break

Tests

Test Career: 2005
Cap Number: 67
Tests Played: 6

Test Batting
Innings:	12	Runs:	29
Highest Score:	12	Average:	2.63
No. 50s:	0	No. 100s:	0

Test Bowling & Fielding
Wickets:	13	Runs:	595
Best Bowling:	3/86	Average:	45.76
5 WI:	0	10 WM:	0
Catches:	3	Stumpings:	0

A promising right arm leg spinner who came through the Under 19 ranks, Cremer has been serviceable in his six Tests to date after making his debut against Bangladesh at Chittagong in 2005.

CROCKER, Gary John

Born:	May 16, 1962
Batting:	Left handed
Bowling:	Left arm medium-fast

Tests

Test Career:	1992
Cap Number:	5
Tests Played:	3

Test Batting

Innings:	4	Runs:	69
Highest Score:	33	Average:	23.00
No. 50s:	0	No. 100s:	0

Test Bowling & Fielding

Wickets:	3	Runs:	217
Best Bowling:	2/65	Average:	72.33
5 WI:	0	10 WM:	0
Catches:	0	Stumpings:	0

One Day Internationals

ODI Career:	1992-93
ODIs Played:	6

ODI Batting

Innings:	5	Runs:	98
Highest Score:	50	Average:	24.50
No. 50s:	1	No. 100s:	0

ODI Bowling & Fielding

Wickets:	7	Runs:	208
Best Bowling:	4/26	Average:	29.71
5 WM:	0	Catches:	1
Stumpings:	0		

A left arm medium-fast bowler from Bulawayo, Gary Crocker was a member of Zimbabwe's inaugural Test team that played against India at Harare in 1992. Crocker scored a useful 23 not out, batting at number eight and took 1/41. Played just the three Tests in total.

CURRAN, Kevin Malcolm

Born:	September 7, 1959
Batting:	Right handed
Bowling:	Right arm medium-fast

One Day Internationals

ODI Career:	1983-87
ODIs Played:	11

ODI Batting

Innings:	11	Runs:	287
Highest Score:	73	Average:	26.09
No. 50s:	2	No. 100s:	0

ODI Bowling & Fielding

Wickets:	9	Runs:	398
Best Bowling:	3/65	Average:	44.22
5 WM:	0	Catches:	1
Stumpings:	0		

A pioneer of Zimbabwe cricket, Kevin Curran was a right arm pace bowler and handy middle order batsman who made his international debut in the 1983 World Cup against Australia at Trent Bridge. In what was supposed to be an innocuous event, Zimbabwe, who were playing their inaugural (official) ODI, caused arguably the biggest boil over in international cricket when they toppled the unbackable Australians by 13 runs. Curran was an integral part of the history making victory as he and captain Duncan Fletcher put on 70 runs for the sixth wicket. Curran had contributed a handy 27 coming in at number seven and then took the important wicket of Allan Border when the Aussies were chasing 240 for victory. Playing in 11 ODI's Curran missed out on the opportunity to play at Test level for his country. He played domestic cricket in England both prior and after his international career and after retiring took on a coaching role with Namibia. In mid 2005 he was appointed national coach of Zimbabwe.

DABENGWA, Keith Mbusi

Born:	August 17, 1980
Batting:	Left handed
Bowling:	Left arm off-break

Tests

Test Career:	2005
Cap Number:	71
Tests Played:	3

Test Batting

Innings:	6	Runs:	90
Highest Score:	35	Average:	15.00
No. 50s:	0	No. 100s:	0

Test Bowling & Fielding

Wickets:	5	Runs:	249
Best Bowling:	3/127	Average:	49.80
5 WI:	0	10 WM:	0
Catches:	1	Stumpings:	0

One Day Internationals

ODI Career:	2005-06
ODIs Played:	6

ODI Batting

Innings:	4	Runs:	33
Highest Score:	21*	Average:	11.00
No. 50s:	0	No. 100s:	0

ODI Bowling & Fielding

Wickets:	3	Runs:	171
Best Bowling:	2/17	Average:	57.00
5 WM:	0	Catches:	3
Stumpings:	0		

A left arm all rounder, Keith Dabengwa made his Test debut against New Zealand at Bulawayo in 2005. He played in Zimbabwe's victorious Tri-Nation Tournament final against Bermuda in the West Indies, but to date it has been a slow pregression. Considered a long term project player.

DAVIES, Sean Gerard

Born:	October 15, 1973
Batting:	Left handed
Bowling:	Right arm fast

One Day Internationals

ODI Career:	1996
ODIs Played:	4

ODI Batting

Innings:	4	Runs:	67
Highest Score:	45	Average:	16.75
No. 50s:	0	No. 100s:	0

ODI Bowling & Fielding			
Wickets:	0	Runs:	0
Best Bowling:		Average:	0.00
5 WM:	0	Catches:	0
Stumpings:	0		

A strong left hand middle order batsman who made his ODI debut against New Zealand at Auckland in 1996. While serviceable, Davies was unable to break into the Test side during his short career.

DEKKER, Mark Hamilton

Born:	December 5, 1969
Batting:	Left handed
Bowling:	Left arm medium

Tests

Test Career:	1993-96		
Cap Number:	17		
Tests Played:	14		

Test Batting

Innings:	22	Runs:	333
Highest Score:	68	Average:	15.85
No. 50s:	2	No. 100s:	0

Test Bowling & Fielding

Wickets:	0	Runs:	15
Best Bowling:	0/15	Average:	0.00
5 WI:	0	10 WM:	0
Catches:	12	Stumpings:	0

One Day Internationals

ODI Career:	1992-96		
ODIs Played:	23		

ODI Batting

Innings:	22	Runs:	379
Highest Score:	79	Average:	18.95
No. 50s:	2	No. 100s:	0

ODI Bowling & Fielding

Wickets:	9	Runs:	290
Best Bowling:	2/16	Average:	32.22
5 WM:	0	Catches:	5
Stumpings:	0		

A left hand opener who had a forgettable Test debut against Pakistan, at Karachi, in 1993, where he was dismissed leg before, in both innings, by Man of the Match, Waqar Younis. Dekker continued to work hard to establish himself as a Test player but could only manage modest performances over his 14 match career.

DUERS, Kevin Gary

Born:	June 30, 1960
Batting:	Right handed
Bowling:	Right arm medium-fast

One Day Internationals

ODI Career:	1992		
ODIs Played:	6		

ODI Batting

Innings:	2	Runs:	7
Highest Score:	5	Average:	7.00
No. 50s:	0	No. 100s:	0

ODI Bowling & Fielding

Wickets:	3	Runs:	256
Best Bowling:	1/17	Average:	85.33
5 WM:	0	Catches:	2
Stumpings:	0		

A right arm medium-fast bowler from Lusaka who made little impact at international level taking just the three wickets in six ODI's.

DUFFIN, Terrence

Born:	March 20, 1982
Batting:	Left handed
Bowling:	Right arm medium

Tests

Test Career:	2005		
Cap Number:	73		
Tests Played:	2		

Test Batting

Innings:	4	Runs:	80
Highest Score:	56	Average:	20.00
No. 50s:	1	No. 100s:	0

Test Bowling & Fielding

Wickets:	0	Runs:	0
Best Bowling:		Average:	0.00
5 WI:	0	10 WM:	0
Catches:	1	Stumpings:	0

One Day Internationals

ODI Career:	2006		
ODIs Played:	13		

ODI Batting

Innings:	13	Runs:	248
Highest Score:	60	Average:	19.07
No. 50s:	2	No. 100s:	0

ODI Bowling & Fielding

Wickets:	0	Runs:	0
Best Bowling:		Average:	0.00
5 WM:	0	Catches:	4
Stumpings:	0		

A technically correct, left-handed opening batsman, Terry Duffin made a great start to his Test career when he scored 56 on debut against India, at Bulawayo, in 2005. Interestingly enough, Duffin was appointed captain of Zimbabwe's One Day side in his first ODI against Kenya, in early 2006. He also led the side to victory in the final of the Tri-Nation Tournament (against Bermuda) in West Indies later that year.

EBRAHIM, Dion Digby

Born:	August 7, 1980
Batting:	Right handed
Bowling:	Right arm medium

Tests

Test Career:	2001-05		
Cap Number:	49		
Tests Played:	29		

Test Batting

Innings:	55	Runs:	1,225
Highest Score:	94	Average:	22.68
No. 50s:	10	No. 100s:	0

Test Bowling & Fielding

Wickets:	0	Runs:	0
Best Bowling:		Average:	0.00
5 WI:	0	10 WM:	0
Catches:	16	Stumpings:	0

One Day Internationals

ODI Career:	2001-05		
ODIs Played:	82		

ODI Batting

Innings:	76	Runs:	1,443
Highest Score:	121	Average:	20.61
No. 50s:	4	No. 100s:	1

ODI Bowling & Fielding

Wickets:	0	Runs:	11
Best Bowling:	0/11	Average:	0.00
5 WM:	0	Catches:	23
Stumpings:	0		

A highly talented batsman who was versatile enough to bat anywhere in the order, Dion Ebrahim made his Test debut against Bangladesh at Bulawayo in 2001 but failed to make an early impact. After an inconsistent 12 months, Ebrahim started to amass runs, compiling several fifties in succession and thus established himself as regular Test player after 2002. By 2005, Ebrahim had registered 10 fifties alongside his name without scoring a Test hundred - his personal best, 94, against India at Delhi. By the end of 2005, Ebrahim was another victim of the in-house turmoil and like a few of his team mates, headed to England to continue his career.

ERVINE, Sean Michael

Born:	December 6, 1982
Batting:	Left handed

Tests

Test Career:	2003-04
Cap Number:	57
Tests Played:	5

Test Batting

Innings:	8	Runs:	261
Highest Score:	86	Average:	32.62
No. 50s:	3	No. 100s:	0

Test Bowling & Fielding

Wickets:	9	Runs:	388
Best Bowling:	4/146	Average:	43.11
5 WI:	0	10 WM:	0
Catches:	7	Stumpings:	0

One Day Internationals

ODI Career:	2001-04
ODIs Played:	42

ODI Batting

Innings:	34	Runs:	698
Highest Score:	100	Average:	25.85
No. 50s:	2	No. 100s:	1

ODI Bowling & Fielding

Wickets:	41	Runs:	1,561
Best Bowling:	3/29	Average:	38.07
5 WM:	0	Catches:	5
Stumpings:	0		

A member of the 2003 World Cup squad, Sean Ervine broke into the Test side that same year when he made his debut against England at Lords. He didn't make much of an impact on debut but scored three fifties in succession shortly afterwards to justify a permanent place in the Test eleven. But before long he was considered a better prospect at the shorter version of the game, and went on to play 42 ODI's in just on three years. Ervine scored the one century at ODI level, a dashing 100 against India, during the one Day triangular series in Australia in 2003/04. Ironically, it would be Australia that he call home shortly afterwards when he became yet another player who could not see 'eye to eye' with the Zimbabwe Cricket Union over contractual issues.

ESSOP-ADAM, Ebrahim Ali (Eboo)

Born:	November 16, 1968
Batting:	Right handed
Bowling:	Right arm off-break

One Day Internationals

ODI Career:	1992
ODIs Played:	1

ODI Batting

Innings:	1	Runs:	14
Highest Score:	14*	Average:	14.00
No. 50s:	0	No. 100s:	0

ODI Bowling & Fielding

Wickets:	0	Runs:	0
Best Bowling:		Average:	0.00
5 WM:	0	Catches:	2
Stumpings:	0		

Eboo Essop-Adam played his maiden and only ODI against New Zealand, at Harare in 1992.

EVANS, Craig Neil

Born:	November 29, 1969
Batting:	Right handed
Bowling:	Right arm medium-fast

Tests

Test Career:	1996-03
Cap Number:	30
Tests Played:	3

Test Batting

Innings:	6	Runs:	52
Highest Score:	22	Average:	8.66
No. 50s:	0	No. 100s:	0

Test Bowling & Fielding

Wickets:	0	Runs:	35
Best Bowling:		Average:	0.00
5 WI:	0	10 WM:	0
Catches:	1	Stumpings:	0

One Day Internationals

ODI Career:	1992-02
ODIs Played:	53

ODI Batting

Innings:	47	Runs:	764
Highest Score:	96*	Average:	18.19
No. 50s:	2	No. 100s:	0

ODI Bowling & Fielding

Wickets:	21	Runs:	848
Best Bowling:	3/11	Average:	40.38
5 WM:	0	Catches:	12
Stumpings:	0		

An all rounder who played his first Test against Sri Lanka at Colombo in 1996. He suited more of a One Day specialist and thus found himself being called up for ODI duties on a regular basis while his Test appearances were limited to three. A highly gifted sportsman, Evans was a competant golfer and rugby player.

EWING, Gavin Mackie

Born: January 21, 1981
Batting: Right handed
Bowling: Right arm off-break

Tests
Test Career: 2003-05
Cap Number: 58
Tests Played: 3

Test Batting
Innings:	6	Runs:	108
Highest Score:	71	Average:	18.00
No. 50s:	1	No. 100s:	0

Test Bowling & Fielding
Wickets:	2	Runs:	260
Best Bowling:	1/27	Average:	130.00
5 WI:	0	10 WM:	0
Catches:	1	Stumpings:	0

One Day Internationals
ODI Career: 2004-05
ODIs Played: 7

ODI Batting
Innings:	7	Runs:	97
Highest Score:	46	Average:	13.85
No. 50s:	0	No. 100s:	0

ODI Bowling & Fielding
Wickets:	5	Runs:	236
Best Bowling:	3/31	Average:	47.20
5 WM:	0	Catches:	3
Stumpings:	0		

Touted as a promising all-rounder, Gavin Ewing was one of the 15 players who were subsequently dubbed "rebels" by the Zimbabwe Cricket Union in 2004 when both parties disagreed about the treatment of former captain Heath Streak amongst other issues. While several have moved abroad to resurrect their careers, Ewing was one of the few that was able to eventually negotiate with the Board and resumed his international career later that year. Ewing has made one Test 50 - 71 against Bangladesh and has the opportunity to become a permanet fixture in both forms of the game.

FERREIRA, Neil Robert

Born: June 3, 1979
Batting: Left handed
Bowling: Right arm off-break
Wicket Keeper

Tests
Test Career: 2005
Cap Number: 70
Tests Played: 1

Test Batting
Innings:	2	Runs:	21
Highest Score:	16	Average:	10.50
No. 50s:	0	No. 100s:	0

Test Bowling & Fielding
Wickets:	0	Runs:	0
Best Bowling:		Average:	0.00
5 WI:	0	10 WM:	0
Catches:	0	Stumpings:	0

Although a wicket-keeper by trade, Neil Ferreira played his only Test to date as an opening batsman. The future of the promising keeper is still uncertain as the Managing Director of Zimbabwe Cricket, Ozias Bvute, stated, in late 2005, that 'the doors were closed' on Ferriera and three other cricketers due to contractual disputes.

FLETCHER, Duncan Andrew Gwynne

Born: September 27, 1948
Batting: Left handed
Bowling: Right arm medium-fast

One Day Internationals
ODI Career: 1983
ODIs Played: 6

ODI Batting
Innings:	6	Runs:	191
Highest Score:	71*	Average:	47.75
No. 50s:	2	No. 100s:	0

ODI Bowling & Fielding
Wickets:	7	Runs:	221
Best Bowling:	4/42	Average:	31.57
5 WM:	0	Catches:	0
Stumpings:	0		

A talented and competitive all rounder Duncan Fletcher became Zimbabwe's inaugural captain at International level when he led his country against Australia at Trent Bridge during the 1983 World Cup. What was to follow was a fairy-tale for Fletcher and his band of 'amateurs' and arguably Australia's most embarrassing moment in their long and proud history. Fletcher was nothing short of inspirational. He scored an unbeaten 69 as Zimbabwe set the Aussies 240 from 60 overs and then almost single handedly went about destroying the highly rated Australian batting line up. He took 4/42 from 11 overs and was aptly named 'Man of the Match' as Zimbabwe pulled off an amazing 13 run victory. And while that would be Zimbabwe's only win for the series, Fletcher, a brilliant fielder, continued to show the world that he had what it takes to compete with cricket's elite when he scored an unbeaten 71 against the powerful pace attack of the West Indies. But it was timing, not talent that deprived Fletcher from playing further internationals and Test cricket for his nation as he was 35 by the time the 1983 World Cup concluded. In 1999 he became coach of England, an unprecedented selection as he was the first non Englishman and non-Test player to be appointed the role.

FLOWER, Andrew (Andy)

Born: April 28, 1968
Batting: Left handed
Bowling: Right arm off-break
Wicket Keeper

Tests
Test Career: 1992-02
Cap Number: 6
Tests Played: 63

Test Batting
Innings:	112	Runs:	4,794
Highest Score:	232*	Average:	51.54
No. 50s:	27	No. 100s:	12

Test Bowling & Fielding			
Wickets:	0	Runs:	4
Best Bowling:	0/4	Average:	0.00
5 WI:	0	10 WM:	0
Catches:	151	Stumpings:	9

One Day Internationals

ODI Career:	1992-03		
ODIs Played:	213		

ODI Batting

Innings:	208	Runs:	6,786
Highest Score:	145	Average:	35.34
No. 50s:	55	No. 100s:	4

ODI Bowling & Fielding

Wickets:	0	Runs:	23
Best Bowling:	0/23	Average:	0.00
5 WM:	0	Catches:	141
Stumpings:	32		

The undisputed greatest player in Zimbabwe's history, Andy Flower was the face of Zimbabwean cricket for a good part of a decade. A member of the inaugural Test side that played against India at Harare in 1992, Flower was also his country's first wicket-keeper. And in addition to keeping wickets on debut, he made a dashing 59 coming in at number seven, thus setting the scene for what would become a stellar career as both batsman and keeper. The older brother of Grant, the brothers represented Zimbabwe in 130 Tests and over 430 ODI's between them. Flower was unsurprisingly appointed captain in 1993 and lead the side to their first Test victory against Pakistan in 1994/95. In all, he captained Zimbabwe in 20 Tests, and for the greater part of Zimbabwe's formative years, Flower was arguably their only batsman of world class quality. All up he scored 27 fifties and a dozen centuries, his first, a solid 115 against India at Delhi in 1993. He then followed up with a stunning 156 against Pakistan in Harare where he and brother Grant added 269 for the fourth wicket. Grant's 201 not out was not enough to earn him the Man of the Match award outright, thus it was shared between the siblings. As to whose mantle-piece it would reside upon was an issue for the brothers to sort out. In November 2000, and with eight Test centuries alongside his name, Andy Flower clocked up his first double century when he amassed his highest score of 232 not out against India at Nagpur. While Grant did play a supporting role with his 106 not out in the first innings, Man of the Match rights were not shared on this occasion. Andy not only picked up the award but was also named the 'Man of the Series', even though India won the series 1-0. Whilst in the twilight of his career, Flower's best was not behind him. Less than a year later, Flower took on the might of the South African bowling attack and scored two centuries in the first Test at Harare. His 142 in the first innings was followed up by an unbeaten 199 not out. Unfortunately for Flower he ran out of partners just one run short of registering his second double century. Flower's brilliance was not restricted to the Test arena. He scored four centuries at ODI level including a highest score of 145 against India during an ICC Champions Trophy match at Colombo. He was a member of four World Cup campaigns - 1992, 96, 99 & 2003. And while he let his form do the talking throughout his career, he will be remembered and admired by many for the stance he took alongside team mate Henry Olonga when the two of them wore black arm bands in a protest dubbed the "death of democracy" in Zimbabwe. Flower retired shortly after the World Cup but walked away with just about every conceivable record and accolade pertaining to Zimbabwean cricket. He has played in more Tests (67) than any other Zimbabwean cricketer. He is Zimbabwe's highest Test run scorer with 4,794 runs and holds the highest Test average of 51.54 which is an amazing achievement for a bona fide wicket-keeper batsman. His 232 not out is the second highest Test score by a Zimbabwean and has scored the most runs at ODI level, 6,786 at 35.34, the second highest average in one day cricket. A fine ambassador, Andy Flower leaves the game having earned the respect of the cricket community world wide.

FLOWER, Grant William

Born:	December 20, 1970
Batting:	Right handed
Bowling:	Left arm off-break

Tests

Test Career:	1992-04
Cap Number:	7
Tests Played:	67

Test Batting

Innings:	123	Runs:	3,457
Highest Score:	201*	Average:	29.54
No. 50s:	15	No. 100s:	6

Test Bowling & Fielding

Wickets:	25	Runs:	1,537
Best Bowling:	4/41	Average:	61.48
5 WI:	0	10 WM:	0
Catches:	43	Stumpings:	0

One Day Internationals

ODI Career:	1992-04
ODIs Played:	219

ODI Batting

Innings:	212	Runs:	6,536
Highest Score:	142*	Average:	33.69
No. 50s:	40	No. 100s:	6

ODI Bowling & Fielding

Wickets:	104	Runs:	4,187
Best Bowling:	4/32	Average:	40.25
5 WM:	0	Catches:	86
Stumpings:	0		

While he may be the younger brother of Zimbabwe's greatest ever cricketer - Andy Flower - Grant Flower by no means lived in his brother shadow. A highly talented batsman, brilliant fielder and left arm off-spinner, Grant Flower carved out a career that earned him respect and recognition in his own right. A member of Zimbabwe's inaugural Test side who played against India at Harare in 1993, Flower opened the Zimbabwean innings with veteran Kevin Arnott. He became the first Zimbabwean to notch up a Test fifty as he went to score an impressive 82 on debut while facing the likes of Srinath, Kapil Dev, Kumble and Probhakar. Such was the stand out form of the Flower brothers in Zimbabwe's formative years, they became the unofficial ambassadors of Zimbabwean cricket as many followers outside Zimbabwe would have had trouble naming any other player within the squad. In a career spanning just over 12 years, Flower was a doyen of the Zimbabwean batting line up scoring 15 fifties and six centuries. His most memorable was his unbeaten 201 against Pakistan at Harare, in 1995, which was the catalyst in setting up Zimbabwe's first ever Test win. On what was a historic win, he shared 'Man of the Match' honours with brother Andy who had scored 156 and the paid had added a record breaking 269 for the fourth wicket. As a one day player, Grant was not found wanting either. His patient demeanor as Test player would be substituted for a more hard hitting approach. Just like his Test record, he scored half a dozen centuries in ODI's with a highest score of 142 not out against Bangladesh, at Bulawayo, in 2001. On this occasion he not only secured the 'Man of the Match' award outright, but also accepted the 'Man of Series' prize. In 2004 he announced his retirement from international cricket with 3457 Test runs alongside his name - the second highest all time (Zimbabwean) run scorer, headed only by big brother Andy!

FRIEND, Travis John

Born:	January 7, 1981
Batting:	Right handed
Bowling:	Right arm medium-fast

Tests

Test Career:	2001-04
Cap Number:	51
Tests Played:	13

Test Batting

Innings:	19	Runs:	447
Highest Score:	81	Average:	29.80
No. 50s:	3	No. 100s:	0

Test Bowling & Fielding

Wickets:	25	Runs:	1,090
Best Bowling:	5/31	Average:	43.60
5 WI:	1	10 WM:	0
Catches:	2	Stumpings:	0

One Day Internationals

ODI Career:	2000-04
ODIs Played:	51

ODI Batting

Innings:	39	Runs:	548
Highest Score:	91	Average:	16.11
No. 50s:	3	No. 100s:	0

ODI Bowling & Fielding

Wickets:	37	Runs:	1,779
Best Bowling:	4/55	Average:	48.08
5 WM:	0	Catches:	17
Stumpings:	0		

A genuine pace bowler, Travis 'Chunks' Friend made his Test debut against India at Harare in 2001. The strongly built and highly competitive paceman endured a back injury shortly after his debut but returned later that year snaring a personal best 5/31 against Bangladesh. A capable lower order batsman, Friend has scored 50's at both versions of the game and was developing into a handy quasi all-rounder until he too became involved in the dispute following the sacking of Heath Streak. Like many of the other 14 'rebels', he too sought to resurrect his career abroad.

GOODWIN, Murray William

Born:	December 11, 1972
Batting:	Right handed
Bowling:	Right arm leg-break

Tests

Test Career:	1998-00
Cap Number:	37
Tests Played:	19

Test Batting

Innings:	37	Runs:	1,414
Highest Score:	166*	Average:	42.84
No. 50s:	8	No. 100s:	3

Test Bowling & Fielding

Wickets:	0	Runs:	69
Best Bowling:		Average:	0.00
5 WI:	0	10 WM:	0
Catches:	10	Stumpings:	0

One Day Internationals

ODI Career:	1998-00
ODIs Played:	71

ODI Batting

Innings:	70	Runs:	1,818
Highest Score:	112*	Average:	27.13
No. 50s:	8	No. 100s:	2

ODI Bowling & Fielding

Wickets:	4	Runs:	210
Best Bowling:	1/12	Average:	52.50
5 WM:	0	Catches:	20
Stumpings:	0		

A prolific run scorer Murray Goodwin was born in Zimbabwe but spent most of his formative years in Western Australia. After returning to Zimbabwe, Goodwin caught the eyes of the selectors and was selected for the tour of Sri Lanka in 1998. After a nervous start, Goodwin made 70 in the second innings and from there became recognised as an accomplished batsman. He scored three Test tons, his first a sensational 166 not out against Pakistan at Bulawayo, in 1998. In 2000, he added two more centuries to his name when he was run out for 113 against the West Indies at Jamaica, and followed up with an entertaining 148 not out against England at Trent Bridge which earned him the 'Man of the Match' award.

Goodwin played just the 19 Tests and could have played many more if not for personal reasons. His Test average of 42.84 remains the third highest in Zimbabwean cricket.

GRIPPER, Trevor Raymond

Born:	December 28, 1975
Batting:	Right handed
Bowling:	Right arm off-break

Tests
Test Career:	1999-04
Cap Number:	41
Tests Played:	20

Test Batting
Innings:	38	Runs:	809
Highest Score:	112	Average:	21.86
No. 50s:	5	No. 100s:	1

Test Bowling & Fielding
Wickets:	6	Runs:	509
Best Bowling:	2/91	Average:	84.83
5 WI:	0	10 WM:	0
Catches:	14	Stumpings:	0

One Day Internationals
ODI Career:	2001-03
ODIs Played:	8

ODI Batting
Innings:	8	Runs:	80
Highest Score:	26	Average:	10.00
No. 50s:	0	No. 100s:	0

ODI Bowling & Fielding
Wickets:	2	Runs:	76
Best Bowling:	2/28	Average:	38.00
5 WM:	0	Catches:	4
Stumpings:	0		

A right hand opening batsman who plied his trade with a great deal of patience, Trevor Gripper made his Test debut against Australia at Harare in 1999, batting at number seven. After failing miserably in the first innings, Gripper opened the batting in the second dig where he scored a superb 60. Gripper went on to score a further four fifties and one century (112 v Bangladesh, Chittagong, 2001) in a Test career spanning just over five years. His batting style restricted him from playing anymore than a handful of One Day Internationals.

HERON, Jack Gunner

Born:	November 8, 1948
Batting:	Right handed

One Day Internationals
ODI Career:	1983
ODIs Played:	6

ODI Batting
Innings:	6	Runs:	50
Highest Score:	18	Average:	8.33
No. 50s:	0	No. 100s:	0

ODI Bowling & Fielding
Wickets:	0	Runs:	0
Best Bowling:		Average:	0.00
5 WM:	0	Catches:	0
Stumpings:	0		

Jack Heron was part of Zimbabwe's inaugural One Day International team that embarrassed Australia in the 1983 World Cup. Although a recognised opener, he batted at number three in all six of his ODI appearances during the tournament.

HIGGINS, Ryan Shaun

Born:	March 24, 1988
Batting:	Right handed
Bowling:	Right arm leg-break

One Day Internationals
ODI Career:	2006
ODIs Played:	9

ODI Batting
Innings:	6	Runs:	8
Highest Score:	5	Average:	1.60
No. 50s:	0	No. 100s:	0

ODI Bowling & Fielding
Wickets:	13	Runs:	316
Best Bowling:	4/21	Average:	24.30
5 WM:	0	Catches:	4
Stumpings:	0		

Touted as a likely all rounder Ryan Higgins has bowled exceptionally well in his role as leg spinner but has failed to make any impact with the bat in his short career to date. But the young does have talent and time on his side.

HOGG, Vincent Richard

Born:	July 3, 1952
Batting:	Right handed
Bowling:	Right arm medium-fast

One Day Internationals
ODI Career:	1983
ODIs Played:	2

ODI Batting
Innings:	1	Runs:	7
Highest Score:	7*	Average:	7.00
No. 50s:	0	No. 100s:	0

ODI Bowling & Fielding
Wickets:	0	Runs:	49
Best Bowling:		Average:	0.00
5 WM:	0	Catches:	0
Stumpings:	0		

A genuine pace bowler from Harare, Vince Hogg opened the bowling for Zimbabwe in their inaugural One Day International against Australia, during the 1983 World Cup at Trent Bridge. It was hailed as one of the biggest boilovers in cricket history as the semi professional Zimbabwe eleven defeated a full strength Australia by 13 runs. While Hogg didn't capture any wickets during the history making event, he did return the respectable figures of 0/15 from six overs. He was to play just the one more ODI which was also against Australia later in the tournament.

HONDO, Douglas Tafadzwa

Born:	July 7, 1979
Batting:	Right handed
Bowling:	Right arm medium-fast

HONDO, Douglas *(implied)*

Tests
Test Career:	2001-05		
Cap Number:	54		
Tests Played:	9		

Test Batting
Innings:	15	Runs:	83
Highest Score:	19	Average:	9.22
No. 50s:	0	No. 100s:	0

Test Bowling & Fielding
Wickets:	21	Runs:	774
Best Bowling:	6/59	Average:	36.85
5 WI:	1	10 WM:	0
Catches:	5	Stumpings:	0

One Day Internationals
ODI Career:	2001-05		
ODIs Played:	56		

ODI Batting
Innings:	29	Runs:	127
Highest Score:	17	Average:	7.47
No. 50s:	0	No. 100s:	0

ODI Bowling & Fielding
Wickets:	61	Runs:	2,171
Best Bowling:	4/37	Average:	35.59
5 WM:	0	Catches:	15
Stumpings:	0		

An exciting right arm swing bowler who entered the international scene in 2001 with a great deal of anticipation, Douglas Hondo has not lived up to expectations. Various injuries have hindered his progress and to date, has played just the nine Tests. But when he is 'on', Hondo is an excitement machine as demonstrated when he tore through the Bangladesh top order taking a career best 6/59 at Dhaka, in 2005.

HOUGHTON, David Laud

Born: June 23, 1957
Batting: Right handed
Bowling: Right arm off-break
Wicket Keeper

Tests
Test Career:	1992-97		
Cap Number:	8		
Tests Played:	22		

Test Batting
Innings:	36	Runs:	1,464
Highest Score:	266	Average:	43.05
No. 50s:	4	No. 100s:	4

Test Bowling & Fielding
Wickets:	0	Runs:	0
Best Bowling:		Average:	0.00
5 WI:	0	10 WM:	0
Catches:	16	Stumpings:	0

One Day Internationals
ODI Career:	1983-97		
ODIs Played:	63		

ODI Batting
Innings:	60	Runs:	1,530
Highest Score:	142	Average:	26.37
No. 50s:	12	No. 100s:	1

ODI Bowling & Fielding
Wickets:	1	Runs:	19
Best Bowling:	1/19	Average:	19.00
5 WM:	0	Catches:	29
Stumpings:	2		

A batsman of the highest quality, who started as a wicket-keeper, Dave Houghton was crowned Zimbabwe's first ever Test captain and scored 121 in the first innings of Zimbabwe's inaugural Test, against India at Harare in 1992/93. He followed up with 41 not out in the second innings, and from there established himself as one of Zimbabwe's greatest ever players. He scored four Test centuries with a reputable average of 43.05. In 1994/95 Houghton scored a sensational 266 against Sri Lanka at Bulawayo, which remains a Zimbabwean Test record.

HUCKLE, Adam George

Born: September 21, 1971
Batting: Right handed
Bowling: Right arm leg-break

Tests
Test Career:	1997-98		
Cap Number:	35		
Tests Played:	8		

Test Batting
Innings:	14	Runs:	74
Highest Score:	28*	Average:	6.72
No. 50s:	0	No. 100s:	0

Test Bowling & Fielding
Wickets:	25	Runs:	872
Best Bowling:	6/109	Average:	34.88
5 WI:	2	10 WM:	1
Catches:	3	Stumpings:	0

One Day Internationals
ODI Career:	1997-99		
ODIs Played:	19		

ODI Batting
Innings:	8	Runs:	9
Highest Score:	5*	Average:	2.25
No. 50s:	0	No. 100s:	0

ODI Bowling & Fielding
Wickets:	7	Runs:	661
Best Bowling:	2/27	Average:	94.42
5 WM:	0	Catches:	7
Stumpings:	0		

A former South African Under-24 representative, leg spinner Adam Huckle returned to Zimbabwe in 1997 where he was selected against the touring Kiwis at Harare. His two wickets in the first innings was followed up by three in the second thus doing enough to impress for future selection. Although Huckle played quite a few ODI's, including matches during the 1999 World Cup tournament, he was far more suited to Test cricket where he took 25 wickets at 34.88 including a career best 6/109 against New Zealand at Bulawayo in 1997.

IRELAND, Anthony John

Born: August 30, 1984
Batting: Right handed
Bowling: Right arm medium

One Day Internationals
ODI Career:	2005-06
ODIs Played:	11

ODI Batting

Innings:	5	Runs:	10
Highest Score:	8	Average:	5.00
No. 50s:	0	No. 100s:	0

ODI Bowling & Fielding

Wickets:	17	Runs:	486
Best Bowling:	3/46	Average:	28.58
5 WM:	0	Catches:	1
Stumpings:	0		

An all rounder from the Midlands who made his ODI debut against New Zealand at Bulawayo where he took 2/52. Has been a solid performer in his 11 appearances to date.

JAMES, Wayne Robert

Born:	August 27, 1965
Batting:	Right handed
	Wicket Keeper

Tests

Test Career:	1993-94
Cap Number:	22
Tests Played:	4

Test Batting

Innings:	4	Runs:	61
Highest Score:	33	Average:	15.25
No. 50s:	0	No. 100s:	0

Test Bowling & Fielding

Wickets:	0	Runs:	0
Best Bowling:		Average:	0.00
5 WI:	0	10 WM:	0
Catches:	16	Stumpings:	0

One Day Internationals

ODI Career:	1992-96
ODIs Played:	11

ODI Batting

Innings:	8	Runs:	101
Highest Score:	29	Average:	14.42
No. 50s:	0	No. 100s:	0

ODI Bowling & Fielding

Wickets:	0	Runs:	0
Best Bowling:		Average:	0.00
5 WM:	0	Catches:	6
Stumpings:	0		

A talented wicket-keeper who played four Tests between 1993 & 94 but could not consolidate a regular spot due to Andy Flower's dual role as keeper-batsman.

JARVIS, Malcolm Peter

Born:	December 6, 1955
Batting:	Right handed
Bowling:	Left arm medium-fast

Tests

Test Career:	1992-94
Cap Number:	9
Tests Played:	5

Test Batting

Innings:	3	Runs:	4
Highest Score:	2*	Average:	2.00
No. 50s:	0	No. 100s:	0

Test Bowling & Fielding

Wickets:	11	Runs:	393
Best Bowling:	3/30	Average:	35.72
5 WI:	0	10 WM:	0
Catches:	2	Stumpings:	0

One Day Internationals

ODI Career:	1987-95
ODIs Played:	12

ODI Batting

Innings:	5	Runs:	37
Highest Score:	17	Average:	18.50
No. 50s:	0	No. 100s:	0

ODI Bowling & Fielding

Wickets:	9	Runs:	451
Best Bowling:	2/37	Average:	50.11
5 WM:	0	Catches:	1
Stumpings:	0		

One of the pioneers of early Zimbabwean cricket, Malcolm 'Mallie' Jarvis played in Zimbabwe's inaugural Test match against India in 1992, just a couple of months short of his 37th birthday. A left-arm seamer, Jarvis toiled hard every time he represented his country and was a fine mentor and example for the younger players in the side.

JOHNSON, Neil Clarkson

Born:	January 24, 1970
Batting:	Left handed
Bowling:	Right arm medium-fast

Tests

Test Career:	1998-00
Cap Number:	40
Tests Played:	13

Test Batting

Innings:	23	Runs:	532
Highest Score:	107	Average:	24.18
No. 50s:	4	No. 100s:	1

Test Bowling & Fielding

Wickets:	15	Runs:	594
Best Bowling:	4/77	Average:	36.60
5 WI:	0	10 WM:	0
Catches:	12	Stumpings:	0

One Day Internationals

ODI Career:	1998-00
ODIs Played:	48

ODI Batting

Innings:	48	Runs:	1,679
Highest Score:	132*	Average:	36.50
No. 50s:	11	No. 100s:	4

ODI Bowling & Fielding

Wickets:	35	Runs:	1,220
Best Bowling:	4/42	Average:	34.85
5 WM:	0	Catches:	19
Stumpings:	0		

A talented all rounder who opened the batting in one dayers, Neil Johnson made his Test debut against India at Harare in 1998. An agressive left handed batsman, Johnson scored centuries in both forms of the game - his one and only Test century came in 1998 when he made 107, against Pakistan at Peshawar, coming in at number seven and thus earning the Man of the Match award. Johnson performed admirably in the 1999 World Cup, where he picked up a further three Man of the Match awards - his best effort, a dour 76 against the old foe, South Africa, where Zimbabwe recorded a memorable 48 run victory.

LOCK, Alan Charles Ingram

Born: September 10, 1962
Batting: Right handed
Bowling: Right arm medium-fast

Tests

Test Career:	1995		
Cap Number:	28		
Tests Played:	1		

Test Batting

Innings:	2	Runs:	8
Highest Score:	8*	Average:	8.00
No. 50s:	0	No. 100s:	0

Test Bowling & Fielding

Wickets:	5	Runs:	105
Best Bowling:	3/68	Average:	21.00
5 WI:	0	10 WM:	0
Catches:	0	Stumpings:	0

One Day Internationals

ODI Career:	1996		
ODIs Played:	8		

ODI Batting

Innings:	3	Runs:	8
Highest Score:	5	Average:	8.00
No. 50s:	0	No. 100s:	0

ODI Bowling & Fielding

Wickets:	8	Runs:	219
Best Bowling:	5/44	Average:	27.37
5 WM:	1	Catches:	1
Stumpings:	0		

Called up to make his Test debut against South Africa at Harare in 1995, Charlie Lock was aged 33 and suffering a broken finger. With the odds of an impressive first up performance well and truly against him, Lock took five wickets for the match and seemed destined for somewhat of a 'cameo' Test career. However his maiden Test was to be his last but he was selected in the World Cup squad of 1996 where he performed admirably when opening the bowling with Heath Streak.

MACKAY, Angus James (Gus)

Born: June 13, 1967
Batting: Right handed
Bowling: Right arm medium-fast

One Day Internationals

ODI Career:	2001		
ODIs Played:	3		

ODI Batting

Innings:	0	Runs:	0
Highest Score:	0	Average:	0.00
No. 50s:	0	No. 100s:	0

ODI Bowling & Fielding

Wickets:	0	Runs:	137
Best Bowling:		Average:	0.00
5 WM:	0	Catches:	1
Stumpings:	0		

A genuine seam bowler and hard hitting lower order batsman, Gus Mackay made his ODI debut against New Zealand at Wellington, just a few months prior to his 34th birthday. Unfortunately he never got the chance to display his much anticipated batting wares during any of his three ODI's.

MADONDO, Trevor Nyasha

Born: January 22, 1976
Batting: Right handed
Bowling: Right arm medium
Wicket Keeper

Tests

Test Career:	1998-00		
Cap Number:	38		
Tests Played:	3		

Test Batting

Innings:	4	Runs:	90
Highest Score:	74*	Average:	30.00
No. 50s:	1	No. 100s:	0

Test Bowling & Fielding

Wickets:	0	Runs:	0
Best Bowling:		Average:	0.00
5 WI:	0	10 WM:	0
Catches:	1	Stumpings:	0

One Day Internationals

ODI Career:	1998-01		
ODIs Played:	13		

ODI Batting

Innings:	13	Runs:	191
Highest Score:	71	Average:	15.91
No. 50s:	1	No. 100s:	0

ODI Bowling & Fielding

Wickets:	0	Runs:	0
Best Bowling:		Average:	0.00
5 WM:	0	Catches:	2
Stumpings:	0		

A talented all round cricketer Trevor Madondo impressed the selectors with his ability as a wicket-keeper but rarely got the chance to display his skills with the gloves at Test level. A more than capable batsman he scored a vauable 74 not out against New Zealand at Wellington in what would be his last Test. Madondo died of malaria some six months later, aged 24.

MAHWIRE, Ngonidzashe Blessing

Born: July 31, 1982
Batting: Right handed
Bowling: Right arm medium-fast

Tests

Test Career:	2002-05		
Cap Number:	55		
Tests Played:	10		

Test Batting

Innings:	17	Runs:	147
Highest Score:	50*	Average:	13.36
No. 50s:	1	No. 100s:	0

Test Bowling & Fielding

Wickets:	18	Runs:	915
Best Bowling:	4/92	Average:	50.83
5 WI:	0	10 WM:	0
Catches:	1	Stumpings:	0

One Day Internationals

ODI Career:	2004-06		
ODIs Played:	18		

ODI Batting

Innings:	16	Runs:	100
Highest Score:	22*	Average:	11.11
No. 50s:	0	No. 100s:	0

ODI Bowling & Fielding
Wickets:	17	Runs:	602
Best Bowling:	3/29	Average:	35.41
5 WM:	0	Catches:	6
Stumpings:	0		

A right arm pace bowler, Blessing Mahwire made his Test debut against Pakistan at Harare in 2002. While he seemed to have all the attributes of a world class bowler, he rarely caused concern to any of the world's elite batsmen. His form, especially his batting, improved throughout 2005 and his performance was promising in the 2006 Tri-Nation Tournament held in the West Indies, between Zimbabwe, Bermuda and Canada.

MAREGWEDE, Alester

Born:	August 5, 1981
Batting:	Right handed
	Wicket Keeper

Tests
Test Career:	2004
Cap Number:	62
Tests Played:	2

Test Batting
Innings:	4	Runs:	74
Highest Score:	28	Average:	18.50
No. 50s:	0	No. 100s:	0

Test Bowling & Fielding
Wickets:	0	Runs:	0
Best Bowling:		Average:	0.00
5 WI:	0	10 WM:	0
Catches:	1	Stumpings:	0

One Day Internationals
ODI Career:	2003-05
ODIs Played:	11

ODI Batting
Innings:	11	Runs:	124
Highest Score:	37	Average:	12.40
No. 50s:	0	No. 100s:	0

ODI Bowling & Fielding
Wickets:	0	Runs:	0
Best Bowling:		Average:	0.00
5 WM:	0	Catches:	2
Stumpings:	0		

A wicket-keeper and handy middle order batsman, Alester Maregwede had a less than memorable ODI debut against West Indies at Harare where he made a duck. A few months later, Maregwede donned the whites for the first time when he was selected in the starting eleven against Sri Lanka. And again things didn't go according to plan as the youngster was caught plumb in front by Murali without troubling the scorers. However things turned around in the second innings when Maregwede compiled a well made 22. He managed scores in the 20's in both innings of his second Test but that was not enough to convince the selectors that he was worth another try at Test level. He went on to play in 11 ODI's.

MARILLIER, Douglas Anthony

Born:	April 24, 1978
Batting:	Right handed
Bowling:	Right arm off-break
	Wicket Keeper

Tests
Test Career:	2000-02
Cap Number:	47
Tests Played:	5

Test Batting
Innings:	7	Runs:	186
Highest Score:	73	Average:	31.00
No. 50s:	2	No. 100s:	0

Test Bowling & Fielding
Wickets:	11	Runs:	322
Best Bowling:	4/57	Average:	29.27
5 WI:	0	10 WM:	0
Catches:	2	Stumpings:	0

One Day Internationals
ODI Career:	2000-03
ODIs Played:	48

ODI Batting
Innings:	41	Runs:	672
Highest Score:	100	Average:	18.16
No. 50s:	3	No. 100s:	1

ODI Bowling & Fielding
Wickets:	30	Runs:	1,235
Best Bowling:	4/38	Average:	41.16
5 WM:	0	Catches:	12
Stumpings:	0		

Another disillusioned talent lost to Zimbabwean cricket due to the ongoing turmoil at board level. Dougie Marillier, an accomplished wicket-keeper was selected for his first Test against New Zealand at Wellington, as an all-rounder with bat and ball rather than a specialist gloveman. In limited overs competition Mariller usually opened the batting and because he rarely got the chance to keep wicket, he developed into an effective off break bowler taking a personal best of 4/38 against England. Like a few of his peers, Marillier looked to further his career abroad.

MARTIN, Gary Christopher

Born:	May 30, 1966
Batting:	Right handed
Bowling:	Right arm medium-fast

One Day Internationals
ODI Career:	1994-95
ODIs Played:	5

ODI Batting
Innings:	4	Runs:	31
Highest Score:	16	Average:	7.75
No. 50s:	0	No. 100s:	0

ODI Bowling & Fielding
Wickets:	2	Runs:	95
Best Bowling:	1/15	Average:	47.50
5 WM:	0	Catches:	0
Stumpings:	0		

A right arm medium pacer from Marondera who made his ODI debut against Sri Lanka at Harare in 1994.

MASAKADZA, Hamilton

Born: August 9, 1983
Batting: Right handed
Bowling: Right arm leg-break

Tests
Test Career:	2001-05		
Cap Number:	53		
Tests Played:	15		

Test Batting
Innings:	30	Runs:	785
Highest Score:	119	Average:	27.06
No. 50s:	3	No. 100s:	1

Test Bowling & Fielding
Wickets:	2	Runs:	39
Best Bowling:	1/9	Average:	19.50
5 WI:	0	10 WM:	0
Catches:	8	Stumpings:	0

One Day Internationals
ODI Career:	2001-06		
ODIs Played:	21		

ODI Batting
Innings:	21	Runs:	344
Highest Score:	66	Average:	17.20
No. 50s:	3	No. 100s:	0

ODI Bowling & Fielding
Wickets:	3	Runs:	96
Best Bowling:	2/26	Average:	32.00
5 WM:	0	Catches:	10
Stumpings:	0		

Hamilton Masakadza is a promising right hand batsman who made his Test debut at age 17, against West Indies at Harare where he became the youngest Zimbabwean to score a Test century on debut. He has played 15 Tests while trying to balance his commitment to both sporting and academic disciplines.

MATAMBANADZO, Everton Zvikomborero

Born: April 13, 1976
Batting: Right handed
Bowling: Right arm medium-fast

Tests
Test Career:	1996-99		
Cap Number:	32		
Tests Played:	3		

Test Batting
Innings:	5	Runs:	17
Highest Score:	7	Average:	4.25
No. 50s:	0	No. 100s:	0

Test Bowling & Fielding
Wickets:	4	Runs:	250
Best Bowling:	2/62	Average:	62.50
5 WI:	0	10 WM:	0
Catches:	0	Stumpings:	0

One Day Internationals
ODI Career:	1996-97		
ODIs Played:	7		

ODI Batting
Innings:	5	Runs:	8
Highest Score:	5*	Average:	4.00
No. 50s:	0	No. 100s:	0

ODI Bowling & Fielding
Wickets:	11	Runs:	217
Best Bowling:	4/32	Average:	19.72
5 WM:	0	Catches:	1
Stumpings:	0		

A genuine pace bowler, Everton Matambanadzo was set to take the cricketing world by storm when he took the wickets of openers Saeed Anwar and Aamer Sohail in his maiden Test against Pakistan at Faisalabad in 1996. However the promising youngster was plagued by injuries and his international career ended after only three years.

MATSIKENYERI, Stuart

Born: May 3, 1983
Batting: Right handed
Bowling: Right arm off-break

Tests
Test Career:	2003-05		
Cap Number:	59		
Tests Played:	8		

Test Batting
Innings:	16	Runs:	351
Highest Score:	57	Average:	23.40
No. 50s:	2	No. 100s:	0

Test Bowling & Fielding
Wickets:	2	Runs:	345
Best Bowling:	1/58	Average:	172.50
5 WI:	0	10 WM:	0
Catches:	7	Stumpings:	0

One Day Internationals
ODI Career:	2002-05		
ODIs Played:	45		

ODI Batting
Innings:	43	Runs:	658
Highest Score:	73	Average:	16.04
No. 50s:	2	No. 100s:	0

ODI Bowling & Fielding
Wickets:	11	Runs:	554
Best Bowling:	2/33	Average:	50.36
5 WM:	0	Catches:	14
Stumpings:	0		

Another talented youth who was caught up in contractual disputes with the Zimbabwe Cricket Union. A right hand opening batsman, Stuart Matsikenyeri was a member of the 2003 World Cup squad and made an impressive start to his Test career when, batting at number six, scored 57 on debut against West Indies at Harare, and then followed up with an unbeaten 46 in the second innings. In early 2006 he headed over to the UK and it's unclear as to whether Matsikenyeri will ever again don the Zimbabwean colours.

MBANGWA, Mpumelelo (Pommie)

Born: June 26, 1976
Batting: Right handed
Bowling: Right arm medium-fast

Tests
Test Career:	1996-00		
Cap Number:	33		
Tests Played:	15		

Test Batting

Innings:	25	Runs:	34
Highest Score:	8	Average:	2.00
No. 50s:	0	No. 100s:	0

Test Bowling & Fielding

Wickets:	32	Runs:	1,006
Best Bowling:	3/23	Average:	31.43
5 WI:	0	10 WM:	0
Catches:	2	Stumpings:	0

One Day Internationals

ODI Career:	1996-02
ODIs Played:	29

ODI Batting

Innings:	13	Runs:	34
Highest Score:	11	Average:	4.85
No. 50s:	0	No. 100s:	0

ODI Bowling & Fielding

Wickets:	11	Runs:	1,140
Best Bowling:	2/24	Average:	103.63
5 WM:	0	Catches:	3
Stumpings:	0		

Pommie Mbangwa was a surprise selection for Zimbabwe's tour of Pakistan in 1996. He made his debut in the 2nd Test of that series where he took 2/67 in the first innings. Mbangwa's accuracy was an ongoing problem and before too long found himself on the fringes of the Test side. He played some serviceable games in One Day competitions but never really established himself at the elite level.

MEMAN, Mohammed Ahmed (Babu)

Born:	June 26, 1952
Batting:	Right handed
Bowling:	Right arm off-break

One Day Internationals

ODI Career:	1987
ODIs Played:	1

ODI Batting

Innings:	1	Runs:	19
Highest Score:	19	Average:	19.00
No. 50s:	0	No. 100s:	0

ODI Bowling & Fielding

Wickets:	0	Runs:	34
Best Bowling:	0/34	Average:	0.00
5 WM:	0	Catches:	0
Stumpings:	0		

Babu Meman was a right arm off spinner who played just the solitary ODI against India during the 1987 World Cup where he took 0/34 and was run out for 19.

METH, Keegan Orry

Born:	February 8, 1988
Batting:	Right handed
Bowling:	Right arm medium

One Day Internationals

ODI Career:	2005-06
ODIs Played:	5

ODI Batting

Innings:	3	Runs:	73
Highest Score:	53	Average:	24.33
No. 50s:	1	No. 100s:	0

ODI Bowling & Fielding

Wickets:	1	Runs:	96
Best Bowling:	1/6	Average:	96.00
5 WM:	0	Catches:	0
Stumpings:	0		

A talented younster, handy with both bat and ball who has already scored a 50 at ODI level.

MPOFU, Christopher Bobby

Born:	November 27, 1985
Batting:	Right handed
Bowling:	Right arm medium-fast

Tests

Test Career:	2005
Cap Number:	68
Tests Played:	6

Test Batting

Innings:	12	Runs:	17
Highest Score:	7	Average:	2.83
No. 50s:	0	No. 100s:	0

Test Bowling & Fielding

Wickets:	8	Runs:	556
Best Bowling:	4/109	Average:	69.50
5 WI:	0	10 WM:	0
Catches:	0	Stumpings:	0

One Day Internationals

ODI Career:	2004-05
ODIs Played:	11

ODI Batting

Innings:	6	Runs:	9
Highest Score:	3*	Average:	4.50
No. 50s:	0	No. 100s:	0

ODI Bowling & Fielding

Wickets:	10	Runs:	444
Best Bowling:	3/59	Average:	44.00
5 WM:	0	Catches:	0
Stumpings:	0		

A tall and athletic seam bowler, Christopher Mpofu was given the opportunity at international level following the departure of the senior players who became disillusioned with the Zimbabwe Cricket Union. After making his Test debut against Bangladesh at Chittagong in 2005, Mpofu has been a valuable contributor in his six Tests and 11 ODI's. His raw talent suggests a promising career looms.

MUPARIWA, Tawanda

Born:	April 16, 1985
Batting:	Right handed
Bowling:	Right arm medium-fast

Tests

Test Career:	2004
Cap Number:	66
Tests Played:	1

Test Batting

Innings:	2	Runs:	15
Highest Score:	14	Average:	15.00
No. 50s:	0	No. 100s:	0

Test Bowling & Fielding

Wickets:	0	Runs:	136
Best Bowling:		Average:	0.00
5 WI:	0	10 WM:	0
Catches:	0	Stumpings:	0

One Day Internationals

ODI Career:	2004-06		
ODIs Played:	13		

ODI Batting

Innings:	12	Runs:	92
Highest Score:	21	Average:	11.50
No. 50s:	0	No. 100s:	0

ODI Bowling & Fielding

Wickets:	25	Runs:	545
Best Bowling:	3/19	Average:	21.80
5 WM:	0	Catches:	4
Stumpings:	0		

A right arm swing bowler with a smooth action, Tawanda Mupariwa has surprisingly played just the one Test to date, against Sri Lanka at Bulawayo in 2004, where he was rushed into the side because of the ongoing exodus of senior players who had rebelled against the Zimbabwean Cricket Union. Mupariwa was used as a first change bowler but like many of his inexperienced team mates, struggled to make an impact. Nevertheless he became a regular in the One Day side and in 2006 took three wickets in Zimbabwe's victorious final against Bermuda in the Tri-Nation Tournament in West Indies.

MURPHY, Brian Andrew

Born:	December 1, 1976
Batting:	Right handed
Bowling:	Right arm leg-break

Tests

Test Career:	2000-01		
Cap Number:	44		
Tests Played:	11		

Test Batting

Innings:	15	Runs:	123
Highest Score:	30	Average:	10.25
No. 50s:	0	No. 100s:	0

Test Bowling & Fielding

Wickets:	18	Runs:	1,113
Best Bowling:	3/32	Average:	61.83
5 WI:	0	10 WM:	0
Catches:	11	Stumpings:	0

One Day Internationals

ODI Career:	2000-03		
ODIs Played:	31		

ODI Batting

Innings:	17	Runs:	72
Highest Score:	20*	Average:	8.00
No. 50s:	0	No. 100s:	0

ODI Bowling & Fielding

Wickets:	29	Runs:	1,130
Best Bowling:	3/43	Average:	38.96
5 WM:	0	Catches:	11
Stumpings:	0		

A right arm leg-spinner who possessed a useful googly in his armory, Brian Murphy was selected on the tour of the Caribbean in 2000. He made his debut in the first Test at Port of Spain, Trinidad, and did quite well taking four wickets for the match. Although an obvious talent, Murphy was quite expensive and had to often gamble with runs in order to capture wickets. After only two years on the international scene, Murphy was awarded the captaincy after Heath Streak stood down from the job in 2002. He captained his country in just the one Test - a draw against Bangladesh - and a handful of ODI's before resigning from the post shortly afterwards.

MUTENDERA, David Travolta

Born:	January 25, 1979
Batting:	Right handed

Tests

Test Career:	2000		
Cap Number:	46		
Tests Played:	1		

Test Batting

Innings:	2	Runs:	10
Highest Score:	10	Average:	5.00
No. 50s:	0	No. 100s:	0

Test Bowling & Fielding

Wickets:	0	Runs:	29
Best Bowling:		Average:	0.00
5 WI:	0	10 WM:	0
Catches:	0	Stumpings:	0

One Day Internationals

ODI Career:	1999-01		
ODIs Played:	9		

ODI Batting

Innings:	4	Runs:	20
Highest Score:	10	Average:	10.00
No. 50s:	0	No. 100s:	0

ODI Bowling & Fielding

Wickets:	9	Runs:	334
Best Bowling:	3/23	Average:	37.11
5 WM:	0	Catches:	1
Stumpings:	0		

A tall, right arm pace bowler, David Mutendera played just the one Test against New Zealand at Bulawayo, in 2000.

MWAYENGA, Waddington

Born:	June 20, 1984
Batting:	Right handed
Bowling:	Right arm medium-fast

Tests

Test Career:	2005		
Cap Number:	74		
Tests Played:	1		

Test Batting

Innings:	2	Runs:	15
Highest Score:	14*	Average:	15.00
No. 50s:	0	No. 100s:	0

Test Bowling & Fielding

Wickets:	1	Runs:	79
Best Bowling:	1/79	Average:	79.00
5 WI:	0	10 WM:	0
Catches:	0	Stumpings:	0

One Day Internationals

ODI Career:	2002-04		
ODIs Played:	3		

ODI Batting

Innings:	2	Runs:	1
Highest Score:	1	Average:	0.50
No. 50s:	0	No. 100s:	0

ODI Bowling & Fielding
Wickets:	1	Runs:	157
Best Bowling:	1/61	Average:	157.00
5 WM:	0	Catches:	2
Stumpings:	0		

A promising right arm pace bowler who made his Test debut against India at Harare in 2005. Took the one wicket, that of Sourav Ganguly and has shown enough to suggest that he could develop into a permanent front line bowler for his country.

NKALA, Mluleki Luke

Born:	April 1, 1981
Batting:	Right handed
Bowling:	Right arm medium-fast

Tests
Test Career:	2000-05		
Cap Number:	45		
Tests Played:	10		

Test Batting
Innings:	15	Runs:	187
Highest Score:	47	Average:	14.38
No. 50s:	0	No. 100s:	0

Test Bowling & Fielding
Wickets:	11	Runs:	727
Best Bowling:	3/82	Average:	66.09
5 WI:	0	10 WM:	0
Catches:	4	Stumpings:	0

One Day Internationals
ODI Career:	1998-05		
ODIs Played:	47		

ODI Batting
Innings:	32	Runs:	288
Highest Score:	47	Average:	10.66
No. 50s:	0	No. 100s:	0

ODI Bowling & Fielding
Wickets:	22	Runs:	1,557
Best Bowling:	3/12	Average:	70.77
5 WM:	0	Catches:	6
Stumpings:	0		

A right arm pace bowler from Bulawayo, Mluleki Nkala got his opportunity at the elite level when he was selected to play in an ODI against India in front of his home crowd. In fairytale fashion, Nkala, with his second delivery, took the prize wicket of Sachin Tendulkar and from then on Nkala became a regular member of the ODI side and in 2000 was eventually capped as a Test player. He made an impressive debut against England at Trent Bridge, taking five wickets for the match while opening the bowling with Heath Streak. While he is in the side purely as a bowler, Nkala's continue improvement with the bat saw the once recognised 'tail ender' elevated up the order.

OLONGA, Henry Khaaba

Born:	July 3, 1976
Batting:	Right handed
Bowling:	Right arm fast

Tests
Test Career:	1995-02		
Cap Number:	25		
Tests Played:	30		

Test Batting
Innings:	45	Runs:	184
Highest Score:	24	Average:	5.41
No. 50s:	0	No. 100s:	0

Test Bowling & Fielding
Wickets:	68	Runs:	2,620
Best Bowling:	5/70	Average:	38.52
5 WI:	2	10 WM:	0
Catches:	10	Stumpings:	0

One Day Internationals
ODI Career:	1995-03		
ODIs Played:	50		

ODI Batting
Innings:	27	Runs:	95
Highest Score:	31	Average:	7.30
No. 50s:	0	No. 100s:	0

ODI Bowling & Fielding
Wickets:	58	Runs:	1,977
Best Bowling:	6/19	Average:	34.08
5 WM:	2	Catches:	13
Stumpings:	0		

An exciting fast bowler, Henry Olonga was the first black cricketer to represent Zimbabwe and being a few months shy of his 19th birthday he was also the youngest player to represent his country at the elite level. In his first Test appearance against Pakistan at Harare in 1995, he took the wicket of Saeed Anwar in his first over but was called for throwing shortly afterwards. Olonga was forced to refine his action and with the help of Australian bowling great, Dennis Lillee, rectified the problem and promptly returned to the international circuit. Although inaccurate at times, Olonga caused concern for many of the world's best batsmen when his radar was on. He took 68 wickets at Test level at unflattering 38.52 and took five wickets in an innings on two occassions - his best haul of 5/70 was against West Indies at Harare, in 1998, which earned him 'Man of the Match' honours. Along with the early controversy surrounding his bowling action, Olonga caused headlines during the 2003 World Cup when he and Andy Flower displayed black armbands in protest against the "death of democracy" in Zimbabwe. Sadly Olonga fled Zimbabwe and set up home in England. Some claim that Olonga never lived up to his unlimited potential but it is undisputed that Zimbabwean cricket is much the richer having had the popular pace bowler in its best eleven for just under a decade.

OMARSHAH, Ali Hassimshah

Born:	August 7, 1959
Batting:	Left handed
Bowling:	Right arm medium

OMARSHAH, Ali

Tests
Test Career:	1992-96
Cap Number:	12
Tests Played:	3

Test Batting
Innings:	5	Runs:	122
Highest Score:	62	Average:	24.39
No. 50s:	1	No. 100s:	0

Test Bowling & Fielding
Wickets:	1	Runs:	125
Best Bowling:	1/46	Average:	125.00
5 WI:	0	10 WM:	0
Catches:	0	Stumpings:	0

One Day Internationals
ODI Career:	1983-96
ODIs Played:	28

ODI Batting
Innings:	28	Runs:	437
Highest Score:	60*	Average:	16.80
No. 50s:	1	No. 100s:	0

ODI Bowling & Fielding
Wickets:	18	Runs:	812
Best Bowling:	3/33	Average:	45.11
5 WM:	0	Catches:	6
Stumpings:	0		

Ali Omarshah played his first international for Zimabawe in their memorable boilover win against Australia in the 1983 World Cup. Although a recognised all rounder, Omarshah opened the batting on that particular occassion and then became a regular member of Zimbabwe's ODI side. He missed out in playing in Zimbabwe's inaugural Test side due to a foot injury.

PANYANGARA, Tinashe

Born:	October 21, 1985
Batting:	Right handed
Bowling:	Right arm medium-fast

Tests
Test Career:	2004-05
Cap Number:	63
Tests Played:	3

Test Batting
Innings:	6	Runs:	128
Highest Score:	40*	Average:	32.00
No. 50s:	0	No. 100s:	0

Test Bowling & Fielding
Wickets:	8	Runs:	286
Best Bowling:	3/28	Average:	35.75
5 WI:	0	10 WM:	0
Catches:	0	Stumpings:	0

One Day Internationals
ODI Career:	2004-05
ODIs Played:	23

ODI Batting
Innings:	19	Runs:	90
Highest Score:	16*	Average:	6.00
No. 50s:	0	No. 100s:	0

ODI Bowling & Fielding
Wickets:	8	Runs:	286
Best Bowling:	3/28	Average:	35.75
5 WM:	0	Catches:	3
Stumpings:	0		

A tall and athletically built all rounder Tinashe Panyangara was another who was fast tracked into the national side due to the mass exodus of senior players unfairly dubbed the 'rebel 15'. He subsequently made his Test debut against Sri Lanka at Harare in 2004. Batting at number eleven, Panyangara scored a very impressive 34 not out in a 50 run, last wicket partnership with Douglas Hondo. Once the innings came to a close the pair opened the bowling and while the Sri Lankans dominated proceedings, the new kid on the block captured three wickets. Panyangara and Hondo again were the shining lights in the second innings as Zimbabwe's batting line up crumbled around them. However, Panyangara and Hondo's 30 run partnership was not enough to make the Sri Lankans bat again, but was enough for the selectors to sit up and take notice of the debutante's undoubted potential. Panyangara has already played over 20 ODI's and has done enough to suggest that he should be considered for further Test selection in the immediate future.

PATERSON, Grant Andrew

Born:	June 9, 1960
Batting:	Right handed

One Day Internationals
ODI Career:	1983-87
ODIs Played:	10

ODI Batting
Innings:	10	Runs:	123
Highest Score:	27	Average:	12.30
No. 50s:	0	No. 100s:	0

ODI Bowling & Fielding
Wickets:	0	Runs:	0
Best Bowling:		Average:	0.00
5 WM:	0	Catches:	2
Stumpings:	0		

A right handed opener who was part of Zimbabwe's inaugural ODI team that shocked the cricketing world when they defeated Australia in their World Cup opener in 1983. Grant Paterson contributed a valuable 27 which was to remain his highest score in international cricket. Patterson went on to represent Zimbabwe in the following World Cup campaign in 1987 held in India and Pakistan, but his career had ended by the time Zimbabwe gained Test status recognition.

PEALL, Stephen Guy

Born:	September 2, 1969
Batting:	Left handed
Bowling:	Right arm off-break

Tests
Test Career:	1993-94
Cap Number:	18
Tests Played:	4

Test Batting
Innings:	6	Runs:	60
Highest Score:	30	Average:	15.00
No. 50s:	0	No. 100s:	0

Test Bowling & Fielding
Wickets:	4	Runs:	303
Best Bowling:	2/89	Average:	75.75
5 WI:	0	10 WM:	0
Catches:	1	Stumpings:	0

One Day Internationals
ODI Career:	1992-96
ODIs Played:	21

ODI Batting
Innings:	15	Runs:	91
Highest Score:	21	Average:	6.50
No. 50s:	0	No. 100s:	0

ODI Bowling & Fielding
Wickets:	8	Runs:	678
Best Bowling:	3/54	Average:	84.75
5 WM:	0	Catches:	1
Stumpings:	0		

An strongly built off-spinner who made a 'pair' on debut against Pakistan at Karachi in 1993 but took a credible 2/89. Peall struggled to trouble high quality batsmen at the elite level and thus his international appearances were limited to just the four Tests.

PECKOVER, Gerald Edward
Born:	June 2, 1955
Batting:	Right handed
	Wicket Keeper

One Day Internationals
ODI Career:	1983
ODIs Played:	3

ODI Batting
Innings:	3	Runs:	33
Highest Score:	16*	Average:	16.50
No. 50s:	0	No. 100s:	0

ODI Bowling & Fielding
Wickets:	0	Runs:	0
Best Bowling:		Average:	0.00
5 WM:	0	Catches:	0
Stumpings:	0		

A wicket-keeper who represented his country in three ODI's during the 1983 World Cup.

PRICE, Raymond William
Born:	June 12, 1976
Batting:	Right handed
Bowling:	Left arm slow

Tests
Test Career:	1999-04
Cap Number:	43
Tests Played:	18

Test Batting
Innings:	30	Runs:	224
Highest Score:	36	Average:	9.73
No. 50s:	0	No. 100s:	0

Test Bowling & Fielding
Wickets:	69	Runs:	2,475
Best Bowling:	6/73	Average:	35.86
5 WI:	5	10 WM:	1
Catches:	3	Stumpings:	0

One Day Internationals
ODI Career:	2002-04
ODIs Played:	26

ODI Batting
Innings:	12	Runs:	90
Highest Score:	20*	Average:	12.85
No. 50s:	0	No. 100s:	0

ODI Bowling & Fielding
Wickets:	15	Runs:	917
Best Bowling:	2/16	Average:	61.13
5 WM:	0	Catches:	1
Stumpings:	0		

The nephew of golfer and 1994 British Open winner Nick, Ray Price made an uneventful Test debut against Sri Lanka at Harare in 1999. However, the left arm spinner followed up with seven wickets in his next Test which was some 14 months later against Bangladesh, at Harare in 2001. Capturing an impressive five wickets in an innings on five occassions (best bowling of 6/73 v West Indies at Harare, 2003) Price remains third on Zimbabwe's all time Test wicket takers list.

PYCROFT, Andrew John
Born:	June 6, 1956
Batting:	Right handed
Bowling:	Right arm off-break

Tests
Test Career:	1992
Cap Number:	10
Tests Played:	3

Test Batting
Innings:	5	Runs:	152
Highest Score:	60	Average:	30.39
No. 50s:	1	No. 100s:	0

Test Bowling & Fielding
Wickets:	0	Runs:	0
Best Bowling:		Average:	0.00
5 WI:	0	10 WM:	0
Catches:	2	Stumpings:	0

One Day Internationals
ODI Career:	1983-92
ODIs Played:	20

ODI Batting
Innings:	19	Runs:	295
Highest Score:	61	Average:	17.35
No. 50s:	2	No. 100s:	0

ODI Bowling & Fielding
Wickets:	0	Runs:	0
Best Bowling:		Average:	0.00
5 WM:	0	Catches:	6
Stumpings:	0		

A technically correct right hand batsman who preferred to play off the back foot, Andy Pycroft played in Zimbabwe's inaugural Test, against India at Harare in 1992, where he scored 39 and 46 on debut. As he was 36 at the time, and in the twilight of his first class career, he could only manage just two more Test appearances thereafter. Later he became Zimbabwe's coach for a short period.

RAINSFORD, Edward Charles

Born: December 14, 1984
Batting: Right handed
Bowling: Right arm medium-fast

One Day Internationals
ODI Career: 2004-06
ODIs Played: 11

ODI Batting

Innings:	7	Runs:	23
Highest Score:	9*	Average:	5.75
No. 50s:	0	No. 100s:	0

ODI Bowling & Fielding

Wickets:	11	Runs:	395
Best Bowling:	3/16	Average:	35.90
5 WM:	0	Catches:	0
Stumpings:	0		

A tall and athletically built right-arm seamer who first represented Zimbabwe at ODI level as a 19 year old when the home side took on the powerful Australians at Harare in 2004. As his first few ODI's didn't yield any memorable performances, Rainsford was subsequently dropped. However due to the instability of cricket in the nation, he was recalled to the national team to tour the West Indies in 2006.

RANCHOD, Ujesh

Born: May 17, 1969
Batting: Right handed
Bowling: Right arm off-break

Tests
Test Career: 1993
Cap Number: 15
Tests Played: 1

Test Batting

Innings:	2	Runs:	8
Highest Score:	7	Average:	4.00
No. 50s:	0	No. 100s:	0

Test Bowling & Fielding

Wickets:	1	Runs:	45
Best Bowling:	1/45	Average:	45.00
5 WI:	0	10 WM:	0
Catches:	0	Stumpings:	0

One Day Internationals
ODI Career: 1992-93
ODIs Played: 3

ODI Batting

Innings:	1	Runs:	3
Highest Score:	3*	Average:	3.00
No. 50s:	0	No. 100s:	0

ODI Bowling & Fielding

Wickets:	1	Runs:	130
Best Bowling:	1/44	Average:	130.00
5 WM:	0	Catches:	1
Stumpings:	0		

A right arm off-spinner who played just the one Test against India at Delhi in 1993. His one and only Test scalp was the prize wicket of Sachin Tendulkar.

RAWSON, Peter Walter Edward

Born: May 25, 1957
Batting: Right handed
Bowling: Right arm medium-fast

One Day Internationals
ODI Career: 1983-87
ODIs Played: 10

ODI Batting

Innings:	8	Runs:	80
Highest Score:	24*	Average:	16.00
No. 50s:	0	No. 100s:	0

ODI Bowling & Fielding

Wickets:	12	Runs:	427
Best Bowling:	3/47	Average:	35.58
5 WM:	0	Catches:	4
Stumpings:	0		

A right arm pace bowler who, with Vincent Hogg, opened the bowling in Zimbabwe's inaugural ODI against Australia during the 1983 World Cup. While both he and Hogg did not take a wicket between them, Zimbabwe caused one of the most memorable upsets on record when they downed the unbackable Australians by 13 runs. Rawson was a consistent performer for the remainder of the tournament and went on to represent Zimbabwe in the following World Cup in 1987.

RENNIE, Gavin James

Born: January 12, 1976
Batting: Left handed
Bowling: Left arm off-break

Tests
Test Career: 1997-02
Cap Number: 36
Tests Played: 23

Test Batting

Innings:	46	Runs:	1,023
Highest Score:	93	Average:	22.73
No. 50s:	7	No. 100s:	0

Test Bowling & Fielding

Wickets:	1	Runs:	84
Best Bowling:	1/40	Average:	84.00
5 WI:	0	10 WM:	0
Catches:	13	Stumpings:	0

One Day Internationals
ODI Career: 1996-03
ODIs Played: 40

ODI Batting

Innings:	37	Runs:	617
Highest Score:	76	Average:	19.90
No. 50s:	2	No. 100s:	0

ODI Bowling & Fielding

Wickets:	2	Runs:	75
Best Bowling:	1/17	Average:	37.50
5 WM:	0	Catches:	16
Stumpings:	0		

Younger brother of John Rennie, Gavin, a left handed opener, made his Test debut against New Zealand at Harare in 1997 where he opened the batting with Grant Flower. After a respectable 23, Rennie followed up with his maiden half century, 57, in the second innings. He was to score seven half centuries in his career, but fell seven runs short of reaching a Test century.

RENNIE, John Alexander

Born: July 29, 1970
Batting: Right handed
Bowling: Right arm medium-fast

Tests
Test Career: 1993-97
Cap Number: 19
Tests Played: 4

Test Batting
Innings:	6	Runs:	62
Highest Score:	22	Average:	12.40
No. 50s:	0	No. 100s:	0

Test Bowling & Fielding
Wickets:	3	Runs:	293
Best Bowling:	2/22	Average:	97.66
5 WI:	0	10 WM:	0
Catches:	1	Stumpings:	0

One Day Internationals
ODI Career: 1993-00
ODIs Played: 44

ODI Batting
Innings:	27	Runs:	201
Highest Score:	27	Average:	13.40
No. 50s:	0	No. 100s:	0

ODI Bowling & Fielding
Wickets:	34	Runs:	1,564
Best Bowling:	3/27	Average:	46.00
5 WM:	0	Catches:	12
Stumpings:	0		

After making his Test debut against Pakistan in 1993, it was quite evident early on that swing bowler John Rennie was far suited to the shorter version of the game. A keen competitor, Rennie was more than serviceable and gave his all for his country every time he donned the Zimbabwean colours.

RINKE, Harry Piet

Born: November 5, 1981
Batting: Right handed
Bowling: Right arm medium-fast

One Day Internationals
ODI Career: 2006
ODIs Played: 13

ODI Batting
Innings:	13	Runs:	292
Highest Score:	72	Average:	22.46
No. 50s:	3	No. 100s:	0

ODI Bowling & Fielding
Wickets:	5	Runs:	149
Best Bowling:	2/11	Average:	29.80
5 WM:	0	Catches:	0
Stumpings:	0		

A nuggety all rounder, Piet Rinke opens the batting as well as bowling some useful medium-pace. He made his ODI debut against Kenya at Bulawayo where he compiled a well made 42.

ROGERS, Barney Guy

Born: August 20, 1982
Batting: Left handed
Bowling: Right arm off-break

Tests
Test Career: 2005
Cap Number: 69
Tests Played: 4

Test Batting
Innings:	8	Runs:	90
Highest Score:	29	Average:	11.25
No. 50s:	0	No. 100s:	0

Test Bowling & Fielding
Wickets:	0	Runs:	17
Best Bowling:	0/17	Average:	0.00
5 WI:	0	10 WM:	0
Catches:	1	Stumpings:	0

One Day Internationals
ODI Career: 2002-05
ODIs Played: 15

ODI Batting
Innings:	15	Runs:	478
Highest Score:	84	Average:	31.86
No. 50s:	5	No. 100s:	0

ODI Bowling & Fielding
Wickets:	6	Runs:	321
Best Bowling:	2/55	Average:	53.50
5 WM:	0	Catches:	7
Stumpings:	0		

A left handed middle order batsman who surprisingly opened the innings on his Test debut against Bangladesh in 2005. Rogers has struggled in his four Tests to date but has been more productive in limited overs competition. He was initially sacked, along with 14 team mates, by the Zimbabwe Cricket Union, but was later offered a contract which should see him continue to push for national selection.

SIBANDA, Vusimuzi

Born: October 10, 1983
Batting: Right handed
Bowling: Right arm medium-fast

Tests
Test Career: 2003-05
Cap Number: 60
Tests Played: 3

Test Batting
Innings:	6	Runs:	48
Highest Score:	18	Average:	8.00
No. 50s:	0	No. 100s:	0

Test Bowling & Fielding
Wickets:	0	Runs:	0
Best Bowling:		Average:	0.00
5 WI:	0	10 WM:	0
Catches:	4	Stumpings:	0

One Day Internationals
ODI Career: 2003-06
ODIs Played: 34

ODI Batting
Innings:	33	Runs:	616
Highest Score:	116	Average:	19.25
No. 50s:	4	No. 100s:	1

ODI Bowling & Fielding
Wickets:	2	Runs:	87
Best Bowling:	1/12	Average:	43.50
5 WM:	0	Catches:	10
Stumpings:	0		

A promising right-handed opening batsman who made his Test debut against the West Indies at Harare, in 2003. Yet to establish himself as a genuine Test batsman, Sibanda has been more successful at One Day level where he has scored four fifties and an important 116 against Bermuda in the final of the Tri-Nation Tournament, held in the West Indies in 2006, which earnt him the Man of the Match award.

SIMS, Richard William

Born:	July 23, 1979
Batting:	Right handed
Bowling:	Right arm off-break

One Day Internationals

ODI Career:	2002-03		
ODIs Played:	3		

ODI Batting

Innings:	2	Runs:	31
Highest Score:	24	Average:	31.00
No. 50s:	0	No. 100s:	0

ODI Bowling & Fielding

Wickets:	0	Runs:	127
Best Bowling:		Average:	0.00
5 WI:	0	Catches:	1
Stumpings:	0		

A right arm off-break bowler who was used sparingly during his three ODI's. Made his highest score of 24, batting at number seven, in his last ODI against South Africa in 2003.

STRANG, Bryan Colin

Born:	June 9, 1972
Batting:	Right handed
Bowling:	Left arm medium

Tests

Test Career:	1995-01		
Cap Number:	26		
Tests Played:	26		

Test Batting

Innings:	45	Runs:	465
Highest Score:	53	Average:	12.91
No. 50s:	1	No. 100s:	0

Test Bowling & Fielding

Wickets:	56	Runs:	2,203
Best Bowling:	5/101	Average:	39.33
5 WI:	1	10 WM:	0
Catches:	11	Stumpings:	0

One Day Internationals

ODI Career:	1995-01		
ODIs Played:	49		

ODI Batting

Innings:	26	Runs:	92
Highest Score:	18	Average:	5.11
No. 50s:	0	No. 100s:	0

ODI Bowling & Fielding

Wickets:	46	Runs:	1,718
Best Bowling:	6/20	Average:	37.35
5 WM:	1	Catches:	15
Stumpings:	0		

The younger brother of the highly decorated Paul, Bryan Strang was a left arm medium pace seamer who made his Test debut against Pakistan at Bulawayo in 1995 where he took five wickets for the match. Strang soon became the regular bowling partner of Heath Streak and the two worked in tandem for just under six years. Strang bowled with a lot of heart and took a career best of 5/101 against South Africa at Harare in 1995. But his best performance occurred in a ODI against Bangladesh, at Nairobi in 1997, where he captured an amazing 6/20 from his allotted ten overs. Although not considered as handy with the bat as his brother, Strang did score a Test fifty in his career. While injury impacted on his career, in 2004 he was banned by the Zimbabwean Cricket Union after he made comments suggesting that Zimbabwe should have not hosted World Cup matches in 2003 on moral grounds. He attempted a comeback in 2005 and was selected for a Zimbabwe 'A' side but any thoughts of a recall to the senior squad were short lived when he was formerly advised by the Zimbabwean board that his services were no longer required.

STRANG, Paul Andrew

Born:	July 28, 1970
Batting:	Right handed
Bowling:	Right arm leg-break

Tests

Test Career:	1994-01		
Cap Number:	23		
Tests Played:	24		

Test Batting

Innings:	41	Runs:	839
Highest Score:	106*	Average:	27.06
No. 50s:	2	No. 100s:	1

Test Bowling & Fielding

Wickets:	70	Runs:	2,522
Best Bowling:	8/109	Average:	36.02
5 WI:	4	10 WM:	1
Catches:	15	Stumpings:	0

One Day Internationals

ODI Career:	1994-01		
ODIs Played:	95		

ODI Batting

Innings:	73	Runs:	1,090
Highest Score:	47	Average:	22.24
No. 50s:	0	No. 100s:	0

ODI Bowling & Fielding

Wickets:	96	Runs:	3,173
Best Bowling:	5/21	Average:	33.05
5 WM:	2	Catches:	30
Stumpings:	0		

One of Zimbabwe's greatest stalwarts, Paul Strang was a quality all-rounder who made his Test debut against Sri Lanka at Harare in 1994. In a game where he was used a third change bowler he took the credible figures of 3/65 with a fine display of leg spin bowling. Strang would go on to become a regular in the Test eleven taking five wickets in an innings on four occasions including a career best 8/109 against New Zealand at Bulawayo in 2001. An excellent fielder, and arguably Zimbabwe's finest, Strang was also a valuable component of the One Day side even though it was not generally viewed as a game suited to leg spinners - until the emergence of Shane Warne. Although he usually batted down the order, Strang averaged a respectable 27 in Tests. Against Pakistan at Sheikhapura in 1996, he scored his maiden Test century, 106 not out, coming in at number eight, in addition to his five wickets in the first innings. Paul Strang is the older brother of Bryan Strang who also represented Zimbabwe at both Test and ODI level.

STREAK, Heath Hilton

Born:	March 16, 1974
Batting:	Right handed
Bowling:	Right arm medium-fast

Tests
Test Career:	1993-05		
Cap Number:	20		
Tests Played:	65		

Test Batting
Innings:	107	Runs:	1,990
Highest Score:	127*	Average:	22.35
No. 50s:	11	No. 100s:	1

Test Bowling & Fielding
Wickets:	216	Runs:	6,079
Best Bowling:	6/73	Average:	28.14
5 WI:	7	10 WM:	0
Catches:	17	Stumpings:	0

One Day Internationals
ODI Career:	1993-05		
ODIs Played:	189		

ODI Batting
Innings:	159	Runs:	2,943
Highest Score:	79*	Average:	28.29
No. 50s:	13	No. 100s:	0

ODI Bowling & Fielding
Wickets:	239	Runs:	7,129
Best Bowling:	5/32	Average:	29.82
5 WM:	1	Catches:	46
Stumpings:	0		

A powerful fast bowler who provided the Zimbabwean bowling attack with genuine 'teeth' after making his debut against Pakistan at Karachi back in 1993. A fierce competitor who could bowl all day, Streak's outswingers could trouble even the world best batsmen and became the first Zimbabwean to reach the 100 Test wicket milestone. Although he started his career as a pace bowler, Streak was soon dubbed an all rounder due to his power hitting in both forms of the game. He scored 11 fifties and a superb 127 not out against West Indies at Harare, in 2003, when coming in at number eight. Streak was awarded the captaincy in 2000, but resigned shortly afterwards to concentrate on his own form. But just two years later, the popular figure was coaxed into leading the national side again. Due to the ongoing, off field political turmoil, Streak resigned from the role in 2004 and after a highly publicised dispute with the Zimbabwean cricket board, Streak was deemed to be 'retired'. He subsequently returned to the Test side in early 2005 and immediately showed the cricketing world that his natural ability had not deserted him during his short hiatus when he captured a career best 6/73 against India at Harare - his final Test to date.

STRYDOM, Gregory Mark

Born:	March 26, 1984
Batting:	Right handed
Bowling:	Right arm medium

One Day Internationals
ODI Career:	2006		
ODIs Played:	10		

ODI Batting
Innings:	8	Runs:	85
Highest Score:	48	Average:	10.62
No. 50s:	0	No. 100s:	0

ODI Bowling & Fielding
Wickets:	1	Runs:	52
Best Bowling:	1/28	Average:	52.00
5 WM:	0	Catches:	4
Stumpings:	0		

South African born Strydom has the hallmarks of a player suited to the shorter version of the game but has yet to make an impact on the game at an international level since making his debut against Kenya at Bullawayo.

TAIBU, Tatenda

Born:	May 14, 1983
Batting:	Right handed
Bowling:	Right arm off-break
	Wicket Keeper

Tests
Test Career:	2001-05		
Cap Number:	52		
Tests Played:	24		

Test Batting
Innings:	46	Runs:	1,273
Highest Score:	153	Average:	29.60
No. 50s:	9	No. 100s:	1

Test Bowling & Fielding
Wickets:	1	Runs:	27
Best Bowling:	1/27	Average:	27.00
5 WI:	0	10 WM:	0
Catches:	48	Stumpings:	4

One Day Internationals
ODI Career:	2001-05		
ODIs Played:	84		

ODI Batting
Innings:	71	Runs:	1,410
Highest Score:	96*	Average:	25.17
No. 50s:	7	No. 100s:	0

ODI Bowling & Fielding
Wickets:	2	Runs:	61
Best Bowling:	2/42	Average:	30.50
5 WM:	0	Catches:	73
Stumpings:	8		

A diminutive and enthusiastic wicket-keeper Tatenda Taibu's early form clearly indicated that he would be the appropriate successor to Andy Flower as Zimbabwe's number one gloveman. Zimbabwe had experimented with various up and coming keepers with limited success and after just two years on the international scene and at the tender age of 19, the board appointed Taibu as vice captain. A useful batsman with an unorthodox style, Taibu enjoyed taking on the bowling at both Test and One Day level and quite often frustrated quality bowlers with his cross bat technique. He was selected as part of the 2003 World Cup squad and in 2004 Taibu was appointed captain due to the highly publicised resignation of Heath Streak. In early 2005, Taibu scored his first Test century, 153 in the second innings against Bangladesh at Dhaka. He had followed on from an inspiring 85 not out in the first innings which earned him the 'Man of the Match' award. Later that year a disillusioned Taibu resigned as captain and subsequently from international cricket. He decided to move to England to play County cricket and becomes yet another talented Zimbabwean forced to pursue their career abroad.

TAYLOR, Brendan Ross Murray

Born:	February 6, 1986
Batting:	Right handed
Bowling:	Right arm off-break
	Wicket Keeper

Tests

Test Career:	2004-05
Cap Number:	64
Tests Played:	10

Test Batting

Innings:	20	Runs:	422
Highest Score:	78	Average:	21.10
No. 50s:	3	No. 100s:	0

Test Bowling & Fielding

Wickets:	0	Runs:	38
Best Bowling:		Average:	0.00
5 WI:	0	10 WM:	0
Catches:	7	Stumpings:	0

One Day Internationals

ODI Career:	2004-06
ODIs Played:	42

ODI Batting

Innings:	42	Runs:	1,156
Highest Score:	98	Average:	28.90
No. 50s:	8	No. 100s:	0

ODI Bowling & Fielding

Wickets:	8	Runs:	224
Best Bowling:	3/54	Average:	28.00
5 WM:	0	Catches:	20
Stumpings:	3		

Another youngster who was propelled into the international arena because of the 2004 player revolt, Brendan Taylor, a wicket-keeper by trade made his Test debut against Sri Lanka, at Harare in 2004 as an opener. The fact that he shared his debut amongst four others in Chigumbura, Maregwede, Panyangara, and Utseya clearly indicated the plight of Zimbabwean cricket at the time. Taylor soon became a regular in both forms of the game and while he didn't get much of opportunity to keep wickets because of current captain Tatenda Taibu presence in the side, Taylor has been used as a part time off-spinner with moderate success. In 2006 he was part of the Zimbabwe's One Day side that won the final of the Tri-Nation Tournament (against Bermuda) held in the West Indies. On this particular occasion, Taylor was the designated keeper.

TRAICOS, Athanasios John

Born:	May 17, 1947
Batting:	Right handed
Bowling:	Right arm off-break

Tests

Test Career:	1970-93
Cap Number:	11
Tests Played:	7

Test Batting

Innings:	10	Runs:	19
Highest Score:	5*	Average:	3.16
No. 50s:	0	No. 100s:	0

Test Bowling & Fielding

Wickets:	18	Runs:	769
Best Bowling:	5/86	Average:	42.72
5 WI:	1	10 WM:	0
Catches:	8	Stumpings:	0

One Day Internationals

ODI Career:	1983-93
ODIs Played:	27

ODI Batting

Innings:	17	Runs:	88
Highest Score:	19	Average:	11.00
No. 50s:	0	No. 100s:	0

ODI Bowling & Fielding

Wickets:	19	Runs:	987
Best Bowling:	3/35	Average:	51.94
5 WM:	0	Catches:	3
Stumpings:	0		

A player with an unusual history. John Traicos was born in Egypt, raised in South Africa, and played his first Test for that nation in 1969/70 - South Africa's final series before they were banned from participating in international cricket. Traicos, a clever off-spinner returned to the international arena almost 23 years later, this time representing neighboring Zimbabwe in their inaugural Test against India at Harare. Traicos, who was 45 years old, showed that he had got better with age when he took 5/86 in his first outing. He went on to play in another three Tests for Zimbabwe, taking his overall tally to seven.

UTSEYA, Prosper

Born:	March 26, 1985
Batting:	Right handed
Bowling:	Right arm off-break

Tests

Test Career:	2004
Cap Number:	65
Tests Played:	1

Test Batting

Innings:	2	Runs:	45
Highest Score:	45	Average:	22.50
No. 50s:	0	No. 100s:	0

The Encyclopedia of International Cricketers - Zimbabwe

Test Bowling & Fielding			
Wickets:	0	Runs:	55
Best Bowling:		Average:	0.00
5 WI:	0	10 WM:	0
Catches:	2	Stumpings:	0

One Day Internationals

ODI Career:	2004-06		
ODIs Played:	39		
ODI Batting			
Innings:	30	Runs:	168
Highest Score:	31	Average:	9.88
No. 50s:	0	No. 100s:	0
ODI Bowling & Fielding			
Wickets:	27	Runs:	1,262
Best Bowling:	3/35	Average:	46.74
5 WM:	0	Catches:	11
Stumpings:	0		

A talented young off-spinner who was fast tracked into the national side due to the withdrawal of the 'rebel' players who were at odds with the Zimbabwean Cricket Union. Utseya made his Test debut against Sri Lanka at Harare and while the youngster couldn't make an impact with the ball, he scored 45 batting at number eight. However the selectors could not find enough merit in his performance to give him another taste of Test cricket and from then on Utseya was selected primarily for ODI's.

VERMEULEN, Mark Andrew

Born:	March 2, 1979
Batting:	Right handed
Bowling:	Right arm off-break

Tests

Test Career:	2002-04		
Cap Number:	56		
Tests Played:	8		
Test Batting			
Innings:	16	Runs:	414
Highest Score:	118	Average:	25.87
No. 50s:	2	No. 100s:	1
Test Bowling & Fielding			
Wickets:	0	Runs:	5
Best Bowling:	0/5	Average:	0.00
5 WI:	0	10 WM:	0
Catches:	6	Stumpings:	0

One Day Internationals

ODI Career:	2000-04		
ODIs Played:	32		
ODI Batting			
Innings:	32	Runs:	583
Highest Score:	79	Average:	20.82
No. 50s:	4	No. 100s:	0
ODI Bowling & Fielding			
Wickets:	0	Runs:	0
Best Bowling:		Average:	0.00
5 WM:	0	Catches:	9
Stumpings:	0		

Tall, blonde and athletic, Mark Vermeulen had all the hallmarks of the perfect cricketer. He made his Test debut opening the batting against Pakistan at Bulawayo in 2002. After succumbing to Shoaib Akhtar in the first innings, he followed up with a well composed 26 in the second. Vermeulen started finding his feet thereafter and in 2003 recorded his first (and only) Test century when, batting at number three, he scored 118 against the West Indies at Bulawayo. An excellent fielder, Vermeulen was unsurprisingly suited to the shorter version of the game and was selected for the 2003 World Cup squad. All up he played in eight Tests and 32 ODI's and surprisingly was not offered a contract by the Zimbabwe Cricket Union at the end of 2005.

VILJOEN, Dirk Peter

Born:	March 11, 1977
Batting:	Left handed
Bowling:	Left arm off-break

Tests

Test Career:	1998-00		
Cap Number:	39		
Tests Played:	2		
Test Batting			
Innings:	4	Runs:	57
Highest Score:	38	Average:	14.25
No. 50s:	0	No. 100s:	0
Test Bowling & Fielding			
Wickets:	1	Runs:	65
Best Bowling:	1/14	Average:	65.00
5 WI:	0	10 WM:	0
Catches:	1	Stumpings:	0

One Day Internationals

ODI Career:	1997-01		
ODIs Played:	53		
ODI Batting			
Innings:	43	Runs:	512
Highest Score:	63*	Average:	14.22
No. 50s:	2	No. 100s:	0
ODI Bowling & Fielding			
Wickets:	44	Runs:	1,639
Best Bowling:	3/20	Average:	37.25
5 WM:	0	Catches:	18
Stumpings:	0		

A promising youngster, the left handed Dirk Viljoen was viewed as an all rounder of the future by the selectors. Unfortunately his much awaited Test debut was to be somewhat of an anti climax as he made a pair when opening the batting with Grant Flower. While his performance in his second Test was far more palatable, Viljoen was quickly pigeon-holed as a one day specialist where he went on to represent his country in over 50 ODI's.

WALLER, Andrew Christopher

Born:	September 25, 1959
Batting:	Right handed
Bowling:	Right arm medium

Tests

Test Career:	1996		
Cap Number:	34		
Tests Played:	2		
Test Batting			
Innings:	3	Runs:	69
Highest Score:	50	Average:	23.00
No. 50s:	1	No. 100s:	0

731

Test Bowling & Fielding

Wickets:	0	Runs:	0
Best Bowling:		Average:	0.00
5 WI:	0	10 WM:	0
Catches:	1	Stumpings:	0

One Day Internationals

ODI Career: 1987-97
ODIs Played: 39

ODI Batting

Innings:	38	Runs:	818
Highest Score:	83*	Average:	23.37
No. 50s:	4	No. 100s:	0

ODI Bowling & Fielding

Wickets:	0	Runs:	0
Best Bowling:		Average:	0.00
5 WM:	0	Catches:	10
Stumpings:	0		

A highly regarded One Day player, Waller represented Zimbabwe in the World Cup sides of 1987, 1992 and 1996. He finally made his Test debut in 1996, aged 37, when Zimbabwe took on England at Bulawayo.

WATAMBWA, Brighton Tonderai

Born: June 9, 1977
Batting: Right handed
Bowling: Right arm medium-fast

Tests

Test Career: 2001-02
Cap Number: 50
Tests Played: 6

Test Batting

Innings:	8	Runs:	11
Highest Score:	4*	Average:	3.66
No. 50s:	0	No. 100s:	0

Test Bowling & Fielding

Wickets:	14	Runs:	490
Best Bowling:	4/64	Average:	35.00
5 WI:	0	10 WM:	0
Catches:	0	Stumpings:	0

A blistering fast bowler, Brighton Watambwa was hailed as the 'next best thing' when he made his debut against Bangladesh, at Bulawayo, in 2001. And while it was looking that the young hopeful would become a household name before too long, Watambwa's career was over just as quick as it began when he refused to sign a contract with the Zimbabwe Cricket Board. Watambwa headed for the United States where he played for Palm Beach, Miami, and hoped to one day play in a World Cup with his adopted country although ironically, Watambwa is one of the very few Zimbabwean cricketers that has not played in a One Day International. With the US missing out on inclusion to the 2007 World Cup, Watambwa's dream was relatively short lived.

WHITTALL, Andrew Richard

Born: March 28, 1973
Batting: Right handed
Bowling: Right arm off-break

Tests

Test Career: 1996-99
Cap Number: 31
Tests Played: 10

Test Batting

Innings:	18	Runs:	114
Highest Score:	17	Average:	7.60
No. 50s:	0	No. 100s:	0

Test Bowling & Fielding

Wickets:	7	Runs:	736
Best Bowling:	3/73	Average:	105.14
5 WI:	0	10 WM:	0
Catches:	8	Stumpings:	0

One Day Internationals

ODI Career: 1996-00
ODIs Played: 63

ODI Batting

Innings:	35	Runs:	168
Highest Score:	29	Average:	7.63
No. 50s:	0	No. 100s:	0

ODI Bowling & Fielding

Wickets:	45	Runs:	2,251
Best Bowling:	3/23	Average:	50.02
5 WM:	0	Catches:	21
Stumpings:	0		

The cousin of Guy Whittall, Andy Whittall, made his Test debut against Sri Lanka at Colombo in 1996. Whittall just made it to double figures in Test appearances but showed that he was more than competant at One Day level where he represented Zimbabwe on 63 ocassions - including the 1999 World Cup.

WHITTALL, Guy James

Born: September 5, 1972
Batting: Right handed
Bowling: Right arm medium

Tests

Test Career: 1993-02
Cap Number: 21
Tests Played: 46

Test Batting

Innings:	82	Runs:	2,207
Highest Score:	203*	Average:	29.42
No. 50s:	10	No. 100s:	4

Test Bowling & Fielding

Wickets:	51	Runs:	2,088
Best Bowling:	4/18	Average:	40.94
5 WI:	0	10 WM:	0
Catches:	19	Stumpings:	0

One Day Internationals

ODI Career: 1993-03
ODIs Played: 147

ODI Batting

Innings:	142	Runs:	2,705
Highest Score:	83	Average:	22.54
No. 50s:	11	No. 100s:	0

ODI Bowling & Fielding

Wickets:	88	Runs:	3,481
Best Bowling:	4/35	Average:	39.55
5 WM:	0	Catches:	36
Stumpings:	0		

Guy Whittall was just about the complete cricketer. A fine fielder, hard hitting middle order batsmen, and a useful seam bowler, Whittall, by the time his career came to a close in 2003, was regarded as a genuine all rounder. He made his Test debut against Pakistan at Karachi in 1993 where he made an impressive 33 before being run out. Just over 12 months later, Whittall chalked up his first Test century against Pakistan in Zimbabwe's first Test win at Harare in 1995. In 1997 he scored his first double century, a remarkable 203 not out against New Zealand at Bulawayo. Whittall was just as impressive in the shorter version of the game having represented his country 147 times, including three World Cup campaigns.

WILLIAMS, Sean Colin

Born: September 26, 1986
Batting: Left handed
Bowling: Left arm off-break

One Day Internationals
ODI Career: 2005
ODIs Played: 4

ODI Batting
Innings:	4	Runs:	54
Highest Score:	33*	Average:	18.00
No. 50s:	0	No. 100s:	0

ODI Bowling & Fielding
Wickets:	0	Runs:	89
Best Bowling:		Average:	0.00
5 WM:	0	Catches:	0
Stumpings:	0		

A talented left handed batsman who got his opportunity in 2005. After a relatively quiet debut against South Africa at Johannesburg, Williams showed promise in his following three ODI's. He captained the national under 19's team in the World Cup in Sri Lanka, but upon his return in early 2006, Williams refused to sign a contract with the Zimbabwe Cricket Board as he had received offers to play cricket in both England and South Africa. Regardless of where he settles, Williams has the potential and the ability to become an elite cricketer over the next decade.

WISHART, Craig Brian

Born: January 9, 1974
Batting: Right handed
Bowling: Right arm off-break

Tests
Test Career: 1995-05
Cap Number: 29
Tests Played: 27

Test Batting
Innings:	50	Runs:	1,098
Highest Score:	114	Average:	22.40
No. 50s:	5	No. 100s:	1

Test Bowling & Fielding
Wickets:	0	Runs:	0
Best Bowling:		Average:	0.00
5 WI:	0	10 WM:	0
Catches:	15	Stumpings:	0

One Day Internationals
ODI Career: 1996-05
ODIs Played: 90

ODI Batting
Innings:	82	Runs:	1,719
Highest Score:	172*	Average:	23.22
No. 50s:	5	No. 100s:	2

ODI Bowling & Fielding
Wickets:	0	Runs:	12
Best Bowling:	0/12	Average:	0.00
5 WM:	0	Catches:	26
Stumpings:	0		

A talented right hand batsman who smashed a memorable 172 not out against Namibia during the 2003 World Cup. Wishart was another who was more suited to the one day game, as he scored just the one Test century from 50 starts. Unfortunately, Wishart, like a few of his team mates at the time, was affected by the controversy surrounding the sacking of Heath Streak in 2004, and subsequently his international career ended prematurely.

Bermuda

BORDEN, Delyone Charles
Born: March 4, 1985
Batting: Right handed

One Day Internationals
ODI Career: 2006
ODIs Played: 1

ODI Batting
Innings:	1	Runs:	24
Highest Score:	24	Average:	24.00
No. 50s:	0	No. 100s:	0

ODI Bowling & Fielding
Wickets:	1	Runs:	16
Best Bowling:	1/16	Average:	16.00
5 WM:	0	Catches:	0
Stumpings:	0		

Debut v Canada, Toronto, 2006.

CANN, Lionel
Born: October 3, 1972
Batting: Right handed
Bowling: Right arm medium

One Day Internationals
ODI Career: 2006
ODIs Played: 2

ODI Batting
Innings:	2	Runs:	72
Highest Score:	40	Average:	72.00
No. 50s:	0	No. 100s:	0

ODI Bowling & Fielding
Wickets:	0	Runs:	0
Best Bowling:		Average:	0.00
5 WM:	0	Catches:	2
Stumpings:	0		

Debut v Canada, Port of Spain 2006.

DURHAM, Hasan
Born: August 14, 1971
Batting: Right handed

One Day Internationals
ODI Career: 2006
ODIs Played: 3

ODI Batting
Innings:	3	Runs:	10
Highest Score:	8	Average:	5.00
No. 50s:	0	No. 100s:	0

ODI Bowling & Fielding
Wickets:	4	Runs:	118
Best Bowling:	2/31	Average:	29.50
5 WM:	0	Catches:	2
Stumpings:	0		

Debut v Canada, Port of Spain 2006.

GIBBONS, Treadwell
Born: December 10, 1985
Batting: Left handed

One Day Internationals
ODI Career: 2006
ODIs Played: 2

ODI Batting
Innings:	2	Runs:	33
Highest Score:	33	Average:	16.50
No. 50s:	0	No. 100s:	0

ODI Bowling & Fielding
Wickets:	0	Runs:	0
Best Bowling:		Average:	0.00
5 WM:	0	Catches:	0
Stumpings:	0		

Debut v Zimbabwe, Port of Spain 2006

HURDLE, Kevin
Born: December 30, 1976
Batting: Right handed
Bowling: Right arm fast

One Day Internationals
ODI Career: 2006
ODIs Played: 1

ODI Batting
Innings:	0	Runs:	0
Highest Score:	0	Average:	0.00
No. 50s:	0	No. 100s:	0

ODI Bowling & Fielding
Wickets:	2	Runs:	66
Best Bowling:	2/66	Average:	33.00
5 WM:	0	Catches:	0
Stumpings:	0		

Debut v Zimbabwe, Port of Spain 2006

LEVEROCK, Dwayne
Born: July 14, 1971
Batting: Right handed
Bowling: Left arm off-break

One Day Internationals
ODI Career: 2006
ODIs Played: 2

ODI Batting
Innings:	1	Runs:	2
Highest Score:	2	Average:	2.00
No. 50s:	0	No. 100s:	0

ODI Bowling & Fielding
Wickets:	1	Runs:	64
Best Bowling:	1/14	Average:	64.00
5 WM:	0	Catches:	0
Stumpings:	0		

Debut v Canada, Port of Spain 2006

MINORS, Dean
Born: January 6, 1970
Batting: Left handed
Wicket Keeper

One Day Internationals
ODI Career:	2006		
ODIs Played:	3		

ODI Batting
Innings:	3	Runs:	87
Highest Score:	46*	Average:	87.00
No. 50s:	0	No. 100s:	0

ODI Bowling & Fielding
Wickets:	0	Runs:	0
Best Bowling:		Average:	0.00
5 WM:	0	Catches:	2
Stumpings:	2		

Debut v Canada, Port of Spain 2006

MORGAN, Daniel
Born:	February 13, 1974
Batting:	Right handed

One Day Internationals
ODI Career:	2006		
ODIs Played:	2		

ODI Batting
Innings:	2	Runs:	2
Highest Score:	1	Average:	1.00
No. 50s:	0	No. 100s:	0

ODI Bowling & Fielding
Wickets:	0	Runs:	0
Best Bowling:		Average:	0.00
5 WM:	0	Catches:	0
Stumpings:	0		

Debut v Canada, Port of Spain 2006

MUKUDDEM, Saleem
Born:	January 20, 1972
Batting:	Right handed
Bowling:	Right arm medium

One Day Internationals
ODI Career:	2006		
ODIs Played:	3		

ODI Batting
Innings:	3	Runs:	30
Highest Score:	25	Average:	10.00
No. 50s:	0	No. 100s:	0

ODI Bowling & Fielding
Wickets:	2	Runs:	129
Best Bowling:	2/35	Average:	64.50
5 WM:	0	Catches:	1
Stumpings:	0		

Debut v Canada, Port of Spain 2006

O'BRIEN, George
Born:	September 16, 1984
Batting:	Right handed
Bowling:	Right arm medium-fast

One Day Internationals
ODI Career:	2006		
ODIs Played:	2		

ODI Batting
Innings:	1	Runs:	16
Highest Score:	16	Average:	16.00
No. 50s:	0	No. 100s:	0

ODI Bowling & Fielding
Wickets:	4	Runs:	83
Best Bowling:	2/41	Average:	20.75
5 WM:	0	Catches:	0
Stumpings:	0		

Debut v Canada, Port of Spain 2006

OUTERBRIDGE, Steven Davonne
Born:	May 20, 1983
Batting:	Right handed
Bowling:	Right arm off-break

One Day Internationals
ODI Career:	2006		
ODIs Played:	2		

ODI Batting
Innings:	2	Runs:	38
Highest Score:	23	Average:	19.00
No. 50s:	0	No. 100s:	0

ODI Bowling & Fielding
Wickets:	0	Runs:	0
Best Bowling:		Average:	0.00
5 WM:	0	Catches:	0
Stumpings:	0		

Debut v Canada, Toronto, 2006.

PITCHER, Azeem
Born:	July 31, 1980
Batting:	Left handed

One Day Internationals
ODI Career:	2006		
ODIs Played:	3		

ODI Batting
Innings:	3	Runs:	6
Highest Score:	3	Average:	2.00
No. 50s:	0	No. 100s:	0

ODI Bowling & Fielding
Wickets:	0	Runs:	0
Best Bowling:		Average:	0.00
5 WM:	0	Catches:	1
Stumpings:	0		

Debut v Canada, Port of Spain 2006

ROMAINE, Irvine
Born:	August 8, 1972
Batting:	Right handed
Bowling:	Right arm off-break

One Day Internationals
ODI Career:	2006		
ODIs Played:	3		

ODI Batting
Innings:	3	Runs:	110
Highest Score:	62	Average:	36.66
No. 50s:	1	No. 100s:	0

ODI Bowling & Fielding
Wickets:	3	Runs:	78
Best Bowling:	2/22	Average:	26.00
5 WM:	0	Catches:	0
Stumpings:	0		

Debut v Canada, Port of Spain 2006

SMITH, Clay James
Born:	January 15, 1971
Batting:	Right handed
Bowling:	Right arm off-break

One Day Internationals
ODI Career:	2006		
ODIs Played:	2		

ODI Batting
Innings:	2	Runs:	62
Highest Score:	38	Average:	31.00
No. 50s:	0	No. 100s:	0

ODI Bowling & Fielding
Wickets:	0	Runs:	0
Best Bowling:		Average:	0.00
5 WM:	0	Catches:	0
Stumpings:	0		

Debut v Canada, Toronto, 2006.

STEEDE, Ryan

Born:	November 9, 1975
Batting:	Right handed
Bowling:	Right arm medium-fast

One Day Internationals
ODI Career:	2006
ODIs Played:	1

ODI Batting
Innings:	0	Runs:	0
Highest Score:	0	Average:	0.00
No. 50s:	0	No. 100s:	0

ODI Bowling & Fielding
Wickets:	1	Runs:	68
Best Bowling:	1/68	Average:	68.00
5 WM:	0	Catches:	0
Stumpings:	0		

Debut v Zimbabwe, Port of Spain 2006

TUCKER, Janeiro

Born:	March 15, 1975
Batting:	Right handed
Bowling:	Right arm medium

One Day Internationals
ODI Career:	2006
ODIs Played:	3

ODI Batting
Innings:	3	Runs:	46
Highest Score:	17	Average:	15.33
No. 50s:	0	No. 100s:	0

ODI Bowling & Fielding
Wickets:	4	Runs:	128
Best Bowling:	2/29	Average:	32.00
5 WM:	0	Catches:	0
Stumpings:	0		

Debut v Canada, Port of Spain 2006

TUCKER, Kwame

Born:	September 28, 1976
Batting:	Right handed
	Wicket Keeper

One Day Internationals
ODI Career:	2006
ODIs Played:	3

ODI Batting
Innings:	3	Runs:	13
Highest Score:	5	Average:	6.50
No. 50s:	0	No. 100s:	0

ODI Bowling & Fielding
Wickets:	0	Runs:	0
Best Bowling:		Average:	0.00
5 WM:	0	Catches:	3
Stumpings:	0		

Debut v Canada, Port of Spain, 2006

Canada

ALI, Qaiser
Born: December 20, 1978
Batting: Right handed
Bowling: Right arm off-break

One Day Internationals
ODI Career: 2006
ODIs Played: 2

ODI Batting
Innings:	2	Runs:	7
Highest Score:	7	Average:	3.50
No. 50s:	0	No. 100s:	0

ODI Bowling & Fielding
Wickets:	0	Runs:	23
Best Bowling:		Average:	0.00
5 WM:	0	Catches:	0
Stumpings:	0		

Debut v Kenya, Toronto, 2006

BAGAI, Ashish
Born: January 26, 1982
Batting: Right handed
Wicket Keeper

One Day Internationals
ODI Career: 2003-06
ODIs Played: 8

ODI Batting
Innings:	8	Runs:	80
Highest Score:	28*	Average:	11.42
No. 50s:	0	No. 100s:	0

ODI Bowling & Fielding
Wickets:	0	Runs:	0
Best Bowling:		Average:	0.00
5 WM:	0	Catches:	11
Stumpings:	2		

Debut v Bangladesh, Durban 2003

BAKSH, Charles
Born: March 15, 1940
Batting: Right handed

One Day Internationals
ODI Career: 1979
ODIs Played: 1

ODI Batting
Innings:	1	Runs:	0
Highest Score:	0	Average:	0.00
No. 50s:	0	No. 100s:	0

ODI Bowling & Fielding
Wickets:	0	Runs:	0
Best Bowling:		Average:	0.00
5 WM:	0	Catches:	0
Stumpings:	0		

Debut v Australia, Edgbaston 1979

BARNETT, Geoff
Born: February 3, 1984
Batting: Left handed

One Day Internationals
ODI Career: 2006
ODIs Played: 2

ODI Batting
Innings:	2	Runs:	1
Highest Score:	1	Average:	0.50
No. 50s:	0	No. 100s:	0

ODI Bowling & Fielding
Wickets:	0	Runs:	0
Best Bowling:		Average:	0.00
5 WM:	0	Catches:	1
Stumpings:	0		

Debut v Zimbabwe, Port of Spain 2006

BHATTI, Umar
Born: January 4, 1984
Batting: Left handed
Bowling: Left arm medium

One Day Internationals
ODI Career: 2006
ODIs Played: 1

ODI Batting
Innings:	1	Runs:	9
Highest Score:	9	Average:	9.00
No. 50s:	0	No. 100s:	0

ODI Bowling & Fielding
Wickets:	0	Runs:	35
Best Bowling:		Average:	0.00
5 WM:	0	Catches:	0
Stumpings:	0		

Debut v Zimbabwe, Port of Spain 2006

BILLCLIFF, Ian
Born: October 26, 1972
Batting: Right handed
Bowling: Right arm medium

One Day Internationals
ODI Career: 2003
ODIs Played: 6

ODI Batting
Innings:	6	Runs:	147
Highest Score:	71	Average:	24.50
No. 50s:	1	No. 100s:	0

ODI Bowling & Fielding
Wickets:	0	Runs:	0
Best Bowling:		Average:	0.00
5 WM:	0	Catches:	0
Stumpings:	0		

Debut v Bangladesh, Durban 2003

CALLENDER, Robert
Born: November 2, 1950
Batting: Right handed
Bowling: Right arm medium-fast

One Day Internationals

ODI Career: 1979
ODIs Played: 2

ODI Batting
Innings:	2	Runs:	0
Highest Score:	0	Average:	0.00
No. 50s:	0	No. 100s:	0

ODI Bowling & Fielding
Wickets:	1	Runs:	26
Best Bowling:	1/14	Average:	26.00
5 WM:	0	Catches:	0
Stumpings:	0		

Debut v England, Old Trafford 1979

CHAPPELL, Christopher James David
Born: July 15, 1955
Batting: Right handed

One Day Internationals
ODI Career: 1979
ODIs Played: 3

ODI Batting
Innings:	3	Runs:	38
Highest Score:	19	Average:	12.66
No. 50s:	0	No. 100s:	0

ODI Bowling & Fielding
Wickets:	0	Runs:	0
Best Bowling:		Average:	0.00
5 WM:	0	Catches:	0
Stumpings:	0		

Debut v Pakistan, Headingly, 1979

CHUMNEY, Desmond
Born: January 8, 1968
Batting: Right handed
Bowling: Right arm off-break

One Day Internationals
ODI Career: 2003-06
ODIs Played: 6

ODI Batting
Innings:	6	Runs:	69
Highest Score:	28	Average:	11.50
No. 50s:	0	No. 100s:	0

ODI Bowling & Fielding
Wickets:	0	Runs:	0
Best Bowling:		Average:	0.00
5 WM:	0	Catches:	1
Stumpings:	0		

Debut v Bangladesh, Durban 2003

CODRINGTON, Austin
Born: August 22, 1975
Batting: Right handed
Bowling: Right arm medium-fast

One Day Internationals
ODI Career: 2003
ODIs Played: 5

ODI Batting
Innings:	5	Runs:	28
Highest Score:	16	Average:	5.60
No. 50s:	0	No. 100s:	0

ODI Bowling & Fielding
Wickets:	6	Runs:	129
Best Bowling:	5/27	Average:	21.50
5 WM:	1	Catches:	0
Stumpings:	0		

Debut v Bangladesh, Durban 2003

CODRINGTON, George
Born: November 26, 1966
Batting: Right handed

One Day Internationals
ODI Career: 2006
ODIs Played: 1

ODI Batting
Innings:	1	Runs:	45
Highest Score:	45*	Average:	0.00
No. 50s:	0	No. 100s:	0

ODI Bowling & Fielding
Wickets:	0	Runs:	23
Best Bowling:		Average:	0.00
5 WM:	0	Catches:	0
Stumpings:	0		

Debut v Bermuda, Port of Spain 2006

DAVISON, John
Born: May 9, 1970
Batting: Right handed
Bowling: Right arm off-break

One Day Internationals
ODI Career: 2003-06
ODIs Played: 8

ODI Batting
Innings:	8	Runs:	249
Highest Score:	111	Average:	31.12
No. 50s:	1	No. 100s:	1

ODI Bowling & Fielding
Wickets:	14	Runs:	246
Best Bowling:	3/15	Average:	17.57
5 WM:	0	Catches:	2
Stumpings:	0		

Debut V Bangladesh, Durban 2003

DE GROOT, Nicholas
Born: October 22, 1975
Batting: Right handed
Bowling: Right arm medium

One Day Internationals
ODI Career: 2003
ODIs Played: 6

ODI Batting
Innings:	6	Runs:	44
Highest Score:	17	Average:	7.33
No. 50s:	0	No. 100s:	0

ODI Bowling & Fielding
Wickets:	3	Runs:	88
Best Bowling:	2/45	Average:	29.33
5 WM:	0	Catches:	0
Stumpings:	0		

Debut V Bangladesh, Durban 2003

DENNIS, Franklyn Anthony
Born: September 26, 1947
Batting: Right handed

One Day Internationals
ODI Career: 1979
ODIs Played: 3

ODI Batting
Innings:	3	Runs:	47
Highest Score:	25	Average:	15.66
No. 50s:	0	No. 100s:	0

ODI Bowling & Fielding
Wickets:	0	Runs:	0
Best Bowling:		Average:	0.00
5 WM:	0	Catches:	0
Stumpings:	0		

Debut v Pakistan, Headingley 1979

DHANIRAM, Sunhil
Born:	October 17, 1968
Batting:	Left handed
Bowling:	Left arm off-break

One Day Internationals
ODI Career:	2006		
ODIs Played:	2		

ODI Batting
Innings:	2	Runs:	26
Highest Score:	14	Average:	13.00
No. 50s:	0	No. 100s:	0

ODI Bowling & Fielding
Wickets:	2	Runs:	51
Best Bowling:	2/34	Average:	25.50
5 WM:	0	Catches:	0
Stumpings:	0		

Debut V Zimbabwe, Port of Spain 2006

DHILLON, Haninder
Born:	October 27, 1976
Batting:	Right handed
Bowling:	Right arm slow

One Day Internationals
ODI Career:	2006		
ODIs Played:	2		

ODI Batting
Innings:	2	Runs:	14
Highest Score:	13	Average:	7.00
No. 50s:	0	No. 100s:	0

ODI Bowling & Fielding
Wickets:	0	Runs:	0
Best Bowling:		Average:	0.00
5 WM:	0	Catches:	0
Stumpings:	0		

Debut V Zimbabwe, Port of Spain 2006

HARRIS, Joe
Born:	August 16, 1965
Batting:	Right handed
Bowling:	Right arm off-break

One Day Internationals
ODI Career:	2003		
ODIs Played:	6		

ODI Batting
Innings:	6	Runs:	91
Highest Score:	31	Average:	15.16
No. 50s:	0	No. 100s:	0

ODI Bowling & Fielding
Wickets:	0	Runs:	0
Best Bowling:		Average:	0.00
5 WM:	0	Catches:	1
Stumpings:	0		

Debut v Bangladesh, Durban 2003

HEANEY, Stewart
Born:	October 17, 1980
Batting:	Right handed
Bowling:	Right arm off-break

One Day Internationals
ODI Career:	2006		
ODIs Played:	2		

ODI Batting
Innings:	2	Runs:	21
Highest Score:	19	Average:	10.50
No. 50s:	0	No. 100s:	0

ODI Bowling & Fielding
Wickets:	0	Runs:	0
Best Bowling:		Average:	0.00
5 WM:	0	Catches:	1
Stumpings:	0		

Debut V Zimbabwe, Port of Spain 2006

HENRY, Cornelius
Born:	September 16, 1956
Batting:	Right handed
Bowling:	Right arm medium

One Day Internationals
ODI Career:	1979		
ODIs Played:	2		

ODI Batting
Innings:	2	Runs:	6
Highest Score:	5	Average:	6.00
No. 50s:	0	No. 100s:	0

ODI Bowling & Fielding
Wickets:	2	Runs:	53
Best Bowling:	2/27	Average:	26.50
5 WM:	0	Catches:	0
Stumpings:	0		

Debut v Pakistan, Headingley 1979

IFILL, Nicholas
Born:	November 24, 1968
Batting:	Right handed
Bowling:	Right arm medium

One Day Internationals
ODI Career:	2003		
ODIs Played:	3		

ODI Batting
Innings:	2	Runs:	16
Highest Score:	9	Average:	8.00
No. 50s:	0	No. 100s:	0

ODI Bowling & Fielding
Wickets:	0	Runs:	88
Best Bowling:		Average:	0.00
5 WM:	0	Catches:	1
Stumpings:	0		

Debut V West Indies, Centurion 2003

JAVED, Tariq
Born:	June 12, 1949
Batting:	Right handed
Bowling:	Right arm leg-break

One Day Internationals
ODI Career:	1979		
ODIs Played:	3		

ODI Batting
Innings:	3	Runs:	15
Highest Score:	8	Average:	5.00
No. 50s:	0	No. 100s:	0

ODI Bowling & Fielding
Wickets:	0	Runs:	0
Best Bowling:		Average:	0.00
5 WM:	0	Catches:	0
Stumpings:	0		

Debut v Pakistan, Headingley 1979

JOSEPH, Davis
Born:	July 31, 1963
Batting:	Right handed
Bowling:	Right arm medium-fast

One Day Internationals
ODI Career: 2003
ODIs Played: 4

ODI Batting
Innings:	3	Runs:	13
Highest Score:	9*	Average:	0.00
No. 50s:	0	No. 100s:	0

ODI Bowling & Fielding
Wickets:	5	Runs:	170
Best Bowling:	2/42	Average:	34.00
5 WM:	0	Catches:	0
Stumpings:	0		

Debut V Bangladesh, Durban 2003

JYOTI, Sandeep
Born:	December 14, 1973
Batting:	Right handed
Bowling:	Right arm off-break

One Day Internationals
ODI Career: 2006
ODIs Played: 1

ODI Batting
Innings:	1	Runs:	17
Highest Score:	17	Average:	17.00
No. 50s:	0	No. 100s:	0

ODI Bowling & Fielding
Wickets:	0	Runs:	0
Best Bowling:		Average:	0.00
5 WM:	0	Catches:	0
Stumpings:	0		

Debut v Bermuda, Toronto, 2006

MARAJ, Ishwar
Born:	January 26, 1969
Batting:	Left handed
Bowling:	Right arm off-break

One Day Internationals
ODI Career: 2003
ODIs Played: 6

ODI Batting
Innings:	6	Runs:	98
Highest Score:	53*	Average:	19.60
No. 50s:	1	No. 100s:	0

ODI Bowling & Fielding
Wickets:	0	Runs:	22
Best Bowling:		Average:	0.00
5 WM:	0	Catches:	2
Stumpings:	0		

Debut v Bangladesh, Durban 2003

MARSHALL, Cecil
Born:	September 13, 1939
Batting:	Right handed
Bowling:	Right arm medium

One Day Internationals
ODI Career: 1979
ODIs Played: 2

ODI Batting
Innings:	2	Runs:	10
Highest Score:	8	Average:	5.00
No. 50s:	0	No. 100s:	0

ODI Bowling & Fielding
Wickets:	0	Runs:	0
Best Bowling:		Average:	0.00
5 WM:	0	Catches:	0
Stumpings:	0		

Debut v Pakistan, Headingley 1979

MAURICETTE, Bryan
Born:	September 4, 1946
Batting:	Right handed
	Wicket Keeper

One Day Internationals
ODI Career: 1979
ODIs Played: 3

ODI Batting
Innings:	3	Runs:	20
Highest Score:	15	Average:	6.66
No. 50s:	0	No. 100s:	0

ODI Bowling & Fielding
Wickets:	0	Runs:	0
Best Bowling:		Average:	0.00
5 WM:	0	Catches:	0
Stumpings:	0		

Debut v Pakistan, Headingley 1979

MAXWELL, Don
Born:	February 23, 1971
Batting:	Right handed
Bowling:	Right arm medium-fast

One Day Internationals
ODI Career: 2006
ODIs Played: 1

ODI Batting
Innings:	1	Runs:	12
Highest Score:	12	Average:	12.00
No. 50s:	0	No. 100s:	0

ODI Bowling & Fielding
Wickets:	0	Runs:	0
Best Bowling:		Average:	0.00
5 WM:	0	Catches:	0
Stumpings:	0		

Debut V Bermuda, Port of Spain 2006

OSINDE, Henry
Born:	October 17, 1978
Batting:	Right handed
Bowling:	Right arm medium-fast

One Day Internationals
ODI Career: 2006
ODIs Played: 2

ODI Batting
Innings:	2	Runs:	11
Highest Score:	11*	Average:	11.00
No. 50s:	0	No. 100s:	0

ODI Bowling & Fielding
Wickets:	2	Runs:	58
Best Bowling:	1/19	Average:	29.00
5 WM:	0	Catches:	0
Stumpings:	0		

Debut V Zimbabwe, Port of Spain 2006

PATEL, Ashish
Born: July 31, 1975
Batting: Right handed
Bowling: Right arm medium

One Day Internationals
ODI Career: 2003
ODIs Played: 2

ODI Batting
Innings:	1	Runs:	25
Highest Score:	25	Average:	25.00
No. 50s:	0	No. 100s:	0

ODI Bowling & Fielding
Wickets:	3	Runs:	73
Best Bowling:	3/41	Average:	24.33
5 WM:	0	Catches:	0
Stumpings:	0		

Debut V South Africa, East London 2003

PATEL, Jitendra
Born: November 26, 1945
Batting: Left handed
Bowling: Left arm off-break

One Day Internationals
ODI Career: 1979
ODIs Played: 3

ODI Batting
Innings:	3	Runs:	3
Highest Score:	2	Average:	1.00
No. 50s:	0	No. 100s:	0

ODI Bowling & Fielding
Wickets:	0	Runs:	47
Best Bowling:		Average:	0.00
5 WM:	0	Catches:	0
Stumpings:	0		

Debut v Pakistan, Headingley, 1979

SAMAD, Abdool
Born: May 3, 1979
Batting: Right handed
Bowling: Right arm off-break
Wicket Keeper

One Day Internationals
ODI Career: 2003
ODIs Played: 1

ODI Batting
Innings:	1	Runs:	12
Highest Score:	12	Average:	12.00
No. 50s:	0	No. 100s:	0

ODI Bowling & Fielding
Wickets:	0	Runs:	0
Best Bowling:		Average:	0.00
5 WM:	0	Catches:	0
Stumpings:	0		

Debut V New Zealand, Benoni 2003

SANDHER, Kevin
Born: July 16, 1980
Batting: Right handed
Bowling: Left arm off-break

One Day Internationals
ODI Career: 2006
ODIs Played: 2

ODI Batting
Innings:	2	Runs:	11
Highest Score:	9	Average:	11.00
No. 50s:	0	No. 100s:	0

ODI Bowling & Fielding
Wickets:	3	Runs:	76
Best Bowling:	2/32	Average:	25.33
5 WM:	0	Catches:	0
Stumpings:	0		

Debut V Zimbabwe, Port of Spain 2006

SATTAUR, Fazil
Born: April 6, 1965
Batting: Right handed
Wicket Keeper

One Day Internationals
ODI Career: 2003
ODIs Played: 3

ODI Batting
Innings:	3	Runs:	20
Highest Score:	13	Average:	6.66
No. 50s:	0	No. 100s:	0

ODI Bowling & Fielding
Wickets:	0	Runs:	0
Best Bowling:		Average:	0.00
5 WM:	0	Catches:	2
Stumpings:	0		

Debut V Bangladesh, Durban 2003

SEALY, Glenroy
Born: June 11, 1940
Batting: Right handed
Bowling: Right arm medium

One Day Internationals
ODI Career: 1979
ODIs Played: 3

ODI Batting
Innings:	3	Runs:	73
Highest Score:	45	Average:	24.33
No. 50s:	0	No. 100s:	0

ODI Bowling & Fielding
Wickets:	0	Runs:	21
Best Bowling:		Average:	0.00
5 WM:	0	Catches:	0
Stumpings:	0		

Debut v Pakistan, Headingley 1979

SEEBARAN, Barry
Born: September 12, 1972
Batting: Right handed
Bowling: Left arm off-break

One Day Internationals
ODI Career: 2003
ODIs Played: 4

ODI Batting
Innings:	3	Runs:	4
Highest Score:	4*	Average:	4.00
No. 50s:	0	No. 100s:	0

ODI Bowling & Fielding
Wickets:	1	Runs:	130
Best Bowling:	1/61	Average:	130.00
5 WM:	0	Catches:	1
Stumpings:	0		

Debut V Sri Lanka, Paarl 2003

SEERAJ, Surendra
Born: September 7, 1973
Batting: Right handed
Wicket Keeper

One Day Internationals
ODI Career: 2006
ODIs Played: 1

ODI Batting
Innings:	1	Runs:	13
Highest Score:	13*	Average:	13.00
No. 50s:	0	No. 100s:	0

ODI Bowling & Fielding
Wickets:	0	Runs:	0
Best Bowling:		Average:	0.00
5 WM:	0	Catches:	0
Stumpings:	0		

Debut v Bermuda, Toronto, 2006.

SORAINE, Durand
Born: September 11, 1983
Batting: Right handed
Bowling: Right arm medium

One Day Internationals
ODI Career: 2006
ODIs Played: 1

ODI Batting
Innings:	1	Runs:	5
Highest Score:	5	Average:	5.00
No. 50s:	0	No. 100s:	0

ODI Bowling & Fielding
Wickets:	0	Runs:	0
Best Bowling:		Average:	0.00
5 WM:	0	Catches:	0
Stumpings:	0		

Debut v Bermuda, Toronto, 2006

STEAD, Martin
Born: June 1, 1958
Batting: Right handed
Bowling: Right arm medium

One Day Internationals
ODI Career: 1979
ODIs Played: 2

ODI Batting
Innings:	2	Runs:	10
Highest Score:	10	Average:	5.00
No. 50s:	0	No. 100s:	0

ODI Bowling & Fielding
Wickets:	0	Runs:	24
Best Bowling:		Average:	0.00
5 WM:	0	Catches:	0
Stumpings:	0		

Debut V Pakistan, Headingley 1979

THURAISINGAM, Sanjayan
Born: September 11, 1969
Batting: Right handed
Bowling: Right arm medium-fast

One Day Internationals
ODI Career: 2003-06
ODIs Played: 5

ODI Batting
Innings:	5	Runs:	37
Highest Score:	13	Average:	7.40
No. 50s:	0	No. 100s:	0

ODI Bowling & Fielding
Wickets:	5	Runs:	169
Best Bowling:	2/53	Average:	33.80
5 WM:	0	Catches:	1
Stumpings:	0		

Debut V Bangladesh, Durban 2003

VALENTINE, John
Born: September 20, 1954
Batting: Left handed
Bowling: Left arm medium

One Day Internationals
ODI Career: 1979
ODIs Played: 3

ODI Batting
Innings:	2	Runs:	3
Highest Score:	3*	Average:	0.00
No. 50s:	0	No. 100s:	0

ODI Bowling & Fielding
Wickets:	3	Runs:	66
Best Bowling:	1/18	Average:	22.00
5 WM:	0	Catches:	1
Stumpings:	0		

Debut V Pakistan, Headingley 1979

VAUGHAN, John
Born: June 8, 1945
Batting: Right handed
Bowling: Right arm medium-fast

One Day Internationals
ODI Career: 1979
ODIs Played: 3

ODI Batting
Innings:	3	Runs:	30
Highest Score:	29	Average:	10.00
No. 50s:	0	No. 100s:	0

ODI Bowling & Fielding
Wickets:	0	Runs:	36
Best Bowling:		Average:	0.00
5 WM:	0	Catches:	0
Stumpings:	0		

Debut V Pakistan, Headingley 1979

WELSH, Steven Richard
Born: March 16, 1974
Batting: Right handed
Bowling: Right arm medium-fast

One Day Internationals
ODI Career: 2006
ODIs Played: 1

ODI Batting
Innings:	1	Runs:	2
Highest Score:	2	Average:	2.00
No. 50s:	0	No. 100s:	0

ODI Bowling & Fielding
Wickets:	0	Runs:	68
Best Bowling:		Average:	0.00
5 WM:	0	Catches:	0
Stumpings:	0		

Debut v Bermuda, Toronto, 2006. Born in Australia.

East Africa

ALI, Frasat
Born: July 31, 1949
Batting: Right handed
Bowling: Right arm medium

One Day Internationals
ODI Career: 1975
ODIs Played: 3

ODI Batting
Innings:	3	Runs:	57
Highest Score:	45	Average:	19.00
No. 50s:	0	No. 100s:	0

ODI Bowling & Fielding
Wickets:	0	Runs:	107
Best Bowling:		Average:	0.00
5 WM:	0	Catches:	0
Stumpings:	0		

Debut V New Zealand, Birmingham, 1975

ALI, Zulfiqar
Batting: Right handed
Bowling: Right arm medium

One Day Internationals
ODI Career: 1975
ODIs Played: 3

ODI Batting
Innings:	3	Runs:	39
Highest Score:	30	Average:	19.50
No. 50s:	0	No. 100s:	0

ODI Bowling & Fielding
Wickets:	4	Runs:	166
Best Bowling:	3/63	Average:	41.50
5 WM:	0	Catches:	1
Stumpings:	0		

Debut v New Zealand, Birmingham, 1975

BADAT, Yunus
Batting: Right handed

One Day Internationals
ODI Career: 1975
ODIs Played: 2

ODI Batting
Innings:	2	Runs:	1
Highest Score:	1	Average:	0.50
No. 50s:	0	No. 100s:	0

ODI Bowling & Fielding
Wickets:	0	Runs:	0
Best Bowling:		Average:	0.00
5 WM:	0	Catches:	0
Stumpings:	0		

Debut V India, Headingley, 1975

McLEOD, Hamish
Batting: Right handed

One Day Internationals
ODI Career: 1975
ODIs Played: 2

ODI Batting
Innings:	2	Runs:	5
Highest Score:	5	Average:	2.50
No. 50s:	0	No. 100s:	0

ODI Bowling & Fielding
Wickets:	0	Runs:	0
Best Bowling:		Average:	0.00
5 WM:	0	Catches:	0
Stumpings:	0		

Debut V New Zealand, Birmingham, 1975

MEHTA, Praful
Batting: Left handed
Wicket Keeper

One Day Internationals
ODI Career: 1975
ODIs Played: 1

ODI Batting
Innings:	1	Runs:	12
Highest Score:	12	Average:	12.00
No. 50s:	0	No. 100s:	0

ODI Bowling & Fielding
Wickets:	0	Runs:	0
Best Bowling:		Average:	0.00
5 WM:	0	Catches:	0
Stumpings:	0		

Debut V India, Headingley, 1975

NAGENDA, John
Born: April 25, 1938
Batting: Right handed
Bowling: Right arm medium-fast

One Day Internationals
ODI Career: 1975
ODIs Played: 1

ODI Batting
Innings:	0	Runs:	0
Highest Score:	0	Average:	0.00
No. 50s:	0	No. 100s:	0

ODI Bowling & Fielding
Wickets:	1	Runs:	50
Best Bowling:	1/50	Average:	50.00
5 WM:	0	Catches:	0
Stumpings:	0		

Debut V New Zealand, Edgbaston, 1975

NANA, P
Batting: Right handed
Bowling: Left arm slow

One Day Internationals
ODI Career: 1975
ODIs Played: 3

ODI Batting
Innings:	3	Runs:	9
Highest Score:	8*	Average:	9.00
No. 50s:	0	No. 100s:	0

The Encyclopedia of International Cricketers - East Africa

ODI Bowling & Fielding
Wickets:	1	Runs:	116
Best Bowling:	1/34	Average:	116.00
5 WM:	0	Catches:	2
Stumpings:	0		

Debut V New Zealand, Birmingham, 1975

PRINGLE, Don
Born:	May 1, 1932
Batting:	Right handed

One Day Internationals
ODI Career:	1975		
ODIs Played:	2		

ODI Batting
Innings:	2	Runs:	5
Highest Score:	3	Average:	2.50
No. 50s:	0	No. 100s:	0

ODI Bowling & Fielding
Wickets:	0	Runs:	55
Best Bowling:		Average:	0.00
5 WM:	0	Catches:	0
Stumpings:	0		

Debut V India, Headingley, 1975

QUARAISHY, Mehmood
Born:	February 4, 1942
Batting:	Right handed

One Day Internationals
ODI Career:	1975		
ODIs Played:	3		

ODI Batting
Innings:	3	Runs:	41
Highest Score:	19	Average:	20.50
No. 50s:	0	No. 100s:	0

ODI Bowling & Fielding
Wickets:	3	Runs:	94
Best Bowling:	2/55	Average:	31.33
5 WM:	0	Catches:	0
Stumpings:	0		

Debut V New Zealand, Birmingham, 1975

SETHI, Ramesh
Born:	September 4, 1941
Batting:	Right handed
Bowling:	Right arm off-break

One Day Internationals
ODI Career:	1975		
ODIs Played:	3		

ODI Batting
Innings:	3	Runs:	54
Highest Score:	30	Average:	18.00
No. 50s:	0	No. 100s:	0

ODI Bowling & Fielding
Wickets:	1	Runs:	100
Best Bowling:	1/51	Average:	100.00
5 WM:	0	Catches:	1
Stumpings:	0		

Debut V New Zealand, Birmingham, 1975

SHAH, Harilal
Born:	April 14, 1943
Batting:	Right handed
Bowling:	Right arm medium

One Day Internationals
ODI Career:	1975		
ODIs Played:	3		

ODI Batting
Innings:	3	Runs:	6
Highest Score:	6	Average:	2.00
No. 50s:	0	No. 100s:	0

ODI Bowling & Fielding
Wickets:	0	Runs:	0
Best Bowling:		Average:	0.00
5 WM:	0	Catches:	0
Stumpings:	0		

Debut V New Zealand, Birmingham, 1975

SHAH, Jawahir
Batting:	Right handed

One Day Internationals
ODI Career:	1975		
ODIs Played:	3		

ODI Batting
Innings:	3	Runs:	46
Highest Score:	37	Average:	15.33
No. 50s:	0	No. 100s:	0

ODI Bowling & Fielding
Wickets:	0	Runs:	0
Best Bowling:		Average:	0.00
5 WM:	0	Catches:	0
Stumpings:	0		

Debut V New Zealand, Birmingham, 1975

SUMAR, Shiraz
Batting:	Right handed

One Day Internationals
ODI Career:	1975		
ODIs Played:	1		

ODI Batting
Innings:	1	Runs:	4
Highest Score:	4	Average:	4.00
No. 50s:	0	No. 100s:	0

ODI Bowling & Fielding
Wickets:	0	Runs:	0
Best Bowling:		Average:	0.00
5 WM:	0	Catches:	0
Stumpings:	0		

Debut V New Zealand, Birmingham, 1975

WALUSIMBI, Samuel
Batting:	Right handed
Bowling:	Left arm medium

One Day Internationals
ODI Career:	1975		
ODIs Played:	3		

ODI Batting
Innings:	3	Runs:	38
Highest Score:	16	Average:	12.66
No. 50s:	0	No. 100s:	0

ODI Bowling & Fielding
Wickets:	0	Runs:	0
Best Bowling:		Average:	0.00
5 WM:	0	Catches:	0
Stumpings:	0		

Debut V New Zealand, Birmingham, 1975

Holland

APONSO, Goniamalimage John Anthony Flavian
Born: October 28, 1952
Batting: Left handed
Bowling: Right arm off-break

One Day Internationals
ODI Career: 1996
ODIs Played: 5

ODI Batting
Innings:	4	Runs:	120
Highest Score:	58	Average:	30.00
No. 50s:	1	No. 100s:	0

ODI Bowling & Fielding
Wickets:	2	Runs:	257
Best Bowling:	1/57	Average:	128.50
5 WM:	0	Catches:	0
Stumpings:	0		

Debut v New Zealand, Vadodara, 1996.

BAKKER, Paul-Jan
Born: August 19, 1957
Batting: Right handed
Bowling: Right arm medium-fast

One Day Internationals
ODI Career: 1996
ODIs Played: 5

ODI Batting
Innings:	4	Runs:	1
Highest Score:	1*	Average:	1.00
No. 50s:	0	No. 100s:	0

ODI Bowling & Fielding
Wickets:	3	Runs:	215
Best Bowling:	2/51	Average:	71.66
5 WM:	0	Catches:	0
Stumpings:	0		

Debut v New Zealand, Vadodara, 1996

BORREN, Peter William
Born: August 21, 1983
Batting: Right handed
Bowling: Right arm medium

One Day Internationals
ODI Career: 2006
ODIs Played: 2

ODI Batting
Innings:	2	Runs:	36
Highest Score:	34	Average:	18.00
No. 50s:	0	No. 100s:	0

ODI Bowling & Fielding
Wickets:	2	Runs:	138
Best Bowling:	1/44	Average:	69.00
5 WM:	0	Catches:	1
Stumpings:	0		

Debut v Sri Lanka, Amstelveen, 2006. Born in Christchurch, New Zealand.

CANTRELL, Peter
Born: October 28, 1962
Batting: Right handed
Bowling: Right arm off-break

One Day Internationals
ODI Career: 1996
ODIs Played: 5

ODI Batting
Innings:	5	Runs:	160
Highest Score:	47	Average:	32.00
No. 50s:	0	No. 100s:	0

ODI Bowling & Fielding
Wickets:	3	Runs:	170
Best Bowling:	1/18	Average:	56.66
5 WM:	0	Catches:	0
Stumpings:	0		

Debut v New Zealand, Vadodara, 1996. Australian born and raised who appeared as a substitute fielder for Australia during the 'Gabba Test of 1990. Cantrell represented his home State, Queensland in Sheffield Shield competition.

CLARKE, Nolan
Born: June 22, 1948
Batting: Right handed

One Day Internationals
ODI Career: 1996
ODIs Played: 5

ODI Batting
Innings:	5	Runs:	50
Highest Score:	32	Average:	10.00
No. 50s:	0	No. 100s:	0

ODI Bowling & Fielding
Wickets:	0	Runs:	0
Best Bowling:		Average:	0.00
5 WM:	0	Catches:	3
Stumpings:	0		

Debut v New Zealand, Vadodara, 1996

DE GROOTH, Tom Nico
Born: May 15, 1979
Batting: Right handed
Bowling: Right arm off-break

One Day Internationals
ODI Career: 2006
ODIs Played: 1

ODI Batting
Innings:	1	Runs:	32
Highest Score:	32	Average:	32.00
No. 50s:	0	No. 100s:	0

ODI Bowling & Fielding
Wickets:	0	Runs:	0
Best Bowling:		Average:	0.00
5 WM:	0	Catches:	0
Stumpings:	0		

Debut v Scotland, Ayr, 2006.

DE LEEDE, Tim
Born: January 25, 1968
Batting: Right handed
Bowling: Right arm medium

One Day Internationals
ODI Career: 1996-06
ODIs Played: 15

ODI Batting
Innings:	15	Runs:	297
Highest Score:	58*	Average:	21.21
No. 50s:	2	No. 100s:	0

ODI Bowling & Fielding
Wickets:	12	Runs:	556
Best Bowling:	4/35	Average:	46.33
5 WM:	0	Catches:	5
Stumpings:	0		

Debut v New Zealand, Vadodara, 1996

ESMEIJER, Jacob-Jan
Born: May 28, 1972
Batting: Right handed
Bowling: Left arm off-break

One Day Internationals
ODI Career: 2002-03
ODIs Played: 6

ODI Batting
Innings:	5	Runs:	10
Highest Score:	7	Average:	2.50
No. 50s:	0	No. 100s:	0

ODI Bowling & Fielding
Wickets:	0	Runs:	208
Best Bowling:		Average:	0.00
5 WM:	0	Catches:	3
Stumpings:	0		

Debut v Sri Lanka, Colombo, 2002

GOUKA, Eric
Born: January 29, 1970
Batting: Right handed
Bowling: Right arm medium

One Day Internationals
ODI Career: 1996
ODIs Played: 3

ODI Batting
Innings:	2	Runs:	19
Highest Score:	19	Average:	19.00
No. 50s:	0	No. 100s:	0

ODI Bowling & Fielding
Wickets:	1	Runs:	51
Best Bowling:	1/32	Average:	51.00
5 WM:	0	Catches:	0
Stumpings:	0		

Debut v New Zealand, Vadodara, 1996

GRANDIA, Victor D
Born: January 10, 1979
Batting: Right handed
Bowling: Right arm medium

One Day Internationals
ODI Career: 2002
ODIs Played: 1

ODI Batting
Innings:	1	Runs:	0
Highest Score:	0	Average:	0.00
No. 50s:	0	No. 100s:	0

ODI Bowling & Fielding
Wickets:	1	Runs:	40
Best Bowling:	1/40	Average:	40.00
5 WM:	0	Catches:	0
Stumpings:	0		

Debut v Sri Lanka, Colombo, 2002

JANSEN, Floris
Born: June 10, 1962
Batting: Right handed
Bowling: Right arm medium

One Day Internationals
ODI Career: 1996
ODIs Played: 2

ODI Batting
Innings:	0	Runs:	0
Highest Score:	0	Average:	0.00
No. 50s:	0	No. 100s:	0

ODI Bowling & Fielding
Wickets:	1	Runs:	62
Best Bowling:	1/40	Average:	62.00
5 WM:	0	Catches:	1
Stumpings:	0		

Debut v England, Peshawar, 1996

KASHIF, Mohammad
Born: December 3, 1984
Batting: Right handed
Bowling: Left arm off-break

One Day Internationals
ODI Career: 2006
ODIs Played: 1

ODI Batting
Innings:	1	Runs:	0
Highest Score:	0	Average:	0.00
No. 50s:	0	No. 100s:	0

ODI Bowling & Fielding
Wickets:	2	Runs:	79
Best Bowling:	2/79	Average:	39.50
5 WM:	0	Catches:	0
Stumpings:	0		

Debut v Sri Lanka, Amstelveen, 2006

KERVEZEE, Alexei Nicolaas
Born: September 11, 1989
Batting: Right handed
Bowling: Right arm off-break

One Day Internationals
ODI Career: 2006
ODIs Played: 2

ODI Batting
Innings:	2	Runs:	65
Highest Score:	47	Average:	32.50
No. 50s:	0	No. 100s:	0

ODI Bowling & Fielding
Wickets:	0	Runs:	0
Best Bowling:		Average:	0.00
5 WM:	0	Catches:	0
Stumpings:	0		

Debut v Sri Lanka, Amstelveen, 2006

KLOPPENBURG, Jan Feiko
Born: June 19, 1974
Batting: Right handed
Bowling: Right arm medium

One Day Internationals
ODI Career: 2002-03
ODIs Played: 6

ODI Batting
Innings:	6	Runs:	165
Highest Score:	121	Average:	27.50
No. 50s:	0	No. 100s:	1

ODI Bowling & Fielding
Wickets:	8	Runs:	191
Best Bowling:	4/42	Average:	23.87
5 WM:	0	Catches:	1
Stumpings:	0		

Debut v Pakistan, Colombo, 2002

LEFEBVRE, Roland
Born: February 7, 1963
Batting: Right handed
Bowling: Right arm medium

One Day Internationals
ODI Career: 1996-03
ODIs Played: 11

ODI Batting
Innings:	11	Runs:	171
Highest Score:	45	Average:	28.50
No. 50s:	0	No. 100s:	0

ODI Bowling & Fielding
Wickets:	9	Runs:	346
Best Bowling:	2/38	Average:	38.44
5 WM:	0	Catches:	4
Stumpings:	0		

Debut v New Zealand, Vadodara, 1996

LUBBERS, Steven
Born: March 24, 1953
Batting: Right handed
Bowling: Right arm off-break

One Day Internationals
ODI Career: 1996
ODIs Played: 4

ODI Batting
Innings:	4	Runs:	24
Highest Score:	9	Average:	8.00
No. 50s:	0	No. 100s:	0

ODI Bowling & Fielding
Wickets:	5	Runs:	187
Best Bowling:	3/48	Average:	37.40
5 WM:	0	Catches:	1
Stumpings:	0		

Debut v New Zealand, Vadodara, 1996

MOL, Hendrik-Jan
Born: March 29, 1977
Batting: Left handed
Bowling: Left arm medium

One Day Internationals
ODI Career: 2002-03
ODIs Played: 5

ODI Batting
Innings:	4	Runs:	38
Highest Score:	23	Average:	9.50
No. 50s:	0	No. 100s:	0

ODI Bowling & Fielding
Wickets:	2	Runs:	89
Best Bowling:	1/24	Average:	44.50
5 WM:	0	Catches:	2
Stumpings:	0		

Debut v Pakistan, Colombo, 2002

RAJA, Adeel K
Born: August 15, 1980
Batting: Right handed
Bowling: Right arm off-break

One Day Internationals
ODI Career: 2002-03
ODIs Played: 5

ODI Batting
Innings:	4	Runs:	9
Highest Score:	5	Average:	3.00
No. 50s:	0	No. 100s:	0

ODI Bowling & Fielding
Wickets:	8	Runs:	204
Best Bowling:	4/42	Average:	25.50
5 WM:	0	Catches:	1
Stumpings:	0		

Debut v Sri Lanka, Colombo, 2002

REEKERS, Darron John
Born: May 26, 1973
Batting: Right handed
Bowling: Right arm medium

One Day Internationals
ODI Career: 2006
ODIs Played: 2

ODI Batting
Innings:	2	Runs:	84
Highest Score:	45	Average:	42.00
No. 50s:	0	No. 100s:	0

ODI Bowling & Fielding
Wickets:	4	Runs:	136
Best Bowling:	3/54	Average:	34.00
5 WM:	0	Catches:	1
Stumpings:	0		

Debut v Sri Lanka, Amstelveen, 2006. Born in New Zealand.

SCHEWE, Marcel
Born: May 10, 1969
Batting: Right handed
Wicket Keeper

One Day Internationals
ODI Career: 1996
ODIs Played: 5

ODI Batting
Innings:	4	Runs:	49
Highest Score:	20	Average:	16.33
No. 50s:	0	No. 100s:	0

ODI Bowling & Fielding
Wickets:	0	Runs:	0
Best Bowling:		Average:	0.00
5 WM:	0	Catches:	2
Stumpings:	1		

Debut v New Zealand, Vadodara, 1996

SCHIFERLI, Edgar
Born: May 17, 1976
Batting: Right handed
Bowling: Right arm medium-fast

One Day Internationals
ODI Career: 2002-03
ODIs Played: 8

ODI Batting
Innings:	8	Runs:	90
Highest Score:	22	Average:	11.25
No. 50s:	0	No. 100s:	0

ODI Bowling & Fielding
Wickets:	4	Runs:	327
Best Bowling:	2/43	Average:	81.75
5 WM:	0	Catches:	1
Stumpings:	0		

Debut v Sri Lanka, Colombo, 2002

SCHOLTE, Reinout Hans
Born: August 10, 1967
Batting: Right handed, Wicket Keeper

One Day Internationals
ODI Career: 2002-03
ODIs Played: 5

ODI Batting
Innings:	5	Runs:	39
Highest Score:	12	Average:	7.80
No. 50s:	0	No. 100s:	0

ODI Bowling & Fielding
Wickets:	0	Runs:	0
Best Bowling:		Average:	0.00
5 WM:	0	Catches:	0
Stumpings:	0		

Debut v Sri Lanka, Colombo, 2002

SEELAAR, Pieter Marinus
Born: July 2, 1987
Batting: Right handed
Bowling: Left arm off-break

One Day Internationals
ODI Career: 2006
ODIs Played: 2

ODI Batting
Innings:	2	Runs:	1
Highest Score:	1*	Average:	1.00
No. 50s:	0	No. 100s:	0

ODI Bowling & Fielding
Wickets:	0	Runs:	50
Best Bowling:		Average:	0.00
5 WM:	0	Catches:	1
Stumpings:	0		

Debut v Sri Lanka, Amstelveen, 2006.

SMITS, Jeroen
Born: June 21, 1972
Batting: Right handed, Wicket Keeper

One Day Internationals
ODI Career: 2003-06
ODIs Played: 8

ODI Batting
Innings:	7	Runs:	59
Highest Score:	26	Average:	14.75
No. 50s:	0	No. 100s:	0

ODI Bowling & Fielding
Wickets:	0	Runs:	0
Best Bowling:		Average:	0.00
5 WM:	0	Catches:	5
Stumpings:	1		

Debut v India, Paarl, 2003

STATHAM, Nick A
Born: March 15, 1975
Batting: Right handed
Bowling: Right arm off-break

One Day Internationals
ODI Career: 2003
ODIs Played: 2

ODI Batting
Innings:	2	Runs:	7
Highest Score:	7	Average:	3.50
No. 50s:	0	No. 100s:	0

ODI Bowling & Fielding
Wickets:	0	Runs:	0
Best Bowling:		Average:	0.00
5 WM:	0	Catches:	0
Stumpings:	0		

Debut v England, East London, 2003

STELLING, William Frederick
Born: June 30, 1969
Batting: Right handed
Bowling: Right arm medium-fast

One Day Internationals
ODI Career: 2006
ODIs Played: 2

ODI Batting
Innings:	2	Runs:	41
Highest Score:	28	Average:	41.00
No. 50s:	0	No. 100s:	0

ODI Bowling & Fielding
Wickets:	4	Runs:	168
Best Bowling:	2/77	Average:	42.00
5 WM:	0	Catches:	2
Stumpings:	0		

Debut v Sri Lanka, Amstelveen, 2006

SZWARCZYNSKI, Eric Stefan
Born: February 13, 1983
Batting: Right handed

One Day Internationals
ODI Career: 2006
ODIs Played: 1

ODI Batting
Innings:	1	Runs:	10
Highest Score:	10	Average:	10.00
No. 50s:	0	No. 100s:	0

ODI Bowling & Fielding
Wickets:	0	Runs:	0
Best Bowling:		Average:	0.00
5 WM:	0	Catches:	0
Stumpings:	0		

Debut v Sri Lanka, Amstelveen, 2006

TEN DOESCHATE, Ryan Neil
Born: June 30, 1980
Batting: Right handed
Bowling: Right arm medium-fast

ODI Career: 2006
ODIs Played: 2

ODI Batting
Innings:	2	Runs:	95
Highest Score:	56*	Average:	95.00
No. 50s:	1	No. 100s:	0

ODI Bowling & Fielding
Wickets:	3	Runs:	86
Best Bowling:	2/51	Average:	28.66
5 WM:	0	Catches:	0
Stumpings:	0		

Debut v Sri Lanka, Amstelveen, 2006

VAN BUNGE, Daan Lodewjk Samuel

Born: October 19, 1982
Batting: Right handed
Bowling: Right arm slow

One Day Internationals
ODI Career: 2002-06
ODIs Played: 10

ODI Batting
Innings:	9	Runs:	189
Highest Score:	62	Average:	21.00
No. 50s:	1	No. 100s:	0

ODI Bowling & Fielding
Wickets:	5	Runs:	85
Best Bowling:	3/16	Average:	17.00
5 WM:	0	Catches:	2
Stumpings:	0		

Debut v Sri Lanka, Colombo, 2002

VAN NOORTWIJK, Klaas-Jan

Born: July 10, 1970
Batting: Right handed
Bowling: Right arm medium

One Day Internationals
ODI Career: 1996-03
ODIs Played: 9

ODI Batting
Innings:	9	Runs:	322
Highest Score:	134*	Average:	46.00
No. 50s:	1	No. 100s:	1

ODI Bowling & Fielding
Wickets:	0	Runs:	0
Best Bowling:		Average:	0.00
5 WM:	0	Catches:	0
Stumpings:	0		

Debut v New Zealand, Vadodara, 1996

VAN OOSTEROM, Robert Frank

Born: October 16, 1968
Batting: Right handed

One Day Internationals
ODI Career: 1996-02
ODIs Played: 3

ODI Batting
Innings:	3	Runs:	7
Highest Score:	5*	Average:	7.00
No. 50s:	0	No. 100s:	0

ODI Bowling & Fielding
Wickets:	0	Runs:	0
Best Bowling:		Average:	0.00
5 WM:	0	Catches:	2
Stumpings:	0		

Debut v United Arab Emirates, Lahore, 1996

VAN TROOST, Lucas Petrus

Born: December 28, 1969
Batting: Left handed
Bowling: Left arm medium

One Day Internationals
ODI Career: 2002-06
ODIs Played: 10

ODI Batting
Innings:	10	Runs:	155
Highest Score:	40	Average:	17.22
No. 50s:	0	No. 100s:	0

ODI Bowling & Fielding
Wickets:	1	Runs:	123
Best Bowling:	1/42	Average:	123.00
5 WM:	0	Catches:	1
Stumpings:	0		

Debut v Sri Lanka, Colombo, 2002

ZUIDERENT, Bas

Born: March 3, 1977
Batting: Right handed
Bowling: Right arm medium

One Day Internationals
ODI Career: 1996-06
ODIs Played: 15

ODI Batting
Innings:	15	Runs:	164
Highest Score:	54	Average:	1,171.00
No. 50s:	1	No. 100s:	0

ODI Bowling & Fielding
Wickets:	0	Runs:	0
Best Bowling:		Average:	0.00
5 WM:	0	Catches:	11
Stumpings:	0		

Debut v New Zealand, Vadodara, 1996

Ireland

BOTHA, Andre
Born:	September 12, 1975
Batting:	Left handed
Bowling:	Right arm medium

One Day Internationals
ODI Career:	2006
ODIs Played:	1

ODI Batting
Innings:	1	Runs:	52
Highest Score:	52	Average:	52.00
No. 50s:	1	No. 100s:	0

ODI Bowling & Fielding
Wickets:	0	Runs:	0
Best Bowling:		Average:	0.00
5 WM:	0	Catches:	1
Stumpings:	0		

Debut V England, Belfast 2006

BRAY, Jeremy
Born:	November 30, 1973
Batting:	Left handed
	Wicket Keeper

One Day Internationals
ODI Career:	2006
ODIs Played:	1

ODI Batting
Innings:	1	Runs:	22
Highest Score:	22	Average:	22.00
No. 50s:	0	No. 100s:	0

ODI Bowling & Fielding
Wickets:	0	Runs:	0
Best Bowling:		Average:	0.00
5 WM:	0	Catches:	0
Stumpings:	0		

Debut V England, Belfast 2006

GILLESPIE, Peter
Born:	May 11, 1974
Batting:	Right handed
Bowling:	Right arm medium

One Day Internationals
ODI Career:	2006
ODIs Played:	1

ODI Batting
Innings:	1	Runs:	0
Highest Score:	0	Average:	0.00
No. 50s:	0	No. 100s:	0

ODI Bowling & Fielding
Wickets:	0	Runs:	0
Best Bowling:		Average:	0.00
5 WM:	0	Catches:	0
Stumpings:	0		

Debut V England, Belfast 2006

JOHNSTON, Trent
Born:	April 29, 1974
Batting:	Right handed
Bowling:	Right arm medium-fast

One Day Internationals
ODI Career:	2006
ODIs Played:	1

ODI Batting
Innings:	1	Runs:	5
Highest Score:	5	Average:	5.00
No. 50s:	0	No. 100s:	0

ODI Bowling & Fielding
Wickets:	0	Runs:	59
Best Bowling:		Average:	0.00
5 WM:	0	Catches:	1
Stumpings:	0		

Debut V England, Belfast 2006

JOYCE, Dominick
Born:	June 14, 1981
Batting:	Right handed

One Day Internationals
ODI Career:	2006
ODIs Played:	1

ODI Batting
Innings:	1	Runs:	0
Highest Score:	0	Average:	0.00
No. 50s:	0	No. 100s:	0

ODI Bowling & Fielding
Wickets:	0	Runs:	0
Best Bowling:		Average:	0.00
5 WM:	0	Catches:	1
Stumpings:	0		

Debut V England, Belfast 2006

LANGFORD-SMITH, Dave
Born:	December 7, 1976
Batting:	Right handed
Bowling:	Right arm medium-fast

One Day Internationals
ODI Career:	2006
ODIs Played:	1

ODI Batting
Innings:	1	Runs:	12
Highest Score:	12	Average:	12.00
No. 50s:	0	No. 100s:	0

ODI Bowling & Fielding
Wickets:	3	Runs:	63
Best Bowling:	3/63	Average:	21.00
5 WM:	0	Catches:	0
Stumpings:	0		

Debut V England, Belfast 2006

McCALLAN, Kyle
Born: August 27, 1975
Batting: Right handed
Bowling: Right arm off-break

One Day Internationals
ODI Career: 2006
ODIs Played: 1

ODI Batting
Innings:	1	Runs:	24
Highest Score:	24	Average:	24.00
No. 50s:	0	No. 100s:	0

ODI Bowling & Fielding
Wickets:	0	Runs:	26
Best Bowling:		Average:	0.00
5 WM:	0	Catches:	0
Stumpings:	0		

Debut V England, Belfast 2006

MOONEY, John
Born: February 10, 1982
Batting: Left handed
Bowling: Right arm medium

One Day Internationals
ODI Career: 2006
ODIs Played: 1

ODI Batting
Innings:	1	Runs:	30
Highest Score:	30*	Average:	0.00
No. 50s:	0	No. 100s:	0

ODI Bowling & Fielding
Wickets:	3	Runs:	79
Best Bowling:	3/79	Average:	26.33
5 WM:	0	Catches:	0
Stumpings:	0		

Debut V England, Belfast 2006

MOONEY, Paul
Born: October 15, 1976
Batting: Right handed
Bowling: Right arm medium

One Day Internationals
ODI Career: 2006
ODIs Played: 1

ODI Batting
Innings:	1	Runs:	11
Highest Score:	11*	Average:	0.00
No. 50s:	0	No. 100s:	0

ODI Bowling & Fielding
Wickets:	0	Runs:	17
Best Bowling:		Average:	0.00
5 WM:	0	Catches:	2
Stumpings:	0		

Debut V England, Belfast 2006

MORGAN, Eoin Joseph Gerard
Born: September 10, 1986
Batting: Left handed
Bowling: Right arm medium
Wicket Keeper

One Day Internationals
ODI Career: 2006
ODIs Played: 1

ODI Batting
Innings:	1	Runs:	99
Highest Score:	99	Average:	99.00
No. 50s:	1	No. 100s:	0

ODI Bowling & Fielding
Wickets:	0	Runs:	0
Best Bowling:		Average:	0.00
5 WM:	0	Catches:	0
Stumpings:	0		

Debut v Scotland, Ayr, 2006.

O'BRIEN, Kevin J
Born: March 4, 1984
Batting: Right handed
Bowling: Right arm medium-fast

One Day Internationals
ODI Career: 2006
ODIs Played: 1

ODI Batting
Innings:	1	Runs:	35
Highest Score:	35	Average:	35.00
No. 50s:	0	No. 100s:	0

ODI Bowling & Fielding
Wickets:	1	Runs:	47
Best Bowling:	1/47	Average:	47.00
5 WM:	0	Catches:	2
Stumpings:	0		

Debut v England, Belfast 2006

O'BRIEN, Niall John
Born: November 8, 1981
Batting: Left handed
Wicket Keeper

One Day Internationals
ODI Career: 2006
ODIs Played: 2

ODI Batting
Innings:	2	Runs:	85
Highest Score:	53	Average:	42.50
No. 50s:	1	No. 100s:	0

ODI Bowling & Fielding
Wickets:	0	Runs:	0
Best Bowling:		Average:	0.00
5 WM:	0	Catches:	3
Stumpings:	1		

Debut v Scotland, Ayr, 2006.

PORTERFIELD, William Thomas Stuart
Born: September 6, 1984
Batting: Left handed

One Day Internationals
ODI Career: 2006
ODIs Played: 2

ODI Batting
Innings:	2	Runs:	59
Highest Score:	48	Average:	29.50
No. 50s:	0	No. 100s:	0

ODI Bowling & Fielding
Wickets:	0	Runs:	0
Best Bowling:		Average:	0.00
5 WM:	0	Catches:	0
Stumpings:	0		

Debut v Scotland, Ayr, 2006.

WHITE, Andrew

Born: July 3, 1980
Batting: Right handed
Bowling: Right arm off-break

One Day Internationals

ODI Career: 2006
ODIs Played: 1

ODI Batting
Innings:	1	**Runs:**	40
Highest Score:	40	**Average:**	40.00
No. 50s:	0	**No. 100s:**	0

ODI Bowling & Fielding
Wickets:	0	**Runs:**	0
Best Bowling:		**Average:**	0.00
5 WM:	0	**Catches:**	0
Stumpings:	0		

Debut V England, Belfast 2006

Kenya

AGA, Rageb Gul
Born: July 10, 1984
Batting: Right handed
Bowling: Right arm medium-fast

One Day Internationals
ODI Career: 2004
ODIs Played: 2

ODI Batting
Innings:	2	Runs:	1
Highest Score:	1	Average:	0.50
No. 50s:	0	No. 100s:	0

ODI Bowling & Fielding
Wickets:	2	Runs:	87
Best Bowling:	2/17	Average:	43.50
5 WM:	0	Catches:	0
Stumpings:	0		

Debut v India, Southhampton, 2004

ALI, Rajab Wazir
Born: November 19, 1965
Batting: Right handed
Bowling: Right arm medium-fast

One Day Internationals
ODI Career: 1996-97
ODIs Played: 9

ODI Batting
Innings:	3	Runs:	7
Highest Score:	6*	Average:	2.00
No. 50s:	0	No. 100s:	0

ODI Bowling & Fielding
Wickets:	11	Runs:	255
Best Bowling:	3/17	Average:	23.18
5 WM:	0	Catches:	1
Stumpings:	0		

Debut v India, Cuttack, 1996

ANGARA, Joseph Oduol
Born: November 8, 1971
Batting: Right handed
Bowling: Right arm medium-fast

One Day Internationals
ODI Career: 1997-03
ODIs Played: 17

ODI Batting
Innings:	17	Runs:	23
Highest Score:	6	Average:	3.83
No. 50s:	0	No. 100s:	0

ODI Bowling & Fielding
Wickets:	14	Runs:	569
Best Bowling:	3/30	Average:	40.64
5 WM:	0	Catches:	2
Stumpings:	0		

Debut v Zimbabwe, Nairobi, 1997

CHUDASAMA, Dipak Nanalal
Born: May 20, 1963
Batting: Right handed

One Day Internationals
ODI Career: 1996-99
ODIs Played: 20

ODI Batting
Innings:	19	Runs:	434
Highest Score:	122	Average:	22.84
No. 50s:	1	No. 100s:	1

ODI Bowling & Fielding
Wickets:	0	Runs:	0
Best Bowling:		Average:	0.00
5 WM:	0	Catches:	0
Stumpings:	0		

Debut v India, Cuttack, 1996

GUPTA, Sandeep Kumar
Born: April 7, 1967
Batting: Right handed
Wicket Keeper

One Day Internationals
ODI Career: 1996-01
ODIs Played: 10

ODI Batting
Innings:	10	Runs:	1
Highest Score:	41	Average:	13.44
No. 50s:	0	No. 100s:	0

ODI Bowling & Fielding
Wickets:	0	Runs:	0
Best Bowling:		Average:	0.00
5 WM:	0	Catches:	0
Stumpings:	0		

Debut v Sri Lanka, Nairobi, 1996

IQBAL, I Tariq
Born: April 3, 1964
Batting: Right handed
Wicket Keeper

One Day Internationals
ODI Career: 1996
ODIs Played: 3

ODI Batting
Innings:	2	Runs:	17
Highest Score:	16	Average:	8.50
No. 50s:	0	No. 100s:	0

ODI Bowling & Fielding
Wickets:	0	Runs:	0
Best Bowling:		Average:	0.00
5 WM:	0	Catches:	2
Stumpings:	0		

Debut v Zimbabwe, Patna, 1996

KAMANDE, James Kabatha
Born: December 12, 1978
Batting: Right handed
Bowling: Right arm medium-fast

One Day Internationals
ODI Career: 1999-06
ODIs Played: 24

ODI Batting
Innings:	20	Runs:	224
Highest Score:	32*	Average:	16.00
No. 50s:	0	No. 100s:	0

ODI Bowling & Fielding
Wickets:	6	Runs:	478
Best Bowling:	1/16	Average:	79.66
5 WM:	0	Catches:	1
Stumpings:	0		

Debut v Zimbabwe, Taunton, 1999

KARIM, Aasif Yusuf
Born: December 15, 1963
Batting: Right handed
Bowling: Left arm off-break

One Day Internationals
ODI Career: 1996-03
ODIs Played: 34

ODI Batting
Innings:	24	Runs:	228
Highest Score:	53	Average:	12.66
No. 50s:	1	No. 100s:	0

ODI Bowling & Fielding
Wickets:	27	Runs:	1,114
Best Bowling:	5/33	Average:	41.25
5 WM:	1	Catches:	0
Stumpings:	0		

Debut v India, Cuttack, 1996

MIGAI, Thomas Odoyo
Born: May 12, 1978
Batting: Right handed
Bowling: Right arm medium-fast

One Day Internationals
ODI Career: 1996-06
ODIs Played: 74

ODI Batting
Innings:	69	Runs:	1,284
Highest Score:	54	Average:	21.04
No. 50s:	3	No. 100s:	0

ODI Bowling & Fielding
Wickets:	74	Runs:	2,536
Best Bowling:	4/28	Average:	34.27
5 WM:	0	Catches:	17
Stumpings:	0		

Debut v India, Cuttack, 1996

MISHRA, Tanmay
Born: December 22, 1986
Batting: Right handed
Bowling: Right arm medium-fast

One Day Internationals
ODI Career: 2006
ODIs Played: 8

ODI Batting
Innings:	8	Runs:	196
Highest Score:	48	Average:	24.50
No. 50s:	0	No. 100s:	0

ODI Bowling & Fielding
Wickets:	0	Runs:	6
Best Bowling:		Average:	0.00
5 WM:	0	Catches:	5
Stumpings:	0		

Debut v Zimbabwe, Bulawayo, 2006

MODI, Hitesh Subhash
Born: October 13, 1971
Batting: Left handed
Bowling: Right arm off-break

One Day Internationals
ODI Career: 1996-06
ODIs Played: 59

ODI Batting
Innings:	52	Runs:	1,085
Highest Score:	78*	Average:	24.65
No. 50s:	5	No. 100s:	0

ODI Bowling & Fielding
Wickets:	0	Runs:	27
Best Bowling:		Average:	0.00
5 WM:	0	Catches:	9
Stumpings:	0		

Debut v India, Cuttack, 1996

NGOCHE, Lameck Onyango
Born: September 22, 1973
Batting: Right handed
Bowling: Right arm medium

One Day Internationals
ODI Career: 1996-02
ODIs Played: 5

ODI Batting
Innings:	5	Runs:	2
Highest Score:	23	Average:	10.00
No. 50s:	0	No. 100s:	0

ODI Bowling & Fielding
Wickets:	1	Runs:	130
Best Bowling:	1/45	Average:	130.00
5 WM:	0	Catches:	1
Stumpings:	0		

Debut v Sri Lanka, Kandy, 1996

NGOCHE, Nehemiah Odhiambo
Born: August 7, 1983
Batting: Right handed
Bowling: Right arm medium-fast

One Day Internationals
ODI Career: 2006
ODIs Played: 1

ODI Batting
Innings:	1	Runs:	0
Highest Score:	0	Average:	0.00
No. 50s:	0	No. 100s:	0

ODI Bowling & Fielding
Wickets:	0	Runs:	29
Best Bowling:		Average:	0.00
5 WM:	0	Catches:	0
Stumpings:	0		

Debut v Zimbabwe, Bulawayo, 2006

OBUYA, Collins Omondi
Born: July 27, 1981
Batting: Right handed
Bowling: Right arm leg-break

One Day Internationals
ODI Career: 2001-06
ODIs Played: 32
ODI Batting
Innings:	24	Runs:	336
Highest Score:	45	Average:	16.00
No. 50s:	0	No. 100s:	0

ODI Bowling & Fielding
Wickets:	25	Runs:	1,177
Best Bowling:	5/24	Average:	47.08
5 WM:	1	Catches:	10
Stumpings:	0		

Debut v West Indies, Nairobi, 2001

OBUYA, David Oluoch
Born: August 14, 1979
Batting: Right handed
Wicket Keeper

One Day Internationals
ODI Career: 2001-06
ODIs Played: 29
ODI Batting
Innings:	29	Runs:	317
Highest Score:	57	Average:	11.74
No. 50s:	1	No. 100s:	0

ODI Bowling & Fielding
Wickets:	0	Runs:	0
Best Bowling:		Average:	0.00
5 WM:	0	Catches:	22
Stumpings:	4		

Debut v West Indies, Nairobi, 2001

OBUYA, Kennedy Otieno
Born: March 11, 1972
Batting: Right handed
Wicket Keeper

One Day Internationals
ODI Career: 1996-06
ODIs Played: 71
ODI Batting
Innings:	69	Runs:	1,622
Highest Score:	144	Average:	23.85
No. 50s:	10	No. 100s:	2

ODI Bowling & Fielding
Wickets:	0	Runs:	5
Best Bowling:		Average:	0.00
5 WM:	0	Catches:	35
Stumpings:	14		

Debut v India, Cuttack, 1996

ODUMBE, Edward Oluoch
Born: May 19, 1965
Batting: Right handed
Bowling: Right arm medium

One Day Internationals
ODI Career: 1996
ODIs Played: 8
ODI Batting
Innings:	7	Runs:	61
Highest Score:	20	Average:	10.16
No. 50s:	0	No. 100s:	0

ODI Bowling & Fielding
Wickets:	6	Runs:	137
Best Bowling:	2/8	Average:	22.83
5 WM:	0	Catches:	4
Stumpings:	0		

Debut v India, Cuttack, 1996

ODUMBE, Maurice Omondi
Born: June 15, 1969
Batting: Right handed
Bowling: Right arm off-break

One Day Internationals
ODI Career: 1996-03
ODIs Played: 61
ODI Batting
Innings:	59	Runs:	1,409
Highest Score:	83	Average:	26.09
No. 50s:	11	No. 100s:	0

ODI Bowling & Fielding
Wickets:	39	Runs:	1,807
Best Bowling:	4/38	Average:	46.33
5 WM:	0	Catches:	12
Stumpings:	0		

Debut v India, Cuttack, 1996

ONDIK, Otieno Suji
Born: February 5, 1976
Batting: Right handed
Bowling: Right arm medium

One Day Internationals
ODI Career: 1996-06
ODIs Played: 51
ODI Batting
Innings:	40	Runs:	459
Highest Score:	67	Average:	13.90
No. 50s:	1	No. 100s:	0

ODI Bowling & Fielding
Wickets:	18	Runs:	1,083
Best Bowling:	2/16	Average:	60.16
5 WM:	0	Catches:	14
Stumpings:	0		

Debut v Pakistan, Nairobi, 1996

ONGONDO, Peter Jimmy Carter
Born: February 10, 1977
Batting: Right handed
Bowling: Right arm medium-fast

One Day Internationals
ODI Career: 1999-06
ODIs Played: 30
ODI Batting
Innings:	27	Runs:	211
Highest Score:	36	Average:	10.55
No. 50s:	0	No. 100s:	0

ODI Bowling & Fielding
Wickets:	25	Runs:	833
Best Bowling:	4/14	Average:	33.32
5 WM:	0	Catches:	4
Stumpings:	0		

Debut v South Africa, Nairobi, 1999

OUMA, Maurice Akumu
Born: November 8, 1982
Batting: Right handed
Bowling: Right arm off-break
Wicket Keeper

One Day Internationals
ODI Career: 2004-06
ODIs Played: 8

ODI Batting

Innings:	8	Runs:	110
Highest Score:	49	Average:	13.75
No. 50s:	0	No. 100s:	0

ODI Bowling & Fielding

Wickets:	0	Runs:	0
Best Bowling:		Average:	0.00
5 WM:	0	Catches:	2
Stumpings:	0		

Debut v India, Southampton, 2004

PATEL, Brijal Jagdish

Born: November 14, 1977
Batting: Right handed
Bowling: Left arm off-break

One Day Internationals

ODI Career: 2001-06
ODIs Played: 28

ODI Batting

Innings:	22	Runs:	330
Highest Score:	44	Average:	17.36
No. 50s:	0	No. 100s:	0

ODI Bowling & Fielding

Wickets:	4	Runs:	163
Best Bowling:	2/20	Average:	40.75
5 WM:	0	Catches:	7
Stumpings:	0		

Debut v West Indies, Nairobi, 2001

PATEL, Kalpesh Ashok

Born: July 18, 1985
Batting: Right handed
Bowling: Right arm medium

One Day Internationals

ODI Career: 2006
ODIs Played: 2

ODI Batting

Innings:	2	Runs:	1
Highest Score:	1*	Average:	1.00
No. 50s:	0	No. 100s:	0

ODI Bowling & Fielding

Wickets:	0	Runs:	34
Best Bowling:		Average:	0.00
5 WM:	0	Catches:	0
Stumpings:	0		

Debut v Bangladesh, Khulna, 2006

PATEL, Malhar L.

Born: November 27, 1983
Batting: Right handed

One Day Internationals

ODI Career: 2004
ODIs Played: 1

ODI Batting

Innings:	1	Runs:	0
Highest Score:	0	Average:	0.00
No. 50s:	0	No. 100s:	0

ODI Bowling & Fielding

Wickets:	0	Runs:	0
Best Bowling:		Average:	0.00
5 WM:	0	Catches:	0
Stumpings:	0		

Debut v Pakistan, Birmingham, 2004

SHAH, Ravindu Dhirajlal

Born: August 28, 1972
Batting: Right handed
Bowling: Right arm medium-fast

One Day Internationals

ODI Career: 1998-04
ODIs Played: 44

ODI Batting

Innings:	44	Runs:	1,125
Highest Score:	71	Average:	25.56
No. 50s:	10	No. 100s:	0

ODI Bowling & Fielding

Wickets:	0	Runs:	72
Best Bowling:		Average:	0.00
5 WM:	0	Catches:	11
Stumpings:	0		

Debut v Bangladesh, Hyderabad, 1998

SHEIKH, Mohammad

Born: August 29, 1980
Batting: Left handed
Bowling: Left arm leg-break

One Day Internationals

ODI Career: 1997-00
ODIs Played: 21

ODI Batting

Innings:	15	Runs:	68
Highest Score:	15*	Average:	6.80
No. 50s:	0	No. 100s:	0

ODI Bowling & Fielding

Wickets:	19	Runs:	625
Best Bowling:	4/36	Average:	32.89
5 WM:	0	Catches:	7
Stumpings:	0		

Debut v Bangladesh, Nairobi, 1997

SORONGO, Alfred Luseno

Born: December 20, 1981
Batting: Right handed
Bowling: Right arm medium

One Day Internationals

ODI Career: 2003-06
ODIs Played: 6

ODI Batting

Innings:	5	Runs:	17
Highest Score:	8*	Average:	17.00
No. 50s:	0	No. 100s:	0

ODI Bowling & Fielding

Wickets:	2	Runs:	190
Best Bowling:	1/42	Average:	95.00
5 WM:	0	Catches:	1
Stumpings:	0		

Debut v Sri Lanka, Shariah, 2003

SORONGO, Josephat Ababu

Born: April 15, 1980
Batting: Right handed
Bowling: Right arm medium-fast

One Day Internationals

ODI Career: 1999-06
ODIs Played: 7

ODI Batting

Innings:	3	Runs:	29
Highest Score:	17	Average:	9.66
No. 50s:	0	No. 100s:	0

ODI Bowling & Fielding				
Wickets:	2	Runs:	180
Best Bowling:	1/26	Average:	90.00
5 WM:	0	Catches:	1
Stumpings:	0		

Debut v Zimbabwe, Nairobi, 1999

SUJI, Martin Armon
Born: June 2, 1971
Batting: Right handed
Bowling: Right arm medium-fast

One Day Internationals

ODI Career:	1996-06
ODIs Played:	64

ODI Batting

Innings:	52	Runs:	247
Highest Score:	16	Average:	8.23
No. 50s:	0	No. 100s:	0

ODI Bowling & Fielding

Wickets:	43	Runs:	2,190
Best Bowling:	4/24	Average:	50.93
5 WM:	0	Catches:	11
Stumpings:	0		

Debut v India, Cuttack, 1996

TIKOLO, Lazaro Openda
Born: December 27, 1964
Batting: Right handed
Bowling: Right arm medium

One Day Internationals

ODI Career:	1996
ODIs Played:	3

ODI Batting

Innings:	2	Runs:	36
Highest Score:	25	Average:	0.00
No. 50s:	0	No. 100s:	0

ODI Bowling & Fielding

Wickets:	0	Runs:	55
Best Bowling:		Average:	0.00
5 WM:	0	Catches:	2
Stumpings:	0		

Debut v India, Cuttack, 1996

TIKOLO, Stephen Ogonji
Born: June 25, 1971
Batting: Right handed
Bowling: Right arm medium

One Day Internationals

ODI Career:	1996-06
ODIs Played:	74

ODI Batting

Innings:	72	Runs:	1,984
Highest Score:	106*	Average:	28.34
No. 50s:	16	No. 100s:	1

ODI Bowling & Fielding

Wickets:	45	Runs:	1,669
Best Bowling:	3/14	Average:	37.08
5 WM:	0	Catches:	26
Stumpings:	0		

Debut v India, Cuttack, 1996

VADHER, Alpesh Vallabhdas
Born: September 7, 1974
Batting: Right handed

One Day Internationals

ODI Career:	1997-99
ODIs Played:	18

ODI Batting

Innings:	16	Runs:	278
Highest Score:	73*	Average:	27.80
No. 50s:	2	No. 100s:	0

ODI Bowling & Fielding

Wickets:	0	Runs:	0
Best Bowling:		Average:	0.00
5 WM:	0	Catches:	6
Stumpings:	0		

Debut v Bangladesh, Nairobi, 1997

VARAIYA, Hiren Ashok
Born: April 9, 1984
Batting: Right handed
Bowling: Left arm off-break

One Day Internationals

ODI Career:	2006
ODIs Played:	3

ODI Batting

Innings:	1	Runs:	2
Highest Score:	2	Average:	2.00
No. 50s:	0	No. 100s:	0

ODI Bowling & Fielding

Wickets:	7	Runs:	82
Best Bowling:	4/25	Average:	11.71
5 WM:	0	Catches:	2
Stumpings:	0		

Debut v Canada, Toronto, 2006.

Scotland

ALLINGHAM, Mike
Born: January 6, 1965
Batting: Right handed
Bowling: Right arm medium

One Day Internationals
ODI Career: 1999
ODIs Played: 3

ODI Batting
Innings:	3	Runs:	11
Highest Score:	6	Average:	3.66
No. 50s:	0	No. 100s:	0

ODI Bowling & Fielding
Wickets:	0	Runs:	0
Best Bowling:		Average:	0.00
5 WM:	0	Catches:	1
Stumpings:	0		

Debut v Australia, Worcester 1999

BLAIN, John
Born: January 4, 1979
Batting: Right handed
Bowling: Right arm medium-fast

One Day Internationals
ODI Career: 1999-06
ODIs Played: 6

ODI Batting
Innings:	6	Runs:	15
Highest Score:	9	Average:	3.00
No. 50s:	0	No. 100s:	0

ODI Bowling & Fielding
Wickets:	10	Runs:	251
Best Bowling:	4/37	Average:	25.10
5 WM:	0	Catches:	1
Stumpings:	0		

Debut V Australia, Worcester 1999

BRINKLEY, James
Born: March 13, 1974
Batting: Right handed
Bowling: Right arm medium-fast

One Day Internationals
ODI Career: 1999
ODIs Played: 5

ODI Batting
Innings:	5	Runs:	52
Highest Score:	23	Average:	10.40
No. 50s:	0	No. 100s:	0

ODI Bowling & Fielding
Wickets:	2	Runs:	117
Best Bowling:	1/29	Average:	58.50
5 WM:	0	Catches:	1
Stumpings:	0		

Debut V Australia, Worcester 1999

BROWN, Douglas Robert
Born: October 29, 1969
Batting: Right handed
Bowling: Right arm medium-fast

One Day Internationals
ODI Career: 1997-06
ODIs Played: 11

ODI Batting
Innings:	10	Runs:	114
Highest Score:	21	Average:	19.00
No. 50s:	0	No. 100s:	0

ODI Bowling & Fielding
Wickets:	9	Runs:	344
Best Bowling:	2/28	Average:	38.22
5 WM:	0	Catches:	1
Stumpings:	0		

Scottish born Dougie Brown made his ODI debut for England against India at Sharjah in 1997. As a promising pace bowler, he played in nine ODI's for England between 1997 and 1998 and after an eight year hiatus made his ODI debut for Scotland in August 2006.

BUTT, Asim
Born: October 24, 1967
Batting: Right handed
Bowling: Left arm medium-fast

One Day Internationals
ODI Career: 1999
ODIs Played: 5

ODI Batting
Innings:	4	Runs:	23
Highest Score:	11	Average:	5.75
No. 50s:	0	No. 100s:	0

ODI Bowling & Fielding
Wickets:	4	Runs:	148
Best Bowling:	2/24	Average:	37.00
5 WM:	0	Catches:	0
Stumpings:	0		

Debut V Australia, Worcester 1999

DAVIES, Alec
Born: August 14, 1962
Batting: Right handed
Wicket Keeper

One Day Internationals
ODI Career: 1999
ODIs Played: 5

ODI Batting
Innings:	5	Runs:	83
Highest Score:	32	Average:	20.75
No. 50s:	0	No. 100s:	0

The Encyclopedia of International Cricketers - Scotland

ODI Bowling & Fielding
Wickets:	0	Runs:	0
Best Bowling:		Average:	0.00
5 WM:	0	Catches:	2
Stumpings:	1		

Debut V Australia, Worcester 1999

DYER, Nick
Born:	June 10, 1969
Batting:	Right handed
Bowling:	Right arm off-break

One Day Internationals
ODI Career:	1999
ODIs Played:	5

ODI Batting
Innings:	4	Runs:	3
Highest Score:	2*	Average:	3.00
No. 50s:	0	No. 100s:	0

ODI Bowling & Fielding
Wickets:	5	Runs:	117
Best Bowling:	2/26	Average:	23.40
5 WM:	0	Catches:	2
Stumpings:	0		

Debut V Australia, Worcester 1999

HAMILTON, Gavin Mark
Born:	September 16, 1974
Batting:	Left handed
Bowling:	Right arm medium-fast

One Day Internationals
ODI Career:	1999-06
ODIs Played:	6

ODI Batting
Innings:	6	Runs:	226
Highest Score:	76	Average:	45.20
No. 50s:	2	No. 100s:	0

ODI Bowling & Fielding
Wickets:	3	Runs:	149
Best Bowling:	2/36	Average:	49.66
5 WM:	0	Catches:	1
Stumpings:	0		

Debut V Australia, Worcester 1999

HOFFMANN, Paul
Born:	January 14, 1970
Batting:	Right handed
Bowling:	Right arm medium-fast

One Day Internationals
ODI Career:	2006
ODIs Played:	1

ODI Batting
Innings:	1	Runs:	0
Highest Score:	0	Average:	0.00
No. 50s:	0	No. 100s:	0

ODI Bowling & Fielding
Wickets:	3	Runs:	22
Best Bowling:	3/22	Average:	7.33
5 WM:	0	Catches:	1
Stumpings:	0		

Debut V Pakistan, Edinburgh 2006

HUSSAIN, Rana Omer
Born:	December 3, 1984
Batting:	Left handed
	Wicket Keeper

One Day Internationals
ODI Career:	2006
ODIs Played:	2

ODI Batting
Innings:	2	Runs:	16
Highest Score:	14	Average:	8.00
No. 50s:	0	No. 100s:	0

ODI Bowling & Fielding
Wickets:	0	Runs:	0
Best Bowling:		Average:	0.00
5 WM:	0	Catches:	0
Stumpings:	0		

Debut v Ireland, Ayr, 2006.

LOCKHART, Douglas
Born:	January 19, 1976
Batting:	Right handed
	Wicket Keeper

One Day Internationals
ODI Career:	2006
ODIs Played:	1

ODI Batting
Innings:	1	Runs:	25
Highest Score:	25*	Average:	0.00
No. 50s:	0	No. 100s:	0

ODI Bowling & Fielding
Wickets:	0	Runs:	0
Best Bowling:		Average:	0.00
5 WM:	0	Catches:	1
Stumpings:	0		

Debut V Pakistan, Edinburgh 2006

LYONS, Ross
Born:	December 8, 1984
Batting:	Left handed
Bowling:	Left arm off-break

One Day Internationals
ODI Career:	2006
ODIs Played:	1

ODI Batting
Innings:	0	Runs:	0
Highest Score:	0	Average:	0.00
No. 50s:	0	No. 100s:	0

ODI Bowling & Fielding
Wickets:	1	Runs:	44
Best Bowling:	1/44	Average:	44.00
5 WM:	0	Catches:	1
Stumpings:	0		

Debut V Pakistan, Edinburgh 2006

MACRAE, Neil
Born:	March 25, 1972
Batting:	Right handed

One Day Internationals
ODI Career:	2006
ODIs Played:	1

ODI Batting
Innings:	1	Runs:	2
Highest Score:	2	Average:	2.00
No. 50s:	0	No. 100s:	0

ODI Bowling & Fielding
Wickets:	0	Runs:	0
Best Bowling:		Average:	0.00
5 WM:	0	Catches:	0
Stumpings:	0		

McCALLUM, Neil
Born: November 22, 1977
Batting: Right handed

One Day Internationals
ODI Career: 2006
ODIs Played: 1

ODI Batting
Innings:	1	Runs:	68
Highest Score:	68	Average:	68.00
No. 50s:	1	No. 100s:	0

ODI Bowling & Fielding
Wickets:	0	Runs:	0
Best Bowling:		Average:	0.00
5 WM:	0	Catches:	0
Stumpings:	0		

Debut V Pakistan, Edinburgh 2006

NEL, Dewald
Born: June 6, 1980
Batting: Right handed
Bowling: Right arm medium-fast

One Day Internationals
ODI Career: 2006
ODIs Played: 1

ODI Batting
Innings:	1	Runs:	3
Highest Score:	3*	Average:	0.00
No. 50s:	0	No. 100s:	0

ODI Bowling & Fielding
Wickets:	1	Runs:	40
Best Bowling:	1/40	Average:	40.00
5 WM:	0	Catches:	0
Stumpings:	0		

Debut V Pakistan, Edinburgh 2006

PATTERSON, Bruce
Born: January 29, 1965
Batting: Right handed

One Day Internationals
ODI Career: 1999
ODIs Played: 3

ODI Batting
Innings:	3	Runs:	10
Highest Score:	10	Average:	3.33
No. 50s:	0	No. 100s:	0

ODI Bowling & Fielding
Wickets:	0	Runs:	0
Best Bowling:		Average:	0.00
5 WM:	0	Catches:	0
Stumpings:	0		

Debut V Australia, Worcester 1999

PHILIP, Ian
Born: June 9, 1958
Batting: Right handed
Bowling: Left arm off-break
Wicket Keeper

One Day Internationals
ODI Career: 1999
ODIs Played: 3

ODI Batting
Innings:	3	Runs:	20
Highest Score:	17	Average:	6.66
No. 50s:	0	No. 100s:	0

ODI Bowling & Fielding
Wickets:	0	Runs:	0
Best Bowling:		Average:	0.00
5 WM:	0	Catches:	4
Stumpings:	0		

Debut V Australia, Worcester 1999

POONIA, Navdeep Singh
Born: May 11, 1986
Batting: Right handed

One Day Internationals
ODI Career: 2006
ODIs Played: 1

ODI Batting
Innings:	1	Runs:	26
Highest Score:	26	Average:	26.00
No. 50s:	0	No. 100s:	0

ODI Bowling & Fielding
Wickets:	0	Runs:	0
Best Bowling:		Average:	0.00
5 WM:	0	Catches:	1
Stumpings:	0		

Debut v Ireland, Ayr, 2006.

SALMOND, George
Born: December 1, 1969
Batting: Right handed
Bowling: Right arm medium

One Day Internationals
ODI Career: 1999
ODIs Played: 5

ODI Batting
Innings:	5	Runs:	57
Highest Score:	31	Average:	11.40
No. 50s:	0	No. 100s:	0

ODI Bowling & Fielding
Wickets:	0	Runs:	0
Best Bowling:		Average:	0.00
5 WM:	0	Catches:	1
Stumpings:	0		

Debut V Australia, Worcester 1999

SMITH, Colin
Born: September 27, 1972
Batting: Right handed
Wicket Keeper

One Day Internationals
ODI Career: 2006
ODIs Played: 1

ODI Batting
Innings:	1	Runs:	0
Highest Score:	0	Average:	0.00
No. 50s:	0	No. 100s:	0

ODI Bowling & Fielding
Wickets:	0	Runs:	0
Best Bowling:		Average:	0.00
5 WM:	0	Catches:	1
Stumpings:	0		

Debut V Pakistan, Edinburgh 2006

SMITH, Mike
Born: March 30, 1966
Batting: Right handed
Bowling: Right arm medium

One Day Internationals
ODI Career: 1999
ODIs Played: 5

ODI Batting
Innings:	5	Runs:	19
Highest Score:	13	Average:	3.80
No. 50s:	0	No. 100s:	0

ODI Bowling & Fielding
Wickets:	0	Runs:	0
Best Bowling:		Average:	0.00
5 WM:	0	Catches:	0
Stumpings:	0		

Debut V Australia, Worcester 1999

STANGER, Ian
Born: October 5, 1971
Batting: Right handed
Bowling: Right arm medium

One Day Internationals
ODI Career: 1999-06
ODIs Played: 5

ODI Batting
Innings:	5	Runs:	50
Highest Score:	27	Average:	10.00
No. 50s:	0	No. 100s:	0

ODI Bowling & Fielding
Wickets:	0	Runs:	56
Best Bowling:		Average:	0.00
5 WM:	0	Catches:	2
Stumpings:	0		

Debut V Pakistan, Chester-le-Street 1999

WATSON, Ryan
Born: November 12, 1976
Batting: Right handed
Bowling: Right arm medium

One Day Internationals
ODI Career: 2006
ODIs Played: 1

ODI Batting
Innings:	1	Runs:	80
Highest Score:	80	Average:	80.00
No. 50s:	1	No. 100s:	0

ODI Bowling & Fielding
Wickets:	0	Runs:	54
Best Bowling:		Average:	0.00
5 WM:	0	Catches:	1
Stumpings:	0		

Debut V Pakistan, Edinburgh 2006

WATTS, David Fraser
Born: June 5, 1979
Batting: Right handed

One Day Internationals
ODI Career: 2006
ODIs Played: 1

ODI Batting
Innings:	1	Runs:	2
Highest Score:	2	Average:	2.00
No. 50s:	0	No. 100s:	0

ODI Bowling & Fielding
Wickets:	0	Runs:	0
Best Bowling:		Average:	0.00
5 WM:	0	Catches:	1
Stumpings:	0		

Debut v Netherlands, Ayr, 2006

WILLIAMSON, Greg
Born: December 20, 1968
Batting: Right handed
Bowling: Right arm medium

One Day Internationals
ODI Career: 1999
ODIs Played: 2

ODI Batting
Innings:	2	Runs:	11
Highest Score:	10	Average:	5.50
No. 50s:	0	No. 100s:	0

ODI Bowling & Fielding
Wickets:	0	Runs:	0
Best Bowling:		Average:	0.00
5 WM:	0	Catches:	0
Stumpings:	0		

Debut V West Indies, Leicester 1999

WRIGHT, Craig McIntyre
Born: April 28, 1974
Batting: Right handed
Bowling: Right arm medium

One Day Internationals
ODI Career: 2006
ODIs Played: 2

ODI Batting
Innings:	2	Runs:	33
Highest Score:	18	Average:	33.00
No. 50s:	0	No. 100s:	0

ODI Bowling & Fielding
Wickets:	4	Runs:	55
Best Bowling:	3/32	Average:	13.75
5 WM:	0	Catches:	0
Stumpings:	0		

Debut v Ireland, Ayr, 2006

UAE

ABBASI, Imtiaz
Born: February 6, 1968
Batting: Right handed
Wicket Keeper

One Day Internationals
ODI Career: 1994-96
ODIs Played: 7

ODI Batting
Innings:	6	Runs:	12
Highest Score:	6*	Average:	6.00
No. 50s:	0	No. 100s:	0

ODI Bowling & Fielding
Wickets:	0	Runs:	0
Best Bowling:		Average:	0.00
5 WM:	0	Catches:	4
Stumpings:	2		

Debut V India, Sharjah, 1994

AL-SAFFAR, Saeed
Born: July 31, 1968
Batting: Right handed
Bowling: Left arm medium-fast

One Day Internationals
ODI Career: 1996
ODIs Played: 1

ODI Batting
Innings:	0	Runs:	0
Highest Score:	0	Average:	0.00
No. 50s:	0	No. 100s:	0

ODI Bowling & Fielding
Wickets:	0	Runs:	25
Best Bowling:		Average:	0.00
5 WM:	0	Catches:	1
Stumpings:	0		

Debut V Netherlands, Lahore, 1996

ALI, Arshad
Born: April 6, 1976
Batting: Right handed
Bowling: Right arm medium

One Day Internationals
ODI Career: 2004
ODIs Played: 2

ODI Batting
Innings:	2	Runs:	7
Highest Score:	7	Average:	3.50
No. 50s:	0	No. 100s:	0

ODI Bowling & Fielding
Wickets:	1	Runs:	5
Best Bowling:	1/5	Average:	5.00
5 WM:	0	Catches:	0
Stumpings:	0		

Debut v India, Dambulla, 2004

ALI, Asghar
Born: September 3, 1971
Batting: Right handed
Wicket Keeper

One Day Internationals
ODI Career: 2004
ODIs Played: 2

ODI Batting
Innings:	2	Runs:	14
Highest Score:	14	Average:	7.00
No. 50s:	0	No. 100s:	0

ODI Bowling & Fielding
Wickets:	0	Runs:	0
Best Bowling:		Average:	0.00
5 WM:	0	Catches:	0
Stumpings:	0		

Debut V India, Dambulla, 2004

ALTAF, Shehzad
Born: October 6, 1957
Batting: Right handed
Bowling: Right arm medium

One Day Internationals
ODI Career: 1996
ODIs Played: 2

ODI Batting
Innings:	0	Runs:	0
Highest Score:	0	Average:	0.00
No. 50s:	0	No. 100s:	0

ODI Bowling & Fielding
Wickets:	1	Runs:	37
Best Bowling:	1/15	Average:	37.00
5 WM:	0	Catches:	0
Stumpings:	0		

Debut V South Africa, Rawalpindi, 1996

ASAD, Ali
Born: December 6, 1976
Batting: Right handed
Bowling: Right arm medium-fast

One Day Internationals
ODI Career: 2004
ODIs Played: 2

ODI Batting
Innings:	2	Runs:	21
Highest Score:	12	Average:	21.00
No. 50s:	0	No. 100s:	0

ODI Bowling & Fielding
Wickets:	2	Runs:	73
Best Bowling:	2/35	Average:	36.50
5 WM:	0	Catches:	0
Stumpings:	0		

Debut V India, Dambulla, 2004

ASLAM, Mohammad
Born: September 7, 1961
Batting: Right handed
Bowling: Right arm medium-fast

One Day Internationals
ODI Career: 1996
ODIs Played: 4

ODI Batting
Innings:	4	Runs:	38
Highest Score:	23	Average:	9.50
No. 50s:	0	No. 100s:	0

ODI Bowling & Fielding
Wickets:	0	Runs:	0
Best Bowling:		Average:	0.00
5 WM:	0	Catches:	0
Stumpings:	0		

Debut V South Africa, Rawalpindi, 1996

ASLAM, Naeemuddin
Born: May 31, 1982
Batting: Right handed

One Day Internationals
ODI Career: 2004
ODIs Played: 2

ODI Batting
Innings:	2	Runs:	12
Highest Score:	12	Average:	6.00
No. 50s:	0	No. 100s:	0

ODI Bowling & Fielding
Wickets:	0	Runs:	0
Best Bowling:		Average:	0.00
5 WM:	0	Catches:	0
Stumpings:	0		

Debut V India, Dambulla, 2004

BUTT, Sohail
Born: June 6, 1966
Batting: Right handed
Bowling: Right arm medium-fast

One Day Internationals
ODI Career: 1994
ODIs Played: 2

ODI Batting
Innings:	2	Runs:	8
Highest Score:	6*	Average:	8.00
No. 50s:	0	No. 100s:	0

ODI Bowling & Fielding
Wickets:	2	Runs:	79
Best Bowling:	2/52	Average:	39.50
5 WM:	0	Catches:	0
Stumpings:	0		

Debut V India, Sharjah, 1994

DUKANWALA, Shaukat
Born: January 21, 1957
Batting: Right handed
Bowling: Right arm off-break

One Day Internationals
ODI Career: 1996
ODIs Played: 5

ODI Batting
Innings:	4	Runs:	84
Highest Score:	40*	Average:	42.00
No. 50s:	0	No. 100s:	0

ODI Bowling & Fielding
Wickets:	6	Runs:	153
Best Bowling:	5/29	Average:	25.50
5 WM:	1	Catches:	2
Stumpings:	0		

Debut V South Africa, Rawalpindi, 1996

HUSSAIN, Mazhar
Born: October 25, 1967
Batting: Right handed
Bowling: Right arm leg-break

One Day Internationals
ODI Career: 1994-96
ODIs Played: 7

ODI Batting
Innings:	7	Runs:	179
Highest Score:	70	Average:	25.57
No. 50s:	1	No. 100s:	0

ODI Bowling & Fielding
Wickets:	0	Runs:	60
Best Bowling:		Average:	0.00
5 WM:	0	Catches:	1
Stumpings:	0		

Debut V India, Sharjah, 1994

ISHAQ, Mohammad
Born: March 7, 1963
Batting: Right handed
Bowling: Right arm medium

One Day Internationals
ODI Career: 1994-96
ODIs Played: 5

ODI Batting
Innings:	5	Runs:	98
Highest Score:	51*	Average:	24.50
No. 50s:	1	No. 100s:	0

ODI Bowling & Fielding
Wickets:	0	Runs:	0
Best Bowling:		Average:	0.00
5 WM:	0	Catches:	1
Stumpings:	0		

Debut V India, Sharjah, 1994

KHAN, Khurram
Born: June 21, 1971
Batting: Left handed
Bowling: Left arm slow

One Day Internationals
ODI Career: 2004
ODIs Played: 2

ODI Batting
Innings:	2	Runs:	13
Highest Score:	8	Average:	6.50
No. 50s:	0	No. 100s:	0

ODI Bowling & Fielding
Wickets:	5	Runs:	80
Best Bowling:	4/32	Average:	16.00
5 WM:	0	Catches:	0
Stumpings:	0		

Debut V India, Dambulla, 2004

LAEEQ, Arshad
Born: November 28, 1970
Batting: Right handed
Bowling: Right arm medium-fast

One Day Internationals
ODI Career: 1994-96
ODIs Played: 6

ODI Batting
Innings:	6	Runs:	101
Highest Score:	43*	Average:	20.20
No. 50s:	0	No. 100s:	0

ODI Bowling & Fielding
Wickets:	1	Runs:	198
Best Bowling:	1/25	Average:	198.00
5 WM:	0	Catches:	1
Stumpings:	0		

Debut V India, Sharjah, 1994

LATIF, Rizwan
Born: October 5, 1973
Batting: Right handed
Bowling: Left arm slow

One Day Internationals
ODI Career: 2004
ODIs Played: 1

ODI Batting
Innings:	1	Runs:	0
Highest Score:	0	Average:	0.00
No. 50s:	0	No. 100s:	0

ODI Bowling & Fielding
Wickets:	2	Runs:	69
Best Bowling:	2/69	Average:	34.50
5 WM:	0	Catches:	0
Stumpings:	0		

Debut V India, Dambulla, 2004

MAQSOOD, Syed
Born: March 11, 1975
Batting: Right handed
Bowling: Right arm medium

One Day Internationals
ODI Career: 2004
ODIs Played: 2

ODI Batting
Innings:	2	Runs:	18
Highest Score:	13	Average:	9.00
No. 50s:	0	No. 100s:	0

ODI Bowling & Fielding
Wickets:	1	Runs:	84
Best Bowling:	1/60	Average:	84.00
5 WM:	0	Catches:	1
Stumpings:	0		

Debut V India, Dambulla, 2004

MEHRA, Vijay
Born: October 17, 1963
Batting: Right handed
Wicket Keeper

One Day Internationals
ODI Career: 1994-96
ODIs Played: 6

ODI Batting
Innings:	6	Runs:	92
Highest Score:	43	Average:	18.40
No. 50s:	0	No. 100s:	0

ODI Bowling & Fielding
Wickets:	0	Runs:	0
Best Bowling:		Average:	0.00
5 WM:	0	Catches:	1
Stumpings:	0		

Debut V India, Sharjah, 1994

MYLVAGANAM, Ganesh
Born: August 1, 1966
Batting: Right handed

One Day Internationals
ODI Career: 1996
ODIs Played: 3

ODI Batting
Innings:	3	Runs:	36
Highest Score:	23	Average:	12.00
No. 50s:	0	No. 100s:	0

ODI Bowling & Fielding
Wickets:	0	Runs:	0
Best Bowling:		Average:	0.00
5 WM:	0	Catches:	1
Stumpings:	0		

Debut V South Africa, Rawalpindi, 1996

POONAWALA, Riaz
Born: May 8, 1961
Batting: Right handed
Bowling: Right arm off-break

One Day Internationals
ODI Career: 1994
ODIs Played: 2

ODI Batting
Innings:	2	Runs:	44
Highest Score:	22	Average:	22.00
No. 50s:	0	No. 100s:	0

ODI Bowling & Fielding
Wickets:	0	Runs:	0
Best Bowling:		Average:	0.00
5 WM:	0	Catches:	1
Stumpings:	0		

Debut V India, Sharjah, 1994

RAI, Ramveer
Born: December 1, 1987
Batting: Right handed
Bowling: Left arm slow

One Day Internationals
ODI Career: 2004
ODIs Played: 1

ODI Batting
Innings:	1	Runs:	39
Highest Score:	39	Average:	39.00
No. 50s:	0	No. 100s:	0

ODI Bowling & Fielding
Wickets:	0	Runs:	0
Best Bowling:		Average:	0.00
5 WM:	0	Catches:	0
Stumpings:	0		

Debut V Sri Lanka, Dambulla, 2004

RAZA, Saleem
Born: July 5, 1964
Batting: Right handed
Bowling: Right arm off-break

One Day Internationals
ODI Career: 1994-96
ODIs Played: 6

ODI Batting

Innings:	6	Runs:	159
Highest Score:	84	Average:	26.50
No. 50s:	1	No. 100s:	0

ODI Bowling & Fielding

Wickets:	3	Runs:	179
Best Bowling:	1/17	Average:	59.66
5 WM:	0	Catches:	0
Stumpings:	0		

Debut V India, Sharjah, 1994

REHMAN, Abdul

Born: January 2, 1987
Batting: Right handed
 Wicket Keeper

One Day Internationals

ODI Career: 2004
ODIs Played: 1

ODI Batting

Innings:	1	Runs:	1
Highest Score:	1	Average:	1.00
No. 50s:	0	No. 100s:	0

ODI Bowling & Fielding

Wickets:	0	Runs:	0
Best Bowling:		Average:	0.00
5 WM:	0	Catches:	0
Stumpings:	0		

Debut V India, Dambulla, 2004

SAEED, Asim

Born: October 5, 1979
Batting: Right handed
Bowling: Left arm medium

One Day Internationals

ODI Career: 2004
ODIs Played: 2

ODI Batting

Innings:	2	Runs:	12
Highest Score:	12	Average:	6.00
No. 50s:	0	No. 100s:	0

ODI Bowling & Fielding

Wickets:	1	Runs:	40
Best Bowling:	1/25	Average:	40.00
5 WM:	0	Catches:	0
Stumpings:	0		

Debut V India, Dambulla, 2004

SAEED, Azhar

Born: December 25, 1970
Batting: Left handed
Bowling: Left arm slow

One Day Internationals

ODI Career: 1994-96
ODIs Played: 7

ODI Batting

Innings:	7	Runs:	61
Highest Score:	32	Average:	8.71
No. 50s:	0	No. 100s:	0

ODI Bowling & Fielding

Wickets:	6	Runs:	213
Best Bowling:	3/45	Average:	35.50
5 WM:	0	Catches:	2
Stumpings:	0		

Debut V India, Sharjah, 1994

SAMARASEKERA, Johanne

Born: February 22, 1968
Batting: Right handed
Bowling: Right arm medium-fast

One Day Internationals

ODI Career: 1994-96
ODIs Played: 7

ODI Batting

Innings:	6	Runs:	124
Highest Score:	47*	Average:	31.00
No. 50s:	0	No. 100s:	0

ODI Bowling & Fielding

Wickets:	4	Runs:	236
Best Bowling:	1/17	Average:	59.00
5 WM:	0	Catches:	1
Stumpings:	0		

Debut V India, Sharjah, 1994

TAUQIR, Mohammad

Born: June 21, 1971
Batting: Right handed
Bowling: Right arm off-break

One Day Internationals

ODI Career: 2004
ODIs Played: 2

ODI Batting

Innings:	2	Runs:	61
Highest Score:	55	Average:	30.50
No. 50s:	0	No. 100s:	0

ODI Bowling & Fielding

Wickets:	1	Runs:	80
Best Bowling:	1/46	Average:	80.00
5 WM:	0	Catches:	1
Stumpings:	0		

Debut V India, Dambulla, 2004

USMAN, Fahad

Born: October 2, 1976
Batting: Left handed
Bowling: Left arm leg-break

One Day Internationals

ODI Career: 2004
ODIs Played: 2

ODI Batting

Innings:	2	Runs:	9
Highest Score:	9	Average:	4.50
No. 50s:	0	No. 100s:	0

ODI Bowling & Fielding

Wickets:	0	Runs:	0
Best Bowling:		Average:	0.00
5 WM:	0	Catches:	1
Stumpings:	0		

Debut V India, Dambulla, 2004

ZARAWANI, Sultan

Born: January 24, 1961
Batting: Right handed
Bowling: Right arm leg-break

One Day Internationals

ODI Career: 1994-96
ODIs Played: 7

ODI Batting

Innings:	6	Runs:	26
Highest Score:	13	Average:	4.33
No. 50s:	0	No. 100s:	0

ODI Bowling & Fielding
Wickets:	5	**Runs:**	257
Best Bowling:	2/49	**Average:**	51.40
5 WM:	0	**Catches:**	1
Stumpings:	0		

Debut V India, Sharjah, 1994

ZIA, Sameer

Born:	September 8, 1981
Batting:	Right handed

One Day Internationals

ODI Career:	2004
ODIs Played:	1

ODI Batting
Innings:	1	**Runs:**	2
Highest Score:	2*	**Average:**	0.00
No. 50s:	0	**No. 100s:**	0

ODI Bowling & Fielding
Wickets:	1	**Runs:**	44
Best Bowling:	1/44	**Average:**	44.00
5 WM:	0	**Catches:**	2
Stumpings:	0		

Debut V Sri Lanka, Dambulla, 2004

USA

ALEXANDER, Rohan
Born: February 20, 1973
Batting: Left handed
Bowling: Right arm off-break

One Day Internationals
ODI Career: 2004
ODIs Played: 2

ODI Batting
Innings:	2	Runs:	34
Highest Score:	26	Average:	17.00
No. 50s:	0	No. 100s:	0

ODI Bowling & Fielding
Wickets:	0	Runs:	0
Best Bowling:		Average:	0.00
5 WM:	0	Catches:	0
Stumpings:	0		

Debut v New Zealand, The Oval 2004

ALI, Aijaz
Born: June 20, 1968
Batting: Right handed
Bowling: Right arm medium-fast

One Day Internationals
ODI Career: 2004
ODIs Played: 2

ODI Batting
Innings:	2	Runs:	5
Highest Score:	4	Average:	2.50
No. 50s:	0	No. 100s:	0

ODI Bowling & Fielding
Wickets:	0	Runs:	0
Best Bowling:		Average:	0.00
5 WM:	0	Catches:	1
Stumpings:	0		

Debut V New Zealand, The Oval 2004

BLAKE, Donovan
Born: December 4, 1961
Batting: Right handed
Bowling: Right arm medium-fast

One Day Internationals
ODI Career: 2004
ODIs Played: 1

ODI Batting
Innings:	1	Runs:	0
Highest Score:	0	Average:	0.00
No. 50s:	0	No. 100s:	0

ODI Bowling & Fielding
Wickets:	0	Runs:	7
Best Bowling:		Average:	0.00
5 WM:	0	Catches:	0
Stumpings:	0		

Debut V Australia, Southampton 2004

DESAI, Jignesh
Born: April 18, 1974
Batting: Left handed
Bowling: Right arm off-break

One Day Internationals
ODI Career: 2004
ODIs Played: 1

ODI Batting
Innings:	1	Runs:	16
Highest Score:	16	Average:	16.00
No. 50s:	0	No. 100s:	0

ODI Bowling & Fielding
Wickets:	0	Runs:	0
Best Bowling:		Average:	0.00
5 WM:	0	Catches:	0
Stumpings:	0		

Debut V New Zealand, The Oval 2004

JAVED, Nasir
Born: June 21, 1966
Batting: Right handed

One Day Internationals
ODI Career: 2004
ODIs Played: 1

ODI Batting
Innings:	1	Runs:	2
Highest Score:	2*	Average:	0.00
No. 50s:	0	No. 100s:	0

ODI Bowling & Fielding
Wickets:	0	Runs:	0
Best Bowling:		Average:	0.00
5 WM:	0	Catches:	0
Stumpings:	0		

Debut V Australia, Southampton 2004

JOHNSON, Howard
Born: August 16, 1964
Batting: Right handed
Bowling: Right arm medium-fast

One Day Internationals
ODI Career: 2004
ODIs Played: 2

ODI Batting
Innings:	2	Runs:	9
Highest Score:	9	Average:	9.00
No. 50s:	0	No. 100s:	0

ODI Bowling & Fielding
Wickets:	1	Runs:	69
Best Bowling:	1/26	Average:	69.00
5 WM:	0	Catches:	0
Stumpings:	0		

Debut V New Zealand, The Oval 2004

JOHNSON, Mark
Born: October 28, 1963
Batting: Left handed
Wicket Keeper

The Encyclopedia of International Cricketers - USA

One Day Internationals
ODI Career:	2004		
ODIs Played:	2		

ODI Batting
Innings:	2	Runs:	20
Highest Score:	20	Average:	10.00
No. 50s:	0	No. 100s:	0

ODI Bowling & Fielding
Wickets:	0	Runs:	0
Best Bowling:		Average:	0.00
5 WM:	0	Catches:	1
Stumpings:	0		

Debut V New Zealand, The Oval 2004

LAMBERT, Clayton
Born:	February 10, 1962
Batting:	Left handed
Bowling:	Right arm off-break

One Day Internationals
ODI Career:	1990-04		
ODIs Played:	12		

ODI Batting
Innings:	12	Runs:	407
Highest Score:	119	Average:	33.91
No. 50s:	2	No. 100s:	1

ODI Bowling & Fielding
Wickets:	0	Runs:	74
Best Bowling:		Average:	0.00
5 WM:	0	Catches:	0
Stumpings:	0		

A former West Indian Test and ODI player who made his ODI debut for USA against New Zealand at The Oval in 2004, aged 42.

MASSIAH, Steve
Born:	June 21, 1979
Batting:	Right handed
Bowling:	Right arm off-break

One Day Internationals
ODI Career:	2004		
ODIs Played:	2		

ODI Batting
Innings:	2	Runs:	23
Highest Score:	23	Average:	11.50
No. 50s:	0	No. 100s:	0

ODI Bowling & Fielding
Wickets:	0	Runs:	0
Best Bowling:		Average:	0.00
5 WM:	0	Catches:	0
Stumpings:	0		

Debut V New Zealand, The Oval 2004

REID, Tony
Born:	April 9, 1962
Batting:	Right handed
Bowling:	Right arm medium

One Day Internationals
ODI Career:	2004		
ODIs Played:	2		

ODI Batting
Innings:	2	Runs:	8
Highest Score:	6	Average:	4.00
No. 50s:	0	No. 100s:	0

ODI Bowling & Fielding
Wickets:	1	Runs:	63
Best Bowling:	1/37	Average:	63.00
5 WM:	0	Catches:	0
Stumpings:	0		

Debut V New Zealand, The Oval 2004

ROMERO, Leon
Born:	December 29, 1974
Batting:	Right handed
Bowling:	Right arm medium
	Wicket Keeper

One Day Internationals
ODI Career:	2004		
ODIs Played:	2		

ODI Batting
Innings:	2	Runs:	1
Highest Score:	1	Average:	0.50
No. 50s:	0	No. 100s:	0

ODI Bowling & Fielding
Wickets:	1	Runs:	52
Best Bowling:	1/52	Average:	52.00
5 WM:	0	Catches:	1
Stumpings:	0		

Debut V New Zealand, The Oval 2004

STAPLE, Richard
Born:	November 25, 1969
Batting:	Right handed
Bowling:	Right arm off-break

One Day Internationals
ODI Career:	2004		
ODIs Played:	2		

ODI Batting
Innings:	2	Runs:	4
Highest Score:	4	Average:	2.00
No. 50s:	0	No. 100s:	0

ODI Bowling & Fielding
Wickets:	2	Runs:	76
Best Bowling:	2/76	Average:	38.00
5 WM:	0	Catches:	0
Stumpings:	0		

Debut V New Zealand, The Oval 2004

ZIA, Rashid
Born:	April 6, 1974
Batting:	Right handed
Bowling:	Right arm off-break
	Wicket Keeper

One Day Internationals
ODI Career:	2004		
ODIs Played:	2		

ODI Batting
Innings:	2	Runs:	9
Highest Score:	8	Average:	4.50
No. 50s:	0	No. 100s:	0

ODI Bowling & Fielding
Wickets:	0	Runs:	69
Best Bowling:		Average:	0.00
5 WM:	0	Catches:	0
Stumpings:	0		

Debut V New Zealand, The Oval 2004